BUS 140: Business Information and Oral Proficiency

University of Scranton

| PEARSON COLLECTIONS |

PEARSON

Cover Art: Courtesy of Photodisc/Getty Images

3 16

Attention bookstores: For permission to return any unsold stock, contact us at pe-uscustomreturns@pearson.com

Pearson Learning Solutions, 501 Boylston Street, Suite 900, Boston, MA 02116

A Pearson Education Company
www.pearsoned.com

ISBN 10: 1323514511

ISBN 13: 9781323514511

Printed in the USA

Table of Contents

Introduction to PowerPoint

From PowerPoint Chapter 1 of *Microsoft® Office 2016, Volume 1*. Mary Anne Poatsy, Mulbery, Krebs, Hogan, Cameron, Davidson, Lau, Lawson, Williams, and Robert T. Grauer.
Download student resources at http://www.pearsonhighered.com/exploring.

PowerPoint

Introduction to PowerPoint

LEARNING OUTCOME You will plan, create, navigate, and print a basic presentation.

OBJECTIVES & SKILLS: After you read this chapter, you will be able to:

Work with PowerPoint

OBJECTIVE 1: OPEN AND VIEW A POWERPOINT PRESENTATION
View a Presentation in Normal View, Use PowerPoint Views Effectively

OBJECTIVE 2: TYPE A SPEAKER NOTE
Use the Notes Pane

OBJECTIVE 3: SAVE AS A POWERPOINT SLIDE SHOW
Save a Presentation in PowerPoint Show Mode

HANDS-ON EXERCISE 1:
Introduction to PowerPoint

Presentation Creation

OBJECTIVE 4: PLAN AND PREPARE A PRESENTATION
Use a Storyboard, Choose a Theme

OBJECTIVE 5: ADD PRESENTATION CONTENT
Use Slide Layouts, Create a Title Slide and an Introduction, Create Key Point Slides, End with a Summary or Conclusion Slide

OBJECTIVE 6: REVIEW THE PRESENTATION
Check Spelling, Use the Thesaurus, Check Slide Show Elements, Reorder Slides

HANDS-ON EXERCISE 2:
Presentation Creation

Presentation Enhancement

OBJECTIVE 7: ADD A TABLE
Add a Table

OBJECTIVE 8: INSERT MEDIA OBJECTS
Insert Media Objects

OBJECTIVE 9: APPLY TRANSITIONS AND ANIMATIONS
Apply Transitions, Animate Objects

OBJECTIVE 10: INSERT A HEADER OR FOOTER
Insert a Header or Footer

HANDS-ON EXERCISE 3:
Presentation Enhancement

Navigation and Printing

OBJECTIVE 11: NAVIGATE A SLIDE SHOW
Navigate a Slide Show, Annotate a Slide Show

OBJECTIVE 12: PRINT IN POWERPOINT
Print a Full Page Slide, Print Handouts, Print Notes Pages, Print Outlines

HANDS-ON EXERCISE 4:
Navigation and Printing

CASE STUDY | Be a Trainer

You teach employee training courses for the Training and Development department of your State Department of Human Resources. You begin each course by presenting your objectives for the course using a Microsoft Office PowerPoint 2016 presentation. You create a slide show to help you organize your content and to help your audience retain the information.

Because of the exceptional quality of your presentations, the director of the State Department of Human Resources has asked you to prepare a new course on presentation skills. In the Hands-On Exercises for this chapter, you will work with two presentations for this course. One presentation will focus on the benefits of using PowerPoint, and the other will focus on the preparation for a slide show, including planning, organizing, and delivering.

Creating a Basic Presentation

The Essence of PowerPoint

- You
  - Focus on content and enter your information
  - Add additional elements to create interest
  - Motivate your audience while presenting
- PowerPoint
  - Helps you organize your thoughts
  - Provides tools to make slide show creation easy
  - Allows flexibility in delivery and presentation

FIGURE 1 Be a Trainer Slide

CASE STUDY | Be A Trainer

Starting File	Files to be Submitted
p01h1Intro	**p01h1Intro_LastFirst** **p01h1Intro_LastFirst.ppsx** **p01h4Content_LastFirst**

Work with PowerPoint

You can use Microsoft Office PowerPoint 2016 to create an electronic slide show or other materials for use in a professional presentation. A ***slide*** is the most basic element of PowerPoint (similar to a page being the most basic element of Microsoft Word). A collection of slides is referred to as a ***deck*** of slides. The slides may be easily arranged just as cards can be easily shuffled in a deck of cards. The arranged slides displayed onscreen for an audience is a ***slide show***, often referred to as a presentation. A ***PowerPoint presentation*** is an electronic slide show that can be edited or delivered in a variety of ways: you can project the slide show on a screen as part of a presentation, run it automatically at a kiosk or from a DVD, display it on the World Wide Web, email it, or create printed handouts.

Figure 2 shows the first four slides of a PowerPoint presentation. The slides contain different types of content, such as text, an online picture, and a table. The presentation has a consistent color scheme. It is easy to create presentations with consistent and attractive designs using PowerPoint.

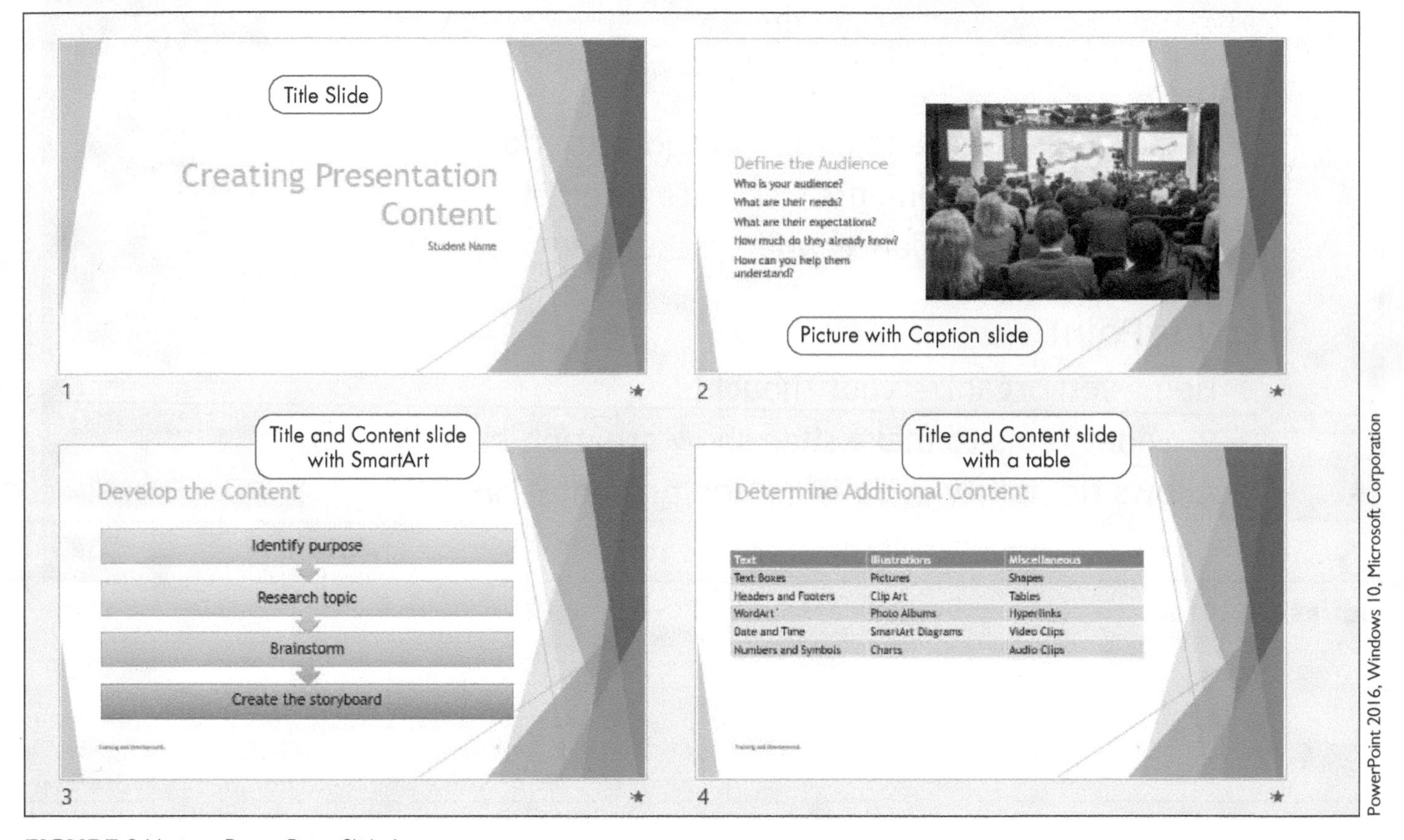

FIGURE 2 Various PowerPoint Slide Layouts

In this section, you will start your exploration of PowerPoint by opening and viewing a previously completed presentation. You will modify the presentation by adding identifying information, examining different PowerPoint views to discover the advantages of each, and saving the presentation.

Opening and Viewing a PowerPoint Presentation

STEP 1 When you open a new presentation or a previously created presentation, you see the default PowerPoint workspace, ***Normal view***. Figure 3 shows Normal view, which displays the Ribbon and other common interface components as well as two panes that provide maximum flexibility in working with the presentation. The pane on the left side of the screen, the ***Slides pane***, shows the slide deck with ***thumbnails*** (slide miniatures) representing the location of the slides. The slides are numbered to help you select the slide you want to edit. The large pane on the right side of the screen, the ***Slide pane***, is the main workspace and displays the currently selected slide.

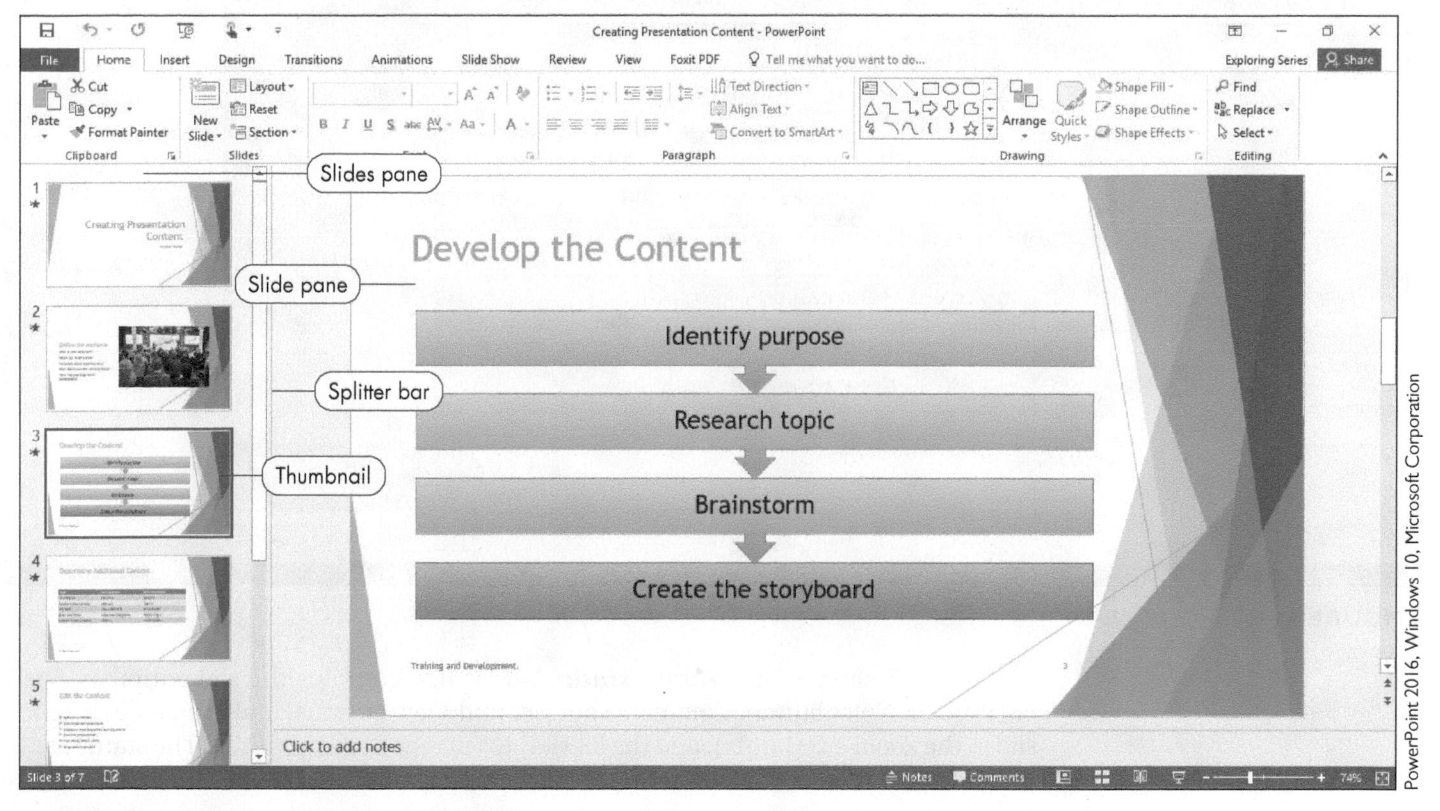

FIGURE 3 Normal View (Default PowerPoint View)

> **TIP: ADD-INS TAB**
> You may see an Add-Ins tab on the Ribbon. This tab indicates that additional functionality, such as an updated Office feature or an Office-compatible program, has been added to your system. Add-Ins are designed to increase your productivity.

While in Normal view, you can hide the left pane that displays the thumbnails. Doing so will expand the workspace so you can see more detail while editing slide content. To hide the pane with the thumbnails, drag the border that separates the panes one from another to the left until you see the word Thumbnails appear on the left side. Figure 4 shows an individual slide in Normal view with the Slides pane closed. You can quickly restore the view by clicking the arrow above Thumbnails or you can click the View tab and click Normal in the Presentation Views group. You can also widen the Slides pane to show more detail by dragging the splitter bar to the right.

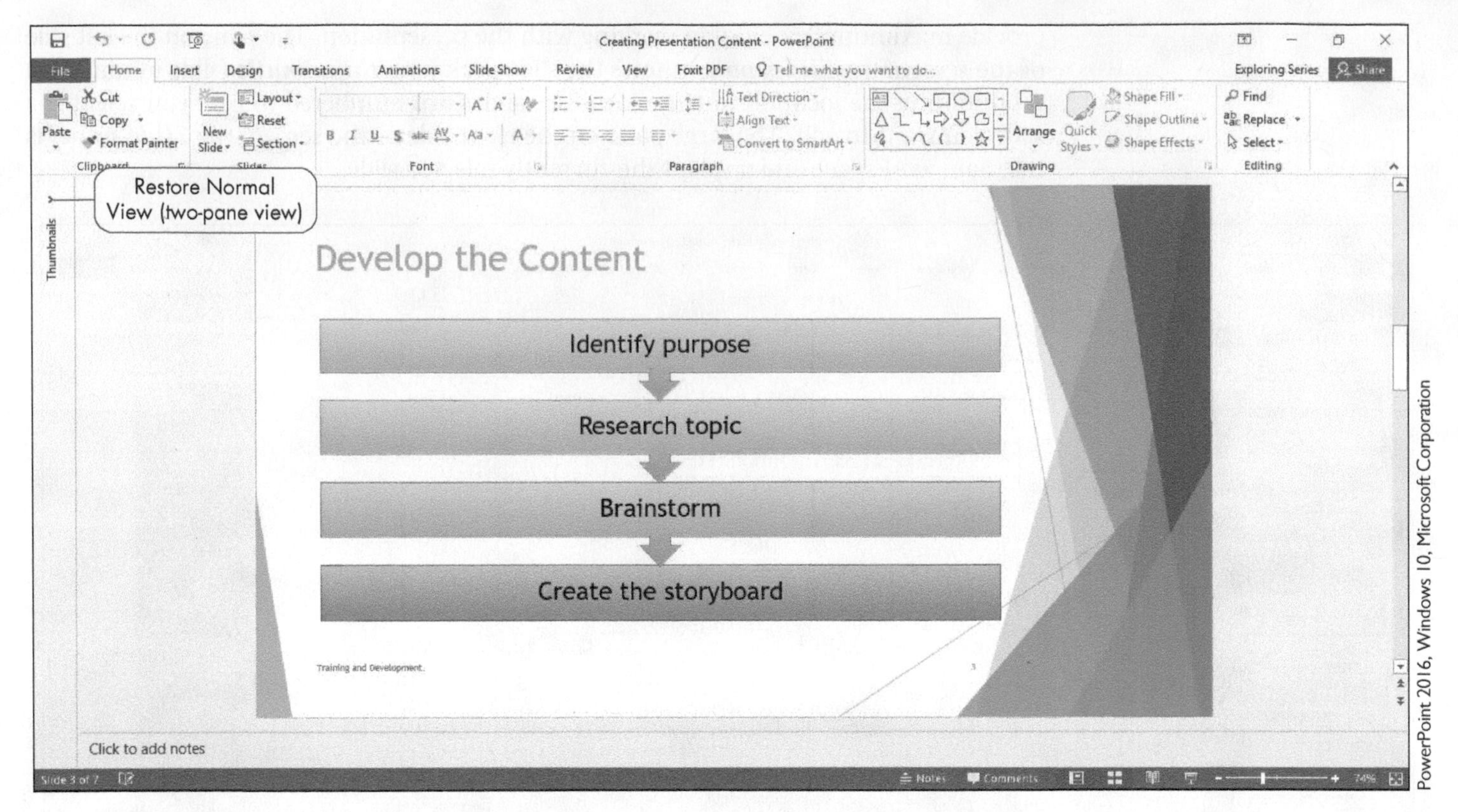

FIGURE 4 Individual Slide View

Figure 5 shows PowerPoint's ***status bar***, which contains the slide number, Spell check icon, Notes button, Comments button, and View buttons. It also includes a Zoom slider, the Zoom level button, and the Fit slide to current window button. The status bar is located at the bottom of your screen and can be customized.

To customize the status bar, complete the following steps:

1. Right-click the status bar.
2. Select the options to display from the Customize Status Bar list.
3. Click off the Customize Status Bar list to return to editing.

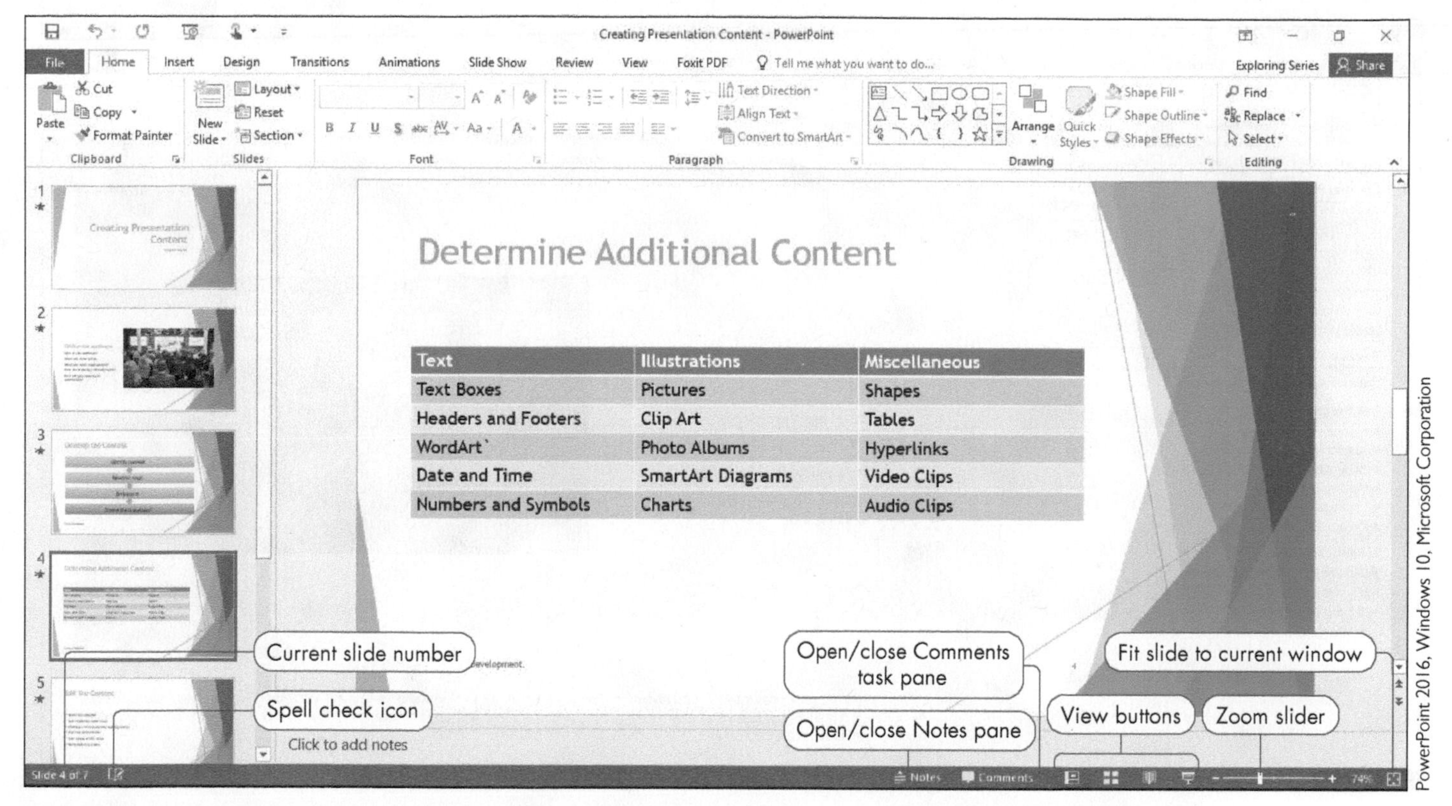

FIGURE 5 PowerPoint Status Bar

Use PowerPoint Views Effectively

In addition to Normal view, PowerPoint offers specialty views to enable you to work effectively and efficiently with your slides. The Presentation Views group on the View tab enables you to access these views:

- Normal
- Outline View
- Slide Sorter
- Notes Page
- Reading View

Use ***Outline View*** when you would like to enter text into your presentation using an outline. In other words, rather than having to enter the text into each placeholder on each slide separately, you can type the text directly into an outline. Figure 6 shows an example of Outline View.

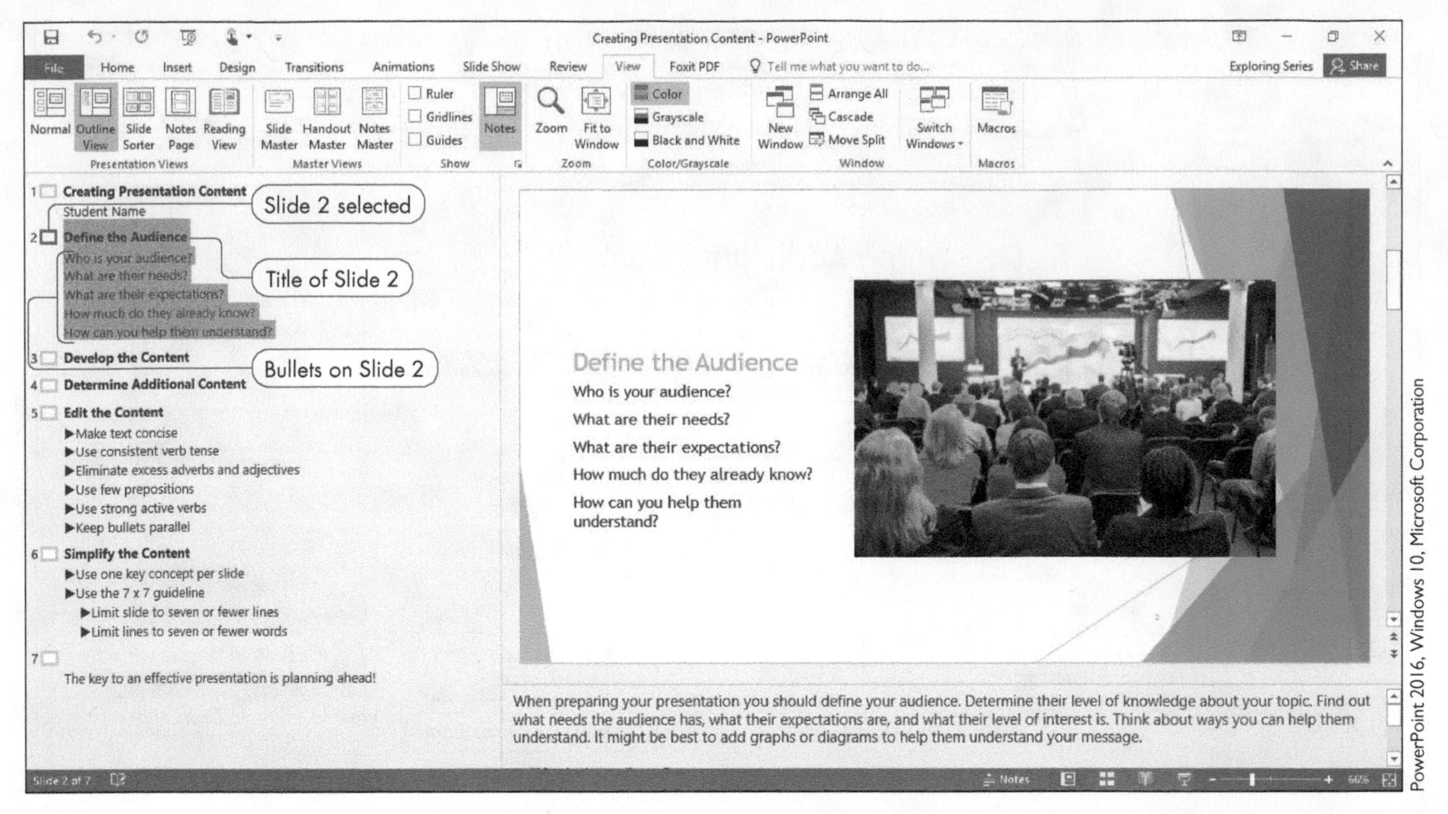

FIGURE 6 Outline View

Slide Sorter view displays thumbnails of your presentation slides, which enables you to view multiple slides simultaneously (see Figure 7). This view is helpful when you want to change the order of the slides, or to delete one or more slides. You can set transition effects (the way the slides transition from one to another) for multiple slides in Slide Sorter view. If you are in Slide Sorter view and double-click a slide thumbnail, PowerPoint displays the selected slide in Normal view.

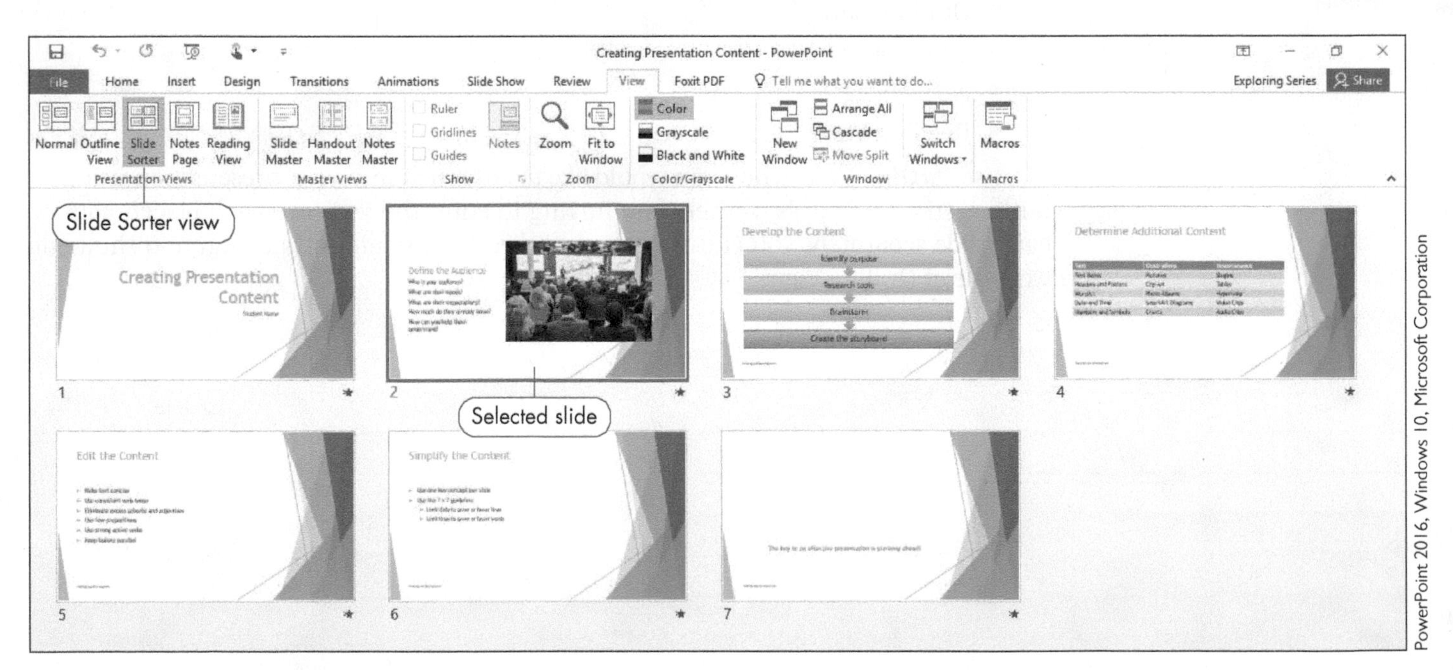

FIGURE 7 Slide Sorter View

To rearrange slides in Slide Sorter view, complete the following steps:

1. Move the pointer over the slide thumbnail of the slide you want to move.
2. Drag the slide to the new location.

Use ***Notes Page view*** when you need to enter and edit large amounts of text that you can refer to when presenting. Slides should contain just key points and you should elaborate on the key points verbally as you deliver the presentation. Consequently, speaker notes can be a most useful tool when giving a presentation. Notes do not display when the presentation is shown (except when Presenter view is used), but are intended to help the speaker remember the key points or additional information about each slide. Figure 8 shows an example of Notes Page view.

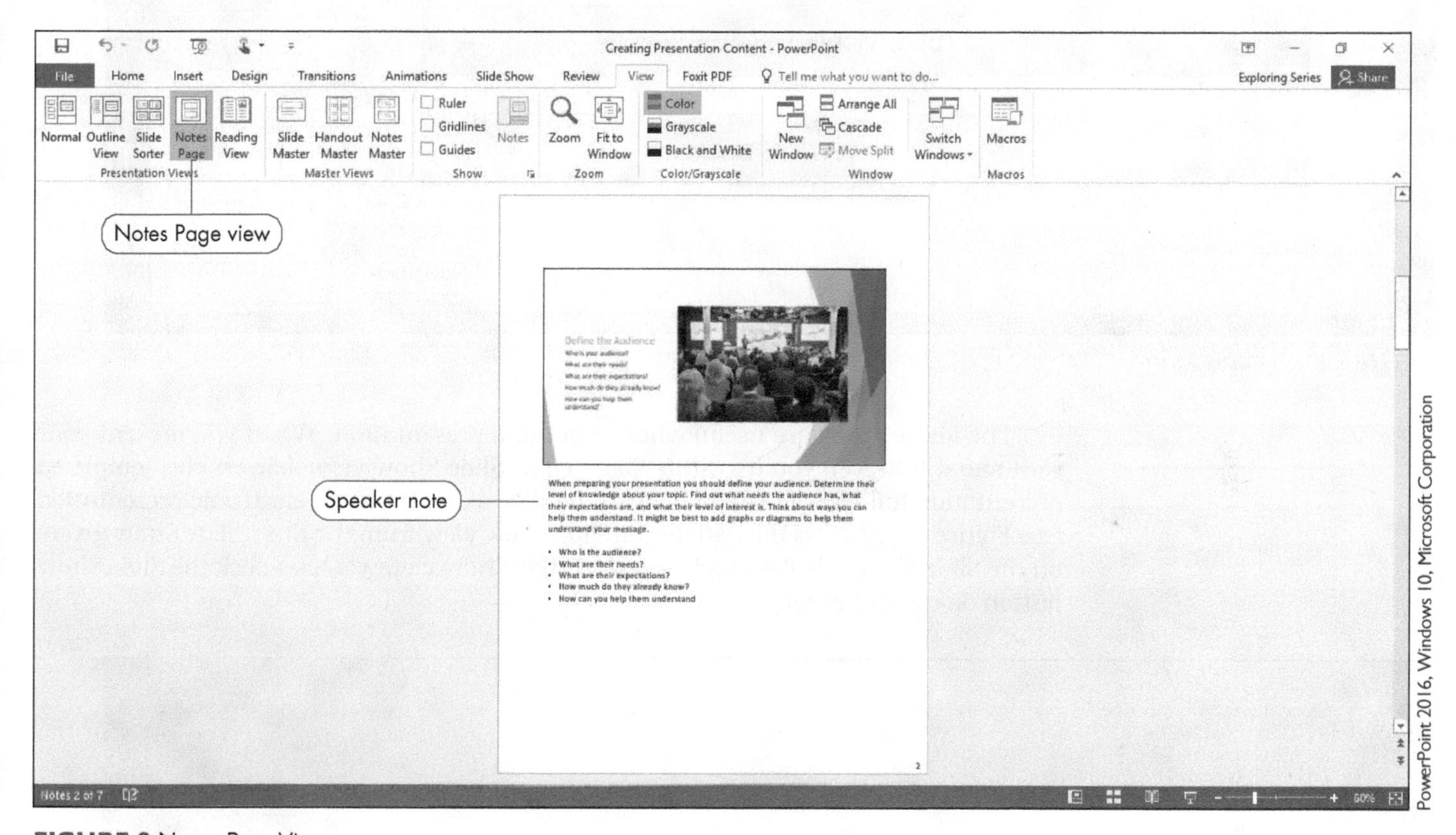

FIGURE 8 Notes Page View

PowerPoint 2016, Windows 10, Microsoft Corporation

Use ***Reading View*** to view the slide show full screen, one slide at a time. Animations and transitions are active in Reading View. A title bar, including the Minimize, Maximize/Restore Down (which changes its name and appearance depending on whether the window is maximized or at a smaller size), and Close buttons, is visible, as well as a modified status bar (see Figure 9). In addition to View buttons, the status bar includes navigation buttons for moving to the next or previous slide, as well as a menu for accomplishing common tasks such as printing. Press Esc to return quickly to the previous view.

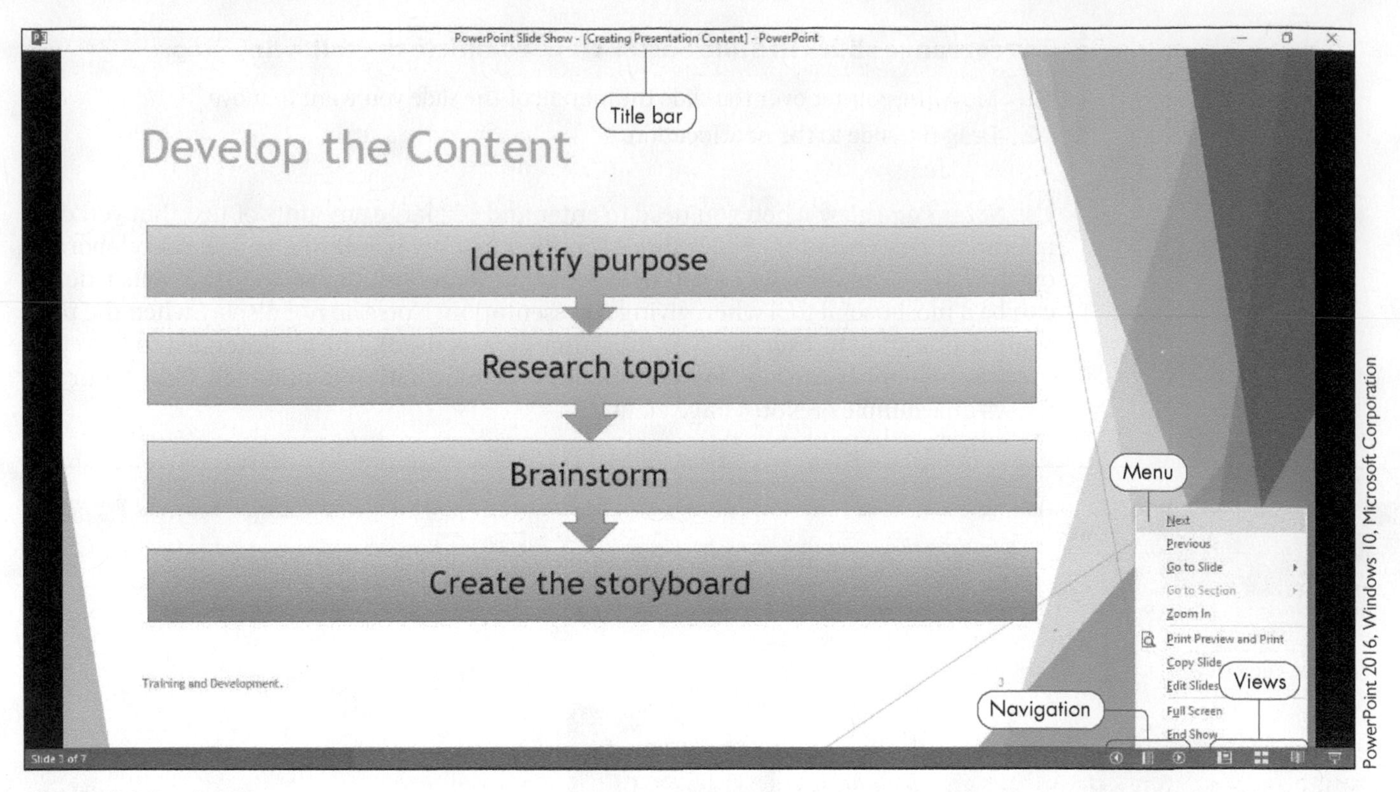

FIGURE 9 Reading View

The above views are useful when creating a presentation. When you present your slide show, however, you use ***Slide Show view***. Slide Show view delivers the completed presentation full screen to an audience, one slide at a time, as an electronic presentation (see Figure 10). Access the options for Slide Show view from the Start Slide Show group on the Slide Show tab. For quick access to Slide Show view, you can click the Slide Show button on the status bar.

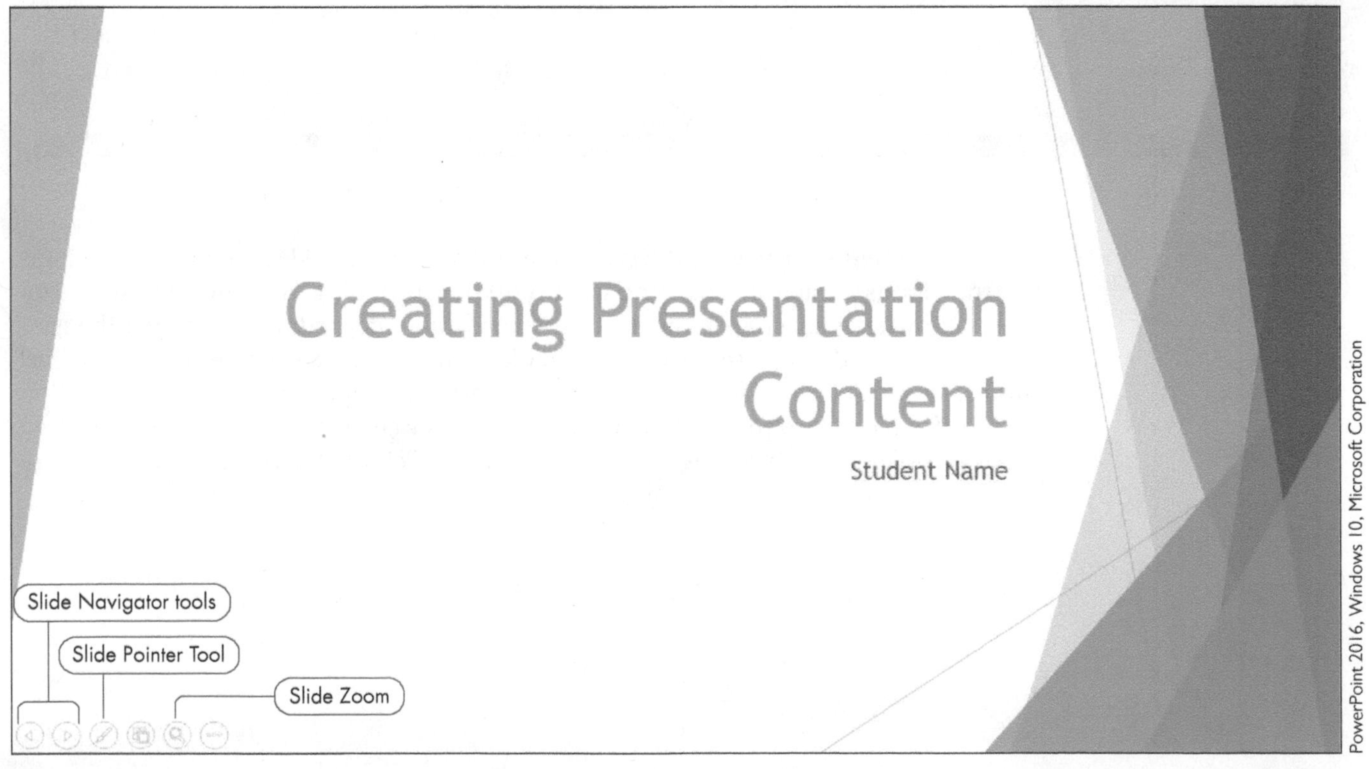

FIGURE 10 Slide Show View

The slide show can be presented manually, where you click the mouse to move from one slide to the next, or automatically, where each slide stays on the screen for a predetermined amount of time, after which the next slide appears. A slide show can contain a combination of both methods. To end the slide show, press Esc. This view also includes pointer tools, Slide Navigator that enables you to move between slides as needed without leaving Slide Show view, and Slide Zoom that you can use to focus your audience on your ideas.

Presenter view, accessed from the Monitors group on the Slide Show tab, is an especially valuable view that lets you deliver a presentation using two monitors simultaneously. Typically, one monitor is a projector that delivers the full-screen presentation to the audience; the other monitor is a laptop or computer that displays the presentation in Presenter view. Presenter view includes a slide, a thumbnail image of the next slide, and any speaker notes you have created. The view options are displayed on the second monitor so the presenter can control them. This view includes a timer that displays the time elapsed since the presentation began so you can keep track of the presentation length. Figure 11 shows the audience view on the right side of the figure and the Presenter view on the left side.

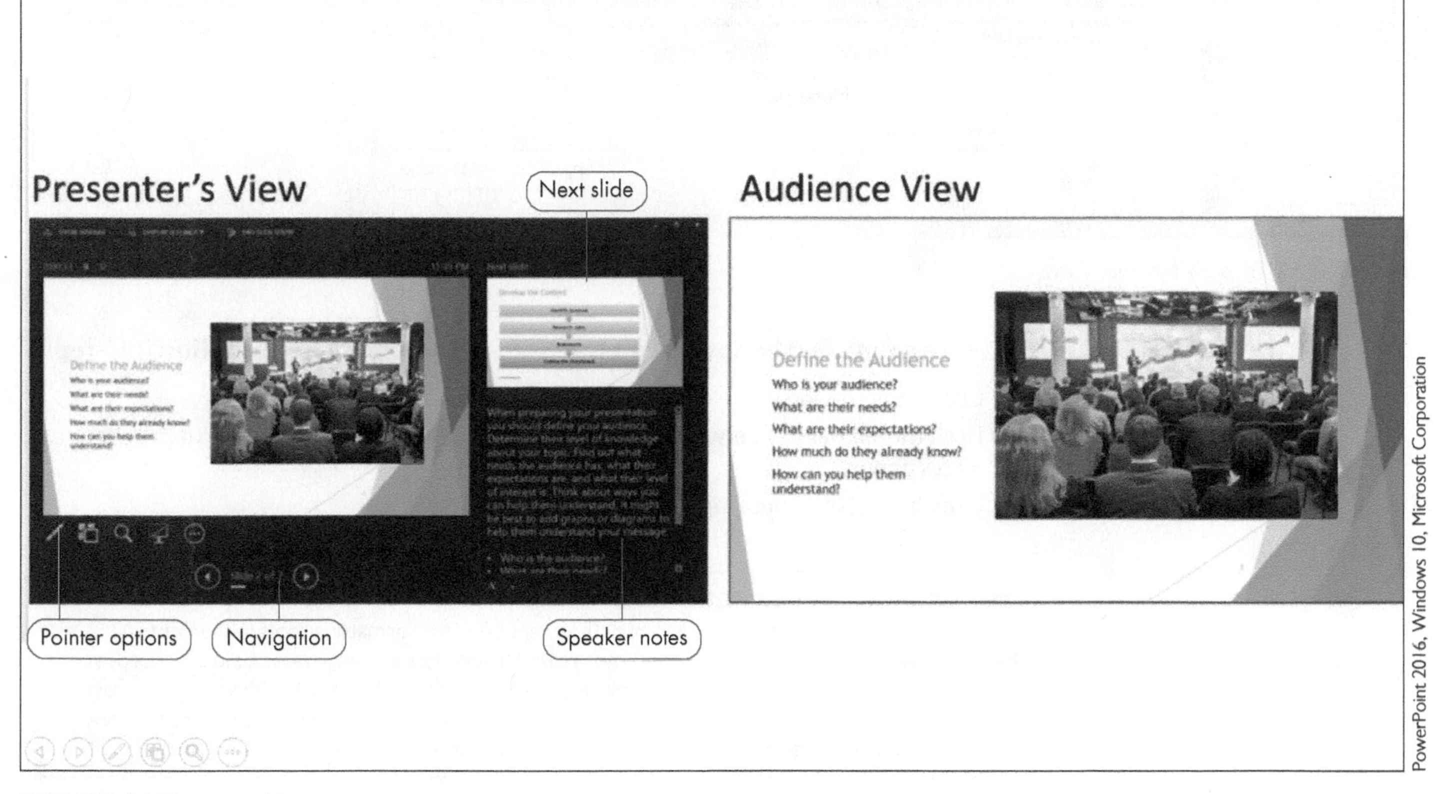

FIGURE 11 Presenter View

Typing a Speaker Note

STEP 2 Rather than change your view to Notes Page view to type speaker notes, you can change Normal view from a two-paned view to a three-paned view as shown in Figure 12. To display the Notes pane, click Notes on the status bar. The Notes pane will display below the Slide Pane, the main working area.

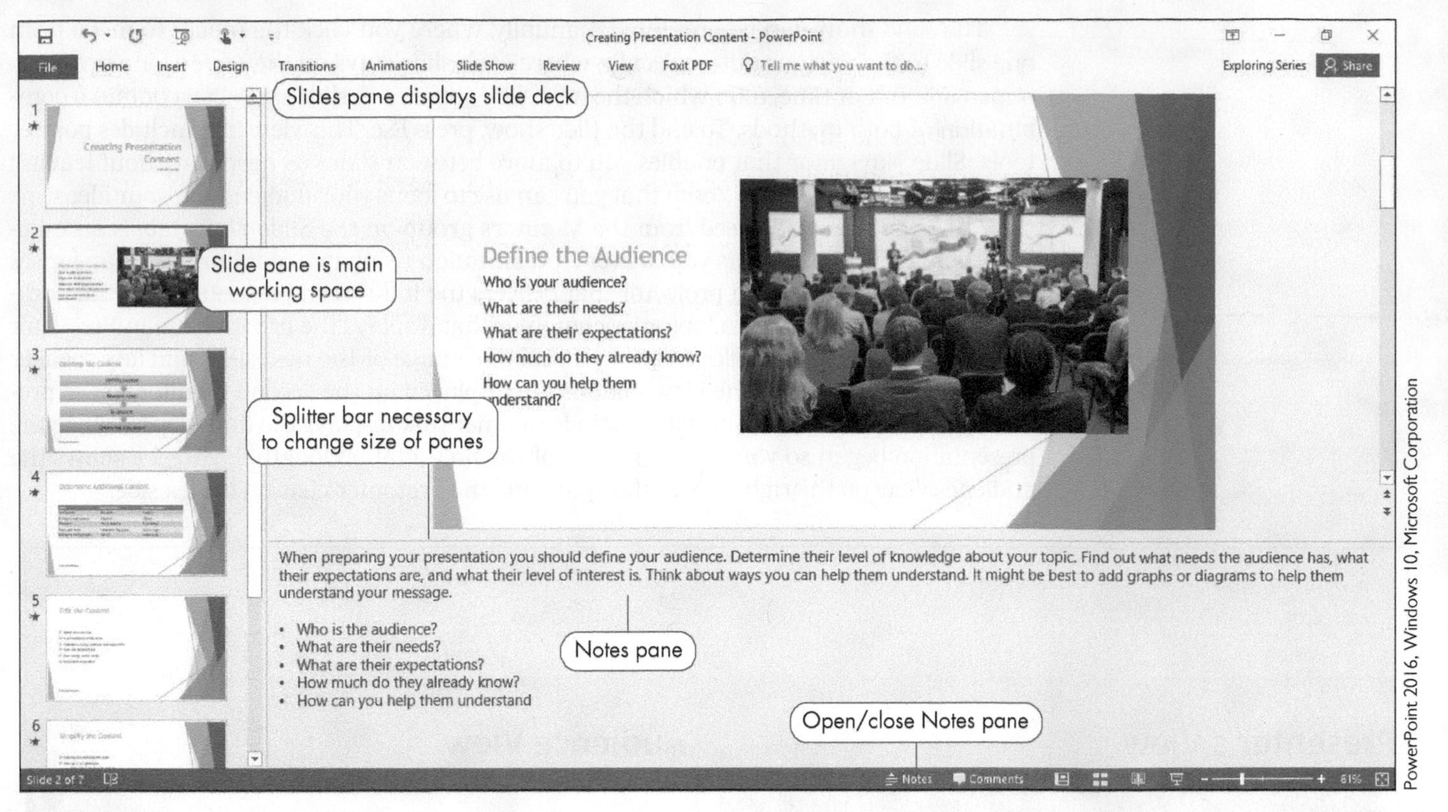

FIGURE 12 Tri-pane Normal View

To create a note for the speaker in the Notes pane, complete the following steps:

1. Click Notes on the status bar if the Notes pane is not visible.
2. Drag the splitter bar between the Slide pane and the Notes pane up to expand the Notes pane.
3. Click in the Notes pane and begin typing.

TIP: FORMAT A SPEAKER NOTE

Notes can be formatted much like a Word document using the formatting tools in the Font and Paragraph groups on the Home tab. You can create bulleted lists and italicize or bold key words you want to feature, among other things, to help you stay organized and on track with your presentation. Not all text modifications will be visible in Normal view or in Presenter view. To see modifications such as font and font size, images, and charts, switch to Notes Page view.

Saving as a PowerPoint Show

STEP 3 When you save a ***PowerPoint presentation***, by default it is saved with a .pptx file extension. Then, when you open the file, it opens to Normal view, or edit mode, so that you can make changes to the presentation. If you use Save As and save the presentation as a ***PowerPoint show*** with a .ppsx extension, the presentation opens in Slide Show view. You will not see the PowerPoint interface; the presentation is in play mode. This is valuable when you are ready to present and do not want your audience to see the PowerPoint interface. You double-click the PowerPoint show file with a .ppsx extension in File Explorer to open the presentation in Slide Show view. PowerPoint presentations are often saved as .ppsx files for distributing to others, too. Although a .ppsx file cannot be changed while viewing, you can open the file in PowerPoint and edit it.

1. Describe the main advantage for using each of the following views: Normal view, Notes Page view, Slide Sorter view, and Slide Show view.
2. Discuss the purpose of a speaker note.
3. Explain the difference between a PowerPoint presentation (.pptx) and a PowerPoint show (.ppsx).

Hands-On Exercises

Skills covered: View a Presentation in Normal View • Use the Notes Pane • Save a Presentation in PowerPoint Show Mode

1 Work with PowerPoint

You have been asked to create a presentation on the benefits of PowerPoint for the Training and Development department. You decide to view an existing presentation to determine if it contains material you can adapt for your presentation. You view the presentation, add a speaker note, and then save the presentation as a PowerPoint presentation and as a PowerPoint show.

STEP 1 » OPEN AND VIEW A POWERPOINT PRESENTATION

You open a presentation created by your colleague. You experiment with various methods of advancing to the next slide and then return to Normal view. As you use the various methods of advancing to the next slide, you find the one that is most comfortable to you and then use that method as you view slide shows in the future. An audio clip of audience applause will play when you view Slide 4: The Essence of PowerPoint. You will want to wear a headset if you are in a classroom lab so that you do not disturb classmates. Refer to Figure 13 as you complete Step 1.

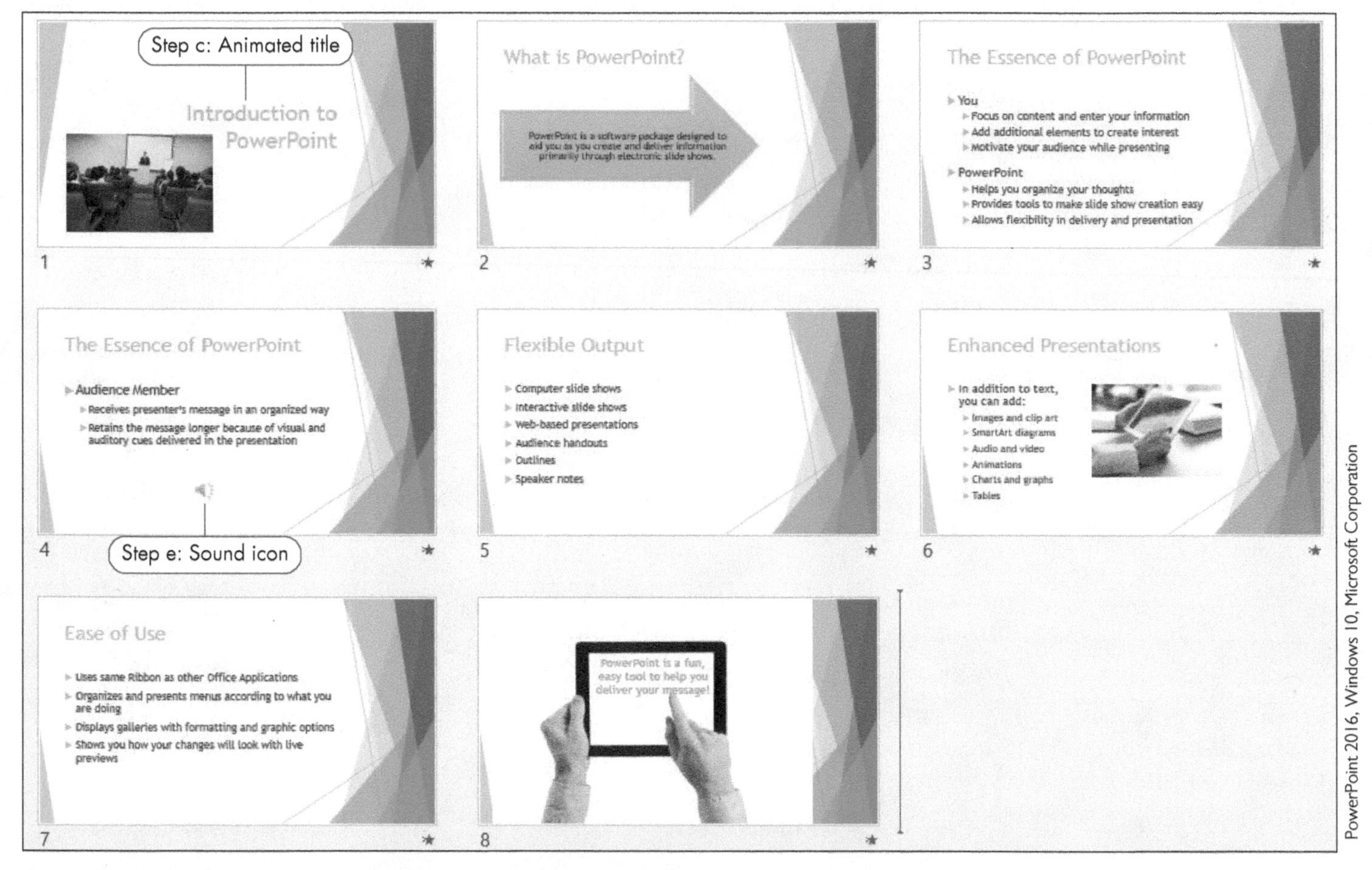

FIGURE 13 Introduction to PowerPoint Presentation

a. Start PowerPoint and open the *p01h1Intro* file. Save the file as **p01h1Intro_LastFirst**. When you save files, use your last and first names. For example, as the PowerPoint author, I would name my presentation "p01h1Intro_KrebsCynthia".

> **TROUBLESHOOTING:** If you make any major mistakes in this exercise, you can close the file, open *p01h1Intro* again, and then start this exercise over.

b. Click **Slide Show** on the status bar.

The presentation begins with the title slide, the first slide in all slide shows. The title has an animation assigned, so it displays automatically.

c. Press **Spacebar** to advance to the second slide and read the slide.

The title animation on the second slide automatically wipes down, and the arrow wipes to the right.

d. Position the pointer in the lower-left corner side of the slide, and click the **right arrow** in the Navigation bar to advance to the next slide. Click to read the animated slide content.

The text on the third slide, and all following slides, has the same animation applied to create consistency in the presentation.

e. Press the **left mouse button** to advance to the fourth slide, which has a sound icon displayed on the slide.

The sound icon on the slide indicates sound has been added. The sound has been set to start automatically so you do not need to click anything for the sound to play.

> **TROUBLESHOOTING:** If you do not hear the sound, your computer may not have a sound card or your sound may be muted.

f. Continue to navigate through the slides until you come to the end of the presentation (a black screen).

g. Press **Esc** to return to Normal view.

STEP 2 » TYPE A SPEAKER NOTE

You add a speaker note to a slide to help you remember to mention some of the many objects that can be added to a slide. You also view the note in Notes view to see how it will print. Refer to Figure 14 as you complete Step 2.

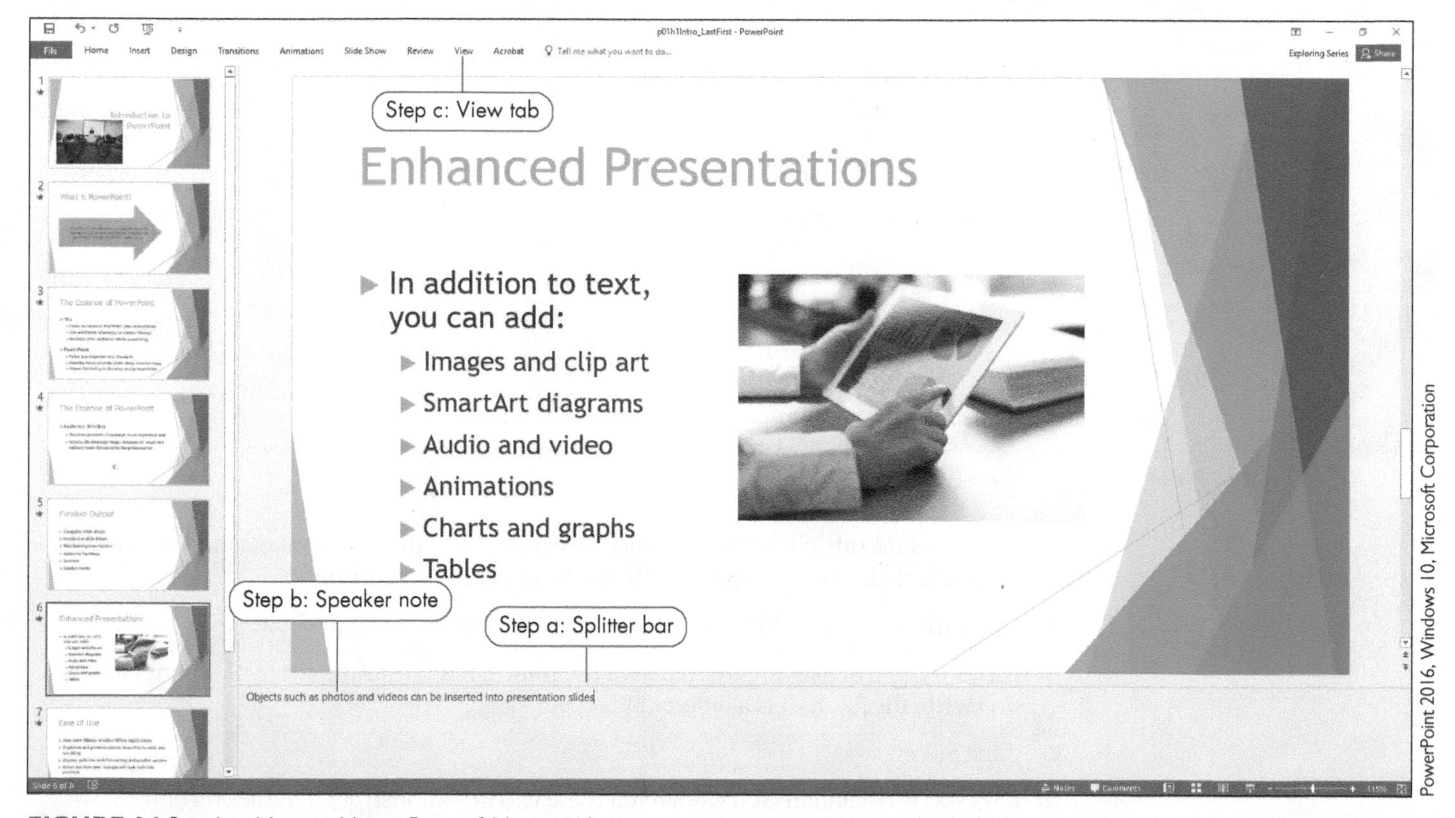

FIGURE 14 Speaker Note in Notes Pane of Normal View

a. Click the **Slide 6 thumbnail** and then drag the border between the Slide pane and the Notes pane up to expand the Notes pane.

   Slide 6 is selected, and the slide displays in the Slide pane.

> **TROUBLESHOOTING:** If the Notes pane is not visible, click Notes on the status bar.

b. Type **Objects such as pictures and videos can be inserted into presentation slides.** in the Notes pane.

c. Click the **View tab** and click **Notes Page** in the Presentation Views group.

   The slide is shown at a reduced size and the speaker note is shown below the slide.

d. Click **Normal** in the Presentation Views group.

   This displays the presentation in Normal view.

e. Save the presentation.

STEP 3 » SAVE AS A POWERPOINT SHOW

You want to save the slide show as a PowerPoint show so that it opens automatically in Slide Show view rather than Normal view. Refer to Figure 15 as you complete Step 3.

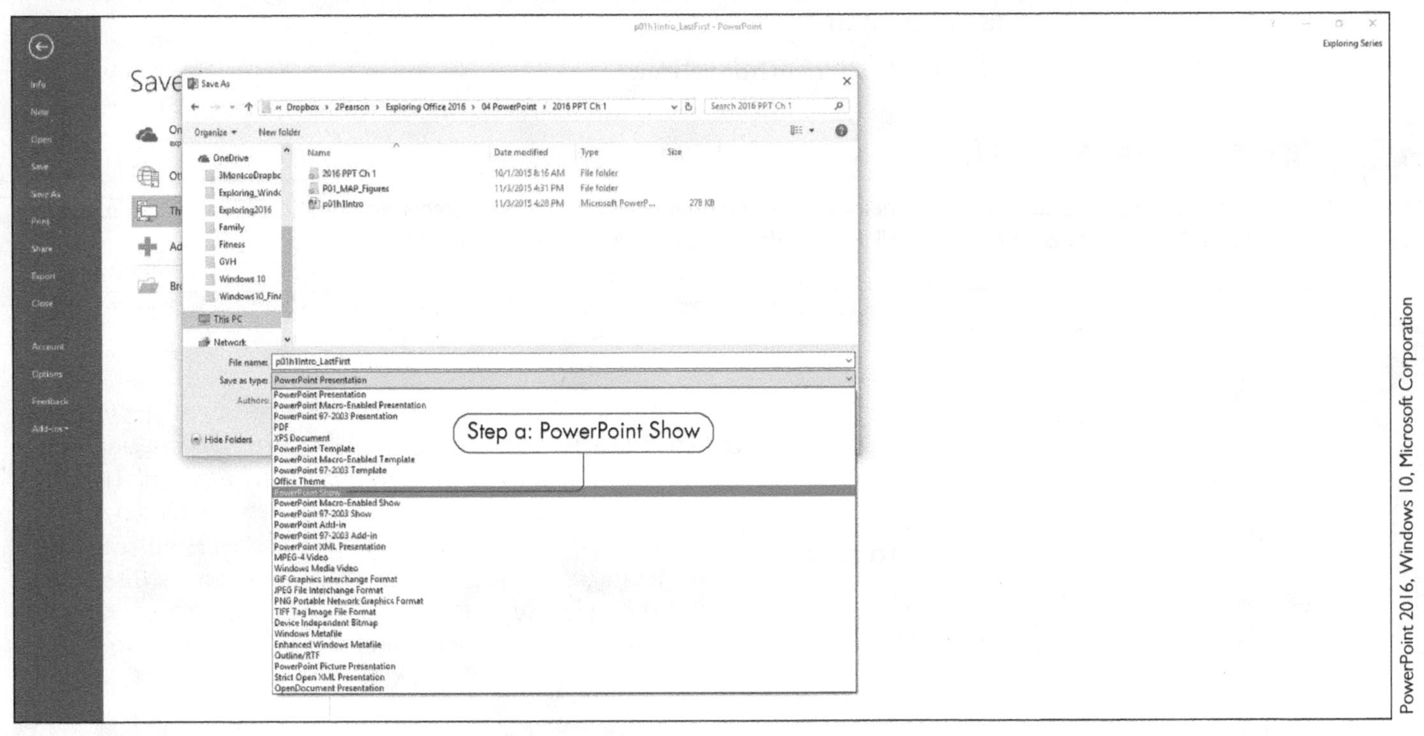

FIGURE 15 Saving a Presentation as a PowerPoint Show

a. Click the **File tab**, click **Save As**, click **Browse**, select the file location where the file is to be saved, click **Save as type**, and then select **PowerPoint Show**.

b. Leave the file name **p01h1Intro_LastFirst** for the PowerPoint show.

   Although you are saving this file with the same file name as the presentation, it will not overwrite the file, as it is a different file type.

c. Click **Save**.

d. Close the presentation. You will submit these files to your instructor at the end of the last Hands-On Exercise.

Presentation Creation

You are ready to create your own presentation by choosing a theme, adding content, and applying formatting. You create the presentation by adding the content first and then applying formatting so that you can concentrate on your message and its structure without getting distracted by the formatting of the presentation.

In this section, you will create a visual plan called a storyboard. You will also learn to polish your presentation by using layouts, applying design themes, and reviewing your presentation for errors.

Planning and Preparing a Presentation

Creating an effective presentation requires advance planning. First, determine the purpose of your presentation. An informative presentation could notify the audience about a change in policy or procedure. An educational presentation could teach an audience about a subject or a skill. Sales presentations are often persuasive calls to action to encourage the purchase of a product, but they can also be used to sell an idea or process. A goodwill presentation could be used to recognize an employee or acknowledge an organization. You could even create a certificate of appreciation using PowerPoint.

Next, research your audience—determine their level of knowledge about your topic. Find out what needs the audience has, what their expectations are, and what their level of interest is.

After determining your purpose and researching your audience, brainstorm how to deliver your message. Before using your computer, you may want to sketch out your thoughts on paper to help you organize them. After organizing your key points, add them as content to the slide show, and then format the presentation.

Use a Storyboard

A ***storyboard*** is a visual plan for your presentation that helps you map out the direction of your presentation. It can be a very rough draft that you sketch out while brainstorming, or it can be an elaborate plan that includes the text and objects drawn as they would appear on a slide.

A simple PowerPoint storyboard is divided into sections representing individual slides. The first block in the storyboard is used for the title slide. Subsequent blocks are used to introduce the topics, develop the topics, and then summarize the information. Figure 16 shows a working copy of a storyboard for planning presentation content. The storyboard is in rough-draft form and shows changes made during the review process. A blank copy of the document in Figure 16 has been included with your student files should you want to use this for presentation planning. The PowerPoint presentation shown in Figure 17 incorporates the changes to the storyboard made during the review process.

Purpose: [ ] Informative [X] Educational [ ] Persuasive [ ] Goodwill [ ] Other

Audience: IAAP Membership
Location: Marriott Hotel
Date and Time: September 16, 2019

Content	Layout	Visual Element(s)
(Title slide) **Title Slide** Planning ~~Before Creating~~ Presentation Content	Title Slide	O Shapes O Chart O Table O WordArt O Picture O Video O Clip Art O Sound O SmartArt O ______ *Description:*
(Introduction) **Introduction (Key Pont, Quote, Image, Other)** A good plan is like a road map: It shows the final destination and usually the best ways to get there. M. Stanley Judd	Section Header	O Shapes O Chart O Table O WordArt ⊗ Picture O Video O Clip Art O Sound O SmartArt O ______ *Description:*
(Key topics with main points) **Key Point #1** Identify the Purpose ~~Selling (e-commercial)~~, Persuasive, Informative, Good Will, ~~Entertaining~~, Educational, Motivational	Title + ~~Two~~ Content	O Shapes O Chart O Table O WordArt O Picture O Video O Clip Art O Sound O SmartArt ⊗ Text *Description:*
Key Point #2 Define the Audience Who is ~~going to be~~ in the audience What are their ~~audience~~ needs? What are their expectations? How much do they already know?	Title + ~~Two~~ Content	O Shapes O Chart O Table O WordArt ⊗ Picture O Video O Clip Art O Sound O SmartArt O ______ *Description:*
Key Point #3 Develop the Content • Identify purpose • Research topic • Brainstorm • Create the storyboard	Title and Content + SmartArt	O Shapes O Chart O Table O WordArt O Picture O Video O Clip Art O Sound ⊗ SmartArt O ______ *Description:*
Key Point #4 Simplify the Content Make text concise, Use consistent verb tense, Eliminate excess adverbs and adjectives, Use few prepositions, Use strong active verbs, Keep bullets parallel	Title and Content	O Shapes O Chart O Table O WordArt O Picture O Video O Clip Art O Sound O SmartArt O ______ *Description:*
Summary (Restatement of Key Points, Quote, Other) Quote: The key to an effective presentation is planning ahead!	Section Header	O Shapes O Chart O Table O WordArt ⊗ Picture O Video O Clip Art O Sound O SmartArt O ______ *Description:*

PowerPoint 2016, Windows 10, Microsoft Corporation

FIGURE 16 Rough-Draft Storyboard

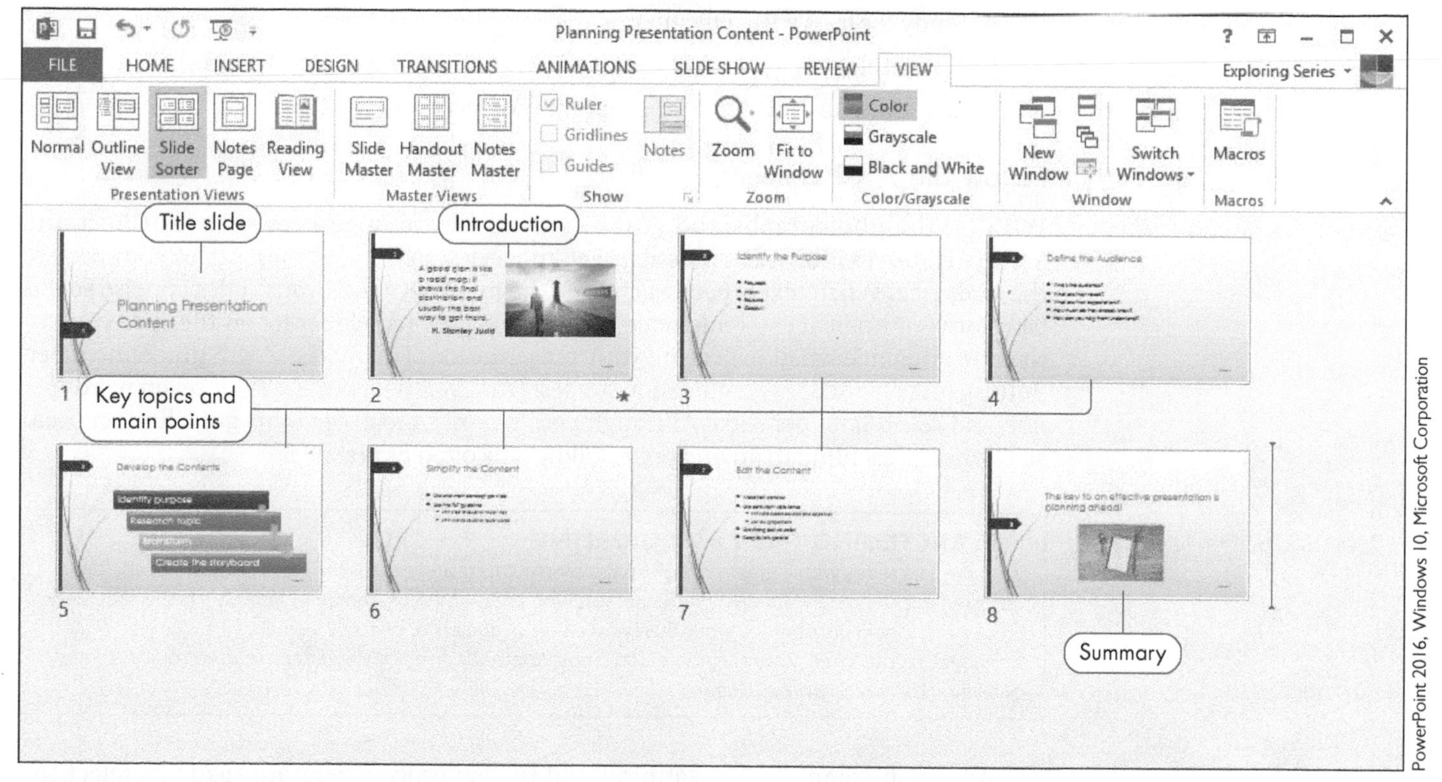

PowerPoint 2016, Windows 10, Microsoft Corporation

FIGURE 17 Slide Show Based on Storyboard

After you create the storyboard, review what you wrote.

Use Short Phrases

Shorten complete sentences to phrases that you can use as bulleted points by eliminating excess adverbs and adjectives and using only a few prepositions. Think like a newspaper editor writing a headline and distill the content into the most important words. For example, "Good computer skills are required of each student attending the CIS 150 course" could be shortened to "CIS 150 course requires good computer skills."

Use Active Voice

Edit the phrases so they begin with active voice when possible to involve the viewer. When using active voice, the subject of the phrase performs the action expressed in the verb. In phrases using passive voice, the subject is acted upon. Passive voice needs more words to communicate your ideas and can make your presentation seem flat. The following is an example of the same thought written in active voice and passive voice:

- Active Voice: Students need good computer skills.
- Passive Voice: Good computer skills are needed by students.

Use Parallel Construction

Use parallel construction so that your bullets are in the same grammatical form to help your audience see the connection between your phrases. If you start your first bullet with a noun, start each successive bullet with a noun; if you start your first bullet with a verb, continue starting your bullets with verbs. Parallel construction also gives each bullet an equal level of importance and promotes balance in your message. In the following example, the fourth bullet is not parallel to the first three bullets because it does not begin with a verb. The fifth bullet shows the bullet in parallel construction.

- Find a good place to study.
- Organize your study time.

- Study for tests with a partner.
- Terminology is important so learn how to use it properly. (Incorrect)
- Learn and use terminology properly. (Correct)

Follow the 7 × 7 Guideline

With all the photographs and graphics available, and features such as Chart and SmartArt, use as little text as possible. Let imagery support your message as you speak to the audience. When text is necessary, keep the information on your slides concise so it is easy for your audience to remember. You can explain and elaborate on the slide content to your audience when delivering your presentation. Follow the 7 × 7 guideline when putting text on a slide. This guideline suggests that you use no more than seven words per line and seven lines per slide. Although you may need to exceed this guideline on occasion when presenting to an audience, follow it as often as possible.

TIP: EXCEEDING THE 7 × 7 GUIDELINE
You may see slides with a great deal of text, multiple charts and graphs, or a combination of multiple objects. This is typically done when the person who created the presentation intends for the slide deck to be printed and distributed rather than viewed by an audience, or to be viewed on a monitor by an individual in control of advancing the slides. These methods give the viewer ample time to absorb any detailed information on the slide.

After you complete the planning and review process, you are ready to select the "look" of your presentation.

Choose a Theme

STEP 1 »» When you first open PowerPoint you are provided the opportunity to choose from various design themes. A ***theme*** is a designer-quality look that includes coordinating colors, matching fonts, and effects such as shadows. The Blank Presentation uses the Office theme.

To create a new presentation, complete the following steps:

1. Click File, and then click New.
2. Click the design theme you want to use.
3. Click Create and a new file will open with the design theme you selected.

You can always change the theme from the one that you initially choose. You can even select a variant for the theme. A ***variant*** is a variation of the theme design you have chosen. Each variant uses different color palettes and font families. Figure 18 shows the Ion theme with four variant options for this theme.

FIGURE 18 Ion Theme with Variant Options

To change a theme or apply a theme variant, complete the following steps:

1. Click the Design tab to display thumbnail previews in the Themes and Variants groups.
2. Click More to see all of the available themes.
3. Point to different themes to see a Live Preview of the theme applied to your presentation.
4. Click a theme to apply it to your presentation.
5. Click a variant in the Variants group to apply it to your presentation.

Adding Presentation Content

After you complete the planning and review process, you are ready to prepare the slide deck you will use during your presentation. To prepare the slide deck, you need to understand PowerPoint's use of slide layouts.

Use Slide Layouts

PowerPoint provides a set of predefined slide ***layouts*** that determine the position of placeholders in various locations. ***Placeholders*** are objects that hold specific content, such as titles, subtitles, or images. Placeholders determine the position of the objects on the slide. Some layouts also include a small palette of icons that you can use to insert a variety of objects.

When you click the New Slide arrow on the Home tab, a gallery from which you can choose a layout displays. Figure 19 shows the Layout Gallery available for you to use when you have selected Blank presentation with the Office theme. Table 1 describes some of the most common slide layouts.

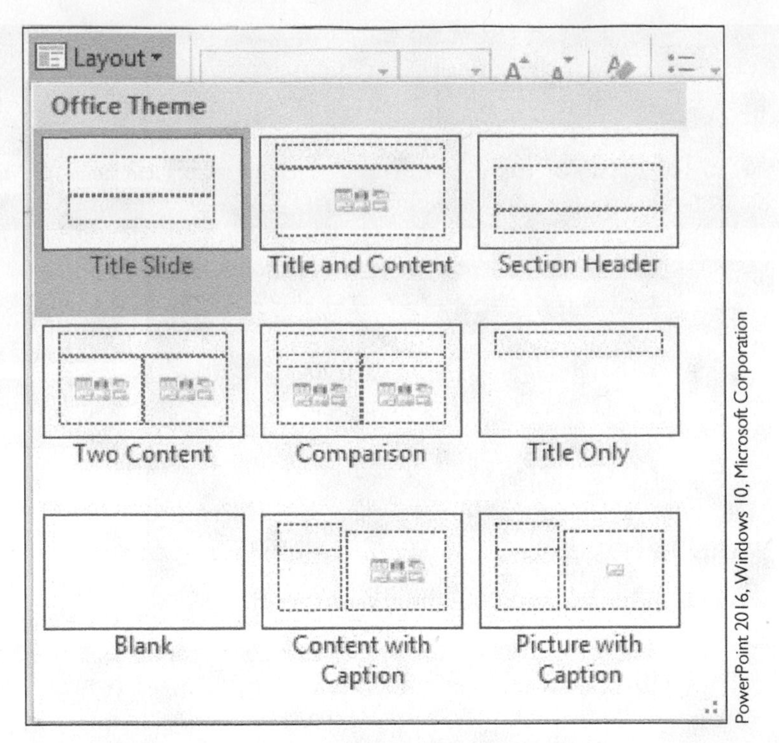

FIGURE 19 Layout Gallery for Office Theme

TABLE 1 Common Layout Options

Slide Layout	Description
Title Slide	A new, blank presentation opens to a title slide layout. This slide includes a placeholder for a title and a placeholder for a subtitle.
Title and Content	In addition to a placeholder for the title, this layout includes a content placeholder. Click and type in the content placeholder and you create a bulleted list. Or, click one of the icons on the palette in the center of the placeholder to insert objects such as a table, chart, SmartArt graphic, picture, online picture, or video.
Section Header	The Section Header layout enables you to separate different sections or main topics similar to how a tabbed page separates sections in a notebook.
Two Content	This layout includes two content placeholders which you can use to create two columns on the slide. Often this layout is used to put text on one side of the slide and graphic content on the other side. A title placeholder is also included.
Comparison	Use this layout to make a comparison between two points by listing supporting detail in columns. In addition to having two content placeholders, this layout also includes a heading placeholder over each content placeholder and a title placeholder.
Title Only	Only a title placeholder is included on the slide which gives you a lot of empty area you can use to insert any type of object such as shapes, WordArt, pictures, charts, etc.
Blank	The blank layout contains no placeholders making it ideal for content that will cover the entire slide, such as a picture.
Content with Caption	The left side of this layout includes a placeholder for a title and a placeholder for text. The right side includes a placeholder for content such as a chart or picture.
Picture with Caption	The top of the slide includes a large placeholder for a picture. Beneath the picture placeholder is a placeholder for a caption and a placeholder for descriptive text.

After you select a layout, click a placeholder. The border of the placeholder becomes a dashed line and you are able to enter content. If you click the dashed line placeholder border, the placeholder and all of its content are selected. The border changes to a solid line. Once selected, you can drag the placeholder to a new position, resize it, format the contents of the placeholder, or delete the placeholder. To format the contents of the placeholder, click the placeholder border and use the controls on the Home tab to format the text. If you only want to change a portion of the text, select the text and then use the controls on the Home tab to format the text.

TIP: UNUSED PLACEHOLDERS
It is not necessary to delete unused placeholders on a slide. Unused placeholders in a slide layout do not show when you display a slide show.

Create a Title Slide and an Introduction

STEP 2 The title placeholder should be used for a short title that indicates the purpose of the presentation. Try to capture the title in two to five words. The subtitle placeholder should be used for information such as the speaker's name and title, the speaker's organization, the organization's logo, and the date of the presentation. To add this information to the placeholders, click in the placeholder and begin typing.

After the title slide, you should include an introduction slide that will get the audience's attention. The introduction could be a list of topics covered in the presentation, a thought-provoking quotation or question, or an image that relates to the topic. Introduction slides can also be used to distinguish between topics or sections of the presentation.

Create Key Point Slides

After you create the title slide and introduction, you should create a slide for each of the key points you outlined in your storyboard.

To add a slide, complete the following steps:

1. Click the New Slide arrow on the Home tab.
2. Click the layout that you want for your new slide in the gallery of layouts.

The New Slide button has two parts, the New Slide button and the New Slide arrow. Click the New Slide arrow when you want to choose a layout from the gallery. Click New Slide, which appears above the New Slide arrow, to quickly insert a new slide. If you click New Slide when the title slide is selected, the new slide uses the Title and Content layout. If the current slide uses any layout other than Title Slide, the subsequent new slide uses the same layout.

Each key point should be on a separate slide with the details needed to support it. The Title and Content layout is a very common layout used for presenting a key point and its supporting details. List the key point in the title placeholder, and then create a bulleted list in the content placeholder. To increase or decrease levels, or indents, for bulleted items, click Increase List Level or Decrease List Level in the Paragraph group on the Home tab. You can press Tab as a shortcut to increase a level, or Shift+Tab as a shortcut to decrease a level.

End with a Summary or Conclusion Slide

To give closure to your presentation, end with a summary slide that reiterates your presentation's key points. Or, create a conclusion slide that restates the purpose of the presentation or invokes a call to action. You may also want to repeat your contact information at the end of the presentation so the audience knows how to follow-up with any questions or needs.

Reviewing the Presentation

After you create the presentation, check for spelling errors, incorrect word usage, and inconsistent capitalization. Nothing is more embarrassing or can make you appear more unprofessional than a misspelled word enlarged on a big screen. Also view the slide show to ensure that the content is presented in the proper order, that the layouts provide the content in an effective manner, and that all transitions and animations work.

Check Spelling

STEP 3 Use a five-step method for checking spelling in PowerPoint. Although proofreading five times may seem excessive, it will help ensure your presentation is professional.

To check spelling, complete the following steps:

1. Read the slide content as you type it looking for wavy red underlines that indicate a potential typographical error or a repeated word. Read each slide after typing its information.
2. Use the Spelling feature located on the Review tab to check the entire presentation.
3. Ask a friend or colleague to review the presentation.
4. Display the presentation in ReadingView and read each word out loud.
5. Correct all spelling or word usage errors found.

TIP: PROOFING OPTIONS

The Spelling feature, by default, does not catch contextual errors like *to*, *too*, and *two*, but you can set the proofing options to help you find and fix this type of error. To modify the proofing options, click File and click Options. Click Proofing in the PowerPoint Options window and click Check Grammar with Spelling. With this option selected, the spelling checker will flag contextual mistakes with a red wavy underline. To correct the error, right-click the flagged word and select the proper word choice.

Use the Thesaurus

As you create and edit your presentation, you may notice that you are using one word too often, especially at the beginning of bullets. Use the Thesaurus to help you make varied word choices. Access the Thesaurus from the Proofing group on the Review tab.

Check Slide Show Elements

STEP 4 After checking the wording on the individual slides, it is helpful to view the presentation in Slide Show view to see if the elements you have incorporated are effective. Check the order of the information to make sure the content is presented in a logical order and that the layout showcases the information effectively. Make sure that the transitions and animations are working. Examine any media to make sure it supports the message.

To check the slide show elements, complete the following steps:

1. Click the Slide Show tab.
2. Click From Beginning in the Start Slide Show group.
3. Advance through each slide checking layouts, transitions, and animations.
4. End the slide show and return to Normal view.
5. Change any layouts, placeholder locations, transitions, and animations as needed.

Reorder Slides

As you review your presentation, you may realize that you need to reorder your slides. This can easily be done using Slide Sorter view.

To reorder slides, complete the following steps:

1. Click the View tab.
2. Click Slide Sorter in the Presentation Views group.
3. Select the slide you want to move and drag the slide to the new location.
4. Double-click any slide to return to Normal view.

4. Identify the three advanced planning steps you should follow before adding content to a slide show.
5. Define storyboard and describe how a storyboard aids you in creating a slide show.
6. Describe two guidelines you should follow when assessing your slide content.
7. Explain the purpose of using a presentation theme.

Hands-On Exercises

Watch the Video for this Hands-On Exercise!

MyITLab®
HOE2 Training

Skills covered: Choose a Theme • Add Presentation Content • Check Spelling • Use the Thesaurus • Check Slide Show Elements • Reorder Slides

2 Presentation Creation

To help state employees learn the process for presentation creation, you decide to give them guidelines for determining content, structuring a slide show, and assessing content. You have previously created a storyboard, and now you create the slide show to deliver these guidelines.

STEP 1 » PLAN AND PREPARE A PRESENTATION

You are creating a Training and Development presentation for the employees from a previously created storyboard. You begin by selecting a theme, and as you progress through the steps you will add and edit several slides. You begin by choosing the Retrospect theme with a specific variation color and creating the Title Slide content. Figure 20 displays the storyboard used to plan the presentation.

Storyboard

Step a: Purpose

Purpose: [X] Informative [ ] Educational [ ] Persuasive [ ] Goodwill [ ] Other

Audience: Training and Development
Location: CS 601A
Date and Time: July 1, 2019

Content	Layout	Visual Element(s)
Title Slide Creating Presentation Content	Title Slide	O Shapes O Chart O Table O WordArt O Picture O Video O Clip Art O Sound O SmartArt O ______ *Description:*
Key Point #1 Define the Audience Who is the audience: What are their needs? What are their expectations? How much do they already know? How can you help them understand?	Two Content	O Shapes O Chart O Table O WordArt X Picture O Video O Clip Art O Sound O SmartArt O ______ *Description:* People at presentation
Key Point #2 Develop the Content • Identify purpose • Research topic • Brainstorm • Create the storyboard	Title and Content	O Shapes O Chart O Table O WordArt O Picture O Video O Clip Art O Sound O SmartArt O ______ *Description:*
Key Point #3 Determine Additional Content List types of text, illustrations, and other content	Title and Content	O Shapes O Chart X Table O WordArt O Picture O Video O Clip Art O Sound O SmartArt O ______ *Description:*
Key Point #4 Edit the Content Make text concise, Use consistent verb tense, Eliminate excess adverbs and adjectives, Use few prepositions, Use strong active verbs, Keep bullets parallel	Title and Content	O Shapes O Chart O Table O WordArt O Picture O Video O Clip Art O Sound O SmartArt O ______ *Description:*
Key Point #5 Simplify the Content Make text concise, Use consistent verb tense, Eliminate excess adverbs and adjectives, Use few prepositions, Use strong active verbs, Keep bullets parallel	Title and Content	O Shapes O Chart O Table O WordArt O Picture O Video O Clip Art O Sound O SmartArt O ______ *Description:*
Summary (Restatement of Key Points, Quote, Other) Quote: The key to an effective presentation is planning ahead!	Section Header	O Shapes O Chart O Table O WordArt O Picture O Video O Clip Art O Sound O SmartArt O ______ *Description:*

Step a: Introduction slide

Step a: Summary slide

Step a: Key point slides

PowerPoint 2016, Windows 10, Microsoft Corporation

FIGURE 20 Storyboard for Creating Presentation Content Slide Show

a. Review the storyboard displayed in Figure 20. Note the purpose, introduction, key points, and summary.

b. Open PowerPoint. Select the **Retrospect theme**. Select the first theme variant, the **Orange variant**, and click **Create**.

c. Save the presentation as **p01h2Content_LastFirst**.

d. Click in the **title placeholder** on the Title Slide and type **Creating Presentation Content**.

e. Type your name in the **subtitle placeholder**.

f. Click **Notes** on the status bar. Type **Training and Development** in the Notes pane.

g. Save the presentation.

STEP 2 ›› ADD PRESENTATION CONTENT

You continue creating your presentation by adding a second slide with the Title and Content layout. After adding a title to the slide, you create a bulleted list to develop your topic. After adding the presentation content, you proofread the presentation to ensure no errors exist. Refer to Figure 21 as you complete Step 2.

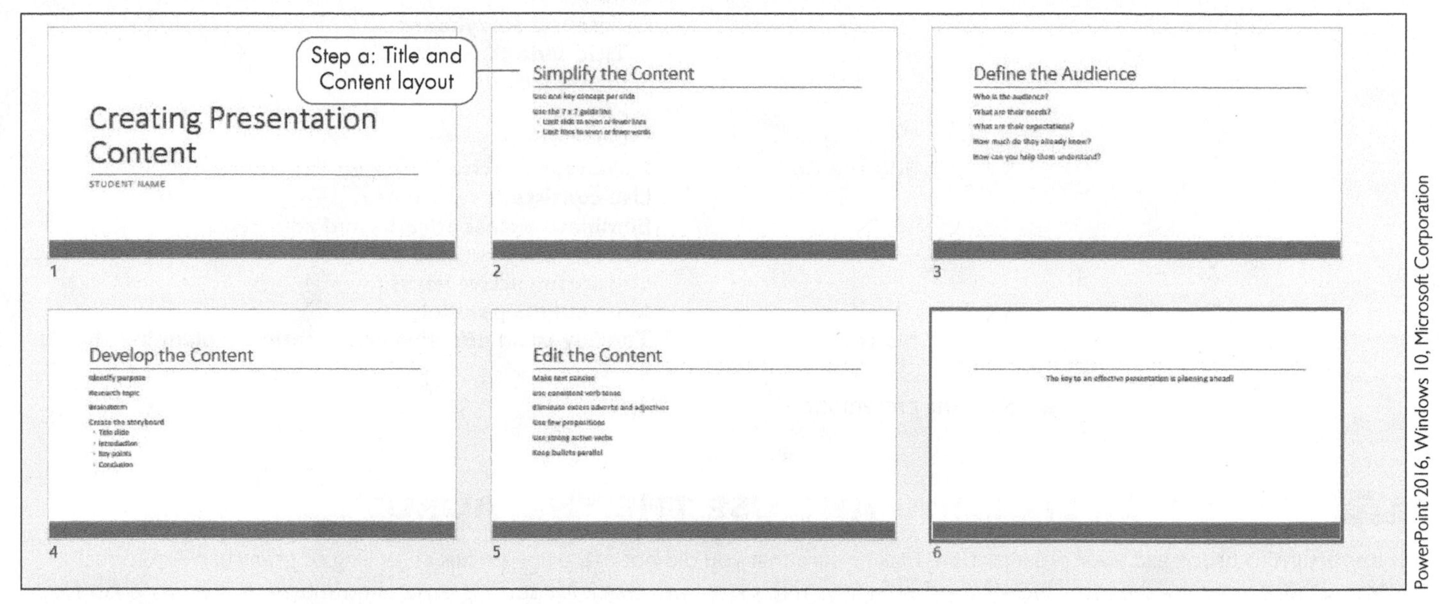

FIGURE 21 New Slides with Content in Slide Sorter View

a. Click **New Slide** in the Slides group on the Home tab.

Because you clicked the top half of New Slide, the new slide uses the Title and Content layout which is the default slide layout after a Title Slide layout. The new Slide 2 contains two placeholders: one for the title and one for body content.

b. Type **Simplify the Content** in the title placeholder.

c. Click in the **content placeholder** below the title placeholder, type **Use one main concept per slide**, and then press **Enter**.

By default, the list level is the same as the previous level. Note that the Retrospect theme does not automatically place bullets into the body of the presentation.

d. Type **Use the 7 × 7 guideline** and press **Enter**.

e. Click **Increase List Level** in the Paragraph group.

The list level indents and the font size is reduced indicating this is a subset of the main level.

f. Type **Limit slide to seven or fewer lines** and press **Enter**.

g. Type **Limit lines to seven or fewer words**. (Do not include the period.)

By default, the list level is the same as the previous level.

h. Click **New Slide** in the Slides group four times to create four more slides with the Title and Content layout.

To move between slides in the slide deck, click the thumbnail of the slide you want to edit in the Slide pane.

i. Type the following text in the appropriate slide. Use Increase List Level and Decrease List Level in the Paragraph group to change levels.

Slide	Slide Title	Content Data
3	Define the Audience	Who is the audience?
		What are their needs?
		What are their expectations?
		How much do they already know?
		How can you help them understand?
4	Develop the Content	Identify purpose
		Research topic
		Brainstorm
		Create the storyboard
		Title slide
		Introduction
		Key points
		Conclusion
5	Edit the Content	Make text concise
		Use consistent verb tense
		Eliminate excess adverbs and adjectives
		Use few prepositions
		Use strong active verbs
		Keep bullets parallel
6	No title	The key to an effective presentation is planning ahead!

j. Save the presentation.

STEP 3 » CHECK SPELLING AND USE THE THESAURUS

It is important to proofread your presentation, making sure that you did not make any errors in spelling or grammar. Additionally, it is important not to use the same words too frequently. In this step, you check for spelling errors and substitute the word *key* for the word *main*.

a. Click **Spelling** in the Proofing group on the Review tab and correct any errors. Carefully proofread each slide.

The result of the spelling check depends on how accurately you entered the text of the presentation.

b. Click **Slide 2**, use the Thesaurus to change *main* in the first bulleted point to **key** and click **Close (X)** on the Thesaurus.

c. Save the presentation.

STEP 4 » CHECK SLIDE SHOW ELEMENTS

You view the slide show and decide that the concluding statement emphasizing the importance of planning can be improved by modifying the layout of the slide. Refer to Figure 22 as you complete Step 4.

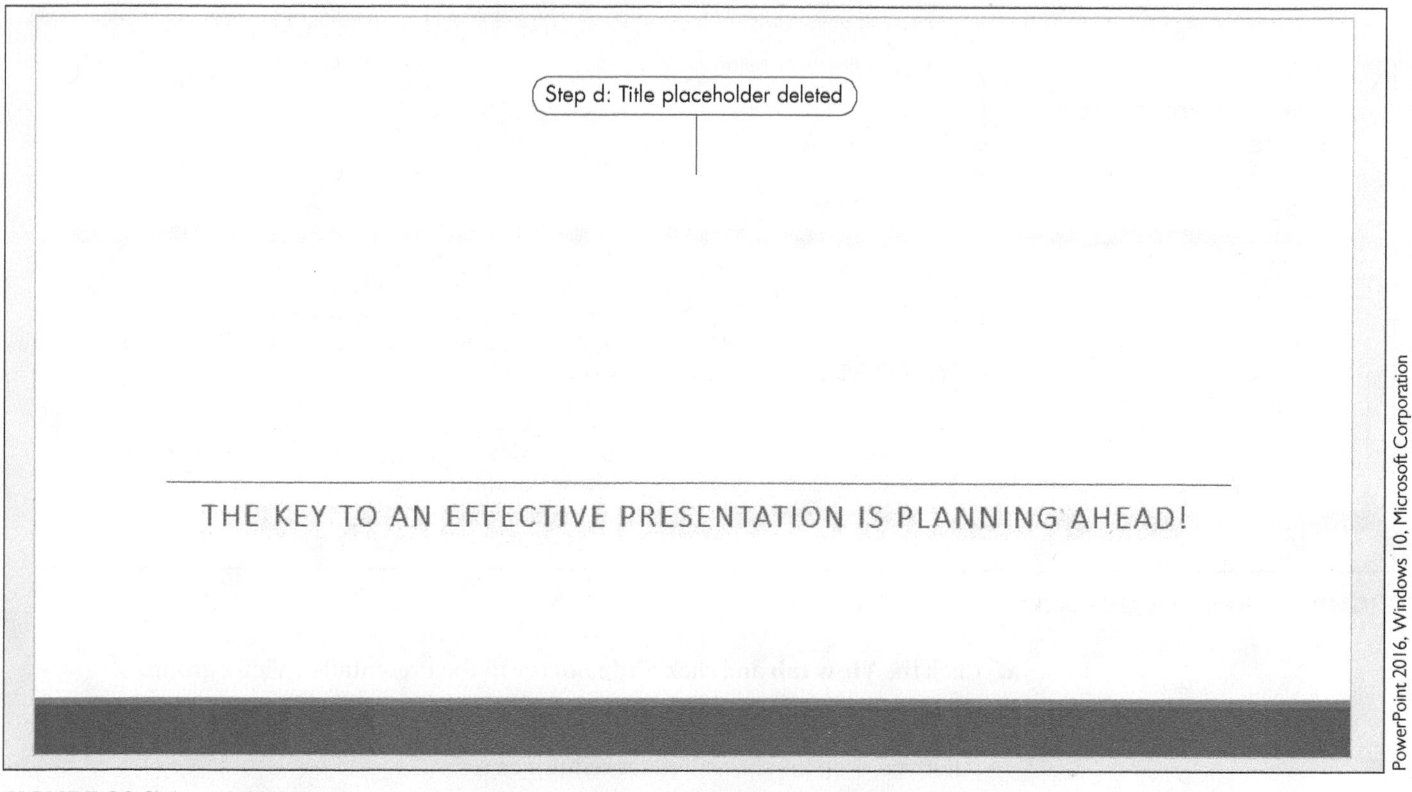

FIGURE 22 Slide with Modified Layout

a. View the presentation in Slide Show view and then return to Normal view.

b. Click the **Slide 6 thumbnail** in the Slides pane. Click the **Home tab** and click **Layout** in the Slides group.

c. Click **Section Header** from the Layout gallery.

The layout for Slide 6 changes to the Section Header layout. The Section Header layout adds emphasis to the statement on Slide 6.

d. Click the border of the title placeholder and press **Delete**.

The dotted line border becomes a solid line, which indicates the placeholder is selected. Pressing Delete removes the placeholder and the content of that placeholder. It is not necessary to delete the placeholder because empty placeholders do not display in Slide Show view, but deleting the placeholder gives you a cleaner look in Normal view.

e. Click the **subtitle placeholder** and click **Center** in the Paragraph group on the Home tab.

The layout of Slide 6 has now been modified.

f. Save the presentation.

STEP 5 » REORDER SLIDES

You notice that the slides do not follow a logical order. You change the slide positions in Slide Sorter view. Refer to Figure 23 as you complete Step 5.

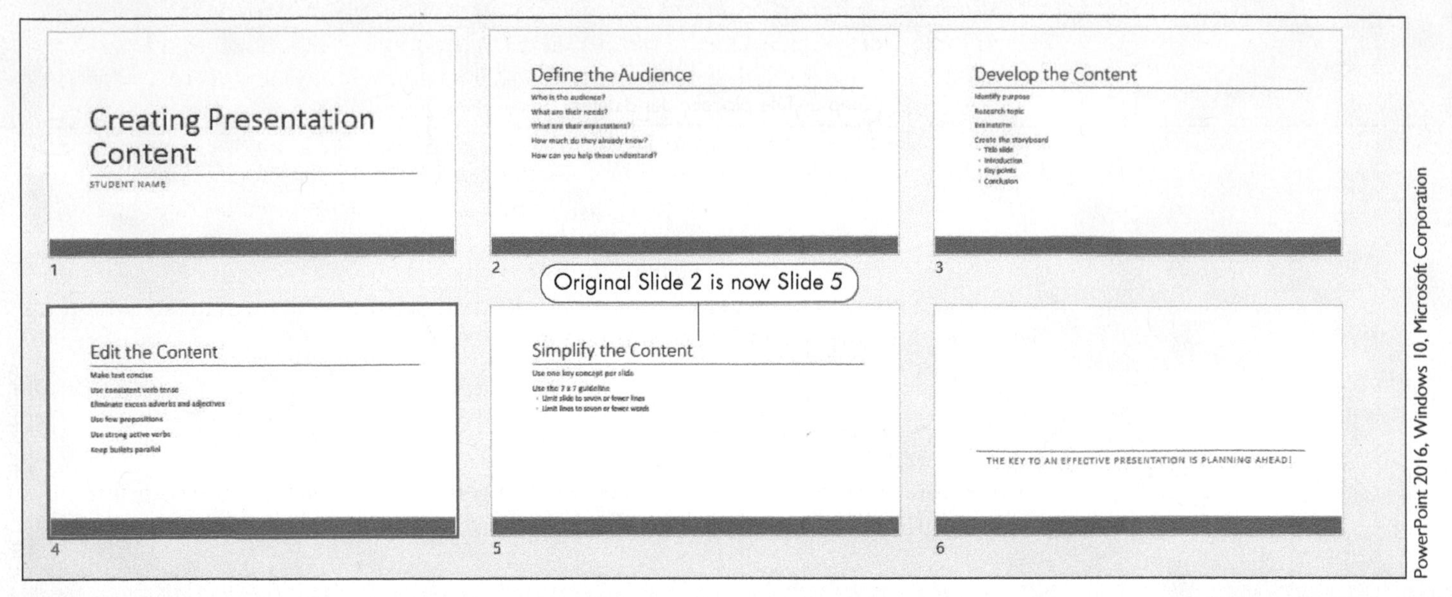

FIGURE 23 Reordered Slide Deck

a. Click the **View tab** and click **Slide Sorter** in the Presentation Views group.

b. Select **Slide 2** and drag it before the conclusion (last) slide so that it becomes Slide 5.

After you drop the slide, all slides renumber.

c. Double-click **Slide 6**.

Your presentation returns to Normal view.

d. Save the presentation. Keep the presentation open if you plan to continue with the next Hands-On Exercise. If not, close the presentation and exit PowerPoint.

Presentation Enhancement

You can strengthen your slide show by adding objects that support the message. PowerPoint enables you to include a variety of visual objects to add impact to your presentation. You can add tables, charts, and SmartArt diagrams created in PowerPoint, or you can insert objects that were created in other applications, such as a chart from Microsoft Excel or a table from Microsoft Word. You can add images, WordArt (stylized letters), sound, animated clips, and video clips to increase your presentation's impact. You can add animations and transitions to catch the audience's attention. You can also add identifying information to slides or audience handouts by adding headers and footers.

In this section, you will add a table to a slide to organize data in columns and rows. You will insert an online picture that relates to your topic and then you will move and resize the picture. You will apply transitions to control how one slide changes to another and add animations to text and pictures to add visual interest. You will finish by adding identifying information in a header and footer.

Adding a Table

STEP 1 ›› A ***table*** organizes information in columns and rows. Tables can be simple and include just a few words or images, or they can be more complex and include structured numerical data.

To create a table on a new slide, complete the following steps:

1. Create a new slide using any layout.
2. Click the Insert tab, and then click Table in the Tables group.
3. Drag over the grid to highlight the number of rows and columns that you need, and then click.
4. Type your information into the table cells.

You can also click the Insert Table icon on any slide layout that includes the icon. Figure 24 shows a table added to a slide. Once a table is created, you can resize a column or a row by positioning the pointer over the border you wish to resize and then dragging the border to the desired position.

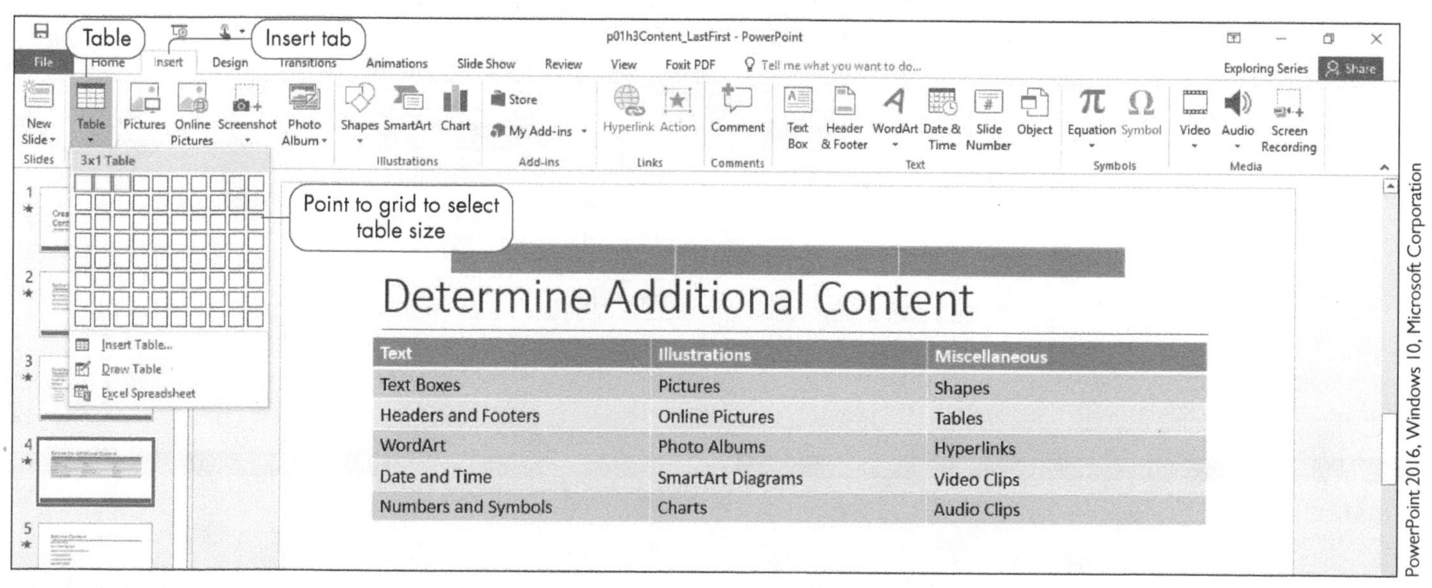

FIGURE 24 Slide with Table

TIP: MOVEMENT WITHIN A TABLE

The insertion point will show you where the text you type will appear in the table. Use the arrow keys or click anywhere in the table to move the insertion point to a new cell. You can also use the Tab key to move the insertion point. Press Tab to move to the next cell or press Shift+Tab to move to the previous cell. Pressing Ctrl+Tab inserts an indent within the cell. Pressing Tab in the last cell of a table creates a new blank row at the end of the table.

Inserting Media Objects

Adding media objects such as pictures, online pictures, audio, and/or video is especially important in PowerPoint, as PowerPoint is a visual medium. Use the Insert tab to insert media objects in any layout. The following layouts include a palette of icons you can use to quickly insert objects:

- Title and Content
- Two Content
- Comparison
- Content with Caption
- Picture with Caption

Clicking the Pictures icon in the content placeholder (or Pictures on the Insert tab) opens a dialog box you can use to browse for picture files on any computer or device to which you are connected. Clicking Online Pictures opens the Insert Pictures dialog box that enables you to search Bing images or your OneDrive account. Figure 25 displays the icons for inserting objects on the slide.

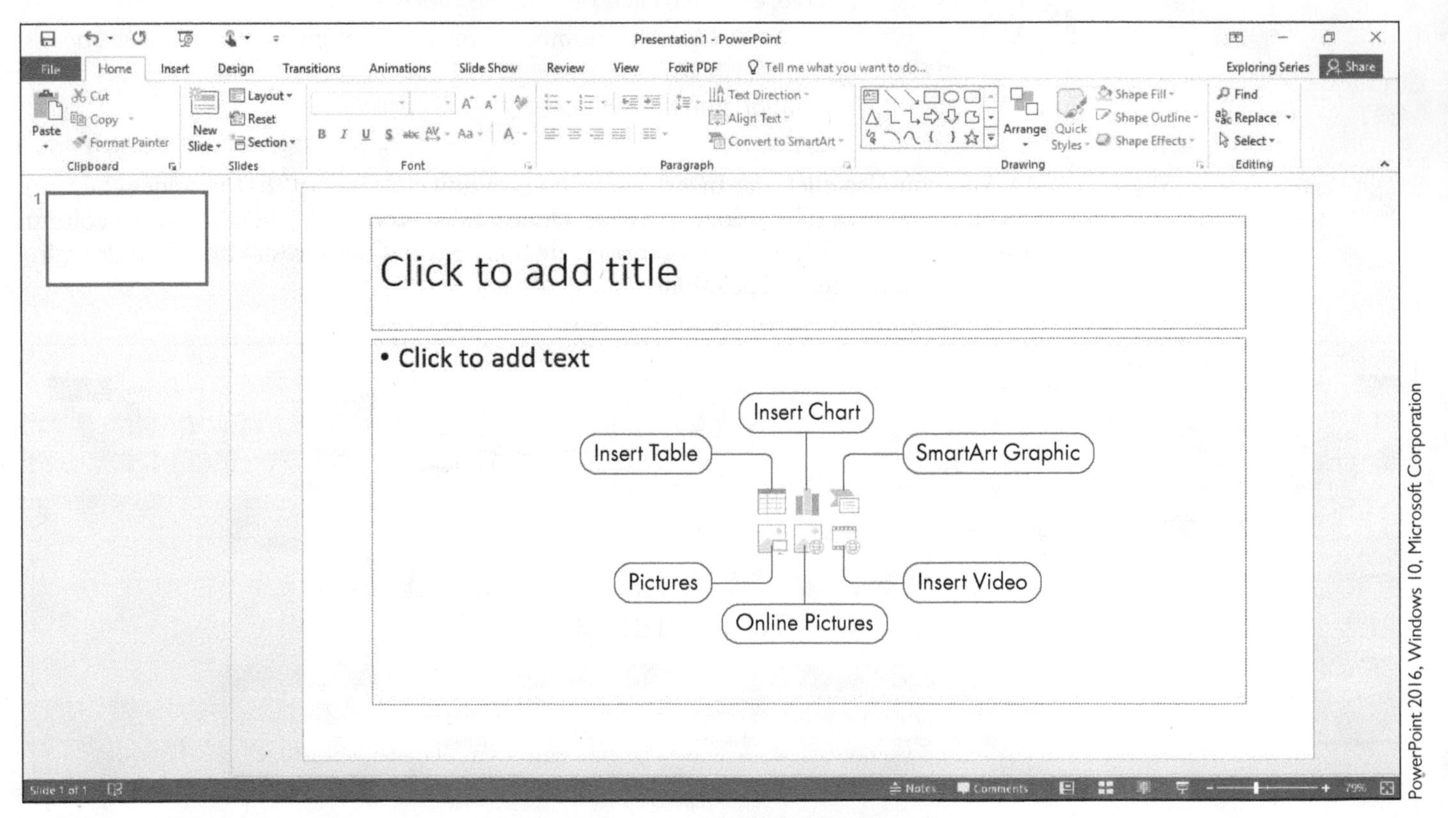

FIGURE 25 Layout Palette Icons

Applying Transitions and Animations

A ***transition*** is a visual effect that takes place when one slide is replaced by another slide while the presentation is displayed in Slide Show view or Reading View. An ***animation*** is motion that you can apply to text and objects. Animating text and objects can help focus attention on an important point, control the flow of information on a slide, and help you keep the audience's attention.

Apply Transitions

STEP 3 A transition is a specific type of animation that is used to provide visual interest as a slide is replaced by another slide. You can select from the basic transitions displayed on the Ribbon, or from the Transition gallery available in the Transition to This Slide group on the Transitions tab. You can control whether the transition applies to all the slides or just the current slide. Figure 26 displays the Transition gallery.

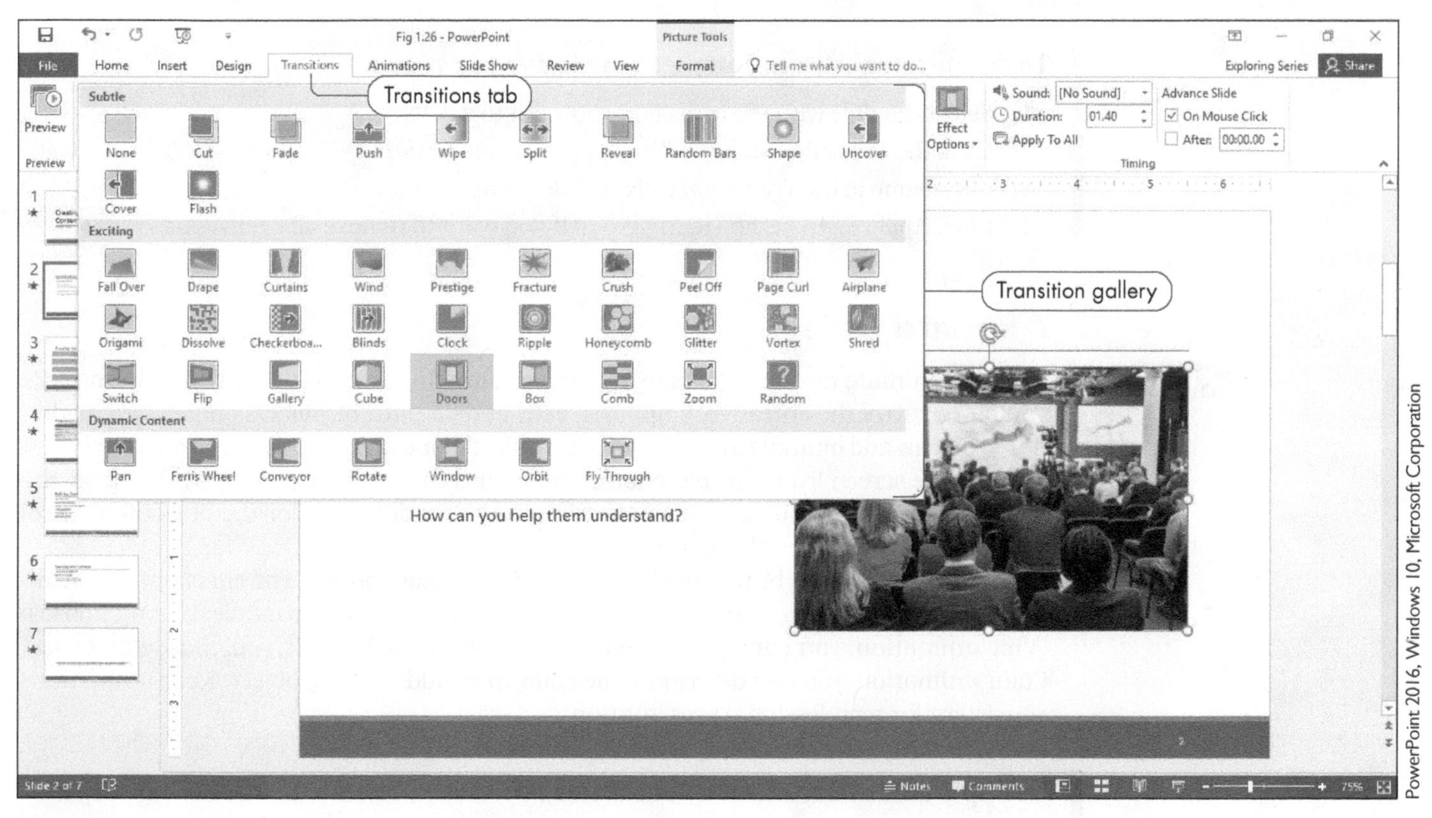

FIGURE 26 Transition Gallery

To apply a transition to a slide, complete the following steps:

1. Select the slide to which you want to add a transition.
2. Click the Transitions tab.
3. Click the More button in the Transition to This Slide group.
4. Select a transition from one of the following groups: Subtle, Exciting, and Dynamic Content.
5. Click Preview to see the transition applied to the slide.

TIP: SLIDE SORTER VIEW AND TRANSITIONS

Transition effects and transition effect options can also be applied from Slide Sorter view. Applying transitions in Slide Sorter view is helpful when you want to apply the same transition to multiple slides. To select multiple contiguous slides, press and hold the Shift key, click the first slide you want to select, and then click the last. To select multiple non-contiguous slides, press and hold the Ctrl key and then click each of the slides you want to include.

After you choose a transition effect, you can select a sound to play when the transition occurs. You can choose the duration of the transition in seconds, which controls how quickly the transition takes place. The sound can be added by choosing an option in the Sound menu found in the Timing group on the Transitions tab.

Another determination you must make is how you want to start the transition process. Use the Advance Slide options in the Timing group to determine whether you want to manually click or press a key to advance to the next slide, or you want the slide to automatically advance after a specified number of seconds. You can set the number of seconds for the slide to display in the same area.

To delete a transition, complete the following steps:

1. Select the slide with the transition you want to delete.
2. Click the Transitions tab.
3. Click None in the Transition to This Slide group.
4. Click Apply to All in the Timing group if you want to remove all transitions.

Animate Objects

STEP 4 You can animate text or objects using an assortment of animations. Using animation, you can control the entrance, emphasis, exit, and/or path of objects on a slide. In addition, you can add multiple animations to an object. For example, you could have an object fly onto the screen from the left, change color, and then exit the screen by flying off the screen to the right. You can even create your own motion path for the object to control the pattern it follows on the screen.

An animation can be modified by changing its effect options. The effect options available for animations are determined by the animation type. For example, if you choose a Wipe animation, you can determine the direction of the wipe. If you choose an Object Color animation, you can determine the color to be added to the object. Keep animations consistent for a professional presentation.

To apply an animation to text or other objects, complete the following steps:

1. Select the object you want to animate.
2. Click the Animations tab.
3. Click More in the Animation group to display the Animation gallery.
4. Select the animation type.
5. Click Effect Options to display any available options related to the selected animation type.

The slide in Figure 27 shows an animation effect added to a quote and an attribution. A tag with the number 1 is attached to the quote to show that it will run first. The attribution has a number 2 to show that it will play after the first animation. The Fly In animation in the gallery is shaded pink to show that it is the selected animation. Click Preview in the Preview group to see all animations on the slide play. You can also see the animations play in Reading View and in Slide Show view. Slides that include an animation display a star icon beneath the slide when viewed in Slide Sorter view or the Slides tab in Normal view.

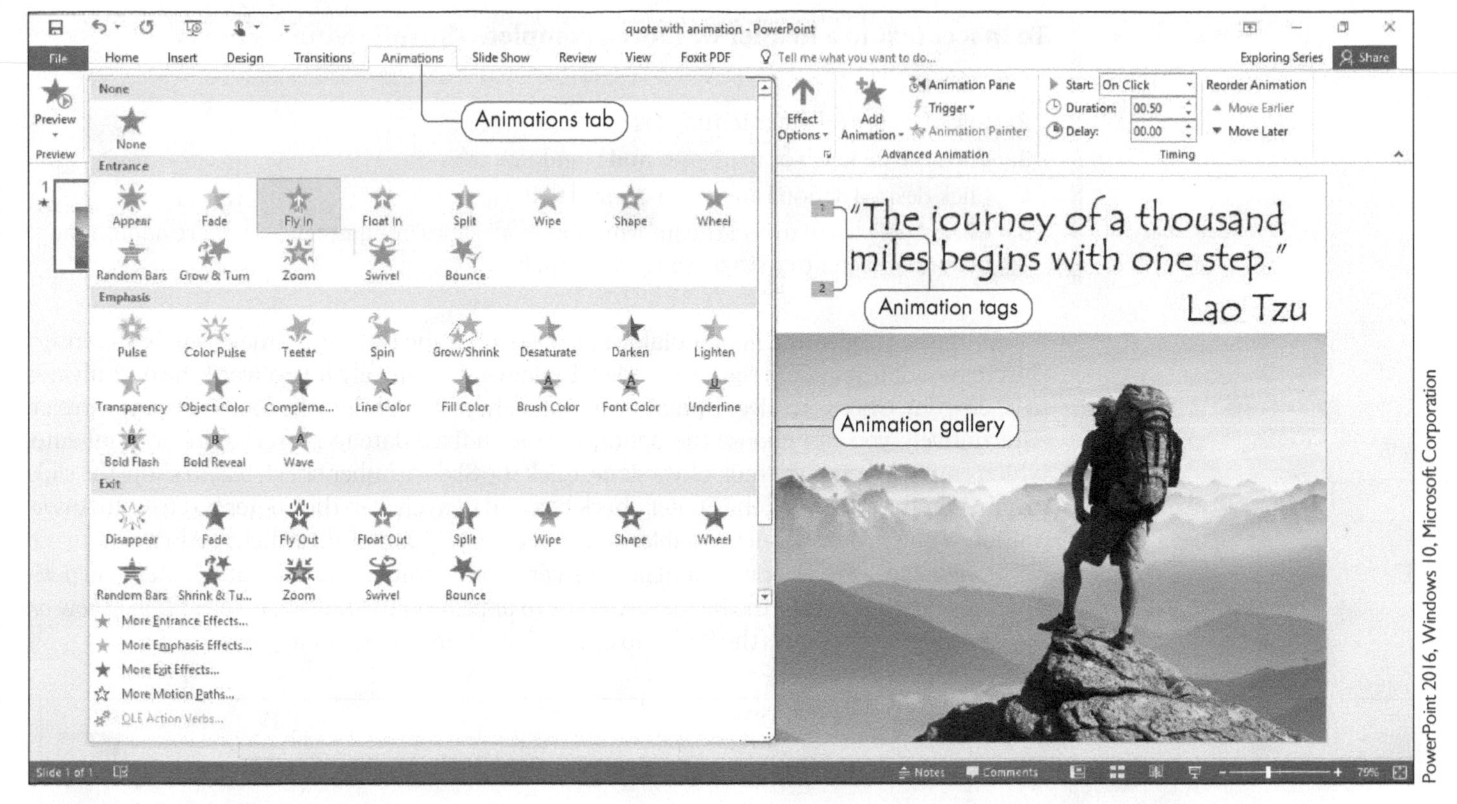

FIGURE 27 Animation Gallery

PowerPoint's Animation Painter feature enables you to copy an animation from one object to another. Animation Painter picks up the animation from the first object and applies it to the second on the same slide or a different slide.

To apply an animation to text or other objects, complete the following steps:

1. Select the object that has the animation effect you want to copy to another object.
2. Click Animation Painter in the advanced Animation group on the Animations tab.
3. Click the text or object to which you want to apply the animation.

TIP: EFFECTIVELY ADDING TRANSITIONS, ANIMATIONS, AND SOUND

When you select transitions, sounds, and animations, remember that too many sounds, transitions, and animations can be distracting. The audience will be wondering what is coming next rather than paying attention to your message. The speed of the transition is important, too—very slow transitions will lose the interest of your audience. Too many sound clips can be annoying. Consider whether you need to have the sound of applause with the transition of every slide. Is a typewriter sound necessary to keep your audience's attention, or will it grate on their nerves if it is used on every word? Ask someone to review your presentation and let you know of any annoying or jarring elements.

Inserting a Header or Footer

STEP 5 » The date of the presentation, the presentation audience, a logo, a company name, and other identifying information are very valuable, and you may want such information to appear on every slide, handout, or notes page. Use the Header and Footer feature to do this. The header generally appears at the top of pages in a handout or on a notes page, while a footer generally appears at the bottom of slides in a presentation or at the bottom of pages in a handout or on a notes page. Because the theme controls the placement of the header/footer elements, you may find headers and footers in various locations on the slide.

To insert text in a header or footer, complete the following steps:

1. Click the Insert tab.
2. Click Header & Footer in the Text group.
3. Click the Slide tab or the Notes and Handouts tab.
4. Click desired options and enter desired text.
5. Click Apply to All to add the information to all slides or pages, or if you are adding the header or footer to a single slide, click Apply.

With the Header and Footer dialog box open, click the Date and time check box to insert the current date and time signature. Click Update automatically if you want the date always to be current. Once you select Update automatically, you can select the date format you prefer. Alternatively, you can choose the option to enter a fixed date to preserve the original date, which can help you keep track of versions. Click the Slide number check box to show the slide number on the slide. Click the Footer check box and then click in the Footer box to enter information. The Preview window enables you to see the position of these fields. Always note the position of the fields, as PowerPoint layouts vary considerably in header and footer field positions. If you do not want the header or footer to appear on the title slide, select *Don't show on title slide.* Figure 28 shows the Slide tab of the Header and Footer dialog box.

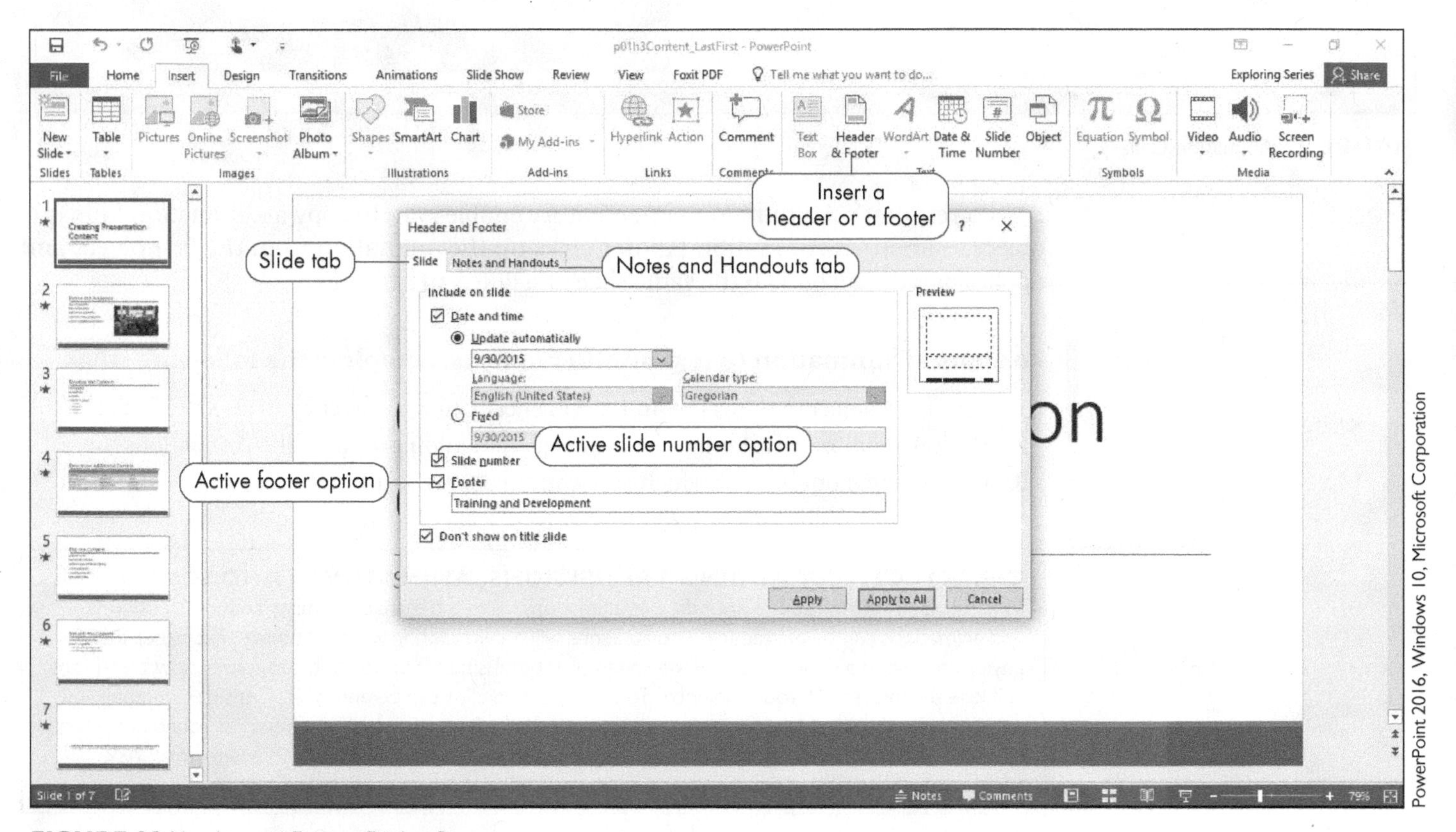

FIGURE 28 Header and Footer Dialog Box

The Notes and Handouts tab contains the same date/time options as the Slide tab, but it also gives you an option for a header. As you activate the fields, the Preview window shows the location of the fields. The header field is located in the upper-left corner of the printout. The date and time are located on the upper-right. The footer field is on the lower-left and the page number is located on the lower-right.

8. Explain why adding media objects to a PowerPoint slide show is important.
9. How does a table organize information?
10. Describe three benefits that can occur when objects are animated in a slide show.
11. Give an example of when you would use the Update automatically option in the Header and Footer feature. When would you use the Fixed date option?

Hands-On Exercises

Watch the Video
for this Hands-On
Exercise!

MyITLab®
HOE3 Training

Skills covered: Add a Table • Insert Media Objects • Apply Transitions • Animate Objects • Insert a Footer

3 Presentation Enhancement

You decide to strengthen the slide show by adding a table and an online picture that will help state employees stay interested in the presentation and retain the information longer. You insert a table, add a picture, apply a transition, and animate the picture you have included. Finally, you create a slide footer and a Notes and Handouts header and footer.

STEP 1 ›› ADD A TABLE

To organize the list of objects that can be added to a PowerPoint slide, you create a table on a new slide. Listing these objects as bullets would take far more space than a table takes. Refer to Figure 29 as you complete Step 1.

Step e: 3 columns

Determine Additional Content

Text	Illustrations	Miscellaneous
Text Boxes	Pictures	Shapes
Headers and Footers	Online Pictures	Tables
WordArt	Photo Albums	Hyperlinks
Date and Time	SmartArt Diagrams	Video Clips
Numbers and Symbols	Charts	Audio Clips

Step e: 6 rows

TRAINING AND DEVELOPMENT 4

PowerPoint 2016, Windows 10, Microsoft Corporation

FIGURE 29 PowerPoint Table

a. Open *p01h2Content_LastFirst* if you closed it after the last Hands-On Exercise and save it as **p01h3Content_LastFirst**, changing h2 to h3.

b. Click **Slide 5** and click **New Slide** in the Slides group.

A new slide with the Title and Content layout is inserted after Slide 5.

c. Click the **title placeholder** and type **Determine Additional Content**.

d. Click **Insert Table** in the content placeholder in the center of the slide.

The Insert Table dialog box opens.

e. Set the number of columns to **3** and the number of rows to **6** and click **OK**.

PowerPoint creates the table and positions it on the slide. The first row is formatted differently from the other rows so that it can be used for column headings.

f. Type **Text** in the upper-left cell of the table. Press **Tab** to move to the next cell and type **Illustrations**. Press **Tab**, type **Miscellaneous**, and then press **Tab** to move to the next row.

g. Type the following text in the remaining table cells, pressing **Tab** after each entry.

Text Boxes	**Pictures**	**Shapes**
Headers and Footers	**Online Pictures**	**Tables**
WordArt	**Photo Albums**	**Hyperlinks**
Date and Time	**SmartArt Diagrams**	**Video Clips**
Numbers and Symbols	**Charts**	**Audio Clips**

h. Save the presentation.

STEP 2 ›› INSERT MEDIA OBJECTS

In this step, you insert a picture and then resize it to better fit the slide. The picture you insert relates to the topic and adds visual interest. Refer to Figure 30 as you complete Step 2.

FIGURE 30 Online Picture Inserted

a. Display **Slide 2**, click **Layout** in the Slides group on the Home tab, and then click the **Two Content layout**.

Changing the layout for this slide will better accommodate the photo you will add in the next step.

b. Click the **Pictures icon** in the right content placeholder, navigate to the folder containing your student data files, and then select *p01h3Audience*. Refer to Figure 30 for a sample image. Click **Insert**.

c. Save the presentation.

APPLY TRANSITIONS

To add motion when one slide changes into another, you apply a transition to all slides in the presentation. You select a transition that is not distracting but that adds emphasis to the slide show. You will also include a sound as the transition occurs. Refer to Figure 31 as you complete Step 3.

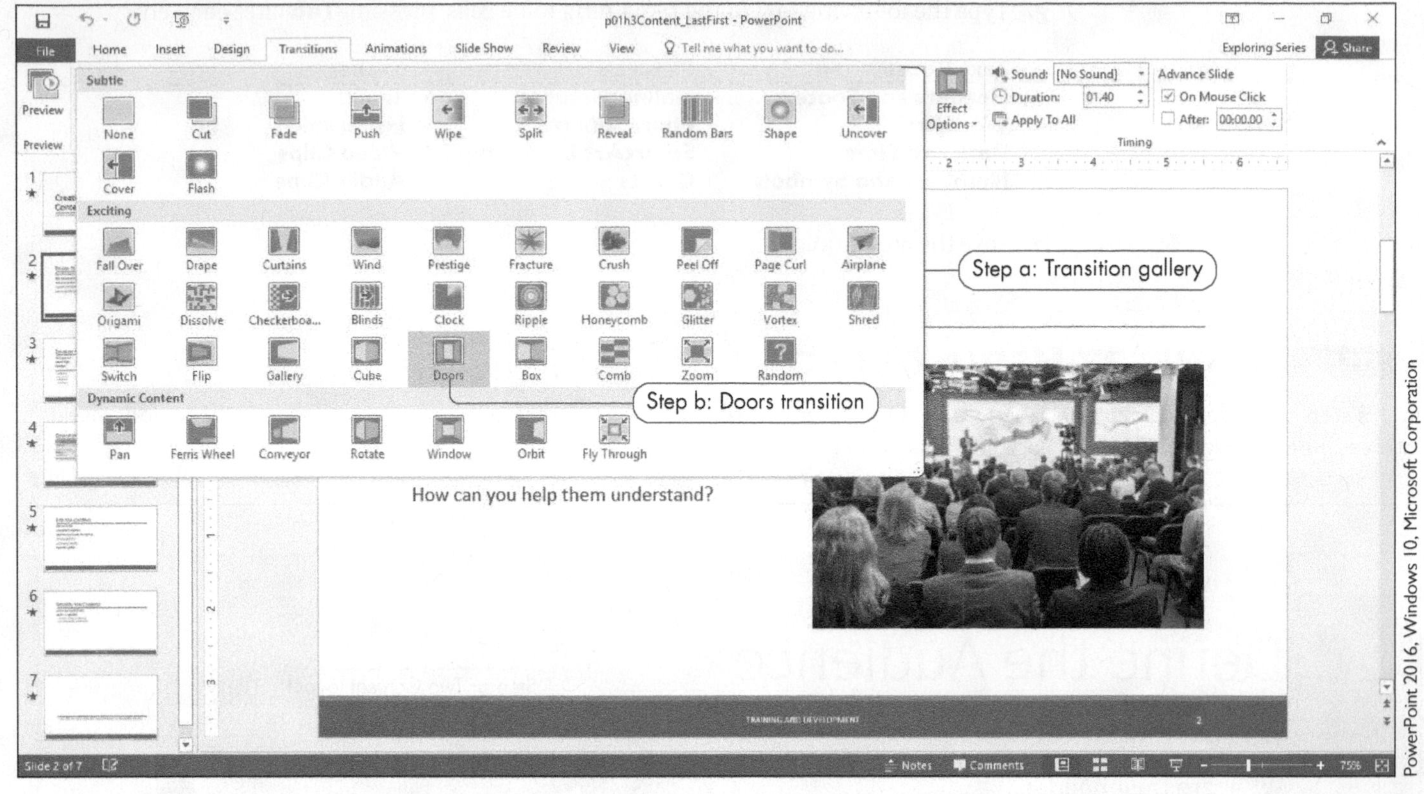

FIGURE 31 Transition Gallery

a. Click the **Transitions tab** and click **More** in the Transition to This Slide group.

The Transition gallery displays.

b. Click **Doors** under Exciting.

c. Click **Apply to All** in the Timing group.

The transition effect will apply to all of the slides in the presentation. Notice that a star has been added next to the thumbnail of each slide where a transition has been applied.

d. Select the **Slide 1 thumbnail**, click the **Sound arrow** in the Timing group, and then select **Push**.

The Push sound will play as Slide 1 enters when in Slide Show view.

e. Click **Preview**.

The Transition effect will play along with the sound for the first slide.

> **TROUBLESHOOTING:** If you are completing this activity in a classroom lab, you may need to plug in headphones or turn on speakers to hear the sound.

f. Save the presentation.

STEP 4 » ANIMATE AN OBJECT

You add animation to your slide show by controlling how individual objects such as lines of text or images enter or exit the slides. Refer to Figure 32 as you complete Step 4.

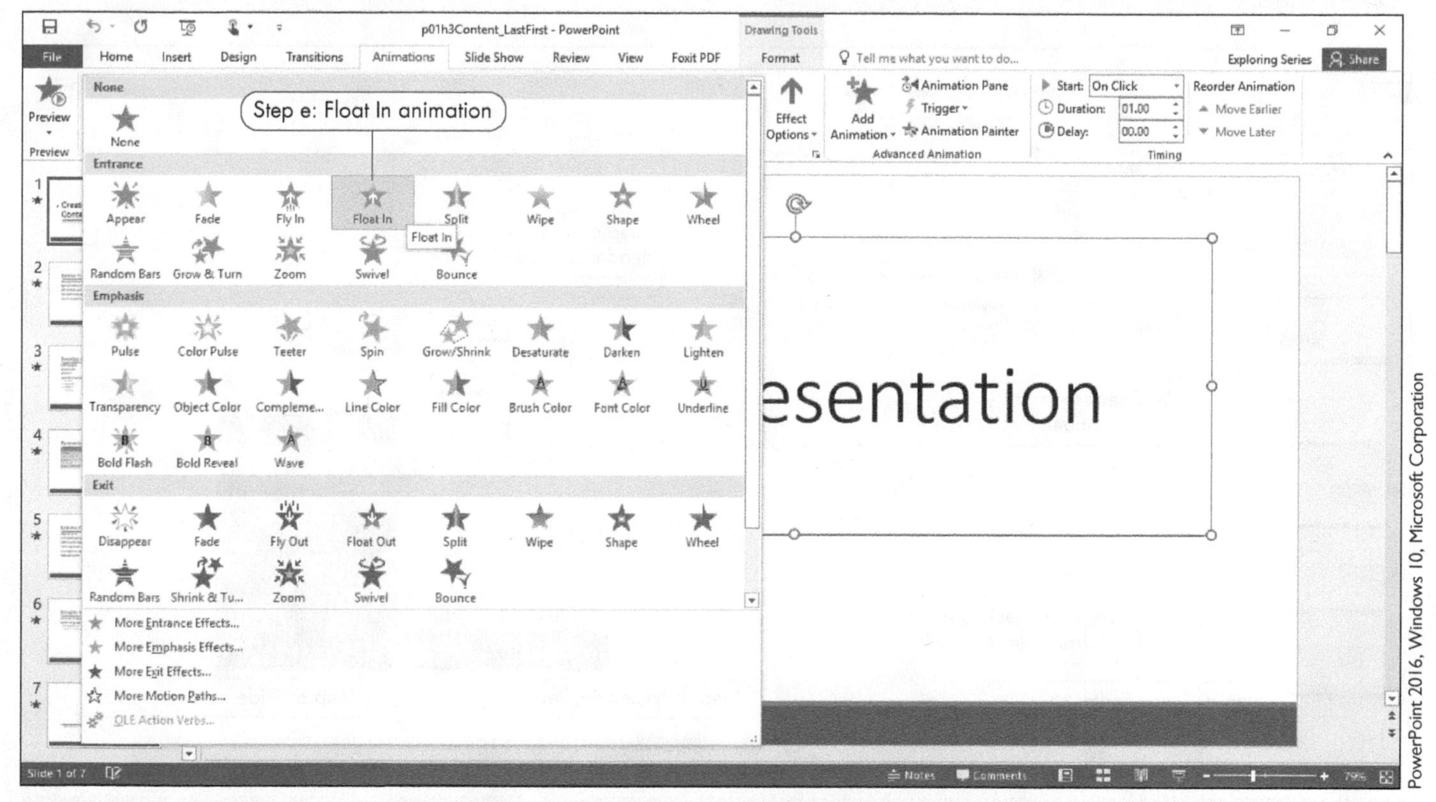

FIGURE 32 Title Placeholder with Animation

a. Select the **title placeholder** on Slide 1.

b. Click the **Animations tab** and click **More** in the Animation group.

c. Click **Float In** (under Entrance).

The Float In animation is applied to the title placeholder.

d. Select the **picture** on Slide 2.

You decide to apply and modify the Zoom animation and change the animation speed.

e. Click **More** in the Animation group and click **Zoom** (under Entrance).

f. Click **Effect Options** in the Animation group and select **Slide Center**.

The picture now grows and zooms from the center of the slide.

g. Save the presentation.

STEP 5 ›› CREATE A HANDOUT FOOTER

Because you are creating this presentation for the Training and Development department, you include this identifying information in a slide footer. You also decide to include your personal information in a Notes and Handouts header and footer. Refer to Figure 33 as you complete Step 5.

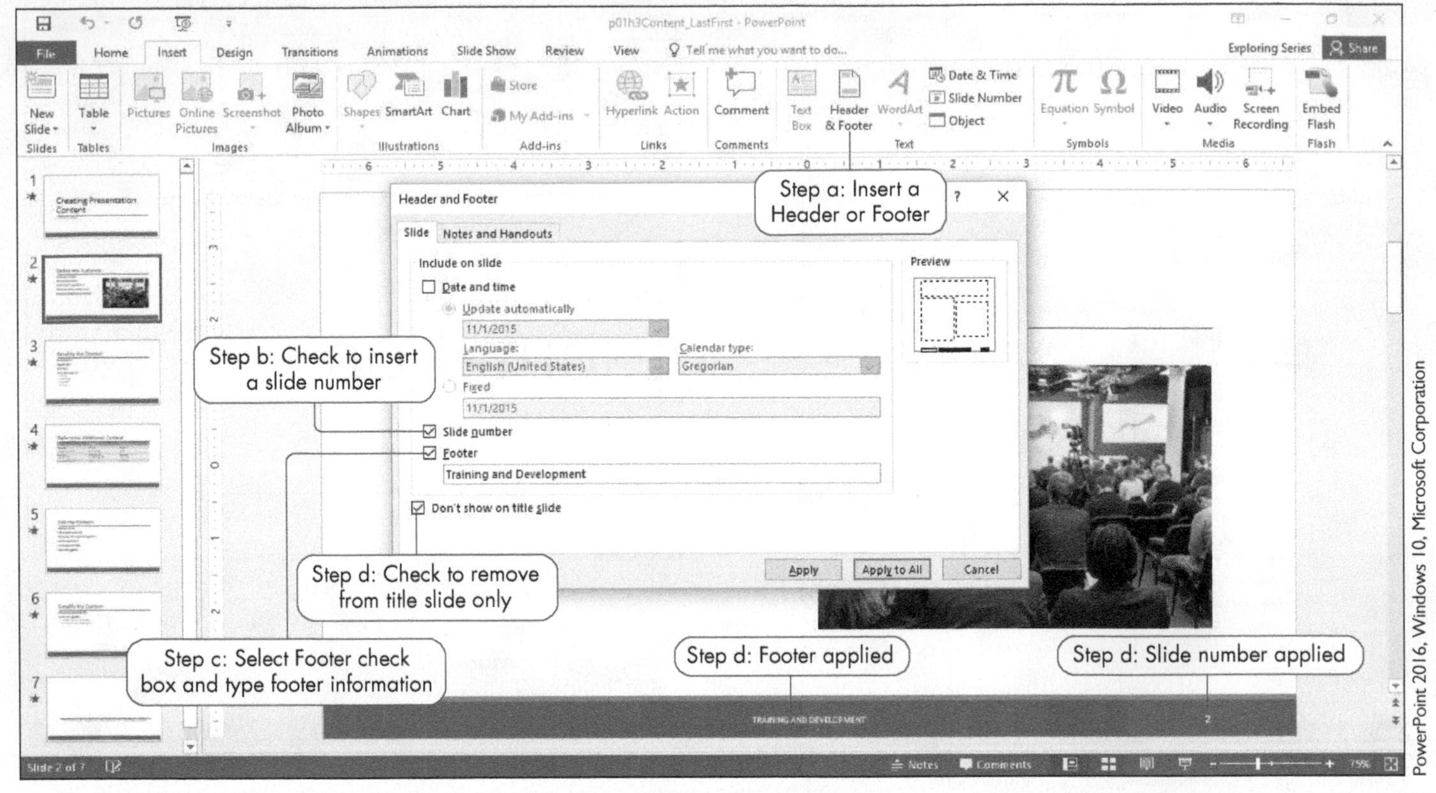

FIGURE 33 Slide Footer

a. Click the **Insert tab** and click **Header & Footer** in the Text group.

The Header and Footer dialog box opens, with the Slide tab active.

b. Click **Slide number check box** to select it.

The slide number will now appear on each slide. Note the position of the slide number in the Preview window: lower-right corner of the slide. The theme determined the position of the slide number.

c. Click the **Footer check box** to select it and type **Training and Development**.

Training and Development will appear on each slide. Note the position of the footer in the Preview window: bottom center of the slide.

d. Click the **Don't show on title slide** check box to select it and click **Apply to All**.

The slide footer and page number appear on all slides except the title slide.

e. Save the presentation. Keep the presentation open if you plan to continue with the next Hands-On Exercise. If not, close the presentation and exit PowerPoint.

Navigation and Printing

In the beginning of this chapter, you opened a slide show and advanced one by one through the slides by clicking the mouse. Audiences may ask questions that can be answered by going to another slide in the presentation. As you respond to the questions, you may find yourself jumping back to a previous slide or moving forward to a future slide. You may even find that during your presentation you wish to direct your audience's attention to a single area of a slide. PowerPoint's navigation options enable you to maneuver through a presentation easily.

To help your audience follow your presentation, you can choose to provide them with a handout. Various options are available for audience handouts. Be aware of the options, and choose the one that best suits your audience's needs. You may distribute handouts at the beginning of your presentation for note taking or provide your audience with the notes afterward.

In this section, you will run a slide show and navigate within the show. You will practice a variety of methods for advancing to new slides or returning to previously viewed slides. You will annotate a slide during a presentation and will change from screen view to black-screen view. Finally, you will print handouts of the slide show.

Navigating a Slide Show

STEP 1 »» PowerPoint provides multiple methods to advance through the slide show. You can also go back to a previous slide or jump to a specific slide, if needed. Use Table 2 to identify navigation options, and then experiment with each navigation method. Find the method that you are most comfortable using and stay with that method.

TABLE 2 Navigation Options

Navigation Option	Mouse	Keyboard	On-Screen
Advance to next slide or animation	Left-click	Press spacebar Press Page Down Press N Press down or right arrow Press Enter	Click right arrow
Return to previous slide or animation	Right-click, choose Previous	Press Backspace Press Page Up Press P Press up or left arrow	Click left arrow
End slide show	Right-click, choose End Show	Press Esc Press Ctrl+Break	Click ... , choose End Show
Go to specific slide	Right-click, click See All Slides, click slide	Type slide number, press Enter	Click <art> select slide.
Zoom in	Right-click, click Zoom In, move pointer to highlight area, click	+ or Ctrl ++	Click Magnifying glass icon, move pointer to highlight area, click
Zoom out	Right-click	Press Esc	

> **TIP: SLIDE SHOW CONTROLS**
> While displaying a slide show, point at the lower-left corner of a slide to display controls for navigating through the show. In addition to these controls, you can also press F1 at any time during your presentation to see a list of slide show controls. Familiarize yourself with these controls before you present to a group.

The See All Slides command displays all of your slides so you can easily identify and select the slide to which you want to go. You can access the See All Slides command in the navigation controls on the lower-left corner of the screen. Once you see all of the slides, you can click the slide of your choice.

To move to a specific slide on the screen using the See All Slides command, complete the following steps:

1. Right-click a slide while in Slide Show view.
2. Click See All Slides.
3. Click the slide you want to display.

If an audience member asks you a question that is best explained by a chart or diagram you have on a slide in your presentation, you can zoom in on a single section of the slide to answer the question. Figure 34 displays a slide in Slide Show view with an area highlighted for zooming on the left and a slide with the zoomed area on the right.

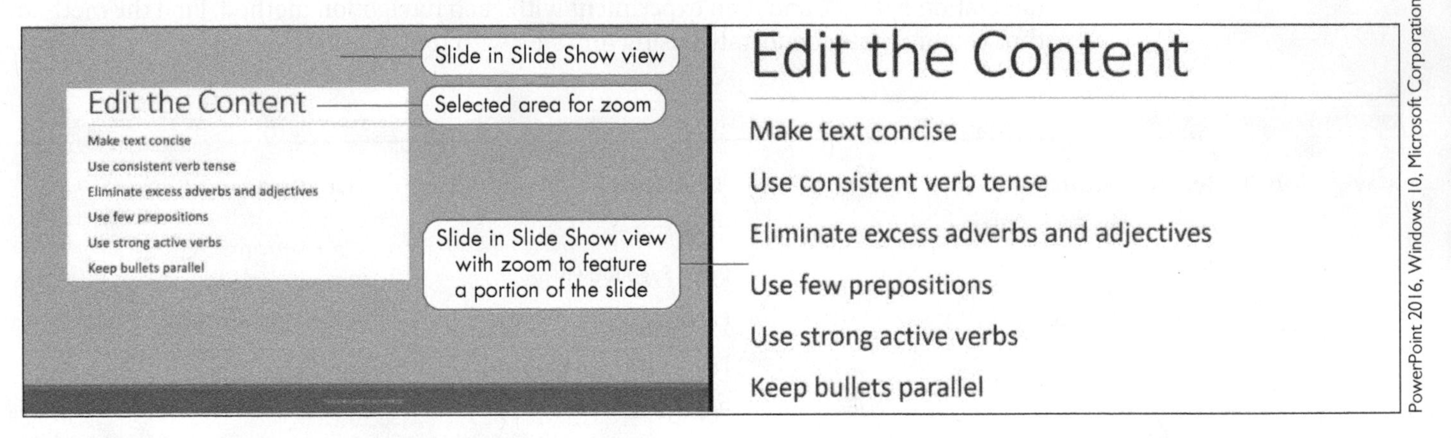

FIGURE 34 Zoom to Emphasize Part of a Slide

To enlarge a section of a slide on the screen, complete the following steps:

1. Navigate to the slide.
2. Point to the lower-left side of the screen to display the navigation controls.
3. Click the magnifying glass icon in the navigation controls on the lower-left corner. This will display a highlighted rectangular area on your slide.
4. Move the rectangular box over the area of the slide you want to emphasize. (Figure 34 shows the rectangular box.)
5. Click Esc to return to Normal view.

After the last slide in your slide show displays, the audience sees a black slide. This slide has two purposes: It enables you to end your show without having your audience see the PowerPoint design screen, and it cues the audience to expect the room lights to brighten. If you need to blacken the screen at any time during your presentation, you can press B. (If you blacken the screen in a darkened room, you must be prepared to quickly brighten some lights.) When you are ready to start your slide show again, simply press B again.

If you prefer bringing up a white screen, press W. White is much harsher on your audience's eyes, however. Only use white if you are in an extremely bright room. Whether using black or white, you are enabling the audience to concentrate on you, the speaker, without the slide show interfering.

Annotate the Slide Show

STEP 2 You may find it helpful to add ***annotations*** (notes or drawings) to your slides during a presentation. You can draw directly on your slide using the Pen tool. You can underline or circle words to call attention to them, draw an arrow to an object, or draw a simple illustration.

To add annotations, complete the following steps:

1. Point to the lower-left side of the slide to display the slide show controls.
2. Click the Pen tool to display the options for annotating a slide, or right-click a slide in Slide Show view.
3. Point to Pointer Options.
4. Click Pen or Highlighter.
5. Press and hold the left mouse button and write or draw on the screen.

To change the ink color for the Pen or Highlighter, complete the following steps:

1. Right-click on a slide to display the shortcut menu.
2. Point to Pointer Options.
3. Click Ink Color.
4. Click the color of your choice.

To erase what you have drawn, press E. With each slide, you must again activate the drawing pointer, in order to avoid accidentally drawing on your slides. The annotations you create are not permanent unless you save the annotations when exiting the slide show and then save the changes upon exiting the file. You may want to save the annotated file with a different file name from the original presentation so that you have both versions of the presentation.

Rather than annotate a slide, you may simply want to point to a specific section of the screen. The laser pointer feature enables you to do this.

To use the laser pointer, complete the following steps:

1. Right-click a slide in Slide Show view.
2. Point to Pointer Options.
3. Click Laser Pointer.
4. Move the pointer to the desired position.
5. Press Esc to end the laser pointer.

TIP: ANNOTATING SHORTCUTS

Press Ctrl+P to change the pointer to a drawing pointer while presenting, and click and draw on the slide, much the same way your favorite football announcer diagrams a play. Use Page Down and Page Up to move forward and backward in the presentation while the annotation is in effect. Press Ctrl+A to return the pointer to an arrow.

Printing in PowerPoint

A printed copy of a PowerPoint slide show can be used to display speaker notes for reference during the presentation, for audience handouts or a study guide, or as a means to deliver the presentation if there were an equipment failure. A printout of a single slide with text on it can be used as a poster or banner. Figure 35 shows the print options. Depending on your printer and printer settings, the names may vary.

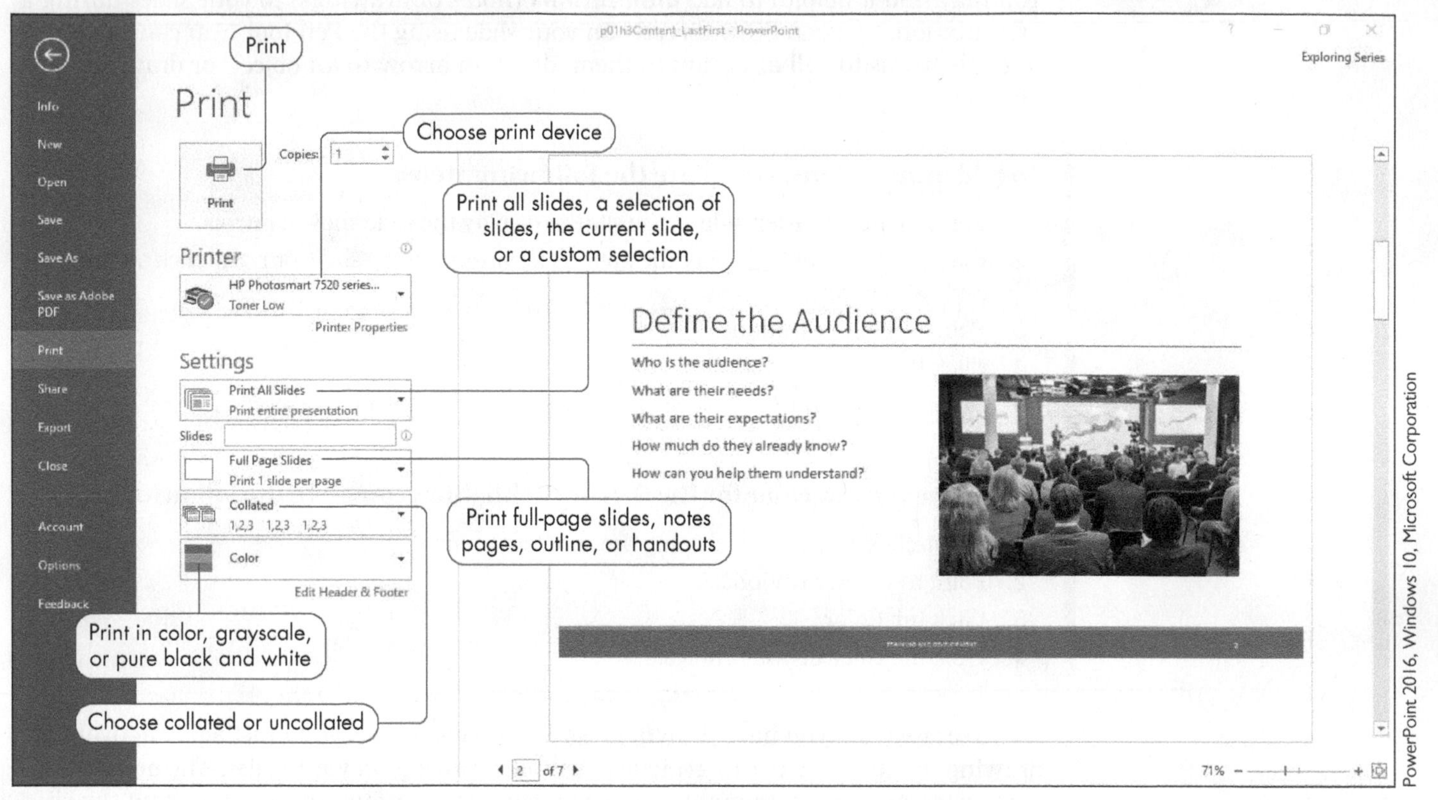

FIGURE 35 Print Options

To print a copy of the slide show using the default PowerPoint settings, complete the following steps:

1. Click the File tab and click Print.
2. Click the currently displayed printer to choose the print device you want to use.
3. Click Print All Slides and then select one of the options for the print area or for a custom range.
4. Click Full Page Slides to select the layout of the printout.
5. Click to select Collated or Uncollated.
6. Click Color to select Color, Grayscale, or Pure Black and White.
7. Click Print.

Print Full Page Slides

Use the Full Page Slides option to print the slides for use as a backup or when the slides contain a great deal of detail the audience needs to examine. You will be grateful for the backup if your projector bulb blows out or if your computer quits working during a presentation.

If you are printing the slides on paper smaller than the standard size, be sure to change the slide size and orientation before you print. By default, PowerPoint sets the slides for landscape orientation for printing so that the width is greater than the height (11" × 8 1/2"). If you are going to print a flyer or overhead transparency, however, you need to set PowerPoint to portrait orientation, to print so that the height is greater than the width (8 1/2" × 11").

To change your slide orientation, complete the following steps:

1. Click the Design tab.
2. Click Slide Size in the Customize group.
3. Click Customize Slide Size.
4. Click Portrait or Landscape in the Slides sized for section. You can also change the size of the slide as well as the orientation in this dialog box. If you want to create a custom size of paper to print, enter the height and width.

When you click Full Page Slides, several print options become available:

- Frame Slides: puts a black border around the slides in the printout, giving the printout a more polished appearance.
- Scale to Fit Paper: ensures that each slide prints on one page even if you have selected a custom size for your slide show, or if you have set up the slide show so that it is larger than the paper on which you are printing.
- High Quality: ensures that the shadows print if you have applied shadows to text or objects.
- Print Comments and Ink Markup: prints any comments or annotations; this option is active only if you have used added annotations to the slides.

After you click the File tab and click Print, you can determine the color option with which to print.

- Color: prints your presentation in color if you have a color printer or grayscale if you are printing on a black-and-white printer.
- Grayscale: prints in shades of gray, but be aware that backgrounds do not print when using the Grayscale option. By not printing the background, you make the text in the printout easier to read and you save ink or toner.
- Pure Black and White: prints in black and white only, with no gray color.

Print Handouts

STEP 3 ›› The principal purpose for printing handouts is to give your audience something they can use to follow and take notes on during the presentation. With your handout and their notes, the audience has an excellent resource for the future. Handouts can be printed with one, two, three, four, six, or nine slides per page. Printing three slides per page is a popular option because it places thumbnails of the slides on the left side of the printout and lines on which the audience can write on the right side of the printout. Figure 36 shows the option set to Handouts and the Slides per page option set to 6.

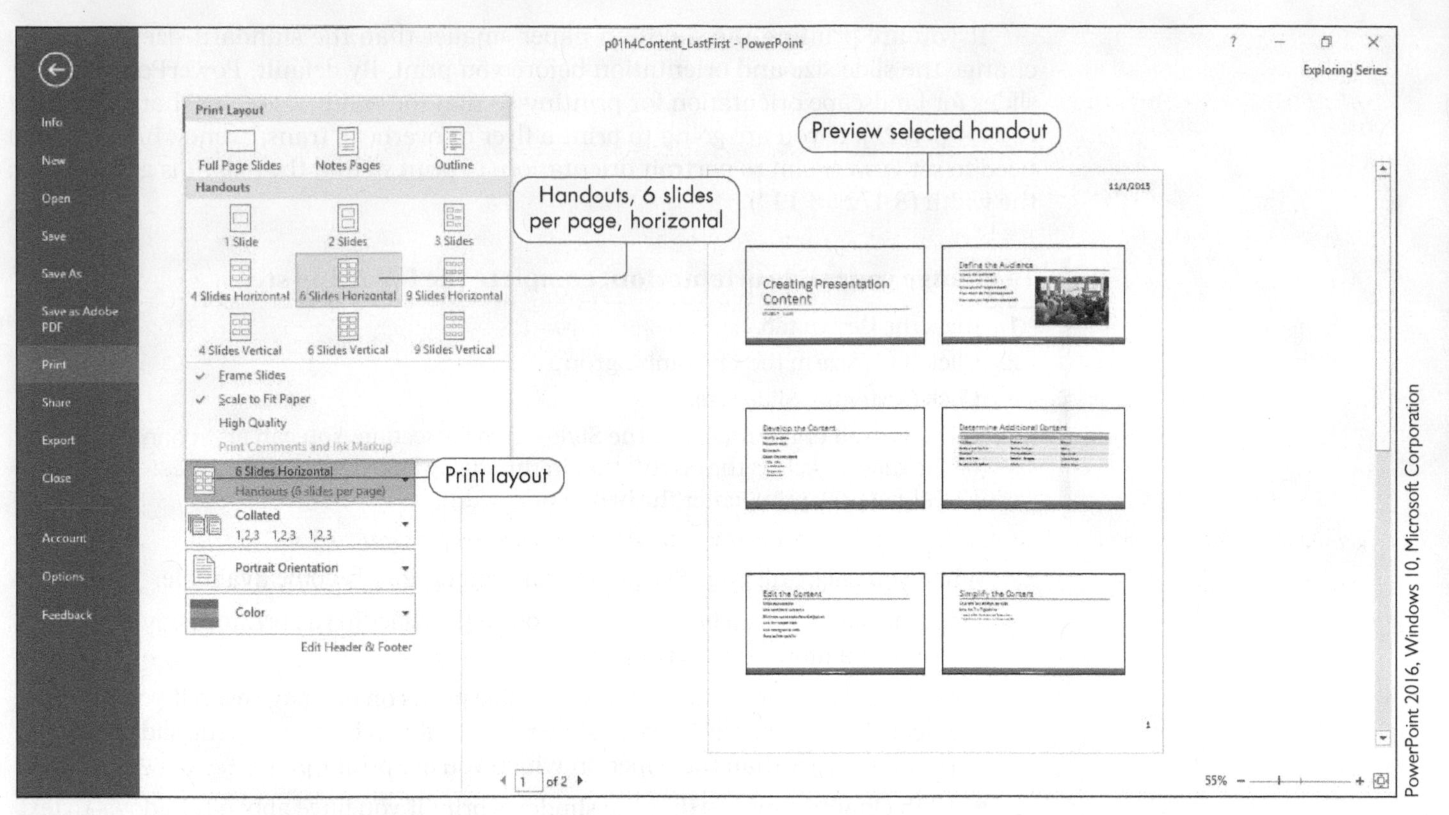

FIGURE 36 Setting Print Options

Print Notes Pages

If you include charts, technical information, or references in a speaker note, print a Notes Page if you want the audience to have a copy. To print a specific notes page, change the print layout to Notes Pages and click the Print All Slides arrow. Click Custom Range and enter the specific slide numbers to print.

Print Outlines

You may print your presentation as an outline made up of the slide titles and main text from each of your slides if you only want to deal with a few pages while presenting. The outline generally gives you enough detail to keep you on track with your presentation, but does not display speaker notes.

Remember, you, the speaker, are the most important part of any presentation. Do not rely on slides or handouts to get your message to the audience. These are supplemental materials for your presentation. The audience is there to hear YOU! Poor delivery will ruin even the best presentation. Speak slowly and clearly, maintain eye contact with your audience, and only use the information on the slides to guide you. Refer to the delivery tips in Table 3 before presenting.

TABLE 3 Practice the following delivery tips to gain confidence and polish your delivery

Before the presentation:

- Practice or rehearse your PowerPoint presentation until you are comfortable with the material and its corresponding slides.
- Know your material thoroughly. Glance at your notes infrequently.
- Arrive early to set up so you do not keep the audience waiting while you manage equipment.
- Have a backup in case the equipment does not work: Handouts work well.
- If appropriate, prepare handouts for your audience so they can relax and participate in your presentation rather than scramble taking notes.
- Make sure your notes pages acknowledge quotes, notes, data, and sources.

During the presentation:

- Speak naturally. Do not read from a prepared script or your PowerPoint Notes.
- Never post a screen full of small text and then torture your audience by saying, "I know you can't read this, so I will …"
- Speak to the person farthest away from you to be sure the people in the last row can hear you. Speak slowly and clearly.
- Vary your delivery. Show emotion or enthusiasm for your topic. If you do not care about your topic, why should the audience?
- Pause to emphasize key points when speaking.
- Look at the audience, not at the screen, as you speak to open communication and gain credibility.
- Use the three-second guide: Look into the eyes of a member of the audience for three seconds and then scan the entire audience. Continue doing this throughout your presentation. Use your eye contact to keep members of the audience involved.
- Blank the screen by pressing B or W at any time during your presentation when you want to solicit questions, comments, or discussion.
- Be judicious. Do not overwhelm your audience with your PowerPoint animations, sounds, and special effects. These features should enhance your message.

After the presentation:

- Thank the audience for their attention and participation. Leave on a positive note.

12. How do you go to a specific slide when displaying a slide show?
13. Describe at least three uses for a printed copy of a PowerPoint slide show.
14. Discuss three things you should do while delivering a presentation and why you think doing these things strengthens your presentation.

Hands-On Exercises

Skills covered: Navigate a Slide Show • Annotate a Slide Show • Print Handouts

4 Navigation and Printing

To prepare for your presentation to Training and Development department employees, you practice displaying the slide show and navigating to specific slides. You also annotate a slide and print audience handouts.

STEP 1 » NAVIGATE A SLIDE SHOW

In this step, you practice various slide navigation techniques to become comfortable with their use. You also review the Slide Show Help feature to become familiar with navigation shortcuts. Refer to Figure 37 as you complete Step 1.

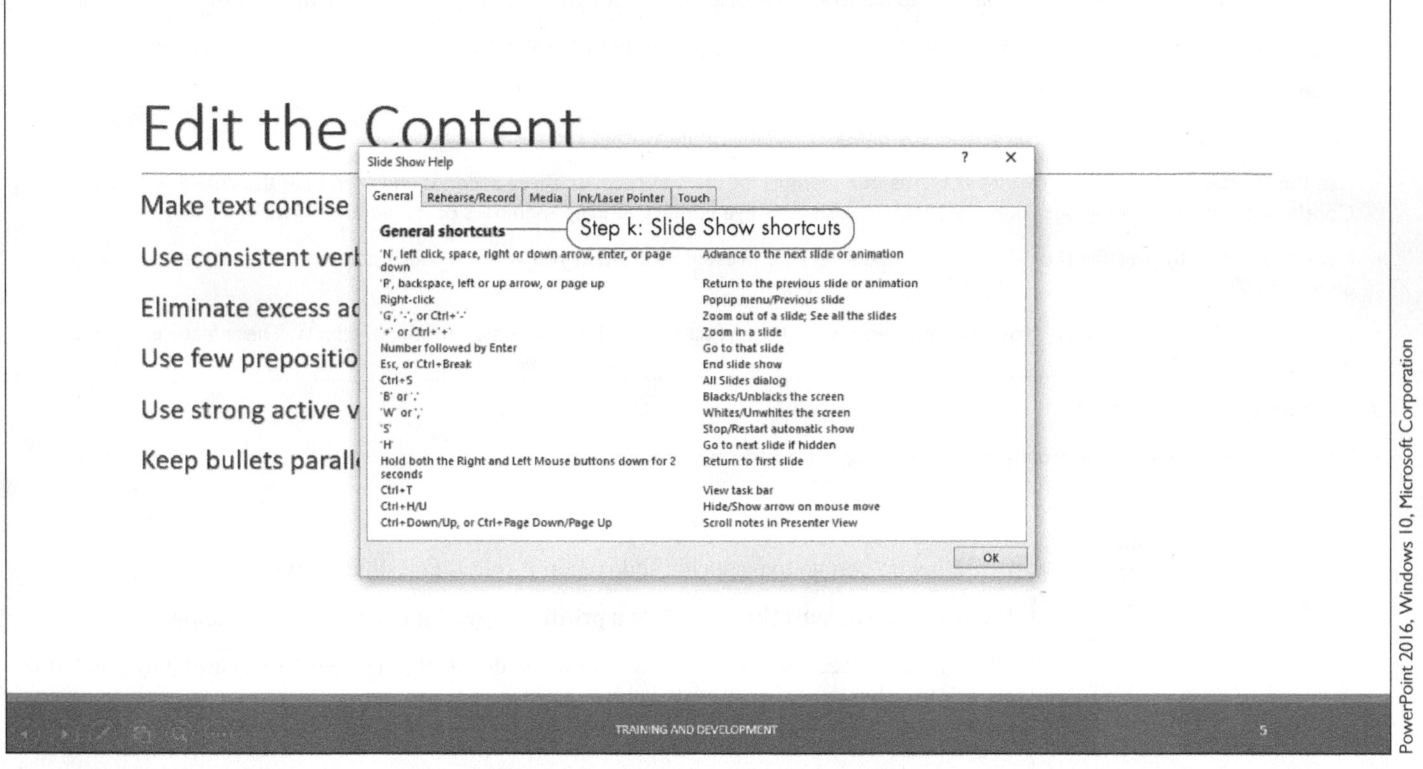

FIGURE 37 Slide Show Help

a. Open *p01h3Content_LastFirst* if you closed it at the end of Hands-On Exercise 3 and save it as **p01h4Content_LastFirst**, changing h3 to h4.

b. Click the **Slide Show tab** and click **From Beginning** in the Start Slide Show group.

   Note the transition effect and sound you applied in Hands-On Exercise 3.

c. Press **Spacebar** to display the animated title.

d. Press the **left mouse button** to advance to Slide 2.

e. Press **Spacebar** to play the animation.

   Note that the picture animation plays on click.

f. Click the **Magnifying glass icon** and zoom in only on the text for Slide 2.

g. Press **Enter** to advance to Slide 3.

h. Press **N** to advance to Slide 4.

i. Press **Backspace** to return to Slide 3.

j. Press the number **5** and press **Enter**.

Slide 5 displays.

k. Press **F1** and read the Slide Show Help window showing the shortcut tips that are available during the display of a slide show.

TROUBLESHOOTING: If you are using a laptop, press FN+F1.

l. Close the Help window. Practice moving between slides using the shortcuts shown in Help.

STEP 2 » ANNOTATE A SLIDE

You practice annotating a slide using a pen, and then you remove the annotations. You practice darkening the screen and returning to the presentation from the dark screen. Refer to Figure 38 as you complete Step 2.

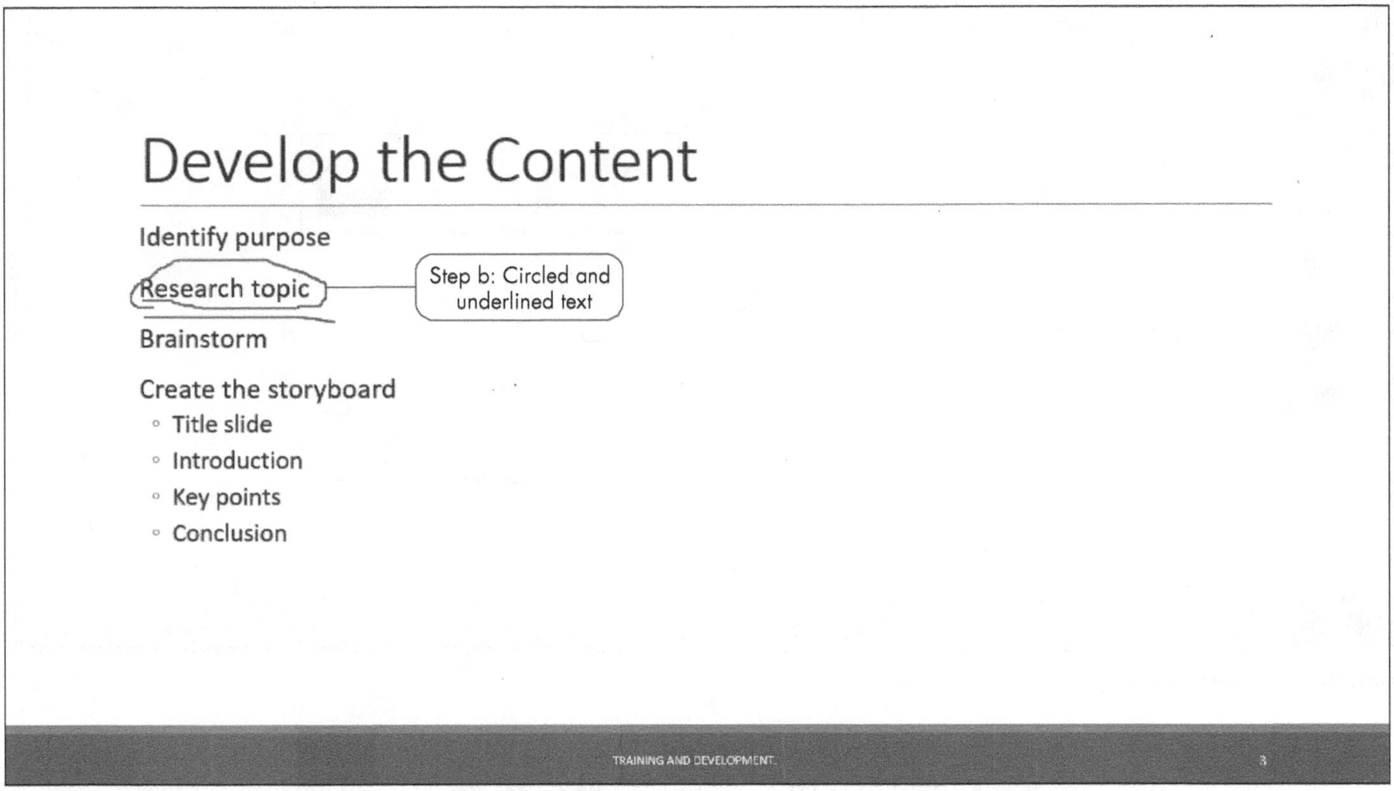

PowerPoint 2016, Windows 10, Microsoft Corporation

FIGURE 38 Annotated Slide

a. Go to Slide 3 and then press **Ctrl+P**.

The pointer becomes a pen.

b. Circle and underline the words *Research topic* on the slide.

c. Press **E**.

The annotations erase.

d. Draw a box around *storyboard*.

e. Press **B**.

The screen blackens.

f. Press **B** again.

The slide show displays again.

g. Press **Esc** to end annotations.

h. Press **Esc** to end the slide show.

i. Save the presentation.

STEP 3 » PRINT HANDOUTS

To enable your audience to follow along during your presentation, you print handouts of your presentation. You know that audience members may want to keep your handouts for future reference. Refer to Figure 39 as you complete Step 3.

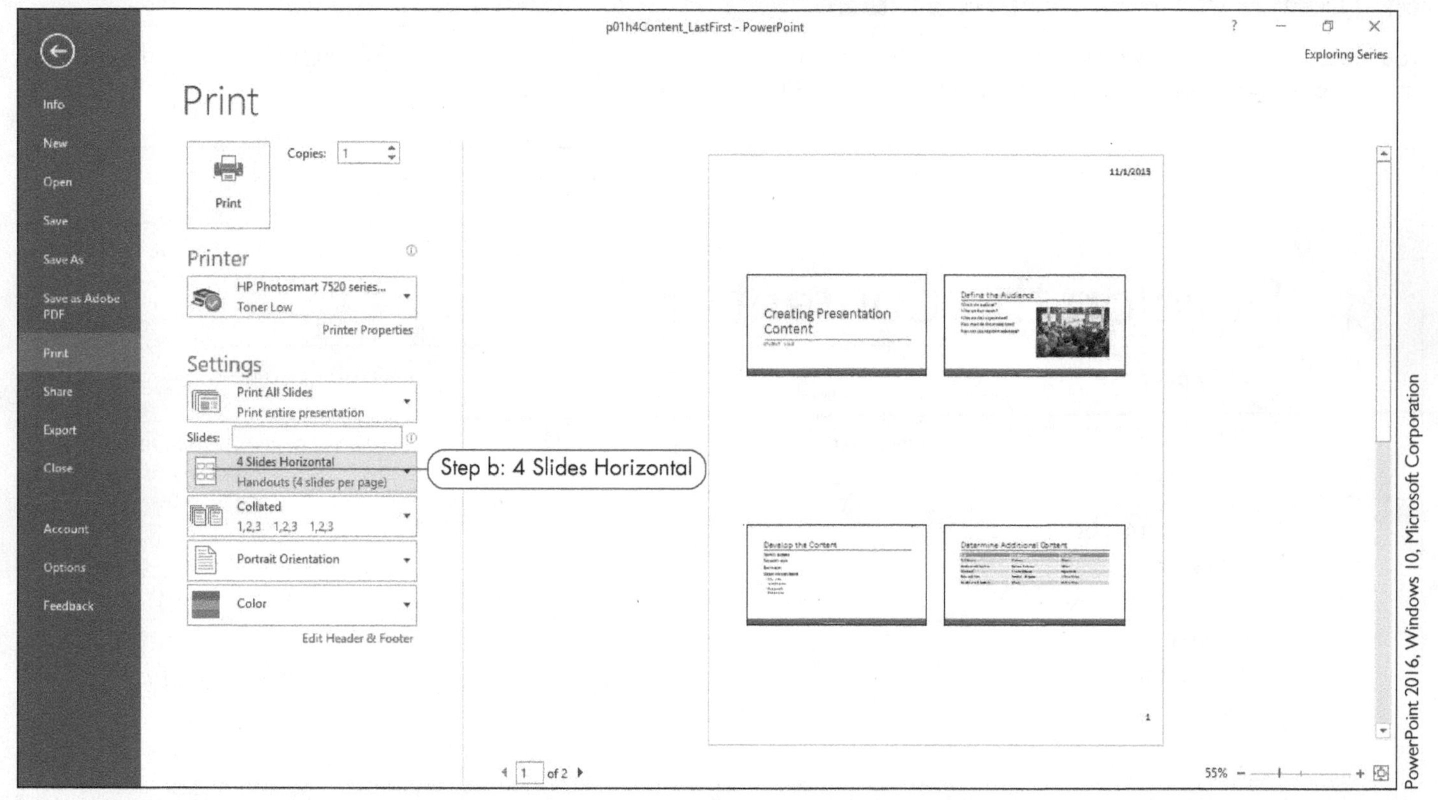

FIGURE 39 Audience Handout

a. Click **File** and then click **Print**.

b. Click **Full Page Slides** and select **4 Slides Horizontal** in the Handouts section.

> **TROUBLESHOOTING:** If you have previously selected a different print layout, Full Page Slides will be changed to that layout. Click the arrow next to the displayed layout option to select a different layout..

c. Click **Print** to print the presentation if requested by your instructor.

d. Save and close the file. Based on your instructor's directions, submit the following:

p01h1Intro_LastFirst

p01h1Intro_LastFirst.ppsx

p01h4Content_LastFirst

Chapter Objectives Review

After reading this chapter, you have accomplished the following objectives:

1. Open and view a PowerPoint presentation.

- Slide shows are electronic presentations that enable you to advance through slides containing content that will help your audience understand your message.
- Normal view, PowerPoint's default view, displays the slide deck in the Slides pane and the workspace in the Slide pane. A third pane, the Notes pane, may be displayed.
- Use PowerPoint views effectively: The Presentation Views group on the View tab enables you to access specialty views designed to help you work effectively and efficiently.
- Slide Sorter view displays thumbnails of slides to enable you to organize your presentation.
- Outline View enables you to easily create a presentation from an outline or view the outline of a presentation you have created.
- Notes Page view displays a thumbnail of the slide and any speaker notes that have been created.
- Slide Show view displays the slide show in full-screen view for an audience.
- Presenter view gives the presenter additional options while presenting, whereas the audience views the full-screen presentation.

2. Type a speaker note.

- Slides should contain only a minimum amount of information, and the speaker should deliver the majority of the information throughout the presentation.
- Speaker notes can be added to the PowerPoint presentation to provide the speaker with additional notes, data, or other comments to refer to during the presentation.

3. Save as a PowerPoint Show.

- By default, when you save a presentation it is saved with the file extension .pptx and, when opened, the presentation opens in Normal view for editing.
- You can save a presentation as a slide show, so that if you open it from a File Explorer winder, the file opens in Slide Show mode. Slide shows are saved with the file extension .ppsx.

4. Plan and prepare a presentation.

- Use a storyboard: Organize your ideas on a storyboard, and then create your presentation in PowerPoint.
- Review the storyboard to ensure that you use active voice, parallel construction, and follow the 7 × 7 guideline.
- Choose a theme: A theme applies coordinating colors, matching fonts, and effects to provide your presentation with a designer-quality look.

5. Add presentation content.

- Use slide layouts: When you add a slide, you can choose from a set of predefined slide layouts that determine the position of the objects or content on a slide.
- Placeholders hold content and determine the position of the objects on the slide.
- Create a title slide and introduction: The title slide should have a short title that indicates the purpose. An introduction slide will get the audience's attention.
- Create key point slides: The content of your presentation follows the title slide and the introduction. Create a slide for each of the key points in the storyboard.
- End with a summary or conclusion slide: The final slide of your presentation reviews the main points, restates the purpose, or invokes a call to action.

6. Review the presentation.

- Check spelling: Read each slide after typing its information, use the spelling feature, ask others to proofread the presentation, and display the presentation in Reading View then read each word out loud. Correct all spelling or word usage errors found for a professional presentation.
- Use the Thesaurus: The Thesaurus helps you make varied word choices.
- Check slide show elements: View the presentation in Slide Show view and check slide layouts, transitions, and animations to ensure that slides present information in a clear and orderly manner. Make changes as needed.
- Reorder slides: Change the order of the slides by dragging them to a new location in Slide Sorter view.

7. Add a table.

- Tables organize information in rows and columns to present structured data.

8. Insert media objects.

- Media objects such as online pictures, images, movies, and sound can be added to enhance the message of your slides and to add visual interest.

9. Apply animations and transitions.

- Apply transitions: Use transitions to control the movement of slides as one slide changes to another.
- Animate objects: Apply animation to objects to control the movement of an object on one slide.

10. Insert a header or footer.

- Headers and footers are used for identifying information on the slide or on handouts and notes pages. Header and footer locations vary depending on the theme applied.

11. Navigate a slide show.

- Various navigation methods advance the slide show, return to previously viewed slides, or go to specific slides.
- Annotate the slide show: Annotations are useful for adding comments to slides.

12. Print in PowerPoint.

- Print full page slides: Print full page slides for use as a backup or when the slides contain a great deal of detail the audience needs to examine.
- Print handouts: Handouts print miniatures of the slides using 1, 2, 3, 4, 6, or 9 slide thumbnails per page. Handouts are useful to an audience.
- Print notes pages: The Notes Page method prints a single thumbnail of a slide with its associated notes per page.
- Print outlines: Outline View prints the titles and main points of the presentation in outline format.

Key Terms Matching

Match the key terms with their definitions. Write the key term letter by the appropriate numbered definition.

a. Animation
b. Annotation
c. Layout
d. Normal view
e. Notes Page view
f. Placeholder
g. PowerPoint presentation
h. PowerPoint show
i. Presenter view
j. Reading View
k. Slide
l. Slide show
m. Slide Show view
n. Slide Sorter view
o. Status bar
p. Storyboard
q. Theme
r. Thumbnail
s. Transition
t. Variant

1. _______ Defines containers, positioning, and formatting for all of the content that appears on a slide.

2. _______ The default PowerPoint view, containing two panes that provide maximum flexibility in working with the presentation.

3. _______ A container that holds content.

4. _______ The movement applied to an object or objects on a slide.

5. _______ The most basic element of PowerPoint, analogous to a page in a Word document.

6. _______ A note or drawing added to a slide during a presentation.

7. _______ Located at the bottom of the screen in Normal view, this contains the slide number, spelling check, Notes, and Comments buttons, and options that control the view of your presentation.

8. _______ Used to view a slide show full screen, one slide at a time, for performing a thorough review of the slides without the full interface onscreen.

9. _______ A presentation saved with a .pptx extension.

10. _______ An electronic method to deliver your message using multiple slides.

11. _______ Used if the speaker needs to enter and edit large amounts of text for reference in the presentation.

12. _______ Uses a .ppsx extension.

13. _______ A specialty view that delivers a presentation on two monitors simultaneously.

14. _______ A variation of the theme you have chosen, using different color palettes and font families.

15. _______ The view used to deliver a completed presentation full screen to an audience, one slide at a time.

16. _______ A slide miniature.

17. _______ A specific animation that is applied when a previous slide is replaced by a new slide.

18. _______ Displays thumbnails of your presentation slides, allowing you to view multiple slides simultaneously.

19. _______ A visual design that helps you plan the direction of your presentation slides.

20. _______ A collection of formatting choices that includes colors, fonts, and special effects.

Multiple Choice

1. Which of the following features enable you to change the color of objects in your slide show without changing text?

(a) Themes
(b) Insert
(c) Format Variants
(d) Slide Color

2. Which of the following statements is *not* accurate about placeholders?

(a) Placeholders may be resized.
(b) All of the content contained in a placeholder is selected when the border of the placeholder is double-clicked.
(c) Placeholder positions are determined by the slide layout and may not be changed.
(d) Placeholders can contain text, pictures, tables, and more.

3. What is the term for theme alternatives using different color palettes and font families?

(a) Palettes
(b) Designs
(c) Variants
(d) Layouts

4. Which print method provides lined space for note taking by the audience?

(a) Handout, 6 Slides Horizontal
(b) Outline
(c) Notes Pages
(d) Handout, 3 Slides

5. Which of the following components are contained in Normal view?

(a) Slide Sorter pane, Slides tab, and Reading pane
(b) Slides pane and Slide pane
(c) Slides tab, Slide pane, and Reading pane
(d) Slide pane, Notes pane, and Slide Sorter pane

6. What view is the best choice if you want to reorder the slides in a presentation?

(a) Slide Sorter view
(b) Presenter view
(c) Reading View
(d) Slide Show view

7. Which of the following layouts is most commonly used when introducing the topic of the presentation and the speaker?

(a) Blank
(b) Title Slide
(c) Comparison
(d) 3 column

8. In reference to content development, which of the following points is *not* in active voice and is not parallel to the others?

(a) Identify the purpose of the presentation.
(b) Sketch out your thoughts on a storyboard.
(c) Brainstorm your thoughts.
(d) Your topic should be researched thoroughly.

9. Which feature will enable you to apply motion as one slide exits and another enters?

(a) Transition
(b) Timing
(c) Animation
(d) Advance

10. During a slideshow, which of the following would *not* focus audience attention on a specific object?

(a) Put nothing on the slide but the object.
(b) Apply an animation to the object.
(c) Use the Pen tool to circle the object.
(d) Apply a transition to the object.

Practice Exercises

1 Managing Your Stress

FROM SCRATCH

The slide show you create in this practice exercise covers concepts and skills that will help you manage your stress as a college student. You create a title slide, an introduction, four slides containing main points of the presentation, and a conclusion slide. Then, you review the presentation and edit a slide so that the text of the bulleted items is parallel. Finally, you print a title page to use as a cover and notes pages to staple together as a reference. Refer to Figure 40 as you complete the exercise.

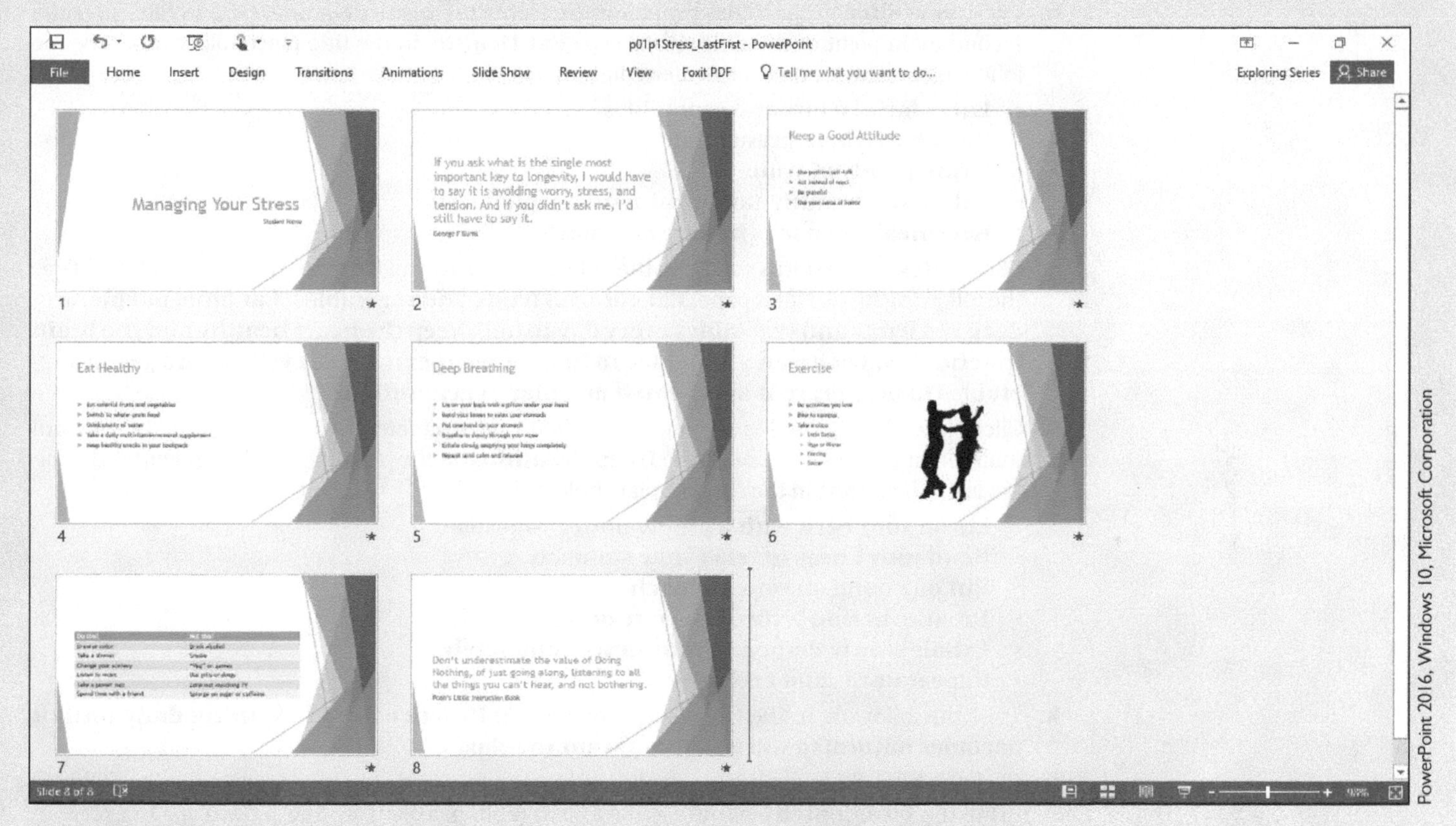

FIGURE 40 Managing Your Stress

PowerPoint 2016, Windows 10, Microsoft Corporation

a. Click **File** and click **New**.

b. Click the **Facet theme**. Click the variant with the blue color (upper-right corner) and click **Create**.

c. Save the presentation as **p01p1Stress_LastFirst**.

d. Click the **Insert tab**, click **Header & Footer** in the Text group, and then click the **Notes and Handouts tab** in the Header and Footer dialog box. Make the following changes:
   - Select the **Date and time check box** and ensure that *Update automatically* is selected.
   - Click to select the **Header check box** and type your name in the **Header box**.
   - Click the **Footer check box** and type your instructor's name and your class name in the **Footer box**. Click **Apply to All**.

e. Click in the **title placeholder** and type **Managing Your Stress**. Click in the **subtitle placeholder** and type your name.

f. Click the **New Slide arrow** in the Slides group on the Home tab to create a new slide (Slide 2) using the **Section Header layout** for the introduction of the slide show. You use a quote for the introduction. Type **Don't underestimate the value of Doing Nothing, of just going along, listening to all the things you can't hear, and not bothering.** in the title placeholder. Type **Pooh's Little Instruction Book** in the subtitle placeholder.

g. Click the **New Slide arrow** in the Slides group on the Home tab to create a new slide (Slide 3) using the **Title and Content layout** for the first main point of the slide show. Type **Keep a Good Attitude** in the title placeholder and type the following bulleted text in the content placeholder:

- **Use positive self-talk**
- **Instead of reacting, act**
- **Be thankful**
- **Use your sense of humor**

h. Click **New Slide** in the Slides group on the Home tab to create a new slide (Slide 4) for the second main point of the slide show. Type **Eat Healthy** in the title placeholder and type the following bulleted text in the content placeholder:

- **Eat colorful fruits and vegetables**
- **Switch to whole-grain food**
- **Drink plenty of water**
- **Take a daily multivitamin/mineral supplement**
- **Keep healthy snacks in your backpack**

i. Click **Notes** on the status bar. Drag the Splitter bar up to provide more room for note text. Type the following in the Notes pane: **Eat colorful fruits and vegetables. Eat blue, purple, and deep red fruits and vegetables every day to help keep the heart healthy and the brain functioning. Eat green vegetables to help prevent cancer. Eat yellow and green vegetables to help prevent age-related macular degeneration.**

j. Click **New Slide** in the Slides group on the Home tab to create a new slide (Slide 5) for the third main point of the slide show. Type **Deep Breathing** in the title placeholder and enter the following bulleted text in the content placeholder:

- **Lie on your back with a pillow under your head**
- **Bend your knees to relax your stomach**
- **Put one hand on your stomach**
- **Breathe in slowly through your nose**
- **Exhale slowly, emptying your lungs completely**
- **Repeat until calm and relaxed**

k. Type the following in the Notes pane for Slide 5: **Practice deep breathing daily until it becomes natural to you when you want to relax.**

l. Click the **New Slide arrow** in the Slides group on the Home tab to create a new slide (Slide 6) using the **Two Content layout** for the fourth main point of the slide show. Type **Exercise** in the title placeholder and enter the following text in the content placeholder on the left side of the slide following the title:

- **Do activities you love**
- **Bike to campus**
- **Take a class**
  - **Latin Dance**
  - **Yoga or Pilates**
  - **Fencing**
  - **Soccer**

m. Click the **Online Pictures icon** in the content placeholder on the right side of the slide. Type **Latin dancing** in the search box for Bing images. Press **Enter**. Click an image of dancers and then click **Insert** to insert the image.

> **TROUBLESHOOTING:** If you cannot locate an image of dancers that you like, use one of the other suggested classes from Step l as your search string.

n. Type the following in the Notes pane: **Learning more about an activity you are interested in gets you moving and is a good stress reliever.**

o. Click the **New Slide arrow** in the Slides group on the Home tab. Click **Title and Content** to create a new slide (Slide 7) for the last main point of the slide show. Select the **title placeholder** and press **Delete**.

p. Click the **Insert Table icon** in the content placeholder. Set Number of columns to **2** and Number of rows to **7**. Click **OK**. Type the following text in the columns, pressing **Tab** after each entry except the last:

Do this!	**Not this!**
Draw or color	**Drink alcohol**
Take a shower	**Smoke**
Change your scenery	**"Veg" on games**
Listen to music	**Use pills or drugs**
Take a power nap	**Zone out watching TV**
Spend time with a friend	**Splurge on sugar or caffeine**

q. Type the following in the Notes pane for Slide 7: **Use healthy activities to relieve your stress. Many activities students use to relieve stress actually cause them a great deal more stress.**

r. Click the **New Slide arrow** in the Slides group on the Home tab and add a new slide (Slide 8) using the **Section Header layout**. You use a quote for the conclusion slide of the slide show. Type **If you ask what is the single most important key to longevity, I would have to say it is avoiding worry, stress, and tension. And if you didn't ask me, I'd still have to say it.** in the title placeholder and then type **George F Burns** in the subtitle placeholder.

s. Click Slide 3. Note that the slide bullets are not in parallel construction. The second bulleted point needs to be changed to active voice. Select *Instead of reacting, act* and type **Act instead of react**.

t. Click **thankful** in the third bullet. Click the **Review tab** and click **Thesaurus**. Click **grateful** in the Thesaurus. Click the **arrow** and then click **Insert**.

u. Click the **Transitions tab** and click **More** in the Transition to This Slide group. Click **Push** in the Transition gallery. Click **Apply to All** in the Timing Group.

v. Click the **View tab**, and click **Slide Sorter** in the Presentation Views group. Drag **Slide 8**, the George Burns quote, so that it becomes **Slide 2**. Drag the new **Slide 3**, the Pooh quote, so that it becomes **Slide 8**.

w. Click the **File tab**, click **Print**, and then click **Full Page Slides**. Click **Full Page Slides** and select **Notes Pages**, click **Frame Slides**, and click **Print**, if your instructor asks you to submit printed slides.

x. Click the **Review tab** and click **Spelling**. Correct any errors.

y. Click the **File tab** and click **Save** to save the presentation as a normal PowerPoint presentation type.

z. Click the **File tab** and click **Save As**. In the Save As dialog box, change the Save as type to **PowerPoint Show** and click **Save**. Close the file. Based on your instructor's directions, submit the following:

p01p1Stress_LastFirst.pptx

p01p1Stress_LastFirst.ppsx

2 Tips for a Successful Presentation

FROM SCRATCH

Your employer is a successful business person who has been asked by the local Chamber of Commerce to give tips for presenting successfully using a PowerPoint presentation. She created a storyboard of her presentation and has asked you to create the presentation from the storyboard. Refer to Figure 41 as you complete this exercise.

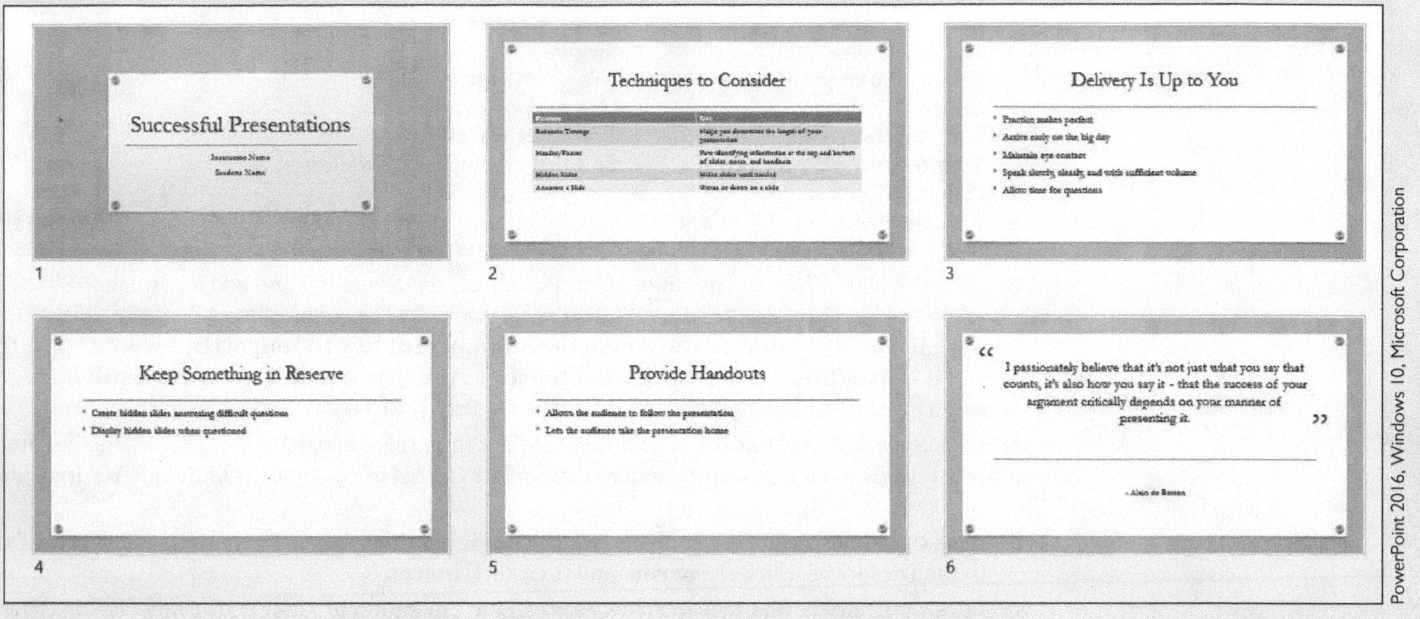

FIGURE 41 Successful Presentations

a. Click **File** and then click **New**.

b. Select **Organic**, select the variant in the lower-right corner, and then click **Create**.

c. Save the presentation as **p01p2Presenting_LastFirst**.

d. Click the **Insert tab**, click **Header & Footer**, and then click the **Notes and Handouts tab** in the Header and Footer dialog box.

- Click to select the **Date and time check box** and click **Update automatically**.
- Click to select the **Header check box** and type your name in the **Header box**.
- Click to select the **Footer check box** and type your instructor's name and your class name. Click **Apply to All**.

e. Click in the **title placeholder** on Slide 1, and type **Successful Presentations**. Click in the **subtitle placeholder** and type your instructor's name. Press **Enter**. On the new line, type your name.

f. Click the **Home tab** and click **New Slide** in the Slides group.

g. Click in the **title placeholder** and type **Techniques to Consider**.

h. Click the **Insert Table icon** in the content placeholder and enter **2** columns and **5** rows.

i. Type the following information in the table cells, pressing **Tab** after each item except the last:

Feature	**Use**
Rehearse Timings	**Helps you determine the length of your presentation**
Header/Footer	**Puts identifying information on the top and bottom of slides, notes, and handouts**
Hidden Slides	**Hides slides until needed**
Annotate a Slide	**Writes or draws on a slide**

j. Click the **Home tab** and click **New Slide** in the Slides group. Type **Delivery Is Up to You** in the title placeholder.

k. Click in the **content placeholder** and type the following bulleted text:
   - **Practice makes perfect**
   - **Arrive early on the big day**
   - **Maintain eye contact**
   - **Speak slowly, clearly, and with sufficient volume**
   - **Allow time for questions**

l. Click **New Slide** and type **Keep Something in Reserve** in the title placeholder.

m. Click in the **content placeholder** and type the following bulleted text:
   - **Create hidden slides answering difficult questions**
   - **Display hidden slides when questioned**

n. Click **New Slide** and type **Provide Handouts** in the title placeholder.

o. Click in the **content placeholder** and type the following bulleted text:
   - **Allows the audience to follow the presentation**
   - **Lets the audience take the presentation home**

p. Click the **New Slide arrow** and click **Quote with Caption.**

q. Type **I passionately believe that it's not just what you say that counts, it's also how you say it — that the success of your argument critically depends on your manner of presenting it.** in the title placeholder.

r. Click the **center placeholder** and press **Delete**.

s. Type **- Alain de Botton** in the bottom placeholder.

t. Select the **bottom placeholder** and then click the **Animations tab**. Click **Fly In** in the Animations group.

u. Click the **Review tab** and click **Spelling** in the Proofing group. Accept *Lets* in Slide 5. Review the presentation in Slide Show view to fix any spelling errors.

v. Click the **Slide Show tab** and click **From Beginning** in the Start Slide Show group. Press **Page Down** to advance through the slides. When you reach the last slide of the slide show, press the number **3** and press **Enter** to return to Slide 3.

w. Right-click, point to **Pointer Options**, and then click **Highlighter**. Highlight **Speak slowly, clearly, and with sufficient volume**.

x. Press **Page Down** to advance through the remainder of the presentation. Press **Esc** when you reach the black slide at the end of the slide show and click **Keep** to keep your slide annotations.

y. Click the **File tab**, click **Print**, and then click **Full Page Slides**. Click **Outline** and click **Print**, if your instructor asks you to submit printed slides.

z. Save and close the file. Based on your instructor's directions, submit p01p2Presenting_LastFirst.

Mid-Level Exercises

1 Planning Presentation Content

You received a high-definition mini action cam for Christmas and you have been using it to video your snowboarding, paddle boarding, and fishing trips. A friend who has seen your videos asked you to present a workshop on characteristics of HD mini action cams and why they are becoming commonly used, popular models, as well as tips for use. You create a slide show for your audience to view as you present.

a. Create a new presentation, applying the design theme of your choice to the presentation. Save the presentation as **p01m1Cam_LastFirst**.

b. Create a title slide that includes **Using a Mini Action Cam** as the title and your name and class in the subtitle placeholder.

c. Create a Title and Content slide using **Popular Models** as the title. Create the following two-column table in the content placeholder.

GoPros	**Muvis**
Garmins	**Rolleis**
Ghosts	**iVues**
Sonys	**Panasonics**
iONs	**HTCs**

d. Create a slide using the Content with Caption layout. Type **Characteristics** as the title, and list the following in the content placeholder on the left side of the slide: **Small, Lightweight, Tough, Attachable, POV video, Fish-eye perspective**. Insert an online picture of a mini action camera in the content placeholder on the right side of the slide.

e. Create a slide using the Two Content layout. Type **Popular Features** as the title. List the following in the content placeholder on the left side of the slide: **Slow motion, GPS tracking, Wrist remote, Waterproof casing**. List the following in the content placeholder on the right side of the slide: **Box cam style, Bullet cam style, Sunglasses mount, WiFi connectivity**.

f. Create a slide using the Title and Content layout. Type **Tips** as the title, and then type this list in the content placeholder:

- **Know your mount**
- **Practice running the camera by touch**
- **Get the light right**
- **Avoid water spots on the lens**

g. Create a slide using the Title and Content layout. Type **Sample Video** as the title. Use the Insert Video button on the palette of content options to insert the video *p01m1Video* located in your student files.

h. Change the view to Slide Sorter view, and then move Slide 3 (Characteristics) so that it becomes Slide 2. While in Slide Sorter view, assign the transition of your choice to all slides in the slide show. Note the star that appears under each slide that indicates the slide has a transition attached.

i. Double-click **Slide 2** to return to Normal view. Select the content placeholder that contains the list of characteristics. Apply the Wipe animation.

j. Change the view to Notes Page view. Add the notes for the speaker's reference as follows:

Slide	Note
2	**Action cameras are small, lightweight cameras that are designed to attach to objects like helmets, surf or paddle boards, cars, sticks, and other objects to create point of view (POV) video.**
4	**When purchasing a mini action camera, determine how you are most likely to use the camera, then look at cameras that will provide those features.**

5 • **Check to see where the mount is steadiest so you don't get a choppy video while getting the shot you want.**
• **Practice until you can operate the camera by touch, as different mounts make it impossible to see the buttons.**
• **Use camera settings for different lighting conditions.**
• **Apply an anti-beading solution to the lens to prevent water spots from forming.**

k. Add a slide number in the footer to all of the slides except the title slide. (Note: The slide number position on the slide will depend on the theme you selected.)

l. Review the slide show in Slide Show view to check spelling and word usage. Adjust layouts and placeholder location until all elements fit attractively and professionally on the slide.

m. Print notes pages.

n. Save and close the file. Based on your instructor's directions, submit p01m1Cam_LastFirst.

2 Wireless Network Safety

You volunteer at the local community center. You have been asked to present to a group of young teens about staying safe when using wireless computer networks. You have researched the topic and using your notes you are ready to prepare your presentation.

a. Start a new presentation. Apply the Banded theme. Apply the black, blue, and green variant. Save the presentation as **p01m2Wifi_LastFirst**.

b. Add **Wi-Fi Safety** as a footer on all slides except the title slide. Also include an automatically updated date and time and a slide number.

c. Create a Notes and Handouts header with your name and a footer with your instructor's name and your class name. Apply to all.

d. Add the title **WiFi Safety** in the title placeholder. Type **Keeping Your Personal Information Safe** in the subtitle placeholder.

e. Insert a new slide using the Two Content layout. Type **Wireless Fidelity (WiFi)** as the title.

f. Type the following into the left content placeholder:

- **Uses radio waves to exchange data wirelessly via a computer network**
- **Commonly found at coffee shops and other public places**
- **Also called hotspots**

g. Add an online picture to the right content placeholder: Search for **WiFi photo** in the search box. Insert the photo of your choosing.

h. Insert a new slide using the **Title and Content layout** as the third slide in the presentation. Type **WiFi Hotspot Security** as the title.

i. Type the following into the content placeholder:

- **Avoid unsecured networks if possible**
- **Don't access confidential information**
- **Set network locations to "Public"**
- **Keep firewall and antivirus software up-to-date**

j. Click **Notes** on the status bar. Add the following text to the Notes pane:

Although a number of threats exist when using public WiFi hotspots, there are several ways you can protect yourself and your computer.

k. Insert a new slide using the Blank layout as the fourth slide in the presentation.

l. Click the **Insert tab**, click **Table**, and then insert a table with four rows and two columns. Type the following text in the table:

Threat	Explanation
Identity Theft	Criminal act involving the use of your personal information for financial gain.
Hacking	Unauthorized access to a computer or network.
Malware	Software programs that are designed to be harmful. A virus is a type of malware.

m. Position the table at the approximate center of the slide.

n. Apply the **Fade transition** from the Subtle category to all slides in the slide show.

DISCOVER

o. Add the **Bounce animation** from the Entrance category to the content placeholder and then to the image on Slide 2. Start the animation for the image with the previous animation so they start at the same time.

p. Move Slide 4 so that it becomes Slide 3.

q. Review the presentation and correct any errors you find.

r. Print the handouts, three per page, framed.

s. Save and close the file. Based on your instructor's directions, submit p01m2Wifi_LastFirst.

3 Creating a Free Website and Blog for Your PowerPoint Experiences

COLLABORATION CASE

FROM SCRATCH

Web 2.0 technologies make it easy for people to interact using the Internet. Web applications often combine functions to help us create our online identity, share information, collaborate on projects, and socialize. In this exercise, you will create an online identity for your use in your PowerPoint class, share information about your PowerPoint experience with others, and get to know a few of your classmates. You will create a website for use during your PowerPoint class, add information to the pages in your website, and then share the address of your site with others. You will also visit the websites of others in your class.

a. Open a Web browser and search for a site that enables you to create a free website or blog. For example: Google Sites, Web.com, Weebly, or any other free site.

b. Register for the site and then begin creating your site.

c. Enter a title for your website as follows: use your first name and last name followed by PPT to indicate this is your PowerPoint site.

d. Use whatever free design elements the site provides to create the look of your site.

e. Add a blog to your site. Add an entry to your blog that explains your previous experience with PowerPoint and why you have registered for this class. Search YouTube for a video about PowerPoint or presentation skills. Create a second blog entry about what you learned and include the link for others to view if interested.

f. Publish your website.

g. Exchange website addresses with at least three other students in your class. Visit your classmates' websites and leave a comment to indicate you have visited. Then, revisit your website to see what comments your classmates entered.

h. Email your instructor your website address so your instructor can visit your site.

Beyond the Classroom

Using Creative Commons

GENERAL CASE

FROM SCRATCH

Research copyright law as it applies in education, and then research the nonprofit organization Creative Commons (CC). Prepare a slide show to present to others that explains what Creative Commons is and how it enables you to legally use online media in your slide show. Create a storyboard on paper outlining your slide show. Then, create a PowerPoint presentation named **p01b1CC_LastFirst** based on your storyboard. Include a title slide and at least four slides related to this topic. Choose a theme, transitions, and animations. Insert at least one appropriate online picture with an attribution to its creator. Include speaker notes on most slides as necessary. Create a handout header with your name and the current date. Include a handout footer with your instructor's name and your class name. Review the presentation to ensure there are no errors and that your transition and animations work by viewing each slide in Slide Show view. Print as full page slides, or as directed by your instructor. Save and close the file. Based on your instructor's directions, submit p01b1CC_LastFirst.

Polishing a Business Presentation

A neighbor has created a slide show to present to a local business explaining his company's services. He has asked you to refine the slide show so it has a more professional appearance. Open *p01b2Green* and save the file as **p01b2Green_LastFirst**. View the slide show. Note that the text is difficult to read because of a lack of contrast with the background, there are capitalization errors and spelling errors, the bulleted points are not parallel, and images are positioned and sized poorly. Select and apply a design theme and a variant. Modify text following the guidelines presented throughout this chapter. Reposition placeholders as needed. Size and position the images in the presentation or replace them with your choice of images. Text may be included in speaker notes to emphasize visuals, if desired. Apply a transition to all slides. Add a minimum of two animations. Make other changes you choose. Create a handout header with your name and the current date. Include a handout footer with your instructor's name and your class name. Review the presentation to ensure there are no errors by viewing each slide in Slide Show view. Save your file and then save it again as a PowerPoint show. Close the file. Print notes pages if directed by your instructor. Based on your instructor's directions, submit the following:

p01b2Green_LastFirst
p01b2Green_LastFirst.ppsx

Capstone Exercise

Want'n Waffles is a small, successful mobile food business. The company was started by two culinary arts students and their families as a way to finance the students' college education. A year later they own three food trucks that sell breakfast waffles, waffle sandwiches, and dessert waffles. Street-food lovers line up around the block when the food trucks park in their neighborhood. The truck locations are advertised via Twitter and on Facebook so waffle lovers can follow the trucks from place to place. The business has increased its revenue and profits and the owners are looking to expand their operation by offering franchises in other college cities. They need to prepare a presentation for an important meeting with financiers.

Create a Title Slide

You add your name to the title slide, apply a theme, and create a slide for the Want'n Waffles mission statement.

a. Open *p01c1Waffles* and save it as **p01c1Waffles_LastFirst**.

b. Create a Notes and Handouts header with your name and a footer with your instructor's name and your class name. Include the date and time, updated automatically. Apply to all.

c. Replace YOUR NAME in the **subtitle placeholder** on Slide 1 with your name.

d. Apply the **Retrospect theme**.

Add Content

You add the information about your business as content slides.

a. Create a new slide after Slide 1 using the **Section Header layout**. Type the following in the title placeholder: **Want'n Waffles provides gourmet quality food prepared on the spot in a clean mobile truck.**

b. Double-click the border of the title placeholder, then change the font size to **60 pt** and apply **Italic**.

c. Add the following speaker note to Slide 3: **We can sell inexpensive breakfasts, lunches, and desserts because our overhead is low. We don't have to pay for a "brick and mortar" restaurant with all of the expenses of a building. Because we don't have to pay for servers, prices stay down while sales increase. Our trucks are a favorite with employees because they get quick service, excellent food, and the convenience of a location close to them. We are mobile so we can change location as needed to increase sales. Best of all, our food is FUN!**

Create Tables

You create a table to show the increase in sales from last year to this year and a table showing a few of your waffle specialties.

a. Create a table of four columns and seven rows in the content placeholder on Slide 4. Type the data from the table below in your table.

TABLE 1

Category	Last Year	This Year	Increase
Breakfast waffles	$125,915	$255,856	$129,941
Breakfast crepes	45,404	97,038	51,634
Waffle-wiches	61,510	138,555	77,045
Waffle cookies	22,100	43,200	21,100
Dessert waffles	151,012	246,065	95,053
Totals	$405,941	$780,714	$374,773

b. Apply the **Medium Style 2 – Accent 2** Table Style to the table.

c. Format the table text font to **18 pt**. Center align the column headings and right align all numbers.

d. Add a new slide after Slide 4 that uses the **Comparison layout**. Type **Want'n Waffle Specialties** as the title of the slide, use **Luncheon Waffles** as the heading for the left column, and type **Dessert Waffles** as the heading for the right column. Type the data from Table 2 below in your table and apply the same formatting to this table that you applied in Step c.

TABLE 2

Chicken and Waffle Grilled Cheese	Waffle Confetti Cake
PB&J Waffle Panini	Waffled Banana Bread
Zucchini-Parmesan Waffle	Chocolate Chip Waffle Cookies
Maple Bacon Waffle	Waffled Carrot Cake
Margherita Waffle Pizza	Waffle Sundae

e. View the slide show in Slide Sorter view.

f. Move Slide 5 (A Natural Franchise) so that it becomes Slide 3.

g. Note that Slide 2 includes the mission statement as the introduction slide, Slides 3 through 7 cover the key points of the presentation and include supporting data, and Slide 8 uses a plan for the future as the conclusion (summary) slide.

Add an Online Picture and Animate Content

You want to include a picture of a waffle creation to inspire interest in the franchise. To emphasize the profits the business has realized, you add animations. To help the audience absorb the next steps on the summary slide, you animate the text.

a. Display Slide 3. Use the content placeholder on the right side to open Online Pictures. Use **waffles** as your search keyword in the search box. Locate an image of a waffle and insert it in the placeholder.

b. Use the same online picture of a waffle on the last slide of your slide show. Position the image in the lower-right portion of your slide, and size it appropriately.

c. Select the **Our first year was profitable box** on Slide 5 and apply the **Fly In entrance animation**.

d. Select the **Our second year was significantly better box** and apply the **Fly In entrance animation**. Change the Start option to **After Previous**.

e. Apply the **Fly In entrance animation** to the text content placeholder on Slide 8.

f. Check the spelling in the slide show, and review the presentation for any other errors. Fix anything you think is necessary.

Navigate and Print

You proofread the presentation in Slide Show view and check the animations. You notice an error on a slide and correct it. When all errors have been corrected, you print a handout with four slides per page.

a. Start the slide show and navigate through the presentation, experimenting with various navigation methods.

b. Note the parallel construction error on Slide 4. The third bulleted point, *Profits are increasing*, does not start with an active verb as the other bulleted points do.

c. Annotate the conclusion slide, *The Next Steps*, by underlining **detailed financial proposal** and circling **two** and **ten** with a red pen.

d. Exit the presentation and keep the annotations.

e. Use the Slides pane in Normal view to navigate to Slide 4. Modify the third bulleted point as follows: **Increase profits.**

f. Print a handout with four slides, horizontal per page if directed to print by your instructor.

g. Save the file as a presentation and as a show. Close the file. Based on your instructor's directions, submit the following:

p01c1Waffles_LastFirst
p01c1Waffles_LastFirst.ppsx

Glossary

Animation A motion applied to text and objects.

Annotation A written note or drawing on a slide for additional commentary or explanation

Deck A collection of slides.

Layout Determines the position of the objects or content on a slide.

Normal view The default PowerPoint workspace.

Notes Page view Used for entering and editing large amounts of text to which the speaker can refer when presenting.

Outline View Shows the presentation in an outline format displayed in levels according to the points and any subpoints on each slide.

Placeholder A container that holds text, images, graphs, or other objects to be used in a presentation.

PowerPoint presentation An electronic slide show that can be edited or delivered in a variety of ways.

PowerPoint show An unchangeable electronic slide show format used for distribution.

Presenter view Specialty view that delivers a presentation on two monitors simultaneously.

Reading View Displays the slide show full screen, one slide at a time, complete with animations and transitions.

Slide pane The main workspace in PowerPoint, that displays the currently selected slide

Slide Show view Displays the completed presentation full screen to an audience as an electronic presentation.

Slide show A series of slides displayed onscreen for an audience.

Slide Sorter view Displays thumbnails of presentation slides enabling a view of multiple slides.

Slides pane Pane on the left side of Normal view that shows the slide deck with thumbnails.

Slide The most basic element of PowerPoint, similar to a page in Word.

Status bar A bar at the bottom of the PowerPoint window that contains the slide number, Spell check button, Notes button, Comments button, View buttons, Zoom slider, Zoom level button, and Fit slide to current window button.

Storyboard A visual plan of a presentation that displays the content of each slide in the slide show.

Table A grid of columns and rows that organizes data.

Theme A collection of design choices that includes colors, fonts, and special effects used to give a consistent look to a presentation.

Thumbnail A miniature view of a slide that appears in the Slidespane and Slide Sorter view.

Transition A specific animation that is applied as na previous slide is repladed by a new slide while displayed in Slide Show view or Reading view.

Variant A variation on a chosen design theme.

Presentation Development

PowerPoint

Presentation Development

LEARNING OUTCOME You will apply tools to create and modify a presentation.

OBJECTIVES & SKILLS: After you read this chapter, you will be able to:

Templates

OBJECTIVE 1: CREATE A PRESENTATION USING A TEMPLATE
Create a New Presentation Based on a Template

OBJECTIVE 2: MODIFY A PRESENTATION BASED ON A TEMPLATE
Modify a Placeholder, Modify a Layout, Add Pictures and Modify a Caption

HANDS-ON EXERCISE 1:
Templates

Outlines

OBJECTIVE 3: CREATE A PRESENTATION IN OUTLINE VIEW
Use Outline View, Edit in Outline View

OBJECTIVE 4: MODIFY AN OUTLINE STRUCTURE
Edit the Outline

OBJECTIVE 5: PRINT AN OUTLINE
Modify the Outline Structure and Print

HANDS-ON EXERCISE 2:
Outlines

Data Imports

OBJECTIVE 6: IMPORT AN OUTLINE
Import a Rich Text Format Outline

OBJECTIVE 7: REUSE SLIDES FROM AN EXISTING PRESENTATION
Reuse Slides from Another Presentation

HANDS-ON EXERCISE 3:
Data Imports

Design

OBJECTIVE 8: USE SECTIONS
Create Sections

OBJECTIVE 9: EXAMINE SLIDE SHOW DESIGN PRINCIPLES
Apply Design Principles

OBJECTIVE 10: MODIFY A THEME
Modify a Theme

OBJECTIVE 11: MODIFY THE SLIDE MASTER
Modify a Slide Master

HANDS-ON EXERCISE 4:
Design

CASE STUDY | The Wellness Education Center

The Wellness Education Center at your school promotes overall good health to students and employees. The director of the Center asked you to create two slide shows that she can use to deliver presentations to the campus community.

You create a presentation to inform campus groups about the Center by downloading a template with a wellness theme from Microsoft Office Online. You modify several of the layouts the template provides to customize the template to your needs. To concentrate on the content of the slides, you use Outline view to enter slide text and edit the presentation outline.

You create a second presentation for the Center using an outline the director created in Microsoft Word. You import the outline, supplement it with slides you reuse from another presentation, and divide the presentation into sections. Using standard slide show design guidelines, polish the presentation by editing the content and the theme.

Wavebreakmedia/
Shutterstock

Planning and Preparing a Presentation

Dedicated to Promoting Healthy Lifestyles!
Wellness Education Center

PowerPoint 2016, Windows 10, Microsoft Corporation

FIGURE 1 Wellness Education Center Slide

CASE STUDY | The Wellness Education Center

Starting Files	Files to be Submitted
Blank presentation **p02h3MedOutline** **p02h3Wellness** **p02h4Logo**	**p02h2Center_LastFirst** **p02h4Mission_LastFirst**

Templates

One of the hardest things about creating a presentation is getting started. You may have a general idea of what you want to say but not how to organize your thoughts. Or you may know what you want to say but need help designing the look for the slides. PowerPoint's templates enable you to create professional-looking presentations and may even include content to help you decide what to say.

In this section, you will learn how to create a presentation using a template that you modify to fit your needs.

Creating a Presentation Using a Template

STEP 1 Templates and themes are not the same thing. A theme is a collection of design choices that includes colors, fonts, and special theme effects. A ***template*** is a file that includes the formatting elements like a background, a theme with a color scheme and font selections for titles and text boxes, and slide layouts that position content placeholders. Some templates include suggestions for how to modify the template, whereas others include ideas about what you could say to inform your audience about your topic. These suggestions can help you learn to use many of the features in PowerPoint.

PowerPoint offers templates online for you to use. You can quickly and easily download additional professional templates in a variety of categories. These templates were created by Microsoft, a Microsoft partner, or a member of the Microsoft community. You can select a suggested search term or type your own search term in the Search box. Then you can filter by category to narrow your search further. For example, you can download a template for a renewable energy presentation created by a Microsoft partner, an active listening presentation created by a Microsoft community member, or a business financial report created by Microsoft. Figure 2 shows four PowerPoint templates.

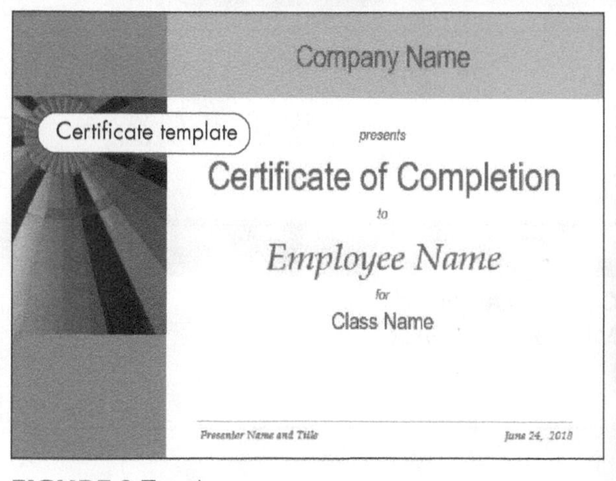

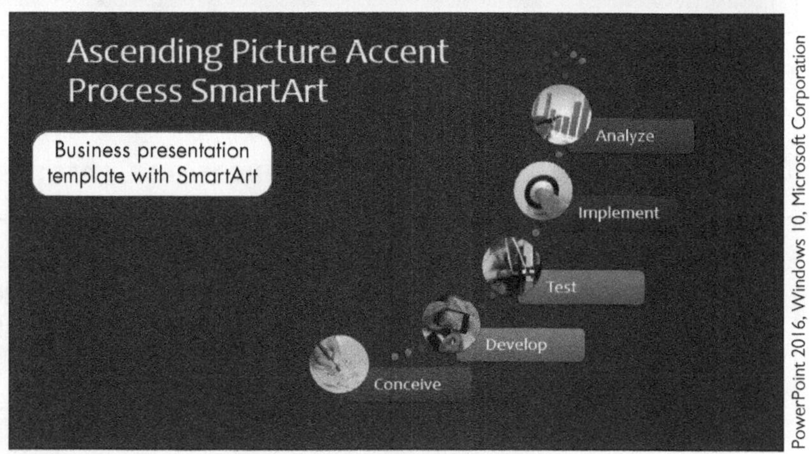

PowerPoint 2016, Windows 10, Microsoft Corporation

FIGURE 2 Templates

TIP: SEARCHING FOR A TEMPLATE

With Office, templates are not installed on your computer with the program but rather are located online. Consequently, your computer must be connected to the Internet to search for Office 2016 templates.

When you open PowerPoint you are presented with a variety of design themes from which to choose. If you want to use a template with suggested content or additional design themes, you need to search online.

To begin a presentation using a template, complete the following steps:

1. Start PowerPoint.
2. Click one of the suggested search terms, or click in the search box and type the text for which you would like to search. Press Enter. For example, you may want to search for Marketing templates, and thus you would type Marketing as your search term.
3. Click a template or theme to preview it in a new window.
4. Click Create to download the template. A new presentation file is created based on the template.

Figure 3 displays some of the templates available and where to search for templates and themes described in Step 2 above. Your view may show different template options, as Microsoft frequently updates the available templates.

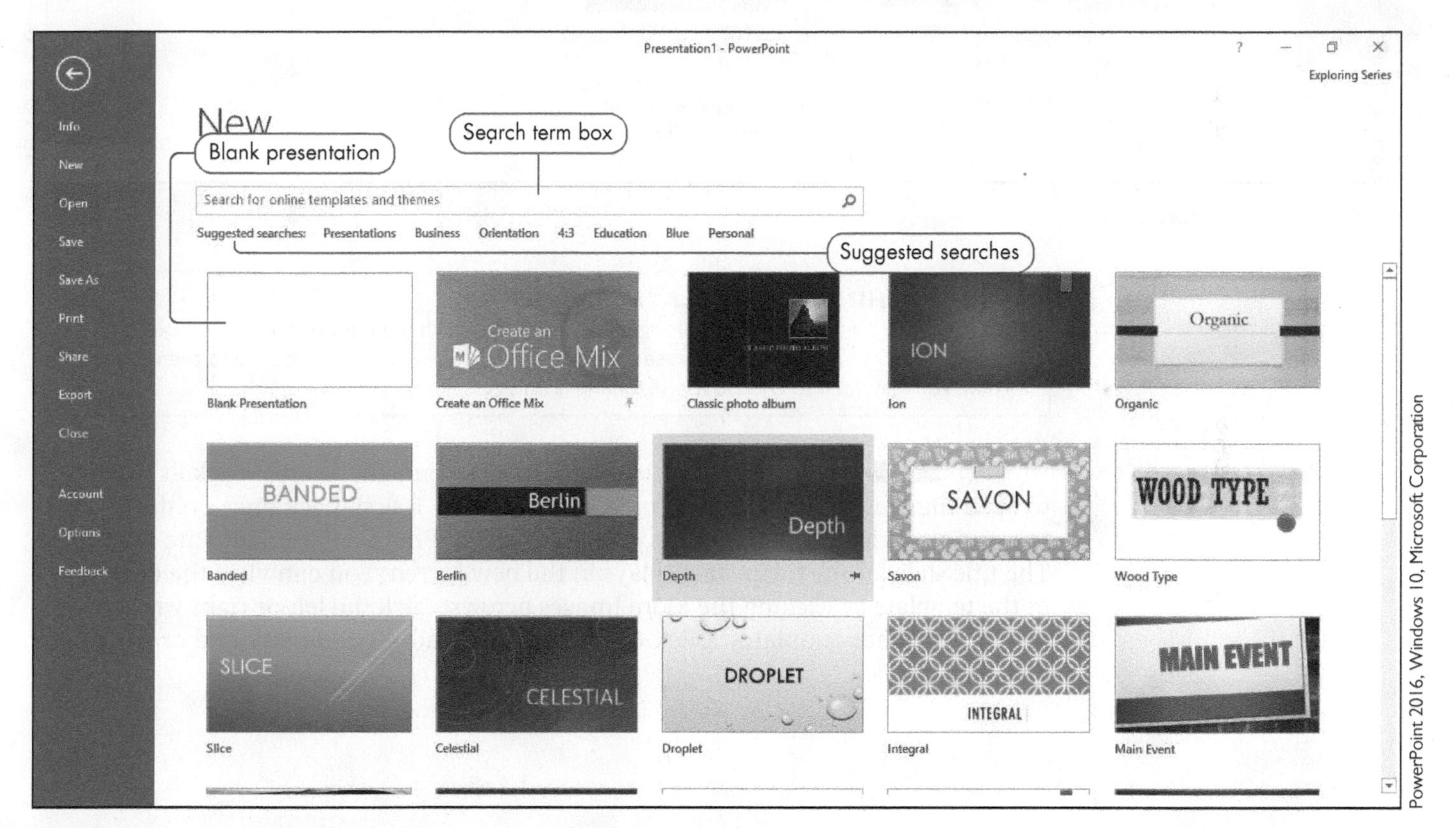

FIGURE 3 Templates and Themes

You can filter your results further by using one of the categories on the right side of the screen. For example, Figure 4 shows the search results for a search for Photo Albums. The column on the right shows several of the categories. Depending on your search criteria, you may also see non-PowerPoint templates in your search results.

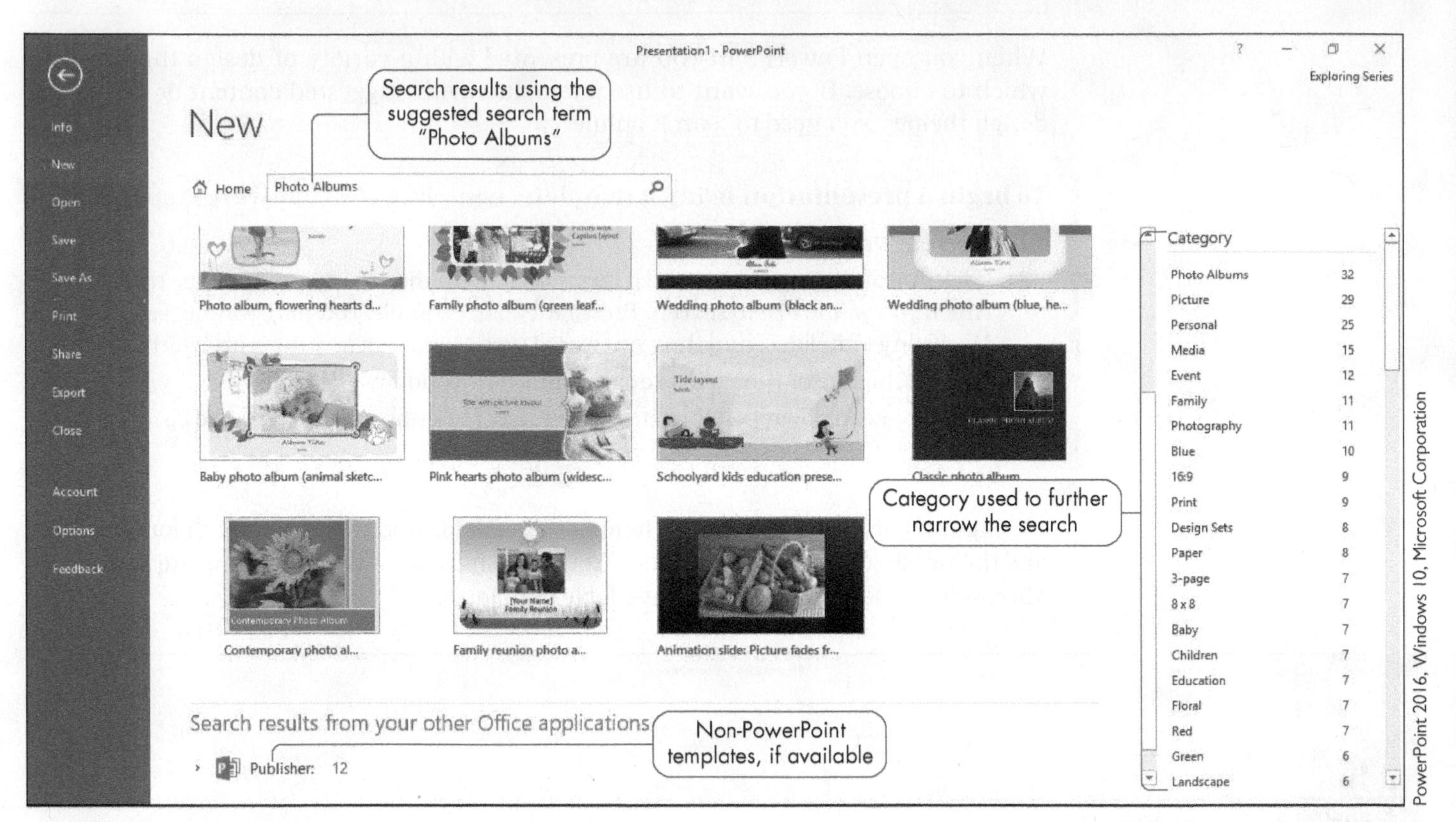

FIGURE 4 Template Categories

> **TIP: SEARCHING BY TEMPLATE DIMENSIONS**
> In the category list, you can search using 4:3 for templates with the typical screen dimensions or 16:9 for widescreen templates. Because most screens and televisions have moved to the widescreen format, you may want to choose the 16:9 dimension size.

If you know you want to work with a particular template, double-click its thumbnail to open the presentation. If you would like to preview it first, click once on the template to open a preview window. In Figure 5, the Classic Photo Album template is selected. The title slide for the template displays in the new screen. You can view the other slides in the template by clicking the More Images arrows. Click the left or right white arrows to preview other templates. Click Create to download the template and create a new presentation file.

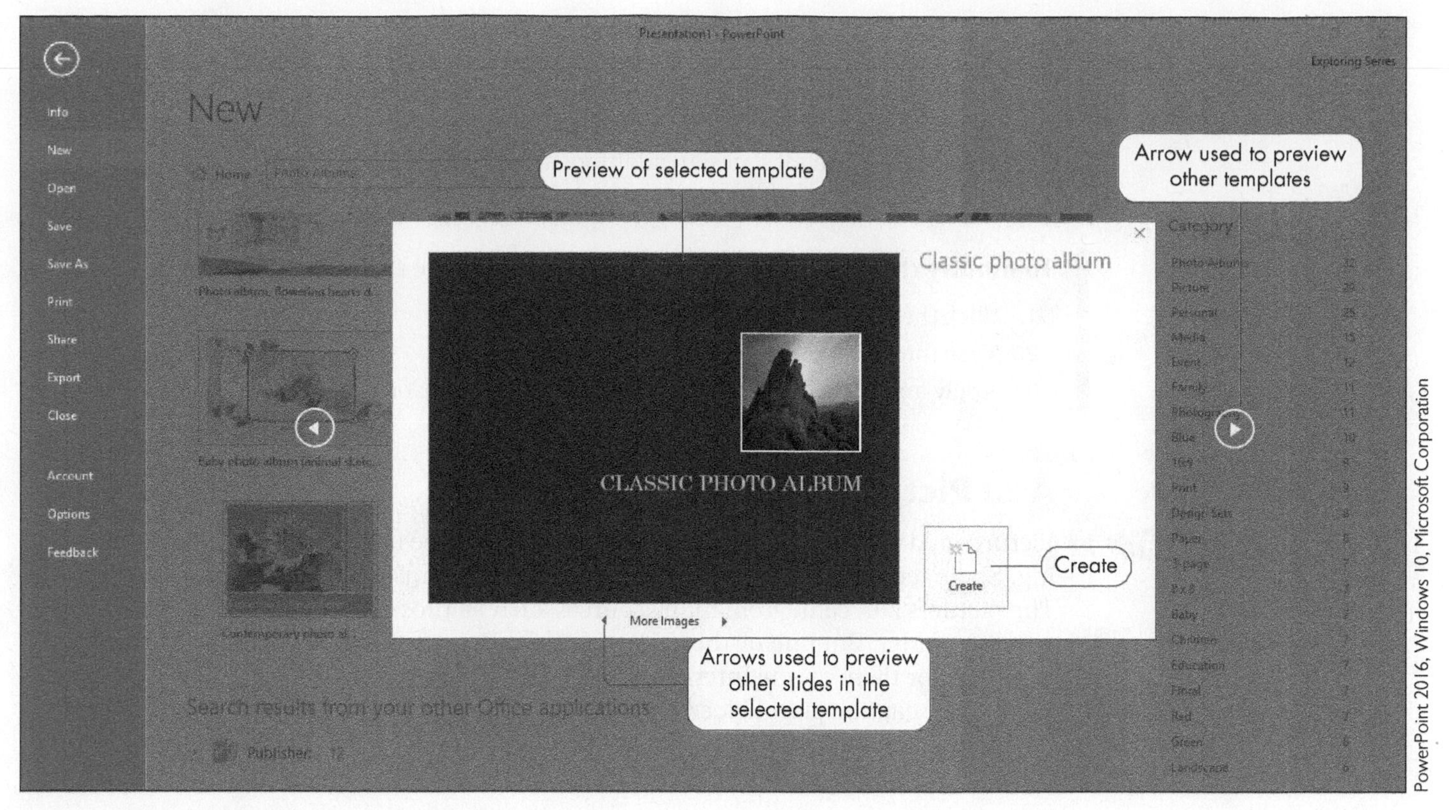

FIGURE 5 Template Preview

Modifying a Presentation Based on a Template

STEP 2 The templates you download may have custom slide layouts unique to that particular template. After you download a template, you can modify it, perhaps by changing a font style or size, moving or deleting a placeholder, or moving an object on the slide. After you modify the presentation, you can save it and use it repeatedly. The ability to save these changes as a new template can save you a tremendous amount of time, because you will not have to redo your modifications the next time you use the presentation.

Modify a Placeholder and Layout

STEP 3 A template may be customized in several ways. Slide layouts, also called layouts, are an obvious point at which to customize a template. You can change the layout by clicking the Layout arrow in the Slides group and selecting a new layout from those listed there. You can also change the layout by moving title, subtitle, or picture placeholders to a new position on individual slides. The placeholders can be resized or deleted.

To modify a layout by moving or resizing a placeholder, complete the following steps:

1. Advance to the slide that you would like to modify.
2. Click the placeholder's border.
3. Drag the placeholder to a different part of the slide to change the position, or drag the border to resize the placeholder.

The colors and background fill for placeholders can be changed to visually carry out a theme. For example, the recruiters at your school may have a presentation developed that is used to explain to prospective students the types of support and academic services that are available at your school. The presentation's theme displays your school's colors in its placeholders on all slides. In addition, although the placeholders for a template may be assigned a default font type, size, or color, these characteristics are easily modified.

To modify the text within a placeholder, complete the following steps:

1. Click the placeholder text.
2. Type the text and then select it.
3. Apply any of the features available in the Font group on the Home tab.

Add Pictures and Captions

Pictures add visual interest to a presentation and can be used to effectively convey meaning. Some templates include slide layouts with placeholders for both pictures and text. The pictures can come from many sources such as those you have taken and stored on your computer. But one of the easiest methods to get pictures for your presentation is to search for them on the Internet and then add them to your slide in the picture placeholder. The caption placeholder can be used for additional information to explain or support the picture or idea. Note that some pictures located on the Internet may not be used without permission or license from the creator.

To locate pictures from the Internet to add to your template, complete the following steps:

1. Advance to a slide where you want to add a picture.
2. Select the picture placeholder.
3. Click Online Pictures in the Insert tab.
4. Type your search term into the Bing Image Search box.

1. Are a template and a theme the same thing? Why or why not?
2. Why might someone use a template rather than start from a blank presentation?
3. What are some of the Suggested searches templates available in PowerPoint? What are some of the categories used to filter one of the Suggested searches?

Hands-On Exercises

Skills covered: Create a New Presentation Based on a Template • Modify a Placeholder • Modify a Layout • Add Pictures and Modify a Caption

1 Templates

To promote the Wellness Education Center at your school, you decide to create a presentation that can be shown to campus groups and other organizations to inform them about the Center and its mission.

STEP 1 » CREATE A NEW PRESENTATION BASED ON A TEMPLATE

You begin the Wellness Education Center presentation by looking for a template that is upbeat and that represents the idea that being healthy makes you feel good. You locate the perfect template (a photo album with warm sunflowers on the cover) from the Photo Albums Suggested search that you conduct. You open a new presentation based on the template and save the presentation. Refer to Figure 6 as you complete Step 1.

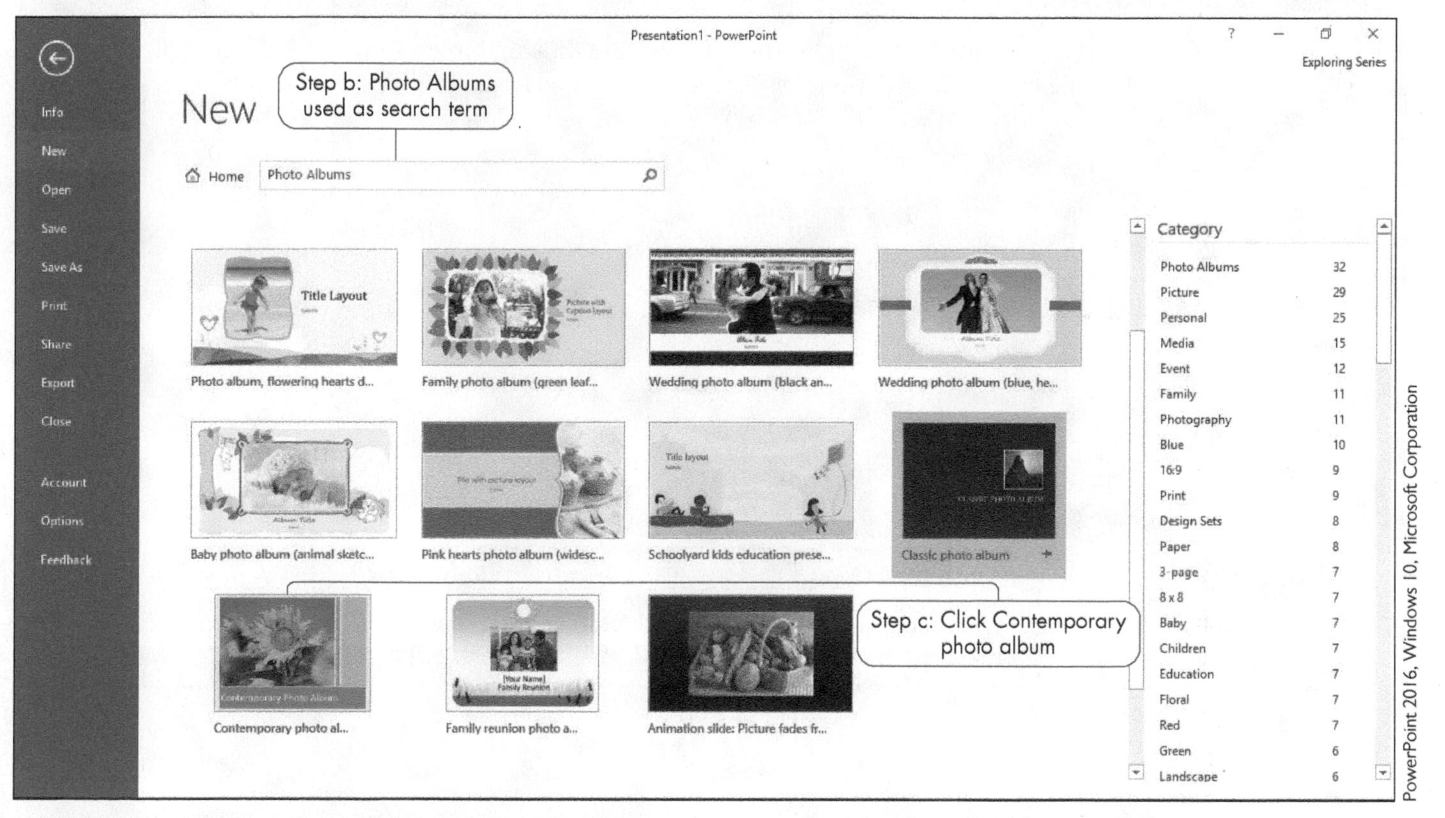

FIGURE 6 New Presentation Dialog Box

a. Start PowerPoint.

b. Type **Photo Albums** in the Search box and press **Enter**.

Thumbnails of sample Photo Album templates will display. The exact results may vary.

c. Scroll to locate, and then click **Contemporary photo album.** Click **Create** in the Preview window.

d. View the slide show and read each of the instructions included in the template.

Templates may include instructions for their use or tips on the content that may be added to create a specific presentation. For example, Slide 2 includes instructions to follow for adding your own pages to the album.

e. Click the **Insert tab** and click **Header & Footer** in the Text group. Click the **Notes and Handouts tab** in the Header and Footer dialog box. Create a handout header with your name and a handout footer with your instructor's name and your class. Include the current date. The page number feature can remain active. Click **Apply to All**.

f. Save the presentation as **p02h1Center_LastFirst**.

STEP 2 » MODIFY A PLACEHOLDER

The template you selected and downloaded consists of a Title Slide layout you like, but the text in the placeholders needs to be changed to the Wellness Education Center information. You edit the title slide to include the Center's name and slogan. You also modify the title placeholder to make the Center's name stand out. Refer to Figure 7 as you complete Step 2.

FIGURE 7 Edited Title Slide

a. Click **Slide 1**, select the text **Contemporary Photo Album** in the title placeholder, and type **Wellness Education Center**.

> **TROUBLESHOOTING:** If you make any major mistakes in this exercise, you can close the file, open *p02h1Center_LastFirst* again and then start this exercise over.

b. Select the title text, and click **Italic** and **Text Shadow** in the Font group on the Home tab.

You modify the template's title placeholder to make the title text stand out.

c. Click the **subtitle text,** *Click to add date or details,* and type **Dedicated to Promoting Healthy Lifestyles!**

d. Save the presentation.

STEP 3 ›› MODIFY A LAYOUT

The Contemporary Photo Album template includes many layouts designed to create an interesting photo album. Although the layout you selected conveys the warm feeling you desire, the layouts will be modified to fit your needs. You modify a section layout and add a new slide with the layout of your choice. You also delete unnecessary slides. Refer to Figure 8 as you complete Step 3.

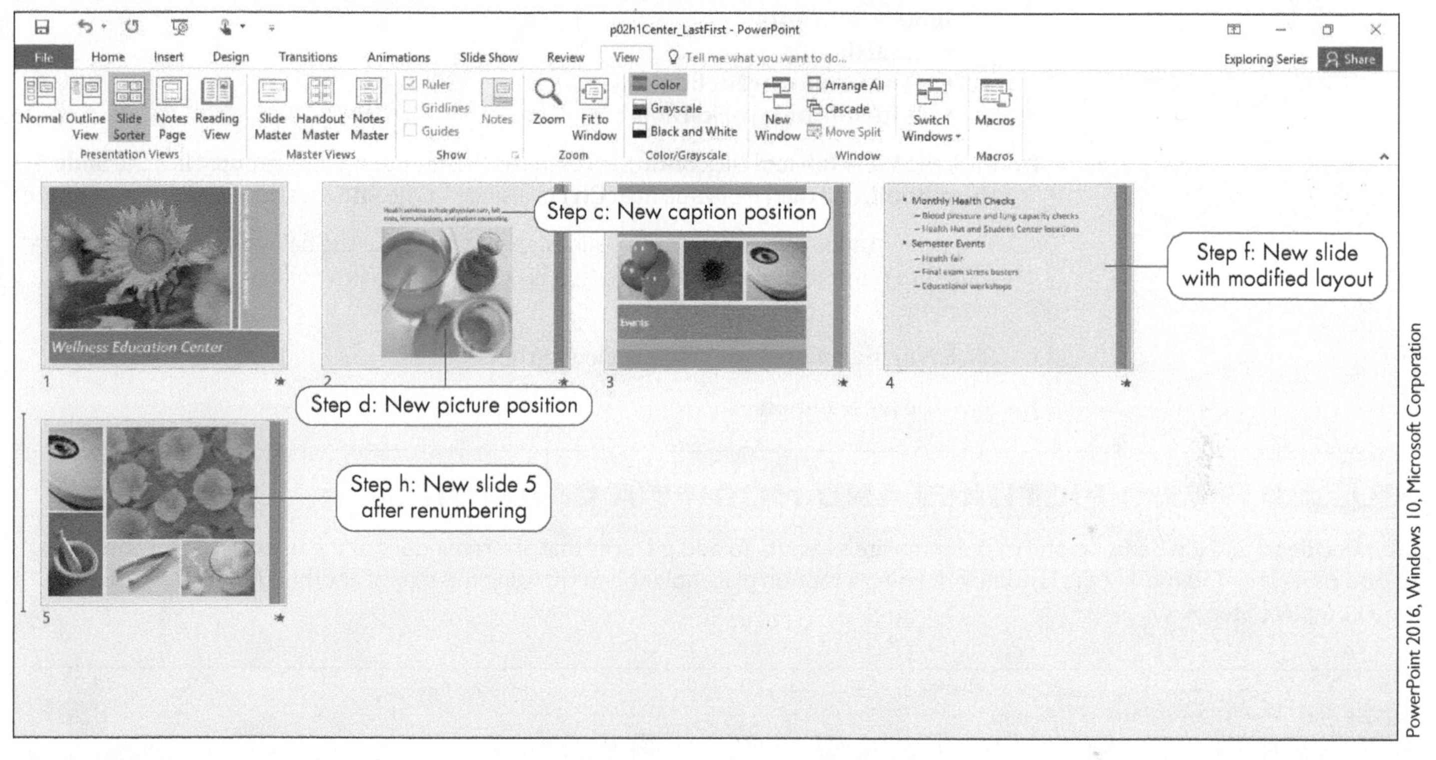

FIGURE 8 Title and Content Layout

a. Click **Slide 2**, replace the sample text with **Health services include physician care, lab tests, immunizations, and patient counseling.**

b. Click **Layout** in the Slides group and click the **Square with Caption layout**.

Note that the Contemporary photo album template has many more layouts than the default Office Theme template. The number of layouts provided with a template varies, so always check to see your options.

c. Select the caption, and drag it to the top of the picture (not above it).

As you drag, you will notice red line guides appear to help you as you move the object. You can press and hold Shift to constrain the movement of the caption as you drag for additional control.

d. Select the picture and drag the picture below the caption.

The location of the placeholder is modified to show the caption above the picture.

e. Click **Slide 3**, select the placeholder text **Choose a layout**, and type **Events**. Delete the subtitle text.

When you delete existing text in a new template placeholder, it is replaced with instructional text such as *Click to add subtitle*. It is not necessary to delete this text, as it will not display when the slide show is viewed.

f. Click the **New Slide arrow** and click the **Title and Content layout**.

> **TROUBLESHOOTING:** Clicking the New Slide arrow opens the Layout gallery for you to select a layout. Clicking New Slide directly above the New Slide arrow creates a new slide using the layout of the current slide.

g. Delete the title placeholder and drag the content placeholder to the top of the slide. Type the following information:

- **Monthly Health Checks**
  - **Blood pressure and lung capacity checks**
  - **Health Hut and Student Center locations**
- **Semester Events**
  - **Health fair**
  - **Final exam stress busters**
  - **Educational workshops**

h. Click the **View tab** and click **Slide Sorter** in the Presentation Views group. Click the **Slide 5 thumbnail**, and then press and hold **Ctrl** to also select the **Slide 6 thumbnail**. Press **Delete**.

The presentation now contains five slides. After you make the deletions, the remaining slides are renumbered, and the slide that becomes Slide 5 is a collage of images from the template.

i. Click **Normal** in the Presentation Views group.

j. Save the presentation.

STEP 4 ›› ADD PICTURES AND MODIFY A CAPTION

You decide to add a slide using one of the template's layouts to add pictures that are reminders of the importance of controlling blood pressure. You modify the layout by deleting a caption placeholder and changing the size of another. Refer to Figure 9 as you complete Step 4.

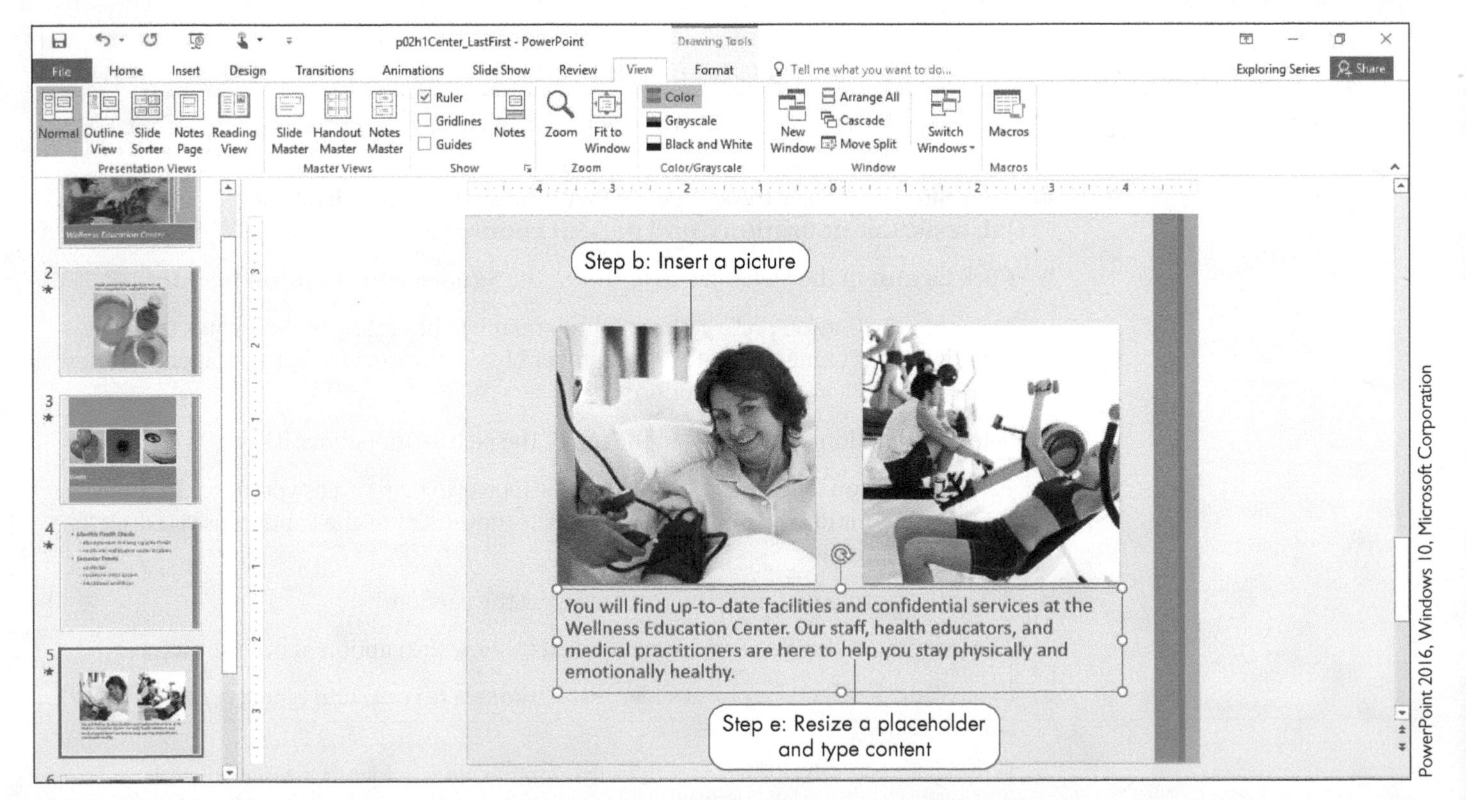

FIGURE 9 Edited Slide

a. Ensure that Slide 4 is the active slide, click the **New Slide arrow** on the Home tab, and then click **2-Up Landscape with Captions.**

A new slide is created. The layout includes two picture placeholders and two caption placeholders.

b. Select the **left picture placeholder** and click **Online Pictures** on the Insert tab. In the Bing Image Search box, type **blood pressure check**, press **Enter**, and then insert a picture of your choice.

The image is added to the placeholder.

TROUBLESHOOTING: Clicking the icon in the center of the picture placeholder will open the Insert Picture dialog box. If this happens, click Cancel. Click somewhere in the white space around the icon to select the placeholder. Once the placeholder is selected, you will be able to continue with the instructions for adding an Online Picture.

c. Select the **right picture placeholder** and click **Online Pictures** on the Insert tab. In the Bing Image Search box, type **gym**, press **Enter**, and then insert a picture of your choice.

d. Delete the right caption placeholder and select the remaining caption placeholder. Click the **Format tab.** In the Size group, change the Width to **9"**. The caption placeholder is now the width of both pictures.

e. Type the following in the caption placeholder: **You will find up-to-date facilities and confidential services at the Wellness Education Center. Our staff, health educators, and medical practitioners are here to help you stay physically and emotionally healthy.**

f. Left align the text and then run the spelling checker. Save the presentation. Keep the presentation open if you plan to continue with the next Hands-On Exercise. If not, close the presentation, and exit PowerPoint.

Outlines

An ***outline*** organizes text using a ***hierarchy*** with main points and subpoints to indicate the levels of importance of the text. When you use a storyboard to determine your content, you create a basic outline. An outline is the fastest way to enter or edit text for a presentation. Think of an outline as the road map you use to create your presentation. Rather than having to enter the text in each placeholder on each slide separately, you can type the text directly into an outline, and it will populate into the slides automatically.

In this section, you will learn how to add content to a presentation using Outline view. After creating the presentation, you will modify the outline structure. Finally, you will print the outline.

Creating a Presentation in Outline View

To create an outline for your presentation you must be in Outline view. ***Outline view*** shows the presentation in an outline format displayed in levels according to the points and subpoints on each slide. There are two panes in Outline view, the outline and an image of the active slide. Instead of the slide thumbnails displayed in Normal view, the presentation is displayed as a hierarchy of the titles and text for each individual slide. Each slide is denoted by a slide number and a slide icon, followed by the slide title if the slide contains a title placeholder. The slide title is formatted as bold. Slide text is indented under the slide title. A slide with only an image (no text) will not have a title in the outline and will display only the slide number and icon.

Use Outline View

To change to Outline view, complete the following steps:

1. Click the View tab.
2. Click Outline View in the Presentation Views group.

STEP 1 »

One benefit of working in Outline view is that you get a good overview of your presentation without the distraction of design elements, and you can move easily from one slide to the next. You can copy text or bullets from one slide to another and rearrange the order of the slides or bullets. Outline view makes it easy to see relationships between points and to determine where information belongs. Figure 10 shows a portion of a presentation in Outline view.

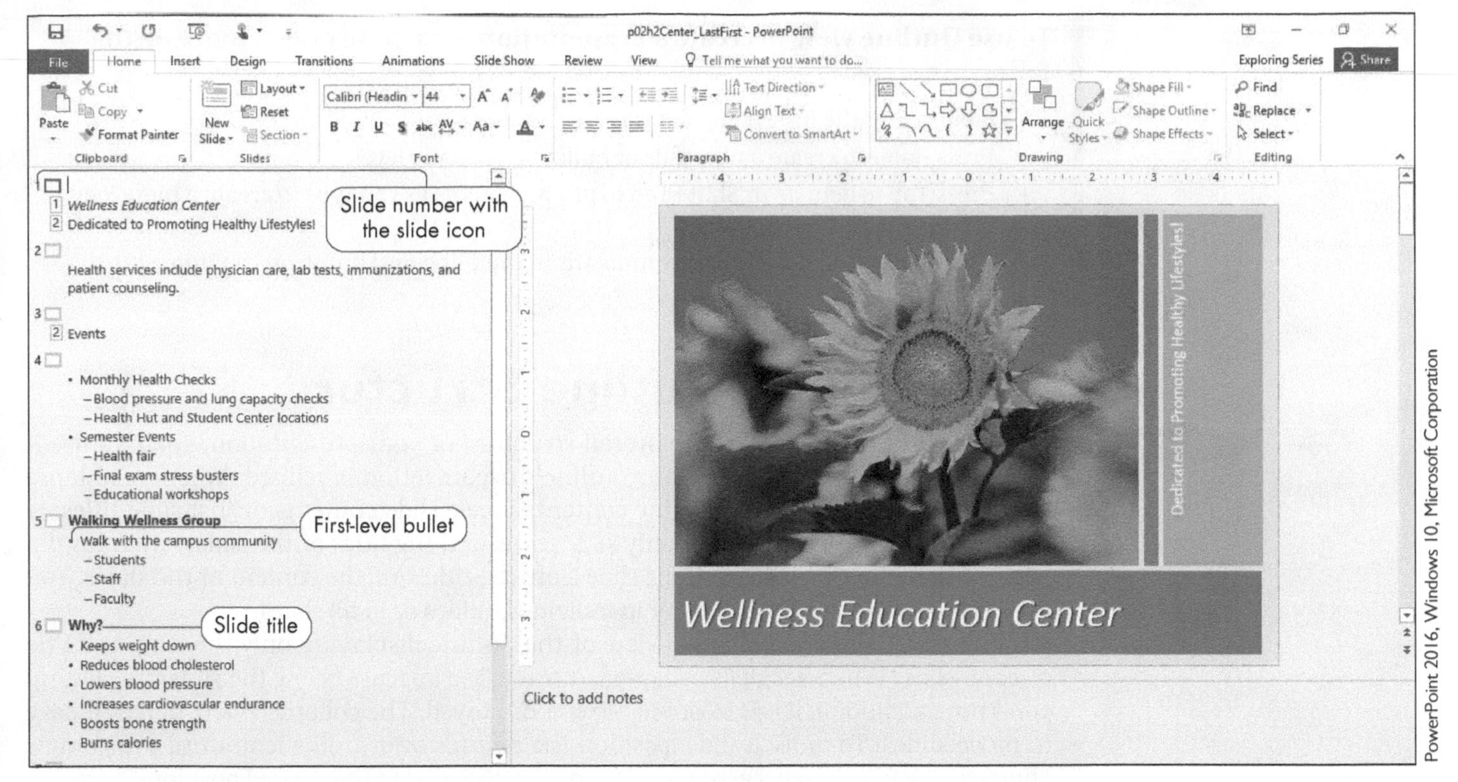

FIGURE 10 Outline View

Edit in Outline View

STEP 2 PowerPoint accommodates nine levels of indentation, although you will likely only use two or three per slide as a design best practice. Levels make it possible to show hierarchy or relationships between the information on your slides. The main points appear on Level 1; subsidiary items are indented below the main point to which they apply, and their font size is decreased.

You can promote any item to a higher level or demote it to a lower level, either before or after the text is entered, by clicking Increase List Level or Decrease List Level in the Paragraph group on the Home tab. When designing your slides, consider the number of subsidiary or lower-level items you add to a main point; too many levels within a single slide make the slide difficult to read or understand because the text size becomes smaller with each additional level.

TIP: CHANGING LIST LEVELS IN AN OUTLINE

As a quick alternative to using Increase and Decrease List Level commands on the Home tab, press Tab to demote an item or press Shift+Tab to promote an item.

Outline view can be an efficient way to create and edit text in a presentation.

To use Outline view to create a presentation, complete one or more of the following steps:

- Ensure that the insertion point is in the Outline pane located on the left.
- Press Enter to create a new slide or bullet at the same level.
- Press Tab to demote or Shift+Tab to promote items as you type to create a hierarchy of information on each slide.
- Use the Cut, Copy, and Paste commands in the Clipboard group on the Home tab to move and copy selected text.

Modifying an Outline Structure

STEP 3 ›› Because Outline view shows the overall structure of your presentation, you can use it to move bullets or slides until your outline's organization is refined. You can collapse or expand your view of the outline contents to see slide contents or just slide titles. A ***collapsed outline*** view displays only slide icons and the titles of the slides, whereas the ***expanded outline*** view displays the slide icon, the title, and the content of the slides. You can collapse or expand the content in individual slides or in all slides.

Figure 11 shows a collapsed view of the outline displaying only the icon and title of each slide. When a slide is collapsed, a wavy line appears below the slide title, letting you know additional levels exist but are not displayed. The collapsed view makes it easy to move slides. To move a slide, position the pointer over a slide icon until the pointer changes to a four-headed arrow, and then drag the icon to the desired position.

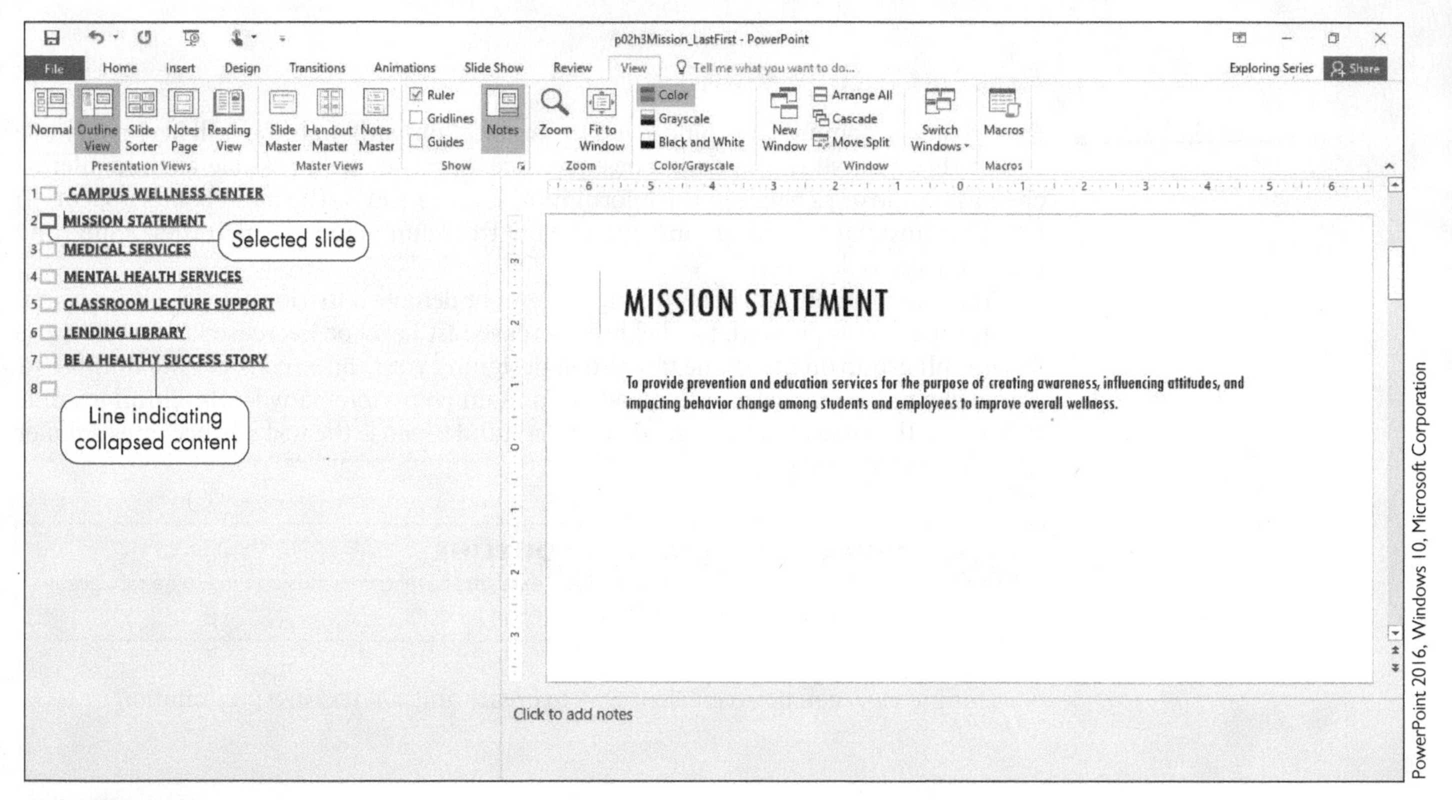

FIGURE 11 Collapsed Outline View

> **To collapse or expand a slide, complete the following steps:**
>
> 1. Double-click the slide icon in the Outline pane. Doing this action collapses or expands the slide contents in the pane.
> 2. Right-click the text following an icon to display Expand or Collapse. Pointing to either will display the shortcut menu with options for collapsing or expanding the selected slides or all slides (see Figure 12).

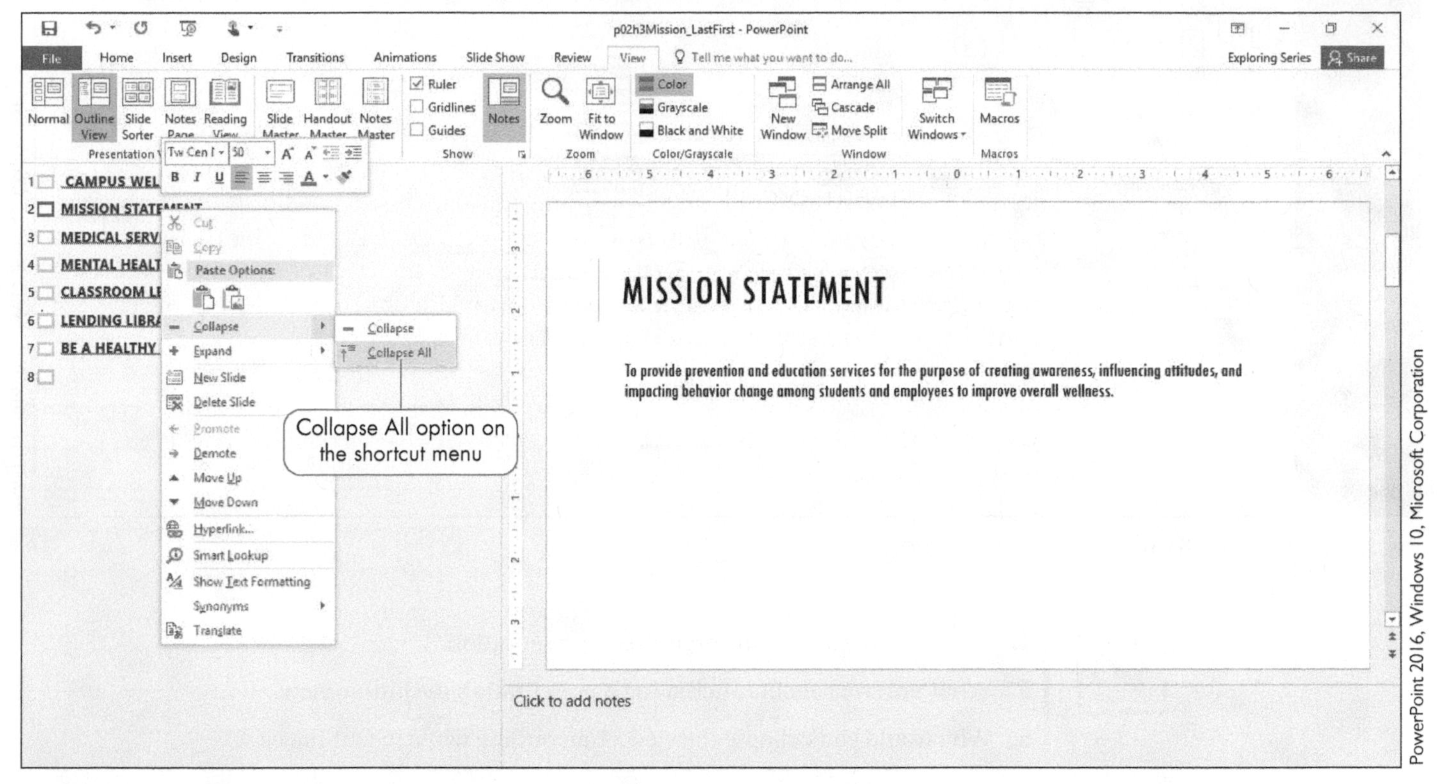

FIGURE 12 Collapse Outline Process

Printing an Outline

You can print an outline in either expanded or collapsed view. Figure 13 displays a preview of an expanded view of the outline ready to print. The slide icon and slide number will print with the outline.

> **To print the outline, complete the following steps:**
>
> 1. Click the File tab and click Print.
> 2. Click Full Page Slides, Notes Pages, or Outline (whichever displays) to open a gallery of printing choices.
> 3. Click Outline.
> 4. Click Print.

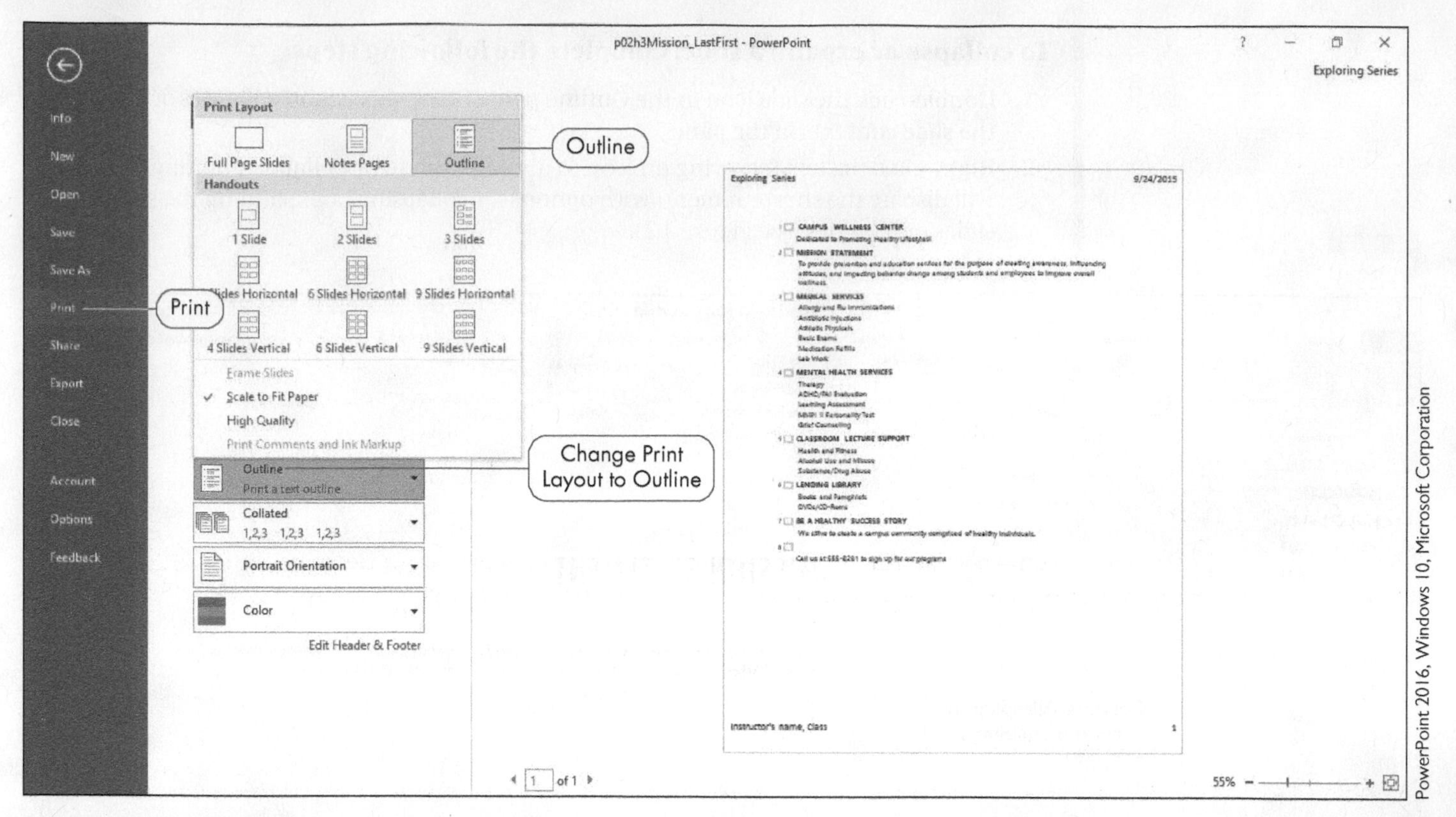

FIGURE 13 Outline Printing

4. Describe how an outline organizes a presentation.
5. What are two benefits of creating a presentation in Outline view?
6. Why would you collapse the view of an outline while in Outline view?

Hands-On Exercises

Skills covered: Use Outline View • Edit in Outline View • Modify the Outline Structure and Print

2 Outlines

The Wellness Education Center sponsors a Walking Wellness group to help campus members increase their physical activity and cardiovascular fitness. The director of the Wellness Education Center believes that joining a group increases a member's level of commitment and provides an incentive for the member to stay active. She asks you to edit the slide show you created in Hands-On Exercise 1 to include information about the walking group.

STEP 1 » USE OUTLINE VIEW

Because you want to concentrate on the information in the presentation rather than the design elements, you use Outline view. You add the information about the walking group as requested by the director. Refer to Figure 14 as you complete Step 1.

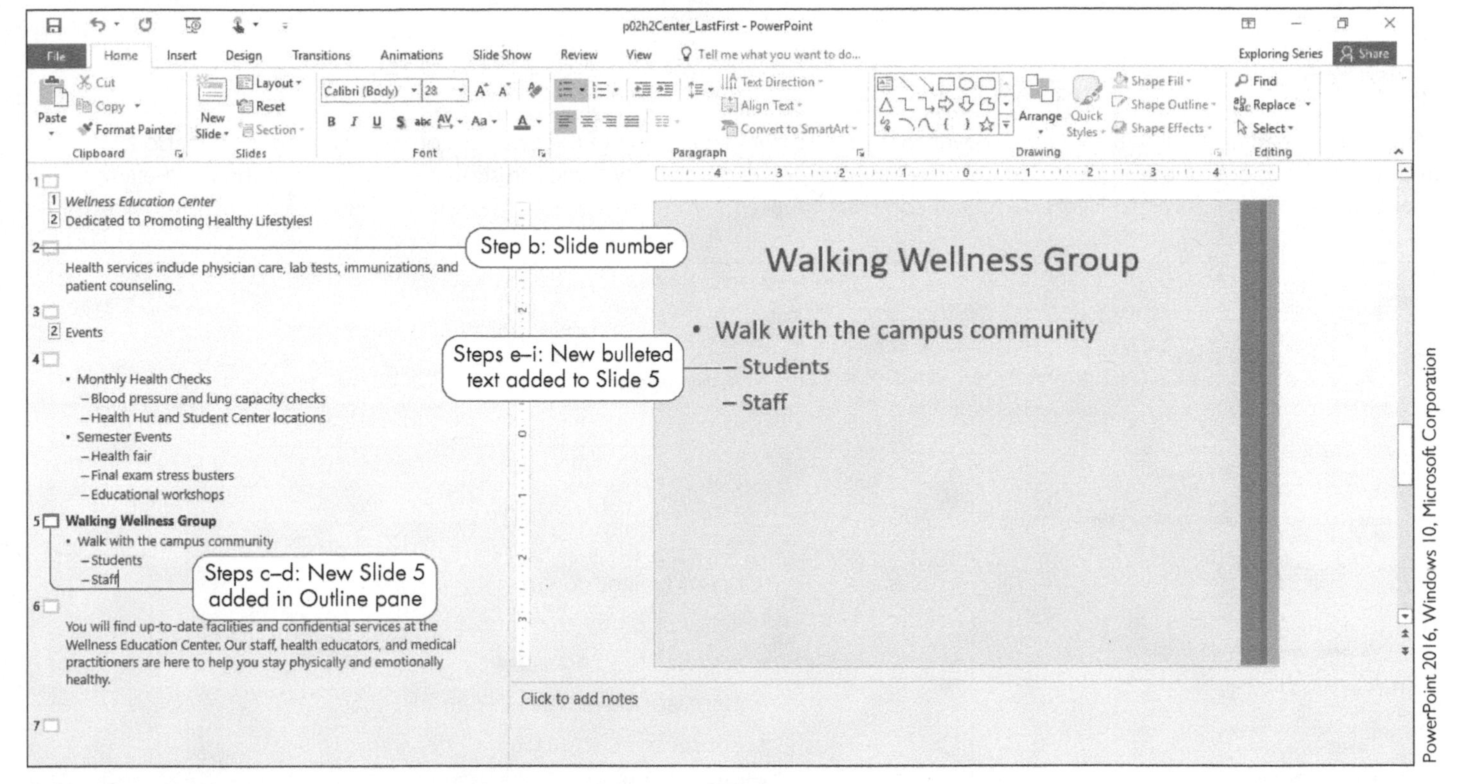

FIGURE 14 Revised Outline

a. Open *p02h1Center_LastFirst* if you closed it at the end of Hands-On Exercise 1, and save it as **p02h2Center_LastFirst**, changing h1 to h2.

b. Click the **View tab** and click **Outline View** in the Presentation Views group.

Note that each slide in the presentation is numbered and has a slide icon. Slides 1 through 5 include text on the slides. Slide 6 contains images only, so no text is displayed in the outline. None of the slides has a title. The text in the Outline pane on the left is also displayed on the slide in the Slide pane on the right.

c. Click at the end of the last bullet for Slide 4 in the Outline pane and press **Enter**.

The insertion point is now positioned to enter text at the same level as the previous bullet point. To create a new slide at a higher level, you must decrease the indent level.

d. Click **Decrease List Level** in the Paragraph group on the Home tab twice.

A new Slide 5 is created, the previous Slide 5 is renumbered as Slide 6, and Slide 6 is renumbered as Slide 7.

e. Type **Walking Wellness Group** and press **Enter**.

Pressing Enter moves the insertion point to the next line and creates a new slide, Slide 6. The title is bold in the Outline.

f. Press **Tab** to demote the text in the outline.

The insertion point is now positioned to enter bulleted text on Slide 5.

g. Type **Walk with the campus community** and press **Enter**.

h. Press **Tab** to demote the bullet and type **Students**.

Students becomes Level 3 text.

i. Press **Enter** and type **Staff**.

j. Save the presentation.

STEP 2 » EDIT THE OUTLINE

While proofreading your outline, you discover that you did not identify one of the campus community groups. You also notice that you left out one of the most important slides in your presentation: why someone should walk. You edit the outline and make these changes. Refer to Figure 15 as you complete Step 2.

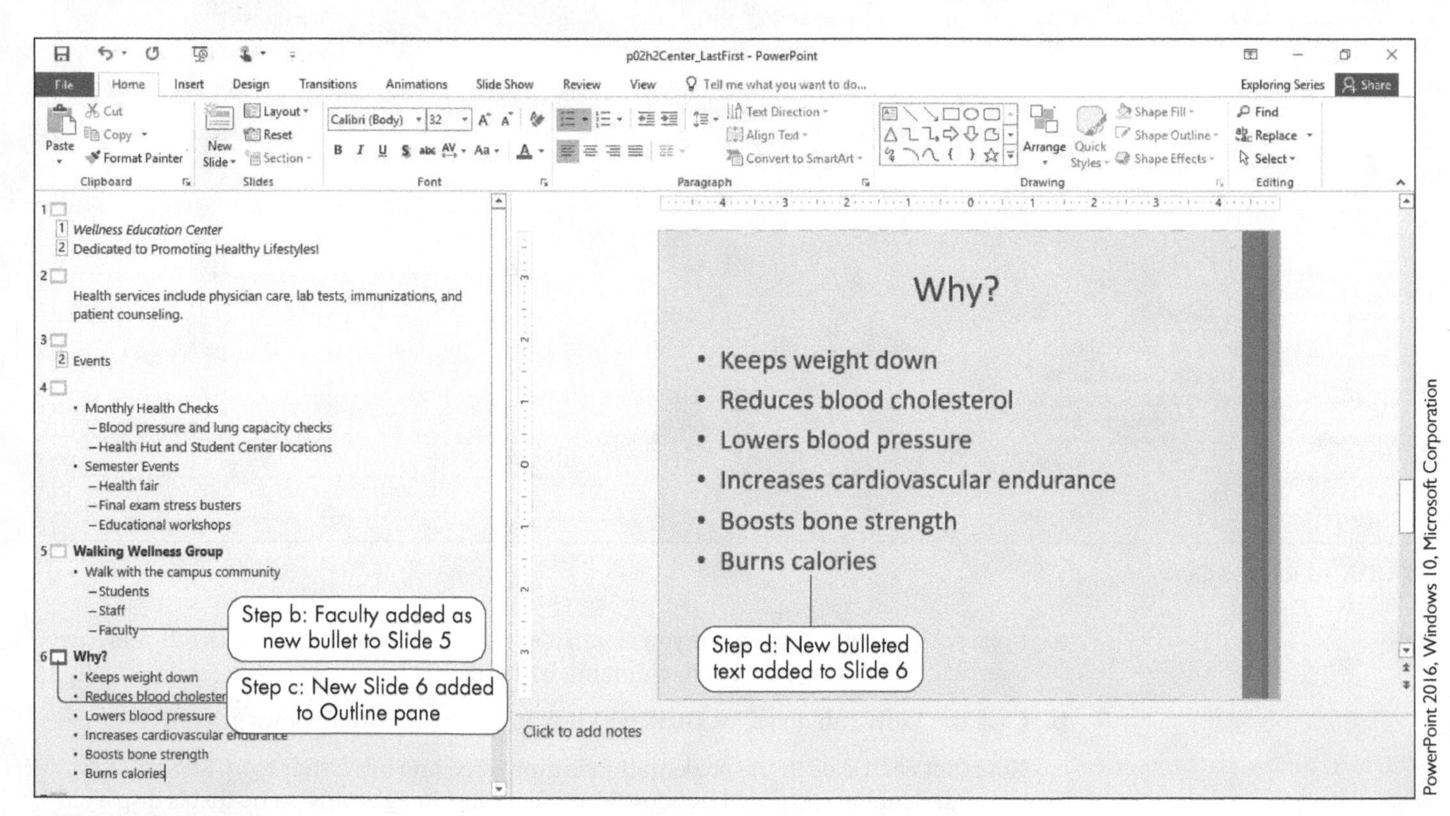

FIGURE 15 Edited Outline

a. Ensure that the word *Staff* on Slide 5 is selected in the outline.

b. Press **Enter** and type **Faculty.**

> **TROUBLESHOOTING:** If your text does not appear in the correct position, check to see if the insertion point was in the wrong location. To enter a blank line for a new bullet, the insertion point must be at the end of an existing bullet point, not at the beginning.

c. Press **Enter** and press **Shift+Tab** twice.

Pressing Shift+Tab promotes the text to create a new Slide 6.

d. Use the Outline pane to type the information for Slide 6 as shown below:

Why?

- **Keeps weight down**
- **Reduces blood cholesterol**
- **Lowers blood pressure**
- **Increases cardiovascular endurance**
- **Boosts bone strength**
- **Burns calories**

e. Save the presentation.

STEP 3 » MODIFY THE OUTLINE STRUCTURE AND PRINT

The director of the Wellness Education Center has reviewed the slide show and made several suggestions about its structure. She feels that keeping weight down belongs at the bottom of the list of reasons for walking and asks you to reposition it. Refer to Figure 16 as you complete Step 3.

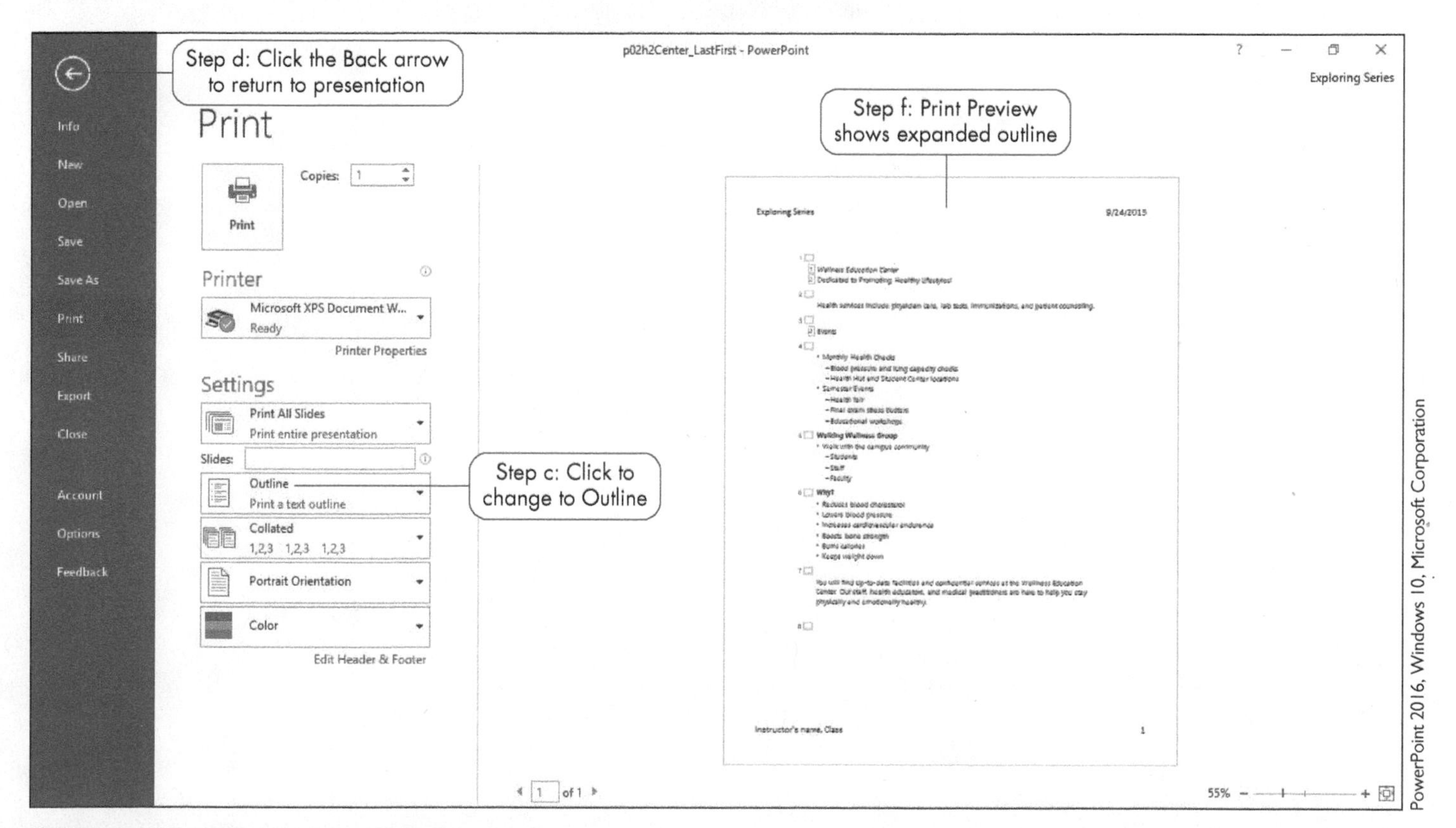

FIGURE 16 Expanded Outline in Print Preview

a. Position the pointer over the first bullet, *Keeps weight down*, on Slide 6 in the outline. When the pointer looks like a four-headed arrow, click and drag the text until it becomes the last bullet on the slide.

b. Right-click anywhere in the Slide 6 text, point to **Collapse**, and then click **Collapse All**.

   Only the slide titles will be shown in the Outline.

c. Click the **File tab**, click **Print**, and then click the **Full Page Slides arrow**. Click **Outline**.

   A preview of the collapsed outline shows in the Preview pane. Because so few slides contain titles, the collapsed outline is not helpful.

d. Click the **Back arrow** to return to the presentation.

   The Outline pane is once again visible.

e. Right-click any text visible in the Outline pane, point to **Expand**, and then select **Expand All**.

f. Click the **File tab** and click **Print**.

   The Outline Print Layout is retained from Step c and the expanded outline shows in the Preview pane.

g. Click the **Back arrow** to return to the presentation.

h. Check spelling in the presentation. Save and close the presentation. You will submit this file to your instructor at the end of the last Hands-On Exercise.

Data Imports

You can add slides to a presentation in several ways if the content exists in other formats, such as an outline in Word or slides from other presentations. PowerPoint can create slides based on Microsoft Word outlines (.docx or .doc formats) or outlines saved in another word-processing format that PowerPoint recognizes (.rtf format). You can import data into a slide show to add existing slides from a previously created presentation. This is a very efficient way to add content to a slide show.

In this section, you will learn how to import an outline into a PowerPoint presentation and how to add slides from another presentation into the current presentation.

Importing an Outline

STEP 1 » Outlines created using Outline view in Microsoft Word can be imported to quickly create a PowerPoint presentation. To create an outline in Word, you must click the View tab, click Outline, and then type your text.

PowerPoint also recognizes outlines created in Word and saved in ***Rich Text Format (.rtf)***, a file format you can use to transfer formatted text documents between applications such as word-processing programs and PowerPoint. You can even transfer documents between different platforms such as Mac and Windows. The structure and most of the text formatting are retained when you import the outline into PowerPoint.

To create a new presentation from an outline, complete the following steps:

1. Click the New Slide arrow on the Home tab.
2. Click Slides from Outline.
3. Locate and select the file and click Insert.

Solve Problems While Importing Word Outlines

You may encounter problems when trying to import an outline. For example, a list using the numbered list or bullet feature in the Paragraph group on the Home tab in Word (that was not created in Outline view) will not import easily to PowerPoint.

If you import a Word document that appears to be an outline and after importing, each line of the Word document becomes a title for a new slide, the Word document is actually a bulleted list rather than an outline. These two features are separate and distinct in Word and do not import into PowerPoint in the same manner. Open the bulleted list in Word, apply outline heading styles, save the file, and then re-import it to PowerPoint.

PowerPoint also recognizes outlines created and saved in a ***plain text format*** (which uses the file extension ***.txt***), a file format that retains text without any formatting. But because .txt outlines have no saved hierarchical structure, each line of the outline becomes a slide. Avoid saving outlines you create in this format. If you receive an outline in a .txt format, you can create a hierarchy in PowerPoint without having to retype the text by simply moving the text around to create the structure.

Reusing Slides from an Existing Presentation

STEP 2 » You can reuse slides from an existing PowerPoint presentation when creating a new presentation without having to open the other file. The imported slides display in a pane on the right so that you can select the slides you want to import into your existing presentation. This feature can save you considerable time.

To import existing slides without having to open the other file, complete the following steps:

1. Click the New Slide arrow in the Slides group on the Home tab.
2. Click Reuse Slides.
3. Click Browse, click Browse File, and then navigate to the folder containing the presentation that has the slides you want to use.
4. Click Open.
5. Select each slide individually to add it to the presentation. Or right-click any slide and click Insert All Slides to add all of the slides to the presentation.
6. Close the Reuse Slides pane.

By default, when you insert a slide into the presentation, it takes on the formatting of the open presentation. If the new slides do not take on the formatting of the open presentation, select the imported text in Outline view and click Clear all Formatting in the Font group of the Home tab. It will format the slides using the active theme. If you wish to retain the formatting of the original presentation, click the Keep source formatting check box at the bottom of the Reuse Slides pane, shown in Figure 17.

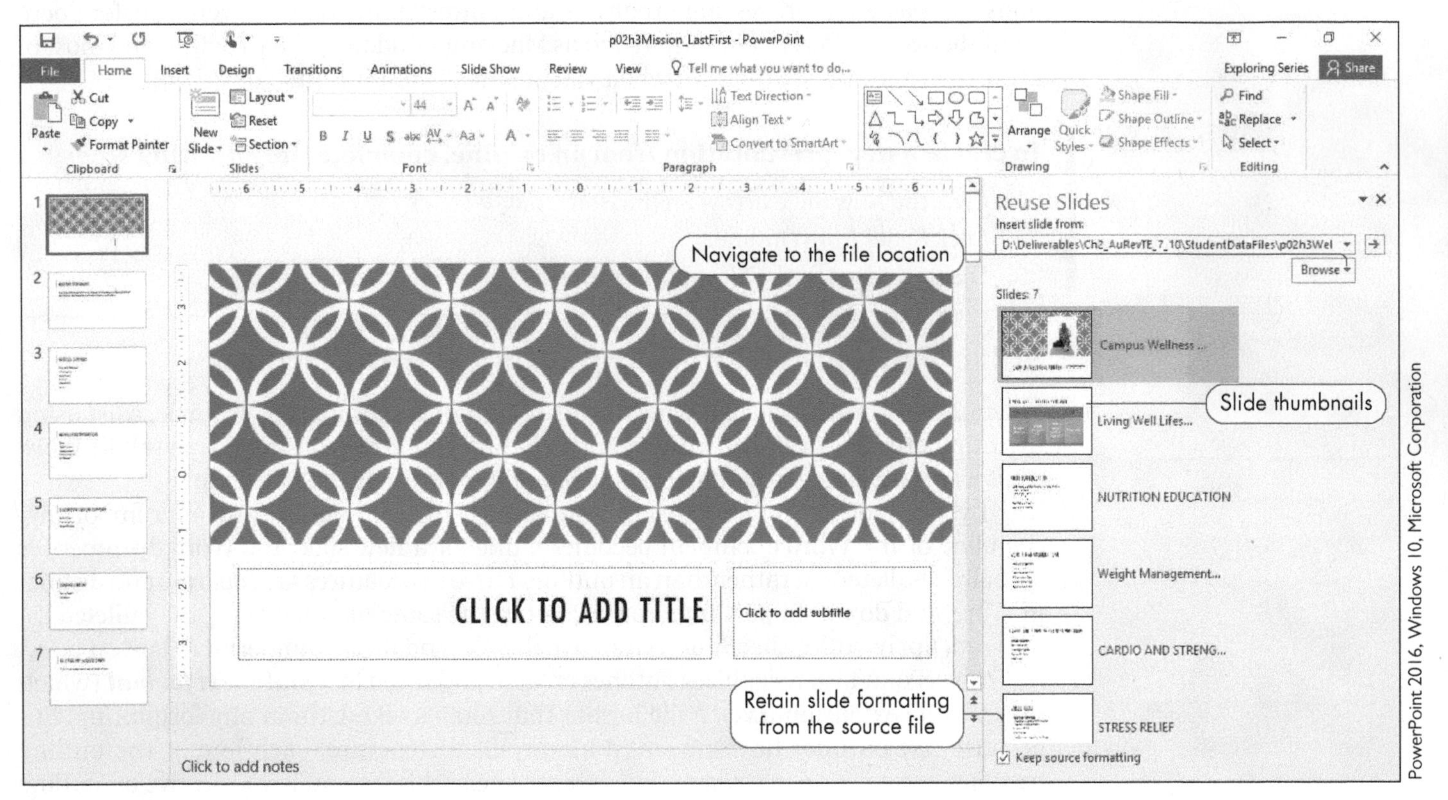

FIGURE 17 Reuse Slides Pane

Quick Concepts

7. Describe two problems and their solutions that you may encounter when importing an outline into PowerPoint.
8. Describe how you would use slides from another presentation in your current presentation.
9. When you insert a slide into a presentation, what formatting does it use? How would you change this default setting?

Hands-On Exercises

Skills covered: Import a Rich Text Format Outline • Reuse Slides from Another Presentation

3 Data Imports

The director of the Wellness Education Center is impressed with the center's overview presentation you created. She gives you an electronic copy of an outline she created in a word-processing software package and asks if you can convert it into a slide show. You create a slide show from the outline and then supplement it with content from another slide show.

STEP 1 ›› IMPORT A RICH TEXT FORMAT OUTLINE

The director of the Wellness Education Center saves an outline for a presentation in Rich Text Format. You import the outline into PowerPoint to use as the basis for a presentation about the center, its mission, and the services it provides to students, staff, and faculty. Refer to Figure 18 as you complete Step 1.

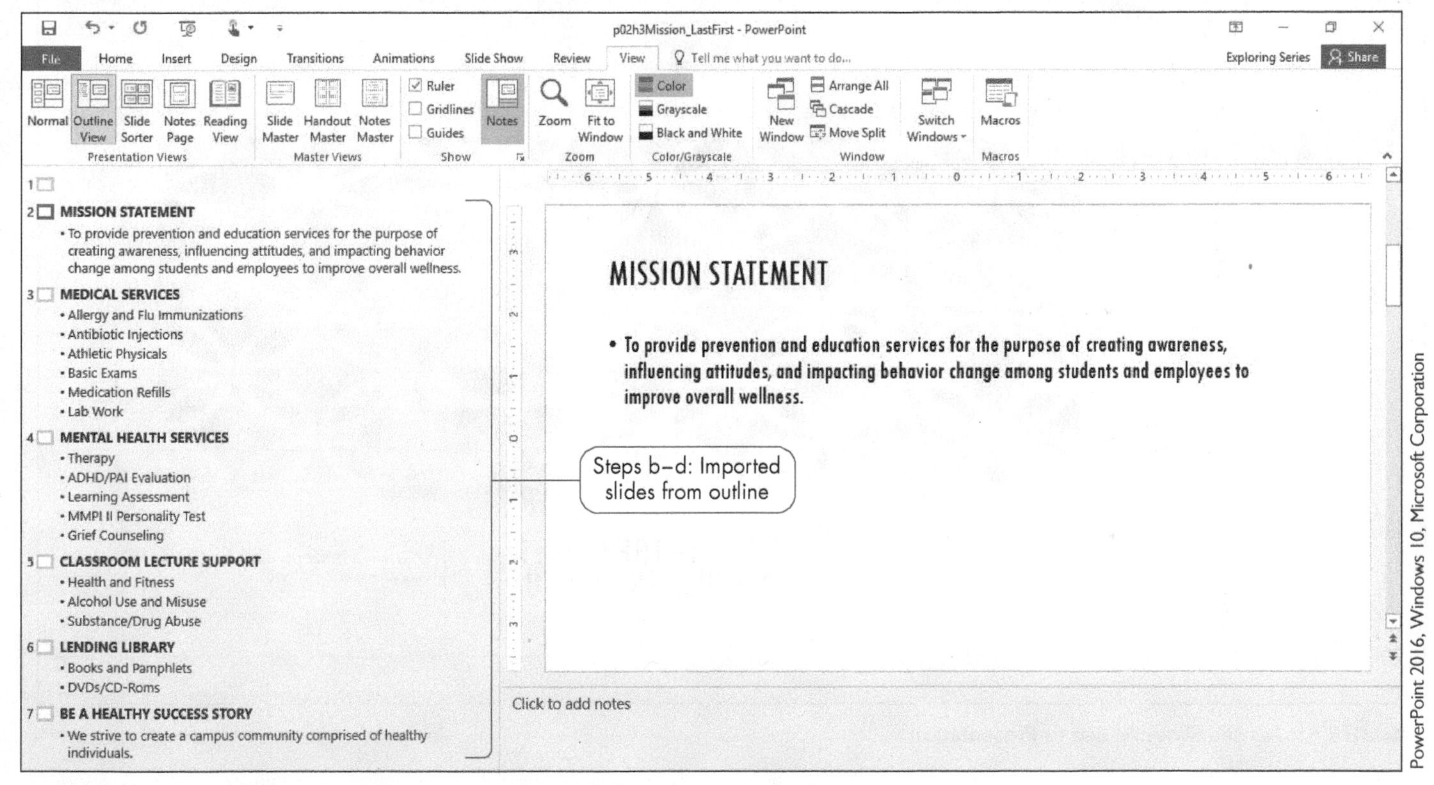

FIGURE 18 New Presentation Based on an Outline

a. Click the **File tab**, click **New**, and then double-click **Blank Presentation**. Save the presentation as **p02h3Mission_LastFirst**.

A new blank presentation opens and is saved.

b. Click the **New Slide arrow** on the Insert tab, click **Slides from Outline**, and then navigate to the location of your student data files.

c. Browse and insert file *p02h3MedOutline*.

The outline is opened and new slides are added to the presentation.

d. Click the **View tab** and click **Outline View** in the Presentation Views group.

Because the file was created in Word with heading styles applied and saved in Rich Text Format, the outline retains its hierarchy. Each slide has a title and bulleted text.

e. Create a handout header with your name and a handout footer with your instructor's name and your class. Include the current date.

f. Apply the **Integral theme** to all slides.

The Integral theme adds a subtle blue line next to the title.

g. Save the presentation.

STEP 2 » REUSE SLIDES FROM ANOTHER PRESENTATION

While reviewing the Wellness Education Center presentation, you realize you do not have a title slide or a final slide inviting students to contact the Center. You reuse slides from another presentation created for the Center containing slides that would fit well in this presentation. Refer to Figure 19 as you complete Step 2.

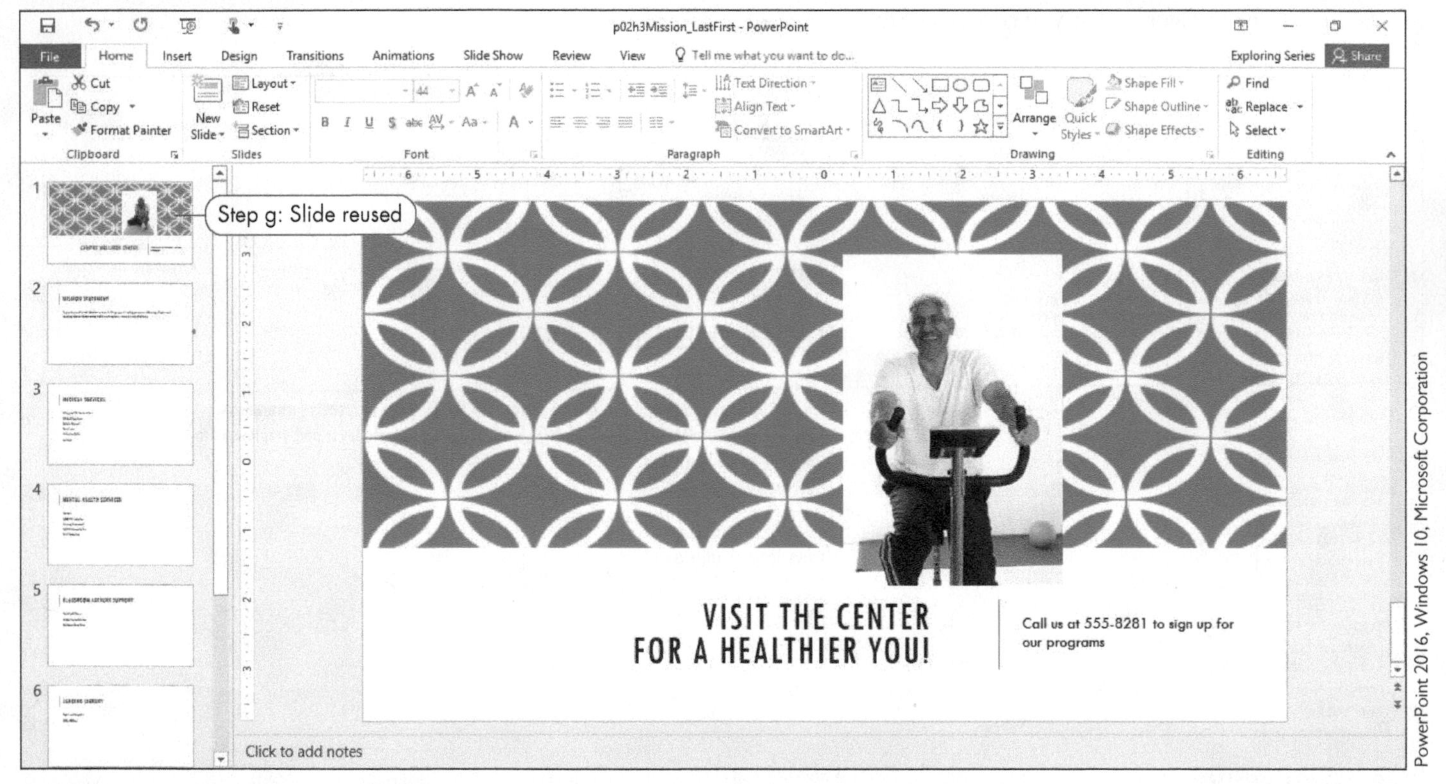

FIGURE 19 Reused Slides Added to Presentation

a. Switch to **Normal view**. Click **Slide 1**, click the **New Slide arrow** in the Slides group on the Home tab, and then click **Reuse Slides** at the bottom of the New Slides gallery.

b. Click **Browse**, click **Browse File**, and then locate your student data files. Select *p02h3Wellness*, and then click **Open**.

> **TROUBLESHOOTING:** If you do not see the *p02h3Wellness* file, click Files of type and select All PowerPoint Presentations.

c. Click to select the **Keep source formatting check box** at the bottom of the Reuse Slides pane.

With *Keep source formatting* selected, the images and design of the slides you reuse will transfer with the slide.

d. Click the **first slide**, *Campus Wellness*, in the Reuse Slides pane.

The slide is added to your presentation after the current slide, Slide 1.

e. Delete the blank title slide that is currently Slide 1.

The newly reused slide will be in the Slide 1 position to serve as the title slide of your presentation.

f. Select the **Slide 7 icon**, *BE A HEALTHY SUCCESS STORY*, in the Slides pane of the original presentation.

g. Click **Slide 7** in the Reuse Slides pane and close the Reuse Slides pane.

h. Save the presentation. Keep the presentation open if you plan to continue with the next Hands-On Exercise. If not, close the presentation, and exit PowerPoint.

Design

After you are satisfied with the content, then you can consider the visual aspects of the presentation. You should evaluate many aspects when considering the visual design of your presentation. Those aspects include layout, background, typography, color, and animation, as well as dividing the content into sections. Sections can help you effectively organize and manage the parts of the presentation.

In this section, you will work with tools that allow you to create well-designed presentations. Using these features, you can create a slide show using a professional template and themes and then modify it to reflect your own preferences. Before doing so, however, you need to consider some basic visual design principles for PowerPoint. Finally, you will customize the slide master and slide layouts controlled by the slide master.

Using Sections

STEP 1 »» Content divided into ***sections*** can help you group slides meaningfully. This is similar to how tabs help to organize a binder. These sections provide organization to a presentation by giving a point at which to collapse or expand the slide hierarchy.

When you create a section, it is given the name Untitled Section. You will want to change this to a meaningful name, which enables you to jump to a section quickly. For example, you may be creating a slide show for a presentation on geothermal energy. You could create sections for Earth, plate boundaries, plate tectonics, and thermal features.

TIP: USING A SECTION HEADER

It is easy to confuse term *section* with *section header.* If you need to create a visual break in the presentation, such as stopping to pose questions for the audience, then you will want to use a section header slide instead of a section. Section header slides can be added through Slide Master view.

Use either Normal view or Slide Sorter view to create sections. Figure 20 shows a section added to a presentation in Normal view. Slide sections can be collapsed or expanded. The collapsed view makes it easier to move groups of slides around to reorganize a presentation.

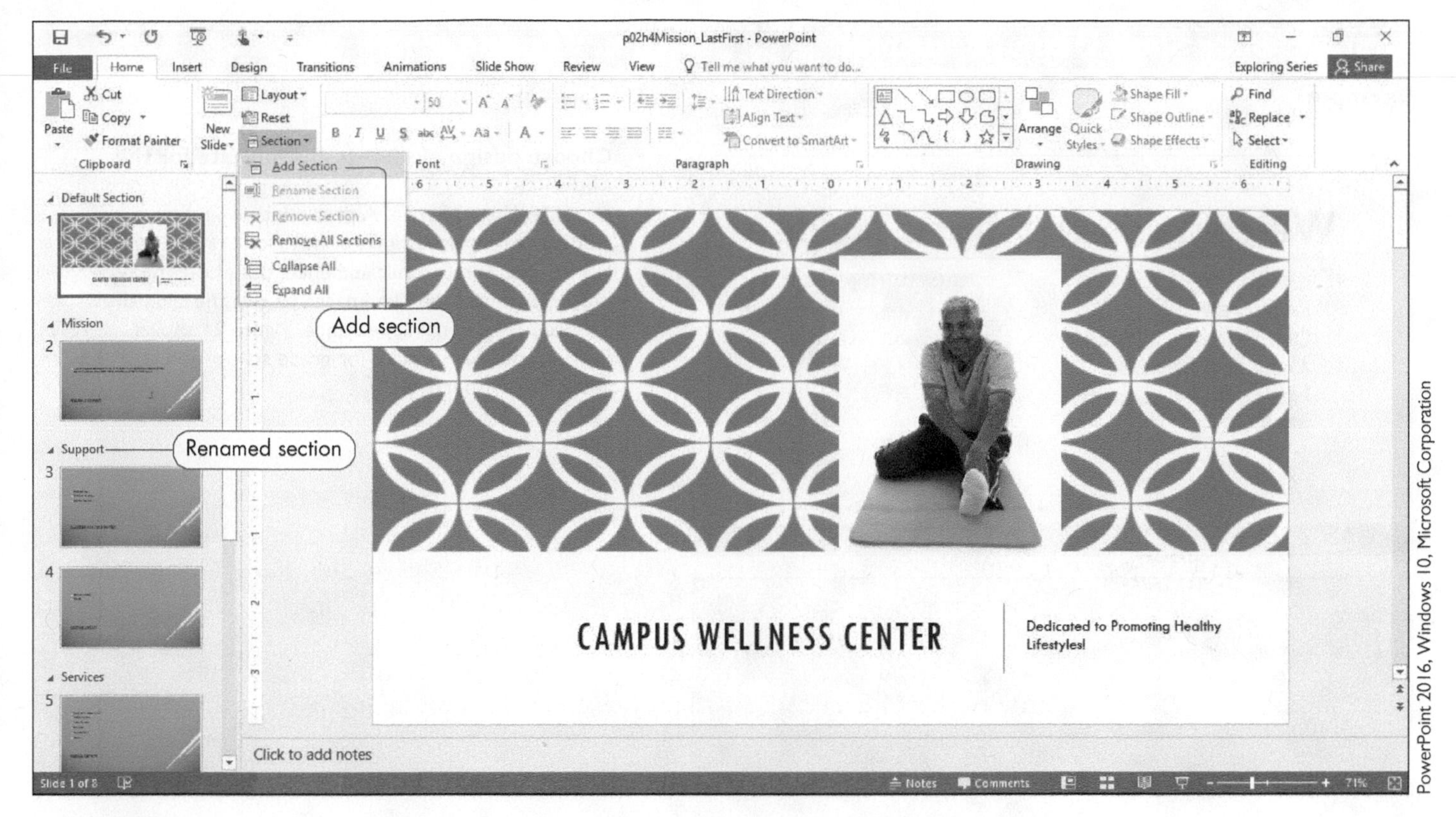

FIGURE 20 Using Sections

To create a section, complete the following steps:

1. Select the first slide of the new section.
2. Click Section in the Slides group on the Home tab.
3. Click Add Section.
4. Right-click Untitled Section and select Rename Section.
5. Type a new name for the section.

Examining Slide Show Design Principles

When applied to a project, universally accepted design principles can increase its appeal and professionalism. Some design aspects may be applied in specific ways to the various types of modern communications: communicating through print media such as flyers or brochures, through audio media such as narrations or music, or through a visual medium such as a slide show. Table 1 focuses on principles that apply to slide shows and examines examples of slides that illustrate these principles.

TABLE 1 Slide Show Design Principles

<table>
<tr><th>Example</th><th>Design Tip</th></tr>
<tr><td>

PowerPoint 2016, Windows 10, Microsoft Corporation
FIGURE 21 Examples of Templates Appropriate for Different Audiences
</td><td>

- Choose design elements appropriate for the audience.
Consider the audience. A presentation to elementary students might use bright, primary colors and cartoon-like images. For an adult audience, use photographs rather than cartoon-like images to give the slide show a more professional appearance. Figure 21 shows design examples suitable for grade school and business audiences, respectively.
</td></tr>
<tr><td>

PowerPoint 2016, Windows 10, Microsoft Corporation
FIGURE 22 Example of a Clean Design
</td><td>

- Keep the design neat and clean.
Avoid using multiple fonts and font colors on a slide. Avoid using multiple images. Use white space (empty space) to open up your design. Figure 22 shows an example of a clean design.
</td></tr>
</table>

TABLE 1 Continued

Example	Design Tip
Delivery Tips • Rehearse timings • Arrive early • Maintain eye contact • Know your audience **FIGURE 23** Example of an Effective Focal Point	• **Create a focal point that leads the viewer's eyes to the critical information on the slide.** The focal point should be the main area of interest. Pictures should always lead the viewer's eyes to the focal point, not away from it. Images should not be so large that they detract from the focal point, unless your goal is to make the image the focal point. Figure 23 illustrates examples of an effective focal point.
 Consistent Style CAT DOG HORSE BIRD **FIGURE 24** Example of Unified Design Elements	• **Use unified design elements for a professional look.** Visual unity creates a harmony between the elements of the slide and between the slides in the slide show. Unity gives the viewer a sense of order and peace. Create unity by repeating colors and shapes. Use images in only one style such as all photographs or all line art throughout the presentation. Figure 24 shows a disjointed and a unified design.
Sans Serif  **FIGURE 25** Sans Serif (left) and Serif (right) Fonts	• **Choose fonts appropriate for the output of your presentation.** If a presentation is to be delivered through a projection device, consider using sans serif fonts with short text blocks. If your presentation will be delivered as a printout, consider using serif fonts. Figure 25 displays an example of sans serif and serif fonts.

TABLE 1 Continued

Example	Design Tip
Text Guidelines • Do not underline text. • DO NOT USE ALL CAPS. • Use **bold** and *italics* sparingly. • Avoid text that leaves one word on a line on its own. • Avoid using multiple spaces after punctuation. Space once after punctuation in a text block. Spacing more can create rivers of white. The white "river" can be very distracting. The white space draws the eye from the message. It can throb when projected. PowerPoint 2016, Windows 10, Microsoft Corporation **FIGURE 26** Appropriate and Inappropriate Text Examples	• **Do not use underlined text.** Underlined text is harder to read, and it is generally assumed that underlined text is a hyperlink. • **Avoid using all capital letters.** In addition to being difficult to read, words or phrases in all caps are considered to be "yelling" at the audience. • **Use italics and bold sparingly.** Too much emphasis through the use of italics and bold is confusing and makes it difficult to determine what is important. • **Avoid leaving a single word hanging on a line of its own.** Modify the placeholder size so that more than one word is on a subsequent line. Or use Shift+Enter to create a soft break. • **Use just one space after punctuation in text blocks.** Using more than one space can create distracting white space in the text block. Figure 26 illustrates these principles.

Pearson Education, Inc.

Remember that these design principles are guidelines. For example, the use of all capital letters is found for headings and titles in certain themes. You may choose to avoid applying one or more of the principles, but you should be aware of the principles and carefully consider why you are not following them. If you are in doubt about your design, ask a classmate or colleague to review the design and make suggestions. Fresh eyes can see things you might miss.

Modifying a Theme

Themes can be modified once they have been applied. You can change the variants, colors, fonts, and effects used in the theme. You can even change the background styles. Each of these options is on the Design tab, and each has its own gallery. Figure 27 shows the locations for accessing the galleries.

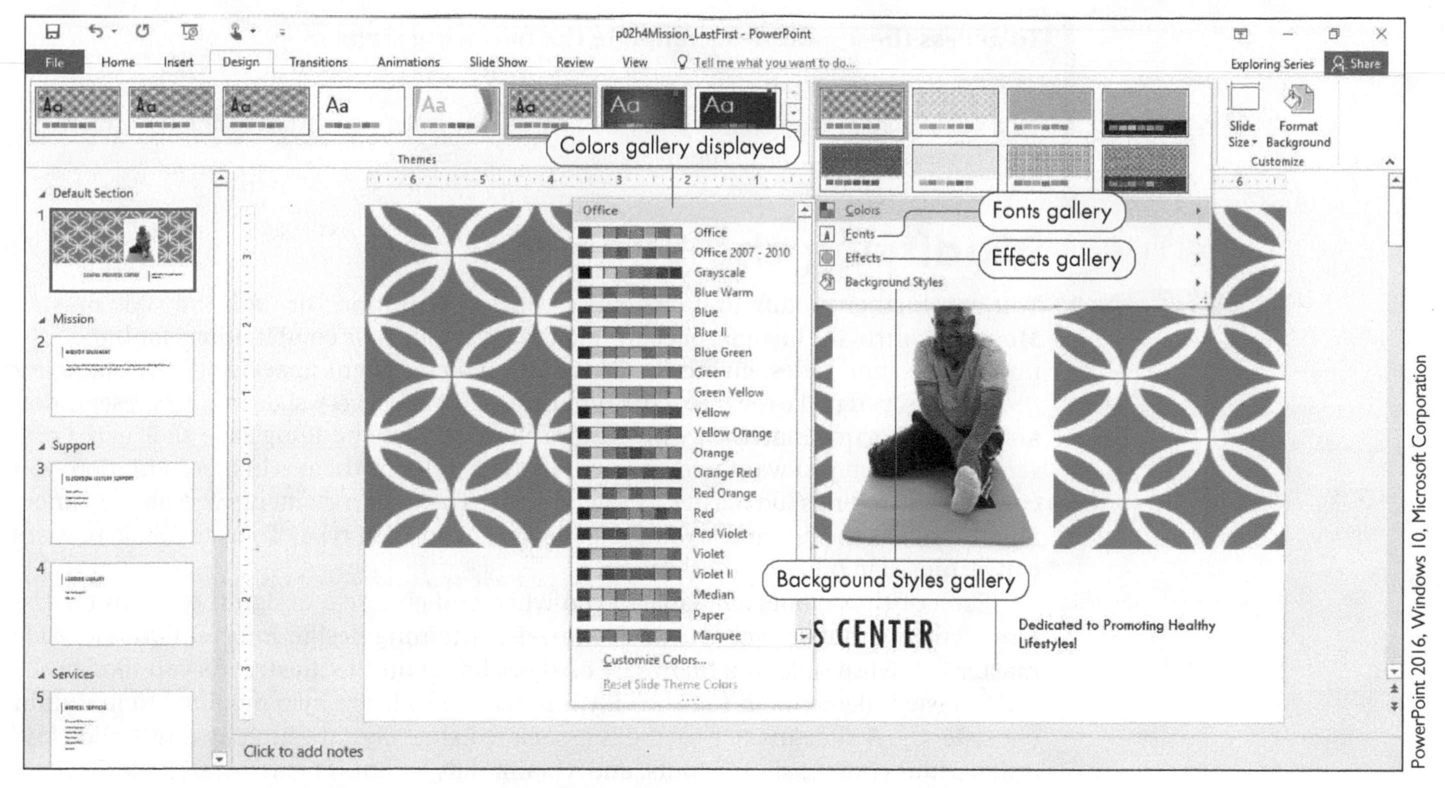

FIGURE 27 Design Galleries

Each PowerPoint theme includes a ***Colors gallery***, a gallery that provides a set of colors with each color assigned to a different element in the theme design. Once the theme is selected, you can change the colors by displaying the Colors gallery. Use Live Preview as you move the pointer along the various color sets to see how each color theme applies to your slides. You can even customize one or more of the colors in each color set.

Selecting a font for the title and another for the bullets or body text of your presentation can be difficult. Without a background in typography, determining which fonts go together well is difficult. The ***Fonts gallery*** is a gallery that pairs a title font and a body font. Click any of the samples in the Fonts gallery, and the font pair is applied to your theme.

The ***Effects gallery*** displays a full range of special effects that can be applied to all shapes in the presentation. Using effects aids you in maintaining a consistency to the appearance of your presentation. The gallery uses effects such as a soft glow, soft edges, shadows, or three-dimensional (3-D) look.

You can change the background style of the theme by accessing the ***Background Styles gallery***, a gallery containing backgrounds consistent with the selected theme colors. Simply changing your background style can liven up a presentation and give it your individual style.

Some of the themes include background shapes to create the design. If the background designs interfere with other objects on the slide, such as tables, images, or charts, you can select Format Background in the Customize group of the Design tab, and then click Hide Background Graphics by clicking so that the background shapes will not display for that slide.

To access these galleries, complete the following steps:

1. Click the Design tab.
2. Click More in the Variants group and choose the gallery you want to change (Colors, Fonts, Effects, or Background Styles.

Modifying the Slide Master

STEP 4 You can further modify and customize your presentation through the slide master. ***Masters*** control the layouts, background designs, and color combinations for handouts, notes pages, and slides, giving the presentation a consistent appearance. By changing the masters, you make universal style changes that affect every slide in your presentation and the supporting materials. This is more efficient than changing each slide in the presentation. When you want two or more different styles or themes in a presentation, you can add a different slide master for each theme. The design elements you already know about, such as themes and layouts, can be applied to each type of master. Slide masters can be reused in other presentations.

Each of the layouts available to you when you choose a design theme has consistent elements that are set by a ***slide master*** containing design information. The slide master is the top slide in a hierarchy of slides based on the master. As you modify the slide master, elements in the slide layouts related to it are also modified to maintain consistency. A slide master includes associated slide layouts such as a title slide layout, various content slide layouts, and a blank slide layout. The associated slide layouts designate the location of placeholders and other objects on slides as well as formatting information.

To modify a slide master or slide layout based on a slide master, complete the following steps:

1. Click the View tab.
2. Click Slide Master in the Master Views group.
3. Click the slide master at the top of the list or click one of the associated layouts.
4. Make modifications.
5. Click Close Master View in the Close group.

In Slide Master view, the slide master is the larger, top slide thumbnail shown in the left pane that coordinates with the Title and Content Layout. The Title Slide Layout is the second slide in the pane. The number of slides following it varies depending upon the template. Figure 28 shows the Integral Theme Slide Master and its related slide layouts. The ScreenTip for the slide master indicates it is used by one slide because the slide show is a new slide show composed of a single title slide.

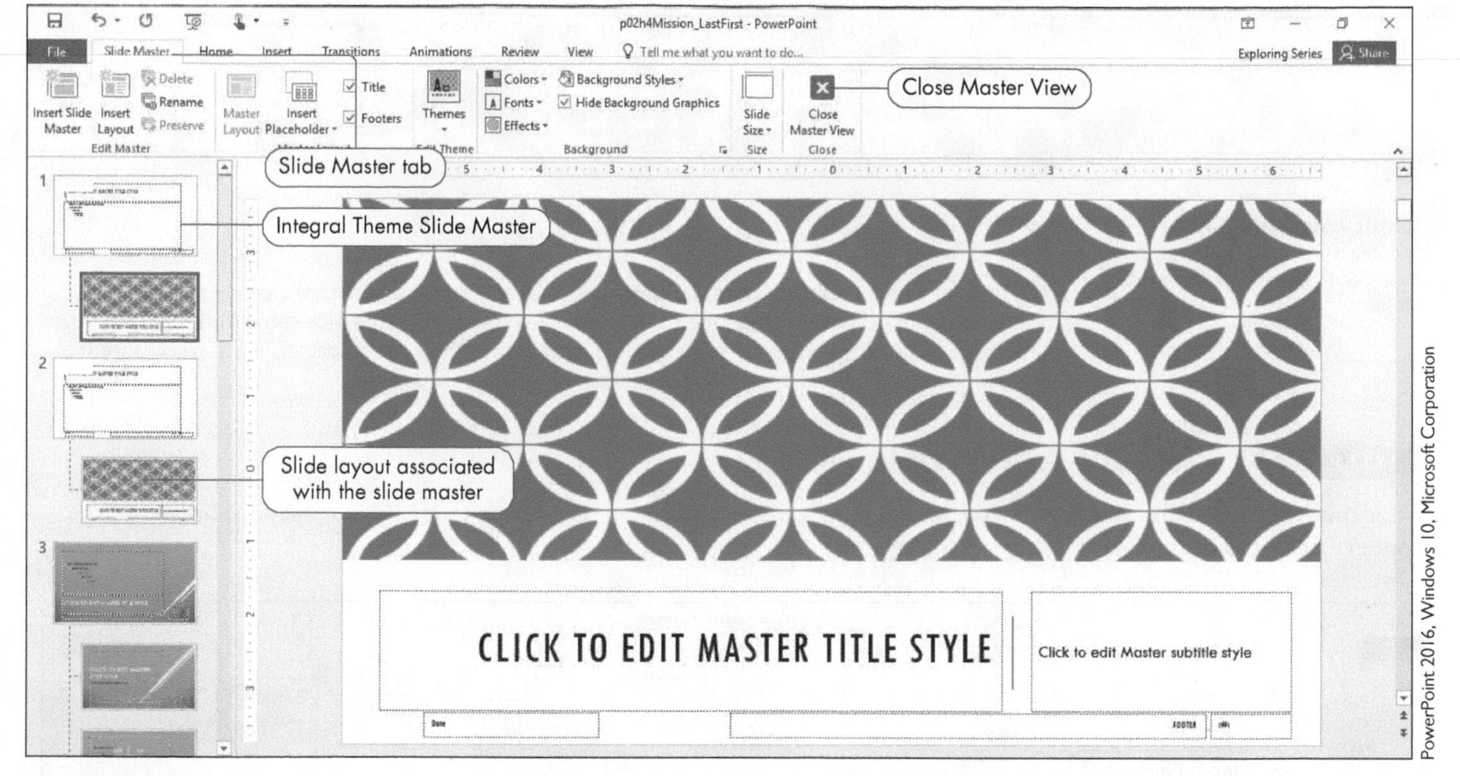

FIGURE 28 Slide Master View

The slide master is the most efficient way of setting the fonts, color scheme, and effects for the entire slide show. For example, you may wish to add a small company logo to the right corner of all slides. To set this choice, click the slide master thumbnail in the slide pane to display the slide master. The main pane shows the placeholders for title style, text styles, a date field, a footer field, and a page number field. Double-click the text in the Master title style or any level of text in the Master text styles placeholder and insert the logo.

You can move and size the placeholders on the slide master. The modifications in position and size will be reflected on the associated slide layouts. This may conflict with some of the slide layout placeholders, however. The placeholders can be moved on the individual slide layouts as needed.

10. How are sections in a presentation similar to tabs in a binder?
11. Why is it important to have unified design elements in a presentation?
12. Which elements of a theme can be modified? Where do you access these elements to make the change?
13. In what ways can a slide master give a consistent appearance to presentations?

Hands-On Exercises

Skills covered: Create Sections • Apply Design Principles • Modify a Theme • Modify a Slide Master

4 Design

The director of the Wellness Education Center plans to add more content to the center's mission presentation. To help her organize the content, you create sections in the slide show. You apply your knowledge of design principles to make the text more professional and readable. Finally, you change the theme and make modifications to the presentation through the slide master.

STEP 1 » CREATE SECTIONS

After reviewing the Campus Wellness Education Center mission slide show, you decide to create four sections organizing the content. Refer to Figure 29 as you complete Step 1.

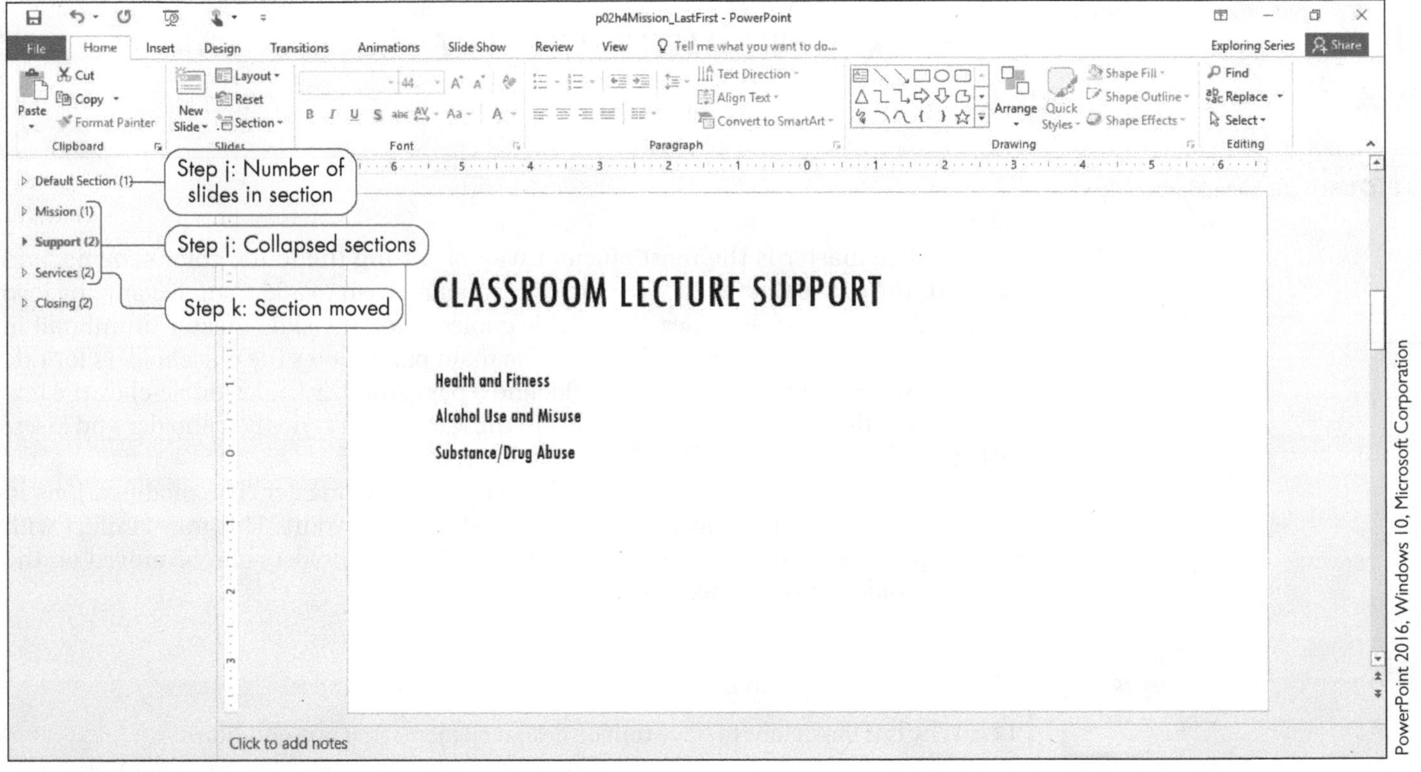

FIGURE 29 Content Divided into Sections

a. Open *p02h3Mission_LastFirst* if you closed it at the end of Hands-On Exercise 3, and save it as **p02h4Mission_LastFirst**, changing h3 to h4.

b. Click the **View tab**, click **Normal**, and then click the **Slide 2 thumbnail**.

c. Click **Section** in the Slides group on the Home tab and select **Add Section**.

A section divider is positioned between Slide 1 and Slide 2 in the Slides tab. It is labeled *Untitled Section.*

d. Right-click the **Untitled Section divider** and select **Rename Section**.

The Rename Section dialog box opens.

e. Type **Mission** in the Section name box and click **Rename**.

The section divider name changes and displays in the Slides tab.

f. Create a new section between Slides 2 and 3.

g. Right-click **Untitled Section**, click **Rename Section**, and then name the section **Services**.

h. Right-click between Slide 4 and Slide 5, click **Add Section**, and then rename the section **Support**.

i. Right-click between Slide 6 and Slide 7 and create a section named **Closing**.

The slide show content is divided into logical sections.

j. Right-click any section divider and select **Collapse All**.

The Slides tab shows the four sections you created: Mission, Services, Support, and Closing, as well as the Default section. Each section divider displays the section name and the number of slides in the section.

k. Right-click the **Support section** and click **Move Section Up**.

The Support section and all its associated slides are moved above the Services section.

l. Right-click any section divider and click **Expand All**.

m. Click the **View tab** and click **Slide Sorter** in the Presentation Views group.

Slide Sorter view displays the slides in each section.

n. Click **Normal** in the Presentation Views group. Save the presentation.

STEP 2 » APPLY DESIGN PRINCIPLES

You note that several of the slides in the presentation do not use slide show text design principles. You edit these slides so they are more readable. Refer to Figure 30 as you complete Step 2.

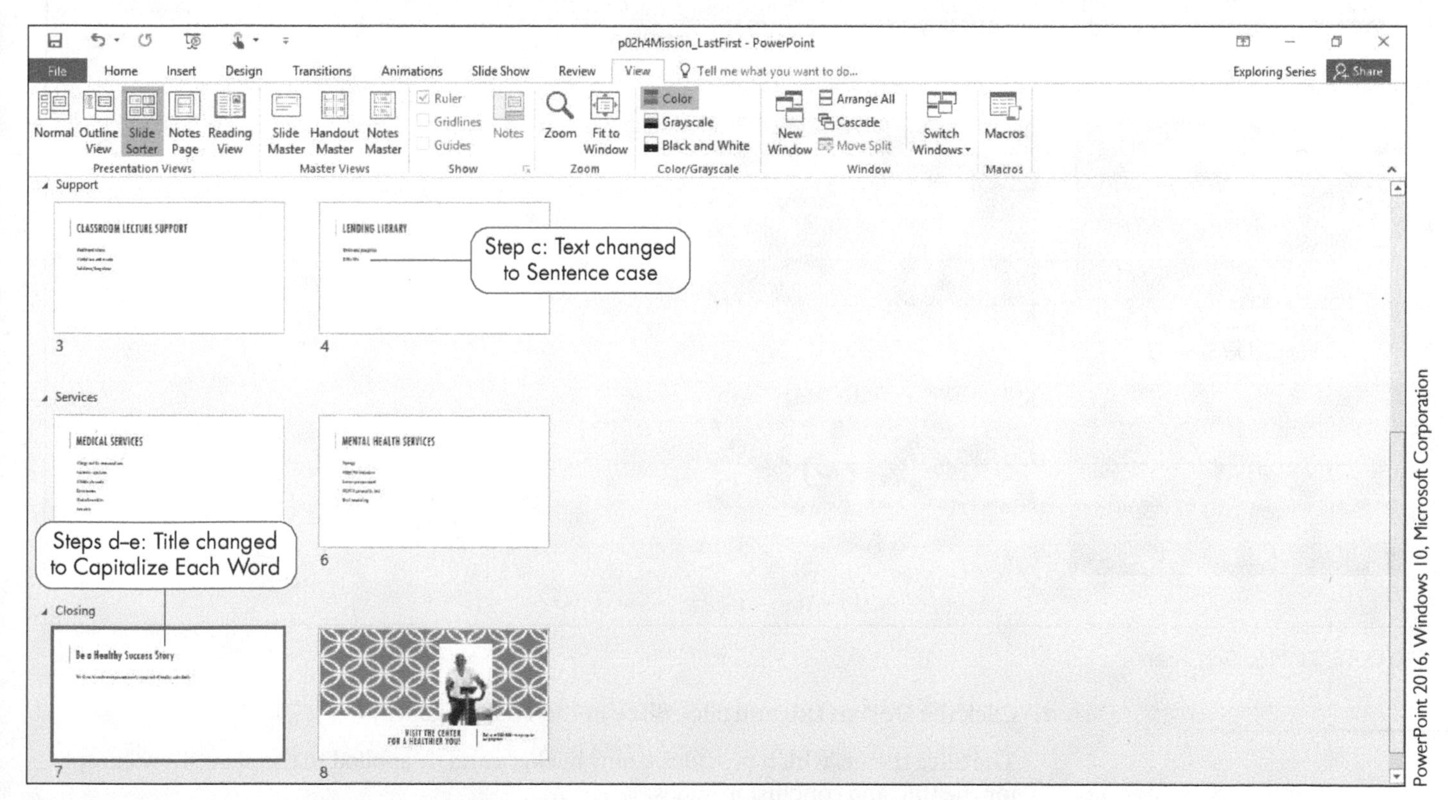

FIGURE 30 Portion of Slide Show in Slide Sorter View

a. Click **Slide 3**, select the text below the title placeholder, click the **Change Case arrow** in the Font group on the Home tab, and then select **Sentence case**.

The text now meets the guideline and is more readable.

b. Change the text below the titles in Slides 4, 5, and 6 to **Sentence case.**

c. Click **Slide 4**, change the second line to **DVDs/CDs.**

Always proofread to ensure that the case feature accurately reflects proper capitalization.

d. Click **Slide 7**, select the **title text**, click **Change Case** in the Font group, and then click **Capitalize Each Word.**

Each word in the title begins with a capital letter.

e. Change the uppercase *A* in the title to a lowercase *a*.

Title case capitalization guidelines state that only significant parts of speech of four or more letters should be capitalized. Minor parts of speech including articles and words shorter than four letters should not be capitalized.

f. Click the **View tab** and click **Slide Sorter** in the Presentation Views group.

Note the sentence case in the Services section.

g. Save the presentation.

STEP 3 » MODIFY A THEME

Although you are satisfied with the opening and closing slides, you think the main body of slides should be enhanced. You decide to change the theme and then modify the new theme to customize it. Refer to Figure 31 as you complete Step 3.

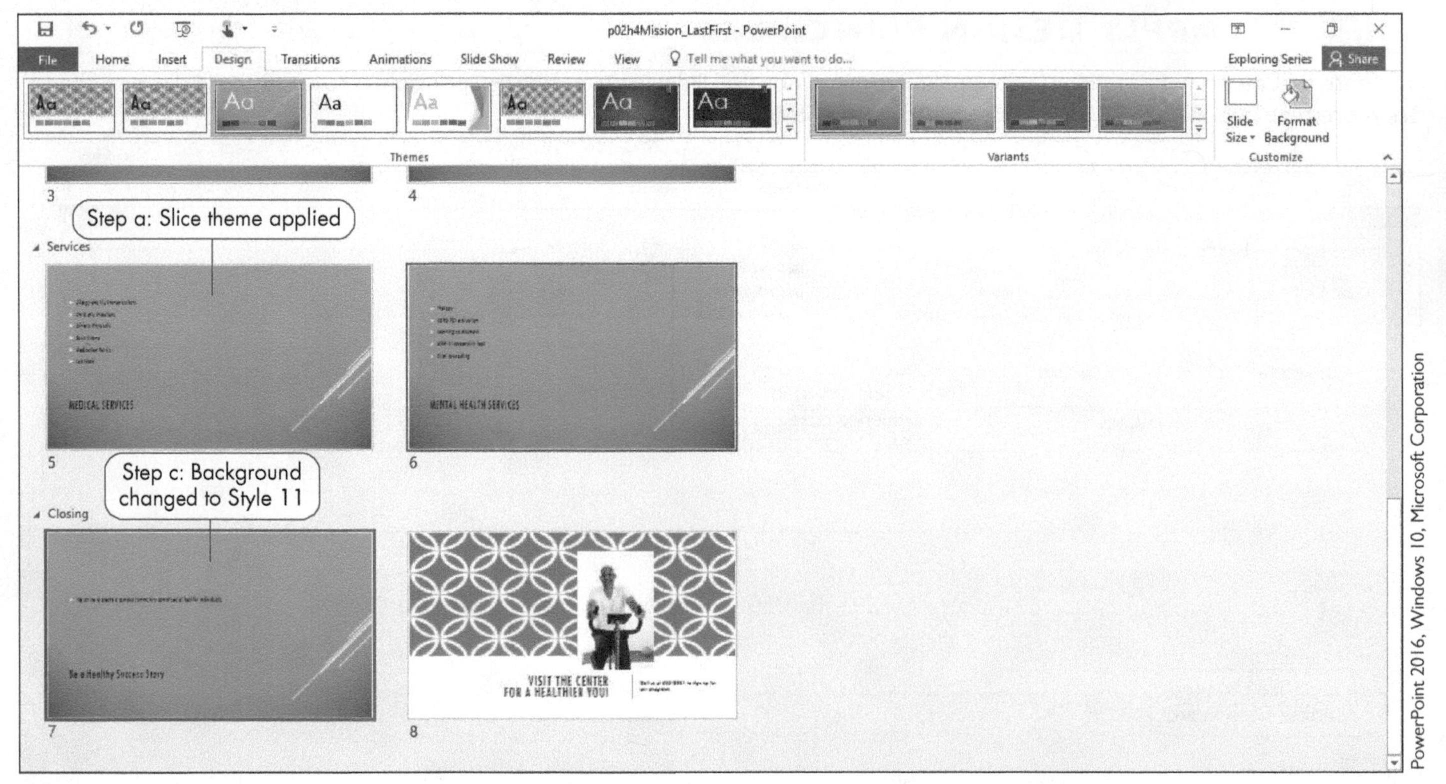

FIGURE 31 Modified Theme

a. Click the **Design tab** and click **Slice** in the Themes gallery.

The Slice theme, which provides a new background, is applied to the slide show except for the title and conclusion slides.

b. Click the **Design tab** and click **More** in the Variants group.

The Variants Gallery opens.

c. Select **Background Styles** and click **Style 11.**

d. Save the presentation.

STEP 4 » MODIFY A SLIDE MASTER

You want to add the Wellness Education Center's logo to slides 2 through 7 using the slide master. Refer to Figure 32 as you complete Step 4.

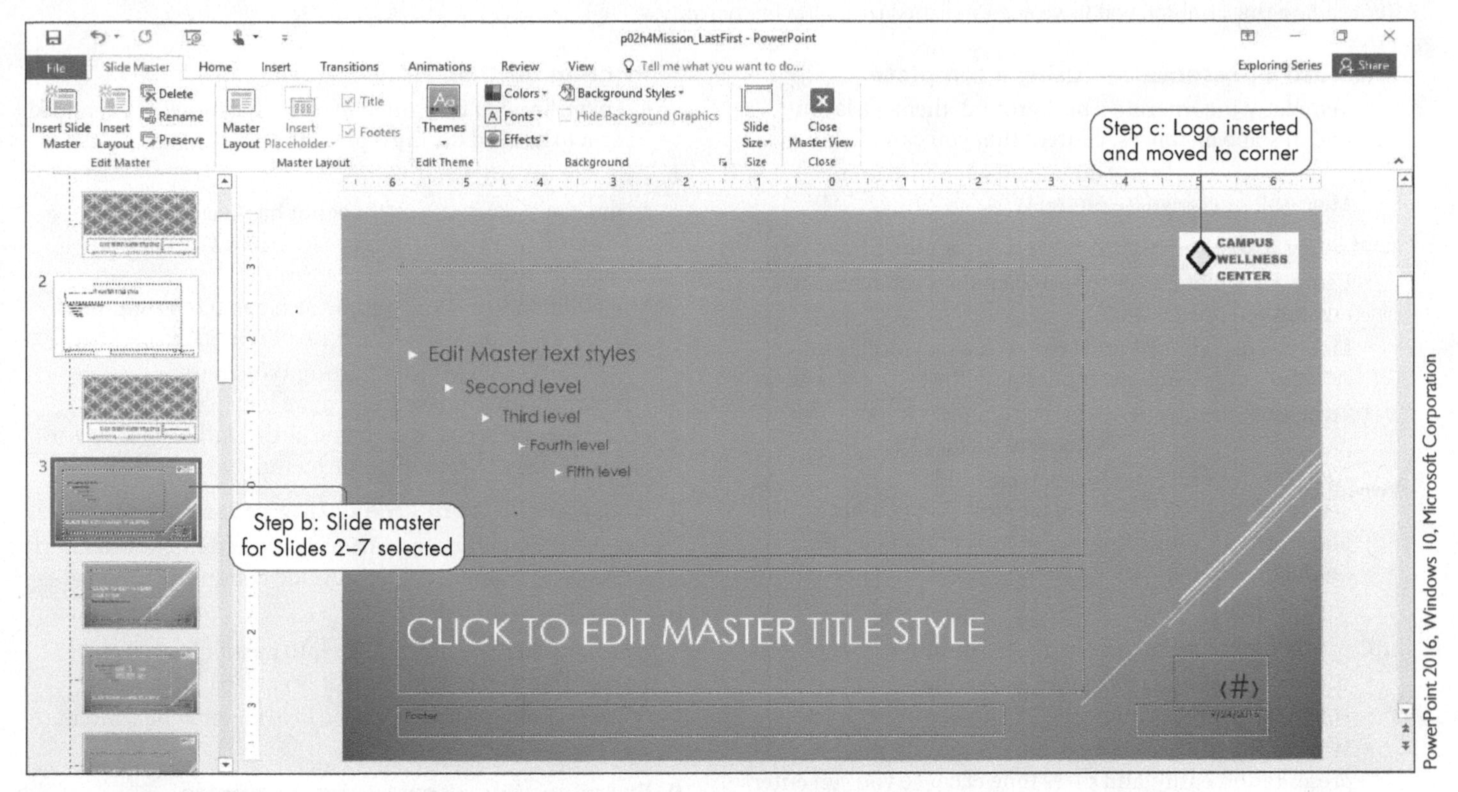

FIGURE 32 Modified Slide Master

a. Click the **View tab** and click **Slide Master** in the Master Views group. Scroll to the top of the slide pane.

   Note the masters labeled 1 and 2. These masters control the first and last slides of the presentation.

b. Click the **slide master thumbnail** next to the number 3.

   The third slide master controls slides 2 through 7.

c. Click the **Insert tab** and click **Pictures**. Locate the *p02h4Logo* picture file in the student files folder and click **Insert**.

   The logo is inserted. The logo will display in the slide pane thumbnails and slide show, but not on the full slide in Normal view.

d. Move the logo to the top right corner of the slide master.

e. Click the **Slide Master tab**. Click **Close Master View** in the Close group.

   Observe that the logo has been inserted on Slides 2 through 7 in the presentation.

f. Check spelling in the presentation. Save and close the file. Based on your instructor's directions, submit the following:

   p02h2Center_LastFirst

   p02h4Mission_LastFirst.

Chapter Objectives Review

After reading this chapter, you have accomplished the following objectives:

1. Create a presentation using a template.

- Templates incorporate a background, theme, a layout, and in some instances, content that you can modify.
- You can search for and download templates from Microsoft or elsewhere on the Web.

2. Modify a presentation based on a template.

- Using a template saves time and enables you to create a customized presentation.
- Modify a placeholder and layout: You can modify the structure of a template by changing the layout of a slide.
- To change the layout, resize placeholders or drag placeholders to new locations on a slide.
- Add pictures and captions: You can add visual interest to your presentation by adding pictures that you have taken and stored on your computer or by searching for them on the Internet and then saving and inserting them into your presentation.

3. Create a presentation in Outline view.

- When you use a storyboard to determine your content, you create a basic outline.
- Working in Outline view enables you to edit the presentation easily, and saves time because you can enter information efficiently without moving from placeholder to placeholder on slides.
- Use Outline view: Entering your presentation in Outline view enables you to organize the content of the presentation in a hierarchy of main points and subpoints.
- Edit in Outline view: Levels of indention makes it easy to show the relationships between information on the slide. You can promote or demote either before or after the information is entered on the slide.

4. Modify an outline structure.

- Because Outline view helps you see the structure of the presentation, you are able to see where content needs to be strengthened or where the flow of information needs to be revised.
- If you decide a slide contains content that would be presented better in another location in the slide show, use the Collapse and Expand features to easily move it.
- After collapsing the slide content, you can drag the slide to a new location and then expand it.
- To move individual bullet points, cut and paste the bullet points, or drag and drop them.

5. Print an outline.

- An outline can be printed in either collapsed or expanded form to be used during a presentation.

6. Import an outline.

- You can import any outline that has been saved in a format PowerPoint can read, such as a Word outline (.doc or .docx).
- In addition to a Word outline, you can use a common generic format such as Rich Text Format (.rtf).
- Solve problems while importing Word outlines: Importing outlines saved in plain text (.txt) can be problematic because each line of the outline becomes a slide instead of retaining the hierarchy.

7. Reuse slides from an existing presentation.

- Slides that have been previously created can be reused in new slide shows for efficiency and continuity.

8. Use sections.

- Sections help organize slides into meaningful groups of slides that can be collapsed or organized.
- Each section can be named to help identify the contents of the sections.

9. Examine slide show design principles.

- Using basic slide show principles and applying the guidelines make presentations more polished and professional.

10. Modify a theme.

- A template includes themes that define its font attributes, colors, and backgrounds.
- Using galleries, you can change a template's theme colors, fonts, effects and backgrounds.

11. Modify the slide master.

- A slide master controls the layouts, background designs, and color combinations associated with the handouts, notes pages, and slides in a presentation.
- By changing the slide master, you make changes that affect every slide in a presentation.

Key Terms Matching

Match the key terms with their definitions. Write the key term letter by the appropriate numbered definition.

a. Background Styles gallery
b. Collapsed outline
c. Colors gallery
d. Effects gallery
e. Expanded outline
f. Fonts gallery
g. Hierarchy
h. Master
i. Outline
j. Outline view
k. Plain text format (.txt)
l. Rich text format (.rtf)
m. Section
n. Slide master
o. Template

1. _______ A file that incorporates a theme, a layout, and content that can be modified.

2. _______ A method of organizing text in a hierarchy to depict relationships.

3. _______ A method used to organize text into levels of importance in a structure.

4. _______ A view showing the presentation in an outline format displayed in levels according to the points and any subpoints on each slide.

5. _______ An Outline view that displays only the slide number, icon, and title of each slide in Outline view.

6. _______ An Outline view that displays the slide number, icon, title, and content of each slide in the Outline view.

7. _______ A Word outline saved in this format can be used when transferring documents between platforms.

8. _______ A file format that retains only text but no formatting when transferring documents between applications or platforms.

9. _______ A set of colors available for every theme.

10. _______ A gallery that pairs a title font with a body font.

11. _______ A range of special effects for shapes used in the presentation.

12. _______ A gallery providing both solid color and background styles for application to a theme.

13. _______ The top slide in a hierarchy of slides based on the master.

14. _______ A slide view where the control of the layouts, background designs, and color combinations for handouts, notes pages, and slides can be set giving a presentation a consistent appearance.

15. _______ A division to presentation content that groups slides meaningfully.

Multiple Choice

1. A widescreen template that can be used for display on most screens and televisions is found in the category:

(a) 4:3.
(b) 11:17.
(c) 16:9.
(d) 20:20.

2. To add pictures to a presentation, you can:

(a) Use your own photos.
(b) Search for and insert pictures from Bing Image Search.
(c) Use the default images that came with the template.
(d) Use any of the above options.

3. What is the advantage to collapsing the outline so only the slide titles are visible?

(a) Transitions and animations can be added.
(b) Graphical objects become visible.
(c) More slide titles are displayed at one time, making it easier to rearrange the slides in the presentation.
(d) All of the above.

4. Which of the following is *true?*

(a) The slide layout can be changed after the template has been chosen.
(b) Themes applied to a template will not be saved with the slide show.
(c) Placeholders downloaded with a template cannot be modified.
(d) Slides cannot be added to a presentation after a template has been chosen.

5. In Outline view, levels of indentation showing the hierarchy of information *cannot* be created by:

(a) Pressing TAB to demote a bullet point from the first level to the second level.
(b) Pressing SHIFT+TAB to promote a bullet point from the second level to the first level.
(c) Pressing ALT+TAB to demote a bullet point from the first level to the second level.
(d) Pressing Decrease List Level to demote a bullet point from the first level to the second level.

6. Which of the following is the easiest method for adding existing content to a presentation?

(a) Import an outline using heading styles created in Word.
(b) Import a numbered list created in Word.
(c) Import a bulleted list created in Word.
(d) Import a document saved in plain text format.

7. How is formatting affected when reusing slides from an existing presentation?

(a) The slide being reused takes on the formatting of the open presentation.
(b) You can click Clear All Formatting to format slides using the active theme.
(c) The original presentation's formatting can be retained by clicking Keep Source Formatting.
(d) Any of the above may happen.

8. Which of the following is *not* true of sections?

(a) Sections can be renamed.
(b) Sections can be created in Normal view or Slide Sorter view.
(c) Sections can be collapsed.
(d) A slide show can be divided into only six logical sections.

9. Which of the following formats *cannot* be imported to use as an outline for a presentation?

(a) .jpg
(b) .docx
(c) .txt
(d) .rtf

10. You own a small business and decide to institute an Employee of the Month award program. Which of the following would be the fastest way to create the award certificate with a professional look?

(a) Enter the text in the title placeholder of a slide, change the font for each line, and then drag several images of awards onto the slide.
(b) Select a theme, modify the placeholders, and then enter the award text information.
(c) Create a table, enter the award text in the table, and then add images.
(d) Search for online templates and themes and download an Award certificate template.

Practice Exercises

1 Classic Photo Album

FROM SCRATCH

You enjoy using your digital camera to record nature shots during trips you take on weekends. You decide to store these pictures in an electronic slide show that you can display for your family. You use the Classic Photo Album template. Refer to Figure 33 as you complete this exercise.

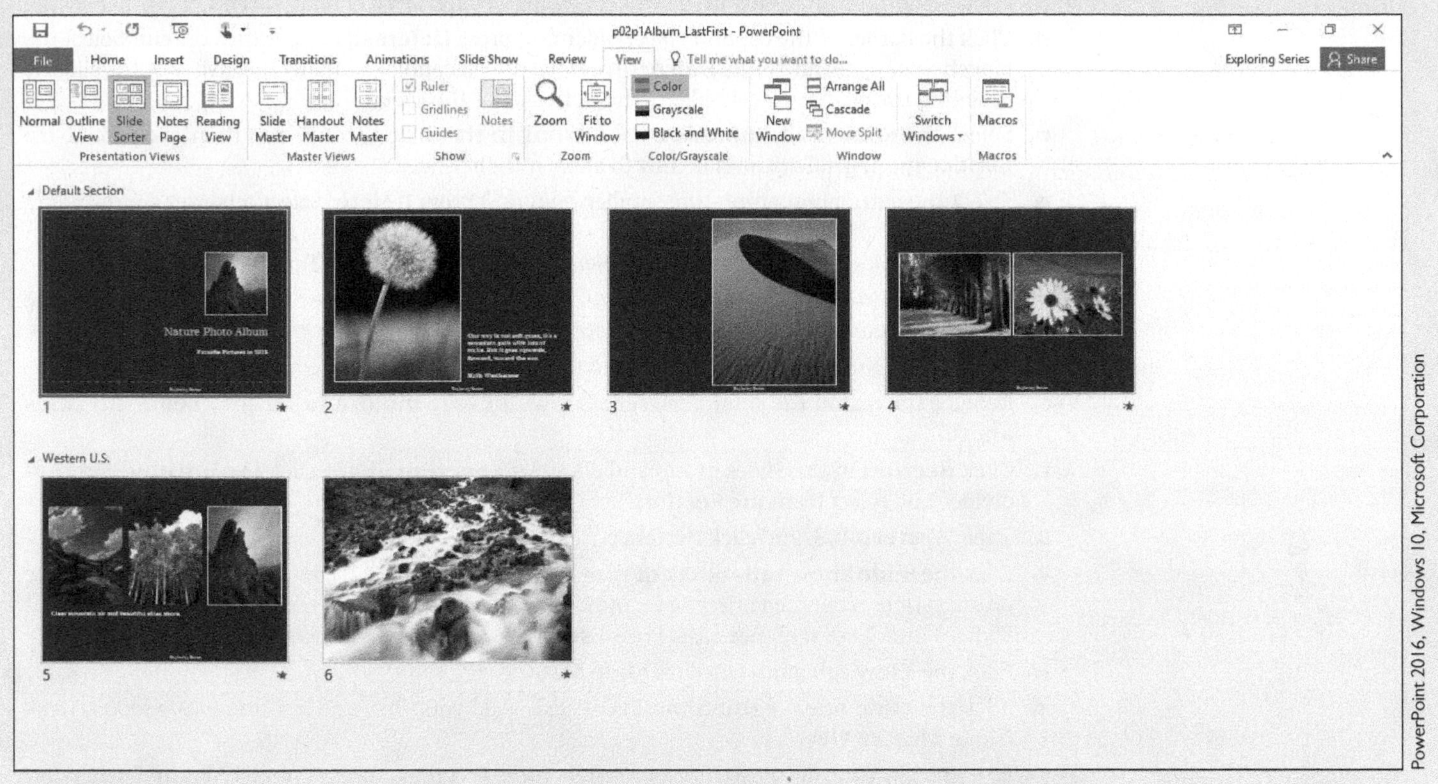

FIGURE 33 Classic Photo Album in Slide Sorter View

a. Start PowerPoint.

b. Type **Photo Albums** in the Search box and press **Enter**.

Thumbnails of sample templates will display.

c. Click **Classic photo album** and click **Create**.

d. Save the presentation file as **p02p1Album_LastFirst**.

e. Create a Notes and Handouts header with your name and a footer with your instructor's name and your class. Include the current date set to update automatically. The page number feature can remain active. Click **Apply to All**.

f. Select the word **CLASSIC** in the title placeholder of the first slide and type **Nature**.

g. Change the case of the title to **Capitalize Each Word**.

h. Replace the text in the **subtitle placeholder**, *Click to add date and other details*, with **Favorite Pictures in 2018**.

i. Click the **New Slide arrow** to display the Layout gallery.

j. Click the **Portrait with Caption layout** to add a new Slide 2.

k. Click the **Picture icon**, locate the image *p02p1Nature* from your student data files, and then click **Insert**.

l. Click in the **caption placeholder** and type **Our way is not soft grass, it's a mountain path with lots of rocks. But it goes upwards, forward, toward the sun.** Press **Enter** twice and type **Ruth Westheimer**.

m. Click **Slide 3**, read the text in the placeholder, and click anywhere in the text.

n. Click the border of the caption placeholder and press **Delete** to remove the content. Select the placeholder again and press **Delete** to remove the placeholder. Modify the layout of the slide by dragging the picture placeholder to the right side of the slide.

o. Select the **Slide 4 thumbnail**, click **Layout** in the Slides group, and then click the **2-Up Landscape with Captions layout** to apply it to the slide.

p. Select the extra photograph (the smaller one) and press **Delete**. Select a border surrounding one of the caption placeholders and press **Delete**. Repeat selecting and deleting until all caption placeholders have been deleted. Delete the CHOOSE A LAYOUT placeholder.

q. Select the **Slide 5 thumbnail**, press and hold **Ctrl**, and select the **Slide 7 thumbnail** in the Slides tab, and then press **Delete** to delete Slides 5 and 7 entirely.

r. Ensure that Normal view is selected, and then click **Slide 5**.

s. Replace the text in the subtitle placeholder with **Clear mountain air and beautiful skies above.**

t. Click **Section** in the Slides group and click **Add Section**. Right-click the **Untitled Section** divider and select **Rename Section**.

u. Type **Western U.S.** and click **Rename**.

v. Click the **Slide Show tab** and click **From Beginning** in the Start Slide Show group to view the presentation. Note the variety of layouts. Proofread to ensure all text is in serif font and that Slides 2 and 5 use sentence case. Press **Esc** when you are finished viewing the presentation.

w. Click the **View tab**, and then click **Slide Master**.

x. Click the **slide master thumbnail** labeled 1. Add your first and last name as a footer. Click **Close Master View**.

y. Save and close the file. Based on your instructor's directions, submit p02p1Album_LastFirst.

2 A Guide to Successful Presentations

Your community's Small Business Development Center (SBDC) asks you to provide training to local small business owners on preparing and delivering presentations. You create an outline and then supplement it by reusing slides from another presentation and by adding slides from an outline. Because the slides come from different sources, they have different fonts, and you change the fonts to match one of the design principles discussed in the chapter. You create sections to organize the presentation and then polish the presentation by adding and modifying a theme. Refer to Figure 34 as you complete this exercise.

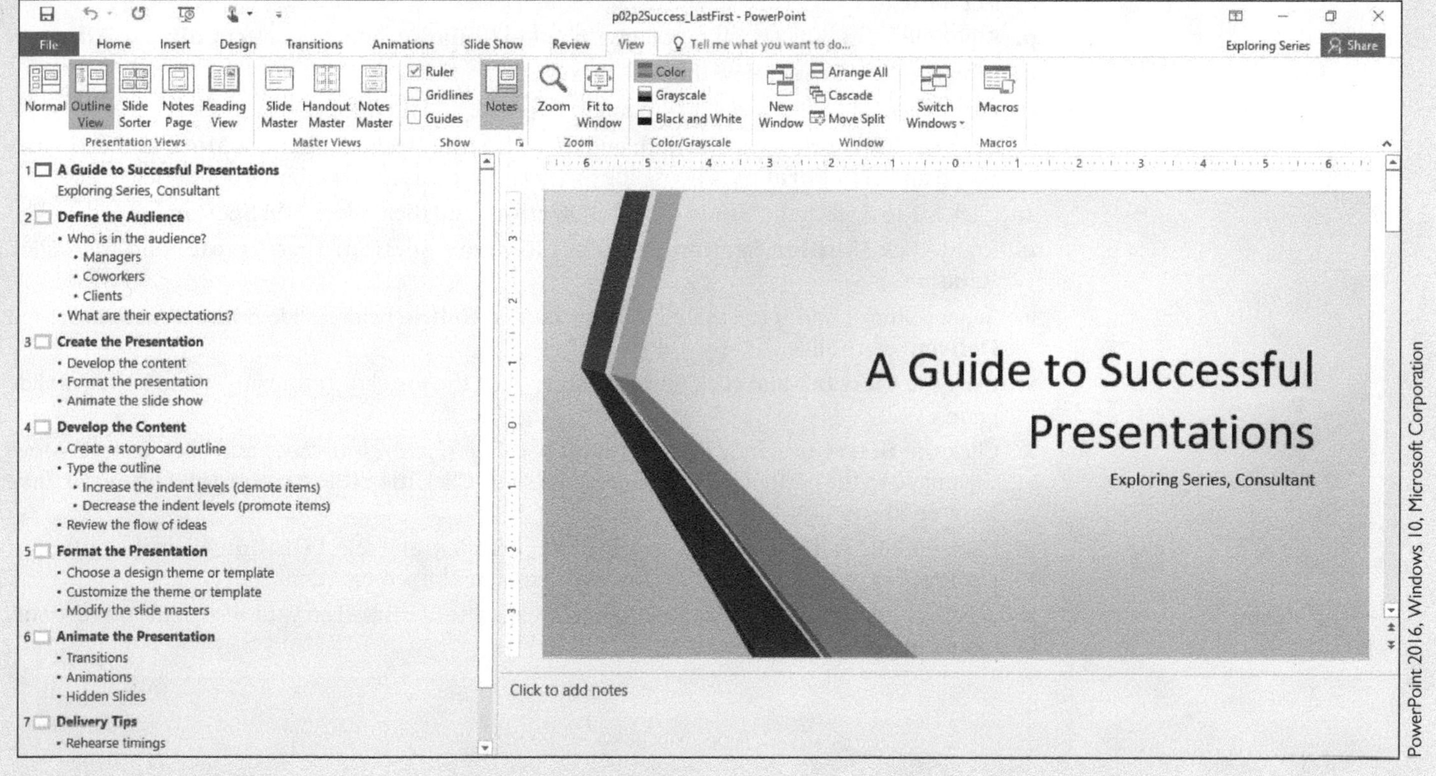

FIGURE 34 Presentation Created from an Outline and Reused Slides

a. Create a new, blank presentation. Click the **View tab** and click **Outline View**. Click next to the Slide 1 icon and type **A Guide to Winning Presentations**. Press **Enter** and press **Tab**. Type your name and add the title **Consultant**.

b. Save the new presentation as **p02p2Success_LastFirst**.

c. Create a Notes and Handouts header with your name and a footer with your instructor's name and your class. Include the current date set to update automatically. The page number feature can remain active.

d. Click the **New Slide arrow** in the Slides group on the Home tab, click **Slides from Outline**, locate *p02p2TipsOutline* in your student data files, and then click **Insert**.

e. Select the word **Winning** on Slide 1 while in Outline view, and type **Successful**.

f. Click at the end of the last bulleted text on Slide 3, press **Enter**, and then press **Shift+Tab** to create a new Slide 4. Type **Develop the Content** and press **Enter**.

g. Press **Tab**, type **Create a storyboard outline**, and then press **Enter**.

h. Type **Type the outline** and press **Enter**.

i. Press **Tab** to create a subpoint and type **Increase the indent levels (demote items)**. Press **Enter**.

j. Type **Decrease the indent levels (promote items)** and press **Enter**.

k. Press **Shift+Tab** to return to the previous level and type **Review the flow of ideas**.

l. Click at the end of the last bulleted text on Slide 4 and click the **New Slide arrow** in the Slides group.

m. Click **Reuse Slides** at the bottom of the gallery to open the Reuse Slides pane. Click **Browse**, click **Browse File**, select *p02p2Reuse*, and then click **Open**.

n. Double-click each of the slides in the Reuse Slides pane to insert the slides into the slide show. Close the Reuse Slides pane.

o. Press **Ctrl+A** to select all text in the outline, change the font to **Calibri (Body)**, and then deselect the text.

p. Right-click any bullet point to collapse, point to **Collapse**, and then select **Collapse All**.

q. Drag the Slide 5 icon below the Slide 7 icon.

r. Right-click one of the slide titles, point to **Expand**, and then select **Expand All**.

s. Click the **View tab**, click **Normal**, and then click the **Design tab**. Click **More** in the Themes group and click **Parallax**. Choose the Green variant (the third variant from the left).

t. Click **Slide 2**, click the **Home tab**, click **Section**, and then select **Add Section**.

u. Right-click **Untitled Section** and select **Rename Section**. Type **Create**, and then click **Rename**.

v. Repeat Steps t and u to create a section named **Refine** before Slide 5 and a section named **Deliver** before Slide 7.

w. Click the **View tab** and click **Slide Master**. Click the top slide (numbered Slide 1) in the slide pane.

x. Click the **Insert tab** and click **Pictures**. Locate *p02p2PresenterLogo* and click **Insert**. Move the image to the bottom-right corner of the slide. Click the **Slide Master tab** and click **Close Master View**.

y. Click the **File tab**, click **Print**, click **Full Page Slides**, and select **Outline**. View the outline in the Preview pane and then press **Back** to return to the presentation.

z. Check spelling in the presentation. Save and close the file. Based on your instructor's directions, submit p02p2Success_LastFirst.

Mid-Level Exercises

1 Nutrition Guide

You have been asked to help create a presentation for a local Girl Scout troop that is featuring good nutrition as its theme for the month. You locate a template online for nutrition that has some fun colors that you think the young girls will enjoy. Since you have given similar presentations, you decide to reuse basic slide content you have previously created on standard nutritional guidelines supported by the U.S. Department of Agriculture. Lastly, you modify the presentation using the slide master so all the changes are easily implemented to all slides.

a. Start PowerPoint, and in the *Search for online templates and themes* box, type **Nutrition**.
b. Select **Fresh food presentation** and click **Create**.
c. Save the presentation as **p02m1Food_LastFirst**.
d. Create a Notes and Handouts header with your name and a footer with your instructor's name and your class. Include the current date.
e. View the slides in Slide Show view.
f. Review the presentation, noting the several types of slide layouts.
g. Click **Slide 1**, replace the Title layout text with **Nutritional Guide**. Replace the subtitle with **June 2018**.
h. Click **Slide 6** and replace the title text with **Food!** Type **Make Good Choices** as the subtitle text.
i. Make the following changes to Slide 2:
   - Replace Title of the Presentation with **Great Nutritional Choices**.
   - Add three bullets: **Colorful fruits and vegetables, Fresh food over processed foods, Reasonable portions.**
j. Delete Slides 3 through 5 and then delete all remaining blank slides.
k. Click the **New Slide arrow** in the Slides group of the Home tab and select **Reuse Slides**.
l. Browse to locate and select the *p02m1Diet* presentation from the student data files in the Reuse Slides pane.
m. Select all seven slides in the Reuse Slides pane. Close the Reuse Slides pane.
n. Move Slide 3 so it becomes the last slide of the presentation.
o. Click the **View tab** and click **Slide Master** from the Master Views group.

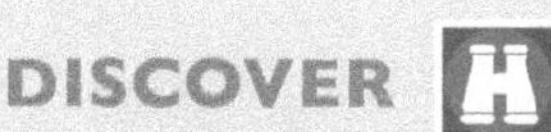

p. Click the third slide in the left pane and make the following changes to the Title and Content Layout slide master:
   - Select the five levels of text in the content placeholder, click the **Font Color arrow** in the Mini toolbar, select the **Eyedropper**, and then click the orange rectangle in the upper-left corner to select one of the colors found in the graphics.
   - Select the text in the title **Click to edit Master title style**, click the **Font Color arrow** in the Mini toolbar, and then select **Dark Green, Accent 6** (theme color, last column).
   - Increase the font size of the slide title to **40**.
   - Close the Slide Master.
q. View Slides 2 through 9 to ensure the changes in the slide master are reflected in the slides.
r. Select Slide 10 and make the following changes:
   - Replace *Food!* with **Food is fun for everyone!**
s. Run the spelling checker and proofread the presentation. Save and close the file. Based on your instructor's directions, submit p02m1Food_LastFirst.

2 Go Digital

The local senior citizens' center asked you to speak on photography. The center has many clients interested in learning about digital photography. You decide to create a presentation with sections on learning the advantages of a digital camera, choosing a camera, taking pictures with a digital camera, and printing and sharing photos. In this exercise, you begin the presentation by importing data from an outline and then complete it by reusing some slides from another presentation.

a. Create a new blank PowerPoint presentation and create slides from the *p02m2Outline* outline. Save the slide show as **p02m2Digital_LastFirst**.

b. Apply the **Wisp theme** to the slides.

c. Delete the blank Slide 1 and change the layout of the new Slide 1 to **Title Slide**. Add your name in the subtitle.

d. Review the presentation in PowerPoint's Outline view and add the following information as the last bullets on Slide 2:

- **Instant feedback**
- **Sharing**

e. Promote the text **Free Experimentation** on Slide 4 so that it creates a new slide.

> **TROUBLESHOOTING:** If you cannot select a bullet, place your insertion point at the end of the bullet and click to select the bulleted line.

f. Select all text in Outline view and click **Clear All Formatting** in the Font group on the Home tab.

g. Open the Reuse Slides pane and browse to locate and open the *p02m2Slides* presentation. Click the last slide in the original presentation in the Outline pane. Right-click any slide in the Reuse Slides pane and click **Insert All Slides**. The new slides should be inserted as Slides 6 and 7. Close the Reuse Slides pane.

h. Select **More** in the Variants Gallery on the Design tab and change the presentation font to **Corbel**. Using the Colors gallery, change the presentation colors to **Red**. Apply **Background Style 10**.

i. Return to Normal view.

j. Create a section between Slides 1 and 2 named **Advantages**.

k. Create a section after Slide 7 named **Choosing a Digital Camera**.

l. Use the Web to research things to consider when purchasing a digital camera. Be sure to include the major types of cameras available.

m. Insert a new Slide 8 in the **Choosing a Digital Camera** section to explain your findings.

n. Create a Notes and Handouts header with your name and a footer with your instructor's name and your class. Include the current date.

o. Save and close the file. Based on your instructor's directions, submit p02m2Digital_LastFirst.

3 Using Social Technologies for Ideas and Resources

COLLABORATION CASE

FROM SCRATCH

Social networking enables us to connect with others who share common interests via the Internet. Social networking also helps businesses connect with their customers. In this exercise, you will give an overview of some of the popular social media technologies such as Facebook, Twitter, LinkedIn, etc. and discuss how businesses can utilize them to engage their customers. Choose a business that interests you and discuss which social media technologies it uses and how they are used to connect with its customers. You will visit Microsoft's Office.com website, download a template from the Design Gallery, modify the template with your information, and then post the PowerPoint presentation you create to a location where others can view and comment on it.

a. Access the Internet and go to **http://templates.office.com**. Click **PowerPoint**. Click to see all available PowerPoint 2016 templates.

b. Click several of the thumbnails to see further details about the presentation.

c. Select one of the templates and download the slides to the location you use to store your files for this class. Save the file as **p02m3Resources_GroupName**. Open the saved slide show and modify the slides so they reflect your information and ideas. Be sure to follow the design principles discussed in the chapter. Your presentation should be approximately six to nine slides in length, including the title and credit slides. Delete any unnecessary slides found in the template. Make sure you create a final slide that credits the source for the template design. Provide the URL for the location from where you downloaded the template.

d. Load your edited presentation to an online location for others to review. Upload your presentation to your Microsoft OneDrive account or use another method for sharing your presentation with your instructor and classmates. (If you do not already have a OneDrive account, you can create a free account at https://onedrive.live.com.)

e. Invite three classmates to view the presentation you saved at the site, and then add a comment about your presentation. If using OneDrive to add comments, click the **Comment button** in PowerPoint Online. If you saved to another online storage location, share the location with three classmates and ask them to download the presentation. After viewing the presentation, ask them to email you with their comments.

f. Visit three of your classmates' presentations from their storage locations. Leave a comment about their presentations or email your classmates, sharing a comment about their presentations.

g. Review the comments of your classmates.

h. Save and close the file. Based on your instructor's directions, submit p02m3Resources_GroupName.

Beyond the Classroom

Social Media Marketing

You have a bright, creative, and energetic personality, and you are using these talents in college as a senior majoring in marketing. You hope to work in social media marketing. The Marketing 405 course you are taking this semester requires every student to create a social media marketing plan for a fictional company and to present an overview of the company to the class. This presentation should include the company purpose, the company's history, and past and present projects—all of which you are to "creatively invent."

Search http://templates.office.com for an appropriate template to use in creating your presentation. Save your presentation as **p02b1Marketing_LastFirst**. Research what a social media marketing campaign entails, and use what you learn to add your own content to comply with the case requirements. Add images, transitions, and animations as desired. Organize using sections. Create a handout header with your name and a handout footer with your instructor's name and your class. Include the current date and page number. Save and close the file. Based on your instructor's directions, submit p02b1Marketing_LastFirst.

Michigan, My State

Your sister spent a lot of time researching and creating a presentation on the state of Michigan for a youth organization leader and team members. She does not like the presentation's design and has asked for your help. You show her how to download the state history report presentation template from Office.com, Presentations category, Education subcategory. Save the new presentation as **p02b2State_LastFirst**. Reuse her slides, which are saved as *p02b2Michigan*. Cut and paste the images she gathered into the correct placeholders and move bulleted text to the correct slide. Resize placeholders as needed. You tell your sister that mixing cartoons and drawings with photos is contributing to the cluttered look. Choose one format based on your preference. Create new slides with appropriate layouts as needed. You remind her that although federal government organizations allow use of their images in an educational setting, your sister should give proper credit if she is going to use their data. Give credit to the State of Michigan's website for the information obtained from Michigan.gov (http://michigan.gov/kids). Give credit to the U.S. Census Bureau (http://www.census.gov) for the Quick Facts. Finalize the presentation by deleting unneeded slides, adding appropriate sections, modifying themes, checking spelling, proofreading, and applying transitions. Create a handout header with your name and a handout footer with your instructor's name and your class. Include the current date. Print the outline as directed by your instructor. Save and close the file. Based on your instructor's directions, submit p02b2State_LastFirst.

Capstone Exercise

You are developing a report for your sociology class about the roles of women in the science, technology, engineering, and mathematics (STEM) fields. After doing some research, you begin to see that throughout history, women have had very few opportunities in these areas for historical and societal reasons. You want to demonstrate to your classmates the key and increasingly important role women have played in STEM advances. You will use your PowerPoint presentation to inform them of some key contributors in the STEM areas. In this capstone project, you concentrate on developing the content of the presentation.

Design Template

You download a template from http://templates.office.com to create the basic design and structure for your presentation, save the presentation, and create the title slide.

- **a.** Create a new presentation using one of the available templates. Search for the template using the search term **Technology** and locate and download the **Technology at work design slides template**.
- **b.** Save the presentation as **p02c1Women_LastFirst**.
- **c.** Type **Women in STEM** as the title on the title slide.
- **d.** Type the subtitle **Science, Technology, Engineering, and Mathematics** and change the font size to 20.
- **e.** Insert 6 blank new slides.
- **f.** Create a handout header with your name and a handout footer with your instructor's name and your class. Include the current date. Apply to all slides.

Outline and Modifications

Based on the storyboard you created after researching women in STEM on the Internet, you type the outline of your presentation. As you create the outline, you also modify the outline structure.

- **a.** Open Outline view.
- **b.** Type **Name 3 women in STEM** as the title for Slide 2.
- **c.** Type each of the following as Level 1 bullets for Slide 2: **My biology teacher**, **My computer applications teacher**, **My math teacher**.
- **d.** Type **Think on a bigger scale** as the title for Slide 3. Enter each of the following as Level 1 bullets for Slide 3: **National names?**, and **International names?**
- **e.** Add this speaker note to Slide 3: **These may be hard questions to answer quickly because there are relatively few women in these fields.**
- **f.** Type **Here are some names to get you started** as the title for Slide 4.
- **g.** Type each of the following as Level 1 bullets for Slide 4: **Sally Ride**, **Christa McAuliffe**.
- **h.** Add this speaker note to Slide 4: **For different reasons, both of these women were important in the development of the aerospace industry.**

Imported Outline

You have an outline on women in STEM that was created in Microsoft Word and also a slide show on that topic. You reuse this content to build your slide show.

- **a.** Position the insertion point at the end of the outline after Slide 4.
- **b.** Use the **Slides from Outline option** to insert the *p02c1Stem* outline.
- **c.** Delete Slide 5 and any blank slides.
- **d.** Demote the last two bullets on the new Slide 5.
- **e.** Click the first bullet on Slide 6. Cut and paste the text after the name and date from the bullet point to the Notes pane. Replace *She* with **Hypatia**. Repeat for the remaining two bullets.
- **f.** Delete all text after *physics* for the first bullet of Slide 7. Replace the comma with a period.
- **g.** Position the insertion point at the end of the outline.
- **h.** Reuse Slides 2 and 3, using the same order, from *p02c1Work* to add two slides to the end of the presentation.
- **i.** Modify the outline structure by reversing slides 8 and 9.

Design

The content of some of the imported slides does not fit well and the font colors are not uniform across all of the slides. You want to adjust the layout and font color to create a well-designed presentation. Then you decide to view a slide show to verify your changes.

- **a.** Switch to Normal view. Change the layout of Slide 9 to Blank.
- **b.** Check Slides 5–7 to ensure the title placeholder font is Arial Black (Heading) with the color set to Black, Text 2. Check the subtitle font to Arial Body with the color set to Grey 80%, Text 1.
- **c.** Use the spelling checker and proofread the presentation.
- **d.** View a slide show from the beginning.
- **e.** Move Slide 5 to just before Slide 8.

Sections

To facilitate organization of the presentation and moving between the slides, you create sections.

a. Add a section before Slide 2 and rename it **Quiz**.

b. Add a section before Slide 5 and rename it **History**.

c. Add a section before Slide 7 and rename it **Reasoning**.

d. Print the outline as directed by your instructor.

e. Save and close the file. Based on your instructor's directions, submit p02c1Women_LastFirst.

Glossary

Background Styles gallery A gallery providing both solid color and background styles for application to a theme.

Collapsed outline An Outline view that displays only the slide number, icon, and title of each slide in Outline view.

Colors gallery A set of colors available for every theme.

Effects gallery A range of special effects for shapes used in the presentation.

Expanded outline An Outline view that displays the slide number, icon, title, and content of each slide in the Outline view.

Fonts gallery A gallery that pairs a title font with a body font.

Hierarchy A method used to organize text into levels of importance in a structure.

Master A slide view where the control of the layouts, background designs, and color combinations for handouts, notes pages, and slides can be set giving a presentation a consistent appearance.

Outline A method of organizing text in a hierarchy to depict relationships.

Outline view (PowerPoint) A view showing the presentation in an outline format displayed in levels according to the points and any subpoints on each slide.

Plain text format (.txt) A file format that retains only text but no formatting when you transfer documents between applications or platforms.

Rich Text Format (.rtf) A file format that retains structure and most text formatting when transferring documents between applications or platforms.

Section A division to presentation content that groups slides meaningfully.

Slide master The top slide in a hierarchy of slides based on the master.

Template A predesigned file that incorporates formatting elements, such as theme and layouts, and may include content that can be modified.

Introduction to Word

Word

Introduction to Word

LEARNING OUTCOME **You will develop a document using features of Microsoft Word.**

OBJECTIVES & SKILLS: After you read this chapter, you will be able to:

Introduction to Word Processing

OBJECTIVE 1: BEGIN AND EDIT A DOCUMENT
Create a Document, Reuse Text, Use a Template, Save a Document, Open a Document, Insert Text and Navigate a Document, Review Spelling and Grammar

OBJECTIVE 2: CUSTOMIZE WORD
Explore Word Options, Customize the Ribbon, Customize the Quick Access Toolbar

HANDS-ON EXERCISE 1:
Introduction to Word Processing

Document Organization

OBJECTIVE 3: USE FEATURES THAT IMPROVE READABILITY
Insert Headers and Footers, Adjust Margins, Change Page Orientation, Insert a Watermark, Insert a Symbol

OBJECTIVE 4: VIEW A DOCUMENT IN DIFFERENT WAYS
Select a Document View, Change the Zoom Setting, View a Document, Manage Page Flow

HANDS-ON EXERCISE 2:
Document Organization

Document Settings and Properties

OBJECTIVE 5: MODIFY DOCUMENT PROPERTIES
Customize Document Properties, Print Document Properties

OBJECTIVE 6: PREPARE A DOCUMENT FOR DISTRIBUTION
Ensure Document Compatibility, Understand Backup Options, Run the Document Inspector, Select Print Options

HANDS-ON EXERCISE 3:
Document Settings and Properties

CASE STUDY | Swan Creek National Wildlife Refuge

You are fascinated with wildlife in its natural habitat. For that reason, you are excited to work with Swan Creek National Wildlife Refuge, assigned the task of promoting the refuge's educational outreach programs. Emily Traynom, Swan Creek's site director, is concerned that children in the city have little opportunity to interact with nature. She fears that a generation of children will mature into adults with little appreciation of the role of our country's natural resources in the overall balance of nature. Her passion is encouraging students to visit Swan Creek and become actively involved in environmental activities.

Ms. Traynom envisions summer day camps where children explore the wildlife refuge and participate in learning activities. She asked you to use your expertise in Microsoft Word to produce documents such as flyers, brochures, memos, contracts, and letters. You will design and produce an article about a series of summer camps available to children from 5th through 8th grades. From a rough draft, you will create an attractive document for distribution to schools.

Organizing a Document

Emily Traynom[illegible] Director
Swan Creek National Wildlife Refuge
89667 Mill Creek Road
Hastings, PA 19092

July 22, 2018

RE: Summer Day Camp Program at Swan Creek

As an educator in our community, you are sure to be interested in an opportunity for your students to learn at Swan Creek National Wildlife Refuge this summer. I hope you will encourage your students who are rising 5th through 8th graders to join us for a few days this summer. The day camp program, which is described on the following page, is an effort to instill an appreciation for our environment, all in an engaging and fun atmosphere. Funded through a grant from the Nature Federation, the program is free to campers; however, space is limited, so please encourage early registration.

I, or a member of my staff, will be happy to visit your classroom to promote the refuge and to answer questions or accept registration for the summer day camp program. Feel free to copy and distribute the article on the following page. We hope to hear from you soon and look forward to working with your students this summer!

Swan Creek National Wildlife Refuge

What: Swan Creek National Wildlife Refuge Day Camp

When: Week-Long Day Camps from July 5-August 21, 2018

Where: Swan Creek National Wildlife Refuge (at the headquarters)

Open to: 5th through 8th Grade Students

When was the last time you spent an afternoon immersed in nature, experiencing sights and sounds you could never enjoy in the city? Did you know there are 38 different types of birds native to our area, all of which you can find at Swan Creek National Wildlife Refuge? The refuge backwaters are home to beavers, mallard ducks, geese, largemouth bass, and slider turtles, among many other inhabitants. What better way to spend a few days this summer than with us at the refuge, experiencing nature at its finest?

Swan Creek National Wildlife Refuge is offering a series of week-long day camps this summer, designed for children who are rising fifth through eighth graders. The series of wildlife camps will begin on June 15, with the last camp ending on August 6. Children will participate in informative seminars and nature observations led by wildlife rangers. On nature hikes through the refuge, camp participants will explore a native forest comprised of trees and forestry indigenous to the area. Other activities include hiking along the raised boardwalk through the sunken forest, identifying wildlife from the refuge observation center, and participating in nature photography classes. The first 50 campers to register will receive a Striker™ backpack, compliments of Swan Creek!

Explore nature

Learn to identify native plants and wildlife

Take digital photos

Participate in nature seminars

Enjoy relaxing days at the refuge

For further information, or to register, please contact:

Melinda Gifford, Events Coordinator

(660) 555-5578

mgifford@scnwf.org

U.S. Fish and Wildlife Service
w01h3Refuge_LastFirst.docx

DRAFT

FIGURE 1 Swan Creek Documents

CASE STUDY | Swan Creek National Wildlife Refuge

Starting Files	Files to be Submitted
Blank document w01h1Camps w01h2Letter w01h3NewEmployee	w01h1Planner_LastFirst w01h2Flyer_LastFirst w01h3NewEmployee_LastFirst w01h3Refuge_LastFirst

Introduction to Word Processing

Word processing software, often called a word processor, is one of the most commonly used types of software in homes, schools, and businesses. People around the world—students, office assistants, managers, and professionals in all fields—use word processing programs such as ***Microsoft Word*** for a variety of tasks. Microsoft Word 2016, included in the Microsoft Office suite of software, is the most current version of the popular word processor. You can create letters, reports, research papers, newsletters, brochures, and all sorts of documents with Word. You can even create and send email, produce webpages, post to social media sites, and update blogs with Word. Figure 2 shows examples of documents created in Word. If a project requires collaboration online or between offices, Word makes it easy to share documents, track changes, view comments, and efficiently produce a document to which several authors can contribute. By using Word to create a research paper, you can easily create citations, a bibliography, a table of contents, a cover page, an index, and other reference pages. To enhance a document, you can change colors, add interesting styles of text, insert graphics, and use tables to present data. With emphasis on saving documents to the cloud, Word enables you to share these documents with others or access them from any device. Word is a comprehensive word processing solution, to say the least.

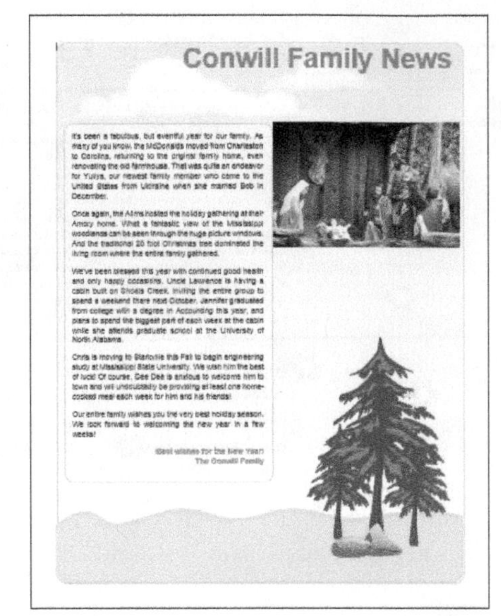

Conwill Family News

It's been a fabulous, but eventful year for our family. As many of you know, the McDonalds moved from Charleston to Carolina, returning to the original family home, even renovating the old farmhouse. That was quite an endeavor for Yuliya, our newest family member who came to the United States from Ukraine when she married Bob in December.

Once again, the Alms hosted the holiday gathering at their Amory home. What a fantastic view of the Mississippi woodlands can be seen through the huge picture windows. And the traditional 20 foot Christmas tree dominated the living room where the entire family gathered.

We've been blessed this year with continued good health and only happy occasions. Uncle Lawrence is having a cabin built on Shoals Creek, inviting the entire group to spend a weekend there next October. Jennifer graduated from college with a degree in Accounting this year, and plans to spend the biggest part of each week at the cabin while she attends graduate school at the University of North Alabama.

Chris is moving to Starkville this Fall to begin engineering study at Mississippi State University. We wish him the best of luck! Of course, Dee Dee is anxious to welcome him to town and will undoubtedly be providing at least one home-cooked meal each week for him and his friends!

Our entire family wishes you the very best holiday season. We look forward to welcoming the new year in a few weeks!

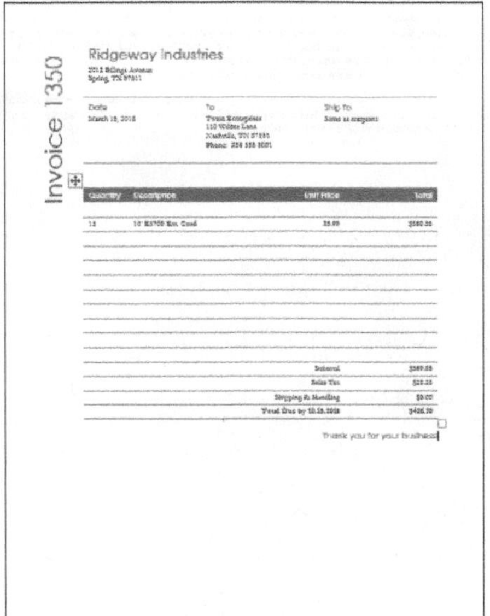

Invoice 1350

Ridgeway Industries

Quantity	Description	Unit Price	Total

Thank you for your business!

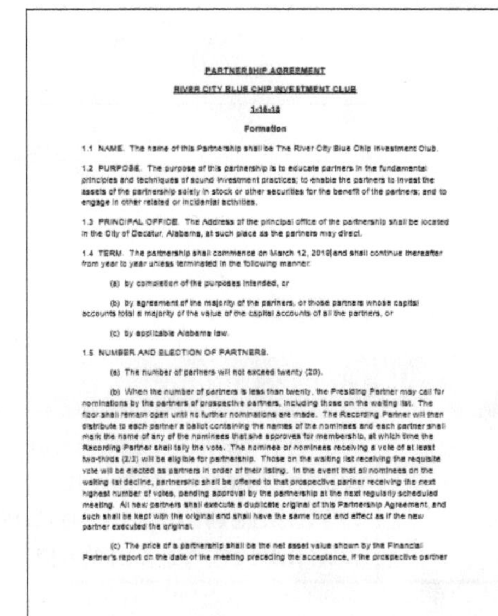

PARTNERSHIP AGREEMENT

RIVER CITY BLUE CHIP INVESTMENT CLUB

1-16-18

Formation

1.1 NAME. The name of this Partnership shall be The River City Blue Chip Investment Club.

1.2 PURPOSE. The purpose of this partnership is to educate partners in the fundamental principles and techniques of sound investment practices; to enable the partners to invest the assets of the partnership solely in stock or other securities for the benefit of the partners; and to engage in other related or incidental activities.

1.3 PRINCIPAL OFFICE. The Address of the principal office of the partnership shall be located in the City of Decatur, Alabama, at such place as the partners may direct.

1.4 TERM. The partnership shall commence on March 12, 2018 and shall continue thereafter from year to year unless terminated in the following manner:

(a) by completion of the purposes intended, or

(b) by agreement of the majority of the partners, or those partners whose capital accounts total a majority of the value of the capital accounts of all the partners, or

(c) by applicable Alabama law.

1.5 NUMBER AND ELECTION OF PARTNERS.

(a) The number of partners will not exceed twenty (20).

(b) When the number of partners is less than twenty, the Presiding Partner may call for nominations by the partners of prospective partners, including those on the waiting list. The floor shall remain open until no further nominations are made. The Recording Partner will then distribute to each partner a ballot containing the names of the nominees and each partner shall mark the name of any of the nominees that she approves for membership, at which time the Recording Partner shall tally the vote. The nominee or nominees receiving a vote of at least two-thirds (2/3) will be eligible for partnership. Those on the waiting list receiving the requisite vote will be elected as partners in order of their listing. In the event that all nominees on the waiting list decline, partnership shall be offered to that prospective partner receiving the next highest number of votes, pending approval by the partnership at the next regularly scheduled meeting. All new partners shall execute a duplicate original of this Partnership Agreement, and such shall be kept with the original and shall have the same force and effect as if the new partner executed the original.

(c) The price of a partnership shall be the net asset value shown by the Financial Partner's report on the date of the meeting preceding the acceptance, if the prospective partner

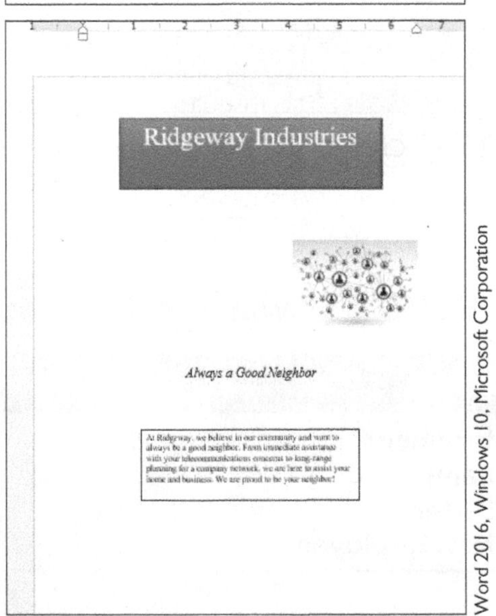

Ridgeway Industries

Always a Good Neighbor

At Ridgeway, we believe in our community and want to always be a good neighbor. From immediate assistance with your telecommunications concerns to long-range planning for a company network, we are here to assist your home and business. We are proud to be your neighbor!

Word 2016, Windows 10, Microsoft Corporation

FIGURE 2 Sample Word Processing Documents

Communicating through the written word is an important, in fact, vital, task for any business or organization. Word processing software, such as Word, simplifies the technical task of preparing documents, but a word processor does not replace the writer. Be careful when phrasing a document so you are sure it is appropriate for the intended audience. Always remember that once you distribute a document, either on paper or electronically, you cannot retract the words. Therefore, you should never send a document that you have not carefully checked several times to be sure it conveys your message in the best way possible. Also, you cannot depend completely on a word processor to identify all spelling and grammatical errors, so be sure to proofread every document you create closely. Although several word processors, including Word, provide predesigned documents (called templates) that include basic layouts for various tasks, it is ultimately up to you to compose well-worded documents. The role of business communication, including the written word, in the success or failure of a business cannot be overemphasized.

In this section, you will explore Word's interface, learn how to create and save a document, explore the use of templates, and perform basic editing operations. You will learn how to move around in a document and to review spelling and word usage. Using Word options, you will explore ways to customize Word to suit your preferences, and you will learn to customize the Ribbon and the Quick Access Toolbar.

Beginning and Editing a Document

When you open Word, your screen will be similar to Figure 3. You can create a blank document, or you can select from several categories of templates. Recently viewed files are shown on the left, for ease of access should you want to open any again.

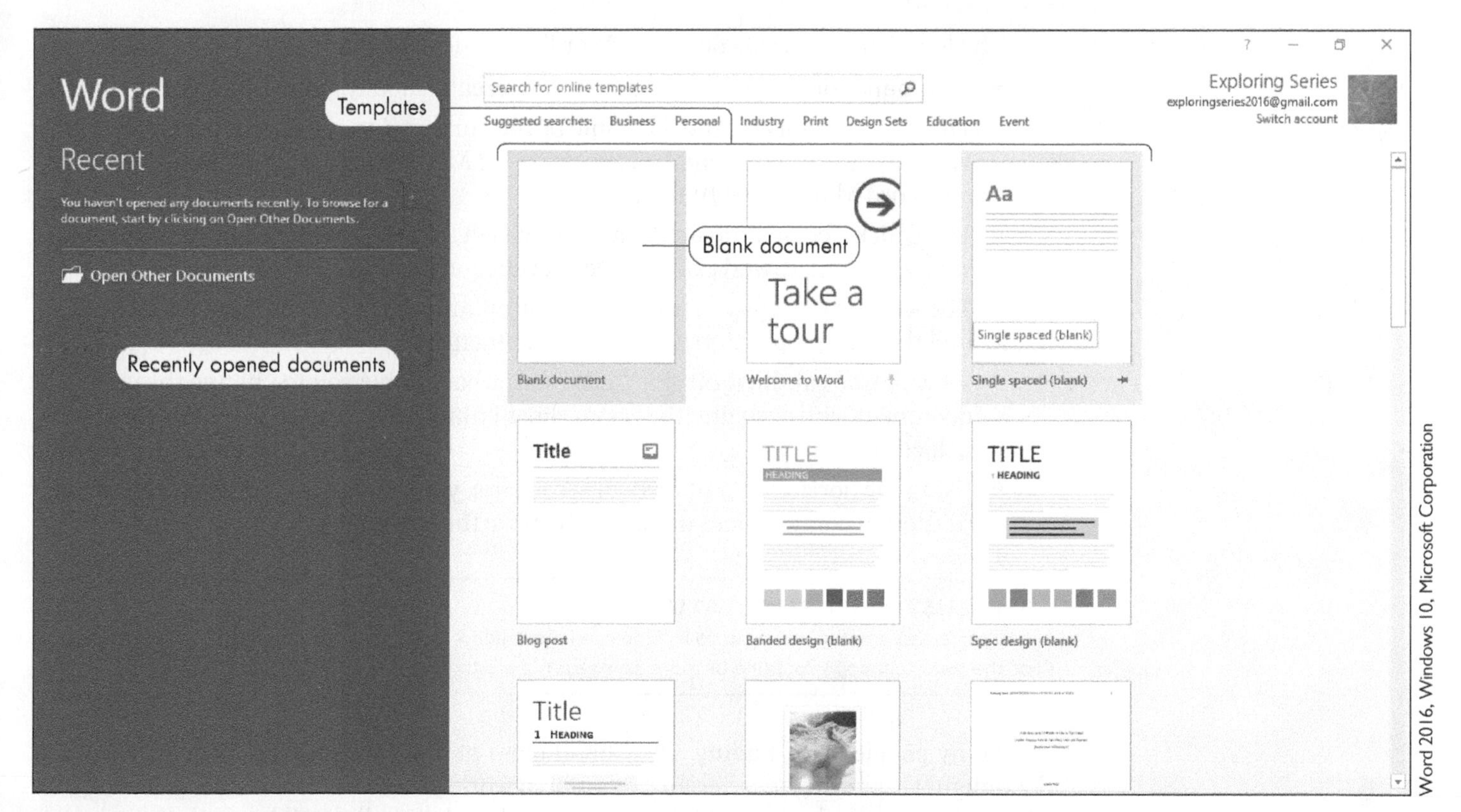

FIGURE 3 Word Document Options

To begin a blank document, click Blank document (or simply press Enter, if Blank document is selected). Word provides a clean, uncluttered area in which to type, with minimal distraction at the sides and across the top. Word provides a large, almost borderless area for your document. Figure 4 shows a typical Word document.

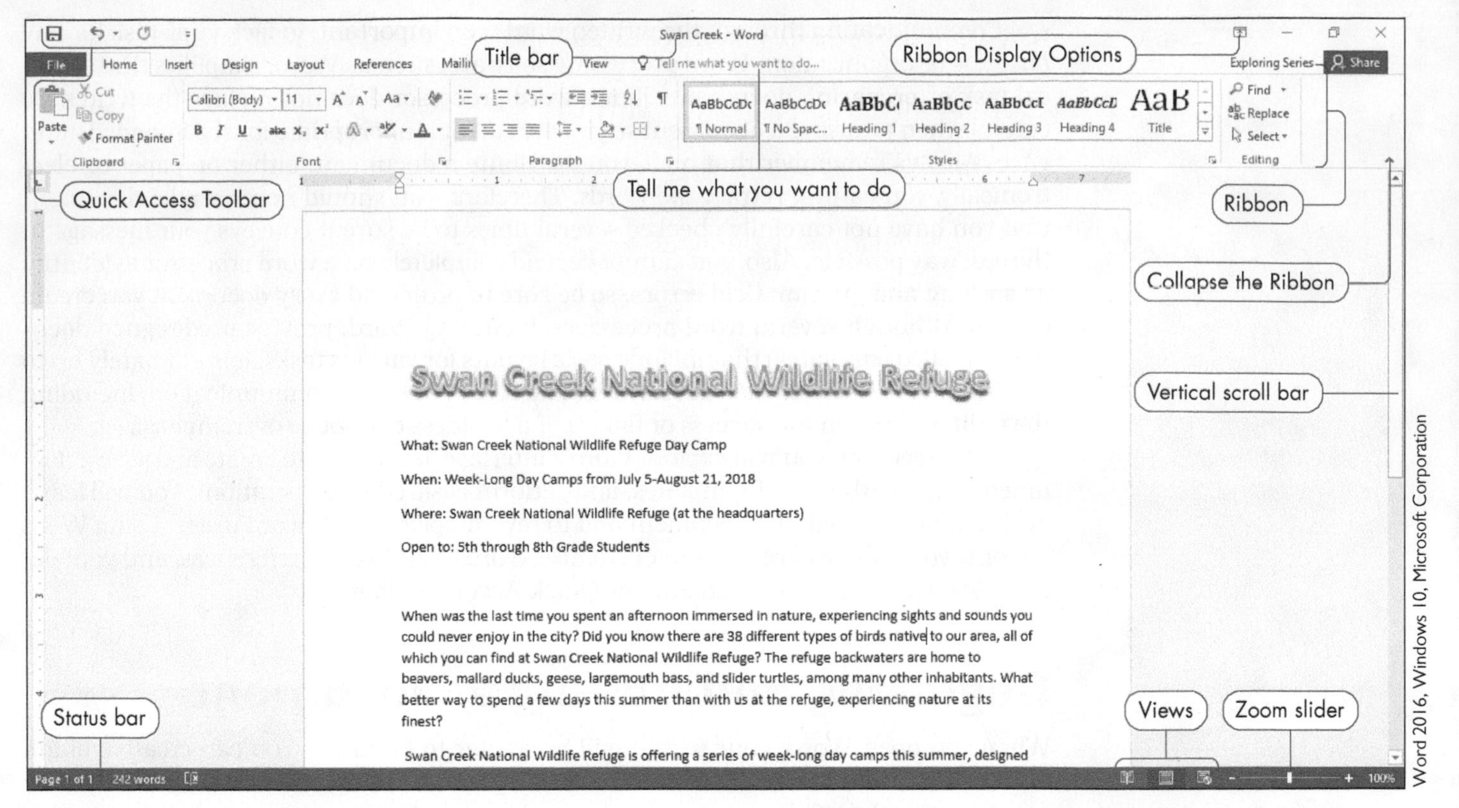

FIGURE 4 Word Components

The following list briefly describes Word's basic features:

- Commands on the Ribbon enable you to create, modify, and enhance documents.
- The title bar indicates the file name of the current document and includes Windows control buttons and access to *Tell Me*, a search tool that enables you to tell Word what you want to do.
- The Quick Access Toolbar, located on the left side of the title bar, makes it easy to save a document, and undo or redo recent commands.
- The status bar keeps you apprised of information such as word and page count, and the current position within the document.
- View buttons at the right side of the status bar enable you to change the view of a document, and dragging the Zoom slider enlarges or reduces the onscreen size of a document.
- Using the horizontal and vertical scroll bars, you can scroll through a document (although doing so does not actually move the insertion point).

TIP: CUSTOMIZE THE STATUS BAR

You can customize the status bar to include even more items of information. Right-click an empty area of the status bar and select one or more items from the list.

Many people enjoy having the Ribbon close at hand when developing or editing a document. Others might prefer an uncluttered workspace, free of distractions. When the Ribbon is removed from view, tabs remain displayed, but all detail beneath them is hidden, resulting in a large amount of uncluttered typing space.

To temporarily remove the Ribbon from view, complete one of the following steps:

- Click Collapse the Ribbon (refer to Figure 4).
- Double-click a tab on the Ribbon.

To display the Ribbon again, complete one of the following steps:

- Click Ribbon Display Options and click Show Tabs and Commands.
- Double-click a tab on the Ribbon.

TIP: USE THE TELL ME FEATURE

New to Microsoft Word 2016, the Tell Me feature not only provides support on how to do something, it can actually do it for you. For example, if you want to check spelling in a document, but do not know how, you can type *check spelling* in the Tell me what you want to do box (refer to Figure 4) and then select the command from a subsequent menu. Word actually checks spelling at that point.

Ribbon Display Options (refer to Figure 4) enables you to adjust the Ribbon view. You can choose to hide the Ribbon, providing a clear document space in which to edit or read a document. Click at the top of the Ribbon to show it again. You can also choose to show only the Ribbon tabs. Click a tab to display its options. Finally, you can choose to show all Ribbon tabs and commands, which is the default.

Create a Document

To create a blank document, click Blank document when Word opens (refer to Figure 3). As you type text, you will not need to think about how much text can fit on one line or how sentences progress from one line to the next. Word's ***word wrap*** feature automatically pushes words to the next line when you reach the right margin.

Word wrap is closely associated with another concept: the hard return and soft return. A hard return is created when you press Enter at the end of a line or paragraph. A soft return is created by Word as it wraps text from one line to the next. The locations of soft returns change automatically as text is inserted or deleted, or as page features or settings, such as objects or margins, are added or changed. Soft returns are not considered characters and cannot be deleted. However, a hard return is actually a nonprinting character, that you can delete, if necessary. To display nonprinting characters, such as hard returns (also called paragraph marks) and tabs, click Show/Hide ¶ (see Figure 5). Just as you delete any other character by pressing Backspace or Delete (depending on whether the insertion point is positioned to the right or left of the item to remove), you can delete a paragraph mark. To remove the display of nonprinting characters, click Show/Hide again.

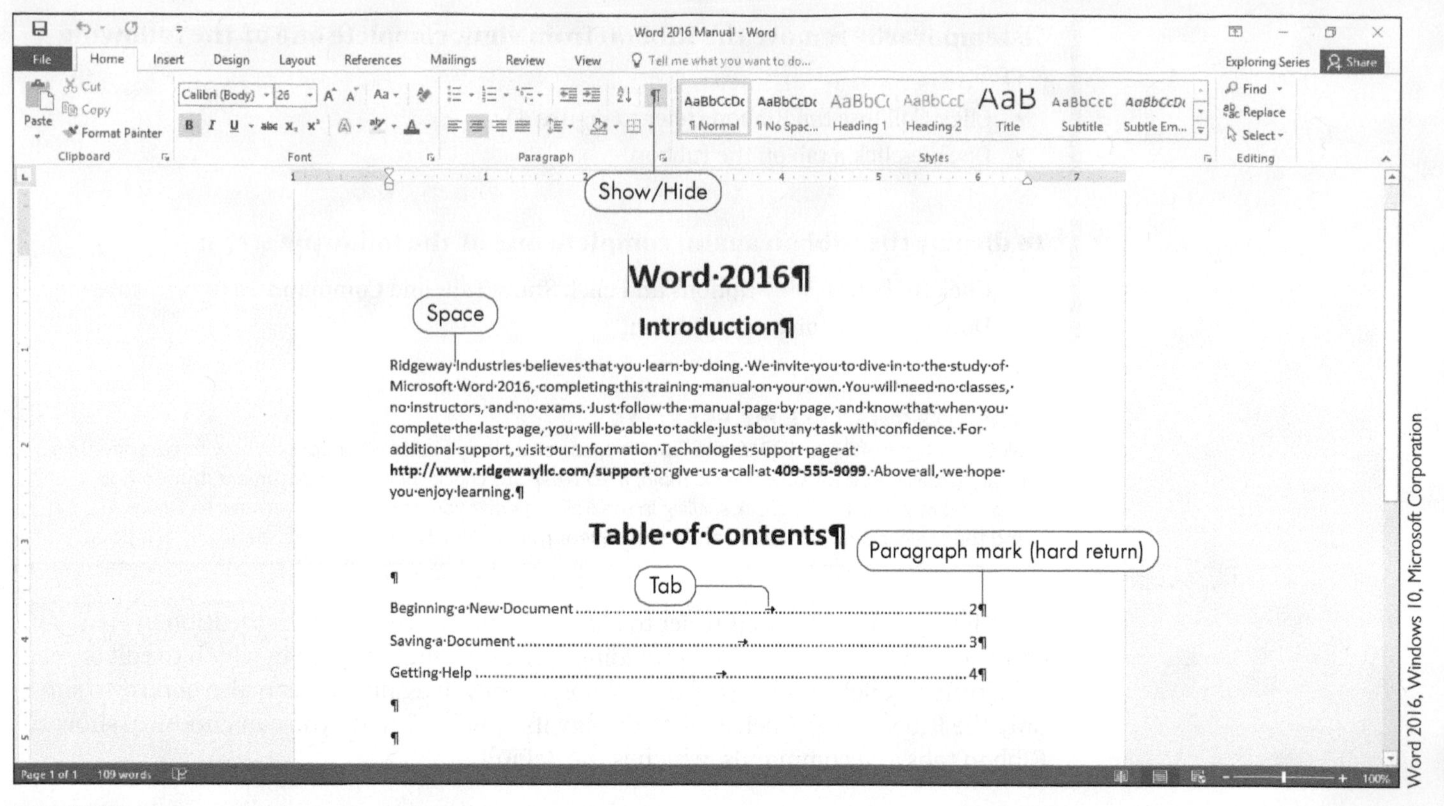

FIGURE 5 Displaying Nonprinting Characters

As you work with Word, you must understand that Word's definition of a paragraph and your definition are not likely to be the same. You would probably define a paragraph as a related set of sentences, which is correct in a literary sense. When the subject or direction of thought changes, a new paragraph begins. However, Word defines a paragraph as text that ends in a hard return. Even a blank line, created by pressing Enter, is considered a paragraph. Therefore, as a Word student, you will consider every line that ends in a hard return a paragraph. When you press Enter, a paragraph mark is displayed in the document if you choose to show nonprinting characters (refer to Figure 5).

In addition to the nonprinting mark that Word inserts when you press Enter, other nonprinting characters are inserted when you press keys such as Tab or the Spacebar. Click Show/Hide in the Paragraph group on the Home tab to reveal all nonprinting characters in a document. Why would you want to display nonprinting characters? Nonprinting characters are generally not viewed when working in a document and will not be included when a document is printed, but they can assist you with troubleshooting a document and modifying its appearance before printing or distributing. For example, if lines in a document end awkwardly, some not even extending to the right margin, you can click Show/Hide to display nonprinting characters and check for the presence of poorly placed, or perhaps unnecessary, hard returns. Deleting the hard returns might realign the document so that lines end in better fashion.

Reuse Text

STEP 1 You might find occasion to reuse text from a previously created document. For example, a memo to employees describing new insurance benefits might borrow wording from another document describing the same benefits to company retirees. In that case, you would simply insert text from a saved document into the new memo.

To insert text from another document, complete the following steps:

1. Position the insertion point where the inserted text is to be placed.
2. Click the Insert tab. Click the Object arrow (see Figure 6).
3. Click Text from File.
4. Navigate to the location of the source document and double-click the file name.

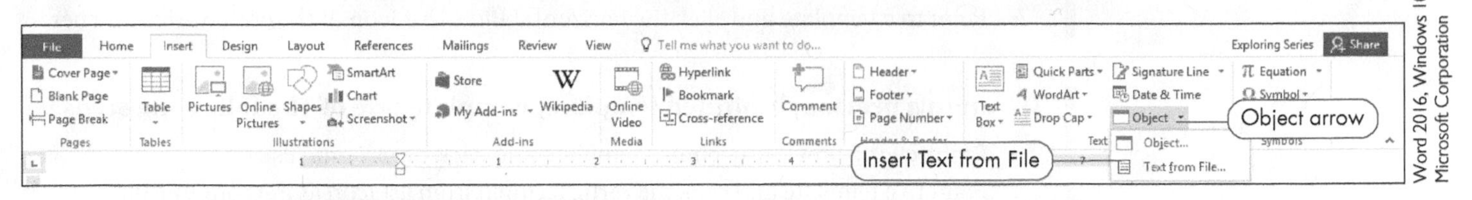

FIGURE 6 Inserting Text from Another File

Use a Template

STEP 2 Developing a new document can be difficult. With that in mind, the developers of Word have included a library of ***templates*** from which you can select a predesigned document. You can then modify the document to suit your needs. Categories of templates are displayed when you first open Word, or when you click the File tab and click New. In addition to local templates—those that are available offline with a typical Word installation—Microsoft provides many more online. All of those templates are displayed or searchable within Word, as shown in Figure 7. Microsoft continually updates content in the template library, so you are assured of having access to all the latest templates each time you open Word.

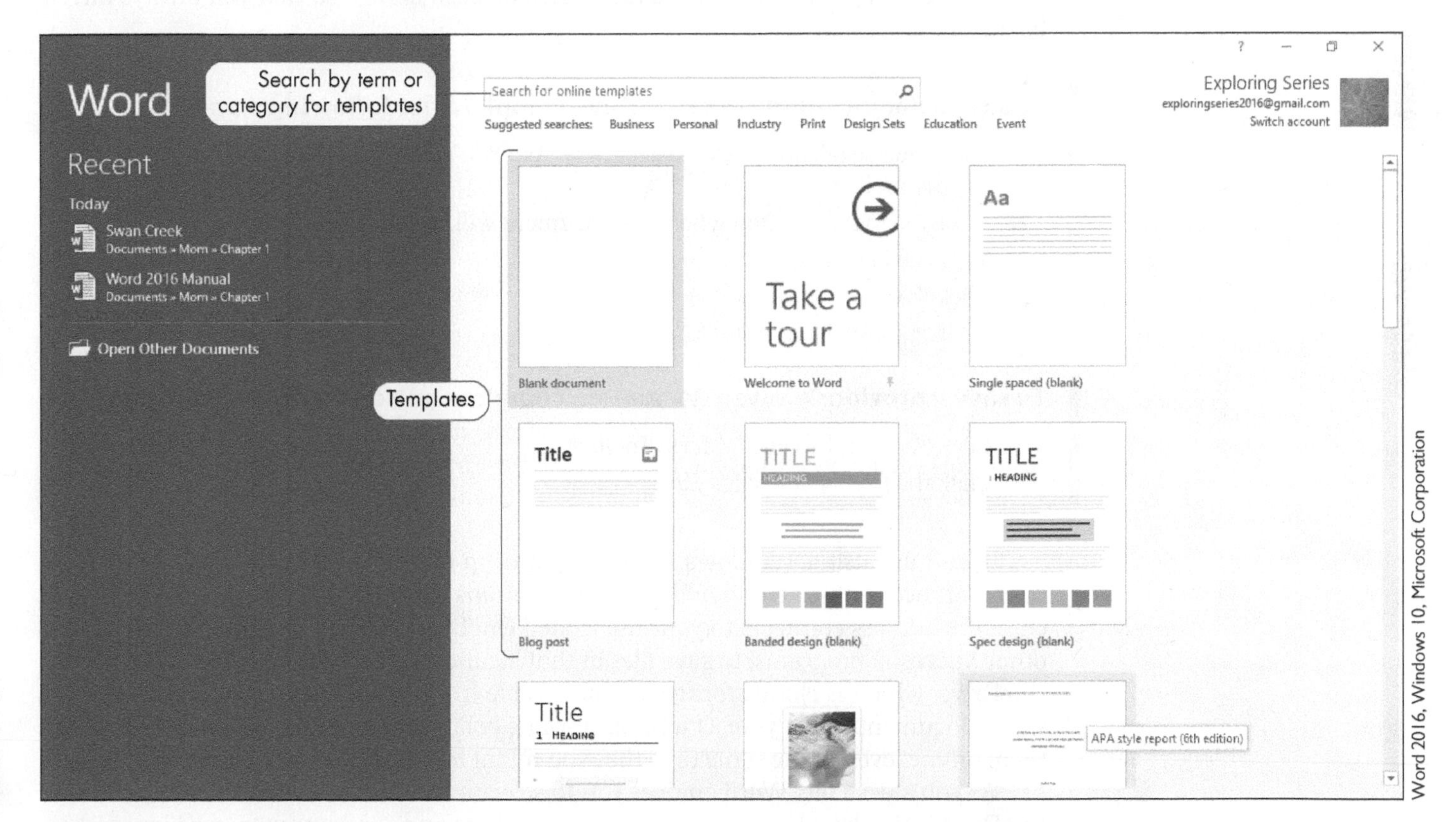

FIGURE 7 Working with Templates

Some templates are likely to become your favorites. Because you will want quick access to those templates, you can pin them to the top of the templates menu so they will always be available.

To pin a template, complete one of the following steps:

- Right-click a favorite template and click Pin to list.
- Point to a template and click the horizontal Pin to list icon at the bottom-right corner.

To unpin a previously pinned template, complete one of the following steps:

- Right-click a previously pinned template and click Unpin from list.
- Point to a template and click the vertical Unpin from list icon at the bottom-right corner.

Save a Document

Saving a document makes it possible for you to access it later for editing, sharing, or printing. In fact, it is a good idea not to wait until a document is complete to save it, but to save a document periodically as you develop it. That way, you risk losing only what you created or edited since the last save operation if you experience a disruption of power. Word recognizes not only the need to save files, but also the need to make them available on any device you might have access to and the need to share documents with others so you can collaborate on projects. To make that possible, Word encourages you to save documents to the cloud. It is always a good idea, however, to save an important document in several places—perhaps a hard drive or flash drive—so that you always have a backup copy.

To save a document for the first time, complete the following steps:

1. Click the File tab and click Save (or Save As). You can instead click Save on the Quick Access Toolbar.
2. Navigate to the location where the document will be saved.
3. Type the file name.
4. Click Save.

To save a previously saved document, complete one of the following steps:

- Click Save on the Quick Access Toolbar.
- Click the File tab and click Save.

If you are using Windows as your operating system, you most likely provided a Microsoft account, or email address, when you installed the operating system. In that case, the address connects to your associated OneDrive storage and enables Word, and other Microsoft programs, to save files in that location by default. Files that are saved on OneDrive, which is cloud storage, are accessible from mobile devices. If you choose to share documents from your OneDrive storage, collaborators can easily access and edit them online, even at the same time that you might be editing the document online.

As you save a file, Word enables you to select a location to which to save. Although OneDrive is the default, you can select another drive on your computer (see Figure 8).

Correcting each error by right-clicl the mistakes are many. In that case, W each identified error so that you can dete

To check an entire document for sp the following steps:

1. Click the Review tab and click Spellin Figure 11).
2. Review each error as it is presented, s error if it is actually correct (as might correct spelling is not presented, and make the correction.

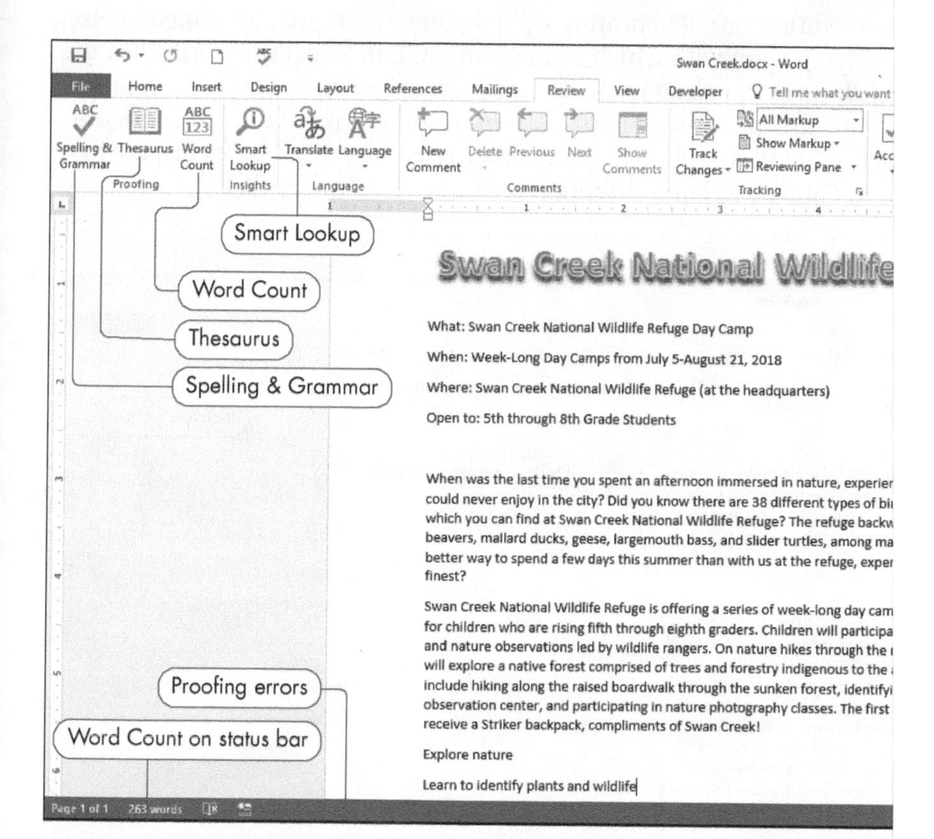

FIGURE 11 Options for Proofing a Document

For even quicker error identification bar (refer to Figure 11). By default, Wor ment for spelling, grammatical, and word errors icon if errors are found. Click the all errors, one at a time. If, instead, you se document appears to be error free. The d cated by the X on the Proofing errors icon

Never depend completely on Word to yourself. For example, typing the word *fe* that Word would typically catch, because flagged as a word usage error, depending

Words do not always come easily. Occ word with the same meaning as another) ***thesaurus*** for just such an occasion.

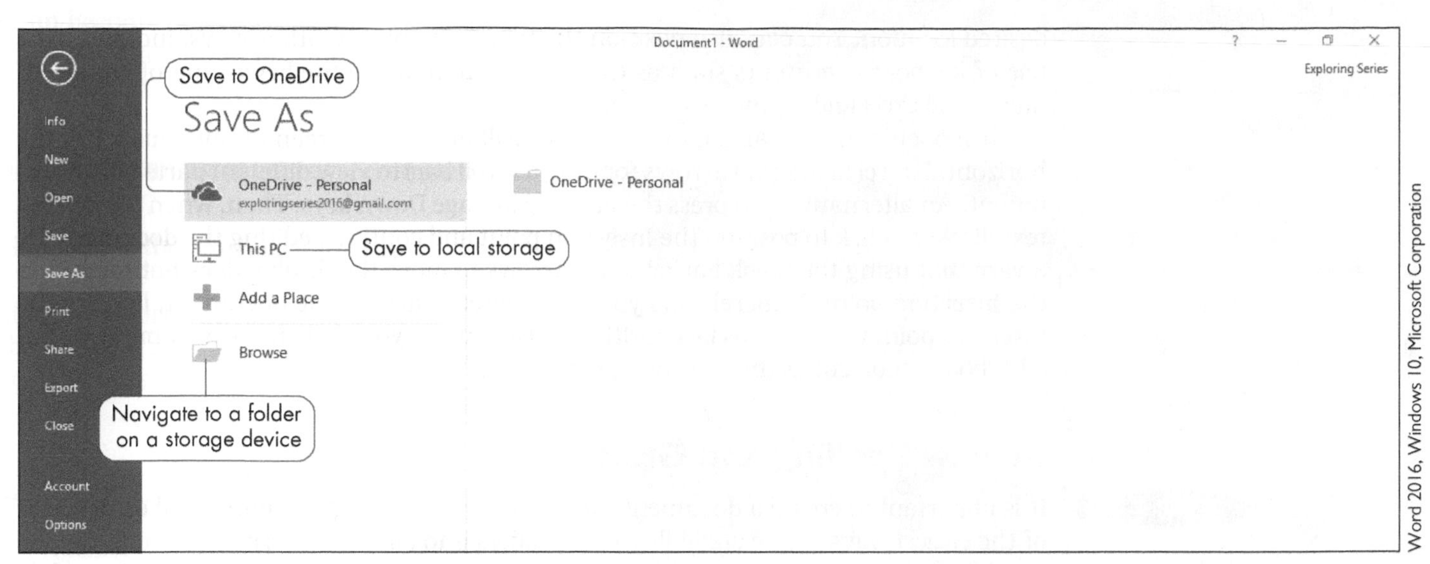

FIGURE 8 Saving a Word Document

Open a Document

After saving a document, you can open it later when you start Word and either select the document from the Recent list, or click Open Other Documents and navigate to the saved file. Word remembers the position of the insertion point when you previously saved the file and suggests that you return to that same location (see Figure 9). Just click the link to return, or ignore it if you want to work somewhere else in the document.

FIGURE 9 Returning to a Previous Position

Insert Text and Navigate a Document

The ***insertion point*** indicates where the text you type will be placed. It is important to remain aware of the location of the insertion point and to know how to move it to control where text is typed. Most often, you will move the insertion point by simply clicking the

desired location. You can also positioi
use of keyboard shortcuts such as Ct
ment) and Ctrl+End (to move to the er

If a document contains more text
horizontal or vertical scroll arrows (or
ument. An alternative is to press the P
text displays, click to position the inser
aware that using the scroll bar or scr
the insertion point. It merely lets you
insertion point where it was last positic
a keyboard shortcut, is the insertion p

Review Spelling and Gram

STEP 4 It is important to create a document th
of the easiest ways to lose credibility wi
words that are appropriate and that bes
ument. Word provides tools on the Revi
ment for errors, identifying proper word

A word considered by Word to be
possible grammatical mistake or word
errors are shown in Figure 10.

**To correct possible spelling, gramm
document, right-click an underlin
steps:**

- Select the correct spelling from one
- Ignore the misspelled word.
- Add the word to the Office dictionar

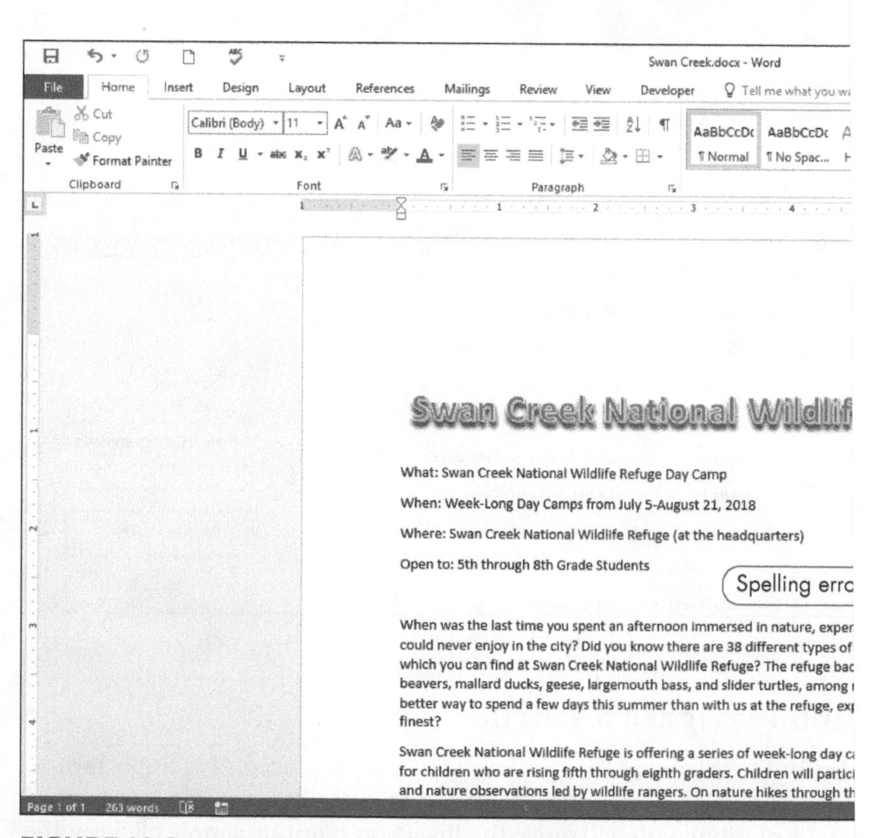

FIGURE 10 Correcting Spelling and Grammatical Errors

To select a synonym, complete one of the following steps:

- Select a word in a document and click the Review tab. Click Thesaurus (refer to Figure 11), click the arrow beside a synonym, and then click Insert.
- Right-click a word and click Synonyms. Select from a group of synonyms.

TIP: COUNTING WORDS

Occasionally, you might need to know how many words are included in a document, or in a selected portion of a document. For example, your English instructor might require a minimum word count for an essay. Click the Review tab and click Word Count (refer to Figure 11) to get a quick summary of words, characters, lines, pages, and paragraphs. Document word count is often displayed on the status bar as well.

Especially when editing or collaborating on a document created by someone else, you might come across a word with which you are unfamiliar. Select the word; click the Review tab and click Smart Lookup in the Insights group (refer to Figure 11). Smart Lookup opens the Insights pane (see Figure 12). ***Insights*** is a pane that presents outside resources, such as images, definitions, and other references. Resources display in a sidebar, as shown in Figure 12. For a definition of the selected word, click Define in the Insights pane.

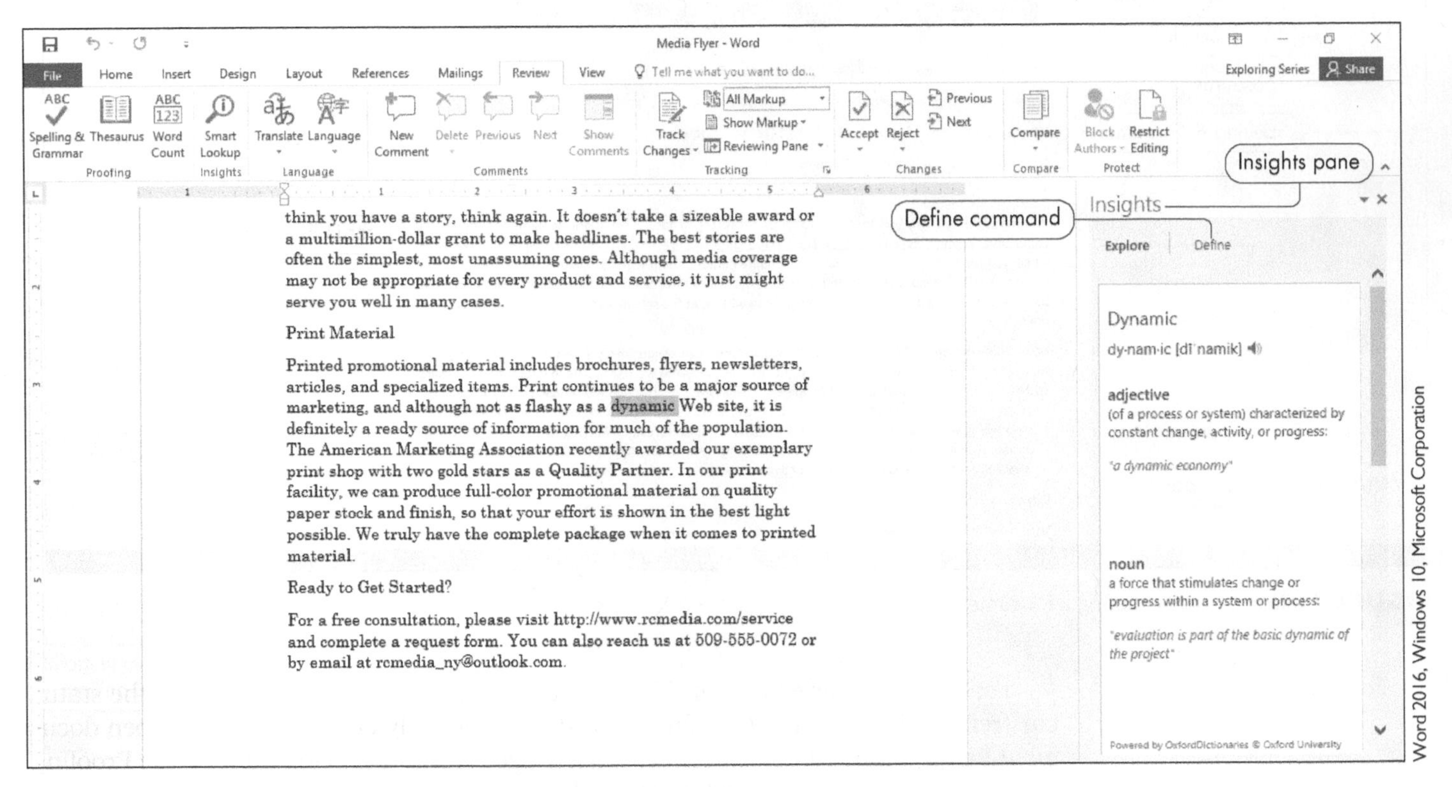

FIGURE 12 Using the Insights Pane

Customizing Word

As installed, Word is immediately useful. However, you might find options that you would prefer to customize, add, or remove from the document window. You might prefer that the Ribbon be organized differently, or it might be helpful to add frequently used commands to the Quick Access Toolbar for ease of access. These and other options are available for customization within Word.

Explore Word Options

STEP 5 »» By default, certain Word settings are determined and in place when you begin a Word document. For example, unless you specify otherwise, Word will automatically check spelling as you type. Similarly, the Mini toolbar will automatically display when text is selected. Although those and other settings are most likely what you will prefer, there may be occasions when you want to change them. When you change Word options, you change them for all documents—not just the currently open file.

TIP: SETTING WORD OPTIONS

Word options that you change will remain in effect until you change them again, even after Word is closed and reopened. Keep in mind that if you are working in a school computer lab, you might not have permission to change options permanently.

To modify Word options, complete the following steps:

1. Click the File tab and click Options.
2. Select from categories and options, as shown in Figure 13.

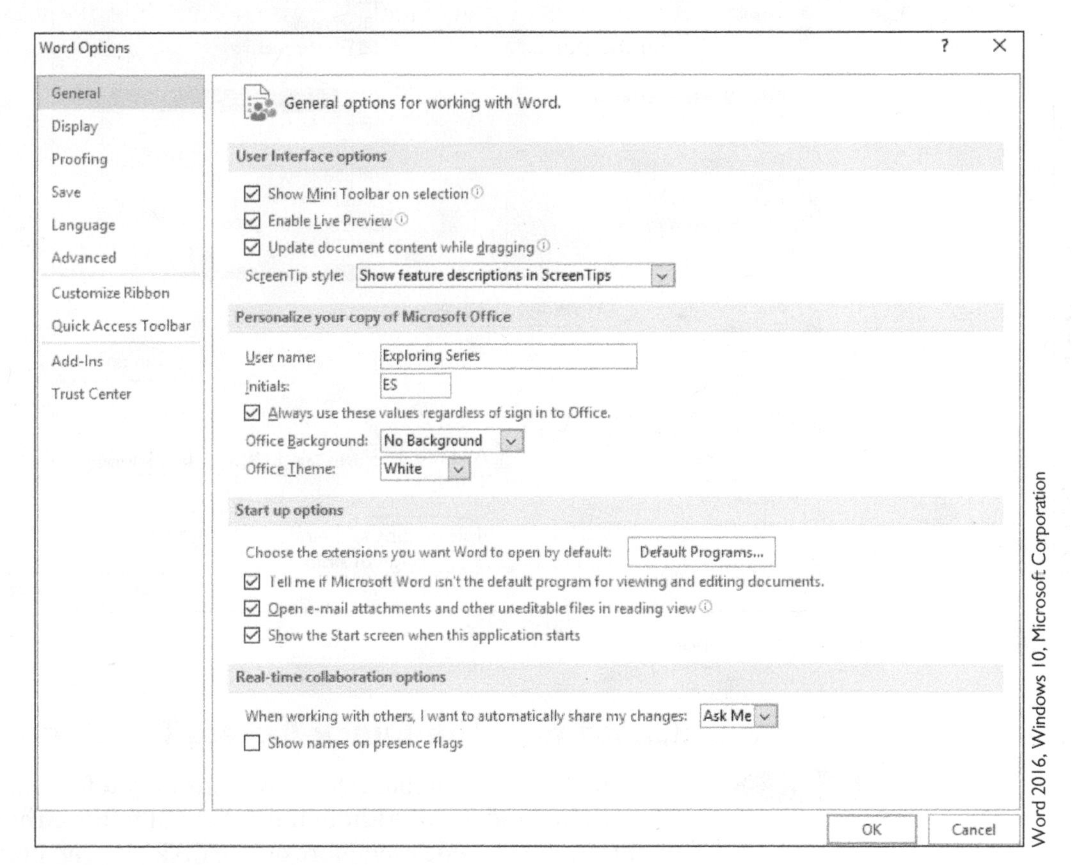

FIGURE 13 Accessing Word Options

Customize the Ribbon

STEP 6 »» The Word Ribbon provides access to commands that make it easy to develop, edit, save, share, and print documents. If necessary, you can add and remove Ribbon tabs, as well as rename them.

To customize the Ribbon, complete the following steps:

1. Click the File tab and click Options.
2. Click Customize Ribbon.
3. Choose from the following options, as shown in Figure 14:
   - To add or remove a tab, select or deselect the tab name check box.
   - To change the name of a current tab, click Rename.
   - To reset the Ribbon to the original tabs, click Reset, and then click Reset all customizations.

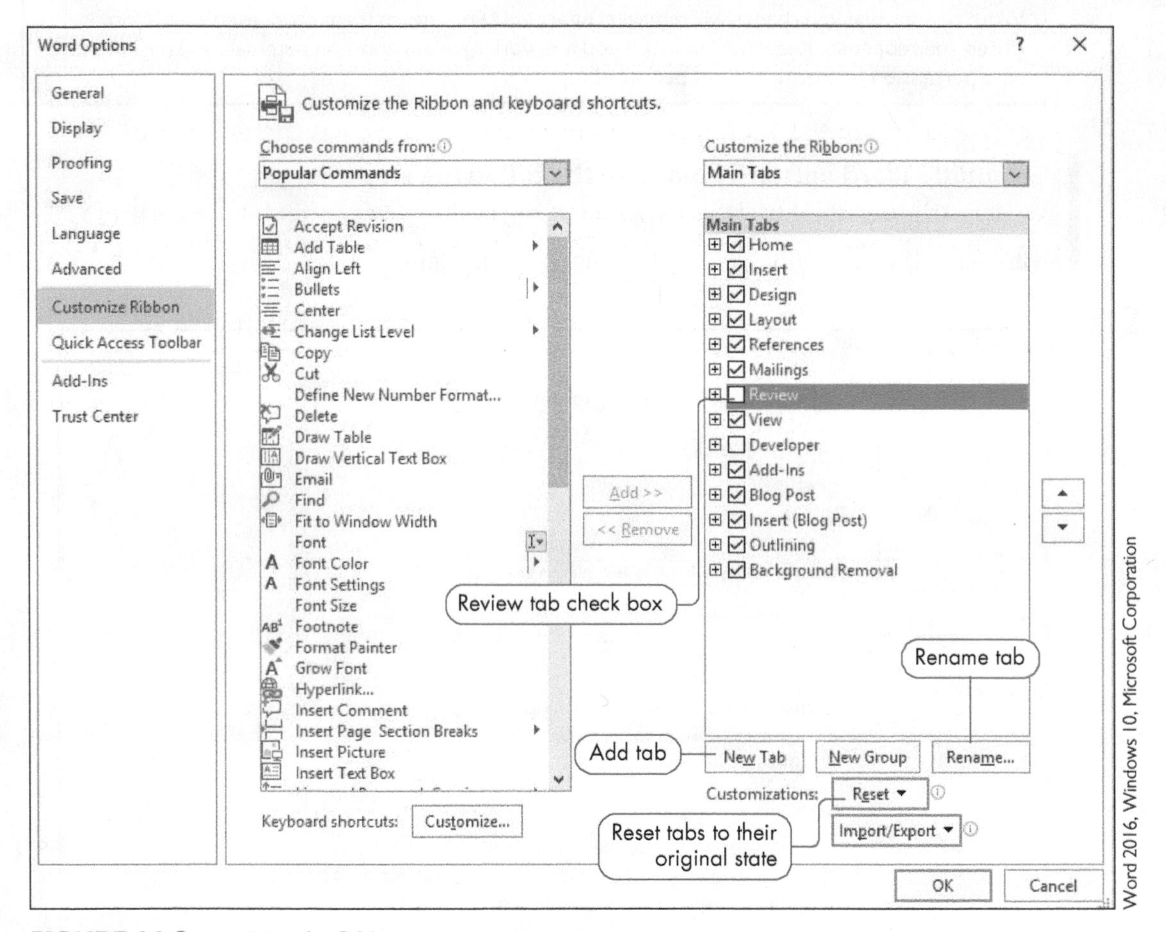

FIGURE 14 Customizing the Ribbon

Customize the Quick Access Toolbar

The Quick Access Toolbar (QAT) contains only a few commands by default, including Save, Undo, and Redo. Although it is helpful to have those options close at hand, you might want to include even more on the QAT. You can even remove commands that you do not use often.

To customize the QAT, complete one of the following steps:

- Click Customize Quick Access Toolbar (see Figure 15) and select from a menu of options.
- Right-click a Ribbon command and click Add to Quick Access Toolbar.

To remove a command from the QAT, right-click the command on the QAT and select Remove from Quick Access Toolbar.

Customize Quick Access Toolbar

Word 2016, Windows 10, Microsoft Corporation

FIGURE 15 Customizing the Quick Access Toolbar

1. Explain how the way you are likely to define a paragraph and the way Word defines a paragraph can differ.
2. Provide at least two advantages of using OneDrive as a storage location for your documents.
3. It is very important to check a document for spelling, grammatical, and word usage errors. However, Word might not identify every error in a document. Why not? Provide an example of an error that Word might not identify.
4. Describe an advantage of using Word templates to begin document production.

Hands-On Exercises

Skills covered: Create a Document • Save a Document • Use a Template • Insert Text and Navigate a Document • Review Spelling and Grammar • Explore Word Options • Customize the Ribbon • Customize the Quick Access Toolbar

1 Introduction to Word Processing

As an office assistant working with the wildlife refuge, you prepare a document publicizing the summer day camps at Swan Creek. Your supervisor provided a few paragraphs that you modify, creating an article for distribution to schools in the area. You also open a document from a template, and create an event planner. Because you plan to use the office computer for future projects as well, you explore ways to customize Word for ease of use.

STEP 1 » CREATE AND SAVE A DOCUMENT

As you create a new document, you insert text provided by your supervisor and then save the document for later editing. Refer to Figure 16 as you complete Step 1.

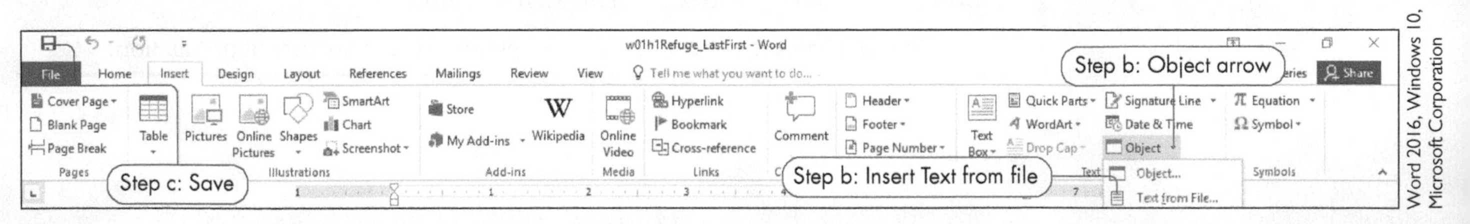

FIGURE 16 Beginning a Document

a. Open Word. Click **Blank document**. Click **Save** on the Quick Access Toolbar. In the right pane, click the location where you save your files, or click **Browse** and navigate to the location. Change the file name to **w01h1Refuge_LastFirst**. Click **Save**.

When you save files, use your last and first names. For example, as the Word author, I would name my document "w01h1Refuge_HoganLynn."

b. Click the **Insert tab** and click the **Object arrow**. Click **Text from File**. Navigate to your student data files for this chapter and double-click *w01h1Camps*. Press **Ctrl+Home** to move the insertion point to the beginning of the document.

c. Click **Save** on the Quick Access Toolbar.

This saves the document without changing the name or the location where it is saved.

d. Click the **File tab** and click **Close**.

You close the document. You will use this document again later in this Hands-On Exercise.

STEP 2 ›› USE A TEMPLATE

As a multitasker, you are accustomed to working with several projects at once. Ms. Traynom, your supervisor, asks that you print an event planner. She must often juggle tasks, and needs a document that will help organize them. You know that Word provides event planner templates, so you locate one. Refer to Figure 17 as you complete Step 2.

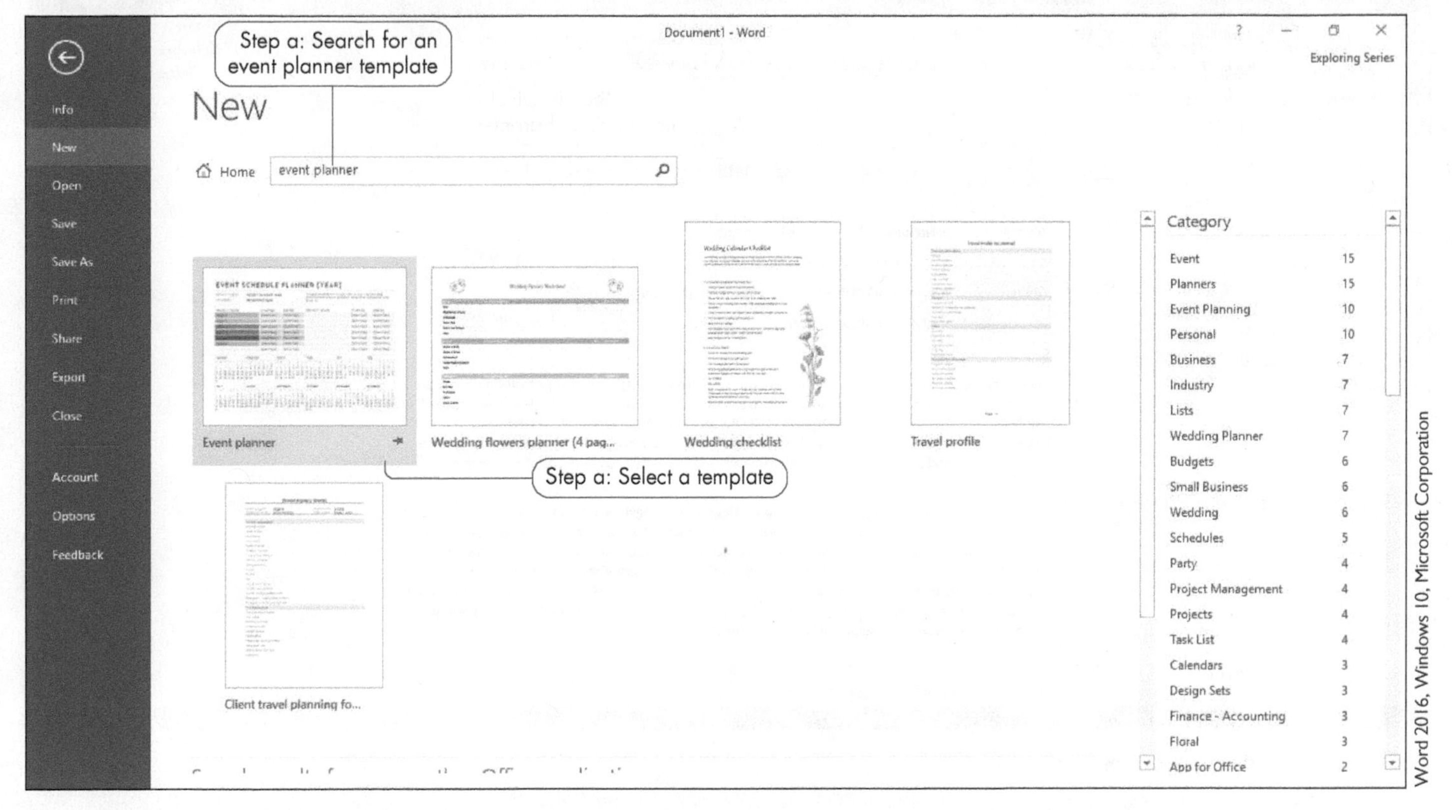

FIGURE 17 Working with a Template

a. Click the **File tab** and click **New**. Click the **Search for online templates box** and type **event planner**. Press **Enter**. Click **Event Planner**.

> **TROUBLESHOOTING:** The event planner template is only available if you are currently connected to the Internet.

b. Click **Create**. Click **OK**, repeatedly if necessary, to accept settings from any subsequent dialog boxes related to scheduling that may open. Save the planner as **w01h1Planner_LastFirst**.

c. Click the **File tab** and click **Close**.

STEP 3 » INSERT TEXT AND NAVIGATE A DOCUMENT

Although Ms. Traynom provided you with a good start, you add a bit more detail to the w01h1Refuge_LastFirst article. Refer to Figure 18 as you complete Step 3.

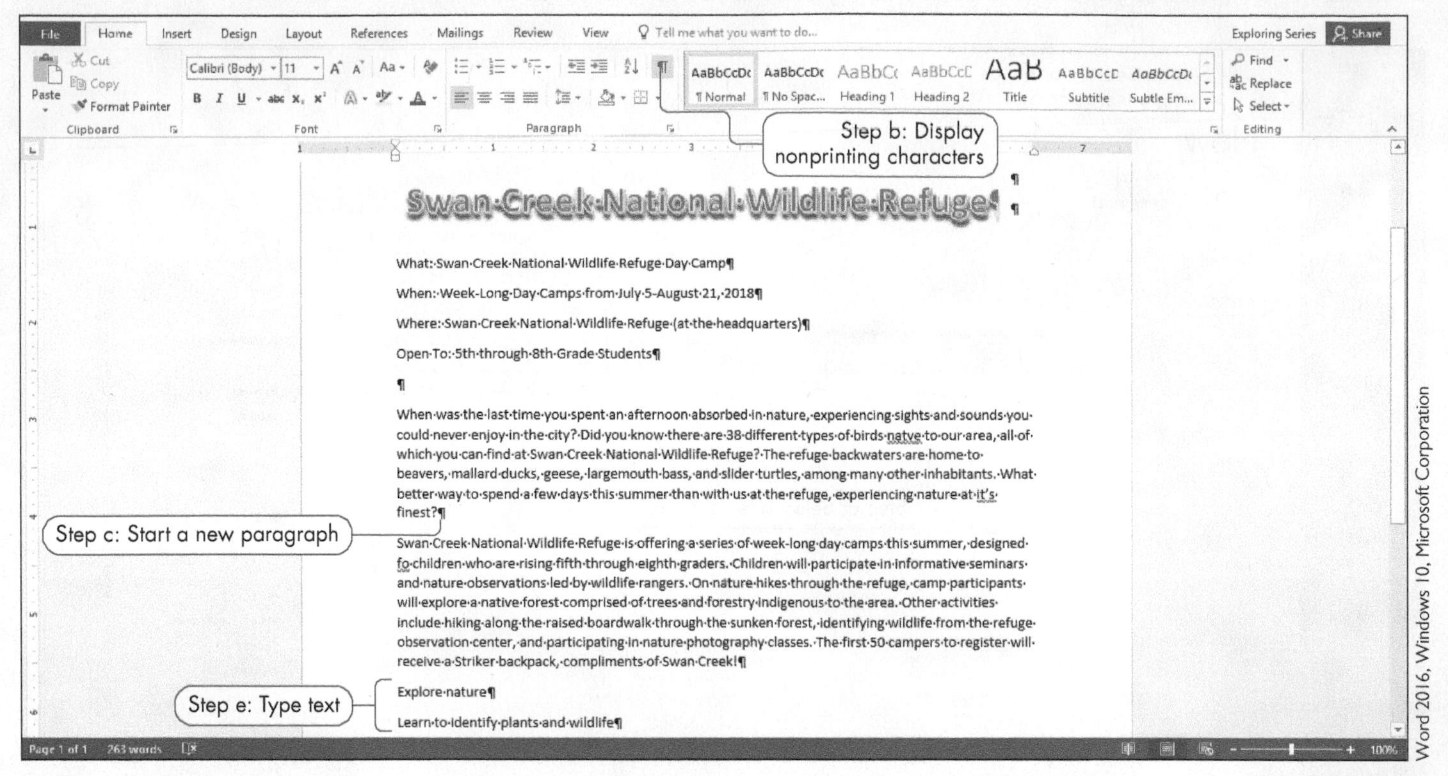

FIGURE 18 Editing a Document

a. Click the **File tab** and click **Open**. In the Recent list, click **w01h1Refuge_LastFirst**.

b. Click **Show/Hide** in the Paragraph group to display nonprinting formatting marks (unless they are already displayed).

c. Click after the sentence ending in *finest?*—immediately after the question mark and before the nonprinting space character at the end of the fourth sentence in the body text. Press **Enter**. Press **Delete**.

> **TROUBLESHOOTING:** There will be no space before Swan if you clicked after the space instead of before it when you pressed Enter. In that case, there is no space to delete, so leave the text as is.

d. Scroll down and click after *Creek!*—immediately after the exclamation point after the second body paragraph—and press **Enter**.

e. Type the following text, pressing **Enter** at the end of each line:

   explore nature

   learn to identify native plants and wildlife

   take digital photos

   participate in nature seminars

   enjoy relaxing days at the refuge

   As you type each line, the first letter is automatically capitalized.

f. Press **Ctrl+End**. Press **Delete**.

   The final paragraph mark is deleted and the second blank page is removed.

g. Save the document.

STEP 4 ›› REVIEW SPELLING AND GRAMMAR

As you continue to develop the article, you check for spelling, grammar, and word usage mistakes. You also identify a synonym and get a definition. Refer to Figure 19 as you complete Step 4.

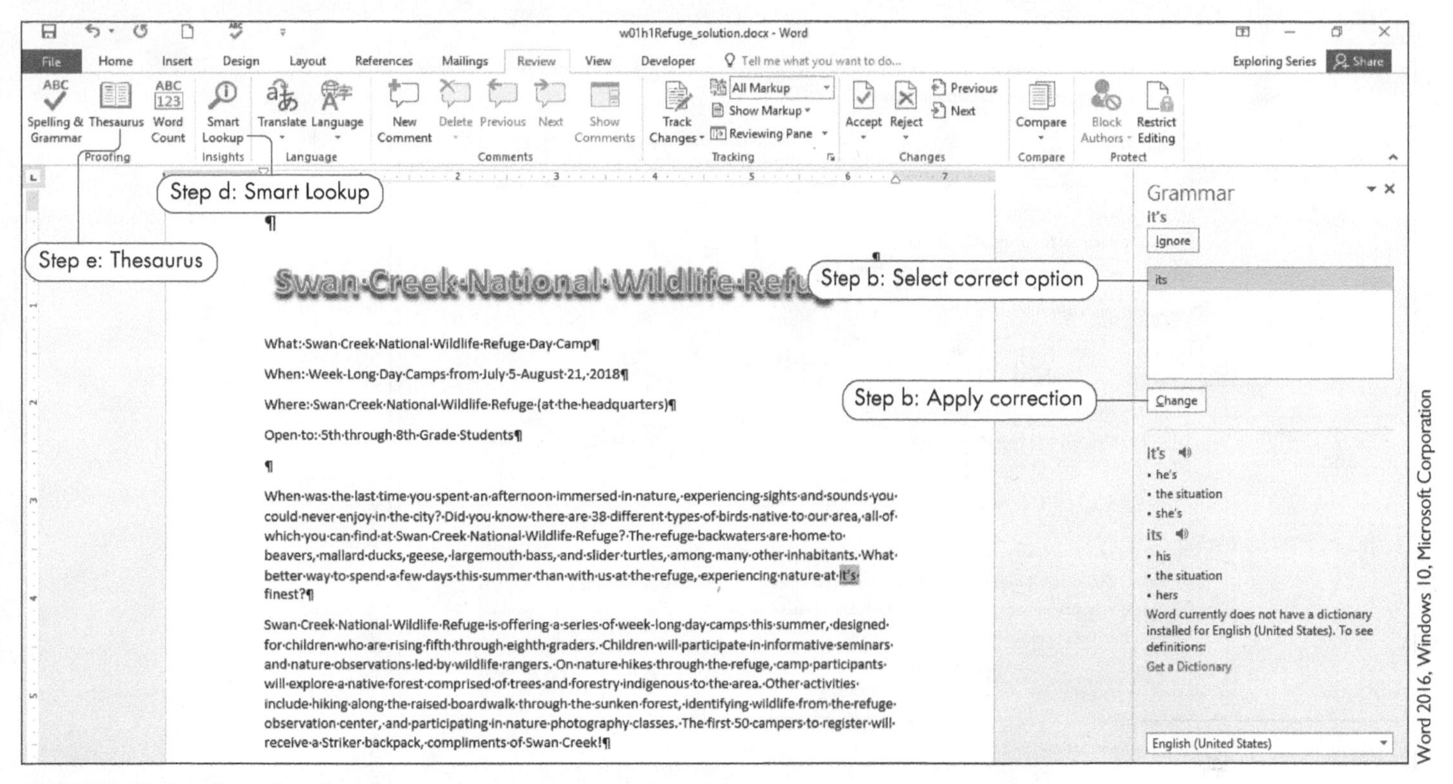

FIGURE 19 Proofing a Document

a. Press **Ctrl+Home**. Right-click the red underlined word **natve** in the second line of the first body paragraph in the document. Click **native** on the shortcut menu.

b. Click the **Review tab** and click **Spelling & Grammar** in the Proofing group. As each error is presented, click to select the correct option. The word *birds* is not possessive, so ignore the suggested error. The word **it's** should not include an apostrophe, so ensure the correct option is selected (refer to Figure 19) and click **Change**. The word *fo* should be **for**. Click **OK** when the check is complete.

c. Read through the document. At least one error in the document is not identified as a spelling or word usage error by Word. Identify and correct the error.

d. Select the word *immersed* in the first sentence of the first body paragraph. Click **Smart Lookup** in the Insights group. Click **Define** in the Insights pane.

Resources related to the selected word are shown in the Insights pane on the right. A definition is also available.

> **TROUBLESHOOTING:** If the Insights pane has not been used before, you may have to respond to a privacy prompt before the Insights pane will open.

e. Close the Insights pane. With the word *immersed* still selected, click **Thesaurus** in the Proofing group. Point to the word *absorbed*, click the arrow at the right, and then select **Insert**.

> **TROUBLESHOOTING:** If you click the word *absorbed* instead of the arrow at the right, you will be presented with related word choices, but the word will not be inserted. Click the back arrow at the top of the Thesaurus pane, and repeat step e.

f. Close the Thesaurus pane. Save the document.

STEP 5 » EXPLORE WORD OPTIONS

You explore some Word options that enable you to customize the computer assigned to you at the refuge. Such customization ensures that Word is configured to suit your preferences. Refer to Figure 20 as you complete Step 5.

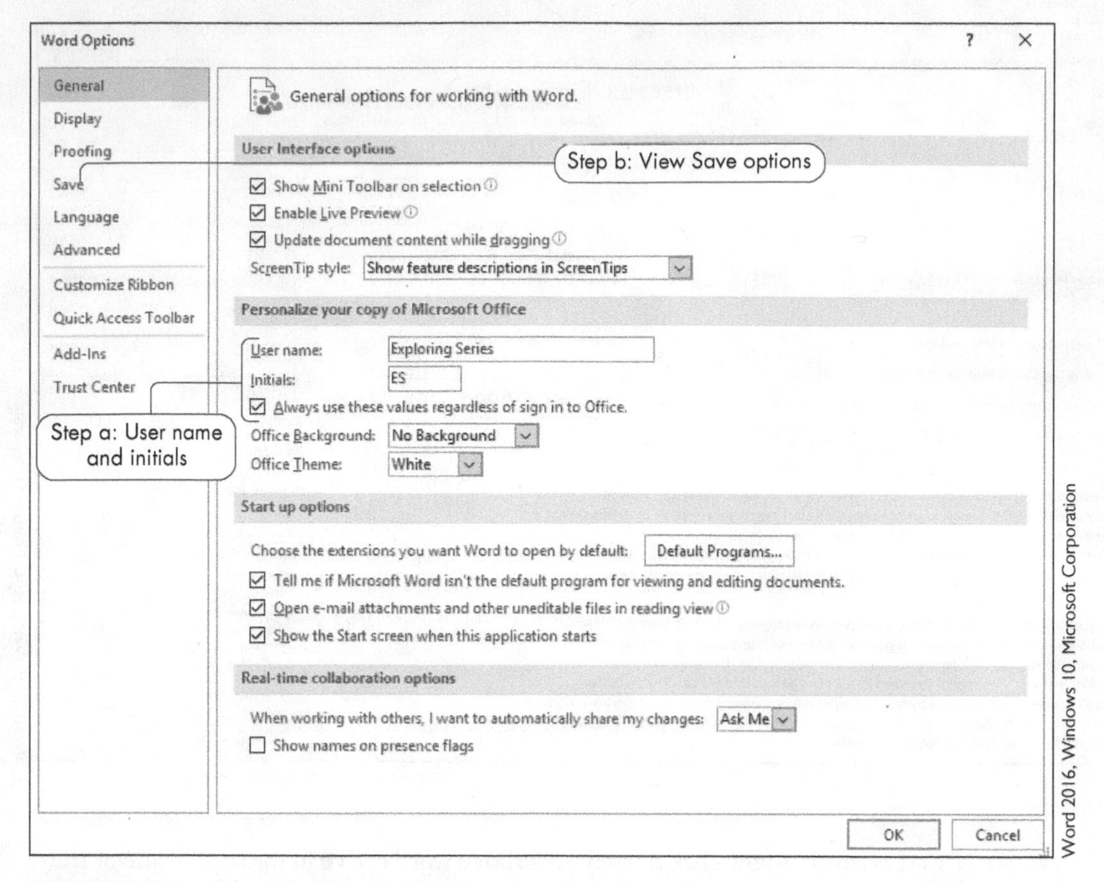

FIGURE 20 Exploring Word Options

a. Click the **File tab** and click **Options**. Ensure that the General category in the left pane is selected.

Note that you can change the User name and Initials that identify you as the author of documents you create. Because you might be working in a computer lab, you do not actually change anything at this time.

b. Click **Save** in the left pane of the Word Options dialog box.

Note that you can adjust the AutoRecover time, a feature covered later in this chapter, by typing in the text box, replacing existing text, or by clicking the up or down arrow repeatedly.

c. Click **Cancel**, so you do not actually make changes.

STEP 6 ›› CUSTOMIZE THE RIBBON

As you continue to explore ways to customize Word preferences, you identify Ribbon tabs that you can add or remove. Refer to Figure 21 as you complete Step 6.

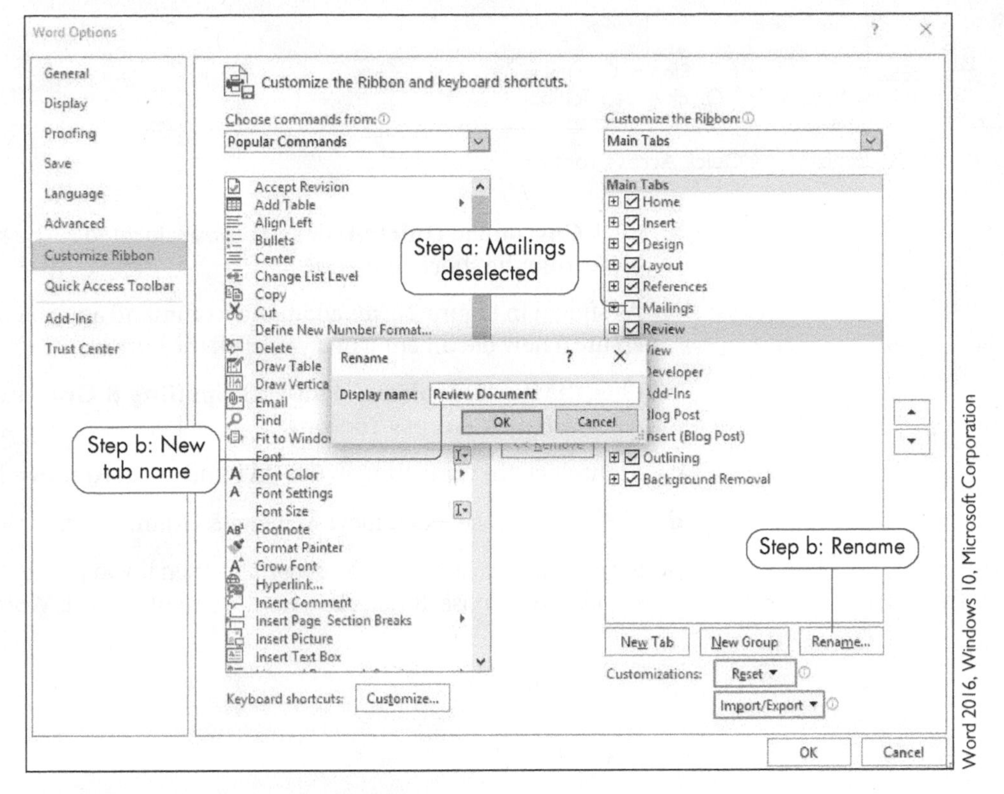

FIGURE 21 Customizing the Ribbon

a. Click the **File tab** and click **Options**. Click **Customize Ribbon** in the left pane. Click the **Mailings check box** under Main Tabs to deselect the item.

> **TROUBLESHOOTING:** If Mailings is not deselected, you clicked the word Mailings instead of the check box next to it. Click the Mailings check box.

b. Click **Review** under Main Tabs (click the word **Review**, not the check mark beside the word). Click **Rename** (located beneath the list of Main Tabs) and type **Review Document**—but do not click OK.

c. Click **Cancel**, so that changes to the Ribbon are not saved to a lab computer. Click **Cancel** again.

STEP 7 » CUSTOMIZE THE QUICK ACCESS TOOLBAR

You customize the Quick Access Toolbar to include commands that you use often. Refer to Figure 22 as you complete Step 7.

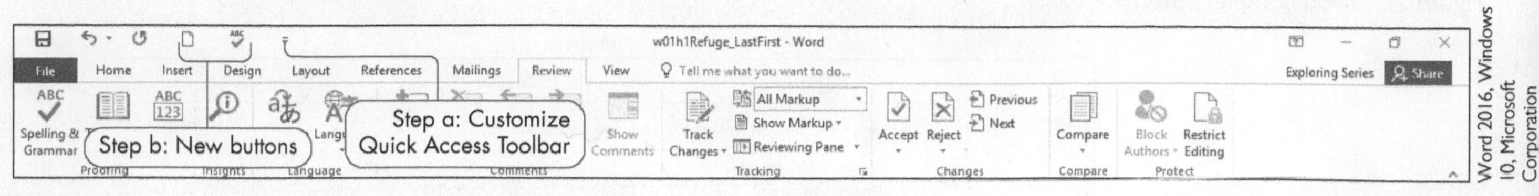

Word 2016, Windows 10, Microsoft Corporation

FIGURE 22 Customizing the Quick Access Toolbar

a. Click **Customize Quick Access Toolbar**, located at the right side of the QAT, and select **New** from the shortcut menu.

As shown in Figure 22, an additional command appears on the QAT, enabling you to create a new document when you click the button.

b. Click the **Review tab** and right-click **Spelling & Grammar** in the Proofing group. Click **Add to Quick Access Toolbar**.

c. Right-click the **New** icon on the QAT and select **Remove from Quick Access Toolbar**.

d. Repeat the process to remove Spelling & Grammar from the Quick Access Toolbar.

e. Save the document. Keep the document open if you plan to continue with the next Hands-On Exercise. If not, close the document and exit Word.

Document Organization

Most often, the reason for creating a document is for others to read; therefore, the document should be designed to meet the needs of the reading audience. It should not only be well worded and structured, but also might include features that better identify it, such as headers, footers, and watermarks. A watermark is text or graphics that displays behind text. In addition, adjusting margins and changing page orientation might better suit a document's purposes and improve its readability. Depending on its purpose, a document might need to fit on one page, or it could be very lengthy.

Before printing or saving a document, review it to ensure that it is attractive and appropriately organized. Word has various views, including Read Mode, Print Layout, Web Layout, Outline, and Draft, that you can use to get a good feel for the way the entire document looks, regardless of its length. The view selected can also give a snapshot of overall document organization so you can be assured that the document is well structured and makes all points. Using options on the View tab on the Ribbon, you can display a document in various ways, showing all pages, only one page, or zooming to a larger view, among other selections.

In this section, you will explore features that improve readability, and you will learn to change the view of a document.

Using Features That Improve Readability

Choosing your words carefully will result in a well-worded document. However, no matter how well worded, a document that is not organized in an attractive manner so that it is easy to read and understand is not likely to impress an audience. Consider not only the content, but also how a document will look when printed or displayed. Special features that can improve readability, such as headers, footers, and symbols, are located on Word's Insert tab. Other settings, such as margins, page orientation, and paper size, are found on the Layout tab. The Design tab provides access to watermarks, which can help convey the purpose or originator of a document.

Insert Headers and Footers

STEP 1 »» ***Headers*** and ***footers*** can give a professional appearance to a document. A header consists of one or more lines at the top of each page. A footer displays at the bottom of each page. Typically, the purpose of including a header or footer is to better identify the document. As a header, you might include an organization name or a class number so that each page identifies the document's origin or purpose. A page number is a typical footer, although it could just as easily be included as a header.

One advantage of using headers and footers is that you have to specify the content only once, after which it displays automatically on all pages. Although you can type the text yourself at the top or bottom of every page, it is time-consuming, and the possibility of making a mistake is great.

To insert a header or footer, complete one of the following steps:

- Click the Insert tab and click Header (or Footer) in the Header & Footer group. Select from a gallery of predefined header or footer styles or click Edit Header (or Edit Footer) as shown in Figure 23 to create an unformatted header or footer.
- Double-click in the header or footer area to open a header or footer.

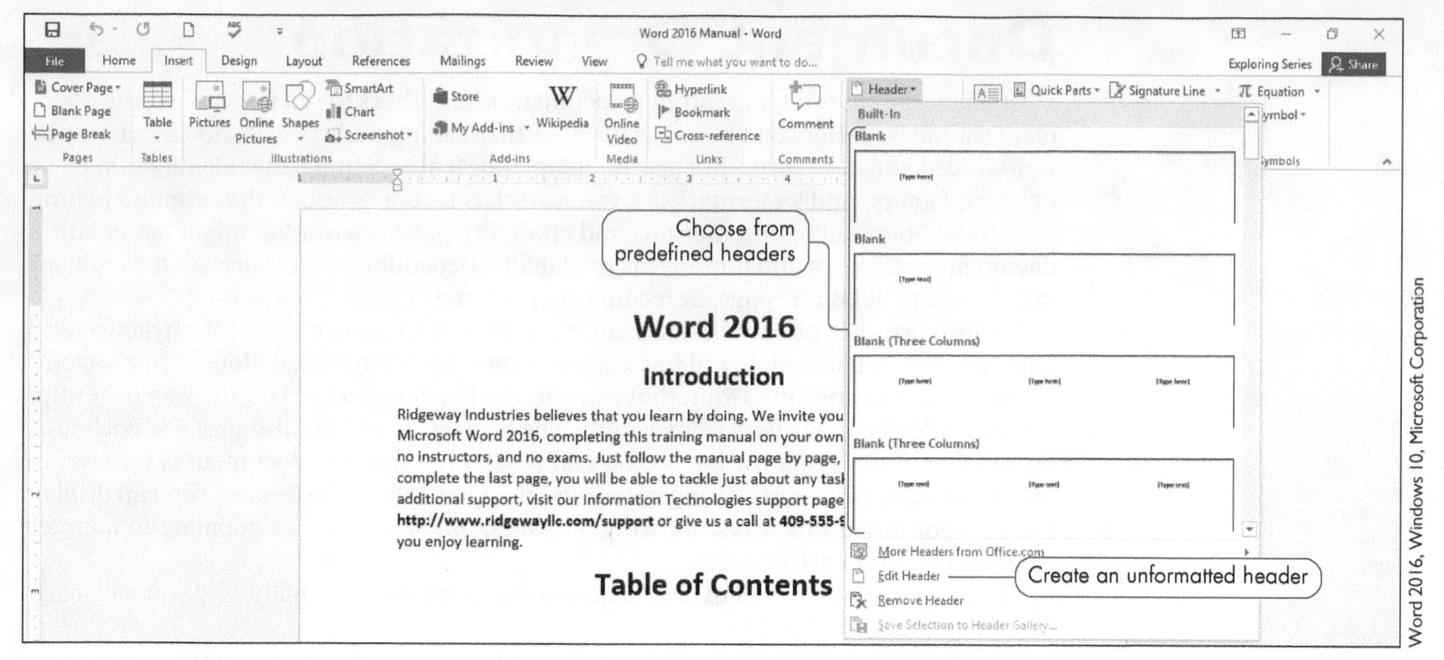

FIGURE 23 Inserting a Header

To close a header or footer, complete one of the following steps:

- Click Close Header and Footer to leave the header and footer area and return to the document (see Figure 24).
- Double-click in the document.

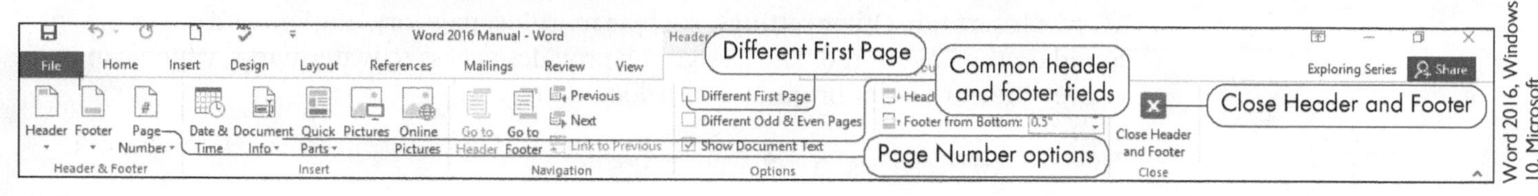

FIGURE 24 Header and Footer Fields and Options

A header or footer can be formatted like any other text. It can be center-, left-, or right-aligned, and formatted in any font or font size. When working with a header or footer, the main body text of the document is grayed out temporarily. When you return to the document, the body text is active, but the header or footer text is dim.

Word provides fields, such as author, date, and file name, that you can include in headers and footers. Some header and footer fields, such as page numbers, will actually change from one page to the next. Other fields, such as author name and date, will remain constant. Regardless, selecting fields (instead of typing the actual data) simplifies the task of creating headers and footers. Some of the most frequently accessed fields, such as Date & Time and Page Number, are available on the Header & Footer Tools Design contextual tab as separate commands (refer to Figure 24). Others, including Author, File Name, and Document Title, are available when you click Document Info in the Insert group (see Figure 25). Depending on the field selected, you might have to indicate a specific format and/or placement. For example, you could display the date as Monday, August 12, 2018, or you might direct that a page number is centered. Document Info also includes a Field option, which provides access to a complete list of fields from which to choose. The same fields are available when you click Quick Parts in the Insert group and click Field.

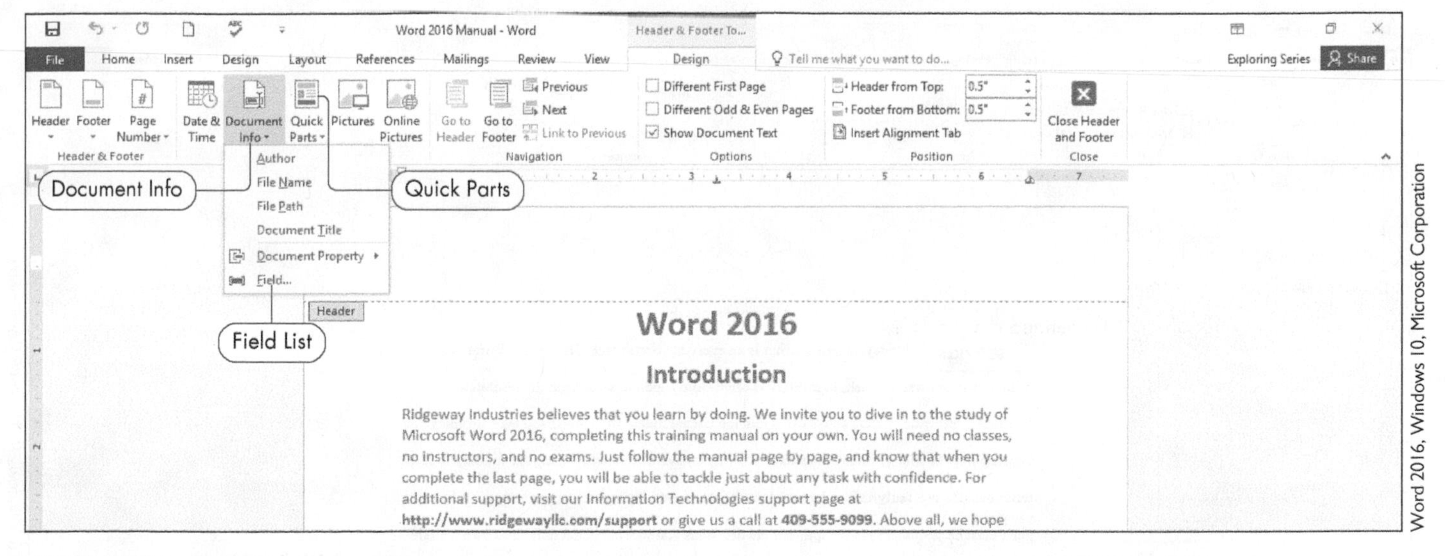

FIGURE 25 Inserting Header and Footer Fields

> **TIP: REMOVING A HEADER FROM THE FIRST PAGE**
> Occasionally, you will want a header or footer on all pages except the first, such as when the first page is a report's cover page. In that case, select Different First Page (refer to Figure 24) in the Options group on the Header & Footer Tools Design tab (when a header or footer is selected).

Adjust Margins

STEP 2 Although a 1" margin all around the document is the default setting, you can easily adjust one or more margins for a particular document. You might adjust margins for several reasons. You can change a document's appearance and readability, perhaps even causing it to fit attractively on one page, by changing margins. Also, a style manual, such as you might use in an English class, will require certain margins for the preparation of papers and publications.

To change margins, complete one of the following steps:

- Click the Layout tab and click Margins in the Page Setup group. Select from one of the predefined margin settings (see Figure 26) or click Custom Margins to adjust each margin (left, right, top, and bottom) individually.
- Click the File tab and click Print. Click Normal Margins (or the previous margin setting) to change one or more margins.

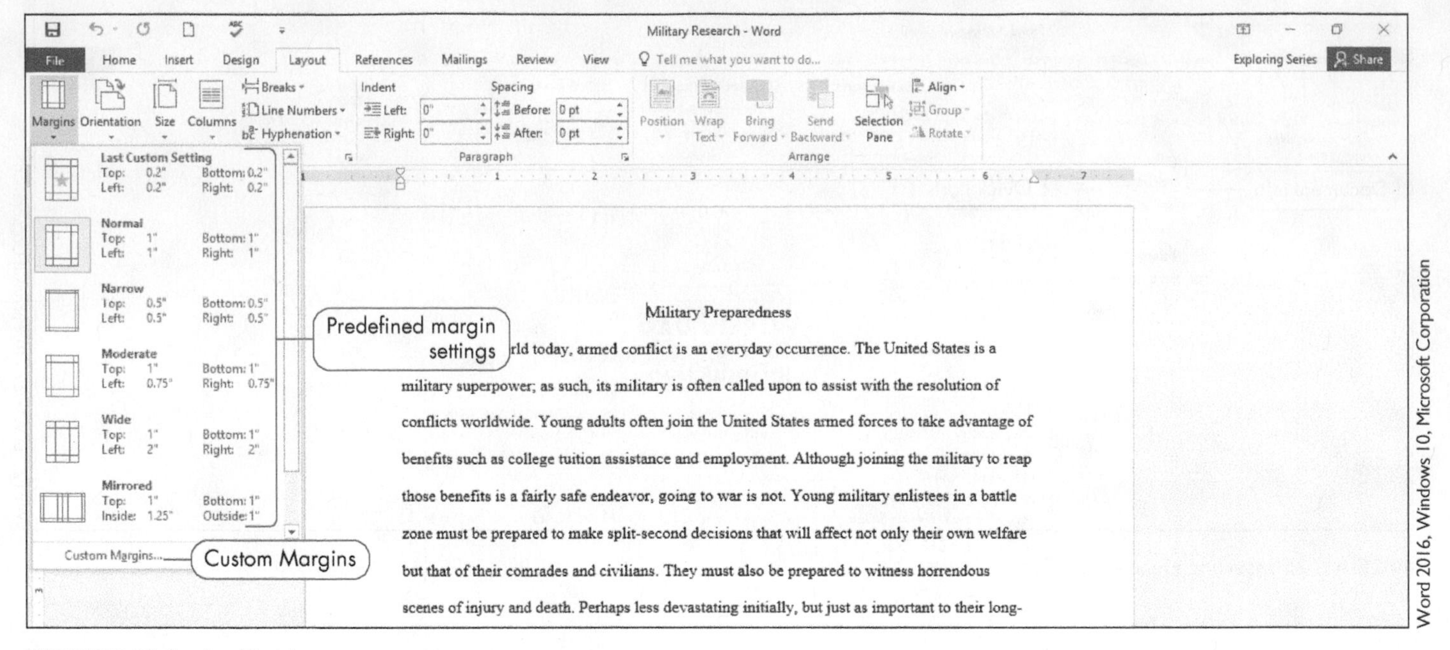

FIGURE 26 Setting Margins

Change Page Orientation

STEP 3 Some documents are better suited for portrait orientation, whereas others are more attractive in landscape. For example, certificates are typically designed in landscape orientation; letters and memos are more often in portrait orientation.

To change orientation, complete one of the following steps:

- Click Orientation on the Layout tab to select either Portrait or Landscape.
- Click Margins on the Layout tab and click Custom Margins to display the Page Setup dialog box (see Figure 27). Select either Portrait or Landscape.
- Click the File tab, click Print, and then click Portrait Orientation (or Landscape Orientation if the document is in landscape orientation). Select either Portrait Orientation or Landscape Orientation.

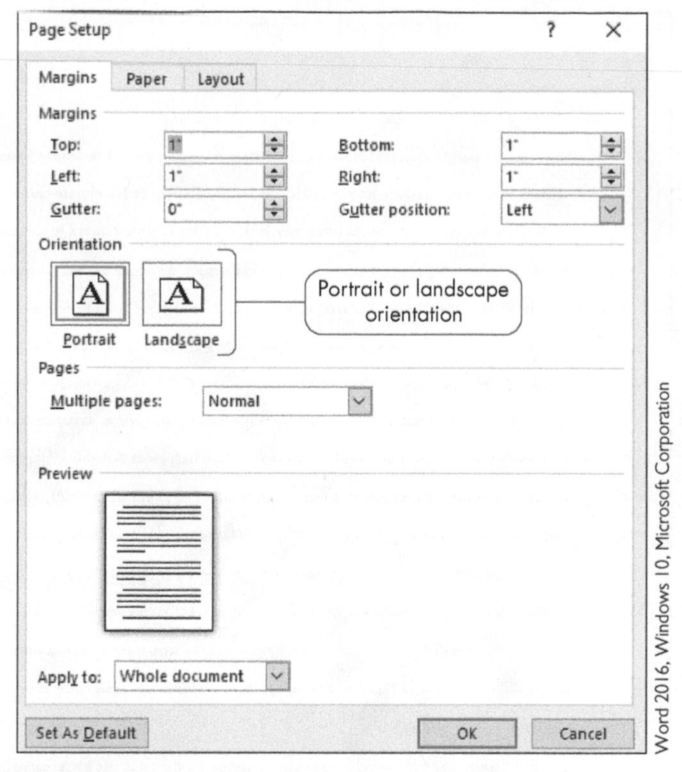

FIGURE 27 Changing Page Orientation

Insert a Watermark

STEP 4 A ***watermark***, which is text or a graphic that displays behind text on a page, is often used to include a very light, washed-out logo for a company within a document, or to indicate the status of the document. For example, a watermark displaying Draft indicates that the document is not in final form. The document shown in Figure 28 contains a watermark. Watermarks do not display on a document that is saved as a webpage, nor will they display in Word's Web Layout view (discussed later in this chapter).

To insert a watermark, complete the following steps:

1. Click the Design tab and click Watermark in the Page Background group.
2. Select from predesigned styles or click Custom Watermark to create your own.

To remove a previously created watermark (for example, when a draft becomes final), complete the following steps:

1. Click the Design tab and click Watermark in the Page Background group.
2. Click Remove Watermark.

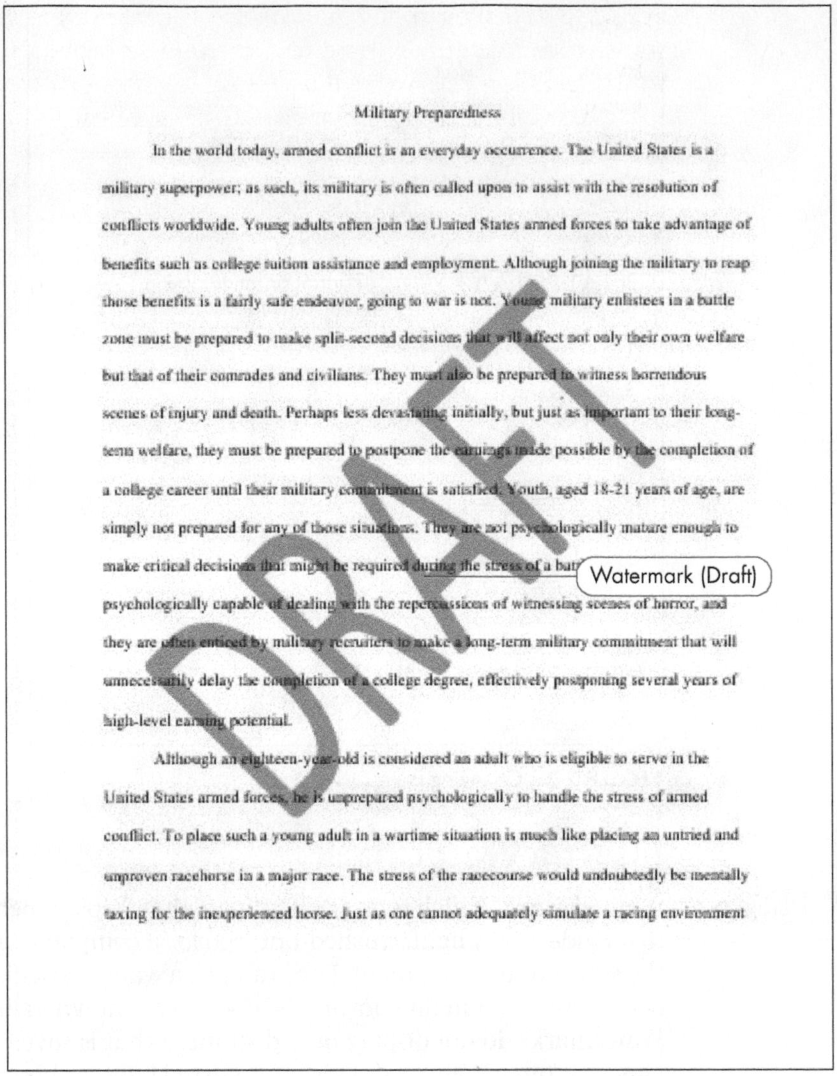

Military Preparedness

In the world today, armed conflict is an everyday occurrence. The United States is a military superpower; as such, its military is often called upon to assist with the resolution of conflicts worldwide. Young adults often join the United States armed forces to take advantage of benefits such as college tuition assistance and employment. Although joining the military to reap those benefits is a fairly safe endeavor, going to war is not. Young military enlistees in a battle zone must be prepared to make split-second decisions that will affect not only their own welfare but that of their comrades and civilians. They must also be prepared to witness horrendous scenes of injury and death. Perhaps less devastating initially, but just as important to their long-term welfare, they must be prepared to postpone the earnings made possible by the completion of a college career until their military commitment is satisfied. Youth, aged 18-21 years of age, are simply not prepared for any of those situations. They are not psychologically mature enough to make critical decisions that might be required during the stress of a bat[...] psychologically capable of dealing with the repercussions of witnessing scenes of horror, and they are often enticed by military recruiters to make a long-term military commitment that will unnecessarily delay the completion of a college degree, effectively postponing several years of high-level earning potential.

Although an eighteen-year-old is considered an adult who is eligible to serve in the United States armed forces, he is unprepared psychologically to handle the stress of armed conflict. To place such a young adult in a wartime situation is much like placing an untried and unproven racehorse in a major race. The stress of the racecourse would undoubtedly be mentally taxing for the inexperienced horse. Just as one cannot adequately simulate a racing environment

DRAFT

Watermark (Draft)

Word 2016, Windows 10, Microsoft Corporation

FIGURE 28 Using a Watermark

> **TIP: FORMATTING A WATERMARK**
> In designing a custom watermark, you can select or change a watermark's color, size, font, and text. In addition, you can include a picture as a watermark.

Insert a Symbol

STEP 5 A ***symbol*** is text, a graphic, or a foreign language character that can be inserted into a document. Some symbols, such as $ and #, are located on the keyboard; however, others are only available from Word's collection of symbols. Symbols such as © and ™ can be an integral part of a document; in fact, those particular symbols are necessary to properly acknowledge a source or product. Because they are typically not located on the keyboard, you need to find them in Word's library of symbols or use a shortcut key combination, if available.

Some symbols serve a very practical purpose. For example, it is unlikely you will want a hyphenated word to be divided between lines in a document. In that case, instead of typing a simple hyphen between words, you can insert a nonbreaking hyphen, which is available as a symbol. Similarly, you can insert a nonbreaking space when you do not want words divided between lines. For example, a person's first name on one line followed by the last name on the next line is not a very attractive placement. Instead, make the space between the words a nonbreaking space by inserting the symbol, so the names are never divided. Mathematical symbols, foreign currency marks, and popular emoticons are also available in Word's symbol library.

A typical Microsoft Office installation includes a wide variety of fonts. Depending upon the font selected (normal text is shown in Figure 29), your symbol choices will vary. Fonts such as Wingdings, Webdings, and Symbol contain a wealth of special symbols, many of which are actually pictures.

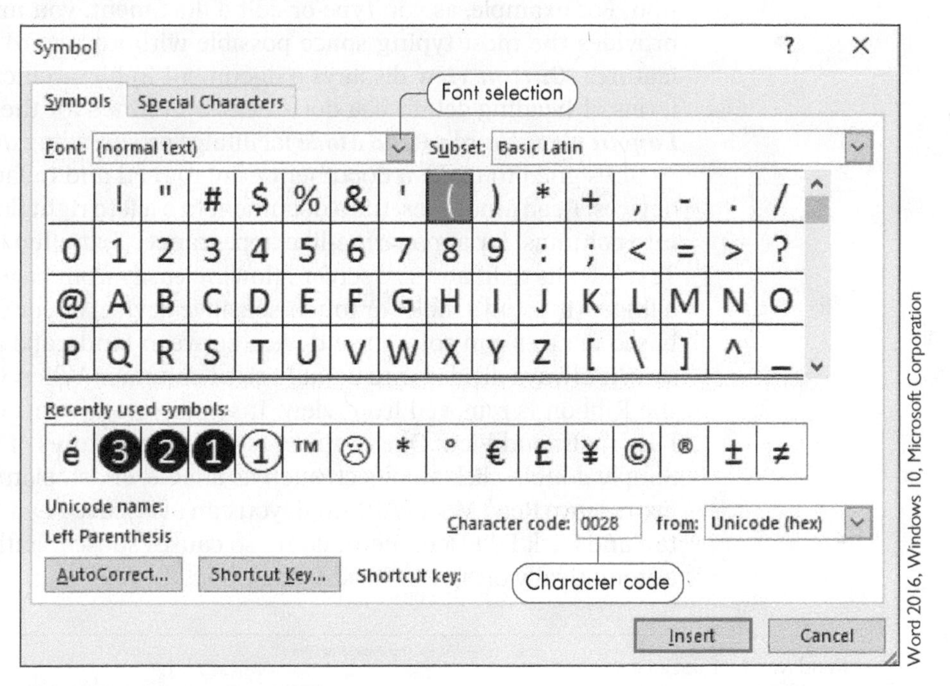

FIGURE 29 Selecting a Symbol

To select and insert a symbol, complete the following steps:

1. Click the Insert tab and click Symbol in the Symbols group.
2. Click More Symbols.
3. Select a symbol or click Special Characters and select from the list.
4. Click Insert. Click Close to close the dialog box.

Each symbol is assigned a character code. If you know the character code, you can type the code (refer to Figure 29) instead of searching for the symbol itself.

TIP: USING SYMBOL SHORTCUTS

Some symbols, such as © and ™, are included in Word's list of AutoCorrect entries. When you type (c), Word will automatically "correct" it to display ©. Type (tm), and Word shows ™.

Viewing a Document in Different Ways

Developing a document is a creative process. As you create, edit, or review a project, you will want to view the document in various ways. Word provides a view that enables you to see a document as it will print, as well as views that maximize typing space by removing page features. You might review a document in a magazine-type format for ease of reading, or perhaps a hierarchical view of headings and subheadings would help you better understand and proof the structure of a document. The ability to zoom in on text and objects can make a document easier to proofread, while viewing a document page by page helps you manage page flow—perhaps drawing attention to awkward page endings or beginnings. Taking advantage of the various views and view settings in Word, you will find it easy to create attractive, well-worded, and error-free documents.

Select a Document View

When you begin a new document, you see the top, bottom, left, and right margins. The default document view is called ***Print Layout view***. You can choose to view a document differently, which is something you might do if you are at a different step in its production. For example, as you type or edit a document, you might prefer ***Draft view***, which provides the most typing space possible without regard to margins and special page features. ***Outline view*** displays a document in hierarchical fashion, clearly delineating levels of heading detail. If a document is destined for the Web, you can view it in ***Web Layout view***. Word's ***Read Mode*** facilitates proofreading and comprehension.

Designed to make a document easy to read and to facilitate access across multiple devices, Read Mode presents a document in a left to right flow, automatically splitting text into columns, for a magazine-like appearance. Text often displays in a two-page format. Text adjusts to fit any size screen, flowing easily from page to page with a simple flick of a finger (if using a tablet or touch-sensitive device) or click of the mouse. Users of touch-based devices can rotate the device between landscape and portrait modes, with the screen always divided into equally sized columns. When in Read Mode (see Figure 30), the Ribbon is removed from view. Instead, you have access to only three menu items: File, Tools, and View. One of the most exciting features of Read Mode is object zooming. Simply double-click an object, such as a table, chart, picture, or video, to zoom in. Press Esc to leave Read Mode. Although you can also leave Read Mode when you click the View tab and click Edit Document, doing so causes subsequently opened Word documents to automatically display in Read Mode when opened.

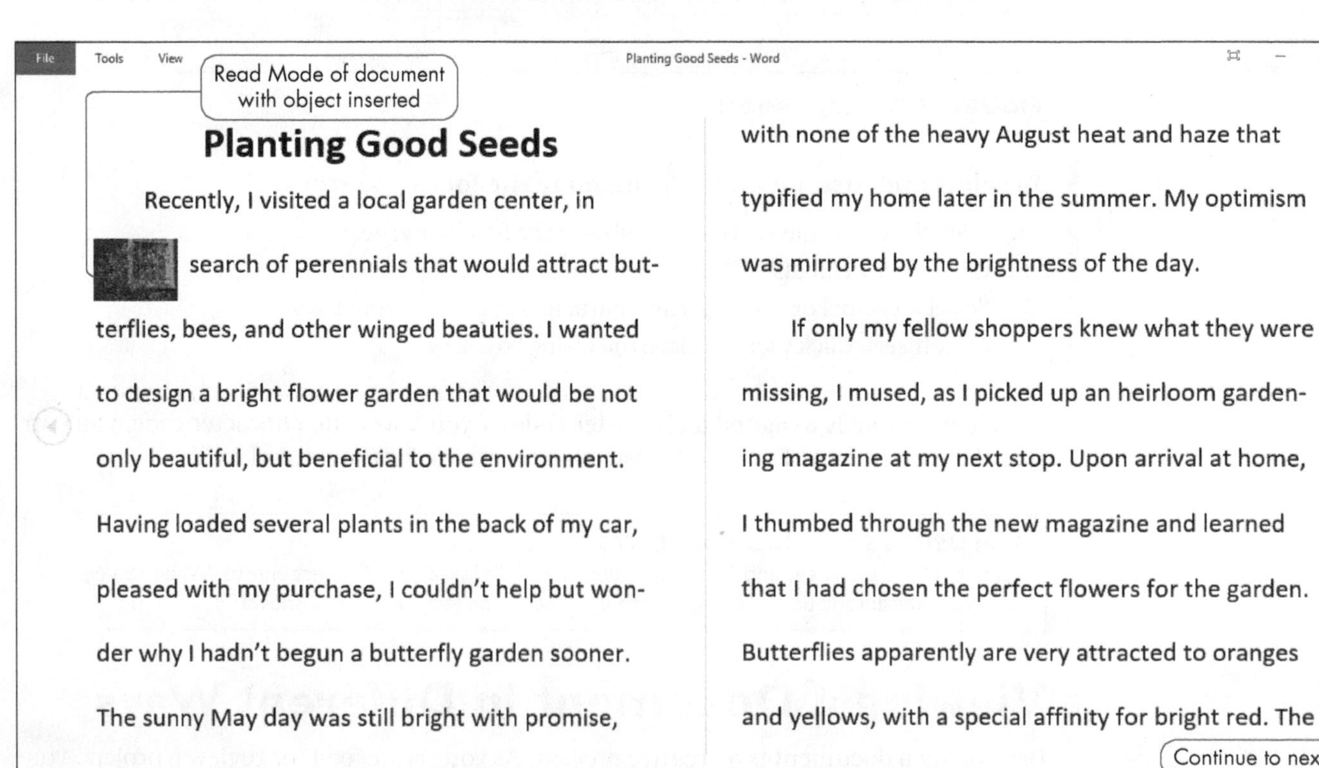

FIGURE 30 Word's Read Mode

To change a document's view, click the View tab and select a view from the Views group (see Figure 31). Although slightly more limited in choice, the status bar also provides views to choose from (Read Mode, Print Layout, and Web Layout). Word views are summarized in Table 1.

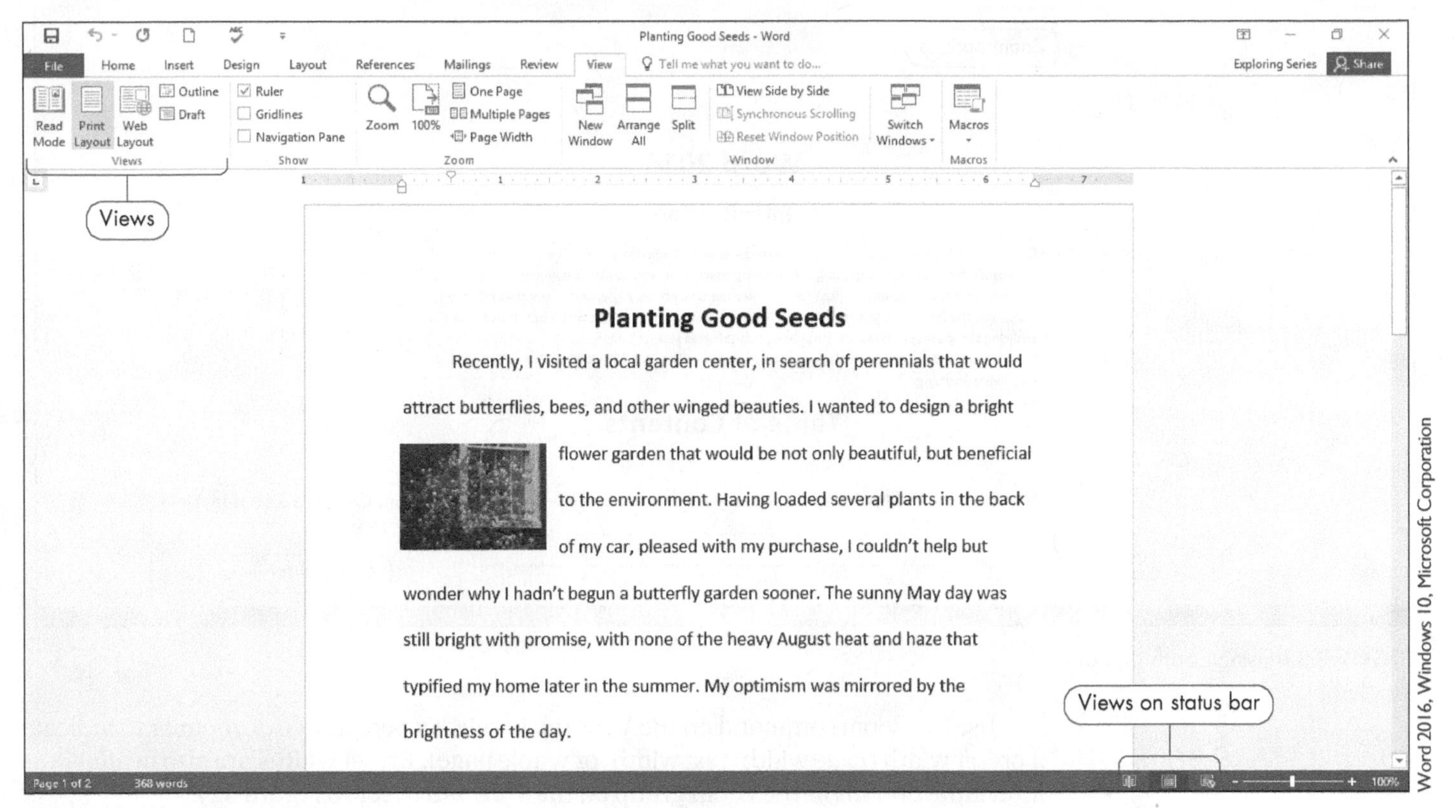

FIGURE 31 Word Views

TABLE 1 Word Views

View	Appearance
Read Mode	Primarily used for reading, with a document shown in pages, much like a magazine. The Ribbon is hidden, with only a limited number of menu selections shown.
Print Layout	Shows margins, headers, footers, graphics, and other page features—much like a document will look when printed.
Web Layout	Shows a document as it would appear on a webpage.
Outline	Shows level of organization and detail. You can collapse or expand detail to show only what is necessary. Often used as a springboard for a table of contents or a PowerPoint summary.
Draft	Provides the most space possible for typing. It does not show margins, headers, or other features, but it does include the Ribbon.

Change the Zoom Setting

Regardless of the view selected, you can use Word's zoom feature to enlarge or reduce the view of text. Unlike zooming in on an object in Read Mode, the zoom feature available on the View tab enables you to enlarge text, not objects or videos. Enlarging text might make a document easier to read and proofread. However, changing the size of text onscreen does not actually change the font size of a document. Zooming in or out is simply a temporary change to the way a document appears onscreen. The View tab includes options that change the onscreen size of a document (see Figure 32). You can also enlarge or reduce the view of text by dragging the Zoom slider on the status bar. Click Zoom In and Zoom Out on the status bar to change the view incrementally by 10% for each click.

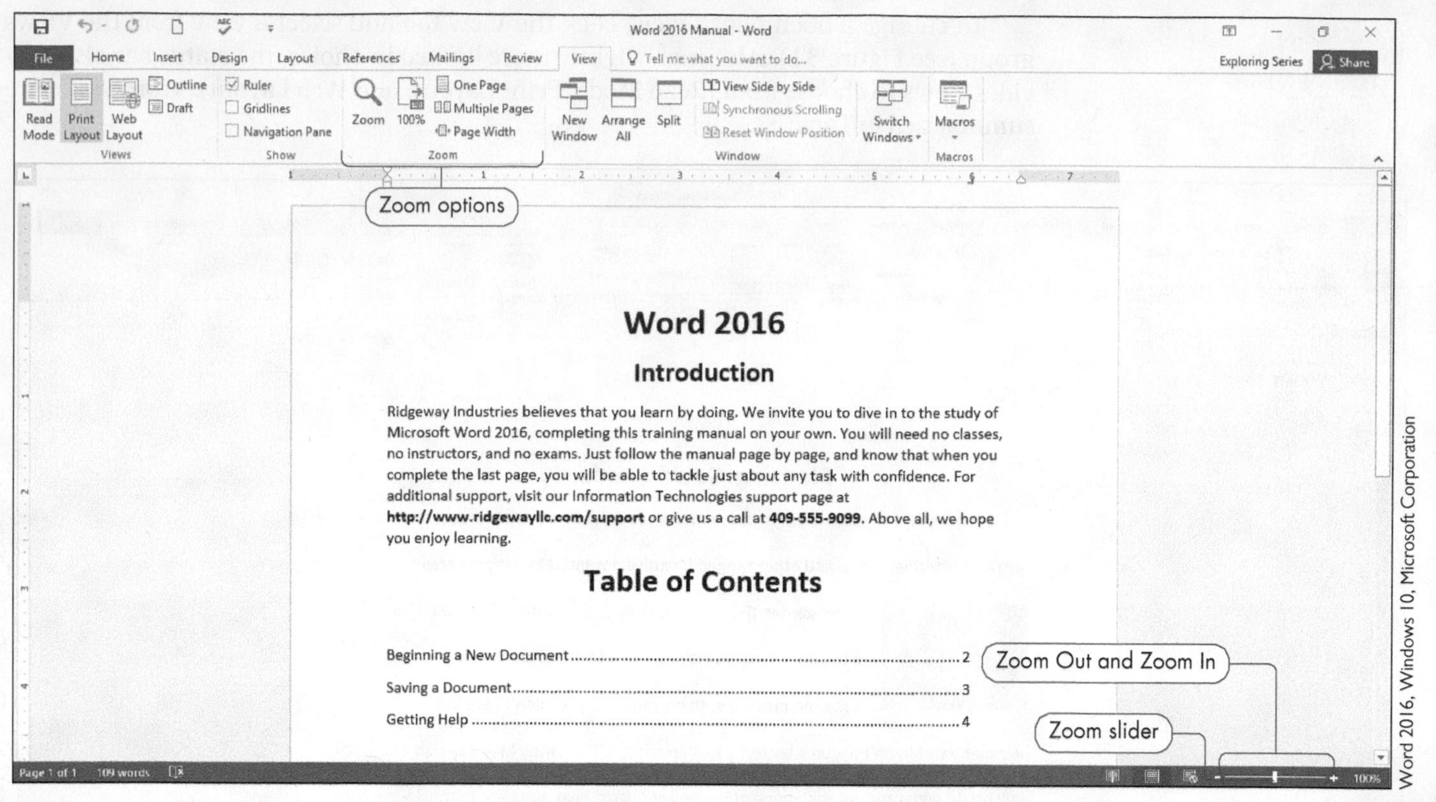

FIGURE 32 Using Zoom Options

Use the Zoom command on the View tab to select a percentage of zoom or to indicate a preset width (page width, text width, or whole page). Preset widths are also available as individual options in the Zoom group on the View tab (refer to Figure 32).

View a Document and Manage Page Flow

STEP 6 Document lengths can vary greatly. A research paper might span 20 pages, whereas a memo is seldom more than a few pages (most often, only one). Obviously, it is easier to view a memo onscreen than an entire research paper. Even so, Word enables you to get a good feel for the way a document will look when printed or distributed, regardless of document length.

Before printing, it is a good idea to view a document in its entirety. One way to do that is to click the File tab and click Print. A document is shown one page at a time in Print Preview (see Figure 33). Click the Next Page or Previous Page navigation arrow to proceed forward or backward in pages. You can also view a document by using options on the View tab (refer to Figure 32). Clicking One Page provides a snapshot of the current page, while Multiple Pages shows pages of a multiple-page document side by side (and on separate rows, in the case of more than two pages).

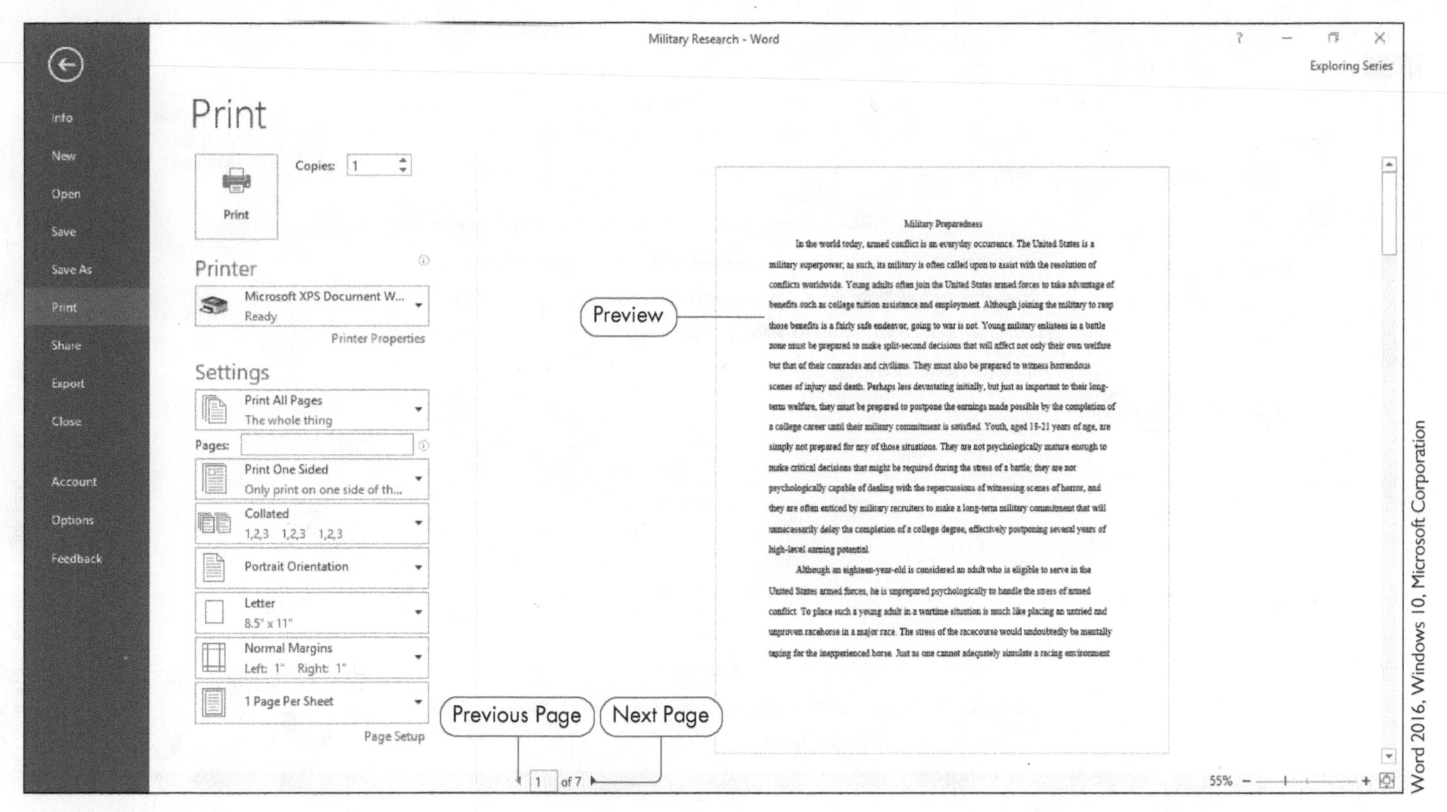

FIGURE 33 Previewing a Document

Word 2016, Windows 10, Microsoft Corporation

Occasionally, a page will end poorly—perhaps with a heading shown alone at the bottom of a page or with a paragraph split awkwardly between pages. Or perhaps it is necessary to begin a new page after a table of contents, so that other pages follow in the order they should. In those cases, you must manage page flow by forcing a page break where it would not normally occur.

To insert a page break, click where the page break is to be placed and complete one of the following:

- Press Ctrl+Enter.
- Click the Layout tab, click Breaks, and then select Page.

With nonprinting characters shown, you will see the Page Break designation (see Figure 34). To remove a page break, click the Page Break indicator and press Delete.

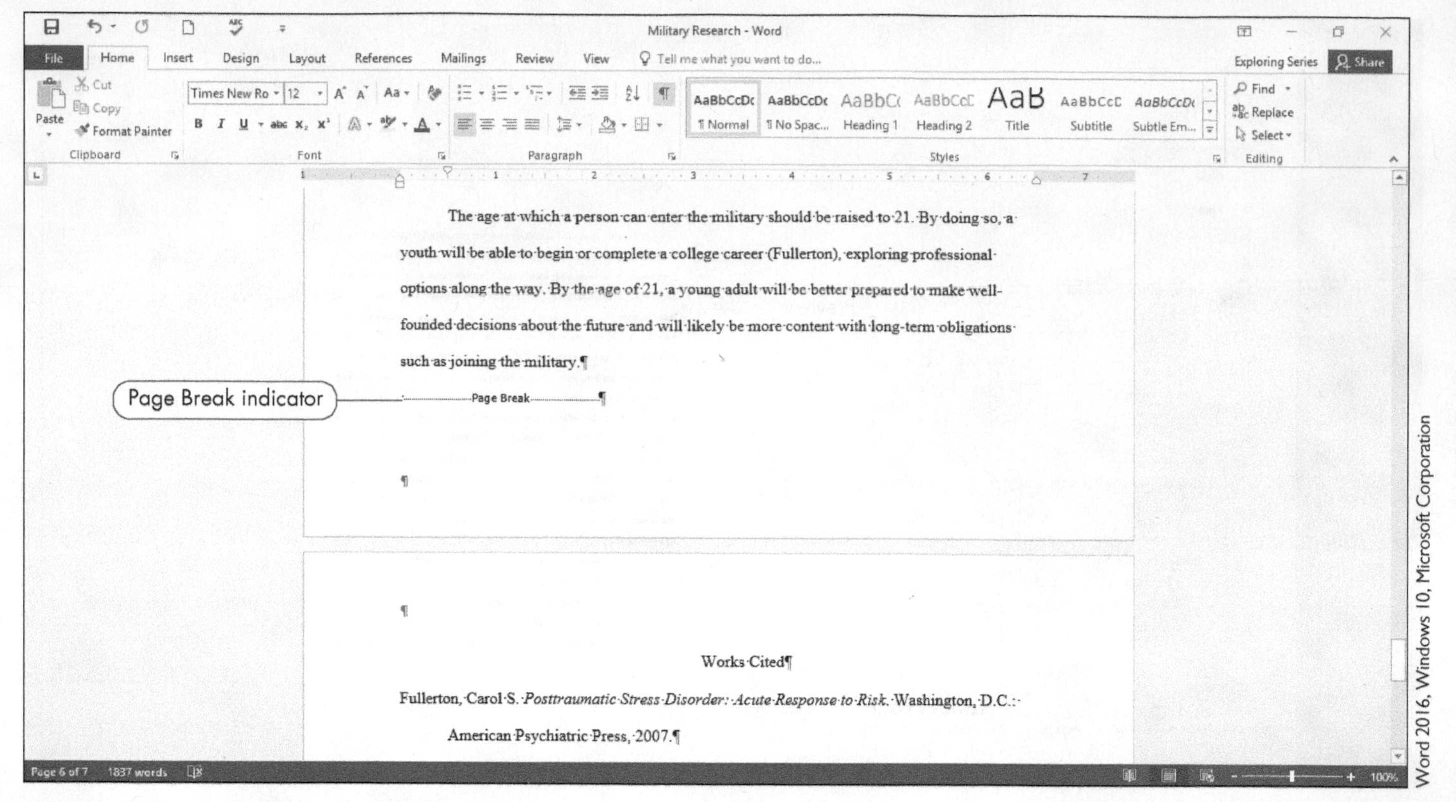
Military Research - Word
The age at which a person can enter the military should be raised to 21. By doing so, a youth will be able to begin or complete a college career (Fullerton), exploring professional options along the way. By the age of 21, a young adult will be better prepared to make well-founded decisions about the future and will likely be more content with long-term obligations such as joining the military.¶
Page Break
Works Cited¶
Fullerton, Carol S. *Posttraumatic Stress Disorder: Acute Response to Risk.* Washington, D.C.: American Psychiatric Press, 2007.¶
Page 6 of 7
1837 words

Page Break indicator

FIGURE 34 Inserting a Page Break

Quick Concepts

5. Some header and footer items, such as author name and file name, serve to identify the document and its origin. Other header and footer fields portray data that changes. Provide at least two examples of fields that contain variable data. When would you want to exclude headers and footers from the first page of a document, and how would you do that?
6. A watermark is often in the form of text, such as the word Draft, which indicates that a document is not in its final form. What other text and/or graphic watermarks might you include in a document?
7. The status bar includes selections that change a document view. Compare and contrast the view selections on the status bar.
8. Before printing a multiple-page research paper, you will check it onscreen to determine how text flows from one page to the next, assuring attractive page endings (no heading shown alone at the end of a page, for example). How would you force a page break before a solo heading that occurs at the bottom of a page?

Hands-On Exercises

Skills covered: Insert Headers and Footers • Adjust Margins • Change Page Orientation • Insert a Watermark • Insert a Symbol • Select a Document View • View a Document • Change the Zoom Setting • Manage Page Flow

2 Document Organization

You are almost ready to submit a draft of the summer day camp article to your supervisor for approval. After inserting a footer to identify the document as originating with the U.S. Fish and Wildlife Service, you adjust the margins and determine the best page orientation for the document. Next, you insert a watermark to indicate it is a draft document. Finally, you review the document for overall appearance and page flow.

STEP 1 » INSERT HEADERS AND FOOTERS

You insert a footer to identify the article as a publication of the U.S. Fish and Wildlife Service. The footer also includes the file name. Refer to Figure 35 as you complete Step 1.

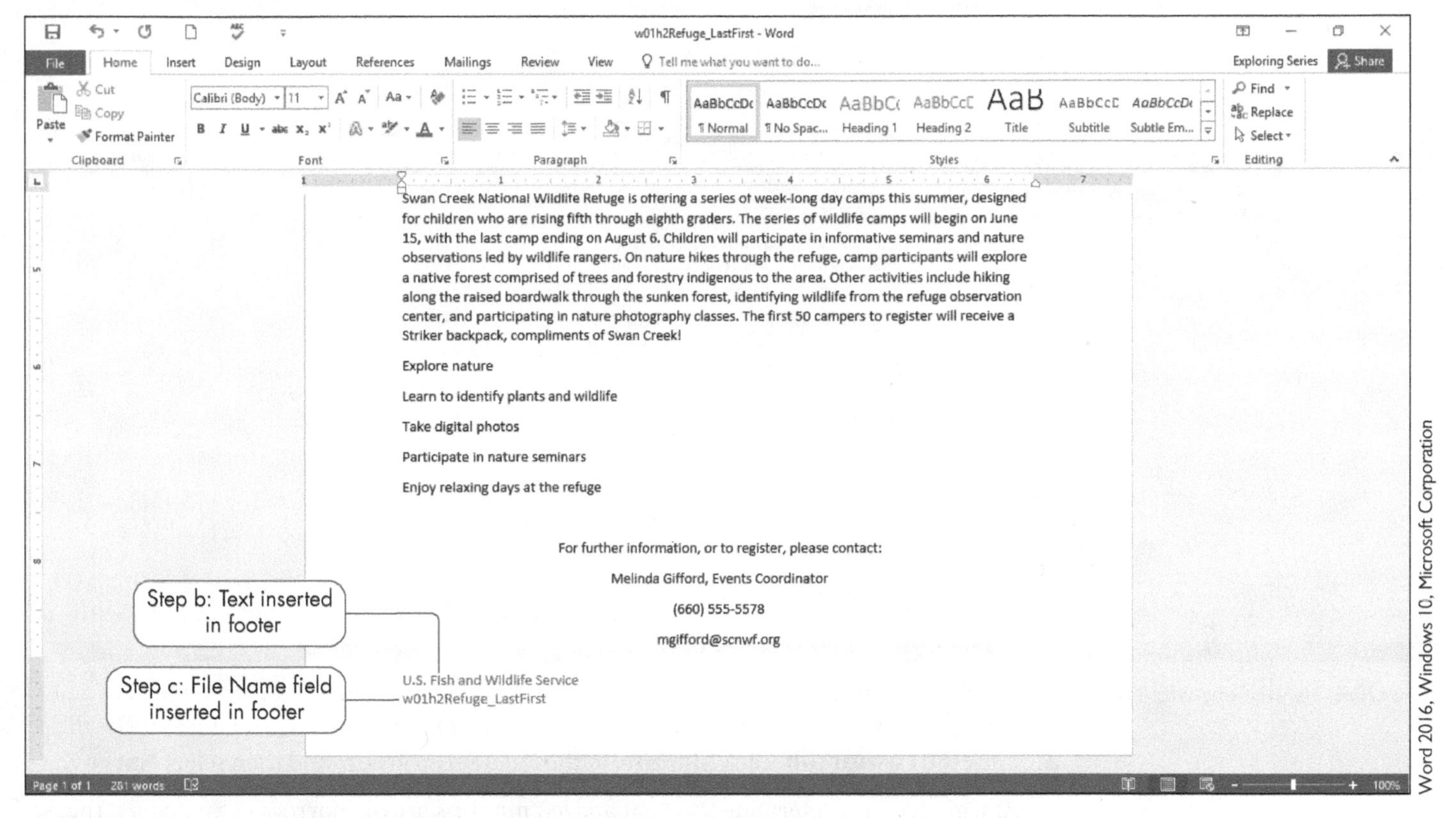

Word 2016, Windows 10, Microsoft Corporation

FIGURE 35 Designing a Footer

a. Open *w01h1Refuge_LastFirst* if you closed it at the end of Hands-On Exercise 1 and save it as **w01h2Refuge_LastFirst**, changing h1 to h2.

> **TROUBLESHOOTING:** If you make any major mistakes in this exercise, you can close the file, open *w01h1Refuge_LastFirst* again, and then start this exercise over.

b. Click the **Insert tab**, click **Footer** in the Header & Footer group, and then select **Edit Footer**. Type **U.S. Fish and Wildlife Service**. Press **Enter**.

> **TROUBLESHOOTING:** If you selected a predefined footer instead of clicking Edit Footer, click Undo on the Quick Access Toolbar and repeat Step b.

c. Click **Document Info** in the Insert group and select **File Name**.

d. Click **Close Header and Footer** in the Close group.

e. Click after the first sentence of the second body paragraph, ending with *through eighth graders*. Be sure to click after the period ending the sentence. Press **Spacebar** and type the following sentence: **The series of wildlife camps will begin on June 15, with the last camp ending on August 6.**

f. Save the document.

STEP 2 ›› ADJUST MARGINS

The article fits on one page, but you anticipate adding text. You suspect that with narrower margins, you might be able to add text while making sure the article requires only one page. You experiment with a few margin settings. Refer to Figure 36 as you complete Step 2.

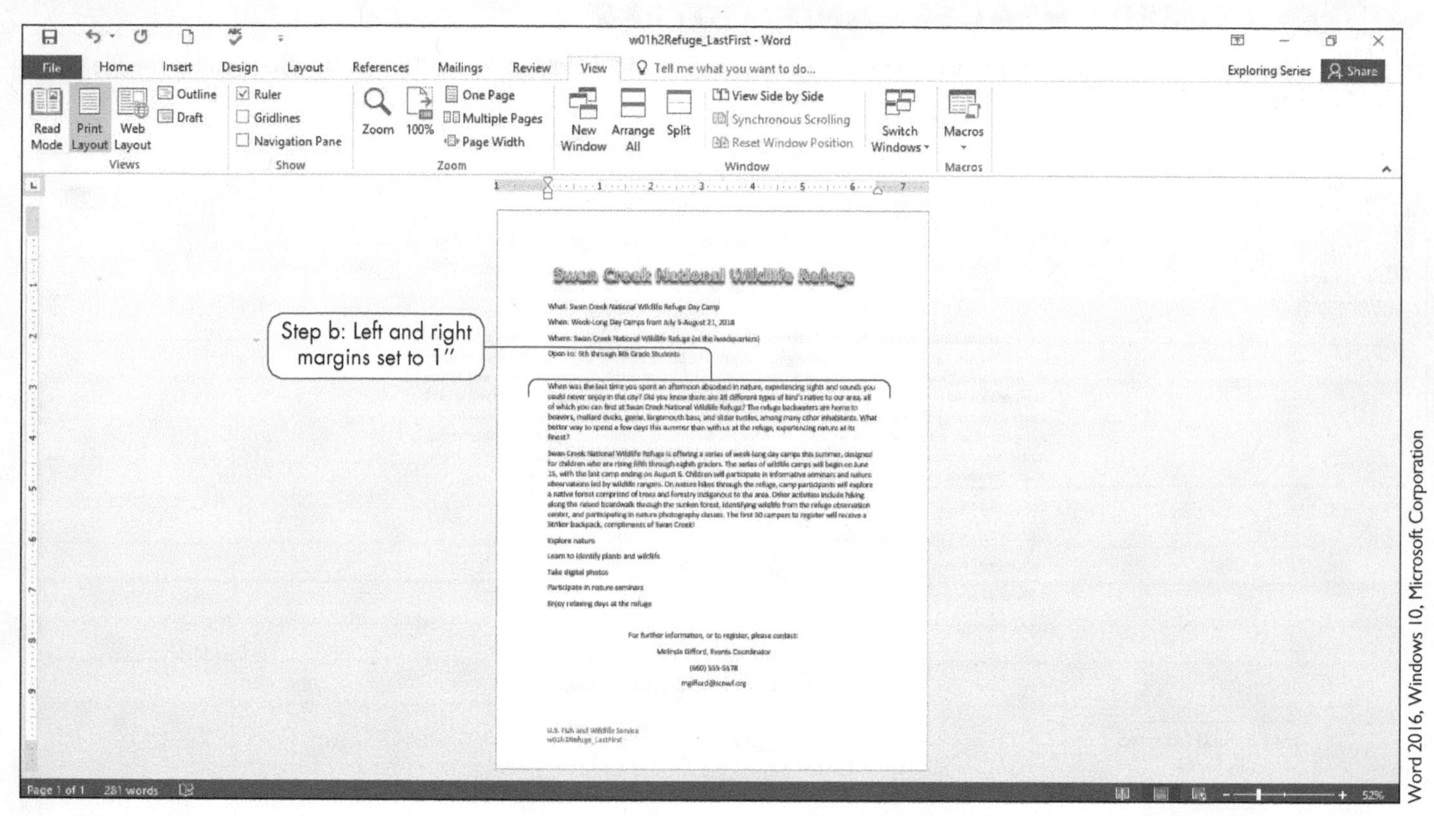

FIGURE 36 Working with Margins

a. Click the **Layout tab**, click **Margins** in the Page Setup group, and then select **Narrow**.

   At a glance, you determine the right and left margins are too narrow, so you adjust them.

b. Click **Margins** and select **Custom Margins**. Adjust the Left and Right margins to **1"** and click **OK**.

c. Click the **View tab** and click **One Page** in the Zoom group.

   The document appears to be well positioned on the page, with room for a small amount of additional text, if necessary.

d. Save the document.

STEP 3 ›› CHANGE PAGE ORIENTATION

Ms. Traynom asked you to prepare an abbreviated version of the article, retaining only the most pertinent information. You prepare and save the shortened version, but you also retain the lengthier version. The shortened article provides a snapshot of the summer activity in an at-a-glance format. Refer to Figure 37 as you complete Step 3.

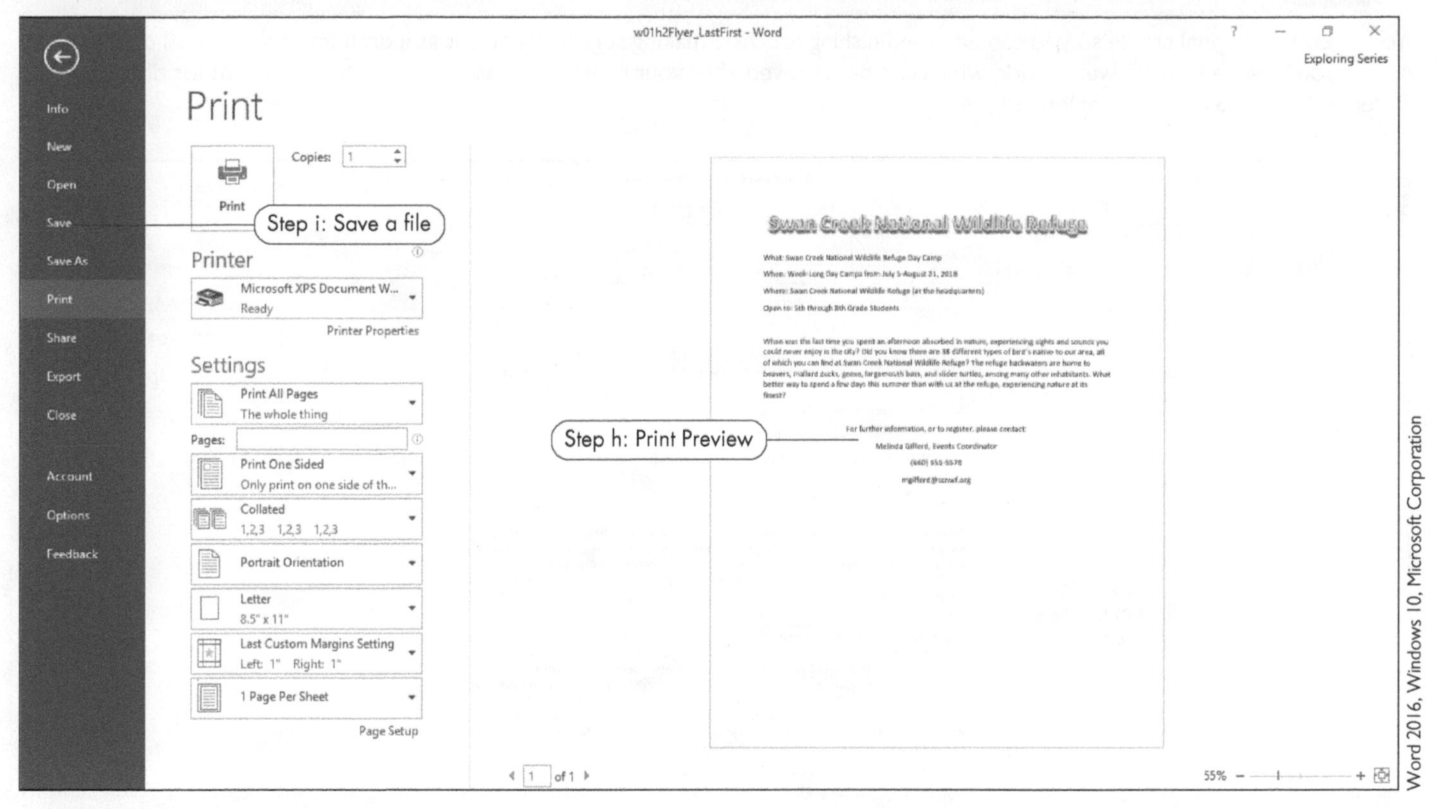

FIGURE 37 Previewing a Document

a. Click **100%** in the Zoom group on the View tab.

b. Ensure that nonprinting characters display. If they do not, click **Show/Hide** in the Paragraph group on the Home tab.

c. Triple-click in the second body paragraph, beginning with *Swan Creek National Wildlife Refuge is offering*, to select the entire paragraph and press **Delete** to remove the paragraph.

d. Delete the single-line paragraphs near the end of the document, beginning with *Explore nature* and ending with *Enjoy relaxing days at the refuge*.

e. Click the **File tab** and click **Save As**. Save the file as **w01h2Flyer_LastFirst**.

Because the document is a shortened version of the original, you save it with a different name.

f. Click the **Layout tab** and click **Orientation** in the Page Setup group. Click **Landscape**. Click the **View tab** and click **One Page**. Click **Undo** on the Quick Access Toolbar.

You had suspected the shortened document would be more attractive in landscape orientation. However, since the appearance did not improve, you return to portrait orientation.

g. Select **100%**. Scroll down and double-click in the footer area. Select both footer lines and press **Delete** to remove the footer. Double-click in the document to close the footer.

The flyer does not require a footer so you remove it.

h. Click the **File tab** and click **Print**. Check the document preview to confirm that the footer is removed.

i. Click **Save** in the left pane. Click the **File tab** and click **Close**.

You close the flyer without exiting Word.

STEP 4 » INSERT A WATERMARK

You open the original article so you can add the finishing touches, making sure to identify it as a draft and not the final copy. To do so, you insert a DRAFT watermark, which can be removed after your supervisor has approved the document for distribution. Refer to Figure 38 as you complete Step 4.

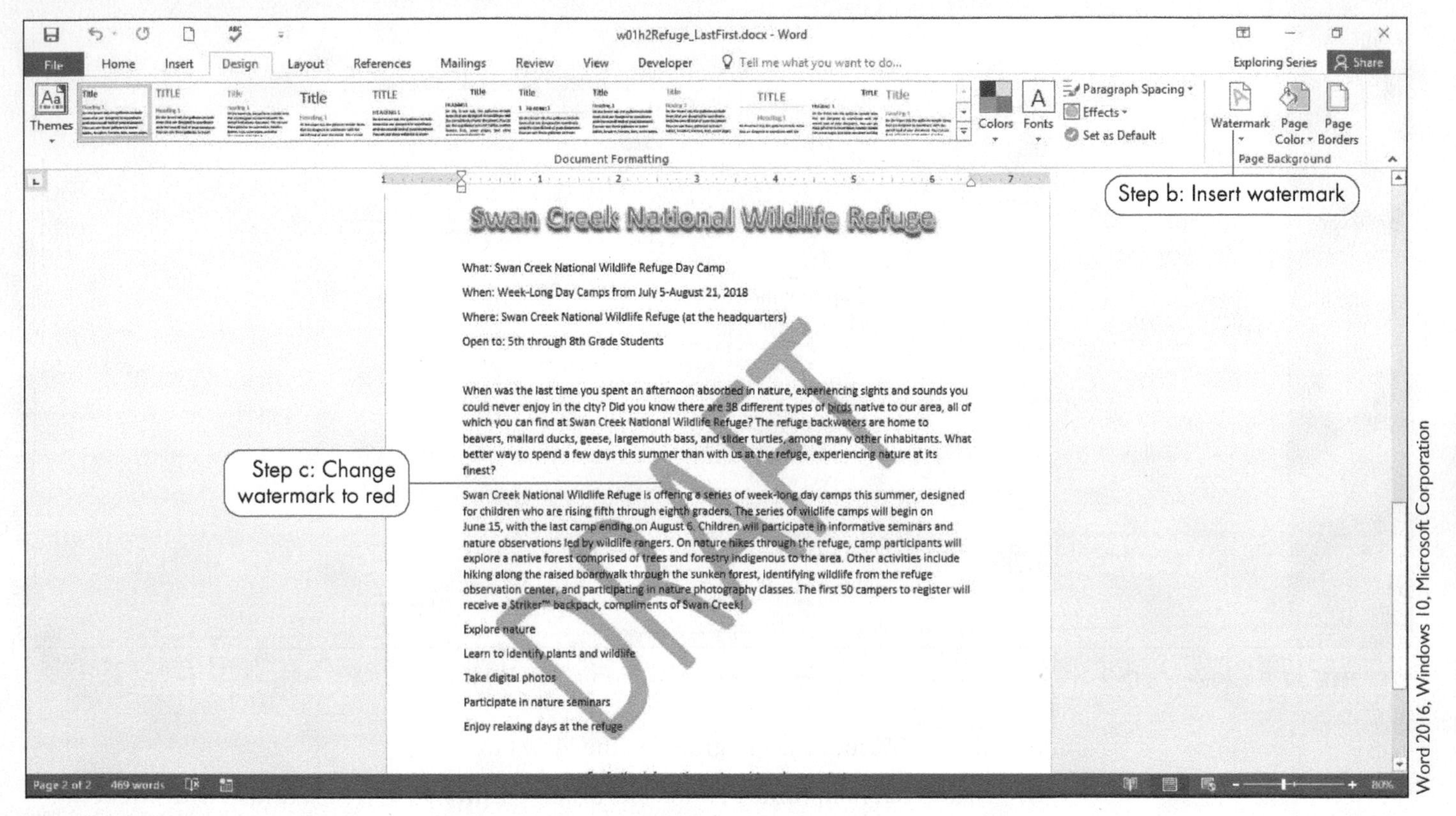

FIGURE 38 Inserting a Watermark

a. Click the **File tab** and click **Open**. Select **w01h2Refuge_LastFirst** in the list of Recent Documents.

b. Click the **Design** tab and click **Watermark** in the Page Background group. Scroll through the gallery of watermarks and click **DRAFT 1** (under Disclaimers).

c. Click **Watermark** again and select **Custom Watermark**. Click the **Color arrow** in the Printed Watermark dialog box and click **Red** (under Standard Colors). Click **OK**.

The watermark is not as visible as you would like, so you change the color.

d. Save the document.

STEP 5 » INSERT A SYMBOL AND SELECT A DOCUMENT VIEW

The article you are preparing will be placed in numerous public venues, primarily schools. Given the widespread distribution of the document, you must consider any legality, such as appropriate recognition of name brands or proprietary mentions, by inserting a trademark symbol. You also ensure that words flow as they should, with no awkward or unintended breaks between words that should remain together. Refer to Figure 39 as you complete Step 5.

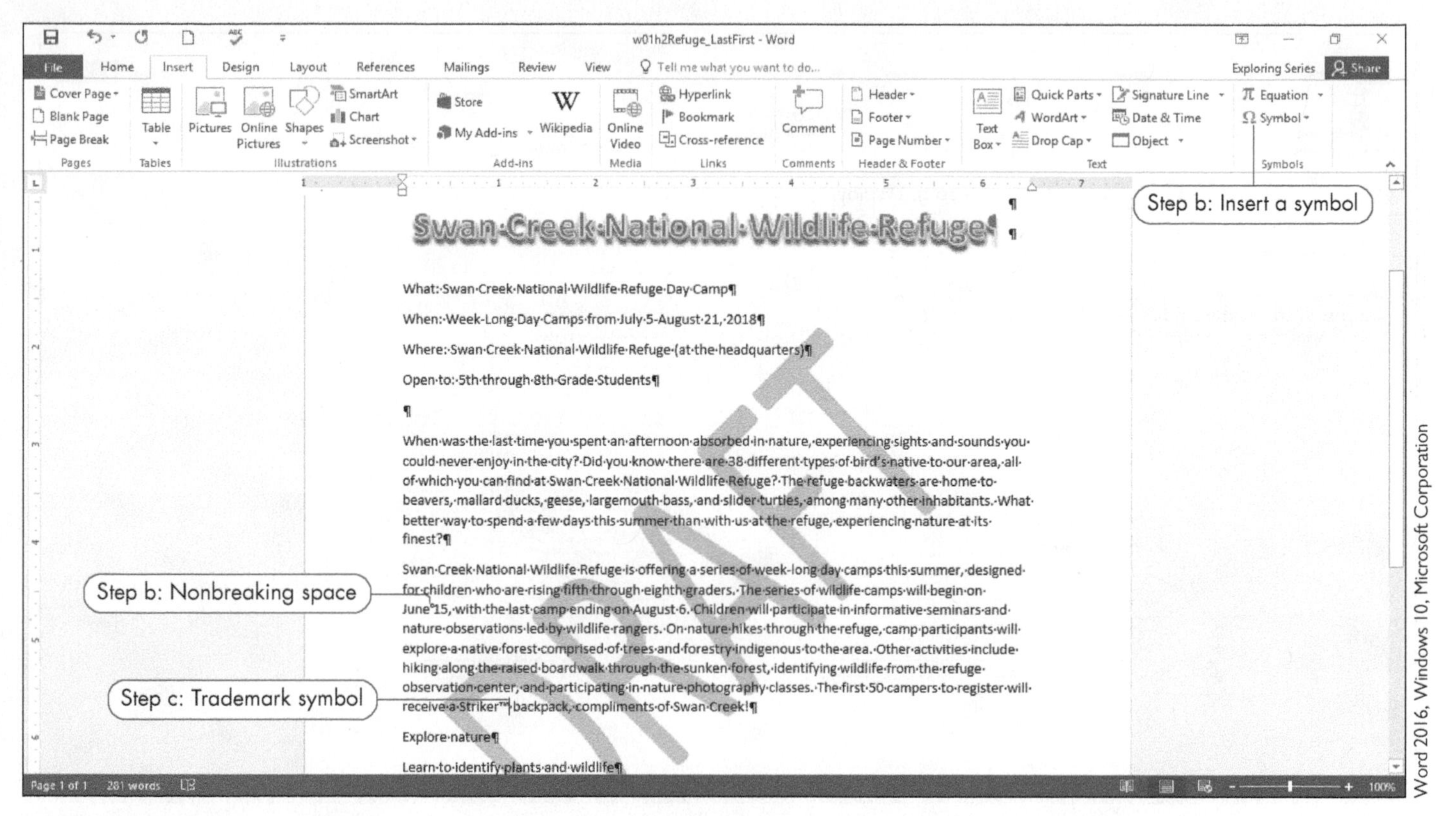

FIGURE 39 Working with Symbols

a. Click after the word *June* on the second line in the second body paragraph. Make sure you have placed the insertion point before the space following the word *June*. Press **Delete** to remove the space.

b. Click the **Insert tab** and click **Symbol** in the Symbols group. Click **More Symbols**. Click the **Special Characters tab**. Click **Nonbreaking Space**. Click **Insert** and click **Close**.

Regardless of where the line ends, you want to make sure the phrase June 15 is not separated, with the month on one line and the day on the following line. Therefore, you insert a nonbreaking space.

c. Click after the word *Striker* in the last sentence of the same paragraph. Click **Symbol** in the Symbols group and click **More Symbols**. Click **Special Characters**. Click **Trademark** to insert the Trademark symbol. Click **Insert** and click **Close**.

You use the Trademark symbol to indicate that Striker is a brand name.

d. Save the document.

STEP 6 » VIEW A DOCUMENT, CHANGE THE ZOOM SETTING, AND MANAGE PAGE FLOW

Ms. Traynom provided you with a cover letter to include with the article. You incorporate the letter text into the article as the first page, remove the footer from the first page, proofread the document, and ensure that both pages are attractively designed. Refer to Figure 40 as you complete Step 6.

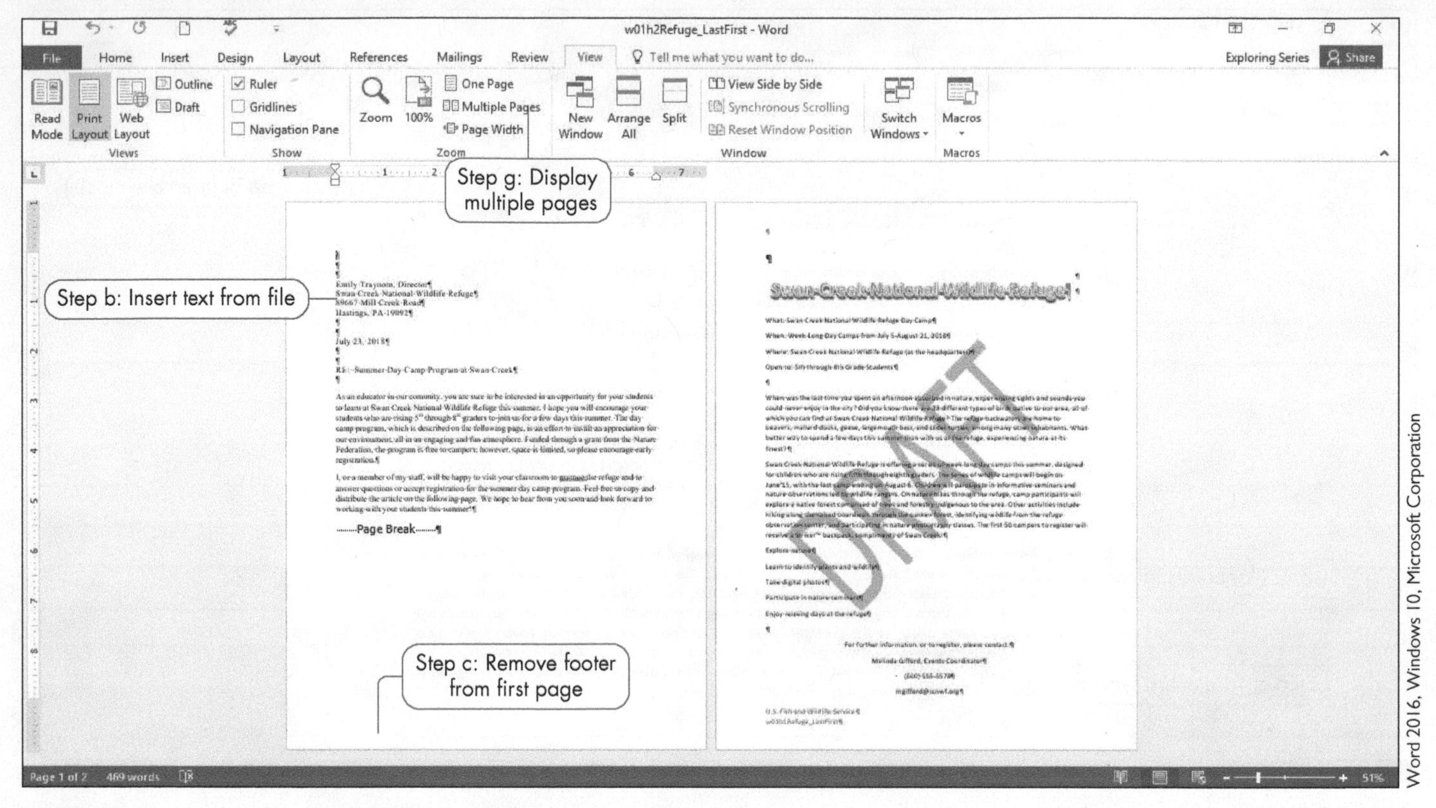

FIGURE 40 Modifying and Viewing a Multi-Page Document

a. Press **Ctrl+Home** to position the insertion point at the top of the article. Press **Ctrl+Enter** to insert a blank page at the top. Press **Ctrl+Home** to move to the top of the new page.

Note that both the watermark and the footer display on the new page. That is because those features are designed to appear by default on all pages of a document.

b. Click the **Insert tab** and click the **Object arrow** in the Text group. Click **Text from File**. Navigate to *w01h2Letter* in your student data files and double-click the file name.

c. Double-click in the footer area of the first page. Click **Different First Page** in the Options group of the Header & Footer Tools Design tab.

You indicate that the watermark and footer are not to appear on the first page, but will remain on all others.

d. Click **Close Header and Footer** in the Close group.

e. Press **Ctrl+Home**. Click the **View tab** and click **Zoom** in the Zoom group. Click in the **Percent box** and change the Zoom to **125%**. Click **OK**.

f. Scroll through the document, proofreading for spelling and grammatical errors. Right-click any underlined error and either correct or ignore it. Manually correct any errors that Word has not flagged. Press **Ctrl+Home**.

g. Click **Multiple Pages** in the Zoom group.

h. Click the **File tab** and click **Print**. Click **Next Page** (the arrow that follows 1 of 2 at the bottom of the screen) to view the article. Click **Previous Page** to return to the letter.

i. Click **Back** to return to the document. Click **100%** in the Zoom group. Ensure the insertion point is at the top of the document, and press **Enter** three times to move the text down the page.

The letter appears to be too high on the page, so you move the text down a bit.

j. Click the **File tab** and click **Print**.

The first page is better situated on the page, with additional space at the top.

k. Save the document. Keep the document open if you plan to continue with the next Hands-On Exercise. If not, close the document and exit Word.

Document Settings and Properties

After you organize your document and make all the formatting changes you desire, you save the document in its final form and prepare it for use by others. You can take advantage of features in Word that enable you to manipulate the file in a variety of ways, such as identifying features that are not compatible with older versions of Word, saving in a format that is compatible with older versions, and including information about the file that does not display in the document. For example, you can include an author name, subject, and even keywords—all information that does not display in the content of the document but further identifies the file, and can be used as a basis on which to search for or categorize the document later. Because you are well aware of the importance of saving files, and even making backup copies of those files, you will explore backup options.

In this section, you will explore ways to prepare a document for distribution, including saving in a format compatible with earlier versions of Word, converting a file created in an earlier version to Office 2016, checking for sensitive information included in a file, making backup copies of important documents, and working with print options. In addition, you will learn to customize and print document properties.

Modifying Document Properties

Occasionally, you might want to include information to identify a document, such as author, document purpose, intended audience, or general comments. Those data elements, or ***document properties***, are saved with the document, but do not appear in the document as it displays onscreen or is printed. You can easily modify document properties to include identifying or descriptive information. Using a document property as a search keyword, or tag, you can even search for a particular file. For example, suppose you apply a keyword of *CIS 225* to all documents you create that are associated with that particular college class. Later, you can use that keyword as a search term, locating all associated documents.

Customize Document Properties

STEP 1 »» For statistical information related to the current document, click the File tab. Data such as file size, number of pages, and total words are presented in the right pane on the Info window (see Figure 41). You can modify some document information in this view, such as adding a title, tags, or comments, but for more possibilities, click Properties and click Advanced Properties (see Figure 42). You can then navigate through the Advanced Properties dialog box, adding or modifying properties. When you save the document, Word saves this information with the document.

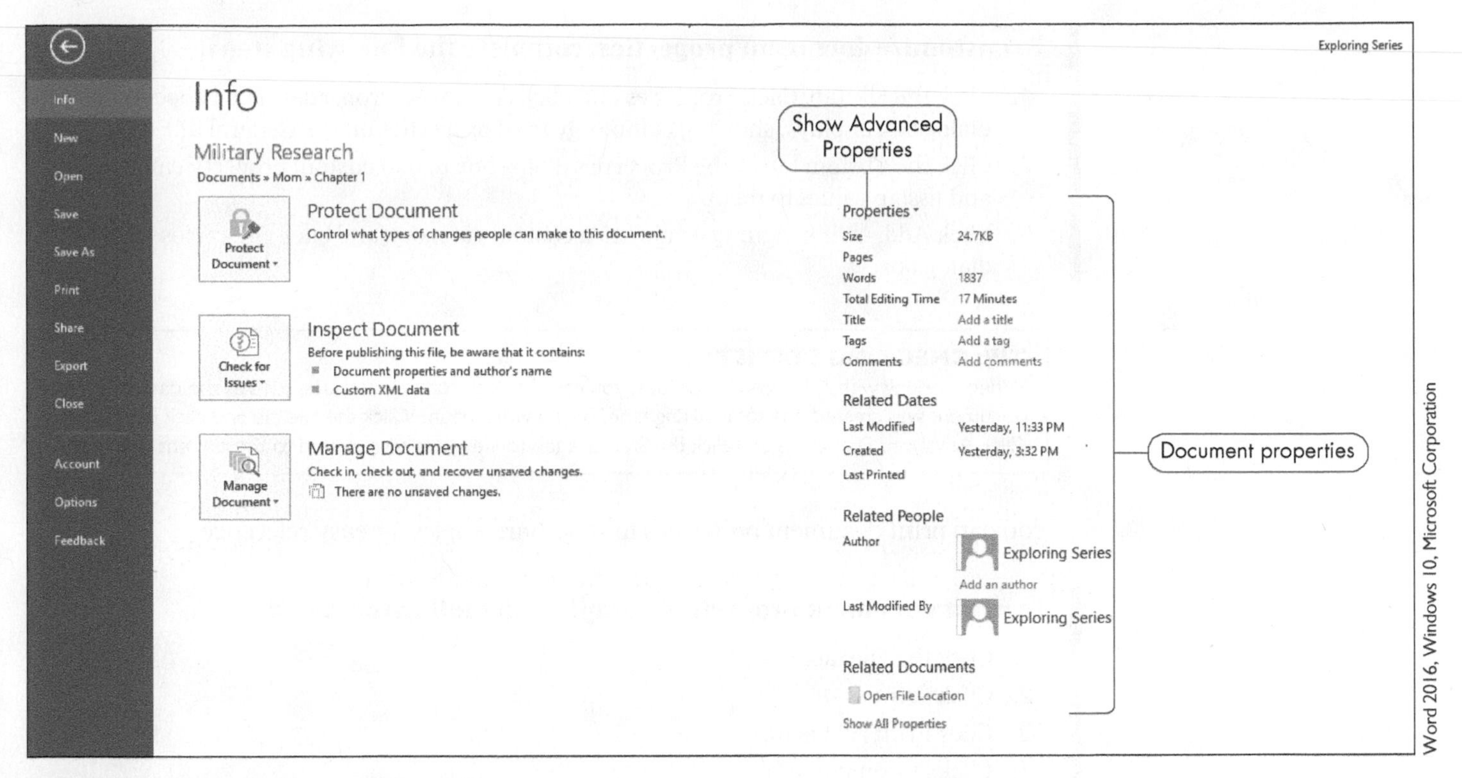

FIGURE 41 Displaying Document Properties

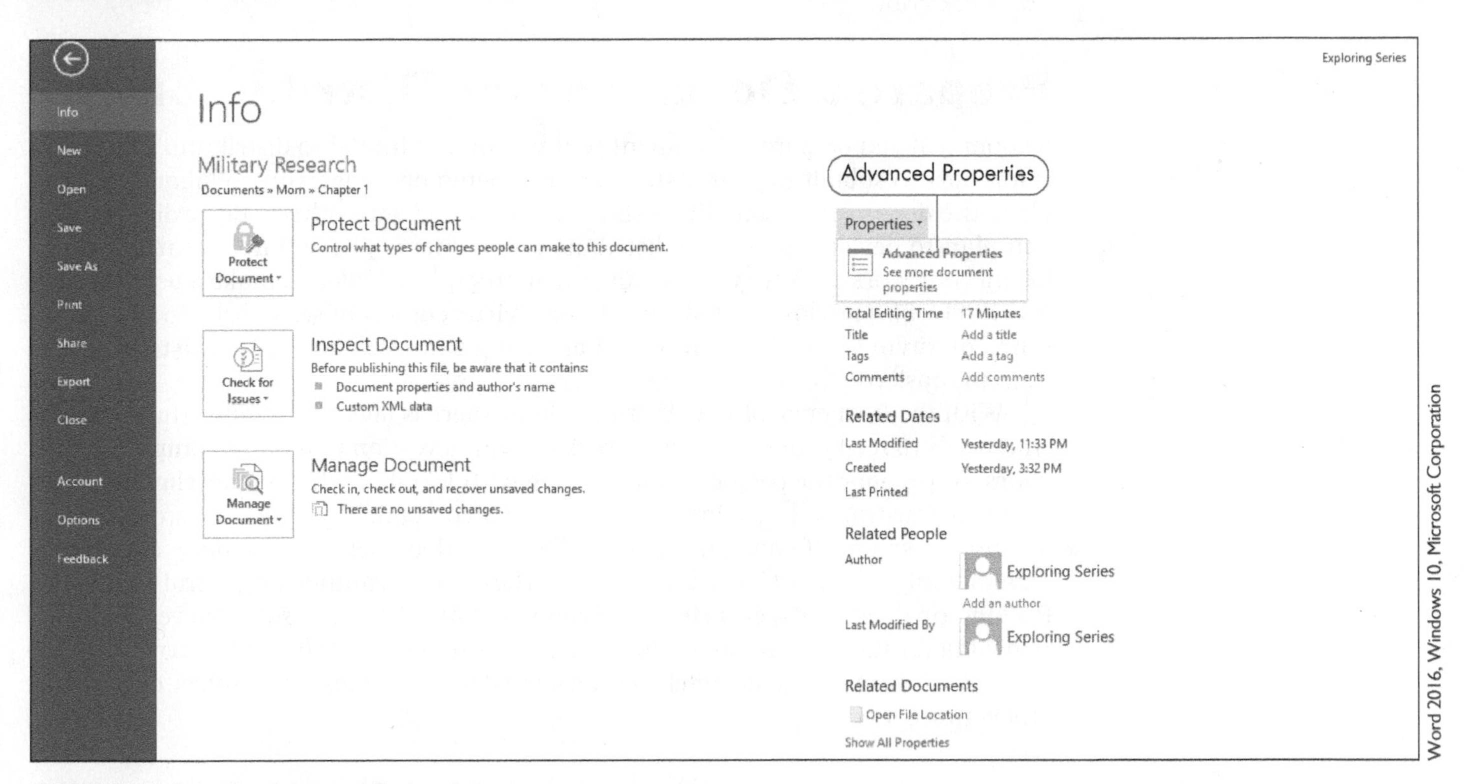

FIGURE 42 Selecting Advanced Properties

You may want to add or change document properties by including specific items such as a subject, department, or a particular project name. For example, you could add a *Date completed* property and specify an exact date for reference. This date would reflect the completion date, not the date the file was last saved. You also might create a field to track company information such as warehouse location or product numbers.

To customize document properties, complete the following steps:

1. Click the File tab. Click Properties and click Advanced Properties. The Properties dialog box displays, showing commonly used properties on the General tab.
2. Click the Custom tab of the Properties dialog box to add custom property categories and assign values to them.
3. Click Add, after assigning a value to a custom category, and click OK to close the dialog box.

TIP: CHECKING STATISTICS
When working with Advanced Properties, you can check document statistics, such as the date the document was created, the total editing time, or the word count. Click the File tab and click Properties. Click Advanced Properties and click the Statistics tab to view statistics related to the current document.

You can print document properties to store hard copies for easy reference.

To print document properties, complete the following steps:

1. Click the File tab.
2. Click Print.
3. Click Print All Pages.
4. Click Document Info.
5. Click Print.

Prepare a Document for Distribution

Seldom will you prepare a document that you do not intend to distribute. Whether it is a report to submit to your instructor or a memo on which you collaborated, most likely the document is something that will be shared with others. Regardless of how you plan to develop, save, and distribute a document, you will not want to chance losing your work because you did not save it properly or failed to make a backup copy. Inevitably, files are lost, systems crash, or a virus compromises a disk. So the importance of saving work frequently and ensuring that backup copies exist cannot be overemphasized.

With the frequency of new Word versions, there is always a chance that someone who needs to read your document is working with a version that is not compatible with yours, or perhaps the person is not working with Word at all. You can eliminate that source of frustration by saving a document in a compatible format before distributing it. Another source of concern when distributing a document is the hidden or personal data that might be stored in document properties, such as author, or general comments. Backing up documents, ensuring their compatibility with other software versions, and removing document information that is either unnecessary or has the potential for too much disclosure should definitely be considered before finalizing a project or allowing others to see it.

Ensure Document Compatibility

STEP 2 »» If you plan to distribute a Word document to others, you should ensure that they will be able to open the document regardless of which version of Word they are using. Users of Word 2007-2013 will be able to open a document saved in Word 2016 format, but some Word 2016 features might be disabled. In that case, you can check a document for compatibility, to determine which features, if any, will be unavailable in an earlier version. If the recipient of a document you are distributing is using Word 2003 or earlier, you can save the document in a Word format that the earlier version can open. You might also consider saving a file in Rich Text Format (RTF) or Portable Document Format (PDF), which adds even more flexibility, as such a file can be opened by other software in addition to Word. Be aware, however, that doing so might compromise the document somewhat because other software versions might not be able to accommodate all of the current Word version's special features.

To save a Word 2016 document as another document type, complete the following steps:

1. Click the File tab and click Save As.
2. Navigate to the location to which you want to save the document.
3. Provide a file name and click the Save as type arrow (see Figure 43).
4. Select another file format and click Save.

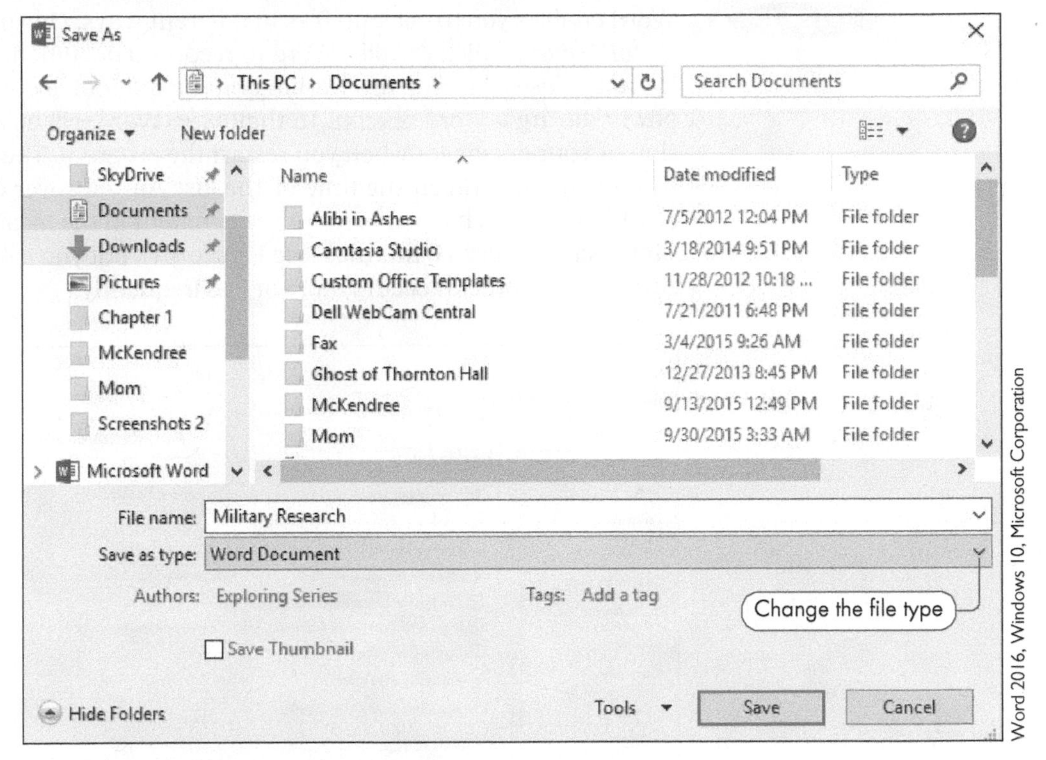

FIGURE 43 Saving as a Different File Type

Occasionally, you might receive a Word document that was created in an earlier Word version. In that case, the words *Compatibility Mode* are included in the title bar, advising you that some of Word 2016's features will not be available or viewable in the document. While in Compatibility Mode, you might not be able to use new and enhanced features of the most current Word version; by keeping the file in Compatibility Mode, you ensure that people with earlier Word versions will still have full editing capability when they receive the document. Word simplifies the process of converting a Word document to the newest version.

To convert a document to Word 2016, complete the following steps:

1. Click the File tab.
2. Click Convert (beside Compatibility Mode). The Convert option will not be displayed if the file is currently in Office 2016 format.
3. Click OK.

Before distributing a document, you can check it for compatibility, ensuring that it can be read in its entirety by users of earlier Word versions.

To check a document for compatibility, complete the following steps:

1. Click the File tab.
2. Click Check for Issues (beside Inspect Document).
3. Click Check Compatibility.
4. Click *Select versions to show* and then select one or more versions of Word to check (or simply leave them all selected). Click *Select versions to show* again to close the list.
5. Read the summary of features that are incompatible, and click OK.

Understand Backup Options

STEP 3 Word enables you to back up files in different ways. One option is to use a feature called ***AutoRecover***, which enables Word to recover a document if an application error causes Word to close while you are working on the original document or if your computer loses power during a Word session. In that case, Word will be able to recover a previous version of your document when you restart the program. The only work you will lose is anything you did between the time of the last AutoRecover operation and the time of the crash, unless you happen to save the document in the meantime. By default, file information is saved every 10 minutes (see Figure 44), but you can adjust the setting so that the AutoRecover process occurs more or less frequently.

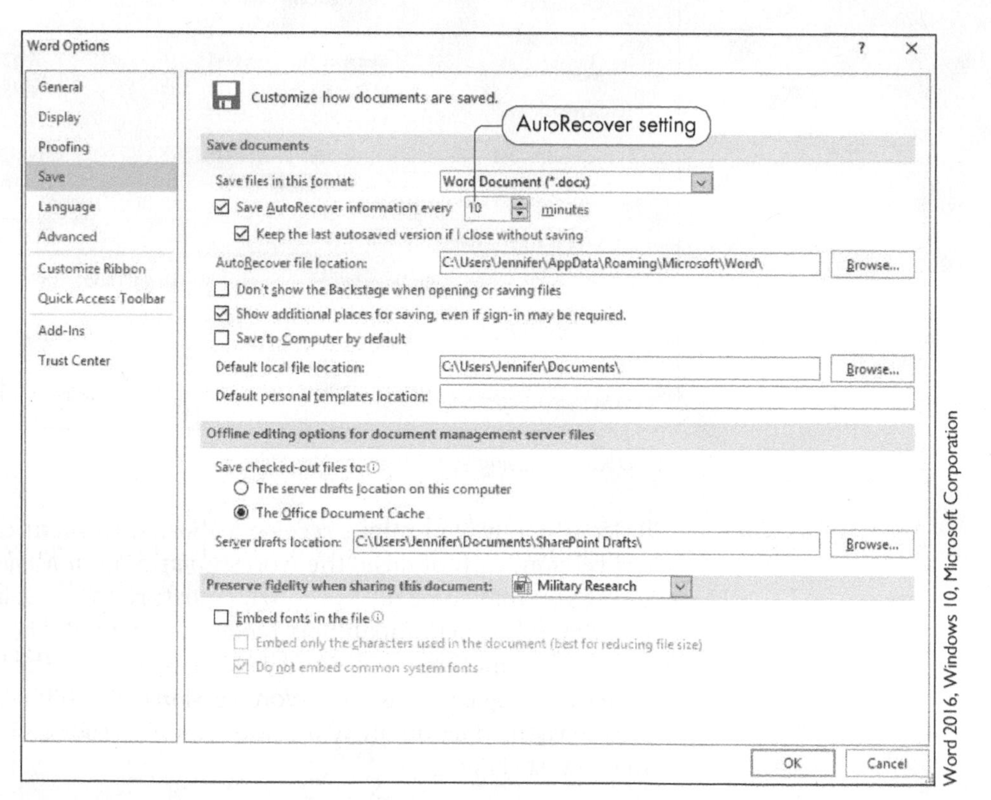

FIGURE 44 The AutoRecover Feature

You can also configure Word to create a backup copy each time a document is saved. Although the setting to always create a backup copy is not enabled by default, you can enable it from Word Options in the Advanced category. Even so, creating frequent backup copies can slow your system and may not be altogether necessary, given the excellent File History facility provided by Windows 10. As an additional safety net, though, you can certainly enable Word to create backup copies of documents.

To enable an automatic backup, complete the following steps:

1. Click the File tab.
2. Click Options.
3. Click Advanced.
4. Scroll to the Save group and select *Always create backup copy*. Click OK.

Run the Document Inspector

STEP 4 Before you send or give a document to another person, you should run the ***Document Inspector*** to reveal any hidden or personal data in the file. For privacy or security reasons, you might want to remove certain items contained in the document such as author name, comments made by one or more people who have access to the document, or document server locations. Word's Document Inspector will check for and enable you to remove various types of identifying information, including:

- Comments, revisions, versions, and annotations
- Document properties and personal information
- Custom XML data
- Headers, footers, and watermarks
- Invisible content
- Hidden text

Because some information removed by the Document Inspector cannot be recovered with the Undo command, you should save a copy of your original document, using a different name, prior to inspecting the document.

To inspect a document, complete the following steps:

1. Click the File tab.
2. Click Check for Issues.
3. Click Inspect Document.
4. Respond if a dialog box appears, by clicking Yes if you have not saved the file and want to do so (or clicking No if you have already saved the file).
5. Confirm the types of content you want to check in the Document Inspector dialog box (see Figure 45). Deselect any categories you do not want to check.
6. Click Inspect to begin the process. When the check is complete, Word lists the results and enables you to choose whether to remove the content from the document. For example, if you are distributing a document to others, you might want to remove all document properties and personal information. In that case, you can instruct the Document Inspector to remove such content.

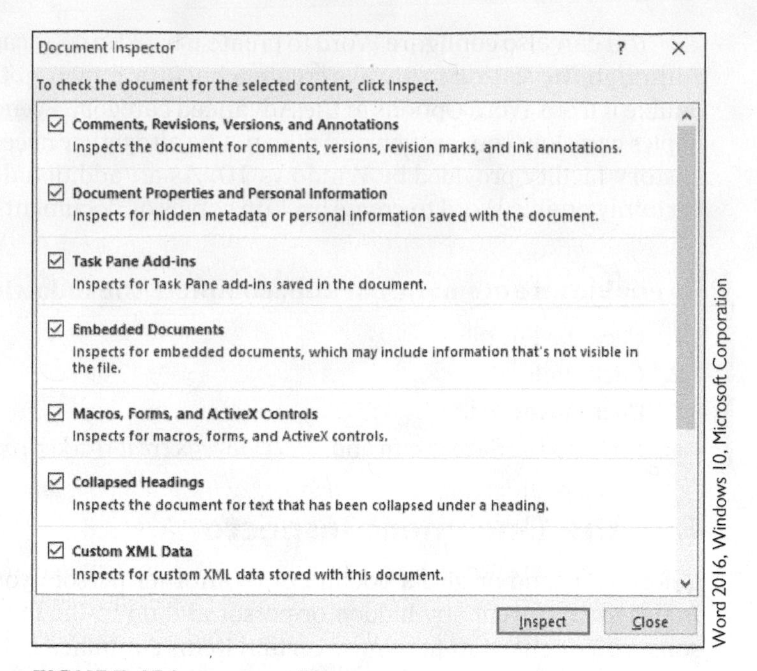

FIGURE 45 Inspecting a Document

Select Print Options

Although by default, Word prints one copy of an entire document, you might find it necessary to print multiple copies, or only a few pages. Those settings and others are available when you click the File tab and click Print. The Print settings shown in Figure 46 enable you to select the number of copies, the pages or range of pages to print, the printer to use, whether to collate pages, whether to print on only one side of the paper, and how many pages to print per sheet. In addition, you can adjust page orientation, paper size, and even customize a document's margins—all by paying attention to print options. Please note that the wording of some print options will vary, depending on whether you have previously selected the option and indicated a custom setting.

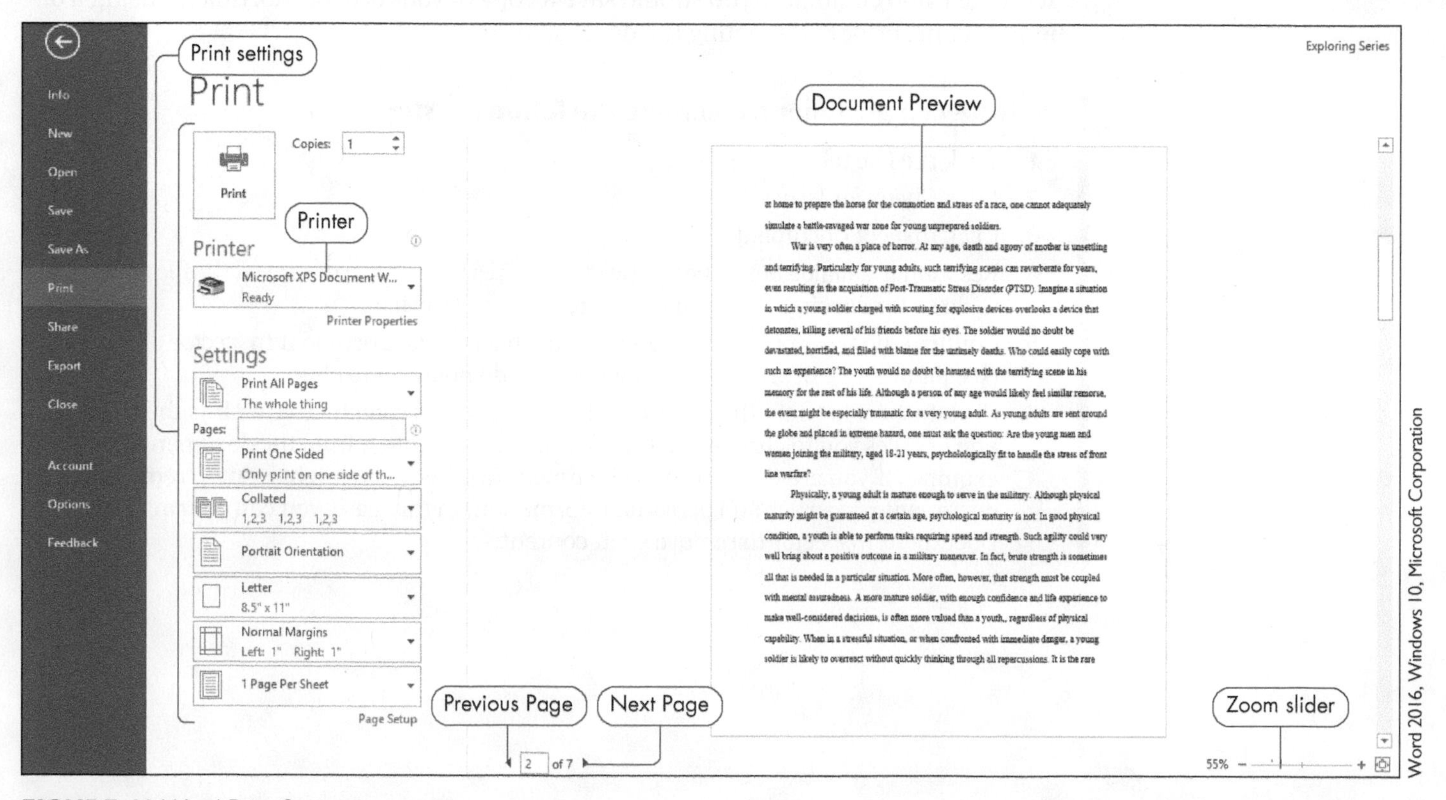

FIGURE 46 Word Print Settings

Print options display to the left of the document preview (refer to Figure 46). You can click the Next Page or Previous Page navigation arrow to move among pages in the document preview. You can also drag the Zoom slider to enlarge or reduce the size of the document preview.

9. A coworker who uses Office 2007 has sent you a document for review. When you open the document, the words *[Compatibility Mode]* display in the title bar after the file name. Is there any reason you might want to remove the document from Compatibility Mode? And if so, how would you convert the document to the format used by Word 2016?
10. Describe the process of using Word options to ensure that backup copies are automatically created.
11. Before distributing a document, how would you remove any personally identifying information, such as author and comments?
12. Before printing pages 3 through 5 of the current document, you want to preview the document and then print only those pages. In a separate print procedure, you also want to print document properties that are associated with the current document. What steps would you follow to preview and print those pages?

Hands-On Exercises

Skills covered: Customize Document Properties • Print Document Properties • Ensure Document Compatibility • Understand Backup Options • Run the Document Inspector • Select Print Options

3 Document Settings and Properties

As the office assistant for Swan Creek National Wildlife Refuge, you are responsible for the security, management, and backup of the organization's documents. The article promoting the summer day camps is ready for final approval. Before that happens, however, you will check it one last time, making sure it is saved in a format that others can read. You will also ensure that you have sufficient backup copies. You also want to include appropriate document properties for additional identification, and you will consider print options. Privacy and security are to be considered as well, so you check for identifiers that should be removed before distributing the document.

STEP 1 » CUSTOMIZE AND PRINT DOCUMENT PROPERTIES

You assign document properties to the summer camp document to identify its author and purpose. You also create an additional property to record a project identifier. Finally, you prepare to print document properties. Refer to Figure 47 as you complete Step 1.

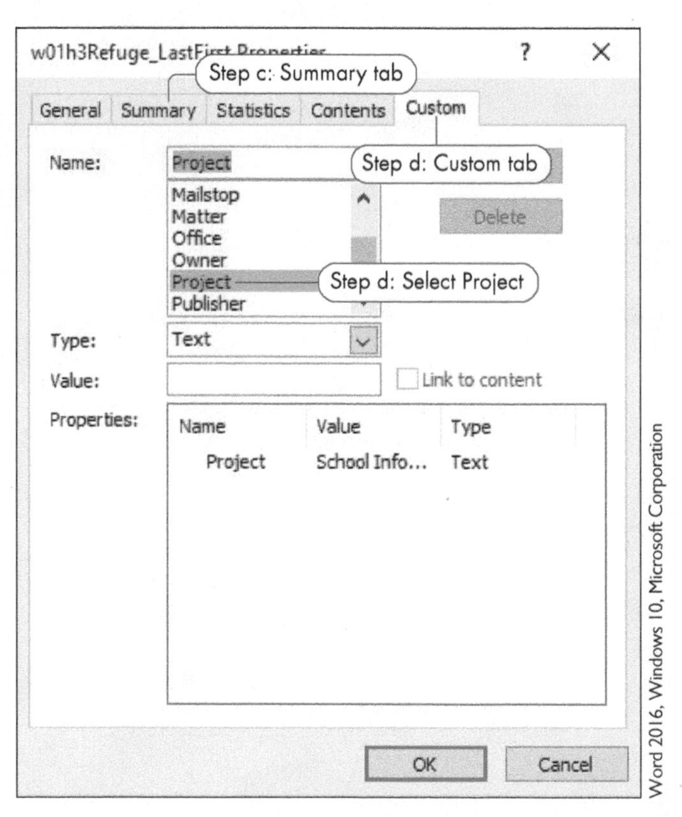

FIGURE 47 Customizing Document Properties

a. Open *w01h2Refuge_LastFirst* if you closed it at the end of Hands-On Exercise 2 and save it as **w01h3Refuge_LastFirst**, changing h2 to h3.

b. Click the **File tab**, click **Properties** in the right pane, and then click **Advanced Properties**.

The Properties dialog box displays.

c. Click the **Summary tab**. Ensure that the Author box contains your name. Click one time in the **Comments box** and type **Summer Camp Information**.

d. Create a custom property by completing the following steps:

- Click the **Custom tab** and scroll to select **Project** in the **Name list**.
- Type **School Information** in the **Value box**, as shown in Figure 47, and click **Add**.
- Click **OK** to close the dialog box.

You want to catalog the documents you create for Swan Creek National Wildlife Refuge, and one way to do that is to assign a project identifier using the custom properties that are stored with each document. Because you set up a custom field, you can later perform searches and find all documents in that Project category.

e. Click **Print**, click **Print All Pages**, and then click **Document Info** (under the Document Info heading). If your computer is in communication with, or connected to, a printer, click **Print**. Otherwise, continue without printing.

STEP 2 ›› ENSURE DOCUMENT COMPATIBILITY

You know Ms. Traynom is anxious to review a copy of this document; however, she has not yet upgraded to Office 2016. Instead, her office computer has Office 2007 installed. To make sure she can open and read the document, you check the document for compatibility with earlier Word versions. Refer to Figure 48 as you complete Step 2.

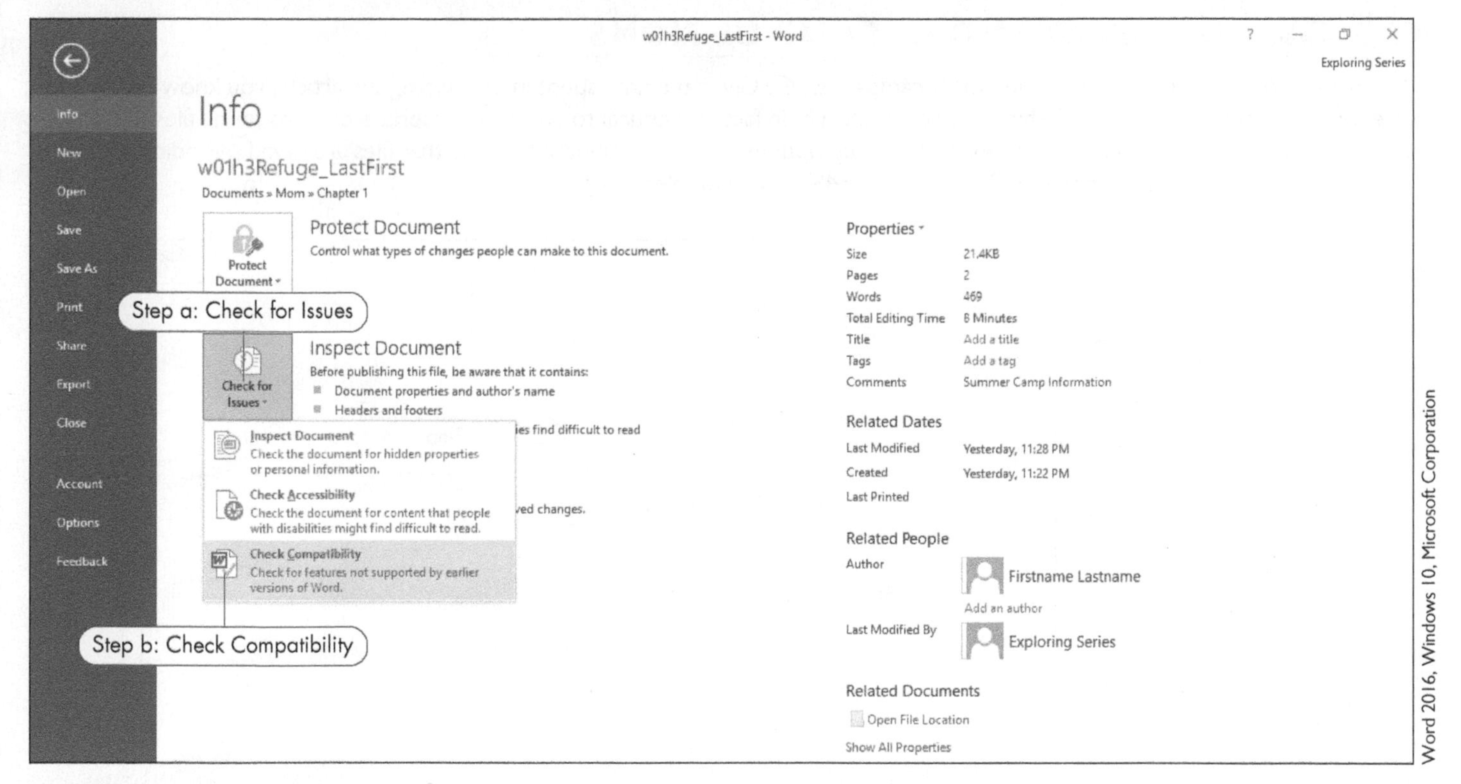

FIGURE 48 Check for Compatibility

a. Click the **File tab**, if necessary. Ensure that the Info window is displayed and click **Check for Issues** (beside Inspect Document).

b. Click **Check Compatibility**. Click **Select versions to show** and deselect **Word 97-2003** to ensure only Word 2007 and Word 2010 are selected.

Note that some formatting features are not supported and will not be available in the version you are preparing for Ms. Traynom.

c. Click **OK**. Save the document.

Because the compatibility issues are few and are restricted to what appear to be minor text effects, you feel confident that Ms. Traynom will be able to open the document in Word 2007.

d. Click the **File tab** and click **Close**.

The personnel director has prepared a draft of a memo introducing a new employee. He asked you to proof the document and prepare it for printing. However, he created and saved the memo using Word 2007.

e. Open *w01h3NewEmployee* from the student data files.

The title bar displays [Compatibility Mode] following the file name *w01h3NewEmployee*, indicating that it is not a file saved with a recent version of Word.

f. Click the **File tab** and click **Convert** (beside Compatibility Mode). A message box displays explaining the consequences of upgrading the document. Click **OK**.

The file is converted to the newest Word format. The Compatibility Mode designation is removed from the title bar.

g. Save the document as **w01h3NewEmployee_LastFirst.**

STEP 3 » UNDERSTAND BACKUP OPTIONS

The timeline for preparing for the summer day camps is short. Given the time spent in developing the article, you know that if it were lost, recreating it in a timely fashion would be difficult. In fact, it is critical to ensure appropriate backups for all files for which you are responsible at Swan Creek. You explore backup options on your computer to verify that files are saved periodically and that backups are automatically created. Refer to Figure 49 as you complete Step 3.

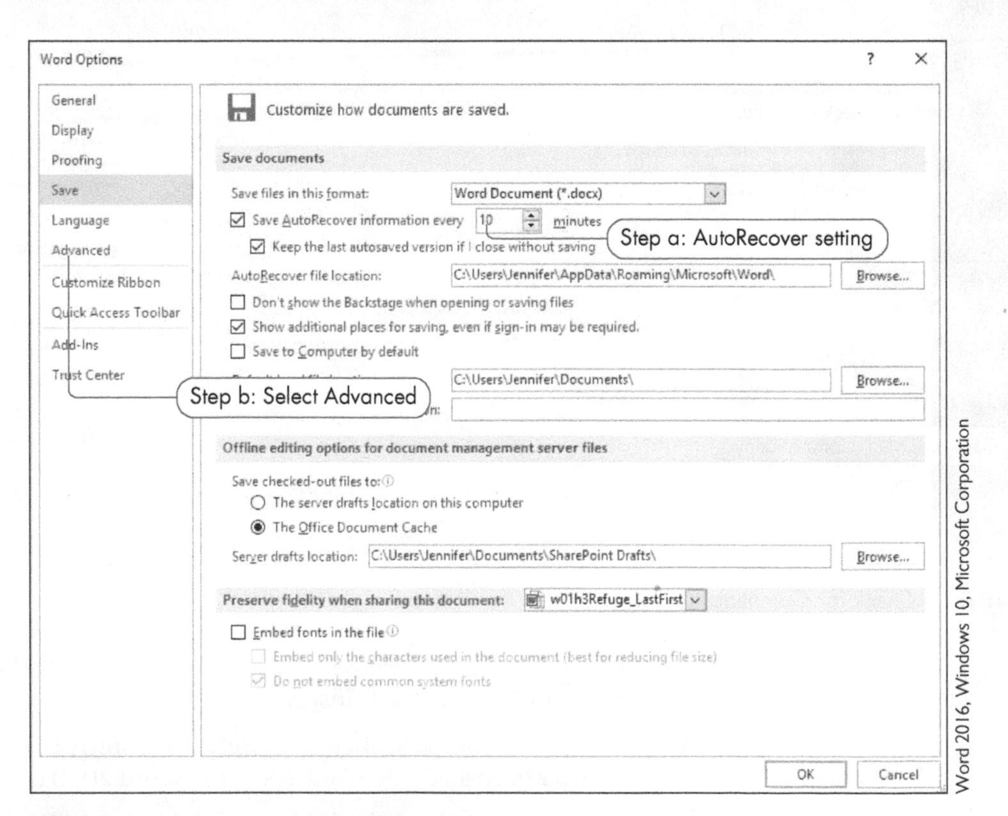

Word 2016, Windows 10, Microsoft Corporation

FIGURE 49 Exploring Backup and Save Options

a. Click the **File tab** and click **Options**. Click **Save** in the left pane of the Word Options dialog box. If *Save AutoRecover information every* is checked, note the number of minutes between saves.

b. Click **Advanced** in the left pane. Scroll to the Save area and ensure that *Always create backup copy* is not selected.

You do not select the setting at this time because you are likely to be in a school computer lab.

c. Click **Cancel**. Close the document.

STEP 4 » RUN THE DOCUMENT INSPECTOR AND SELECT PRINT OPTIONS

Before distributing the article, you run the Document Inspector to identify any information that should first be removed. You also prepare to print the document. Refer to Figure 50 as you complete Step 4.

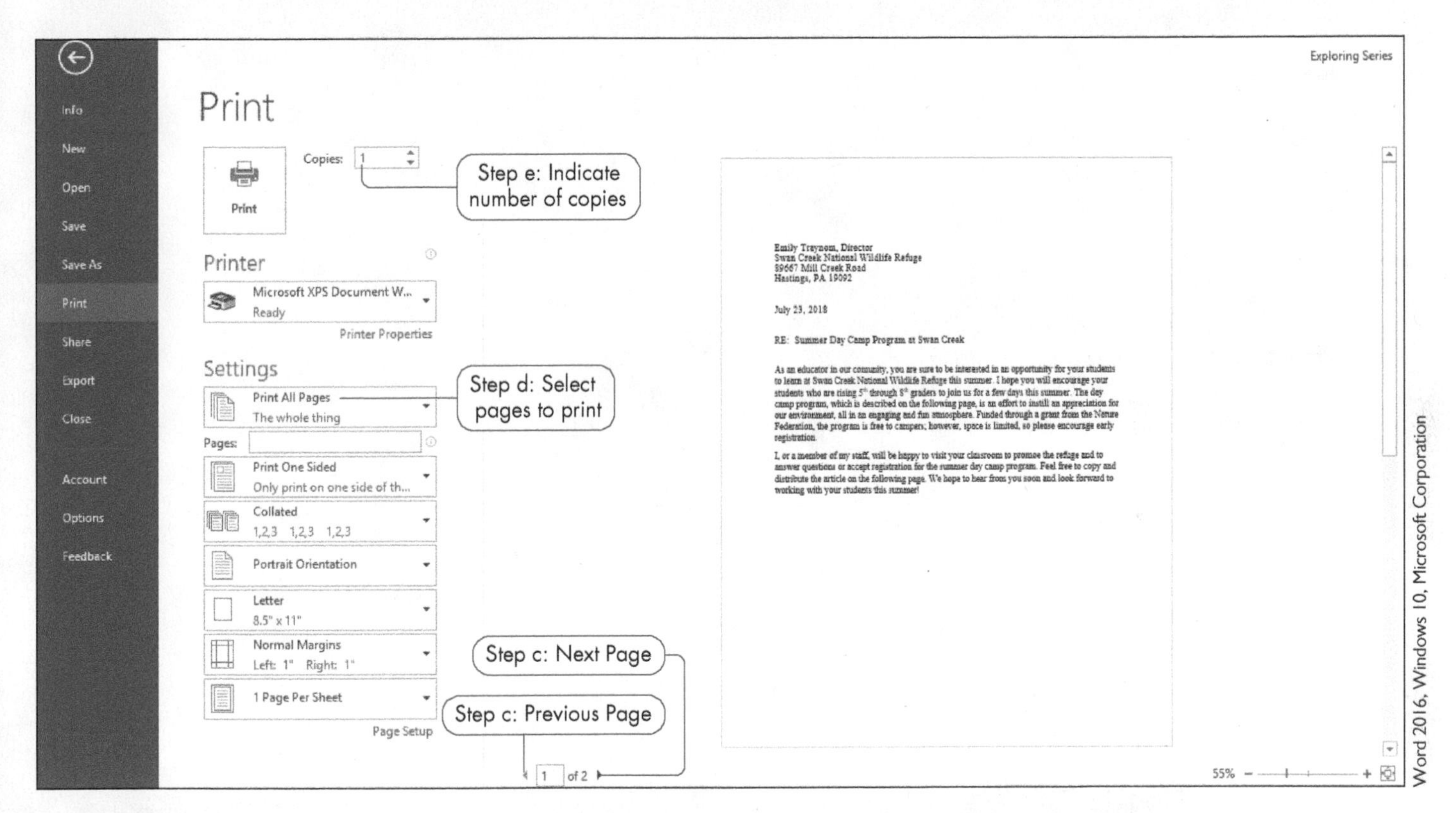

FIGURE 50 Working with Print Options

a. Open *w01h3Refuge_LastFirst*. Click the **File tab** and click **Check for Issues** (beside Inspect Document). Click **Inspect Document**. Click **Inspect**.

You check for document areas that might display sensitive information. The inspection suggests that the category of Document Properties and Personal Information contains identifying data, as does that of Headers, Footers, and Watermarks.

b. Click **Remove All** beside Document Properties and Personal Information. Click **Close**.

You determine that it would be best to remove all document properties, but you leave headers, footers, and watermarks.

c. Click **Print**. Click **Next Page** to view the next page. Click **Previous Page** to return to the first page.

d. Click in the **Pages box** below **Print All Pages**. Type **2**.

You indicate that you want to print page 2 only.

e. Click the **Copies up arrow** repeatedly to print five copies.

You indicate that you want to print five copies of page 2.

f. Press **Esc** to return to the document without printing.

g. Save and close the file. Based on your instructor's directions, submit the following:
w01h3Refuge_LastFirst
w01h1Planner_LastFirst
w01h2Flyer_LastFirst
w01h3NewEmployee_LastFirst

Chapter Objectives Review

After reading this chapter, you have accomplished the following objectives:

1. Begin and edit a document.

- Use a template: Predesigned documents save time by providing a starting point.
- Create a document: Create a blank document by clicking Blank document when Word opens.
- Reuse text: Text from previously created documents can be inserted in another document.
- Save a document: Saving a document makes it possible to access it later for editing, sharing, or printing.
- Open a document: Open a saved document by selecting the document from the Recent Documents list or browsing for other documents.
- Insert text and navigate a document: The insertion point indicates where the text you type will be placed. Use scroll bars or keyboard shortcuts to move around in a document.
- Review spelling and grammar: Use the Review tab to make sure all documents are free of typographical and grammatical errors.

2. Customize Word.

- Explore Word options: Word options are global settings you can select, such as whether to check spelling automatically, or where to save a file by default.
- Customize the Ribbon: Customize the Ribbon, using Word Options, to add, remove, or rename Ribbon tabs and commands.
- Customize the Quick Access Toolbar: The Quick Access Toolbar contains a few commands by default, but you can add more.

3. Use features that improve readability.

- Insert headers and footers: Headers and footers provide information, such as page number and organization name, in the top and bottom margins of a document.
- Adjust margins: You can change margins, selecting predefined settings or creating your own.
- Change page orientation: Select Landscape to show a document that is wider than it is tall, or Portrait to show a document taller than it is wide.
- Insert a watermark: A watermark is text or a graphic that displays behind text to identify such items as a document's purpose, owner, or status.
- Insert a symbol: A symbol is typically a character or graphic that is not found on the keyboard, such as ©.

4. View a document in different ways.

- Select a document view: A view is the way a document displays onscreen; available Word views include Print Layout, Read Mode, Outline, Web Layout, and Draft.
- Change the zoom setting: By changing the zoom setting, you can enlarge or reduce text size onscreen.
- View a document and manage page flow: Forcing a page break is useful to divide document sections (for example, to separate a cover page from other report pages), or to better manage page flow so that pages do not end awkwardly.

5. Modify document properties.

- Customize document properties: Document properties are items you can add to a document to further describe it, such as author, keywords, and comments.

6. Prepare a document for distribution.

- Ensure document compatibility: Using Word 2016, you can convert documents to the most recent version and you can also ensure a document's compatibility with earlier versions.
- Understand backup options: Backup options include AutoRecover and the ability always to create a backup copy of a saved document.
- Run the Document Inspector: Word's Document Inspector reveals any hidden or personal data in a file and enables you to remove sensitive information.
- Select print options: Using Word's print options, you can specify the pages to print, the number of copies, and various other print selections.

Key Terms Matching

Match the key terms with their definitions. Write the key term letter by the appropriate numbered definition.

a. AutoRecover
b. Document Inspector
c. Draft view
d. Header and Footer
e. Insertion point
f. Insights
g. Microsoft Word
h. Outline view
i. Print Layout view
j. Read Mode
k. Symbol
l. Template
m. Thesaurus
n. Watermark
o. Word processing software
p. Word wrap

1. _______ Text or graphic that displays behind text.

2. _______ A structural view of a document or presentation that can be collapsed or expanded as necessary.

3. _______ The feature that automatically moves words to the next line if they do not fit on the current line.

4. _______ The feature that enables Word to recover a previous version of a document.

5. _______ A computer application, such as Microsoft Word, used primarily with text to create, edit, and format documents.

6. _______ View in which text reflows to screen-sized pages to make it easier to read.

7. _______ Word processing application included in the Microsoft Office software suite.

8. _______ A predesigned document that may include formats that can be modified.

9. _______ View that closely resembles the way a document will look when printed.

10. _______ A character or graphic not normally included on a keyboard.

11. _______ A feature that checks for and removes certain hidden and personal information from a document.

12. _______ Information that displays at the top or bottom of each document page.

13. _______ View that shows a great deal of document space, but no margins, headers, footers, or other special features.

14. _______ Blinking bar that indicates where text that you next type will appear.

15. _______ Pane that displays when you click Smart Lookup, enabling you to access outside resources, such as images, definitions, and other items for a selected word.

16. _______ Tool that enables you to find a synonym for a selected word.

Multiple Choice

1. The view that presents a document in screen-sized pages with two shown at a time, for ease of comprehension and sharing, is:

(a) Read Mode.
(b) Print Layout view.
(c) Draft view.
(d) Full Screen Mode.

2. The Document Inspector is useful when you want to:

(a) Troubleshoot a document, identifying and adjusting nonprinting characters.
(b) Reveal any hidden or personal data in the file so that it can be removed, if necessary.
(c) Check the document for spelling and grammatical errors.
(d) Adjust page layout.

3. To keep a date, such as June 15, from being separated between lines of a document, where the word June might display on one line, with 15 on the next, you could:

(a) Insert a soft return between June and 15.
(b) Insert an Em dash symbol before the word June.
(c) Insert a hard return after 15.
(d) Insert a nonbreaking space symbol between June and 15.

4. The pane that displays images, resources, and definitions of a selected word is:

(a) Insights.
(b) Thesaurus.
(c) Document Properties.
(d) Read Mode.

5. Suppose you find that a heading within a report is displayed at the end of a page, with remaining text in that section placed on the next page. To keep the heading with the text, you would position the insertion point before the heading and then:

(a) Press Ctrl+Enter.
(b) Click the Layout tab, click Breaks, and then select Line Numbers.
(c) Insert a soft return.
(d) Press Ctrl+Page Down.

6. You need to generate a printed calendar quickly. You can use Word to accomplish that by using a predesigned document called a:

(a) Pattern.
(b) View.
(c) Template.
(d) Shell.

7. One reason to display nonprinting characters is to:

(a) Simplify the process of converting a document to an earlier Word version.
(b) Enable spell checking on the document.
(c) Enable document properties to be added to a document.
(d) Assist with troubleshooting a document and modifying its appearance.

8. You have just opened a document provided by a coworker, and the title bar includes not only the file name but also the words Compatibility Mode. What does that mean?

(a) The file was created in an earlier version of Word but saved as a Word 2016 file.
(b) The file was created using another operating system, but opened under a version of Windows.
(c) Word has placed the document in read-only mode, which means you will not be able to edit it.
(d) The file was created in an earlier version of Word and might not be able to accommodate newer Word 2016 features unless you convert it.

9. To identify a document as a draft, and not in final form, which of the following would you mostly likely add to the document?

(a) Symbol
(b) Watermark
(c) Template
(d) Document property

10. One reason to use a header or footer is because:

(a) The header or footer becomes a document property that can be used to search for the document later.
(b) You only have to specify the content once, after which it displays automatically on all pages.
(c) Most writing style guides require both headers and footers.
(d) Headers and footers are required for all professional documents.

Practice Exercises

1 River City Media

Having recently graduated from college with a marketing degree, you are employed by River City Media as a marketing specialist. River City Media provides promotional material in a variety of ways, including print, Web communications, photography, and news releases. It is your job to promote River City Media so that it attracts a large number of new and recurring contracts seeking support with the marketing of products and services. One of your first tasks is updating printed material that describes the specific services that River City Media offers to prospective clients. You modify a brief description of services, first converting the document from an earlier version of Word, in which it was originally saved, to the most current. Refer to Figure 51 as you complete this exercise.

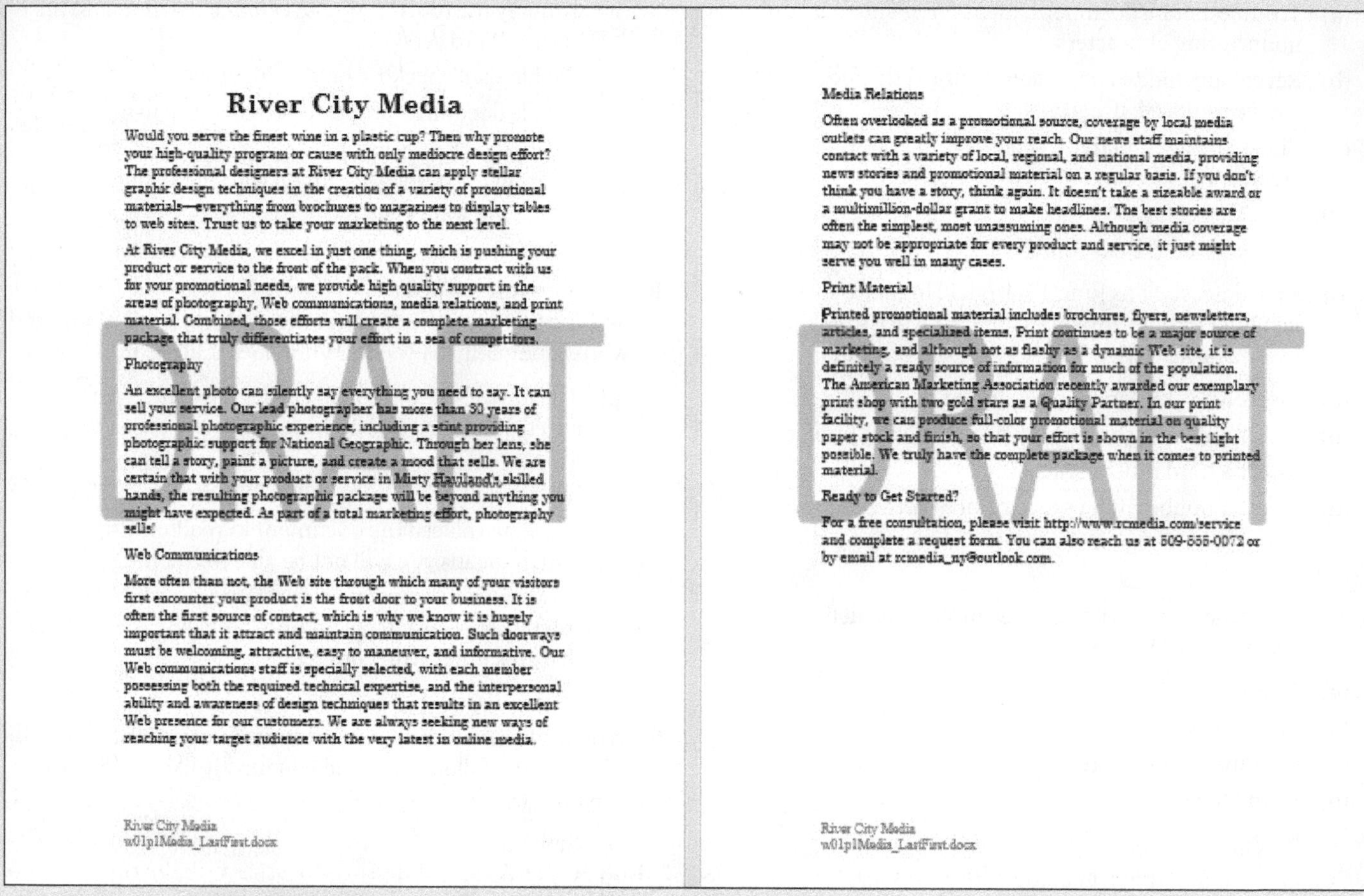

River City Media

Would you serve the finest wine in a plastic cup? Then why promote your high-quality program or cause with only mediocre design effort? The professional designers at River City Media can apply stellar graphic design techniques in the creation of a variety of promotional materials—everything from brochures to magazines to display tables to web sites. Trust us to take your marketing to the next level.

At River City Media, we excel in just one thing, which is pushing your product or service to the front of the pack. When you contract with us for your promotional needs, we provide high quality support in the areas of photography, Web communications, media relations, and print material. Combined, those efforts will create a complete marketing package that truly differentiates your effort in a sea of competitors.

Photography

An excellent photo can silently say everything you need to say. It can sell your service. Our lead photographer has more than 30 years of professional photographic experience, including a stint providing photographic support for National Geographic. Through her lens, she can tell a story, paint a picture, and create a mood that sells. We are certain that with your product or service in Misty Haviland's skilled hands, the resulting photographic package will be beyond anything you might have expected. As part of a total marketing effort, photography sells!

Web Communications

More often than not, the Web site through which many of your visitors first encounter your product is the front door to your business. It is often the first source of contact, which is why we know it is hugely important that it attract and maintain communication. Such doorways must be welcoming, attractive, easy to maneuver, and informative. Our Web communications staff is specially selected, with each member possessing both the required technical expertise, and the interpersonal ability and awareness of design techniques that results in an excellent Web presence for our customers. We are always seeking new ways of reaching your target audience with the very latest in online media.

River City Media
w01p1Media_LastFirst.docx

Media Relations

Often overlooked as a promotional source, coverage by local media outlets can greatly improve your reach. Our news staff maintains contact with a variety of local, regional, and national media, providing news stories and promotional material on a regular basis. If you don't think you have a story, think again. It doesn't take a sizeable award or a multimillion-dollar grant to make headlines. The best stories are often the simplest, most unassuming ones. Although media coverage may not be appropriate for every product and service, it just might serve you well in many cases.

Print Material

Printed promotional material includes brochures, flyers, newsletters, articles, and specialized items. Print continues to be a major source of marketing, and although not as flashy as a dynamic Web site, it is definitely a ready source of information for much of the population. The American Marketing Association recently awarded our exemplary print shop with two gold stars as a Quality Partner. In our print facility, we can produce full-color promotional material on quality paper stock and finish, so that your effort is shown in the best light possible. We truly have the complete package when it comes to printed material.

Ready to Get Started?

For a free consultation, please visit http://www.rcmedia.com/service and complete a request form. You can also reach us at 509-555-0072 or by email at rcmedia_ny@outlook.com.

River City Media
w01p1Media_LastFirst.docx

DRAFT

FIGURE 51 River City Media Draft

a. Open the *w01p1Media* document.

The words [*Compatibility Mode*] in the title bar inform you the document was created in an earlier version of Word.

b. Click the **File tab**, and then click **Save As**. Change the file name to **w01p1Media_LastFirst**. Click in the **Save as type box** and select **Word Document**. Click **Save**. You will be presented with a dialog box letting you know the document will be upgraded to the newest file format. Click **OK**.

c. Ensure that nonprinting characters are displayed by clicking Show/Hide in the paragraph group on the Home tab. Press **Ctrl+Home** to ensure that the insertion point is at the beginning of the document. Check the document for errors:

- Click the **Review tab** and click **Spelling & Grammar** in the Proofing group. The photographer's name is Haviland, so it is not misspelled. Click **Ignore**.
- Correct any identified spelling or grammatical errors. Click **OK** when the check is complete.
- Review the document again, checking for errors the spell check might have missed.

d. Double-click to select the word **maneuver** in the paragraph under the *Web Communications* heading. Click **Smart Lookup** in the Insights group. Scroll through the Insights pane to view information related to the selected word. Close the Insights pane.

e. Double-click **capable** in the paragraph under the *Photography* heading. Click **Thesaurus** in the Proofing group. Locate the word *skilled* in the Thesaurus pane, click its arrow, and then click **Insert**. Close the Thesaurus pane.

f. Make the following edits in the document:

- Select the words **When they are** from the second body paragraph on the first page and press **Delete**.
- Capitalize the word *Combined* in the same sentence.
- Rearrange the words *We at River City Media* in the same paragraph, so they read **At River City Media, we** (including a comma after the word *Media*).

g. Click after the word **materials** in the first body paragraph on the first page. Delete the following hyphen. Click the **Insert tab** and click **Symbol** in the Symbols group. Click **More Symbols**. Click the **Special Characters tab**. Ensure that Em Dash is selected. Click **Insert** and click **Close**. Click after the word **National** in the paragraph under the *Photography* heading and delete the following space. Press **Ctrl+Shift+Space** to insert a nonbreaking space, ensuring that the magazine title will not be divided between lines. Similarly, insert a nonbreaking space between **Misty** and **Haviland** so the photographer's name will not be divided between lines.

h. Click the **Design tab** and click **Watermark** in the Page Background group. Scroll through the watermarks and click **Draft 2**. Click **Watermark**, click **Custom Watermark**, and then click the **Semitransparent check box** to deselect it. Click **Color**, select **Blue Accent 5** (first row, ninth column under Theme Colors), and then click **OK**. You have inserted a watermark that indicates the document is not yet final.

i. Set up a footer:

- Click the **Insert tab** and click **Footer** in the Header & Footer group.
- Click **Edit Footer**. Type **River City Media** and press **Enter**.
- Click **Document Info** on the Header & Footer Tools Design tab and select **File Name**.
- Click **Close Header and Footer** (or double-click in the body of the document).

j. Adjust the left and right margins:

- Click the **Layout tab** and click **Margins** in the Page Setup Group.
- Click **Custom Margins**.
- Change the left and right margins to **1.5"**. Click **OK**.
- Click the **View tab** and click **Multiple Pages** in the Zoom group to see how the text is lining up on the pages.

k. Click before the **Media Relations** heading at the bottom of the first page and press **Ctrl+Enter** to insert a page break.

l. Press **Ctrl+Home**. Click **Read Mode** in the Views group. Click the arrow on the right to move from one page to the next. Press **Esc** to return to the previous document view. Click **100%** in the Zoom group. Save the document.

m. Click the **File tab** and click **Check for Issues**. Click **Inspect Document** and click **Inspect**. Click **Remove All** beside Document Properties and Personal Information and click **Close**.

n. Check the document for compatibility with earlier Word versions:

- Click **Check for Issues** and click **Check Compatibility**.
- Click **Select versions to show** and make sure that all earlier Word versions are selected.
- Click **Select versions to show** again to close the list. No compatibility issues are found.
- Click **OK**.

o. Click **Save** on the Quick Access Toolbar to save the document.

p. Close the file. Based on your instructor's directions, submit w01p1Media_LastFirst.

2 Working Space

You and a friend formed a partnership in which you help small businesses and independent workers procure temporary office space. Called Working Space, your company relies heavily on social media to advertise the business and obtain clients. As the company grows, and you hire more employees, you are finding it necessary to delegate much of the social media contact to others. Even so, you know that it is very important that the company maintain an appropriate and effective social media presence. Therefore, you use Word to develop a brief summary of expectations related to the use of social media to promote the business. Refer to Figure 52 as you complete this exercise.

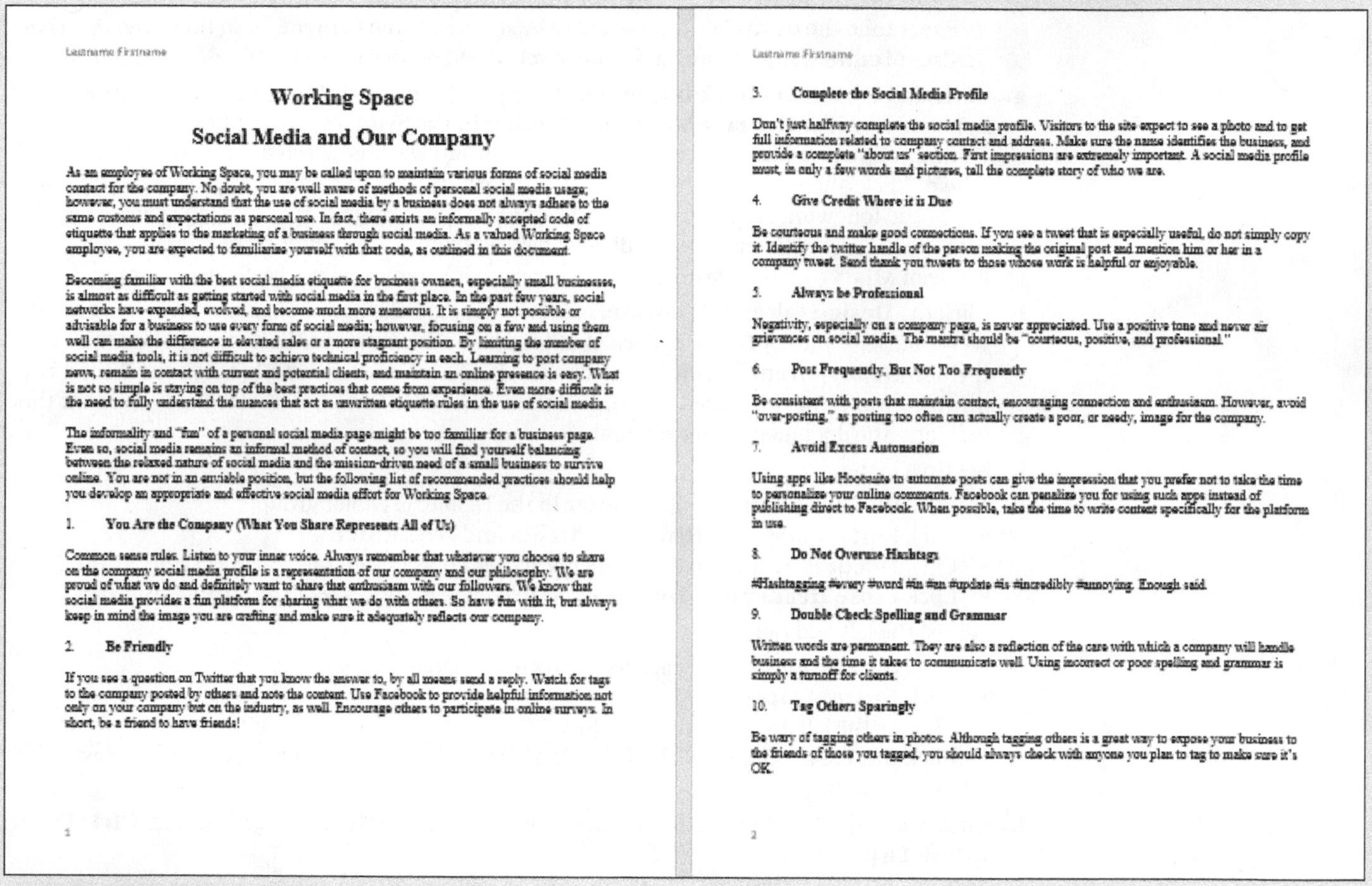

Lastname Firstname

Working Space

Social Media and Our Company

As an employee of Working Space, you may be called upon to maintain various forms of social media contact for the company. No doubt, you are well aware of methods of personal social media usage; however, you must understand that the use of social media by a business does not always adhere to the same customs and expectations as personal use. In fact, there exists an informally accepted code of etiquette that applies to the marketing of a business through social media. As a valued Working Space employee, you are expected to familiarize yourself with that code, as outlined in this document.

Becoming familiar with the best social media etiquette for business owners, especially small businesses, is almost as difficult as getting started with social media in the first place. In the past few years, social networks have expanded, evolved, and become much more numerous. It is simply not possible or advisable for a business to use every form of social media; however, focusing on a few and using them well can make the difference in elevated sales or a more stagnant position. By limiting the number of social media tools, it is not difficult to achieve technical proficiency in each. Learning to post company news, remain in contact with current and potential clients, and maintain an online presence is easy. What is not so simple is staying on top of the best practices that come from experience. Even more difficult is the need to fully understand the nuances that act as unwritten etiquette rules in the use of social media.

The informality and "fun" of a personal social media page might be too familiar for a business page. Even so, social media remains an informal method of contact, so you will find yourself balancing between the relaxed nature of social media and the mission-driven need of a small business to survive online. You are not in an enviable position, but the following list of recommended practices should help you develop an appropriate and effective social media effort for Working Space.

1. **You Are the Company (What You Share Represents All of Us)**

Common sense rules. Listen to your inner voice. Always remember that whatever you choose to share on the company social media profile is a representation of our company and our philosophy. We are proud of what we do and definitely want to share that enthusiasm with our followers. We know that social media provides a fun platform for sharing what we do with others. So have fun with it, but always keep in mind the image you are crafting and make sure it adequately reflects our company.

2. **Be Friendly**

If you see a question on Twitter that you know the answer to, by all means send a reply. Watch for tags to the company posted by others and note the content. Use Facebook to provide helpful information not only on your company but on the industry, as well. Encourage others to participate in online surveys. In short, be a friend to have friends!

1

Lastname Firstname

3. **Complete the Social Media Profile**

Don't just halfway complete the social media profile. Visitors to the site expect to see a photo and to get full information related to company contact and address. Make sure the name identifies the business, and provide a complete "about us" section. First impressions are extremely important. A social media profile must, in only a few words and pictures, tell the complete story of who we are.

4. **Give Credit Where it is Due**

Be courteous and make good connections. If you see a tweet that is especially useful, do not simply copy it. Identify the twitter handle of the person making the original post and mention him or her in a company tweet. Send thank you tweets to those whose work is helpful or enjoyable.

5. **Always be Professional**

Negativity, especially on a company page, is never appreciated. Use a positive tone and never air grievances on social media. The mantra should be "courteous, positive, and professional."

6. **Post Frequently, But Not Too Frequently**

Be consistent with posts that maintain contact, encouraging connection and enthusiasm. However, avoid "over-posting," as posting too often can actually create a poor, or needy, image for the company.

7. **Avoid Excess Automation**

Using apps like Hootsuite to automate posts can give the impression that you prefer not to take the time to personalize your online comments. Facebook can penalize you for using such apps instead of publishing direct to Facebook. When possible, take the time to write content specifically for the platform in use.

8. **Do Not Overuse Hashtags**

#Hashtagging #every #word #in #an #update #is #incredibly #annoying. Enough said.

9. **Double Check Spelling and Grammar**

Written words are permanent. They are also a reflection of the care with which a company will handle business and the time it takes to communicate well. Using incorrect or poor spelling and grammar is simply a turnoff for clients.

10. **Tag Others Sparingly**

Be wary of tagging others in photos. Although tagging others is a great way to expose your business to the friends of those you tagged, you should always check with anyone you plan to tag to make sure it's OK.

2

Word 2016, Windows 10, Microsoft Corporation

FIGURE 52 Working Space Document

a. Open *w01p2Social* and save it as **w01p2Social_LastFirst**.

b. Press **Ctrl+End** to move the insertion point to the end of the document. Press **Enter**. Click the **Insert tab** and click the **Object arrow** in the Text group. Click **Text from File**. Locate and double-click *w01p2Tips*.

c. Click the **View tab** and click **Multiple Pages** in the Zoom group. Note that very little text is shown on the last page.

d. Adjust the margins:

- Click the **Layout tab**. Click **Margins** in the Page Setup group.
- Click **Custom Margins**.
- Change the left and right margins to **0.5"**. Click **OK**. Confirm that the document now fits on two pages.
- Click the **View tab** and click **100%** in the Zoom group.

e. Insert a footer:

- Click the **Insert tab** and click **Footer** in the Header & Footer group.
- Click **Edit Footer**.
- Click **Page Number** in the Header & Footer group, point to **Current Position**, and then click **Plain Number**.
- Double-click in the current page of the document to close the footer.

f. Press **Ctrl+Home** to move to the beginning of the document and double-click in the Header area (top margin). Type your first name and last name. Double-click in the current page of the document to close the header.

g. Click the **File tab** and click **Print**. Click **Next Page** to view the next page. Click **Previous Page**. Note that the last line on the first page is a numbered item that is separated from its contents on the next page. Click **Back** (the arrow at the top left) to return to the document.

h. Ensure that nonprinting characters are displayed. Click before the number 3 on the last line of the first page. Press **Ctrl+Enter** to insert a page break.

i. Edit the text as follows:

- Remove the words *develop or* from the first sentence of the first body paragraph on the first page. Ensure that only one space remains between the words *to* and *maintain*.
- Locate the words *also are* in the paragraph under the heading *Double Check Spelling and Grammar* on the second page. Reverse those words so the sentence reads **are also** instead of *also are*.

j. Press **Ctrl+Home**. Click the **Review tab** and click **Spelling & Grammar** in the Proofing group. Correct any identified errors, if they are actual errors. The words *Hootsuite* and *Hashtagging* are correct and should not be changed. Click **OK** when the spelling check is complete.

k. Press **Ctrl+Home**. Click the **View tab** and click **Multiple Pages** in the Zoom group.

l. Adjust the left and right margins:

- Click **100%** in the Zoom group.
- Click the **Layout tab** and click **Margins** in the Page Setup group.
- Click **Moderate**.

m. Preview the document. Press **Ctrl+End** and delete the blank paragraph mark that is forcing a third page. Ensure that the document now spans only two pages. Save the document.

n. Click the **File tab**, click **Check for Issues**, and then click **Check Compatibility**. Ensure that all versions of Word are checked. There are no compatibility issues with earlier Word versions, so click **OK**.

o. Click the **File tab**. Click **Check for Issue**s, click **Inspect Document**, click **No**, and then click **Inspect**. Click **Close** after you view the results.

p. Click **Print**. Click in the **Pages box** under Print All Pages and type **2** to indicate that you want to print only the second page. Because you are likely in a lab setting, you will not print the pages.

q. Press **Esc** to return to the document. Save and close the file. Based on your instructor's direction, submit w01p2Social_LastFirst.

Mid-Level Exercises

1 Runners at Heart

A local cross-country team, Runners at Heart, is comprised of people who are recovering from a heart ailment or who support the cause of fitness for former heart patients. A half marathon is coming up in five months, and the Runners at Heart cross-country team wants to be prepared. A half marathon is a run/walk of 13.1 miles. You and others have researched tips on preparing for a half marathon and compiled a brief guide. You have begun a document containing a few of those tips, and have collected ideas from other club members as well. You finalize the document and make it available in plenty of time for the runners to prepare.

a. Open *w01m1Running* and save it as **w01m1Running_LastFirst**.

b. Move to the end of the document and press **Enter**. Insert text from *w01m1Guide*.

c. Display nonprinting characters if they are not already shown. View each page of the document and note that the first page ends awkwardly, with a single heading at the bottom. Insert a page break before the *What to wear* heading.

d. Correct any headings that are not capitalized appropriately. Headings should be changed to **Choose a Plan**, **Run Quality Miles**, **Cross-train**, **Prepare Mentally**, **Train with Others**, **Do Your Research**, **Rest**, and **What to Wear**.

e. Insert a hard return before each heading except What To Wear (beginning with *Choose a Plan* and ending with *Rest*) to increase the space between them.

f. Remove the page break before the *What to Wear* heading.

g. View the document and insert a page break, wherever a heading stands alone.

h. Identify synonyms for the word *regimen* in the *Choose a Plan* section. Insert the word **schedule**. Close the Thesaurus pane. Check for spelling and word usage errors, correcting any that are identified. The brand of clothing is correctly spelled *Dri-Fit*. Proofread the document carefully to identify any errors that Word might have missed. Review the word *resistance* in the *Cross-train* section using the Smart Lookup tool. Close the Insights pane.

i. Insert a page number footer as a **Plain Number** in the current position (on the left side of the footer). As a header, include the file name as a field.

j. Select the hyphen between the words *long* and *distance* in the paragraph following *Training Tips for a Half Marathon*. Insert a Nonbreaking Hyphen. Insert a trademark symbol immediately after the words *Nike Dri-Fit* (before the period) in the *What to Wear* section.

k. Add a horizontal draft watermark. The watermark should be clearly visible (not semitransparent), and colored **Dark Blue**.

l. Change the page orientation to **Landscape**. Preview the document to determine if the orientation is appropriate. Delete the page break before the *Do Your Research* heading. Remove one of the blank paragraphs before the *Do Your Research* heading. Change the zoom to **100%**. Save the document.

m. Access Advanced Properties and replace the current author with your first and last names. In the Comments section, type **Tips for a Half Marathon**. Remove any information in the Company box.

n. Preview the document. Print the document properties if approved by your instructor.

o. Save and close the file. Based on your instructor's directions, submit w01m1Running_LastFirst.

2 Backyard Bonanza

With a degree in horticulture, you have recently been employed to work with Backyard Bonanza, a local outdoor living business specializing in garden gifts, statuary, outdoor fireplaces, landscaping materials, and pavers. The first Friday of each month, Backyard Bonanza participates in a downtown event in which vendors, artists, and musicians set up areas to perform or display products. To encourage those passing by to visit the store, you prepare a document describing a few do-it-yourself backyard projects—all of which can be completed with the help of products sold at Backyard

Bonanza. The document is well underway, but you modify it slightly, making sure it is attractive and ready for distribution at the next event.

a. Open *w01m2Backyard*. The document was originally saved in an earlier version of Word, so you should save it as a Word Document with the file name of **w01m2Backyard_LastFirst**. Agree that the upgrade should proceed, if asked.
b. Display nonprinting characters. Preview the document to get a feel for the text flow. Change the orientation to **Portrait**. Change the view to **One Page**.
c. Return to **100%** view. Add a page number footer. The page number should be placed at the **Bottom** with the **Plain Number 2** selection. Close the footer.
d. Insert text from *w01m2Fish* at the end of the document.
e. Scroll to the top of page 2. Change the word *Create* to **Build**.
f. Check the document for spelling and grammatical errors. The word *Delite* is not misspelled as it is a brand name. Because there is no correct suggestion for the misuse of the word *layer*, you will need to manually change it. (Hint: You can ignore the error and then return to manually correct the mistake.) Proofread the document to identify and correct errors that Word might have missed.
g. Preview the document and note the small amount of text on page 3. Change margins to **Narrow**.
h. Insert a page break so that *Build a Backyard Fish Pond* begins on a new page.
i. View the document in Read Mode. Return to Print Layout view. Display the document in **100%** zoom.
j. Click after the word **noticed** on page 2 and before the comma in the third sentence of the first body paragraph of directions. Remove the comma and the following space, and insert an **Em Dash**. On page 1, click after the words **Paving Delite**, but before the closing parenthesis (in the first paragraph of directions under *What to do:*). Insert a trademark symbol.

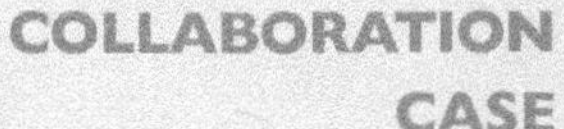

k. Add a watermark with the text **Backyard Bonanza** shown in Red. The watermark should be horizontal and semitransparent.
l. List **Backyard Bonanza** as the author in Document Properties. The subject is **Backyard Projects**.
m. Run the Compatibility Checker to make sure the file is compatible with earlier Word versions.
n. Save and close the file. Based on your instructor's directions, submit w01m2Backyard_LastFirst.

3 College Events

COLLABORATION CASE

FROM SCRATCH

You and a group of your fellow students are assigned the project of preparing a document describing several upcoming events at your college or university. Identify a few events to highlight, and assign each event to a student. Although each student will conduct independent research on an event, all event descriptions will be collected and combined into one document for submission to your instructor. To complete the project:

a. Identify a unique name for the group (perhaps assigned by your instructor).
b. Identify events (perhaps conduct research online) and assign one event to each student.
c. Each student will collect information on the event (general description, location, cost, etc.).
d. Compose a cover letter to the instructor, identifying group members and noting events to be included in the document. The cover letter should be attractive and error free.
e. Insert a page break at the end of the cover letter so that the first event description begins on a new page.
f. Save the document to OneDrive as **w01m3Events_GroupName** (replacing GroupName with the actual group name). Go to http://onedrive.live.com, sign in, and then open *w01m3Events_GroupName*. Click **Share** and click **Get a link**. Click **Shorten link** to get a shorter version of the URL. Provide the URL to group members so each member can access and edit the file.

g. Each group member will access the file from the URL. When the document opens, click **Edit Document**, and then click **Edit in Word**. Click Yes, if advised of a possibility of viruses. Enter any login information (Microsoft account credentials) and edit the document to add event information. When a description is complete, insert a hard return so that the next description begins on a new page. Click **Save** on the Quick Access Toolbar to save the document back to OneDrive.

h. Based on your instructor's directions, submit w01m3Events_GroupName.

Beyond the Classroom

Dream Destination

GENERAL CASE 

FROM SCRATCH

You work with a local radio station that will award a dream vacation of one week in a resort area to a lucky listener. Select a destination and conduct some research to determine approximately how much it will cost your employer to make the vacation available. What travel arrangements are possible? What type of accommodations do you recommend? What activities are there to enjoy in the area, and what are some outstanding restaurants? Prepare a one- to two-page document, outlining what you think are the best selling points for the area and approximately how much the travel and hotel accommodations will cost the radio station. Because the document is for internal distribution in draft format, you do not need to be overly concerned with format. However, you should use skills from this chapter to properly identify the document (headers, footers, and watermarks) and to position it on the page. The document should be error free. Modify document properties to include yourself as the author. Save the file as **w01b1Vacation_LastFirst**. Close the file and based on your instructor's directions, submit w01b1Vacation_LastFirst.

Logo Policy

Open *w01b2Policy* and save it as a Word 2016 file with the file name **w01b2Policy_LastFirst**. The document was started by an office assistant, but was not finished. You must complete the document, ensuring that it is error free and attractive. The current header includes a page number at the top right. Remove the page number from the header and create a footer with a centered page number instead. Remove the word *copyright* anywhere it appears in the document and replace it with the copyright symbol. Show nonprinting characters and remove any unnecessary or improperly placed paragraph marks. Insert hard returns where necessary to better space paragraphs. The hyphenated word *non-Association* should not be divided between lines, so use a nonbreaking hyphen. Modify document properties to include yourself as the author and assign relevant keywords. Finally, use a watermark to indicate that the document is not in final form. Save the document as a Word 2016 file and as a separate Word 97-2003 document with the same file name. Based on your instructor's directions, submit w01b2Policy_LastFirst.doc and w01b1Policy_LastFirst.docx.

Capstone Exercise

As a travel editor for a regional magazine, you are responsible for the preparation of material related to destinations and special events. Your staff often prepares material on specific areas, and you edit and combine the submissions into attractive documents for publication. In this case, you collect information to spotlight a couple of destinations in the Southeast. A deadline is looming so you use Word to produce an attractive article.

Spelling, Margins, Watermarks, and Editing

Nothing detracts from content more than spelling and grammatical errors. Since this article is destined for print, it must be error free. You check it for errors and manually proofread it. Additionally, you find it necessary to adjust margins to improve readability and you edit the content. Finally, a watermark indicates that this is not the final version.

a. Open *w01c1Travel* and save it as **w01c1Travel_LastFirst**.

b. Position the insertion point at the end of the document. On a new line, insert text from *w01c1Texas*.

c. Use Word's Spelling & Grammar checker to identify any spelling or word usage errors. All names are spelled correctly, so ignore any errors related to a name. Select the word *quaint* in the third paragraph on the first page. Use the thesaurus to identify synonyms. Insert the word **charming** instead. Close the Thesaurus pane. Proofread the document to ensure that there are no other errors.

d. Change the left and right margins to **1"**.

e. Insert a diagonal watermark that displays **Draft**. Color the watermark blue and leave semitransparency on.

f. Display nonprinting characters. Remove the hard return at the end of the third paragraph on the first page (ending in *guest rooms*). Insert a space. Change the number *200* in the sixth paragraph on the first page to *300*. Change the word *offer* in the last paragraph on the first page to **feature**. Change the word *it's* in the last paragraph on the second page to **it is**. The fourth paragraph on the first page incorrectly describes *The Cloister* as *The Cloisters*. Edit the paragraph to remove the *s* from the end of the resort name each place it occurs in the paragraph.

Headers, Footers, Symbols, and Features That Improve Readability

You number the pages and include a descriptive header. You also ensure that each destination appears on its own page (or set of pages). Finally, you use several symbols to improve readability and to ensure proper credit.

a. Create a page number footer, centered at the bottom of each page. Create a header with **Southeastern Living** on the left. On a second line in the header, insert the document file name.

b. Edit the header to include a copyright symbol before the words *Southeastern Living*.

c. At a couple of locations throughout the document, a hyphenated phrase is incorrectly separated at the end of a line. Replace the dash separating those divided words with a nonbreaking hyphen. Similarly, replace the space after the first name *Addison* with a nonbreaking space so that the full name is not divided.

d. Insert a page break before the fifth paragraph on the first page.

e. View the document as Multiple Pages to get a feel for the flow of text. Because the text is a bit too high on the page, change the top margin to **2"**. Return the view to **100%**. Save the document.

Set Properties and Finalize Document

As the document nears completion, you adjust document properties to include yourself as the author and to apply descriptive keywords. You also save the document in a format that ensures others will be able to read it. Finally you ensure compatibility with earlier Word versions.

a. Save the document in Rich Text Format as **w01c1Travel_LastFirst**. Save the document again as a Word Document with the same file name. Replace the existing file and agree to the upgrade.

b. Save the document. Run the Compatibility Checker for all previous Word versions. Inspect the document and remove all document properties and personal information.

c. Add **Travel**, **Texas**, and **Georgia** to the Keywords field in the document properties. List your first name and last name as the Author.

d. Preview the document.

e. Save and close the file. Based on your instructor's directions, submit w01c1Travel_LastFirst (the RTF document) and w01c1Travel_LastFirst (the Word document).

Glossary

AutoRecover A feature that enables Word to recover a previous version of a document.

Document Inspector Checks for and removes certain hidden and personal information from a document.

Document properties Data elements that identify a document, such as author or comments.

Draft view View that shows a great deal of document space, but no margins, headers, footers, or other special features.

Footer Information that displays at the bottom of a document page.

Header Information that generally displays at the top of a document page.

Insertion point Blinking bar that indicates where text that you next type will appear.

Insights A pane that presents outside resources, such as images, definitions, and other references.

Microsoft Word A word processing software application used to produce all sorts of documents, including memos, newsletters, forms, tables, and brochures.

Outline view A structural view of a document that can be collapsed or expanded as necessary.

Print Layout view View that closely resembles the way a document will look when printed.

Read Mode View in which text reflows automatically between columns to make it easier to read.

Symbol A character or graphic not normally included on a keyboard.

Template A predesigned file that incorporates formatting elements, such as theme and layouts, and may include content that can be modified.

Thesaurus A tool used to quickly find a synonym (a word with the same meaning as another).

Watermark Text or graphics that display behind text.

Web Layout view View that displays the way a document will look when posted on the Internet.

Word processing software A computer application, such as Microsoft Word, used primarily with text to create, edit, and format documents.

Word wrap The feature that automatically moves words to the next line if they do not fit on the current line.

Document Presentation

Word

Document Presentation

LEARNING OUTCOME **You will modify a Word document with formatting, styles, and objects.**

OBJECTIVES & SKILLS: After you read this chapter, you will be able to:

Text and Paragraph Formatting

OBJECTIVE 1: APPLY FONT ATTRIBUTES
Select Font Options, Change Text Appearance

OBJECTIVE 2: FORMAT A PARAGRAPH
Select Paragraph Alignment, Select Line and Paragraph Spacing, Select Indents, Set Tab Stops, Apply Borders and Shading, Create Bulleted and Numbered Lists

HANDS-ON EXERCISE 1:
Text and Paragraph Formatting

Document Appearance

OBJECTIVE 3: FORMAT A DOCUMENT
Select a Document Theme, Work with Sections, Format Text into Columns

OBJECTIVE 4: APPLY STYLES
Select and Modify Styles, Use a Style Set, Create a New Style from Text, Use Outline View

HANDS-ON EXERCISE 2:
Document Appearance

Objects

OBJECTIVE 5: INSERT AND FORMAT OBJECTS
Insert a Picture; Move, Align, and Resize a Picture; Modify a Picture; Insert a Text Box; Modify, Move, and Resize a Text Box; Insert WordArt

HANDS-ON EXERCISE 3:
Objects

CASE STUDY | Phillips Studio L Photography

Having recently opened your own photography studio, you are engaged in marketing the business. Not only do you hope to attract customers from the local community who want photos of special events, but you will also offer classes in basic photography for interested amateur photographers. In addition, you have designed a website to promote the business and to provide details on upcoming events and classes. The business is not large enough yet to employ an office staff, so much of the work of developing promotional material falls on you.

Among other projects, you are currently developing material to include in a quarterly mailing to people who have expressed an interest in upcoming studio events. You have prepared a rough draft of a newsletter describing photography basics—a document that must be formatted and properly organized before it is distributed to people on your mailing list. You will modify the document to ensure attractive line and paragraph spacing, and you will format text to draw attention to pertinent points. Formatted in columns, the document will be easy to read. The newsletter is somewhat informal, and you will make appropriate use of color, borders, and pictures so that it is well received by your audience.

Editing and Formatting

Basics of Photography

Camera Body

[illegible]

Lens

[illegible]

Juxtaposition

[illegible]

Rule of Thirds

[illegible]

Depth of Field

[illegible]

Blurry Images

[illegible]

[illegible]

Word 2016, Windows 10, Microsoft Corporation

FIGURE 1 Phillips Studio L Photography Document

CASE STUDY | Phillips Studio L Photography

Starting File	File to be Submitted
w02h1Studio	w02h3Studio_LastFirst

Text and Paragraph Formatting

When you format text, you change the way it looks. Your goal in designing a document is to ensure that it is well received and understood by an audience of readers. Seldom will your first attempt at designing a document be the only time you work with it. Inevitably, you will identify text that should be reworded or emphasized differently, paragraphs that might be more attractive in another alignment, or the need to bold, underline, or use italics to call attention to selected text. As you develop a document, or after reopening a previously completed document, you can make all these modifications and more. That process is called ***formatting***.

In this section, you will learn to change font and font size, and format text with character attributes, such as bold, underline, and italics. At the paragraph level, you will adjust paragraph and line spacing, set tab stops, change alignment, and apply bullets and numbering.

Applying Font Attributes

A ***font*** is a combination of typeface and type style. The font you select should reinforce the message of the text without calling attention to itself, and it should be consistent with the information you want to convey. For example, a paper prepared for a professional purpose, such as a resume, should have a standard font, such as Times New Roman, instead of one that looks casual or frilly, such as Freestyle Spirit or French Script MT. Additionally, you will want to minimize the variety of fonts in a document to maintain a professional look. Typically, you should use three or fewer fonts within a document. Headings might be formatted in one font, while body text is shown in another. This arrangement is the default for Word. However, Word allows you to format text in a variety of ways. Not only can you change a font, but you can apply text attributes, such as bold, italic, or underline, to selected text, or to text that you are about to type. Several of the most commonly used text formatting commands are located in the Font group on the Home tab.

Select Font Options

When you begin a new, blank document, the default font for the body of the document is Calibri 11 pt, which you can change for the current document if you like. To change the font for selected text, or for a document you are beginning, click the Font arrow and select a font from those displayed (see Figure 2). Each font shown is a sample of the actual font. With text selected, you can point to any font in the list, without clicking, to see a preview of the way selected text will look in that particular font. ***Live Preview*** enables you to select text and see the effects without clicking.

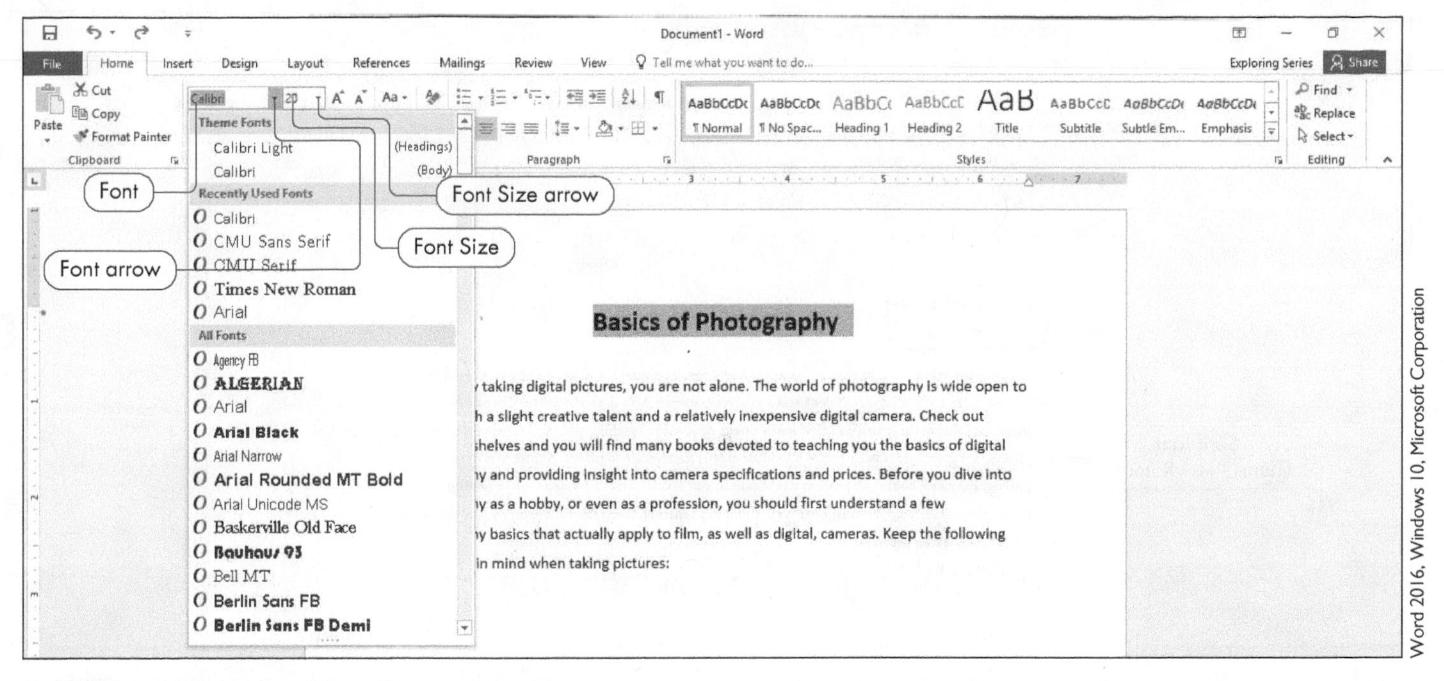

FIGURE 2 Select a Font and Font Size

You can also change font size when you click the Font Size arrow (refer to Figure 2) and select a point size. Each point size is equivalent to 1/72 of an inch; therefore, the larger the point size, the larger the font. A document often contains various sizes of the same font. For example, a document that includes levels of headings and subheadings might have major headings formatted in a larger point size than lesser headings.

A definitive characteristic of any font is the presence or absence of serifs, thin lines that begin and end the main strokes of each letter. A ***serif font*** contains a thin line or extension at the top and bottom of the primary strokes on characters. Times New Roman is an example of a serif font. A ***sans serif font*** (*sans* from the French word meaning *without*) does not contain the thin lines on characters. Calibri is a sans serif font.

Serifs help the eye connect one letter with the next and generally are used with large amounts of text. The paragraphs in this text, for example, are set in a serif font. Body text of newspapers and magazines is usually formatted in a serif font, as well. A sans serif font, such as Calibri, Arial, or Verdana, is more effective with smaller amounts of text such as titles, headlines, corporate logos, and webpages. For example, the heading *Select Font Options*, at the beginning of this section, is set in a sans serif font. Web developers often prefer a sans serif font because the extra strokes that begin and end letters in a serif font can blur or fade into a webpage, making it difficult to read. Examples of serif and sans serif fonts are shown in Figure 3.

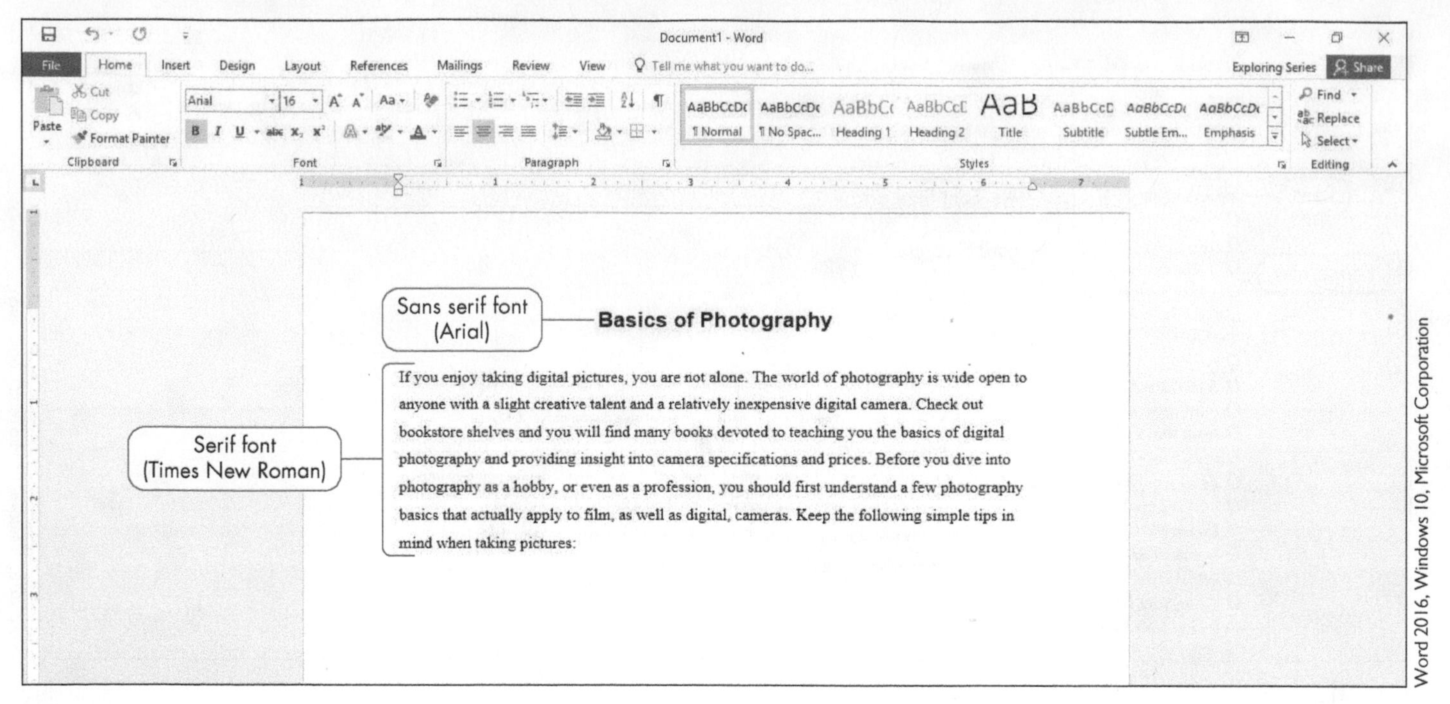

FIGURE 3 Serif and Sans Serif Fonts

> **TIP: FONT FOR BUSINESS DOCUMENTS**
> Most business documents are best formatted in 11- or 12-point serif font. A good choice is Times New Roman. A document designed for display on the Web is attractive in a blocky sans serif font, such as Arial, regardless of point size.

A second characteristic of a font is whether it is monospaced or proportional. A monospaced font (such as Courier New) uses the same amount of horizontal space for every character regardless of its width. Monospaced fonts are used in tables and financial projections where text must be precisely aligned, one character underneath another. A proportional font (such as Times New Roman or Arial) allocates space according to the width of the character. For example, the lowercase *m* is wider than the lowercase *i*. Proportional fonts create a professional appearance and are appropriate for most documents, such as research papers, status reports, and letters.

A typical Word installation includes support for TrueType and OpenType fonts. A TrueType font can be scaled to any size. Any output device, such as a printer, that Windows supports can recognize a TrueType font. An OpenType font is an advanced form of font that is designed for all platforms, including Windows and Macintosh. OpenType fonts incorporate a greater extension of the basic character set. Most fonts included in a typical Word installation are OpenType.

Change Text Appearance

STEP 1 Commonly accessed commands related to font settings are located in the Font group on the Home tab (see Figure 4). Word enables you to bold, underline, and italicize text, apply text highlighting, change font color, and work with various text effects and other formatting options from commands in the Font group. For even more choices, click the Font Dialog Box Launcher in the Font group and select from additional formatting commands available in the Font dialog box (see Figure 5). With text selected, you will see the Mini toolbar (see Figure 6) when you move the pointer near the selection, making it more convenient to quickly select a format (instead of locating it on the Ribbon or using a keyboard shortcut).

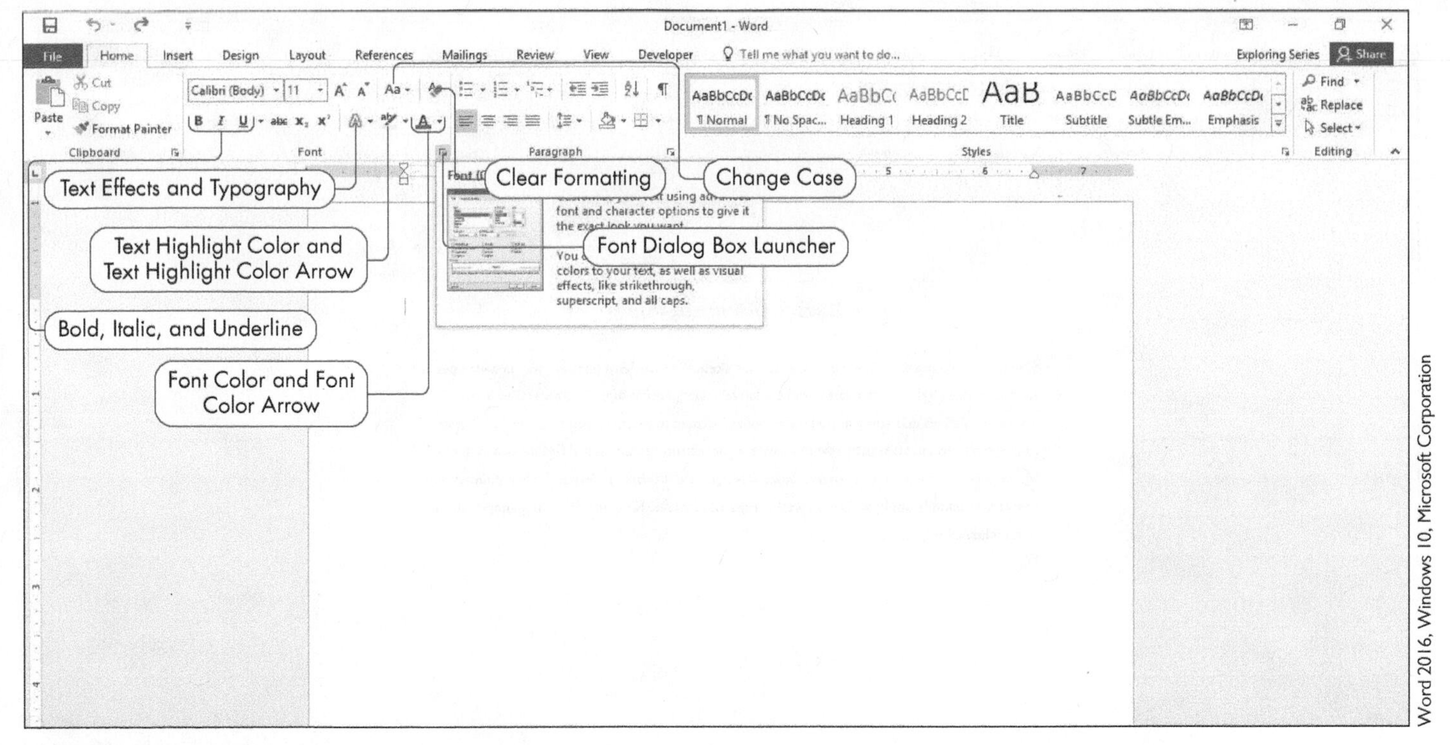

Word 2016, Windows 10, Microsoft Corporation

FIGURE 4 Font Commands

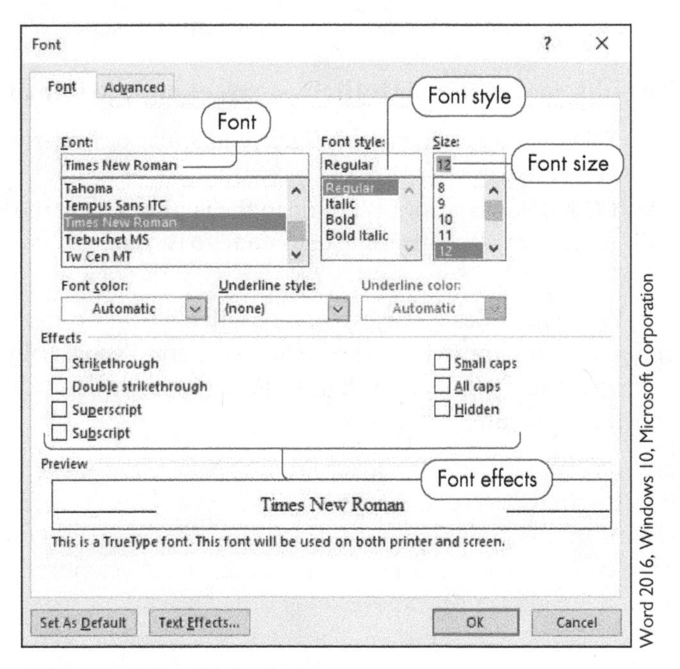

Word 2016, Windows 10, Microsoft Corporation

FIGURE 5 Font Dialog Box

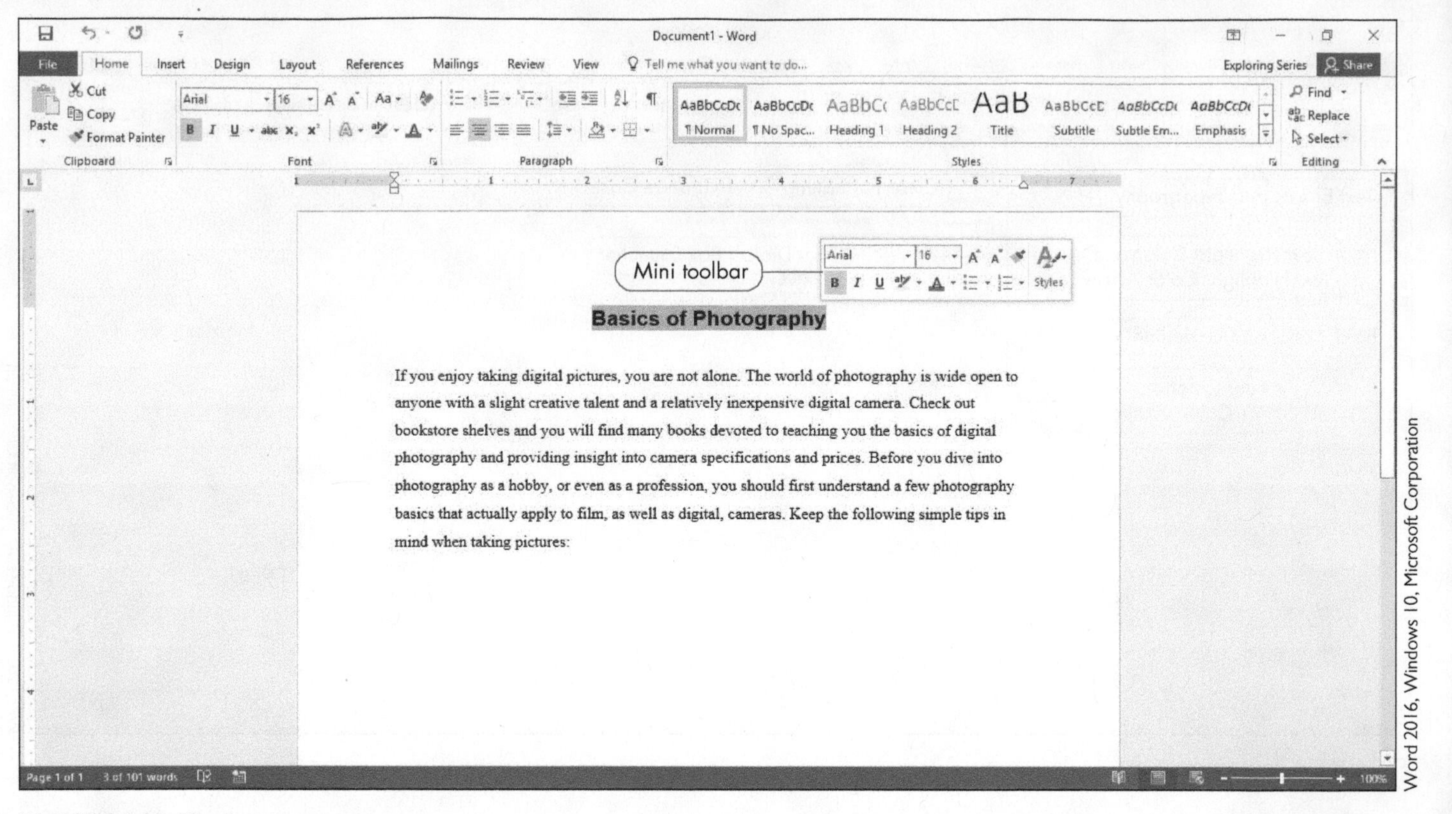

FIGURE 6 Mini Toolbar

To bold, underline, or italicize text, complete one of the following steps:

- Select text to be formatted. Click Bold, Italic, or Underline in the Font group on the Home tab.
- Click Bold, Italic, or Underline in the Font group on the Home tab and type text to be formatted. Click the same command to turn off the formatting effect.

Word includes a variety of text effects that enable you to add a shadow, outline, reflection, or glow to text. The Text Effects and Typography gallery (see Figure 7) provides access to those effects as well as to WordArt styles, number styles, ligatures, and stylistic sets that you can apply to text.

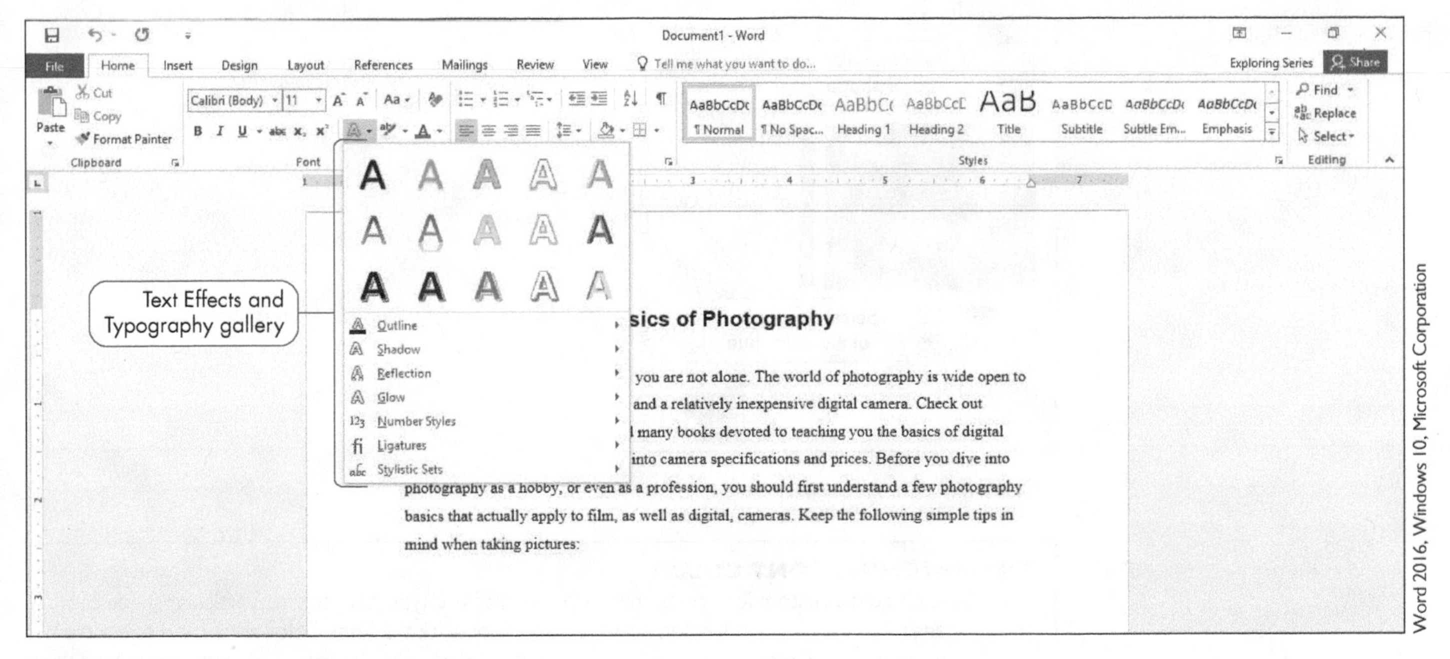

FIGURE 7 Text Effects and Typography Gallery

A ligature is two letters that are crafted together into a single character, or glyph. For example, you often see the letters *f* and *i* bound together in a ligature. A stylistic set is a collection of letter styles that you can apply to OpenType fonts. Some fonts include more stylistic sets than others. To explore advanced font settings, click the Font Dialog Box Launcher (refer to Figure 4) and click the Advanced tab (refer to Figure 5). Select a ligature and stylistic set. Stylistic sets and ligatures are often used in the preparation of formal documents such as wedding invitations.

As a student, you are likely to highlight important parts of textbooks, magazine articles, and other documents. You probably use a highlighting marker to shade parts of text you want to remember or to which you want to draw attention. Word provides an equivalent tool with which you can highlight text you want to stand out or to locate easily—the Text Highlight Color command, located in the Font group on the Home tab (refer to Figure 4).

To highlight text *before* selecting it, complete the following steps:

1. Click Text Highlight Color to select the current highlight color or click the Text Highlight Color arrow and choose another color. The pointer resembles a pen when you move it over the document.
2. Drag across text to highlight it.
3. Click Text Highlight Color or press Esc to stop highlighting.

To highlight text *after* selecting it, click Text Highlight Color or click the Text Highlight Color arrow and choose another color. You can remove highlights in the same manner, except that you will select No Color.

When creating a document, you must consider when and how to capitalize. Titles are occasionally in all caps, sentences begin with a capital letter, and headings typically capitalize each key word. Use the Change Case option in the Font group on the Home tab to quickly change the capitalization of document text (refer to Figure 4).

By default, text is shown in black as you type a document. For a bit of interest, or to draw attention to text within a document, you can change the font color of previously typed text or of text that you are about to type. Click the Font Color arrow (refer to Figure 4) and select from a gallery of colors. For even more choices, click More Colors and select from a variety of hues or shades. As shown in Figure 8, you can click the Custom tab in the Colors dialog box and click to select a color hue, while honing in on a variation of that hue by dragging along a continuum.

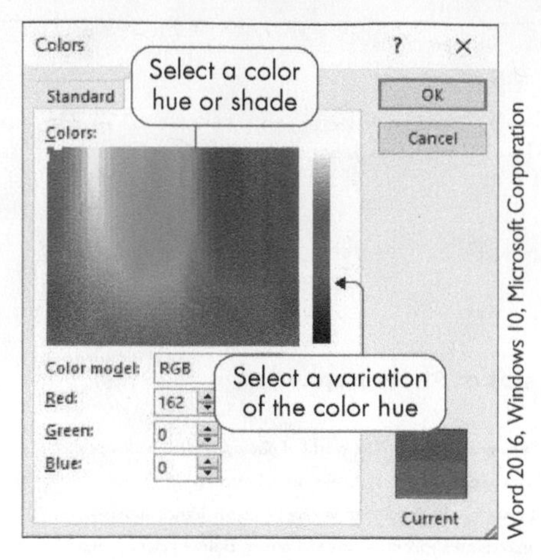

FIGURE 8 Apply a Custom Color

> **TIP: MATCHING FONT COLOR**
> If you have created a custom font color, matching text that you type later to that particular shade can be a challenge. It is easy to match color, however, when you click the Font Color arrow and select the shade from the Recent Colors area.

Formatting a Paragraph

Formatting selected text is only one way to alter the appearance of a document. You can also change the alignment, indentation, tab stops, or line spacing for any paragraph within the document. Recall that Word defines a paragraph as text followed by a hard return, or even a hard return on a line by itself (indicating a blank paragraph). You can include borders or shading for added emphasis around selected paragraphs, and you can number paragraphs or enhance them with bullets. The Paragraph group on the Home tab contains several paragraph formatting commands (see Figure 9). If you are formatting only one paragraph, you do not have to select the entire paragraph. Simply click to place the insertion point within the paragraph and apply a paragraph format. However, if you are formatting several paragraphs, you must select them before formatting.

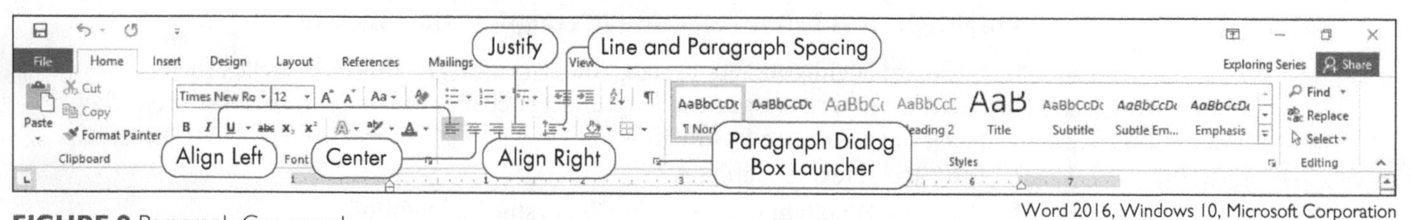

Word 2016, Windows 10, Microsoft Corporation

FIGURE 9 Paragraph Commands

Select Paragraph Alignment

Alignment refers to how the text is positioned relative to the margins. ***Left alignment*** is the most common alignment, often seen in letters, reports, and memos. When you begin a new blank Word document, paragraphs are left aligned by default. Text begins evenly at the left margin and ends in an uneven ("ragged") right edge. The opposite of left alignment is ***right alignment***, a setting in which text is aligned at the right margin with a ragged left edge. Short lines including dates, figure captions, and headers are often right aligned. A ***center alignment*** positions text horizontally in the center of a line, with an equal distance from both the left and right margins. Report titles and major headings are typically centered. Finally, ***justified alignment*** spreads text evenly between the left and right margins so that text begins at the left margin and ends uniformly at the right margin. Newspaper and magazine articles are often justified. Such text alignment often causes awkward spacing as text is stretched to fit evenly between margins. Figure 10 shows examples of paragraph alignments.

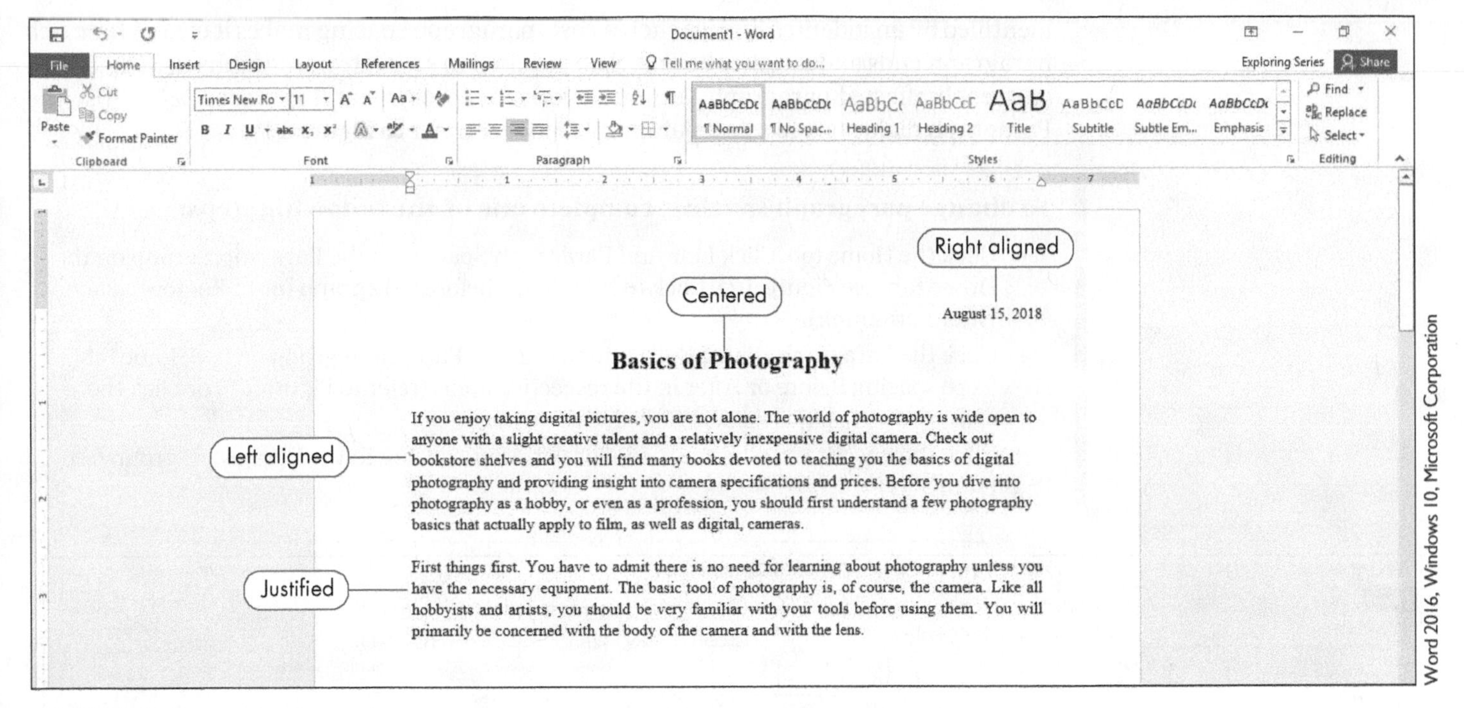

FIGURE 10 Paragraph Alignment

To change paragraph alignment, select text (or click to position the insertion point in a paragraph, if only one paragraph is to be affected) and select an alignment from the Paragraph group on the Home tab (refer to Figure 9). You can also change alignment by making a selection from the Paragraph dialog box (see Figure 11), which opens when you click the Paragraph Dialog Box Launcher (refer to Figure 9).

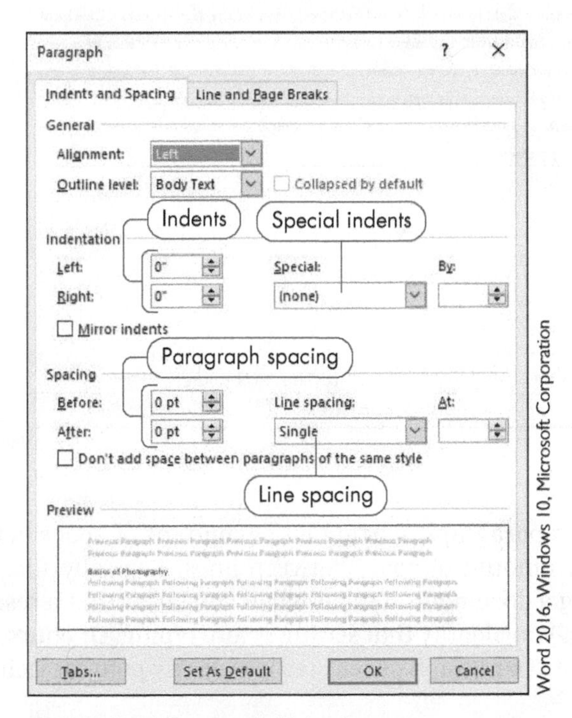

FIGURE 11 Paragraph Dialog Box

Select Line and Paragraph Spacing

Paragraph spacing is the amount of space between paragraphs, measured in points. (Recall that one point is 1/72 of an inch.) Paragraph spacing is a good way to differentiate between paragraphs, especially if the beginning of each paragraph is not clearly identified by an indented line. In such a case, paragraph spacing makes it clear where one paragraph ends and another begins. Spacing used to separate paragraphs usually comes *after* each affected paragraph, although you can specify that it is placed *before*. Use the Paragraph dialog box to select paragraph spacing (refer to Figure 11).

To change paragraph spacing, complete one of the following steps:

- Click the Home tab. Click Line and Paragraph Spacing in the Paragraph group on the Home tab (see Figure 12). Click to Add Space Before Paragraph (or to Remove Space After Paragraph).
- Click the Paragraph Dialog Box Launcher in the Paragraph group on the Home tab. Type spacing Before or After in the respective areas (refer to Figure 11) or click the spin arrows to adjust spacing. Click OK.
- Click the Layout tab. Change the Before or After spacing in the Paragraph group (see Figure 13).

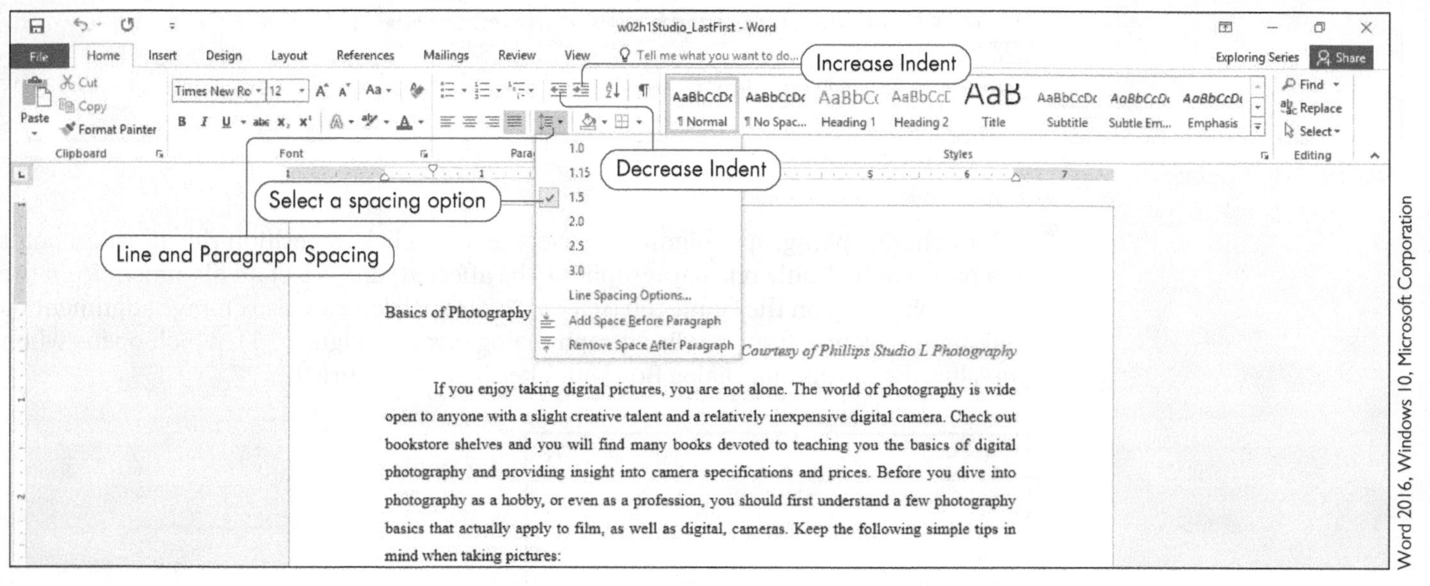

FIGURE 12 Spacing Options

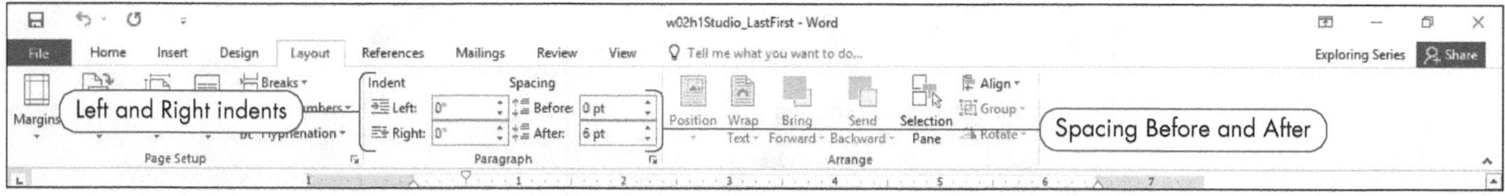

FIGURE 13 Paragraph Spacing and Indents

Just as paragraph spacing is the amount of space between paragraphs, ***line spacing*** is the amount of space between lines. Typically, line spacing is determined before beginning a document, such as when you know that a research paper should be double-spaced, so you identify that setting before typing. Of course, you can change line spacing of a current paragraph or selected text at any point as well.

To change the line spacing, complete one of the following steps:

- Click the Home tab. Click Line and Paragraph Spacing (refer to Figure 12). Select the line spacing you want to use or click Line Spacing Options for more choices.
- Click the Paragraph Dialog Box Launcher on the Home tab. Click the Line spacing arrow and select spacing (refer to Figure 11). Click OK.

The most common line spacing options are single, double, or 1.5 lines. Word provides those options and more. From the Paragraph dialog box (refer to Figure 11), you can select Exactly, At Least, or Multiple. To specify an exact point size for spacing, select Exactly. If you select At Least, you will indicate a minimum line spacing size while allowing Word to adjust the height, if necessary, to accommodate such features as drop caps (oversized letters that sometimes begin paragraphs). The Multiple setting enables you to select a line spacing interval other than single, double, or 1.5 lines.

Select Indents

STEP 2 »» An ***indent*** is a setting associated with how part of a paragraph is distanced from one or more margins. One of the most common indents is a ***first line indent***, in which the first line of each paragraph is set off from the left margin. For instance, your English instructor might require that the first line of each paragraph in a writing assignment is indented 0.5" from the left margin, which is a typical first line indent. If you have ever prepared a bibliography for a research paper, you have most likely specified a ***hanging indent***, where the first line of a source begins at the left margin, but all other lines in the source are indented. Indenting an entire paragraph from the left margin is a ***left indent***, while indenting an entire paragraph from the right margin is a ***right indent***. A lengthy quote is often set apart by indenting from both the left and right margins.

Using the Paragraph dialog box (refer to Figure 11), you can select an indent setting for one or more paragraphs. First line and hanging indents are considered special indents. You can select left and right indents from either the Paragraph dialog box or from the Paragraph group on the Layout tab (refer to Figure 13).

You can use the Word ruler to set indents. If the ruler does not display above the document space, click the View tab and click Ruler (see Figure 14). The three-part indicator at the left side of the ruler enables you to set a left indent, a hanging indent, or a first line indent. Drag the desired indent along the ruler to apply the indent to the current paragraph (or selected paragraphs). Figure 14 shows the first line indent moved to the 0.5" mark, resulting in the first line of a paragraph being indented by 0.5".

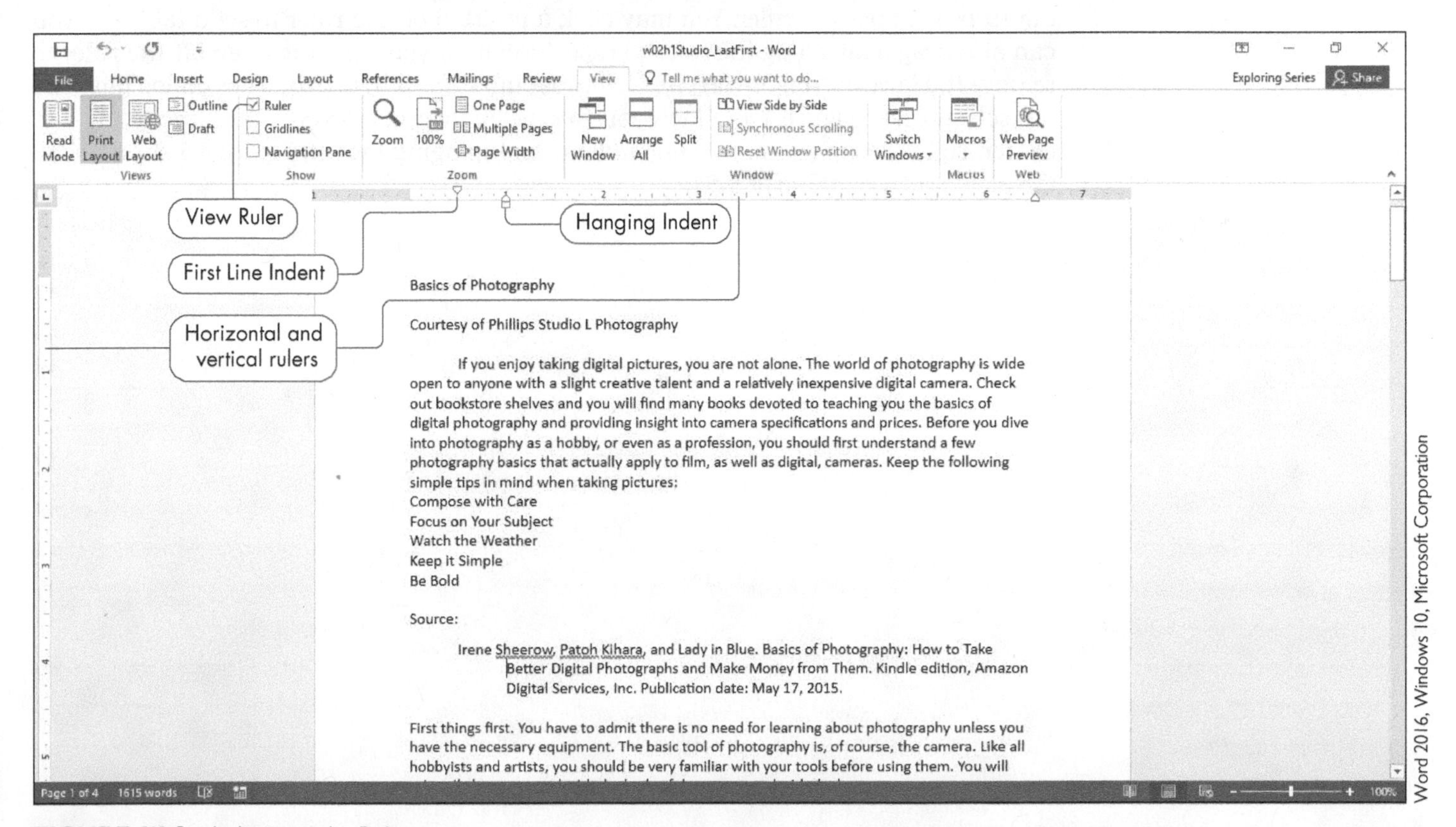

FIGURE 14 Set Indents on the Ruler

Set Tab Stops

STEP 3 ›› A ***tab stop*** is a marker that specifies a position for aligning text. By using tab stops, you can easily arrange text in columns or position text a certain distance from the left or right margins. Tabs enable you to add organization to a document, arranging text in easy-to-read columns. A table of contents is an example of tabbed text, as is a restaurant menu. The most common tab stops are left, right, center, and decimal. By default, a left tab is set every 0.5" when you start a new document. Each time you press Tab on the keyboard, the insertion point will move to the right by 0.5". Typically, you would set a first line indent or simply press Tab to indent the first line of each new paragraph within a document. Table 1 describes the types of tabs.

TABLE 1 Tab Markers

Tab Icon on Ruler	Type of Tab	Function
∟	Left	Sets the start position on the left, so as you type text moves to the right of the tab setting.
⊥	Center	Sets the middle point of the text you type. Whatever you type will be centered on that tab setting.
┘	Right	Sets the start position on the right, so as you type text moves to the left of that tab setting and aligns on the right.
⊥.	Decimal	Aligns numbers on a decimal point. Regardless of how long the number, each number lines up with the decimal point in the same position.
|	Bar	This tab does not position text or decimals but inserts a vertical bar at the tab setting. This bar is useful as a separator for text printed on the same line.

Tab stops that you set override default tabs. For example, suppose you set a left tab at 1". That means the default tab of 0.5" is no longer in effect. The easiest way to set tab stops is to use the ruler. You may click a position on the ruler to set a tab stop. You can also drag a tab along the ruler to reposition it, or you can drag a tab off the ruler to remove it. However, a more precise way to set tab stops is to use the Tabs dialog box. The tab selector (see Figure 15) allows you to repeatedly cycle through tabs, including left, center, right, decimal, bar, first line indent, and hanging indent. Figure 15 shows a left tab at 1" and a right tab at 5.5".

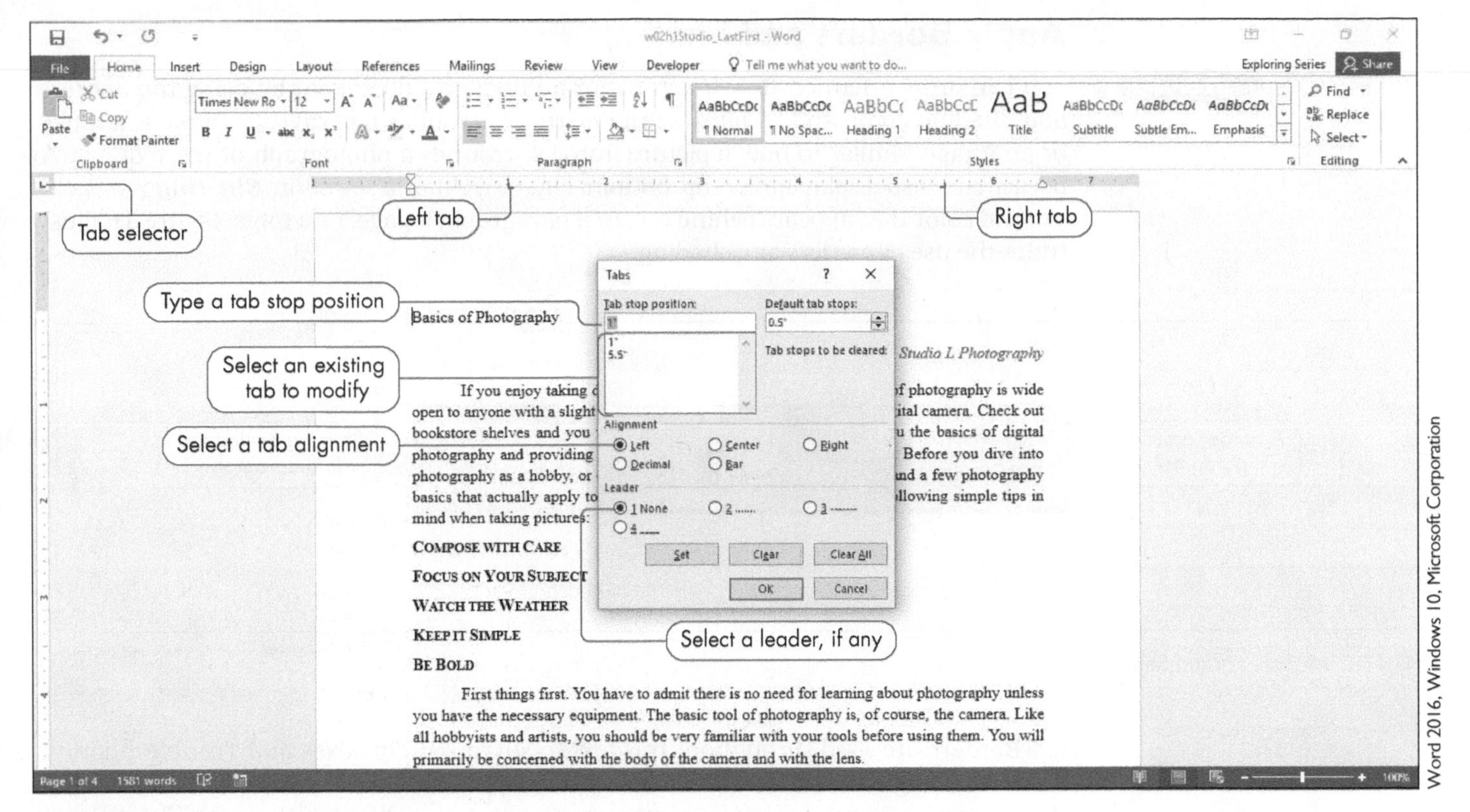

FIGURE 15 Set Tab Stops

> **TIP: MANAGE TAB STOPS**
> Tab stops can be inserted and applied in two ways. First, you can select text and then set the tab stops, which applies tabs to the selected text. Second, you can set a tab stop and then type text, which applies tab stops to text typed after setting tabs.

To include leaders (the series of dots or hyphens that leads the reader's eye across the page to connect two columns of information), use the Tabs dialog box, shown in Figure 15. The row of dots that typically connects a food item with its price on a restaurant menu is an example of a leader.

To set a tab with a leader, complete the following steps:

1. Click the Paragraph Dialog Box Launcher in the Paragraph group on the Home tab and click Tabs from the Indents and Spacing tab. Alternatively, double-click a tab on the ruler.
2. Type the location where you want to set the tab. The number you type is assumed to be in inches, so typing *2* would place a tab at 2".
3. Select a tab alignment (Left, Right, etc.).
4. Specify a leader.
5. Click OK (or click Set and continue specifying tabs).

> **TIP: DELETING TAB STOPS**
> To manually delete a tab stop you have set, select the text first, then simply drag the tab stop off the ruler. An alternative is to click the Paragraph Dialog Box Launcher, click Tabs, select the tab (in the Tab stop position box), and then click Clear. Click OK.

Apply Borders and Shading

You can draw attention to a document or an area of a document by using the Borders and Shading command. A ***border*** is a line that surrounds a paragraph, a page, a table, or an image, similar to how a picture frame surrounds a photograph or piece of art. A border can also display at the top, bottom, left, or right of a selection. ***Shading*** is a background color that appears behind text in a paragraph, a page, or a table. Figure 16 illustrates the use of borders and shading.

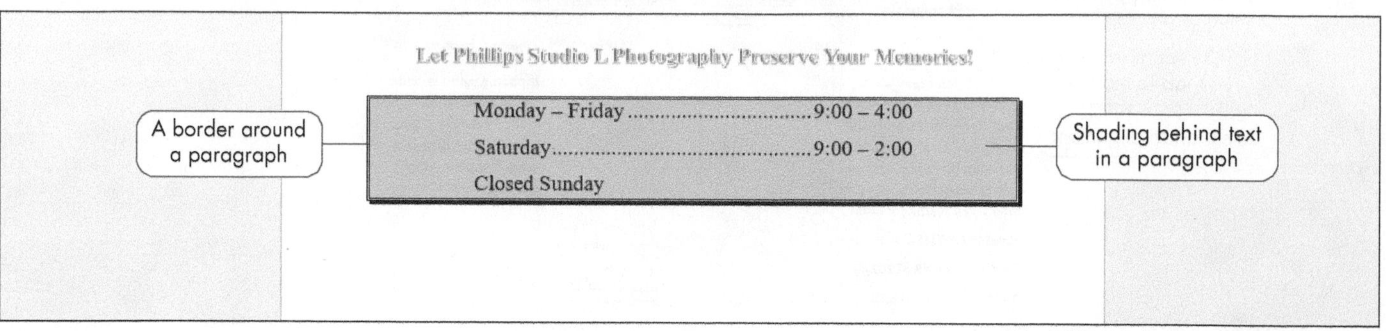

FIGURE 16 Borders and Shading

Borders are used throughout this text to surround Tip boxes and Troubleshooting areas. You might surround a particular paragraph with a border, possibly even shading the paragraph, to set it apart from other text on the page, drawing the reader's attention to its contents. You must first select all paragraphs to which you will apply the border or shading formats. If you have not selected text, any border or shading you identify will be applied to the paragraph in which the insertion point is located.

When you click the Borders arrow in the Paragraph group on the Home tab and select Borders and Shading, the Borders and Shading dialog box displays (see Figure 17). There are three tabs in the dialog box: Borders, Page Border, and Shading. The paragraph border settings are on the Borders tab. Besides the None setting, you can format your borders using a Box, Shadow, 3-D, or Custom format. A Box border places a uniform border around a paragraph. A Shadow border places thicker lines at the right and bottom of the bordered area. The 3-D border, on the other hand, adds more dimension to the border. The Custom border enables the user to select a specific style, color, width, and side. The Preview area displays a diagram of the border options that you select.

To apply a paragraph border to selected text, complete the following steps:

1. Select text. Click the Borders arrow in the Paragraph group on the Home tab.
2. Click Borders and Shading. Ensure that the Borders tab is selected.
3. Select the border setting of your choice (see Figure 17).
4. Select the style of the line of your choice.
5. Select the color for the border.
6. Select the width of the border.
7. Click OK.

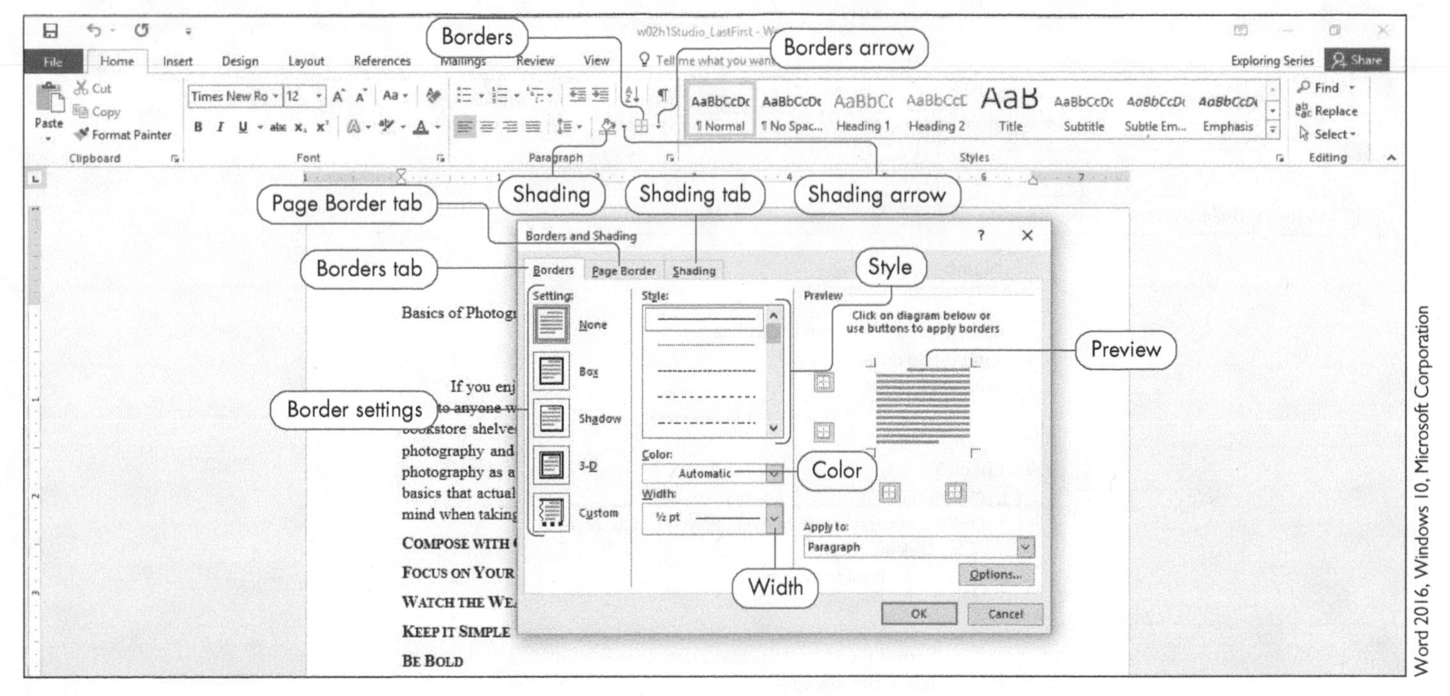

FIGURE 17 Select a Border

The Page Border tab in the Borders and Shading dialog box provides controls that you use to place a decorative border around one or more selected pages. As with a paragraph border, you can place the border around the entire page, or you can select one or more sides. The Page Border tab also provides an additional option to use a preselected image as a border instead of ordinary lines. Note that it is appropriate to use page borders on documents such as flyers, newsletters, and invitations, but not on formal documents such as research papers and professional reports.

To apply shading to one or more selected paragraphs, complete the following steps:

1. Click the Shading arrow in the Paragraph group on the Home tab.
2. Select a solid color, or a lighter or darker variation of the color, for the shaded background. Or, click More Colors for even more selections. You can also select shading from the Shading tab of the Borders and Shading dialog box (see Figure 17).
3. Click OK.

Create Bulleted and Numbered Lists

STEP 5 A list organizes information by topic or in a sequence. Use a ***numbered list*** if the list is a sequence of steps. If the list is not of a sequential nature, but is a simple itemization of points, use a ***bulleted list*** (see Figure 18). The numerical sequence in a numbered list is automatically updated to accommodate additions or deletions, which means that if you add or remove items, the list items are renumbered. A multilevel list extends a numbered or bulleted list to several levels, and it, too, is updated automatically when topics are added or deleted. You create each of these lists from the Paragraph group on the Home tab.

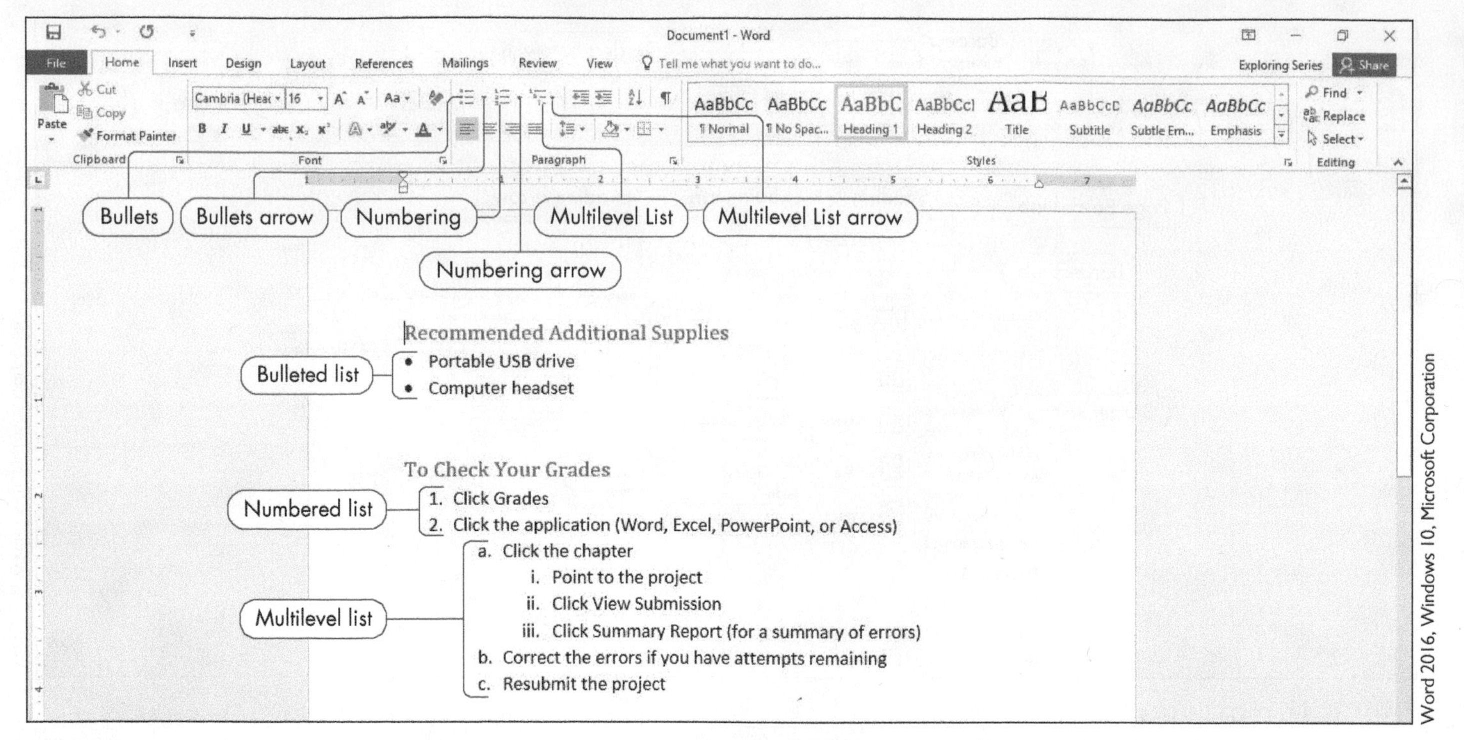

FIGURE 18 Bullets and Numbering

To apply bullets, numbering, or multiple levels to a list, complete the following steps:

1. Select the items to be bulleted or numbered.
2. Complete one of the following steps:
   - Click Bullets (or Numbering) to apply the default bullet or numbering style.
   - Click the Bullets (or Numbering) arrow in the Paragraph group on the Home tab and point to one of the predefined symbols or numbering styles in the library. A preview of the style will display in your document. Click the style you want to use.
   - Click Multilevel List and select a style to apply multiple levels to a list.

You can also apply bullets or numbering before you type the items by clicking Bullets (or Numbering), typing the list items, and clicking Bullets (or Numbering) again to turn off the toggle.

To define a new bullet or customize the formatting (such as color or special effect) of a selected bullet, complete the following steps:

1. Click the Bullets arrow in the Paragraph group on the Home tab.
2. Click Define New Bullet.
3. Make selections from the Define New Bullet dialog box.
4. Click OK.

TIP: RENUMBERING A LIST

Especially when creating several numbered lists in a document, you might find that Word continues the numbering sequence from one list to the next, when your intention was to begin numbering each list at 1. To restart numbering at a new value, right-click the item that is not numbered correctly, and click Restart at 1. Alternatively, you can click the Numbering arrow and select Set Numbering Value. Indicate a starting value in the subsequent dialog box and click OK.

1. Describe the difference between a serif and sans serif font. Give examples of when you might use each.
2. What could cause the larger space between lines of bullets, and how would you correct it so that the bulleted items are single spaced?
3. If you use Word to create a restaurant menu, what type of tabs would you use, and approximately how would you space them?
4. You are preparing a document with a list of items to bring for an upcoming camping trip. What Word feature could you use to draw attention to the list?

Hands-On Exercises

Skills covered: Select Font Options • Change Text Appearance • Select Paragraph Alignment • Select Paragraph Spacing • Select Indents • Set Tab Stops • Apply Borders and Shading • Create Bulleted and Numbered Lists

1 Text and Paragraph Formatting

The newsletter you are developing needs a lot of work. You want to format it so it is much easier to read. After selecting an appropriate font and font size, you will emphasize selected text with bold and italic text formatting. Paragraphs must be spaced so they are easy to read. You know that to be effective, a document must capture the reader's attention while conveying a message. You will begin the process of formatting and preparing the newsletter in this exercise.

STEP 1 » SELECT FONT OPTIONS AND CHANGE TEXT APPEARANCE

The newsletter will be printed and distributed by mail. As a printed document, you know that certain font options are better suited for reading. Specifically, you want to use a serif font in an easy-to-read size. Refer to Figure 19 as you complete Step 1.

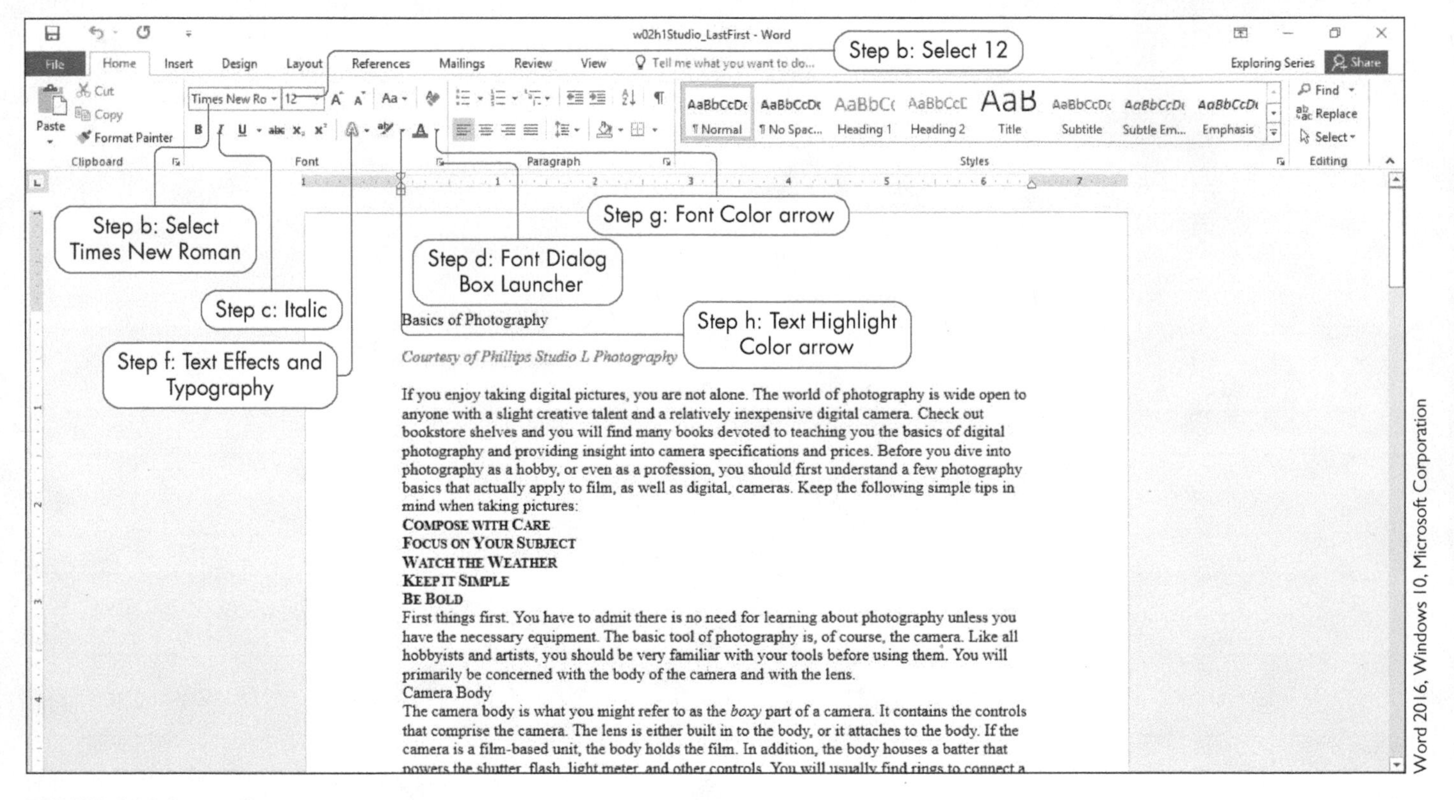

FIGURE 19 Format Text

a. Open *w02h1Studio* and save it as **w02h1Studio_LastFirst**.

> **TROUBLESHOOTING:** If you make any major mistakes in this exercise, you can close the file, open *w02h1Studio* again, and then start this exercise over.

b. Press **Ctrl+A** to select all of the text in the document. Click the **Font arrow** in the Font group on the Home tab and scroll to select **Times New Roman**. Click the **Font Size arrow** in the Font group and select **12**.

You use a 12-pt serif font on the whole document because it is easier to read in print.

c. Select the second paragraph in the document, *Courtesy of Phillips Studio L Photography*. Click **Italic** on the Mini toolbar. Locate and double-click **boxy** in the paragraph below Camera Body. Click **Italic** in the Font group.

> **TROUBLESHOOTING:** If the Mini toolbar does not display or disappears, click Italic in the Font group on the Home tab.

d. Select the five paragraphs beginning with *Compose with Care* and ending with *Be Bold*. Click the **Font Dialog Box Launcher** in the Font group.

   The Font dialog box displays with font options.

e. Ensure that the Font tab is displayed in the Font dialog box, and click **Bold** in the Font style box. Click to select the **Small caps check box** under Effects. Click **OK**.

f. Press **Ctrl+End** to move the insertion point to the end of the document. Select the last paragraph in the document, *Let Phillips Studio L Photography Preserve Your Memories!* Click **Text Effects and Typography** in the Font group. Select **Fill – Blue, Accent 1, Outline – Background 1, Hard Shadow – Accent 1** (third row, third column). Change the font size of the selected text to **16**. Click anywhere to deselect the text.

g. Press **Ctrl+Home** to position the insertion point at the beginning of the document. Select the second paragraph in the document, *Courtesy of Phillips Studio L Photography*. Click the **Font Color arrow** and select **Blue, Accent 5, Darker 25%** (fifth row, ninth column).

h. Select the words *you should consider how to become a better photographer* in the paragraph under the *Composition* heading. Click the **Text Highlight Color arrow** and select **Yellow**.

i. Press **Ctrl+Home**. Click the **Review tab** and click **Spelling & Grammar** in the Proofing group to check spelling and grammar. Ignore any possible grammatical errors, but correct spelling mistakes.

j. Save the document.

STEP 2 ›› SELECT PARAGRAPH ALIGNMENT, SPACING, AND INDENT

The lines of the newsletter are too close together. It is difficult to tell where one paragraph ends and the next begins, and the layout of the text is not very pleasing. Overall, you will adjust line and paragraph spacing, and apply indents where necessary. Refer to Figure 20 as you complete Step 2.

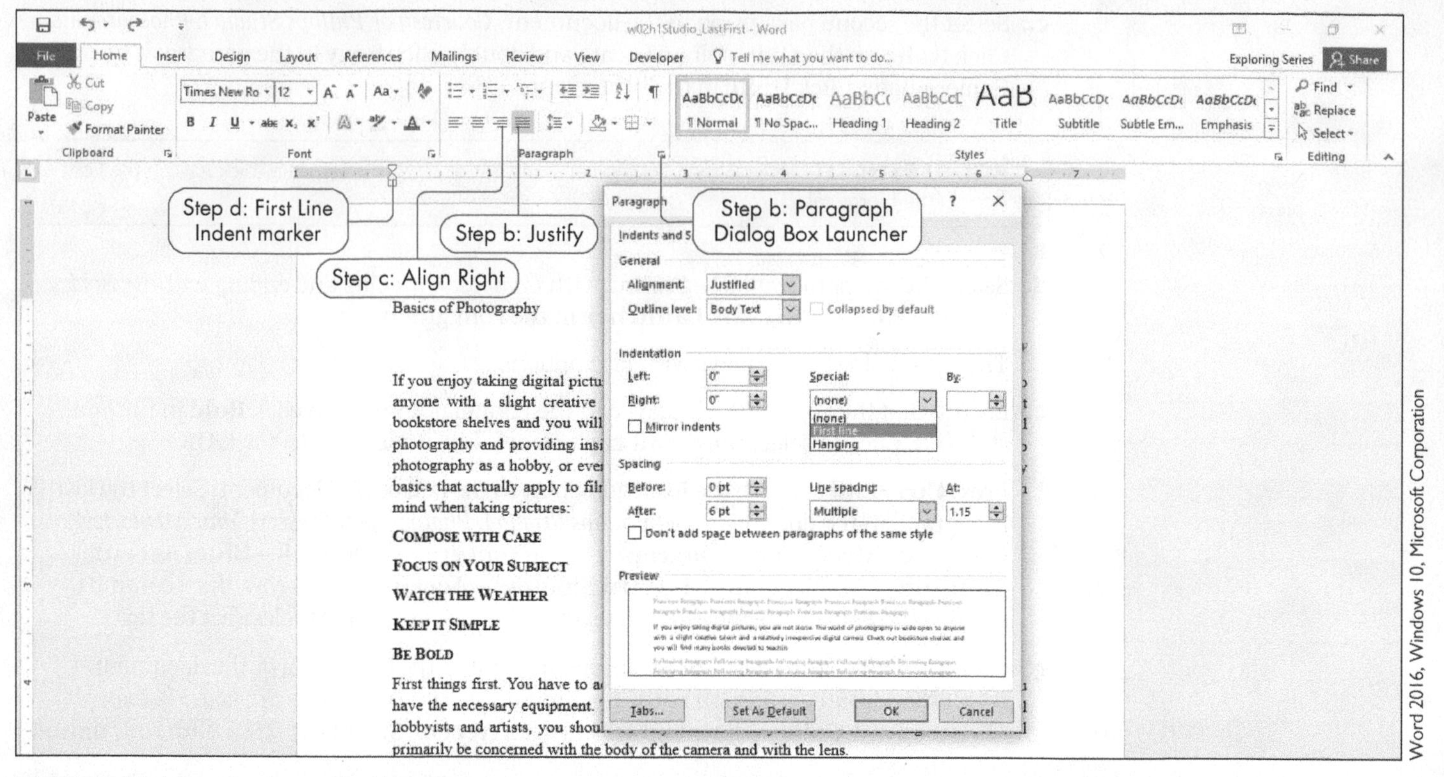

FIGURE 20 Adjust Spacing and Indents

a. Select most of the document beginning with the sentence *If you enjoy taking digital pictures* and ending with *emotion expressed before even greeting Santa.* Click the **Home tab**. Click **Line and Paragraph Spacing** in the Paragraph group. Select **1.15**. Do not deselect the text.

All lines within the selected text are spaced by 1.15.

b. Click **Justify** in the Paragraph group. Click the **Paragraph Dialog Box Launcher**. With the Indents and Spacing tab selected, click the **After spin arrow** in the Spacing section to increase spacing after to **6 pt**. Click **OK**. Click anywhere to deselect the text.

You have placed 6 pt spacing after each paragraph in the selected area. Selected paragraphs are also aligned with justify, which means text is evenly distributed between the left and right margins.

c. Press **Ctrl+End**. Click anywhere on the last paragraph in the document, *Let Phillips Studio L Photography Preserve Your Memories!* Click **Center** in the Paragraph group. Press **Ctrl+Home**. Click anywhere on the second line of text in the document, *Courtesy of Phillips Studio L Photography*. Click **Align Right** in the Paragraph group.

d. Click the **View tab**, and click the **Ruler check box** in the Show group to select it. Click anywhere in the first body paragraph, beginning with *If you enjoy taking digital pictures*. Click the **Home tab**, and click the **Paragraph Dialog Box Launcher**. Click the **Special arrow** in the Indentation group and select **First line**. Click **OK**. Click anywhere in the paragraph beginning with *First things first*. Position the pointer on the First Line Indent marker on the ruler and drag the marker to the **0.5"** mark on the horizontal ruler.

The first line of both multiline paragraphs that begin the document are indented by 0.5 inches.

e. Save the document.

STEP 3 ›› SET TAB STOPS

You realize that you left off the studio hours and want to include them at the end of the document. Refer to Figure 21 as you complete Step 3.

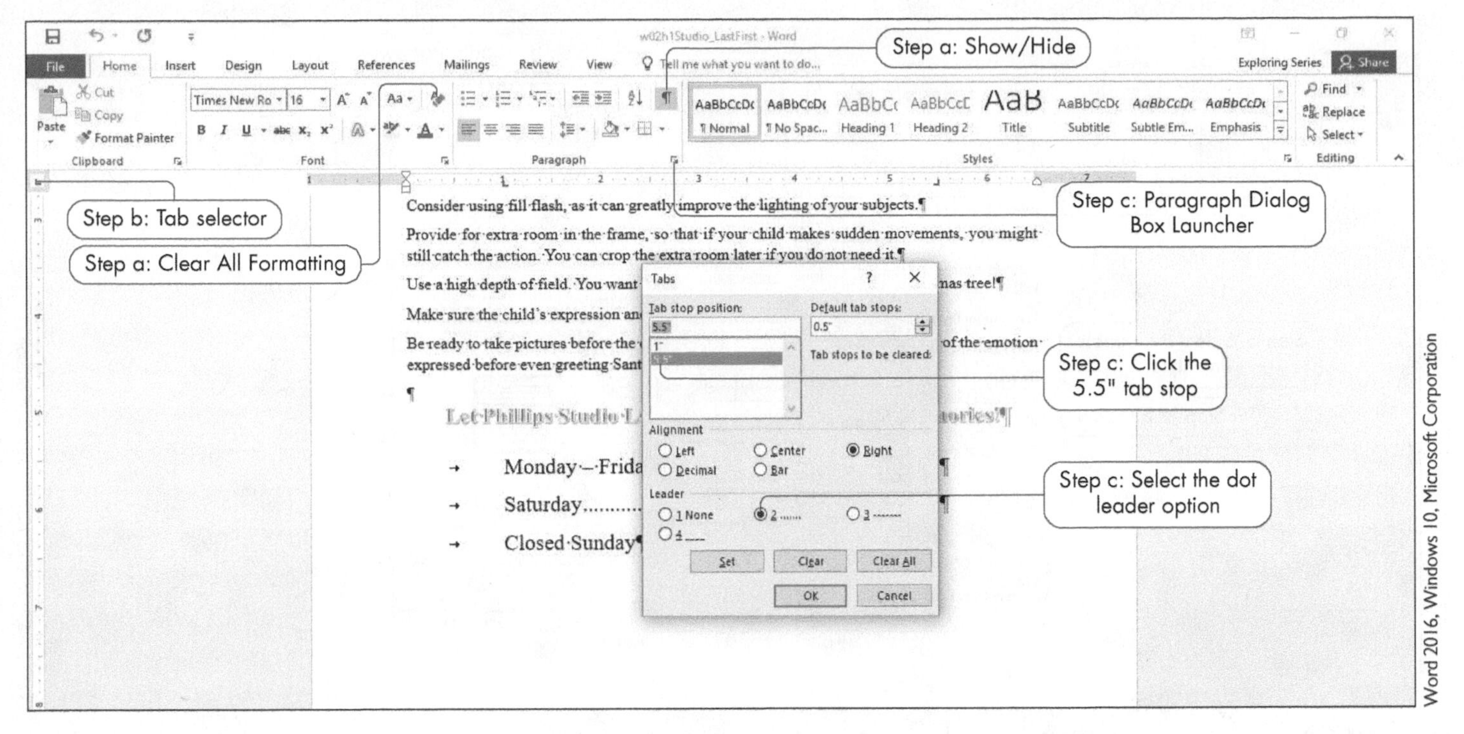

FIGURE 21 Set Tab Stops

a. Press **Ctrl+End**. Click **Show/Hide** in the Paragraph group to display nonprinting characters. Press **Enter** twice. Click **Clear All Formatting** in the Font group on the Home tab. Select **Times New Roman font** and **16 pt size**.

You clicked Clear All Formatting so that the text effect formatting from the line above the insertion point is not carried forward to text that you will type next.

b. Ensure the tab selector (shown at the top of the vertical ruler) specifies a Left Tab and click at **1"** on the ruler. Click the **tab selector** twice to select a Right Tab and click at **5.5"** on the ruler.

You set a left tab at 1" and a right tab at 5.5".

> **TROUBLESHOOTING:** If the tabs you set are incorrectly placed on the ruler, click Undo in the Quick Access Toolbar and repeat Step b. You can also simply drag a tab off the ruler to remove it, or drag it along the ruler to reposition it.

c. Click the **Paragraph Dialog Box Launcher** and click **Tabs** at the bottom-left corner. Click **5.5"** in the Tab stop position box. Click **2** in the Leader section and click **OK**.

You modified the right tab to include dot leaders, which means dots will display before text at the right tab.

d. Press **Tab**. Type **Monday – Friday** and press **Tab**. Type **9:00 – 4:00**. Press **Enter**. Press **Tab**. Type **Saturday** and press **Tab**. Type **9:00 – 2:00**. Press **Enter**. Press **Tab**. Type **Closed Sunday**.

e. Save the document.

STEP 4 » APPLY BORDERS AND SHADING

To draw attention to the business hours, you will shade and border the information you typed. Refer to Figure 22 as you complete Step 4.

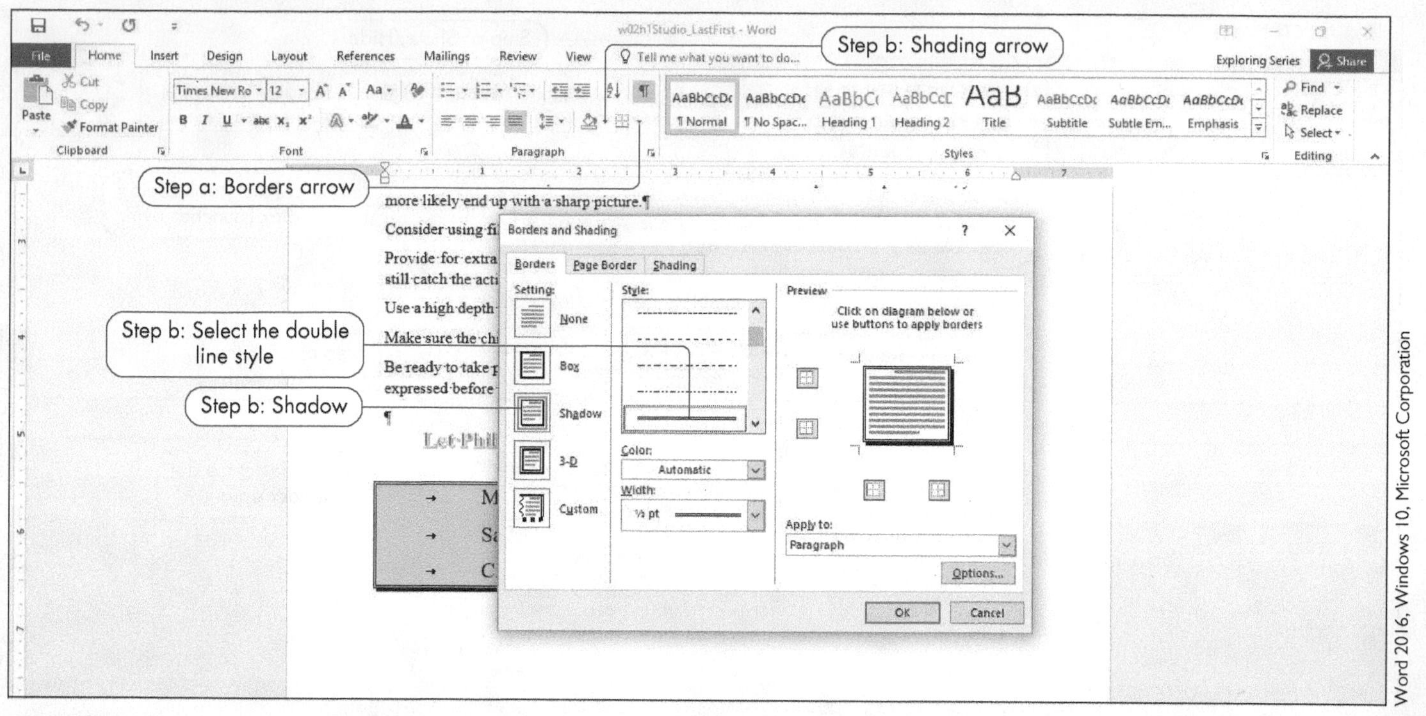

FIGURE 22 Apply Borders and Shade Text

a. Select the three paragraphs at the end of the document, beginning with *Monday – Friday* and ending with *Closed Sunday*. Click the **Borders arrow** in the Paragraph group on the Home tab and select **Borders and Shading**.

> **TROUBLESHOOTING:** If you click Borders instead of the Borders arrow, you will not see the Borders and Shading dialog box and the most recent border will be applied to selected text. Click Undo on the Quick Access Toolbar, click the Borders arrow, and then click Borders and Shading.

b. Click **Shadow** in the Setting section. Scroll through the Style box and select the seventh style—**double line**. Click **OK**. Do not deselect the text. Click the **Shading arrow** and select **Blue, Accent 1, Lighter 60%** (third row, fifth column). Click anywhere to deselect the text.

   Studio hours are bordered and shaded.

c. Save the document.

STEP 5 ›› CREATE BULLETED AND NUMBERED LISTS

At several points in the newsletter, you include either a list of items or a sequence of steps. You will add bullets to the lists and number the steps. Refer to Figure 23 as you complete Step 5.

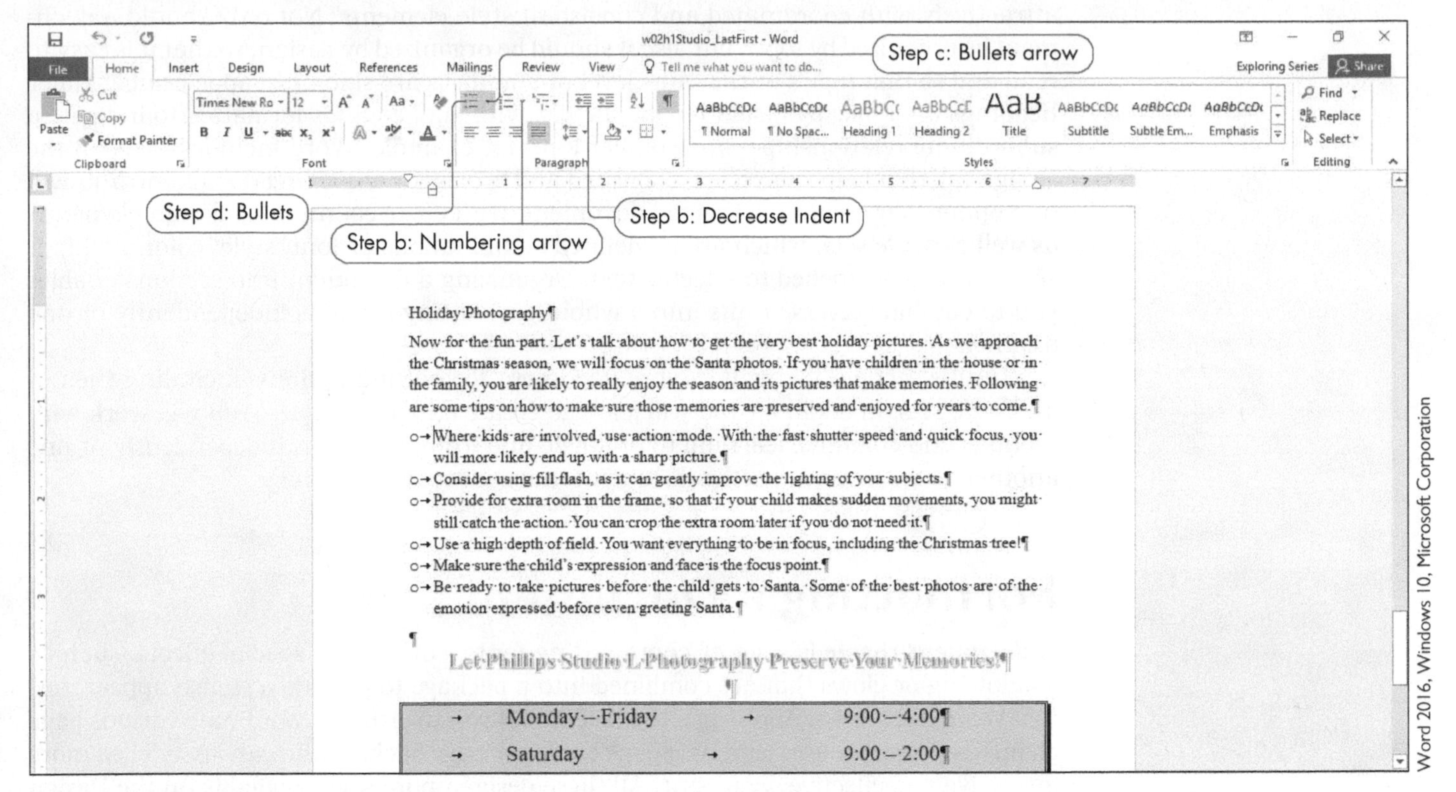

FIGURE 23 Add Bullets and Numbers

a. Press **Ctrl+Home**. Select the five boldfaced paragraphs, beginning with *Compose with Care* and ending with *Be Bold.*

b. Click the **Numbering arrow** and select the **Number Alignment** showing each number followed by a right parenthesis. Click **Decrease Indent** in the Paragraph group to move the numbered items to the left margin. Click anywhere to deselect the text.

c. Scroll to the second page and select the four paragraphs following the sentence *Depth of field is determined by several factors:*, beginning with *Aperture/F-Stop* and ending with *Point of View*. Click the **Bullets arrow** and select the **hollow round bullet**. Decrease the indent to move the selected text to the left margin. Deselect the text.

d. Press **Ctrl+End** and select the six paragraphs above the last line of text, beginning with *Where kids are involved*, and ending with *even greeting Santa*. Click **Bullets** to apply a hollow round bullet to the selected paragraphs. Decrease the indent so the bullets begin at the left margin.

Clicking Bullets applied the most recently selected bullet style to selected text. You did not have to click the Bullets arrow and select from the Bullet Library.

e. Save the document. Keep the document open if you plan to continue with the next Hands-On Exercise. If not, close the document, and exit Word.

Document Appearance

The overall appearance and organization of a document is the first opportunity to effectively convey your message to readers. You should ensure that a document is formatted attractively with coordinated and consistent style elements. Not only should a document be organized by topic, but also it should be organized by design, so that it is easy to read and so that topics of the same level of emphasis are similar in appearance. Major headings are typically formatted identically, with subheadings formatted to indicate a subordinate relationship—in a smaller font, for example. Word includes tools on the Design tab that help you create a polished and professional-looking document. You will find options for creating a themed document, with color-coordinated design elements, as well as ***style sets***, which are predefined combinations of font, style, color, and font size that can be applied to selected text. Organizing a document into sections enables you to combine diverse units into a whole, formatting sections independently of one another.

In this section, you will explore document formatting options, including themes and style sets. In addition, you will learn to create and apply styles. You will work with sections and columns, learning to organize and format sections independently of one another, to create an attractive document that conveys your message.

Formatting a Document

A ***document theme*** is a set of coordinating fonts, colors, and special effects, such as shadowing or glows that are combined into a package to provide a stylish appearance in a Word document. Applying a theme enables you to visually coordinate various page elements. In some cases, adding a page border or page background can also yield a more attractive and effective document. All these design options are available on the Design tab. As you consider ways to organize a document, you might find it necessary to divide it into sections, with each section arranged or formatted independently of others. For example, a cover page (or section) might be centered vertically, while all other pages are aligned at the top. By arranging text in columns, you can easily create an attractive newsletter or brochure. The Layout tab facilitates the use of sections and formatting in columns. When formatting a document, you should always keep in mind the document's purpose and its intended audience. Whereas a newsletter might use more color and playful text and design effects, a legal document should be more conservative. With the broad range of document formatting options available in Word, you can be as playful or conservative as necessary.

Select a Document Theme

STEP 1 ›› When you select a theme for a document, a unified set of design elements, including font style, color, and special effects, is applied to the entire document. The Design tab includes selections related to themes (see Figure 24). A new blank Word document is based on a theme by default—the Office theme.

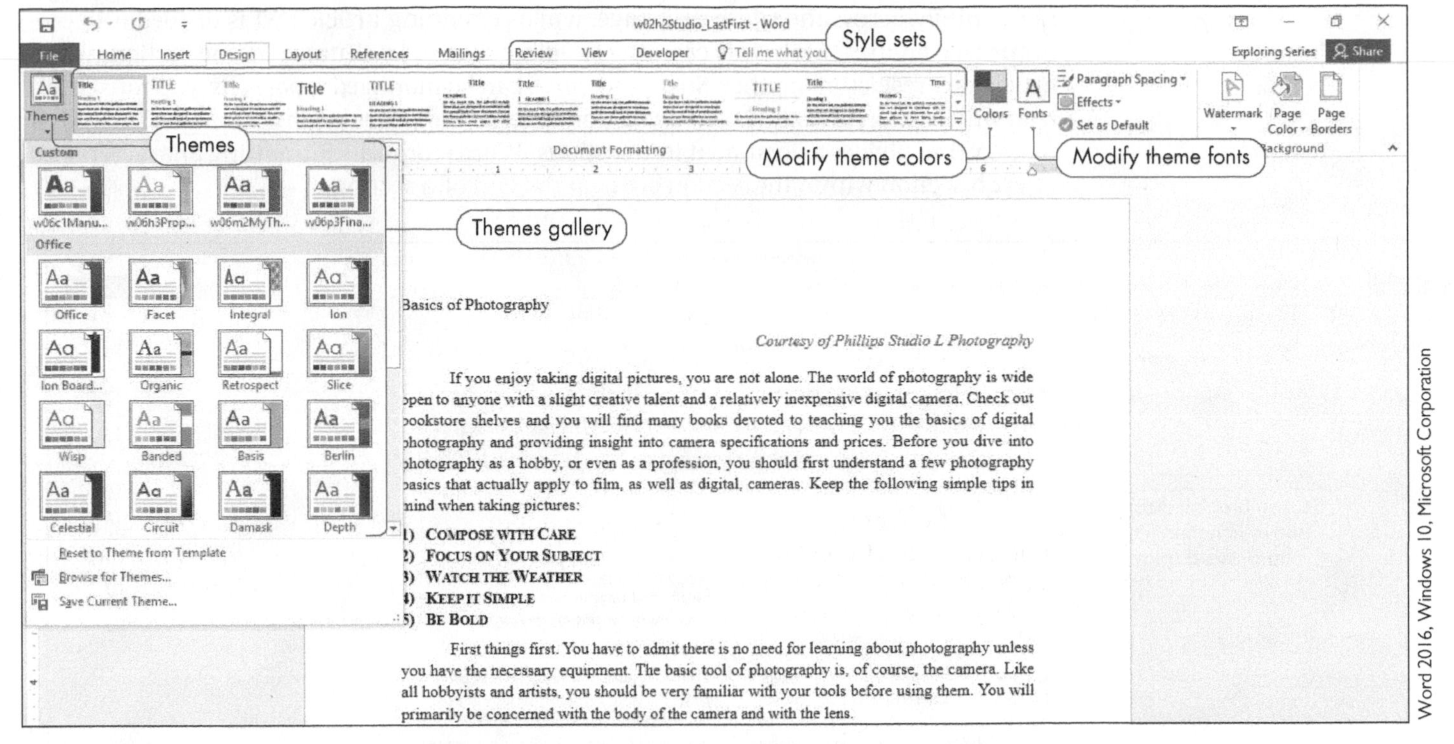

Word 2016, Windows 10, Microsoft Corporation

FIGURE 24 Design Tab

Themes are located in the Document Formatting group on the Design tab (refer to Figure 24). You can choose from a variety of themes from Themes in the Document Formatting group. You can change the style, color, font, paragraph spacing, and effects of any theme by selecting a different option within the Document Formatting group.

To change a document's theme, complete the following steps:

1. Click Themes in the Document Formatting group on the Design tab.
2. Point to each theme in the Themes gallery to display a preview of the effect on the document. Depending on document features and color selections already in place, you might not see an immediate change when previewing a theme.
3. Click a theme to select it.

To modify a color or font selection in a theme, complete the following steps:

1. Click Colors or Fonts in the Document Formatting group on the Design tab. Each group of coordinated colors or font selections is summarized and identified by a unique name.
2. Click to select a color or font group to adjust the selected theme in the document.

To apply theme effects to objects in a document, complete the following steps:

1. Click Effects in the Document Formatting group on the Design tab.
2. Select an effect from the gallery.

Work with Sections

It sometimes becomes necessary to vary the layout of a document within a page or between pages, and incorporate sections into a document. A section is a part of a document that contains its own page format settings, such as those for margins, columns, and orientation. To have text on the same page accommodating both single column and two-column text, break it into sections. For instance, a headline of an article might center horizontally across the width of a page, while remaining article text is divided into columns (see Figure 25). In this case, the headline should be situated in one section, while article text resides in another. So that sections can be managed separately, you must indicate with section breaks where one section ends and another begins. A ***section break*** is a marker that divides a document into sections. Word stores the formatting characteristics of each section within the section break at the end of a section.

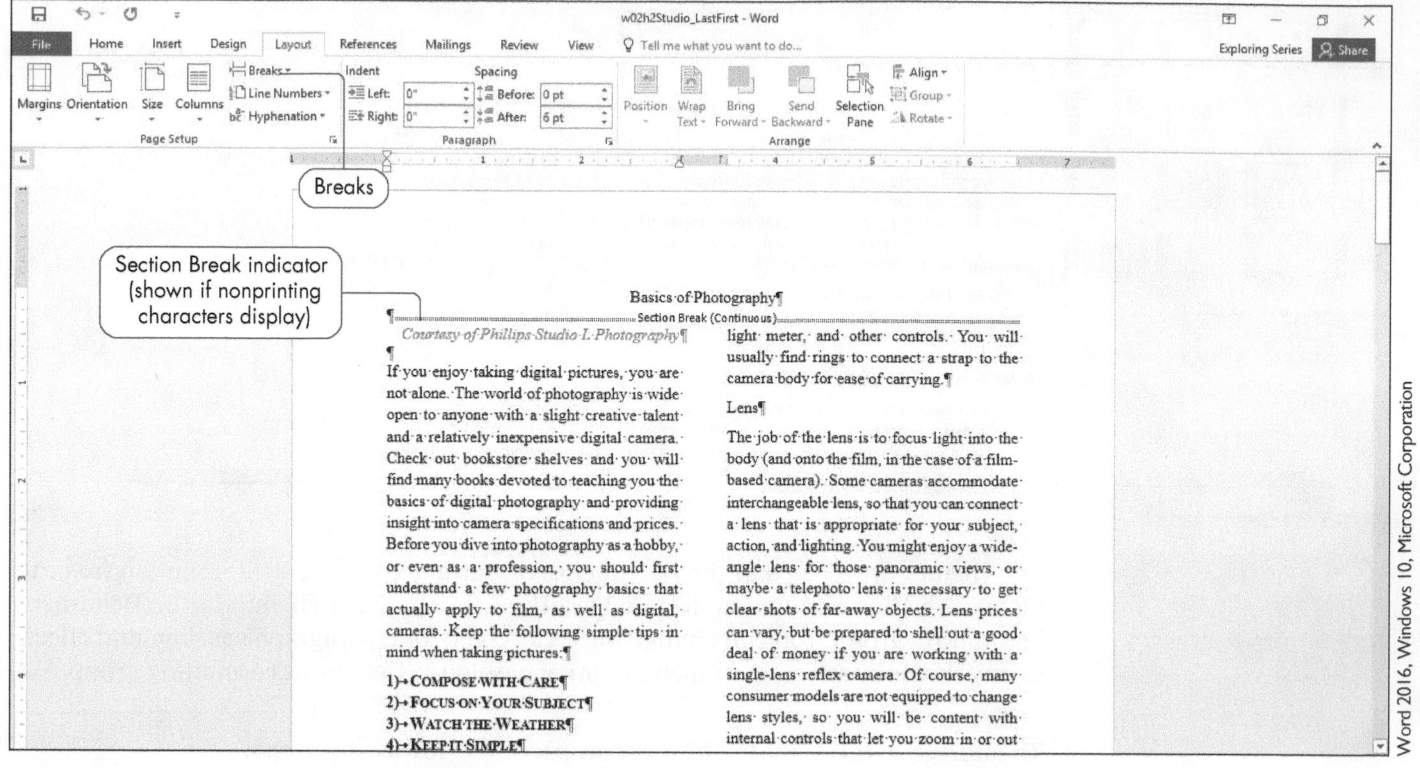

FIGURE 25 Select and Display a Section Break

There are four types of section breaks, as shown in Table 2. Before inserting a break, the insertion point should be at the point where the break is to occur. You can select a section break type from the Layout tab and click Breaks in the Page Setup group to apply the break.

TABLE 2 Section Breaks

Type	Text that follows ...	Use to ...
Next Page	must begin at the top of the next page.	force a chapter to start at the top of a page.
Continuous	can continue on the same page.	format text in the middle of the page into columns.
Even Page	must begin at the top of the next even-numbered page.	force a chapter to begin at the top of an even-numbered page.
Odd Page	must begin at the top of the next odd-numbered page.	force a chapter to begin at the top of an odd-numbered page.

Pearson Education, Inc.

To place a section break in a document, complete the following steps:

1. Click at the location where the section break should occur.
2. Click the Layout tab. Click Breaks in the Page Setup group.
3. Select a section break type (see Table 2). If nonprinting characters display, you will see a section break (refer to Figure 25).

If you delete a section break, you also delete the formatting for that section, causing the text above the break to assume the formatting characteristics of the following section. To delete a section break, click the section break indicator (refer to Figure 25) and press Delete.

Format Text into Columns

STEP 2 ›› ***Columns*** format a document or section of a document into side-by-side vertical blocks in which the text flows down the first column and continues at the top of the next column.

To format text into columns, complete the following steps:

1. Click at the location where you want to start formatting the text into columns.
2. Click the Layout tab and click Columns in the Page Setup group.
3. Specify the number of columns or select More Columns to display the Columns dialog box. The Columns dialog box (see Figure 26) provides options for setting the number of columns and spacing between columns.
4. Click OK.

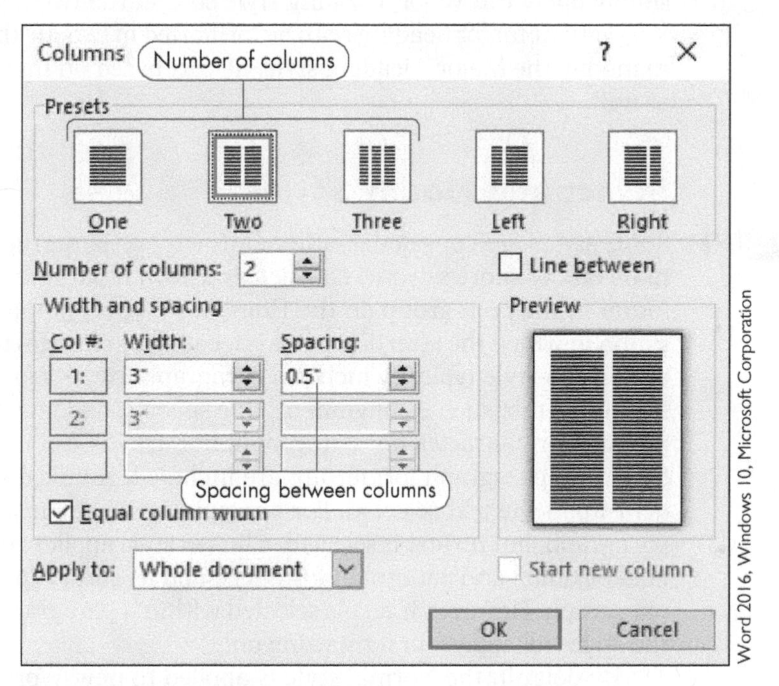

FIGURE 26 Columns Dialog Box

Having created a two-column document, you should preview the document to ensure an attractive arrangement of columns. Try to avoid columns that end awkwardly, such as a column heading at the bottom of one column with remaining text continuing at the top of the next column. In addition, columns should be somewhat balanced, if possible, so that one column is not far more lengthy than the next. To remedy these kinds of issues, a column break may be necessary.

To insert a column break, complete the following steps:

1. Click in the document where the break is to occur.
2. Click the Layout tab, click Breaks, and then click Column in the Page Breaks section.

With nonprinting characters displayed, you will see the Column break indicator at the location where one column ends and the next begins.

Applying Styles

As you complete reports, assignments, and other projects, you probably apply the same text, paragraph, table, and list formatting for similar documents. Instead of formatting each element of each document individually, you can create your own custom format for each element—called a style—to save time in designing titles, headings, and paragraphs. A ***style*** is a named collection of formatting characteristics. A characteristic of a professional document is uniform formatting. All major headings look the same, with uniform subheadings. Even paragraphs can be styled to lend consistency to a document. If styles are appropriately assigned, Word can automatically generate reference pages such as a table of contents and indexes.

Styles automate the formatting process and provide a consistent appearance to a document. It is possible to store any type of character or paragraph formatting within a style, and once a style is defined, you can apply it to any element within a document to produce identical formatting. Word provides a gallery of styles from which you can choose, or you can create your own style. For example, having formatted a major report heading with various settings, such as font type, color, and size, you can create a style from the heading, calling it Major_Heading. The next time you type a major heading, simply apply the Major_Heading style so that the two headings are identical in format. Subsequent major headings can be formatted in exactly the same way. If you later decide to modify the Major_Heading style, all text based on that style will automatically adjust as well.

Select and Modify Styles

STEP 3 » Some styles are considered either character or paragraph styles. A character style formats one or more selected characters within a paragraph, often applying font formats found in the Font group on the Home tab. A paragraph style changes the entire paragraph in which the insertion point is located, or changes multiple selected paragraphs. A paragraph style typically includes paragraph formats found in the Paragraph group on the Home tab, such as alignment, line spacing, indents, tabs, and borders. Other styles are neither character nor paragraph, but are instead linked styles in which both character and paragraph formatting are included. A linked style applies formatting dependent upon the text selected. For example, when the insertion point is located within a paragraph, but no text is selected, a linked style applies both font characteristics (such as bold or italic) and paragraph formats (such as paragraph and line spacing) to the entire paragraph. However, if text is selected within a paragraph when a linked style is applied, the style will apply font formatting only.

By default, the Normal style is applied to new Word documents. Normal style is a paragraph style with specific font and paragraph formatting. If that style is not appropriate for a document you are developing, you can select another style from Word's Style gallery. The most frequently accessed styles are shown in the Styles group on the Home tab (see Figure 27).

To apply a style to selected text or to an existing paragraph, complete the following steps:

1. Select the text or place the insertion point within the paragraph.
2. Click a style in the Styles group on the Home tab. Click the More arrow for more styles.
3. Click the Styles Dialog Box Launcher (see Figure 27) to display the Styles pane for more choices.
4. Click to select a style.

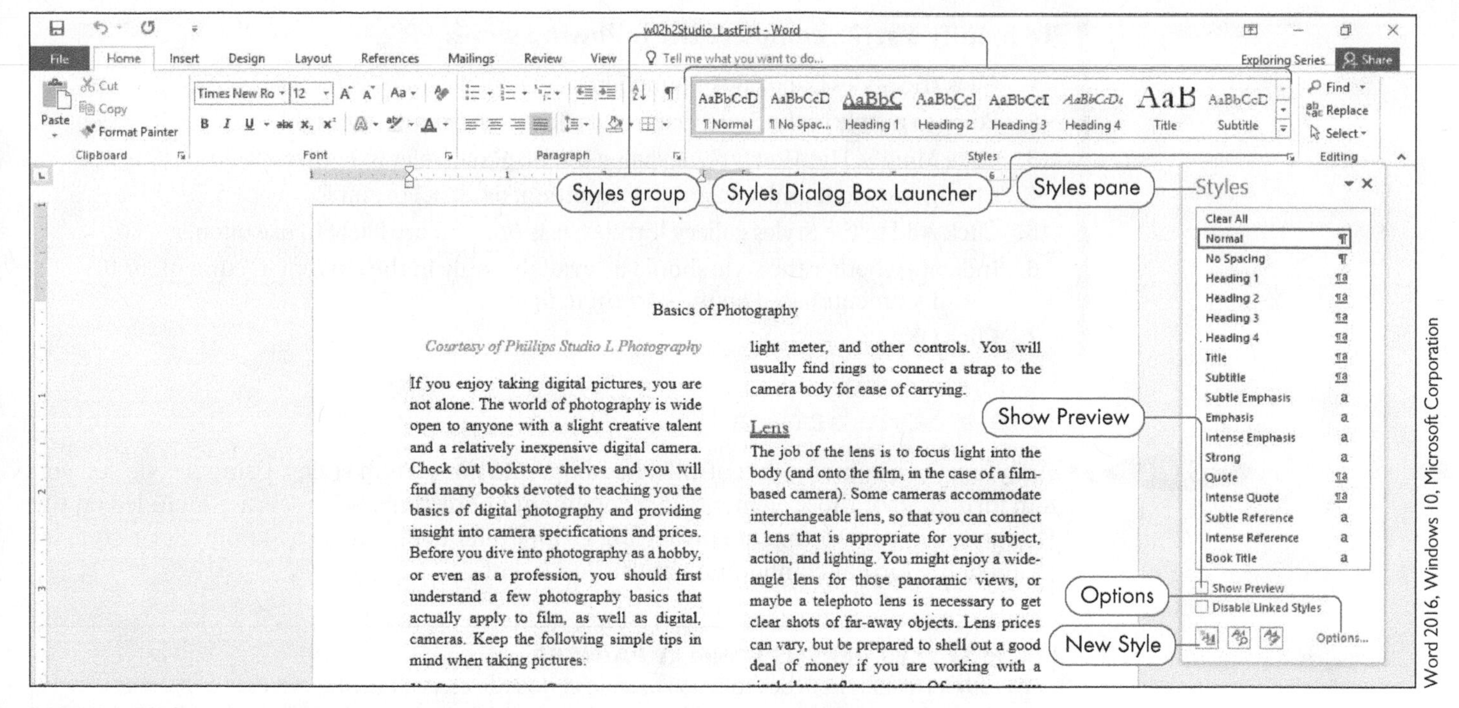

FIGURE 27 Styles

Modifying a style, or even creating a new style, affects only the current document, by default. However, you can cause the style to be available to all documents that are based on the current template when you select *New documents based on this template* in the Modify Style dialog box (see Figure 28). Unless you make that selection, however, the changes are not carried over to new documents you create or to others that you open. As an example, the specifications for the Title style are shown in Figure 28.

Modify Style
Properties
Name: Title
Style type: Linked (paragraph and character)
Style based on: ¶ Normal
Style for following paragraph: ¶ Normal
Formatting
Garamond (Headi | 28 | B I U | Automatic
Basics of Photography
Indicate whether the style is to be included in the current document or in new documents based on the current template
Font: (Default) +Headings (Garamond), 28 pt, Condensed by 0.5 pt, Kern at 14 pt
Line spacing: single, Space
After: 0 pt, Don't add space between paragraphs of the same style, Style: Linked, Show in the Styles gallery, Priority: 11
Add to the Styles gallery | Automatically update
Only in this document | New documents based on this template
Format ▾ | More formatting options | OK | Cancel
Word 2016, Windows 10, Microsoft Corporation

FIGURE 28 Modify a Style

To modify a style, complete the following steps:

1. Click the Styles Dialog Box Launcher.
2. Point to a style in the Styles pane and click the arrow on the right.
3. Click Modify. The Modify Style dialog box displays (refer to Figure 28).
4. Change any font and paragraph formatting, or click Format for even more choices.
5. Click Add to the Styles gallery if the style is one you are likely to use often.
6. Indicate whether the style should be available only in the current document, or in new documents based on the current template.
7. Click OK.

Use a Style Set

STEP 4 A style set is a combination of title, heading, and paragraph styles. Using a style set, you can format all of those elements in a document at one time. Style sets are included on the Design tab in the Document Formatting group (refer to Figure 24). Simply click a style set to apply the format combination to the document.

TIP: STYLES VERSUS FORMAT PAINTER

To copy formatting from one selection to another, you can certainly use Format Painter. Another alternative is to create a new style from the selection and apply it to additional text. Both processes seem to produce the same results. However, unlike changes made using Format Painter, a style remains available in both the current document and in other documents based on the same template, if you indicate that preference when you create the style. That way, the same formatting changes can be applied repeatedly in various documents or positions within the same document, even after a document is closed and reopened. Formatting changes made as a result of using Format Painter are not available later. Also, styles that indicate a hierarchy (such as Heading 1, Heading 2) can be used to prepare a table of contents or outline.

Create a New Style from Text

Having applied several formatting characteristics to text, you might want to repeat that formatting on other selections that are similar in purpose. For example, suppose you format a page title with a specific font size, font color, and bordering. Subsequent page titles should be formatted identically. You can select the formatted page title and create a new style based on the formatting of the selected text. Then select the next title to which the formatting should be applied and choose the newly created style name from the Styles group or from the Styles pane.

To create a new style from existing text, complete the following steps:

1. Select the text from which the new style should be created or click in a paragraph containing paragraph characteristics you want to include in the new style.
2. Click the Styles Dialog Box Launcher (refer to Figure 27) to open the Styles pane.
3. Click New Style, located in the bottom-left corner of the Styles pane (refer to Figure 27).
4. Type a name for the new style. Do not use the name of an existing style.
5. Click the Style type arrow and select a style type (Paragraph, Character, or Linked, among others).
6. Adjust any other formatting to fit your needs.
7. Click OK.

Use Outline View

STEP 5 ❯❯ One benefit of applying styles to headings in a long document is the ability to use those headings to view the document in Outline view, making it easier to view and modify the organization of a long document. Outline view in Word displays a document in various levels of detail, according to heading styles applied in a document. Figure 29 shows Outline view of a document in which major headings were formatted in Heading 1 style, with subheadings in Headings 2 and 3 style. You can modify the heading styles to suit your preference. To select a level to view, perhaps only first-level headings, click All Levels (beside Show Level) and select a level. You can display the document in Outline view by clicking the View tab, and clicking Outline in the Views group.

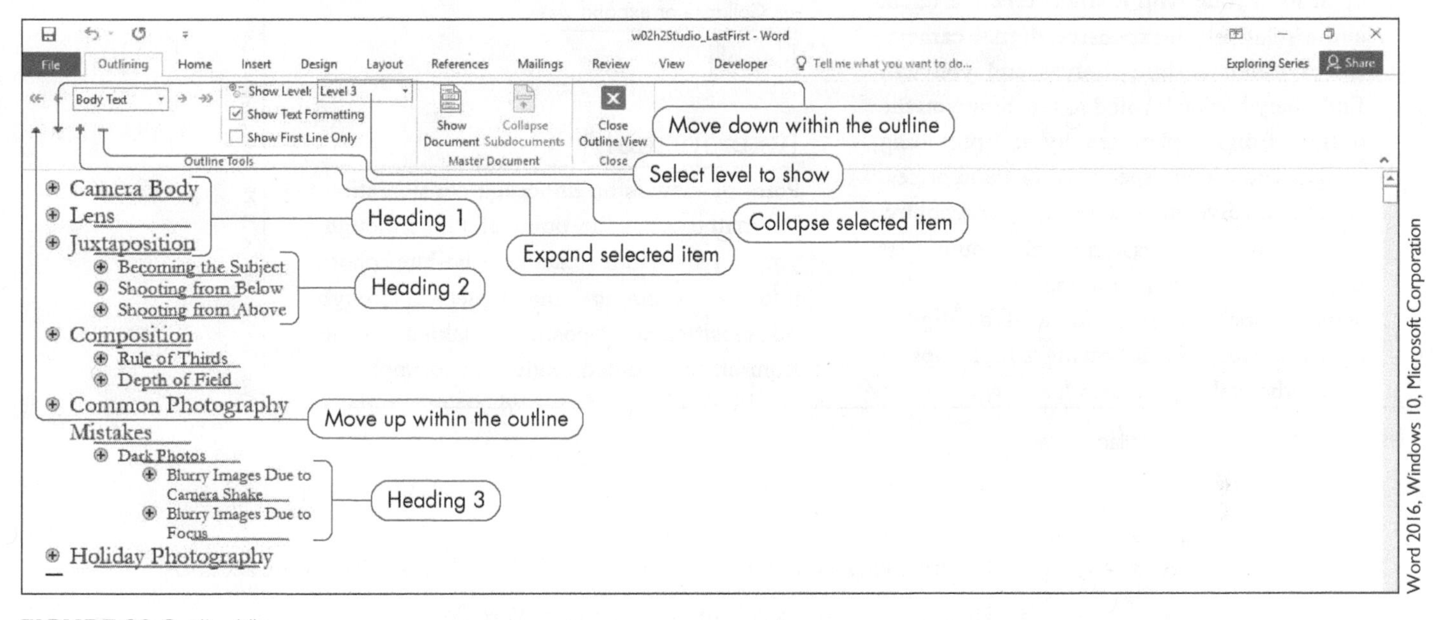

FIGURE 29 Outline View

Use Outline view to glimpse or confirm a document's structure. Especially when developing lengthy reports, you will want to make sure headings are shown at the correct level of detail. A document shown in Outline view can also be easily converted to a PowerPoint presentation, with Heading 1 becoming the slide titles, and lower levels becoming bullets on each slide. Also, a table of contents is automatically generated when you click Table of Contents on the References tab.

To collapse or expand a single heading, click the heading in Outline view and click the plus (+) sign (to expand) or the minus (–) sign (to collapse) on the Ribbon. For example, having clicked text formatted as Heading 1, click + to show any lower-level headings associated with the particular heading (refer to Figure 29). Text other than that associated with the selected heading will remain unaffected. As shown in Figure 29, you can move a heading (along with all associated subheadings) up or down in the document. In Outline view, you can also drag the plus (+) or minus (–) sign beside a heading to move the entire group, including all sublevels, to another location.

You can quickly move through a document in Outline view and to restructure a document. If the levels are collapsed so that body text does not display, you will click a heading to move quickly to that section, and change the view to Print Layout or another view. The document will expand, and the insertion point will be in the section identified by the heading you clicked. Using Outline view to move through a lengthy document can save a great deal of time because it is not necessary to page through a document looking for a particular section heading. You can also use Outline view to restructure a document. Simply drag and drop a heading to reposition it within a document, or use the Move Up or Move Down buttons. If subheadings are associated, they will move with the heading as well.

In Print Layout view, you can quickly collapse everything except the section with which you want to work. Point to a heading and click the small triangle that displays beside the heading (see Figure 30) to collapse or expand the following body text and sublevels. Collapsing text in that manner is a handy way to provide your readers with a summary.

¶ Section Break (Continuous)

Courtesy of Phillips Studio L Photography¶

¶

If you enjoy taking digital pictures, you are not alone. The world of photography is wide open to anyone with a slight creative talent and a relatively inexpensive digital camera. Check out bookstore shelves and you will find many books devoted to teaching you the basics of digital photography and providing insight into camera specifications and prices. Before you dive into photography as a hobby, or even as a profession, you should first understand a few photography basics that actually apply to film, as well as digital, cameras. Keep the following simple tips in mind when taking pictures:¶

houses a batter that powers the shutter, flash, light meter, and other controls. You will usually find rings to connect a strap to the camera body for ease of carrying.¶

Collapse or expand view

Lens¶

Juxtaposition¶

Point of view is an important consideration. No matter what the point of view, though, you can sometimes change a ho-hum photo into a stunning masterpiece through juxtaposition. Juxtaposition is taking a photo from an unexpected angle. For example, an eye-level photo of a bird is much more

Word 2016, Windows 10, Microsoft Corporation

FIGURE 30 Expand and Collapse Detail

Quick Concepts

5. Describe why a document may need to be divided into two or more sections.
6. How do you insert a column break into a Word document?
7. What is the benefit of using styles when formatting several different areas of text?
8. How is the concept of styles related to Outline view?

Hands-On Exercises

Skills covered: Select a Document Theme • Work with Sections • Format Text into Columns • Select and Modify Styles • Use a Style Set • Create a New Style from Text • Use Outline View

2 Document Appearance

The next step in preparing the photography newsletter for distribution is to apply document formatting to several areas of the document that will make it easier to read. By applying a theme and formatting the document in columns, you will add to the visual appeal. Using styles, you can ensure consistent formatting of document text. Finally, you will check the document's organization by viewing it in Outline view.

STEP 1 » SELECT A DOCUMENT THEME

A document theme provides color and font coordination, simplifying your design task. You will apply a document theme to the newsletter as a simple way to ensure that yours is an attractive document with well-coordinated features. Refer to Figure 31 as you complete Step 1.

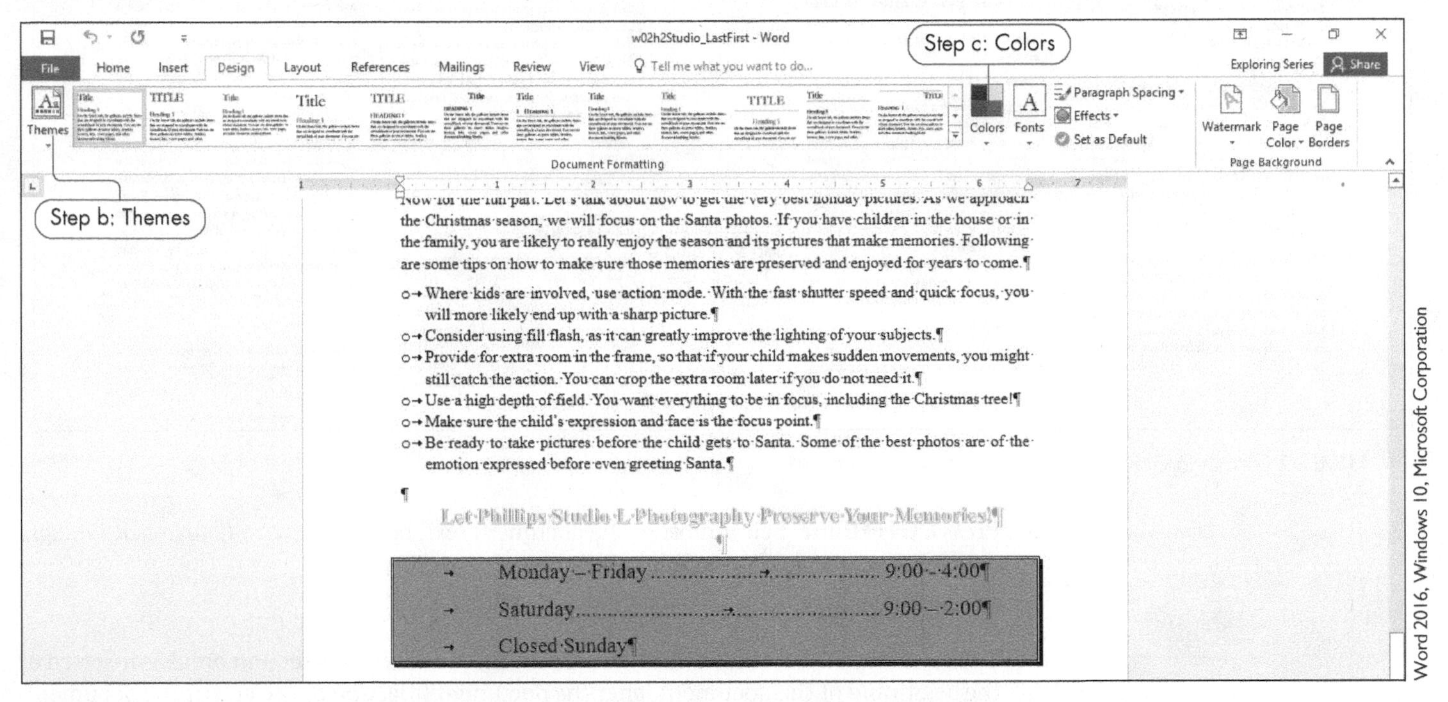

FIGURE 31 Apply a Document Theme

a. Open *w02h1Studio_LastFirst* if you closed it at the end of Hands-On Exercise 1, and save it as **w02h2Studio_LastFirst**, changing h1 to h2.

b. Press **Ctrl+Home**. Click the **Design tab** and click **Themes** in the Document Formatting group. Select **Organic**.

Note the color change applied to the second paragraph of the document, *Courtesy of Phillips Studio L Photography*.

c. Click **Colors** in the Document Formatting group and select **Violet II**.

The second paragraph of the document, *Courtesy of Phillips Studio L Photography*, has changed colors because you selected a new color scheme within the theme. The table of studio hours on the last page of the document also changed colors.

d. Save the document.

STEP 2 » WORK WITH SECTIONS AND FORMAT TEXT INTO COLUMNS

The document should be formatted as a newsletter. Most often, newsletters display in columns, so you will apply columns to the newsletter. A few items, such as the newsletter heading and the store hours at the end of the document, should be centered horizontally across the page instead of within a column. Using sections, you will format those items differently from column text. Refer to Figure 32 as you complete Step 2.

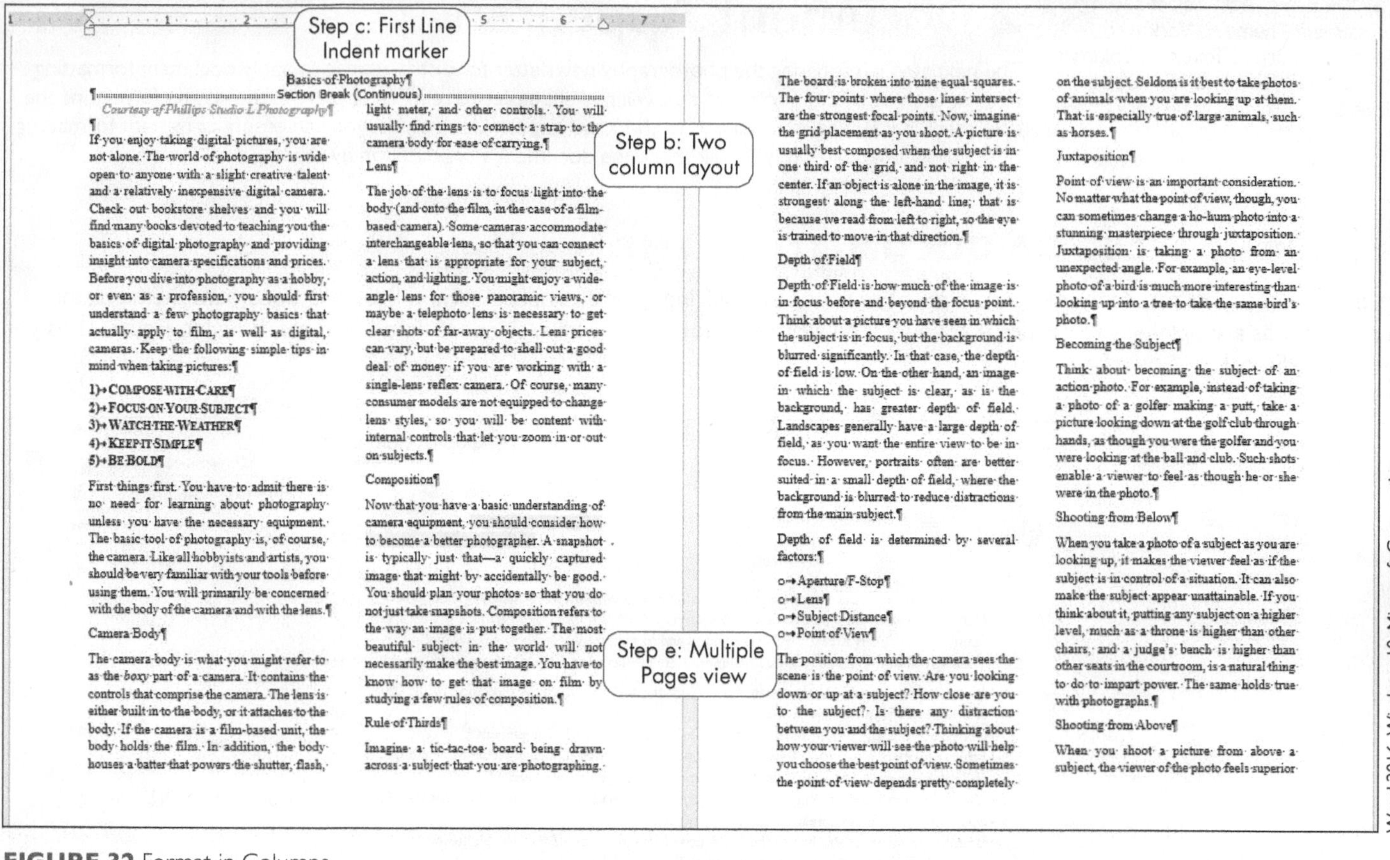

FIGURE 32 Format in Columns

a. Press **Ctrl+Home**. Select most of the document text, beginning with *Courtesy of Phillips Studio L Photography* and ending with *before even greeting Santa*.

b. Click the **Layout tab** and click **Columns**. Select **Two**.

   The selected text is formatted into two columns. A continuous section break is inserted at the beginning of the document, after the document title, and at the end of the document (before the line that precedes the shaded box). The document now has three sections: The title, the middle with the two-column text, and the end.

c. Press **Ctrl+Home**. Click anywhere on the line containing *Basics of Photography*. Click the **Home tab** and click **Center** in the Paragraph group. Click anywhere in the paragraph beginning with *If you enjoy taking digital pictures*. Drag the **First Line Indent marker** on the ruler back to the left margin.

   The title of the newsletter is centered horizontally. The first line indent is removed from the first multiline paragraph in the newsletter.

d. Click anywhere in the paragraph beginning with *First things first*. Drag the **First Line Indent marker** to the left margin to remove the indent.

e. Click the **View tab** and click **Multiple Pages** in the Zoom group. Scroll down to view all pages, getting an idea of how text is positioned on all pages. Click **100%** in the Zoom group.

f. Save the document.

STEP 3 ›› SELECT AND MODIFY STYLES

The newsletter is improving in appearance, but you note that the headings (Camera Body, Lens, Composition, etc.) are not as evident as they should be. Also, some headings are subordinate to others, and should be identified accordingly. You will apply heading styles to headings in the newsletter to resolve these issues. Refer to Figure 33 as you complete Step 3.

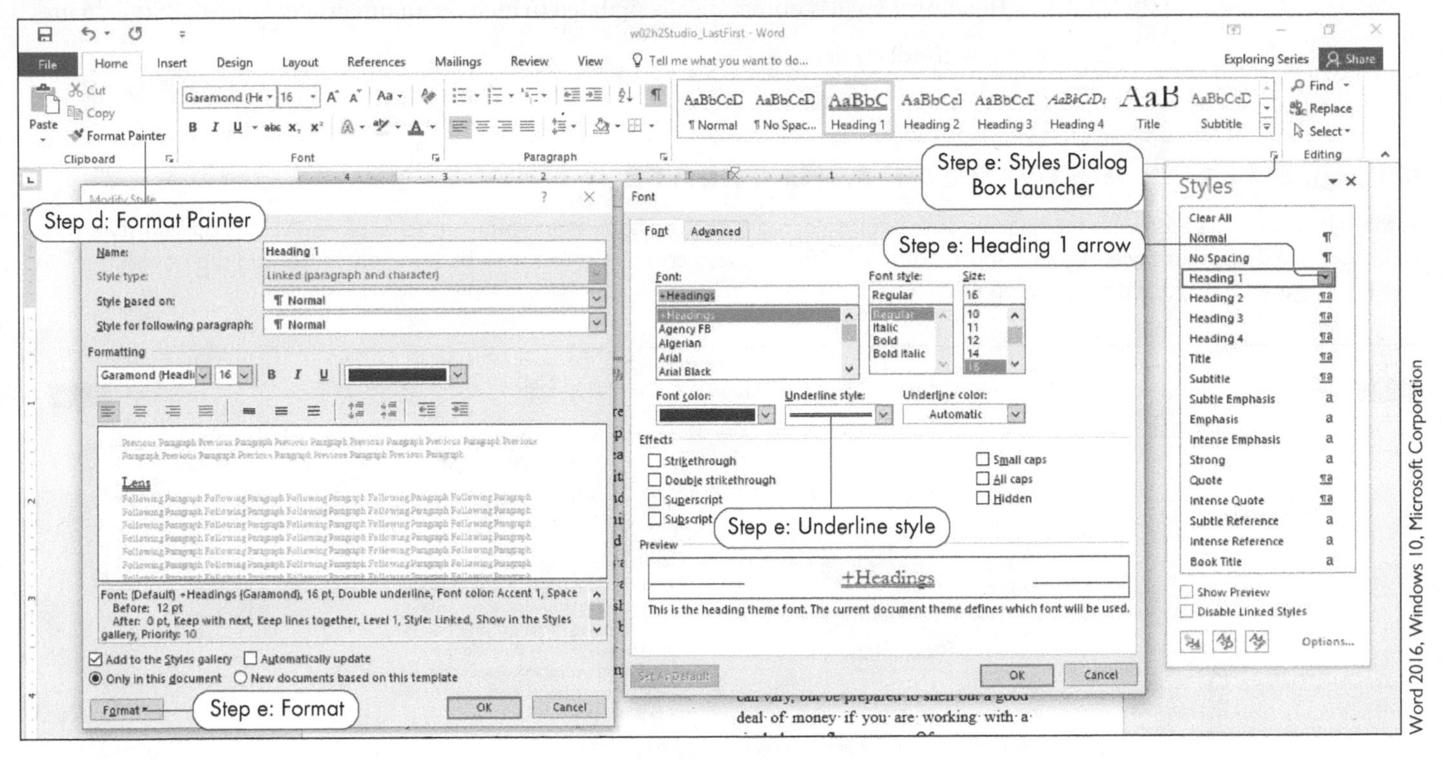

FIGURE 33 Work with Styles

a. Select the text **Camera Body** on the first page of the newsletter. Click the **Home tab** and select **Heading 1** in the Styles group. On the same page, in the column on the right, select **Lens** and apply **Heading 1**. Select **Composition** and apply **Heading 1**.

b. Apply **Heading 1** to *Juxtaposition, Common Photography Mistakes*, and *Holiday Photography* on the second and third pages of the newsletter.

c. Select **Rule of Thirds** on the first page, and press and hold **Ctrl** on the keyboard as you also select **Depth of Field**, **Becoming the Subject**, **Shooting from Below**, and **Shooting from Above** on the second page. Release Ctrl. Click **Heading 2** in the Styles group on the Home tab. Do not deselect text.

d. Double-click **Format Painter** in the Clipboard group. Select **Dark Photos** on the third page. Select **Blurry Images**. Press **Esc**. Select **Blurry Images Due to Focus** on the third page. Click **Heading 3** in the Styles group. Select **Blurry Images Due to Camera Shake** on the third page and apply the **Heading 3** style.

> **TROUBLESHOOTING:** If you do not see Heading 3 in the Styles group, click More in the Styles group and select Heading 3.

Using Format Painter, you copied the format of the Heading 2 style to a few headings. Headings throughout the newsletter are formatted according to their hierarchy, with major headings in Heading 1 style and others in correct order beneath the first level.

e. Click the **Styles Dialog Box Launcher** to display the Styles pane. Point to **Heading 1** and click the **Heading 1 arrow**. Click **Modify**. Click **Format** in the Modify Style dialog box and click **Font**. Click the **Underline style arrow** and click the second underline style (double underline). Click **OK**. Click **OK** again.

You modified Heading 1 style to include a double underline. Every heading formatted in Heading 1 style is automatically updated to include an underline. Close the Styles pane.

f. Save the document.

STEP 4 » USE A STYLE SET AND CREATE A NEW STYLE FROM TEXT

Although you are pleased with the heading styles you selected in the previous step, you want to explore Word's built-in style sets to determine if another style might be more attractive. You will also create a style for all bulleted paragraphs in the newsletter. Refer to Figure 34 as you complete Step 4.

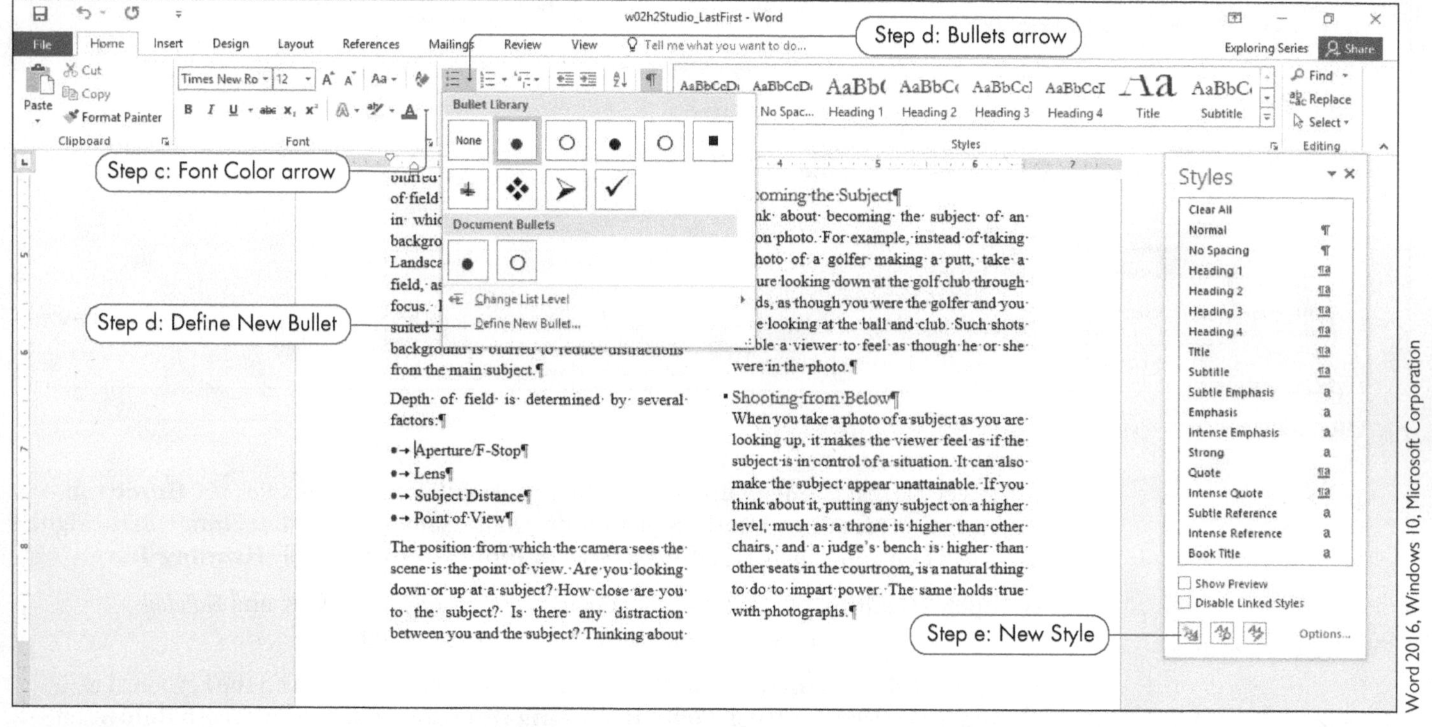

FIGURE 34 Use a Style Set

a. Press **Ctrl+Home**. Click the **Design tab**. Point to any style set in the Document Formatting group, without clicking, to view the effect on the document. Specifically, see how the previewed style affects the Lens heading shown in the right column. Click the **More arrow** beside the style sets and select **Lines (Simple)**.

When you apply a style set, headings are formatted according to the style settings, overriding any formatting characteristics you might have set earlier.

b. Click the **View tab** and click **One Page** in the Zoom group to view the first page.

Note that the format of the major headings—Camera Body, Lens, and Composition—has been modified, removing the underline you set earlier, and now displays the format of the Lines (Simple) style set.

c. Click **100%** in the Zoom group. Select the second paragraph in the document, *Courtesy of Phillips Studio L Photography*. Click the **Home tab**. Click the **Font Color arrow** and select **Plum, Accent 1, Darker 25%** (fifth row, fifth column).

You select a coordinating text color for the second line in the document.

d. Scroll to the second page and click anywhere in the bulleted paragraph containing the text *Aperture/F-Stop*. Click the **Bullets arrow** and select a solid round black bullet. Click the **Bullets arrow** and click **Define New Bullet**. Click **Font**. Click the **Font color arrow** and select **Plum, Accent 1, Darker 25%**. Click **OK**. Click **OK** again.

Having modified the format of one bulleted item, you will create a style from that format to apply to all other bulleted items in the document.

e. Click **New Style** in the Styles pane. Type **Bullet Paragraph** in the Name box and click **OK**.

You should see a new style in the Styles pane titled Bullet Paragraph.

f. Select the three bulleted paragraphs below *Aperture/F-Stop* and click **Bullet Paragraph** in the Styles pane. Scroll to the third page, select the three bulleted paragraphs at the bottom of the right column, and then click **Bullet Paragraph** in the Styles pane. Scroll to the fourth page, select the three bulleted paragraphs at the top of the page (in both columns), and then apply the **Bullet Paragraph style**. Close the Styles pane.

g. Save the document.

STEP 5 » USE OUTLINE VIEW

The newsletter spans four pages, with headings identifying various levels of detail. You will check to make sure you have formatted headings according to the correct hierarchy. To do so, you will view the newsletter in Outline view. Refer to Figure 35 as you complete Step 5.

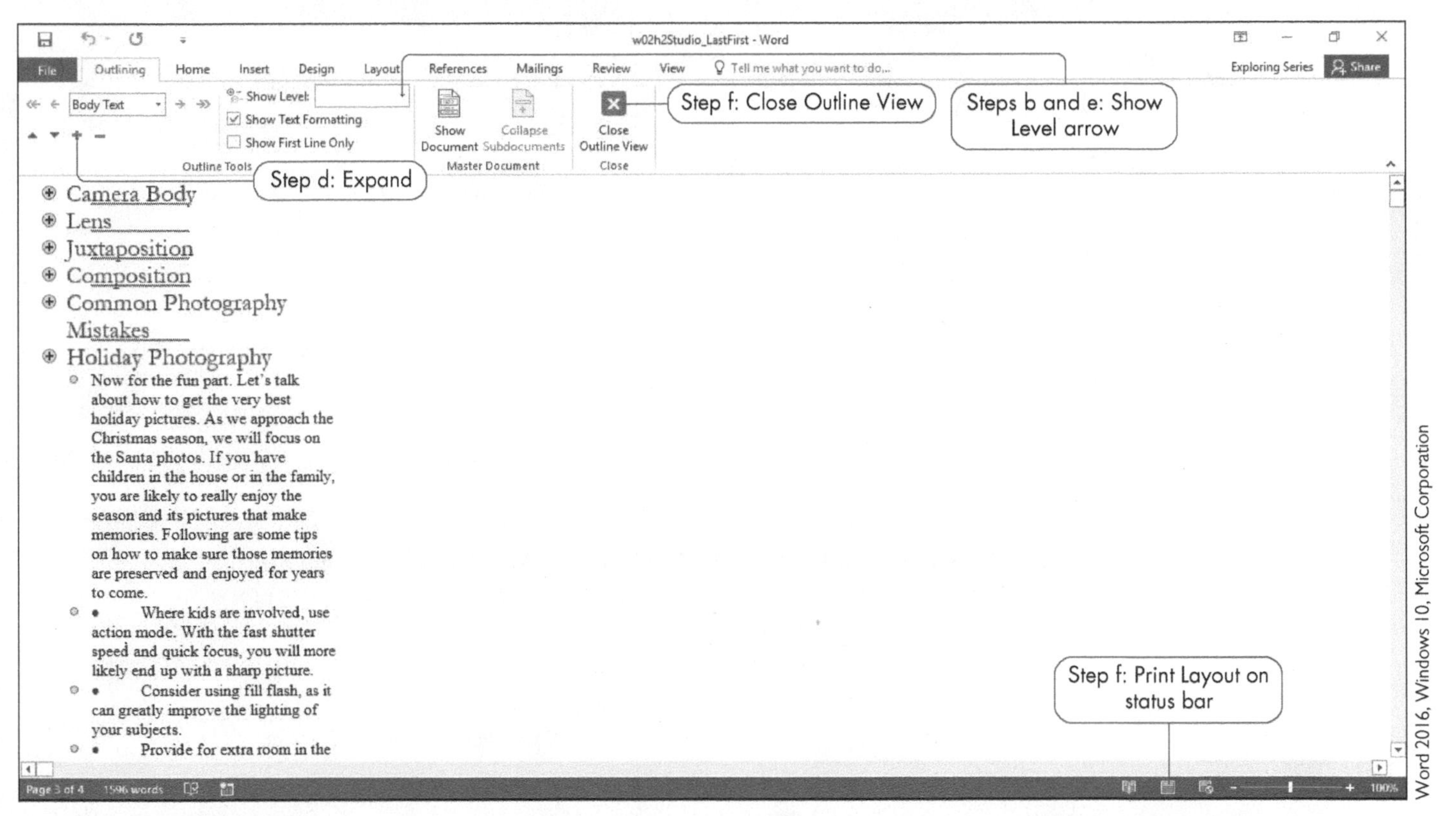

FIGURE 35 View an Outline

a. Press **Ctrl+Home**. Click the **View tab** and click **Outline** in the Views group. Scroll down slightly to see the first major heading (with a plus (+) sign on the left)—Camera Body.

b. Click the **Show Level arrow** and click **Level 3**.

You formatted headings in the newsletter as headings, in three levels of detail. Because you did so, you are able to view the document structure according to the hierarchy of headings.

c. Position the pointer on the plus (+) sign that precedes *Blurry Images Due to Camera Shake* (so the pointer becomes a four-headed arrow). Drag the heading above the preceding level (*Blurry Images Due to Focus*). When you see a small black triangle above the preceding level, release the mouse button to reposition the section.

d. Use the same procedure as in Step c to move the *Juxtaposition* section above *Composition*. Click **Expand** in the Outline Tools group to view the content of the *Juxtaposition* section.

e. Click the **Show Level arrow** and select **Level 1** to display Level 1 headings only. Select **Holiday Photography** and click **Expand** in the Outline Tools group.

The *Holiday Photography* section is expanded. Other Level 1 headings remain collapsed.

f. Click **Close Outline View** in the Close group on the Outlining tab. If both columns do not display, click **Print Layout** on the status bar.

g. Save the document. Keep the document open if you plan to continue with the next Hands-On Exercise. If not, save and close the document, and exit Word.

Objects

An ***object*** is an item that can be individually selected and manipulated within a document. Objects, such as pictures, text boxes, tables, and other graphic types, are often included in documents to add interest or convey a point (see Figure 36). A ***text box*** is a bordered area you can use to draw attention to specific text. Newsletters typically include pictures and other decorative elements to liven up what might otherwise be a somewhat mundane document. As you work with a document, you can conduct a quick search for appropriate pictures and graphics online—all without ever leaving your document workspace.

FIGURE 36 Word Objects

One thing all objects have in common is that they can be selected and worked with independently of surrounding text. You can resize them, add special effects, and even move them to other locations within the document. Word includes convenient text wrapping controls so that you can quickly adjust the way text wraps around an object. With Live Layout and alignment guides, you can easily line up pictures and other diagrams with existing text.

In this section, you will explore the use of objects in a Word document. Specifically, you will learn to include pictures, searching for them online as well as obtaining them from your own storage device. You will learn to create impressive text displays with WordArt. You will create text boxes, as well.

Inserting and Formatting Objects

Objects, such as pictures and illustrations, can be selected from the Web or a storage device. You can create other objects, such as WordArt, text boxes, charts, and tables. When you insert an object, it is automatically selected so that you can manipulate it independently of surrounding text. An additional tab displays on the Ribbon with options related to the selected object, making it easy to quickly modify and enhance an object.

Insert a Picture

A ***picture*** is a graphic image, such as a drawing or photograph. You can insert pictures in a document from your own library of digital pictures you have saved, or you can access abundant picture resources from the Internet. For instance, you can use Bing Image Search in Word to conduct a Web search to locate picture possibilities. Finding and inserting a picture is only the first step in the process. Once incorporated into your document, a picture can be resized and modified with special borders and artistic effects. Other options enable you to easily align a picture with surrounding text, rotate or crop it if necessary, and even recolor it so it blends in with an existing color scheme.

If you do not have a picture already saved on your computer, you can go online to locate a suitable image. The picture is inserted directly from the Web, after which you can resize and reposition it. You can also insert images from Facebook and Flickr.

To insert an online picture, complete the following steps:

1. Click to place the insertion point in the document in the location where the picture is to be inserted.
2. Click the Insert tab and click Online Pictures (see Figure 37).
3. Complete one of the following steps:
   - Use Bing Image Search:
     1. Click in the Bing Image Search box.
     2. Type a search term (for example, type *school* to identify school-related images), and press Enter.
     3. Review any relevant licensing information, if presented, and select an image. Alternatively, click a link to expand the search.
     4. Click Insert.
   - Use OneDrive:
     1. Click Browse.
     2. Navigate to the folder containing the picture you want to insert.
     3. Click the picture and click Insert.

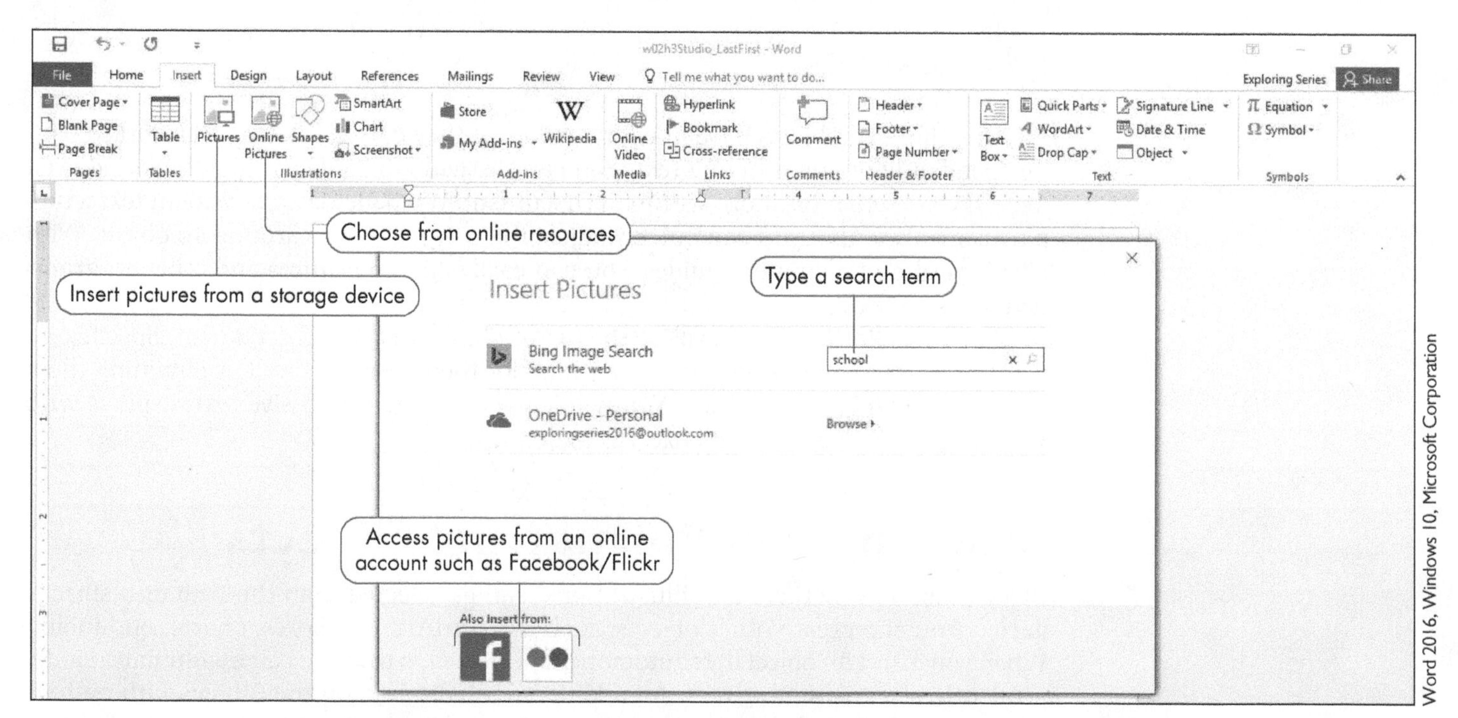

FIGURE 37 Insert an Online Picture

Word 2016, Windows 10, Microsoft Corporation

TIP: INSERT A SCREENSHOT

When describing a process, you might find occasion to include in a document a screenshot of what is displaying on your computer monitor. You can capture a screenshot and insert it in a document as an object. With the item to capture displayed on the computer screen, open the document in which you plan to place the screenshot. Click the Insert tab and click Screenshot in the Illustrations group. Click Screen Clipping. The document is removed from view, leaving the original screen display. Drag to select any part of the screen display. The document displays again, with the selection included as an object.

If you enjoy taking digital pictures, you most likely have a great many of your pictures saved to a storage device you can access with a computer. Suppose you are using Word to prepare a flyer or newsletter. In that case, you might want to insert one or more of your pictures into the document, which is a simple process.

To insert pictures from a storage device, complete the following steps:

1. Position the insertion point in the document where the picture is to be inserted.
2. Click the Insert tab, and click Pictures in the Illustrations group (refer to Figure 37).
3. Navigate to the folder in which your photos are stored.
4. Select a photo to insert, and click Insert.

Move, Align, and Resize a Picture

STEP 2 A new Ribbon tab, with one or more associated tabs beneath it, is added to the Ribbon when you insert and select an object. When a picture is selected, the Format tab displays, and includes settings and selections related to the inserted picture, as shown in Figure 38.

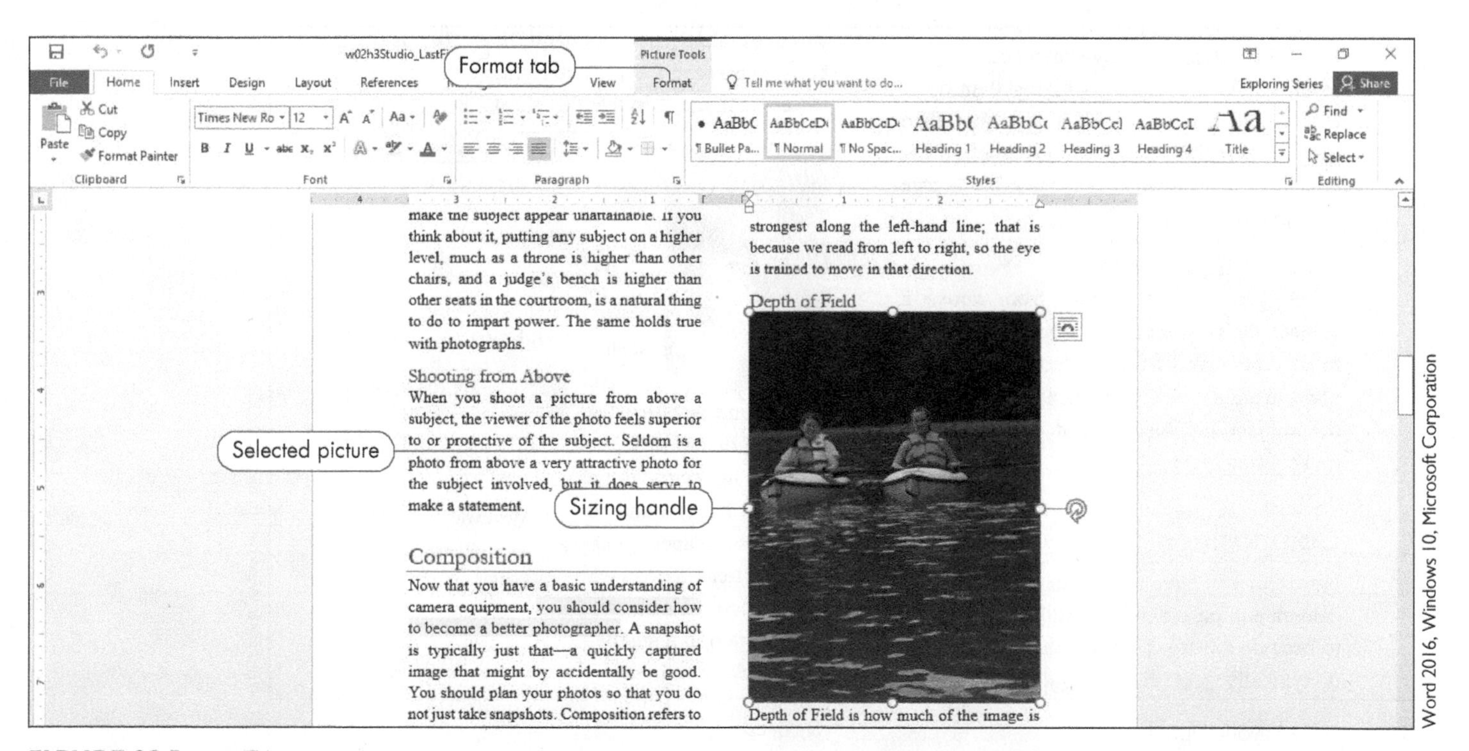

FIGURE 38 Format Tab

Although an inserted picture is considered a separate object, you will want to position it so that it flows well with document text and does not appear to be a separate unit. One way to make that happen is to wrap text around the picture. The Format tab includes Wrap Text in the Arrange group (refer to Figure 38). You can select from the text wrapping styles shown in Table 3 when you click Wrap Text. You can also choose to allow the object to move with text as text is added or deleted, or you can keep the object in the same place on the page, regardless of text changes.

TABLE 2.3 Text Wrap Options

Type	Effect
In Line with Text	The image is part of the line of text in which it is inserted. Typically, text wraps above and below the object.
Square	Text wraps on all sides of an object, following an invisible square.
Tight	Text follows the shape of the object, but does not overlap the object.
Through	Text follows the shape of the object, filling any open spaces in the shape.
Top and Bottom	Text flows above and below the borders of the object.
Behind Text	The object is positioned behind text. Both the object and text are visible (unless the fill color exactly matches the text color).
In Front of Text	The object is positioned in front of text, often obscuring the text.

Word has a feature that simplifies text wrapping around an object—Layout Options. Located next to a selected object, the Layout Options control (see Figure 39) includes the same selections shown in Table 3. The close proximity of the control to the selected object makes it easy to quickly adjust text wrapping.

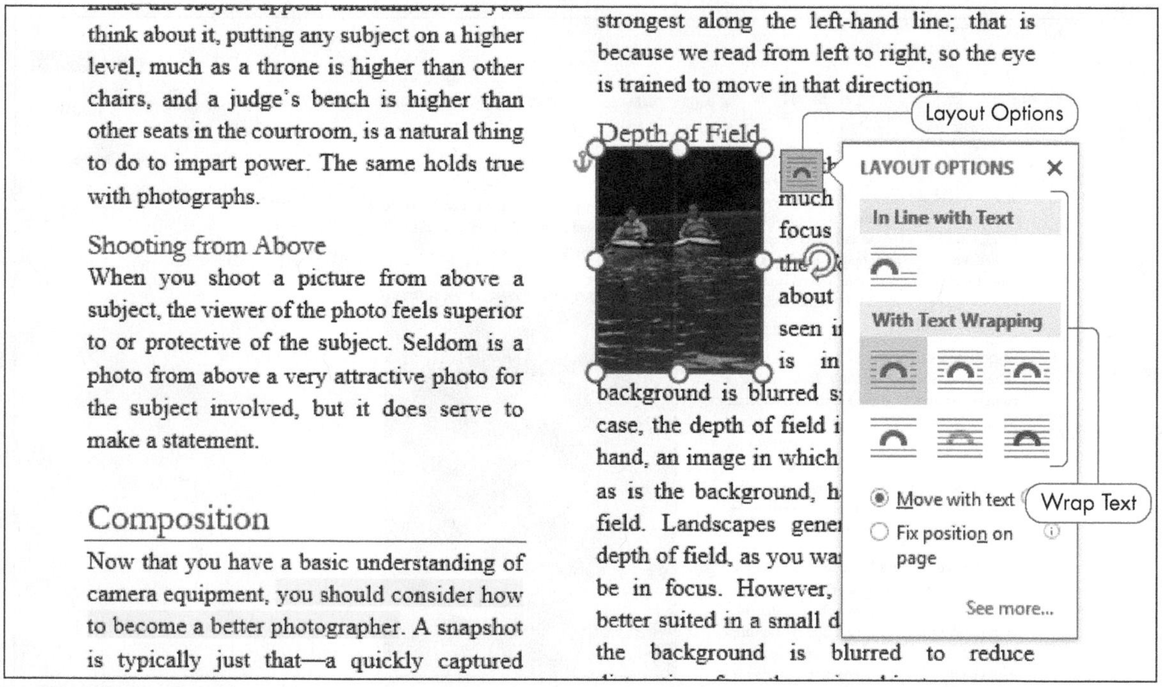

FIGURE 39 Layout Options

Word has two interesting features to assist you as you wrap text: Live Layout and alignment guides. ***Live Layout*** enables you to watch text flow around an object as you move it, so you can position the object exactly as you want it. ***Alignment guides*** are horizontal or vertical green bars that appear as you drag an object, so you can line up an object with text or with another object. The green alignment guide shown in Figure 40 helps align the picture object with paragraph text.

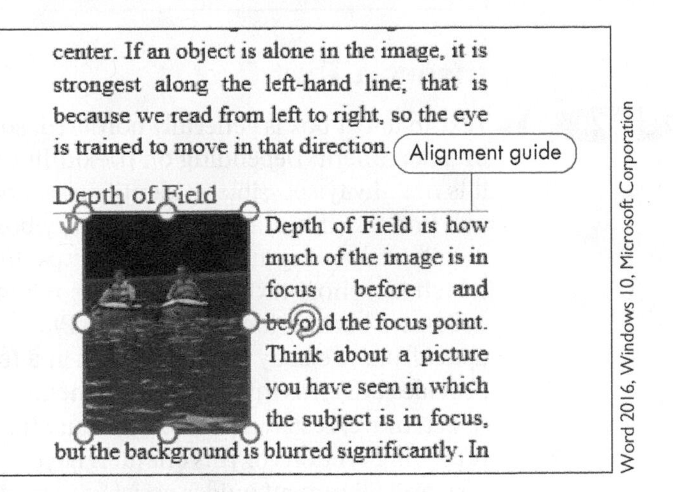

subject is in control of a situation. It can also make the subject appear unattainable. If you think about it, putting any subject on a higher level, much as a throne is higher than other chairs, and a judge's bench is higher than other seats in the courtroom, is a natural thing to do to impart power. The same holds true with photographs.

Shooting from Above

When you shoot a picture from above a subject, the viewer of the photo feels superior to or protective of the subject. Seldom is a photo from above a very attractive photo for the subject involved, but it does serve to

center. If an object is alone in the image, it is strongest along the left-hand line; that is because we read from left to right, so the eye is trained to move in that direction.

Depth of Field

Depth of Field is how much of the image is in focus before and beyond the focus point. Think about a picture you have seen in which the subject is in focus, but the background is blurred significantly. In

FIGURE 40 Alignment Guides

Often, a picture is inserted in a size that is too large or too small for your purposes. To resize a picture, you can drag a corner ***sizing handle***, which is a series of faint dots on the outside border of a selected object. (Resizing a picture by dragging a center sizing handle is generally not recommended, as doing so skews the picture.) You can also resize a picture by adjusting settings in the Size group of the Format tab (refer to Figure 38).

Modify a Picture

STEP 3 The Format tab includes options for modifying a picture. You can apply a picture style or effect, as well as add a picture border, from selections in the Picture Styles group. Click the More arrow (refer to Figure 38) to view a gallery of picture styles. As you point to a style, the style is shown in Live Preview, but the style is not applied until you click it. Options in the Adjust group simplify changing a color scheme, applying creative artistic effects, and even adjusting the brightness, contrast, and sharpness of an image.

If a picture contains more detail than is necessary, you can ***crop*** it, which is the process of trimming edges that you do not want to display. The Crop tool is located on the Format tab (refer to Figure 38). Even though cropping enables you to adjust the amount of a picture that displays, it does not actually delete the portions that are cropped out. Therefore, you can later restore parts of the picture, if necessary. Note that this means also that cropping a picture does not reduce the file size of the picture or of the Word document in which it displays.

Other common adjustments to a picture include contrast and/or brightness. Adjusting contrast increases or decreases the difference in dark and light areas of the image. Adjusting brightness lightens or darkens the overall image. These adjustments often are made on a picture taken with a digital camera in poor lighting or if a picture is too bright or dull to match other objects in your document. The Brightness/Contrast adjustment is available when you click Corrections in the Adjust group on the Format tab (refer to Figure 38).

> **TIP: REMOVING BACKGROUND**
> Word makes it easy to remove the background or portions of a picture you do not want to keep. When you select a picture and click the Remove Background tool in the Adjust group on the Format tab, Word creates a marquee selection area in the picture that determines the background, or area to be removed, and the foreground, or area to be kept. Word identifies the background selection with magenta coloring. Using tools on the Background Removal tab, you can mark areas to keep or mark additional areas to remove. Click Keep Changes to remove the background.

Insert a Text Box

Text in a text box is generally bordered, sometimes shaded, and set apart from other text in a document. Depending on the outline selected, a border might not even be visible, so it is not always possible to identify a text box in a document. In most cases, however, you will find a text box as a conspicuously boxed area of text—usually providing additional details or drawing attention to an important point. A text box could contain a pull quote, which is a short text excerpt that is reinforced from a document, or a text box could be used as a banner for a newsletter. Place any text you want to draw attention to or set apart from the body of a document in a text box. Figure 41 shows a simple text box that provides business information. Remember that a text box is an object. As such, you can select, move, resize, and modify it, much as you learned you could do with pictures in the preceding sections of this chapter. Layout Options enable you to wrap text around a text box, and alignment guides assist with positioning a text box within existing text.

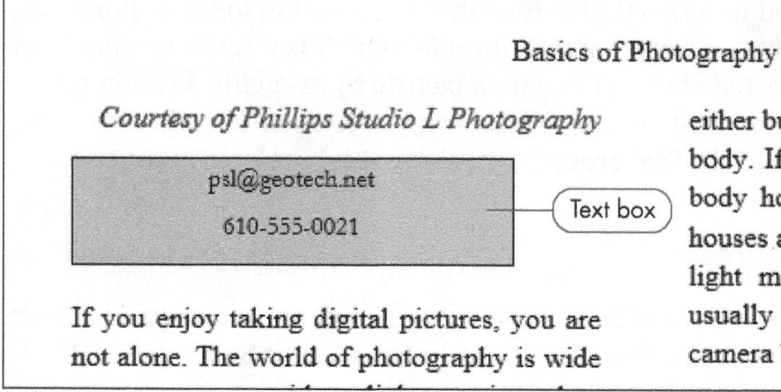

Basics of Photography
Courtesy of Phillips Studio L Photography
psl@geotech.net
610-555-0021
Text box
If you enjoy taking digital pictures, you are not alone. The world of photography is wide
either built in to the body, or it attaches to the body. If the camera is a film-based unit, the body holds the film. In addition, the body houses a batter that powers the shutter, flash, light meter, and other controls. You will usually find rings to connect a strap to the camera body for ease of carrying.

Word 2016, Windows 10, Microsoft Corporation

FIGURE 41 Text Box

> **To insert a text box, complete the following steps:**
>
> 1. Click the Insert tab.
> 2. Click Text Box in the Text group.
> 3. Click Draw Text Box or select a predefined text box style (see Figure 42).
> 4. Drag to draw a box (unless you selected a predefined text box style, in which case, the text box will be automatically drawn). The dimensions of the text box are not that critical, as you can adjust the size using the Ribbon.
> 5. Type text in the text box.

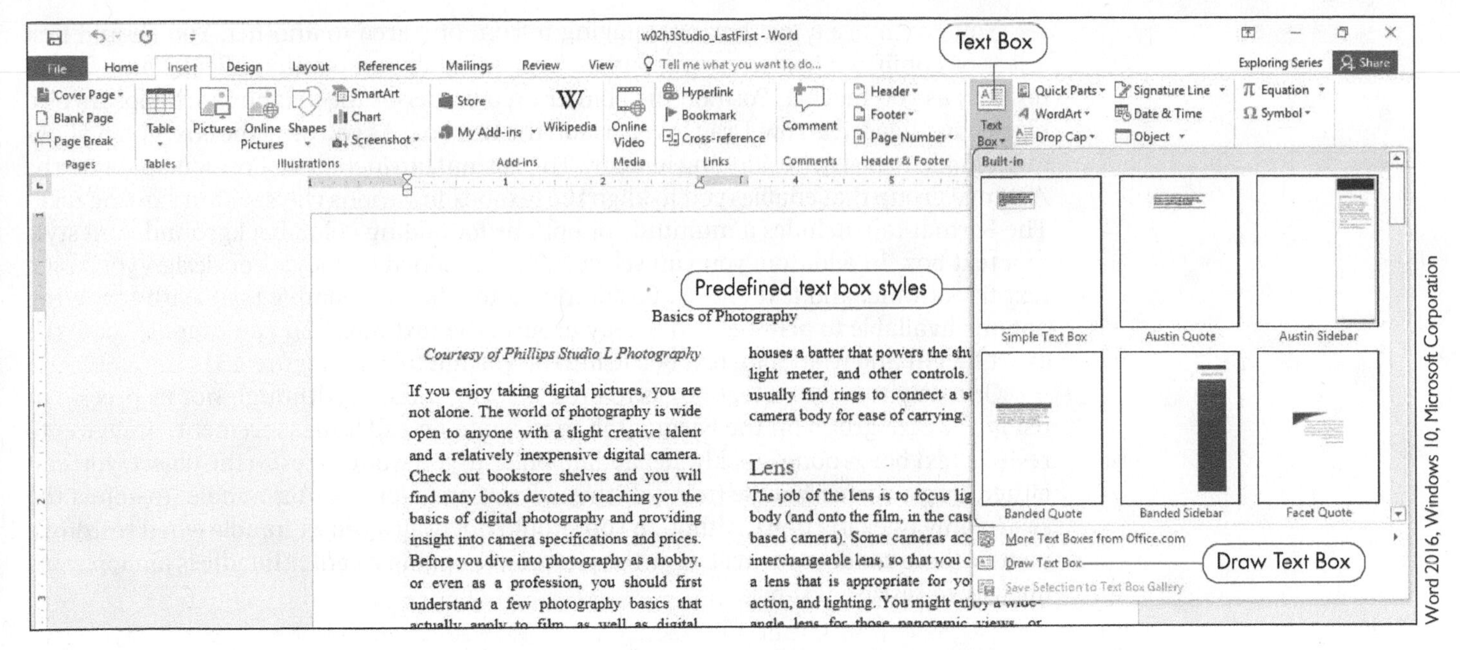

FIGURE 42 Draw a Text Box

> **TIP: FORMATTING TEXT IN A TEXT BOX**
> Before formatting text in a text box, you should select the text to be affected. To do so, drag to select the text to be formatted. Or, if you want to select all text, you might appreciate learning a shortcut. You can select all of the text when you click the dashed border surrounding the text box (when the pointer is a small four-headed shape). The dashed line should become solid, indicating that all text is selected. At that point, any formatting selections you make related to text are applied to all text in the text box.

Modify, Move, and Resize a Text Box

You can be as creative as you like when designing a text box. Options on the Format tab enable you to add color and definition to a text box with shape fill and outline selections, or select from a gallery of shape styles. Select text within a text box and select an alignment option on the Home tab to left-align, right-align, center, or justify text.

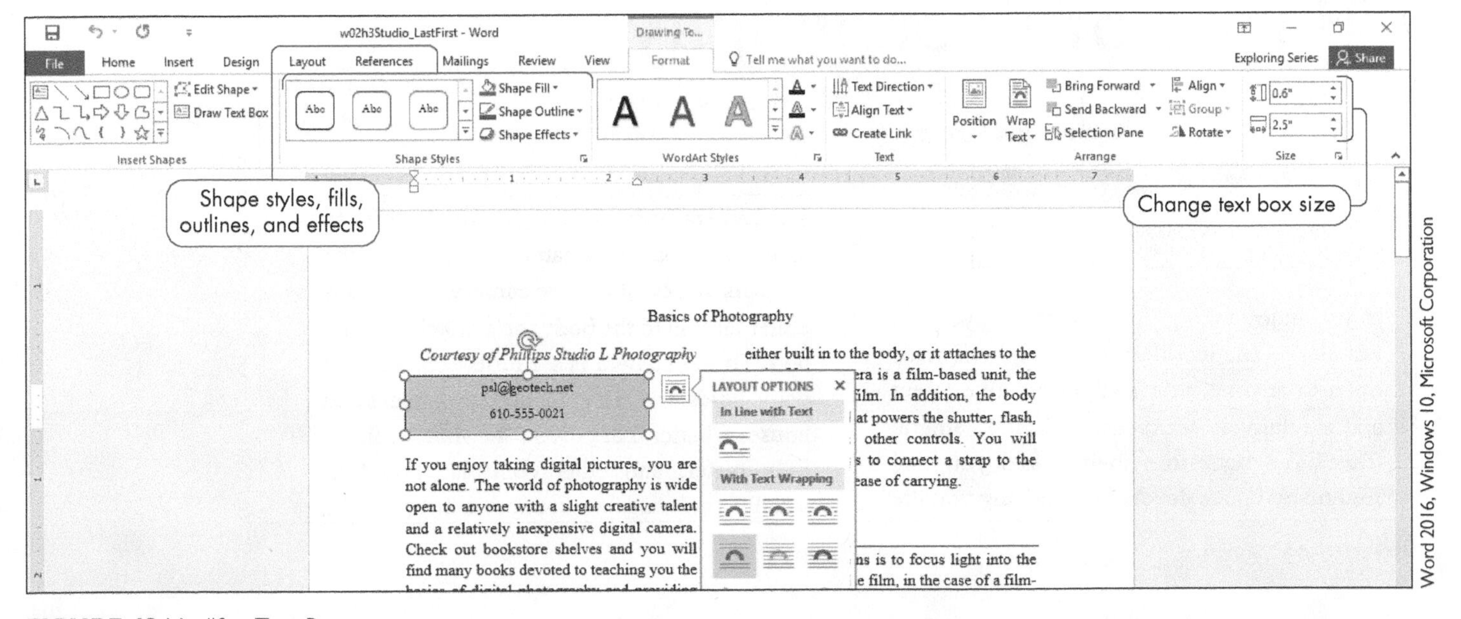

FIGURE 43 Modify a Text Box

You can move a text box by dragging it from one area to another. You should first select or confirm a text wrapping option. Text will then wrap automatically around the text box as you move it. Position the pointer on a border of the text box so it appears as a black, four-headed arrow. Drag to reposition the text box. As you drag the box, green alignment guides assist in positioning it neatly. The Format tab includes a Position option in the Arrange group that enables you to align the text box in various ways within existing text. The Format tab includes a multitude of options for adding color, background, and style to a text box. In addition, you can select from predefined text styles or design your own text fill, outline, and text effects. Positioning a text box is a simple task, with text wrap options available to arrange text evenly around the text box. You can even indicate the exact height and width of a text box using the Format tab (see Figure 43).

One way to resize a text box is to drag a sizing handle. Although not as precise as using the Size group on the Format tab to indicate an exact measurement, dragging to resize a text box is done quickly. Depending on how you want to resize the object, you can either drag a corner handle (to resize two sides at once) or a center handle (to adjust the size in only one direction). Although you should not drag a center handle when resizing a picture (because doing so will skew the picture), dragging a center handle is an appropriate way to resize a text box.

Insert WordArt

STEP 5 **_WordArt_** is a feature that modifies text to include special effects, including colors, shadows, gradients, and 3-D effects (see Figure 44). It is a quick way to format text so that it is vibrant and eye-catching. Of course, WordArt is not appropriate for all documents, especially more conservative business correspondence, but it can give life to newsletters, flyers, and other more informal projects, especially when applied to headings and titles. WordArt is well suited for single lines, such as document headings, where the larger print and text design draws attention and adds style to a document title. However, it is not appropriate for body text, because a WordArt object is managed independently of surrounding text and cannot be formatted as a document (with specific margins, headers, footers, etc.). In addition, if WordArt were incorporated into body text, the more ornate text design would adversely affect the readability of the document.

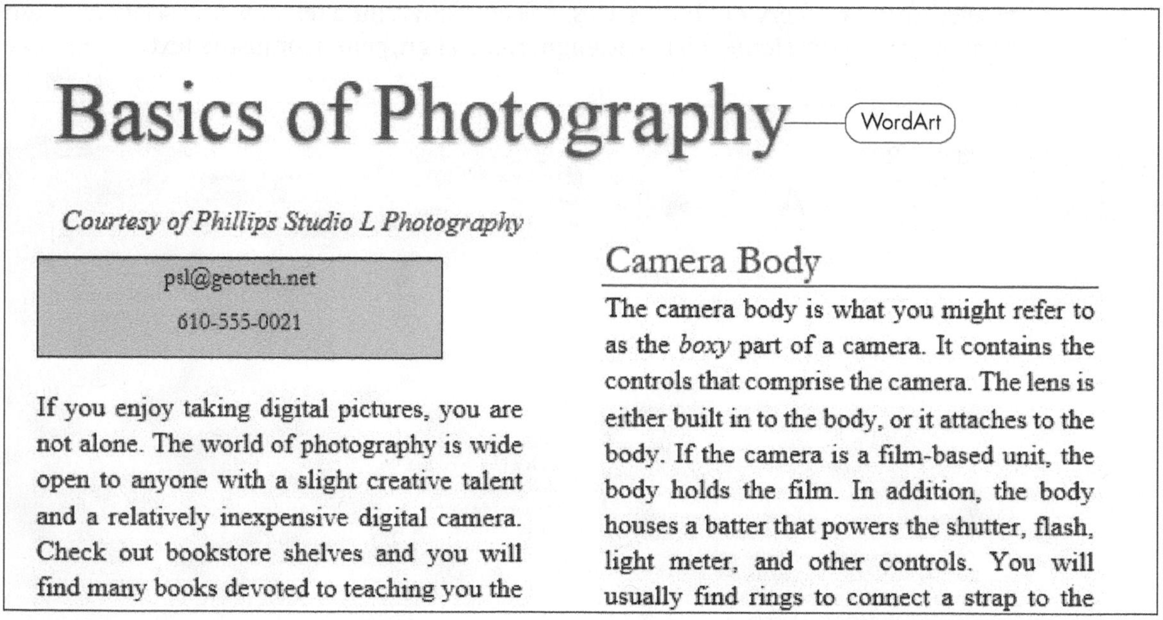

Basics of Photography — WordArt

Courtesy of Phillips Studio L Photography

psl@geotech.net
610-555-0021

If you enjoy taking digital pictures, you are not alone. The world of photography is wide open to anyone with a slight creative talent and a relatively inexpensive digital camera. Check out bookstore shelves and you will find many books devoted to teaching you the

Camera Body

The camera body is what you might refer to as the *boxy* part of a camera. It contains the controls that comprise the camera. The lens is either built in to the body, or it attaches to the body. If the camera is a film-based unit, the body holds the film. In addition, the body houses a batter that powers the shutter, flash, light meter, and other controls. You will usually find rings to connect a strap to the

FIGURE 44 WordArt

You can format existing text as WordArt, or you can insert new WordArt text into a document. WordArt is considered an object; as such, the preceding discussion related to positioning pictures and text boxes applies to WordArt as well. Also, Live Layout and alignment guides are available to facilitate ease of positioning, and you can select a text wrapping style with layout options.

To format existing text as WordArt, complete the following steps:

1. Select text to be formatted.
2. Click the Insert tab.
3. Click WordArt in the Text group.
4. Select a WordArt style.

To insert new text as WordArt, complete the following steps:

1. Place the insertion point at the point where WordArt should appear.
2. Click the Insert tab.
3. Click WordArt in the Text group.
4. Select a WordArt style.
5. Type text.

Depending upon the purpose of a document and its intended audience, objects such as pictures, text boxes, and WordArt can help convey a message and add interest. As you learn to incorporate objects visually within a document so that they appear to flow seamlessly within existing text, you will find it easy to create attractive, informative documents that contain an element of design apart from simple text.

9. How would you determine what type of text wrapping to use when positioning a picture in a document?
10. Describe two methods to modify the height and width of a picture.
11. How does a text box differ from simple shaded text?
12. Why is WordArt most often used to format headings or titles, and not text in the body of a document?

Hands-On Exercises

Skills covered: Insert a Picture • Move, Align, and Resize a Picture • Modify a Picture • Insert a Text Box • Modify, Move, and Resize a Text Box • Insert WordArt

3 Objects

You will add interest to the newsletter by including pictures that illustrate points, a text box with business information, and WordArt that livens up the newsletter heading.

STEP 1 » INSERT A PICTURE

You will include pictures in the newsletter to represent photographs shot from various angles, as well as holiday graphics. The pictures will be formatted with appropriate picture styles and effects and positioned within existing text. Refer to Figure 45 as you complete Step 1.

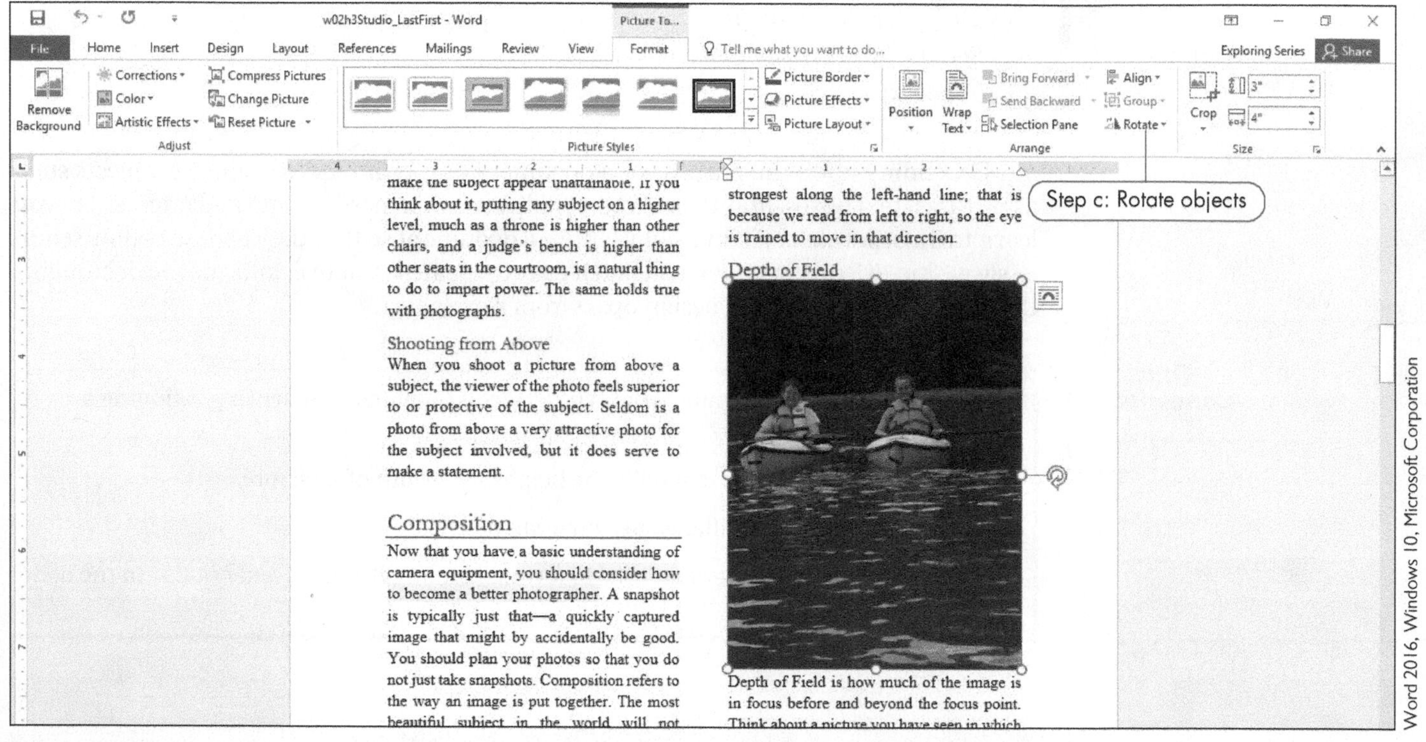

FIGURE 45 Insert and Rotate a Picture

a. Open *w02h2Studio_LastFirst* if you closed it at the end of Hands-On Exercise 2, and save it as **w02h3Studio_LastFirst**, changing h2 to h3.

b. Scroll to the second page of the document and click to place the insertion point before the words *Depth of Field is how much of the image*. Click the **Insert tab** and click **Pictures** in the Illustrations group. Navigate to the location of your student data files and double-click *w02h3Kayak*.

The picture is inserted, but must be rotated.

c. Ensure the picture selected (surrounded by a border and sizing handles), click **Rotate Objects** in the Arrange group on the Format tab, and click **Rotate Right 90°**. Click outside the picture to deselect it.

> **TROUBLESHOOTING:** If you do not see Rotate Objects or the Format tab, click the picture to select it and then click the Format tab.

d. Scroll to the third page and click to place the insertion point before *The most common reason for a blurred image* under the *Blurry Images Due to Focus* heading. Click the **Insert tab**, click **Pictures** in the Illustrations group, and then double-click *w02h3Float* in your student data files. Rotate the picture to the right. Click outside the picture to deselect it.

> **TROUBLESHOOTING:** The placement of the picture will vary, so it is OK if it is not positioned directly below the *Blurry Images Due to Focus* heading. You will move it later.

e. Scroll to the *Holiday Photography* section and click to place the insertion point before *Now for the fun part*. Click the **Insert tab**. Click **Online Pictures** in the Illustrations group. In the Bing Image Search box, type **Ski** and press **Enter**. Select the picture shown in Figure 47 (or one that is very similar). Click **Insert**.

The picture is placed within or very near the *Holiday Photography* section. You will reposition it and resize it later.

f. Save the document.

STEP 2 » MOVE, ALIGN, AND RESIZE A PICTURE

The pictures you inserted are a bit large, so you will resize them. You will also position them within the column and select an appropriate text wrapping style. Refer to Figure 46 and Figure 47 as you complete Step 2.

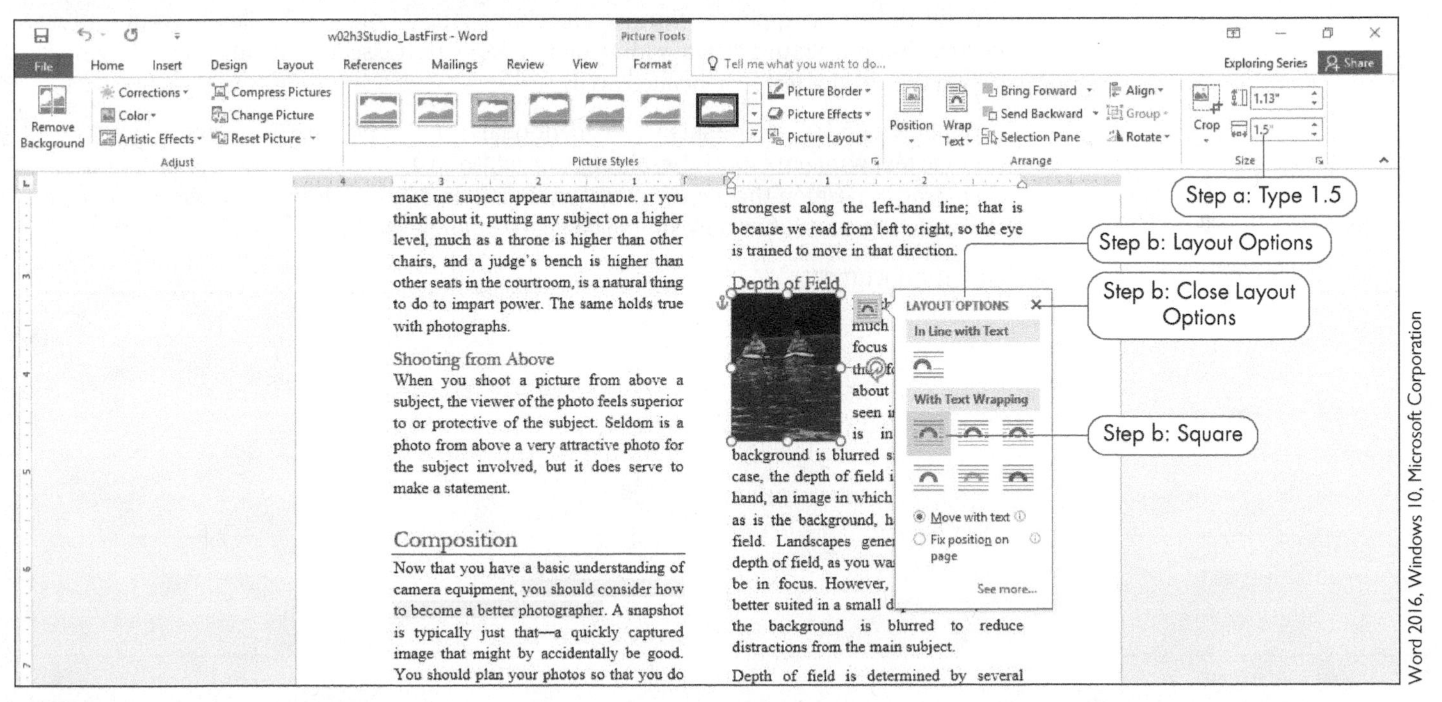

FIGURE 46 Resize, Move, and Align Pictures

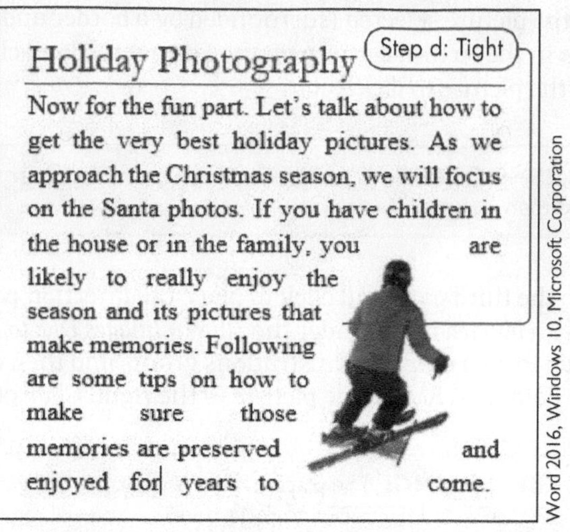

Holiday Photography
Step d: Tight
Now for the fun part. Let's talk about how to get the very best holiday pictures. As we approach the Christmas season, we will focus on the Santa photos. If you have children in the house or in the family, you are likely to really enjoy the season and its pictures that make memories. Following are some tips on how to make sure those memories are preserved and enjoyed for years to come.
Word 2016, Windows 10, Microsoft Corporation

FIGURE 47 Insert and Rotate Pictures

a. Scroll up and click to select the picture near the *Depth of Field* section. Click in the **Width box** in the Size group on the Format tab and type **1.5**. Press **Enter**.

By default, the Lock aspect ratio setting is on, which means that when you change a dimension—either width or height—of a picture, the other dimension is automatically adjusted as well. To confirm or deselect the Lock aspect ratio, click the Size Dialog Box Launcher and adjust the setting in the Layout dialog box. Unless you deselect the setting, you cannot change both width and height distinctly from each other, as that would skew the picture.

b. Click **Layout Options** (beside the selected picture) and select **Square** (first selection under *With Text Wrapping*). Close Layout Options. Check the placement of the image with that shown in Figure 46, and adjust if necessary.

c. Scroll down and select the second picture, near the *Blurry Images Due to Focus* heading. Change the text wrapping to **Square** and change the width to **1.5**. Close Layout Options. Ensure that the picture displays immediately beneath the section heading by dragging it (when the pointer is a four-headed arrow).

d. Scroll down and select the ski picture in, or near, the *Holiday Photography* section. Change text wrapping to **Tight**, change the width to **1.5**, close Layout Options, and then drag to position the picture as shown in Figure 47. Words may not wrap exactly as shown in Figure 47, but they should be approximately as shown.

e. Save the document.

STEP 3 » MODIFY A PICTURE

You will apply a picture style and picture effects to the pictures included in the newsletter. You will also crop a picture to remove unnecessary detail. Refer to Figure 48 and Figure 49 as you complete Step 3.

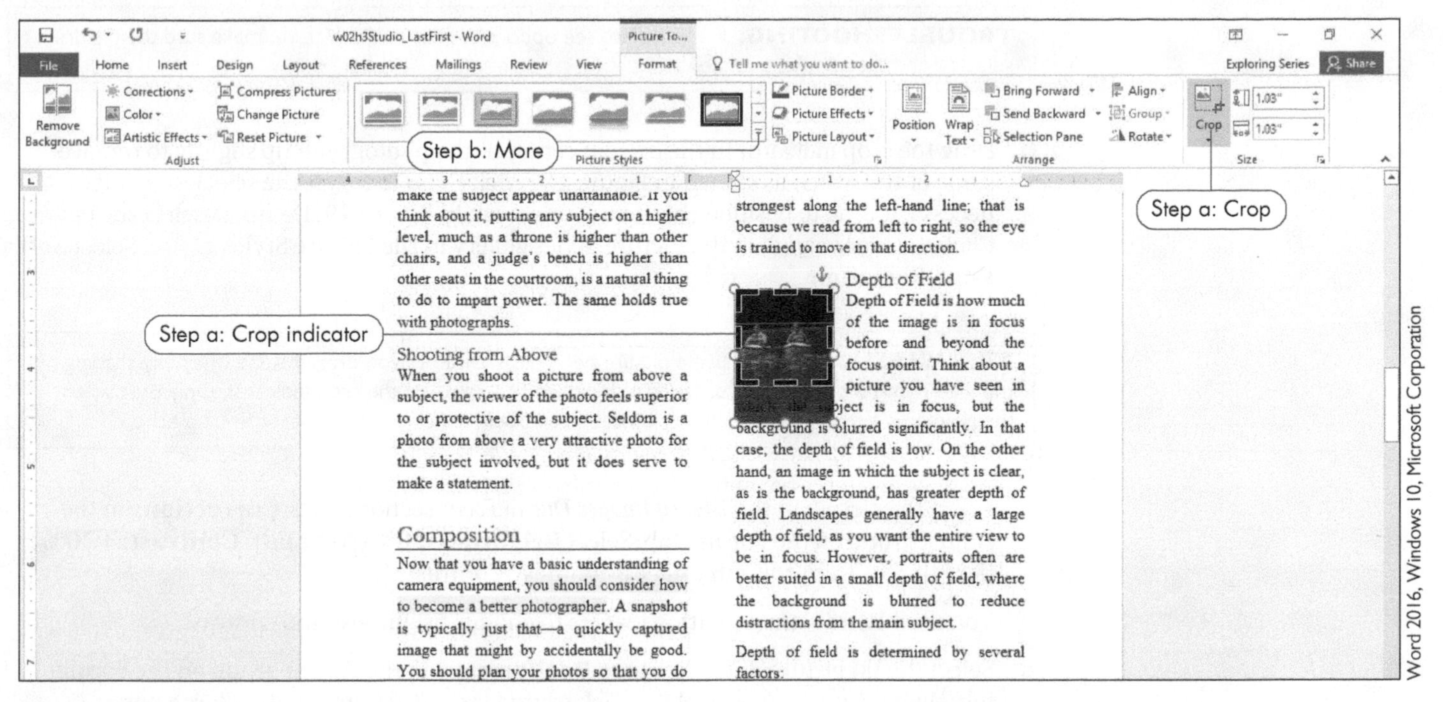

make the subject appear unattainable. If you think about it, putting any subject on a higher level, much as a throne is higher than other chairs, and a judge's bench is higher than other seats in the courtroom, is a natural thing to do to impart power. The same holds true with photographs.

Shooting from Above

When you shoot a picture from above a subject, the viewer of the photo feels superior to or protective of the subject. Seldom is a photo from above a very attractive photo for the subject involved, but it does serve to make a statement.

Composition

Now that you have a basic understanding of camera equipment, you should consider how to become a better photographer. A snapshot is typically just that—a quickly captured image that might by accidentally be good. You should plan your photos so that you do

strongest along the left-hand line; that is because we read from left to right, so the eye is trained to move in that direction.

Depth of Field

Depth of Field is how much of the image is in focus before and beyond the focus point. Think about a picture you have seen in which the subject is in focus, but the background is blurred significantly. In that case, the depth of field is low. On the other hand, an image in which the subject is clear, as is the background, has greater depth of field. Landscapes generally have a large depth of field, as you want the entire view to be in focus. However, portraits often are better suited in a small depth of field, where the background is blurred to reduce distractions from the main subject.

Depth of field is determined by several factors:

Word 2016, Windows 10, Microsoft Corporation

FIGURE 48 Crop a Picture

hands, as though you were the golfer and you were looking at the ball and club. Such shots enable a viewer to feel as though he or she were in the photo.

Shooting from Below

When you take a photo of a subject as you are looking up, it makes the viewer feel as if the subject is in control of a situation. It can also make the subject appear unattainable. If you think about it, putting any subject on a higher level, much as a throne is higher than other chairs, and a judge's bench is higher than other seats in the courtroom, is a natural thing to do to impart power. The same holds true with photographs.

Step b: Soft Edge Rectangle

Shooting from Above

When you shoot a picture from above a subject, the viewer of the photo feels superior to or protective of the subject. Seldom is a photo from above a very attractive photo for the subject involved, but it does serve to make a statement.

Composition

Imagine a tic-tac-toe board being drawn across a subject that you are photographing. The board is broken into nine equal squares. The four points where those lines intersect are the strongest focal points. Now, imagine the grid placement as you shoot. A picture is usually best composed when the subject is in one third of the grid, and not right in the center. If an object is alone in the image, it is strongest along the left-hand line; that is because we read from left to right, so the eye is trained to move in that direction.

Depth of Field

Depth of Field is how much of the image is in focus before and beyond the focus point. Think about a picture you have seen in which the subject is in focus, but the background is blurred significantly. In that case, the depth of field is low. On the other hand, an image in which the subject is clear, as is the background, has greater depth of field. Landscapes generally have a large depth of field, as you want the entire view to

Word 2016, Windows 10, Microsoft Corporation

FIGURE 49 Select a Picture Style

a. Select the picture in the *Depth of Field* section. Click **Crop** in the Size group on the Format tab. (Be sure to click Crop, not the Crop arrow.)

   The crop indicator consists of dark thick lines around the selected picture.

> **TROUBLESHOOTING:** If you do not see options related to the picture, make sure the picture is selected and click the Format tab.

b. Drag the crop indicator in the bottom center of the photograph up slightly to remove some of the water, as shown in Figure 48. Click **Crop** to toggle the selection off. If necessary, drag to position the picture as shown in Figure 49. Do not deselect the picture. Click the More arrow in the Picture Styles gallery in the Picture Styles group. Select **Soft Edge Rectangle**.

> **TROUBLESHOOTING:** If the picture becomes skewed as you drag, instead of simply shading the water to remove, you are dragging a sizing handle instead of the crop indicator. Only drag when the pointer is a thick black T, not a two-headed arrow. Click Undo and repeat the crop action.

c. Select the picture in the *Blurry Images Due to Focus* section. Click **Corrections** in the Adjust group on the Format tab. Select **Brightness: 0% (Normal), Contrast: +20%** (fourth row, third column under Brightness/Contrast).

   You used Word's image editing feature to change brightness and contrast.

d. Select the ski picture. Click **Remove Background** in the Adjust group on the Format tab. Wait a few seconds until the background is shaded in magenta. Click **Keep Changes**. Deselect the picture.

e. Save the document.

STEP 4 » INSERT, MODIFY, MOVE, AND RESIZE A TEXT BOX

By placing text in a text box, you can draw attention to information you want your readers to notice. You will insert a text box, including the studio's contact information, near the beginning of the document. You will then modify the text to coordinate with other page elements. Refer to Figure 50 as you complete Step 4.

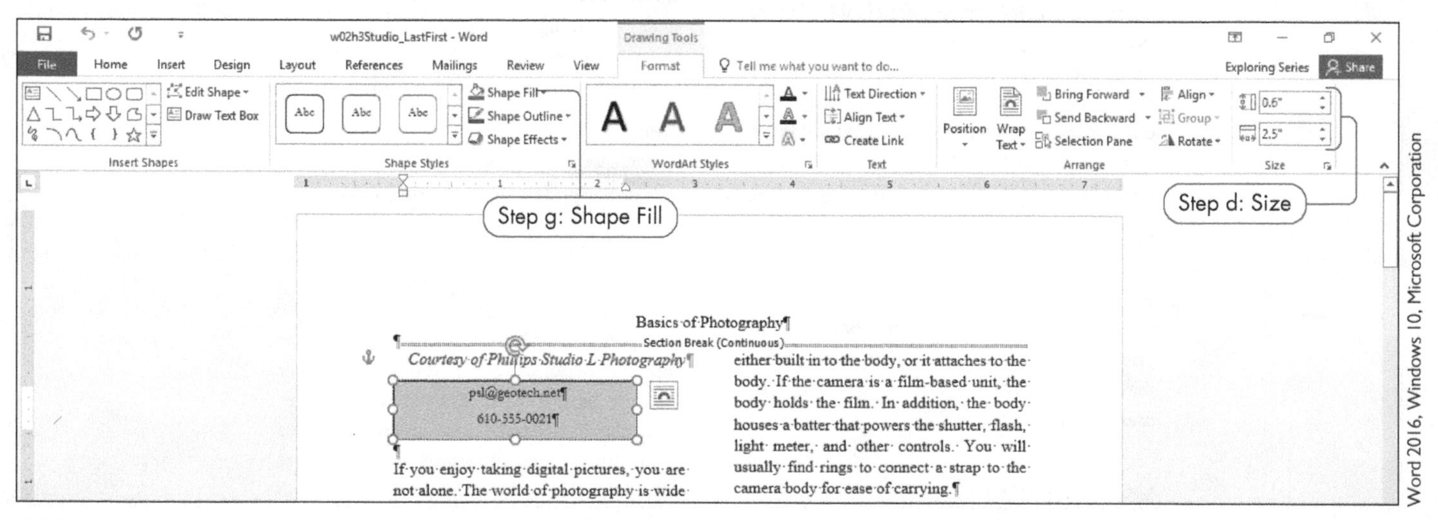

FIGURE 50 Insert a Text Box

a. Press **Ctrl+Home**. Click **Show/Hide** in the Paragraph group on the Home tab to ensure that nonprinting characters display.

b. Click the **Insert tab** and click **Text Box** in the Text group. Click **Draw Text Box**. Point to the blank paragraph mark below *Courtesy of Phillips Studio L Photography* and drag to draw a small box. The dimensions are not important, as you will resize the text box later.

A small text box is drawn in the document.

c. Click **Layout Options** (beside the text box) and select **Top and Bottom** (second row, first column under Text Wrapping). Close Layout Options.

Text wraps above and below the text box.

d. Click the **Height box** in the Size group on the Format tab and type **0.6**. Click the Width box and type **2.5**. Press **Enter**.

e. Click in the text box to position the insertion point. Type **psl@geotech.net** and press **Enter**. Type **610-555-0021**. Right-click the underlined email link in the text box and select **Remove Hyperlink**.

f. Click the dashed line surrounding the text box to make it solid, so that all text in the text box is selected (although it is not shaded). Click the **Home tab** and click **Center** in the Paragraph group.

All text is centered in the text box.

g. Click the **Format tab**. Click **Shape Fill** in the Shape Styles group. Select **Plum, Accent 1, Lighter 80%** (second row, fifth column).

The text box background is shaded to match the document theme.

h. Position the pointer near a border of the text box so that the pointer appears as a four-headed arrow. Drag to the left edge of the column, until the green alignment guide indicates the text box is aligned at that edge. Release the mouse button. The text box should appear as shown in Figure 50.

i. Save the document.

STEP 5 »» INSERT WORDART

The newsletter is near completion, but you need to work with the heading—*Basics of Photography*. You will format the heading with WordArt to add some visual appeal. Refer to Figure 51 as you complete Step 5.

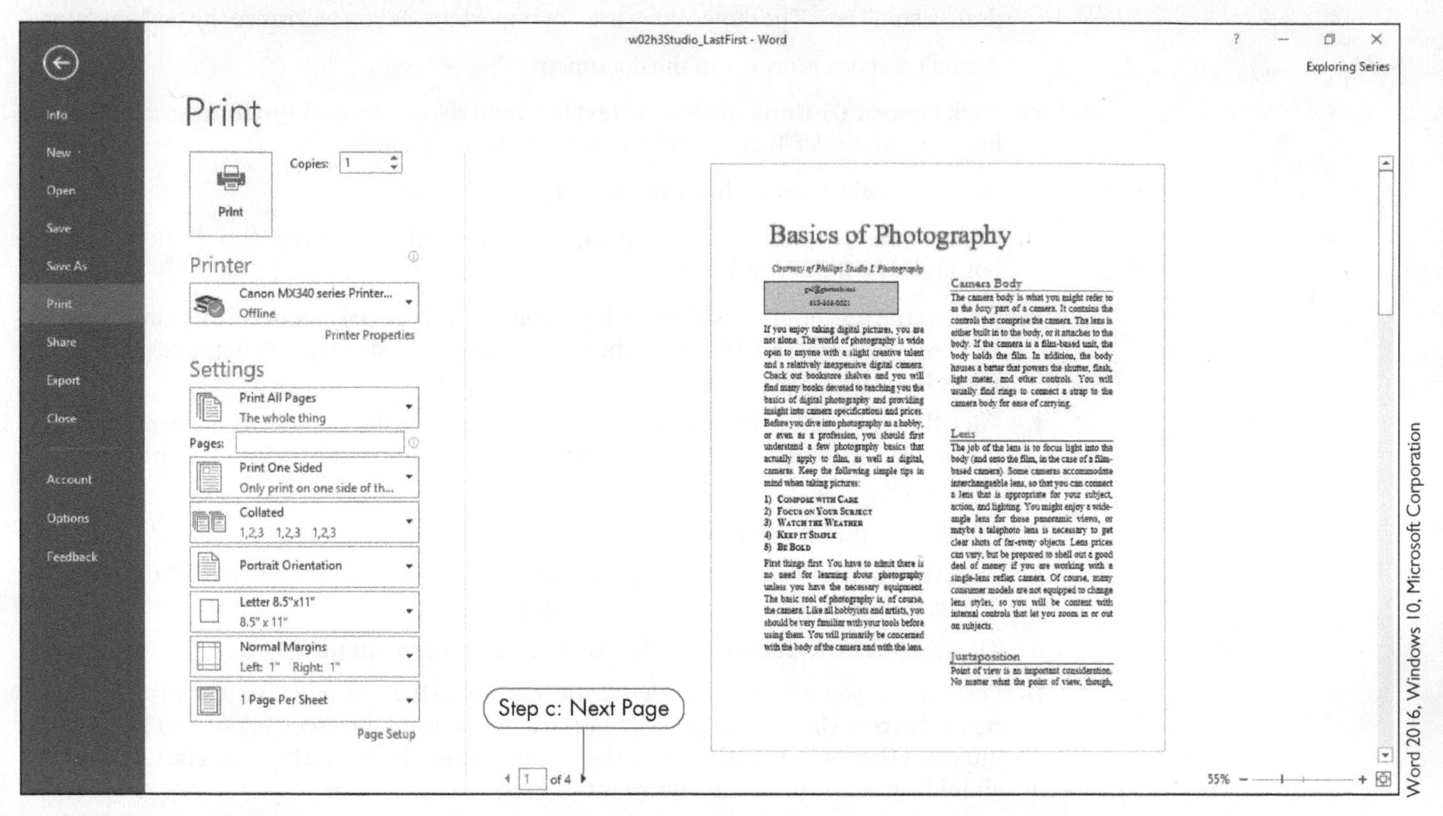

FIGURE 51 Insert WordArt

a. Select *Basics of Photography* on the first line of the newsletter, including the following paragraph mark. Be careful not to select the Section Break indicator following the paragraph mark. Click the **Insert tab** and click **WordArt** in the Text group. Select **Fill – Plum, Accent 1, Shadow** (first row, second column).

> **TROUBLESHOOTING:** If you do not see a Section Break indicator, click Show/Hide in the Paragraph group on the Home tab to display the nonprinting characters.

The heading is formatted in WordArt, in a shade that coordinates with other text formatting in the newsletter.

b. Click **Layout Options** and click **Top and Bottom**. Close Layout Options.

c. Click outside the WordArt object to deselect it. Click the **File tab** and click **Print**. The first page shows in preview in the right pane (refer to Figure 51). Click **Next Page** (at the bottom of the preview page) to move to the next page.

d. Save and close the file. Based on your instructor's directions, submit w02h3Studio_LastFirst.

Chapter Objectives Review

After reading this chapter, you have accomplished the following objectives:

1. Apply font attributes.

- Select font options: Font options include serif or sans serif fonts, as well as monospaced or proportional fonts. The Font group on the Home tab contains all the font selections.
- Change text appearance: Format characters by applying bold, italics, underline, font color, text highlighting, and text effects.

2. Format a paragraph.

- Select paragraph alignment: Align paragraphs to be left or right aligned, centered, or justified.
- Select line and paragraph spacing: Line spacing refers to the amount of space between lines within a paragraph, whereas paragraph spacing is the amount of space between paragraphs.
- Select indents: Options for indenting paragraphs include left indent, right indent, hanging indent, and first line indent.
- Set tab stops: Use tabs to indent the first line of the paragraph, or to arrange text in columns, including leaders if desired.
- Apply borders and shading: Borders and shading draw attention to selected paragraphs.
- Create bulleted and numbered lists: Itemized lists can be set apart from other text with bullets, while sequential lists are formatted with numbers.

3. Format a document.

- Select a document theme: Use a theme to create a color-coordinated document, with page elements based on theme settings.
- Work with sections: Divide a document into sections, so that each area can be formatted independently of others.
- Format text into columns: Some documents, such as newsletters, are formatted in two or more columns.

4. Apply styles.

- Select and modify styles: Styles enable you to apply identical formatting to page features, such as headings. When a style is modified, changes apply to all text formatted in that style.
- Use a style set: Select a style set to quickly format page elements, such as headers and paragraph text.
- Create a new style from text: Format text and create a style from the text so that formatting characteristics can be easily applied to other text in the document.
- Use Outline view: Expand and collapse sections, view document structure, and easily rearrange document sections in Outline view.

5. Insert and format objects.

- Insert a picture: Insert pictures from online sources or from a storage device connected to your computer.
- Move, align, and resize a picture: Reposition objects easily using Live Layout and alignment guides. You can also resize objects and wrap text around objects.
- Modify a picture: Apply a picture style or effect, adjust the color, contrast, and brightness of a picture, and crop a picture to modify a picture's appearance.
- Insert a text box: Include text in a bordered area by inserting a text box. You can format a text box with shape styles and effects, and you can align text within a text box.
- Modify, move, and resize a text box: As an object, a text box can be modified, moved, and resized with options on the Format tab.
- Insert WordArt: A WordArt object displays text with special effects, such as color, size, gradient, and 3-D appearance.

Key Terms Matching

Match the key terms with their definitions. Write the key term letter by the appropriate numbered definition.

a. Alignment guide
b. Border
c. Bulleted list
d. Column
e. Document theme
f. First line indent
g. Font
h. Indent
i. Line spacing
j. Live Preview
k. Object
l. Paragraph spacing
m. Picture
n. Section break
o. Sizing handle
p. Style
q. Style set
r. Tab stop
s. Text box
t. WordArt

1. ______ A feature that modifies text to include special effects, such as color, shadow, gradient, and 3-D appearance.

2. ______ A series of faint dots on the outside border of a selected object; enables the user to adjust the height and width of the object.

3. ______ A list of points that is not sequential.

4. ______ An item, such as a picture or text box, that can be individually selected and manipulated.

5. ______ A unified set of design elements, including font style, color, and special effects, that is applied to an entire document.

6. ______ A typeface or complete set of characters.

7. ______ A named collection of formatting characteristics that can be applied to characters or paragraphs.

8. ______ A mark that indicates the location to indent only the first line in a paragraph.

9. ______ The horizontal or vertical green bar that appears as you move an object, assisting with lining up an object.

10. ______ A combination of title, heading, and paragraph styles that can be used to format all of those elements at one time.

11. ______ A format that separates document text into side-by-side vertical blocks, often used in newsletters.

12. ______ A line that surrounds a paragraph or a page.

13. ______ The amount of space before or after a paragraph.

14. ______ An Office feature that provides a preview of the results of a selection when you point to it.

15. ______ The vertical space between the lines in a paragraph.

16. ______ An indicator that divides a document into parts, enabling different formatting in each section.

17. ______ A boxed object that can be bordered and shaded, providing space for text.

18. ______ A marker that specifies the position for aligning text, sometimes including a leader.

19. ______ A graphic file that is obtained from the Internet or a storage device.

20. ______ A setting associated with the way a paragraph is distanced from one or more margins.

Multiple Choice

1. How does a document theme differ from a style?

(a) A theme applies an overall design to a document, with no requirement that any text is selected. A style applies formatting characteristics to selected text or to a current paragraph.
(b) A theme applies color-coordinated design to selected page elements. A style applies formatting to an entire document.
(c) A theme and a style are actually the same feature.
(d) A theme applies font characteristics, whereas a style applies paragraph formatting.

2. To identify a series of sequential steps to several levels, you could use:

(a) Tabs.
(b) A bulleted list.
(c) A multilevel list.
(d) A numbered list.

3. The feature that is a collection of formatting characteristics that can be applied to text or paragraphs is:

(a) WordArt.
(b) Themes.
(c) Style.
(d) Text box.

4. What kind of indent is often used in preparing a bibliography for a research paper?

(a) First line indent
(b) Hanging indent
(c) Right indent
(d) Left indent

5. To draw attention to such items as contact information or store hours, you could place text in a bordered area called a:

(a) Text box.
(b) Dot leader.
(c) Section.
(d) Tabbed indent.

6. To divide a document into side-by-side vertical blocks so that the text flows down one side and then continues at the top of the other side, you can use a(n):

(a) Column.
(b) Indent.
(c) Section break.
(d) Page break.

7. If you select text and apply a linked style, what happens?

(a) Paragraph formats are applied, but not character formats.
(b) Both paragraph and character formats are applied.
(c) Linked formats are applied.
(d) Character formats are applied, but not paragraph formats.

8. Having applied a particular heading style to several headings within a document, you modify the style to include bold and italic font formatting. What happens to the headings that were previously formatted in that style, and why?

(a) They remain as they are. Changes in style affect only text typed from that point forward.
(b) They remain as they are. You cannot modify a style that has already been applied to text in the current document.
(c) They are updated to reflect the modified heading style settings. When a heading style is modified, all text formatted in that style is updated.
(d) Each heading reverts to its original setting. When you modify styles, you make them unavailable to previously formatted styles.

9. Which of the following statements is FALSE regarding Outline view?

(a) It simplifies the application of formatting to entire sections.
(b) It streamlines the process of applying heading styles to selected text.
(c) It color coordinates various heading levels.
(d) It allows you to easily convert the outline to a PowerPoint presentation.

10. The feature that simplifies text wrapping around an object is:

(a) The alignment guide.
(b) Live Layout.
(c) Live Preview.
(d) Layout Options.

Practice Exercises

1 Campus Safety

You are the office assistant for the police department at a local university. As a service to students, staff, and the community, the police department publishes a campus safety guide, available both in print and online. With national emphasis on homeland security, and local incidents of theft and robbery, it is obvious that the safety guide should be updated and distributed. You will work with a draft document, formatting it to make it more attractive and ready for print. Refer to Figure 52 as you complete this exercise.

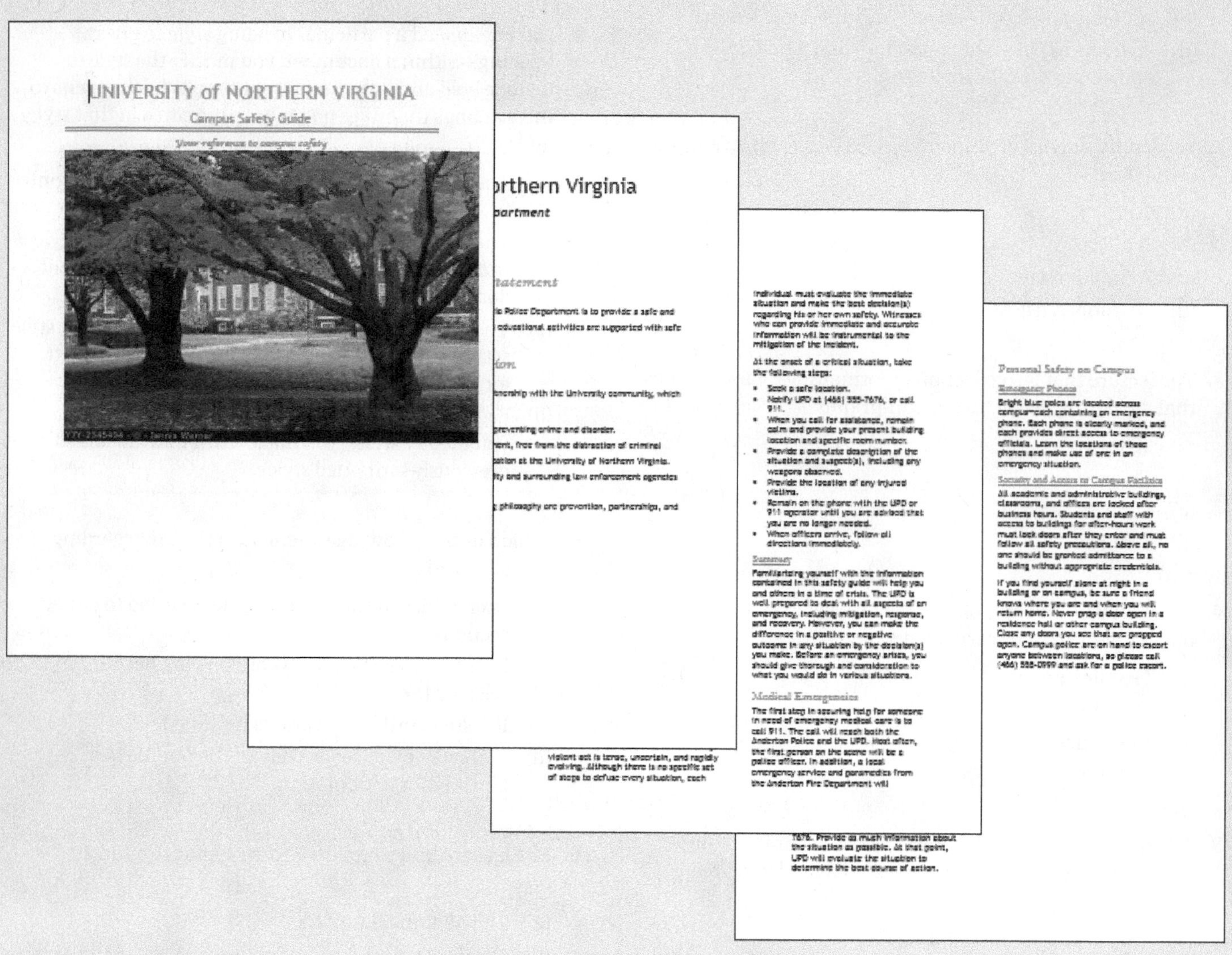

Word 2016, Windows 10, Microsoft Corporation

FIGURE 52 Format a Document

a. Open *w02p1Campus* and save the document as **w02p1Campus_LastFirst**. Click **Show/Hide** in the Paragraph group to ensure nonprinting characters are displayed.

b. Click the **Design tab**. Click **Themes** in the Document Formatting group and select **Ion Boardroom**. Click **Colors** in the Document Formatting group and select **Green Yellow**. Click **Fonts** in the Document Formatting group and select **Garamond TrebuchetMs**.

c. Click the **Home tab**. Select the first line in the document and click **Center** in the Paragraph group. Click the **Font Color arrow** in the Font group and select **Green, Accent 3**. Click the **Font Size arrow** and select **26**. Click **Change Case** in the Font group and select **UPPERCASE**. Double-click **of** in the first line in the document, click **Change Case**, and then select **lowercase**. Select the second line in the document. Center the line, change the font color to **Green, Accent 3**, change the font size to **16**, and then change the case to **Capitalize Each Word**. Do not deselect the text.

d. Click the **Borders arrow** in the Paragraph group and click **Borders and Shading**. Click **Custom** in the Setting section of the Borders and Shading dialog box. Click the **Color arrow** and select **Green, Accent 3**. Scroll through styles in the Style box and select the seventh style (double line). Click the **Width arrow** and select **1 1/2 pt**. Click **Bottom** in the Preview group and click **OK**.

e. Select the line containing the text *Your reference to campus safety*. Click **Font Color** on the Mini toolbar to apply the most recent font color selection. Use either the Mini toolbar or selections on the Home tab to change the font to **Lucida Calligraphy** and center the selection.

f. Click at the end of the currently selected line to position the insertion point immediately after *Your reference to campus safety*. Click the **Insert tab** and click **Pictures** in the Illustrations group. Navigate to the location of your student data files and double-click *w02p1Campus*.

g. Click **Height** in the Size group on the Format tab and type **5**. Press **Enter**. Click **Corrections** in the Adjust group and select **Brightness: 0% (Normal), Contrast: +20%** under Brightness/Contrast.

h. Click before the words *University of Northern Virginia* immediately below the picture and press **Ctrl+Enter** to insert a manual page break. Scroll up and select the first line on page 1 of the document. Click the **Home tab**, and click **Format Painter** in the Clipboard group. Scroll to the second page and select the first line (*University of Northern Virginia*) to copy the formatting. (Note that the Format Painter does not copy the All Caps format.) Change the font color of the selected line to **Black, Text 1**.

i. Select the second line on page 2, containing the text *Police Department*. Apply **Center**, **Bold**, and **Italic** to the selection. Change the font size to **16 pt**. Select text in the document beginning with *Mission Statement* and ending with *prevention, partnerships, and problem solving* (on the same page). Click **Line and Paragraph Spacing** in the Paragraph group and select **1.5**. Click the **Paragraph Dialog Box Launcher** and change Spacing After to **6 pt**. Click **OK**. Click to position the insertion point after the words *Police Department* and press **Enter** twice.

j. Select the *Mission Statement* heading near the top of page 2 and change the font color to **Green, Accent 3**. Center the selection and change the font size to **16** and the font to **Lucida Calligraphy**. Copy the format of the selection to the *Vision* heading on the same page. Insert a page break after the sentence ending with the words *problem solving* on page 2.

k. Select the paragraphs on page 2 beginning with *University police officers are committed to* and ending with *prevention, partnerships, and problem solving*. Click the **Bullets arrow** in the Paragraph group and select the square filled bullet. Click **Decrease Indent** in the Paragraph group to move the bullets to the left margin.

l. Scroll to page 3. Click the **Styles Dialog Box Launcher**. Complete the following steps to apply styles to selected text.

- Click in the line containing *Emergency Notifications*. Click **Heading 1** in the Styles pane. Scroll down and apply the Heading 1 style to the headings *Personal Safety*, *Medical Emergencies*, *Fire Emergencies*, *Homeland Security*, and *Personal Safety on Campus*.
- Click in the line on page 4 containing the text *Summary*. Click **Heading 2** in the Styles pane. Scroll down and apply Heading 2 style to the headings *Security and Access to Campus Facilities* and *Emergency Phones*.

m. Point to Heading 2 in the Styles pane, and click the **Heading 2 arrow**. Click **Modify**. Click **Underline** and click **OK**.

The Heading 2 style is modified to include an underline. All text previously formatted in the Heading 2 style now includes an underline.

n. Scroll to page 3 and select the five paragraphs in the *Emergency Notifications* section, beginning with *Phone* and ending with *provide additional information.* Apply square filled bullets to the selection. Decrease indent to the left margin. Click **New Style** in the Styles pane, type **Bulleted Text** in the Name box, and then click **OK**.

o. Select the seven paragraphs in the *Personal Safety* section, beginning with *Seek a safe location* and ending with *follow all directions immediately.* Click **Bulleted Text** in the Styles pane to apply the style to the selection. Apply the same style to the seven paragraphs in the *Medical Emergencies* section, beginning with *The victim should not be moved* and ending with *information is needed.* Close the Styles pane.

p. Press **Ctrl+Home** to move to the beginning of the document. Spell check the document. The word *of* in the university name is correct in lowercase, so do not correct it.

q. Scroll to page 3 and select all text beginning with *The University of Northern Virginia* and ending at the end of the document. Click the **Layout tab**, click **Columns**, and then select **Two**. Click the **View tab** and click **Multiple Pages** in the Zoom group to view pages of the document. Scroll up or down to check the document for text positioning and any awkward column endings. Click **100%** in the Zoom group.

r. Click **Outline** in the Views group. Click the **Show Level arrow** in the Outline Tools group and click **Level 1**. Click the plus (+) sign beside *Personal Safety on Campus* and click **Expand** in the Outline Tools group. Point to the plus (+) sign beside *Emergency Phones* and drag to position the *Emergency Phones* section above *Security and Access to Campus Facilities.* Click **Print Layout** on the status bar.

s. Press **Ctrl+Home** to move to the beginning of the document. Click **Show/Hide** in the Paragraph group to turn off the nonprinting characters feature. Click the **File tab** and click **Print** to preview the document. Click **Next Page** to move through the pages of the document. Click **Back** at the top-left corner of the screen to leave print preview.

t. Compare your work to Figure 52. Save and close the file. Based on your instructor's directions, submit w02p1Campus_LastFirst.

2 Drug Abuse

The local community center recently received a grant from the state to educate young people on the danger of drug addiction. You have been hired by the local community center to oversee this project. The primary purpose of the project is to develop materials on drug addiction, educate teenagers on the dangers of abusing illegal drugs, and warn them about the long-term repercussions of drug dependency. You will make presentations to various groups around the city, including high schools, civic clubs, and student organizations. Besides a PowerPoint presentation to support your discussions, you will also distribute research articles, flyers, and brochures to help convey the message. One such document, a summary of medical facts regarding drug abuse, is near completion. It is in need of proofreading, formatting, and a few other features that will result in a polished handout for your next presentation. Refer to Figure 53 as you complete this exercise.

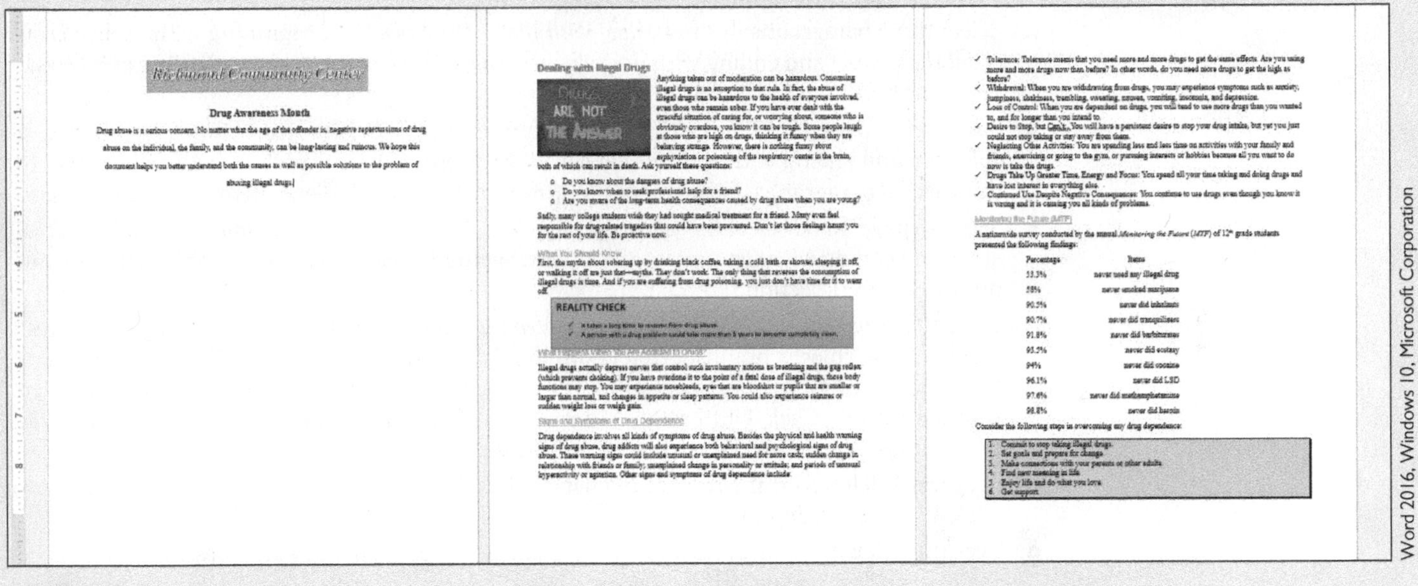

Word 2016, Windows 10, Microsoft Corporation

FIGURE 53 Finish a Handout

a. Open *w02p2Drug* and save it as **w02p2Drug_LastFirst**.

b. Click the **Home tab** and click **Show/Hide** if nonprinting characters are not displayed. Press **Ctrl+A** to select all document text. Click the **Font arrow** and select **Times New Roman**. Click anywhere to deselect the text. Check the document for spelling and grammatical errors. Ignore the identified grammatical mistake on page 2.

c. Press **Ctrl+Home** to move to the beginning of the document. Select the first line in the document, *Richmond Community Center*. Click the **Insert tab** and select **WordArt** in the Text group. Click **Fill – Black, Text 1, Outline – Background 1, Hard Shadow – Background 1** (third row, first column). Ensure that the text is still selected. Click the **Shape Fill arrow** in the Shape Styles group on the Format tab. Select **White, Background 1, Darker 25%** (fourth row, first column). Click the **Home tab** and change the font size to **24**.

d. Click **Layout Options** and click **Top and Bottom**. Close Layout Options. Point to the WordArt object and drag to visually center it. You should drag when the pointer resembles a four-headed arrow.

e. Select the second line in the document, *Drug Awareness Month*. When you select the text, the WordArt is also selected because it is anchored to the selected paragraph. Center and bold the selected text and change the font size to **14**.

f. Click anywhere in the first paragraph that begins *Drug abuse is a serious concern*. Center the paragraph. Click **Line and Paragraph Spacing** in the Paragraph group and select **2.0**. Click before the paragraph mark ending the paragraph that begins *Drug abuse is a serious concern*.

Click the **Layout tab** and click **Breaks**. Click **Next Page** in the Section Breaks group. Press **Delete** to remove the paragraph mark at the top of page 2.

g. Click the **Home tab**. Select the first line on page 2, *Dealing with Illegal Drugs*. Click **Heading 1** in the Styles group. Select *What You Should Know* and select **Heading 2**.

h. Select *What Happens When You Are Addicted to Drugs?* Change the font to **Arial**, click **Underline** in the Font group, click the **Font Color arrow**, and change the font color to **Blue, Accent 1**. Click the **Styles Dialog Box Launcher**. Click **New Style**. Type **Lower Item** in the Name box and click **OK**. Select the heading *Signs and Symptoms of Drug Dependence*. Click **Lower Item** in the Styles pane to apply the newly created style to the selected text. Apply the same format to the heading *Monitoring the Future (MTF)*.

i. Point to Heading 1 in the Styles pane and click the **Heading 1 arrow**. Click **Modify**. Click **Bold** and click **OK**. Scroll up, if necessary, to see that the heading *Dealing with Illegal Drugs* is bold. Close the Styles pane.

j. Select three paragraphs in the *Dealing with Illegal Drugs* section, beginning with *Do you know about the dangers* and ending with *drug abuse when you are young?* Click the **Bullets arrow** and select the hollow round bullet.

k. Select seven paragraphs in the *Signs and Symptoms of Drug Dependence* section, beginning with *Tolerance* and ending with *it is causing you all kinds of problems*. Apply a check mark bullet to the selected paragraphs. Click **Decrease Indent** to move the bulleted items to the left margin.

l. Scroll to page 3 and select the last six paragraphs, beginning with *Commit to stop taking illegal drugs* and ending with *Get support*. Click **Numbering** in the Paragraph group to apply default numbers to the selection.

m. Click after the sentence ending with *presented the following findings*: on the same page. Press **Enter**. If the ruler is not displayed above the document area, click the **View tab** and click **Ruler** in the Show group. Ensure that the tab selector, shown just above the vertical ruler, shows a left tab. Click **1"** to set a left tab. Click **3"** to set another left tab. Press **Tab**. Type **Percentage**. Press **Tab**. Type **Items**. Press **Enter**.

n. Drag the 3" left tab off the ruler to remove it. Click the **tab selector** twice to select a right tab. Click **4"** to set a right tab.

o. Type the following data, pressing **Tab** at the beginning of each entry and pressing **Enter** at the end of each line except the last line:

53.3%	**never used any illegal drug**
58%	**never smoked marijuana**
90.5%	**never did inhalants**
90.7%	**never did tranquilizers**
91.8%	**never did barbiturates**
93.5%	**never did ecstasy**
94%	**never did cocaine**
96.1%	**never did LSD**
97.6%	**never did methamphetamine**
98.8%	**never did heroin**

p. Scroll to page 2 and click before the first sentence in the *Dealing with Illegal Drugs* section. Click the **Insert tab** and click **Online Pictures** in the Illustrations group. Type **say no to drugs** in the Bing Image Search box. Press **Enter**. Double-click the image shown in Figure 53 (or select one very similar if it is unavailable). Change the height of the picture to **1.5** in the Size group on the Format tab. Click **Layout Options** and select **Square**. Close Layout Options. Drag to position the image as shown in Figure 53.

q. Press **Ctrl+End** to move to the end of the document. Select the six numbered paragraphs. Click the **Home tab** and click the **Borders arrow** in the Paragraph group. Click **Borders and Shading**. Click **Shadow** in the Setting section. Click the **Shading tab**. Click the **Color arrow** in the Fill section and select **White, Background 1, Darker 15%**. Click **OK**.

r. Click after the last sentence in the *What You Should Know* section. Click the **Insert tab** and click **Text Box** in the Text group. Click **Draw Text Box**. Drag to draw a box approximately 1" high and 6" wide below the *What You Should Know* section. Adjust the height to **1"** and the width to **6"** exactly in the Size group on the Format tab. Click **Layout Options**. Click **Top and Bottom**. Click to place the insertion point in the text box.

s. Click the **Home tab** and click **Bold** in the Font group. Change the font size to **16**. Type **REALITY CHECK** and press **Enter**. Click **Line and Paragraph Spacing** in the Paragraph group and click **1.0**. Click the **Paragraph Dialog Box Launcher**. Change Paragraph Spacing After to **0 pt**. Click **OK**. Change the font size to **10**. Type the following, pressing **Enter** after each line:

It takes a long time to recover from drug abuse.
A person with a drug problem could take more than 5 years to become completely clean.

t. Apply check mark bullets to the two sentences you just typed. Click the **Format tab**. Click the **More arrow** in the Shape Styles group. Select **Subtle Effect – Blue, Accent 5** (fourth row, sixth column). Point in the text box so that the pointer displays as a four-headed arrow. Drag to position the text box as shown in Figure 53. Click **Show/Hide** in the Paragraph group to turn off the nonprinting characters feature.

u. Save and close the file. Based on your instructor's directions, submit w02p2Drug_LastFirst.

Mid-Level Exercises

1 Balloon Festival

As chair of the Mount Sedona Balloon Festival, you are responsible for promoting the upcoming event. You have begun a document providing details on the festival. You plan to distribute the document both in print and online. First, you must format the document to make it more attractive and well designed. You will use styles, bullets, and line and paragraph spacing to coordinate various parts of the document. In addition, you will add interest by including objects, such as pictures, text boxes, and WordArt.

a. Open *w02m1Balloons* and save it as **w02m1Balloons_LastFirst**.

b. Change the document theme to **Slice**. Select the first line in the document, *Mount Sedona Hot Air Balloon Festival*. Insert WordArt, selecting **Fill – Dark Purple, Accent 2, Outline – Accent 2** (first row, third column). Change the font size of the WordArt object to **20**.

c. Wrap text around the WordArt object as **Top and Bottom**. Format the WordArt object with Shape Style **Subtle Effect – Dark Purple, Accent 2** (fourth row, third column). Visually center the WordArt object on the first line of the document.

d. Select the second line in the document, *See the Canyon From On High!* Center and bold the text and apply a font color of **Dark Purple, Accent 2**.

e. Select the remaining text on page 1, beginning with *May 26-27, 2018* and ending with *on the festival grounds*. Format the selected text into two columns. Insert a page break (not a section break) after the sentence ending with *on the festival grounds*. Change the font of the columned text on page 1 to **Century Schoolbook**.

f. Check spelling and grammar—the word *Ballumination* is not misspelled (for the purposes of this document). Also, ignore *From* in the second paragraph on page 1.

g. Click in the third line on page 1—May 26-27, 2018—and right align it. Select all columned text, including the line containing festival dates, and select a line spacing of **1.5** and paragraph spacing after of **6 pt**. Insert a column break before the paragraph beginning with *And don't forget the dogs!*

h. Click to place the insertion point before the paragraph beginning *As for the kids*. Insert an online picture from Bing Image Search relating to hot air balloons. Size the picture with a height of **1.5"**. Select **Square text wrapping** and a picture style of **Rotated, White**. Position the picture so that it is on the left side of the paragraph beginning with *As for the kids*, but still in the right column.

i. Select the picture and recolor it to coordinate with the purple theme of the document. Choose an artistic effect of **Photocopy**.

j. Scroll to page 3 and select the heading, *When is the best time to see balloons?* Bold the selection and change the font color to **Dark Purple, Accent 2**. Do not deselect the heading. Open the Styles pane and create a new style named **Questions**. Apply the **Questions style** to other questions (headings) on page 3.

k. Scroll to page 4 and apply solid round bullets to the first nine paragraphs on the page. Decrease the indent so the bullets begin at the left margin. With the bulleted items selected, click the **Bullets arrow** and click **Define New Bullet**. Click **Font** and change the font color to **Dark Purple, Accent 2**. Click **OK**. Click **OK** again.

l. Insert a page break (not a section break) before the heading *How can I plan for the best experience?* on page 3.

m. Select the schedule of items under the heading *Saturday (5/26/18)*, beginning with *6:00 AM* and ending with *Balloon Glow*. Set a left tab at **1"**. Press **Tab** twice to move selected paragraphs to the left tab. Select the schedule of items under *Sunday (5/27/18)*, set a left tab at **1"**, and then tab twice for selected paragraphs.

n. Save and close the file. Based on your instructor's directions, submit w02m1Balloons_LastFirst.

2 Johnson Orthodontics

You are the office manager for Dr. Johnson, an orthodontist for children, who periodically conducts informational sessions for his young patients. You have written a letter to children in the neighborhood reminding them about the upcoming monthly session, but you want to make the letter more professional looking. You decide to use paragraph formatting such as alignment, paragraph spacing, borders and shading, and bullets that describe some of the fun activities of the day. You also want to add Dr. Johnson's email address and an appropriate image to the letter.

a. Open the document *w02m2Orthodontics* and save it as **w02m2Orthodontics_LastFirst**.

b. Change the capitalization of the recipient *ms. samantha smith* and her address so that each word is capitalized and the state abbreviation displays in uppercase. Also capitalize her first name in the salutation. Change Dr. Johnson's name to your full name in the signature block. Type your email address (or a fictitious email address) on the next line below your name.

c. Show nonprinting characters, if they are not already displayed. Apply **Justify alignment** to body paragraphs beginning with *On behalf* and ending with *July 12*. At the paragraph mark under the first body paragraph, create a bulleted list, selecting a bullet of your choice. Type the following items in the bulleted list. Do not press Enter after the last item in the list.

Participating in the dental crossword puzzle challenge
Writing a convincing letter to the tooth fairy
Digging through the dental treasure chest
Finding hidden toothbrushes in the dental office

d. Select text from the salutation *Dear Samantha*: through the last paragraph that ends with *seeing you on July 12*. Set **12 pt Spacing After paragraph**. Remove the paragraph mark just after the *Dear Samantha* paragraph.

e. Select *Dr. Johnson Orthodontics Office* in the first paragraph and apply small caps.

f. Select the italicized lines of text that give date, time, and location of the meeting. Remove the italics, do not deselect the text, and then complete the following:

- Increase left and right indents to **1.25** and set **0 pt Spacing After paragraph**.
- Apply a **double-line box border** with the color **Green, Accent 4, Darker 50%** and a line width of **3/4 pt**. Shade selected text with the **Green, Accent 4, Lighter 40% shading color**.
- Delete the extra tab formatting marks to the left of the lines containing *July 12, 2018; 4:00 p.m.*; and *Dr. Johnson Orthodontics Office* to align them with other text in the bordered area.
- Remove the paragraph mark before the paragraph that begins with *Please call our office*.

g. Click the line containing the text *Glen Allen, VA 23059*, and set **12 pt Spacing After** the paragraph. Click the line containing *Sincerely* and set **6 pt Spacing Before** the paragraph. Add **6 pt Spacing Before** the paragraph beginning with the text *Dr. Johnson is pleased to let you know.*

h. Select the entire document and change the font to **12-pt Bookman Old Style**.

i. Move to the beginning of the document. Search online for a picture related to **tooth**. Insert the picture and apply a square text wrap. Position the picture in the top-right corner of the document, just below the header area. Resize the graphic to **1.1"** high. Apply the **Bevel Perspective Left, White picture style** (fourth row, third column).

j. Move to the end of the document. Insert a Next Page section break. Change the orientation to **Landscape**. Change Paragraph Spacing After to **6 pt**. Change the font size to **14**. Center the first line. Type **Lake George Water Park Fun Day!** Press **Enter** and type **July 7, 2018**. Press **Enter** and change the alignment to **Left**. Change the font size to **12**. Set a left tab at **2"** and a right tab at **7"**. Type the following text, with the first column at the 2" tab and the next column at the 7" tab. Do not press Enter after typing the last line.

Check-in	**9:00**
Water slide	**9:30-11:00**
Lunch at the pavilion	**11:00-12:00**
Wave pool	**12:00-2:00**
Bungee	**2:00-3:00**
Parent pickup at the gate	**3:00-3:30**

k. Select **Lake George Water Park Fun Day!** on page 2 and insert WordArt with the style **Fill – Aqua, Accent 1, Outline – Background 1, Hard Shadow – Accent 1** (third row, third column). Wrap text around the WordArt object at **Top and Bottom**, change the font size of the WordArt object to **24**, and drag to center the object horizontally on the first line.

l. Select the tabbed text, beginning with *Check-in* and ending with *3:00-3:30*. Modify the 7" right tab to include a dot leader.

m. Change the theme to **Integral**. Check spelling and grammar, correcting any errors and ignoring those that are not errors. Turn off the nonprinting characters feature.

n. Save and close the file. Based on your instructor's directions, submit w02m2Orthodontics_LastFirst.

3 A Music CD Cover

COLLABORATION CASE

FROM SCRATCH 

You play bass guitar with a local band, Twilight Hour. You love playing with the band, but you also enjoy the business side of music, and plan to pursue a career in music production. To that end, you are completing requirements for a B.S. degree. This semester, you are participating in a seminar on music marketing and production. You are in a group that is required to design the front and back of a CD cover for a band, real or fictitious, and your group decides to create a cover for your band. You will begin a document and share it with members of the group, who will each contribute to the CD cover. Your group will first locate a music CD case to use as a model. The front of the CD typically displays the band or artist name, along with a graphic or background design.

Before continuing with this case, all group members must have a Microsoft account. An account can be obtained at www.outlook.com.

a. One person in your group will complete the following two steps:
- Open a new Word document. Include the group name in the header. Click the **File tab** and click **Share**. Click **Save to Cloud** and click the **OneDrive link**. Select a recently accessed folder, or click **Browse**, and navigate to, or create, another folder.
- Change the file name to **w02m3Cover_GroupName** and click **Save**. Click **Share** and then click **Get a Sharing Link**. Click **Create Link** beside the Edit Link section. Share the link with group members so that they can access the document online.

b. Each group member will enter the link in a browser to access the shared document. When the document opens in Word Online, click **Edit Document** and click **Edit in Word**.
- One or more group members will focus on developing the front cover, including WordArt, pictures, and/or text boxes where appropriate. Use font and paragraph formatting, as needed, to produce an attractive front cover. The front cover should occupy the first page, or first section, of the shared document. Save the document often, ensuring the save location is OneDrive.
- One or more group members will focus on the back cover, including a list of songs, numbered and in two columns. In addition, give attention to the design of text and headings, formatting all items to produce an attractive back cover. The back cover will occupy the second page, or second section, of the shared document. Save the document often, ensuring the save location is OneDrive.
- The dimensions of the final document will not necessarily be that of an actual CD. You are concerned with the design only.

c. The final version of the CD cover should be saved to OneDrive. Close the file. Based on your instructor's directions, submit w02m3Cover_GroupName.

Beyond the Classroom

Invitation

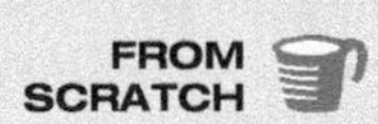

Search the Internet for an upcoming local event at your school or in your community and produce the perfect invitation. You can invite people to a charity ball, a fun run, or a fraternity or sorority party. Your color printer and abundance of fancy fonts, as well as your ability to insert page borders, enable you to do anything a professional printer can do. Save your work as **w02b1Invitation_LastFirst**, and close the file. Based on your instructor's directions, submit w02b1Invitation_LastFirst.

Fundraising Letter

DISASTER RECOVERY

Each year, you update a letter to several community partners soliciting support for an auction. The auction raises funds for your organization, and your letter should impress your supporters. Open *w02b2Auction* and notice how unprofessional and unorganized the document looks so far. You must make changes immediately to improve the appearance. Consider replacing much of the formatting that is in place now and instead using columns for auction items, bullets to draw attention to the list of forms, page borders, and pictures or images—and that is just for starters! Save your work as **w02b2Auction_LastFirst** and close the file. Based on your instructor's directions, submit w02b2Auction_LastFirst.

Capstone Exercise

MyITLab® Grader

This semester you are enrolled in a personal finance course at your local university. One of the assignments is to write a research paper about investing. You conducted research on the various types of investing instruments, and wrote a final draft of the report. Now your research paper requires formatting to enhance readability and important information; and you will use skills from this chapter to format multiple levels of headings, arrange and space text, and insert graphics.

Applying Styles

This document is ready for enhancements, and the Styles feature is a good tool that enables you to add them quickly and easily.

a. Open *w02c1Finance* and save it as **w02c1Finance_LastFirst**.

b. Press **Ctrl+Home**. Create a paragraph style named **Title_Page_1** with these formats: **22-pt** font size and **Dark Blue, Text 2, Darker 50%** font color. Ensure that this style is applied to the first line of the document, *Personal Finance:*.

c. Select the second line, *Understanding the Investment Instruments*. Change the font size to **16** and apply a font color of **Dark Blue, Text 2, Darker 50%**.

d. Click the line following *Updated by:* and type your first and last names. Change the capitalization for your name to uppercase.

e. Select the remainder of the text in the document that follows your name, starting with *Personal Finance*. Justify the alignment of all paragraphs and change line spacing to **1.15**. Place the insertion point on the left side of the title *Personal Finance* (below your name) and insert a page break (not a section break).

f. Apply **Heading 1 style** to *Personal Finance* at the top of page 2. Apply **Heading 2 style** to paragraph headings, including *Introduction, Equity Stocks, Bonds, Mutual Funds, U.S. Treasury Bills, Fixed Deposits, Sources*, and *Conclusion*.

g. Modify the Heading 2 style to use **Dark Red** font color.

Formatting the Paragraphs

Next, you will apply paragraph formatting to the document. These format options will further increase the readability and attractiveness of your document.

a. Apply a bulleted list format for the six-item list in the third paragraph of the *Introduction* section. Use the symbol of a diamond.

b. Select the second body paragraph in the *Introduction* section, which begins with *The best time to prepare for your retirement*, and apply these formats: **0.6"** left and right indents, **6 pt** spacing after the paragraph, **boxed 1 1/2 pt border** using the color **Dark Blue, Text 2, Darker 25%**, and the shading color **Dark Blue, Text 2, Lighter 80%**.

c. Apply the numbered list format (1., 2., 3.) to the three types of bonds in the *Bonds* section.

d. Select the three quotes by Warren Buffet and the *Source:* paragraph in the *Equity Stocks* section and display them in two columns with a line between the columns.

e. Insert the hyperlinks for all the five sources listed in the *Sources* section.

Inserting Graphics

To put the finishing touches on your document, you will add graphics that enhance the explanations given in some paragraphs.

a. Insert the picture file *w02c1Bull* at the beginning of the line that contains *The major stock market* in the *Equity Stocks* section. Change the height of the picture to **3"**. Change text wrapping to **Top and Bottom**. Center the graphic horizontally. Apply the **Rounded Diagonal Corner, White picture style**. Position the picture so that it appears below the *Equity Stocks* heading.

b. Insert the picture file *w02c1Bear* at the beginning of the line that begins with *If you want something a little less risky than stocks* in the *Bonds* section. Change the height of the picture to **3"**. Ensure that text wrapping is **Top and Bottom**, position the picture so it appears immediately above the line beginning *U.S. Treasury bills and government*. Apply **Offset Center Shadow Picture Effect** (second row, second column under *Outer*) to the graphic. Position the picture so that it appears below the *Bonds* heading.

c. Spell check and review the entire document—no author names are misspelled.

d. Display the document in Outline view. Collapse all paragraphs so only lines formatted as Heading 1 or Heading 2 display. Move the *Sources* section to below the *Conclusion* section. Close Outline view.

e. Save and close the file. Based on your instructor's directions, submit w02c1Finance_LastFirst.

Glossary

Alignment guide A horizontal or vertical green bar that appears as you move an object, assisting with aligning the object with text or with another object.

Border A line that surrounds a paragraph, page, or a table or table element.

Bulleted list A graphic element that itemizes and separates paragraph text to increase readability; often used to identify lists.

Center alignment Positions text horizontally in the center of a line, with an equal distance from both the left and right margins.

Column A format that separates document text into side-by-side vertical blocks, often used in newsletters.

Crop The process of reducing an image size by eliminating unwanted portions of an image or other graphical object.

Document theme A set of coordinating fonts, colors, and special effects that gives a stylish and professional look.

First line indent Marks the location to indent only the first line in a paragraph.

Font A combination of typeface and type style.

Formatting The process of modifying text by changing font and paragraph characteristics.

Hanging indent Aligns the first line of a paragraph at the left margin, indenting remaining lines in the paragraph.

Indent A setting associated with the way a paragraph is distanced from one or more margins.

Justified alignment Spreads text evenly between the left and right margins, so that text begins at the left margin and ends uniformly at the right margin.

Left alignment Begins text evenly at the left margin, with a ragged right edge.

Left indent A setting that positions all text in a paragraph an equal distance from the left margin.

Line spacing The vertical spacing between lines in a paragraph.

Live Layout Feature that enables you to watch text flow around an object as you move it, so you can position the object exactly as you want it.

Live Preview An Office feature that provides a preview of the results of a selection when you point to an option in a list or gallery. Using Live Preview, you can experiment with settings before making a final choice.

Numbered list Sequences items in a list by displaying a successive number beside each item.

Object An item, such as a picture or text box, that can be individually selected and manipulated in a document.

Paragraph spacing The amount of space before or after a paragraph.

Picture A graphic file that is retrieved from storage media or the Internet and placed in an Office project.

Right alignment Begins text evenly at the right margin, with a ragged left edge.

Right indent A setting that positions all text in a paragraph an equal distance from the right margin.

Sans serif font A font that does not contain a thin line or extension at the top and bottom of the primary strokes on characters.

Section break An indicator that divides a document into parts, enabling different formatting for each section.

Serif font A font that contains a thin line or extension at the top and bottom of the primary strokes on characters.

Shading A background color that appears behind text in a paragraph, page, or table element.

Sizing handle A series of faint dots on the outside border of a selected object; enables the user to adjust the height and width of the object.

Style A named collection of formatting characteristics that can be applied to text or paragraphs.

Style set A combination of title, heading, and paragraph styles that can be used to format all of those elements in a document at one time.

Tab Stop A marker that specifies the position for aligning text in a column arrangement, often including a dot leader.

Text box A graphical object that contains text.

WordArt A Microsoft Office feature that creates decorative text that can be used to add interest to the text used in a document.

Introduction to Excel

Excel

Introduction to Excel

LEARNING OUTCOME **You will create and format a basic Excel worksheet.**

OBJECTIVES & SKILLS: After you read this chapter, you will be able to:

Introduction to Spreadsheets

OBJECTIVE 1: EXPLORE THE EXCEL WINDOW
Identify Excel Window Elements; Identify Columns, Rows, and Cells; Navigate in and Among Worksheets

OBJECTIVE 2: ENTER AND EDIT CELL DATA
Enter Text, Use Auto Fill to Complete a Sequence, Enter Values, Enter a Date, Clear Cell Contents

HANDS-ON EXERCISE 1:
Introduction to Spreadsheets

Mathematical Operations and Formulas

OBJECTIVE 3: CREATE FORMULAS
Use Cell References in Formulas, Apply the Order of Operations, Use Semi-Selection to Create a Formula, Copy Formulas

OBJECTIVE 4: DISPLAY CELL FORMULAS
Display Cell Formulas

HANDS-ON EXERCISE 2:
Mathematics and Formulas

Worksheet Structure and Clipboard Tasks

OBJECTIVE 5: MANAGE COLUMNS AND ROWS
Insert Cells, Columns, and Rows; Delete Cells, Columns, and Rows; Hide a Column or Row; Adjust Column Width; Adjust Row Height

OBJECTIVE 6: SELECT, MOVE, COPY, AND PASTE DATA
Select a Range, Move a Range, Copy and Paste a Range, Use Paste Options and Paste Special

HANDS-ON EXERCISE 3:
Worksheet Structure and Clipboard Tasks

Worksheet Formatting

OBJECTIVE 7: APPLY CELL STYLES, ALIGNMENT, AND FONT OPTIONS
Apply a Cell Style, Merge and Center Data, Change Cell Alignment, Wrap Text, Increase Indent, Apply a Border, Apply Fill Color

OBJECTIVE 8: APPLY NUMBER FORMATS
Apply Number Formats, Increase and Decrease Decimal Places

HANDS-ON EXERCISE 4:
Worksheet Formatting

Worksheets, Page Setup, and Printing

OBJECTIVE 9: MANAGE WORKSHEETS
Insert a Worksheet, Delete a Worksheet, Copy or Move a Worksheet, Rename a Worksheet, Group Worksheets

OBJECTIVE 10: SELECT PAGE SETUP OPTIONS
Set Page Orientation, Select Scaling Options, Set Margin Options, Create a Header or Footer, Select Sheet Options

OBJECTIVE 11: PREVIEW AND PRINT A WORKSHEET
View in Print Preview, Set Print Options, Print a Worksheet

HANDS-ON EXERCISE 5:
Worksheets, Page Setup, and Printing

CASE STUDY | OK Office Systems

Alesha Bennett, the general manager at OK Office Systems (OKOS), asked you to calculate the retail price, sale price, and profit analysis for selected items on sale this month. Using markup rates provided by Alesha, you will calculate the retail price, the amount OKOS charges its customers for the products. You will calculate sale prices based on discount rates between 10% and 30%. Finally, you will calculate the profit margin to determine the percentage of the final sale price over the cost.

After you create the initial pricing spreadsheet, you will be able to change values and see that the formulas update the results automatically. In addition, you will insert data for additional sale items or delete an item based on the manager's decision. After inserting formulas, you will format the data in the worksheet to have a professional appearance.

Creating and Formatting a Worksheet

Everything possible/ Shutterstock

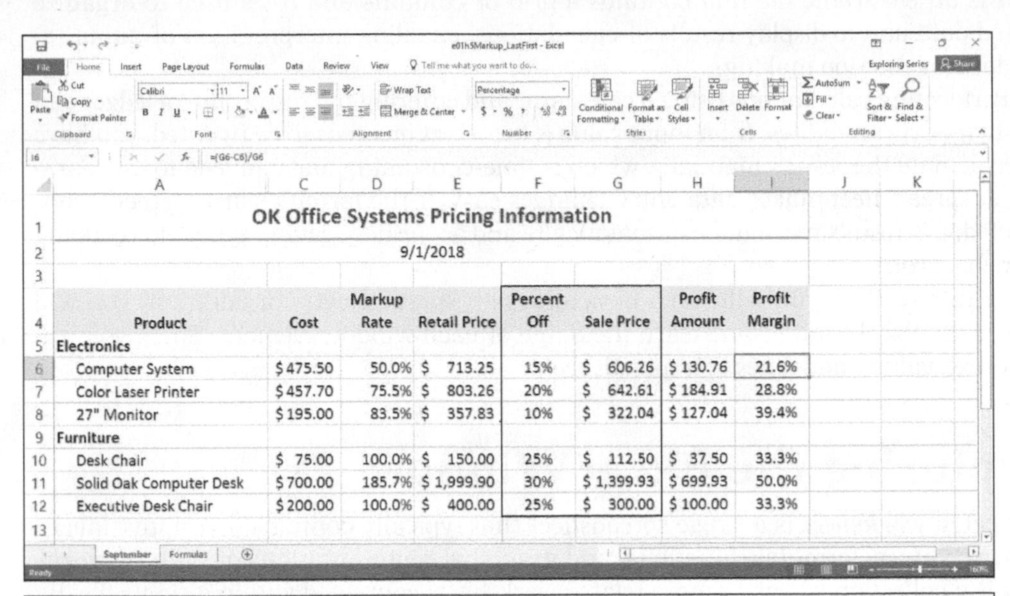

	A	C	D	E	F	G	H	I
1	OK Office Systems Pricing Information							
2	9/1/2018							
3								
4	Product	Cost	Markup Rate	Retail Price	Percent Off	Sale Price	Profit Amount	Profit Margin
5	Electronics							
6	Computer System	$ 475.50	50.0%	$ 713.25	15%	$ 606.26	$ 130.76	21.6%
7	Color Laser Printer	$ 457.70	75.5%	$ 803.26	20%	$ 642.61	$ 184.91	28.8%
8	27" Monitor	$ 195.00	83.5%	$ 357.83	10%	$ 322.04	$ 127.04	39.4%
9	Furniture							
10	Desk Chair	$ 75.00	100.0%	$ 150.00	25%	$ 112.50	$ 37.50	33.3%
11	Solid Oak Computer Desk	$ 700.00	185.7%	$ 1,999.90	30%	$ 1,399.93	$ 699.93	50.0%
12	Executive Desk Chair	$ 200.00	100.0%	$ 400.00	25%	$ 300.00	$ 100.00	33.3%

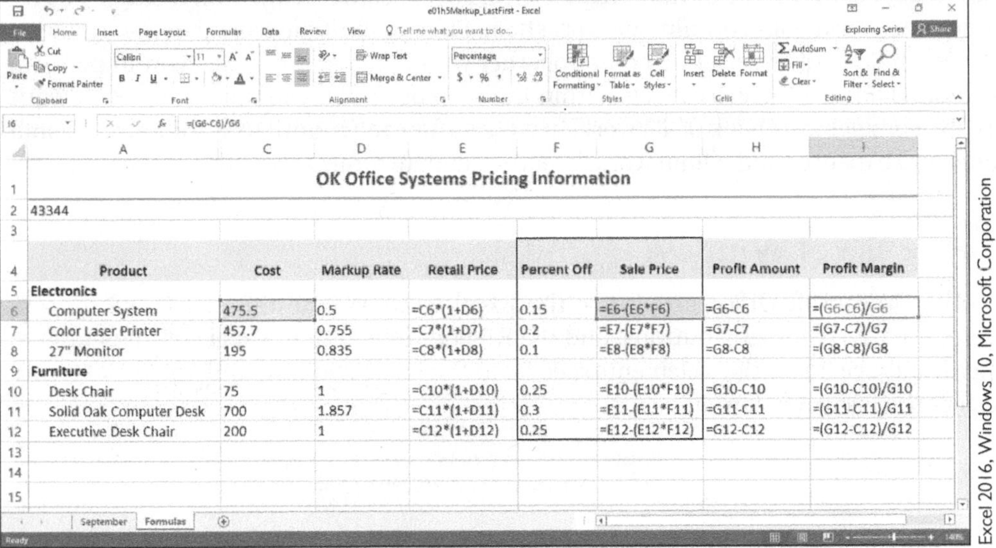

	A	C	D	E	F	G	H	I
1	OK Office Systems Pricing Information							
2	43344							
3								
4	Product	Cost	Markup Rate	Retail Price	Percent Off	Sale Price	Profit Amount	Profit Margin
5	Electronics							
6	Computer System	475.5	0.5	=C6*(1+D6)	0.15	=E6-(E6*F6)	=G6-C6	=(G6-C6)/G6
7	Color Laser Printer	457.7	0.755	=C7*(1+D7)	0.2	=E7-(E7*F7)	=G7-C7	=(G7-C7)/G7
8	27" Monitor	195	0.835	=C8*(1+D8)	0.1	=E8-(E8*F8)	=G8-C8	=(G8-C8)/G8
9	Furniture							
10	Desk Chair	75	1	=C10*(1+D10)	0.25	=E10-(E10*F10)	=G10-C10	=(G10-C10)/G10
11	Solid Oak Computer Desk	700	1.857	=C11*(1+D11)	0.3	=E11-(E11*F11)	=G11-C11	=(G11-C11)/G11
12	Executive Desk Chair	200	1	=C12*(1+D12)	0.25	=E12-(E12*F12)	=G12-C12	=(G12-C12)/G12

Excel 2016, Windows 10, Microsoft Corporation

FIGURE I Completed OKOS Worksheet

CASE STUDY | OK Office Systems

Starting File	File to be Submitted
e01h1Markup	**e01h5Markup_LastFirst**

Introduction to Spreadsheets

Organizing, calculating, and evaluating quantitative data are important skills needed today for personal and managerial decision making. You track expenses for your household budget, maintain a savings plan, and determine what amount you can afford for a house or car payment. Retail managers create and analyze their organizations' annual budgets, sales projections, and inventory records. Charitable organizations track the donations they receive, the distribution of those donations, and overhead expenditures.

You should use a spreadsheet to maintain data and perform calculations. A ***spreadsheet*** is an electronic file that contains a grid of columns and rows used to organize related data and to display results of calculations, enabling interpretation of quantitative data for decision making.

Performing calculations using a calculator and entering the results into a ledger can lead to inaccurate values. If an input value is incorrect or needs to be updated, you have to recalculate the results manually, which is time-consuming and can lead to inaccuracies. A spreadsheet makes data entry changes easy. If the formulas are correctly constructed, the results recalculate automatically and accurately, saving time and reducing room for error.

In this section, you will learn how to design spreadsheets. In addition, you will explore the Excel window and learn the name of each window element. Then, you will enter text, values, and dates in a spreadsheet.

Exploring the Excel Window

In Excel, a ***worksheet*** is a single spreadsheet that typically contains descriptive labels, numeric values, formulas, functions, and graphical representations of data. A ***workbook*** is a collection of one or more related worksheets contained within a single file. By default, new workbooks contain one worksheet. Storing multiple worksheets within one workbook helps organize related data together in one file and enables you to perform calculations among the worksheets within the workbook. For example, you might want to create a budget workbook of 13 worksheets, one for each month to store your personal income and expenses and a final worksheet to calculate totals across the entire year.

Identify Excel Window Elements

Like other Microsoft Office programs, the Excel window contains the Quick Access Toolbar, the title bar, sizing buttons, and the Ribbon. In addition, Excel contains unique elements. Figure 2 identifies elements specific to the Excel window, and Table 1 lists and describes the Excel window elements.

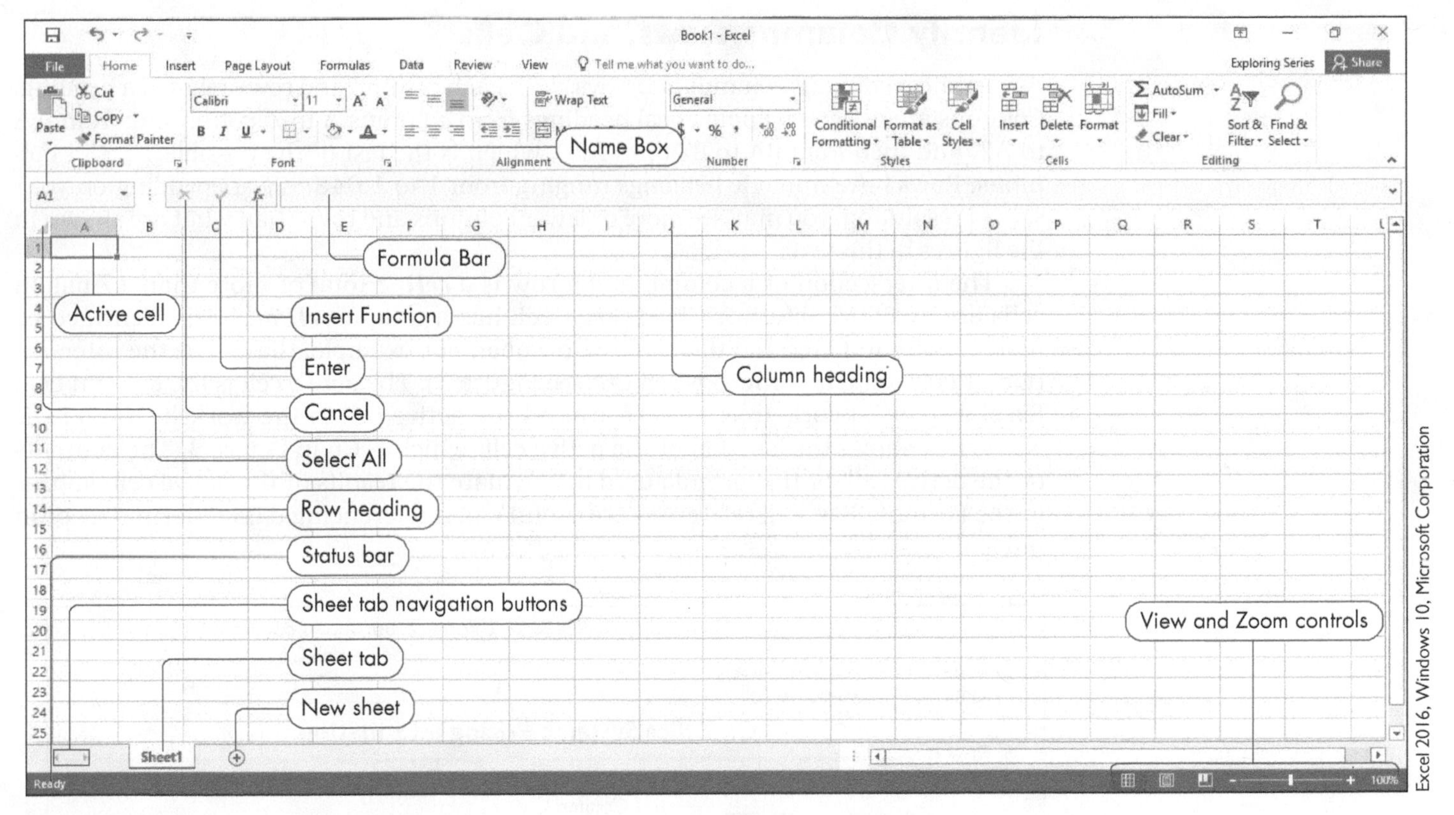

FIGURE 2 Excel Window

TABLE 1 Excel Elements

Element	Description
Name Box	An element located below the Ribbon and displays the address of the active cell. Use the Name Box to go to a cell, assign a name to one or more cells, or select a function.
Cancel	When you enter or edit data, click Cancel to cancel the data entry or edit, and revert back to the previous data in the cell, if any. Cancel changes from gray to red when you position the pointer over it.
Enter	When you enter or edit data, click Enter to accept data typed in the active cell and keep the current cell active. Enter changes from gray to blue when you position the pointer over it.
Insert Function	Click to display the Insert Function dialog box to search for and select a function to insert into the active cell. The Insert Function icon changes from gray to green when you position the pointer over it.
Formula Bar	An element located below the Ribbon and to the right of the Insert Function command. Shows the contents of the active cell. You enter or edit cell contents here or directly in the active cell. Drag the bottom border of the Formula Bar down to increase the height of the Formula Bar to display large amounts of data or a long formula contained in the active cell.
Select All	The triangle at the intersection of the row and column headings in the top-left corner of the worksheet. Click it to select everything contained in the active worksheet.
Column headings	The letters above the columns. For example, B is the letter above the second column.
Row headings	The numbers to the left of the rows, such as 1, 2, 3, and so on. For example, 3 is the row heading for the third row.
Active cell	The current cell, which is indicated by a dark green border.
Sheet tab	A visual label that looks like a file folder tab. A sheet tab shows the name of a worksheet contained in the workbook. When you create a new Excel workbook, the default worksheet is named Sheet1.
New sheet	Click to insert a new worksheet to the right of the current worksheet.
Sheet tab navigation	If your workbook contains several worksheets, Excel may not show all the sheet tabs at the same time. Use the buttons to display the first, previous, next, or last worksheet.
Status bar	The row at the bottom of the Excel window. It displays information about a selected command or operation in progress. For example, it displays *Select destination and press ENTER or choose Paste* after you use the Copy command.
View controls	Icons on the right side of the status bar that control how the worksheet is displayed. Click a view control to display the worksheet in Normal, Page Layout, or Page Break Preview. ***Normal view*** displays the worksheet without showing margins, headers, footers, and page breaks. ***Page Layout view*** shows the margins, header and footer area, and a ruler. ***Page Break Preview*** indicates where the worksheet will be divided into pages.
Zoom control	Drag the zoom control to increase the size of the worksheet onscreen to see more or less of the worksheet data.

Identify Columns, Rows, and Cells

A worksheet contains columns and rows, with each column and row assigned a heading. Columns are assigned alphabetical headings from columns A to Z, continuing from AA to AZ, and then from BA to BZ until XFD, which is the last of the possible 16,384 columns. Rows have numeric headings ranging from 1 to 1,048,576. Depending on your screen resolution, you may see more or fewer columns and rows than what are shown in the figures in this text.

The intersection of a column and a row is a ***cell***; a total of more than 17 billion cells are available in a worksheet. Each cell has a unique ***cell address***, identified by first its column letter and then its row number. For example, the cell at the intersection of column C and row 6 is cell C6 (see Figure 3). The active cell is the current cell. Excel displays a dark green border around the active cell in the worksheet, and the Name Box shows the location of the active cell, which is C6 in Figure 3. The contents of the active cell, or the formula used to calculate the results of the active cell, appear in the Formula Bar. Cell references are useful when referencing data in formulas, or in navigation.

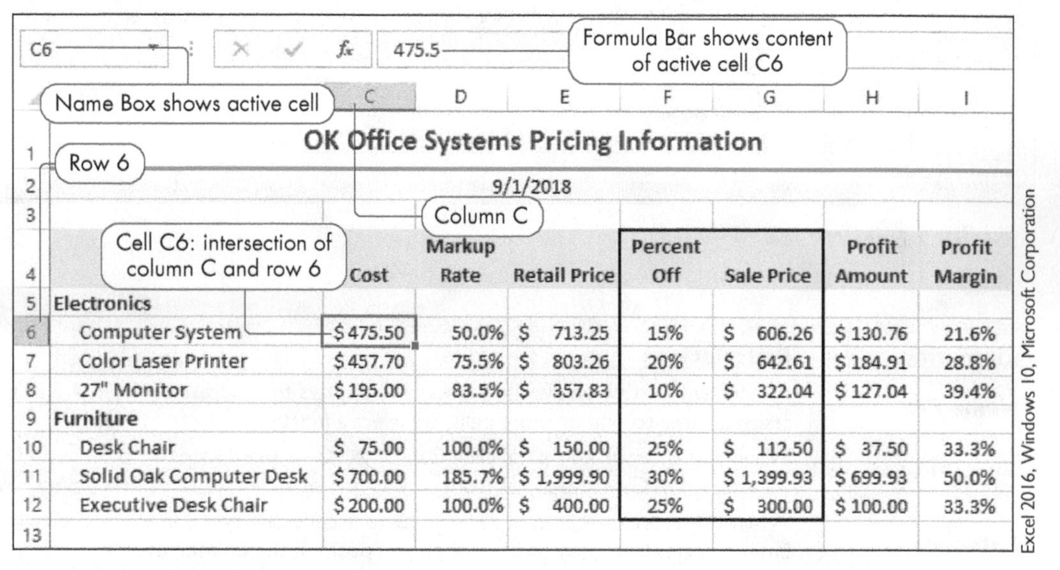

	C	D	E	F	G	H	I
1	OK Office Systems Pricing Information						
2	9/1/2018						
3							
4	Cost	Markup Rate	Retail Price	Percent Off	Sale Price	Profit Amount	Profit Margin
5 Electronics							
6 Computer System	$475.50	50.0%	$ 713.25	15%	$ 606.26	$ 130.76	21.6%
7 Color Laser Printer	$457.70	75.5%	$ 803.26	20%	$ 642.61	$ 184.91	28.8%
8 27" Monitor	$195.00	83.5%	$ 357.83	10%	$ 322.04	$ 127.04	39.4%
9 Furniture							
10 Desk Chair	$ 75.00	100.0%	$ 150.00	25%	$ 112.50	$ 37.50	33.3%
11 Solid Oak Computer Desk	$700.00	185.7%	$ 1,999.90	30%	$ 1,399.93	$ 699.93	50.0%
12 Executive Desk Chair	$200.00	100.0%	$ 400.00	25%	$ 300.00	$ 100.00	33.3%
13							

FIGURE 3 Columns, Rows, and Cells

Navigate in and Among Worksheets

To navigate to a new cell, click it or use the arrow keys on the keyboard. When you press Enter, the next cell down in the same column becomes the active cell. If you work in a large worksheet, use the vertical and horizontal scroll bars to display another area of the worksheet and click in the desired cell to make it the active cell. The keyboard contains several keys that can be used in isolation or in combination with other keys to navigate in a worksheet. Table 2 lists the keyboard navigation methods. The Go To command is helpful for navigating to a cell that is not visible onscreen.

TABLE 2 Keystrokes and Actions	
Keystroke	**Used to**
↑	Move up one cell in the same column.
↓	Move down one cell in the same column.
←	Move left one cell in the same row.
→	Move right one cell in the same row.
Tab	Move right one cell in the same row.
Page Up	Move the active cell up one screen.
Page Down	Move the active cell down one screen.
Home	Move the active cell to column A of the current row.
Ctrl+Home	Make cell A1 the active cell.
Ctrl+End	Make the rightmost, lowermost active corner of the worksheet—the intersection of the last column and row that contains data—the active cell. Does not move to cell XFD1048576 unless that cell contains data.
F5 or Ctrl+G	Display the Go To dialog box to enter any cell address.

To display the contents of another worksheet within the workbook, click the sheet tab at the bottom of the workbook window, above the status bar. After you click a sheet tab, you can then navigate within that worksheet.

Entering and Editing Cell Data

You should plan the structure of a worksheet before you start entering data. Using the OKOS case presented at the beginning of the chapter as an example, use the following steps to plan the worksheet design, enter and format data, and complete the workbook. Refer to Figure 1 for the completed workbook.

Plan the Worksheet Design

1. **State the purpose of the worksheet.** The purpose of the OKOS worksheet is to store data about products on sale and to calculate important details, such as the retail price based on markup, the sales price based on a discount rate, and the profit margin.
2. **Decide what outputs are needed to achieve the purpose of the worksheet.** Outputs are the results you need to calculate. For the OKOS worksheet, the outputs include columns to calculate the retail price (i.e., the selling price to your customers), the sale price, and the profit margin. In some worksheets, you might want to create an ***output area***, the region in the worksheet to contain formulas dependent on the values in the input area.
3. **Decide what input values are needed to achieve the desired output.** Input values are the initial values, such as variables and assumptions. You may change these values to see what type of effects different values have on the end results. For the OKOS worksheet, the input values include the costs OKOS pays the manufacturers, the markup rates, and the proposed discount rates for the sale. In some worksheets, you should create an ***input area***, a specific region in the worksheet to store and change the variables used in calculations. For example, if you applied the same Markup Rate and same Percent Off for all products, it would be easier to create an input area at the top of the worksheet to change the values in one location rather than in several locations.

Enter and Format the Data

4. **Enter the labels, values, and formulas in Excel.** Use the design plan (steps 2–3) as you enter labels, input values, and formulas to calculate the output. In the OKOS worksheet, descriptive labels (the product names) appear in the first column to indicate that the values on a specific row pertain to a specific product. Descriptive labels appear at the top of each column, such as Cost and Retail Price, to describe the values in the respective column. Change the input values to test that your formulas produce correct results. If necessary, correct any errors in the formulas to produce correct results. For the OKOS worksheet, change some of the original costs and markup rates to ensure the calculated retail price, selling price, and profit margin percentage results update correctly.
5. **Format the numerical values in the worksheet.** Align decimal points in columns of numbers and add number formats and styles. In the OKOS worksheet, you will use Accounting Number Format and the Percent Style to format the numerical data. Adjust the number of decimal places as needed.
6. **Format the descriptive titles and labels.** Add bold and color to headings so that they stand out and are attractive. Apply other formatting to headings and descriptive labels. In the OKOS worksheet, you will center the main title over all the columns, bold and center column labels over the columns, and apply other formatting to the headings.

Complete the Workbook

7. **Document the workbook as thoroughly as possible.** Include the current date, your name as the workbook author, assumptions, and purpose of the workbook. Some people provide this documentation in a separate worksheet within the workbook. You can also add some documentation in the Properties section when you click the File tab.
8. **Save and share the completed workbook.** Preview and prepare printouts for distribution in meetings, send an electronic copy of the workbook to those who need it, or upload the workbook on a shared network drive or in the cloud.

Enter Text

Text is any combination of letters, numbers, symbols, and spaces not used in calculations. Excel treats phone numbers, such as 555-1234, and Social Security numbers, such as 123-45-6789, as text entries. You enter text for a worksheet title to describe the contents of the worksheet, as row and column labels to describe data, and as cell data. In Figure 4, the cells in column A contain text, such as Class. Text aligns at the left cell margin by default.

To enter text in a cell, complete the following steps:

1. Make sure the cell is active where you want to enter text.
2. Type the text. If you want to enter a numeric value as text, such as a class section number, type an apostrophe and the number, such as '002.
3. Make another cell the active cell after entering data by completing one of the following steps:
   - Press Enter on the keyboard.
   - Press an arrow key on the keyboard.
   - Press Tab on the keyboard.

   Keep the current cell active after entering data by completing one of the following steps:
   - Press Ctrl+Enter on the keyboard.
   - Click Enter (the check mark between the Name Box and the Formula Bar).

As soon as you begin typing a label into a cell, the ***AutoComplete*** feature searches for and automatically displays any other label in the same column that matches the letters you type. The top half of Figure 4 shows Spreadsheet Apps is typed in cell A3. When you start to type *Sp* in cell A4, AutoComplete displays Spreadsheet Apps because a text entry in the same column already starts with *Sp*. Press Enter to accept the repeated label, or continue typing to enter a different label, such as Spanish II. The bottom half of Figure 4 shows that '002 was entered in cell B4 to start the text with a 0. Otherwise, Excel would have eliminated the zeros in the class section number. Ignore the error message that displays when you intentionally use an apostrophe to enter a number which is not actually a value.

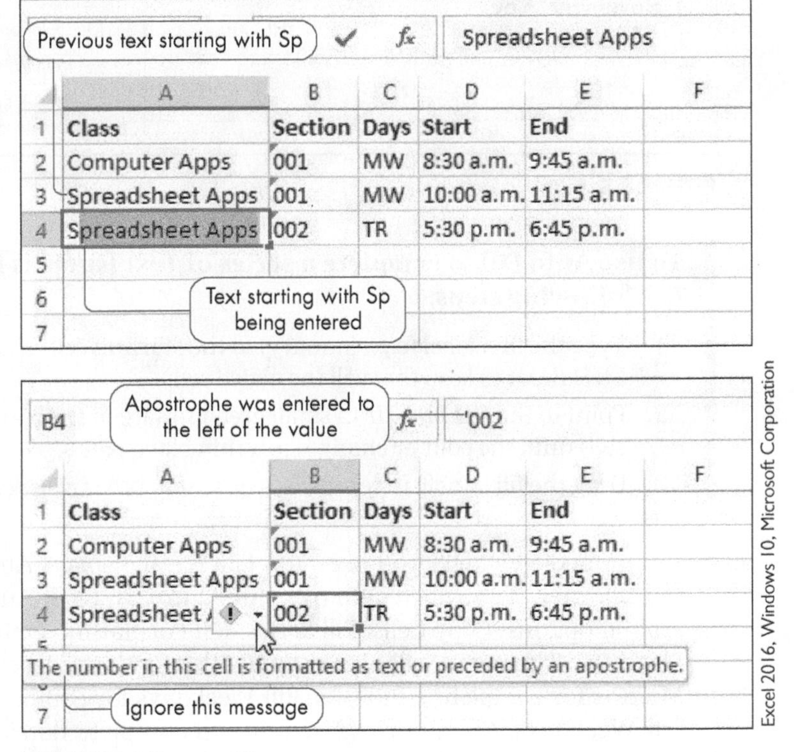

FIGURE 4 Entering Text

Use Auto Fill to Complete a Sequence

STEP 2 While AutoComplete helps to complete a label that is identical to another label in the same column, ***Auto Fill*** is a feature that helps you complete a sequence of words or values. For example, if you enter January in a cell, use Auto Fill to fill in the rest of the months in adjacent cells so that you do not have to type the rest of the month names. Auto Fill can help you complete other sequences, such as quarters (Qtr 1, etc.), weekdays, and weekday abbreviations after you type the first item in the sequence. Figure 5 shows the results of filling in months, abbreviated months, quarters, weekdays, abbreviated weekdays, and increments of 5.

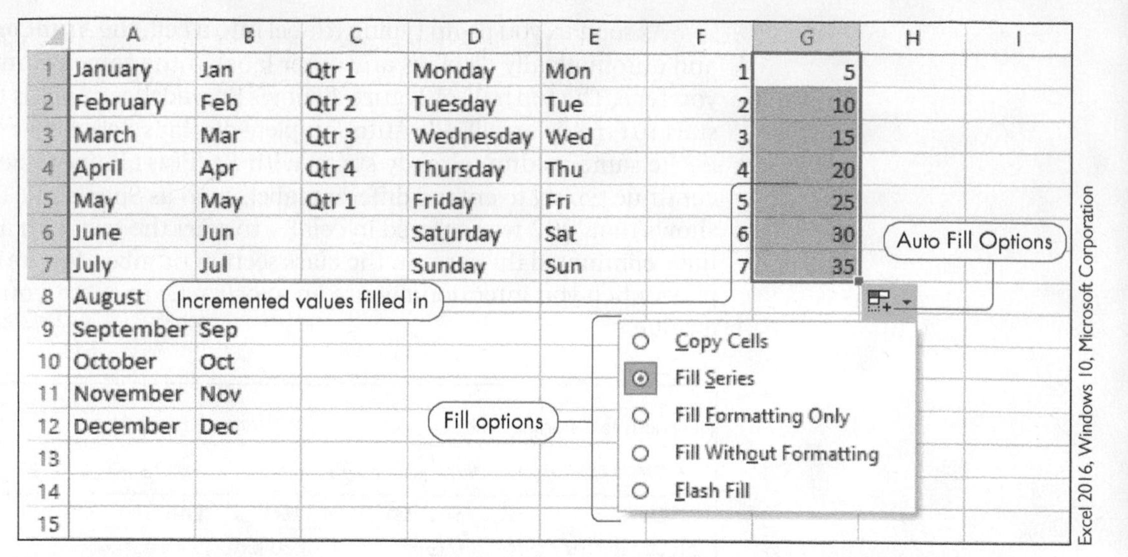

FIGURE 5 Auto Fill Examples

To use Auto Fill to complete a series of text (such as month names), complete the following steps:

1. Type the first label (e.g., January) in the starting cell (e.g., cell A1) and press Ctrl+Enter to keep that cell the active cell.
2. Point to the ***fill handle*** (a small green square in the bottom-right corner of the active cell) until the pointer changes to a thin black plus sign.
3. Drag the fill handle to repeat the content in other cells (e.g., through cell A12).

Immediately after you use Auto Fill, Excel displays Auto Fill Options in the bottom-right corner of the filled data (refer to Figure 5). Click Auto Fill Options to display several fill options: Copy Cells, Fill Series, Fill Formatting Only, Fill Without Formatting, or Flash Fill. The menu will also include other options, depending on the cell content: Fill Months for completing months; Fill Weekdays for completing weekdays; and Fill Days, Fill Weekdays, Fill Months, Fill Years to complete dates. Select Fill Formatting Only when you want to copy the formats but not complete a sequence. Select Fill Without Formatting when you want to complete the sequence but do not want to format the rest of the sequence.

To use Auto Fill to fill a sequence of consecutive numbers (such as 1, 2, 3, etc.), complete the following steps:

1. Type the first number in the starting cell (e.g., cell F1) and press Ctrl+Enter to keep that cell the active cell.
2. Drag the fill handle to fill the content in other cells. Excel will copy the same number for the rest of the cells.
3. Click Auto Fill Options and select Fill Series. Excel will change the numbers to be in sequential order, starting with the original value you typed.

For non-consecutive numeric sequences, you must specify the first two values in sequence. For example, if you want to fill in 5, 10, 15, and so on, you must enter 5 and 10 in two adjacent cells before using Auto Fill so that Excel knows to increment by 5.

To use Auto Fill to fill a sequence of number patterns (such as 5, 10, 15, 20 shown in the range G1:G7 in Figure 5), complete the following steps:

1. Type the first two numbers of the sequence in adjoining cells.
2. Select those two cells containing the starting two values.
3. Drag the fill handle to fill in the rest of the sequence.

TIP: FLASH FILL

Flash Fill is a similar feature to Auto Fill in that it can quickly fill in data for you; however, *Flash Fill* uses data in previous columns as you type in a new label in an adjoining column to determine what to fill in. For example, assume that column A contains a list of first and last names (such as Penny Sumpter in cell A5), but you want to have a column of just first names. To do this, type Penny's name in cell B5, click Fill in the Editing group on the Home tab and select Flash Fill to fill in the rest of column B with people's first names based on the data entered in column A.

Enter Values

STEP 3 ››› ***Values*** are numbers that represent a quantity or a measurable amount. Excel usually distinguishes between text and value data based on what you enter. The primary difference between text and value entries is that value entries can be the basis of calculations, whereas text cannot. In Figure 3, the data below the Cost, Markup Rates, and Percent Off labels are values. Values align at the right cell margin by default. After entering values, align decimal places and apply formatting by adding characters, such as $ or %. Entering values is the same process as entering text: Type the value in a cell and click Enter or press Enter.

TIP: ENTERING VALUES WITH TRAILING ZEROS OR PERCENTAGES

You do not need to type the last 0 in 475.50 shown in cell C6 in Figure 3. Excel will remove or add the trailing 0 depending on the decimal place formatting. Similarly, you do not have to type the leading 0 in a percentage before the decimal point. Type a percent in the decimal format, such as .5 for 50%. You will later format the value.

Enter Dates and Times

››› You can enter dates and times in a variety of formats. You should enter a static date to document when you create or modify a workbook or to document the specific point in time when the data were accurate, such as on a balance sheet or income statement. Later, you will learn how to use formulas to enter dates that update to the current date. In Figure 6, the data in column A contains the date 9/1/2018 but in different formats. Dates are values, so they align at the right side of a cell. The data in column C contains the time 2:30 PM but in different formats.

	A	B	C	D
1	9/1/2018		2:30:00 PM	
2	Saturday, September 1, 2018		14:30	
3	9/1		2:30 PM	
4	9/1/18		14:30:00	
5	09/01/18		2:30:00 PM	
6	1-Sep			
7	1-Sep-18			
8	September 1, 2018			
9				

Excel 2016, Windows 10, Microsoft Corporation

FIGURE 6 Date and Time Examples

Excel displays dates differently from the way it stores dates. For example, the displayed date 9/1/2018 represents the first day in September in the year 2018. Excel stores dates as serial numbers starting at 1 with January 1, 1900, so that you can create formulas, such as to calculate how many days exist between two dates. For example, 9/1/2018 is stored as 43344.

Edit and Clear Cell Contents

After entering data in a cell, you may need to change it. For example, you may want to edit a label to make it more descriptive, such as changing a label from OKC Office Systems Information to OKC Office Systems Pricing Information. Furthermore, you might realize a digit is missing from a value and need to change 500 to 5000.

To edit the contents of a cell, compete the following steps:

1. Click the cell.
2. Click in the Formula Bar or press F2 to put the cell in edit mode. The insertion point displays on the right side of the data in the cell when you press F2.
3. Make the changes to the content in the cell.
4. Click or press Enter.

You may want to clear or delete the contents in a cell if you no longer need data in a cell.

To clear the contents of a cell, complete the following steps:

1. Click the cell.
2. Press Delete or click the cell, click Clear in the Editing group on the Home tab, and select the desired option (see Figure 7).

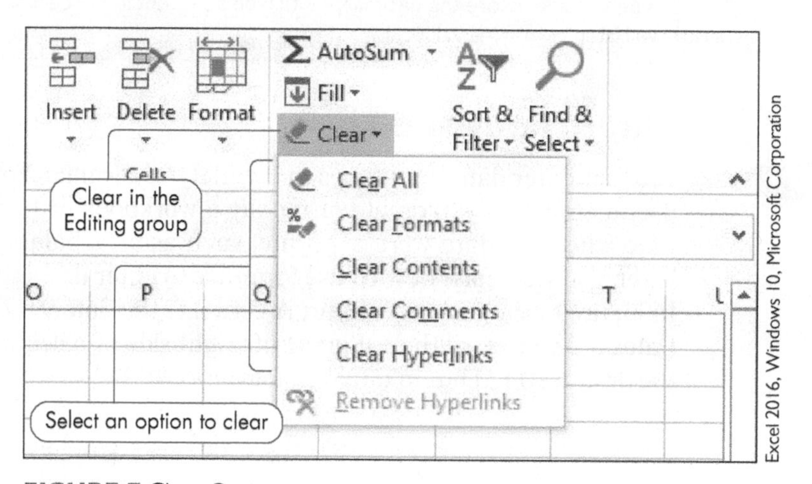

FIGURE 7 Clear Options

1. What are two major advantages of using an electronic spreadsheet instead of a paper-based ledger?
2. What are the visual indicators that a cell is the active cell?
3. What steps should you perform before entering data into a worksheet?
4. What three types of content can you can enter into a cell? Give an example for each type.

Hands-On Exercises

Watch the Video
for this Hands-On
Exercise!

MyITLab®
HOE1 Training

Skills covered: Enter Text • Use Auto Fill to Complete a Sequence • Enter Values • Enter a Date • Clear Cell Contents

1 Introduction to Spreadsheets

As the assistant manager of OKOS, you will create a worksheet that shows the cost (the amount OKOS pays its suppliers), the markup percentage (the amount by which the cost is increased), and the retail selling price. You also will list the discount percentage (such as 25% off) for each product, the sale price, and the profit margin percentage.

STEP 1 » ENTER TEXT

Now that you have planned the OKOS worksheet, you are ready to enter labels for the title, column labels, and row labels. You will type a title in cell A1, product labels in the first column, and row labels in the fourth row. Refer to Figure 8 as you complete Step 1.

	A	B	C	D	E	F	G	H	I
1	OK Office Sys			mation					
2									
3									
4	Product	Code	Cost	Markup Ra	Retail Pric	Percent O	Sale Price	Profit Margin	
5	Computer System					0.15			
6	Color Laser Printer					0.2			
7	Filing Cabinet					0.1			
8	Desk Chair					0.25			
9	Solid Oak Computer Desk					0.3			
10	27" Monitor					0.1			
11									
12									

Step b: Enter text for first product

Steps b and c: Labels extend into empty column B

Step c: Name of products

Excel 2016, Windows 10, Microsoft Corporation

FIGURE 8 Text Entered in Cells

a. Open *e01h1Markup* and save it as **e01h1Markup_LastFirst**.

When you save files, use your last and first names. For example, as the Excel author, I would save my workbook as *e01h1Markup_MulberyKeith*.

> **TROUBLESHOOTING:** If you make any major mistakes in this exercise, you can close the file, open *e01h1Markup* again, and then start this exercise over.

b. Click **cell A5**, type **Computer System**, and then press **Enter**.

When you press Enter, the next cell down—cell A6 in this case—becomes the active cell. The text does not completely fit in cell A5, and some of the text appears in cell B5. If you make cell B5 the active cell, the Formula Bar is empty, indicating that nothing is stored in that cell.

c. Type **Color Laser Printer** in **cell A6** and press **Enter**.

When you start typing C in cell A6, AutoComplete displays a ScreenTip suggesting a previous text entry starting with C—Computer System—but keep typing to enter Color Laser Printer instead.

d. Continue typing the rest of the text in **cells A7** through **A10** as shown in Figure 8. Text in column A appears to flow into column B.

You just entered the product labels to describe the data in each row.

TROUBLESHOOTING: If you make an error, click in the cell containing the error and retype the label, or press F2 to edit the cell contents, move the insertion point using the arrow keys, press Backspace or Delete to delete the incorrect characters, type the correct characters, and press Enter. If you type a label in an incorrect cell, click the cell and press Delete.

e. Click **Save** on the Quick Access Toolbar to save the changes you made to the workbook.

You should develop a habit of saving periodically. That way if your system unexpectedly shuts down, you will not lose everything you worked on.

STEP 2 » USE AUTO FILL TO COMPLETE A SEQUENCE

You want to assign a product code for each product on sale. You will assign consecutive numbers 101 to 106. After typing the first code number, you will use Auto Fill to complete the rest of the series. Refer to Figures 9 and 10 as you complete Step 2.

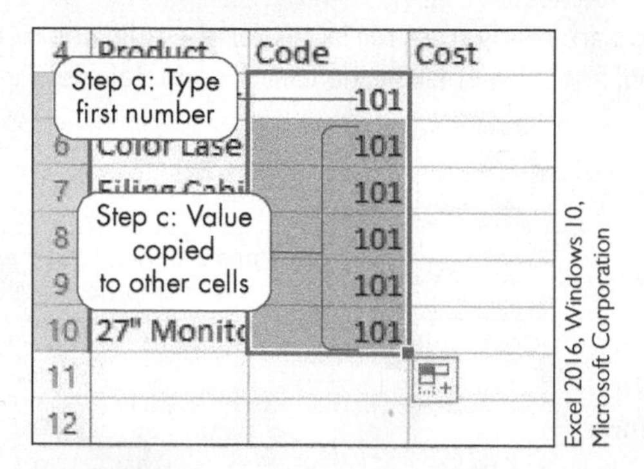

FIGURE 9 Auto Fill Copied Original Value

	A	B	C	D	E	F	G	H	I
1	OK Office Systems Pricing Information								
2									
3									
4	Product	Code	Cost	Markup Ra	Retail Pric	Percent O	Sale Price	Profit Margin	
5	Computer	101				0.15			
6	Color Lase	102				0.2			
7	Filing Cabi	103				0.1			
8	Desk Chair	104				0.25			
9	Solid Oak (	105				0.3			
10	27" Monito	106				0.1			

Copy Cells
Fill Series
Fill Formatting Only
Fill Without Formatting
Flash Fill

Step d: Click Auto Fill Options

Step d: Select Fill Series

Excel 2016, Windows 10, Microsoft Corporation

FIGURE 10 Auto Fill Sequence

a. Click **cell B5**, type **101**, and then press **Ctrl+Enter**.

The product name Computer System no longer overlaps into column B after you enter data into cell B5. The data in cell A5 is not deleted; the rest of the label is hidden until you increase the column width later.

b. Position the pointer on the fill handle in the bottom-right corner of **cell B5**.

The pointer looks like a black plus sign when you point to a fill handle.

c. Double-click the **cell B6 fill handle**.

Excel copies 101 as the item number for the rest of the products. Excel stops inserting item numbers in column B when it detects the last label in cell A10 (refer to Figure 9).

d. Click **Auto Fill Options** and select **Fill Series**. Save the workbook.

Excel changes the duplicate values to continue sequentially in a series of numbers.

STEP 3 ›› ENTER VALUES

Now that you have entered the descriptive labels and item numbers, you will enter the cost and markup rate for each product. Refer to Figure 11 as you complete Step 3.

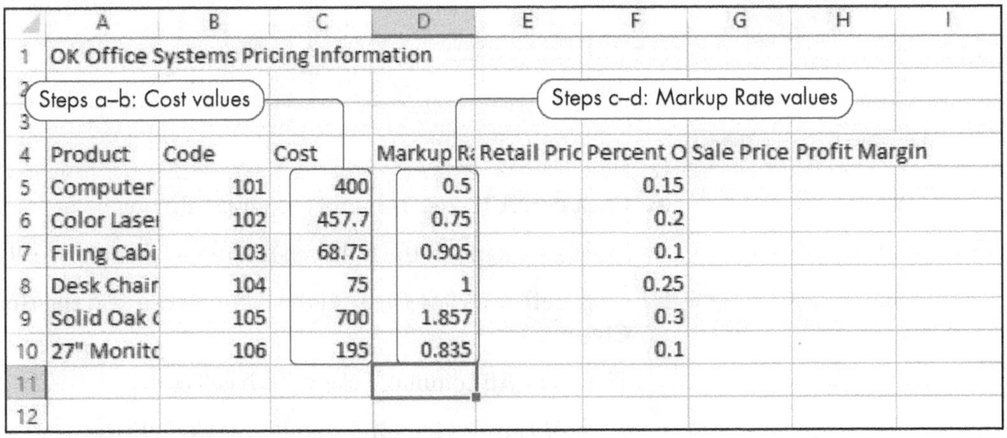

Steps a–b: Cost values

Steps c–d: Markup Rate values

	A	B	C	D	E	F	G	H	I
1	OK Office Systems Pricing Information								
2									
3									
4	Product	Code	Cost	Markup Ra	Retail Pric	Percent O	Sale Price	Profit Margin	
5	Computer	101	400	0.5		0.15			
6	Color Laser	102	457.7	0.75		0.2			
7	Filing Cabi	103	68.75	0.905		0.1			
8	Desk Chair	104	75	1		0.25			
9	Solid Oak (	105	700	1.857		0.3			
10	27" Monitc	106	195	0.835		0.1			
11									
12									

FIGURE 11 Values Entered in Cells

a. Click **cell C5**, type **400**, and then press **Enter**.

b. Type the remaining costs in **cells C6** through **C10** shown in Figure 11.

To improve your productivity, use the number keypad (if available) on the right side of your keyboard. It is much faster to type values and press Enter on the number keypad rather than to use the numbers on the keyboard. Make sure Num Lock is active before using the number keypad to enter values.

c. Click **cell D5**, type **0.5**, and then press **Enter**.

You entered the markup rate as a decimal instead of a percentage. You will apply Percent Style later, but now you will concentrate on data entry.

d. Type the remaining values in **cells D6** through **D10** as shown in Figure 11. Save the workbook.

STEP 4 » ENTER A DATE AND CLEAR CELL CONTENTS

As you review the worksheet, you realize you need to provide a date to indicate when the sale starts. Refer to Figure 12 as you complete Step 4.

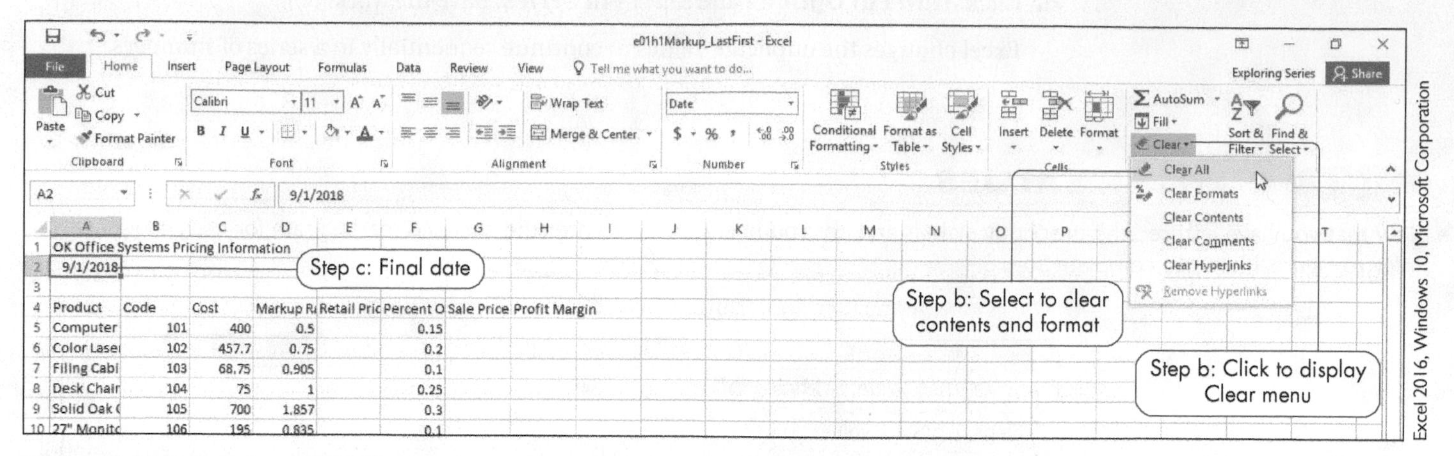

FIGURE 12 Date Entered in a Cell

a. Click **cell A2**, type **9/1**, and then press **Enter**.

The date aligns on the right cell margin by default. Excel displays 1-Sep instead of 9/1.

b. Click **cell A2**, click **Clear** in the Editing group on the Home tab, and then select **Clear All**.

The Clear All command clears both cell contents and formatting in the selected cell(s).

c. Type **9/1/2018** in **cell A2** and press **Ctrl+Enter**.

> **TROUBLESHOOTING:** If you did not use Clear All and typed 9/1/2018 in cell A2, Excel would have retained the previous date format and displayed 1-Sep again.

When you type the month, day, and year such as 9/1/2018, Excel enters the date in that format (unless it has a different date format applied).

d. Save the workbook. Keep the workbook open if you plan to continue with the next Hands-On Exercise. If not, close the workbook, and exit Excel.

Mathematical Operations and Formulas

A ***formula*** combines cell references, arithmetic operations, values, and/or functions used in a calculation. Formulas transform static numbers into meaningful results that update as values change. For example, a payroll manager can build formulas to calculate the gross pay, deductions, and net pay for an organization's employees, or a doctoral student can create formulas to perform various statistical calculations to interpret his or her research data.

In this section, you will learn how to use mathematical operations in Excel formulas. You will refresh your memory of the mathematical order of operations and learn how to construct formulas using cell addresses so that when the value of an input cell changes, the result of the formula changes without you having to modify the formula.

Creating Formulas

Use formulas to help you analyze how results will change as the input data changes. You can change the value of your assumptions or inputs and explore the results quickly and accurately. For example, if your rent increases, how does that affect your personal budget? Analyzing different input values in Excel is easy after you build formulas. Simply change an input value and observe the change in the formula results. In the OKOS product sales worksheet, the results for the Retail Price, Sale Price, and Profit Margin labels were calculated by using formulas (refer to Figure 1).

Use Cell References in Formulas

STEP 1 »

You should use cell references instead of values in formulas where possible. You may include values in an input area—such as dates, salary, or costs—that you will need to reference in formulas. Referencing these cells in your formulas, instead of typing the value of the cell to which you are referring, keeps your formulas accurate if you change values to perform a what-if analysis.

Figure 13 shows a worksheet containing input values and results of formulas. The figure also displays the actual formulas used to generate the calculated results. For example, cell E2 contains the formula =B2+B3. Excel uses the value stored in cell B2 (10) and adds it to the value stored in cell B3 (2). The result (12) appears in cell E2 instead of the actual formula. The Formula Bar displays the formula entered into the active cell.

E2 | fx | =B2+B3

	A	B	C	D	E	F
1	**Description**	**Values**		**Description**	**Results**	**Formulas in Column E**
2	First input value	10		Sum of 10 and 2	12	=B2+B3
3	Second input value	2		Difference between 10 and 2	8	=B2-B3
4				Product of 10 and 2	20	=B2*B3
5				Results of dividing 10 by 2	5	=B2/B3
6				Results of 10 to the 2nd power	100	=B2^B3

FIGURE 13 Formula Results

To enter a formula, complete the following steps:

1. Click the cell.
2. Type an equal sign (=), followed by the arithmetic expression, using cell references instead of values. Do not include any spaces in the formula.
3. Click Enter or press Enter.

TIP: EQUAL SIGN NEEDED
If you type B2+B3 without the equal sign, Excel does not recognize that you entered a formula and stores the "formula" as text.

TIP: UPPER OR LOWERCASE
When you create a formula, type the cell references in uppercase, such as =B2+B3, or lowercase, such as =b2+b3. Excel changes cell references to uppercase automatically.

In Figure 13, cell B2 contains 10, and cell B3 contains 2. Cell E2 contains =B2+B3 but shows the result 12. If you change the value of cell B3 to 5, cell E2 displays the new result, which is 15. However, if you had typed actual values in the formula, =10+2, you would have to edit the formula to =10+5, even though the value in cell B3 was changed to 5. Using values in formulas can cause problems as you might forget to edit the formula or you might have a typographical error if you edit the formula. Always design worksheets in such a way as to be able to place those values that might need to change as input values. Referencing cells with input values in formulas instead of using the values themselves will avoid having to modify your formulas if an input value changes later.

TIP: WHEN TO USE A VALUE IN A FORMULA
Use cell references instead of actual values in formulas, unless the value will never change. For example, if you want to calculate how many total months are in a specified number of years, enter a formula such as =B5*12, where B5 contains the number of years. You might want to change the number of years, so you type that value in cell B5. However, every year always has 12 months, so you can use the value 12 in the formula.

Apply the Order of Operations

The ***order of operations*** (also called order of precedence) are rules that controls the sequence in which arithmetic operations are performed, which affects the result of the calculation. Excel performs mathematical calculations left to right in this order: **P**arentheses, **E**xponentiation, **M**ultiplication or **D**ivision, and finally **A**ddition or **S**ubtraction. Some people remember the order of operations with the phrase ***P****lease* ***E****xcuse* ***M****y* ***D****ear* ***A****unt* ***S****ally*.

Table 3 lists the primary order of operations. Use Help to learn about the complete order of precedence.

TABLE 3 Order of Operations

Order	Description	Symbols
1	Parentheses	( )
2	Exponentiation	^
3	Multiplication and Division	* and / (respectively)
4	Addition and Subtraction	+ and − (respectively)

TIP: PARENTHESES IN FORMULAS
Use parentheses to make sure a lower-order operation occurs first. For example, if you want to add the values stored in cells A1 and A2 and multiply that result by the value stored in cell A3, enclose parentheses around the addition operation: =(A1+A2)*A3. Without parentheses, =A1+A2*A3, the first calculation multiplies the values stored in A2 and A3. That result is then added to the value stored in cell A1 since multiplication has a higher order of operations than addition.

Figure 14 shows formulas, the sequence in which calculations occur, calculations, the description, and the results of each order of operations. The highlighted results are the final formula results. This figure illustrates the importance of symbols and use of parentheses.

	A	B	C	D	E	F
1	Input		Formula	Sequence	Description	Result
2	2		=A2+A3*A4+A5	1	3 (cell A3) * 4 (cell A4)	12
3	3			2	2 (cell A2) + 12 (order 1)	14
4	4			3	14 (order 2) + 5 (cell A5)	19
5	5					
6			=(A2+A3)*(A4+A5)	1	2 (cell A2) + 3 (cell A3)	5
7				2	4 (cell A4) + 5 (cell A5)	9
8				3	5 (order 1) * 9 (order 2)	45
9						
10			=A2/A3+A4*A5	1	2 (cell A2) / 3 (cell A3)	0.666667
11				2	4 (cell A4) * 5 (cell A5)	20
12				3	0.666667 (order 1) + 20 (order 2)	20.66667
13						
14			=A2/(A3+A4)*A5	1	3 (cell A3) + 4 (cell A4)	7
15				2	2 (cell A2) / 7 (order 1)	0.285714
16				3	0.285714 (order 2) * 5 (cell A5)	1.428571
17						
18			=A2^2+A3*A4%	1	4 (cell A4) is converted to percentage	0.04
19				2	2 (cell A2) to the power of 2	4
20				3	3 (cell A3) * 0.04 (order 1)	0.12
21				4	4 (order 2) + 0.12 (order 3)	4.12

FIGURE 14 Formula Results Based on Order of Operations

Use Semi-Selection to Create a Formula

STEP 2 To decrease typing time and ensure accuracy, use ***semi-selection***, a process of selecting a cell or range of cells for entering cell references as you create formulas. Semi-selection is often called ***pointing*** because you use the pointer to select cells as you build the formula. Some people prefer using the semi-selection method instead of typing a formula so that they can make sure they use the correct cell references as they build the formula.

To use the semi-selection technique to create a formula, complete the following steps:

1. Click the cell where you want to create the formula.
2. Type an equal sign (=) to start a formula.
3. Click the cell that contains the value to use in the formula. A moving marquee appears around the cell or range you select, and Excel displays the cell or range reference in the formula.
4. Type a mathematical operator.
5. Continue clicking cells, selecting ranges, and typing operators to finish the formula. Use the scroll bars if the cell is in a remote location in the worksheet, or click a worksheet tab to see a cell in another worksheet.
6. Press Enter to complete the formula.

Copy Formulas

After you enter a formula in a cell, you duplicate the formula without retyping the formula for other cells that need a similar formula. Previously, you learned about the Auto Fill feature that enables you to use the fill handle to fill in a series of values, months, quarters, and weekdays. You can also use the fill handle to copy the formula in the active cell to adjacent cells down a column or across a row, depending on how the data are organized. Cell references in copied formulas adjust based on their relative locations to the original formula.

To copy a formula to other cells using the fill handle, complete the following steps:

1. Click the cell with the content you want to copy to make it the active cell.
2. Point to the fill handle in the bottom-right corner of the cell until the pointer changes to the fill pointer (a thin black plus sign).
3. Drag the fill handle to copy the formula.

Displaying Cell Formulas

Excel shows the result of the formula in the cell (see the top half of Figure 15); however, you might want to display the formulas instead of the calculated results in the cells (see the bottom half of Figure 15). Displaying the cell formulas may help you double-check all your formulas at one time or troubleshoot a problem with a formula instead of clicking in each cell containing a formula and looking at just the Formula Bar.

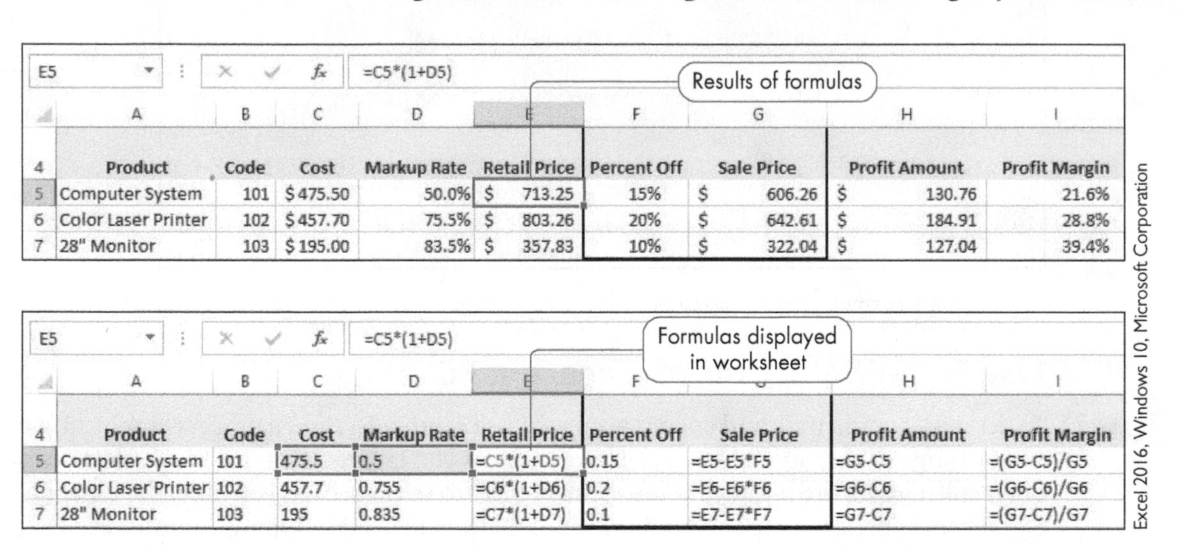

	A	B	C	D	E	F	G	H	I
4	Product	Code	Cost	Markup Rate	Retail Price	Percent Off	Sale Price	Profit Amount	Profit Margin
5	Computer System	101	$ 475.50	50.0%	$ 713.25	15%	$ 606.26	$ 130.76	21.6%
6	Color Laser Printer	102	$ 457.70	75.5%	$ 803.26	20%	$ 642.61	$ 184.91	28.8%
7	28" Monitor	103	$ 195.00	83.5%	$ 357.83	10%	$ 322.04	$ 127.04	39.4%

	A	B	C	D	E	F	G	H	I
4	Product	Code	Cost	Markup Rate	Retail Price	Percent Off	Sale Price	Profit Amount	Profit Margin
5	Computer System	101	475.5	0.5	=C5*(1+D5)	0.15	=E5-E5*F5	=G5-C5	=(G5-C5)/G5
6	Color Laser Printer	102	457.7	0.755	=C6*(1+D6)	0.2	=E6-E6*F6	=G6-C6	=(G6-C6)/G6
7	28" Monitor	103	195	0.835	=C7*(1+D7)	0.1	=E7-E7*F7	=G7-C7	=(G7-C7)/G7

FIGURE 15 Formulas and Formula Results

To display cell formulas in the worksheet, complete one of the following steps:

- Press Ctrl and the grave accent (`) key, sometimes referred to as the tilde key, in the top-left corner of the keyboard, below the Esc key.
- Click Show Formulas in the Formula Auditing group on the Formulas tab.

To hide the formulas and display the formula results again, repeat the preceding process.

5. What is the order of operations? Provide and explain two examples that use four different operators: one with parentheses and one without.
6. Why should you use cell references instead of typing values in formulas?
7. When would it be useful to display formulas instead of formula results in a worksheet?

Hands-On Exercises

Skills covered: Use Cell References in Formulas • Apply the Order of Operations • Use Semi-Selection to Create a Formula • Copy Formulas • Display Cell Formulas

2 Mathematical Operations and Formulas

In Hands-On Exercise 1, you created the basic worksheet for OKOS by entering text, values, and a date for items on sale. Now you will insert formulas to calculate the missing results—specifically, the retail (before sale) price, sale price, and profit margin. You will use cell addresses in your formulas, so when you change a referenced value, the formula results will update automatically.

STEP 1 » USE CELL REFERENCES IN A FORMULA AND APPLY THE ORDER OF OPERATIONS

The first formula you create will calculate the retail price. The retail price is the price you originally charge. It is based on a percentage of the original cost so that you earn a profit. Refer to Figure 16 as you complete Step 1.

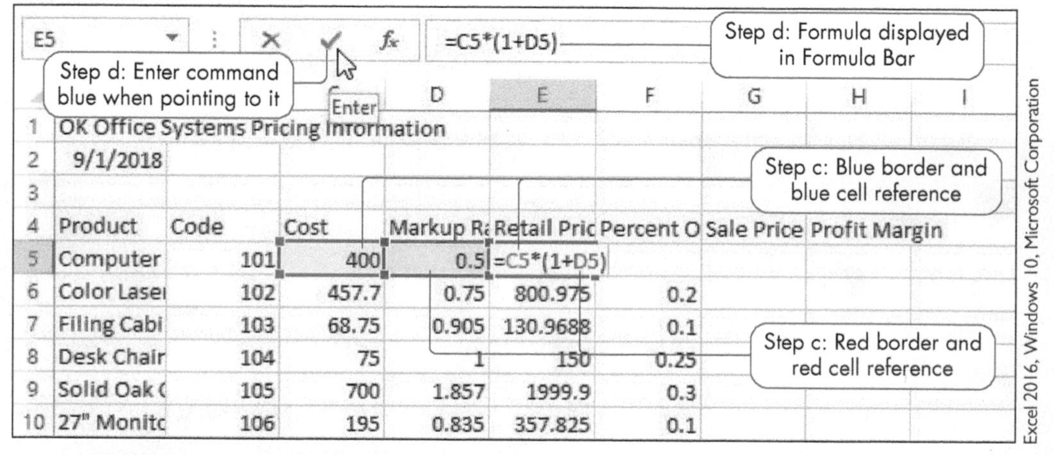

FIGURE 16 Retail Price Formula

a. Open *e01h1Markup_LastFirst* if you closed it at the end of Hands-On Exercise 1 and save it as **e01h2Markup_LastFirst**, changing h1 to h2.

b. Click **cell E5**.

Cell E5 is the cell where you will enter the formula to calculate the retail selling price of the first item.

c. Type **=C5*(1+D5)** and view the formula and the colored cells and borders on the screen.

As you build or edit a formula, each cell address in the formula displays in a specific color, and while you type or edit the formula, the cells referenced in the formula have a temporary colored border. For example, in the formula =C5*(1+D5), C5 appears in blue, and D5 appears in red. Cell C5 has a temporarily blue border and light blue shading, and cell D5 has a temporarily red border with light red shading to help you identify cells as you construct your formulas (refer to Figure 16).

You enclosed 1+D5 in parentheses to control the order of operations so that 1 is added to the value in cell D5 (0.5). The result is 1.5, which represents 150% of the cost. That result is then multiplied by the value in C5 (400). If you did not use the parentheses, Excel would multiply the value in C5 by 1 (which would be 400) and add that result to the value in D5 (0.5) for a final result of 400.5, which would have given you incorrect results.

An alternative formula also calculates the correct retail price: =C5*D5+C5 or =C5+C5*D5. In this formula, 400 (cell C5) is multiplied by 0.5 (cell D5); that result (200) represents the dollar value of the markup. Excel adds the value 200 to the original cost of 400 to obtain 600, the retail price. You were instructed to enter =C5*(1+D5) to demonstrate the order of operations.

d. Click **Enter** ✓ (between the Name Box and the Formula Bar) and view the formula in the Formula Bar to check it for accuracy.

The result of the formula, 600, appears in cell E5, and the formula displays in the Formula Bar. This formula first adds 1 (the decimal equivalent of 100%) to 0.5 (the value stored in cell D5). Excel multiplies that sum of 1.5 by 400 (the value stored in cell C5). This calculation reflects a retail price is 150% of the original cost.

> **TROUBLESHOOTING:** If the result is not correct, click the cell and look at the formula in the Formula Bar. Click in the Formula Bar, edit the formula to match the formula shown in Step c, and click Enter (the check mark between the Name Box and the Formula Bar). Make sure you start the formula with an equal sign.

e. Position the pointer on the **cell E5 fill handle**. When the pointer changes from a white plus sign to a thin black plus sign, double-click the **fill handle**.

Excel copies the retail price formula for the remaining products in your worksheet. Excel detects when to stop copying the formula when it detects the last label in the dataset.

f. Click **cell E6**, the cell containing the first copied retail price formula, look at the Formula Bar, and then save the workbook.

The formula in cell E6 is =C6*(1+D6). It was copied from the formula in cell E5, which is =C5*(1+D5). Excel adjusts the row references in this formula as you copied the formula down a column so that the results are based on each row's data.

> **TROUBLESHOOTING:** The result in cell E7 may show more decimal places than shown in Figure 16. Do not worry about this slight difference.

STEP 2 » USE SEMI-SELECTION AND APPLY THE ORDER OF OPERATIONS TO CREATE A FORMULA

Now that you have calculated the retail price, you will calculate a sale price. This week, the computer is on sale for 15% off the retail price. Refer to Figure 17 as you complete Step 2.

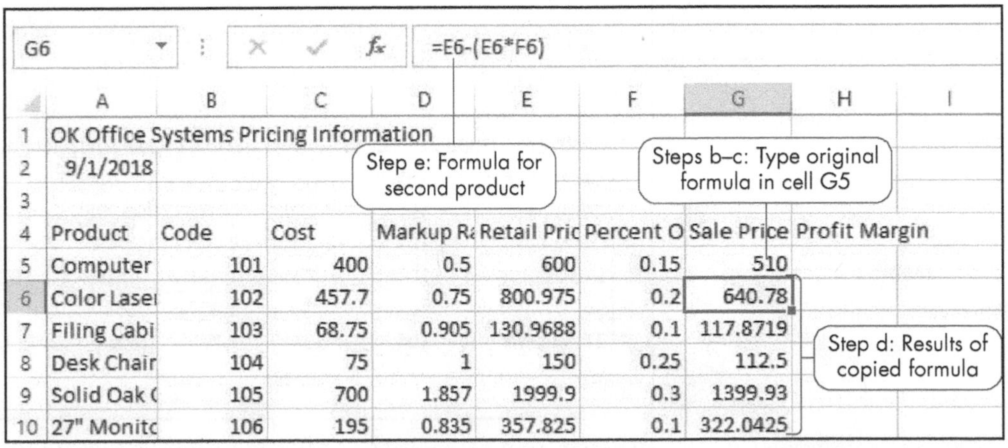

G6 | =E6-(E6*F6)

	A	B	C	D	E	F	G	H	I
1	OK Office Systems Pricing Information								
2	9/1/2018								
3									
4	Product	Code	Cost	Markup Ra	Retail Pric	Percent O	Sale Price	Profit Margin	
5	Computer	101	400	0.5	600	0.15	510		
6	Color Lasei	102	457.7	0.75	800.975	0.2	640.78		
7	Filing Cabi	103	68.75	0.905	130.9688	0.1	117.8719		
8	Desk Chair	104	75	1	150	0.25	112.5		
9	Solid Oak (	105	700	1.857	1999.9	0.3	1399.93		
10	27" Monitc	106	195	0.835	357.825	0.1	322.0425		

Step e: Formula for second product

Steps b–c: Type original formula in cell G5

Step d: Results of copied formula

FIGURE 17 Sale Price Formula

a. Click **cell G5**, the cell where you will enter the formula to calculate the sale price.

b. Type =, click **cell E5**, type -, click **cell E5**, type *, and then click **cell F5**. Notice the color-coding in the cell addresses. Press **Ctrl+Enter** to keep the current cell the active cell.

You used the semi-selection method to enter a formula. The result is 510. Looking at the formula, you might think E5–E5 equals zero; remember that because of the order of operations, multiplication is calculated before subtraction. The product of 600 (cell E5) and 0.15 (cell F5) equals 90, which is then subtracted from 600 (cell E5), so the sale price is 510.

> **TROUBLESHOOTING:** You should check the result for logic. Use a calculator to spot-check the accuracy of formulas. If you mark down merchandise by 15% of its regular price, you are charging 85% of the regular price. You should spot-check your formula to ensure that 85% of 600 is 510 by multiplying 600 by 0.85.

c. Click **cell G5**, type **=E5-(E5*F5)**, and then click **Enter**.

Although the parentheses are not needed because the multiplication occurs before the subtraction, it may be helpful to add parentheses to make the formula easier to interpret.

d. Double-click the **cell G5 fill handle** to copy the formula down column G.

e. Click **cell G6**, the cell containing the first copied sale price formula, view the Formula Bar, and save the workbook.

The original formula was =E5-(E5*F5). The copied formula in cell G6 is adjusted to =E6-(E6*F6) so that it calculates the sales price based on the data in row 6.

STEP 3 ›› USE CELL REFERENCES IN A FORMULA AND APPLY THE ORDER OF OPERATIONS

After calculating the sale price, you want to know the profit margin OKOS will earn. OKOS paid $400 for the computer and will sell it for $510. The profit of $110 is then divided by the $400 cost, which gives OKOS a profit margin of 0.215686, which will be formatted later as a percent 21.6%. Refer to Figure 18 as you complete Step 3.

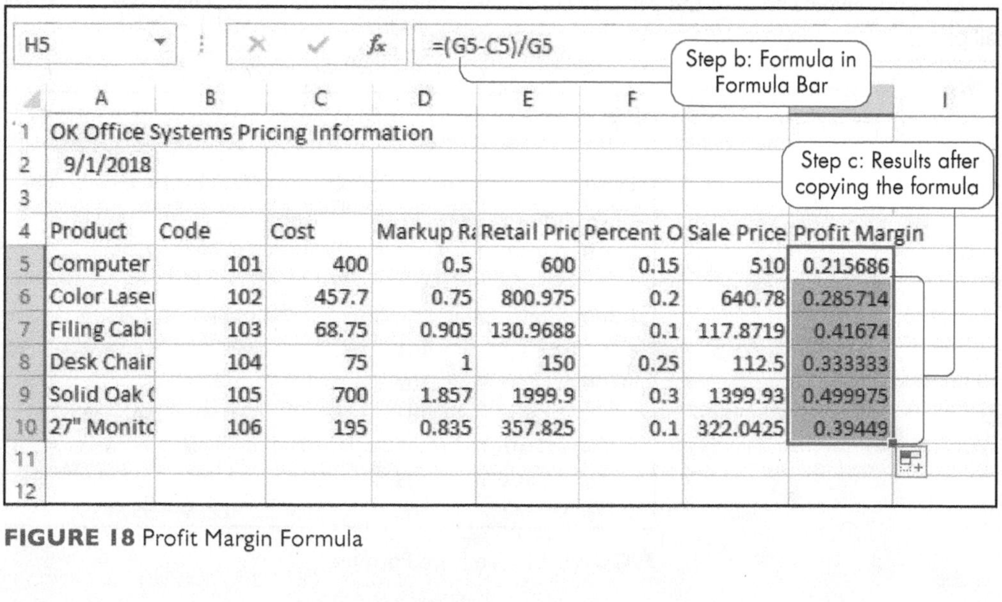

H5 =(G5-C5)/G5

Step b: Formula in Formula Bar

Step c: Results after copying the formula

	A	B	C	D	E	F	G	H	I
1	OK Office Systems Pricing Information								
2	9/1/2018								
3									
4	Product	Code	Cost	Markup Ra	Retail Pric	Percent O	Sale Price	Profit Margin	
5	Computer	101	400	0.5	600	0.15	510	0.215686	
6	Color Lasei	102	457.7	0.75	800.975	0.2	640.78	0.285714	
7	Filing Cabi	103	68.75	0.905	130.9688	0.1	117.8719	0.41674	
8	Desk Chair	104	75	1	150	0.25	112.5	0.333333	
9	Solid Oak (	105	700	1.857	1999.9	0.3	1399.93	0.499975	
10	27" Monitc	106	195	0.835	357.825	0.1	322.0425	0.39449	
11									
12									

FIGURE 18 Profit Margin Formula

a. Click **cell H5**, the cell where you will enter the formula to calculate the profit margin.

The profit margin is the profit (difference in sales price and cost) percentage of the sale price.

b. Type **=(G5-C5)/G5** and notice the color-coding in the cell addresses. Press **Ctrl+Enter**.

The formula must first calculate the profit, which is the difference between the sale price (510) and the original cost (400). The difference (110) is then divided by the sale price (510) to determine the profit margin of 0.215686, or 21.6%.

c. Double-click the **cell H5 fill handle** to copy the formula down the column.

d. Click **cell H6**, the cell containing the first copied profit margin formula, look at the Formula Bar, and then save the workbook.

The original formula was =(G5-C5)/G5, and the copied formula in cell H6 is =(G6-C6)/G6.

STEP 4 » DISPLAY CELL FORMULAS

You want to see how the prices and profit margins are affected when you change some of the original cost values. For example, the supplier might notify you that the cost to you will increase. In addition, you want to see the formulas displayed in the cells temporarily. Refer to Figures 19 and 20 as you complete Step 4.

	A	B	C	D	E	F	G	H	I
1	OK Office Systems Pricing Informatic								
2									
3									
4	Product	Code	Cost	Markup Ra	Retail Pric	Percent O	Sale Price	Profit Margin	
5	Computer	101	475.5	0.5	713.25	0.15	606.2625	0.215686	
6	Color Laser	102	457.7	0.755	803.2635	0.2	642.6108	0.287749	
7	Filing Cabi	103	68.75	0.905	130.9688	0.05	124.4203	0.447437	
8	Desk Chair	104	75	1	150	0.25	112.5	0.333333	
9	Solid Oak (	105	700	1.857	1999.9	0.3	1399.93	0.499975	
10	27" M			0.835	357.825	0.1	322.0425	0.39449	
11									

Step a: Updated results in cells E5, G5, and H5
Step c: Updated results in cells G7 and H7
Step b: New value in cell D6
Step a: New value in cell C5
Step c: New value in cell F7
Excel 2016, Windows 10, Microsoft Corporation

FIGURE 19 Results of Changed Values

	A	B	C	D	E	F	G	H
1	OK Office Systems Pri							
2	43344							
3								
4	Product	Code	Cost	Markup Rate	Retail Price	Percent Off	Sale Price	Profit Margin
5	Computer System	101	475.5	0.5	=C5*(1+D5)	0.15	=E5-(E5*F5)	=(G5-C5)/G5
6	Color Laser Printer	102	457.7	0.755	=C6*(1+D6)	0.2	=E6-(E6*F6)	=(G6-C6)/G6
7	Filing Cabinet	103	68.75	0.905	=C7*(1+D7)	0.05	=E7-(E7*F7)	=(G7-C7)/G7
8	Desk Chair	104	75	1	=C8*(1+D8)	0.25	=E8-(E8*F8)	=(G8-C8)/G8
9	Solid Oak Computer D	105	700	1.857	=C9*(1+D9)	0.3	=E9-(E9*F9)	=(G9-C9)/G9
10	27" Monitor	106	195	0.835	=C10*(1+D10)	0.1	=E10-(E10*F10)	=(G10-C10)/G10

Step d: Values appear left aligned
Step d: Formulas displayed instead of results
Step d: Date displays as a serial number
Excel 2016, Windows 10, Microsoft Corporation

FIGURE 20 Formulas Displayed in the Worksheet

a. Click **cell C5**, type **475.5**, and then press **Enter**.

The results of the retail price, sale price, and profit margin formulas change based on the new cost.

b. Click **cell D6**, type **0.755**, and then press **Enter**.

The results of the retail price, sale price, and profit margin formulas change based on the new markup rate.

c. Click **cell F7**, type **0.05**, and then press **Ctrl+Enter**.

The results of the sale price and profit margin formulas change based on the new markdown rate. Note that the retail price did not change because that formula is not based on the markup rate.

d. Press **Ctrl+`** (the grave accent mark).

The workbook now displays the formulas rather than the formula results (refer to Figure 20). This is helpful when you want to review several formulas at one time. Numbers are left-aligned, and the date displays as a serial number when you display formulas.

e. Press **Ctrl+`** (the grave accent mark).

The workbook now displays the formula results in the cells again.

f. Save the workbook. Keep the workbook open if you plan to continue with the next Hands-On Exercise. If not, close the workbook, and exit Excel.

Worksheet Structure and Clipboard Tasks

Although you plan worksheets before entering data, you might need to insert a new row to accommodate new data, delete a column that you no longer need, hide a column of confidential data before printing worksheets for distribution, or adjust the size of columns and rows so that the data fit better. Furthermore, you may decide to move data to a different location in the same worksheet or even to a different worksheet. Instead of deleting the original data and typing it in the new location, select and move data from one cell to another. In some instances, you might want to create a copy of data entered so that you can explore different values and compare the results of the original data set and the copied and edited data set.

In this section, you will learn how to make changes to columns and rows. Furthermore, you will also learn how to select ranges, move data to another location, copy data to another range, and use the Paste Special feature.

Managing Columns and Rows

As you enter and edit worksheet data, you might need to adjust the row and column structure to accommodate new data or remove unnecessary data. You can add rows and columns to add new data and delete data, columns, and rows that you no longer need. Adjusting the height and width of rows and columns, respectively, can often present the data better.

Insert Cells, Columns, and Rows

STEP 1 »» After you construct a worksheet, you might need to insert cells, columns, or rows to accommodate new data. For example, you might want to insert a new column to perform calculations or insert a new row to list a new product.

To insert a new column or row, complete the following set of steps:

1. Click in the column or row.
2. Click the Insert arrow in the Cells group on the Home tab (see Figure 21).
3. Select Insert Sheet Columns or Insert Sheet Rows.

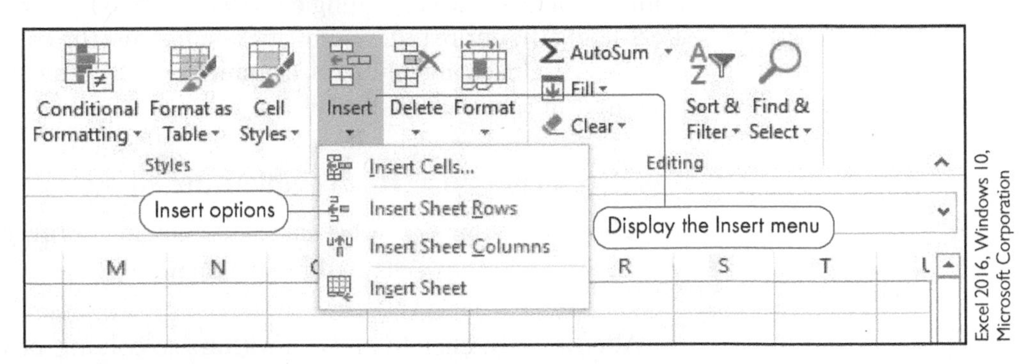

FIGURE 21 Insert Menu

Alternatively, you can use a shortcut menu. Right-click the column (letter) or row (number) heading. Then select Insert from the shortcut menu

Excel inserts new columns to the left of the current column and new rows above the active row. If the current column is column C and you insert a new column, the new column becomes column C, and the original column C data are now in column D. Likewise, if the current row is 5 and you insert a new row, the new row is row 5, and the original row 5 data are now in row 6. When you insert cells, rows, and columns, cell addresses in formulas adjust automatically.

Inserting a cell is helpful when you realize that you left out an entry after you have entered all of the data. Instead of inserting a new row or column, you just want to move the existing content down or over to enter the missing value. You can insert a single cell in a particular row or column.

To insert one or more cells, complete the following steps:

1. Click in the cell where you want the new cell.
2. Click the Insert arrow in the Cells group on the Home tab.
3. Select Insert Cells.
4. Select an option from the Insert dialog box (see Figure 22) to position the new cell and click OK.

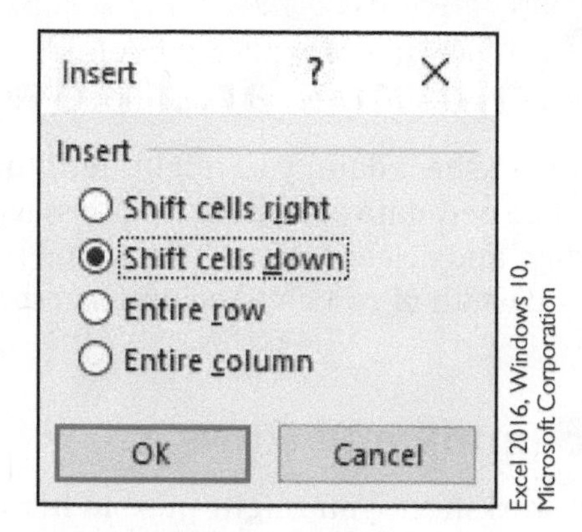

Excel 2016, Windows 10, Microsoft Corporation

FIGURE 22 Insert Dialog Box

Alternatively, click Insert in the Cells group. The default action of clicking Insert is to insert a cell at the current location, which moves existing data down in that column only.

Delete Cells, Columns, and Rows

STEP 2 If you no longer need a cell, column, or row, you should delete it. For example, you might want to delete a row containing a product you no longer carry. In these situations, you are deleting the entire cell, column, or row, not just the contents of the cell to leave empty cells. As with inserting new cells, columns, or rows, any affected formulas adjust the cell references automatically.

To delete a column or row, complete the following sets of steps:

1. Click the column or row heading for the column or row you want to delete.
2. Click Delete in the Cells group on the Home tab.

Alternatively, click in any cell within the column or row you want to delete, click the Delete arrow in the Cells group on the Home tab (see Figure 23), and then select Select Delete Sheet Columns or Delete Sheet Rows. Another alternative is to right-click the column letter or row number for the column or row you want to delete and then select Delete from the shortcut menu.

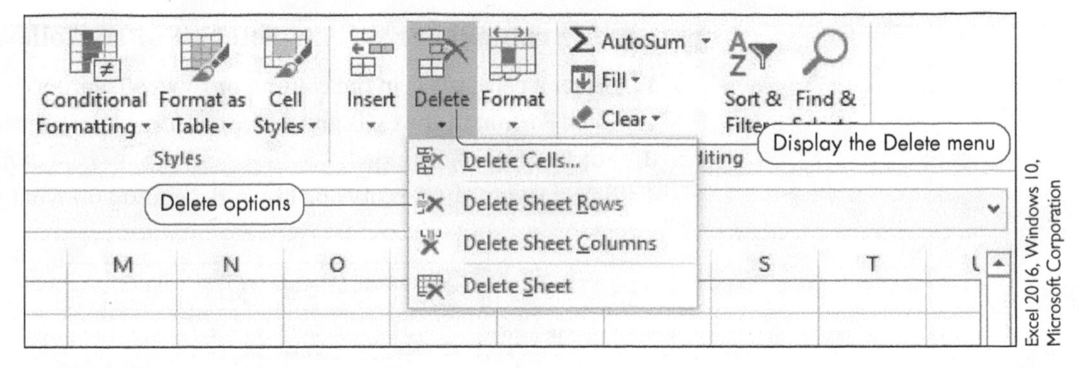

FIGURE 23 Delete Menu

To delete a cell or cells, complete the following steps:

1. Select the cell(s).
2. Click the Delete arrow in the Cells group.
3. Select Delete Cells to display the Delete dialog box (see Figure 24).
4. Click the appropriate option to shift cells left or up and click OK.

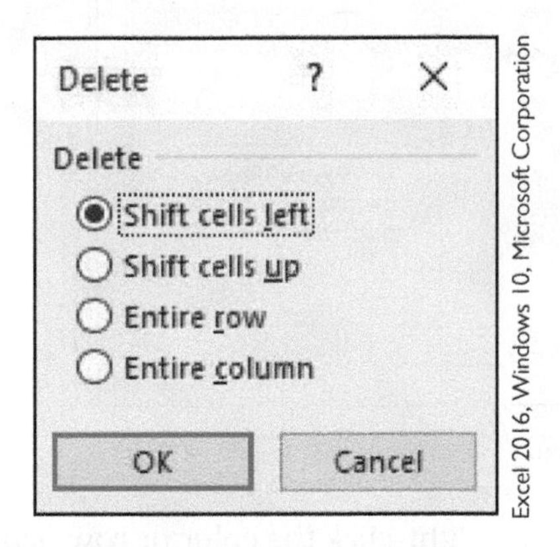

FIGURE 24 Delete Dialog Box

Alternatively, click Delete in the Cells group. The default action of clicking Delete is to delete the active cell, which moves existing data up in that column only.

Hide and Unhide Columns and Rows

If your worksheet contains information you do not want to display, hide some columns and/or rows before you print a copy for public distribution. However, the column or row is not deleted. If you hide column B, you will see columns A and C side by side. If you hide row 3, you will see rows 2 and 4 together. Figure 25 shows that column B and row 3 are hidden. Excel displays a double line between column headings (such as between A and C), indicating one or more columns are hidden, and a double line between row headings (such as between 2 and 4), indicating one or more rows are hidden.

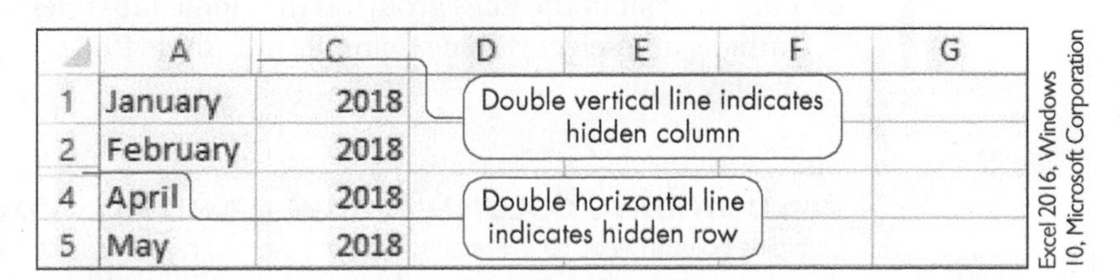

FIGURE 25 Hidden Columns and Rows

> **To hide a column or row, complete one of the following sets of steps:**
>
> 1. Select a cell or cells in the column or row you want to hide.
> 2. Click Format in the Cells group on the Home tab (refer to Figure 26).
> 3. Point to Hide & Unhide.
> 4. Select Hide Columns or Hide Rows, depending on what you want to hide.

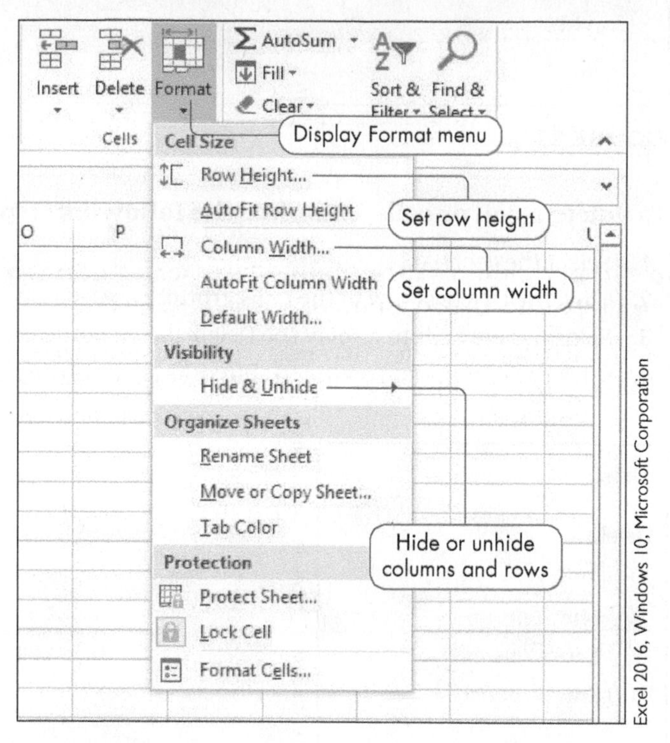

FIGURE 26 Format Menu

Alternatively, you can right-click the color or row heading(s) you want to hide. Then select Hide.

You can hide multiple columns and rows at the same time. To select adjacent columns (such as columns B through E) or adjacent rows (such as rows 2 through 4), drag across the adjacent column or row headings and use the Hide command.

> **To hide nonadjacent columns or rows, complete the following steps:**
>
> 1. Press and hold Ctrl while you click the desired column or row headings.
> 2. Use any acceptable method to hide the selected columns or rows.

> **To unhide a column or row, complete the following steps:**
>
> 1. Select the columns or rows on both sides of the hidden column or row. For example, if column B is hidden, drag across column letters A and C.
> 2. Click Format in the Cells group on the Home tab (refer to Figure 26), point to Hide & Unhide, and select Unhide Columns or Unhide Rows, depending on what you want to display again.

TIP: UNHIDING COLUMN A, ROW 1, AND ALL HIDDEN ROWS/COLUMNS
Unhiding column A or row 1 is different because you cannot select the row or column on either side. To unhide column A or row 1, type A1 in the Name Box and press Enter. Click Format in the Cells group on the Home tab, point to Hide & Unhide, and select Unhide Columns or Unhide Rows to display column A or row 1, respectively. If you want to unhide all columns and rows, click Select All (the triangle above the row 1 heading and to the left of the column A heading) and use the Hide & Unhide submenu.

Adjust Column Width

STEP 3 After you enter data in a column, you often need to adjust the ***column width***—the horizontal measurement of a column in a table or a worksheet. In Excel, column width is measured by the number of characters or pixels. For example, in the worksheet you created in Hands-On Exercises 1 and 2, the labels in column A displayed into column B when those adjacent cells were empty. However, after you typed values in column B, the labels in column A appeared cut off. You will need to widen column A to show the full name of all of your products.

TIP: POUND SIGNS DISPLAYED

Numbers and dates appear as a series of pound signs (######) when the cell is too narrow to display the complete value, and text appears to be truncated.

To widen a column to accommodate the longest label or value in a column, complete one of the following sets of steps:

- Point to the right vertical border of the column heading. When the pointer displays as a two-headed arrow, double-click the border. For example, if column B is too narrow to display the content in that column, double-click the right vertical border of the column B heading.
- Click Format in the Cells group on the Home tab (refer to Figure 26) and select AutoFit Column Width.

To adjust the width of a column to an exact width, complete the following sets of steps:

- Drag the vertical border to the left to decrease the column width or to the right to increase the column width. As you drag the vertical border, Excel displays a ScreenTip specifying the width (see Figure 27) from 0 to 255 characters and in pixels.
- Click Format in the Cells group on the Home tab (refer to Figure 26), select Column Width, type a value that represents the maximum number of characters to display in the Column width box in the Column Width dialog box, and then click OK.

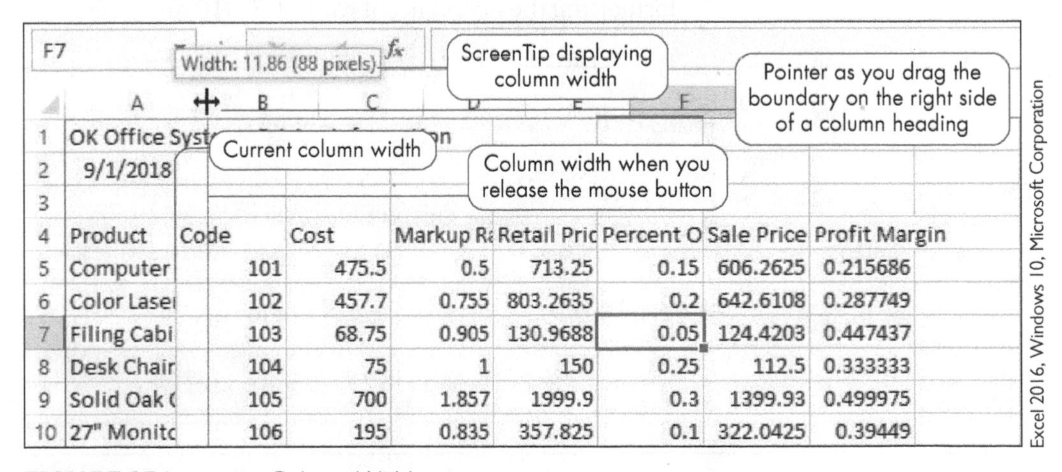

F7
Width: 11.86 (88 pixels)
ScreenTip displaying column width
Pointer as you drag the boundary on the right side of a column heading
Current column width
Column width when you release the mouse button
OK Office Syst
9/1/2018
Product Code Cost Markup Ra Retail Pric Percent O Sale Price Profit Margin
Computer 101 475.5 0.5 713.25 0.15 606.2625 0.215686
Color Laser 102 457.7 0.755 803.2635 0.2 642.6108 0.287749
Filing Cabi 103 68.75 0.905 130.9688 0.05 124.4203 0.447437
Desk Chair 104 75 1 150 0.25 112.5 0.333333
Solid Oak (105 700 1.857 1999.9 0.3 1399.93 0.499975
27" Monitc 106 195 0.835 357.825 0.1 322.0425 0.39449

FIGURE 27 Increasing Column Width

Adjust Row Height

You can adjust the ***row height***—the vertical measurement of the row—in a way similar to how you change column width by double-clicking the border between row numbers or by selecting Row Height or AutoFit Row Height from the Format menu (refer to Figure 26). In Excel, row height is a value between 0 and 409 based on point size (abbreviated as pt) and pixels. Whether you are measuring font sizes or row heights, one point size is equal to 1/72 of an inch. Your row height should be taller than your font size. For example, with an 11-pt font size, the default row height is 15.

> **TIP: MULTIPLE COLUMN WIDTHS AND ROW HEIGHTS**
> You can set the size for more than one column or row at a time to make the selected columns or rows the same size. Drag across the column or row headings for the area you want to format, and set the size using any method.

Selecting, Moving, Copying, and Pasting Data

You may already know the basics of selecting, cutting, copying, and pasting data in other programs, such as Microsoft Word. These tasks are somewhat different when working in Excel.

Select a Range

STEP 4 A ***range*** refers to a group of adjacent or contiguous cells in a worksheet. A range may be as small as a single cell or as large as the entire worksheet. It may consist of a row or part of a row, a column or part of a column, or multiple rows or columns, but will always be a rectangular shape, as you must select the same number of cells in each row or column for the entire range. A range is specified by indicating the top-left and bottom-right cells in the selection. For example, in Figure 28, the date is a single-cell range in cell A2, the Color Laser Printer data are stored in the range A6:H6, the cost values are stored in the range C5:C10, and the sales prices and profit margins are stored in range G5:H10. A ***nonadjacent range*** contains multiple ranges, such as D5:D10 and F5:F10. At times, you will select nonadjacent ranges so that you can apply the same formatting at the same time, such as formatting the nonadjacent range D5:D10 and F5:F10 with Percent Style.

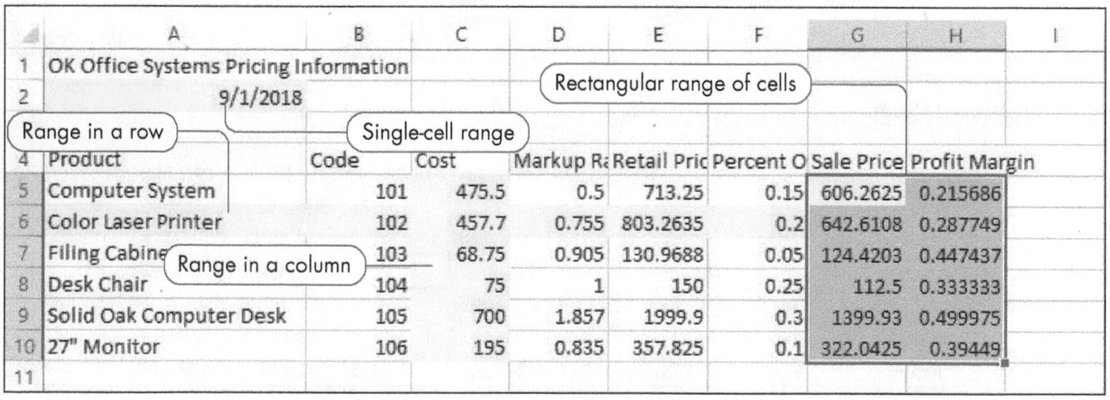

	A	B	C	D	E	F	G	H	I
1	OK Office Systems Pricing Information								
2	9/1/2018								
3									
4	Product	Code	Cost	Markup Ra	Retail Pric	Percent O	Sale Price	Profit Margin	
5	Computer System	101	475.5	0.5	713.25	0.15	606.2625	0.215686	
6	Color Laser Printer	102	457.7	0.755	803.2635	0.2	642.6108	0.287749	
7	Filing Cabine	103	68.75	0.905	130.9688	0.05	124.4203	0.447437	
8	Desk Chair	104	75	1	150	0.25	112.5	0.333333	
9	Solid Oak Computer Desk	105	700	1.857	1999.9	0.3	1399.93	0.499975	
10	27" Monitor	106	195	0.835	357.825	0.1	322.0425	0.39449	
11									

Excel 2016, Windows 10, Microsoft Corporation

FIGURE 28 Sample Ranges

Table 4 lists methods to select ranges, including nonadjacent ranges.

TABLE 4 Selecting Ranges

To Select:	Do This:
A range	Drag until you select the entire range. Alternatively, click the first cell in the range, press and hold Shift, and click the last cell in the range.
An entire column	Click the column heading.
An entire row	Click the row heading.
Current range containing data, including headings	Click in the range of data and press Ctrl+A.
All cells in a worksheet	Click Select All or press Ctrl+A twice.
Nonadjacent range	Select the first range, press and hold Ctrl, and select additional range(s).

A green border appears around a selected range. Any command you execute will affect the entire range. The range remains selected until you select another range or click in any cell in the worksheet.

TIP: NAME BOX
Use the Name Box to select a range by clicking in the Name Box, typing a range address such as B15:D25, and pressing Enter.

Move a Range

You can move cell contents from one range to another. For example, you might want to move an input area from the right side of the worksheet to above the output range. When you move a range containing text and values, the text and values do not change. However, any formulas that refer to cells in that range will update to reflect the new cell addresses.

To move a range, complete the following steps:

1. Select the range.
2. Click Cut in the Clipboard group to copy the range to the Clipboard (see Figure 29). Unlike cutting data in other Microsoft Office applications, the data you cut in Excel remain in their locations until you paste them elsewhere. A moving dashed green border surrounds the selected range and the status bar displays *Select destination and press ENTER or choose Paste.*
3. Ensure the destination range—the range where you want to move the data—is the same size or greater than the size of the cut range.
4. Click in the top-left corner of the destination range, and use the Paste command (see Figure 29). If any cells within the destination range contain data, Excel overwrites that data when you use the Paste command.

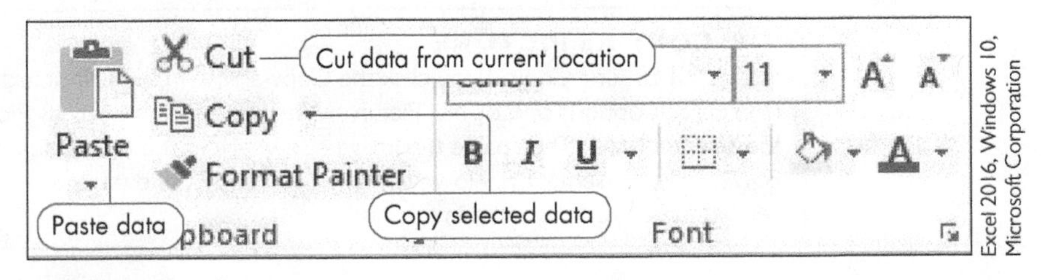

FIGURE 29 Cut, Copy, Paste

Copy and Paste a Range

You may want to copy cell contents from one range to another. When you copy a range, the original data remain in their original locations. For example, you might copy your January budget to another worksheet to use as a model for creating your February budget. Cell references in copied formulas adjust based on their relative locations to the original data. Furthermore, you want to copy formulas from one range to another range. In this situation where you cannot use the fill handle, you will use the Copy and Paste functions to copy the formula.

To copy a range, complete the following steps:

1. Select the range.
2. Click Copy in the Clipboard group (refer to Figure 29) to copy the contents of the selected range to the Clipboard. A moving dashed green border surrounds the selected range and the status bar displays *Select destination and press ENTER or choose Paste.*
3. Ensure the destination range—the range where you want to copy the data—is the same size or greater than the size of the copied range.
4. Click in the top-left corner of the destination range where you want the duplicate data, and click Paste (refer to Figure 29). If any cells within the destination range contain data, Excel overwrites that data when you use the Paste command. The original range still has the moving dashed green border, and the pasted copied range is selected with a solid green border. Figure 30 shows a selected range (A4:H10) and a copy of the range (J4:Q10). Immediately after you click Paste, the ***Paste Options button*** displays in the bottom-right corner of the pasted data. Click the arrow to select a different result for the pasted data.
5. Press Esc to turn off the moving dashed border around the originally selected range.

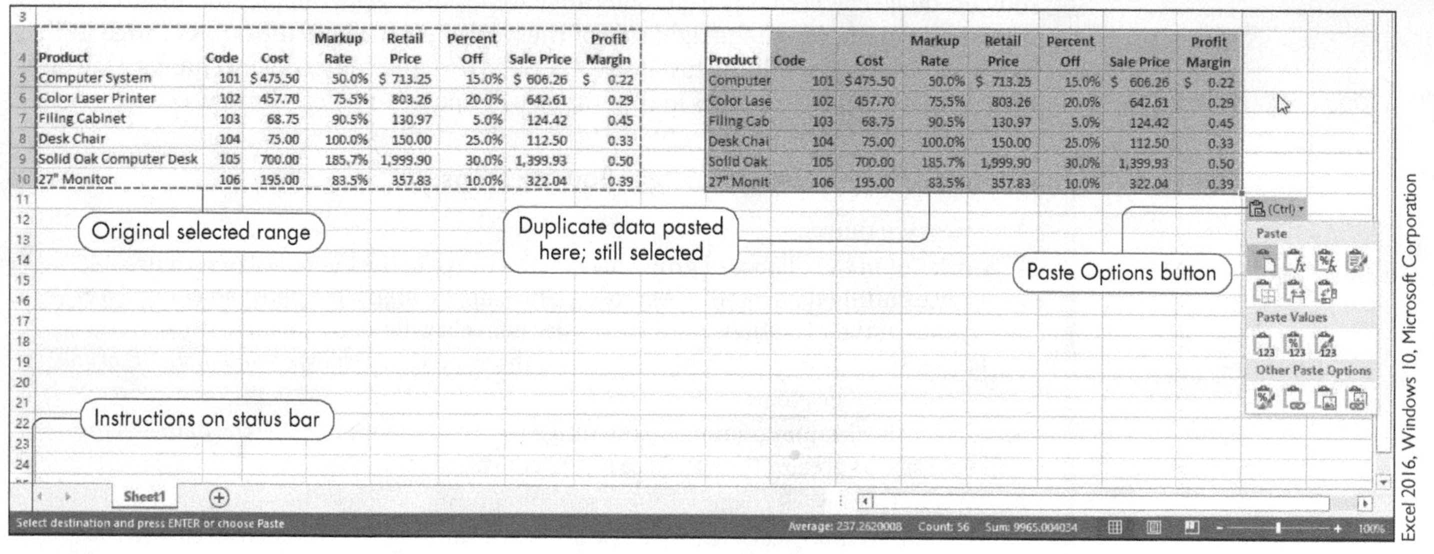

FIGURE 30 Copied and Pasted Range

TIP: COPY AS PICTURE

Instead of clicking Copy, if you click the Copy arrow in the Clipboard group, you can select Copy (the default option) or Copy as Picture. When you select Copy as Picture, you copy an image of the selected data. Then paste the image elsewhere in the workbook or in a Word document or PowerPoint presentation. However, when you copy the data as an image, you cannot edit individual cell data after you paste the image.

Use Paste Options and Paste Special

STEP 6 Sometimes you might want to paste data in a different format than they are in the Clipboard. For example, you might want to preserve the results of calculations before changing the original data. To do this, you can paste the data as values. If you want to copy data from Excel and paste them into a Word document, you can paste the Excel data as a worksheet object, as unformatted text, or in another format.

To paste data from the Clipboard into a different format, complete the following steps:

1. Click the Paste arrow in the Clipboard group (see Figure 31).
2. Point to command to see a ScreenTip and a preview of how the pasted data will look.
3. Click the option you want to apply.

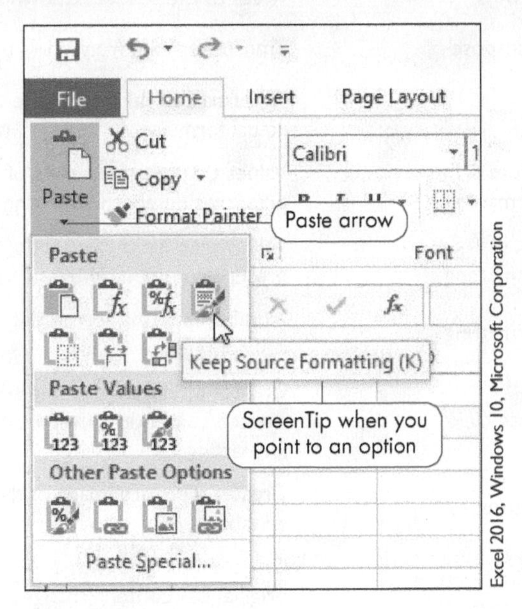

FIGURE 31 Paste Options

Table 5 lists and describes some of the options in the Paste gallery that opens when you click the Paste arrow in the Clipboard or the Paste Options button that displays immediately after you use Paste. Paste options enable you to paste content or attributes, such as a formula or format.

TABLE 5 Paste Options

Icon	Option Name	Paste Description
	Paste	Cell contents and all formatting from copied cells
	Formulas	Formulas, but no formatting, from copied cells
	Formulas & Number Formatting	Formulas and number formatting, such as Currency, but no font formatting, such as font color, fill color, or borders
	Keep Source Formatting	Cell contents and formatting from copied cells
	No Borders	Cell contents, number formatting, and text formatting except borders
	Keep Source Column Widths	Cell contents, number and text formatting, and the column width of the source data when pasting in another column
	Transpose	Transposes data from rows to columns and columns to rows
	Values	Unformatted values that are the results of formulas, not the actual formulas
	Values & Number Formatting	Values that are the results of formulas, not the actual formulas; preserves number formatting but not text formatting
	Values & Source Formatting	Values that are the results of formulas, not the actual formulas; preserves number and text formatting
	Formatting	Number and text formatting only from the copied cells; no cell contents
	Paste Link	Creates a reference to the source cells (such as =$G$15), not the cell contents; preserves number formatting but not text formatting
	Picture	Creates a picture image of the copied data; pasted data is not editable
	Linked Picture	Creates a picture with a reference to the copied cells; if the original cell content changes, so does the picture
	Paste Special	Opens the Paste Special dialog box (see Figure 32)

Paste Special ? X

Paste

- (•) All
- ( ) Formulas
- ( ) Values
- ( ) Formats
- ( ) Comments
- ( ) Validation
- ( ) All using Source theme
- ( ) All except borders
- ( ) Column widths
- ( ) Formulas and number formats
- ( ) Values and number formats
- ( ) All merging conditional formats

Operation

- (•) None
- ( ) Add
- ( ) Subtract
- ( ) Multiply
- ( ) Divide

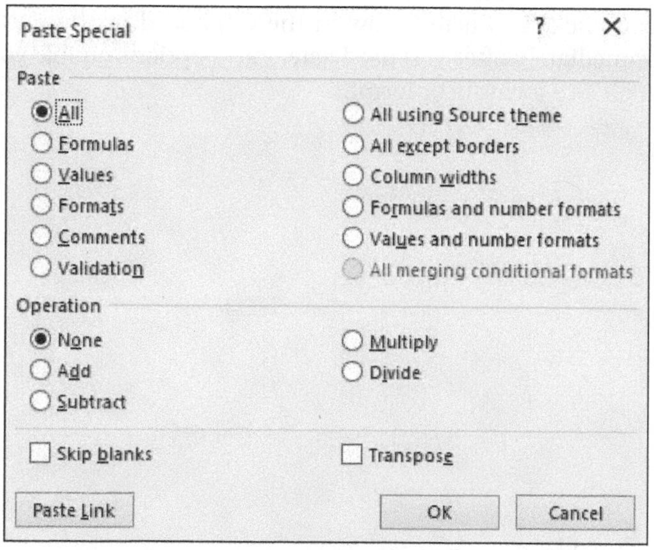

- [ ] Skip blanks
- [ ] Transpose

Paste Link | OK | Cancel

FIGURE 32 Paste Special Dialog Box

TIP: TRANSPOSING COLUMNS AND ROWS

After entering data into a worksheet, you might want to transpose the columns and rows so that the data in the first column appear as column labels across the first row, or the column labels in the first row appear in the first column. Figure 33 shows the original data with the months in column A and the utility costs in columns B, C, and D. In the transposed data, the months are shown in the first row, and each row contains utility information. The original formats (bold and right-aligned) are copied in the transposed data.

	A	B	C	D	E	F	G	H	I	J
1	**Month**	**Gas**	**Electric**	**Water**		**Month**	January	February	March	
2	January	$275	$120	$35		**Gas**	$275	$265	$200	
3	February	$265	$114	$35		**Electric**	$120	$114	$118	
4	March	$200	$118	$35		**Water**	$35	$35	$35	
5										(Ctrl) ▾
6										

FIGURE 33 Transposed Data

Copy Excel Data to Other Programs

You can copy Excel data and use it in other applications, such as in a Word document or in a PowerPoint slide show. For example, you might perform statistical analyses in Excel and copy the data into a research paper in Word. Or, you might want to create a budget in Excel and copy the data into a PowerPoint slide show for a meeting.

After selecting and copying a range in Excel, you must decide how you want the data to appear in the destination application. Click the Paste arrow in the destination application to see a gallery of options or to select the Paste Special option.

8. Give an example of when you would delete a column versus when you would hide a column.
9. When should you adjust column widths instead of using the default width?
10. Why would you use the Paste Special options in Excel?

Hands-On Exercises

Skills covered: Insert Columns and Rows • Delete a Row • Hide a Column • Adjust Column Width • Adjust Row Height • Select a Range • Move a Range • Copy and Paste a Range • Use Paste Special

3 Worksheet Structure and Clipboard Tasks

You want to insert a column to calculate the amount of markup and delete a row containing data you no longer need. You also want to adjust column widths to display the labels in the columns. In addition, your supervisor asked you to enter data for a new product. Because it is almost identical to an existing product, you will copy the original data and edit the copied data to save time. You also want to experiment with the Paste Special option to see the results of using it in the OKOS workbook.

STEP 1 » INSERT A COLUMN AND ROWS

You decide to add a column to display the amount of profit. Because profit is a dollar amount, you want to keep the profit column close to another column of dollar amounts. Therefore, you will insert the profit column before the profit margin (percentage) column. You will insert new rows for product information and category names. Refer to Figure 34 as you complete Step 1.

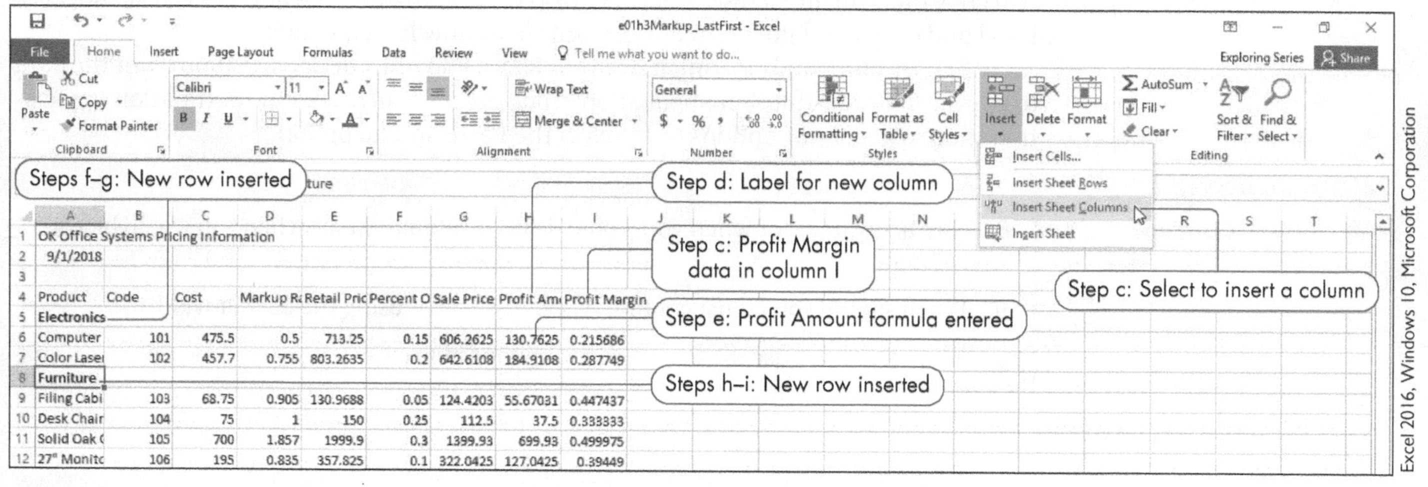

FIGURE 34 Column and Rows Inserted

a. Open *e01h2Markup_LastFirst* if you closed it at the end of Hands-On Exercise 2 and save it as **e01h3Markup_LastFirst**, changing h2 to h3.

b. Click **cell H5** (or any cell in column H).

You want to insert a column between the Sale Price and Profit Margin columns so that you can calculate the profit amount in dollars.

c. Click the **Insert arrow** in the Cells group and select **Insert Sheet Columns**.

You inserted a new blank column H. The data in the original column H are now in column I.

d. Click **cell H4**, type **Profit Amount**, and then press **Enter**.

e. Ensure the active cell is **cell H5**. Type **=G5-C5** and click **Enter**. Double-click the **cell H5 fill handle**.

You calculated the profit amount by subtracting the original cost from the sale price and then copied the formula down the column.

f. Right-click the **row 5 heading** and select **Insert** from the shortcut menu.

You inserted a new blank row 5, which is selected. The original rows of data move down a row each.

g. Click **cell A5**. Type **Electronics** and press **Ctrl+Enter**. Click **Bold** in the Font group on the Home tab.

You typed and applied bold formatting to the category name Electronics above the list of electronic products.

h. Right-click the **row 8 heading** and select **Insert** from the shortcut menu.

You inserted a new blank row 8. The data that was originally on row 8 is now on row 9.

i. Click **cell A8**. Type **Furniture** and press **Ctrl+Enter**. Click **Bold** in the Font group on the Home tab and save the workbook.

You typed and applied bold formatting to the category name Furniture above the list of furniture products.

STEP 2 » DELETE A ROW AND HIDE A COLUMN

You just realized that you do not have enough filing cabinets in stock to offer on sale, so you need to delete the Filing Cabinet row. The item numbers are meaningful to you, but the numbers are not necessary for the other employees. Before distributing the worksheet to the employees, you want to hide column B. Because you might need to see that data later, you will hide it rather than delete it. Refer to Figure 35 as you complete Step 2.

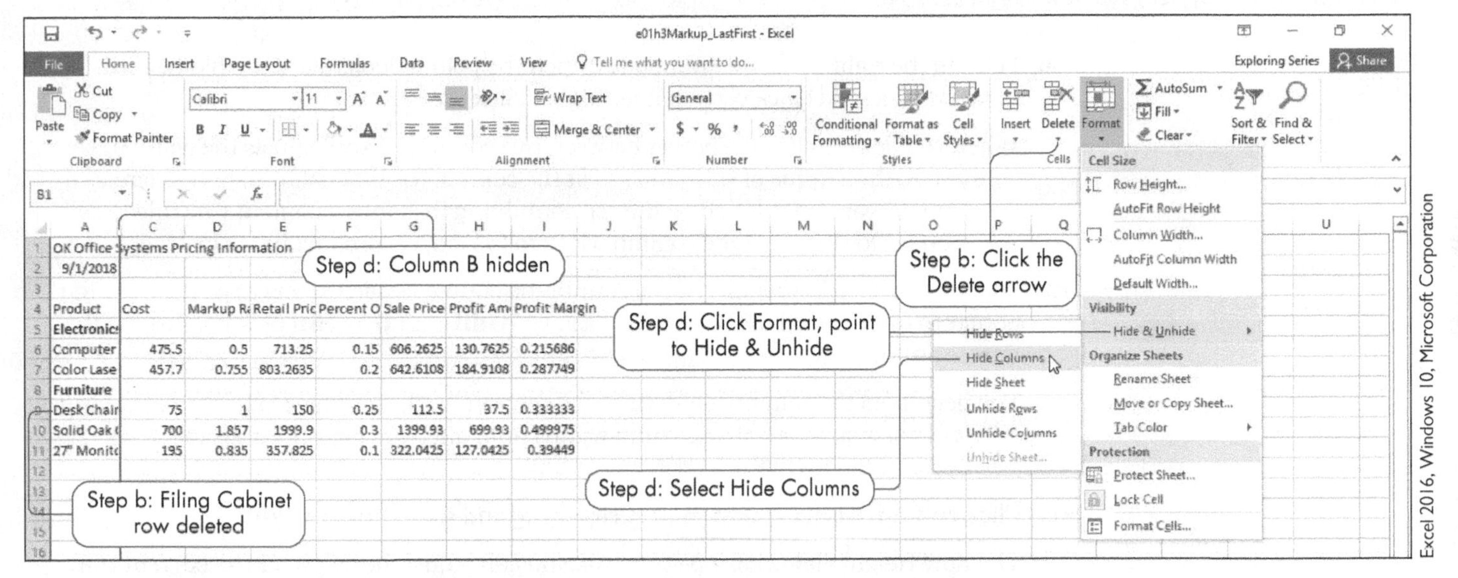

FIGURE 35 Row Deleted and Column Hidden

a. Click **cell A9** (or any cell on row 9), the row that contains the Filing Cabinet data.

b. Click the **Delete arrow** in the Cells group and select **Delete Sheet Rows**.

The Filing Cabinet row is deleted, and the remaining rows move up one row.

> **TROUBLESHOOTING:** If you accidentally delete the wrong row or accidentally selected Delete Sheet Columns instead of Delete Sheet Rows, click Undo on the Quick Access Toolbar to restore the deleted row or column.

c. Click the **column B heading**.

d. Click **Format** in the Cells group, point to **Hide & Unhide**, and then select **Hide Columns**.

Excel hides column B. You see a gap in column heading letters A and C, indicating column B is hidden instead of deleted.

e. Save the workbook.

STEP 3 » ADJUST COLUMN WIDTH AND ROW HEIGHT

As you review your worksheet, you notice that the labels in column A appear cut off. You will increase the width of that column to display the entire product names. In addition, you want to make row 1 taller. Refer to Figure 36 as you complete Step 3.

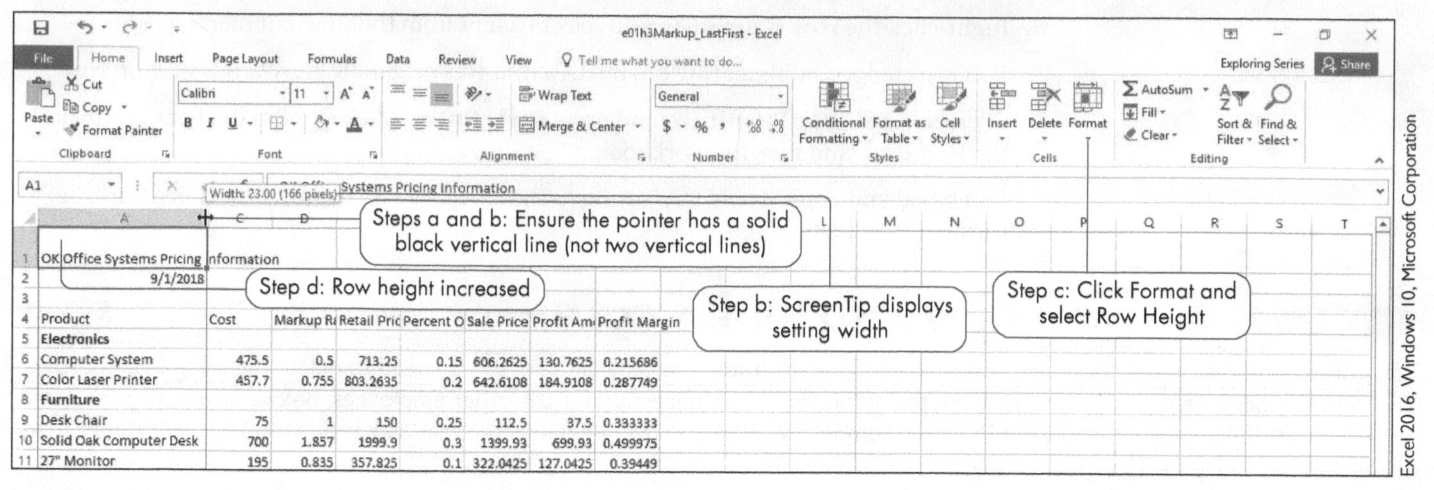

FIGURE 36 Column Width and Row Height Changed

a. Point to the right border of column A. When the pointer looks like a double-headed arrow with a solid black vertical line, double-click the border.

When you double-click the border between two columns, Excel adjusts the width of the column on the left side of the border to fit the contents of that column. Excel increased the width of column A based on the cell containing the longest content (the title in cell A1). You decide to adjust the column width to the longest product name instead.

b. Point to the right border of column A until the double-headed arrow appears. Drag the border to the left until the ScreenTip displays **Width: 23.00 (166 pixels)**. Release the mouse button.

You decreased the column width to 23 for column A. The longest product name is visible. You will not adjust the other column widths until after you apply formats to the column headings in Hands-On Exercise 4.

c. Click **cell A1**. Click **Format** in the Cells group and select **Row Height**.

The Row Height dialog box opens so that you can adjust the height of the current row.

d. Type **30** in the **Row height box** and click **OK**. Save the workbook.

You increased the height of the row that contains the worksheet title so that it is more prominent.

STEP 4 » SELECT A RANGE AND MOVE A RANGE TO A NEW LOCATION

You want to move the 27" Monitor product to be immediately after the Color Laser Printer product. Before moving the 27" Monitor row, you will insert a blank row between the Color Laser Printer and Furniture rows. Refer to Figure 37 as you complete Step 4.

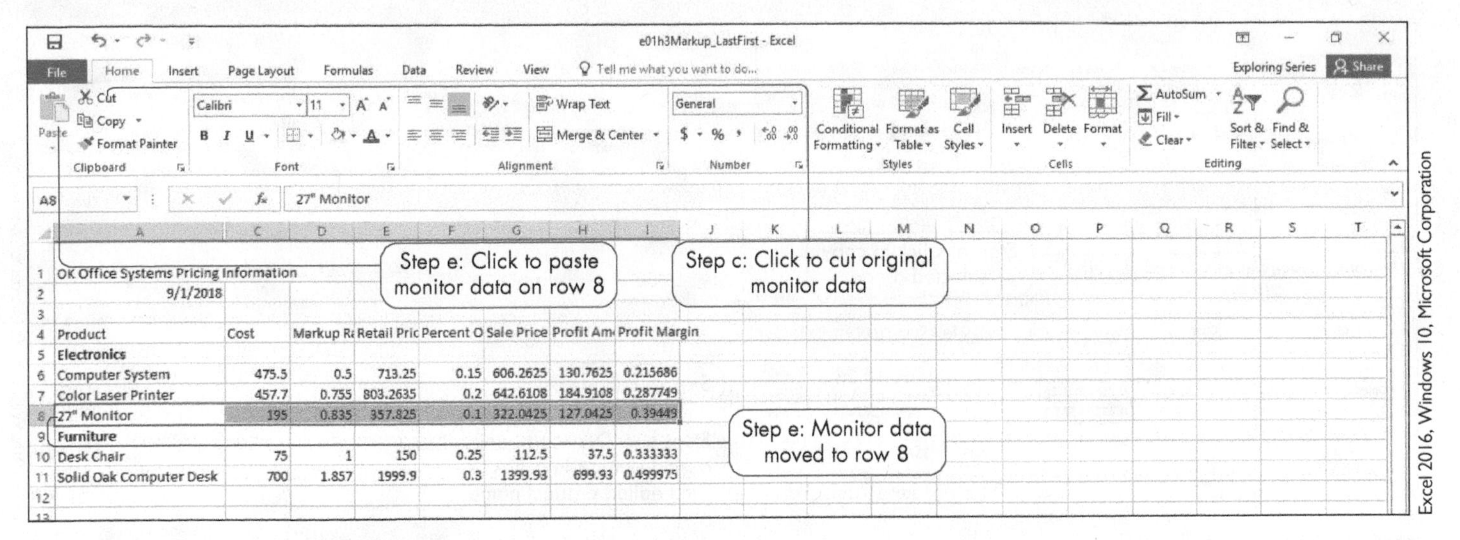

FIGURE 37 Row Moved to New Location

a. Right-click the **row 8 heading** and select **Insert** from the menu.

You will insert a blank row so that you can move the 27" Computer Monitor data to be between the Color Laser Printer and Furniture rows.

b. Select the **range A12:I12**.

You selected the range of cells containing the 27" Monitor data.

c. Click **Cut** in the Clipboard group.

A moving dashed green border outlines the selected range. The status bar displays the message *Select destination and press ENTER or choose Paste.*

d. Click **cell A8**.

This is the first cell in the destination range. If you cut and paste a row without inserting a new row first, Excel will overwrite the original row of data, which is why you inserted a new row in step a.

e. Click **Paste** in the Clipboard group and save the workbook.

The 27" Monitor product data is now located on row 8.

STEP 5 » COPY AND PASTE A RANGE

Alesha told you that a new chair is on its way. She asked you to enter the data for the Executive Desk Chair. Because most of the data is the same as the Desk Chair data, you will copy the original Desk Chair data, edit the product name, and change the cost to reflect the cost of the second chair. Refer to Figure 38 as you complete Step 5.

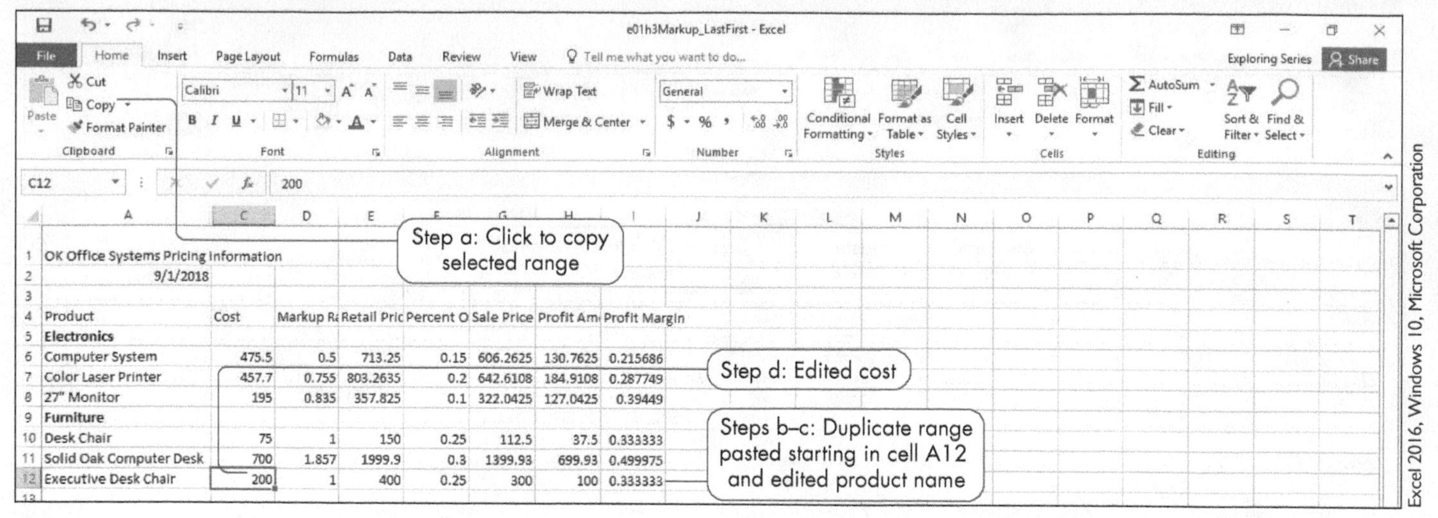

FIGURE 38 Data Copied and Edited

a. Select the **range A10:I10** and click **Copy** in the Clipboard group.

You copied the row containing the Desk Chair product data to the Clipboard.

b. Click **cell A12**, click **Paste** in the Clipboard group, and then press **Esc**.

The pasted range is selected in row 12.

c. Click **cell A12**, press **F2** to activate Edit Mode, press **Home**, type **Executive**, press **Spacebar**, and then press **Enter**.

You edited the product name to display Executive Desk Chair.

d. Change the value in **cell C12** to **200**. Save the workbook.

The formulas calculate the results based on the new cost of 200 for the Executive Desk Chair.

STEP 6 » USE PASTE SPECIAL

During your lunch break, you want to experiment with some of the Paste Special options. Particularly, you are interested in pasting Formulas and Value & Source Formatting. First, you will apply bold and a font color to the title to help you test these Paste Special options. Refer to Figure 39 as you complete Step 6.

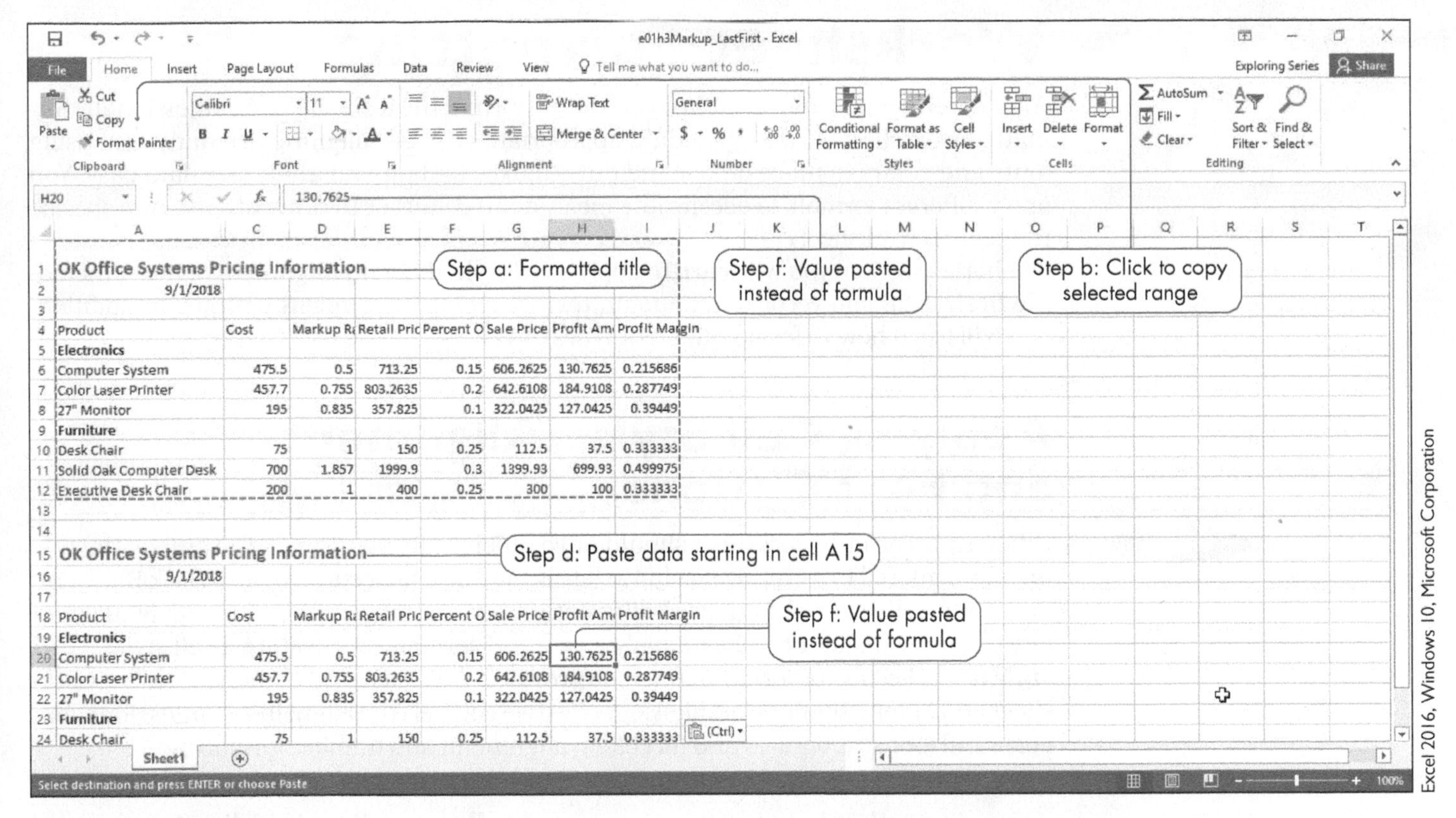

FIGURE 39 Paste Special Results

a. Click **cell A1**. Change the font size to **14**, click **Bold**, click the **Font Color arrow** in the Font group and then select **Gold, Accent 4, Darker 50%**.

You will format text to see the effects of using different Paste Special options.

b. Select the **range A1:I12** and click **Copy** in the Clipboard group.

c. Click **cell A15**, the top-left corner of the destination range.

d. Click the **Paste arrow** in the Clipboard group and point to **Formulas**, the second icon from the left in the Paste group.

Without clicking the command, Excel shows you a preview of what that option would do. The pasted copy would not contain the font formatting you applied to the title or the bold on the two category names. In addition, the pasted date would appear as a serial number. The formulas would be maintained.

e. Position the pointer over **Values & Source Formatting**, the first icon from the right in the Paste Values group.

This option would preserve the formatting, but it would convert the formulas into the current value results.

f. Click **Values & Source Formatting**, click **cell H6** to see a formula, and then click **cell H20**. Press **Esc** to turn off the border.

Cell H6 contains a formula, but in the pasted version, the equivalent cell H20 has converted the formula result into an actual value. If you were to change the original cost on row 20, the contents of cell H20 would not change. In a working environment, this is useful only if you want to capture the exact value in a point in time before making changes to the original data.

g. Save the workbook. Keep the workbook open if you plan to continue with the next Hands-On Exercise. If not, close the workbook and exit Excel.

Worksheet Formatting

After entering data and formulas, you should format the worksheet. A professionally formatted worksheet—through adding appropriate symbols, aligning decimals, and using fonts and colors to make data stand out—makes finding and analyzing data easy. You apply different formats to accentuate meaningful details or to draw attention to specific ranges in a worksheet.

In this section, you will learn to apply a cell style, different alignment options, including horizontal and vertical alignment, text wrapping, and indent options. In addition, you will learn how to format different types of values.

Applying Cell Styles, Alignment, and Font Options

STEP 1 »» Different areas of a worksheet should have different formatting. For example, the title may be centered in 16-pt size; column labels may be bold, centered, and Dark Blue font; and input cells may be formatted differently from output cells. You can apply different formats individually, or you can apply a group of formats by selecting a cell style. A ***cell style*** is a collection of format settings to provide a consistent appearance within a worksheet and among similar workbooks. A cell style controls the following formats: font, font color and font size, borders and fill colors, alignment, and number formatting.

To apply a cell style to a cell or a range of cells, complete the following steps:

1. Click Cell Styles in the Styles group on the Home tab to display the Cell Styles gallery (see Figure 40).
2. Position the pointer over a style name to see a Live Preview of how the style will affect the selected cell or range. The gallery provides a variety of built-in styles to apply to your worksheet data.
3. Click a style to apply it to the selected cell or range.

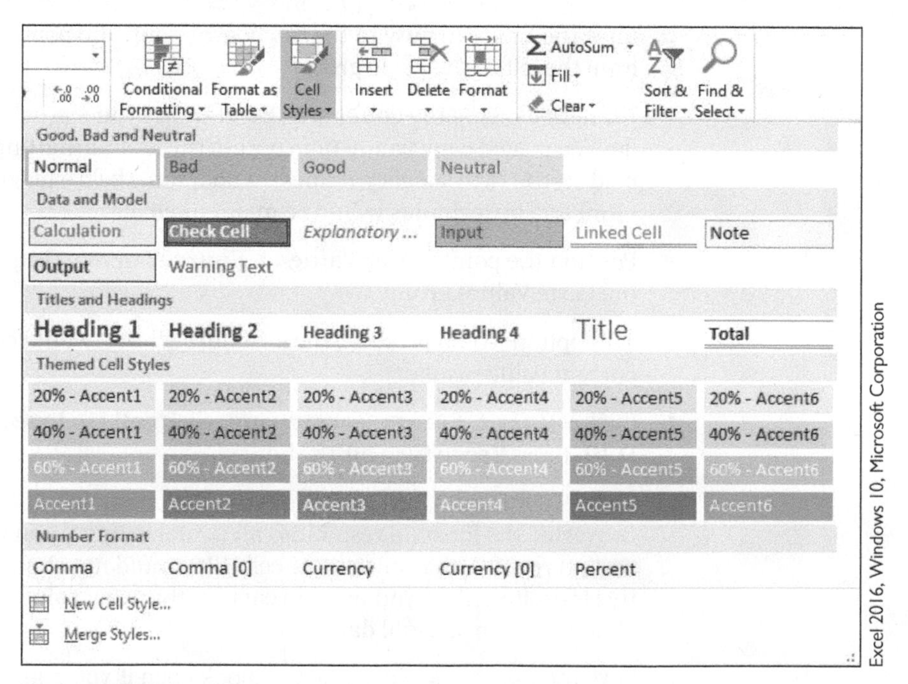

Excel 2016, Windows 10, Microsoft Corporation

FIGURE 40 Cell Styles

Alignment refers to how data are positioned in the boundaries of a cell. Each type of data has a default alignment. Text aligns at the left cell margin, and dates and values align at the right cell margin. You should change the alignment of cell contents to improve the appearance of data within the cells. The Alignment group (see Figure 41) on the Home tab contains several commands to help you align and format data.

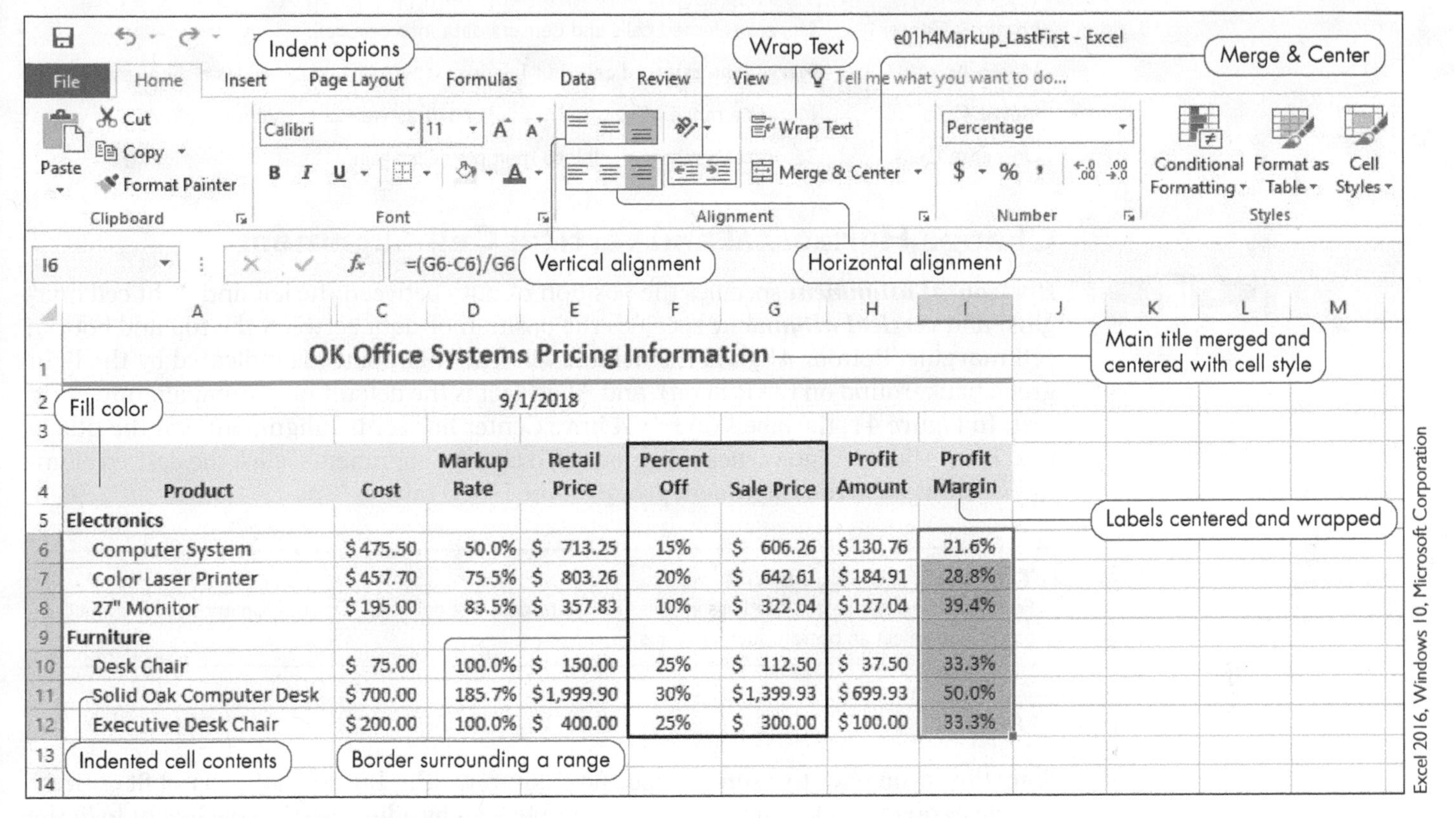

FIGURE 41 Alignment and Font Settings Applied

> **TIP: ALIGNMENT OPTIONS**
> The Format Cells dialog box contains additional alignment options. To open the Format Cells dialog box, click the Dialog Box Launcher in the Alignment group on the Home tab. The Alignment tab in the dialog box contains the options for aligning data.

Merge and Center Labels

STEP 1 You may want to place a title at the top of a worksheet and center it over the columns of data in the worksheet. You can center main titles over all columns in the worksheet, and you can center category titles over groups of related columns. You can also merge cells on adjacent rows.

To merge and center cells, complete the following steps:

1. Enter the text in the top left cell of the range.
2. Select the range of cells across which you want to center the label.
3. Click Merge & Center in the Alignment group on the Home tab.

Only data in the far left cell (or top-right cell) are merged. Any other data in the merged cells are deleted. Excel merges the selected cells together into one cell, and the merged cell address is that of the original cell on the left. The data are centered within the merged cell.

If you want to split a merged cell into multiple cells, click the merged cell and click Merge & Center. Unmerging places the data in the top-left cell.

For additional options, click the Merge & Center arrow. Table 6 lists the four merge options.

TABLE 6 Merge Options	
Option	**Results**
Merge & Center	Merges selected cells and centers data into one cell.
Merge Across	Merges the selected cells but keeps text left aligned or values right aligned.
Merge Cells	Merges a range of cells on multiple rows as well as in multiple columns.
Unmerge Cells	Separates a merged cell into multiple cells again.

Change Horizontal and Vertical Cell Alignment

STEP 2 ›› ***Horizontal alignment*** specifies the position of data between the left and right cell margins, and ***vertical alignment*** specifies the position of data between the top and bottom cell margins. Bottom Align is the default vertical alignment (as indicated by the light green background on the Ribbon), and Align Left is the default horizontal alignment for text. In Figure 41, the labels on row 4 have Center horizontal alignment and the title in row 1 has Middle Align vertical alignment. To change alignments, click the desired alignment setting(s) in the Alignment group on the Home tab.

> **TIP: ROTATE CELL DATA**
> People sometimes rotate headings in cells. To rotate data in a cell, click Orientation in the Alignment group and select an option, such as Angle Clockwise.

Wrap Text

Sometimes you have to maintain specific column widths, but the data do not fit entirely. Use ***wrap text*** to make data appear on multiple lines by adjusting the row height to fit the cell contents within the column width. Excel wraps the text on two or more lines within the cell. In Figure 41, the Markup Rate and Percent Off labels on row 4 are examples of wrapped text.

To wrap text within a cell, complete the following steps:

1. Click the cells or select the range of cells that contain labels that need to be wrapped.
2. Click Wrap Text in the Alignment group.

> **TIP: LINE BREAK IN A CELL**
> If a long text label does not fit well in a cell even after you have applied wrap text, you might want to insert a line break to display the text label on multiple lines within the cell. To insert a line break while you are typing a label, press Alt+Enter where you want to start the next line of text within the cell.

Increase and Decrease Indent

STEP 3 ›› Cell content is left-aligned or right-aligned based on the default data type. However, you can ***indent*** the cell contents to offset the data from its current alignment. For example, text is left-aligned, but you can indent it to offset it from the left side. Indenting helps others see the hierarchical structure of data. Accountants often indent the word Totals in financial statements so that it stands out from a list of items above the total row. Values are right-aligned by default, but you can indent a value to offset it from the right side of the cell. In Figure 41, Computer System and Desk Chair are indented.

To increase or decrease the indent of data in a cell, complete the following steps:

1. Click the cell that contains data.
2. Click Increase Indent or Decrease Indent in the Alignment group.

TIP: INDENTING VALUES

Values are right aligned by default. You should align the decimal places in a column of values. If the column label is wide, the values below it appear too far on the right. To preserve the values aligning at the decimal places, use the Align Right horizontal alignment and click Increase Indent to shift the values over to the left a little for better placement.

Apply Borders and Fill Color

STEP 4 »» You can apply a border or fill color to accentuate data in a worksheet. A ***border*** is a line that surrounds a cell or a range of cells. Use borders to offset some data from the rest of the worksheet data. To apply a border, select the cell or range that you want to have a border, click the Borders arrow in the Font group, and select the desired border type. In Figure 41, a border surrounds the range F4:G12. To remove a border, select No Border from the Borders menu.

Add some color to your worksheets to emphasize data or headers by applying a fill color. ***Fill color*** is a background color that displays behind the data in a cell so that the data stand out. You should choose a fill color that contrasts with the font color. For example, if the font color is Black, Text 1, you might choose Yellow fill color. If the font color is White, Background 1, you might apply Blue or Dark Blue fill color. The color palette contains two sections: Theme Colors and Standard Colors. The Theme Colors section displays variations of colors that match the current theme applied in the worksheet. For example, it contains shades of blue, such as Blue, Accent 5, Lighter 80%. The Standard Colors section contains basic colors, such as Dark Red and Red.

To apply a fill color, complete the following steps:

1. Select the cell or range that you want to have a fill color.
2. Click the Fill Color arrow on the Home tab to display the color palette.
3. Select the color choice from the Fill Color palette. In Figure 41, the column labels in row 4 contain the Blue, Accent 1, Lighter 80% fill color. If you want to remove a fill color, select No Fill from the bottom of the palette. Select More Colors to open the Colors dialog box, click the Standard tab or Custom tab, and then click a color.

For additional border and fill color options, complete the following steps:

1. Click the Dialog Box Launcher in the Font group to display the Format Cells dialog box.
2. Click the Border tab to select border options, including the border line style and color.
3. Click the Fill tab to set the background color, fill effects, and patterns.

Applying Number Formats

Values have no special formatting when you enter data. However, you should apply ***number formats***, settings that control how a value is displayed in a cell. For example, you might want to apply either the Accounting or Currency number format to monetary values. Changing the number format changes the way the number displays in a cell, but the format does not change the stored value. If, for example, you enter 123.456 into a cell and format the cell with the Currency number type, the value shows as $123.46 onscreen, but the actual value 123.456 is used for calculations. When you apply a number format, specify the number of decimal places to display onscreen.

Apply a Number Format

STEP 5 » The default number format is General, which displays values as you originally enter them. General number format does not align decimal points in a column or include symbols, such as dollar signs, percent signs, or commas. Table 7 lists and describes the primary number formats in Excel.

TABLE 7 Number Formats

Format Style	Display
General	A number as it was originally entered. Numbers are shown as integers (e.g., 12345), decimal fractions (e.g., 1234.5), or in scientific notation (e.g., 1.23E+10) if the number exceeds 11 digits.
Number	A number with or without the 1,000 separator (e.g., a comma) and with any number of decimal places. Negative numbers can be displayed with parentheses and/or red.
Currency	A number with the 1,000 separator and an optional dollar sign (which is placed immediately to the left of the number). Negative values are preceded by a minus sign or are displayed with parentheses or in red. Two decimal places display by default.
Accounting Number Format	A number that contains the $ on the left side of the cell and formats the value with a comma for every three digits on the left side of the decimal point and displays two digits to the right of the decimal point. Negative values display in parentheses, and zero values display as hyphens.
Comma Style	A number is formatted with a comma for every three digits on the left side of the decimal point and displays two digits to the right of the decimal point. Used in conjunction with Accounting Number Format to align commas and decimal places.
Date	The date in different ways, such as Long Date (March 14, 2016) or Short Date (3/14/16 or 14-Mar-16).
Time	The time in different formats, such as 10:50 PM or 22:50 (military time).
Percent Style	The value as it would be multiplied by 100 (for display purpose), with the percent symbol. The default number of decimal places is zero if you click Percent Style in the Number group or two decimal places if you use the Format Cells dialog box. However, you should typically increase the number of decimal points to show greater accuracy.
Fraction	A number as a fraction; use when no exact decimal equivalent exists. A fraction is entered into a cell as a formula such as =1/3. If the cell is not formatted as a fraction, the formula results display.
Scientific	A number as a decimal fraction followed by a whole number exponent of 10; for example, the number 12345 would appear as 1.23E+04. The exponent, +04 in the example, is the number of places the decimal point is moved to the left (or right if the exponent is negative). Very small numbers have negative exponents.
Text	The data left aligned; is useful for numerical values that have leading zeros and should be treated as text, such as postal codes or phone numbers. Apply Text format before typing a leading zero so that the zero displays in the cell.
Special	A number with editing characters, such as hyphens in a Social Security number.
Custom	Predefined customized number formats or special symbols to create your own customized number format.

The Number group on the Home tab contains commands for applying ***Accounting Number Format***, ***Percent Style***, and ***Comma Style*** numbering formats. You can click the Accounting Number Format arrow and select other denominations, such as English pounds or euros. For other number formats, click the Number Format arrow and select the numbering format you want to use. For more specific numbering formats than those provided, select More Number Formats from the Number Format menu or click the Number Dialog Box Launcher to open the Format Cells dialog box with the Number tab options readily available. Figure 42 shows different number formats applied to values.

	A	B
1	General	1234.567
2	Number	1234.57
3	Currency	$1,234.57
4	Accounting	$ 1,234.57
5	Comma	1,234.57
6	Percent	12%
7	Short Date	3/1/2018
8	Long Date	Thursday, March 1, 2018

Excel 2016, Windows 10, Microsoft Corporation

FIGURE 42 Number Formats

Increase and Decrease Decimal Places

STEP 5 After applying a number format, you may need to adjust the number of decimal places that display. For example, if you have an entire column of monetary values formatted in Accounting Number Format, Excel displays two decimal places by default. If the entire column of values contains whole dollar values and no cents, displaying *.00* down the column looks cluttered. Decrease the number of decimal places to show whole numbers only.

To change the number of decimal places displayed, complete the following steps:

1. Click the cell or select a range of cells containing values that need to have fewer or more decimal places.
2. Click Increase Decimal in the Number group on the Home tab to display more decimal places for greater precision or Decrease Decimal to display fewer or no decimal places.

Quick Concepts

11. What is the importance of formatting a worksheet?
12. Describe five alignment and font formatting techniques used to format labels that are discussed in this section.
13. What are the main differences between Accounting Number Format and Currency format? Which format has its own command on the Ribbon?

Hands-On Exercises

Skills covered: Apply a Cell Style • Merge and Center Data • Change Cell Alignment • Wrap Text • Increase Indent • Apply a Border • Apply Fill Color • Apply Number Formats • Increase and Decrease Decimal Places

4 Worksheet Formatting

In the first three Hands-On Exercises, you entered data about products on sale, created formulas to calculate markup and profit, and inserted new rows and columns to accommodate the labels Electronics and Furniture to identify the specific products. You are ready to format the worksheet. Specifically, you will center the title, align text, format values, and apply other formatting to enhance the readability of the worksheet.

STEP 1 » APPLY A CELL STYLE AND MERGE AND CENTER THE TITLE

To make the title stand out, you want to apply a cell style and center it over all the data columns. You will use the Merge & Center command to merge cells and center the title at the same time. Refer to Figure 43 as you complete Step 1.

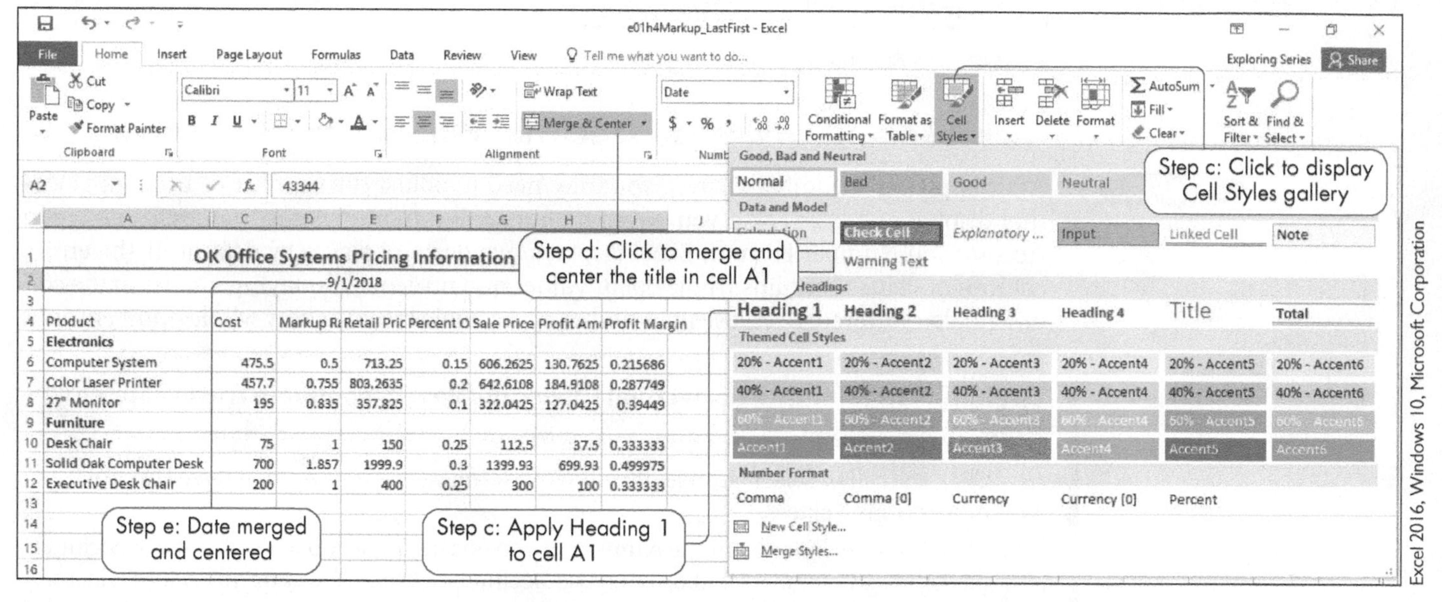

FIGURE 43 Cell Style Applied; Data Merged and Centered

a. Open *e01h3Markup_LastFirst* if you closed it at the end of Hands-On Exercise 3 and save it as **e01h4Markup_LastFirst**, changing h3 to h4.

b. Select the **range A15:I26** and press **Delete**.

You maintained a copy of your Paste Special results in the *e01h3Markup_LastFirst* workbook, but you do not need it to continue.

c. Select the **range A1:I1**, click **Cell Styles** in the Styles group on the Home tab, and then click **Heading 1**.

You applied the Heading 1 style to the range A1:I1. This style formats the contents with 15-pt font size, Blue-Gray, Text 2 font color, and a thick blue bottom border.

d. Click **Merge & Center** in the Alignment group.

Excel merges cells in the range A1:I1 into one cell and centers the title horizontally within the merged cell, which is cell A1.

TROUBLESHOOTING: If you merge too many or not enough cells, unmerge the cells and start again. To unmerge cells, click in the merged cell. The Merge & Center command is shaded in green when the active cell is merged. Click Merge & Center to unmerge the cell. Then select the correct range to merge and use Merge & Center again.

e. Select the **range A2:I2**. Click **Merge & Center** in the Alignment group. Save the workbook.

TROUBLESHOOTING: If you try to merge and center data in the range A1:I2, Excel will keep the top-left data only and delete the date. To merge separate data on separate rows, you must merge and center data separately.

STEP 2 » CHANGE CELL ALIGNMENT

You will wrap the text in the column headings to avoid columns that are too wide for the data, but which will display the entire text of the column labels. In addition, you will horizontally center column labels between the left and right cell margins. Refer to Figure 44 as you complete Step 2.

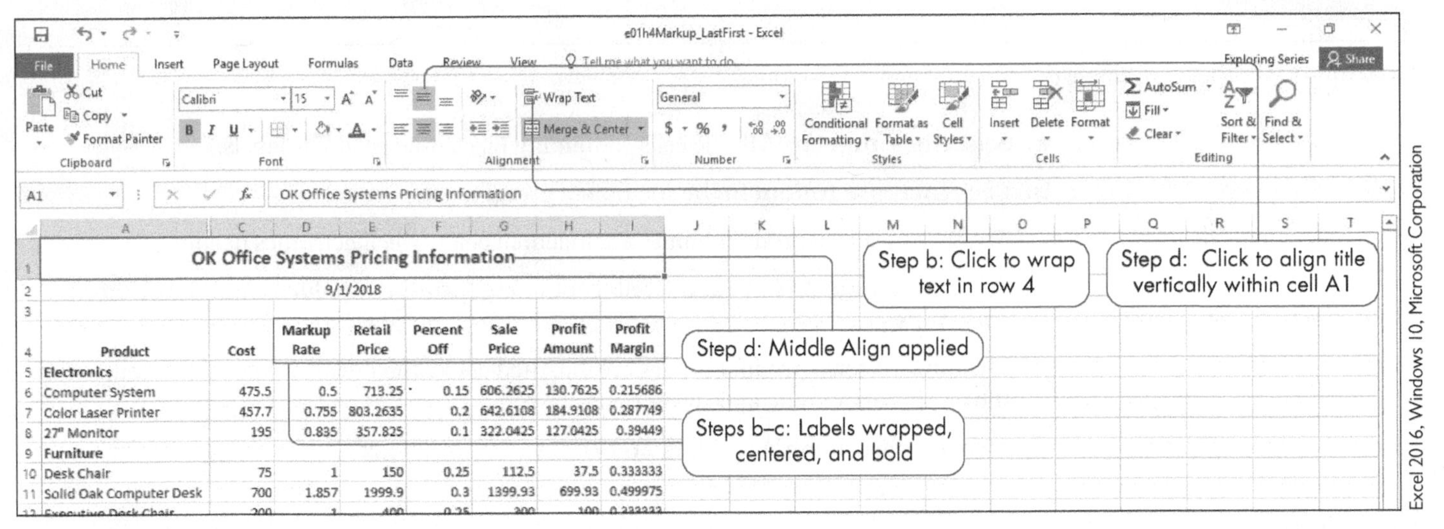

FIGURE 44 Formatted Column Labels

a. Select the **range A4:I4** to select the column labels.

b. Click **Wrap Text** in the Alignment group.

The multiple-word column headings are now visible on two lines within each cell.

c. Click **Center** in the Alignment group and click **Bold** in the Font group to format the selected column headings.

The column headings are centered horizontally between the left and right edges of each cell.

d. Click **cell A1**, which contains the title, click **Middle Align** in the Alignment group, and then save the workbook.

Middle Align vertically centers data between the top and bottom edges of the cell.

STEP 3 » INCREASE INDENT

As you review the first column, you notice that the category names, Electronics and Furniture, do not stand out. You decide to indent the labels within each category to better display which products are in each category. Refer to Figure 45 as you complete Step 3.

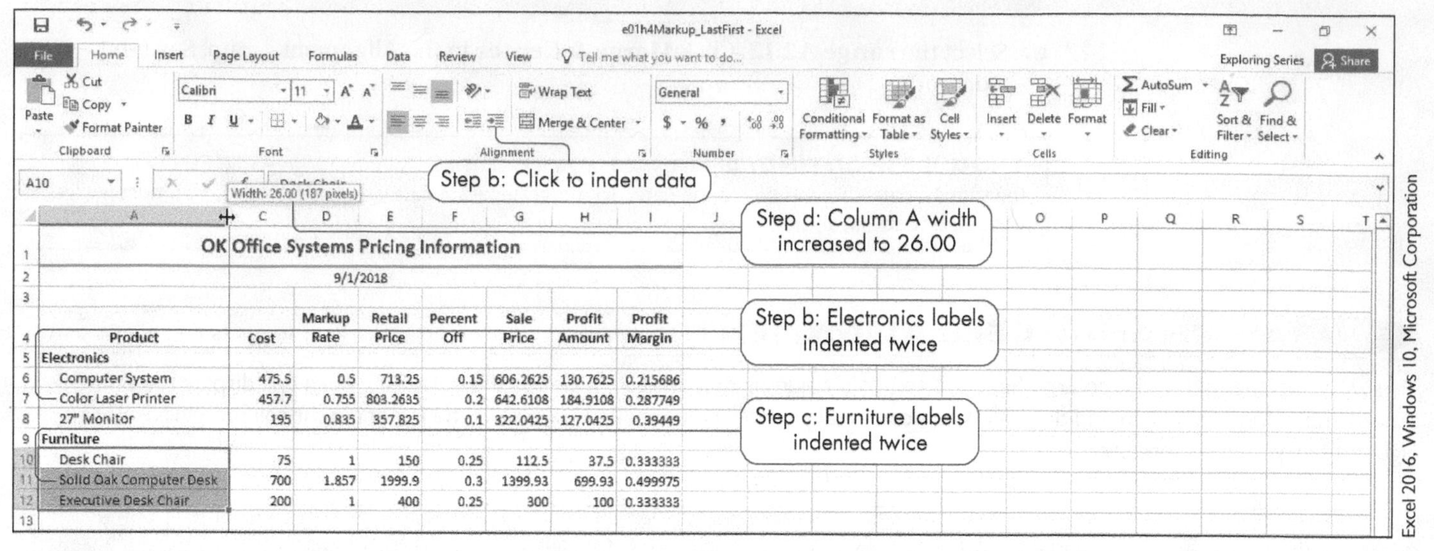

FIGURE 45 Indented Cell Contents

a. Select the **range A6:A8**, the cells containing Electronic products labels.

b. Click **Increase Indent** in the Alignment group twice.

The three selected product names are indented below the Electronics heading.

c. Select the **range A10:A12**, the cells containing furniture products, and click **Increase Indent** twice.

The three selected product names are indented below the Furniture heading. Notice that the one product name appears cut off.

d. Increase the column A width to **26.00**. Save the workbook.

STEP 4 » APPLY A BORDER AND FILL COLOR

You want to apply a light blue fill color to highlight the column headings. In addition, you want to emphasize the percent off and sale prices. You will do this by applying a border around that range. Refer to Figure 46 as you complete Step 4.

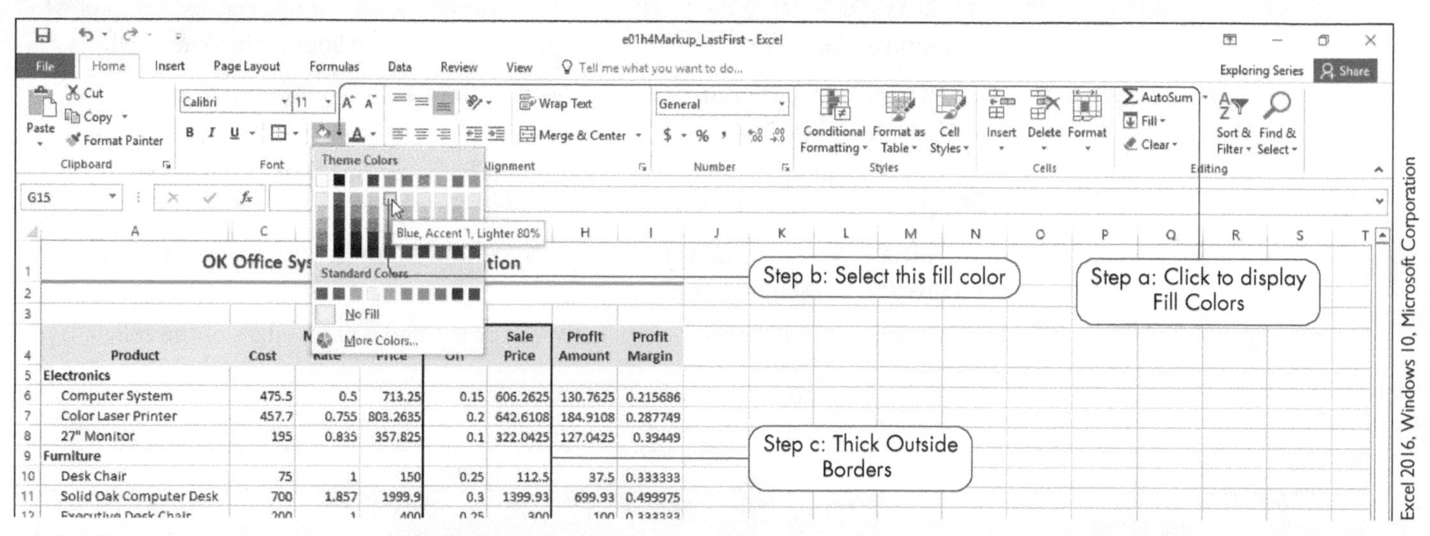

FIGURE 46 Border and Fill Color Applied

a. Select the **range A4:I4** and click the **Fill Color arrow** in the Font group.

b. Click **Blue, Accent 1, Lighter 80%** in the Theme Colors section (second row, fifth column).

You applied a fill color to the selected cells to draw attention to these cells.

c. Select the **range F4:G12**, click the **Border arrow** in the Font group, and then select **Thick Outside Borders**.

You applied a border around the selected cells.

d. Click in an empty cell below the columns of data to deselect the cells. Save the workbook.

STEP 5 » APPLY NUMBER FORMATS AND INCREASE AND DECREASE DECIMAL PLACES

You need to format the values to increase readability and look more professional. You will apply number formats and adjust the number of decimal points displayed. Refer to Figure 47 as you complete Step 5.

Step c: Percent Style with one decimal place

Steps d and f: Percent Style, Align Right, Increase Indent

Steps e–f: Percent Style, Align Right, Increase Decimal, Increase Indents

Step b: Accounting Number Format

	A	C	D	E	F	G	H	I	J
1	OK Office Systems Pricing Information								
2									
3									
4	Product	Cost	Markup Rate	Retail Price	Percent Off	Sale Price	Profit Amount	Profit Margin	
5	Electronics								
6	Computer System	$ 475.50	50.0%	$ 713.25	15%	$ 606.26	$ 130.76	21.6%	
7	Color Laser Printer	$ 457.70	75.5%	$ 803.26	20%	$ 642.61	$ 184.91	28.8%	
8	27" Monitor	$ 195.00	83.5%	$ 357.83	10%	$ 322.04	$ 127.04	39.4%	
9	Furniture								
10	Desk Chair	$ 75.00	100.0%	$ 150.00	25%	$ 112.50	$ 37.50	33.3%	
11	Solid Oak Computer Desk	$ 700.00	185.7%	$1,999.90	30%	$1,399.93	$ 699.93	50.0%	
12	Executive Desk Chair	$ 200.00	100.0%	$ 400.00	25%	$ 300.00	$ 100.00	33.3%	
13									

Excel 2016, Windows 10, Microsoft Corporation

FIGURE 47 Number Formats and Decimal Places

a. Select the **range C6:C12.** Press and hold **Ctrl** as you select the **ranges E6:E12** and **G6:H12.**

Because you want to apply the same format to nonadjacent ranges, you hold down Ctrl while selecting each range.

b. Click **Accounting Number Format** in the Number group. If some cells display pound signs, increase the column widths as needed.

You formatted the selected nonadjacent ranges with the Accounting Number Format. The dollar signs align on the left cell margins and the decimals align.

c. Select the **range D6:D12,** click **Percent Style** in the Number group, and then click **Increase Decimal** in the Number group.

You formatted the values in the selected range with Percent Style and increased the decimal to show one decimal place to avoid misleading your readers by displaying the values as whole percentages.

d. Apply **Percent Style** to the **range F6:F12.**

e. Select the **range I6:I12**, apply **Percent Style**, and then click **Increase Decimal.**

f. Select the **range F6:F12**, click **Align Right**, and then click **Increase Indent** twice. Select the **range I6:I12**, click **Align Right**, and then click **Increase Indent**.

With values, you want to keep the decimal points aligned, but you can then use Increase Indent to adjust the indent so that the values appear more centered below the column labels.

g. Save the workbook. Keep the workbook open if you plan to continue with the next Hands-On Exercise. If not, close the workbook and exit Excel.

Worksheets, Page Setup, and Printing

When you start a new blank workbook in Excel, the workbook contains one worksheet named Sheet1. However, you can add additional worksheets. The text, values, dates, and formulas you enter into the individual worksheets are saved under one workbook file name. Having multiple worksheets in one workbook is helpful to keep related items together.

Although you might distribute workbooks electronically as email attachments or you might upload workbooks to a corporate server, you should prepare the worksheets in case you need to print them or in case others who receive an electronic copy of your workbook want to print the worksheets.

In this section, you will copy, move, and rename worksheets. You will also select options on the Page Layout tab. Specifically, you will use the Page Setup, Scale to Fit, and Sheet Options groups. After selecting page setup options, you will learn how to print your worksheet.

Managing Worksheets

Creating a multiple-worksheet workbook takes some planning and maintenance. Worksheet tab names should reflect the contents of the respective worksheets. In addition, you can insert, copy, move, and delete worksheets within the workbook. You can even apply background color to the worksheet tabs so that they stand out onscreen. Figure 48 shows a workbook in which the sheet tabs have been renamed, colors have been applied to worksheet tabs, and a worksheet tab has been right-clicked so that the shortcut menu appears.

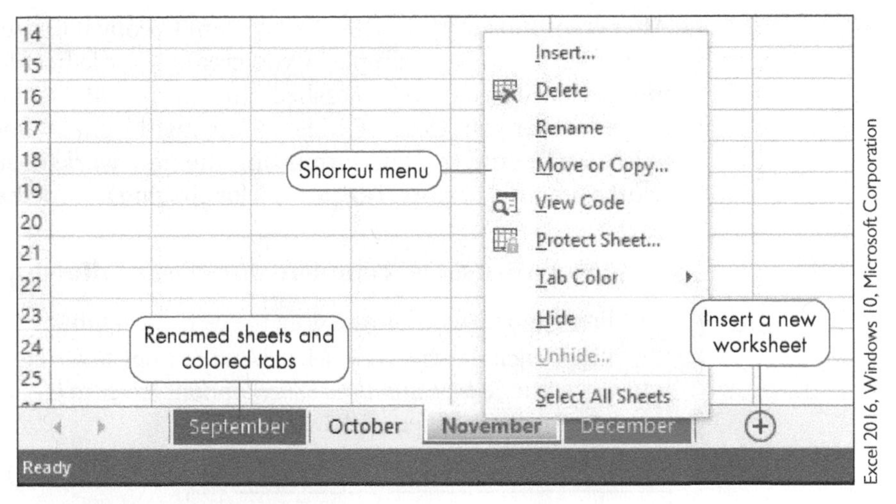

FIGURE 48 Worksheet Tabs

The active sheet tab has a green horizontal bar below the sheet name, and the sheet name is bold and green. If a color (such as Red) has been applied to the sheet tab, the tab shows in the full color when it is not active. When that sheet is active, the sheet tab color is a gradient of the selected color.

Insert and Delete a Worksheet

Sometimes you need more than one worksheet in the workbook. For example, you might want one worksheet for each month to track your monthly income and expenses for one year. When tax time comes around, you have all your data stored in one workbook file. You can insert additional, rename, copy, and move worksheets. Adding worksheets within one workbook enables to you save related sheets of data together.

To insert a new worksheet, complete one of the following sets of steps:

- Click New sheet to the right of the last worksheet tab.
- Click the Insert arrow (either to the right or below Insert) in the Cells group on the Home tab and select Insert Sheet.
- Right-click any sheet tab, select Insert from the shortcut menu (refer to Figure 48), click Worksheet in the Insert dialog box, and click OK.
- Press Shift+F11.

If you no longer need the data in a worksheet, delete the worksheet. Doing so will eliminate extra data in a file and reduce file size.

To delete a worksheet in a workbook, complete one of the following sets of steps:

- Click the Delete arrow (either to the right or below Delete) in the Cells group on the Home tab and select Delete Sheet.
- Right-click any sheet tab and select Delete from the shortcut menu (refer to Figure 48).

If the sheet you are trying to delete contains data, Excel will display a warning: *Microsoft Excel will permanently delete this sheet. Do you want to continue?* Click Delete to delete the worksheet, or click Cancel to keep the worksheet. If you try to delete a blank worksheet, Excel will not display a warning; it will immediately delete the sheet.

Copy or Move a Worksheet

STEP 1 After creating a worksheet, you may want to copy it to use as a template or starting point for similar data. For example, if you create a worksheet for your September budget, you might want to copy the worksheet and easily edit the data on the copied worksheet to enter data for your October budget. Copying the entire worksheet saves you a lot of valuable time in entering and formatting the new worksheet, and it preserves the column widths and row heights. The process for copying a worksheet is similar to moving a sheet.

To copy a worksheet, complete one of the following sets of steps:

- Press and hold Ctrl as you drag the worksheet tab.
- Right-click the sheet tab, select Move or Copy to display the Move or Copy dialog box, select the *To book* and *Before sheet* options (refer to Figure 49), click the *Create a copy* check box, and then click OK.

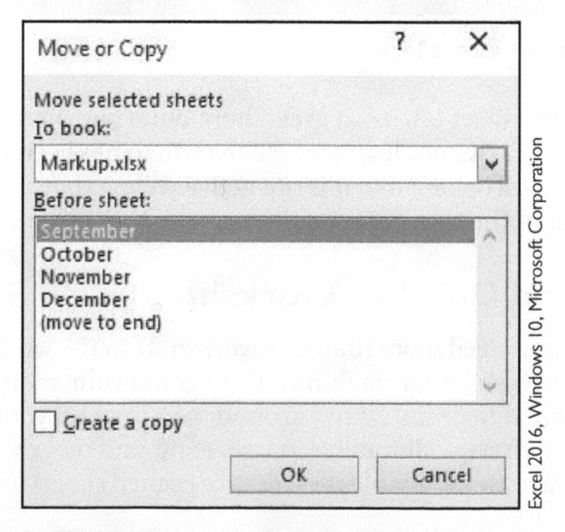

FIGURE 49 Move or Copy Dialog Box

You can arrange the worksheet tabs in a different sequence. For example, if the December worksheet is to the left of the October and November worksheets, move the December worksheet to be in chronological order.

To move a worksheet, complete one of the following sets of steps:

- Drag a worksheet tab to the desired location. As you drag a sheet tab, the pointer resembles a piece of paper. A down-pointing triangle appears between sheet tabs to indicate where the sheet will be placed when you release the mouse button.
- Click Format in the Cells group on the Home tab (refer to Figure 35) and select Move or Copy Sheet.
- Right-click the sheet tab you want to move and select Move or Copy to display the Move or Copy dialog box. You can move the worksheet within the current workbook or to a different workbook. In the *Before sheet* list, select the worksheet you want to come after the moved worksheet and click OK.

Rename a Worksheet

The default worksheet name Sheet1 does not describe the contents of the worksheet. You should rename worksheet tabs to reflect the sheet contents. For example, if your budget workbook contains monthly worksheets, name the worksheets September, October, etc. Although you can have spaces in worksheet names, keep worksheet names relatively short. The longer the worksheet names, the fewer sheet tabs you will see at the bottom of the workbook window without scrolling.

To rename a worksheet, complete one of the following sets of steps:

- Double-click a sheet tab, type the new name, and then press Enter.
- Click the sheet tab for the sheet you want to rename, click Format in the Cells group on the Home tab (refer to Figure 35), select Rename Sheet, type the new sheet name, and then press Enter.
- Right-click the sheet tab, select Rename from the shortcut menu (refer to Figure 48), type the new sheet name, and then press Enter.

TIP: CHANGE TAB COLOR

You can change the color of each worksheet tab to emphasize the difference among the sheets. For example, you might apply red to the September tab and yellow to the October tab. Right-click a sheet tab, select Tab Color, and select a color from the color palette.

Selecting Page Setup Options

The Page Setup group on the Page Layout tab contains options to set the margins, select orientation, specify page size, select the print area, and apply other options (see Figure 50). The Scale to Fit group contains options for adjusting the scaling of the spreadsheet on the printed page. When possible, use the commands in these groups to apply page settings. Table 8 lists and describes the commands in the Page Setup group.

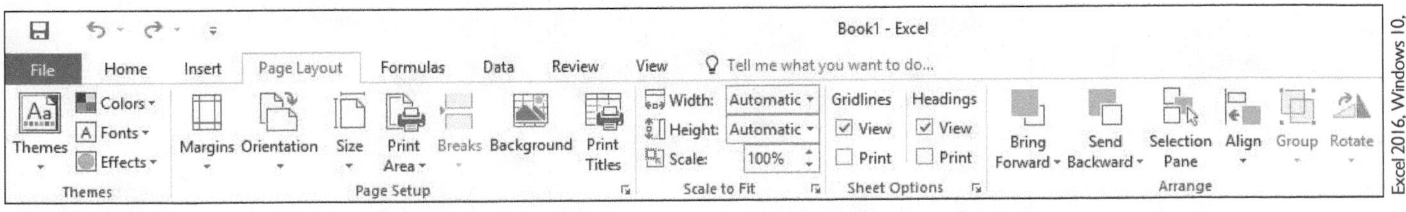

Excel 2016, Windows 10, Microsoft Corporation

FIGURE 50 Page Layout Tab

TABLE 8 Page Setup Commands

Command	Description
Margins	Displays a menu to select predefined margin settings. The default margins are 0.75" top and bottom and 0.7" left and right. You will often change these margin settings to balance the worksheet data better on the printed page. If you need different margins, select Custom Margins.
Orientation	Displays orientation options. The default page orientation is portrait, which is appropriate for worksheets that contain more rows than columns. Select landscape orientation when worksheets contain more columns than can fit in portrait orientation. For example, the OKOS worksheet might appear better balanced in landscape orientation because it has eight columns.
Size	Displays a list of standard paper sizes. The default size is 8 ½" by 11". If you have a different paper size, such as legal paper, select it from the list.
Print Area	Displays a list to set or clear the print area. When you have very large worksheets, you might want to print only a portion of that worksheet. To do so, select the range you want to print, click Print Area in the Page Setup group, and select Set Print Area. When you use the Print commands, only the range you specified will be printed. To clear the print area, click Print Area and select Clear Print Area.
Breaks	Displays a menu to insert or remove page breaks.
Background	Enables you to select an image to appear as the background behind the worksheet data when viewed onscreen (backgrounds do not appear when the worksheet is printed).
Print Titles	Enables you to select column headings and row labels to repeat on multiple-page printouts.

TIP: APPLYING PAGE SETUP OPTIONS TO MULTIPLE WORKSHEETS

When you apply Page Setup Options, those settings apply to the current worksheet only. However, you can apply page setup options, such as margins or a header, to multiple worksheets at the same time. To select adjacent sheets, click the first sheet tab, press and hold Shift, and click the last sheet tab. To select nonadjacent sheets, press and hold Ctrl as you click each sheet tab. Then choose the Page Setup options to apply to the selected sheets. When you are done, right-click a sheet tab and select Ungroup Sheets.

Specify Page Options

STEP 2 To apply several page setup options at once or to access options not found on the Ribbon, click the Page Setup Dialog Box Launcher. The Page Setup dialog box organizes options into four tabs: Page, Margins, Header/Footer, and Sheet. All tabs contain Print and Print Preview buttons. Figure 51 shows the Page tab.

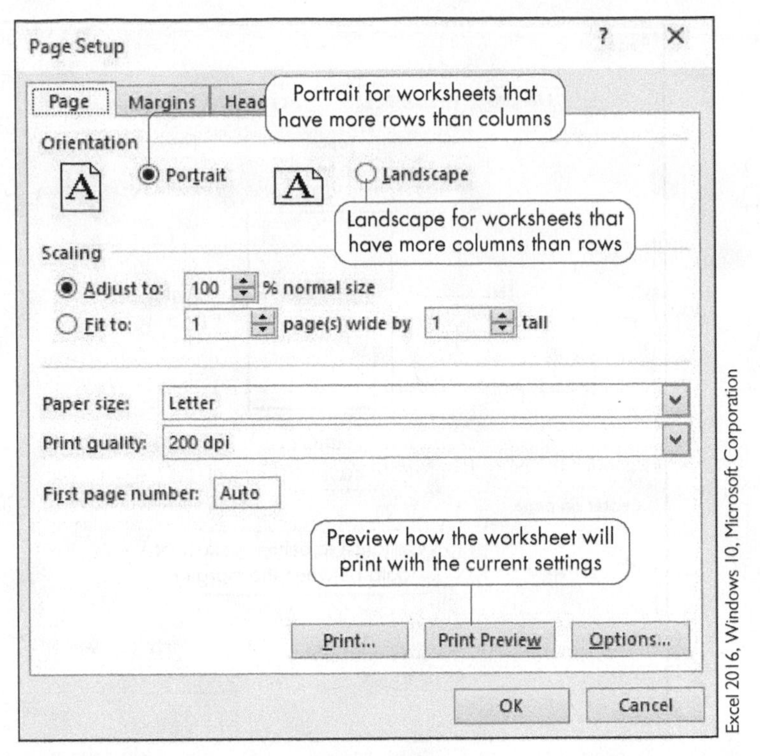

FIGURE 51 Page Setup Dialog Box: Page Tab

The Page tab contains options to select the orientation and paper size. In addition, it contains scaling options that are similar to the options in the Scale to Fit group on the Page Layout tab. You use scaling options to increase or decrease the size of characters on a printed page, similar to using a zoom setting on a photocopy machine. You might want to use the *Fit to* option to force the data to print on a specified number of pages.

Set Margin Options

The Margins tab (see Figure 52) contains options for setting the specific margins. In addition, it contains options to center the worksheet data horizontally or vertically on the page, which are used to balance worksheet data equally between the left and right margins or top and bottom margins, respectively.

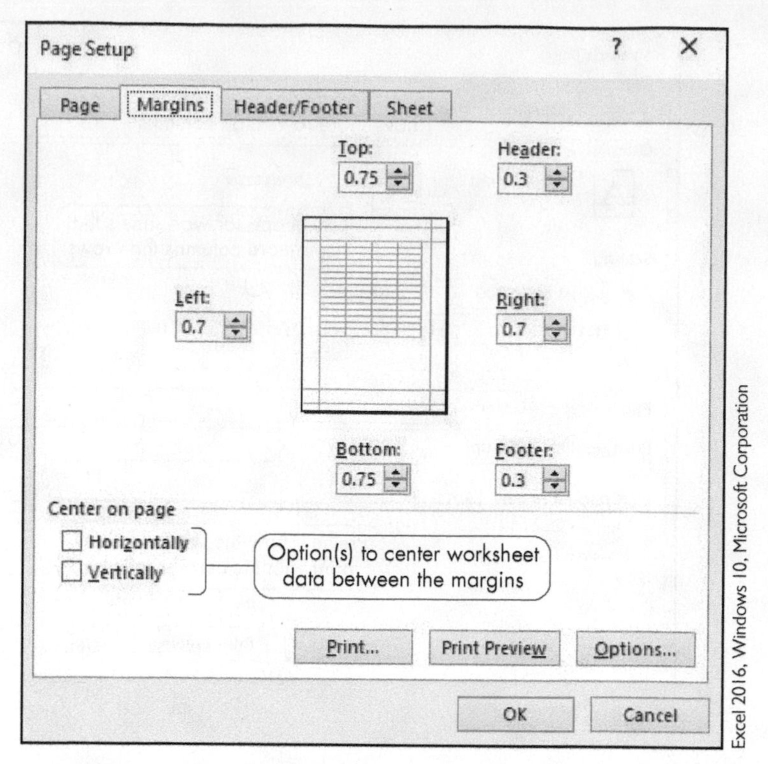

FIGURE 52 Page Setup Dialog Box: Margins Tab

Create Headers and Footers

STEP 3 The Header/Footer tab (see Figure 53) lets you create a header and/or footer that appears at the top and/or bottom of every printed page. Click the arrows to choose from several preformatted entries, or alternatively, click Custom Header or Custom Footer, insert text and other objects, and click the appropriate formatting button to customize the headers and footers. Use headers and footers to provide additional information about the worksheet. You can include your name, the date the worksheet was prepared, and page numbers, for example.

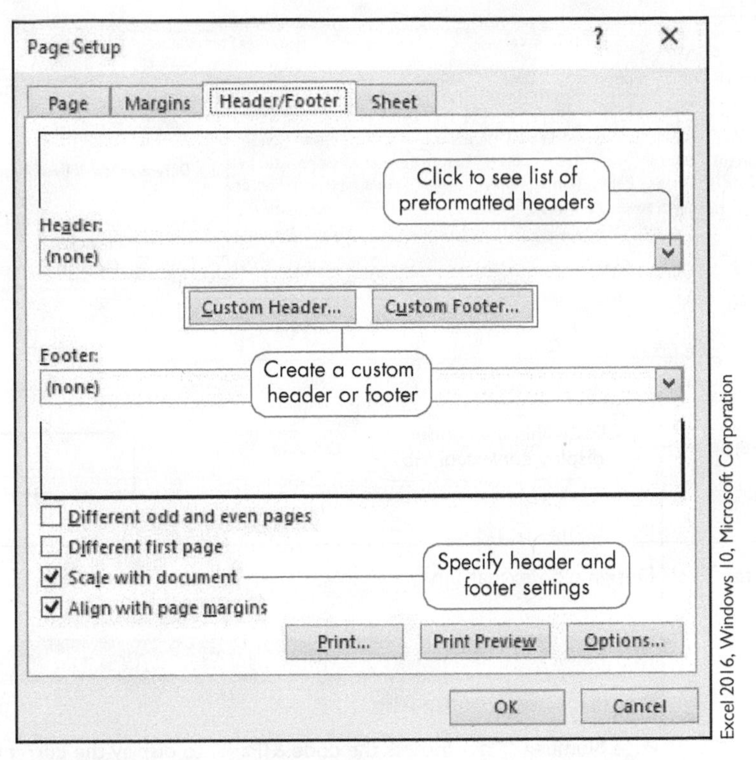

FIGURE 53 Page Setup Dialog Box: Header/Footer Tab

You can create different headers or footers on different pages, such as one header with the file name on odd-numbered pages and a header containing the date on even-numbered pages. Click the *Different odd and even pages* check box to select it in the Page Setup dialog box (see Figure 53).

You might want the first page to have a different header or footer from the rest of the printed pages, or you might not want a header or footer to show up on the first page but want the header or footer to display on the remaining pages. Click the *Different first page* check box to select it in the Page Setup dialog box to specify a different first page header or footer.

Instead of creating headers and footers using the Page Setup dialog box, you can click the Insert tab and click Header & Footer in the Text group. Excel displays the worksheet in Page Layout view with the insertion point in the center area of the header. Click inside the left, center, or right section of a header or footer. When you click inside a section within the header or footer, Excel displays the Header & Footer Tools Design contextual tab (see Figure 54). Enter text or insert data from the Header & Footer Elements group on the tab. Table 9 lists and describes the options in the Header & Footer Elements group. To get back to Normal view, click any cell in the worksheet and click Normal in the Workbook Views group on the View tab.

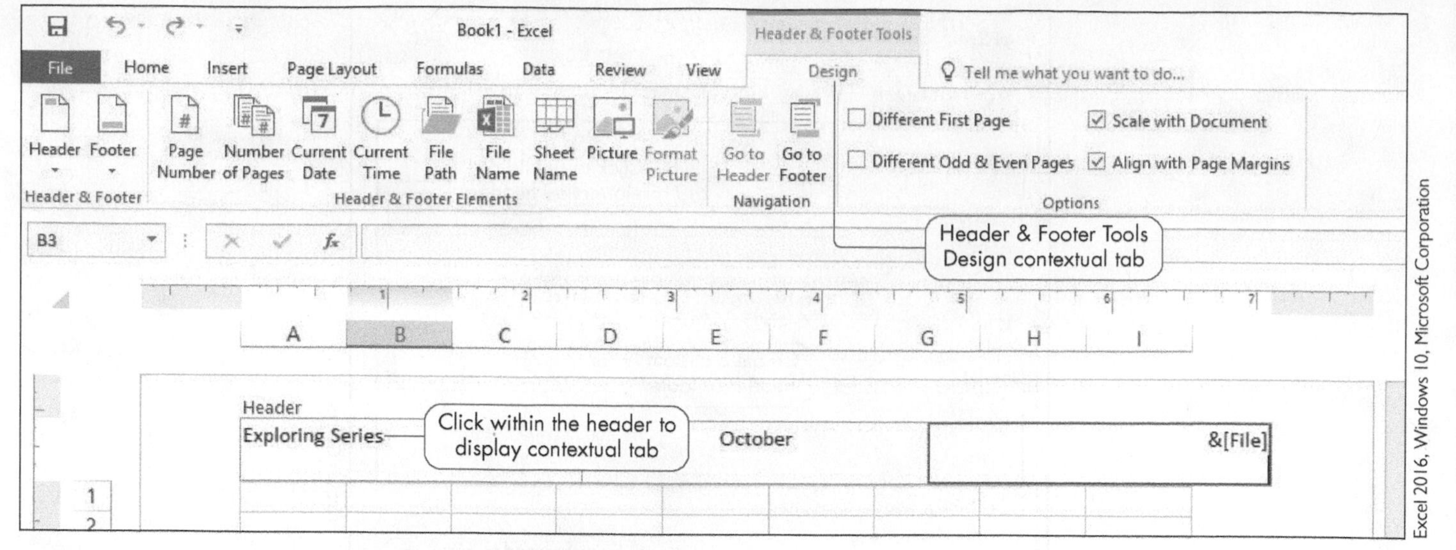

FIGURE 54 Headers & Footer Tools Design Contextual Tab

TABLE 9 Header & Footer Elements Options

Option Name	Result
Page Number	Inserts the code &[Page] to display the current page number.
Number of Pages	Inserts the code &[Pages] to display the total number of pages that will print.
Current Date	Inserts the code &[Date] to display the current date, such as 5/19/2018. The date is updated to the current date when you open or print the worksheet.
Current Time	Inserts the code &[Time] to display the current time, such as 5:15 PM. The time is updated to the current time when you open or print the worksheet.
File Path	Inserts the code &[Path]&[File] to display the path and file name, such as C:\Users\Keith\Documents\e01h4Markup. This information changes if you save the workbook with a different name or in a different location.
File Name	Inserts the code &[File] to display the file name, such as e01h4Markup. This information changes if you save the workbook with a different name.
Sheet Name	Inserts the code &[Tab] to display the worksheet name, such as September. This information changes if you rename the worksheet.
Picture	Inserts the code &[Picture] to display and print an image as a background behind the data, not just the worksheet.
Format Picture	Enables you to adjust the brightness, contrast, and size of an image after you use the Picture option.

TIP: VIEW TAB

If you click the View tab and click Page Layout, Excel displays an area *Click to add header* at the top of the worksheet.

Select Sheet Options

The Sheet tab (see Figure 55) contains options for setting the print area, print titles, print options, and page order. Some of these options are also located in the Sheet Options group on the Page Layout tab.

By default, Excel displays gridlines onscreen to show you each cell's margins, but the gridlines do not print unless you specifically select the Gridlines check box in the Page Setup dialog box or the Print Gridlines check box in the Sheet Options group on the Page Layout tab. In addition, Excel displays row (1, 2, 3, etc.) and column (A, B, C, etc.) headings onscreen. However, these headings do not print unless you click the *Row and column headings* check box in the Page Setup dialog box or click the Print Headings check box in the Sheet Options group on the Page Layout tab. For most worksheets, you do not need to print gridlines and row/column headings. However, when you want to display and print cell formulas instead of formula results, you might want to print the gridlines and row/column headings. Doing so will help you analyze your formulas. The gridlines help you see the cell boundaries, and the headings help you identify what data are in each cell. At times, you might want to display gridlines to separate data on a regular printout to increase readability.

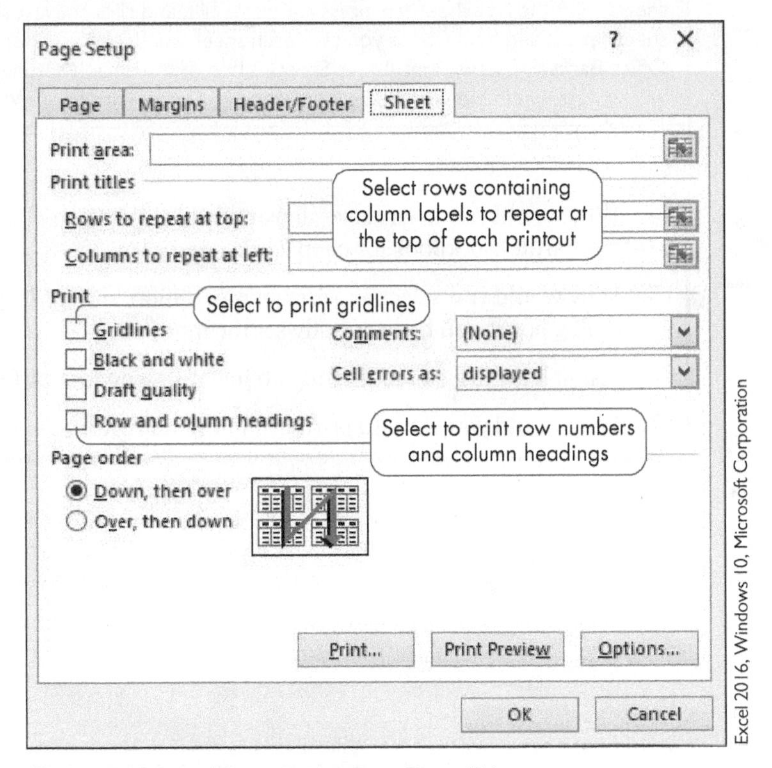

FIGURE 55 Page Setup Dialog Box: Sheet Tab

> **TIP: REPEATING ROWS AND COLUMNS**
> If you have spreadsheet data that would take more than one printed page, open the Page Setup dialog box, click the Sheet tab, click in the *Rows to repeat at top* box, and then select the row(s) containing column labels. That way, when the pages print, the rows containing the descriptive column labels will repeat at the top of each printed page so that you can easily know what data is in each column. Likewise, if the spreadsheet has too many columns to print on one page, you can click in the *Columns to repeat at left* box on the Sheet tab within the Page Setup dialog box and select the column(s) so that the row labels will display on the left side of each printed page.

Previewing and Printing a Worksheet

STEP 4 Microsoft Office Backstage view displays print options and displays the worksheet in print preview mode. Print preview helps you see before printing if the data are balanced on the page or if data will print on multiple pages.

You can specify the number of copies to print and which printer to use to print the worksheet. The first option in the Settings area specifies what to print. The default option is Print Active Sheets. You might want to choose other options, such as Print Entire Workbook or Print Selection, or specify which pages to print. If you are connected to a printer capable of duplex printing, you can print on only one side or print on both sides. You can also collate, change the orientation, specify the paper size, adjust the margins, and adjust the scaling.

The bottom of the Print window indicates how many pages will print. If you do not like how the worksheet will print, click Page Setup at the bottom of the print settings to open the Page Setup dialog box so that you can adjust margins, scaling, column widths, and so on until the worksheet data appear the way you want them to print.

TIP: PRINTING MULTIPLE WORKSHEETS

To print more than one worksheet at a time, select the sheets you want to print. To select adjacent sheets, click the first sheet tab, press and hold Shift, and click the last sheet tab. To select nonadjacent sheets, press and hold Ctrl as you click each sheet tab. When you display the Print options in Microsoft Office Backstage view, Print Active Sheets is one of the default settings. If you want to print all of the worksheets within the workbook, change the setting to Print Entire Workbook.

14. Why would you insert several worksheets of data in one workbook instead of creating a separate workbook for each worksheet?
15. Why would you select a *Center on page* option in the Margins tab within the Page Setup dialog box if you have already set the margins?
16. List at least five elements you can insert in a header or footer.
17. Why would you want to print gridlines and row and column headings?

Hands-On Exercises

Skills covered: Copy or Move a Worksheet • Rename a Worksheet • Group Worksheets • Set Page Orientation • Select Scaling Options • Set Margin Options • Create a Header or Footer • View in Print Preview • Print a Worksheet

5 Worksheets, Page Setup, and Printing

You are ready to complete the OKOS worksheet. You want to copy the existing worksheet so that you display the results on the original sheet and display formulas on the duplicate sheet. Before printing the worksheet for your supervisor, you want to make sure the data will appear professional when printed. You will adjust some page setup options to put the finishing touches on the worksheet.

STEP 1 » COPY, MOVE, AND RENAME A WORKSHEET

You want to copy the worksheet, move it to the right side of the original worksheet, and rename the duplicate worksheet so that you can show formulas on the duplicate sheet. Refer to Figure 56 as you complete Step 1.

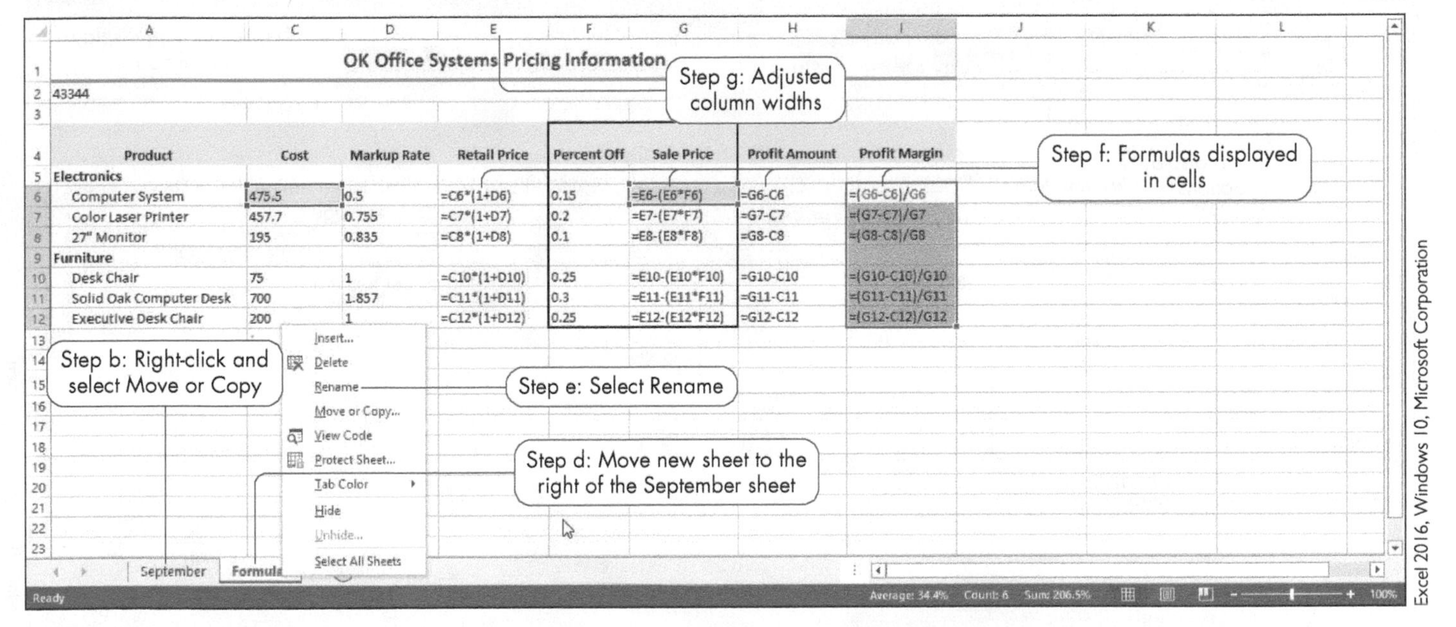

FIGURE 56 Worksheets

a. Open *e01h4Markup_LastFirst* if you closed it at the end of Hands-On Exercise 4 and save it as **e01h5Markup_LastFirst**, changing h4 to h5.

b. Right-click the **Sheet1 tab** at the bottom of the worksheet and select **Move or Copy**.

The Move or Copy dialog box opens so that you can move the existing worksheet or make a copy of it.

c. Click the **Create a copy check box** to select it and click **OK**.

The duplicate worksheet is named Sheet1 (2) and is placed to the left of the original worksheet.

d. Drag the **Sheet1 (2) worksheet tab** to the right of the Sheet1 worksheet tab.

The duplicate worksheet is now on the right side of the original worksheet.

e. Right-click the **Sheet1 sheet tab**, select **Rename**, type **September**, and then press **Enter**. Rename Sheet1 (2) as **Formulas**.

You renamed the original worksheet as September to reflect the September sales data, and you renamed the duplicate worksheet as Formulas to indicate that you will keep the formulas displayed on that sheet.

f. Press **Ctrl+`** to display the formulas in the Formulas worksheet.

g. Change these column widths in the Formulas sheet:

- Column A **(13.00)**
- Columns C and D **(6.00)**
- Columns E, G, H, and I **(7.00)**
- Column F **(5.00)**

You reduced the column widths so that the data will fit on a printout better.

h. Save the workbook.

STEP 2 » SET PAGE ORIENTATION, SCALING, AND MARGIN OPTIONS

Because the worksheet has several columns, you decide to print it in landscape orientation. You want to set a 1" top margin and center the data between the left and right margins. Furthermore, you want to make sure the data fits on one page on each sheet. Currently, if you were to print the Formulas worksheet, the data would print on two pages. Refer to Figure 57 as you complete Step 2.

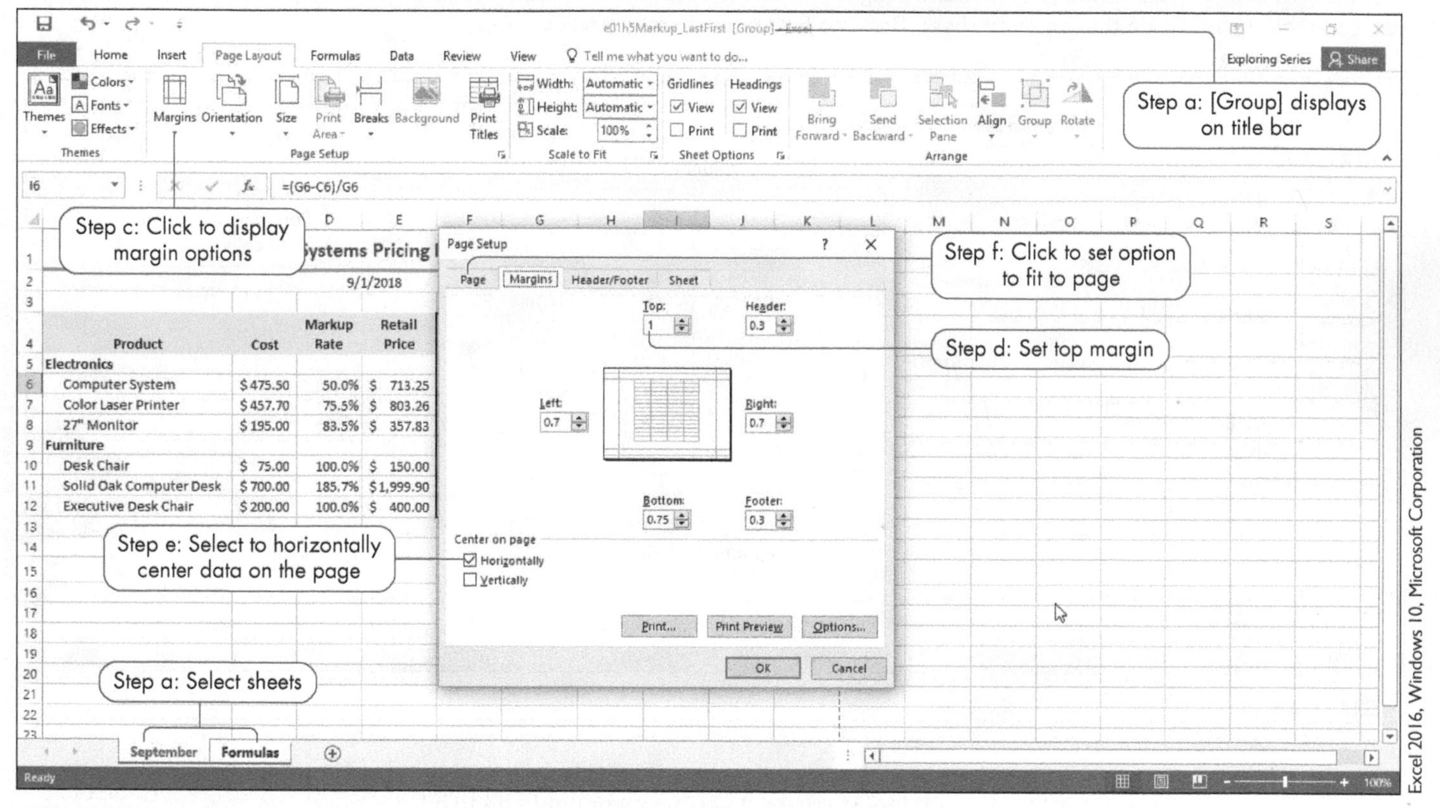

FIGURE 57 Page Setup Options Applied

a. Click the **September sheet tab**, press and hold down **Ctrl**, and then click the **Formulas sheet tab**.

Both worksheets are grouped together as indicated by [Group] after the file name on the title bar. Anything you do on one sheet affects both sheets.

b. Click the **Page Layout tab**, click **Orientation** in the Page Setup group, and then select **Landscape** from the list.

Because both worksheets are grouped, both worksheets are formatted in landscape orientation.

c. Click **Margins** in the Page Setup group on the Page Layout tab and select **Custom Margins**.

The Page Setup dialog box opens with the Margins tab options displayed.

d. Click the **Top spin arrow** to display **1**.

Because both worksheets are grouped, the 1" top margin is set for both worksheets.

e. Click the **Horizontally check box** to select it in the Center on page section.

Because both worksheets are grouped, the data on each worksheet are centered between the left and right margins.

f. Click the **Page tab** within the Page Setup dialog box, click **Fit to** in the Scaling section, and then click **OK**. Save the workbook.

The Fit to option ensures that each sheet fits on one page.

STEP 3 ›› CREATE A HEADER

To document the grouped worksheets, you want to include your name, the sheet name, and the file name in a header. Refer to Figure 58 as you complete Step 3.

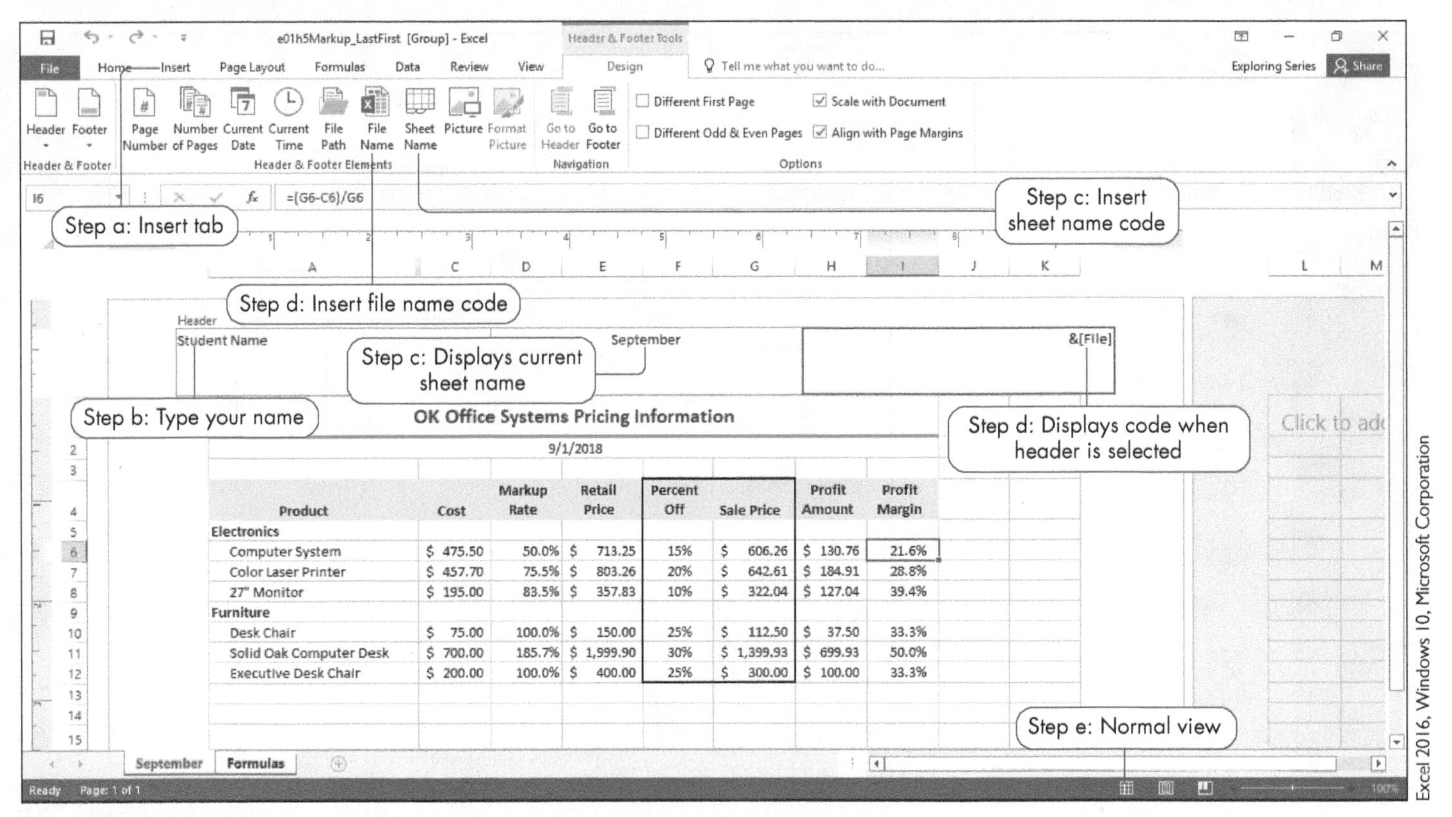

FIGURE 58 Header

a. Ensure the worksheets are still grouped, click the **Insert tab**, and then click **Header & Footer** in the Text group.

Excel displays the Header & Footer Tools Design contextual tab and the worksheet displays in Page Layout view, which displays the header area, margin space, and ruler. The insertion point blinks inside the center section of the header.

b. Click in the left section of the header and type your name.

c. Click in the center section of the header and click **Sheet Name** in the Header & Footer Elements group on the Design tab.

Excel inserts the code &[Tab]. This code displays the name of the worksheet. If you change the worksheet tab name, the header will reflect the new sheet name.

d. Click in the right section of the header and click **File Name** in the Header & Footer Elements group on the Design tab.

Excel inserts the code &[File]. This code displays the name of the file. Because the worksheets were grouped when you created the header, a header will appear on both worksheets. The file name will be the same; however, the sheet names will be different.

e. Click in any cell in the worksheet, click **Normal** on the status bar, and then save the workbook.

Normal view displays the worksheet, but does not display the header or margins.

f. Click the **Review tab** and click **Spelling** in the Proofing group. Correct all errors, if any, and click **OK** when prompted with the message, *Spell check complete. You're good to go!* Save the workbook.

You should always spell-check a workbook before publishing it.

STEP 4 » VIEW IN PRINT PREVIEW AND PRINT

Before printing the worksheets, you should preview it. Doing so helps you detect margin problems and other issues, such as a single row or column of data flowing onto a new page. Refer to Figure 59 as you complete Step 4.

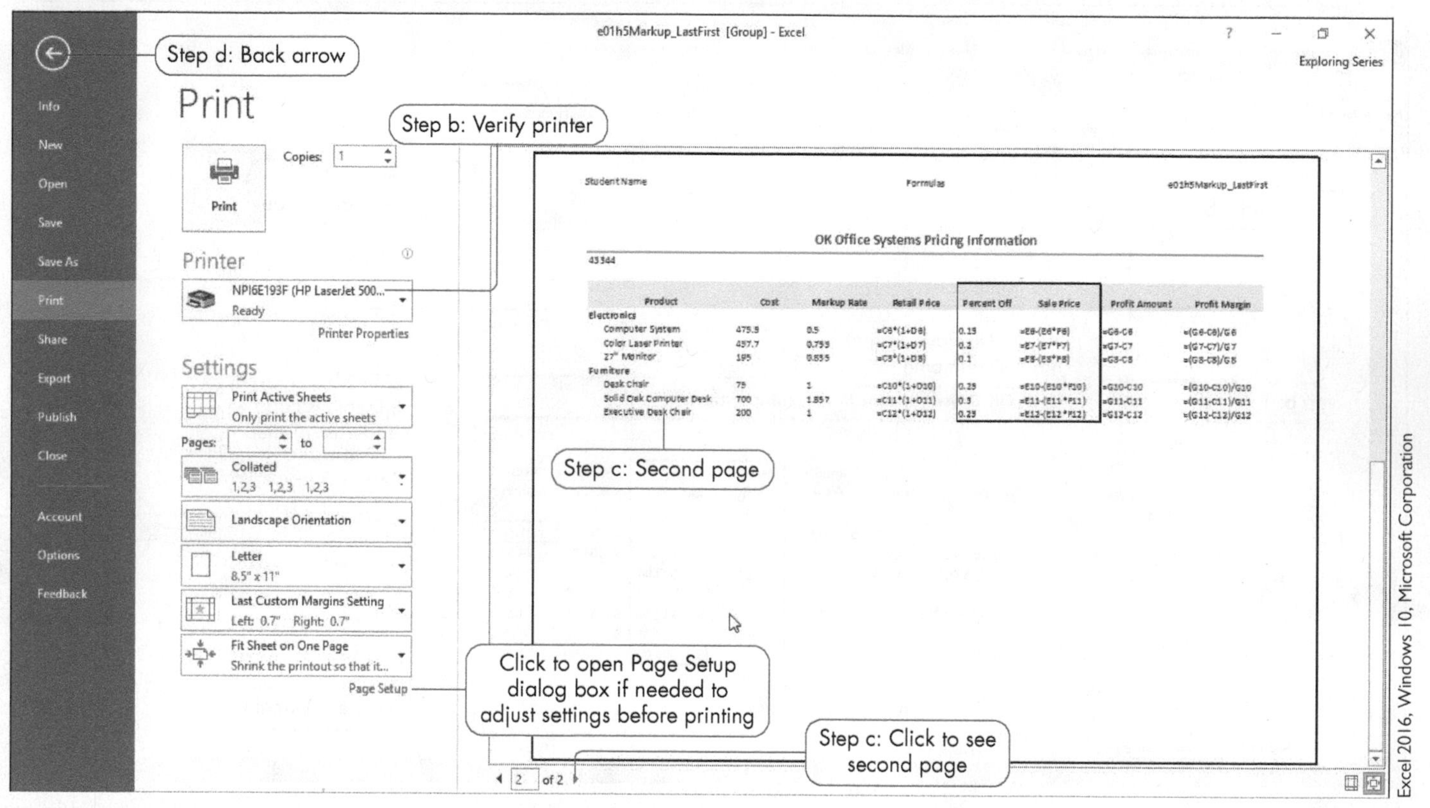

FIGURE 59 Worksheet in Print Preview

a. Click the **File tab** and click **Print**.

The Microsoft Office Backstage view displays print options and a preview of the worksheet.

b. Verify the Printer box displays the printer that you want to use to print your worksheet, and verify the last Settings option displays Fit Sheet on One Page.

The bottom of Backstage shows 1 of 2, indicating two pages will print.

c. Click **Next Page** to see the second page, which is the data on the Formulas worksheet, and verify the last Settings option displays Fit Sheet on One Page.

Check the Print Preview window to make sure the data are formatted correctly and would print correctly.

d. Click the **Back arrow** and save the workbook.

Although you did not print the worksheets, all the print options are saved.

e. Save and close the file. Based on your instructor's directions, submit e01h5Markup_LastFirst. Once the file is closed, the Formulas sheet may not display the formulas when you open the workbook again. If that happens, press **Ctrl+`** again.

Chapter Objectives Review

After reading this chapter, you have accomplished the following objectives:

1. Explore the Excel window.

- A worksheet is a single spreadsheet containing data. A workbook is a collection of one or more related worksheets contained in a single file.
- Identify Excel window elements: The Name Box displays the name of the current cell. The Formula Bar displays the contents of the current cell. The active cell is the current cell. A sheet tab shows the name of the worksheet.
- Identify columns, rows, and cells: Columns have alphabetical headings, such as A, B, C. Rows have numbers, such as 1, 2, 3. A cell is the intersection of a column and row and is indicated with a column letter and a row number.
- Navigate in and among worksheets: Use the arrow keys to navigate within a sheet, or use the Go To command to go to a specific cell. Click a sheet tab to display the contents on another worksheet.

2. Enter and edit cell data.

- You should plan the worksheet design by stating the purpose, deciding what output you need, and then identifying what input values are needed. Next, you enter and format data in a worksheet. Finally, you document, save, and then share a workbook.
- Enter text: Text may contain letters, numbers, symbols, and spaces. Text aligns at the left side of a cell.
- Use Auto Fill to complete a sequence. Auto Fill can automatically fill in sequences, such as month names or values, after you enter the first label or value. Double-click the fill handle to fill in the sequence.
- Enter values: Values are numbers that represent a quantity. Values align at the right side of a cell by default.
- Enter dates and times: Excel stores dates and times as serial numbers so that you can calculate the number of days between dates or times.
- Edit and clear contents: You might want to edit the contents of a cell to correct errors or to make labels more descriptive. Use the Clear option to clear the cell contents and/or formats.

3. Create formulas.

- A formula is used to perform a calculation. The formula results display in the cell.
- Use cell references in formulas: Use references, such as =B5+B6, instead of values within formulas.
- Apply the order of operations: The most commonly used operators are performed in this sequence: Parentheses, exponentiation, multiplication, division, addition, and subtraction.
- Use semi-selection to create a formula: When building a formula, click a cell containing a value to enter that cell reference in the formula.
- Copy formulas with the fill handle: Double-click the fill handle to copy a formula down a column.

4. Display cell formulas.

- By default, the results of formulas appear in cells.
- Display formulas by pressing Ctrl+`.

5. Manage columns and rows.

- Insert cells, columns, and rows: Insert a cell to move the remaining cells down or to the right. Insert a new column or row for data.
- Delete cells, columns, and rows: You should delete cells, columns, and rows you no longer need.
- Hide and unhide columns and rows: Hiding rows and columns protects confidential data from being displayed.
- Adjust column width: Double-click between the column headings to widen a column based on the longest item in that column, or drag the border between column headings to increase or decrease a column width.
- Adjust row height: Drag the border between row headings to increase or decrease the height of a row.

6. Select, move, copy, and paste data.

- Select a range: A range may be a single cell or a rectangular block of cells.
- Move a range to another location: After selecting a range, cut it from its location. Then select the top-left corner of the destination range to make it the active cell and paste the range there.
- Copy and paste a range: After selecting a range, click Copy, click the top-left corner of the destination range, and then click Paste to make a copy of the original range.
- Use Paste Options and Paste Special: The Paste Special option enables you to specify how the data are pasted into the worksheet.
- Copy Excel data to other programs: You can copy Excel data and paste it in other programs, such as in Word or PowerPoint.

7. Apply cell styles, alignment, and font options.

- Cell styles contain a collection of formatting, such as font, font color, font size, fill, and borders. You can apply an Excel cell style to save formatting time.
- Merge and center labels: Type a label in the left cell, select a range including the data you typed, and then click Merge & Center to merge cells and center the label within the newly merged cell.

- Change horizontal and vertical cell alignment: The default horizontal alignment depends on the data entered, and the default vertical alignment is Bottom Align.
- Wrap text: Use the Wrap Text option to present text on multiple lines in order to avoid having extra-wide columns.
- Increase and decrease indent: To indicate hierarchy of data or to offset a label, increase or decrease how much the data are indented in a cell.
- Apply borders and fill colors: Borders and fill colors help improve readability of worksheets.

8. Apply number formats.

- Apply a number format: The default number format is General, which does not apply any particular format to values. Apply appropriate formats to values to present the data with the correct symbols and decimal alignment. For example, Accounting Number Format is a common number format for monetary values.
- Increase and decrease decimal places: After applying a number format, you might want to increase or decrease the number of decimal places displayed.

9. Manage worksheets.

- Insert and delete a worksheet: You can insert new worksheets to include related data within one workbook, or you can delete extra worksheets you do not need.
- Copy or move a worksheet: Drag a sheet tab to rearrange the worksheets. You can copy a worksheet within a workbook or to another workbook.
- Rename a worksheet: The default worksheet tab name is Sheet1, but you should change the name to describe the contents of the worksheet.

10. Select page setup options.

- The Page Layout tab on the Ribbon contains options for setting margins, selecting orientation, specifying page size, selecting the print area, and applying other settings.
- Specify page options: Page options include orientation, paper size, and scaling.
- Set margin options: You can set the left, right, top, and bottom margins. In addition, you can center worksheet data horizontally and vertically on a page.
- Create headers and footers: Insert a header or footer to display documentation, such as your name, date, time, and worksheet tab name.
- Select sheet options: Sheet options control the print area, print titles, print options, and page order.

11. Preview and print a worksheet.

- Before printing a worksheet, you should display a preview to ensure the data will print correctly. The Print Preview helps you see if margins are correct or if isolated rows or columns will print on separate pages.
- After making appropriate adjustments, you can print the worksheet.

Key Terms Matching

Match the key terms with their definitions. Write the key term letter by the appropriate numbered definition.

- **a.** Alignment
- **b.** Auto Fill
- **c.** Cell
- **d.** Column width
- **e.** Fill color
- **f.** Fill handle
- **g.** Formula
- **h.** Formula Bar
- **i.** Input area
- **j.** Name Box
- **k.** Order of operations
- **l.** Output area
- **m.** Range
- **n.** Row height
- **o.** Sheet tab
- **p.** Text
- **q.** Value
- **r.** Workbook
- **s.** Worksheet
- **t.** Wrap text

1. _______ A spreadsheet that contains formulas, functions, values, text, and visual aids.

2. _______ A file containing related worksheets.

3. _______ A range of cells containing values for variables used in formulas.

4. _______ A range of cells containing results based on manipulating the variables.

5. _______ Identifies the address of the current cell.

6. _______ Displays the content (text, value, date, or formula) in the active cell.

7. _______ Displays the name of a worksheet within a workbook.

8. _______ The intersection of a column and row.

9. _______ Includes letters, numbers, symbols, and spaces.

10. _______ A number that represents a quantity or an amount.

11. _______ Rules that control the sequence in which Excel performs arithmetic operations.

12. _______ Enables you to copy the contents of a cell or cell range or to continue a sequence by dragging the fill handle over an adjacent cell or range of cells.

13. _______ A small green square at the bottom-right corner of a cell.

14. _______ The horizontal measurement of a column.

15. _______ The vertical measurement of a row.

16. _______ A rectangular group of cells.

17. _______ The position of data between the cell margins.

18. _______ Formatting that enables a label to appear on multiple lines within the current cell.

19. _______ The background color appearing behind data in a cell.

20. _______ A combination of cell references, operators, values, and/or functions used to perform a calculation.

Multiple Choice

1. Which step is *not* part of planning a worksheet design?
   (a) Decide what input values are needed.
   (b) State the purpose of the worksheet.
   (c) Decide what outputs are needed to achieve the purpose.
   (d) Enter labels, values, and formulas.

2. You just copied a range of data containing formulas. However, you want to preserve the formula results and the original number and text formatting in the pasted range. Which paste option would you select?
   (a) Formulas
   (b) Keep Source Formatting
   (c) Values & Source Formatting
   (d) Values & Number Formatting

3. Given the formula =B1*B2+B3/B4^2, what operation is calculated first?
   (a) B1*B2
   (b) B2+B3
   (c) B3/B4
   (d) B4^2

4. How can you display formulas within the cells instead of the cell results?
   (a) Press Ctrl+G.
   (b) Press Ctrl+`.
   (c) Click Cell References on the Home tab.
   (d) Press Ctrl+C.

5. What is a fast way to apply several formats at one time?
   (a) Click each one individually.
   (b) Apply a cell style.
   (c) Use Auto Fill.
   (d) Use Copy and Paste options.

6. Which of the following is *not* an alignment option?
   (a) Increase Indent
   (b) Merge & Center
   (c) Fill Color
   (d) Wrap Text

7. Which of the following characteristics is *not* applicable to the Accounting Number Format?
   (a) Dollar sign immediately on the left side of the value
   (b) Commas to separate thousands
   (c) Two decimal places
   (d) Zero values displayed as hyphens

8. You selected and copied worksheet data containing formulas. However, you want the pasted copy to contain the current formula results rather than formulas. What do you do?
   (a) Click Paste in the Clipboard group on the Home tab.
   (b) Click the Paste arrow in the Clipboard group and select Formulas.
   (c) Click the Paste arrow in the Clipboard group and select Values & Source Formatting.
   (d) Display the Paste Special dialog box and select Formulas & Number Formatting.

9. Assume that the data on a worksheet consume a whole printed page and a couple of columns on a second page. You can do all of the following *except* what to force the data to print all on one page?
   (a) Decrease the Scale value.
   (b) Increase the left and right margins.
   (c) Decrease column widths if possible.
   (d) Select a smaller range as the print area.

10. What should you do if you see pound signs (###) instead of values or results of formulas?
    (a) Increase the zoom percentage.
    (b) Delete the column.
    (c) Adjust the row height.
    (d) Increase the column width.

Practice Exercises

1 Mathematics Review

You want to brush up on your math skills to test your logic by creating formulas in Excel. You realize that you should avoid values in formulas most of the time. Therefore, you created an input area that contains values you will use in your formulas. To test your knowledge of formulas, you will create an output area that will contain a variety of formulas using cell references from the input area. You will include a formatted title, the date prepared, and your name. After creating and verifying formula results, you will change input values and observe changes in the formula results. You want to display cell formulas, so you will create a picture copy of the formulas view. Refer to Figure 60 as you complete this exercise.

	A	B	C	D	E
1				**Excel Formulas and Order of Precedence**	
2	Date Created:	42614		Student Name	
3					
4	**Input Area:**			**Output Area:**	
5	First Value	2		Sum of 1st and 2nd values	=B5+B6
6	Second Value	4		Difference between 4th and 1st values	=B8-B5
7	Third Value	6		Product of 2nd and 3rd values	=B6*B7
8	Fourth Value	8		Quotient of 3rd and 1st values	=B7/B5
9				2nd value to the power of 3rd value	=B6^B7
10				1st value added to product of 2nd and 4th values and difference between sum and 3rd value	=B5+B6*B8-B7
11				Product of sum of 1st and 2nd and difference between 4th and 3rd values	=(B5+B6)*(B8-B7)
12				Product of 1st and 2nd added to product of 3rd and 4th values	=(B5*B6)+(B7*B8)

Excel 2016, Windows 10, Microsoft Corporation

FIGURE 60 Formula Practice

a. Open *e01p1Math* and save it as **e01p1Math_LastFirst**.

b. Type the current date in **cell B2** in this format: 9/1/2018. Type your first and last names in **cell D2**.

c. Adjust the column widths by doing the following:
- Click in any cell in column A and click **Format** in the Cells group.
- Select **Column Width**, type **12.57** in the Column width box, and then click **OK**.
- Click in any cell in column B and set the width to **11**.
- Click in any cell in column D and set the width to **35.57**.

d. Select the **range A1:E1**, click **Merge & Center** in the Alignment group, click **Bold** in the Font group, and then change the font size to **14**.

e. Select the **range B5:B8** and click **Center** in the Alignment group.

f. Select the **range D10:D12** and click **Wrap Text** in the Alignment group.

g. Enter the following formulas in column E:
- Click **cell E5**. Type **=B5+B6** and press **Enter**. Excel adds the value stored in cell B5 (1) to the value stored in cell B6 (2). The result (3) appears in cell E5, as described in cell D5.
- Enter appropriate formulas in **cells E6:E8**, pressing **Enter** after entering each formula. Subtract to calculate a difference, multiply to calculate a product, and divide to calculate a quotient.
- Type **=B6^B7** in **cell E9** and press **Enter**. Calculate the answer: 2*2*2 = 8.
- Enter **=B5+B6*B8-B7** in **cell E10** and press **Enter**. Calculate the answer: 2*4 = 8; 1+8 = 9; 9-3 = 6. Multiplication occurs first, followed by addition, and finally subtraction.
- Enter **=(B5+B6)*(B8-B7)** in **cell E11** and press **Enter**. Calculate the answer: 1+2 = 3; 4-3 = 1; 3*1 = 3. This formula is almost identical to the previous formula; however, calculations in parentheses occur before the multiplication.
- Enter **=B5*B6+B7*B8** in **cell E12** and press **Enter**. Calculate the answer: 1*2 = 2; 3*4 = 12; 2+12 = 14.

h. Edit a formula and the input values:

- Click **cell E12** and click in the Formula Bar to edit the formula. Add parentheses as shown: **=(B5*B6)+(B7*B8)** and click **Enter** to the left side of the Formula Bar. The answer is still 14. The parentheses do not affect order of operations because multiplication occurred before the addition. The parentheses help improve the readability of the formula.
- Type **2** in **cell B5**, **4** in **cell B6**, **6** in **cell B7**, and **8** in **cell B8**.
- Double-check the results of the formulas using a calculator or your head. The new results in cells E5:E12 should be 6, 6, 24, 3, 4096, 28, 12, and 56, respectively.

i. Double-click the **Sheet1 tab**, type **Results**, and then press **Enter**. Right-click the **Results sheet tab**, select **Move or Copy**, click **(move to end)** in the *Before sheet* section, click the **Create a copy check box** to select it, and click **OK**. Double-click the **Results (2) sheet tab**, type **Formulas**, and then press **Enter**.

j. Ensure that the Formulas sheet tab is active, click the **Formulas sheet tab** and click **Show Formulas** in the Formula Auditing group. Double-click between the column A and column B headings to adjust the column A width. Double-click between the column B and column C headings to adjust the column B width. Set **24.00 width** for column D.

k. Ensure that the Formulas worksheet is active, click the **Page Layout tab**, and do the following:

- Click the **Gridlines Print check box** to select it in the Sheet Options group.
- Click the **Headings Print check box** to select it in the Sheet Options group.

l. Click the **Results sheet tab**, press and hold **Ctrl**, and click the **Formulas sheet tab** to select both worksheets. Do the following:

- Click **Orientation** in the Page Setup group and select **Landscape**.
- Click the **Insert tab**, click **Header & Footer** in the Text group. Click **Go to Footer** in the Navigation group.
- Type your name on the left side of the footer.
- Click in the center section of the footer and click **Sheet Name** in the Header & Footer Elements group.
- Click in the right section of the footer and click **File Name** in the Header & Footer elements group.

m. Click in the worksheet, press **Ctrl+Home**, and click **Normal View** on the status bar.

n. Click the **File tab** and click **Print**. Verify that each worksheet will print on one page. Press **Esc** to close the Print Preview, and right-click the worksheet tab and click **Ungroup Sheets**.

o. Save and close the file. Based on your instructor's directions, submit e01p1Math_LastFirst.

2 Calendar Formatting

You want to create a calendar for July 2018. The calendar will enable you to practice alignment settings, including center, merge and center, and indents. In addition, you will need to adjust column widths and increase row height to create cells large enough to enter important information, such as birthdays, in your calendar. You will create a formula and use Auto Fill to complete the days of the week and the days within each week. To improve the appearance of the calendar, you will add fill colors, font colors, and borders to create a red, white, and blue effect to celebrate Independence Day. Refer to Figure 61 as you complete this exercise.

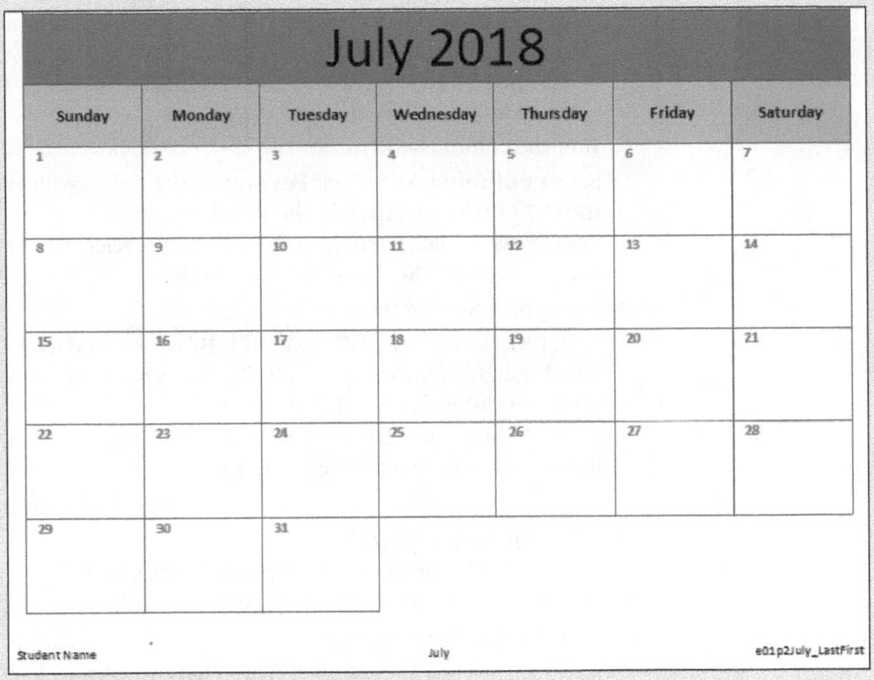

July 2018						
Sunday	Monday	Tuesday	Wednesday	Thursday	Friday	Saturday
1	2	3	4	5	6	7
8	9	10	11	12	13	14
15	16	17	18	19	20	21
22	23	24	25	26	27	28
29	30	31				

Student Name July e01p2July_LastFirst

Excel 2016, Windows 10, Microsoft Corporation

FIGURE 61 Calendar

a. Click the **File tab**, select **New**, and click **Blank workbook**. Save the workbook as **e01p2July_LastFirst**.

b. Type **'July 2018** in **cell A1** and click **Enter** on the left side of the Formula Bar.

> **TROUBLESHOOTING:** If you do not type the apostrophe before July 2018, the cell will display July-18 instead of July 2018.

c. Format the title:
- Select the **range A1:G1** and click **Merge & Center** in the Alignment group.
- Change the font size to **48**.
- Click the **Fill Color arrow** and click **Blue** in the Standard Colors section of the color palette.
- Click **Middle Align** in the Alignment group.

d. Complete the days of the week:
- Type **Sunday** in **cell A2** and click **Enter** to the left side of the Formula Bar.
- Drag the **cell A2 fill handle** across the row through **cell G2** to use Auto Fill to complete the rest of the weekdays.
- Ensure that the **range A2:G2** is selected. Click the **Fill Color arrow** and select **Blue, Accent 1, Lighter 40%** in the Theme Colors section of the color palette.
- Apply bold and change the font size to **14 size** to the selected range.
- Click **Middle Align** and click **Center** in the Alignment group to format the selected range.

e. Complete the days of the month:
- Type **1** in **cell A3** and press **Ctrl+Enter**. Drag the **cell A3 fill handle** across the row through **cell G3**.
- Click **Auto Fill Options** in the bottom-right corner of the copied data and select **Fill Series** to change the numbers to 1 through 7.
- Type **=A3+7** in **cell A4** and press **Ctrl+Enter**. Usually you avoid numbers in formulas, but the number of days in a week is always 7. Drag the **cell A4 fill handle** down through **cell A7** to get the date for each Sunday in July.

- Keep the **range A4:A7** selected and drag the fill handle across through **cell G7**. This action copies the formulas to fill in the days in the month.
- Select the **range D7:G7** and press **Delete** to delete the extra days 32 through 35 because July has only 31 days.

f. Format the columns and rows:
- Select **columns A:G**. Click **Format** in the Cells group, select **Column Width**, type **16** in the Column width box, and then click **OK**.
- Select **row 2**. Click **Format** in the Cells group, select **Row Height**, type **54**, and then click **OK**.
- Select **rows 3:7**. Set the row height to **80**.

g. Apply borders around the cells:
- Select the **range A1:G7**. Click the **Borders arrow** in the Font group and select **More Borders** to display the Format Cells dialog box with the Border tab selected.
- Click the **Color arrow** and select **Red**.
- Click **Outline** and **Inside** in the Presets section. Click **OK**. This action applies a red border inside and outside the selected range.

h. Clear the border formatting around cells that do not have days:
- Select the **range D7:G7**.
- Click **Clear** in the Editing group and select **Clear All**. This action removes the red borders around the cells after the last day of the month.

i. Format the days in the month:
- Select the **range A3:G7**. Click **Top Align** and **Align Left** in the Alignment group.
- Click **Increase Indent** in the Alignment group to offset the days from the border.
- Click **Bold** in the Font group, click the **Font Color arrow** and select **Blue**, and click the **Font Size arrow**, and then select **12**.

j. Double-click the **Sheet1 tab**, type **July**, and then press **Enter**.

k. Deselect the range and click the **Page Layout tab** and do the following:
- Click **Orientation** in the Page Setup group and select **Landscape**.
- Click **Margins** in the Page Setup group and select **Custom Margins**. Click the **Horizontally check box** to select it in the *Center on page* section and click **OK**.

l. Click the **Insert tab** and click **Header & Footer** in the Text group and do the following:
- Click **Go to Footer** in the Navigation group.
- Click in the left side of the footer and type your name.
- Click in the center of the footer and click **Sheet Name** in the Header & Footer Elements group on the Design tab.
- Click in the right side of the footer and click **File Name** in the Header & Footer Elements group on the Design tab.
- Click in any cell in the workbook, press **Ctrl+Home**, and then click **Normal** on the status bar.

m. Save and close the file. Based on your instructor's directions, submit e01p2July_LastFirst.

3 Downtown Theatre

You are the assistant manager at Downtown Theatre, where touring Broadway plays and musicals are performed. You will analyze ticket sales by completing a worksheet that focuses on seating charts for each performance. The spreadsheet will identify the seating sections, total seats in each section, and the number of seats sold for a performance. You will then calculate the percentage of seats sold and unsold. Refer to Figure 62 as you complete this exercise.

	A	B	C	D	E	F
1	Downtown Theatre					
2	Ticket Sales by Seating Section					
3	3/31/2018					
4						
5	Section	Available Seats	Seats Sold	Percentage Sold	Percentage Unsold	
6	Box Seats	25	12	48.0%	52.0%	
7	Front Floor	120	114	95.0%	5.0%	
8	Back Floor	132	108	81.8%	18.2%	
9	Tier 1	40	40	100.0%	0.0%	
10	Mezzanine	144	138	95.8%	4.2%	
11	Balcony	106	84	79.2%	20.8%	

FIGURE 62 Theatre Seating Data

a. Open *e01p3TicketSales* and save it as **e01p3TicketSales_LastFirst**.

b. Double-click the **Sheet1 sheet tab**, type **Seating**, and press **Enter**.

c. Type **3/31/2018** in **cell A3** and press **Enter**.

d. Format the title:
- Select the **range A1:E1** and click **Merge & Center** in the Alignment group.
- Click **Cell Styles** in the Styles group and select **Title** in the Titles and Headings section.
- Click **Bold** in the Font group.

e. Format the subtitle and date:
- Use the Merge & Center command to merge the **range A2:E2** and center the subtitle.
- Use the Merge & Center command to merge the **range A3:E3** and center the date.

f. Select the **range A5:E5**, click **Wrap Text**, click **Center**, and click **Bold** to format the column labels.

g. Right-click the **row 9 heading** and select **Insert** from the shortcut menu to insert a new row. Type the following data in the new row: **Back Floor**, **132**, **108**.

h. Move the Balcony row to be the last row by doing the following:
- Click the **row 6 heading** and click **Cut** in the Clipboard group on the Home tab.
- Right-click the **row 12 heading** and select **Insert Cut Cells** from the menu.

i. Adjust column widths by doing the following:
- Double-click between the column A and column B headings.
- Select **columns B** and **C headings** to select the columns, click **Format** in the Cells group, select **Column Width**, type **9** in the **Column width box**, and then click **OK**. Because columns B and C contain similar data, you set the same width for these columns.
- Set the width of columns D and E to **12**.

j. Select the **range B6:C11**, click **Align Right** in the Alignment group, and then click **Increase Indent** twice in the Alignment group.

k. Click **cell D6** and use semi-selection to calculate and format the percentage of sold and unsold seats by doing the following:
- Type =, click **cell C6**, type /, and then click **cell B6** to enter =C6/B6.
- Press **Tab** to enter the formula and make cell E6 the active cell. This formula divides the number of seats sold by the total number of Box Seats.
- Type **=(B6-C6)/B6** and click **Enter** on the left side of the Formula Bar to enter the formula and keep cell E6 the active cell. This formula must first subtract the number of sold seats from the available seats to calculate the number of unsold seats. The difference is divided by the total number of available seats to determine the percentage of unsold seats.
- Select the **range D6:E6**, click **Percent Style** in the Number group, and then click **Increase Decimal** in the Number group. Keep the range selected.
- Double-click the **cell E6 fill handle** to copy the selected formulas down their respective columns. Keep the range selected.
- Click **Align Right** in the Alignment group and click **Increase Indent** twice in the Alignment group. These actions will help center the data below the column labels. Do not click Center; doing so will center each value and cause the decimal points not to align. Deselect the range.

l. Display and preserve a screenshot of the formulas by doing the following:
- Click **New sheet**, double-click the **Sheet1 sheet tab**, type **Formulas**, and then press **Enter**.
- Click the **View tab** and click **Gridlines** in the Show group to hide the gridlines on the Formulas worksheet. This action will prevent the cell gridlines from bleeding through the screenshot you are about to embed.
- Click the **Seating sheet tab**, click the **Formulas tab** on the Ribbon, and then click **Show Formulas** in the Formula Auditing group to display cell formulas.
- Click **cell A1** and drag down to **cell E11** to select the range of data.
- Click the **Home tab**, click **Copy arrow** in the Clipboard group, select **Copy as Picture**, and then click **OK** in the Copy Picture dialog box.
- Click the **Formulas sheet tab**, click **cell A1**, and then click **Paste**.
- Click the **Page Layout tab**, click **Orientation** in the Page Setup group, and then select **Landscape** to change the orientation for the Formulas sheet.
- Click the **Seating sheet tab**, click the **Formulas tab**, and then click **Show Formulas** in the Formula Auditing group to hide the cell formulas.

m. Click the **Seating sheet tab**, press **Ctrl** and click the **Formulas sheet tab** to group the two sheets. Click the **Page Layout tab**, click **Margins** in the Page Setup group, and then select **Custom Margins**. Click the **Horizontally check box** to select it and click **Print Preview**. Excel centers the data horizontally based on the widest item in each worksheet. Verify that the worksheets each print on one page. If not, go back into the Page Setup dialog box for each worksheet and reapply settings if needed. Press **Esc** to leave the Print Preview mode.

n. Click the **Page Setup Dialog Box Launcher**, click the **Header/Footer tab** in the Page Setup dialog box, click **Custom Footer**, click in the left section of the header and type your name, click in the center section of the header, click **Insert Sheet Name**, click in the **right section of the header**, click **Insert File Name**, and then click **OK** to close the Footer dialog box. Click **OK** to close the Page Setup dialog box.

o. Right-click the **Seating sheet tab** and select **Ungroup Sheets**.

p. Save and close the file. Based on your instructor's directions, submit e01p3TicketSales_LastFirst.

Mid-Level Exercises

1 Guest House Rental Rates

You manage a beach guest house in Ft. Lauderdale containing three types of rental units. Prices are based on peak and off-peak times of the year. You want to calculate the maximum daily revenue for each rental type, assuming all units are rented. In addition, you will calculate the discount rate for off-peak rental times. Finally, you will improve the appearance of the worksheet by applying font, alignment, and number formats.

a. Open *e01m1Rentals* and save it as **e01m1Rentals_LastFirst**.

b. Apply the **Heading 1** cell style to the **range A1:G1** and the **20% - Accent1** cell style to the **range A2:G2**.

c. Merge and center Peak Rentals in the **range C4:D4**, over the two columns of peak rental data. Apply **Dark Red fill color** and **White, Background 1 font color**.

d. Merge and center Off-Peak Rentals in the **range E4:G4** over the three columns of off-peak rental data. Apply **Blue fill color** and **White, Background 1 font color**.

e. Center and wrap the headings on row 5. Adjust the width of columns D and F, if needed. Center the data in the **range B6:B8**.

f. Create and copy the following formulas:
   - Calculate the Peak Rentals Maximum Revenue by multiplying the number of units by the peak rental price per day.
   - Calculate the Off-Peak Rentals Maximum Revenue by multiplying the number of units by the off-peak rental price per day.
   - Calculate the Discount rate for the Off-Peak rental price per day. For example, using the peak and off-peak per day values, the studio apartment rents for 75% of its peak rental rate. However, you need to calculate and display the off-peak discount rate, which is .20 for the Studio Apartment. To calculate the discount rate, divide the off-peak per day rate by the peak per day rate. Subtract that result from 1, which represents 100%.

g. Format the monetary values with **Accounting Number Format**. Format the Discount Rate formula results in **Percent Style** with one decimal place. Adjust column widths if necessary to display the data.

h. Apply **Blue, Accent 1, Lighter 80% fill color** to the **range E5:G8**.

i. Select the **range C5:D8** and apply a custom color with **Red 242**, **Green 220**, and **Blue 219**.

j. Answer the four questions below the worksheet data. If you change any values to answer the questions, change the values back to the original values.

k. Create a copy of the Rental Rates worksheet, place the new sheet to the right side of the original worksheet, and rename the new sheet **Formulas**. Display cell formulas on the Formulas sheet.

l. Group the worksheets and do the following:
   - Select landscape orientation.
   - Set **1"** top, bottom, left, and right margins. Center the data horizontally on the page.
   - Insert a footer with your name on the left side, the sheet name code in the center, and the file name code on the right side.
   - Apply the setting to fit to one page.

m. Click the **Formulas sheet tab** and set options to print gridlines and headings. Adjust column widths.

n. Save and close the file. Based on your instructor's directions, submit e01m1Rentals_LastFirst.

2 Real Estate Sales Report

You are a small real estate agent in Indianapolis. You track the real estate properties you list for clients. You want to analyze sales for selected properties. Yesterday, you prepared a workbook with a worksheet for recent sales data and another worksheet listing several properties you listed. You want to calculate the number of days that the houses were on the market and their sales percentage of the list price. In one situation, the house was involved in a bidding war between two families that really wanted the house. Therefore, the sale price exceeded the list price.

a. Open *e01m2Sales* and save it as **e01m2Sales_LastFirst**.

b. Delete the row that has incomplete sales data. The owners took their house off the market.

c. Type **2018-001** in **cell A5** and use Auto Fill to complete the series to assign a property ID to each property.

d. Calculate the number of days each house was on the market in column C. Copy the formula down that column.

e. Format list prices and sold prices with **Accounting Number Format** with zero decimal places.

f. Calculate the sales price percentage of the list price in cell H5. The second house was listed for $500,250, but it sold for only $400,125. Therefore, the sale percentage of the list price is 79.99%. Format the percentages with two decimal places.

g. Wrap the headings on row 4.

h. Insert a new column between the Date Sold and List Price columns. Do the following:

- Move the Days on Market range C4:C13 to the new column.
- Delete the empty column C.

i. Edit the list date of the 41 Chestnut Circle house to be **4/22/2018**. Edit the list price of the house on Amsterdam Drive to be **$355,000**.

j. Select the property rows and set a **25 row height** and apply **Middle Align**.

k. Apply the **All Borders** border style to the **range A4:H12**. Adjust column widths as necessary.

l. Apply **Align Right** and indent twice the values in the **range E5:E12**.

m. Apply **120% scaling**.

n. Delete the Properties worksheet.

o. Insert a new worksheet and name it **Formulas**.

p. Use the Select All feature to select all data on the Houses Sold worksheet and copy it to the Formulas worksheet.

q. Complete the following steps on the Formulas worksheet:

- Hide the Date Listed and Date Sold columns.
- Display cell formulas.
- Set options to print gridlines and row and column headings.
- Adjust column widths.

r. Group the worksheets and do the following:

- Set landscape orientation.
- Center the page horizontally and vertically between the margins.
- Insert a footer with your name on the left side, the sheet tab code in the center, and the file name code on the right side.

s. Save and close the file. Based on your instructor's directions, submit e01m2Sales_LastFirst.

3 Problem Solving with Classmates

COLLABORATION CASE 

Your instructor wants all students in the class to practice their problem-solving skills. Pair up with a classmate so that you can create errors in a workbook and then see how many errors your classmate can find in your worksheet and how many errors you can find in your classmate's worksheet.

a. Create a folder named **Exploring** on your OneDrive and give access to that drive to a classmate and your instructor.

b. Open *e01h5Markup_LastFirst*, which you created in the Hands-On Exercises, and save it as **e01m3Markup_LastFirst**, changing h5 to m3.

c. Edit each main formula to have a deliberate error (such as a value or incorrect cell reference) in it and then copy the formulas down the columns.

d. Save the workbook to your shared folder on your OneDrive.

e. Open the workbook your classmate saved on his or her OneDrive and save the workbook with your name after theirs, such as *e01m3Markup_MulberyKeith_KrebsCynthia*.

f. Find the errors in your classmate's workbook, insert comments to describe the errors, and then correct the errors.

g. Save the workbook back to your classmate's OneDrive and close the file. Based on your instructor's directions, submit e01m3Markup_LastFirst_LastFirst.

Beyond the Classroom

Tip Distribution

GENERAL CASE

You are a server at a restaurant in Portland. You must tip the bartender 13% of each customer's drink sales and the server assistant 1.75% of the food sales plus 2% of the drink sales. You want to complete a worksheet that shows the sales, tips, and your net tip. Open *e01b1Server* and save it as **e01b1Server_LastFirst**.

Insert a column between the Drinks and Tip Left columns. Type the label **Subtotal** in cell D6. Calculate the food and drinks subtotal for the first customer and copy the formula down the column. In column F, enter a formula to calculate the amount of the tip as a percentage of the subtotal for the first customer's sales. Format the results with Percent Style with one decimal place. Type **13%** in cell G7, type **1.75%** in cell H7, and type **2%** in cell I7. Copy these percentage values down these three columns. Horizontally center the data in the three percentage columns.

In cell J7, calculate the bartender's tip for the first customer, using the rule specified in the first paragraph. In cell K7, calculate the assistant's tip for the first customer, using the rule specified in the first paragraph. In cell L7, calculate your net tip after giving the bartender and server their share of the tips. Copy the formulas from the range J7:L7 down their respective columns. Merge and center **Customer Subtotal and Tip** in the range B5:E5, **Tip Rates** in the range F5:I5, and **Tip Amounts** in the range J5:L5. Apply Currency format to the monetary values. Apply borders around the Tip Rates and Tip Amounts sections similar to the existing border around the Customer Subtotal and Tip section. For the range A6:L6, apply **Orange, Accent 2, Lighter 40%** fill color, center horizontal alignment, and wrap text. Apply **Orange, Accent 2, Lighter 80%** fill color to the values in the Tip Left column and the My Net Tip column.

Set 0.2" left and right margins, select Landscape orientation, and set the scaling to fit to one page. Include a footer with your name on the left footer, the sheet name code in the center, and file name code on the right side. Copy the worksheet and place the copied worksheet on the right side of the original worksheet. Rename the copied worksheet as **Tip Formulas**. On the Tip Formulas worksheet, display cell formulas, print gridlines, print headings, and adjust the column widths. Change the Tips sheet tab color to **Orange, Accent 2**, and change the Tip Formulas sheet tab color to **Orange, Accent 2, Darker 25%**. Save and close the file. Based on your instructor's directions, submit e01b1Server_LastFirst.

Net Proceeds from House Sale

Daryl Patterson is a real estate agent. He wants his clients to have a realistic expectation of how much money they will receive when they sell their houses. Sellers know they have to pay a commission to the agent and pay off their existing mortgages; however, many sellers forget to consider they might have to pay some of the buyer's closing costs, title insurance, and prorated property taxes. The realtor commission and estimated closing costs are based on the selling price and the respective rates. The estimated property taxes are prorated based on the annual property taxes and percentage of the year. For example, if a house sells three months into the year, the seller pays 25% of the property taxes. Daryl created a worksheet to enter values in an input area to calculate the estimated deductions at closing and calculate the estimated net proceeds the seller will receive. However, the worksheet contains errors. Open *e01b2Proceeds* and save it as **e01b2Proceeds_LastFirst**. Review the font formatting and alignment for consistency.

Use Help to learn how to insert comments into cells. As you identify the errors, insert comments in the respective cells to explain the errors. Correct the errors, including formatting errors. Apply Landscape orientation, 115% scaling, 1.5" top margin, and center horizontally. Insert your name on the left side of the header, the sheet name code in the center, and the file name code on the right side. Save and close the file. Based on your instructor's directions, submit e01b2Proceeds_LastFirst.

Capstone Exercise

You are a division manager for a regional hearing-aid company in Cheyenne, Wyoming. Your sales managers travel frequently to some of the offices in the western region. You need to create a travel expense report for your managers to use to record their budgeted and actual expenses for their travel reports. The draft report contains a title, input areas, and a detailed expense area.

Format the Title and Complete the Input Areas

Your first tasks are to format the title and complete the input area. The input area contains two sections: Standard Inputs that are identical for all travelers and Traveler Inputs that the traveler enters based on his or her trip.

a. Open *e01c1Travel* and save it as **e01c1Travel_LastFirst**.

b. Merge and center the title over the **range A1:E1** and set the row height for the first row to **40**.

c. Apply the **Input cell style** to the **ranges B3:B6**, **E3:E4**, and **E6:E7**, and then apply the **Calculation cell style** to **cell E5**. Part of the borders are removed when you apply these styles.

d. Select the **ranges A3:B6** and **D3:E7**. Apply **Thick Outside Borders**.

e. Enter **6/1/2018** in **cell E3** for the departure date, **6/5/2018** in **cell E4** for the return date, **149** in **cell E6** for the hotel rate per night, and **18%** in **cell E7** for the hotel tax rate.

f. Enter a formula in **cell E5** to calculate the number of days between the return date and the departure date.

Insert Formulas

The Detailed Expenses section contains the amount budgeted for the trip, the actual expenses reported by the traveler, percentage of the budget spent on each item, and the amount the actual expense went over or under budget. You will insert formulas for this section. Some budgeted amounts are calculated based on the inputs. Other budgeted amounts, such as airfare, are estimates.

a. Enter the amount budgeted for Mileage to/from Airport in **cell B12**. The amount is based on the mileage rate and roundtrip to the airport from the Standard Inputs section.

b. Enter the amount budgeted for Airport Parking in **cell B13**. This amount is based on the airport parking daily rate and the number of total days traveling (the number of nights + 1) to include both the departure and return dates. For example, if a person departs on June 1 and returns on June 5, the total number of nights at a hotel is 4, but the total number of days the vehicle is parked at the airport is 5.

c. Enter the amount budgeted for Hotel Accommodations in **cell B16**. This amount is based on the number of nights, the hotel rate, and the hotel tax rate.

d. Enter the amount budgeted for Meals in **cell B17**. This amount is based on the daily meal allowance and the total travel days (# of hotel nights + 1).

e. Enter the % of Budget in **cell D12**. This percentage indicates the percentage of actual expenses to budgeted expenses. Copy the formula to the **range D13:D18**.

f. Enter the difference between the actual and budgeted expenses in **cell E12**. Copy the formula to the **range E13:E18**. If the actual expenses exceeded the budgeted expenses, the result should be positive. If the actual expenses were less than the budgeted expense, the result should be negative, indicating under budget.

Add Rows, Indent Labels, and Move Data

The Detailed Expenses section includes a heading Travel to/from Destination. You want to include two more headings to organize the expenses. Then you will indent the items within each category. Furthermore, you want the monetary columns together, so you will insert cells and move the Over or Under column to the right of the Actual column.

a. Insert a new row 15. Type **Destination Expenses** in **cell A15**. Bold the label.

b. Insert a new row 19. Type **Other** in **cell A19**. Bold the label.

c. Indent twice the labels in the **ranges A12:A14**, **A16:A18**, and **A20**.

d. Select the **range D10:D21** and insert cells to shift the selected cells to the right.

e. Cut the **range F10:F21** and paste it in the **range D10:D21** to move the Over or Under data in the new cells you inserted.

Format the Detailed Expenses Section

You are ready to format the values to improve readability. You will apply Accounting Number Format to the monetary values on the first and total rows, Comma Style to the monetary values in the middle rows, and Percent Style for the percentages.

a. Apply **Accounting Number Format** to the **ranges B12:D12** and **B21:D21**.

b. Apply **Comma Style** to the **range B13:D20**.

c. Apply **Percent Style** with one decimal place to the **range E12:E20**.

d. Underline the **range: B20:D20**. Do not use the border feature.

e. Apply the cell style **Bad** to **cell D21** because the traveler went over budget.

f. Select the **range A10:E21** and apply **Thick Outside Borders**.

g. Select the **range A10:E10**, apply **Blue-Gray, Text 2, Lighter 80% fill color**, apply **Center** alignment, and apply **Wrap Text**.

Manage the Workbook

You will apply page setup options, insert a footer, and, then duplicate the Expenses statement worksheet.

a. Spell-check the workbook and make appropriate corrections.

b. Set a **1.5"** top margin and select the margin setting to center the data horizontally on the page.

c. Insert a footer with your name on the left side, the sheet name code in the center, and the file name code on the right side.

d. Copy the Expenses worksheet, move the new worksheet to the end, and rename it **Formulas**.

e. Display the cell formulas on the Formulas worksheet, change to landscape orientation, and adjust column widths. Use the Page Setup dialog box or the Page Layout tab to print gridlines and row and column headings.

f. Save and close the file. Based on your instructor's directions, submit e01c1Travel_LastFirst.

Glossary

Accounting Number Format A number format that displays $ on the left side of a cell, formats a value with a comma for every three digits on the left side of the decimal point, and displays two digits to the right of the decimal point.

Active cell The current cell in a worksheet. It is indicated by a dark green border, and the Name Box shows the location of the active cell.

Alignment The placement of data within the boundaries of a cell. By default, text aligns on the left side, and values align on the right side of a cell.

AutoComplete A feature that searches for and automatically displays any other label in that column that matches the letters you type.

Auto Fill A feature that helps you complete a sequence of months, abbreviated months, quarters, weekdays, weekday abbreviations, or values. Auto Fill also can be used to fill or copy a formula down a column or across a row.

Border A line that surrounds a cell or a range of cells to offset particular data from the rest of the data in a worksheet.

Cancel An icon between the Name Box and Formula Bar. When you enter or edit data, click Cancel to cancel the data entry or edit, and revert back to the previous data in the cell, if any. Cancel changes from gray to red when you position the pointer over it.

Cell The intersection of a column and row in a table, such as the intersection of column B and row 5.

Cell address The unique identifier of a cell, starting with the column letter and then the row number, such as C6.

Cell style A set of formatting applied to a cell to produce a consistent appearance for similar cells within a worksheet.

Column heading The alphabetical letter above a column in a worksheet. For example, B is the column heading for the second column.

Column width The horizontal measurement of a column in a table or a worksheet. In Excel, it is measured by the number of characters or pixels.

Comma Style A number format that formats a value with a comma for every three digits on the left side of the decimal point and displays two digits to the right of the decimal point.

Enter An icon between the Name Box and Formula Bar. When you enter or edit data, click Enter to accept data typed in the active cell and keep the current cell active. Enter changes from gray to blue when you position the pointer over it.

Fill color The background color that displays behind the data in a cell so that the data stands out.

Fill handle A small green square at the bottom-right corner of the active cell. You can position the pointer on the fill handle and drag it to repeat the contents of the cell to other cells or to copy a formula in the active cell to adjacent cells down the column or across the row.

Flash Fill A feature that fills in data or values automatically based on one or two examples you enter using another part of data entered in a previous column in the dataset.

Formula A combination of cell references, operators, values, and/or functions used to perform a calculation.

Formula Bar An element located below the Ribbon and to the right of the Insert Function command. It shows the contents of the active cell. You enter or edit cell contents in the Formula Bar for the active cell.

Horizontal alignment The placement of cell data between the left and right cell margins. By default, text is left-aligned, and values are right-aligned.

Indent A format that offsets data from its default alignment within the margins or cell. For example, if text is left-aligned, the text may be indented or offset from the left side to stand out. If a value is right-aligned, it can be indented or offset from the right side of the cell.

Input area A range of cells in a worksheet used to store and change the variables used in calculations.

Insert Function An icon between the Name Box and Formula Bar. Click Insert Function to open the Insertion Function dialog box to search for and insert a particular function.

Name Box An element located below the Ribbon, which displays the address of the active cell.

New sheet An icon that, when clicked, inserts a new worksheet in the workbook.

Nonadjacent range A collection of multiple ranges (such as D5:D10 and F5:F10) that are not positioned in a contiguous cluster in an Excel worksheet.

Normal view The default view of a worksheet that shows worksheet data but not margins, headers, footers, or page breaks.

Number format A setting that controls how a value appears in a cell.

Order of operations A rule that controls the sequence in which arithmetic operations are performed. Also called the *order of precedence*.

Output area The range of cells in an Excel worksheet that contain formulas dependent on the values in the input area.

Page Break Preview A view setting that displays the worksheet data and page breaks within the worksheet.

Page Layout view A view setting that displays the worksheet data, margins, headers, and footers.

Paste Options button An icon that displays in the bottom-right corner immediately after using the Paste command. It enables the user to apply different paste options.

Percent Style A number format that displays a value as if it was multiplied by 100 and with the % symbol. The default number of decimal places is zero if you click Percent Style in the Number group or two decimal places if you use the Format Cells dialog box.

Pointing The process of using the pointer to select cells while building a formula. Also known as *semi-selection*.

Range A group of adjacent or contiguous cells in a worksheet. A range can be adjacent cells in a column (such as C5:C10), in a row (such as A6:H6), or a rectangular group of cells (such as G5:H10).

Row heading A number to the left side of a row in a worksheet. For example, 3 is the row heading for the third row.

Row height The vertical measurement of the row in a worksheet.

Select All The triangle at the intersection of the row and column headings in the top-left corner of the worksheet. Click it to select everything contained in the active worksheet.

Semi-selection The process of using the pointer to select cells while building a formula. Also known as *pointing*.

Sheet tab A visual label that looks like a file folder tab. In Excel, a sheet tab shows the name of a worksheet contained in the workbook.

Sheet tab navigation Visual elements that help you navigate to the first, previous, next, or last sheet within a workbook.

Spreadsheet An electronic file that contains a grid of columns and rows used to organize related data and to display results of calculations, enabling interpretation of quantitative data for decision making.

Status bar The row at the bottom of the Excel window that displays instructions and other details about the status of a worksheet.

Text Any combination of letters, numbers, symbols, and spaces not used in Excel calculations.

Value A number that represents a quantity or a measurable amount.

Vertical alignment The placement of cell data between the top and bottom cell margins.

View controls Icons on the right side of the status bar that enable you to change to Normal, Page Layout, or Page Break view to display the worksheet.

Workbook A collection of one or more related worksheets contained within a single file.

Worksheet A single spreadsheet that typically contains descriptive labels, numeric values, formulas, functions, and graphical representations of data.

Wrap text An Excel feature that makes data appear on multiple lines by adjusting the row height to fit the cell contents within the column width.

Zoom control A control that enables you to increase or decrease the size of the worksheet data onscreen.

Formulas and Functions

Excel

Formulas and Functions

LEARNING OUTCOME **You will apply formulas and functions to calculate and analyze data.**

OBJECTIVES & SKILLS: After you read this chapter, you will be able to:

Formula Basics

OBJECTIVE 1: USE RELATIVE, ABSOLUTE, AND MIXED CELL REFERENCES IN FORMULAS
Use a Relative Cell Reference, Use an Absolute Cell Reference, Use a Mixed Cell Reference

HANDS-ON EXERCISE 1:
Formula Basics

Function Basics

OBJECTIVE 2: INSERT A FUNCTION
Insert a Function, Insert a Function Using Formula AutoComplete, Use the Insert Function Dialog Box

OBJECTIVE 3: INSERT BASIC MATH AND STATISTICS FUNCTIONS
Use the SUM Function, Use the AVERAGE and MEDIAN Functions, Use the MIN and MAX Functions, Use the COUNT Functions, Perform Calculations with Quick Analysis Tools

OBJECTIVE 4: USE DATE FUNCTIONS
Use the TODAY Function, Use the NOW Function

HANDS-ON EXERCISE 2:
Function Basics

Logical, Lookup, and Financial Functions

OBJECTIVE 5: DETERMINE RESULTS WITH THE IF FUNCTION
Use the IF Function

OBJECTIVE 6: USE LOOKUP FUNCTIONS
Use the VLOOKUP Function, Create the Lookup Table, Use the HLOOKUP Function

OBJECTIVE 7: CALCULATE PAYMENTS WITH THE PMT FUNCTION
Use the PMT Function

HANDS-ON EXERCISE 3:
Logical, Lookup, and Financial Functions

CASE STUDY | Townsend Mortgage Company

You are an assistant to Erica Matheson, a mortgage broker at the Townsend Mortgage Company. Erica spends her days reviewing mortgage rates and trends, meeting with clients, and preparing paperwork. She relies on your expertise in using Excel to help analyze mortgage data.

Today, Erica provided you with sample mortgage data: loan number, house cost, down payment, mortgage rate, and the length of the loan in years. She asked you to perform some basic calculations so that she can check the output provided by her system to verify if it is calculating results correctly. She wants you to calculate the amount financed, the periodic interest rate, the total number of payment periods, the percent of the house cost that is financed, and the payoff year for each loan. In addition, you will calculate totals, averages, and other basic statistics.

Furthermore, she has asked you to complete another worksheet that uses functions to look up interest rates from a separate table, calculate the monthly payments, and determine how much (if any) the borrower will have to pay for private mortgage insurance (PMI).

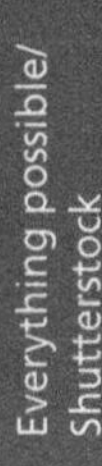

Performing Quantitative Analysis

	A	B	C	D	E	F	G	H	I	J	K	L
1	Townsend Mortgage Company											
2												
3	Input Area											
4	Today's Date:	10/2/2018										
5	Pmts Per Year:	12										
6												
7	Loan #	House Cost	Down Payment	Amount Financed	Mortgage Rate	Rate Per Period	Years	# of Pmt Periods	% Financed	Date Financed	Payoff Year	
8	452786	$ 400,000	$ 80,000	$ 320,000	3.625%	0.302%	25	300	80.0%	5/1/2016	2041	
9	453000	$ 425,000	$ 60,000	$ 365,000	3.940%	0.328%	30	360	85.9%	11/3/2016	2046	
10	453025	$ 175,500	$ 30,000	$ 145,500	3.550%	0.296%	25	300	82.9%	4/10/2017	2042	
11	452600	$ 265,950	$ 58,000	$ 207,950	2.500%	0.208%	15	180	78.2%	10/14/2017	2032	
12	452638	$ 329,750	$ 65,000	$ 264,750	3.250%	0.271%	30	360	80.3%	2/4/2018	2048	
13												
14	Summary Statistics											
15	Statistics	House Cost	Down Payment	Amount Financed								
16	Total	$ 1,596,200	$ 293,000	$ 1,303,200								
17	Average	$ 319,240	$ 58,600	$ 260,640								
18	Median	$ 329,750	$ 60,000	$ 264,750								
19	Lowest	$ 175,500	$ 30,000	$ 145,500								
20	Highest	$ 425,000	$ 80,000	$ 365,000								
21	# of Mortgages	5	5	5								

Details | Payment Info

Ready

Excel 2016, Windows 10, Microsoft Corporation

FIGURE 1 Townsend Mortgage Company Worksheet

CASE STUDY | Townsend Mortgage Company

Starting File	File to be Submitted
e02h1Loans	e02h3Loans_LastFirst

Formula Basics

When you increase your understanding of formulas, you can build robust workbooks that perform a variety of calculations for quantitative analysis. Your ability to build sophisticated workbooks and to interpret the results increases your value to any organization. By now, you should be able to build simple formulas using cell references and mathematical operators and use the order of operations to control the sequence of calculations in formulas.

In this section, you will create formulas in which cell addresses change or remain fixed when you copy them.

Using Relative, Absolute, and Mixed Cell References in Formulas

When you copy a formula, Excel either adjusts or preserves the cell references in the copied formula based on how the cell references appear in the original formula. Excel uses three different ways to reference a cell in a formula: relative, absolute, and mixed. Relative references change when a formula is copied. For example, if a formula containing the cell A1 is copied down one row in the column, the reference would become A2. In contrast, absolute references remain constant, no matter where they are copied. Mixed references are a combination of both absolute and relative, where part will change and part will remain constant.

When you create a formula that you will copy to other cells, ask yourself the following question: Do the cell references contain constant or variable values? In other words, should the cell references be adjusted or always refer to the same cell location, regardless of where the copied formula is located?

Use a Relative Cell Reference

STEP 1 »» A ***relative cell reference*** is the default method of referencing in Excel. It indicates a cell's relative location, such as five rows up and one column to the left, from the original cell containing the formula. When you copy a formula containing a relative cell reference, the cells referenced in the copied formula change relative to the position of the copied formula. Regardless of where you paste the formula, the cell references in the copied formula maintain the same relative distance from the cell containing the copied formula, as the cell references the relative location to the original formula cell.

In Figure 2, the formulas in column F contain relative cell references. When you copy the original formula =D2-E2 from cell F2 down one row to cell F3, the copied formula changes to =D3-E3. Because you copy the formula *down* the column to cell F3, the column letters in the formula stay the same, but the row numbers change to reflect the row to which you copied the formula. Using relative referencing is an effective time saving tool. For example, using relative cell addresses to calculate the amount financed ensures that each borrower's down payment is subtracted from his or her respective house cost.

F2 =D2-E2

Relative cell references in original formula

Original formula entered in cell F2

	A	B	C	D	E	F	G
1	Input Area			House Cost	Down Payment	Amount Financed	Amount Financed Formula
2	# Pmts Per Year	12		$300,000.00	$45,000.00	$ 255,000.00	=D2-E2
3	PMI Rate	0.3%		$250,0[illegible]		212,500.00	=D3-E3
4	Down Pmt Rate	15%		$200,0[illegible]		170,000.00	=D4-E4

Cell reference (row number) adjusted in copied formulas

Excel 2016, Windows 10, Microsoft Corporation

FIGURE 2 Relative Cell References

Use an Absolute Cell Reference

STEP 2 In many calculations there are times in which a value should remain constant, such as an interest rate or payoff date. In these situations absolute cell references are utilized. An ***absolute cell reference*** provides a constant reference to a specific cell. When you copy a formula containing an absolute cell reference, the cell reference in the copied formula does not change, regardless of where you copy the formula. An absolute cell reference appears with a dollar sign before both the column letter and row number, such as $B$4.

In Figure 3, the down payment is calculated by multiplying the house cost by the down payment rate (15%). Each down payment calculation uses a different purchase price and constant down payment rate, therefore an absolute reference is required. Cell E2 contains =D2*$B$4 ($300,000*15.0%) to calculate the first borrower's down payment ($45,000). When you copy the formula down to the next row, the copied formula in cell E3 is =D3*$B$4. The relative cell reference D2 changes to D3 (for the next house cost) and the absolute cell reference $B$4 remains the same to refer to the constant 15.0% down payment rate. This formula ensures that the cell reference to the house cost changes for each row but that the house cost is always multiplied by the rate in cell B4.

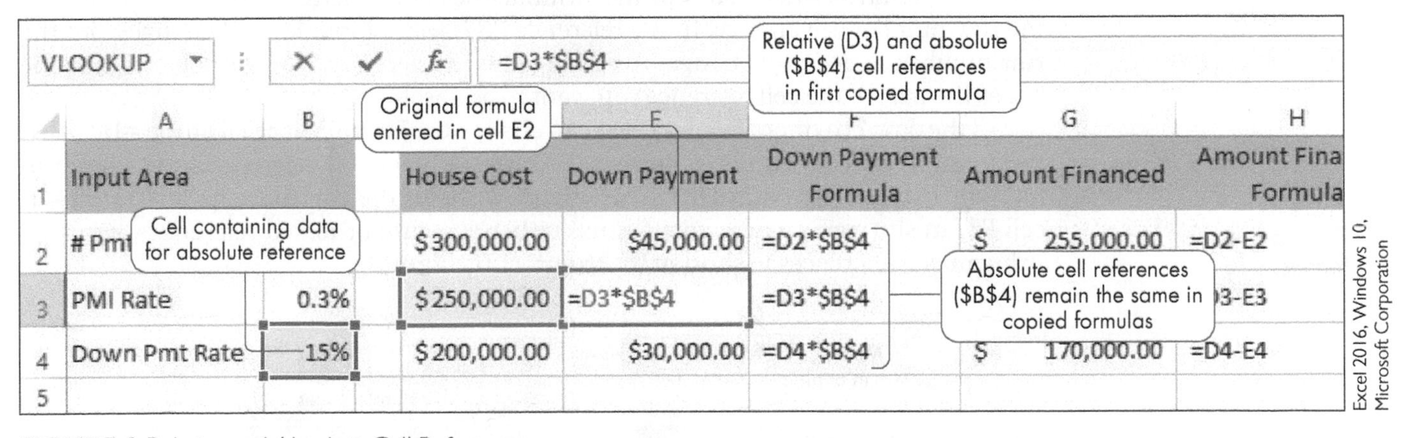

FIGURE 3 Relative and Absolute Cell References

TIP: INPUT AREA AND ABSOLUTE CELL REFERENCES

To illustrate the effect of modifying an assumption (e.g., the down payment rate changes from 15% to 20%), it is efficient to enter the new input value in only one cell (e.g., B4) rather than including the same value in a string of formulas. In Figure 3, values that can be modified, such as the down payment rate, are put in an input area. Generally, formulas use absolute references to the cells in the input area. For example, B4 is an absolute cell reference in all the down payment calculations. If the value in B4 is modified, Excel recalculates the amount of down payment for all the down payment formulas. By using cell references from an input area, you can perform what-if analyses very easily.

When utilizing the fill option to copy a formula, if an error or unexpected result occurs, a good starting point for troubleshooting is checking input values to determine if an absolute or mixed reference is needed. Figure 4 shows what happens if the down payment formula used a relative reference to cell B4. If the original formula in cell E2 is =D2*B4, the copied formula becomes =D3*B5 in cell E3. The relative cell reference to B4 changes to B5 when you copy the formula down. Because cell B5 is empty, the $350,000 house cost in cell D3 is multiplied by 0, giving a $0 down payment, which is not a valid down payment amount.

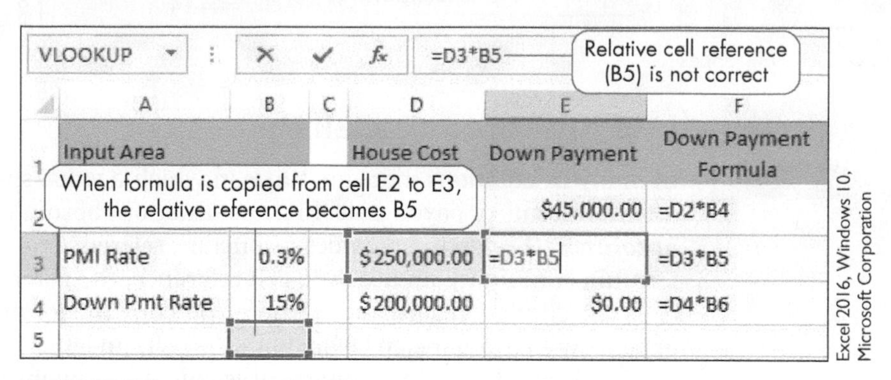

FIGURE 4 Error in Formula

Use a Mixed Cell Reference

STEP 3 A ***mixed cell reference*** combines an absolute cell reference with a relative cell reference. When you copy a formula containing a mixed cell reference, either the column letter or the row number that has the absolute reference remains fixed while the other part of the cell reference that is relative changes in the copied formula. $B4 and B$4 are examples of mixed cell references. In the reference $B4, the column B is absolute, and the row number is relative; when you copy the formula, the column letter B does not change, but the row number will change. In the reference B$4, the column letter B changes, but the row number, 4, does not change. To create a mixed reference, type the dollar sign to the left of the part of the cell reference you want to be absolute.

In the down payment formula, you can change the formula in cell E2 to be =D2*B$4. Because you are copying down the same column, only the row reference 4 must be absolute; the column letter stays the same. Figure 5 shows the copied formula =D3*B$4 in cell E3. In situations where you can use either absolute or mixed references, consider using mixed references to shorten the length of the formula.

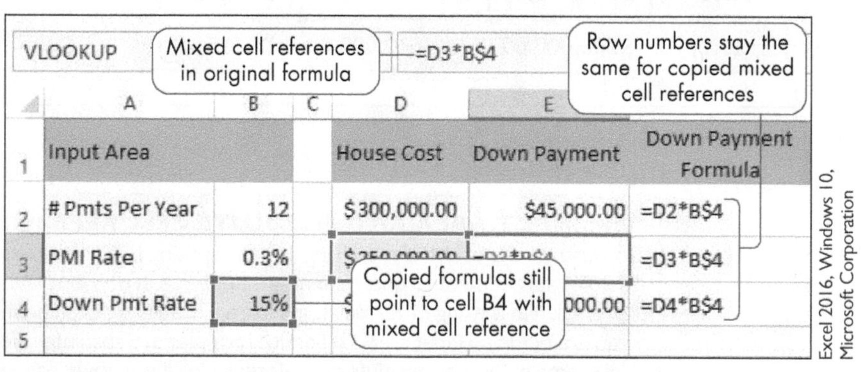

FIGURE 5 Relative and Mixed Cell References

TIP: THE F4 KEY

The F4 key toggles through relative, absolute, and mixed references. Click a cell reference within a formula on the Formula Bar and press F4 to change it. For example, click in B4 in the formula =D2*B4. Press F4 and the relative cell reference (B4) changes to an absolute cell reference ($B$4). Press F4 again and $B$4 becomes a mixed reference (B$4); press F4 again and it becomes another mixed reference ($B4). Press F4 a fourth time and the cell reference returns to the original relative reference (B4).

Quick Concepts

1. What happens when you copy a formula containing a relative cell reference one column to the right?
2. Why would you use an absolute reference in a formula?
3. What is the benefit of using a mixed reference?

Hands-On Exercises

Skills covered: Use a Relative Cell Reference • Use an Absolute Cell Reference • Use a Mixed Cell Reference

1 Formula Basics

Erica prepared a workbook containing data for five mortgages financed with the Townsend Mortgage Company. The data include house cost, down payment, mortgage rate, number of years to pay off the mortgage, and the financing date for each mortgage.

STEP 1 » USE A RELATIVE CELL REFERENCE

You will calculate the amount financed by each borrower by creating a formula with relative cell references that calculates the difference between the house cost and the down payment. After verifying the results of the amount financed by the first borrower, you will copy the formula down the Amount Financed column to calculate the other borrowers' amounts financed. Refer to Figure 6 as you complete Step 1.

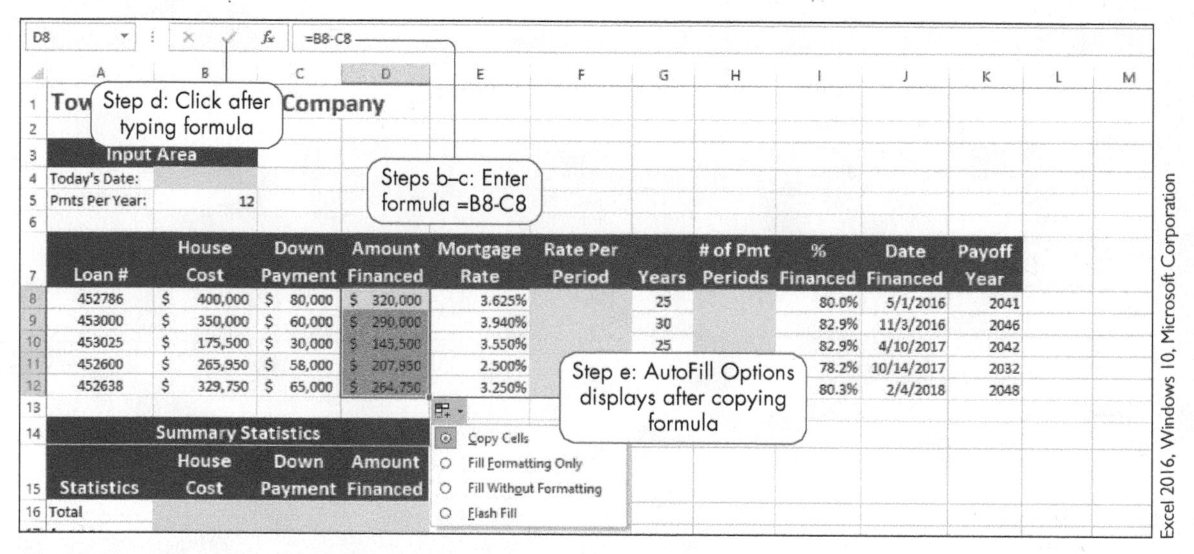

FIGURE 6 Formula Containing Relative Cell Reference Copied

a. Open *e02h1Loans* and save it as **e02h1Loans_LastFirst**.

> **TROUBLESHOOTING:** If you make any major mistakes in this exercise, you can close the file, open *e02h1Loans* again, and then start this exercise over.

The workbook contains two worksheets: Details (for Hands-On Exercises 1 and 2) and Payment Info (for Hands-On Exercise 3). You will enter formulas in the shaded cells.

b. Click **cell D8** in the Details sheet. Type = and click **cell B8**, the cell containing the first borrower's house cost.

c. Type - and click **cell C8**, the cell containing the down payment by the first borrower.

d. Click **Enter** ✓ (the check mark between the Name Box and Formula Bar) to complete the formula.

The first borrower financed (i.e., borrowed) $320,000, the difference between the cost ($400,000) and the down payment ($80,000).

e. Double-click the **cell D8 fill handle**.

You copied the formula down the Amount Financed column for each mortgage row.

f. Click **cell D9** and view the formula in the Formula Bar.

The formula in cell D8 is =B8-C8. The formula copied to cell D9 is =B9-C9. Because the original formula contained relative cell references, when you copy the formula down to the next row, the row numbers for the cell references change. Each result represents the amount financed for that particular borrower.

g. Press ↓ and look at the cell references in the Formula Bar to see how the references change for each formula you copied. Save the workbook with the new formula you created.

STEP 2 » USE AN ABSOLUTE CELL REFERENCE

Column E contains the mortgage rate for each loan. Because the borrowers will make monthly payments, you will modify the given annual interest rate (APR) to a monthly rate by dividing it by 12 (the number of payments in one year) for each borrower. Refer to Figure 7 as you complete Step 2.

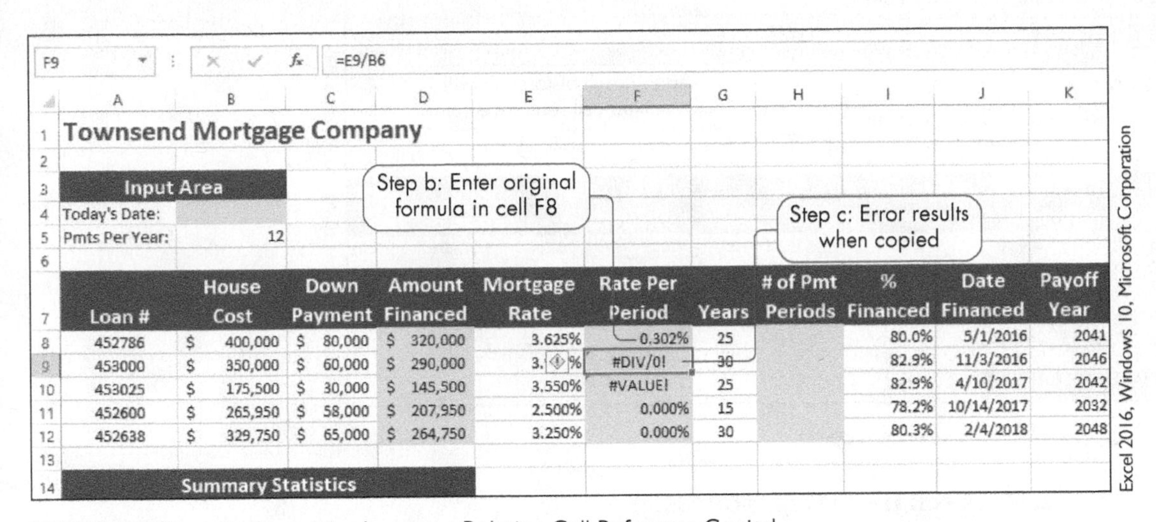

F9 =E9/B6

Townsend Mortgage Company

Input Area	
Today's Date:	
Pmts Per Year:	12

Loan #	House Cost	Down Payment	Amount Financed	Mortgage Rate	Rate Per Period	Years	# of Pmt Periods	% Financed	Date Financed	Payoff Year
452786	$ 400,000	$ 80,000	$ 320,000	3.625%	0.302%	25		80.0%	5/1/2016	2041
453000	$ 350,000	$ 60,000	$ 290,000	3.[illegible]%	#DIV/0!	30		82.9%	11/3/2016	2046
453025	$ 175,500	$ 30,000	$ 145,500	3.550%	#VALUE!	25		82.9%	4/10/2017	2042
452600	$ 265,950	$ 58,000	$ 207,950	2.500%	0.000%	15		78.2%	10/14/2017	2032
452638	$ 329,750	$ 65,000	$ 264,750	3.250%	0.000%	30		80.3%	2/4/2018	2048

Summary Statistics

FIGURE 7 Formula Containing Incorrect Relative Cell Reference Copied

a. Click **cell F8.**

You will create a formula to calculate the monthly interest rate for the first borrower.

b. Type **=E8/B5** and click **Enter** (the check mark between the Name Box and the Formula Bar).

Typically, you should avoid typing values directly in formulas. Therefore, you use a reference to cell B5, where the number of payments per year is placed in the input area, so that the company can change the payment period to bimonthly (24 payments per year) or quarterly (four payments per year) without adjusting the formula.

c. Double-click the **cell F8 fill handle**, click **cell F9**, and then view the results (see Figure 7).

An error icon displays to the left of cell F9, which displays #DIV/0!, and cell F10 displays #VALUE!. The original formula was =E8/B5. Because you copied the formula =E8/B5 down the column, the first copied formula is =E9/B6, and the second copied formula is =E10/B7. Although you want the mortgage rate cell reference (E8) to change (E9, E10, etc.) from row to row, you do not want the divisor (cell B5) to change. You need all formulas to divide by the value stored in cell B5, so you will edit the formula to make B5 an absolute reference.

d. Click **Undo** in the Quick Access Toolbar to undo the AutoFill process. With F8 as the active cell, click to the right of **B5** in the Formula Bar.

e. Press **F4** and click **Enter** (the check mark between the Name Box and the Formula Bar).

Excel changes the cell reference from B5 to $B$5, making it an absolute cell reference.

f. Double-click the fill handle to copy the formula down the Rate Per Period column. Click **cell F9** and view the formula in the Formula Bar.

   The formula in cell F9 is =E9/$B$5. The reference to E9 is relative and the reference to B5 is absolute. The results of all the calculations in the Rate Per Period column are now correct.

g. Save the workbook.

STEP 3 » USE A MIXED CELL REFERENCE

The next formula you create will calculate the total number of payment periods for each loan. Refer to Figure 8 as you complete Step 3.

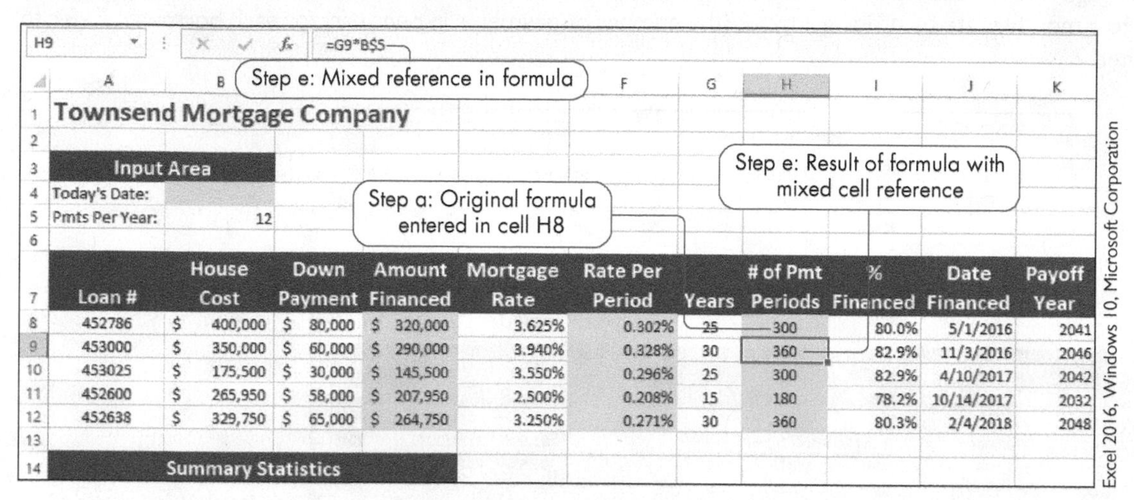

Loan #	House Cost	Down Payment	Amount Financed	Mortgage Rate	Rate Per Period	Years	# of Pmt Periods	% Financed	Date Financed	Payoff Year
452786	$ 400,000	$ 80,000	$ 320,000	3.625%	0.302%	25	300	80.0%	5/1/2016	2041
453000	$ 350,000	$ 60,000	$ 290,000	3.940%	0.328%	30	360	82.9%	11/3/2016	2046
453025	$ 175,500	$ 30,000	$ 145,500	3.550%	0.296%	25	300	82.9%	4/10/2017	2042
452600	$ 265,950	$ 58,000	$ 207,950	2.500%	0.208%	15	180	78.2%	10/14/2017	2032
452638	$ 329,750	$ 65,000	$ 264,750	3.250%	0.271%	30	360	80.3%	2/4/2018	2048

FIGURE 8 Formula Containing Mixed Cell Reference Copied

a. Click **cell H8** and type **=G8*B5**.

   You will multiply the number of years (25) by the number of payment periods in one year (12) using cell references.

b. Press **F4** to make the B5 cell reference absolute and click **Enter**.

   You want B5 to be absolute so that the cell reference remains B5 when you copy the formula. The product of 25 years and 12 months is 300 months or payment periods.

c. Copy the formula down the # of Pmt Periods column.

   The first copied formula is =G9*$B$5, and the result is 360. You want to see what happens if you change the absolute reference to a mixed reference and copy the formula again. Because you are copying down a column, the column letter B can be relative because it will not change either way, but the row number 5 must be absolute.

d. Ensure that cell H8 is the active cell and click **Undo** on the Quick Access Toolbar to undo the copied formulas.

e. Click within the **$B$5 cell reference** in the Formula Bar. Press **F4** to change the cell reference to a mixed cell reference: B$5. Press **Ctrl+Enter** and copy the formula down the # of Pmt Periods column. Click **cell H9**.

   The first copied formula is =G9*B$5 and the result is still 360. In this situation, using either an absolute reference or a mixed reference provides the same results.

f. Save the workbook. Keep the workbook open if you plan to continue with the next Hands-On Exercise. If not, close the workbook and exit Excel.

Function Basics

An Excel ***function*** is a predefined computation that simplifies creating a formula that performs a complex calculation. Excel contains more than 400 functions, which are organized into 14 categories. Table 1 lists and describes the primary function categories used in this chapter.

TABLE 1 Function Categories and Descriptions

Category	Description
Date & Time	Provides methods for manipulating date and time values.
Financial	Performs financial calculations, such as payments, rates, present value, and future value.
Logical	Performs logical tests and returns the value of the tests. Includes logical operators for combined tests, such as AND, OR, and NOT.
Lookup & Reference	Looks up values, creates links to cells, or provides references to cells in a worksheet.
Math & Trig	Performs standard math and trigonometry calculations.
Statistical	Performs common statistical calculations, such as averages and standard deviations.

When using functions, you must adhere to correct ***syntax***, the rules that dictate the structure and components required to perform the necessary calculations. Start a function with an equal sign, followed by the function name, and then its arguments enclosed in parentheses.

- The function name describes the purpose of the function. For example, the function name SUM indicates that the function sums, or adds, values.
- A function's ***arguments*** specify the inputs—such as cells, values, or arithmetic expressions—that are required to complete the operation. In some cases, a function requires multiple arguments separated by commas.

In this section, you will learn how to insert common functions using the keyboard and the Insert Function and Function Arguments dialog boxes.

Inserting a Function

To insert a function by typing, first type an equal sign, and then begin typing the function name. ***Formula AutoComplete*** displays a list of functions and defined names that match letters as you type a formula. For example, if you type =SU, Formula AutoComplete displays a list of functions and names that start with *SU* (see Figure 9). You can double-click the function name from the list or continue typing the function name. You can even point to a list item and see the ScreenTip describing the function.

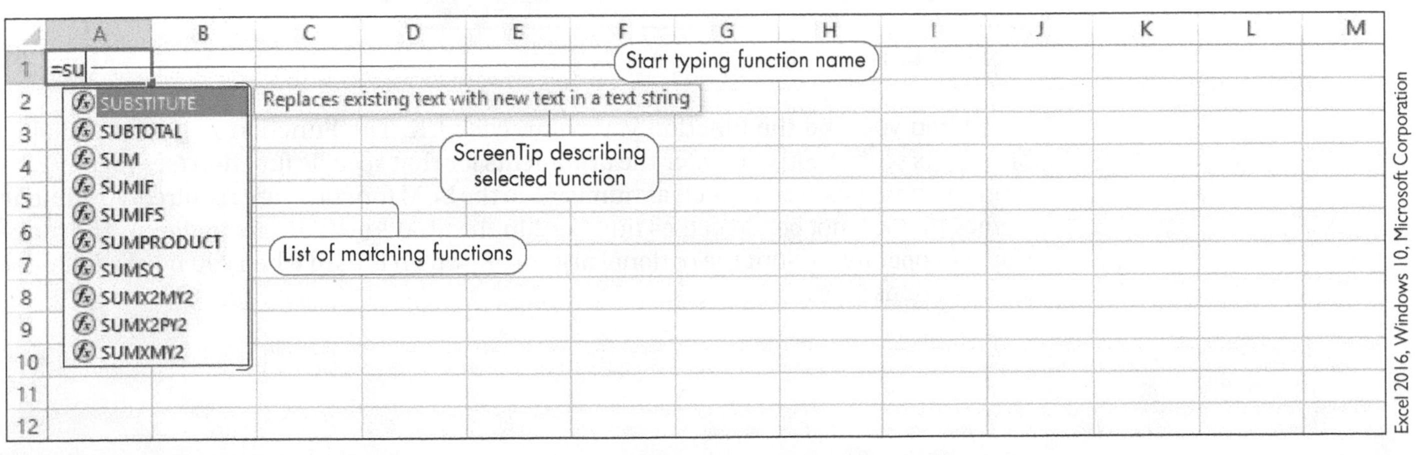

FIGURE 9 Formula AutoComplete

After you type the function name and opening parenthesis, Excel displays the ***function ScreenTip***, a small pop-up description that displays the function's arguments. The argument you are currently entering is bold in the function ScreenTip (see Figure 10). Square brackets indicate optional arguments. For example, the SUM function requires the number1 argument, but the number2 argument is optional. Click the argument name in the function ScreenTip to select the actual argument in the formula you are creating if you want to make changes to the argument.

	A	B	C	D	E	F	G	H	I	J
1	=SUM(									
2	SUM(**number1**, [number2], ...)									
3										

Excel 2016, Windows 10, Microsoft Corporation

FIGURE 10 Function ScreenTip

You can also use the Insert Function dialog box to search for a function, select a function category, and select a function from the list (see Figure 11). The dialog box is helpful if you want to browse a list of functions, especially if you are not sure of the function you need and want to see descriptions.

To display the Insert Function dialog box, click Insert Function *fx* (located between the Name Box and the Formula Bar) or click Insert Function in the Function Library group on the Formulas tab. From within the dialog box, select a function category, such as Most Recently Used, and select a function to display the syntax and a brief description of that function. Click *Help on this function* to display details about the selected function.

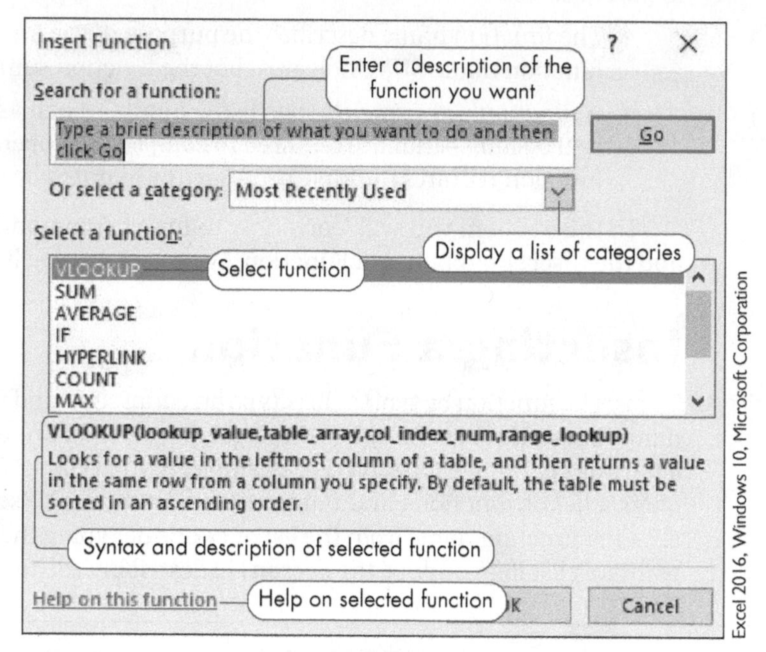

FIGURE 11 Insert Function Dialog Box

When you find the function you want, click OK. The Function Arguments dialog box opens so that you can enter the arguments for that specific function (see Figure 12). Argument names in bold (such as number1 in the SUM function) are required. Argument names that are not bold (such as number2 in the SUM function) are optional. The function can operate without the optional argument, which is used when you need additional specifications to calculate a result.

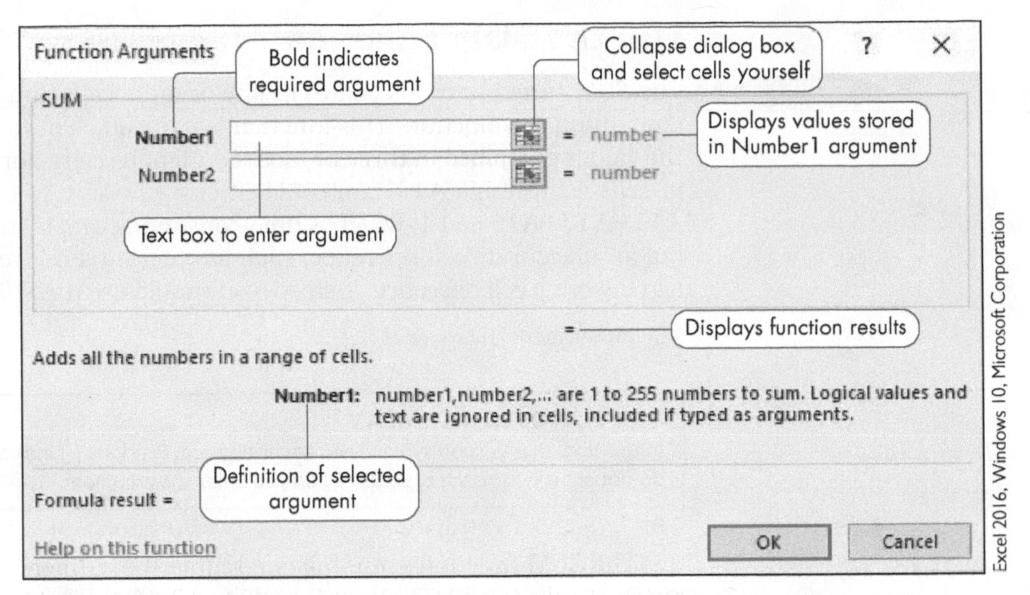

FIGURE 12 Function Arguments Dialog Box

Type the cell references in the argument boxes, or click a collapse button to the right side of an argument box to collapse the dialog box and select the cell or range of cells in the worksheet to designate as that argument. If you click the collapse button to select a range, you need to click the expand button to expand the dialog box again. You also have the ability to manually select the cells for the argument without clicking the collapse button. The collapse button is best used if the desired cells for the arguments view is obstructed. The value, or results, of a formula contained in the argument cell displays on the right side of the argument box (such as 5; 10; 15; 20; 25—the values stored in the range A1:A5 used for the number1 argument). If the argument is not valid, Excel displays an error description on the right side of the argument box.

The bottom of the Function Arguments dialog box displays a description of the function and a description of the argument containing the insertion point. As you enter arguments, the bottom of the dialog box also displays the results of the function, such as 75.

TIP: #NAME?

If you enter a function and #NAME? displays in the cell, you might have mistyped the function name. To avoid this problem, select the function name from the Formula AutoComplete list as you type the function name, or use the Insert Function dialog box. You can type a function name in lowercase letters. If you type the name correctly, Excel converts the name to all capital letters when you press Enter, indicating that you spelled the function name correctly.

Inserting Basic Math and Statistics Functions

Excel includes commonly used math and statistical functions that you can use for a variety of calculations. For example, you can insert functions to calculate the total amount you spend on dining out in a month, the average amount you spend per month purchasing music online, your highest electric bill, and your lowest time to run a mile this week. When using these functions, a change in the values within the ranges referenced will change the results of the function.

Use the SUM Function

STEP 1 The ***SUM function*** totals values in one or more cells and displays the result in the cell containing the function. This function is more efficient to create when you need to add the values contained in three or more contiguous cells. For example, to add the contents of cells A2 through A14, you could enter =A2+A3+A4+A5+A6+A7+A8+A9+A10+A11+A12+A13+A14, which is time-consuming and increases the probability of entering an inaccurate cell reference, such as entering a cell reference twice or accidentally leaving out a cell reference. Instead, you should use the SUM function, =SUM(A2:A14).

=SUM(number1, [number2],...)

> **TIP: FUNCTION SYNTAX**
> In this text, the function syntax lines are highlighted. Brackets [ ] indicate optional arguments; however, do not actually type the brackets when you enter the argument.

The SUM function contains one required argument (number1) that represents a range of cells to add. The range, such as A2:A14, specifies the first and last of an adjacent group of cells containing values to SUM. Excel will sum all cells within that range. The number2 optional argument is used when you want to sum values stored in nonadjacent cells or ranges, such as =SUM(A2:A14,F2:F14). The ellipsis in the function syntax indicates that you can add as many additional ranges as desired, separated by commas.

> **TIP: AVOIDING FUNCTIONS FOR BASIC FORMULAS**
> Do not use a function for a basic mathematical expression. For example, although =SUM(B4/C4) produces the same result as =B4/C4, the SUM function is not needed to perform the basic arithmetic division. Furthermore, someone taking a quick look at that formula might assume it performs addition instead of division. Use the most appropriate, clear-cut formula, =B4/C4.

To insert the SUM function (for example, to sum the values of a range), complete one of the following steps:

- Type =SUM(type the range), and press Enter.
- Type =SUM(drag to select the range, then type the closing) and press Enter.
- Click a cell, click Sum [Σ AutoSum ▾] in the Editing group on the Home tab, press Enter to select the suggested range (or drag to select a range), and then press Enter.
- Click in a cell, click AutoSum in the Function Library group on the Formulas tab, either press Enter to select the suggested range or type the range, and then press Enter.
- Click the cell directly underneath the range you would like to SUM and press Alt=.

Figure 13 shows the result of using the SUM function in cell D2 to total scores (898).

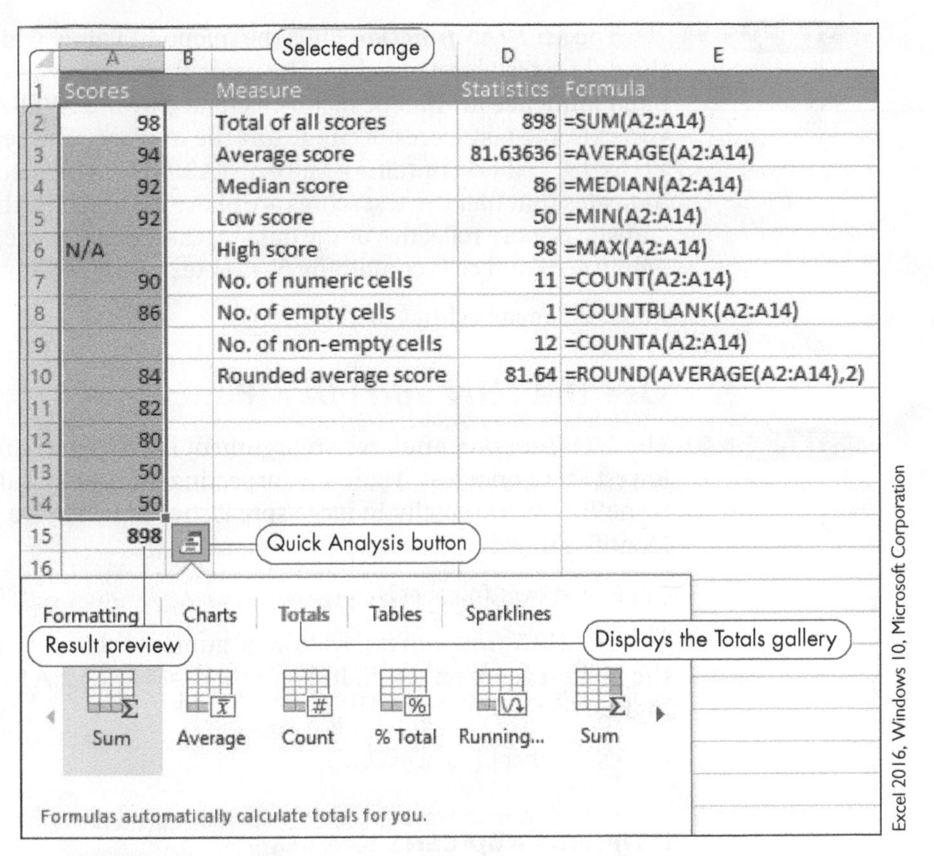

FIGURE 13 Function Results

> **TIP: SUM ARROW**
> If you click Sum in the Editing group on the Home tab or in the Function Library group on the Formulas tab, Excel inserts the SUM function. However, if you click the Sum arrow, Excel displays a list of basic functions to select: Sum, Average, Count Numbers, Max, and Min. If you want to insert another function, select More Functions from the list.

> **TIP: NEST FUNCTIONS AS ARGUMENTS**
> A *nested function* occurs when one function is embedded as an argument within another function. Each function has its own set of arguments that must be included. For example, cell D10 in Figure 13 contains =ROUND(AVERAGE(A2:A14),2). The ROUND function requires two arguments: number (the number to be rounded) and num_digits (the number of decimals to which the number is to be rounded).
>
> The AVERAGE function is used to create the number to be rounded, and is nested in the number argument of the ROUND function. AVERAGE(A2:A14) returns 81.63636. That value is then rounded to two decimal places, indicated by 2 in the num_digits argument. The result is 81.64. If you change the second argument from 2 to 0, such as =ROUND(AVERAGE (A2:A14),0), the result would be 82.

Use the AVERAGE and MEDIAN Functions

STEP 2 People often describe data based on central tendency, which means that values tend to cluster around a central value. Excel provides two functions to calculate central tendency: AVERAGE and MEDIAN. The ***AVERAGE function*** calculates the arithmetic mean, or average, for the values in a range of cells. You can use this function to calculate the class average on a biology test or the average number of points scored per game by a basketball player. In Figure 13, =AVERAGE(A2:A14) in cell D3 returns 81.63636 as the average test score. The AVERAGE function ignores empty cells and cells containing N/A or text.

=AVERAGE (number1,[number2],...)

STEP 3 » The ***MEDIAN function*** finds the midpoint value, which is the value that one half of the data set is above or below. The median is particularly useful because extreme values often influence arithmetic mean calculated by the AVERAGE function. In Figure 13, the two extreme test scores of 50 distort the average. The rest of the test scores range from 80 to 98. Cell D4 contains =MEDIAN(A2:A14). The median for test scores is 86, which indicates that half the test scores are above 86 and half the test scores are below 86. This statistic is more reflective of the data set than the average. The MEDIAN function ignores empty cells and cells containing N/A or text.

=MEDIAN(number1,[number2],...)

Use the MIN and MAX Functions

STEP 4 » The ***MIN function*** analyzes an argument list to determine the lowest value, such as the lowest score on a test. Manually inspecting a range of values to identify the lowest value is inefficient, especially in large spreadsheets. In Figure 13, =MIN(A2:A14) in cell D5 identifies that 50 is the lowest test score.

=MIN(number1,[number2],...)

The ***MAX function*** analyzes an argument list to determine the highest value, such as the highest score on a test. In Figure 13, =MAX(A2:A14) in cell D6 identifies 98 as the highest test score.

=MAX(number1,[number2],...)

TIP: NONADJACENT RANGES

In most basic aggregate functions such as SUM, MIN, MAX, and AVERAGE, you can use multiple ranges as arguments, such as finding the largest number within two nonadjacent (nonconsecutive) ranges. For example, you can find the highest test score where some scores are stored in cells A2:A14 and others are stored in cells K2:K14. Separate each range with a comma in the argument list, so that the formula is =MAX(A2:A14,K2:K14).

Use the COUNT Functions

Excel provides three basic count functions—COUNT, COUNTBLANK, and COUNTA—to count the cells in a range that meet a particular criterion. The ***COUNT function*** tallies the number of cells in a range that contain values you can use in calculations, such as numerical and date data, but excludes blank cells or text entries from the tally. In Figure 13, the selected range spans 13 cells; however, =COUNT(A2:A14) in cell D7 returns 11, the number of cells that contain numerical data. It does not count the cell containing the text *N/A* or the blank cell.

The ***COUNTBLANK function*** tallies the number of cells in a range that are blank. In Figure 13, =COUNTBLANK(A2:A14) in cell D8 identifies that one cell in the range A2:A14 is blank. The ***COUNTA function*** tallies the number of cells in a range that are not blank, that is, cells that contain data, whether a value, text, or a formula. In Figure 13, =COUNTA(A2:A14) in cell D9 returns 12, indicating that the range A2:A14 contains 12 cells that contain some form of data. It does not count the blank cell; however, it will count cells that contain text such as cell A6.

=COUNT(value1,[value2],...)

=COUNTBLANK(range)

=COUNTA(value1,[value2],...)

TIP: STATUS BAR STATISTICS: AVERAGE, COUNT, AND SUM

When you select a range of cells containing values, by default Excel displays the average, count, and sum of those values on the status bar. You can customize the status bar to show other selection statistics, such as the minimum and maximum values for a selected range. To display or hide particular selection statistics, right-click the status bar and select the statistic.

Perform Calculations with Quick Analysis Tools

Quick Analysis is a set of analytical tools you can use to apply formatting, create charts or tables, and insert basic functions. When you select a range of data, the Quick Analysis button displays adjacent to the bottom-right corner of the selected range. Click the Quick Analysis button to display the Quick Analysis gallery and select the analytical tool to meet your needs.

Figure 13 shows the Totals gallery options so that you can sum, average, or count the values in the selected range. Select % Total to display the percentage of the grand total of two or more columns. Select Running Total to provide a cumulative total at the bottom of multiple columns. Additional options can be seen by clicking the right expansion arrow.

TIP: ROUND VERSUS DECREASE DECIMAL POINTS

When you click Decrease Decimal in the Number group to display fewer or no digits after a decimal point, Excel still stores the original value's decimal places so that those digits can be used in calculations. The ROUND function changes the stored value to a specified number of decimal places.

Using Date Functions

In order to maximize the use of dates and date functions in Excel, it is important to understand how they are handled in the program. Excel assigns serial numbers to dates. The date January 1, 1900 is the equivalent to the number 1. The number 2 is the equivalent of January 2, 1900 and so on. Basically, Excel adds 1 to every serial number as each day passes. Therefore the newer the date, the bigger the equivalent serial number. For example, assume today is January 1, 2018, and you graduate on May 6, 2018. To determine how many days until graduation, subtract today's date from the graduation date. Excel uses the serial numbers for these dates (43101 and 43226) to calculate the difference of 125 days.

Insert the TODAY Function

STEP 5 »» The ***TODAY function*** displays the current date in a cell. Excel updates the TODAY function results when you open or print the workbook. The TODAY() function does not require arguments, but you must include the parentheses. If you omit the parentheses, Excel displays #NAME? in the cell with a green triangle in the top-left corner of the cell. When you click the cell, an error icon appears that you can click for more information.

=TODAY()

Insert the NOW Function

The ***NOW function*** uses the computer's clock to display the current date and military time that you last opened the workbook. (Military time expresses time on a 24-hour period where 1:00 is 1 a.m. and 13:00 is 1 p.m.) The date and time will change every time the workbook is opened. Like the TODAY function, the NOW function does not require arguments, but you must include the parentheses. Omitting the parentheses creates a #NAME? error.

=NOW()

> **TIP: UPDATE THE DATE AND TIME**
> Both the TODAY and NOW functions display the date/time the workbook was last opened or last calculated. These functions do not continuously update the date and time while the workbook is open. To update the date and time, press F9 or click the Formulas tab and click *Calculate Now* in the Calculation group.

Quick Concepts

4. What visual features help guide you through typing a function directly in a cell?
5. What type of data do you enter in a Function Arguments dialog box, and what are four things the dialog box tells you?
6. What is the difference between the AVERAGE and MEDIAN functions?
7. What is a nested function, and why would you create one?

Hands-On Exercises

Skills covered: Insert a Function • Insert a Function Using Formula AutoComplete • Use the Insert Function Dialog Box • Use the SUM Function • Use the AVERAGE and MEDIAN Functions • Use the MIN and MAX Functions • Use the COUNT Functions • Use the TODAY Function

2 Function Basics

The Townsend Mortgage Company worksheet contains an area in which you will enter summary statistics. In addition, you will include the current date.

STEP 1 » USE THE SUM FUNCTION

The first summary statistic you calculate is the total value of the houses bought by the borrowers. You will use the SUM function. Refer to Figure 14 as you complete Step 1.

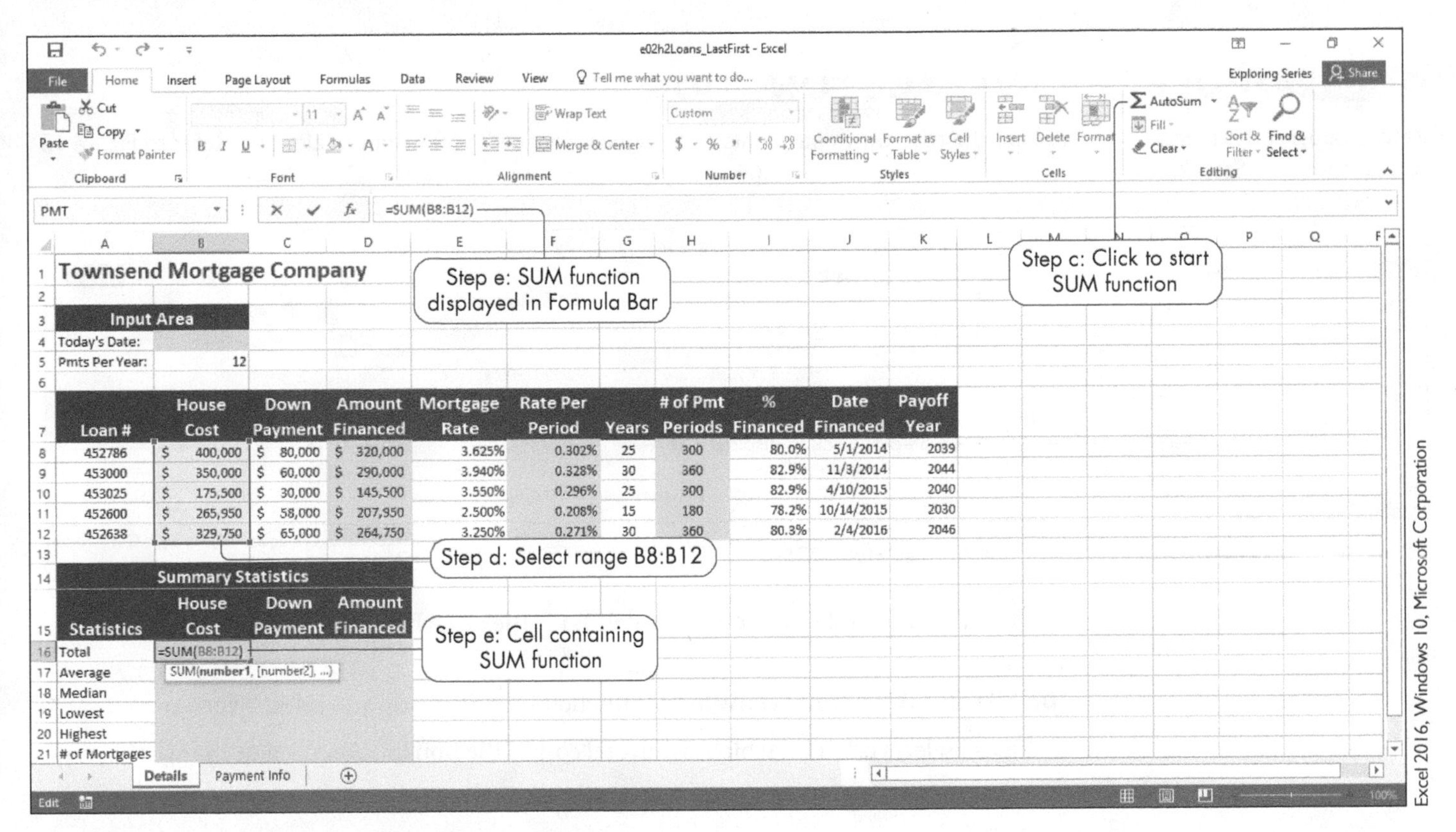

FIGURE 14 SUM Function Calculates Total House Cost

a. Open *e02h1Loans_LastFirst* if you closed it at the end of Hands-On Exercise 1 and save it as **e02h2Loans_LastFirst**, changing h1 to h2.

b. Ensure that the Details worksheet is active and click **cell B16**, the cell where you will enter a formula for the total house cost.

c. Click **AutoSum** [Σ AutoSum] in the Editing group on the Home tab.

   Excel anticipates the range of cells containing values you want to sum based on where you enter the formula—in this case, A8:D15. This is not the correct range, so you must enter the correct range.

> **TROUBLESHOOTING:** AutoSum, like some other commands in Excel, contains two parts: the main command button and an arrow. Click the main command button when instructed to click Sum to perform the default action. Click the arrow when instructed to click the Sum arrow for additional options. If you accidentally clicked the arrow instead of Sum, press Esc to cancel the SUM function from being completed and try Step c again.

d. Select the **range B8:B12**, the cells containing house costs.

As you use the semi-selection process, Excel enters the range in the SUM function.

> **TROUBLESHOOTING:** If you entered the function without changing the arguments, repeat Steps b–d or edit the arguments in the Formula Bar by deleting the default range, typing B8:B12 between the parentheses and pressing Enter.

e. Click **Enter**.

Cell B16 contains the function = SUM(B8:B12), and the result is $1,521,200.

f. Save the workbook.

STEP 2 » USE THE AVERAGE FUNCTION

Before copying the functions to calculate the total down payments and amounts financed, you want to calculate. Refer to Figure 15 as you complete Step 2.

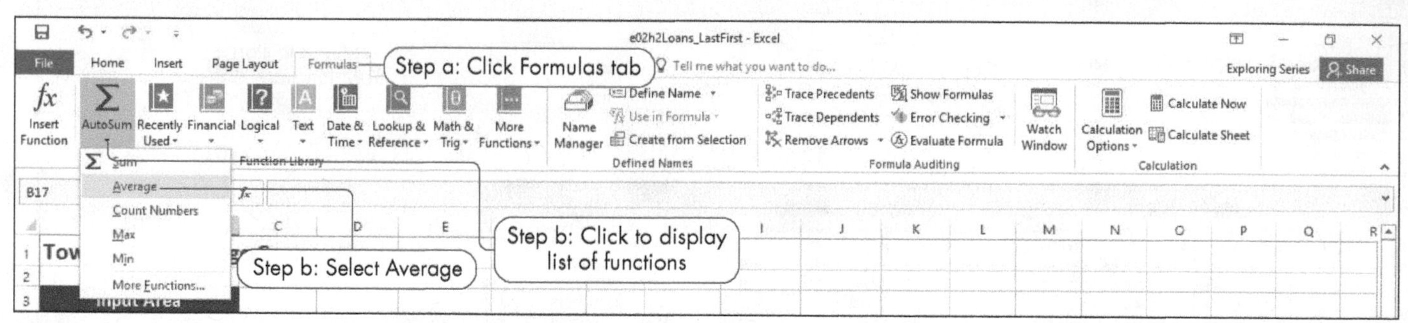

FIGURE 15 AVERAGE Function Calculates Average House Cost

a. Click the **Formulas tab** and click **cell B17**, the cell where you will display the average cost of the houses.

b. Click the **AutoSum arrow** in the Function Library group and select **Average**.

Excel selects cell B16, which is the total cost of the houses. You need to change the range.

c. Select the **range B8:B12**, the cells containing the house costs.

The function is =AVERAGE(B8:B12).

d. Press **Enter**, making cell B18 the active cell.

The average house cost is $304,240.

e. Save the workbook.

STEP 3 ›› USE THE MEDIAN FUNCTION

You realize that extreme house costs may distort the average. Therefore, you decide to identify the median house cost to compare it to the average house cost. Refer to Figure 16 as you complete Step 3.

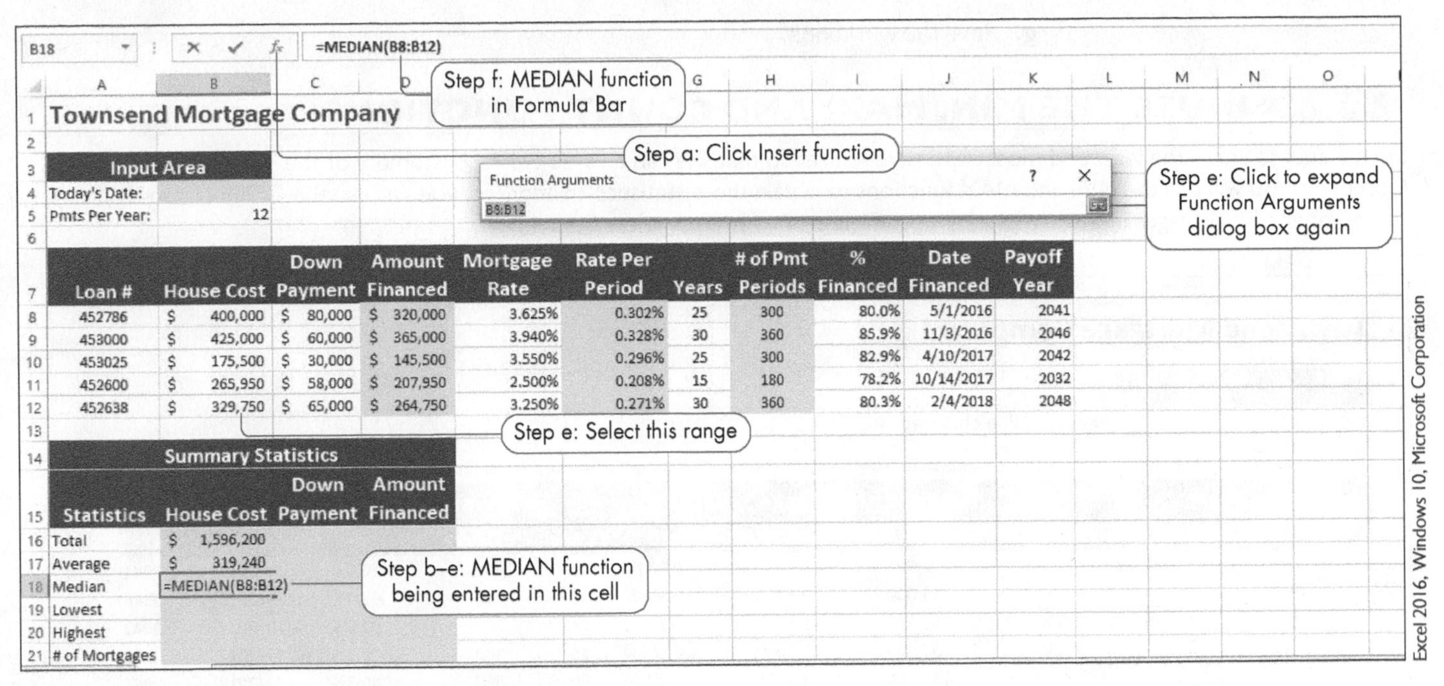

Loan #	House Cost	Down Payment	Amount Financed	Mortgage Rate	Rate Per Period	Years	# of Pmt Periods	% Financed	Date Financed	Payoff Year
452786	$ 400,000	$ 80,000	$ 320,000	3.625%	0.302%	25	300	80.0%	5/1/2016	2041
453000	$ 425,000	$ 60,000	$ 365,000	3.940%	0.328%	30	360	85.9%	11/3/2016	2046
453025	$ 175,500	$ 30,000	$ 145,500	3.550%	0.296%	25	300	82.9%	4/10/2017	2042
452600	$ 265,950	$ 58,000	$ 207,950	2.500%	0.208%	15	180	78.2%	10/14/2017	2032
452638	$ 329,750	$ 65,000	$ 264,750	3.250%	0.271%	30	360	80.3%	2/4/2018	2048

Summary Statistics			
Statistics	House Cost	Down Payment	Amount Financed
Total	$ 1,596,200		
Average	$ 319,240		
Median	=MEDIAN(B8:B12)		
Lowest			
Highest			
# of Mortgages			

FIGURE 16 MEDIAN Function Calculates the Median House Cost

a. Ensure that cell B18 is the active cell. Click **Insert Function** between the Name Box and the Formula Bar, or in the Function Library group on the Formulas tab.

The Insert Function dialog box opens. Use this dialog box to select the MEDIAN function because it is not available on the Ribbon.

b. Type **median** in the *Search for a function box* and click **Go**.

Excel displays a list of functions in the *Select a function* list. The MEDIAN function is selected at the top of the list; the bottom of the dialog box displays the syntax and the description.

c. Read the MEDIAN function description and click **OK**.

The Function Arguments dialog box opens. It contains one required argument, Number1, representing a range of cells containing values. It has an optional argument, Number2, which you can use if you have nonadjacent ranges that contain values.

d. Click **Collapse Dialog Box** to the right of the Number1 box.

You collapsed the Function Arguments dialog box so that you can select the range.

e. Select the **range B8:B12** and click **Expand Dialog Box** in the Function Arguments dialog box.

The Function Arguments dialog box expands, displaying B8:B12 in the Number1 box.

f. Click **OK** to accept the function arguments and close the dialog box.

Half of the houses purchased cost more than the median, $329,750, and half of the houses cost less than this value. Notice the difference between the median and the average: The average is lower because it is affected by the lowest-priced house, $175,500.

g. Save the workbook.

STEP 4 » USE THE MIN, MAX, AND COUNT FUNCTIONS

Erica wants to know the least and most expensive houses so that she can analyze typical customers of the Townsend Mortgage Company. You will use the MIN and MAX functions to obtain these statistics. In addition, you will use the COUNT function to tally the number of mortgages in the sample. Refer to Figure 17 as you complete Step 4.

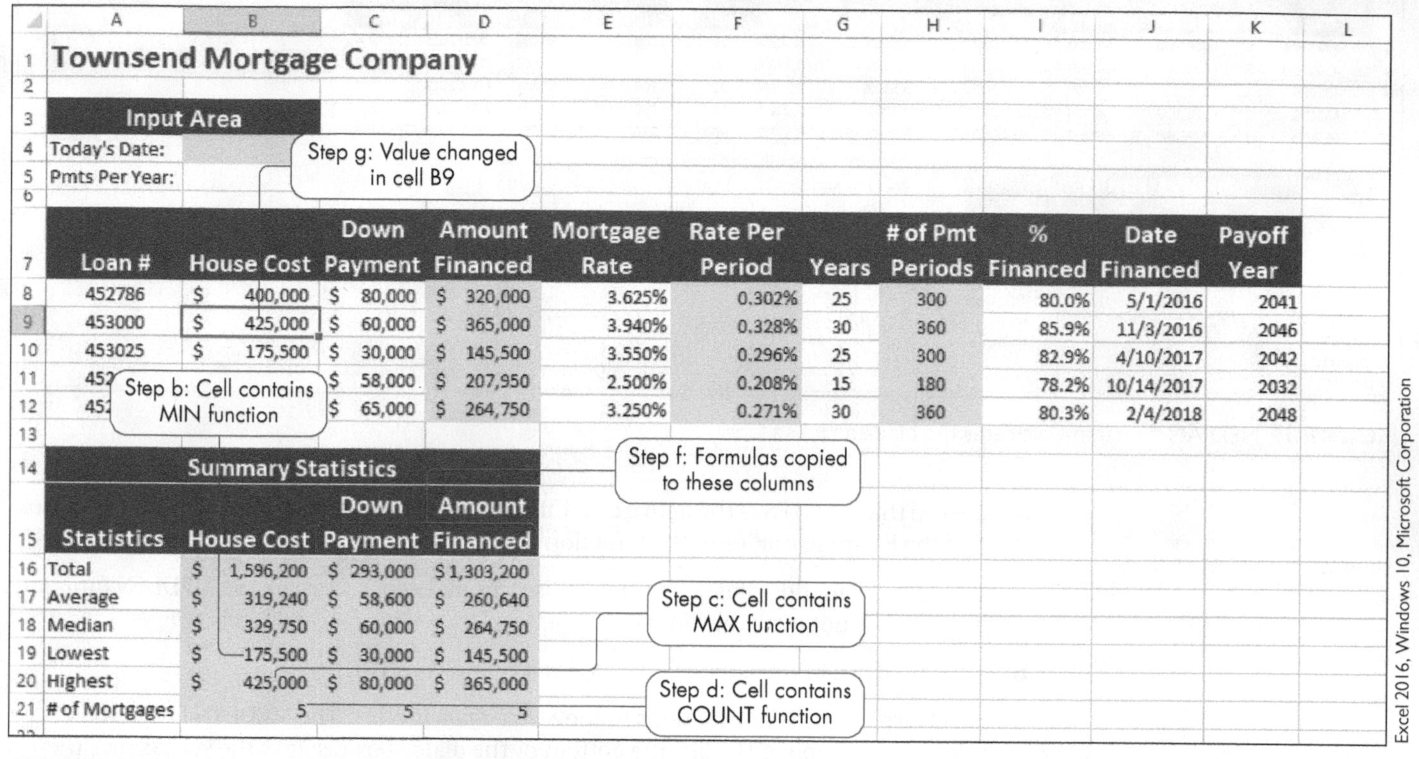

FIGURE 17 MIN, MAX, and COUNT Function Results

a. Click **cell B19**, the cell to display the cost of the lowest-costing house.

b. Click the **AutoSum arrow** in the Function Library group, select **MIN**, select the **range B8:B12**, and then press **Enter**.

The MIN function identifies that the lowest-costing house is $175,500.

c. Click **cell B20**. Click the **AutoSum arrow** in the Function Library group, select **MAX**, select the **range B8:B12**, and then press **Enter**.

The MAX function identifies that the highest-costing house is $400,000.

d. Click **cell B21**. Type **=COUNT(B8:B12)** and press **Enter**.

As you type the letter C, Formula AutoComplete suggests functions starting with C. As you continue typing, the list of functions narrows. After you type the beginning parenthesis, Excel displays the function ScreenTip, indicating the arguments for the function. The range B8:B12 contains five cells.

e. Select the **range B16:B21**.

You want to select the range of original statistics to copy the cells all at one time to the next two columns.

f. Drag the fill handle to the right by two columns to copy to the range C16:D21. Click **cell D21**.

Because you used relative cell references in the functions, the range in the function changes from =COUNT(B8:B12) to =COUNT(D8:D12).

g. Click **cell B9** and, change the cell value to **425000**, and click **Enter**.

The results of all formulas and functions change, including the total, average, and max house costs.

h. Save the workbook.

STEP 5 » USE THE TODAY FUNCTION

Before finalizing the worksheet you will insert the current date. You will use the TODAY function to display the current date. Refer to Figure 18 as you complete Step 5.

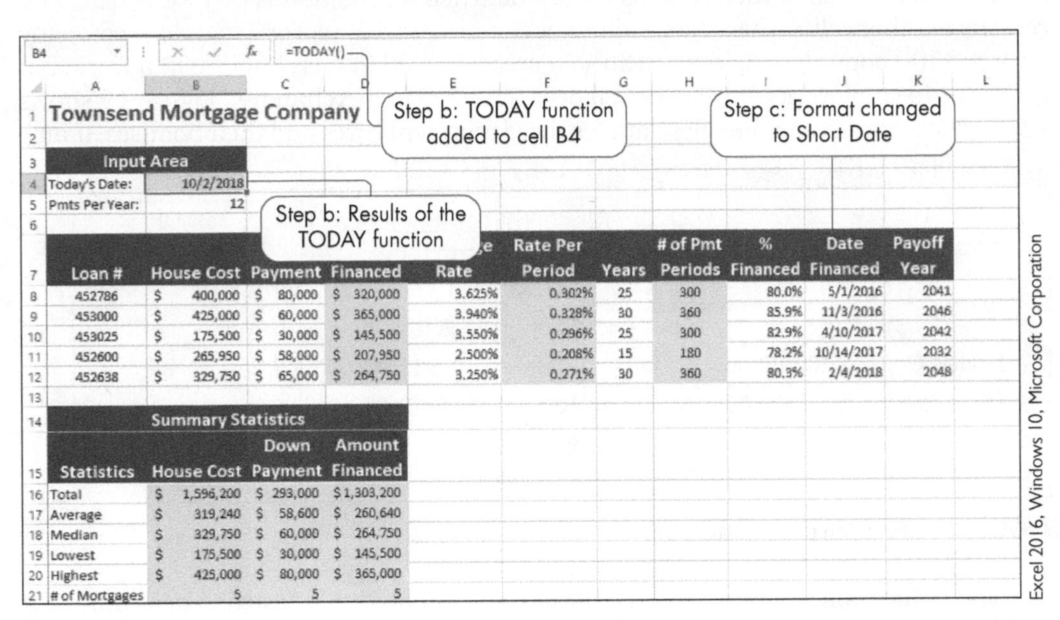

FIGURE 18 Insert the Current Date with the TODAY Function

a. Click **cell B4**, the cell to contain the current date.

b. Click **Date & Time** in the Function Library group, select **TODAY** to display the Function Arguments dialog box, and then click **OK** to close the dialog box.

The Function Arguments dialog box opens, although no arguments are necessary for this function. Excel displays TODAY() in the Edit formula bar, and inserts the current date in Short Date format, such as 6/1/2018, based on the computer system's date.

c. Click the **Format arrow** from the Cells group and select **AutoFit Column Width**.

d. Save the workbook. Keep the workbook open if you plan to continue with the next Hands-On Exercise. If not, close the workbook and exit Excel.

Logical, Lookup, and Financial Functions

As you prepare complex spreadsheets using functions, you will frequently use three function categories: logical, lookup and reference, and finance. Logical functions test the logic of a situation and return a particular result. Lookup and reference functions are useful when you need to look up a value in a list to identify the applicable value. Financial functions are useful to anyone who plans to take out a loan or invest money.

In this section, you will learn how to use the logical, lookup, and financial functions.

Determining Results with the IF Function

STEP 3 ›› The most common logical function is the ***IF function***, which tests specified criteria to see if it is true or false, then returns one value when a condition is met, or is true, and returns another value when the condition is not met, or is false. For example, a company gives a $500 bonus to employees who sold *over* $10,000 in merchandise in a week, but no bonus to employees who did not sell over $10,000 in merchandise. Figure 19 shows a worksheet containing the sales data for three representatives and their bonuses, if any.

F2 =IF(E2>B$2,B$3,0)

	A	B	C	D	E	F	G
1	Input Are			Sales Rep Sales		Bonus	
2	Sales Goal	$10,000.00		Tiffany	$11,000.00	$500.00	
3	Bonus	$ 500.00		Jose	$10,000.00	$ -	
4				Rex	$ 9,000.00	$ -	
5							

Condition to be tested

Result if condition is true

Result if condition is false

Excel 2016, Windows 10, Microsoft Corporation

FIGURE 19 Function to Calculate Bonus

The IF function has three arguments: (1) a condition that is tested to determine if it is either true or false, (2) the resulting value if the condition is true, and (3) the resulting value if the condition is false.

=IF(logical_test,[value_if_true],[value_if_false])

You might find it helpful to create two flowcharts to illustrate an IF function. First, construct a flowchart that uses words and numbers to illustrate the condition and results. For example, the left flowchart in Figure 20 illustrates the condition to see if sales are greater than $10,000, and the $500 bonus if the condition is true or $0 if the condition is false. Then, create a second flowchart—similar to the one on the right side of Figure 20—that replaces the words and values with actual cell references. Creating these flowcharts can help you construct the IF function that is used in cell F2 in Figure 19.

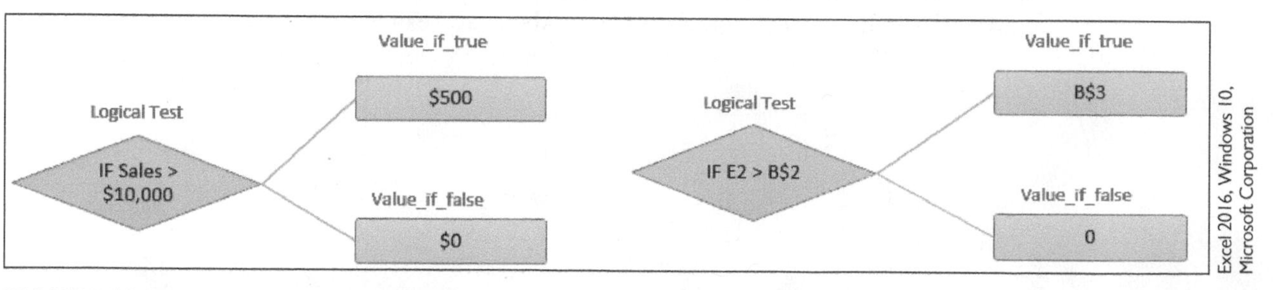

FIGURE 20 Flowcharts Illustrating IF Function

Design the Logical Test

The first argument for the IF function is the logical test. The ***logical test*** contains either a value or an expression that evaluates to true or false. The logical test requires a comparison between at least two variables, such as the values stored in cells E2 and B2. In this example a salesperson receives a bonus IF he or she sells more than the $10,000 quota. The variable of total sales is in cell E2 and the constant of the sales quota is in cell B2. Therefore the logical test IF E2 > B2 translates into the following: if the amount of sales generated is greater than $10,000. Table 2 lists and describes in more detail the logical operators to make the comparison in the logical test.

In Figure 19, cell F2 contains an IF function where the logical test is E2>$B$2 to determine if Tiffany's sales in cell E2 are greater than the sales goal in cell B2. Copying the function down the column will compare each sales representative's sales with the $10,000 value in cell B2.

TABLE 2 Logical Operators

Operator	Description
=	Equal to
<>	Not equal to
<	Less than
>	Greater than
<=	Less than or equal to
>=	Greater than or equal to

Design the Value_If_True and Value_If_False Arguments

The second and third arguments of an IF function are value_if_true and value_if_false. When Excel evaluates the logical test, the result is either true or false. If the logical test is true, the value_if_true argument executes. If the logical test is false, the value_if_false argument executes. Only one of the last two arguments is executed; both arguments cannot be executed, because the logical test is either true or false but not both.

The value_if_true and value_if_false arguments can contain text, cell references, formulas, or constants. In Figure 19, cell F2 contains an IF function in which the value_if_true argument is B$3 and the value_if_false argument is 0. Because the logical test (E2>B$2) is true—that is, Tiffany's sales of $11,000 are greater than the $10,000 goal—the value_if_true argument is executed, and the result displays $500, the value that is stored in cell B3.

Jose's sales of $10,000 are *not* greater than $10,000, and Rex's sales of $9,000 are *not* greater than $10,000. Therefore, the value_if_false argument is executed and returns no bonus in cells F3 and F4.

> **TIP: AT LEAST TWO POSSIBLE RIGHT ANSWERS**
> Every IF function can have at least two right solutions to produce the same results. Since the logical test is a comparative expression, it can be written two ways. For example, comparing whether E2 is greater than B2 can be written using greater than (E2>B2) or the reverse can also be compared to see if B2 is less than E2 (B2<E2). Depending on the logical test, the value if true and value if false arguments will switch.

Figure 21 illustrates several IF functions, how they are evaluated, and their results. The input area contains values that are used in the logical tests and results. You can create this worksheet with the input area and IF functions to develop your understanding of how IF functions work.

	A	B	C
1	Input Values		
2	$ 1,000.00		
3	$ 2,000.00		
4	10%		
5	5%		
6	$ 250.00		
7			
8	IF Function	Evaluation	Result
9	=IF(A2=A3,A4,A5)	$1,000 is equal to $2,000: FALSE	5%
10	=IF(A2<A3,A4,A5)	$1,000 is less than $2,000: TRUE	10%
11	=IF(A2<>A3,"Not Equal","Equal")	$1,000 and $2,000 are not equal: TRUE	Not Equal
12	=IF(A2>A3,A2*A4,A2*A5)	$1,000 is greater than $2,000: FALSE	$ 50.00
13	=IF(A2>A3,A2*A4,MAX(A2*A5,A6))	$1,000 is greater than $2,000: FALSE	$ 250.00
14	=IF(A2*A4=A3*A5,A6,0)	$100 (A2*A4) is equal to $100 (A3*A5): TRUE	$ 250.00

Excel 2016, Windows 10, Microsoft Corporation

FIGURE 21 Sample IF Functions

- **Cell A9.** The logical test A2=A3 compares the values in cells A2 and A3 to see if they are equal. Because $1,000 is not equal to $2,000, the logical test is false. The value_if_false argument is executed, which displays 5%, the value stored in cell A5.
- **Cell A10.** The logical test A2<A3 determines if the value in cell A2 is less than the value in A3. Because $1,000 is less than $2,000, the logical test is true. The value_if_true argument is executed, which displays the value stored in cell A4, which is 10%.
- **Cell A11.** The logical test A2<>A3 determines if the values in cells A2 and A3 are not equal. Because $1,000 and $2,000 are not equal, the logical test is true. The value_if_true argument is executed, which displays the text Not Equal.
- **Cell A12.** The logical test A2>A3 is false. The value_if_false argument is executed, which multiplies the value in cell A2 ($1,000) by the value in cell A5 (5%) and displays $50. The parentheses in the value_if_true (A2*A4) and value_if_false (A2*A5) arguments are optional. They are not required but may help you read the function arguments better.
- **Cell A13.** The logical test A2>A3 is false. The value_if_false argument, which contains a nested MAX function, is executed. The MAX function, MAX(A2*A5,A6), multiplies the values in cells A2 ($1,000) and A5 (5%) and returns the higher of the product ($50) and the value stored in cell A6 ($250).
- **Cell A14.** The logical test A2*A4=A3*A5 is true. The contents of cell A2 ($1,000) are multiplied by the contents of cell A4 (10%) for a result of $100. That result is then compared to the result of A3*A5, which is also $100. Because the logical test is true, the function returns the value of cell A6 ($250).

TIP: TEXT AND NESTED FUNCTIONS IN IF FUNCTIONS

You can use text within a formula. For example, you can build a logical test comparing the contents of cell A1 to specific text, such as A1="Input Values". The IF function in cell A11 in Figure 21 uses "Not Equal" and "Equal" in the value_if_true and value_if_false arguments. When you use text in a formula or function, you must enclose the text in quotation marks. However, do not use quotation marks around formulas, cell references, or values. You can also nest functions in the logical test, value_if_true, and value_if_false arguments of the IF function. When you nest functions as arguments, make sure the nested function contains the required arguments for it to work and that you nest the function in the correct argument to calculate accurate results. For example, cell C13 in Figure 21 contains a nested MAX function in the value_if_false argument.

Using Lookup Functions

You can use lookup and reference functions to quickly find data associated with a specified value. For example, when you order merchandise on a website, the webserver looks up the shipping costs based on weight and distance; or at the end of a semester, your professor uses your average, such as 88%, to look up the letter grade to assign, such as B+. There are numerous lookup functions in Excel, including HLOOKUP, INDEX, LOOKUP, MATCH, and VLOOKUP. Each lookup function can be used to identify and return information based, in part, on how the data is organized.

Use the VLOOKUP function

STEP 1 The ***VLOOKUP function*** accepts a value and looks for the value in the left column of a specified table array and returns another value located in the same row from a specified column. Use VLOOKUP to search for exact matches or for the nearest value that is less than or equal to the search value, such as assigning a B grade for a class average between 80% and 89%. The VLOOKUP function has the following three required arguments and one optional argument: (1) lookup_value, (2) table_array, (3) col_index_num, and (4) range_lookup.

```
=VLOOKUP(lookup_value,table_array,col_index_num,[range_lookup])
```

Figure 22 shows a partial grade book that contains a vertical lookup table, as well as the final scores and letter grades. The function in cell F3 is =VLOOKUP(E3,$A$3:$B$7,2).

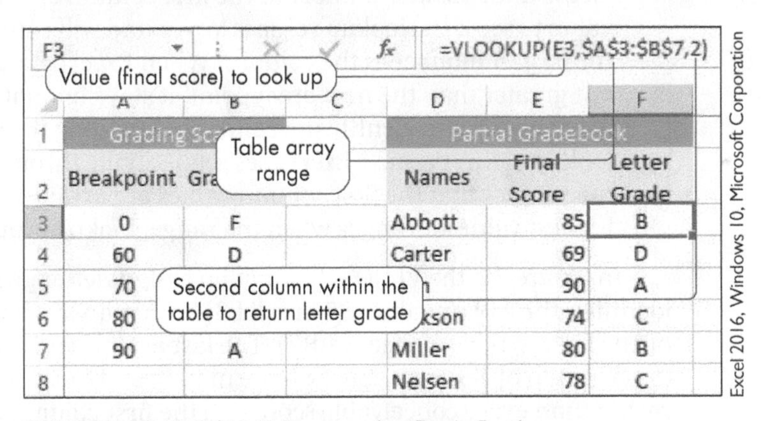

FIGURE 22 VLOOKUP Function for Grade Book

The ***lookup value*** is the cell reference of the cell that contains the value to look up. The lookup value for the first student is cell E3, which contains 85. The ***table array*** is the range that contains the lookup table: $A$3:$B$7. The table array range must be absolute, the value you want to look up must be located in the first column, and cannot include column labels for the lookup table. The ***column index number*** is the column number in the lookup table that contains the return values. In this example, the column index number is 2, which corresponds to the letter grades in column B.

> **TIP: USING VALUES IN FORMULAS**
>
> You know to avoid using values in formulas because the input values in a worksheet cell might change. However, as shown in Figure 22, the value 2 is used in the col_index_number argument of the VLOOKUP function. The 2 refers to a particular column within the lookup table and is an acceptable use of a number within a formula.

The last argument in the VLOOKUP function is the optional ***range_lookup***. This argument determines how the VLOOKUP function handles lookup values that are not an exact match for the data in the lookup table. By default, the range_lookup is set to TRUE, which is appropriate to look up values in a range. Omitting the optional argument or typing TRUE in it enables the VLOOKUP function to find the nearest value that is less than or equal in the table to the lookup value. For this reason, the first column in a VLOOKUP table array should be sorted from smallest to largest (or A to Z alphabetically) when defaulting to TRUE.

To look up an exact match, enter FALSE in the range_lookup argument. For example, if you are looking up product numbers, you must find an exact match to display the price. The function would look like this: =VLOOKUP(D15,$A$1:$B$50,2,FALSE). The function returns a value for the first lookup value that matches the first column of the lookup table. If no exact match is found, the function returns #N/A.

Here is how the VLOOKUP function works:

1. The first argument of the function evaluates the value to be located in the left column of lookup table.
2. Excel searches the first column of the lookup table until it (a) finds an exact match (if possible) or (b) identifies the correct range if an exact match is not required.
3. If Excel finds an exact match, it moves across the table to the column designated by the column index number on that same row, and returns the value stored in that cell. If the last argument is TRUE or omitted, then Excel is looking for an approximate value (NOT an exact value). In this example, if the lookup value is larger than the first number in the first column of the table, it looks to the next value to see if the lookup value is larger and will continue to do so until reaching the largest number in the column. When Excel detects that the lookup value is not greater than the next breakpoint, it stays on that row. It then uses the column index number to identify the column containing the value to return for the lookup value. Because Excel goes sequentially through the breakpoint values, it is mandatory that the first column values are arranged from the lowest value to the highest value for ranges when the range_lookup argument is TRUE or omitted.

In Figure 22, the VLOOKUP function assigns letter grades based on final scores. Excel identifies the lookup value (85 in cell E3) and compares it to the values in the first column of the lookup table (range A3:B7). The last argument is omitted, so Excel tries to find an exact match of 85 or an approximate match; and because the table contains breakpoints rather than every conceivable score and the first column of the lookup table is arranged from the lowest to the highest breakpoints, Excel detects that 85 is greater than 80 but is not greater than 90. Therefore, it stays on the 80 row. Excel looks at the second column (column index number of 2) and returns the letter grade of B. The B grade is then displayed in cell F3.

Create the Lookup Table

A ***lookup table*** is a range containing a table of values and text from which data can be retrieved. The table should contain at least two rows and two columns, not including headings. Figure 23 illustrates a college directory with three columns. The first column contains professors' names. You look up a professor's name in the first column to see his or her office (second column) and phone extension (third column).

Name	Office	Extension
Brazil, Estivan	GT 218b	7243
Fiedler, Zazilia	CS 417	7860
Lam, Kaitlyn	SC 124a	7031
Rodriquez, Lisa	GT 304	7592
Yeung, Braden	CS 414	7314

FIGURE 23 College Directory Lookup Table Analogy

It is important to plan the table so that it conforms to the way in which Excel can utilize the data in it. Excel cannot interpret the structure of Table 3. If the values you look up are exact values, you can arrange the first column in any logical order. However, to look up an approximate value in a range (such as the range 80–89), you must arrange data from the lowest to the highest value and include only the lowest value in the range (such as 80) instead of the complete range (as demonstrated in Table 3). The lowest value for a category or in a series is the ***breakpoint***. Table 4 shows how to construct the lookup table in Excel. The first column contains the breakpoints—such as 60, 70, 80, and 90—or the lowest values to achieve a particular grade. The lookup table contains one or more additional columns of related data to retrieve.

TABLE 3 Grading Scale

Range	Grade
90–100	A
80–89	B
70–79	C
60–69	D
Below 60	F

TABLE 4 Grades Lookup Table

Range	Grade
0	F
60	D
70	C
80	B
90	A

You can nest functions as arguments inside the VLOOKUP function. For example, Figure 24 illustrates shipping amounts that are based on weight and location (Boston or Chicago). In the VLOOKUP function in cell C3, the lookup_value argument looks up the weight of a package in cell A3. That weight (14 pounds) is compared to the data in the table array argument, which is $E$3:$G$5. To determine which column of the lookup table to use, an IF function is nested as the column_index_number argument. The nested IF function compares the city stored in cell B3 to the text Boston. If cell B3 contains Boston, it returns 2 to use as the column_index_number to identify the shipping value for a package that is going to Boston. If cell B3 does not contain Boston (i.e., the only other city in this example is Chicago), the column_index_number is 3.

C3 | fx | =VLOOKUP(A3,$E$3:$G$5,IF(B3="Boston",2,3))

	A	B	C	D	E	F	G	H
1	Customer Data				Lookup Data			
2	Weight	Location	Shipping		Weight	Boston	Chicago	
3	14	Boston	$ 19.95		0	$ 9.95	$ 12.95	
4	4	Chicago	$ 12.95		5	$ 14.95	$ 16.95	
5	8	Boston	$ 14.95		10	$ 19.95	$ 22.95	

FIGURE 24 IF Function Nested in VLOOKUP Function

Use the HLOOKUP Function

Lookup functions are not limited to only vertical tables. In situations in which data is better organized horizontally, you can design a lookup table where the first row contains the values for the basis of the lookup or the breakpoints, and additional rows contain data to be retrieved. With a horizontal lookup table, use the ***HLOOKUP function***. Table 5 shows how quarterly sales data would look in a horizontal lookup table.

TABLE 5 Horizontal Lookup Table

Region	Qtr1	Qtr2	Qtr3	Qtr4
North	3495	4665	4982	5010
South	8044	7692	7812	6252
East	5081	6089	5982	6500
West	4278	4350	4387	7857

The syntax is almost the same as the syntax for the VLOOKUP function, except the third argument is row_index_num instead of col_index_num.

=HLOOKUP(lookup_value,table_array,row_index_num,[range_lookup])

Calculating Payments with the PMT Function

STEP 2 ›› Excel contains several financial functions to help you perform calculations with monetary values. If you take out a loan to purchase a car, you need to know the monthly payment, which depends on the price of the car, the down payment, and the terms of the loan, in order to determine if you can afford the car. The decision is made easier by developing the worksheet in Figure 25 and by changing the various input values as indicated.

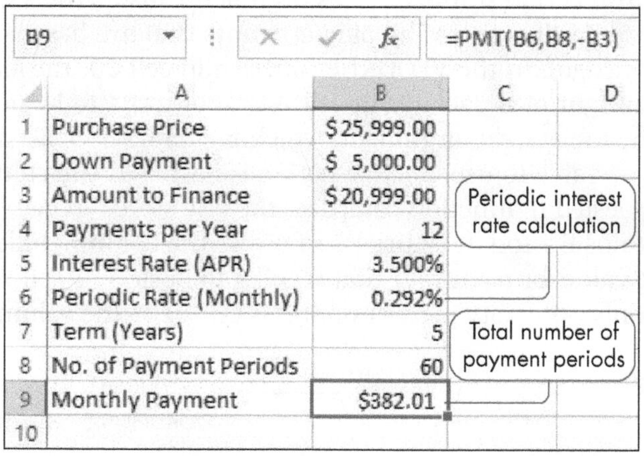

B9 fx =PMT(B6,B8,-B3)

	A	B	C	D
1	Purchase Price	$25,999.00		
2	Down Payment	$ 5,000.00		
3	Amount to Finance	$20,999.00		
4	Payments per Year	12		
5	Interest Rate (APR)	3.500%		
6	Periodic Rate (Monthly)	0.292%		
7	Term (Years)	5		
8	No. of Payment Periods	60		
9	Monthly Payment	$382.01		
10				

Periodic interest rate calculation

Total number of payment periods

FIGURE 25 Car Loan Worksheet

Creating a loan model helps you evaluate options. You realize that the purchase of a $25,999 car is prohibitive because the monthly payment is $382.01. Purchasing a less expensive car, coming up with a substantial down payment, taking out a longer-term loan, or finding a better interest rate can decrease your monthly payments.

The ***PMT function*** calculates payments for a loan with a fixed amount at a fixed periodic rate for a fixed time period. The PMT function uses three required arguments and up to two optional arguments: (1) rate, (2) nper, (3) pv, (4) fv, and (5) type.

```
=PMT(rate,nper,pv,[fv],[type])
```

The ***rate*** is the interest rate per payment period. If the annual percentage rate (APR) is 12% and you make monthly payments, the periodic rate is 1% (12%/12 months). With the same APR and quarterly payments, the periodic rate is 3% (12%/4 quarters). Divide the APR by the number of payment periods in one year. However, instead of calculating the periodic interest rate within the PMT function, you can calculate it in a separate cell and refer to that cell in the PMT function, as is done in cell B6 of Figure 25.

The ***nper*** is the total number of payment periods. The term of a loan is usually stated in years; however, you make several payments per year. For monthly payments, you make 12 payments per year. To calculate the nper, multiply the number of years by the number of payments in one year. You can either calculate the number of payment periods in the PMT function, or calculate the number of payment periods in cell B8 and use that calculated value in the PMT function.

The ***pv*** is the present value of the loan. The result of the PMT function is a negative value because it represents your debt. However, you can display the result as a positive value by typing a minus sign in front of the present value cell reference in the PMT function.

TIP: FINANCIAL FUNCTIONS AND NEGATIVE VALUES

When utilizing the PMT and other financial functions in Excel, you will often receive negative numbers. This happens because Excel understands accounting cash flow and the negative value represents a debt or outgoing monetary stream. It is important to understand why this happens and also to understand in some situations this should be a positive number, for example, if you are the company that granted the loan. In this situation you would receive an incoming cash flow, which should be a positive number. In contrast, if you are the requester of a loan, the payment should be negative as you will have a cash outflow each payment period. This can be manipulated by changing the pv argument of the PMT function between positive and negative values or by adding—in front of the PMT function.

8. Describe the three arguments for an IF function.
9. How should you structure a vertical lookup table if you need to look up values in a range?
10. What are the first three arguments of a PMT function? Why would you divide by or multiply an argument by 12?

Hands-On Exercises

Skills covered: Use the VLOOKUP Function • Use the PMT Function • Use the IF Function

3 Logical, Lookup, and Financial Functions

Erica wants you to complete another model that she might use for future mortgage data analysis. As you study the model, you realize you need to incorporate logical, lookup, and financial functions.

STEP 1 ›› USE THE VLOOKUP FUNCTION

Rates vary based on the number of years to pay off the loan. Erica created a lookup table for three common mortgage years, and she entered the current APR. The lookup table will provide efficiency later when the rates change. You will use the VLOOKUP function to display the correct rate for each customer based on the number of years of the respective loans. Refer to Figure 26 as you complete Step 1.

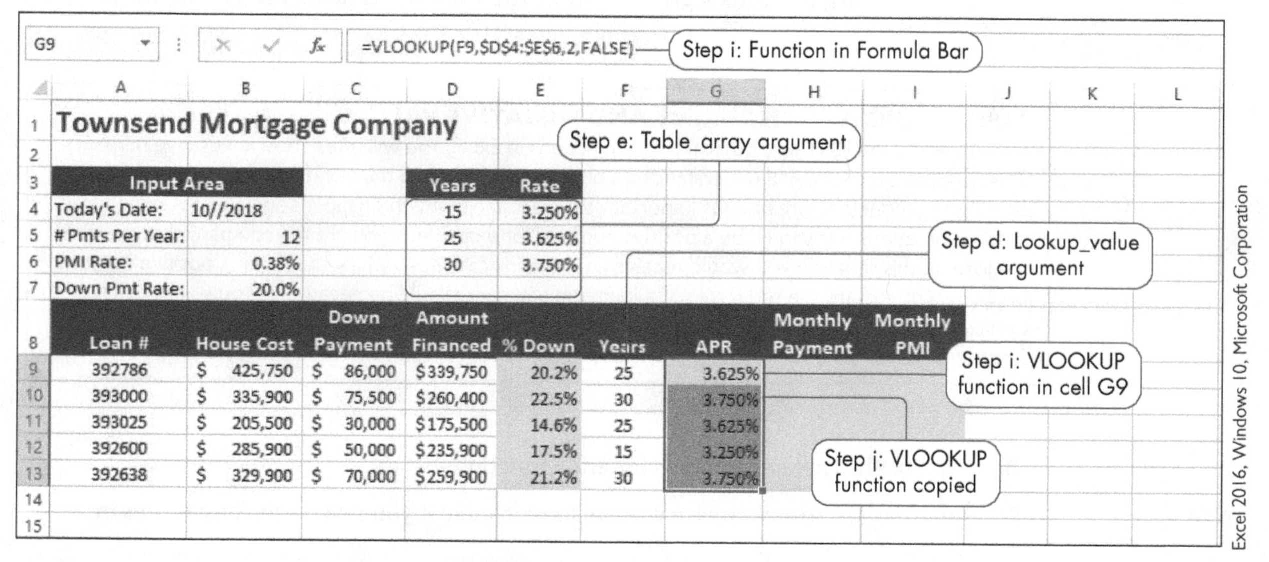

Input Area	
Today's Date:	10//2018
# Pmts Per Year:	12
PMI Rate:	0.38%
Down Pmt Rate:	20.0%

Years	Rate
15	3.250%
25	3.625%
30	3.750%

Loan #	House Cost	Down Payment	Amount Financed	% Down	Years	APR	Monthly Payment	Monthly PMI
392786	$ 425,750	$ 86,000	$339,750	20.2%	25	3.625%		
393000	$ 335,900	$ 75,500	$260,400	22.5%	30	3.750%		
393025	$ 205,500	$ 30,000	$175,500	14.6%	25	3.625%		
392600	$ 285,900	$ 50,000	$235,900	17.5%	15	3.250%		
392638	$ 329,900	$ 70,000	$259,900	21.2%	30	3.750%		

FIGURE 26 VLOOKUP Function to Determine APR

a. Open *e02h2Loans_LastFirst* if you closed it at the end of Hands-On Exercise 2 and save it as **e02h3Loans_LastFirst**, changing h2 to h3.

b. Click the **Payment Info worksheet tab** to display the worksheet containing the data to complete. Click **cell G9**, the cell that will store the APR for the first customer.

c. Click the **Formulas tab**, click **Lookup & Reference** in the Function Library group, and then select **VLOOKUP**.

The Function Arguments dialog box opens.

d. Ensure that the insertion point is in the Lookup_value box, click the **Collapse Dialog Box**, click **cell F9** to enter F9 in the Lookup_value box, and then click the **Expand Dialog Box** to return to Function Arguments dialog box.

Cell F9 contains the value you need to look up from the table: 25 years.

e. Press **Tab**, click **Collapse Dialog Box** to the right of the Table_array box, select the **range D4:E6**, and then click **Expand Dialog Box** to return to the Function Arguments dialog box.

   This is the range that contains that data for the lookup table. The Years values in the table are arranged from lowest to highest. Do *not* select the column labels for the range.

   Anticipate what will happen if you copy the formula down the column. What do you need to do to ensure that the cell references always point to the exact location of the table? If your answer is to make the table array cell references absolute, then you answered correctly.

f. Press **F4** to make the range references absolute.

   The Table_array box now contains $D$4:$E$6.

g. Press **Tab** and type **2** in the Col_index_num box.

   The second column of the lookup table contains the Rates that you want to return and display in the cells containing the formulas.

h. Press **Tab** and type **False** in the Range_lookup box.

   To ensure an exact match to look up in the table, you enter *False* in the optional argument.

i. Click **OK**.

   The VLOOKUP function uses the first loan's term in years (25) to find an exact match in the first column of the lookup table, and then returns the corresponding rate from the second column, which is 3.625%.

j. Copy the formula down the column.

   Spot-check the results to make sure the function returned the correct APR based on the number of years.

k. Save the workbook.

STEP 2 ›› USE THE PMT FUNCTION

The worksheet now has all the necessary data for you to calculate the monthly payment for each loan: the APR, the number of years for the loan, the number of payment periods in one year, and the initial loan amount. You will use the PMT function to calculate the monthly payment, which includes paying back the principal amount with interest. This calculation does not include escrow amounts, such as property taxes or insurance. Refer to Figure 27 as you complete Step 2.

H9 =PMT(G9/$B$5,F9*$B$5,-D9)

Step g: Function in the Formula Bar

Step g: Completed functioned copied down the column

Townsend Mortgage Company

Input Area			Years	Rate
Today's Date:	10/2/2018		15	3.250%
# Pmts Per Year:	12		25	3.625%
PMI Rate:	0.38%		30	3.750%
Down Pmt Rate:	20.0%			

Loan #	House Cost	Down Payment	Amount Financed	% Down	Years	APR	Monthly Payment	Monthly PMI
392786	$ 425,750	$ 86,000	$339,750	20.2%	25	3.625%	$1,723.73	
393000	$ 335,900	$ 75,500	$260,400	22.5%	30	3.750%	$1,205.95	
393025	$ 205,500	$ 30,000	$175,500	14.6%	25	3.625%	$890.40	
392600	$ 285,900	$ 50,000	$235,900	17.5%	15	3.250%	$1,657.60	
392638	$ 329,900	$ 70,000	$259,900	21.2%	30	3.750%	$1,203.64	

Excel 2016, Windows 10, Microsoft Corporation

FIGURE 27 PMT Function to Calculate Monthly Payment

a. Click **cell H9**, the cell that will store the payment for the first customer.

b. Click **Financial** in the Function Library group, scroll through the list, and then select **PMT**.

The Function Arguments dialog box opens.

> **TROUBLESHOOTING:** Make sure you select PMT, not PPMT. The PPMT function calculates the principal portion of a particular monthly payment, not the total monthly payment itself.

c. Type **G9/B5** in the Rate box.

Think about what will happen if you copy the formula. The argument will be G10/B6 for the next customer. Are those cell references correct? G10 does contain the APR for the next customer, but B6 does not contain the correct number of payments in one year. Therefore, you need to make B5 an absolute cell reference because the number of payments per year does not vary.

d. Press **F4** to make the reference to cell B5 absolute.

e. Press **Tab** and type **F9*$B$5** in the Nper box.

You calculate the nper by multiplying the number of years by the number of payments in one year. You must make B5 an absolute cell reference so that it does not change when you copy the formula down the column.

f. Press **Tab** and type **-D9** in the Pv box.

The bottom of the dialog box indicates that the monthly payment is 1723.73008 or $1,723.73.

> **TROUBLESHOOTING:** If the payment displays as a negative value, you probably forgot to type the minus sign in front of the D9 reference in the Pv box. Edit the function and type the minus sign in the correct place.

g. Click **OK**. Copy the formula down the column.

h. Save the workbook.

STEP 3 » USE THE IF FUNCTION

Lenders often want borrowers to have a 20% down payment. If borrowers do not put in 20% of the cost of the house as a down payment, they pay a private mortgage insurance (PMI) fee. PMI serves to protect lenders from absorbing loss if the borrower defaults on the loan, and it enables borrowers with less cash to secure a loan. The PMI fee is about 0.38% of the amount financed. Some borrowers have to pay PMI for a few months or years until the balance owed is less than 80% of the appraised value. The worksheet contains the necessary values in the input area. You use the IF function to determine which borrowers must pay PMI and how much they will pay. Refer to Figure 28 as you complete Step 3.

I9 =IF(E9>=$B$7,0,D9*$B$6/$B$5)

Step f: IF function in cell I9

Townsend Mortgage Company

Input Area			Years	Rate
Today's Date:	10/2/2018		15	3.250%
# Pmts Per Year:	12		25	3.625%
PMI Rate:	0.38%		30	3.750%
Down Pmt Rate:	20.0%			

Loan #	House Cost	Down Payment	Amount Financed	% Down	Years	APR	Monthly Payment	Monthly PMI
392786	$ 425,750	$ 86,000	$339,750	20.2%	25	3.625%	$1,723.73	$ -
393000	$ 335,900	$ 75,500	$260,400	22.5%	30	3.750%	$1,205.95	$ -
393025	$ 205,500	$ 30,000	$175,500	14.6%	25	3.625%	$890.40	$ 55.58
392600	$ 285,900	$ 50,000	$235,900	17.5%	15	3.250%	$1,657.60	$ 74.70
392638	$ 329,900	$ 70,000	$259,900	21.2%	30	3.750%	$1,203.64	$ -

Step f: Results of copied IF function

FIGURE 28 IF Function to Calculate Monthly PMI

a. Click **cell I9**, the cell that will store the PMI, if any, for the first customer.

b. Click **Logical** in the Function Library group and select **IF**.

The Function Arguments dialog box opens. You will enter the three arguments.

c. Type **E9>=$B$7** in the Logical_test box.

The logical test compares the down payment percentage to see if the customer's down payment is at least 20%, the threshold stored in B7, of the amount financed. The customer's percentage cell reference is relative so that it will change when you copy it down the column; however, cell B7 must be absolute because it contains a value that should remain constant when the formula is copied to other cells.

d. Press **Tab** and type **0** in the Value_if_true box.

If the customer makes a down payment that is at least 20% of the purchase price, the customer does not pay PMI, so a value of 0 will display whenever the logical test is true. The first customer paid 20% of the purchase price, so he or she does not have to pay PMI.

e. Press **Tab** and type **D9*$B$6/$B$5** in the Value_if_false box.

If the logical test is false, the customer must pay PMI, which is calculated by multiplying the amount financed (D9) by the periodic PMI rate (the result of dividing the yearly PMI (B6) by the number of payments per year (B5)).

f. Click **OK** and copy the formula down the column.

The first, second, and fifth customers paid 20% of the purchase price, so they do not have to pay PMI. The third and fourth customers must pay PMI because their respective down payments were less than 20% of the purchase price.

> **TROUBLESHOOTING:** If the results are not as you expected, check the logical operators. People often mistype < and > or forget to type = for >= situations. Correct any errors in the original formula and copy the formula again.

g. Set the worksheets to print on one page. Add a footer with your name on the left, sheet code in the middle, and the file name code on the right.

h. Save and close the file. Based on your instructor's directions, submit e02h3Loans_LastFirst.

Chapter Objectives Review

After reading this chapter, you have accomplished the following objectives:

1. Use relative, absolute, and mixed cell references in formulas.

- Use a relative cell address: A relative reference indicates a cell's location relative to the formula cell. When you copy the formula, the relative cell reference changes.
- Use an absolute cell reference: An absolute reference is a permanent pointer to a particular cell, indicated with $ before the column letter and the row number, such as $B$5. When you copy the formula, the absolute cell reference does not change.
- Use a mixed cell reference: A mixed reference contains part absolute and part relative reference, such as $B5 or B$5. Either the column or the row reference changes, while the other remains constant when you copy the formula.

2. Insert a function.

- A function is a predefined formula that performs a calculation. It contains the function name and arguments. Formula AutoComplete, function ScreenTips, and the Insert Function dialog box help you select and create functions. The Function Arguments dialog box guides you through the entering requirements for each argument.

3. Insert basic math and statistics functions.

- Use the SUM function: The SUM function calculates the total of a range of values. The syntax is =SUM(number1,[number2],...).
- Use the AVERAGE and MEDIAN functions: The AVERAGE function calculates the arithmetic mean of values in a range. The MEDIAN function identifies the midpoint value in a set of values.
- Use the MIN and MAX functions: The MIN function identifies the lowest value in a range, whereas the MAX function identifies the highest value in a range.
- Use the COUNT functions: The COUNT function tallies the number of cells in a range, that contain values, whereas the COUNTBLANK function tallies the number of blank cells in a range, and COUNTA tallies the number of cells that are not empty.
- Perform calculations with Quick Analysis tools: With the Quick Analysis tools you can apply formatting, create charts or tables, and insert basic functions.

4. Use date functions.

- Insert the TODAY function: The TODAY function displays the current date.
- Insert the NOW function: The NOW function displays the current date and time.

5. Determine results with the IF function.

- Design the logical test: The IF function is a logical function that evaluates a logical test using logical operators, such as <, >, and =, and returns one value if the condition is true and another value if the condition is false.
- Design the value_if_true and value_if_false arguments: The arguments can contain cell references, text, or calculations. If a logical test is true, Excel executes the value_if_true argument. If a logical test is false, Excel executes the value_if_false argument.
- You can nest or embed other functions inside one or more of the arguments of an IF function to create more complex formulas.

6. Use lookup functions.

- Use the VLOOKUP function: The VLOOKUP function contains the required arguments lookup_value, table_array, and col_index_num and one optional argument, range_lookup.
- Create the lookup table: Design the lookup table using exact values or the breakpoints for ranges. If using breakpoints, the breakpoints must be in ascending order.
- Use the HLOOKUP function: The HLOOKUP function looks up values by row (horizontally) rather than by column (vertically).

7. Calculate payments with the PMT function.

- The PMT function calculates periodic payments for a loan with a fixed interest rate and a fixed term. The PMT function requires the periodic interest rate, the total number of payment periods, and the original value of the loan.

Key Terms Matching

Match the key terms with their definitions. Write the key term letter by the appropriate numbered definition.

a. Absolute cell reference
b. Argument
c. AVERAGE function
d. COUNT function
e. IF function
f. Logical test
g. Lookup table
h. MAX function
i. MEDIAN function
j. MIN function
k. Mixed cell reference
l. NOW function
m. PMT function
n. Relative cell reference
o. SUM function
p. Syntax
q. TODAY function
r. VLOOKUP function

1. ______ A set of rules that governs the structure and components for properly entering a function.

2. ______ Displays the current date.

3. ______ Indicates a cell's specific location; the cell reference does not change when you copy the formula.

4. ______ An input, such as a cell reference or value, needed to complete a function.

5. ______ Identifies the highest value in a range.

6. ______ Tallies the number of cells in a range that contain values.

7. ______ Looks up a value in a vertical lookup table and returns a related result from the lookup table.

8. ______ A range that contains data for the basis of the lookup and data to be retrieved.

9. ______ Calculates the arithmetic mean, or average, of values in a range.

10. ______ Identifies the midpoint value in a set of values.

11. ______ Displays the current date and time.

12. ______ Evaluates a condition and returns one value if the condition is true and a different value if the condition is false.

13. ______ Calculates the total of values contained in two or more cells.

14. ______ Calculates the periodic payment for a loan with a fixed interest rate and fixed term.

15. ______ Indicates a cell's location from the cell containing the formula; the cell reference changes when the formula is copied.

16. ______ Contains both an absolute and a relative cell reference in a formula; the absolute part does not change but the relative part does when you copy the formula.

17. ______ An expression that evaluates to true or false.

18. ______ Displays the lowest value in a range.

Multiple Choice

1. If cell E15 contains the formula =$C$5*J$15, what type of cell reference is the J$15 in the formula?

(a) Relative reference
(b) Absolute reference
(c) Mixed reference
(d) Syntax

2. What function would most efficiently accomplish the same thing as =(B5+C5+D5+E5+F5)/5?

(a) =SUM(B5:F5)/5
(b) =AVERAGE(B5:F5)
(c) =MEDIAN(B5:F5)
(d) =COUNT(B5:F5)

3. When you start to type =AV, what feature displays a list of functions and defined names?

(a) Function ScreenTip
(b) Formula AutoComplete
(c) Insert Function dialog box
(d) Function Arguments dialog box

4. A formula containing the entry =$B3 is copied to a cell one column to the right and two rows down. How will the entry appear in its new location?

(a) =$B3
(b) =B3
(c) =$C5
(d) =$B5

5. Which of the following functions should be used to insert the current date and time in a cell?

(a) =TODAY()
(b) =CURRENT()
(c) =NOW()
(d) =DATE

6. Which of the following is not an argument of the IF function?

(a) value_if_true
(b) value_if_false
(c) logical_test
(d) lookup_value

7. Which of the following is *not* true about the VLOOKUP function?

(a) The lookup table must be in ascending order.
(b) The lookup table must be in descending order.
(c) The default match type is approximate.
(d) The match type must be false when completing an exact match.

8. The function =PMT(C5,C7,-C3) is stored in cell C15. What must be stored in cell C5?

(a) APR
(b) Periodic interest rate
(c) Loan amount
(d) Number of payment periods

9. Which of the following is *not* an appropriate use of the SUM function?

(a) =SUM(B3:B45)
(b) =SUM(F1:G10)
(c) =SUM(A8:A15,D8:D15)
(d) =SUM(D15-C15)

10. What is the keyboard shortcut to create an absolute reference?

(a) F2
(b) F3
(c) F4
(d) Alt

Practice Exercises

1 Hamilton Heights Auto Sales

You are the primary loan manager for Hamilton Heights Auto Sales, an auto sales company located in Missouri. In order to most efficiently manage the auto loans your company finances, you have decided to create a spreadsheet to perform several calculations. You will insert the current date, calculate down payment and interest rates based on credit score, calculate periodic payment amounts, and complete the project with basic summary information. Refer to Figure 29 as you complete this exercise.

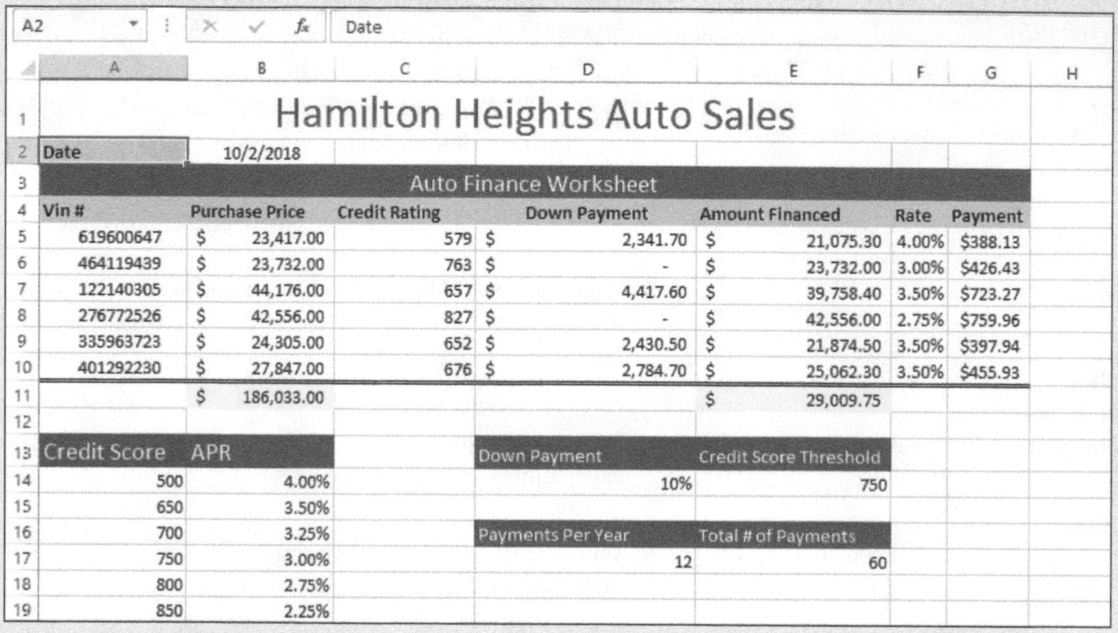

A2 | fx | Date

	A	B	C	D	E	F	G	H
1	Hamilton Heights Auto Sales							
2	Date	10/2/2018						
3	Auto Finance Worksheet							
4	Vin #	Purchase Price	Credit Rating	Down Payment	Amount Financed	Rate	Payment	
5	619600647	$ 23,417.00	579	$ 2,341.70	$ 21,075.30	4.00%	$388.13	
6	464119439	$ 23,732.00	763	$ -	$ 23,732.00	3.00%	$426.43	
7	122140305	$ 44,176.00	657	$ 4,417.60	$ 39,758.40	3.50%	$723.27	
8	276772526	$ 42,556.00	827	$ -	$ 42,556.00	2.75%	$759.96	
9	335963723	$ 24,305.00	652	$ 2,430.50	$ 21,874.50	3.50%	$397.94	
10	401292230	$ 27,847.00	676	$ 2,784.70	$ 25,062.30	3.50%	$455.93	
11		$ 186,033.00			$ 29,009.75			
12								
13	Credit Score	APR		Down Payment	Credit Score Threshold			
14	500	4.00%		10%	750			
15	650	3.50%						
16	700	3.25%		Payments Per Year	Total # of Payments			
17	750	3.00%		12	60			
18	800	2.75%						
19	850	2.25%						

FIGURE 29 Hamilton Heights Auto Sales

a. Open *e02p1AutoSales* and save it as **e02p1AutoSales_LastFirst**.

b. Click **cell B2**, click the **Formulas tab**, click **Date & Time** in the Function Library group, select **NOW**, and then click **OK** to enter today's date in the cell.

c. Click **cell D5** on the Formulas tab, click **Logical** in the Function Library group, and select **IF**.

d. Type **C5<=$E$14** in the Logical_test box, type **$D$14*B5** in the Value_if_true box, type **0** in the Value_if_false box, and then click **OK**.

This uses the IF function to calculate the required down payment based on credit score. If the customer has a credit score higher than 750 a down payment is not required. All clients with credits scores lower than 750 must pay a required 10% down payment in advance.

e. Use the fill handle to copy the contents of **cell D5** down the column, click **Auto Fill Options** to the lower-right of the copied cells, and then click **Fill Without Formatting** to ensure that the **Bottom Double border** remains applied to cell D10.

f. Calculate the Amount Financed by doing the following:

- Click **cell E5** and type **=B5-D5**.
- Use **cell E5's fill handle** to copy the function down the column.
- Apply **Bottom Double border** to cell E10.

g. Calculate the Rate by doing the following:

- Click **cell F5**. Click **Lookup & Reference** in the Function Library group and select **VLOOKUP**.
- Type **C5** in the Lookup_value box, type **$A$14:$B$19** in the Table_array box, type **2** in the Col_index_num box, and then click **OK**
- Double-click **cell F5's fill handle** to copy the function down the column.
- Click **Auto Fill Options**, and click **Fill Without Formatting**.

h. Calculate the required periodic payment by doing the following:
   - Click **cell G5**, click **Financial** in the Function Library Group, and then click **PMT**.
   - Type **F5/$D$17** in the Rate box, type **$E$17** in the Nper box, type **–E5** in the Pv box, and then click **OK**.
   - Double-click **cell G5's** fill handle to copy the function down the column.
   - Click the **Auto Fill Options** button, and click **Fill Without Formatting**.

i. Select the **range B5:B10**, click the **Quick Analysis button**, click **TOTALS**, and select **Sum** from the Quick Analysis Gallery.

j. Click **cell E11** and type **=AVERAGE(E5:E10)** to calculate the average amount financed.

k. Create a footer with your name on the left side, the sheet name code in the center, and the file name on the right side.

l. Save and close the workbook. Based on your instructor's directions, submit e02p1AutoSales_LastFirst.

2 Lockridge Marketing Analytics

As a business analyst for Lockridge Marketing Analytics, you have been tasked with awarding performance bonuses. You prepare a model to calculate employee bonuses based on average customer satisfaction survey results. The survey is based on a scale of 1 to 5 with 5 being the highest rating. Employees with survey results where ratings are between 1 and 2.9 do not receive bonuses, scores between 3 and 3.9 earn a 2% one-time bonus on their monthly salary, and scores of 4 or higher receive a 5% bonus. In addition, you calculate basic summary data for reporting purposes. Refer to Figure 30 as you complete this exercise.

J10

	A	B	C	D	E	F
1	Lockridge Marketing Analytics					
2						
3	Inputs and Constants				Bonus Data	
4	Today:	10/2/2018		Rating	1	3
5	Employees Surveyed	6		Bonus	0%	2%
6						
7						
8						
9	Survey Code	Current Salary	Monthly Salary	Survey Score	Rating Bonus	Monthly Take Home
10	38078	$ 50,000	$ 4,166.67	5	$ 208.33	$ 4,375.00
11	41105	$ 75,250	$ 6,270.83	3.5	$ 125.42	$ 6,396.25
12	39752	$ 67,250	$ 5,604.17	4.2	$ 280.21	$ 5,884.38
13	37872	$ 45,980	$ 3,831.67	3	$ 76.63	$ 3,908.30
14	40616	$ 58,750	$ 4,895.83	4.2	$ 244.79	$ 5,140.63
15	40347	$ 61,000	$ 5,083.33	4.5	$ 254.17	$ 5,337.50
16						
17						
18	Statistics					
19	Lowest Bonus	$ 76.63				
20	Average Bonus	$ 198.26				
21	Highest Bonus	$ 280.21				

Excel 2016, Windows 10, Microsoft Corporation

FIGURE 30 Lockridge Marketing Analytics

a. Open *e02p2Bonus* and save it as **e02p2Bonus_LastFirst**.

b. Click **cell B4**, click the **Formulas tab**, click **Date & Time** in the Function Library group, select **TODAY**, and then click **OK** to enter today's date in the cell.

c. Click **cell B5**, click the **AutoSum arrow** in the Function Library group, and then select **Count Numbers**. Select the **range A10:A15** and press **Enter**.

d. Click **cell C10**, type **=B10/12**, press **Ctrl+Enter**, and double-click the **fill handle**.

e. Enter the Rating Bonus based on survey average by doing the following:

- Click **cell E10** and type **=C10***.
- Click **Lookup & Reference** in the Function Library group and select **HLOOKUP**.
- Type **D10** in the Lookup_value box, type **E$4:G$5** in the Table_array box, type **2** in the Col_index_num box, and then click **OK**.
- Double-click the **cell E10 fill handle** to copy the formula down the Rating Bonus column.

f. Calculate each employee's monthly take-home by doing the following:

- Click **cell F10** and type **=C10+E10**.
- Double-click the **cell F10 fill handle**.

g. Calculate basic summary statistics by doing the following:

- Click **cell B19**, click the **Formulas tab**, click the **AutoSum arrow**, and then select **MIN**.
- Select the **range E10:E15** and then press **Enter**.
- In **cell B20**, click the **AutoSum arrow**, select **AVERAGE**, select the **range E10:E15**, and then press **Enter**.
- In **cell B21**, click the **AutoSum arrow**, select **MAX**, select the **range E10:E15**, and then press **Enter**.

h. Create a footer with your name on the left side, the sheet name in the center, and the file name code on the right side.

i. Save and close the workbook. Based on your instructor's directions, submit e02p2Bonus_LastFirst.

3 Facebook and Blackboard

COLLABORATION CASE

FROM SCRATCH

Social media extends past friendships to organizational and product "fan" pages. Organizations such as Lexus, Pepsi, and universities create pages to provide information about their organizations. Some organizations even provide product details, such as for the Lexus ES350. Facebook includes a wealth of information about Microsoft Office products. People share information, pose questions, and reply with their experiences.

a. Log in to your Facebook account. If you do not have a Facebook account, sign up for one and add at least two classmates as friends. Search for Microsoft Excel 2016 and click **Like**.

b. Review postings on the Microsoft Excel wall. Notice that some people post what they like most about Excel or how much it has improved their productivity. Post a note about one of your favorite features about Excel that you have learned so far or how you have used Excel in other classes or on the job.

c. Click the **Discussions link** on the Microsoft Excel Facebook page and find topics that relate to IF or HLOOKUP functions. Post a response to one of the discussions. Take a screenshot of your posting and insert it into a Word document. Save the Word document **as e02m3_LastFirst**.

d. Create a team of three students. Create one discussion that asks people to describe their favorite use of any of the nested functions used in this chapter. Each team member should respond to the posting. Monitor the discussion and, when you have a few responses, capture a screenshot of the dialogue and insert it into your Word document.

e. Go to www.youtube.com and search for one of these Excel topics: absolute references, mixed references, semi-selection, IF function, VLOOKUP function, or PMT function.

f. Watch several video clips and find one of particular interest to you.

g. Post the URL on your Facebook wall. Specify the topic and describe why you like this particular video.

h. Watch videos from the links posted by other students on their Facebook walls. Comment on at least two submissions. Point out what you like about the video or any suggestions you have for improvement.

i. Insert screenshots of your postings in a Word document, if required by your instructor. Save and close the file. Based on your instructor's directions submit e02m3_LastFirst.

Beyond the Classroom

Auto Finance

GENERAL CASE 

FROM SCRATCH

After graduating from college and obtaining your first job, you have decided to purchase a new vehicle. Before purchasing the car, you want to create a worksheet to estimate the monthly payment based on the purchase price, APR, down payment, and years. Your monthly budget is $500 and you will use conditional logic to automatically determine if you can afford the cars you are evaluating. Open the workbook *e02b1CarLoan* and save it as **e02b1CarLoan_LastFirst**.

Insert a function to automatically enter the current date in cell A4. Starting in cell B12 enter a formula to calculate the down payment for each vehicle price range based on the down payment percentage listed in cell D4. Be sure to use the appropriate absolute or mixed reference and copy the formula to complete range B13:B16. Before calculating the periodic payment for each vehicle, you will need to research the current vehicle interest rates. Conduct an Internet search to determine the current interest rate for a five-year auto loan and enter the value in cell D5. In cell C12 type a function that calculates the periodic payment for the first vehicle based on the input information in range D4:D7. Be sure to use the appropriate absolute or mixed reference and copy the formula to complete range C12:C16. In column D, use an IF function to determine if the first vehicle is financially viable; display either Test Drive or NA based on the criteria in cell D8. Be sure to use the appropriate absolute or mixed reference and copy the formula to complete range D12:D16.

Include a footer with your name on the left side, the date in the center, and the file name on the right side. Save and close the workbook. Based on your instructor's directions, submit e02b1CarLoan_LastFirst.

Park City Condo Rental

DISASTER RECOVERY 

You and some friends are planning a Labor Day vacation to Park City, Utah. You have secured a four-day condominium that costs $1,200. Some people will stay all four days; others will stay part of the weekend. One of your friends constructed a worksheet to help calculate each person's cost of the rental. The people who stay Thursday night will split the nightly cost evenly. To keep the costs down, everyone agreed to pay $30 per night per person for Friday, Saturday, and/or Sunday nights. Depending on the number of people who stay each night, the group may owe more money. Kyle, Ian, Isaac, and Daryl agreed to split the difference in the total rental cost and the amount the group members paid. Open the workbook *e02b2ParkCity*, and save it as **e02b2ParkCity_LastFirst**.

Review the worksheet structure, including the assumptions and calculation notes at the bottom of the worksheet. Check the formulas and functions, making necessary corrections. With the existing data, the number of people staying each night is 5, 8, 10, and 7, respectively. The total paid given the above assumptions is $1,110, giving a difference of $90 to be divided evenly among the first four people. Kyle's share should be $172.50. In the cells containing errors, insert comments to describe the error and fix the formulas. Verify the accuracy of formulas by entering an IF function in cell I1 to ensure that the totals match. Nick, James, and Body inform you they cannot stay Sunday night, and Rob wants to stay Friday night. Change the input accordingly. The updated total paid is now $1,200, and the difference is $150. Include a footer with your name on the left side, the date in the center, and the file name on the right side. Save and close the workbook. Based on your instructor's directions, submit e02b2ParkCity_LastFirst.

Capstone Exercise

You are an account manager for Inland Jewelers, a regional company that makes custom class rings for graduating seniors. Your supervisor requested a workbook to report on new accounts created on payment plans. The report should provide details on total costs to the student as well as payment information. Each ring financed has a base price that can fluctuate based on ring personalization.

Insert Current Date

You open the starting workbook you previously created, and insert the current date and time.

a. Open the *e02c1ClassRing* workbook, and then save it as **e02c1ClassRing_LastFirst**.

b. Insert a function in **cell B2** to display the current date and format as a **Long Date**.

c. Set column B's width to **Autofit**.

Calculate Cost

You are ready to calculate the cost of each class ring ordered. The rings are priced based on their base metal as displayed in the range A15:B19.

a. Insert a lookup function in **cell C5** to display the ring cost for the first student.

b. Copy the function from **cell C5** down through **C11** to complete column C.

c. Apply **Accounting Number Format** to **column C**.

Determine the Total Due

You will calculate the total due for each student's order. The total is the base price of the ring plus an additional charge for personalization if applicable.

a. Insert an IF function in **cell E5** to calculate the total due. If the student has chosen to personalize the ring, there is an additional charge of 5% located in **cell B21** that must be applied; if not, the student pays only the base price. Use appropriate relative and absolute cell references.

b. Copy the function from **cell E5** down through **E11** to complete column E.

c. Apply **Accounting Number Format** to **column E**.

Calculate the Monthly Payment

Your next step is to calculate the periodic payment for each student's account. The payments are based on the years financed in column F and the annual interest rate in cell B22. All accounts are paid on a monthly basis.

a. Insert the function in **cell G5** to calculate the first student's monthly payment, using appropriate relative and absolute cell references.

b. Copy the formula down the column.

c. Apply **Accounting Number Format** to **column G**.

Finalize the Workbook

You perform some basic statistical calculations and finalize the workbook with formatting and page setup options.

a. Calculate totals in **cells C12**, **E12**, and **G12**.

b. Apply **Accounting Number Format** to the **cells C12**, **E12**, and **G12**.

c. Set **0.3"** left and right margins and ensure that the page prints on only one page.

d. Insert a footer with your name on the left side, the sheet name in the center, and the file name on the right side.

e. Save and close the workbook. Based on your instructor's directions, submit e02c1ClassRing_LastFirst.

Glossary

Absolute cell reference A designation that indicates a constant reference to a specific cell location; the cell reference does not change when you copy the formula.

Argument An input, such as a cell reference or value, required to complete a function.

AVERAGE function A predefined formula that calculates the arithmetic mean, or average, of values in a range of cells.

Breakpoint The lowest value for a category or in a series.

Formula AutoComplete A feature that displays a list of functions and defined names that match letters as you type a formula.

Function A predefined computation that simplifies creating a formula that performs a complex calculation.

Function ScreenTip A small pop-up description that displays the function's arguments.

Column index number The column number in the lookup table that contains the return values.

COUNT function A predefined formula that tallies the number of cells in a range that contain values you can use in calculations, such as numerical and date data, but excludes blank cells or text entries from the tally.

COUNTA function A predefined formula that tallies the number of cells in a range that are not blank, that is, cells that contain data, whether a value, text, or a formula.

COUNTBLANK function A predefined formula that tallies the number of cells in a range that are blank.

HLOOKUP function A function that looks for a value in the top row of a specified table array and returns another value located in the same column from a specified row.

IF function A predefined formula that evaluates a condition and returns one value if the condition is true and a different value if the condition is false.

Logical test An expression that evaluates to true or false.

Lookup table A range that contains data for the basis of the lookup and data to be retrieved.

Lookup value The cell reference of the cell that contains the value to look up.

MAX function A predefined formula that identifies the highest value in a range.

MEDIAN function A predefined formula that identifies the midpoint value in a set of values.

MIN function A predefined formula that displays the lowest value in a range.

Mixed cell reference A designation that combines an absolute cell reference with a relative cell reference. The absolute part does not change but the relative part does when you copy the formula.

Nested function A function that contains another function embedded inside one or more of it's arguments.

Nper Total number of payment periods.

NOW function A predefined formula that calculates the current date and military time that you last opened the workbook using the computer's clock.

Pmt function A function that calculates the periodic payment for a loan with a fixed interest rate and a fixed term.

PV A predefined formula that calculates the present value of a loan.

Quick Analysis A set of analytical tools you can use to apply formatting, create charts or tables, and insert basic functions.

Range_lookup An argument that determines how the VLOOKUP and HLOOKUP function handle lookup values that are not an exact match for the data in the lookup table.

Rate The periodic interest rate; the percentage of interest paid for each payment period; the first argument in the PMT function.

Relative cell reference A designation that indicates a cell's relative location from the original cell containing the formula; the cell reference changes when the formula is copied.

SUM function A predefined formula that calculates the total of values contained in one or more cells.

Syntax A set of rules that governs the structure and components for properly entering a function.

Table array The range that contains the lookup table.

TODAY function A predefined formula that displays the current date.

VLOOKUP function A predefined formula that accepts a value, looks the value up in a vertical lookup table with data organized in columns, and returns a result.

Charts

Excel

Charts

LEARNING OUTCOME You will create charts and insert sparklines to represent data visually.

OBJECTIVES & SKILLS: After you read this chapter, you will be able to:

Chart Basics

OBJECTIVE 1: SELECT THE DATA SOURCE
Select an Adjacent Range, Select a Nonadjacent Range

OBJECTIVE 2: CHOOSE A CHART TYPE
Create a Clustered Column Chart, Create a Bar Chart, Change the Chart Type, Create a Line Chart, Create a Pie Chart, Create a Combo Chart, Create an Area Chart, Create a Scatter Chart, Create a Stock Chart

OBJECTIVE 3: MOVE, SIZE, AND PRINT A CHART
Move a Chart to a New Chart Sheet, Move a Chart Within a Worksheet, Size a Chart

HANDS-ON EXERCISE 1:
Chart Basics

Chart Elements

OBJECTIVE 4: ADD, EDIT, AND FORMAT CHART ELEMENTS
Edit and Format Chart Titles; Add and Format Axes Titles; Format Axes; Add, Position, and Format Data Labels; Format and Position the Legend; Apply a Quick Layout; Format the Chart Area; Format the Plot Area; Format a Data Series; Format the Gridlines; Format a Data Point

HANDS-ON EXERCISE 2:
Chart Elements

Chart Design and Sparklines

OBJECTIVE 5: APPLY A CHART STYLE AND COLORS
Apply a Chart Style, Change Colors

OBJECTIVE 6: MODIFY THE DATA SOURCE
Apply Chart Filters, Switch Row and Column Data

OBJECTIVE 7: CREATE AND CUSTOMIZE SPARKLINES
Insert a Sparkline, Customize Sparklines

HANDS-ON EXERCISE 3:
Chart Design and Sparklines

CASE STUDY | Computer Job Outlook

You are an academic advisor for the School of Computing at a private university in Seattle, Washington. You will visit high schools over the next few weeks to discuss the computing programs at the university and to inform students about the job outlook in the computing industry. Your assistant, Doug Demers, researched growing computer-related jobs in the *Occupational Outlook Handbook* published by the Bureau of Labor Statistics on the U.S. Department of Labor's website. In particular, Doug listed seven jobs, the number of those jobs in 2010, the projected number of jobs by 2020, the growth in percentage increase and number of jobs, and the 2010 median pay. This dataset shows an 18%–31% increase in computer-related jobs in that 10-year time period.

To prepare for your presentation to encourage students to enroll in your School of Computing, you will create several charts that depict the job growth in the computer industry. You know that different charts provide different perspectives on the data. After you complete the charts, you will be able to use them in a variety of formats, such as presentations, fliers, and brochures.

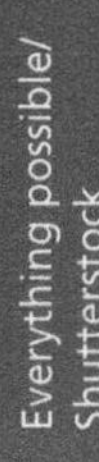

Everything possible/
Shutterstock

Depicting Data Visually

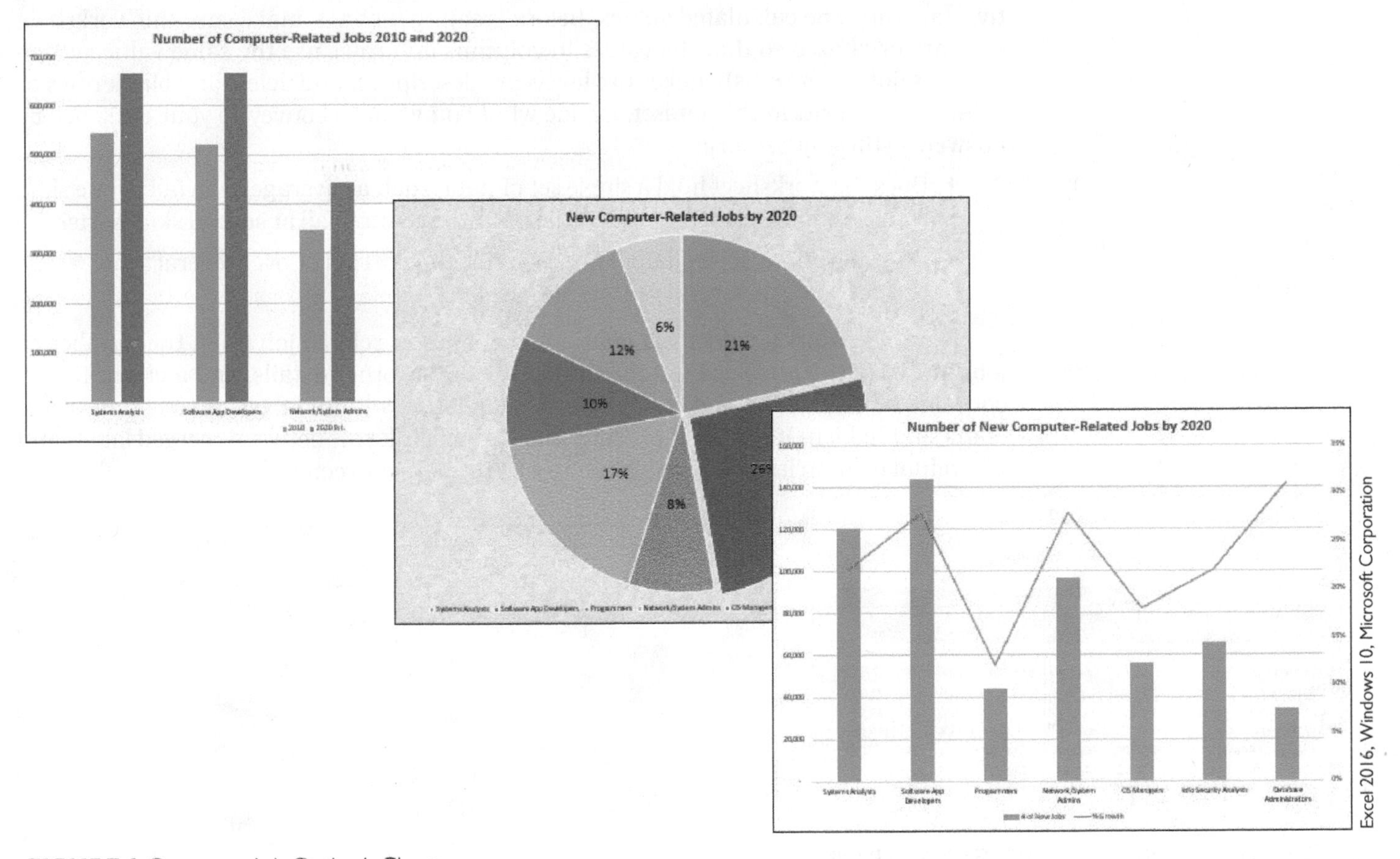

Excel 2016, Windows 10, Microsoft Corporation

FIGURE 1 Computer Job Outlook Charts

CASE STUDY | Computer Job Outlook

Starting File	File to be Submitted
e03h1Jobs	**e03h3Jobs_LastFirst**

Chart Basics

A ***chart*** is a visual representation of numerical data that compares data and reveals trends or patterns to help people make informed decisions. An effective chart depicts data in a clear, easy-to-interpret manner and contains enough data to be useful without overwhelming your audience.

In this section, you will select the data source, choose the best chart type to represent numerical data, and designate the chart's location.

Selecting the Data Source

Look at the structure of the worksheet—the column labels, the row labels, the quantitative data, and the calculated values. Before creating a chart, make sure the worksheet data are organized so that the values in columns and rows use the same value system (such as dollars or units), make sure labels are descriptive, and delete any blank rows or columns that exist in the dataset. Decide what you want to convey to your audience by answering these questions:

- Does the worksheet hold a single set of data, such as average snowfall at one ski resort, or multiple sets of data, such as average snowfall at several ski resorts?
- Do you want to depict data for one specific time period or over several time periods, such as several years or decades?

Figure 2 shows a worksheet containing computer-related job titles, the number of jobs in 2010, the projected number of jobs by 2020, other details, and a chart. Row 3 contains labels merged and centered over individual column labels in row 5. Row 4 is blank and hidden. It is a good practice to insert a blank row between merged labels and individual column labels to enable you to sort the data correctly.

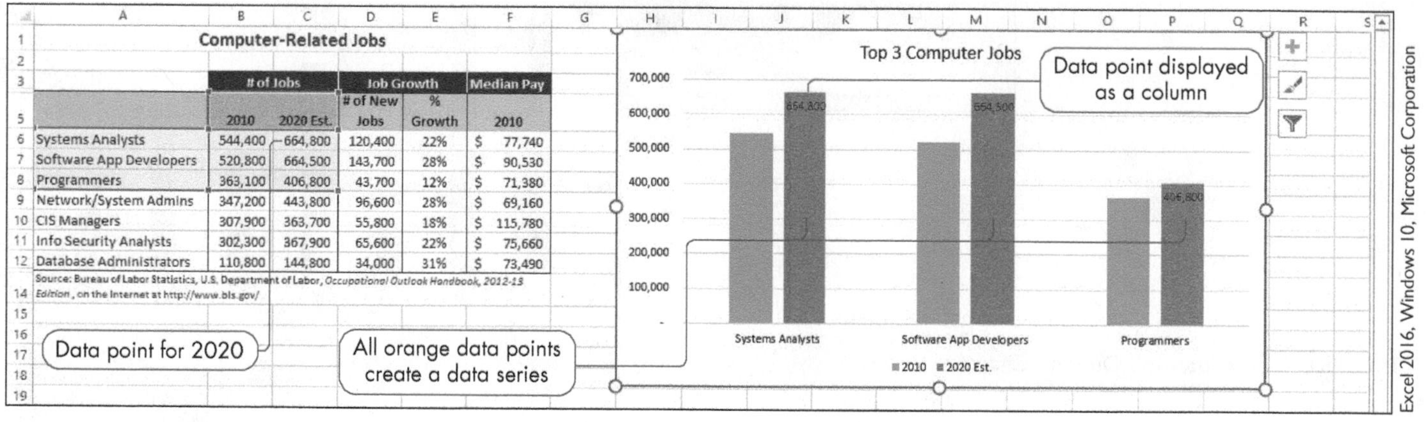

Computer-Related Jobs

	# of Jobs		Job Growth		Median Pay
	2010	2020 Est.	# of New Jobs	% Growth	2010
Systems Analysts	544,400	664,800	120,400	22%	$ 77,740
Software App Developers	520,800	664,500	143,700	28%	$ 90,530
Programmers	363,100	406,800	43,700	12%	$ 71,380
Network/System Admins	347,200	443,800	96,600	28%	$ 69,160
CIS Managers	307,900	363,700	55,800	18%	$ 115,780
Info Security Analysts	302,300	367,900	65,600	22%	$ 75,660
Database Administrators	110,800	144,800	34,000	31%	$ 73,490

Source: Bureau of Labor Statistics, U.S. Department of Labor, *Occupational Outlook Handbook, 2012-13 Edition*, on the Internet at http://www.bls.gov/

FIGURE 2 Dataset and Chart

Each cell containing a value is a ***data point***. For example, the value 664,800 in cell C6 is a data point for the estimated number of Systems Analysts in 2020. Each data point in the worksheet creates an individual data point in the chart. A group of related data points that display in row(s) or column(s) in the worksheet create a ***data series***. For example, the values 664,800, 664,500, and 406,800 comprise the number of estimated jobs by 2020 data series, which is indicated by the orange columns in the chart.

Identify the data range by selecting values and labels that you want to include in the chart. If the values and labels are not stored in adjacent cells, hold Ctrl while selecting the nonadjacent ranges. Do not select worksheet titles or subtitles; doing so would add unnecessary data to the chart. To create the chart in Figure 2, select the range A5:C8. It is important to select parallel ranges. A parallel range is one that consists of the same starting and end point as another similar range. For example, the range C5:C12 is a parallel range to A5:A12. Including the column headings on row 5 (even though cell A5 is blank) is necessary to include the years in the legend at the bottom of the chart area.

TIP: AVOID USING DATA AGGREGATES AND INDIVIDUAL VALUES
Do not include data aggregates (such as totals or averages) *and* individual values. Including aggregates diminishes the effectiveness of comparing individual data points. It distorts each data point because the columns or bars are too small compared to the total.

TIP: SELECTING COLUMN AND ROW LABELS
When you create a column or bar chart, make sure you include the row labels (such as Systems Analysts) and column headings (such as 2010 and 2020 Est.). If you select only the data, such as the range B6:C12, Excel will display *Series 1* and *Series 2* for the color-coded columns or bars. In that case, you would not know what color represents what year.

Excel transforms the selected data into a chart. A chart may include several chart elements or components. Table 1 lists and describes some of these elements. Figure 3 shows a chart area that contains these elements.

TABLE 1 Chart Elements

Chart Element	Description
Chart area	The container for the entire chart and all of its elements.
Plot area	Region containing the graphical representation of the values in the data series. Two axes form a border around the plot area.
X-axis	The horizontal border that provides a frame of reference for measuring data left to right.
Y-axis	The vertical border that provides a frame of reference for measuring data up and down.
Legend	A key that identifies the color, gradient, picture, texture, or pattern assigned to each data series in a chart. For example, blue might represent values for 2010, and orange might represent values for 2020.

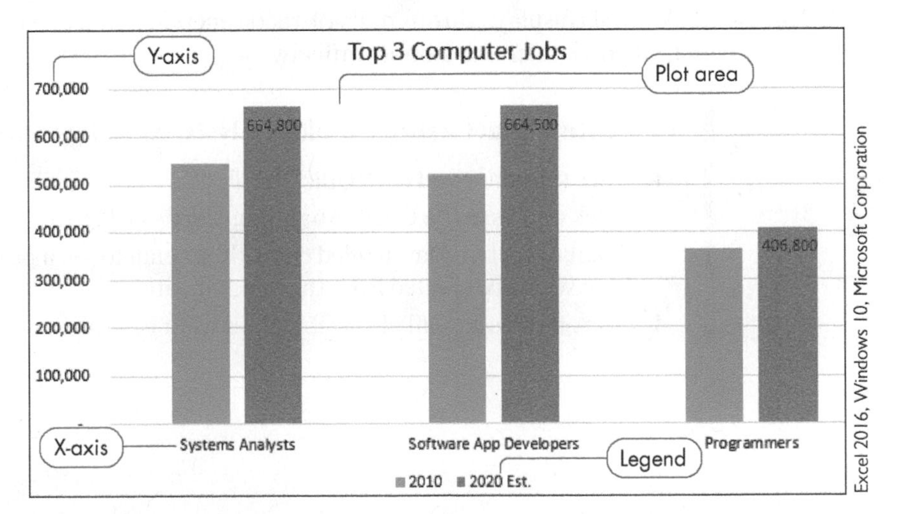

FIGURE 3 Chart Elements

Excel refers to the axes as the category axis and value axis. The ***category axis*** is the axis that displays descriptive labels for the data points plotted in a chart. The category axis labels are typically text contained in the first column of worksheet data (such as job titles) used to create the chart. The ***value axis*** is the axis that displays incremental numbers to identify the approximate values (such as number of jobs or revenue) of data points in a chart.

Choosing a Chart Type

You can create different charts from the same dataset; each chart type tells a different story. Select a chart type that appropriately represents the data and tells a story. For example, one chart might compare the number of computer-related jobs between 2010 and 2020, and another chart might indicate the percentage of new jobs by job title. The most commonly used chart types are column, bar, line, pie, and combo (see Table 2). Each chart type is designed to provide a unique perspective to the selected data.

TABLE 2 Common Chart Types

Chart	Chart Type	Description
	Column	Displays values in vertical columns where the height represents the value; the taller the column, the larger the value. Categories display along the horizontal (category) axis.
	Bar	Displays values in horizontal bars where the length represents the value; the longer the bar, the larger the value. Categories display along the vertical (category) axis.
	Line	Displays category data on the horizontal axis and value data on the vertical axis. Appropriate to show continuous data to depict trends over time, such as months, years, or decades.
	Pie	Shows proportion of individual data points to the total or whole of all those data points.
	Combo	Combines two chart types (such as column and line) to plot different data types (such as values and percentages)

Quick Analysis. When you select a range of adjacent cells (such as the range A5:C12) and position the pointer over that selected range, Excel displays Quick Analysis in the bottom-right corner of the selected area. However, Quick Analysis does not display when you select nonadjacent ranges, such as ranges A6:A12 and D6:D12. Quick Analysis displays thumbnails of recommended charts based on the data you selected so that you can create a chart quickly.

To create a chart using Quick Analysis, complete the following steps:

1. Select the data and click Quick Analysis.
2. Click Charts in the Quick Analysis gallery (see Figure 4).
3. Point to each recommended chart thumbnail to see a preview of the type of chart that would be created from the selected data.
4. Click the thumbnail of the chart you want to create.

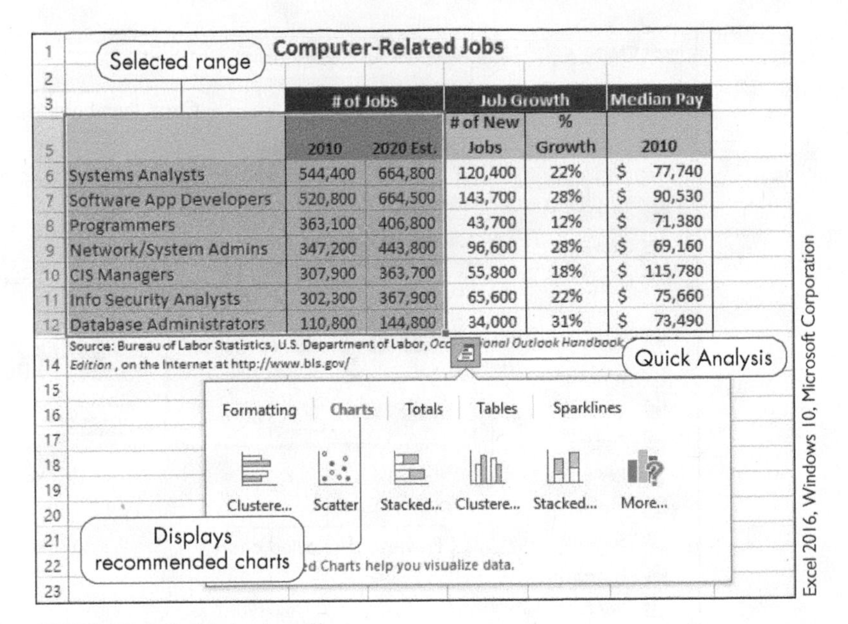

FIGURE 4 Quick Analysis Tool

Insert Tab. The Insert tab contains commands for creating a variety of charts. You must use the Insert tab to create a chart when you select nonadjacent ranges, but you can also use the Insert tab to create a chart when you select adjacent ranges. Clicking a particular chart on the Insert tab displays a gallery of icons representing more specific types of charts.

To create a chart using the Insert tab, complete the following steps:

1. Select the data and click the Insert tab.
2. Complete one of the following steps to select the chart type:
   - Click the chart type (such as Column) in the Charts group and click a chart subtype (such as Clustered Column) from the chart gallery (see Figure 5).
   - Click Recommended Charts in the Charts group to open the Insert Chart dialog box, click a thumbnail of the chart you want in the Recommended Charts tab or click the All Charts tab (see Figure 6) and click a thumbnail, and then click OK.

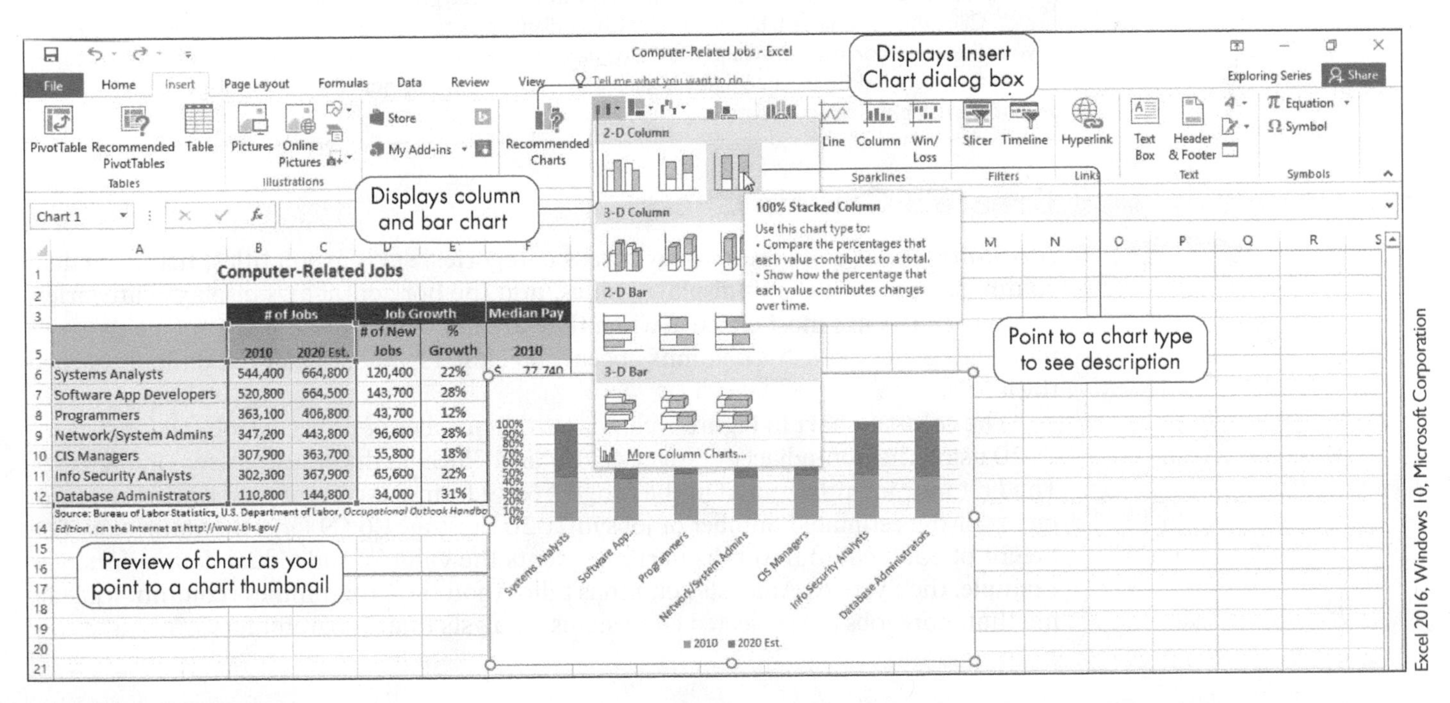

FIGURE 5 Chart Gallery

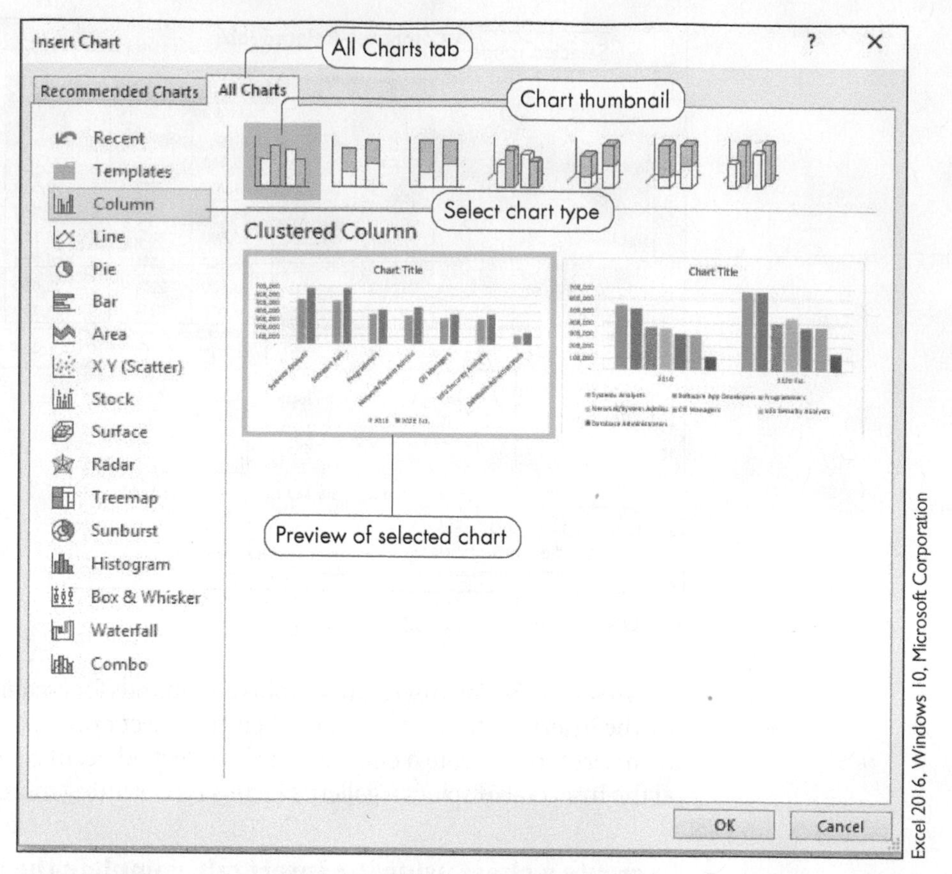

FIGURE 6 Insert Chart Dialog Box

> **TIP: RECOMMENDED VS. LIST OF ALL CHARTS**
> If you are unsure which type of chart would be a good choice for the selected data, click Recommended Charts in the Chart group. Excel will analyze the selected data and display thumbnails of recommended charts in the Insert Chart dialog box. Click a thumbnail to see a larger visualization of how your selected data would look in that chart type. The dialog box displays a message indicating the purpose of the selected chart, such as *A clustered bar chart is used to compare values across a few categories. Use it when the chart shows duration or when the category text is long.*
> Click the All Charts tab in the Insert Chart dialog box to display a list of all chart types. After you click a type on the left side of the dialog box, the top of the right side displays specific subtypes, such as Clustered Column. When you click a subtype, the dialog box displays an image of that subtype using the selected data.

Create a Column Chart

STEP 1 »» A ***column chart*** compares values across categories, such as job titles, using vertical columns. The vertical axis displays values, and the horizontal axis displays categories. Column charts are most effective when they are limited to seven or fewer categories. If more categories exist, the columns appear too close together, making it difficult to read the labels.

The column chart in Figure 7 compares the number of projected jobs by job title for 2020 using the non-adjacent ranges A5:A9 and C5:C9 in the dataset shown in Figure 5. The first four job titles stored in the range A6:A9 form the category axis, and the increments of the estimated number of jobs in 2020 in range C6:C9 form the value axis. The height of each column in the chart represents the value of individual data points. For example, the Systems Analysts column is taller than the Programmers column, indicating that more jobs are projected for Systems Analysts than Programmers.

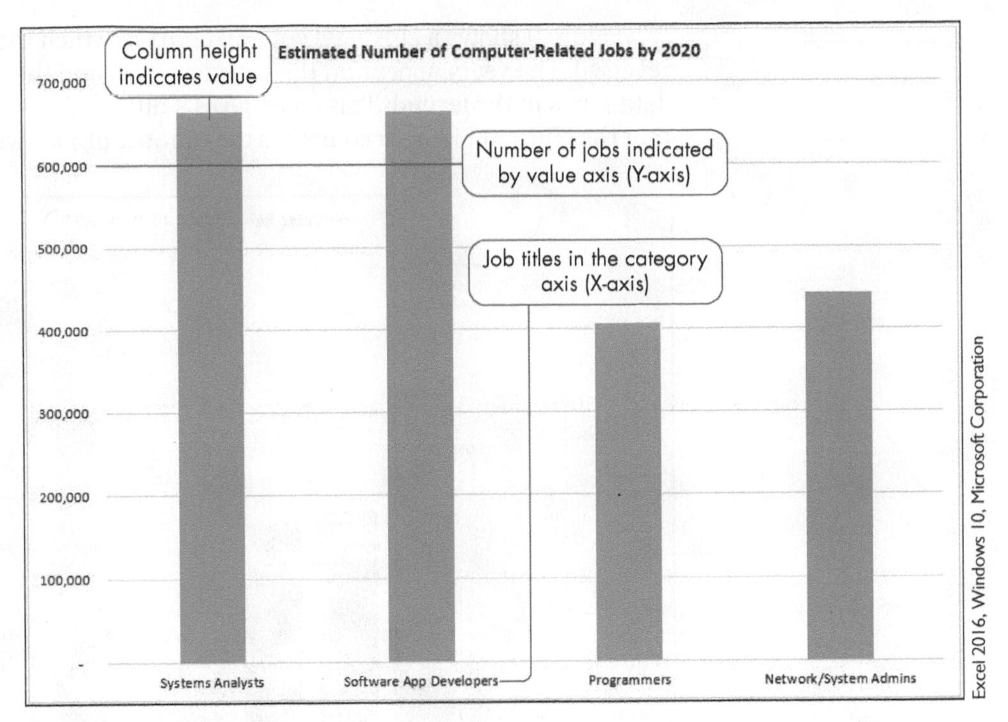

FIGURE 7 Column Chart

A ***clustered column chart*** compares groups—or clusters—of columns set side by side. The clustered column chart facilitates quick comparisons across data series, and it is effective for comparing several data points among categories. Figure 8 shows a clustered column chart created from the adjacent range A5:C9 in the dataset shown in Figure 5. By default, the job titles in the range A6:A9 appear on the category axis, and the yearly data points appear as columns with the value axis showing incremental numbers. Excel assigns a different color to each yearly data series and includes a legend so that you know what color represents which data series. The 2010 data series is light blue, and the 2020 data series is dark blue. This chart makes it easy to compare the predicted job growth from 2010 to 2020 for each job title and then to compare the trends among job titles.

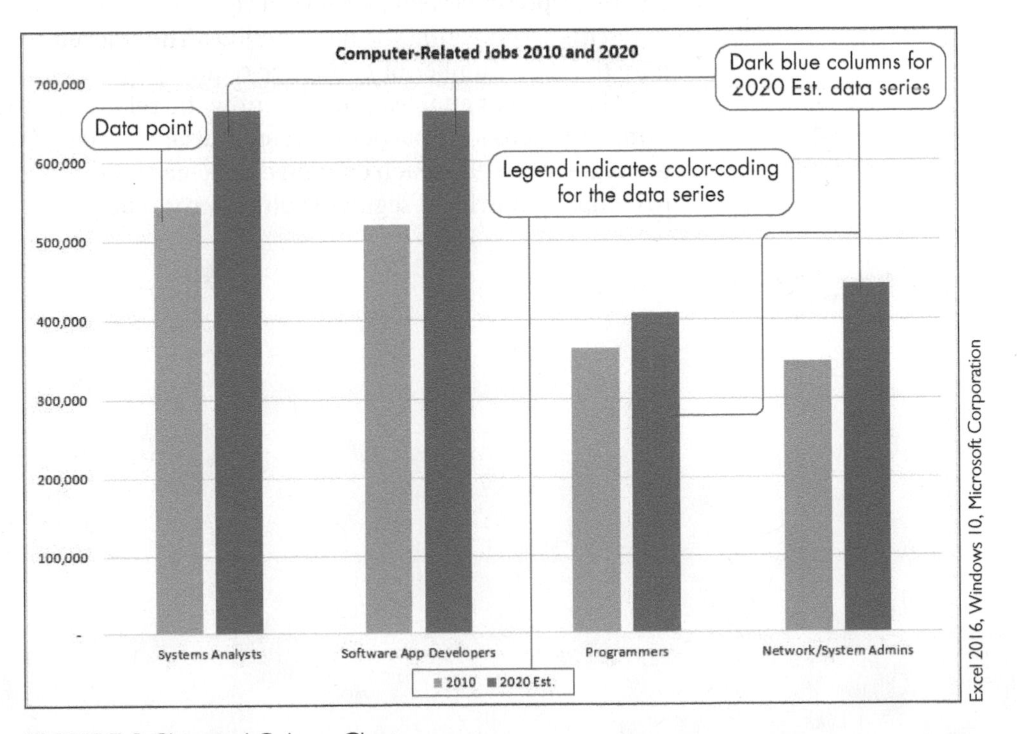

FIGURE 8 Clustered Column Chart

Figure 9 shows a clustered column chart in which the categories and data series are reversed. The years appear on the category axis, and the job titles appear as color-coded data series in the legend. This chart gives a different perspective from that in Figure 8 in that the chart in Figure 9 compares the number of jobs within a given year.

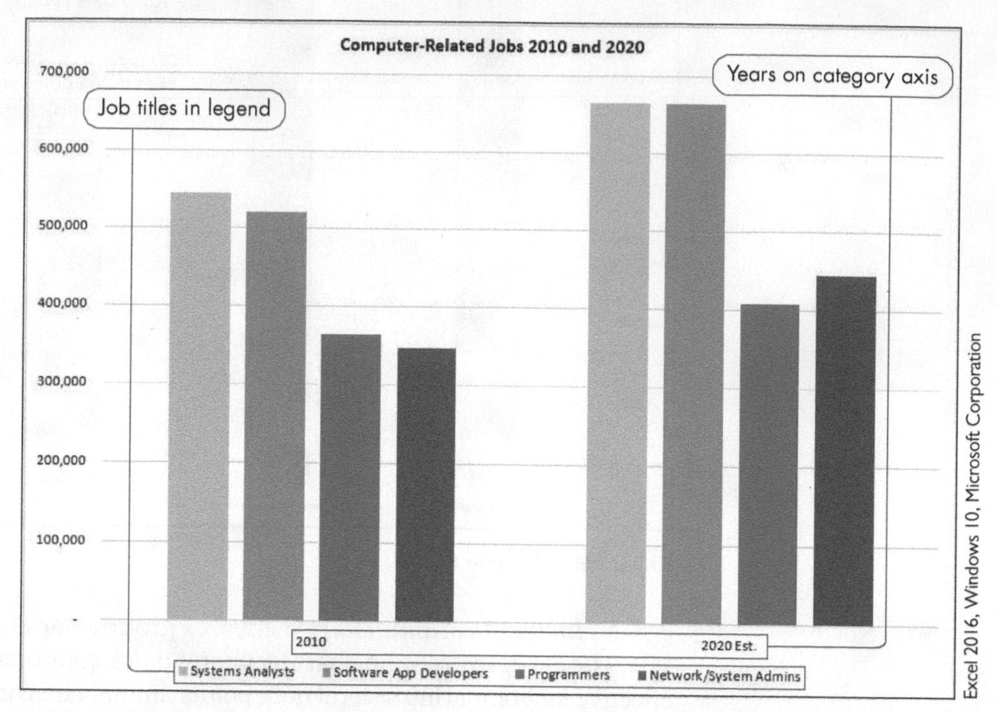

FIGURE 9 Clustered Column Chart: Category Axis and Legend Reversed

A ***stacked column chart*** shows the relationship of individual data points to the whole category. A stacked column chart displays only one column for each category. Each category within the stacked column is color-coded for one data series. Use the stacked column chart when you want to compare total values across categories, as well as to display the individual category values. Figure 10 shows a stacked column chart in which a single column represents each categorical year, and each column stacks color-coded data-point segments representing the different jobs. The stacked column chart enables you to compare the total number of computer-related jobs for each year. The height of each color-coded data point enables you to identify the relative contribution of each job to the total number of jobs for a particular year. A disadvantage of the stacked column chart is that the segments within each column do not start at the same point, making it more difficult to compare individual segment values across categories.

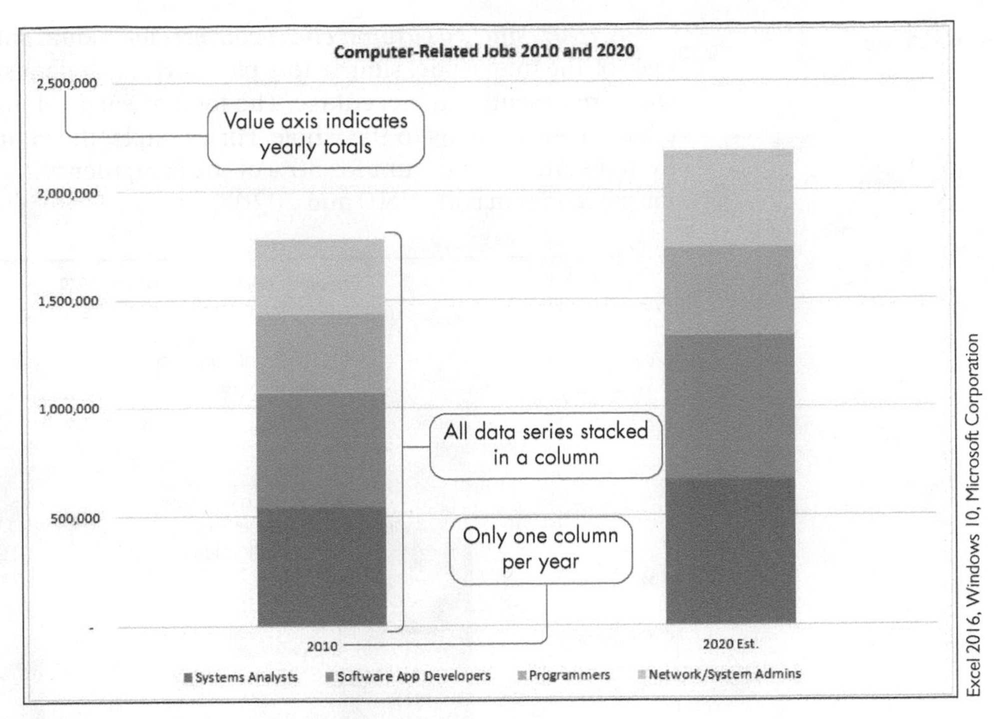

FIGURE 10 Stacked Column Chart

When you create a stacked column chart, make sure data are additive: Each column represents a sum of the data for each segment. Figure 10 correctly uses years as the category axis and the jobs as data series. For each year, Excel adds the number of jobs, and the columns display the total number of jobs. For example, the estimated total number of the four computer-related jobs in 2020 is about 2,180,000. Figure 11 shows a meaningless stacked column chart because the yearly number of jobs by job title is *not* additive. Adding the number of current actual jobs to the number of estimated jobs in the future does not make sense. It is incorrect to state that about 1,200,000 Systems Analysts jobs exist. Be careful when constructing stacked column charts to ensure that they lead to logical interpretation of data.

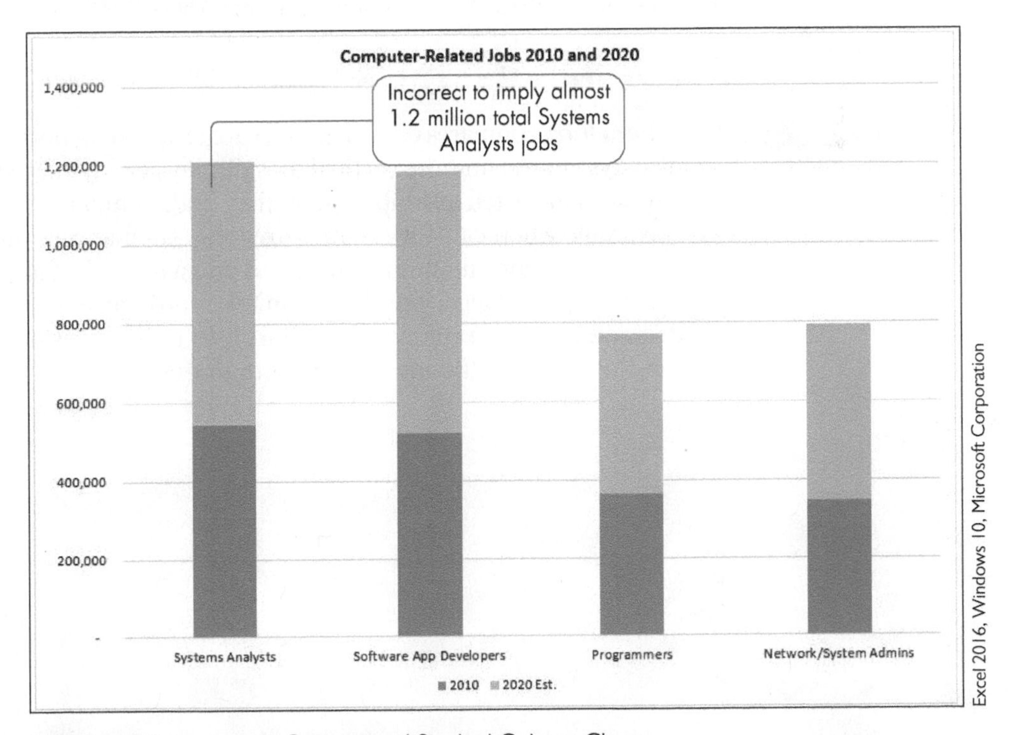

FIGURE 11 Incorrectly Constructed Stacked Column Chart

A ***100% stacked column chart*** converts individual data points (values) into percentages of the total value, similar to a pie chart. Each data series is a different color of the stack, representing a percentage. The total of each column is 100%. This type of chart depicts contributions to the whole. For example, the chart in Figure 12 illustrates that Systems Analysts account for 30% of the computer-related jobs represented by the four job categories in both 2010 and 2020.

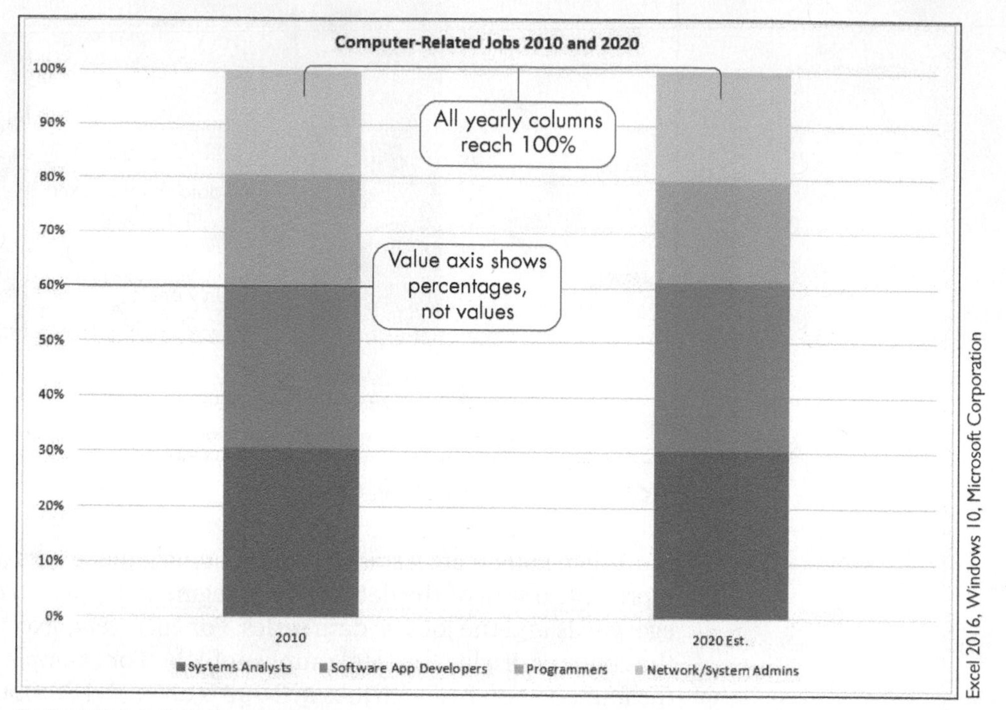

FIGURE 12 100% Stacked Column Chart

> **TIP: AVOID 3-D CHARTS**
> Avoid creating 3-D charts, because the third dimension is a superficial enhancement that usually distorts the charted data. For example, some columns appear taller or shorter than they actually are because of the angle of the 3-D effect, or some columns might be hidden by taller columns in front of them.

Create a Bar Chart

STEP 2 A ***bar chart*** compares values across categories using horizontal bars. The horizontal axis displays values, and the vertical axis displays categories (see Figure 13). Bar charts and column charts tell a similar story: they both compare categories of data. A bar chart is preferable when category names are long, such as *Software App Developers*. A bar chart enables category names to appear in an easy-to-read format, whereas a column chart might display category names at an awkward angle or in a smaller font size. The overall decision between a column and a bar chart may come down to the fact that different data may look better with one chart type than the other.

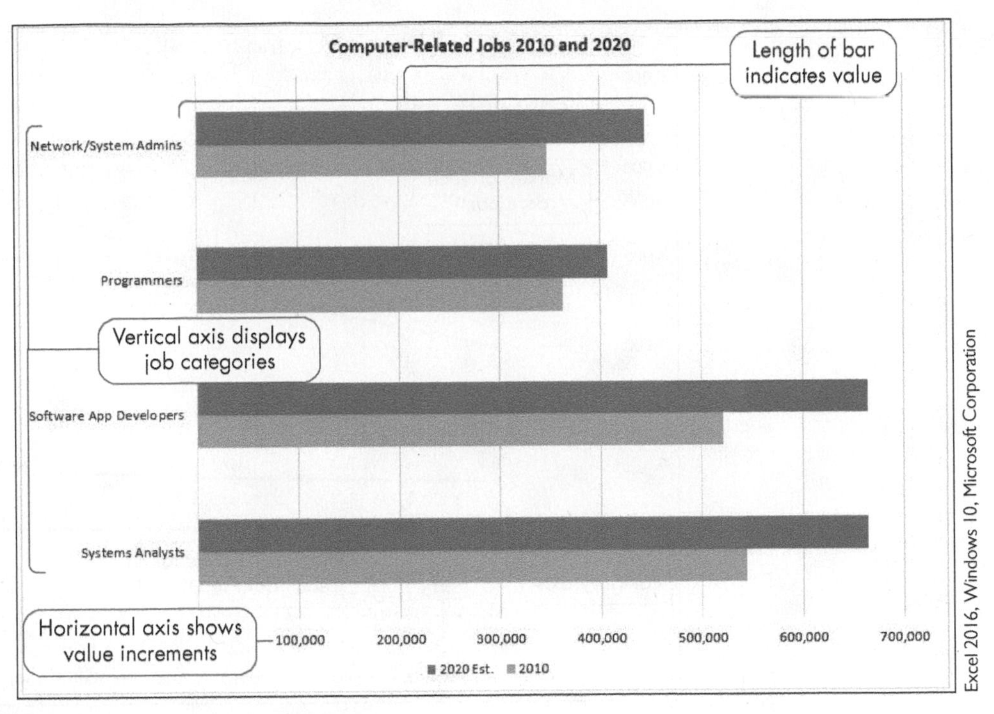

FIGURE 13 Clustered Bar Chart

Change the Chart Type

After you create a chart, you may decide that the data would be better represented by a different type of chart. For example, you might decide a bar chart would display the labels better than a column chart, or you might want to change a clustered bar chart to a stacked bar chart to provide a different perspective for the data. Use the Change Chart Type feature to change a chart to a different type of chart.

To change the type of an existing chart, complete the following steps:

1. Select the chart and click the Design tab.
2. Click Change Chart Type in the Type group to open the Change Chart Type dialog box (which is similar to the Insert Chart dialog box).
3. Click the All Charts tab within the dialog box.
4. Click a chart type on the left side of the dialog box.
5. Click a chart subtype on the right side of the dialog box and click OK.

Create a Line Chart

A ***line chart*** displays lines connecting data points to show trends over equal time periods. Excel displays each data series with a different line color. The category axis (X-axis) represents time, such as 10-year increments, whereas the value axis (Y-axis) represents a value, such as money or quantity. A line chart enables you to detect trends because the line continues to the next data point. To show each data point, choose the Line with Markers chart type. Figure 14 shows a line chart indicating the number of majors from 2005 to 2020 (estimated) at five-year increments. The number of Arts majors remains relatively constant, but the number of Tech & Computing majors increases significantly over time, especially between the years 2010 and 2020.

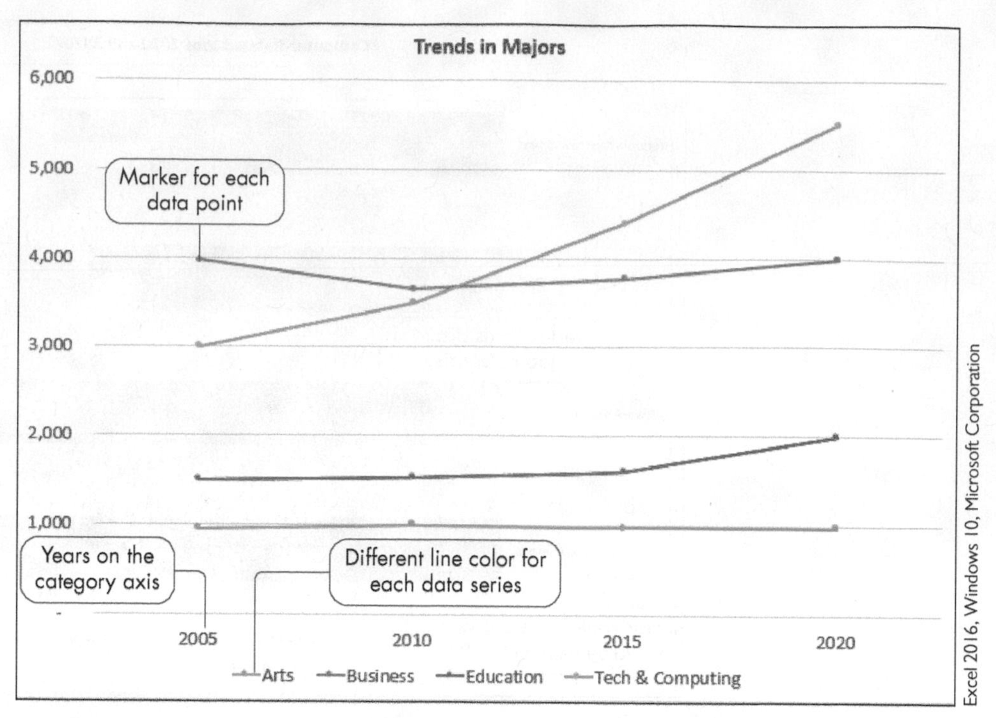

FIGURE 14 Line Chart

Create a Pie Chart

STEP 4 A ***pie chart*** shows each data point as a proportion to the whole data series. The pie chart displays as a circle, or "pie," where the entire pie represents the total value of the data series. Each slice represents a single data point. The larger the slice, the larger percentage that data point contributes to the whole. Use a pie chart when you want to convey percentage. Unlike column, bar, and line charts that typically chart multiple data series, pie charts represent a single data series only.

The pie chart in Figure 15 divides the pie representing the estimated number of new jobs into seven slices, one for each job title. The size of each slice is proportional to the percentage of total computer-related jobs depicted in the worksheet for that year. For example, Systems Analysts account for 21% of the estimated total number of new computer-related jobs in 2020. Excel creates a legend to indicate which color represents which pie slice. When you create a pie chart, limit it to about seven data points. Pie charts with too many slices appear too busy to interpret, or shades of the same color scheme become too difficult to distinguish.

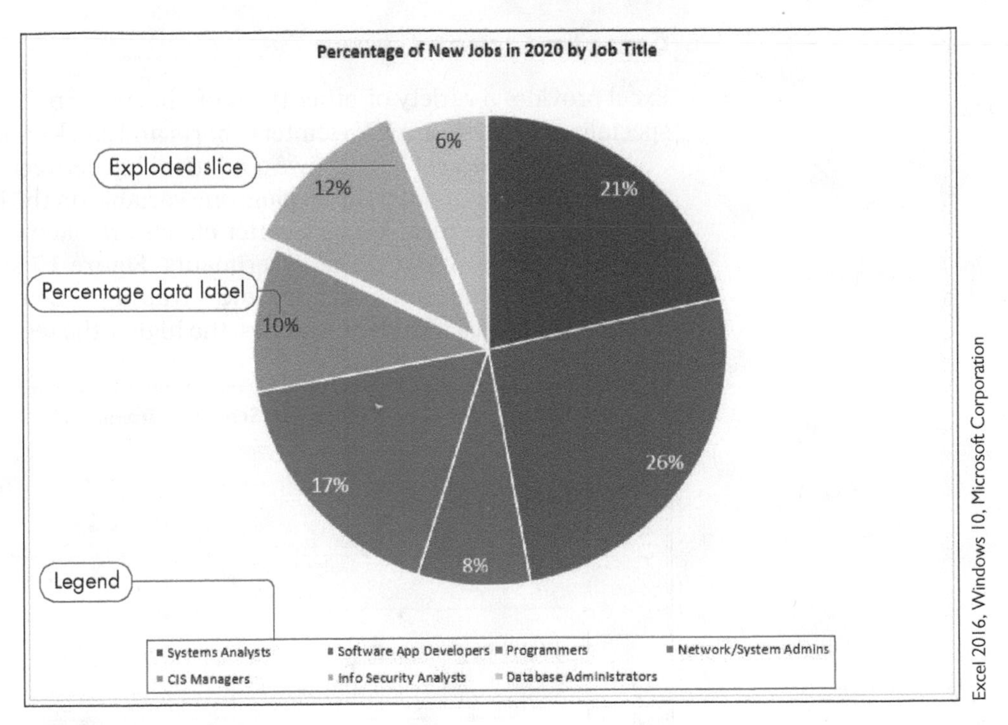

FIGURE 15 Pie Chart

Create a Combo Chart

STEP 5 A ***combo chart*** is a chart that combines two chart types, such as column and line charts. This type of chart is useful to show two different but related data types. For example, you might want to show the number of new jobs in columns and the percentage growth of new jobs in a line within the same chart (see Figure 16). A combo chart has a primary and a secondary axis. The primary axis displays on the left side of the chart. In this case, the primary axis indicates the number of jobs represented in the columns. The secondary axis displays on the right side of the chart. In this case, the secondary axis indicates the percentage of new jobs created as represented by the line.

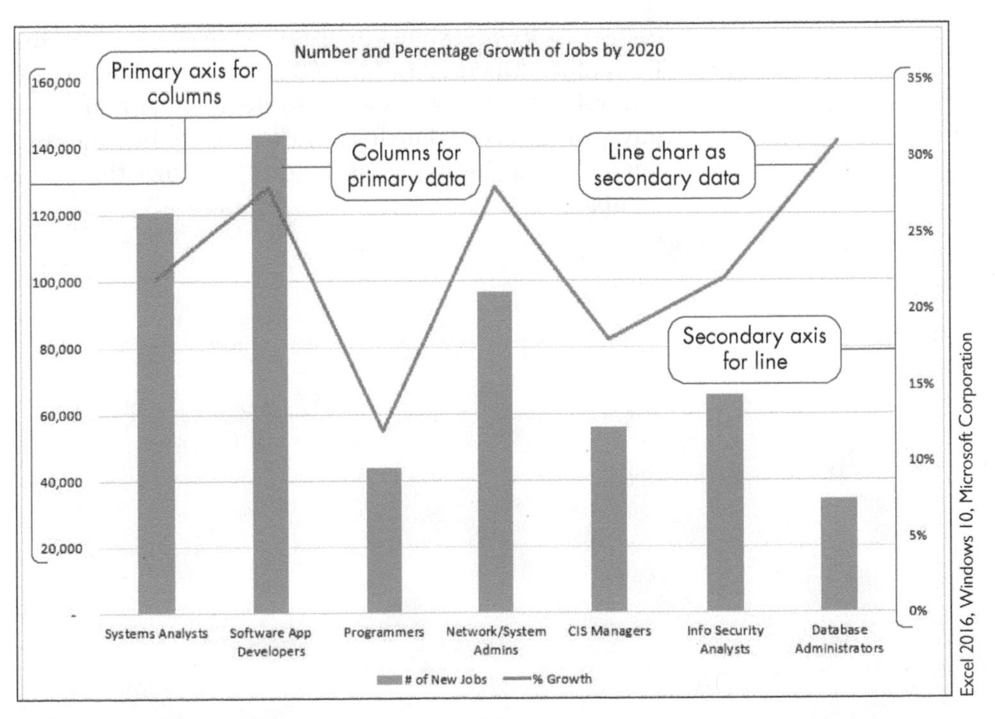

FIGURE 16 Combo Chart

Create Other Chart Types

Excel provides a variety of other types of charts. Two other chart types that are used for specialized analysis are X Y (scatter) charts and stock charts.

An ***X Y (scatter) chart*** shows a relationship between two numerical variables using their X and Y coordinates. Excel plots one variable on the horizontal X-axis and the other variable on the vertical Y-axis. Scatter charts are often used to represent data in educational, scientific, and medical experiments. Figure 17 shows the relationship between the number of minutes students view a training video and their test scores. The more minutes of a video a student watches, the higher the test score.

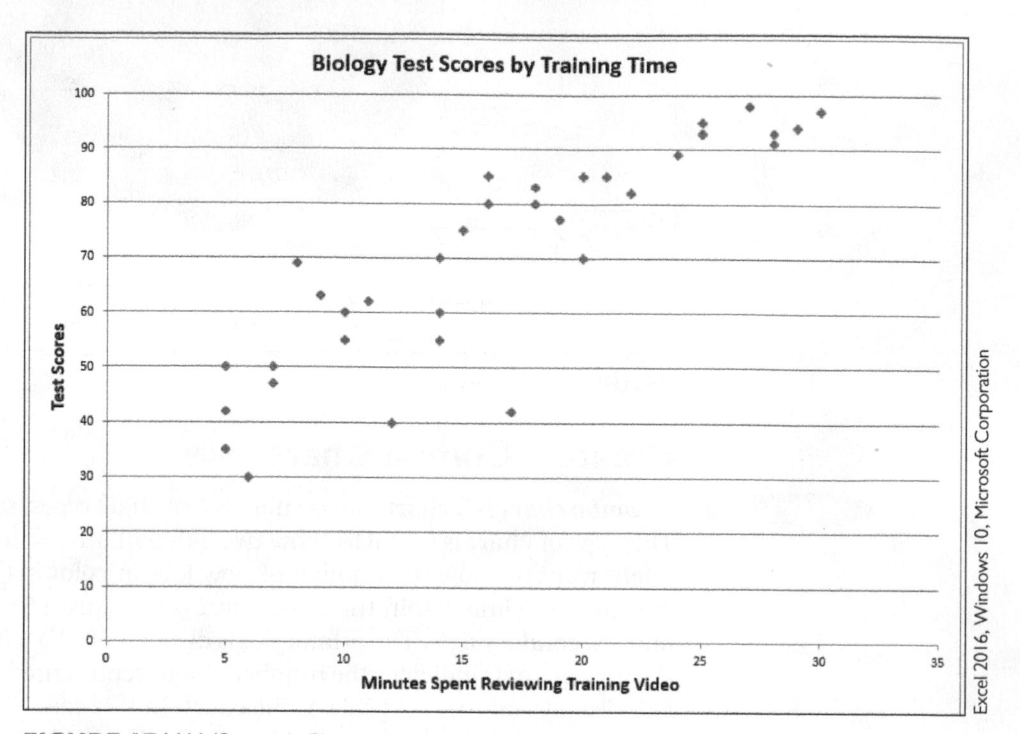

FIGURE 17 X Y (Scatter) Chart

A ***stock chart*** shows fluctuations in stock prices. Excel has four stock subtypes: High-Low-Close, Open-High-Low-Close, Volume-High-Low-Close, and Volume-Open-High-Low-Close. The High-Low-Close stock chart marks a stock's trading range on a given day with a vertical line from the lowest to the highest stock prices. Rectangles mark the opening and closing prices. Figure 18 shows three days of stock prices for a particular company.

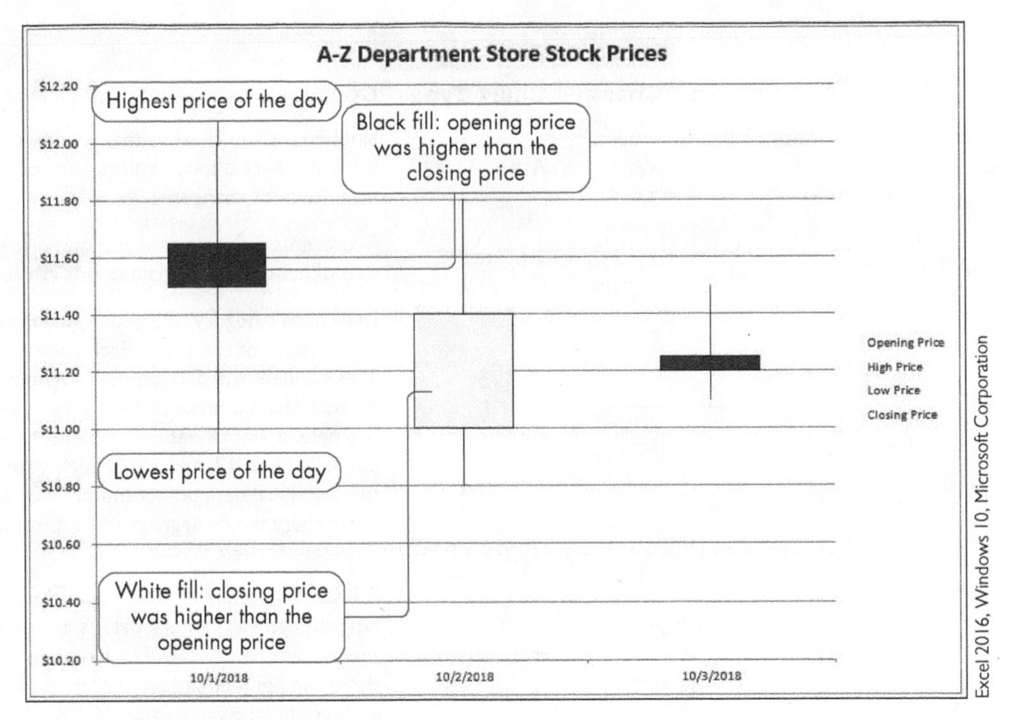

FIGURE 18 Stock Chart

The rectangle represents the difference in the opening and closing prices. If the rectangle has a white fill, the closing price is higher than the opening price. If the rectangle has a black fill, the opening price is higher than the closing price. In Figure 18, on October 1, the opening price was $11.65, and the closing price was $11.50, indicated by the top and bottom of the black rectangle. A line below the rectangle indicates that the lowest trading price is lower than the opening and closing prices. The lowest price was $11.00 on October 1. A line above the rectangle indicates that the highest trading price is higher than the opening and closing prices. The highest price was $12.00 on October 1. If no line exists below the rectangle, the lowest price equals either the opening or closing price, and if no line exists above the rectangle, the highest price equals either the opening or closing price.

TIP: ARRANGE DATA FOR A STOCK CHART

To create an Open-High-Low-Close stock chart, you must arrange data with Opening Price, High Price, Low Price, and Closing Price as column labels in that sequence. If you want to create other variations of stock charts, you must arrange data in a structured sequence required by Excel.

Table 3 lists and describes some of the other types of charts you can create in Excel.

TABLE 3 Other Chart Types

Chart	Chart Type	Description
	Area	Similar to a line chart in that it shows trends over time; however, the area chart displays colors between the lines to help illustrate the magnitude of changes.
	Surface	Represents numeric data and numeric categories. Displays trends using two dimensions on a continuous curve.
	Radar	Uses each category as a spoke radiating from the center point to the outer edges of the chart. Each spoke represents each data series, and lines connect the data points between spokes, similar to a spider web. A radar chart compares aggregate values for several data series. For example, a worksheet could contain the number of specific jobs for 2015, 2016, 2017, and 2018. Each year would be a data series containing the individual data points (number of specific jobs) for that year. The radar chart would aggregate the total number of jobs per year for all four data series.
	Histogram	A histogram is similar to a column chart. The category axis shows bin ranges (intervals) where data is aggregated into bins, and the vertical axis shows frequencies. For example, your professor might want to show the number (frequency) of students who earned a score within each grade interval, such as 60-69, 70-79, 80-89, and 90-100.

Moving, Sizing, and Printing a Chart

STEP 3 Excel inserts the chart as an embedded object in the current worksheet, often to the right of, but sometimes on top of and covering up, the data area. After you insert a chart, you usually need to move it to a different location and adjust its size. If you need to print a chart, decide whether to print the chart only or the chart and its data source.

Move a Chart

When you create a chart, Excel displays the chart in the worksheet, often on top of existing worksheet data. Therefore, you should move the chart so that it does not cover up data. If you leave the chart in the same worksheet, you can print the data and chart on the same page.

To move a chart on an active worksheet, complete the following steps:

1. Point to the chart area to display the Chart Area ScreenTip and the pointer includes the white arrowhead and a four-headed arrow.
2. Drag the chart to the desired location.

You might want to place the chart in a separate worksheet, called a ***chart sheet***. A chart sheet contains a single chart only; you cannot enter data and formulas on a chart sheet. If you want to print or view a full-sized chart, move the chart to its own chart sheet.

To move a chart to another sheet or a chart sheet, complete the following steps:

1. Select the chart.
2. Click the Design tab and click Move Chart in the Location group (or right-click the chart and select Move Chart) to open the Move Chart dialog box (see Figure 19).
3. Select one of these options to indicate where you want to move the chart:
   - Click *New sheet* to move the chart to its own sheet. The default chart sheet for the first chart is Chart1, but you can rename it in the Move Chart dialog box or similarly to the way you rename other sheet tabs.
   - Click *Object in*, click the *Object in* arrow, and select the worksheet to which you want to move the chart.
4. Click OK.

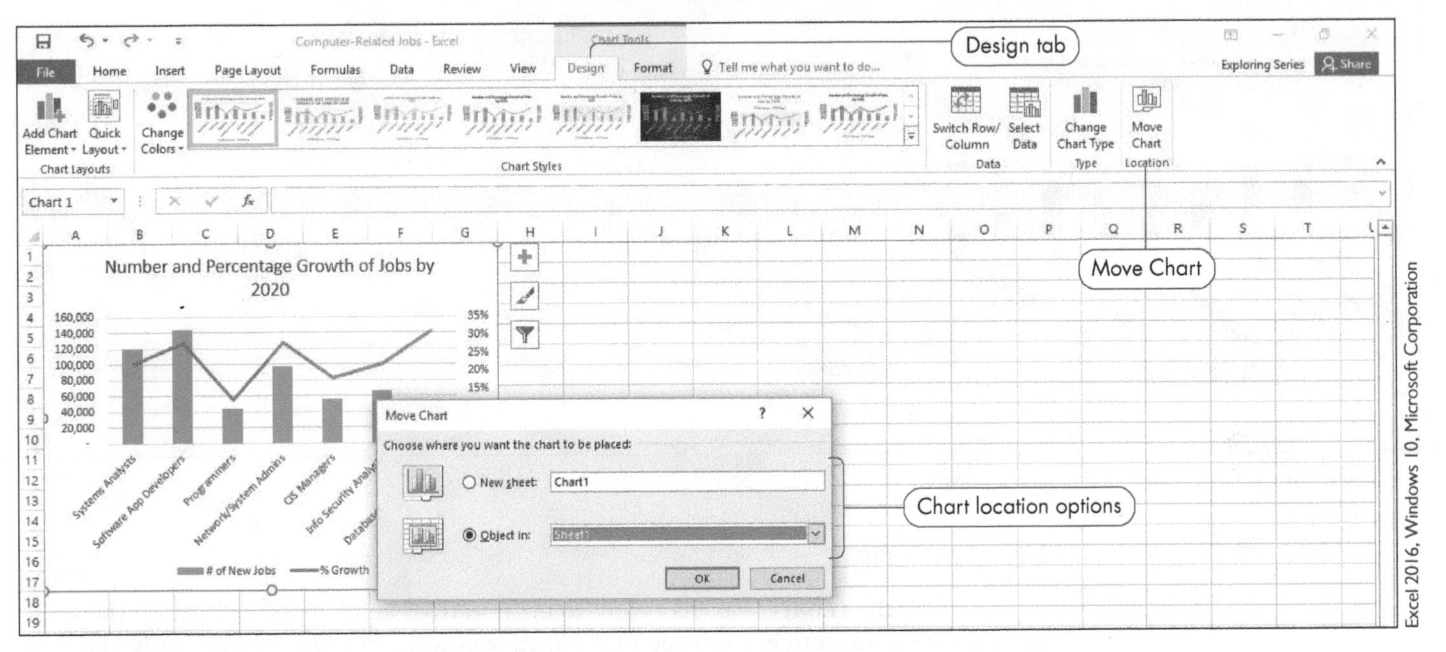

FIGURE 19 Design Tab and Move Chart Dialog Box

Size a Chart

If you move a chart to a chart sheet, the chart is enlarged to fill the entire sheet. If you keep a chart embedded within a worksheet, you might want to size the chart to fit in a particular range or to ensure the chart elements are proportional. Use the sizing handles or the Format tab on the Ribbon to change the size of the chart.

To change the chart size with sizing handles, complete the following steps:

1. Select the chart. Excel displays a line border and sizing handles around the chart when you select it. ***Sizing handles*** are eight circles that display around the four corners and outside middle sections of a chart when you select it.
2. Point to the outer edge of the chart where the sizing handles are located until the pointer changes to a two-headed arrow.
3. Drag the border to adjust the chart's height or width. Drag a corner sizing handle to increase or decrease the height and width of the chart at the same time. Press and hold Shift as you drag a corner sizing handle to change the height and width proportionately.

To change the chart size on the Ribbon, complete the following steps:

1. Select the chart.
2. Click the Format tab.
3. Change the value in the Height and Width boxes in the Size group (see Figure 20).

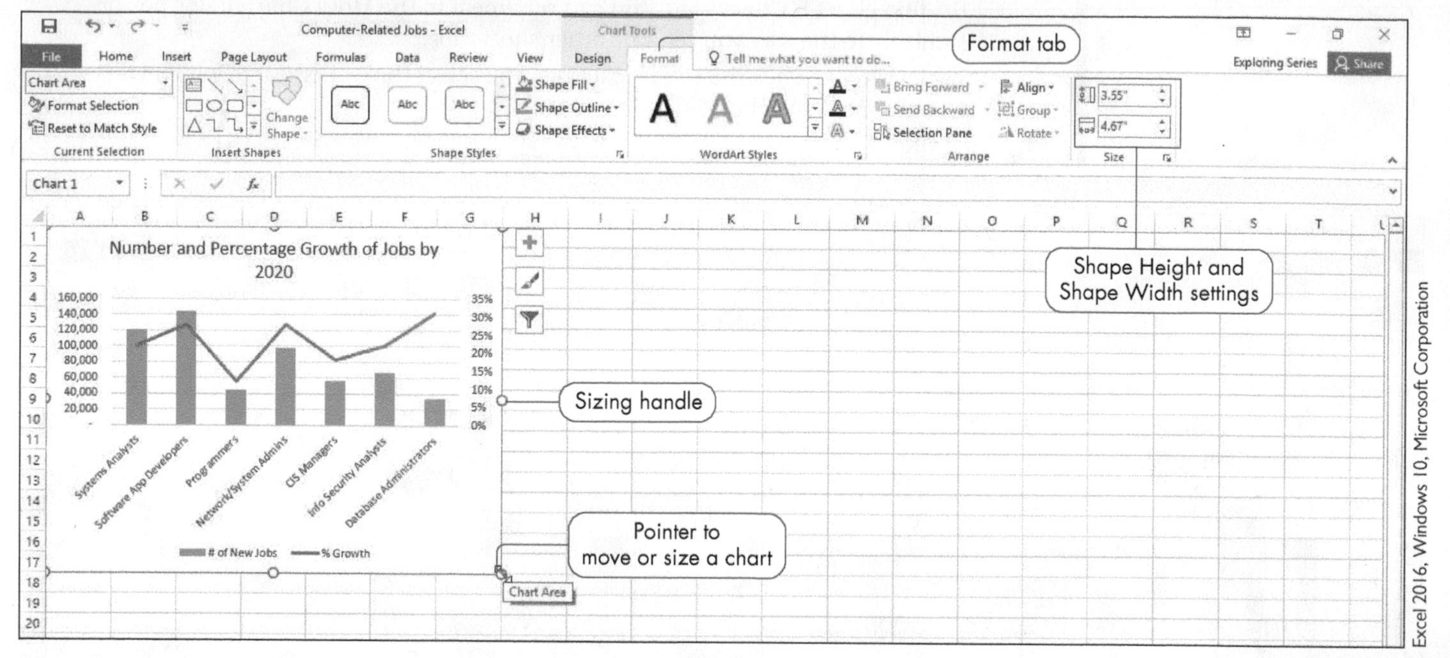

FIGURE 20 Sizing a Chart

Print a Chart

After you create a chart, you may want to print it. If you embedded a chart on the same sheet as the data source, you need to decide if you want to print the data only, the data and the chart, or the chart only.

To print the data only, complete the following steps:

1. Select the data.
2. Click the File tab and click Print.
3. Click the first arrow in the Settings section and select Print Selection.
4. Click Print.

To print only the chart as a full page, complete the following steps:

1. Select the chart if it is on a worksheet that also contains data.
2. Click the File tab and click Print.
3. Make sure the default setting is Print Selected Chart.
4. Click Print.

If the data and chart are on the same worksheet, print the worksheet contents to print both, but do not select either the chart or the data before displaying the Print options. The preview shows you what will print. Make sure it displays what you want to print before clicking Print.

If you moved the chart to a chart sheet, the chart is the only item on that worksheet. When you display the print options, the default is Print Active Sheets, and the chart will print as a full-page chart.

1. Why should you not include aggregates, such as totals or averages, along with individual data points in a chart?
2. Describe the purpose of each of these chart types: (a) column, (b) bar, (c) line, (d) pie, and (e) combo.
3. How can you use Quick Analysis to create a chart?
4. How do you decide whether to move a chart within the worksheet where you created it or move it to a chart sheet?

Hands-On Exercises

Skills covered: Select an Adjacent Range • Create a Clustered Column Chart • Move a Chart to a New Chart Sheet • Select a Nonadjacent Range • Create a Bar Chart • Change the Chart Type • Move a Chart Within a Worksheet • Size a Chart • Create a Pie Chart • Create a Combo Chart

1 Chart Basics

Doug Demers, your assistant, gathered data about seven computer-related jobs from the *Occupational Outlook Handbook* online. He organized the data into a structured worksheet that contains the job titles, the number of jobs in 2010, the projected number of jobs by 2020, and other data. Now you are ready to transform the data into visually appealing charts.

STEP 1 » CREATE A CLUSTERED COLUMN CHART

You want to compare the number of jobs in 2010 to the projected number of jobs in 2020 for all seven computer-related professions that Doug entered into the worksheet. You decide to create a clustered column chart to depict this data. After you create this chart, you will move it to its own chart sheet. You will format the charts in Hands-On Exercise 2. Refer to Figure 21 as you complete Step 1.

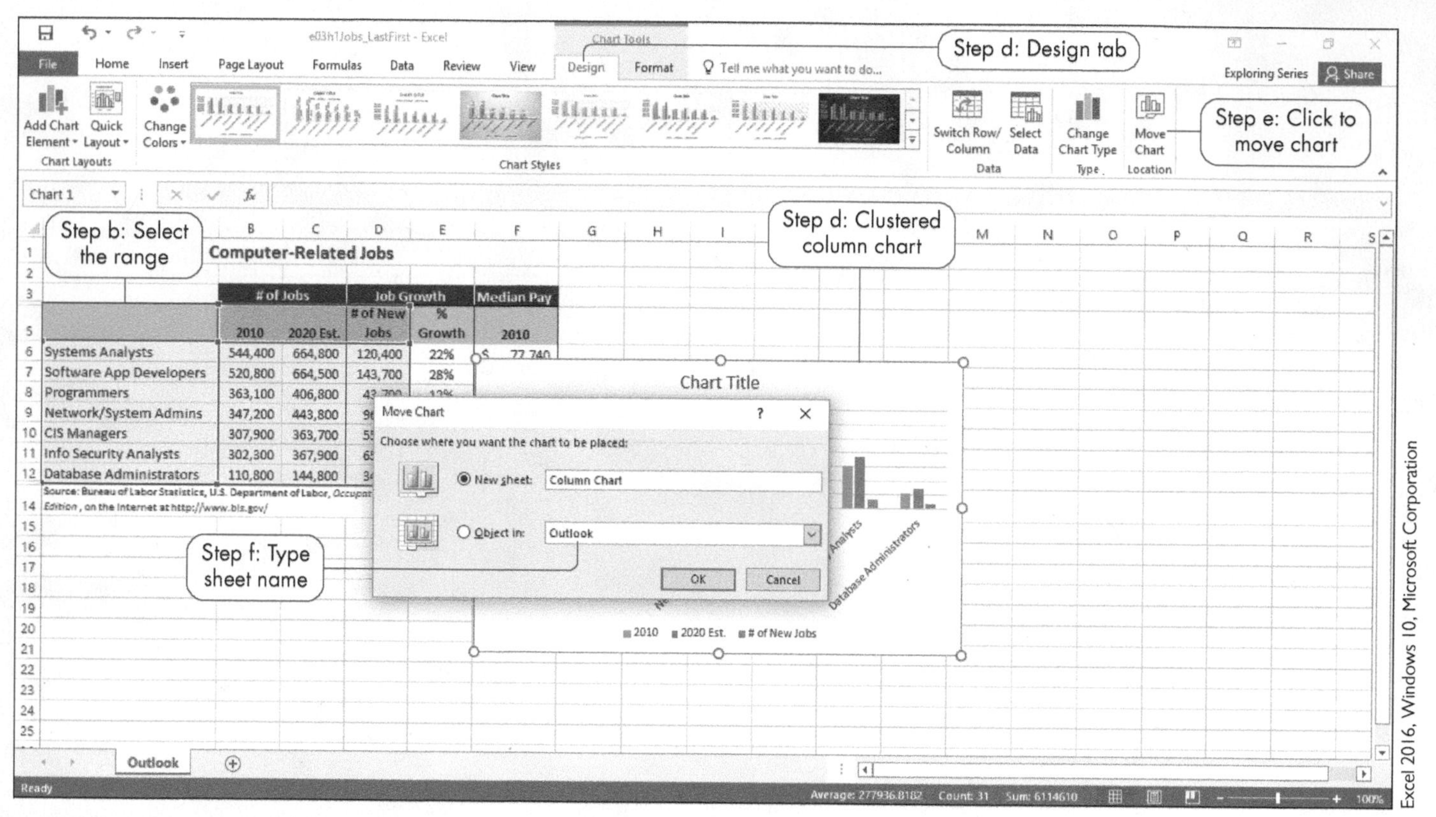

FIGURE 21 Clustered Column Chart

a. Open *e03h1Jobs* and save it as **e03h1Jobs_LastFirst**.

> **TROUBLESHOOTING:** If you make any major mistakes in this exercise, you can close the file, open *e03h1Jobs* again, and then start this exercise over.

b. Select the **range A5:D12.**

You selected the job titles, the number of jobs in 2010, the projected number of jobs in 2020, and the number of new jobs. Because you are selecting three data series (three columns of numerical data), you must also select the column headings on row 5.

c. Click **Quick Analysis** at the bottom-right corner of the selected range and click **Charts.**

The Quick Analysis gallery displays recommended charts based on the selected range.

d. Point to **Clustered Column** (the third thumbnail in the Charts gallery) to see a preview of what the chart would look like and click **Clustered Column.**

Excel inserts a clustered column chart based on the selected data. The Design tab displays on the Ribbon while the chart is selected.

e. Click **Move Chart** in the Location group.

The Move Chart dialog box opens for you to specify where to move the chart.

f. Click **New sheet**, type **Column Chart**, and then click **OK**. Save the workbook.

Excel moves the clustered column chart to a new sheet called Column Chart.

STEP 2 » CREATE A BAR CHART

You want to create a bar chart to depict the number of jobs in 2010 and the number of new jobs that will be created by 2020. Finally, you want to change the chart to a stacked bar chart to show the total jobs in 2020 based on the number of jobs in 2010 and the number of new jobs. Refer to Figure 22 as you complete Step 2.

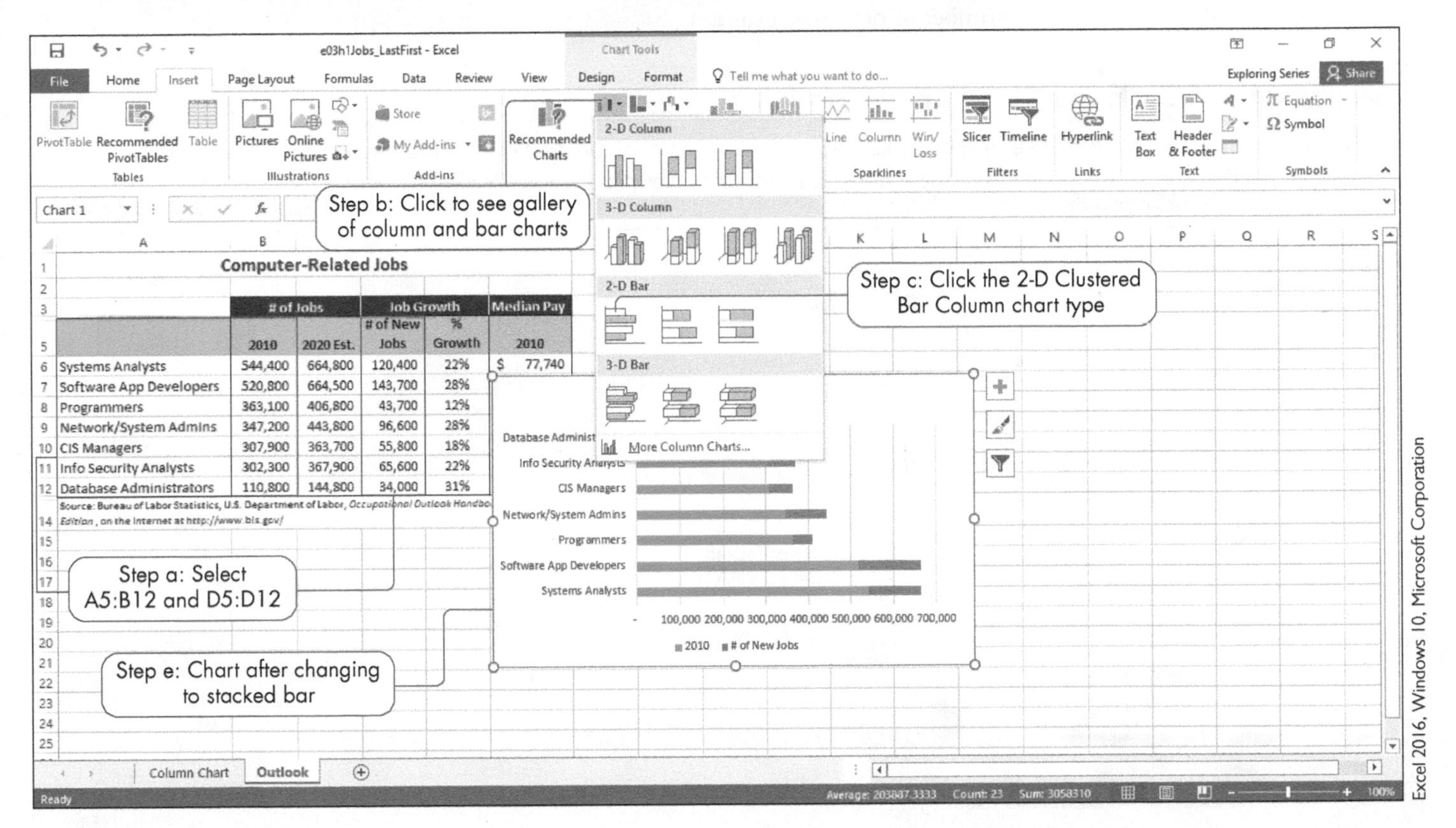

FIGURE 22 Bar Chart

a. Click the **Outlook sheet tab**, select the **range A5:B12**, press and hold **Ctrl**, and then select the **range D5:D12**.

You used Ctrl to select nonadjacent ranges: the job title labels, the number of jobs in 2010, and the number of new jobs.

> **TIP: PARALLEL RANGES**
>
> Nonadjacent ranges should be parallel so that the legend will correctly reflect the data series. This means that each range should contain the same number of related cells. For example, A5:A12, B5:B12, and D5:D12 are parallel ranges. Even though cell A5 is blank, you must select it to have a parallel range with the other two selected ranges that include cells on row 5.

b. Click the **Insert tab** and click **Insert Column or Bar Chart** in the Charts group.

The gallery shows both column and bar chart thumbnails.

c. Click **Clustered Bar** in the 2-D Bar section to create a clustered bar chart.

Excel inserts the clustered bar chart in the worksheet.

d. Click **Change Chart Type** in the Type group on the Design tab.

The Change Chart Type dialog box opens. The left side of the dialog box lists all chart types. The top-right side displays thumbnails of various bar charts, and the lower section displays a sample of the selected chart.

e. Click **Stacked Bar** in the top center of the dialog box and click **OK**. Save the workbook.

Excel displays the number of jobs in 2010 in blue and stacks the number of new jobs in orange into one bar per job title. This chart tells the story of how the total projected number of jobs in 2020 is calculated: the number of existing jobs in 2010 (blue) and the number of new jobs (orange).

STEP 3 » MOVE AND SIZE A CHART

The bar chart is displayed in the middle of the worksheet. You decide to position it below the job outlook data and adjust its size to make it larger so that it is as wide as the dataset and a little taller for better proportions. Refer to Figure 23 as you complete Step 3.

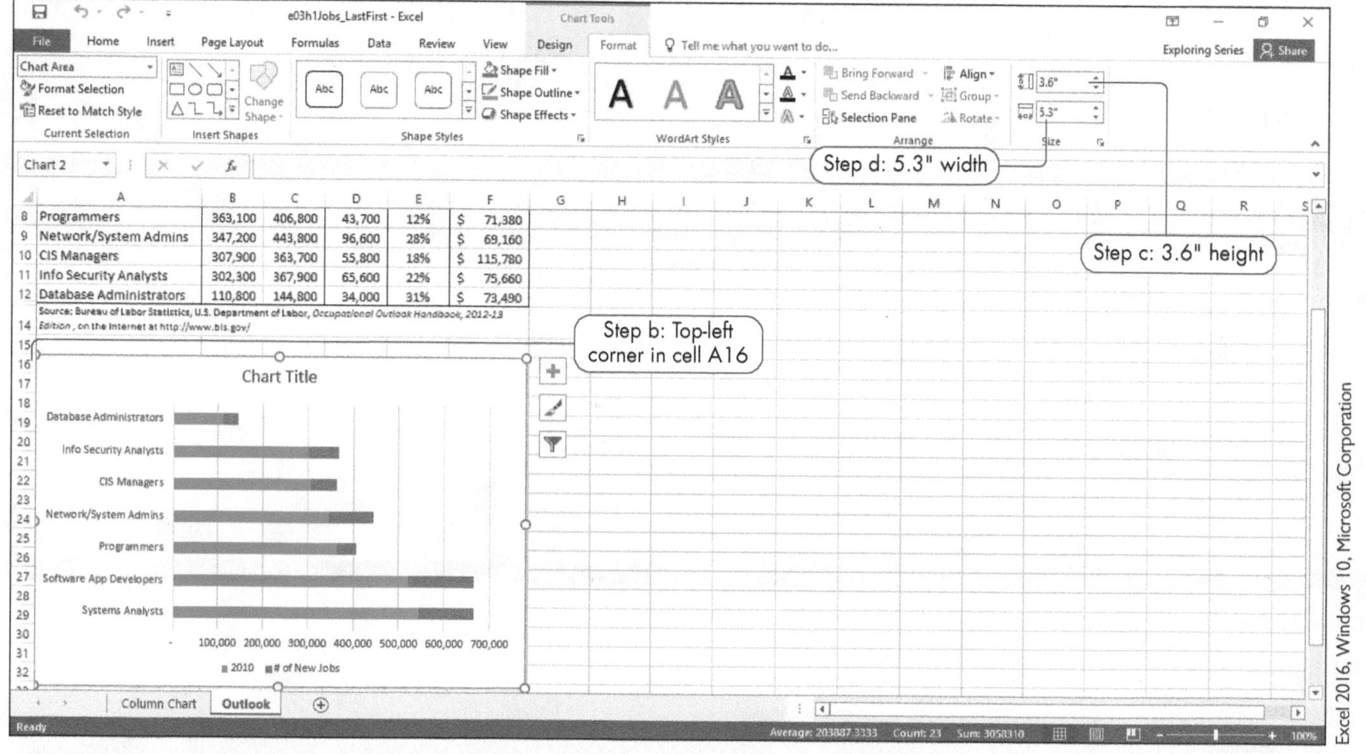

FIGURE 23 Stacked Bar Chart Moved and Sized

a. Point to an empty part of the chart area.

The pointer displays a four-headed arrow with the regular white arrowhead, and the Chart Area ScreenTip displays.

> **TROUBLESHOOTING:** Make sure you see the Chart Area ScreenTip as you perform Step b. If you move the pointer to another chart element—such as the legend—you will move or size that element instead of moving the entire chart.

b. Drag the chart so that the top-left corner of the chart appears in **cell A16**.

You positioned the chart below the worksheet data.

c. Click the **Format tab**, select the value in the **Shape Height box**, type **3.6**, and then press **Enter**.

The chart is now 3.6" tall.

d. Select the value in the **Shape Width box**, type **5.3**, and then press **Enter**. Save the workbook.

The chart is now 5.3" wide.

STEP 4 » CREATE A PIE CHART

You decide to create a pie chart that depicts the percentage of new jobs by job title calculated from the total number of new jobs created for the seven job titles Doug researched. After creating the pie chart, you will move it to its own sheet. Refer to Figure 24 as you complete Step 4.

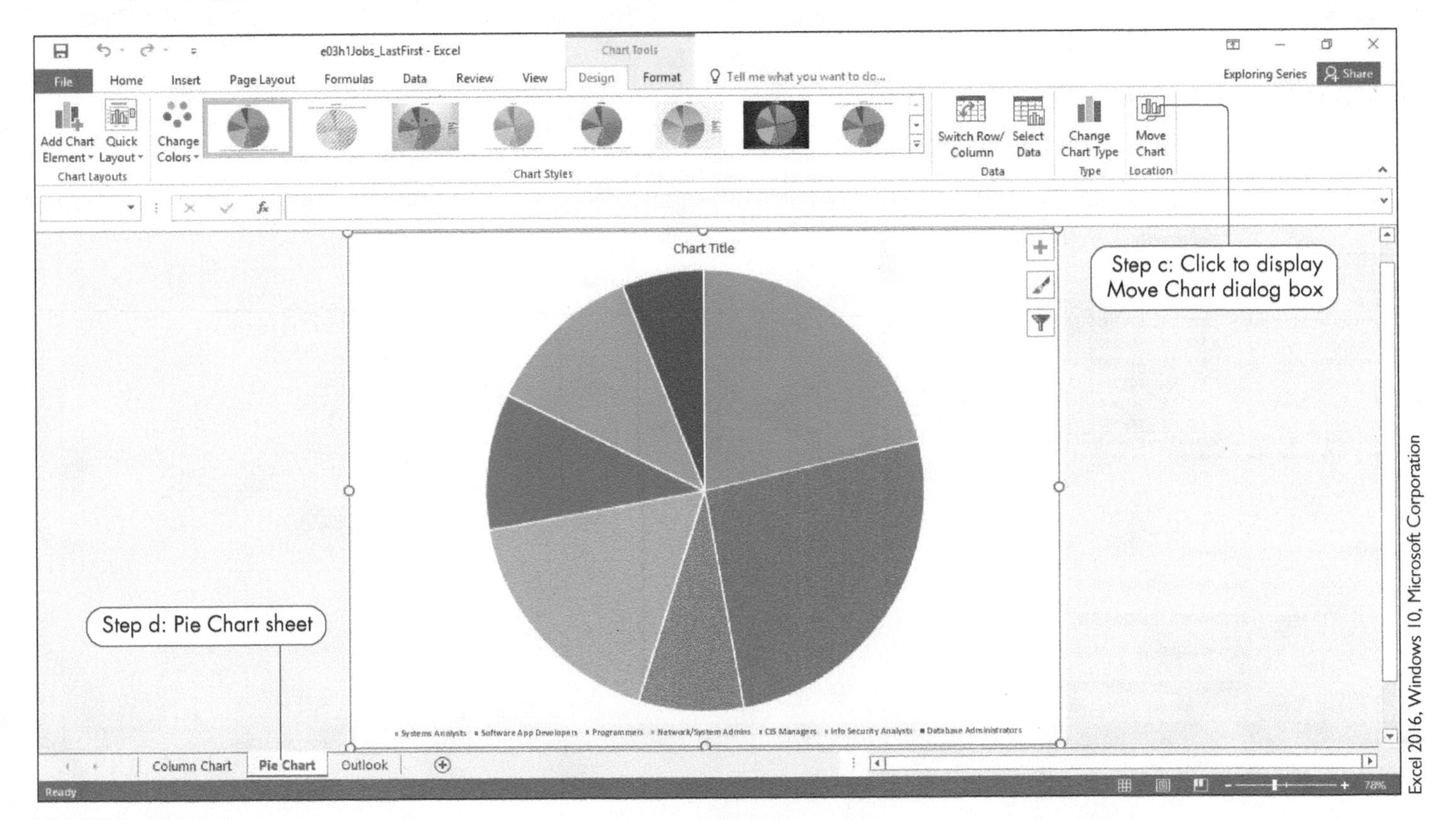

FIGURE 24 Pie Chart

a. Select the **range A6:A12**, press and hold **Ctrl**, then select the **range D6:D12**.

> **TROUBLESHOOTING:** Do not select cells A5 and D5 this time because you are creating a pie chart. When creating a chart from a single data series (e.g., # of New Jobs), you do not need to select the column headings.

b. Click the **Insert tab**, click **Insert Pie or Doughnut Chart** in the Charts group, and then select **Pie** in the 2-D Pie group on the gallery.

   The pie chart displays in the worksheet.

c. Click **Move Chart** in the Location group on the Design tab.

   The Move Chart dialog box opens.

d. Click **New sheet**, type **Pie Chart**, and then click **OK**. Save the workbook.

   Excel creates a new sheet called Pie Chart. The pie chart is the only object on that sheet.

STEP 5 » CREATE A COMBO CHART

You want to create a combo chart that shows the number of new jobs in columns and the percentage of new jobs created in a line on the secondary axis. Although the number of new jobs may appear low as represented by the smallest column (such as 34,000 new database administrators), the actual percentage of new jobs created between 2010 and 2020 may be significant as represented by the steep incline of the orange line (such as 31% growth for database administrators). Refer to Figure 25 as you complete Step 5.

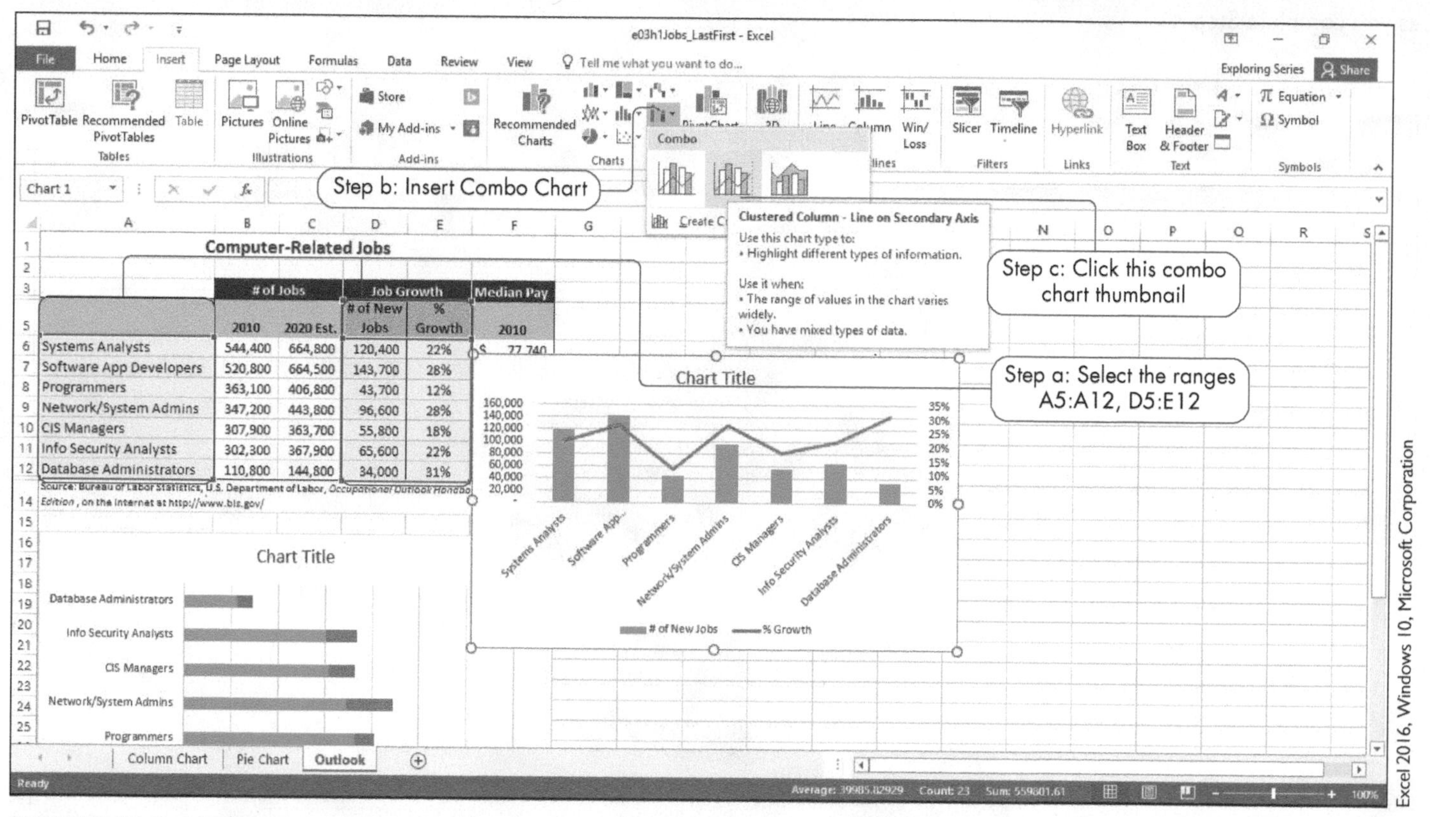

FIGURE 25 Combo Chart

a. Click the **Outlook sheet tab**, select the **range A5:A12**, press and hold **Ctrl**, then select the **range D5:E12**.

b. Click the **Insert tab** and click **Insert Combo Chart** in the Charts group.

The Combo Chart gallery of thumbnails displays.

c. Click the **Clustered Column – Line on Secondary Axis thumbnail**, which is the middle thumbnail.

Excel creates a combo chart based on the thumbnail you selected. The number of new jobs displays in blue columns, and the percentage growth displays as an orange line.

d. Click **Move Chart** in the Location group on the Design tab, click **New sheet**, type **Combo Chart**, and then click **OK**.

e. Save the workbook. Keep the workbook open if you plan to continue with the next Hands-On Exercise. If not, close the workbook, and exit Excel.

Chart Elements

After creating a chart, you should add appropriate chart elements. A ***chart element*** is a component that completes or helps clarify the chart. Some chart elements, such as chart titles, should be included in every chart. Other elements are optional. Table 4 describes the chart elements, and Figure 26 illustrates several chart elements.

TABLE 4 Chart Elements

Element	Description
Axis title	Label that describes the category or value axes. Display axis titles, such as In Millions of Dollars or Top 7 Computer Job Titles, to clarify the axes. Axis titles are not displayed by default.
Chart title	Label that describes the entire chart. It should reflect the purpose of the chart. For example, Houses Sold is too generic, but Houses Sold in Seattle in 2018 indicates the what (Houses), the where (Seattle), and the when (2018). The default text is Chart Title.
Data label	Descriptive label that shows the exact value or name of a data point. Data labels are not displayed by default.
Data table	A grid that contains the data source values and labels. If you embed a chart on the same worksheet as the data source, you might not need to include a data table. Only add a data table with a chart that is on a chart sheet.
Error bars	Visuals that indicate the standard error amount, a percentage, or a standard deviation for a data point or marker. Error bars are not displayed by default.
Gridlines	Horizontal or vertical lines that display in the plot area, designed to help people identify the values plotted by the visual elements, such as a column.
Legend	A key that identifies the color, gradient, picture, texture, or pattern assigned to each data series. The legend is displayed by default for some chart types.
Trendline	A line that depicts trends or helps forecast future data, such as estimating future sales or number of births in a region. Add a trendline to column, bar, line, stock, scatter, and bubble charts. Excel will analyze the current trends and display a line indicating future values based on those trends.

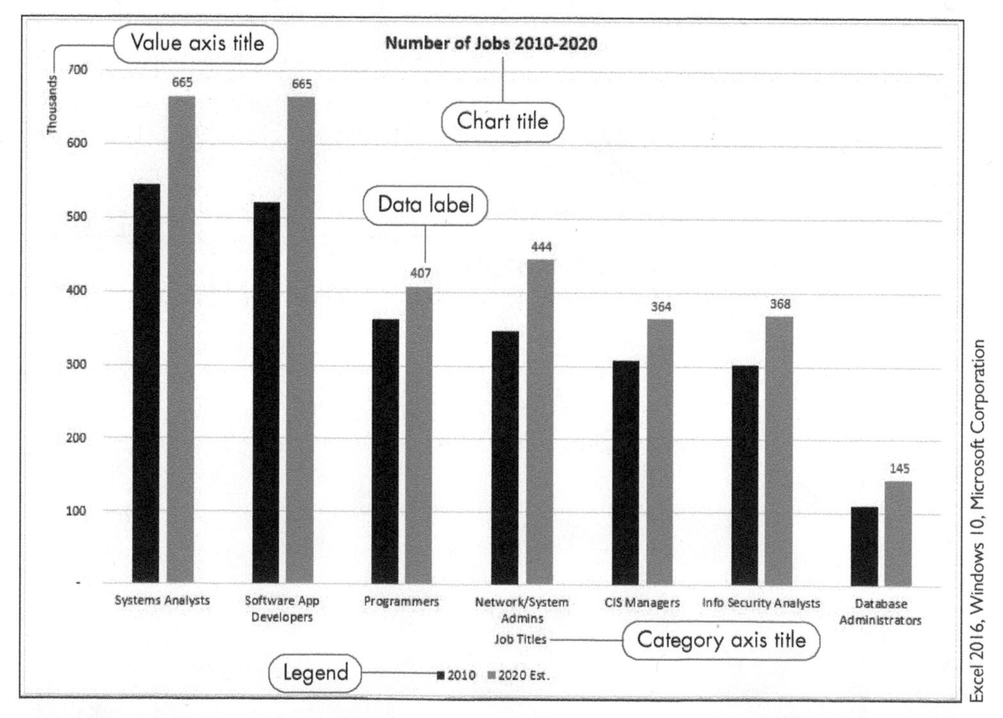

FIGURE 26 Chart Elements

In this section, you will learn how to add, edit, and format chart elements. Specifically, you will learn how to type a chart title, add axis titles, add data labels, and position the legend. Furthermore, you will learn how to format these elements as well as format axes, position the legend, and add gridlines. Finally, you will learn how to format the chart area, plot area, data series, and a data point.

Adding, Editing, and Formatting Chart Elements

After you create a chart, you usually need to add elements to provide labels to describe the chart. Adding descriptive text for labels provides information for the reader to comprehend the chart without knowing or seeing the underlying data. When you create a chart, one or more elements may display by default. For example, when you created the charts in Hands-On Exercise 1, Excel displayed a placeholder for the chart title and displayed a legend so that you know which color represents each data series.

When a chart is selected, three icons display to the right of the chart: Chart Elements, Chart Styles, and Chart Filters. In addition, the Design tab contains the Chart Layouts group that allows you to add and customize chart elements and change the layout of the chart.

When you point to a chart element, Excel displays a ScreenTip with the name of that element. To select a chart element, click it when you see the ScreenTip, or click the Format tab, click the Chart Elements arrow in the Current Selection group, and select the element from the list.

Edit, Format, and Position the Chart Title

STEP 1 »» Excel includes the placeholder text *Chart Title* above the chart. You should replace that text with a descriptive title. In addition, you might want to format the chart title by applying bold and changing the font, font size, font color, and fill color.

To edit and format the chart title, complete the following steps:

1. Select the chart title.
2. Type the text you want to appear in the title and press Enter.
3. Click the Home tab.
4. Apply the desired font formatting, such as increasing the font size and applying bold.
5. Click the chart to deselect the chart title.

TIP: FONT COLOR

The default font color for the chart title, axes, axes titles, and legend is Black, Text 1, Lighter 35%. If you want these elements to stand out, change the color to Black, Text 1 or another solid color.

By default, the chart title displays centered above the plot area. Although this is a standard location for the chart, you might want to position it elsewhere.

To change the position of the chart title, complete the following steps:

1. Select the chart title and click Chart Elements to the right of the chart.
2. Point to the Chart Title and click the triangle on the right side of the menu option, Chart Title (see Figure 27).
3. Select one of the options:
   - Above Chart: Centers the title above the plot area, decreasing the plot area size to make room for the chart title.
   - Centered Overlay: Centers the chart title horizontally without resizing the plot area; the title displays over the top of the plot area.
   - More Options: Opens the Format Chart Title task pane to apply fill, border, and alignment settings. A ***task pane*** is a window of options to format and customize chart elements. The task pane name and options change based on the selected chart element. For example, when you double-click the chart title, the Format Chart Title task pane displays.
4. Click Chart Elements to close the menu.

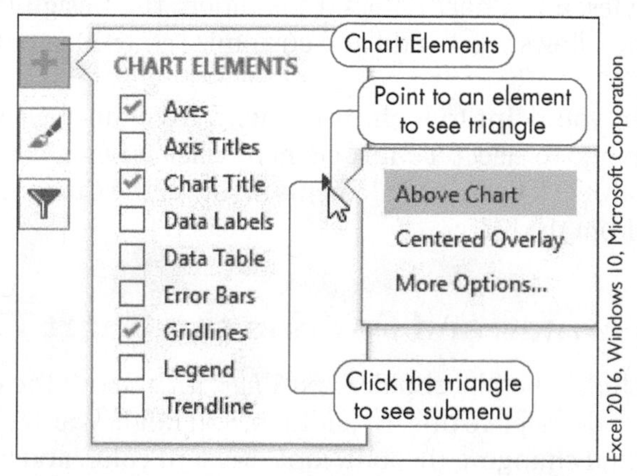

FIGURE 27 Chart Elements List

TIP: LINKING A CHART TITLE OR AN AXIS TITLE TO A CELL

Instead of typing text directly in the Chart Title or Axis Title placeholder, you can link the title to a label in a cell. Click the Chart Title or Axis Title placeholder, type = in the Formula Bar, click the cell containing the label you want for the title, and then press Enter. Excel will enter the sheet name and cell reference, such as =Outlook!$A$1, in the Formula Bar. If you change the worksheet label, Excel will also change the title in the chart.

Add, Format, and Position Axis Titles

STEP 2 »» Axis titles are helpful to provide more clarity about the value or category axis. Axis titles also help you conform to ADA compliance requirements. For example, if the values are abbreviated as 7 instead of 7,000,000 you should indicate the unit of measurement on the value axis as In Millions. You might want to further clarify the labels on the category axis by providing a category axis title, such as Job Titles.

To add an axis title, complete the following steps:

1. Select the chart and click Chart Elements to the right of the chart.
2. Point to Axis Titles and click the triangle on the right side.
3. Select one or more of these options:
   - Primary Horizontal: Displays a title for the primary horizontal axis.
   - Primary Vertical: Displays a title for the primary vertical axis.
   - Secondary Horizontal: Displays a title for the secondary horizontal axis in a combo chart.
   - Secondary Vertical: Displays a title for the secondary vertical axis in a combo chart.
   - More Options: Opens the Format Axis Title task pane to apply fill, border, and alignment settings.
4. Click Chart Elements to close the menu.

To use the Design tab to add a chart element, complete the following steps:

1. Click the Design tab.
2. Click Add Chart Element in the Chart Layouts group.
3. Point to an element and select from that element's submenu (see Figure 28).

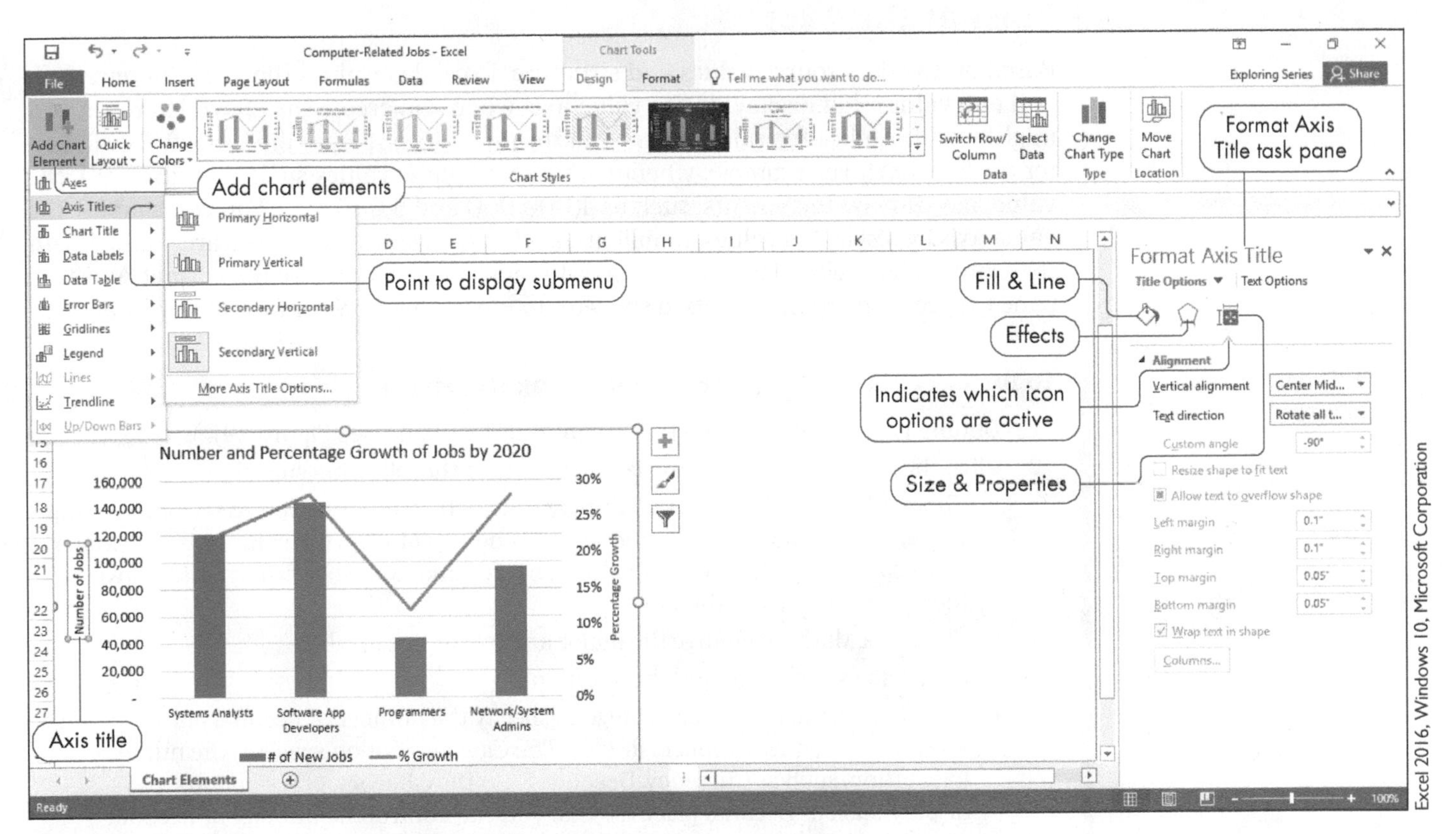

FIGURE 28 Chart Elements Menu and Format Axis Title Task Pane

The horizontal axis title displays below the category labels, and the rotated vertical axis title displays on the left side of the value axis. After including an axis title, click the title, type the text for the title, and then press Enter similarly to editing text for a chart title. You might want to apply font formatting (such as font size and color) to the axis titles similarly to formatting a chart title. Use the Format Axis Title task pane to customize and format the axis title.

To position and format the axis title, complete the following:

1. Double-click the axis title to open the Format Axis Title task pane (refer to Figure 28). Each task pane has categories, such as Title Options and Text Options. Below these categories are icons, such as Fill & Line, Effects, and Size & Properties.
2. Click Title Options and click the Size & Properties icon. The options in the task pane change to display options related to the icon you click. A thin horizontal gray line separates the icons from the options. The line contains a partial triangle that points to the icon that is active to indicate which options are displayed. Figure 28 shows the triangle is pointing to Size & Properties.
3. Change the *Vertical alignment* or *Horizontal alignment* option to the desired position.
4. Click other icons, such as Fill & Line, and select the desired options.
5. Close the Format Axis Title task pane.
6. Click the Home tab and apply font formatting, such as Font Color.

TIP: REMOVE AN ELEMENT

To remove an element, click Chart Elements and click a check box to deselect the check box. Alternatively, click Add Chart Element in the Chart Layouts group on the Chart Tools Design tab, point to the element name, and then select None. You can also select a chart element and press Delete to remove it.

Format the Axes

Based on the data source values and structure, Excel determines the start, incremental, and end values that display on the value axis when you create the chart. However, you might want to adjust the value axis so that the numbers displayed are simplified or fit better on the chart. For example, when working with large values such as 4,567,890, the value axis displays increments, such as 4,000,000 and 5,000,000. You can simplify the value axis by displaying values in millions, so that the values on the axis are 4 and 5 with the word Millions placed by the value axis to indicate the units. Use the Format Axis task pane to specify the bounds, units, display units, labels, and number formatting for an axis.

To format an axis, complete the following steps:

1. Double-click the axis to open the Format Axis task pane (see Figure 29).
2. Click the Axis Options icon, and complete any of the following steps:
   - Change the bounds, units, and display units. The Minimum Bound sets the starting value, and the Maximum Bound sets the ending value on the value axis. The Major Units specifies the intervals of values on the value axis. The Display units converts the values, such as to Millions.
   - Click Tick Marks to change the major and minor tick marks.
   - Click Labels to change the label position.
   - Click Number to change the category, specify the number of decimal places, select how negative numbers display. The Category option specifies the number formatting, such as Currency. Depending on the category, other options may display, such as Decimal places so that you can control the number of decimal places on the value axis.
3. Close the Format Axis task pane.
4. Click the Home tab and apply font formatting, such as Font Color.

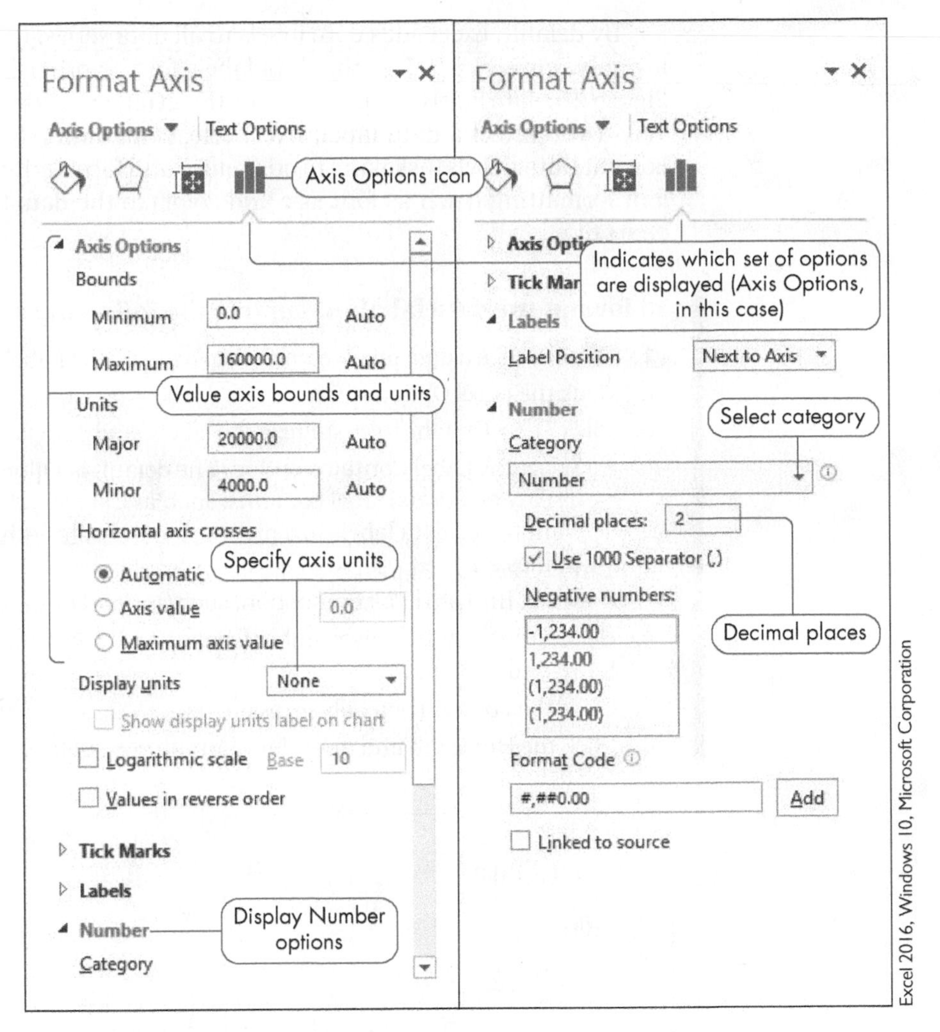

FIGURE 29 Format Axis Task Pane

> **TIP: DISPLAYING OPTIONS WITHIN TASK PANES**
> A diagonal black triangle next to a category, such as Axis Options, indicates that all of a category's options are displayed (expanded). A triangle with a white fill, such as the one next to Tick Marks, indicates that the category options are not displayed (collapsed).

Add, Position, and Format Data Labels

STEP 3 A data label is descriptive text that shows the exact value or name of a data point. Data labels are useful to indicate specific values for data points you want to emphasize. Typically, you would add data labels only to specific data points, and not all data points. Use either Chart Elements or the Design tab to display data labels.

To add and position data labels, complete the following steps:

1. Select the chart and click Chart Elements to the right of the chart.
2. Click the Data Labels check box to display data labels.
3. Click the arrow to the right of the Data Labels item to select the position, such as Center or Outside End.
4. Click Chart Elements to close the menu.

By default, Excel adds data labels to all data series. If you want to display data labels for only one series, select the data labels for the other data series and press Delete. In Figure 26, data labels are included for the 2020 data series but not the 2010 data series. When you select a data label, Excel selects all data labels in that data series. Use the Format Data Labels task pane to customize and format the data labels. You can also apply font formatting (such as font size and color) to the data labels similarly to formatting a chart title.

To format the data labels, complete the following steps:

1. Double-click a data label to open the Format Data Labels task pane (see Figure 30).
2. Click the Label Options icon.
3. Click Label Options to customize the labels, and complete any of the following steps:
   - Select the Label Contains option. The default is Value, but you might want to display additional label contents, such as Category Name. For example, you might want to add data labels to a pie chart to indicate both Percentage and Category Names.
   - Select the Label Position option, such as Center or Inside End.
4. Click Number and apply number formatting if the numeric data labels are not formatted.
5. Close the Format Data Labels task pane.
6. Click the Home tab and apply font formatting, such as Font Color.

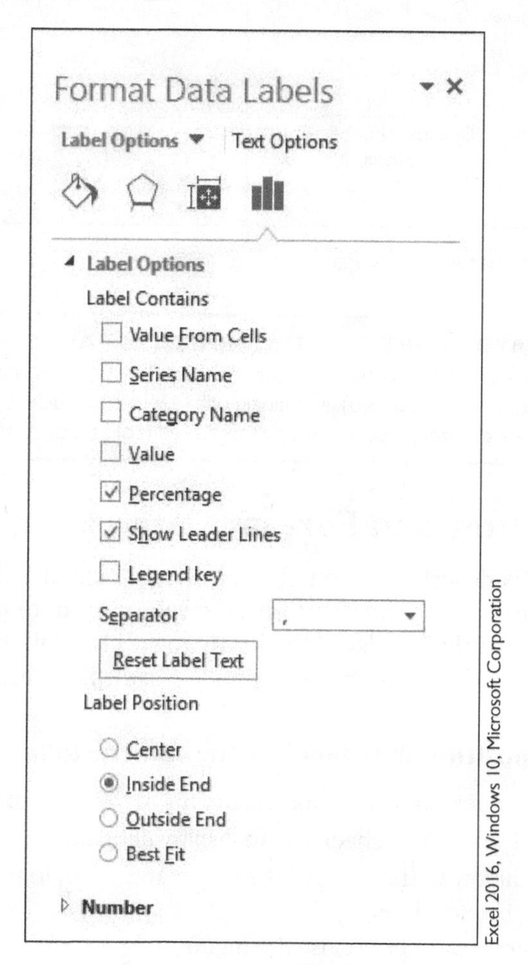

FIGURE 30 Format Data Labels Task Pane

TIP: PIE CHART DATA LABELS

When you first create a pie chart, Excel generates a legend to identify the category labels for the different slice colors, but it does not display data labels. You should display Percentage data labels within or next to each slice. If you also include category labels, remove the legend to avoid duplicating elements. Category data labels are easier to read than the small print in the legend.

Position and Format the Legend

When you create a multiple series chart, the legend displays, providing a key to the color-coded data series. Position the legend to the right, top, bottom, or left of the plot area, similarly to choosing the position for a chart title using Chart Elements. Make sure that the columns, bars, or lines appear proportionate and well balanced after you position the legend. Use the Format Legend task pane to customize and format the legend.

To format the legend, complete the following steps:

1. Double-click the legend to open the Format Legend task pane.
2. Click the Legend Options icon.
3. Select the position of the legend: Top, Bottom, Left, Right, or Top Right.
4. Click the Fill & Line icon, click Border, and set border options if you want to change the border settings for the legend.
5. Close the Format Legend task pane.
6. Click the Home tab and apply font formatting, such as Font Color.

TIP: QUICK LAYOUT

Use Quick Layout to apply predefined layouts to a chart. Specifically, you can apply a layout to add several chart elements at one time. Click Quick Layout in the Chart Layouts group on the Design tab (see Figure 31). When you point to a thumbnail in the gallery, Excel displays a ScreenTip with the layout name, such as Layout 11. After reviewing the gallery, select a layout. Each layout contains predefined chart elements and their positions.

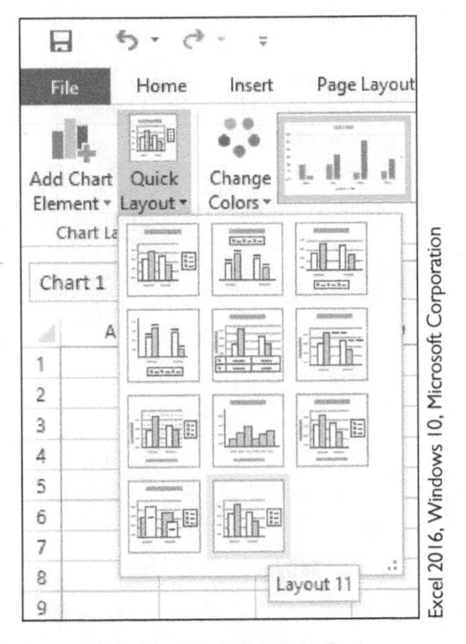

FIGURE 31 Quick Layout Gallery

Add and Format Gridlines

Gridlines are horizontal or vertical lines that span across the plot area of the chart to help people identify the values plotted by the visual elements, such as a column. Excel displays horizontal gridlines for column, line, scatter, stock, surface, and bubble charts and vertical gridlines for bar charts. Click either Chart Elements or Add Chart Elements in the Chart Layouts group on the Design tab to add gridlines.

Format gridlines by double-clicking a gridline to open the Format Major Gridlines task pane. You can change the line type, color, and width of the gridlines.

> **TIP: ALTERNATIVE FOR OPENING FORMAT TASK PANES**
>
> Another way to display a task pane is to right-click the chart element and choose Format <element>, where <element> is the specific chart element. If you do not close a task pane after formatting a particular element, such as gridlines, and then click another chart element, the task pane will change so that you can format that particular chart element.

Format the Chart Area, Plot Area, and Data Series

STEP 4 » Apply multiple settings, such as fill colors and borders, at once using the Format task pane for an element. To open a chart element's task pane, double-click the chart element. Figure 32 displays the Format Chart Area, Format Plot Area, and Format Data Series task panes with different fill options selected to display the different options that result. All three task panes include the same fill and border elements. For example, you might want to change the fill color of a data series from blue to green. After you select a fill option, such as *Gradient fill*, the remaining options change in the task pane.

FIGURE 32 Format Task Panes

TIP: USE IMAGES OR TEXTURES

For less formal presentations, you might want to use images or a texture to fill the data series, chart area, or plot area instead of a solid fill color. To use an image or a texture, click the Fill & Line icon at the top of the task pane, click Fill, and then click *Picture or texture fill*. Click File or Online in the *Insert picture from* section and insert an image file or search online to insert an image. The image is stretched by default, but you might want to select the Stack option to avoid distorting the image. To add a texture, click *Picture or texture fill*, click the Texture arrow, and then select a textured background from the gallery of textures. Generally, do not mix images and textures because doing so would create a cluttered appearance.

TIP: ACCESSIBILITY COMPLIANCE

It is a good practice to apply some features that are accessibility compliant for people who have disabilities, such as vision or cognitive impairments, that may prevent them from seeing or comprehending the visual aid. For charts, it is recommended to assign a name to a chart, such as New Jobs, because the default chart name such as Chart 1 is not meaningful. To name a chart, select it and type a name in the Name Box to the left of the Formula Bar.

In addition, you should provide ***Alt Text***, which is a title and description that provides an alternative text-based interpretation of the visual, such as a chart. A device can read the title and description to the user. To enter Alt Text for a chart, right-click the chart area to open the Format Chart Area task pane, click Alt Text to display its options, type a brief title in the Title box, and type a descriptive interpretation of the chart in the Description box.

Format a Data Point

STEP 4 »

Earlier in this chapter, you learned that a data point reflects a value in a single cell in a worksheet. You can select that single data point in a chart and format it differently from the rest of the data series. Select the data point you want to format, display the Format Data Point task pane, and make the changes you want. For example, you might want to focus a person's attention on a particular slice by separating one or more slices from the rest of the chart in an ***exploded pie chart*** (refer to Figure 15).

To format a pie slice data point, complete the following steps:

1. Click within the pie chart, pause, and then click the particular slice you want to format.
2. Right-click the selected pie slice and select Format Data Point to open the Format Data Point task pane.
3. Click the Fill & Line icon and click the desired option (such as Solid fill) in the Fill category.
4. Click the Color arrow and select a color for a solid fill; select a *Preset gradient*, type, color, and other options for a gradient fill; or insert a picture or select a texture for a picture or texture fill.
5. Click the Series Options icon and drag the Point Explosion to the right to explode the selected pie slice, such as to 12% (see Figure 33).
6. Close the Format Data Point task pane.

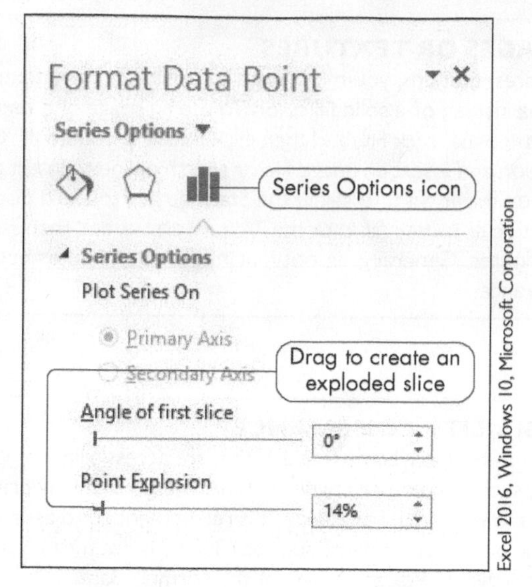

FIGURE 33 Format Data Point Task Pane

TIP: DRAG TO EXPLODE A PIE SLICE
Another way to explode a pie slice is to select the specific slice and then drag it away from the pie.

Use the Chart Tools Format Tab

The Format tab contains options to select a chart element, insert shapes, apply shape styles, apply WordArt styles, arrange objects, and specify the size of an object. Table 5 lists and describes the groups on the Format tab.

TABLE 5 Chart Tools Format Tab

Group	Description
Current Selection	Selects a chart element, displays the task pane to format the selected element, and clears custom formatting of the selected element.
Insert Shapes	Inserts a variety of shapes in a chart.
Shape Styles	Specifies a shape style, fill color, outline color, and shape effect.
WordArt Styles	Adds artistic style, text fill, and text effects to an object.
Arrange	Brings an object forward or backward to layer multiple objects; aligns, groups, and rotates objects.
Size	Adjusts the height and width of the selected object.

5. List at least four types of appropriate labels that describe chart elements. What types of things can you do to customize these labels?
6. What is the purpose of exploding a slice on a pie chart?
7. What are some of the fill options you can apply to a chart area or a plot area?

Hands-On Exercises

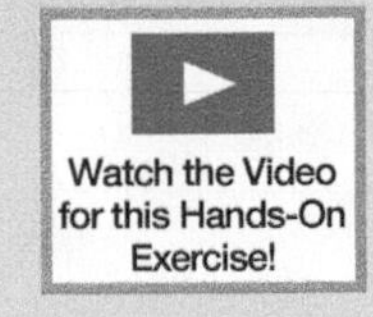

Skills covered: Edit and Format Chart Titles • Add and Format Axes Titles • Format Axes • Add, Position, and Format Data Labels • Format the Chart Area • Format a Data Point

2 Chart Elements

You want to enhance the computer job column, bar, and pie charts by adding some chart elements. In particular, you will enter a descriptive chart title for each chart, add and format axis titles for the bar chart, add and format data labels for the pie chart, and change fill colors in the pie chart.

STEP 1 » EDIT AND FORMAT CHART TITLES

When you created the column, bar, and pie charts in Hands-On Exercise 1, Excel displayed *Chart Title* at the top of each chart. You will add a title that appropriately describes each chart. In addition, you want to format the chart titles by applying bold and enlarging the font sizes. Refer to Figure 34 as you complete Step 1.

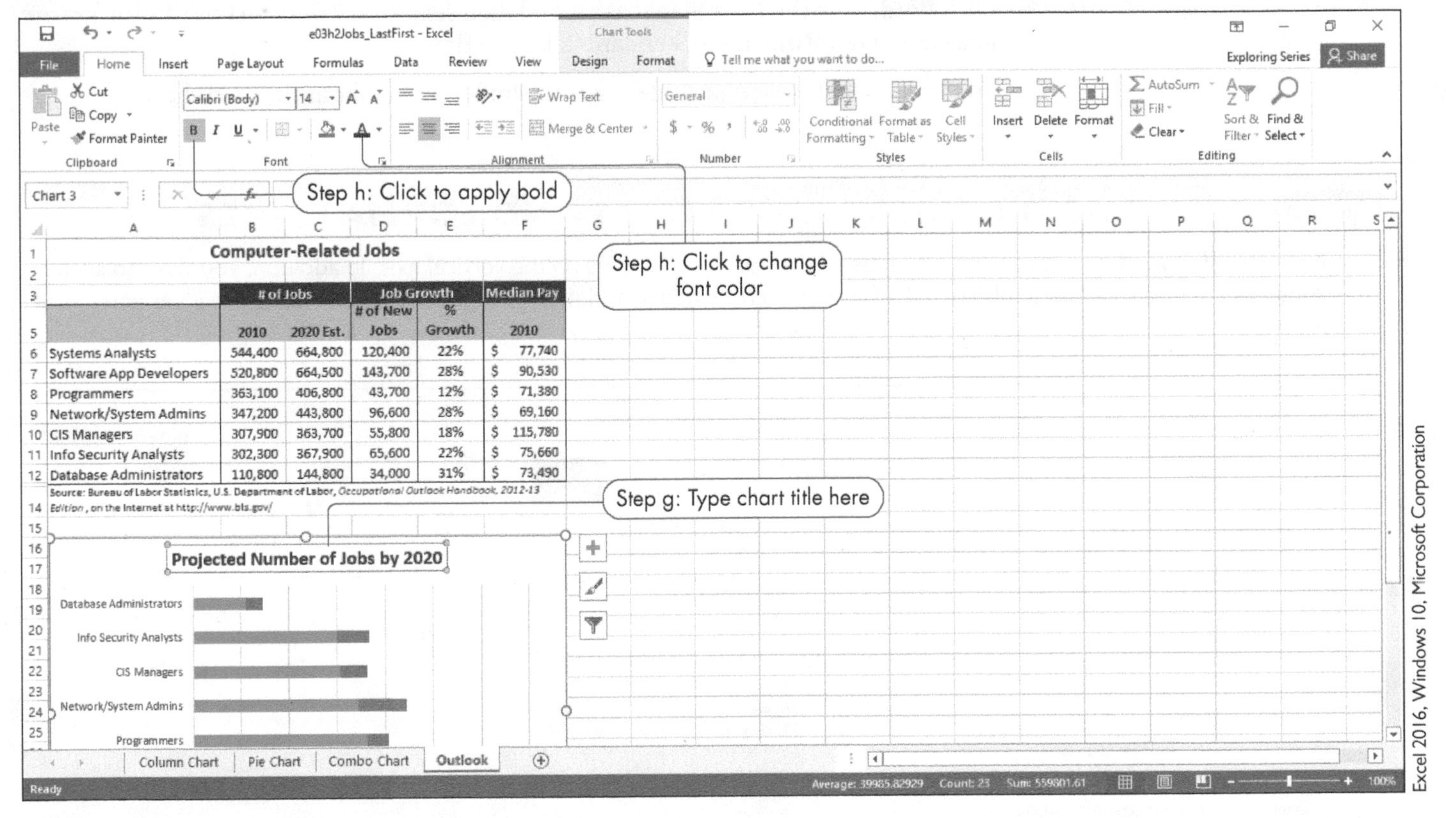

FIGURE 34 Formatted Chart Title

a. Open *e03h1Jobs_LastFirst* if you closed it at the end of the Hands-On Exercise 1, and save it as **e03h2Jobs_LastFirst**, changing h1 to h2.

b. Make sure the Combo Chart sheet is the active sheet, select the **Chart Title** placeholder, type **Number of New Computer-Related Jobs by 2020**, and then press **Enter**.

As you type a chart title, Excel displays the text in the Formula Bar. The text does not appear in the chart title until after you press Enter.

> **TROUBLESHOOTING:** If you double-click a title and type directly into the title placeholder, do not press Enter after typing the new title. Doing so will add a blank line.

c. Click the **Home tab**, click **Bold**, click the **Font Color arrow**, and then select **Black, Text 1**.

You applied font formats so that the chart title stands out.

d. Click the **Pie Chart sheet tab**, select the **Chart Title** placeholder, type **New Computer-Related Jobs by 2020**, and then press **Enter**.

Excel displays the text you typed for the chart title.

e. Click the **Home tab**, click **Bold**, click the **Font Size arrow** and select **18**, and then click the **Font Color arrow** and select **Black, Text 1**.

You formatted the pie chart title so that it stands out.

f. Click the **Column Chart sheet tab**, select the **Chart Title** placeholder, type **Number of Computer-Related Jobs 2010 and 2020**, and then press **Enter**. Click **Bold**, click the **Font Size arrow**, and then select **18**. Click the **Font Color arrow** and click **Black, Text 1** font color to the chart title.

g. Click the **Outlook sheet tab**, select the **Chart Title** placeholder, type **Projected Number of Jobs by 2020**, and then press **Enter**.

h. Click **Bold**, click the **Font Size arrow**, and then select **14**. Click the **Font Color arrow** and click **Dark Blue** in the Standard Colors section. Save the workbook.

You formatted the bar chart title to have a similar font color as the worksheet title.

STEP 2 ›› ADD AND FORMAT AXIS TITLES AND FORMAT AXES

For the bar chart, you want to add and format a title to describe the job titles on the vertical axis. In addition, you want to simplify the horizontal axis values to avoid displaying *,000* for each increment and add the title *Thousands*. Refer to Figure 35 as you complete Step 2.

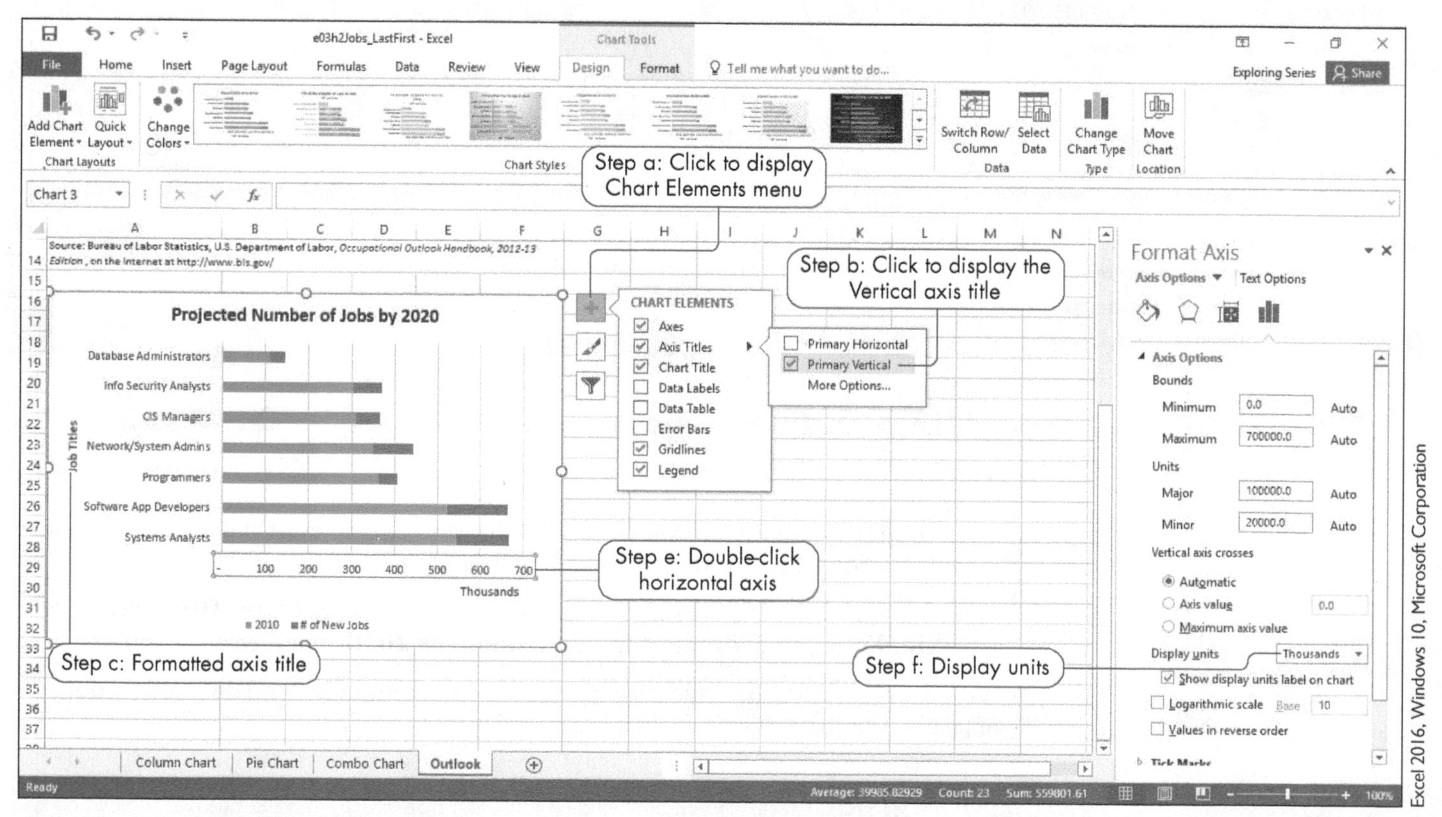

FIGURE 35 Formatted Axis Titles and Axes

a. Ensure that the bar chart is selected in the Outlook worksheet and click **Chart Elements** to the right of the chart.

   Excel displays the Chart Elements menu.

b. Point to **Axis Titles**, click the **Axis Titles arrow**, and then click the **Primary Vertical check box** to select it. Close the menu.

   Excel displays Axis Title on the left side of the vertical axis.

c. Ensure that the Axis Title placeholder is selected, type **Job Titles**, and then press **Enter**.

d. Click **Font Color** to apply the default Dark Blue font color to the selected axis title.

e. Point to the **horizontal axis**. When you see the ScreenTip, Horizontal (Value) Axis, double-click the values on the horizontal axis.

   The Format Axis task pane opens for you to format the value axis.

f. Click the **Display units arrow** and select **Thousands**.

> **TROUBLESHOOTING:** If the Display units is not shown, click the Axis Options icon, and click Axis Options to display the options.

   The axis now displays values such as 700 instead of 700,000. The title Thousands displays in the bottom-right corner of the horizontal axis.

g. Click the **Home tab**, select the title **Thousands**, and then apply **Dark Blue font color** in the Font group. Close the Format Axis task pane. Save the workbook.

STEP 3 ›› ADD AND FORMAT DATA LABELS

The pie chart includes a legend to identify which color represents each computer-related job; however, it does not include numerical labels to help you interpret what percentage of all computer-related jobs will be hired for each position. You want to insert and format percentage value labels. Refer to Figure 36 as you complete Step 3.

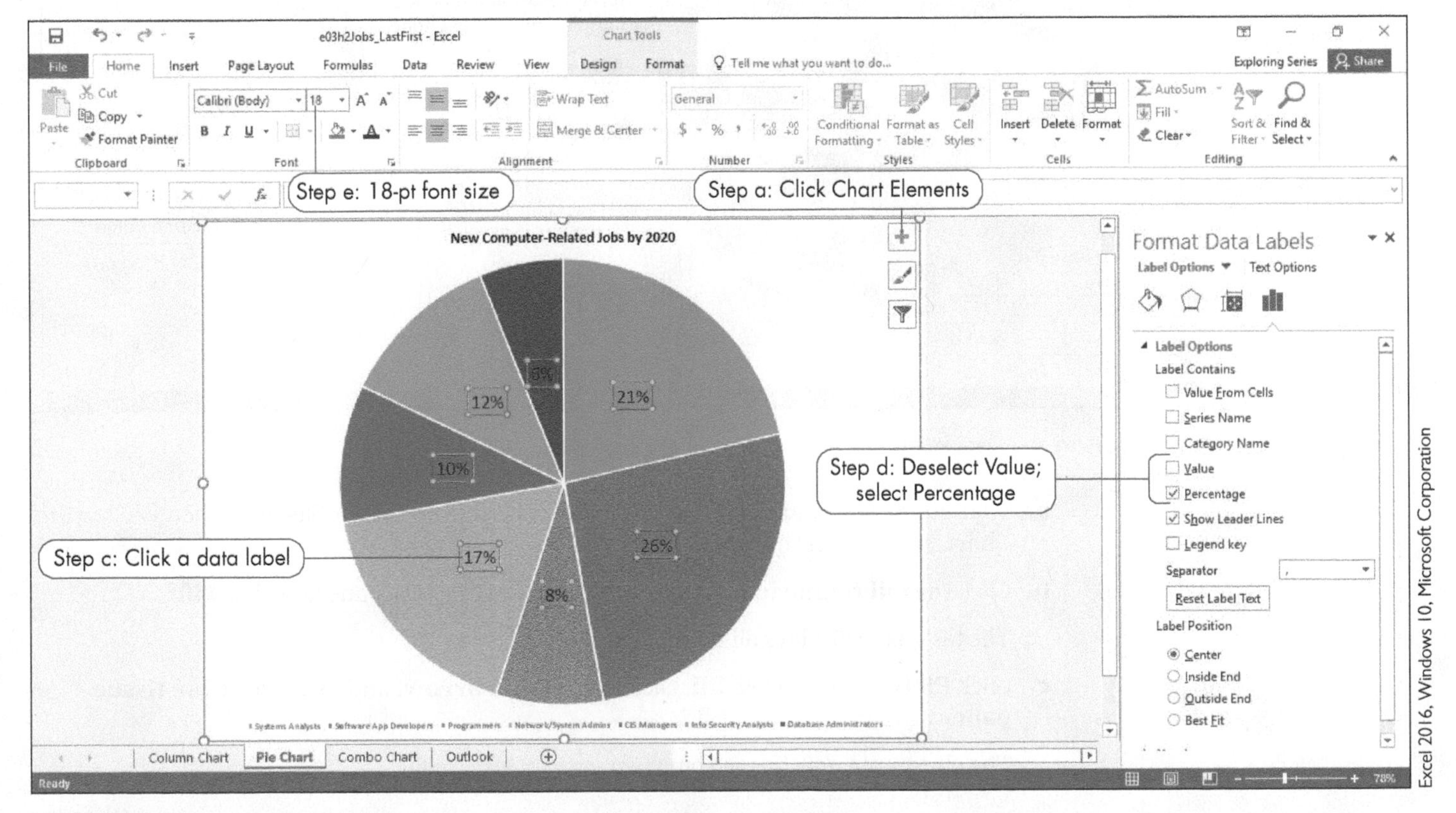

FIGURE 36 Formatted Data Labels

a. Click the **Pie Chart sheet tab** and click **Chart Elements**.

b. Click the **Data Labels arrow** and select **Center**. Close the Chart Elements menu.

You added data labels to the pie slices. The default data labels show the number of new jobs in the pie slices.

c. Right-click one of the data labels and select **Format Data Labels** to open the Format Data Label task pane.

d. Click **Label Options**, click the **Percentage check box** to select it, and then click the **Value check box** to deselect it. Close the Format Data Labels task pane.

Typically, pie chart data labels show percentages instead of values.

e. Change the font size to **18** to make the data labels larger. Save the workbook.

STEP 4 » FORMAT THE CHART AREA AND A DATA POINT

You want to apply a texture fill to the chart area and change the fill colors for the Software Apps Developers and the Database Administrators slices. Refer to Figure 37 as you complete Step 4.

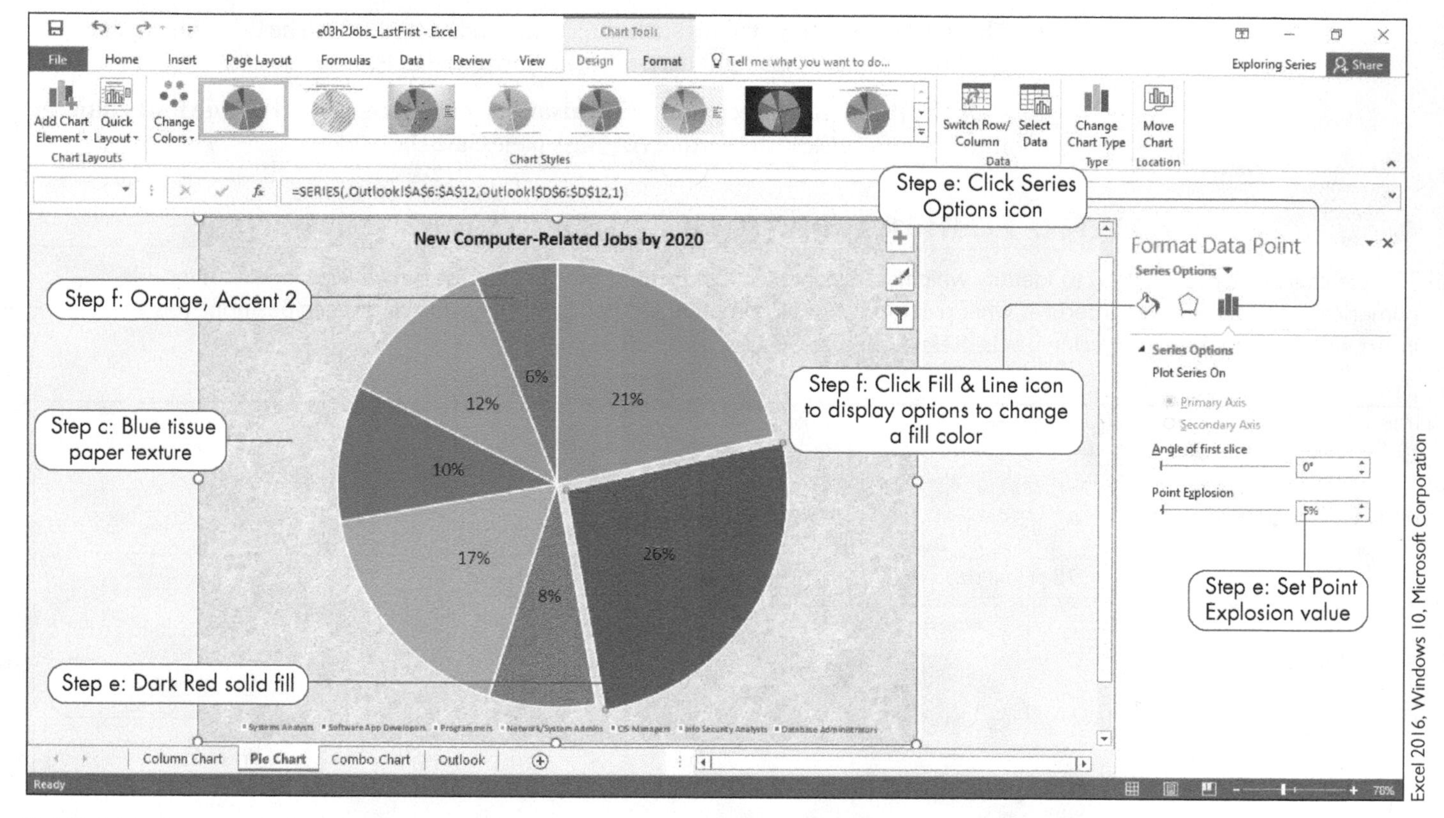

FIGURE 37 Formatted Chart Area and Data Point

a. Point to the **chart area** (the white space in the chart) and double-click when you see the Chart Area ScreenTip.

b. Click the **Fill & Line icon** in the Format Chart Area task pane and click **Fill**.

The task pane displays different fill options.

c. Click **Picture or texture fill**, click the **Texture arrow**, and then click **Blue tissue paper**.

The chart area now has the blue tissue paper texture fill.

d. Click the **26% Orange, Accent 2 slice**, pause, and then click the **26% Orange, Accent 2 slice** again to select just that data point (slice).

The first click selects all slices of the pie. The second click selects only the Software App Developers slice so that you can format that data point. Because you did not close the Format Chart Area task pane after Step c, Excel changes to the Format Data Point task pane when you select a data point.

e. Complete the following steps to format the selected data point:

- Click the **Fill & Line icon**, click **Solid fill**, click the **Color arrow**, and then click **Dark Red** in the Standard Colors section.
- Click the **Series Options icon** in the Format Data Point task pane and click the **Point Explosion increment** to **5%**.

You changed the fill color and exploded the slice for the selected data point.

f. Click the **6% Database Administrators slice**, click the **Fill & Line icon** in the Format Data Point task pane, click **Solid fill**, click the **Color arrow**, and then click **Orange, Accent 2**. Close the Format Data Point task pane.

The new color for the Database Administrators slice makes it easier to read the percentage data label.

g. Save the workbook. Keep the workbook open if you plan to continue with the next Hands-On Exercise. If not, close the workbook and exit Excel.

Chart Design and Sparklines

After you add and format chart elements, you might want to experiment with other features to enhance a chart. The Chart Tools Design tab contains two other groups: Chart Styles and Data. These groups enable you to apply a different style or color scheme to a chart or manipulate the data that are used to build a chart. You can also click Chart Styles and Chart Filters to the right of a chart to change the design of a chart.

At times, you might want to insert small visual chart-like images within worksheet cells to illustrate smaller data series rather than a large chart to illustrate several data points. Excel enables you to create small chart-like images in close proximity to individual data points to help you visualize the data.

In this section, you will learn how to apply chart styles and colors, filter chart data, and insert and customize miniature charts (sparklines) within individual cells.

Applying a Chart Style and Colors

STEP 1 » A ***chart style*** is a collection of formatting that controls the color of the chart area, plot area, and data series. Styles, such as flat, 3-D, or beveled, also affect the look of the data series. Figure 38 shows the options when you click Chart Styles to the right of the chart, and Figure 39 shows the Chart Styles gallery that displays when you click Chart Styles on the Design tab. The styles in the Chart Styles gallery reflect what is available for the currently selected chart, such as a pie chart. If you select a different type of chart, the gallery will display styles for that particular type of chart.

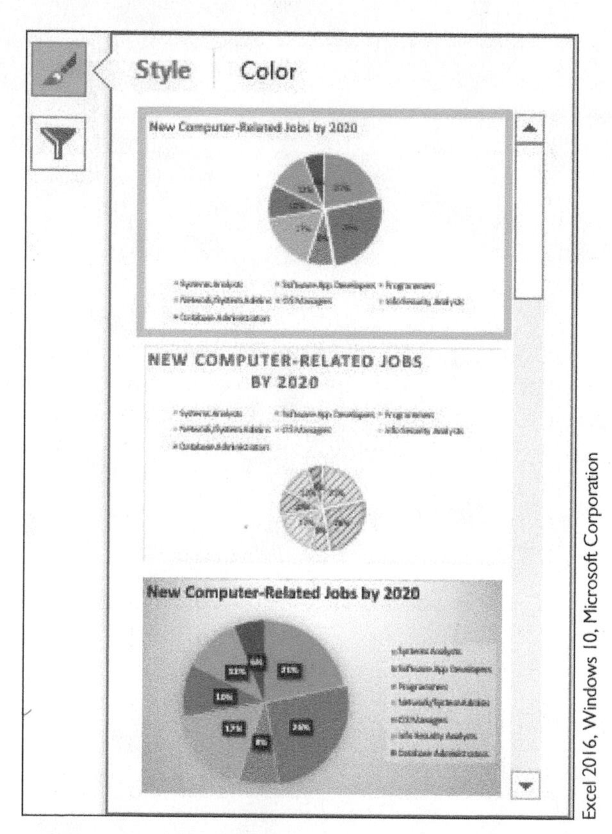

FIGURE 38 Chart Styles

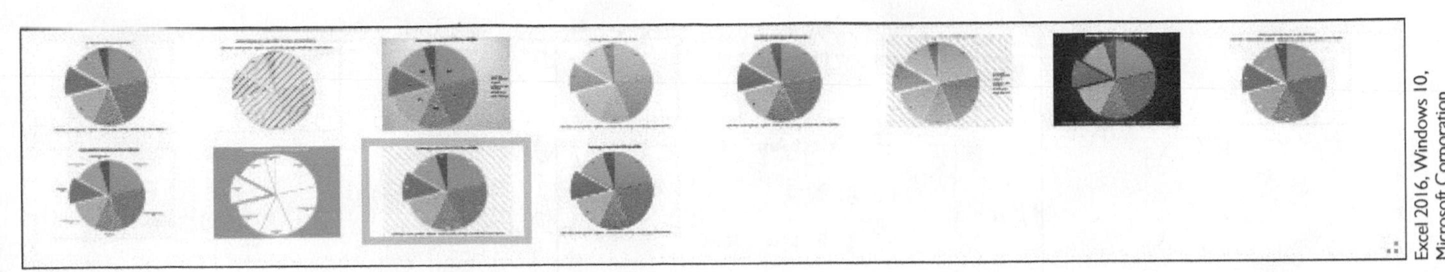

FIGURE 39 Chart Styles Gallery

TIP: CHOOSING APPROPRIATE CHART STYLES
When choosing a chart style, make sure the style complements the chart data and is easy to read. Also, consider whether you will display the chart onscreen in a presentation or print the chart. If you will display the chart in a presentation, consider selecting a style with a black background.

To change the color scheme of the chart, complete the following steps:

1. Click Chart Styles to the right of the chart.
2. Click Color or click Change Colors in the Chart Styles group on the Design tab.
3. Select from the Colorful and Monochromatic sections.

Modifying the Data Source

The data source is the range of worksheet cells that are used to construct a chart. Although you should select the data source carefully before creating a chart, you may decide to alter that data source after you create and format the chart. The Data group on the Design tab is useful for adjusting the data source. Furthermore, you can apply filters to display or hide a data series without adjusting the entire data source.

Apply Chart Filters

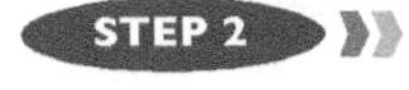

A ***chart filter*** controls which data series and categories are visible in a chart. By default, all the data you selected to create the chart are used to construct the data series and categories. However, you can apply a chart filter to focus on particular data. For example, you might want to focus on just one job title at a time. Click Chart Filters to the right of the chart to display the options (see Figure 40). A check mark indicates the data series or categories currently displayed in the chart. Click a check box to deselect or hide a data series or a category.

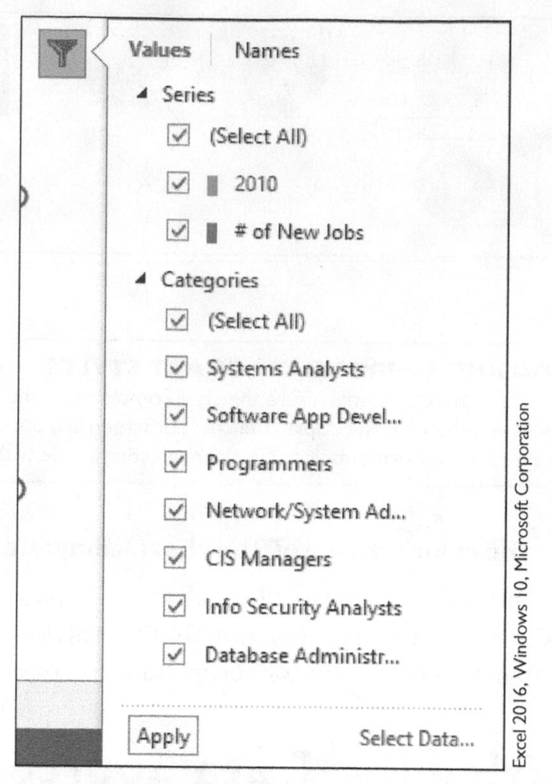

FIGURE 40 Chart Filter Options

Click Select Data in the Data group on the Design tab to open the Select Data Source dialog box (see Figure 41). This dialog box is another way to filter which categories and data series are visible in your chart. Furthermore, this dialog box enables you to change the chart data range, as well as add, edit, or remove data that is being used to create the chart. For example, you might want to add another data series or remove an existing data series from the chart.

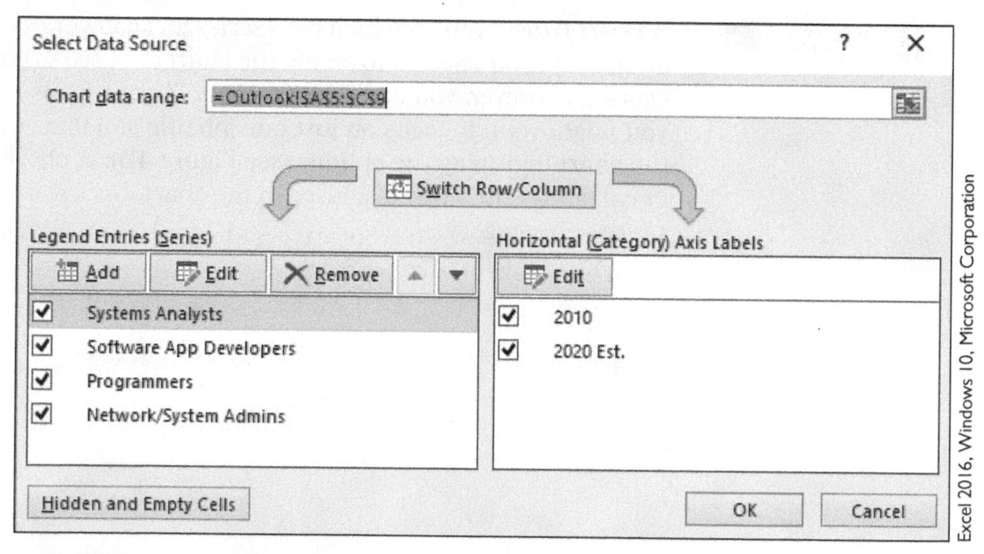

FIGURE 41 Select Data Source Dialog Box

Switch Row and Column Data

You might want to switch data used to create the horizontal axis and the legend to give a different perspective and to change the focus on the data. For example, you might want to display years as data series to compare different years for categories, and then you might want to switch the data to show years on the category axis to compare job titles within the same year. In Figure 42, the chart on the left uses the job titles to build the data series and legend, and the years display on the horizontal axis. The chart on the right shows the results after switching the data: the job titles build the horizontal axis, and the years build the data series and legend.

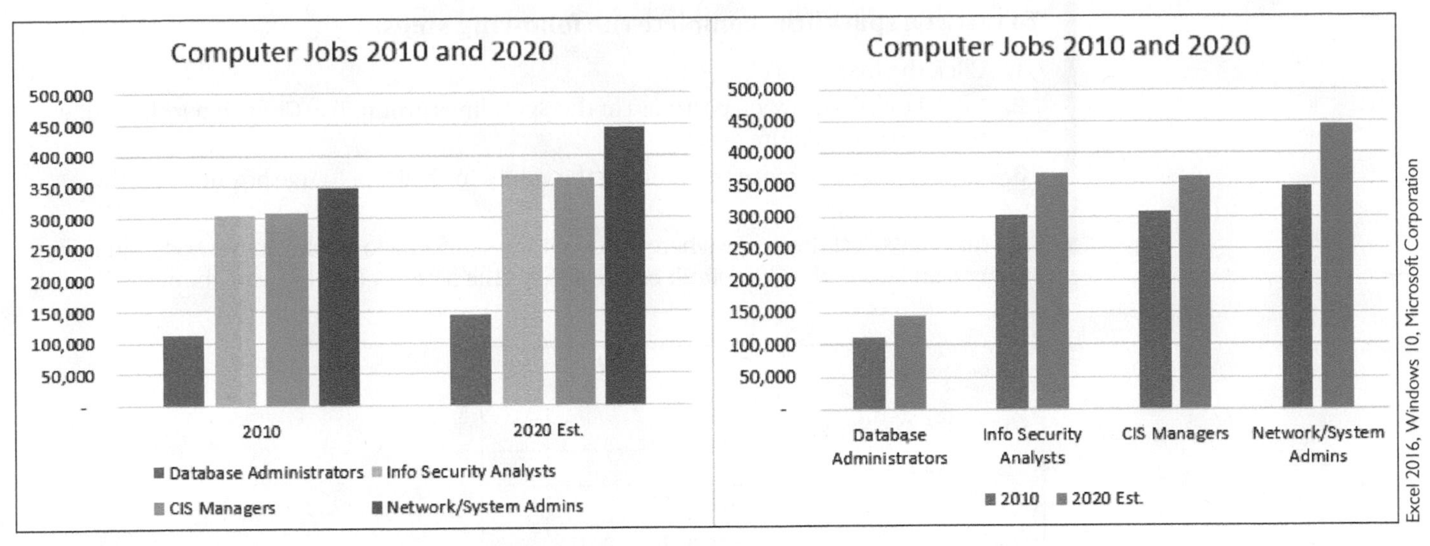

FIGURE 42 Original Chart and Chart with Switched Rows/Columns

To switch the row and column data, complete the following steps:

1. Select the chart.
2. Click Switch Row/Column in the Data group on the Design tab.

Creating and Customizing Sparklines

A ***sparkline*** is a small line, column, or win/loss chart contained in a single cell. The purpose of a sparkline is to present a condensed, simple, succinct visual illustration of data. Unlike a regular chart, a sparkline does not include any of the standard chart labels, such as a chart title, axis label, axis titles, legend, or data labels. Inserting sparklines next to data helps to create a visual "dashboard" to help you understand the data quickly without having to look at a full-scale chart.

Figure 43 shows three sample sparklines: line, column, and win/loss. The line sparkline shows trends over time, such as each student's trends in test scores. The column sparkline compares test averages. The win/loss sparkline depicts how many points a team won or lost each game.

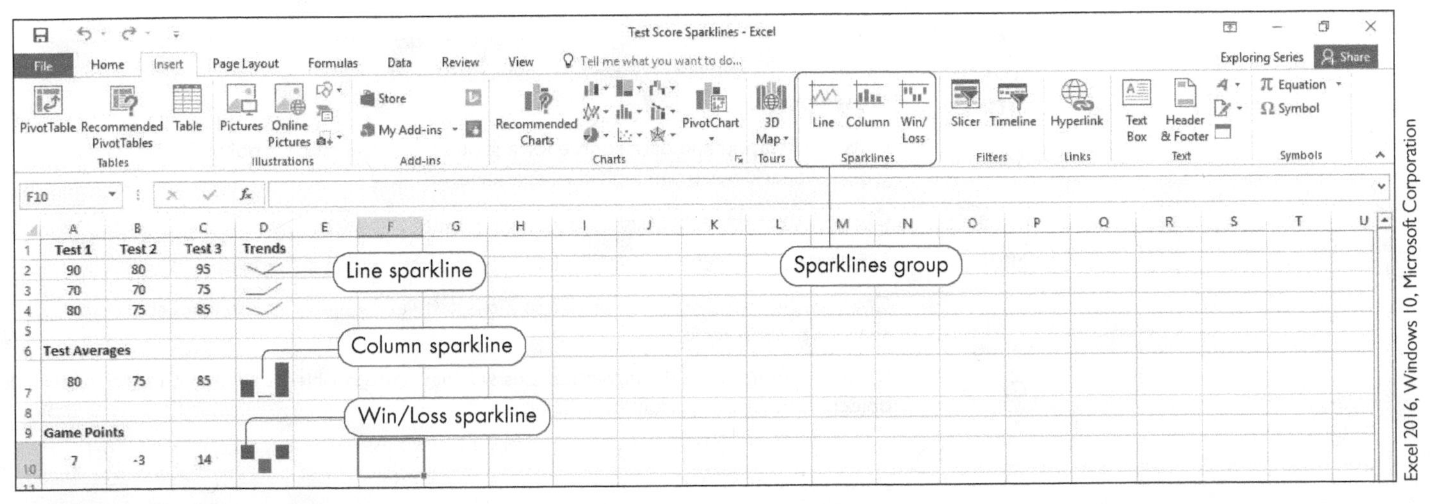

FIGURE 43 Sample Sparklines

Insert a Sparkline

Before creating a sparkline, identify the data range you want to depict (such as A2:C2 for the first person's test score) and where you want to place the sparkline (such as cell D2).

To insert a sparkline, complete the following steps:

1. Click the Insert tab.
2. Click Line, Column, or Win/Loss in the Sparklines group. The Create Sparklines dialog box opens (see Figure 44).
3. Type the cell references containing the values in the Data Range box or select the range.
4. Enter or select the range where you want the sparkline to display in the Location Range box and click OK. The default cell location is the active cell unless you change it.

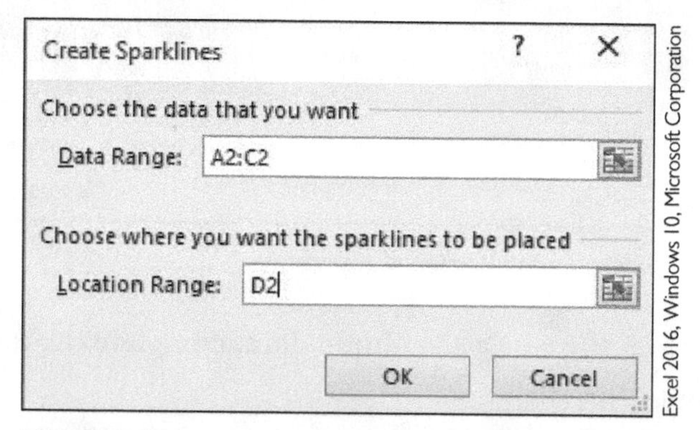

FIGURE 44 Create Sparklines Dialog Box

Customize a Sparkline

After you insert a sparkline, the Sparkline Tools Design tab displays (see Figure 45), with options to customize the sparkline. Table 6 lists and describes the groups on the Sparkline Tools Design tab.

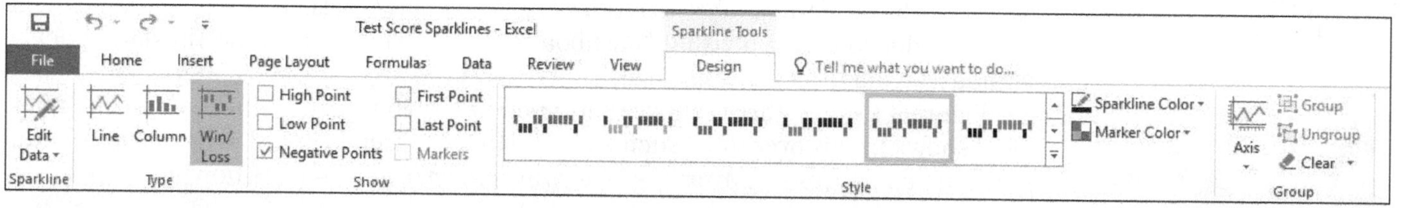

FIGURE 45 Sparkline Tools Design Tab

Excel 2016, Windows 10, Microsoft Corporation

TABLE 6 Sparkline Tools Design Tab

Group	Description
Sparkline	Edits the location and data source for a group or individual data point that generates a group of sparklines or an individual sparkline.
Type	Changes the selected sparkline type (line, column, win/loss).
Show	Displays points, such as the high points, or markers within a sparkline.
Style	Changes the sparkline style, similar to a chart style, changes the sparkline color, or changes the marker color.
Group	Specifies the horizontal and vertical axis settings, groups objects together, ungroups objects, and clears sparklines.

8. What are two ways to change the color scheme of a chart?
9. How can you change a chart so that the data in the legend are on the X-axis and the data on the X-axis are in the legend?
10. What is a sparkline, and why would you insert one?

Hands-On Exercises

Skills covered: Apply a Chart Style • Apply Chart Filters • Insert a Sparkline • Customize Sparklines

3 Chart Design and Sparklines

Now that you have completed the pie chart, you want to focus again on the bar chart. You are not satisfied with the overall design and want to try a different chart style. In addition, you would like to include sparklines to show trends for all jobs between 2010 and 2020.

STEP 1 » APPLY A CHART STYLE

You want to give more contrast to the bar chart. Therefore, you will apply the Style 2 chart style. That style changes the category axis labels to all capital letters and displays data labels inside each segment of each bar. Refer to Figure 46 as you complete Step 1.

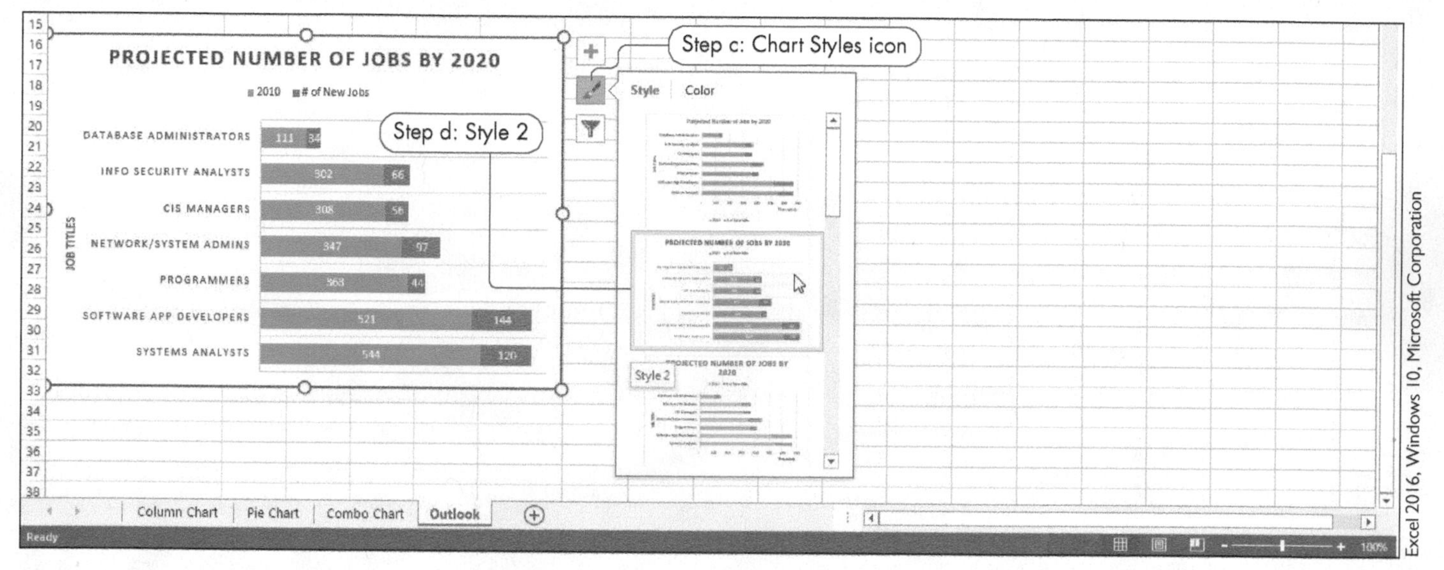

FIGURE 46 Chart Style Applied

a. Open *e03h2Jobs_LastFirst* if you closed it at the end of the Hands-On Exercise 2, and save it as **e03h3Jobs_LastFirst**, changing h2 to h3.

b. Click the **Outlook sheet tab** and click the bar chart to select it.

c. Click **Chart Styles** to the right of the chart.

The gallery of chart styles opens.

d. Point to **Style 2**. When you see the ScreenTip that identifies Style 2, click **Style 2**. Click **Chart Styles** to close the gallery. Save the workbook.

Excel applies the Style 2 chart style to the chart, which displays value data labels in white font color within each stack of the bar chart. The chart title and the category labels display in all capital letters. The legend displays above the plot area.

STEP 2 » APPLY CHART FILTERS

When you first created the clustered column chart, you included the number of new jobs as well as the number of 2010 jobs and the projected number of 2020 jobs. However, you decide that the number of new jobs is implied by comparing the 2010 to the 2020 jobs. Therefore, you want to set a chart filter to exclude the number of new jobs. Refer to Figure 47 as you complete Step 2.

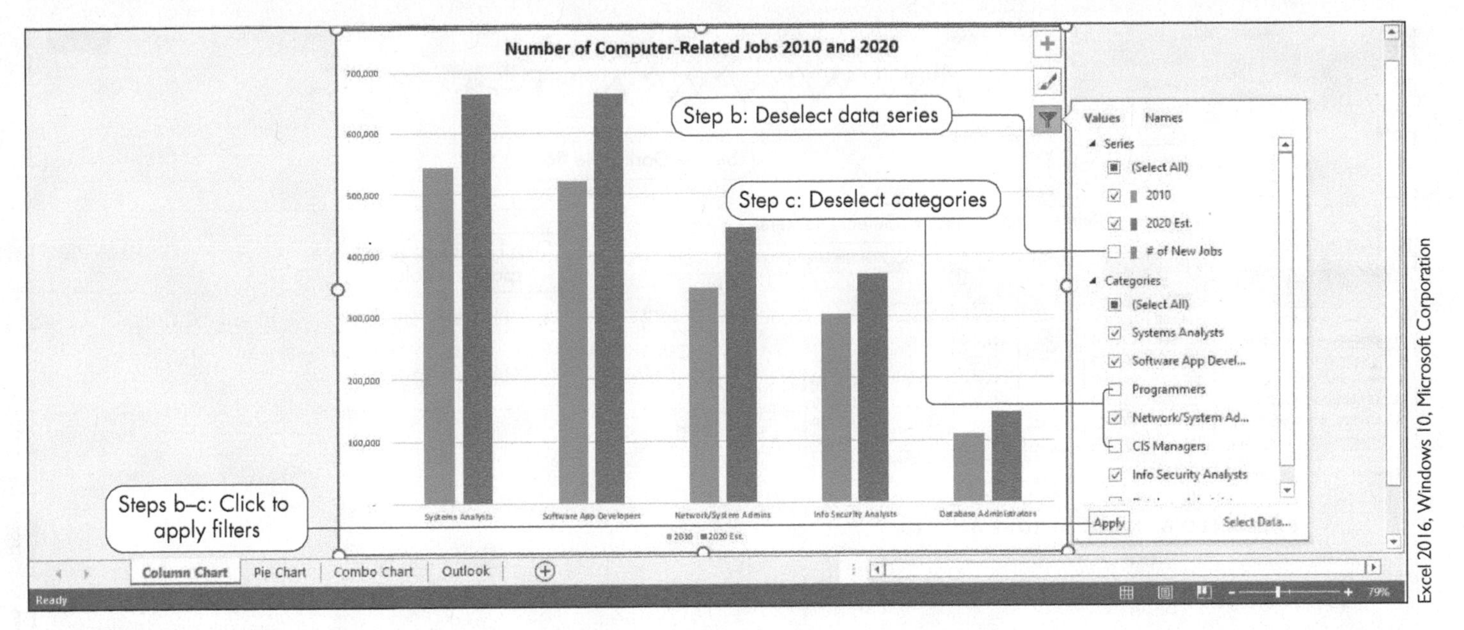

FIGURE 47 Chart Filters

a. Click the **Column Chart sheet tab** and click **Chart Filters** on the right of the chart area.

b. Point to the various filter options to see a preview of the filtered data. Click the **# of New Jobs check box** in the Series group to deselect it and click **Apply** at the bottom of the filter window.

The number of new jobs (gray) data series no longer displays in the clustered column chart.

c. Click the **Programmers check box** to deselect the category, click the **CIS Managers check box** to deselect it, and then click **Apply**. Click **Chart Filters** to close the menu. Save the workbook.

The Programmers and CIS Managers categories no longer display in the clustered column chart.

STEP 3 ›› INSERT AND CUSTOMIZE SPARKLINES

You want to insert sparklines to show the trends between 2010 and 2020. After inserting the sparklines, you want to display the high points to show that all jobs will have major increases by 2020. Refer to Figure 48 as you complete Step 3.

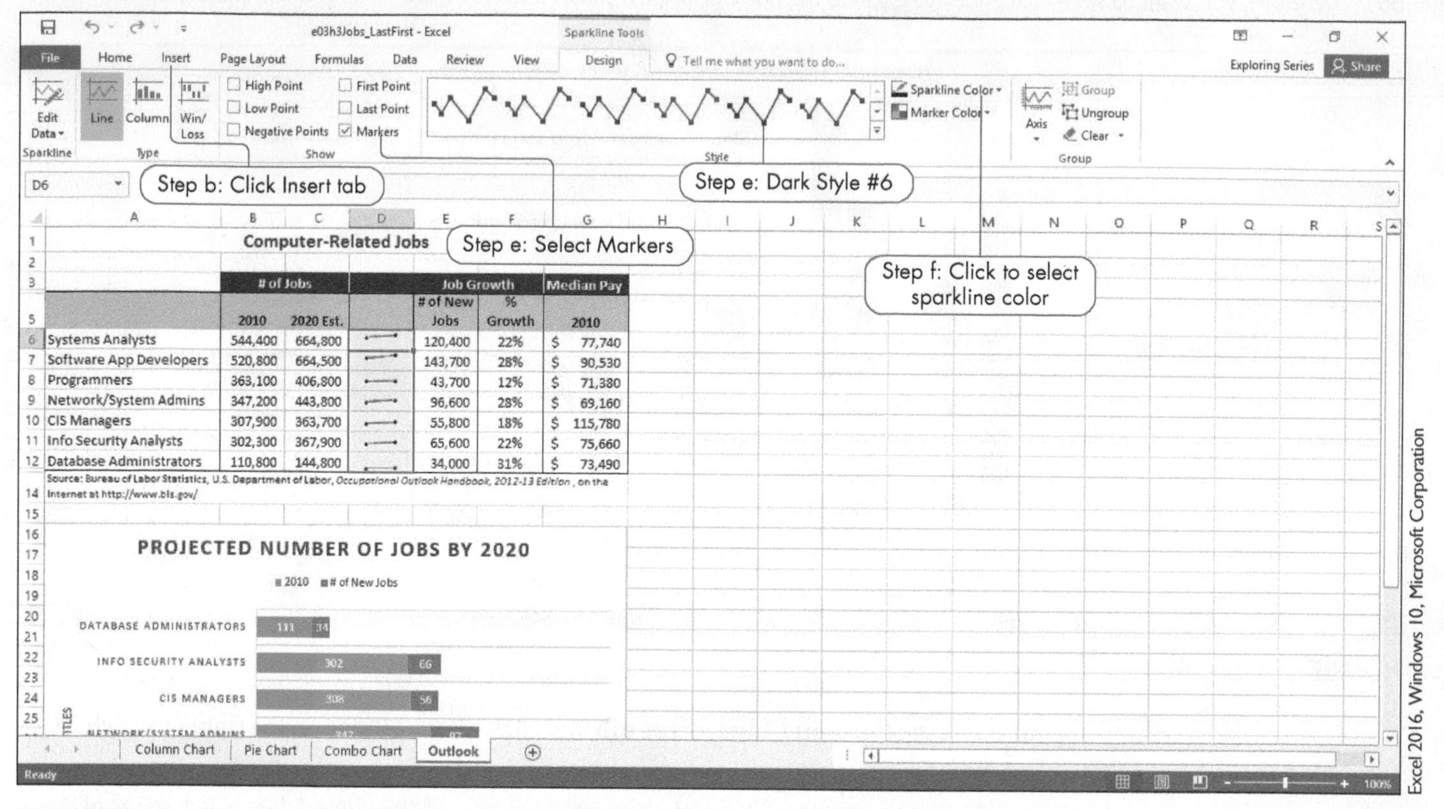

FIGURE 48 Sparkline Tools Design Tab

a. Click the **Outlook sheet tab**, select **cell D6**, click the **Insert arrow** in the Cells group, and then select **Insert Sheet Columns**.

   You inserted a new column so that you can place the sparklines close to the data you want to visualize.

b. Click the **Insert tab** and click **Line** in the Sparklines group.

c. Select the **range B6:C12** to enter that range in the Data Range box.

   You selected multiple rows at one time to create a group of sparklines.

d. Press **Tab** and select the **range D6:D12** to enter that range in the Location Range box. Click **OK**.

   Excel inserts sparklines in the range D6:D12 with each sparkline representing data on its respective row. The Sparkline Tools Design tab displays.

e. Click the **Markers check box** in the Show group to select it and click **Sparkline Style Dark #6** in the Style group.

f. Click **Sparkline Color** in the Style group and click **Red** in the Standard Colors section.

g. Click **Axis** in the Group group and click **Same for All Sparklines** in the Vertical Axis Minimum Value Options section. Click **Axis** again and click **Same for All Sparklines** in the Vertical Axis Maximum Value Options section.

   Because the sparklines look identical in trends, you changed the axis settings to set the minimum and maximum values as relative to the sparkline values in the entire selected range of rows rather than the default setting that bases the minimum and maximum for each row.

h. Save and close the file. Based on your instructor's directions, submit e03h3Jobs_LastFirst.

Chapter Objectives Review

After reading this chapter, you have accomplished the following objectives:

1. Select the data source.

- Decide which data you want to include in a chart. Each value is a data point, and several related data points create a data series in a chart.
- Select the range of data, including appropriate labels. The labels become the legend and the category axis.

2. Choose a chart type.

- After selecting a range, click Quick Analysis and click Charts to display a gallery of recommended chart types.
- Create a column chart: A clustered column chart compares groups of side-by-side columns where the height of the column indicates its value. The taller the column, the larger the value. A stacked column chart shows relationships of individual data points to the whole.
- Create a bar chart: A bar chart compares values across categories using horizontal bars where the width of the bar indicates its value. The wider the bar, the larger the value. A stacked bar chart shows relationships of individual data points to the whole.
- Change the chart type: After creating a chart, you might want to change it to a different type by clicking Change Chart Type in the Type group on the Design tab.
- Create a line chart: A line chart compares trends over time. Values are displayed on the value axis, and time periods are displayed on the category axis.
- Create a pie chart: A pie chart indicates the proportion to the whole for one data series. The size of the slice indicates the size of the value. The larger the pie slice, the larger the value.
- Create a combo chart: A combo chart combines elements of two chart types, such as column and line, to depict different data, such as individual data points compared to averages or percentages.
- Create other chart types: An X Y (scatter) chart shows a relationship between two numerical variables. A stock chart shows fluctuations in prices of stock, such as between the opening and closing prices on a particular day.

3. Move, size, and print a chart.

- Move a chart: The Move Chart dialog box enables you to select a new sheet and name the new chart sheet. To move a chart within a worksheet, click and drag the chart to the desired area.
- Size a chart: Adjust the chart size by dragging a sizing handle or specifying exact measurements in the Size group on the Format tab.
- Print a chart: To print a chart with its data series, the chart needs to be on the same worksheet as the data source. To ensure both the data and the chart print, make sure the chart is not selected. If the chart is on its own sheet or if you select the chart on a worksheet containing other data, the chart will print as a full-sized chart.

4. Add, edit, and format chart elements.

- Click Chart Elements to add elements. Chart elements include a chart title, axis titles, data labels, legend, gridlines, chart area, plot area, data series, and data point.
- Edit, format, and position the chart title: The default chart title is Chart Title, but you should edit it to provide a descriptive title for the chart. Apply font formats, such as bold and font size, to the chart title. Position the chart title above the chart, centered and overlaid, or in other locations.
- Add, format, and position axis titles: Display titles for the value and category axes to help describe the axes better. Apply font formats, such as bold and font size, to the axis titles.
- Format the axes: Change the unit of display for the value axis, such as converting values to In Millions.
- Add, position, and format data labels: Data labels provide exact values for a data series. Select the position of the data labels and the content of the data labels. Apply font formats, such as bold and font size, to the data labels.
- Position and format the legend: Position the legend to the right, top, bottom, or left of the plot area. Change the font size to adjust the label sizes within the legend.
- Add and format gridlines: Gridlines help the reader read across a column chart. Adjust the format of the major and minor gridlines.
- Format the chart area, plot area, and data series: The Format task panes enable you to apply fill colors, select border colors, and apply other settings.
- Format a data point: Format a single data point, such as changing the fill color for a single pie slice or specifying the percentage to explode a slice in a pie chart. Apply font formats, such as bold and font size, to the data points.
- Use the Chart Tools Format tab: Use this tab to select a chart element and insert and format shapes.

5. Apply a chart style and colors.

- Apply a chart style: This feature applies predetermined formatting, such as the background color and the data series color.

6. Modify the data source.

- Add or remove data from the data source to change the data in the chart.
- Apply chart filters: The Select Data Source dialog box enables you to modify the ranges used for the data series. When you deselect a series, Excel removes that series from the chart.
- Switch row and column data: You can switch the way data is used to create a chart by switching data series and categories.

7. Create and customize sparklines.

- Create a sparkline: A sparkline is a miniature chart in a cell representing a single data series.
- Customize a sparkline: Change the data source, location, and style. Display markers and change line or marker colors.

Key Terms Matching

Match the key terms with their definitions. Write the key term letter by the appropriate numbered definition.

a. Axis title
b. Bar chart
c. Category axis
d. Chart area
e. Chart title
f. Clustered column chart
g. Combo chart
h. Data label
i. Data point
j. Data series
k. Gridline
l. Legend
m. Line chart
n. Pie chart
o. Plot area
p. Sizing handle
q. Sparkline
r. Task pane
s. Value axis
t. X Y (scatter) chart

1. _______ Chart that groups columns side by side to compare data points among categories.

2. _______ Miniature chart contained in a single cell.

3. _______ Chart type that shows trends over time in which the value axis indicates quantities and the horizontal axis indicates time.

4. _______ Label that describes the entire chart.

5. _______ Label that describes either the category axis or the value axis.

6. _______ Key that identifies the color, gradient, picture, texture, or pattern fill assigned to each data series in a chart.

7. _______ Chart type that compares categories of data horizontally.

8. _______ Chart that shows each data point in proportion to the whole data series.

9. _______ Numeric value that describes a single value on a chart.

10. _______ Chart that contains two chart types, such as column and line, to depict two types of data, such as individual data points and percentages.

11. _______ A circle that enables you to adjust the height or width of a selected chart.

12. _______ Horizontal or vertical line that extends from the horizontal or vertical axis through the plot area.

13. _______ Chart type that shows the relationship between two variables.

14. _______ Group of related data points that display in row(s) or column(s) in a worksheet.

15. _______ Window of options to format and customize chart elements.

16. _______ Provides descriptive labels for the data points plotted in a chart.

17. _______ Section of a chart that contains graphical representation of the values in a data series.

18. _______ A container for the entire chart and all of its elements.

19. _______ An identifier that shows the exact value of a data point in a chart.

20. _______ Displays incremental numbers to identify approximate values, such as dollars or units, of data points in a chart.

Multiple Choice

1. Which type of chart is the *least* appropriate for depicting yearly rainfall totals for five cities for four years?
   (a) Pie chart
   (b) Line chart
   (c) Column chart
   (d) Bar chart

2. Look at the stacked bar chart in Figure 35. Which of the following is a category on the category axis?
   (a) Thousands
   (b) Job Titles
   (c) CIS Managers
   (d) 700

3. Which of the following is not a type of sparkline?
   (a) Line
   (b) Bar
   (c) Column
   (d) Win-Loss

4. If you want to show exact values for a data series in a bar chart, which chart element should you display?
   (a) Chart title
   (b) Legend
   (c) Value axis title
   (d) Data labels

5. The value axis currently shows increments such as 50,000 and 100,000. What option would you select to display the values in increments of 50 and 100?
   (a) More Primary Vertical Axis Title Options
   (b) Show Axis in Thousands
   (c) Show Axis in Millions
   (d) Show Right to Left Axis

6. You want to create a single chart that shows the proportion of yearly sales for five divisions for each year for five years. Which type of chart can accommodate your needs?
   (a) Pie chart
   (b) Surface chart
   (c) Clustered bar chart
   (d) 100% stacked column chart

7. Currently, a column chart shows values on the value axis, years on the category axis, and state names in the legend. What should you do if you want to organize data with the states on the category axis and the years shown in the legend?
   (a) Change the chart type to a clustered column chart.
   (b) Click Switch Row/Column in the Data group on the Design tab.
   (c) Click Layout 2 in the Chart Layouts group on the Design tab and apply a different chart style.
   (d) Click Legend in the Labels group on the Layout tab and select Show Legend at Bottom.

8. What do you click to remove a data series from a chart so that you can focus on other data series?
   (a) Chart Elements
   (b) Chart Series
   (c) Chart Filters
   (d) Chart Styles

9. Which of the following does not display automatically when you create a clustered column chart?
   (a) Data labels
   (b) Chart title placeholder
   (c) Gridlines
   (d) Legend

10. After you create a line type sparkline, what option should you select to display dots for each data point?
    (a) High Point
    (b) Negative Point
    (c) Sparkline Color
    (d) Markers

Practice Exercises

1 Hulett Family Utility Expenses

Your cousin, Alex Hulett, wants to analyze his family's utility expenses for 2018. He gave you his files for the electric, gas, and water bills for the year. You created a worksheet that lists the individual expenses per month, along with yearly totals per utility type and monthly totals. You will create some charts to depict the data. Refer to Figure 49 as you complete this exercise.

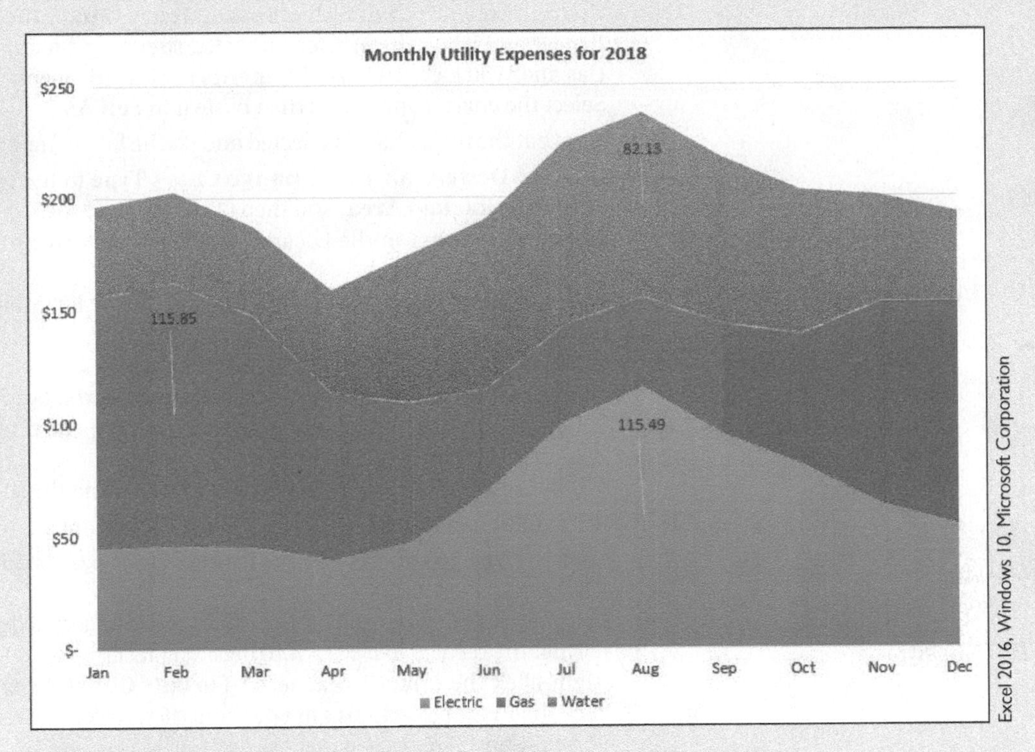

FIGURE 49 Hulett Family Utility Expenses

a. Open *e03p1Utilities* and save it as **e03p1Utilities_LastFirst**.

b. Select the **range A4:E17**, click **Quick Analysis**, click **Charts**, and then click **Clustered Column**.

c. Click **Chart Filters** to the right of the chart and do the following:

- Deselect the **Monthly Totals check box** in the Series group.
- Scroll through the Categories group and deselect the **Yearly Totals check box**.
- Click **Apply** to remove totals from the chart. Click **Chart Filters** to close the menu.

d. Point to the **chart area**. When you see the Chart Area ScreenTip, drag the chart so that the top-left corner of the chart is in **cell A21**.

e. Click the **Format tab** and change the size by doing the following:

- Click in the **Shape Width box** in the Size group, type **6"**, and then press **Enter**.
- Click in the **Shape Height box** in the Size group, type **3.5"**, and then press **Enter**.

f. Click the **Design tab**, click **Quick Layout** in the Chart Layouts group, and then click **Layout 3**.

g. Select the **Chart Title placeholder**, type **Monthly Utility Expenses for 2018**, and then press **Enter**.

h. Click the chart, click the **More button** in the Chart Styles group, and then click **Style 6**.

i. Click **Copy** on the Home tab, click **cell A39**, and then click **Paste**. With the second chart selected, do the following:
   - Click the **Design tab**, click **Change Chart Type** in the Type group, click **Line** on the left side of the dialog box, select **Line with Markers** in the top-center section, and then click **OK**.
   - Click the **Electric data series line** to select it and click the highest marker to select only that marker. Click **Chart Elements** and click **Data Labels**.
   - Repeat and adapt the previous bulleted step to add a data label to the highest markers for Gas and Water. Click **Chart Elements** to close the menu.
   - Select the chart, copy it, and then paste it in **cell A57**.

j. Ensure that the third chart is selected and do the following:
   - Click the **Design tab**, click **Change Chart Type** in the Type group, select **Area** on the left side, click **Stacked Area**, and then click **OK**.
   - Click **Move Chart** in the Location group, click **New sheet**, type **Area Chart**, and then click **OK**.
   - Select each data label and change the font size to **12**. Move each data label up closer to the top of the respective shaded area.
   - Select the value axis and change the font size to **12**.
   - Right-click the value axis and select **Format Axis**. Scroll down in the Format Axis task pane, click **Number**, click in the **Decimal places box**, and then type **0**. Close the Format Axis task pane.
   - Change the font size to **12** for the category axis and the legend.

k. Click the **Expenses sheet tab**, select the line chart, and do the following:
   - Click the **Design tab**, click **Move Chart** in the Location group, click **New sheet**, type **Line Chart**, and then click **OK**.
   - Change the font size to **12** for the value axis, category axis, data labels, and legend.
   - Format the vertical axis with zero decimal places.
   - Right-click the **chart area**, select **Format Chart Area**, click **Fill**, click **Gradient fill**, click the **Preset gradients arrow**, and then select **Light Gradient – Accent 1**. Close the Format Chart Area task pane.

l. Click the **Expenses sheet**, select the **range B5:D16** and do the following:
   - Click the **Insert tab**, click **Line** in the Sparkline group, click in the **Location Range box**, type **B18:D18**, and then click **OK**.
   - Click the **High Point check box** to select it and click the **Low Point check box** to select it in the Show group with all three sparklines selected.

m. Create a footer with your name on the left side, the sheet name code in the center, and the file name code on the right of each sheet.

n. Save and close the file. Based on your instructor's directions, submit e03p1Utilities_LastFirst.

2 Trends in Market Value of Houses on Pine Circle

You live in a house on Pine Circle, a quiet cul-de-sac in a suburban area. Recently, you researched the market value and square footage of the five houses on Pine Circle. Now, you want to create charts to visually depict the data to compare values for the houses in the cul-de-sac. Refer to Figure 50 as you complete this exercise.

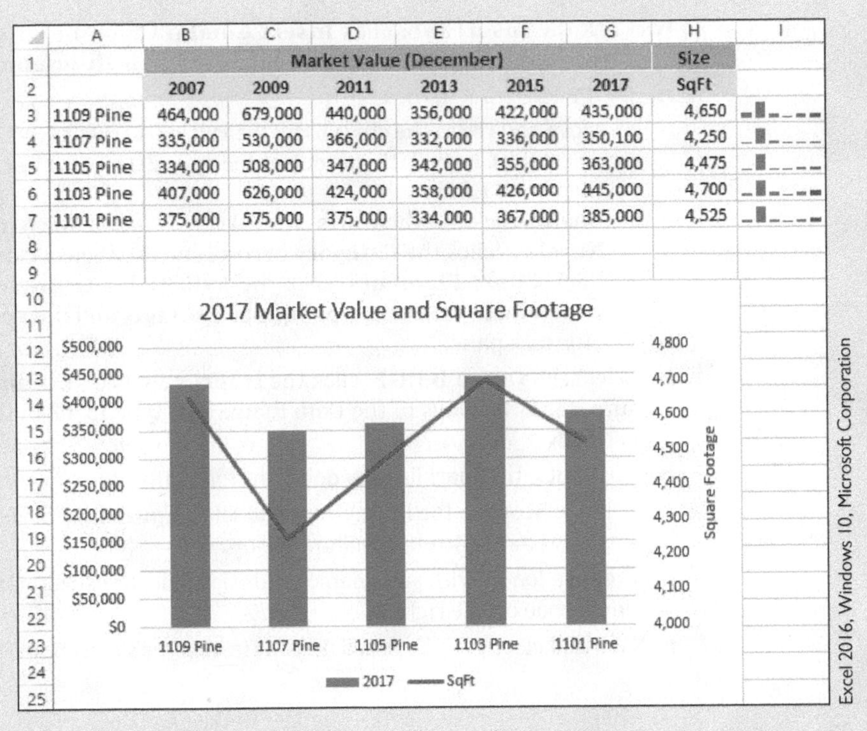

	Market Value (December)						Size
	2007	2009	2011	2013	2015	2017	SqFt
1109 Pine	464,000	679,000	440,000	356,000	422,000	435,000	4,650
1107 Pine	335,000	530,000	366,000	332,000	336,000	350,100	4,250
1105 Pine	334,000	508,000	347,000	342,000	355,000	363,000	4,475
1103 Pine	407,000	626,000	424,000	358,000	426,000	445,000	4,700
1101 Pine	375,000	575,000	375,000	334,000	367,000	385,000	4,525

FIGURE 50 Market Values

a. Open *e03p2Pine* and save it as **e03p2Pine_LastFirst.**

b. Select the **range A2:G7**, click **Quick Analysis**, click **Charts**, and then click **Line**.

c. Click **Move Chart** in the Location group, click **New sheet**, type **Line**, and then click **OK**.

d. Select the **Chart Title placeholder** and do the following:
   - Type **Market Value of Pine Circle Houses** and press **Enter**.
   - Apply bold to the chart title, change the font size to **20**, and then select **Olive Green, Accent 3, Darker 50% font color**.

e. Click the **value axis** on the left side of the chart and do the following:
   - Change the font size to 12 and select **Olive Green, Accent 3, Darker 50% font color**.
   - Double-click the value axis to open the Format Axis task pane.
   - Type **300000** in the Minimum Bounds box and press **Enter**. The Maximum Bounds box should change to 700000 automatically.
   - Scroll down in the Format Axis task pane and click **Number** to display those options.
   - Click the **Category arrow** and select **Currency**.
   - Close the Format Axis task pane.

f. Click **Chart Elements**, click the **Axis Titles triangle**, and then click the **Primary Vertical check box** to select it. Type **December Market Values** in the **Axis Title placeholder** and press **Enter**.

g. Make sure the Chart Elements menu is showing, click the **Gridlines triangle**, and then click the **Primary Minor Horizontal check box** to select it.

h. Click the blue **1109 Pine data series line**, click the **Data Labels check box** to select it, and then click **Chart Elements** to close the menu.

i. Click the data labels you just created, click the **Home tab**, click the **Font Color arrow**, and then select **Blue** in the Standard Colors section.

j. Select the category axis, change the font size to **12**, and select **Olive Green, Accent 3, Darker 50% font color**.

k. Right-click the legend and select **Format Legend**. Click **Top** in the Legend Position section of the Format Legend task pane and close the task pane.

l. Click the **Pine Circle sheet tab** and select the **ranges A2:A7** and **G2:H7**.

m. Click the **Insert tab**, click **Insert Combo Chart** in the Charts group, and then click the **Clustered Column – Line on Secondary Axis thumbnail**.

n. Do the following to the chart:

- Move and resize the chart to fill the **range A10:H25**.
- Select the **Chart Title placeholder**, type **2017 Market Value and Square Footage**, and then press **Enter**.
- Double-click the value axis on the left side, scroll down in the Format Axis task pane, click **Number**, click the **Category arrow**, and then select **Currency**.
- Click **Chart Elements**, click the **Axis Titles triangle**, click the **Secondary Vertical check box** to select it, type **Square Footage**, and then press **Enter**. Close the Format Axis Title task pane.

o. Select the **range B3:G7**, click the **Insert tab**, click **Column** in the Sparklines group, make sure B3:G7 displays in the Data Range box, type **I3:I7** in the Location Range box, and then click **OK**.

p. Customize the sparklines by doing the following:

- Click **More** in the Style group and select **Sparkline Style Accent 6, Darker 25%**.
- Click **Last Point** in the Show group.

q. Create a footer with your name on the left side, the sheet name code in the center, and the file name code on the right of both sheets.

r. Save and close the file. Based on your instructor's directions, submit e03p2Pine_LastFirst.

Mid-Level Exercises

1 Airport Passenger Counts

As an analyst for the airline industry, you track the number of passengers at the top five major U.S. airports: Atlanta, Chicago, Los Angeles, Dallas/Fort Worth, and Denver. You researched passenger data at http://www.aci-na.org. One worksheet you created lists the number of total yearly passengers at the top five airports for a six-year period. To prepare for an upcoming meeting, you need to create a clustered column chart to compare the number of passengers at each airport. Next, you will create a bar chart to compare the passenger count for the latest year of data available and then emphasize the airport with the largest number of passenger traffic. Finally, you want to insert sparklines to visually represent trends in passengers at each airport over the six-year period. You can then refer to the sparklines and clustered column chart to write a paragraph analyzing the trends to detect.

a. Open *e03m1Airports* and save it as **e03m1Airports_LastFirst**.
b. Create a clustered column chart for the **range A4:G9**. Position and resize the chart to fit in the **range A15:G34**.
c. Customize the chart by doing the following:
   - Swap the data on the category axis and in the legend.
   - Apply the **Style 6 chart style**.
   - Select **Color 12** in the Monochromatic section of the Change Colors gallery.
   - Apply the **Light Gradient – Accent 1** preset gradient fill to the chart area.
   - Change the fill color of the 2013 data series to **Dark Blue** and change the fill color of the 2008 data series to **Blue, Accent 5, Lighter 60%**.

   - Use Help and add a solid **Blue border** around the legend.
d. Type **Passengers by Top U.S. Airports** as the chart title. Change the font color to **Blue**.

DISCOVER

e. Adjust the value axis by doing the following:
   - Change the display units to **Millions** for the value axis.
   - Edit the axis title to display **Millions of Passengers**.
f. Display data labels above the columns for the 2013 data series only.
g. Create a clustered bar chart for the **range A5:A9** and **G5:G9** and then do the following:
   - Move the bar chart to a chart sheet named **Bar Chart**.
   - Enter **Passengers at Top 5 U.S. Airports in 2013** as the chart title.
   - Apply the **Style 3 chart style.**
   - Change the font color to **Dark Blue** on the chart title, category axis, and the value axis.
   - Format the Atlanta data point with **Dark Blue fill color**.
h. Display the Passenger worksheet and insert **Line sparklines** in the **range H5:H9** to illustrate the data in the **range B5:G9**. This should insert a sparkline to represent yearly data for each airport.
i. Customize the sparklines by doing the following:
   - Show the high and low points in each sparkline.
   - Apply **Black, Text 1 color** to the high point marker in each sparkline.

   - Apply **Dark Red color** to the low point marker in each sparkline.
j. Click **cell A36** and compose a paragraph that analyzes the trends depicted by the airport sparklines. Notice the overall trends in decreased and increased number of passengers and any unusual activity for an airport. Spell-check the worksheet and correct any errors.
k. Set **0.2"** left and right margins and scale to fit to 1 page for the Passenger worksheet.
l. Insert a footer with your name on the left side, the sheet name code in the center, and the file name code on the right on all worksheets.
m. Save and close the file. Based on your instructor's directions, submit e03m1Airports_LastFirst.

2 Grade Analysis

You are a teaching assistant for Dr. Monica Unice's introductory psychology class. You have maintained her grade book all semester, entering three test scores for each student and calculating the final average. You created a section called Final Grade Distribution that contains calculations to identify the number of students who earned an A, B, C, D, or F. Dr. Unice wants you to create a chart that shows the percentage of students who earn each letter grade. Therefore, you decide to create and format a pie chart. You will also create a bar chart to show a sample of the students' test scores. Furthermore, Dr. Unice wants to see if a correlation exists between attendance and students' final grades; therefore, you will create a scatter chart depicting each student's percentage of attendance with his or her respective final grade average.

a. Open *e03m2Psych* and save it as **e03m2Psych_LastFirst**.

b. Create a pie chart from the Final Grade Distribution data located below the student data in the **range F38:G42** and move the pie chart to its own sheet named **Grades Pie**.

c. Customize the pie chart with these specifications:
- Apply the **Style 7 chart style.**
- Type **PSY 2030 Final Grade Distribution - Fall 2018** for the chart title.
- Explode the B grade slice by **10%.**
- Remove the legend.

d. Add centered data labels and customize the labels with these specifications:
- Display these data labels: **Percentage** and **Category Name**. Remove other data labels.
- Change the font size to **20** and apply **Black, Text 1** font color.

e. Create a clustered bar chart using the **range A7:D12** and move the bar chart to its own sheet named **Students Bar Chart**.

f. Customize the bar chart with these specifications:
- Apply the **Style 5 chart style**.
- Type **Sample Student Test Scores** for the chart title.
- Position the legend on the right side.
- Add data labels in the Outside End position for the Final Exam data series.
- Arrange the categories in reverse order so that Atkin is listed at the top and Ethington is listed at the bottom of the bar chart.

g. Create a scatter chart using the **range E7:F33**, the attendance record and final averages from the Grades worksheet. Move the scatter chart to its own sheet named **Scatter Chart**.

h. Apply these label settings to the scatter chart:
- Remove the legend.
- Type **Attendance-Final Average Relationship** for the chart title.
- Add the following primary horizontal axis title: **Percentage of Attendance**.
- Add the following primary vertical axis title: **Student Final Averages**.

i. Use Help to learn how to apply the following axis settings:
- Vertical axis: 40 minimum bound, 100 maximum bound, 10 major units, and a number format with zero decimal places
- Horizontal axis: 40 minimum bound, 100 maximum bound, automatic units

j. Change the font size to **12** on the vertical axis title, vertical axis, horizontal axis title, and horizontal axis. Bold the chart title and the two axes titles.

k. Add the **Parchment texture fill** to the plot area.

l. Insert a linear trendline.

m. Insert Line sparklines in the **range H8:H33** using the three tests score columns. Change the sparkline color to **Purple** and show the low points.

n. Insert a footer with your name on the left, the sheet name code in the center, and the file name code on the right on all the sheets.

o. Save and close the file. Based on your instructor's directions, submit e03m2Psych_LastFirst.

3 Box Office Movies

COLLABORATION CASE

FROM SCRATCH

You and two of your friends like to follow the popularity of new movies at the theater. You will research current movies that have been showing for four weeks and decide which movies on which to report. Work in teams of three for this activity. After obtaining the data, your team will create applicable charts to illustrate the revenue data. Team members will critique each other's charts.

a. Have all three team members log in to a chat client and engage in a dialogue about which movies are currently playing. Each member should research a different theater to see what is playing at that theater. Decide on six movies that have been in theaters for at least four weeks to research. Save a copy of your instant message dialogue and submit based on your instructor's directions.

b. Divide the six movies among the three team members. Each member should research the revenue reported for two movies for the past four weeks. Make sure your team members use the same source to find the data.

Student 1:

c. Create a new Excel workbook and enter appropriate column labels and the four-week data for all six movies. Name Sheet1 **Data**.

d. Format the data appropriately. Save the workbook as **e03m3Movies_GroupName**. Upload the workbook to a shared location, such as OneDrive, invite the other students to share this location, and send a text message to the next student.

Student 2:

e. Create a line chart to show the trends in revenue for the movies for the four-week period.

f. Add a chart title, format the axes appropriately, select a chart style, and then apply other formatting.

g. Move the chart to its own sheet named **Trends**. Save the workbook, upload it to the shared location, and send a text message to the next student.

Student 3:

h. Add a column to the right of the four-week data and total each movie's four-week revenue.

i. Create a pie chart depicting each movie's percentage of the total revenue for your selected movies.

j. Add a chart title, explode one pie slice, add data labels showing percentages and movie names, and then apply other formatting.

k. Move the chart to its own sheet named **Revenue Chart**. Save the workbook, upload it to the shared location, and send a text message to the next student.

Student 1:

l. Critique the charts. Insert a new worksheet named **Chart Critique** that provides an organized critique of each chart. Type notes that list each team member's name and specify what each student's role was in completing this exercise.

m. Save the workbook, upload it to the shared location, and send a text message to the next student.

Student 2:

n. Read the critique of the line chart and make any appropriate changes for the line chart. On the critique worksheet, provide a response to each critique and why you made or did not make the suggested change.

o. Save the workbook, upload it to the shared location, and send a text message to the next student.

Student 3:

p. Read the critique of the pie chart and make any appropriate changes for the pie chart. On the critique worksheet, provide a response to each critique and why you made or did not make the suggested change.

q. Save and close the file. Based on your instructor's directions, submit e03m3Movies_GroupName.

Beyond the Classroom

Historical Stock Prices

GENERAL CASE ✓

FROM SCRATCH 

You are interested in investing in the stock market. First, you need to research the historical prices for a particular stock. Launch a Web browser, go to finance.yahoo.com, type a company name, such as Apple, and then select the company name from a list of suggested companies. Click the Historical Prices link. Copy the stock data (date, high, low, open, close, volume) for a six-month period and paste it in a new workbook, adjusting the column widths to fit the data. Save the workbook as **e03b1StockData_LastFirst**. Rename Sheet1 **Data**. Display data for only the first date listed for each month; delete rows containing data for other dates. Sort the list from the oldest date to the newest date. Use Help if needed to learn how to sort data and how to create a Volume-Open-High-Low-Close chart. Then rearrange the data columns in the correct sequence. Format the data and column labels.

Insert a row to enter the company name and insert another row to list the company's stock symbol, such as AAPL. Copy the URL from the Web browser and paste it as a source below the list of data and the date you obtained the data. Merge the cells containing the company name and stock symbol through the last column of data and word-wrap the URL.

Create a Volume-Open-High-Low-Close chart on a new chart sheet named **Stock Chart**. Type an appropriate chart title. Set the primary vertical axis (left side) unit measurement to millions and include an axis title **Volume in Millions**. Include a secondary vertical axis (right side) title **Stock Prices**. Apply the Currency number style with 0 decimal places for the secondary axis values. Change the font size to 11 and the font color to Black, Text 1 on the vertical axes and category axis. Hide the legend.

Use Help to research how to insert text boxes. Insert a text box that describes the stock chart: white fill rectangles indicate the closing price was higher than the opening price; black fill rectangles indicate the closing price was lower than the opening price; etc. Create a footer with your name, the sheet name code, and the file name code on both worksheets. Save and close the file. Based on your instructor's directions, submit e03b1StockData_LastFirst.

Harper County Houses Sold

You want to analyze the number of houses sold by type (e.g., rambler, two story, etc.) in each quarter in Harper County. You entered quarterly data for 2018, calculated yearly total number of houses sold by each type, and quarterly total number of houses sold. You asked an intern to create a stacked column chart for the data, but the chart contains a lot of errors.

Open *e03b2Houses* and save it as **e03b2Houses_LastFirst**. Identify the errors and poor design for the chart. Below the chart, list the errors and your corrections in a two-column format. Then correct the problems in the chart. Link the chart title to the cell containing the most appropriate label in the worksheet. Create a footer with your name, the sheet name code, and the file name code. Adjust the margins and scaling to print the worksheet data, including the error list, and the chart on one page. Save and close the file. Based on your instructor's directions, submit e03b2Houses_LastFirst.

Capstone Exercise

You are an analyst for the airline industry. You created a workbook that lists overall airline arrival statistics for several years. In particular, you listed the percentage and number of on-time arrivals, late arrivals, canceled flights, and diverted flights based on information provided by the Bureau of Transportation Statistics. You want to create charts and insert sparklines that show the trends to discuss with airline and airport managers.

Insert and Format Sparklines

The first dataset shows the percentages. You want to insert sparklines that show the trends in the five-year data. The sparklines will help show any trends in on-time arrivals compared to late arrivals, canceled flights, and diverted flights.

a. Open the *e03c1Arrivals* workbook and save it as **e03c1Arrivals_LastFirst**.

b. Insert Line sparklines in the **range G4:G7**, using the data for the five years.

c. Display the high and low points for the sparklines.

d. Change the high point marker color to **Green**.

Create a Pie Chart

You want to focus on the arrival percentages for 2014. Creating a pie chart will help people visualize the breakdown of all operations for that year. After you create the chart, you will move it to its own chart sheet and edit the chart title to reflect 2014 flight arrivals.

a. Select the **range A4:A7** and the **range F4:F7**.

b. Create a pie chart and move it to a chart sheet named **Pie Chart**.

c. Change the chart title to **2014 Flight Arrivals**.

Add and Format Chart Elements

You want to format the chart by applying a different chart style and positioning the legend above the plot area. Furthermore, you need to add data labels so that you will know the percentages for the arrival categories. Finally, you want to emphasize the canceled flights in Dark Red and explode the late arrival pie slice.

a. Apply the **Style 12 chart style** to the pie chart.

b. Format the chart title with **Blue font color**.

c. Position the legend between the chart title and the plot area.

d. Add data labels to the Best Fit position and display.

e. Apply bold to the data labels and change the font size to **12**.

f. Format the Canceled data point with **Dark Red fill color** and format the Late Arrival data point in **Green**.

g. Explode the Late Arrival data point by **5%**.

Create and Size a Column Chart

To provide a different perspective, you will create a clustered column chart using the actual number of flights. The Total Operations row indicates the total number of reported (scheduled) flights. After creating the chart, you will position and size the chart below the source rows.

a. Create a clustered column chart using the **range A10:F15** in the Arrivals sheet.

b. Edit the chart title: **On-Time and Late Flight Arrivals.**

c. Position the clustered column chart so that the top-left corner is in **cell A20**.

d. Change the width to **5.75"** and the height to **3.5"**.

Format the Column Chart

Now that you have created the column chart, you realize that some data seems irrelevant. You will filter out the unneeded data, format the value axis to remove digits, insert a vertical axis title, apply a color change, and format the chart area.

a. Apply chart filters to remove the canceled, diverted, and total operations data.

b. Select the value axis, set **500000** for the Major unit, display the axis units **in Millions**, select category **Number** format with **1** decimal place.

c. Add a primary vertical axis title **Number of Flights.**

d. Apply the **Color 2 chart color** to the chart.

e. Apply the **Light Gradient – Accent 3** fill to the chart area.

Finalizing the Workbook

You want to prepare the workbook in case someone wants to print the data and charts. The margins and scaling have already been set. You just need to insert a footer.

a. Create a footer on each worksheet with your name, the sheet name code, and the file name code.

b. Save and close the file. Based on your instructor's direction, submit e03c1Arrivals_LastFirst.

Glossary

100% stacked column chart A chart type that places (stacks) data in one column per category, with each column the same height of 100%.

Alt text An accessibility compliance feature where you enter text and a description for an objective, such as a table or a chart. A special reader can read the alt text to a user.

Area chart A chart type that emphasizes magnitude of changes over time by filling in the space between lines with a color.

Axis title A label that describes either the category axis or the value axis. Provides clarity, particularly in describing the value axis.

Bar chart A chart type that compares values across categories using horizontal bars where the length represents the value; the longer the bar, the larger the value. In a bar chart, the horizontal axis displays values and the vertical axis displays categories.

Category axis The chart axis that displays descriptive labels for the data points plotted in a chart. The category axis labels are typically text contained in the first column of worksheet data (such as job titles) used to create the chart.

Chart A visual representation of numerical data.

Chart area A container for the entire chart and all of its elements, including the plot area, titles, legends, and labels.

Chart element A component of a chart that helps complete or clarify the chart.

Chart filter A setting that controls what data series and categories are displayed or hidden in a chart.

Chart sheet A sheet within a workbook that contains a single chart and no spreadsheet data.

Chart style A collection of formatting that controls the color of the chart area, plot area, and data series.

Chart title The label that describes the entire chart. The title is usually placed at the top of the chart area.

Clustered column chart A type of chart that groups, or clusters, columns set side by side to compare several data points among categories.

Column chart A type of chart that compares values vertically in columns where the height represents the value; the taller the column, the larger the value. In a column chart, the vertical axis displays values and the horizontal axis displays categories.

Combo chart A chart that combines two chart types, such as column and line, to plot different types of data, such as quantities and percentages.

Data label An identifier that shows the exact value of a data point in a chart. Appears above or on a data point in a chart. May indicate percentage of a value to the whole on a pie chart.

Data point A numeric value that describes a single value in a chart or worksheet.

Data series A group of related data points that display in row(s) or column(s) in a worksheet.

Data table A grid that contains the data source values and labels to plot data in a chart. A data table may be placed below a chart or hidden from view.

Error bars Visual that indicates the standard error amount, a percentage, or a standard deviation for a data point or marker in a chart.

Exploded pie chart A chart type in which one or more pie slices are separated from the rest of the pie chart for emphasis.

Gridline A horizontal or vertical line that extends from the horizontal or vertical axis through the plot area to guide the reader's eyes across the chart to identify values.

Histogram A chart that is similar to a column chart. The category axis shows bin ranges (intervals) where data is aggregated into bins, and the vertical axis shows frequencies.

Legend A key that identifies the color, gradient, picture, texture, or pattern assigned to each data series in a chart.

Line chart A chart type that displays lines connecting data points to show trends over equal time periods, such as months, quarters, years, or decades.

Pie chart A chart type that shows each data point in proportion to the whole data series as a slice in a circle. A pie chart depicts only one data series.

Plot area The region of a chart containing the graphical representation of the values in one or more data series. Two axes form a border around the plot area.

Radar chart A chart type that compares aggregate values of three or more variables represented on axes starting from the same point.

Sizing handles Eight circles that display on the outside border of a chart—one on each corner and one on each middle side—when the chart is selected; enables the user to adjust the height and width of the chart.

Sparkline A small line, column, or win/loss chart contained in a single cell to provide a simple visual illustrating one data series.

Stacked column chart A chart type that places stacks of data in segments on top of each other in one column, with each category in the data series represented by a different color.

Stock chart A chart type that shows fluctuation in stock prices.

Surface chart A chart type that displays trends using two dimensions on a continuous curve.

Task pane A window of options to format and customize chart elements. The task pane name and options change based on the selected chart element.

Trendline A line that depicts trends or helps forecast future data in a chart. For example, if the plotted data includes 2005, 2010, and 2015, a trendline can help forecast values for 2020 and beyond.

Value axis The chart axis that displays incremental numbers to identify approximate values, such as dollars or units, of data points in a chart.

X Y (scatter) chart A chart type that shows a relationship between two variables using their X and Y coordinates. Excel plots one coordinate on the horizontal X-axis and the other variable on the vertical Y-axis. Scatter charts are often used to represent data in education, scientific, and medical experiments.

X-axis The horizontal border that provides a frame of reference for measuring data left to right on a chart.

Y-axis The vertical border that provides a frame of reference for measuring data up and down on a chart.

Introduction to Access

Access

Introduction to Access

LEARNING OUTCOME **You will demonstrate understanding of relational database concepts.**

OBJECTIVES & SKILLS: After you read this chapter, you will be able to:

Databases Are Everywhere

OBJECTIVE 1: OPEN, SAVE, AND ENABLE CONTENT IN A DATABASE
Open a Database, Save a Database with a New Name, Enable Content in a Database

OBJECTIVE 2: RECOGNIZE DATABASE OBJECT TYPES
Examine the Access Interface, Explore Table Datasheet View, Navigate Through Records, Explore Table Design View, Rename and Describe Tables, Understand Relationships Between Tables

OBJECTIVE 3: MODIFY DATA IN TABLE DATASHEET VIEW
Understand the Difference Between Working in Storage and Memory, Change Data in Table Datasheet View

OBJECTIVE 4: ADD RECORDS TO A TABLE
Add Records to a Table

OBJECTIVE 5: DELETE RECORDS FROM A TABLE
Delete Records from a Table

OBJECTIVE 6: USE DATABASE UTILITIES
Back Up a Database, Compact and Repair a Database, Encrypt a Database, Print Information

HANDS-ON EXERCISE 1:
Databases Are Everywhere!

Filters and Sorts

OBJECTIVE 7: WORK WITH FILTERS
Use a Selection Filter to Find Exact Matches, Use a Selection Filter to Find Records Containing a Value, Use Filter By Form

OBJECTIVE 8: PERFORM SORTS
Sort Table Data

HANDS-ON EXERCISE 2:
Filters, Sorts, Relationships, and Sort Table Data

Access Database Creation

OBJECTIVE 9: CREATE A DATABASE
Create a Blank Desktop Database, Create a Desktop Database Using a Template, Add Records to a Downloaded Desktop Database, Explore the Database Objects in a Downloaded Desktop Database Template, Create a Table Using an Application Part, Create a Web App Using a Template

HANDS-ON EXERCISE 3:
Access Database Creation

CASE STUDY | Managing a Business in the Global Economy

Northwind Traders is an international gourmet food distributor that imports and exports specialty foods from around the world. Keeping track of customers, vendors, orders, and inventory is a critical task. The owners of Northwind have just purchased an order-processing database created with Microsoft Access 2016 to help manage their customers, suppliers, products, and orders.

You have been hired to learn, use, and manage the database. Northwind's owners are willing to provide training about their business and Access. They expect the learning process to take about three months. After three months, your job will be to support the order-processing team as well as to provide detail and summary reports to the sales force as needed. Your new job at Northwind Traders will be a challenge, but it is also a good opportunity to make a great contribution to a global company. Are you up to the task?

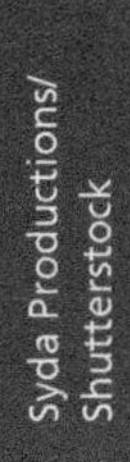

Finding Your Way Through an Access Database

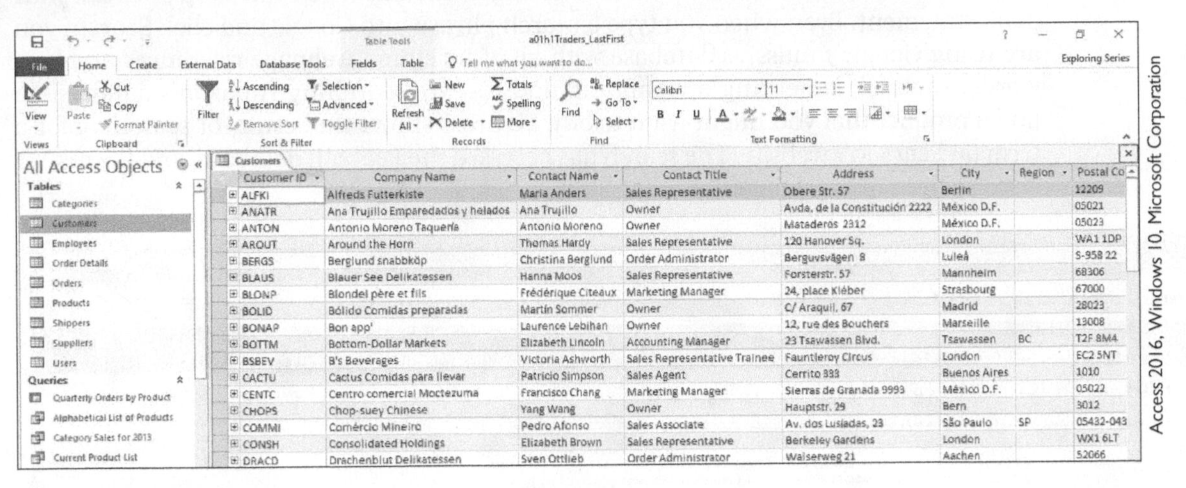

Access 2016, Windows 10, Microsoft Corporation

FIGURE 1 Northwind Traders Database

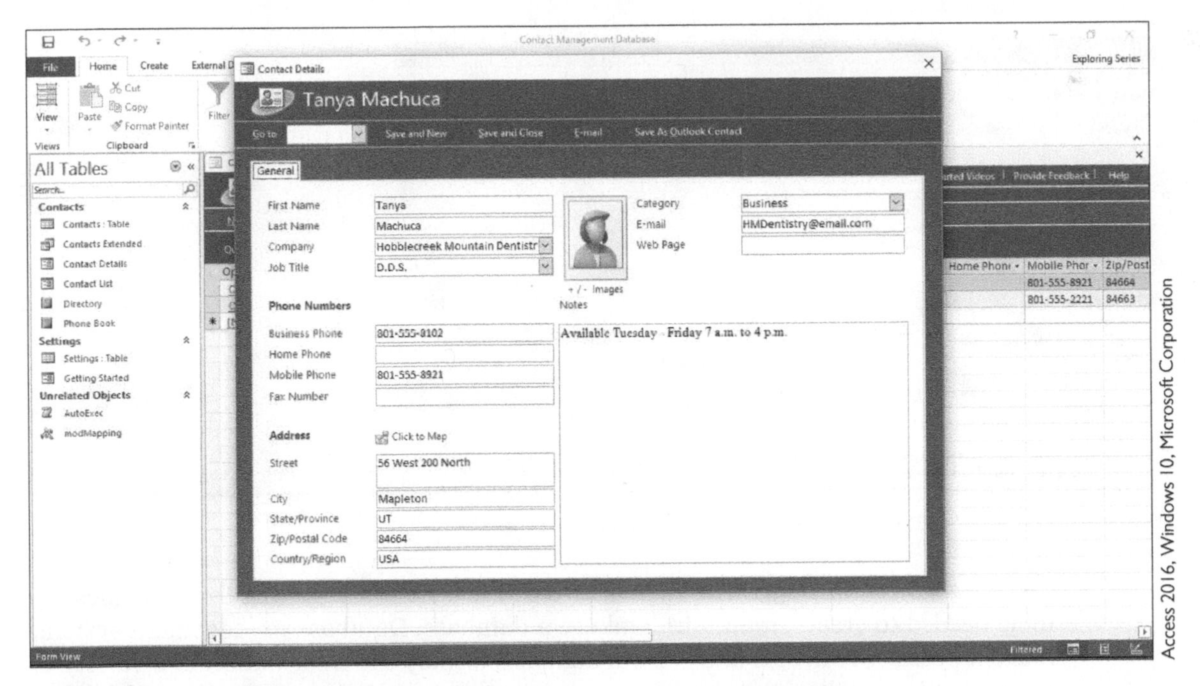

Access 2016, Windows 10, Microsoft Corporation

FIGURE 2 Northwind Traders Contacts Database

CASE STUDY | Managing a Business in the Global Economy

Starting File	Files to be Submitted
a01h1Traders	**a01h1Traders_LastFirst_*CurrentDate*** **a01h2Traders_LastFirst** **a01h3Contacts_LastFirst**

Databases Are Everywhere!

A ***database*** is a collection of data organized as meaningful information that can be accessed, managed, stored, queried, sorted, and reported. You probably participate in data collection and are exposed to databases on a regular basis. Your college or university stores your personal and registration data. When you registered for this course, your data was entered into a database. If you have a bank account, have a Social Security card, have a medical history, or have booked a flight with an airline, your information is stored in a database.

You use databases online without realizing it, such as when you shop or check your bank statement. Even when you type a search phrase into Google and click Search, you are using Google's massive database with all of its stored webpage references and keywords. Look for something on Amazon, and you are searching Amazon's database to find a product that you might want to buy. Figure 3 shows the results of searching for a term on Pearson's website. The search has accessed the Pearson database, and the results are displayed in a webpage.

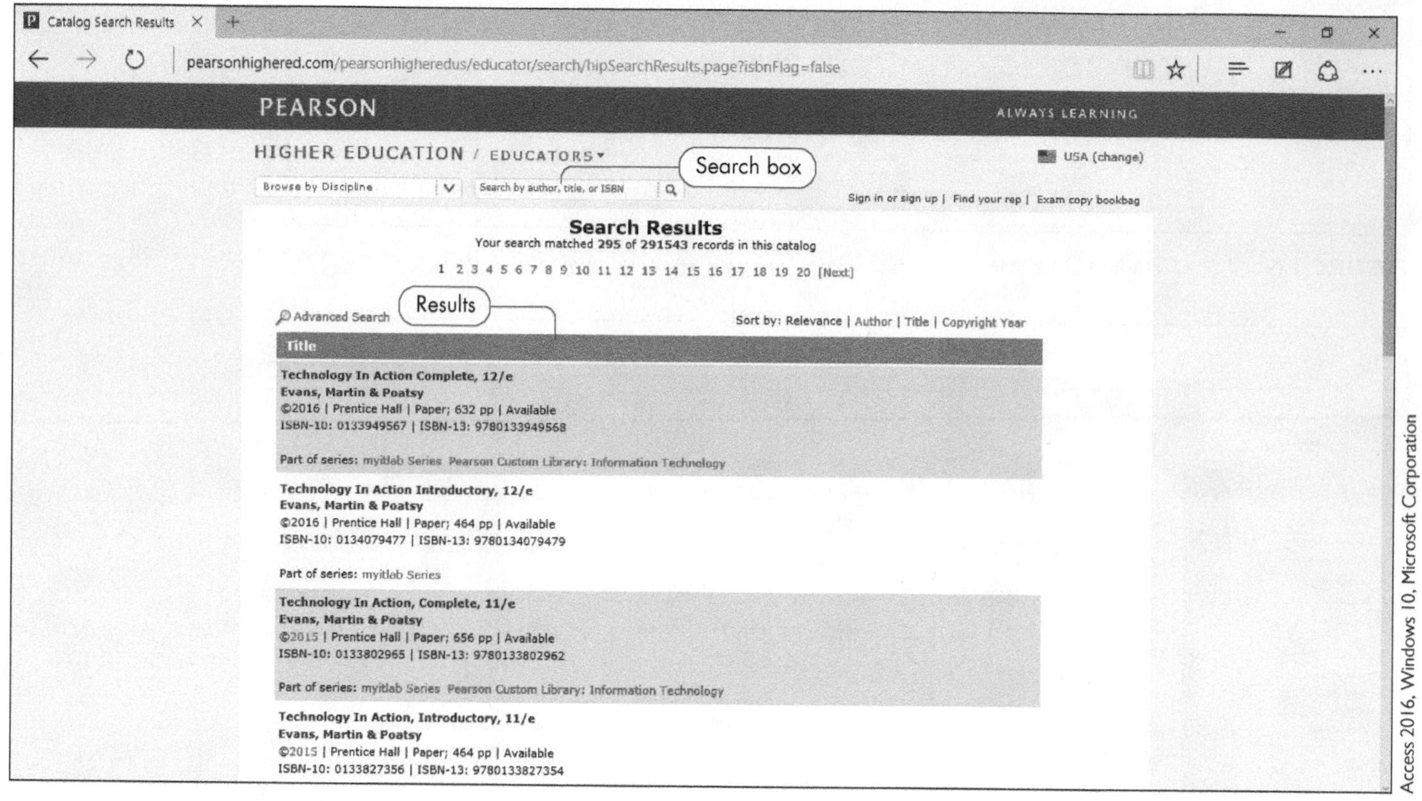

FIGURE 3 Pearson Website Search

A ***database management system (DBMS)*** is a software system that provides the tools needed to create, maintain, and use a database. Database management systems make it possible to access and control data and display the information in a variety of formats. ***Access*** is the database management system included in professional editions of the Office 2016 suite. Access is a valuable decision-making tool used by many organizations. More advanced DBMS packages include Microsoft SQL Server, MySQL, and Oracle.

Organizations from all industries rely on data to conduct daily operations. Businesses maintain and analyze data about their students, customers, employees, orders, volunteers, activities, and facilities. Data and information are two terms that are often used interchangeably. However, when it comes to databases, the two terms mean different things. Data is what is entered into a database. Information is the finished product that is produced by the database. Data is converted to information by selecting, performing calculations, and sorting. Decisions in an organization are usually based on information produced by a database, rather than raw data. For example, the number 55 is just data, because it could mean anything. Only when a label is attached to it (for example, as someone's age) does it take on meaning and become information.

In this section, you will learn the fundamentals of organizing data in a database, explore Access database objects and the purpose of each object, and examine the Access interface.

Opening, Saving, and Enabling Content in a Database

STEP 1 »» As you work through the material in this text, you will frequently be asked to open a database, save it with a new name, and enable content. You can also start by creating a new database if appropriate.

If you have been provided a database, open the file to get started. When you open any database for the first time, you will be presented with a warning that it might contain harmful code. By enabling the content, the database file will be trusted on the computer you are working on. All content from this publisher and associated with this text can be trusted.

To open an existing Access database and enable content, complete the following steps:

1. Start Access 2016. Backstage view displays. (Note: If Access is already open, click the File tab to display Backstage view).
2. Click Open Other Files.
3. Click Browse to open the Open dialog box.
4. Locate and select the database and click Open.
5. Click Enable Content on the message bar (see Figure 4). Access will close and reopen the database, and the security warning disappears and will not appear again for this database.

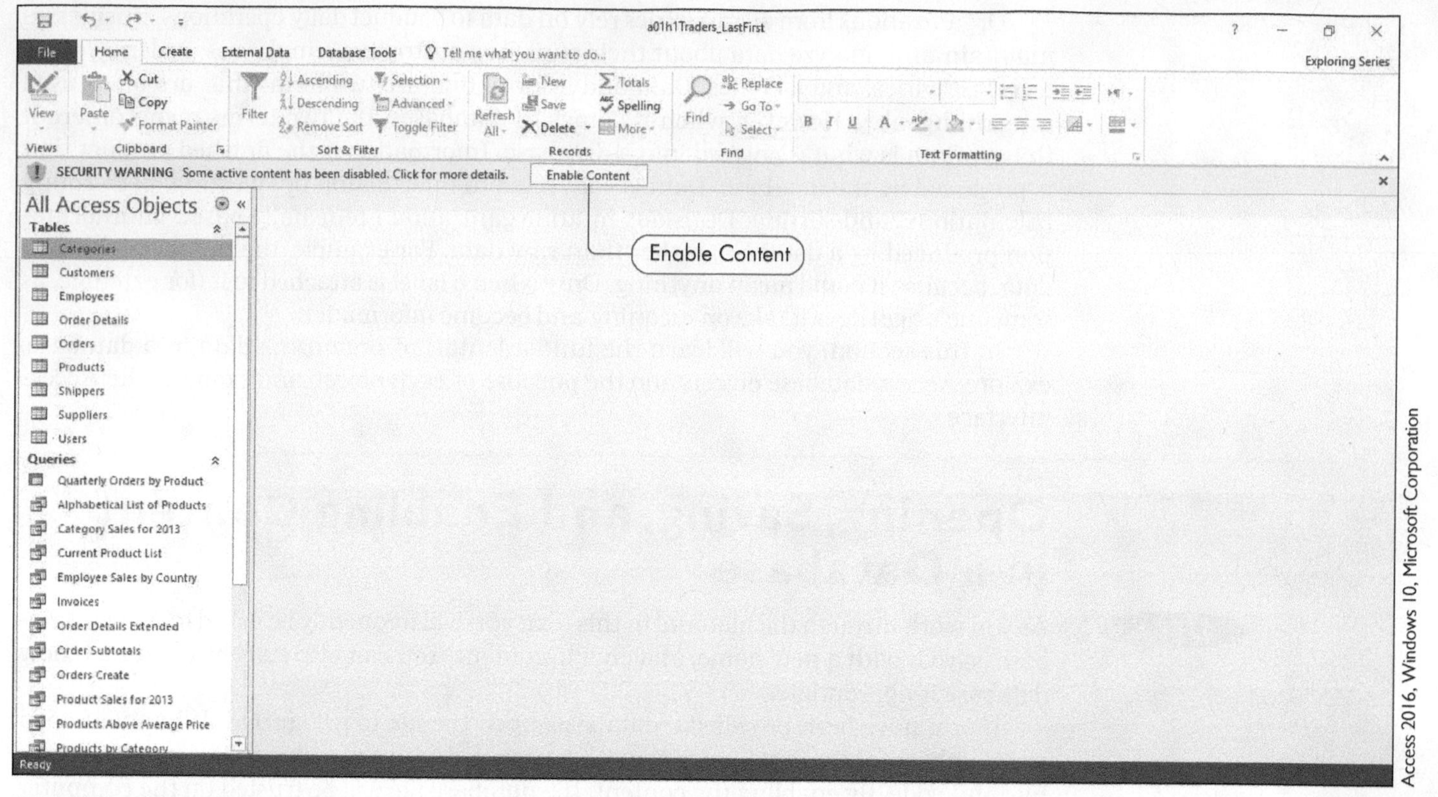

FIGURE 4 Access Security Warning

Backstage view gives you access to the Save As command. Most assignments will have you save the starting database file with a new name.

To save the database with a new name, complete the following steps:

1. Click the File tab.
2. Select Save As.
3. Ensure Save Database As is selected (see Figure 5).
4. Click Save As.
5. Type the new name for your database, and click Save.

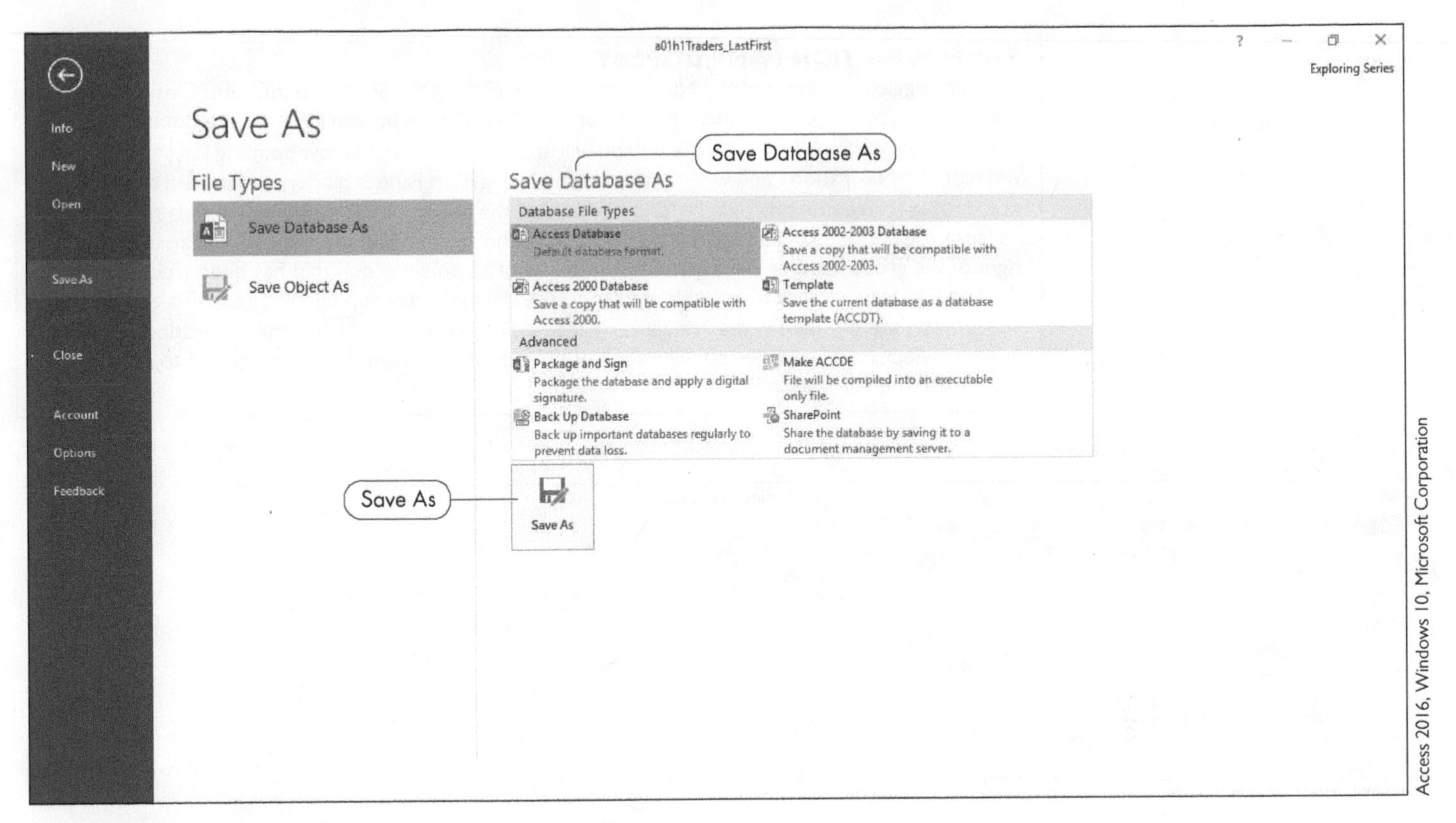

FIGURE 5 Access Save As Options

> **TIP: ALTERNATIVE SAVE FORMAT: ACCESS DATABASE EXECUTABLE**
> Creating an Access Database Executable (ACCDE) file allows users to enter data, but not add, modify, or delete objects. In other words, the only task they can do is data entry. This file format protects against users changing designs or deleting objects.
> To create an Access Database Executable, click the File tab, click Save As, and double-click Make ACCDE. Click Save to save as an Access Database Executable.

Recognizing Database Object Types

Databases must be carefully managed to keep information accurate. Data need to be changed, added, and deleted. Managing a database also requires that you understand when data is saved and when you need to use the Save commands.

In Access, each component created and used to make the database function is known as an ***object***. Objects include tables, queries, forms, and reports, and can be found in the ***Navigation Pane***. The Navigation Pane is an Access interface element that organizes and lists the objects in an Access database. The Navigation Pane appears on the left side of the screen, and displays all objects. You can open any object by double-clicking the object's name in the list.

TIP: NAVIGATION PANE DISPLAY

You can toggle the display of the Navigation Pane by clicking the Shutter Bar Open/Close button at the top-right corner of the pane. The Shutter Bar Open/Close button appears as a double arrow. If the Navigation Pane is shown, the button will appear as a double arrow pointing left « and it will hide the Navigation Pane when clicked. If the Navigation Pane is hidden, the button appears as a double arrow pointing right » and it will show the Navigation Pane when clicked. You can collapse the contents of an object group by clicking the group heading or the double arrows to the right of the group heading. To expand the contents of an object group that has been hidden, click the heading again or click the double arrows to the right of the group heading again. To change the way objects are grouped in the Navigation Pane, click the list arrow on the Navigation Pane title bar and select your preferred configuration of the available options. Refer to Figure 6 to see the features of the Navigation Pane.

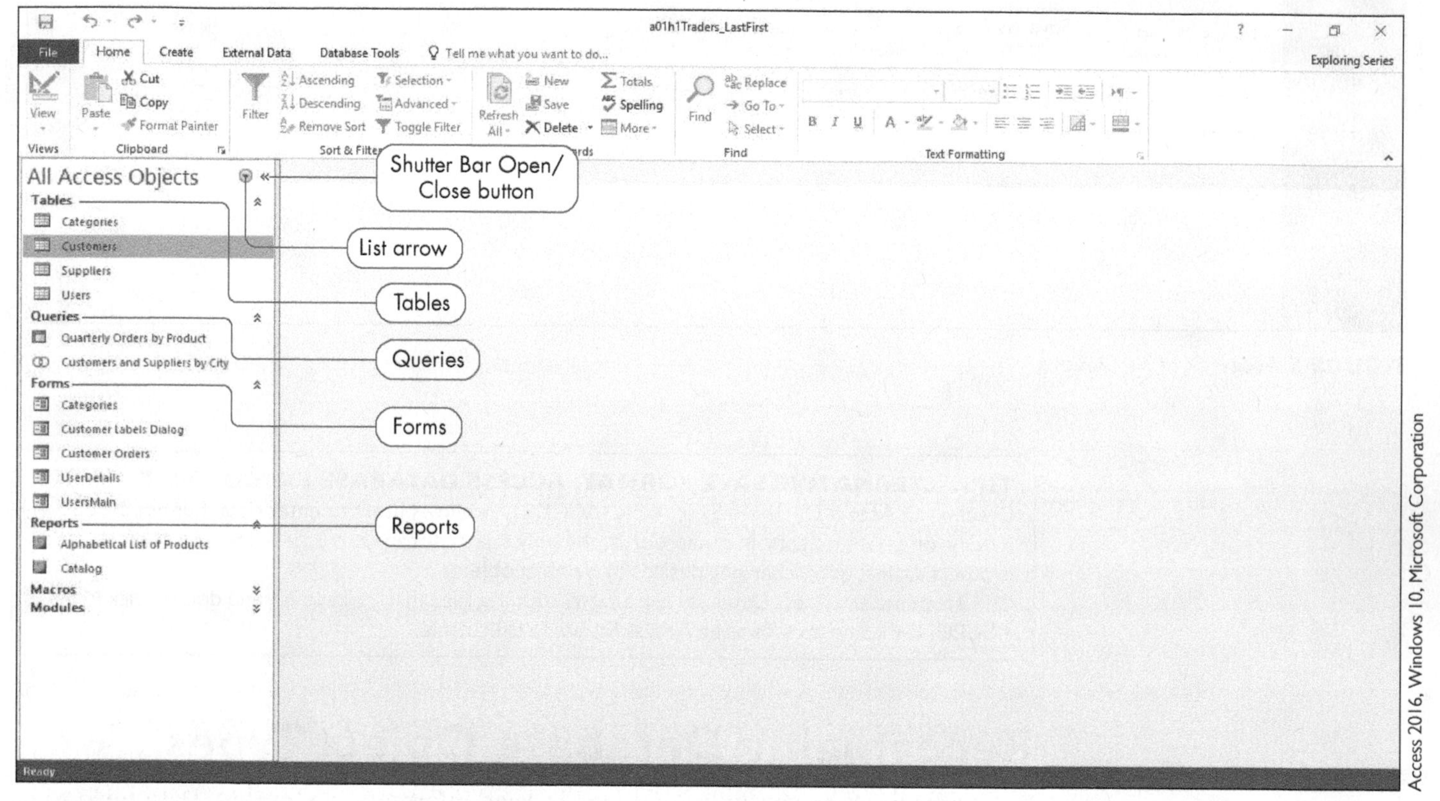

FIGURE 6 Navigation Pane Features

Most databases contain multiple tables. By default, the objects display in groups by object type in the Navigation Pane. In other words, you will see a list of tables, followed by queries, followed by forms, followed by reports. The purpose of each of these objects is described below.

- A ***table*** is where all data is stored in your database, and thus can be said to be the foundation of each database. Tables organize data into columns and rows. Each column represents a ***field***, a category of information we store in a table. For example, in the Northwind database, a table containing customer information would include fields such as Customer ID, Company Name, and City. Each row in a table contains a ***record***, a complete set of all the fields about one person, place, event, or concept. A customer record, for example, would contain all of the fields about a single customer, including the Customer ID, the Company Name, Contact Name, Contact Title, Address, City, etc. Figure 7 shows both fields and records. The ***primary key*** is a field (or combination of fields) that uniquely identifies each record in a table. Common primary keys are driver's license number, government

ID number (such as a Social Security number), passport number, and student ID. Many of these primary keys are generated by a database. Your college or university's database likely assigns a unique identifier to a student as soon as they apply, for example.

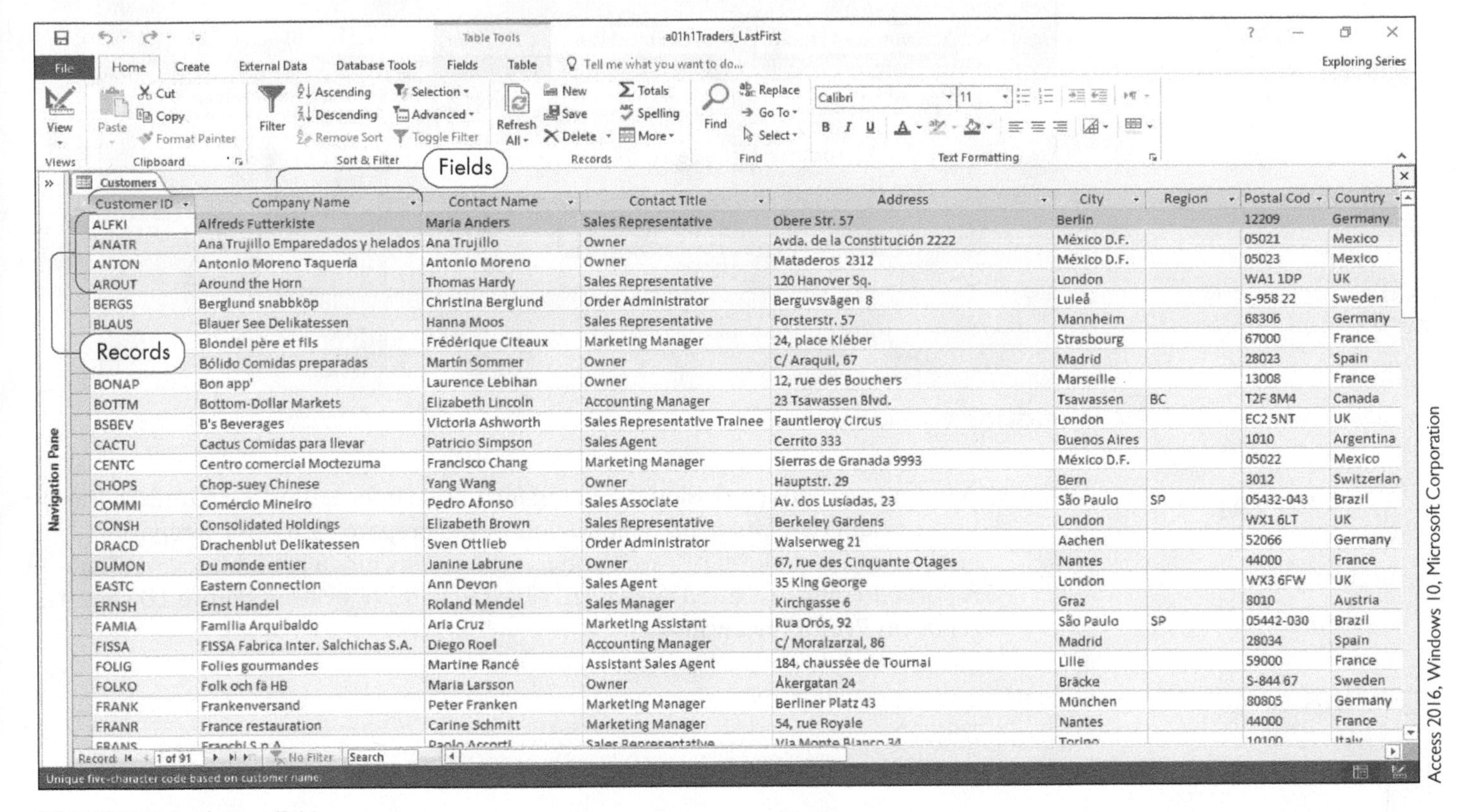

Access 2016, Windows 10, Microsoft Corporation

FIGURE 7 An Access Table

- A ***query*** (or queries, plural) is a question you ask about the data in your database. Notice the word query is similar to the word inquiry, which means question. It produces a subset of data that provides information about the question you have asked. For example, a query may display a list of which customers live in a specific town, or a list of children registered for a specific after-school program. You can double-click a query in the Navigation Pane and you will notice the interface is similar to that of a table, as shown in Figure 8.

Customers in Madrid

Company Name	Contact Name	Country	City	Region	Phone
Bólido Comidas preparadas	Martín Sommer	Spain	Madrid		(91) 555 22 82
FISSA Fabrica Inter. Salchichas S.A.	Diego Roel	Spain	Madrid		(91) 555 94 44
Romero y tomillo	Alejandra Camino	Spain	Madrid		(91) 745 6200

Access 2016, Windows 10, Microsoft Corporation

FIGURE 8 An Access Query

- A ***form*** allows simplified entry and modification of data. Much like entering data on a paper form, a database form enables you to add, modify, and delete table data. Most forms display one record at a time, which helps prevent data entry errors. Forms are typically utilized by the users of the database, while the database designer creates and edits the form structure. Figure 9 shows a form. Notice a single record is displayed.

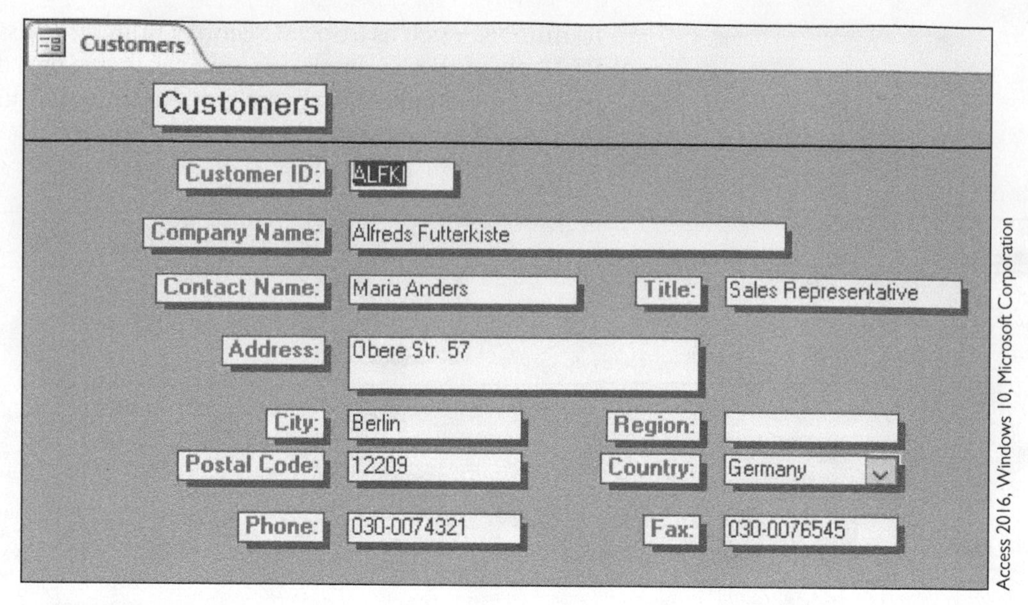

FIGURE 9 An Access Form

- A ***report*** contains professional-looking formatted information from underlying tables or queries. Much like a report you would prepare for a class, a report enables you to perform research and put the results into a readable format. The report can then be viewed on-screen, saved to a file, or printed. Figure 10 shows a report in Print Preview mode.

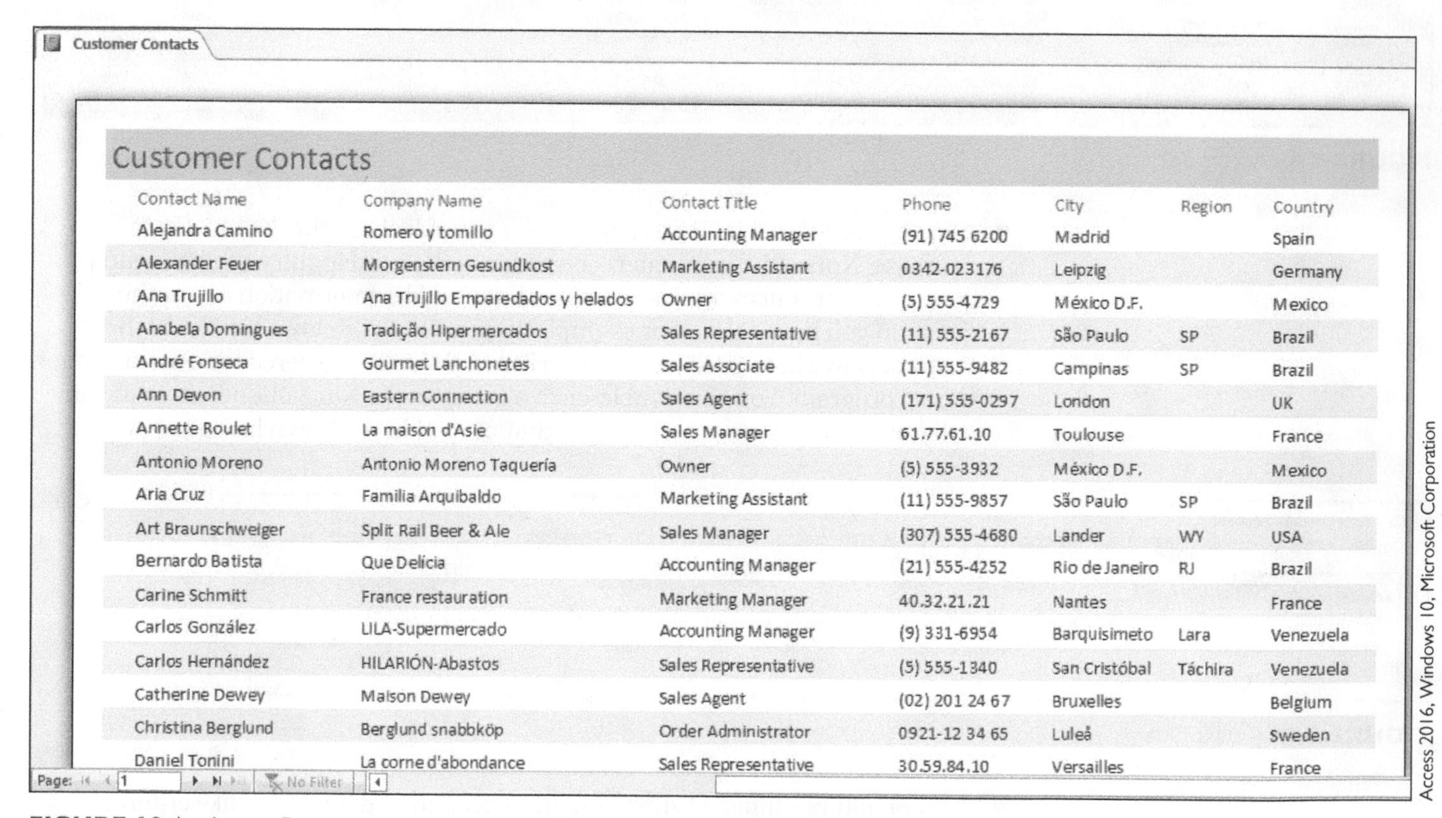
Customer Contacts

Customer Contacts

Contact Name	Company Name	Contact Title	Phone	City	Region	Country
Alejandra Camino	Romero y tomillo	Accounting Manager	(91) 745 6200	Madrid		Spain
Alexander Feuer	Morgenstern Gesundkost	Marketing Assistant	0342-023176	Leipzig		Germany
Ana Trujillo	Ana Trujillo Emparedados y helados	Owner	(5) 555-4729	México D.F.		Mexico
Anabela Domingues	Tradição Hipermercados	Sales Representative	(11) 555-2167	São Paulo	SP	Brazil
André Fonseca	Gourmet Lanchonetes	Sales Associate	(11) 555-9482	Campinas	SP	Brazil
Ann Devon	Eastern Connection	Sales Agent	(171) 555-0297	London		UK
Annette Roulet	La maison d'Asie	Sales Manager	61.77.61.10	Toulouse		France
Antonio Moreno	Antonio Moreno Taquería	Owner	(5) 555-3932	México D.F.		Mexico
Aria Cruz	Familia Arquibaldo	Marketing Assistant	(11) 555-9857	São Paulo	SP	Brazil
Art Braunschweiger	Split Rail Beer & Ale	Sales Manager	(307) 555-4680	Lander	WY	USA
Bernardo Batista	Que Delícia	Accounting Manager	(21) 555-4252	Rio de Janeiro	RJ	Brazil
Carine Schmitt	France restauration	Marketing Manager	40.32.21.21	Nantes		France
Carlos González	LILA-Supermercado	Accounting Manager	(9) 331-6954	Barquisimeto	Lara	Venezuela
Carlos Hernández	HILARIÓN-Abastos	Sales Representative	(5) 555-1340	San Cristóbal	Táchira	Venezuela
Catherine Dewey	Maison Dewey	Sales Agent	(02) 201 24 67	Bruxelles		Belgium
Christina Berglund	Berglund snabbköp	Order Administrator	0921-12 34 65	Luleå		Sweden
Daniel Tonini	La corne d'abondance	Sales Representative	30.59.84.10	Versailles		France

Page: 1 No Filter

FIGURE 10 An Access Report

Figure 11 displays the different object types in Access with the foundation object—the table—in the center of the illustration. The purpose each object serves is explained underneath the object name. The flow of information between objects is indicated by single-arrowhead arrows if the flow is one direction only. Two-arrowhead arrows indicate that the flow goes both directions. For example, you can use forms to view, add, delete, or modify data from tables.

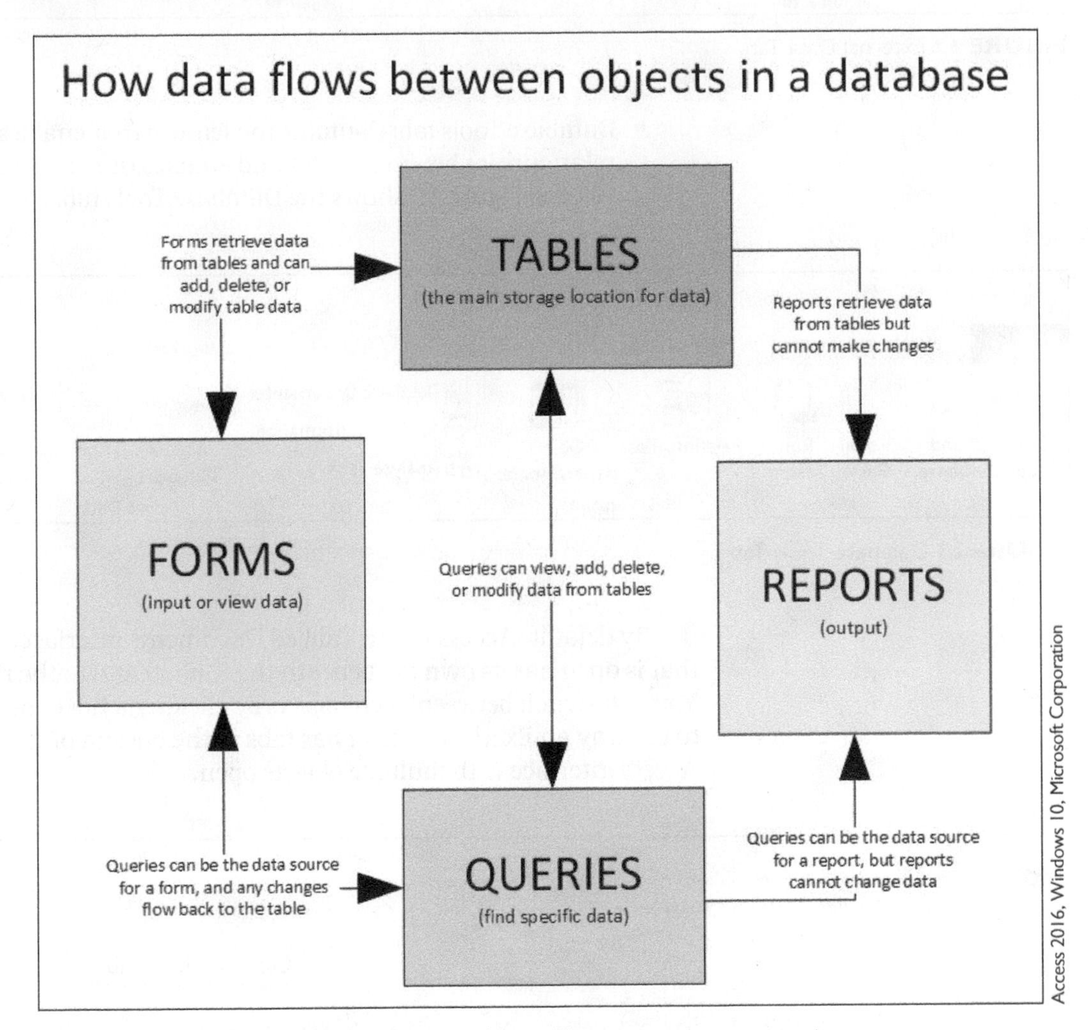
How data flows between objects in a database
TABLES
(the main storage location for data)
Forms retrieve data from tables and can add, delete, or modify table data
Reports retrieve data from tables but cannot make changes
FORMS
(input or view data)
Queries can view, add, delete, or modify data from tables
REPORTS
(output)
Queries can be the data source for a form, and any changes flow back to the table
QUERIES
(find specific data)
Queries can be the data source for a report, but reports cannot change data
Access 2016, Windows 10, Microsoft Corporation

FIGURE 11 Flow of Information Between Object Types

Two other object types, macros and modules, are rarely used by beginning Access users. A ***macro*** object is a stored series of commands that carry out an action. Macros are often used to automate tasks. A ***module*** is an advanced object written using the VBA (Visual Basic® for Applications) programming language. Modules provide more functionality than macros, but are not generally required for even intermediate users.

Examine the Access Interface

While Access includes the standard elements of the Microsoft Office applications interface such as the title bar, the Ribbon, the Home tab, Backstage view, and scroll bars, it also includes elements unique to Access.

The Access Ribbon has five tabs that always display, as well as tabs that appear only when particular objects are open. The two tabs that are unique to Access are:

- External Data tab: Contains all of the operations used to facilitate data import and export. See Figure 12.

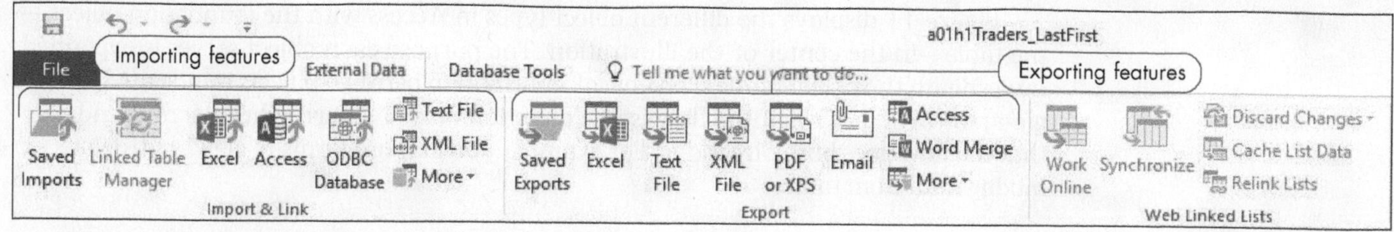

FIGURE 12 External Data Tab

Access 2016, Windows 10, Microsoft Corporation

- Database Tools tab: Contains the feature that enables users to create relationships between tables and enables use of more advanced features of Access. Figure 13 shows the Database Tools tab.

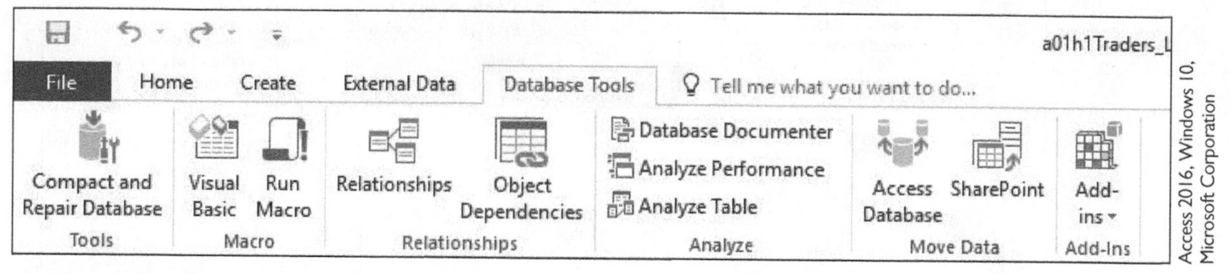

Access 2016, Windows 10, Microsoft Corporation

FIGURE 13 Database Tools Tab

By default, Access uses a Tabbed Documents interface. That means that each object that is open has its own tab beneath the Ribbon and to the right of the Navigation Pane. You can switch between open objects by clicking a tab to make that object active, similar to the way an Excel worksheet has tabs at the bottom of the screen. Figure 14 shows the Access interface with multiple objects open.

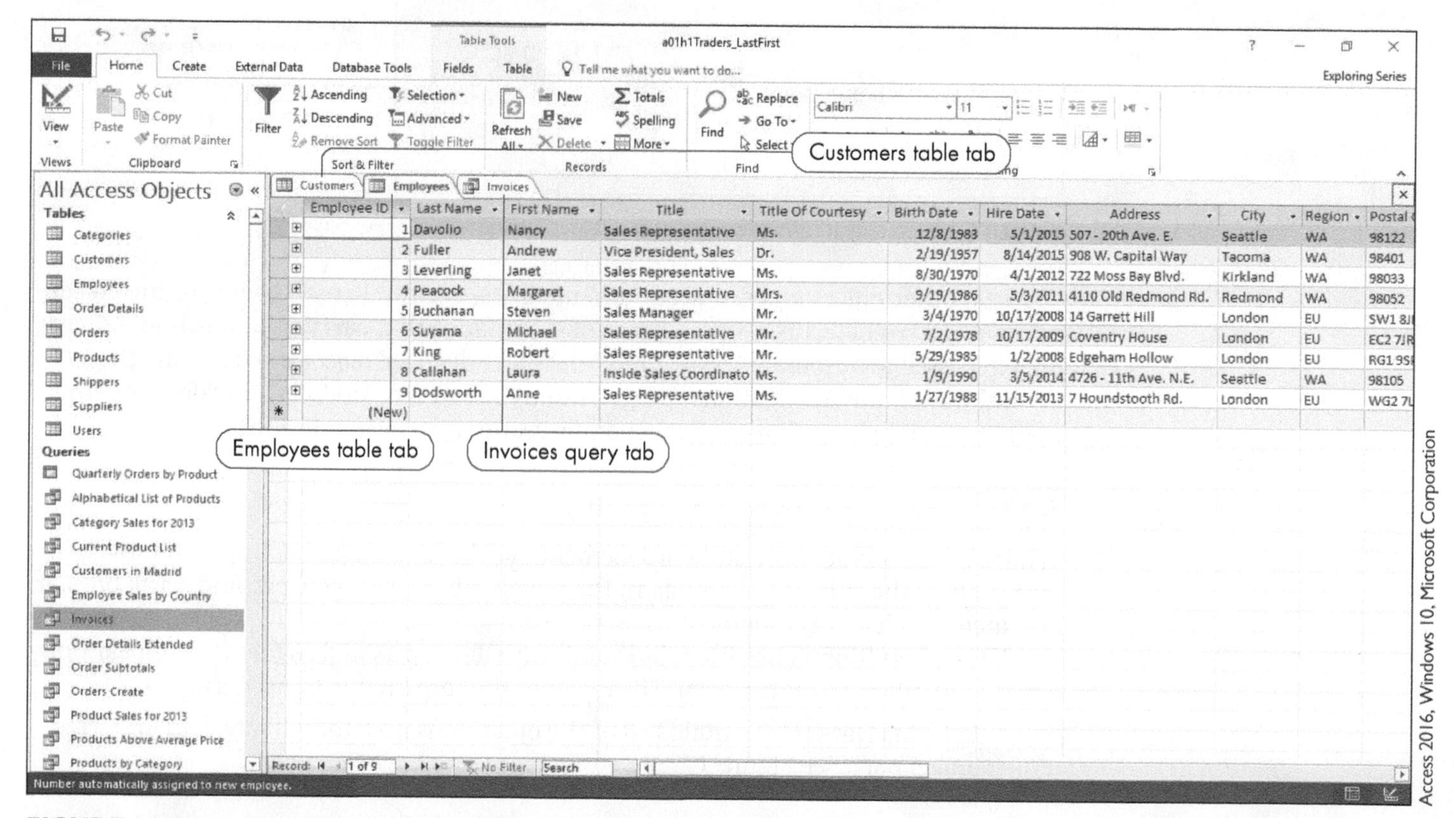

FIGURE 14 Access Database with Multiple Objects Open

Access 2016, Windows 10, Microsoft Corporation

Explore Table Datasheet View

Access provides two different ways to view a table: Datasheet view and Design view. When you double-click a table, Datasheet view displays by default. ***Datasheet view*** is a grid containing fields (columns) and records (rows). You can view, add, edit, and delete records in Datasheet view. Figure 15 shows the Customers table in Datasheet view. Each row contains a record for a specific customer. Click the record selector, or row heading, at the beginning of a row to select the record. Each column represents a field, or one attribute about a customer. Click the field selector, or column heading, to select a field.

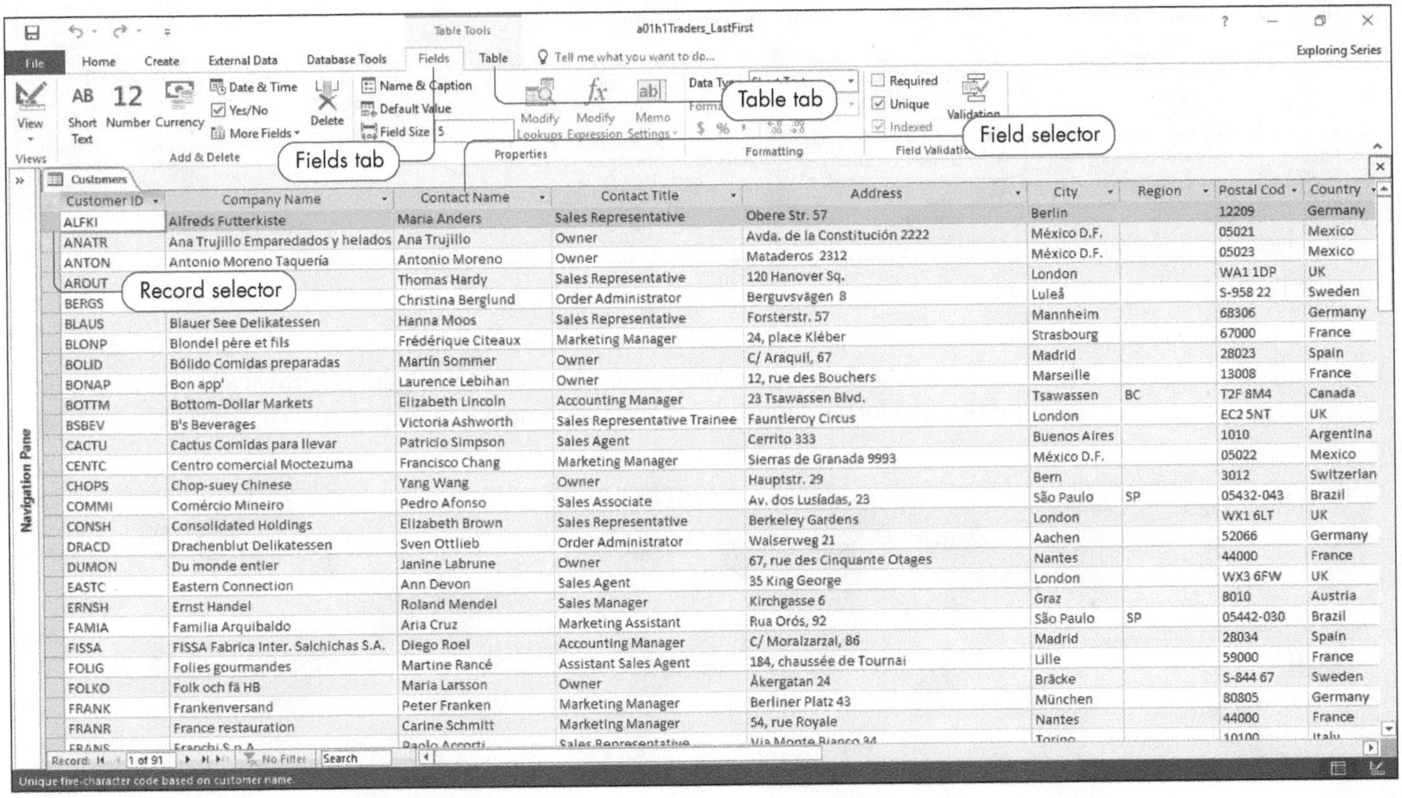

Table tab
Field selector
Fields tab
Record selector

Customer ID	Company Name	Contact Name	Contact Title	Address	City	Region	Postal Cod	Country
ALFKI	Alfreds Futterkiste	Maria Anders	Sales Representative	Obere Str. 57	Berlin		12209	Germany
ANATR	Ana Trujillo Emparedados y helados	Ana Trujillo	Owner	Avda. de la Constitución 2222	México D.F.		05021	Mexico
ANTON	Antonio Moreno Taquería	Antonio Moreno	Owner	Mataderos 2312	México D.F.		05023	Mexico
AROUT		Thomas Hardy	Sales Representative	120 Hanover Sq.	London		WA1 1DP	UK
BERGS		Christina Berglund	Order Administrator	Berguvsvägen 8	Luleå		S-958 22	Sweden
BLAUS	Blauer See Delikatessen	Hanna Moos	Sales Representative	Forsterstr. 57	Mannheim		68306	Germany
BLONP	Blondel père et fils	Frédérique Citeaux	Marketing Manager	24, place Kléber	Strasbourg		67000	France
BOLID	Bólido Comidas preparadas	Martín Sommer	Owner	C/ Araquil, 67	Madrid		28023	Spain
BONAP	Bon app'	Laurence Lebihan	Owner	12, rue des Bouchers	Marseille		13008	France
BOTTM	Bottom-Dollar Markets	Elizabeth Lincoln	Accounting Manager	23 Tsawassen Blvd.	Tsawassen	BC	T2F 8M4	Canada
BSBEV	B's Beverages	Victoria Ashworth	Sales Representative Trainee	Fauntleroy Circus	London		EC2 5NT	UK
CACTU	Cactus Comidas para llevar	Patricio Simpson	Sales Agent	Cerrito 333	Buenos Aires		1010	Argentina
CENTC	Centro comercial Moctezuma	Francisco Chang	Marketing Manager	Sierras de Granada 9993	México D.F.		05022	Mexico
CHOPS	Chop-suey Chinese	Yang Wang	Owner	Hauptstr. 29	Bern		3012	Switzerlan
COMMI	Comércio Mineiro	Pedro Afonso	Sales Associate	Av. dos Lusíadas, 23	São Paulo	SP	05432-043	Brazil
CONSH	Consolidated Holdings	Elizabeth Brown	Sales Representative	Berkeley Gardens	London		WX1 6LT	UK
DRACD	Drachenblut Delikatessen	Sven Ottlieb	Order Administrator	Walserweg 21	Aachen		52066	Germany
DUMON	Du monde entier	Janine Labrune	Owner	67, rue des Cinquante Otages	Nantes		44000	France
EASTC	Eastern Connection	Ann Devon	Sales Agent	35 King George	London		WX3 6FW	UK
ERNSH	Ernst Handel	Roland Mendel	Sales Manager	Kirchgasse 6	Graz		8010	Austria
FAMIA	Familia Arquibaldo	Aria Cruz	Marketing Assistant	Rua Orós, 92	São Paulo	SP	05442-030	Brazil
FISSA	FISSA Fabrica Inter. Salchichas S.A.	Diego Roel	Accounting Manager	C/ Moralzarzal, 86	Madrid		28034	Spain
FOLIG	Folies gourmandes	Martine Rancé	Assistant Sales Agent	184, chaussée de Tournai	Lille		59000	France
FOLKO	Folk och fä HB	Maria Larsson	Owner	Åkergatan 24	Bräcke		S-844 67	Sweden
FRANK	Frankenversand	Peter Franken	Marketing Manager	Berliner Platz 43	München		80805	Germany
FRANR	France restauration	Carine Schmitt	Marketing Manager	54, rue Royale	Nantes		44000	France

Record: 1 of 91 No Filter Search

Unique five-character code based on customer name.

Access 2016, Windows 10, Microsoft Corporation

FIGURE 15 Datasheet View for Customers Table

Notice the Customers table shows records for 91 employees. The customer records contain multiple fields about each customer, including the Company Name, Contact Name, and so on. Occasionally a field does not contain a value for a particular record. For example, many customers do not have a Region assigned. Access shows a blank cell when data is missing.

Navigate Through Records

The navigation bar at the bottom of Figure 16 shows that the Customers table has 91 records and that record number 18 is the current record. The pencil symbol to the left of record 18 indicates that the data in that record is being edited and that changes have not yet been saved. The pencil icon disappears when you move to another record. Access saves data automatically as soon as you move from one record to another. This may seem counterintuitive at first because other Office applications, such as Word and Excel, do not save changes and additions automatically. The navigation arrows enable you to go to the first record, the previous record, the next record, or the last record. Click the right arrow with a yellow asterisk to add a new (blank) record.

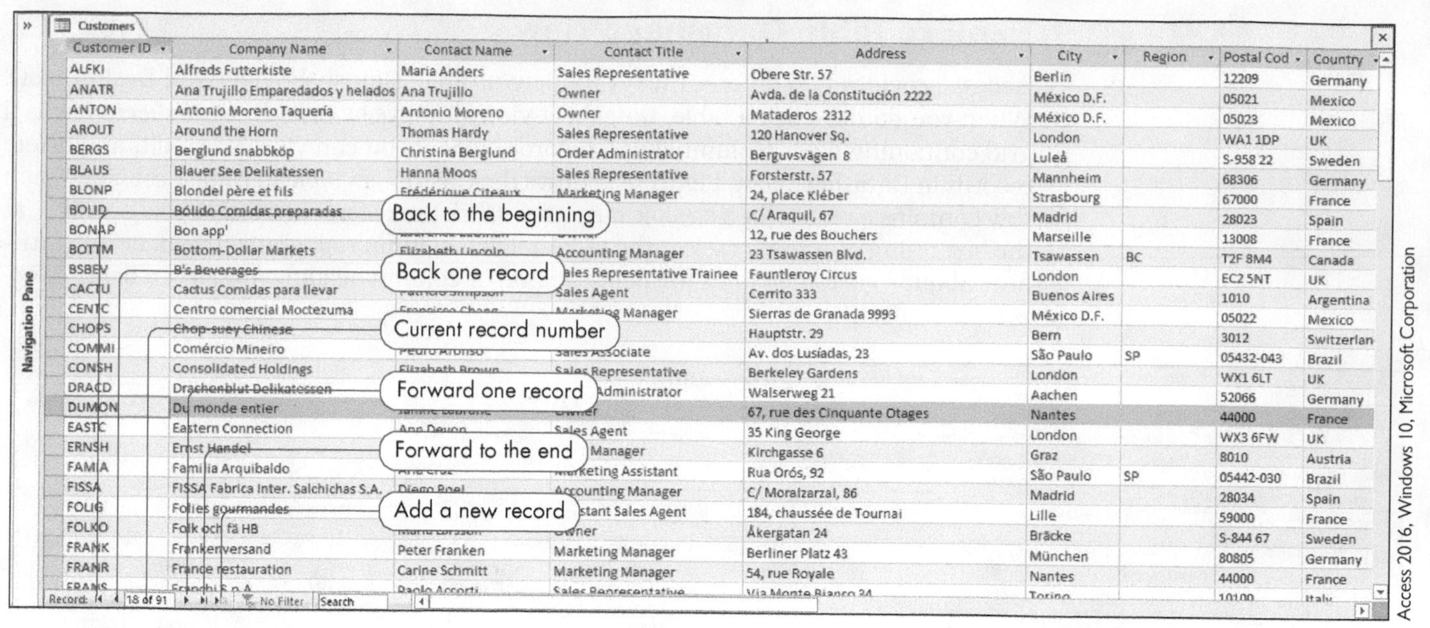

FIGURE 16 Navigation Arrows in a Table

Navigation works for more than just tables. Navigation arrows are also available in queries and forms. Figure 17 shows the same navigation arrows appearing in forms.

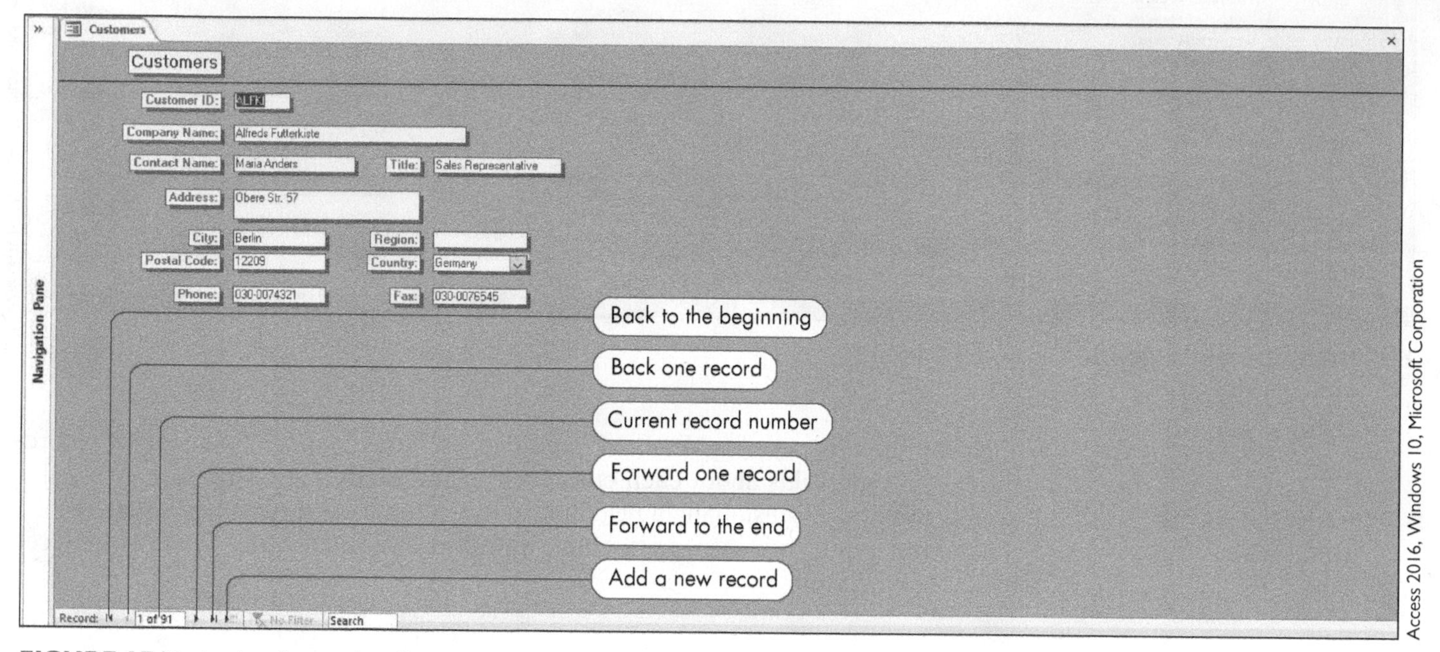

FIGURE 17 Navigation Arrows in a Form

In addition to navigating, you also have access to the Find command. The Find command is located in the Find group on the Home tab, and can be used to locate specific records. You can search for a single field or the entire record, match all or part of the selected field(s), move forward or back in a table, or specify a case-sensitive search.

To find a record using the Find command, complete the following steps:

1. Open the table that contains the data you are searching for. Note that if you want to search a query, form, or report, you can follow the same steps, except open the appropriate object instead of the table.
2. Click any cell within the field you want to search. For example, if you want to search the City field in the Customers table, as shown in Figure 18, click any City value.
3. Ensure the Home tab is selected.
4. Click Find in the Find group.
5. Type the value you are searching for in the Find What box. Note that the entry is not case sensitive.
6. Click Find Next to find the next matching value.

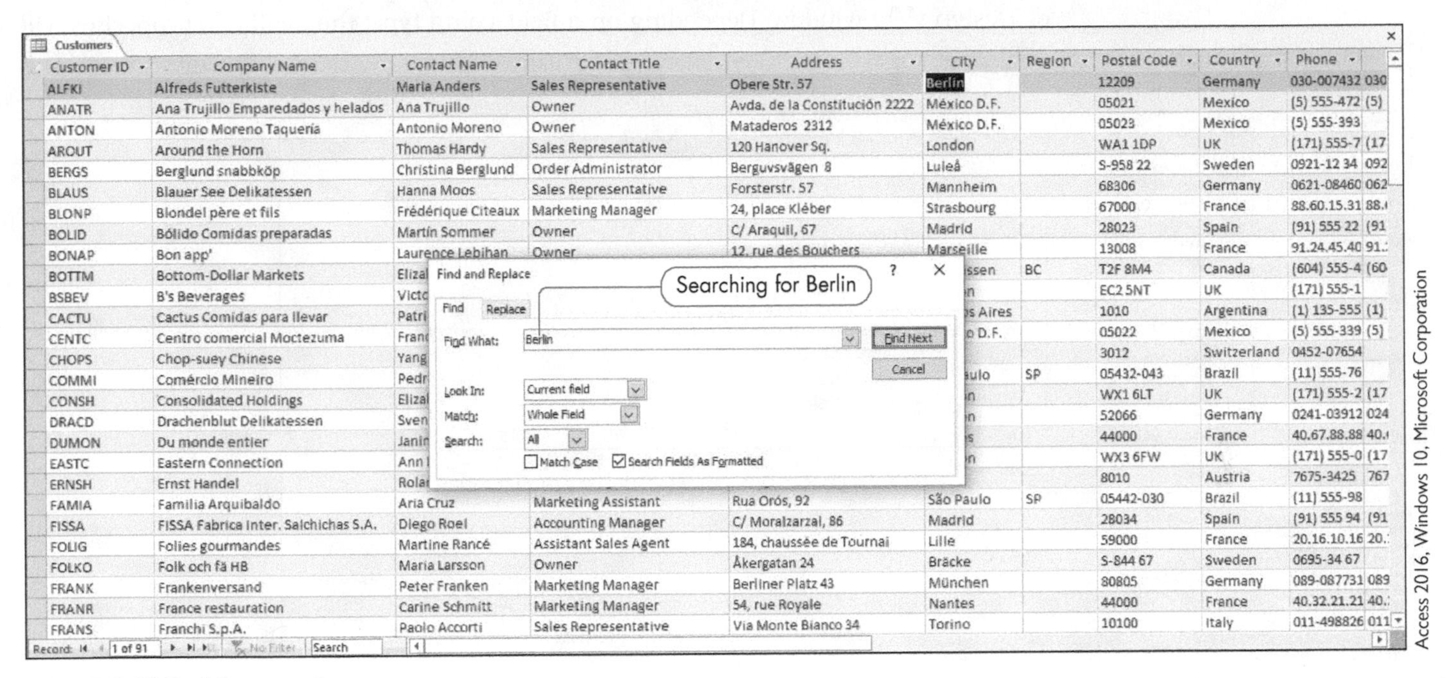

FIGURE 18 Find Command

Explore Table Design View

Design view gives you a detailed view of the table's structure and is used to create and modify a table's design by specifying the fields it will contain, the fields' data types, and their associated properties. When you double-click a table in the Navigation Pane, it will open in Datasheet view, as the design of a table typically does not change frequently.

To switch between Datasheet and Design view, complete the following steps:

1. Click the Home tab.
2. Click View in the Views group to toggle between the current view and the previous view. See Figure 19.

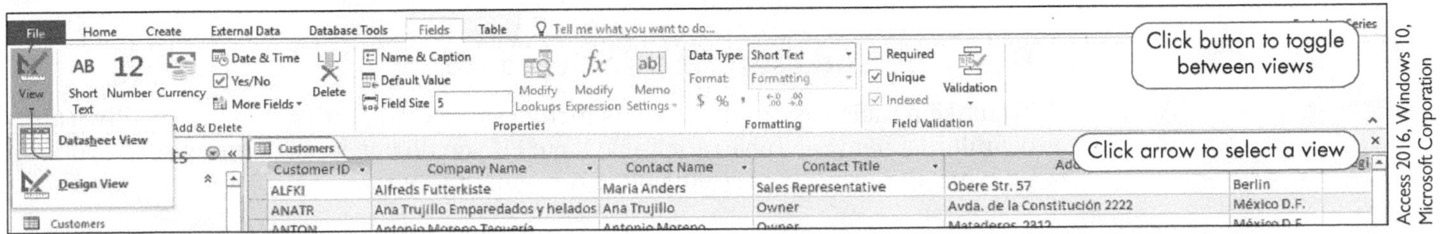

FIGURE 19 View Button

Also notice the arrow that allows you to select either Design or Datasheet view. Either way of performing this task is correct.

Data types define the type of data that will be stored in a field, such as short text, numeric, currency, date/time, etc. For example, if you need to store the hire date of an employee, you would input a field name and select the Date/Time data type. A ***field property*** defines the characteristics of a field in more detail. For example, for the field OrderDate, you could set add validation (the OrderDate must be today's date or later), or choose whether the field is required or not. Though some changes can be made to the field properties in Datasheet view, Design view gives you access to more properties.

Figure 20 shows Design view for the Orders table. In the top portion, each row contains the field name the data type, and an optional description for each field in the table. In the bottom portion, the Field Properties pane contains the properties (details) for a field. Click a field, and the properties for that field display in the Field Properties section of Design view window. Depending on a field's data type, the available properties will change.

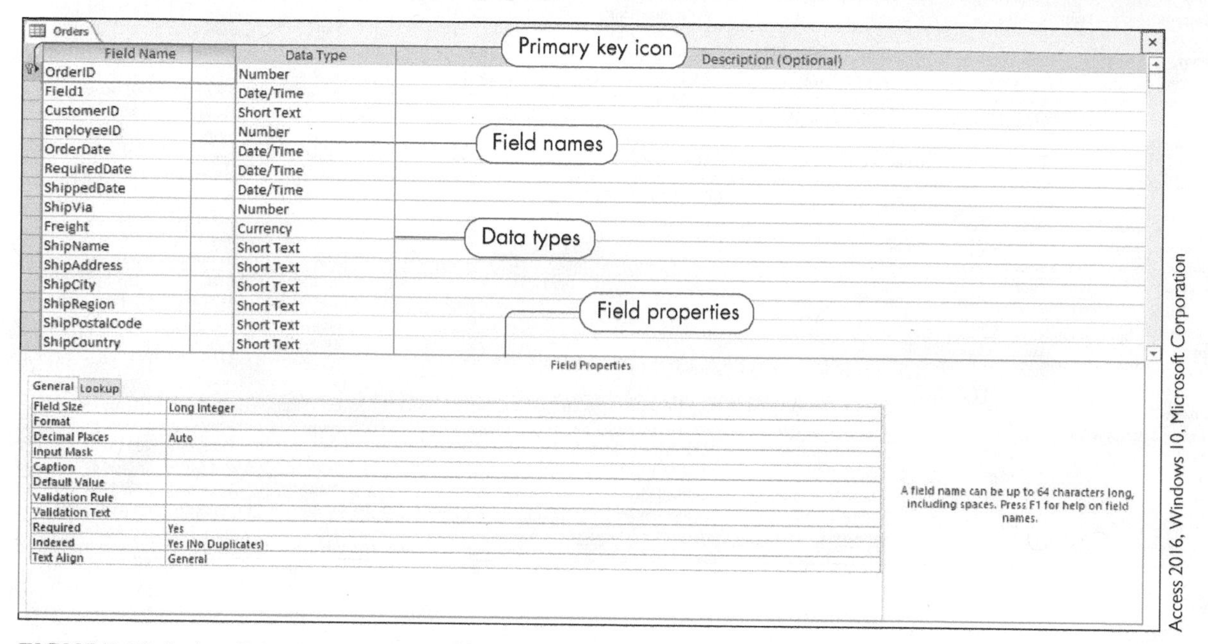

Access 2016, Windows 10, Microsoft Corporation

FIGURE 20 Orders Table Design View

Notice the key icon next to the OrderID field; this denotes this field is the primary key in the Orders table; it ensures that each record in the table is unique and can be distinguished from every other record. You may have multiple orders from the same customer, but you can tell they are different because there are two separate OrderIDs. This is why many companies ask for you to include your account number when you pay a bill. The account number, similar to an OrderID, uniquely identifies you and helps ensure that the payment is not applied to the wrong customer.

In Figure 20, the OrderID field has an AutoNumber data type—a number that is generated by Access and is automatically incremented each time a record is added. Each field's data type determines the type of input accepted.

Rename and Describe Tables

To make a table easy to use, Access includes a few properties you can modify. Tables default to a name of Table1 (or Table2, etc.) if you do not specify otherwise. As you can imagine, this would be very difficult to navigate.

To rename a table, complete the following steps:

1. Verify that the table is closed. If it is not closed, right-click the table tab and select Close. A table cannot be renamed while it is open.
2. Right-click the table name in the Navigation Pane.
3. Select Rename on the shortcut menu.
4. Type the new name over the selected text and press Enter.

Tables also include a description, which can be useful to provide documentation about the contents of a table. For example, most tables in the Northwind database are straightforward. However, just in case, the database comes with predefined descriptions for most tables. This can provide a user with additional clarification regarding the purpose of a table if they know where to look. By default, descriptions are not shown unless you right-click the table and select Table Properties. If you are working with a complex database, adding descriptions can be extremely helpful for new users. Figure 21 shows a table description.

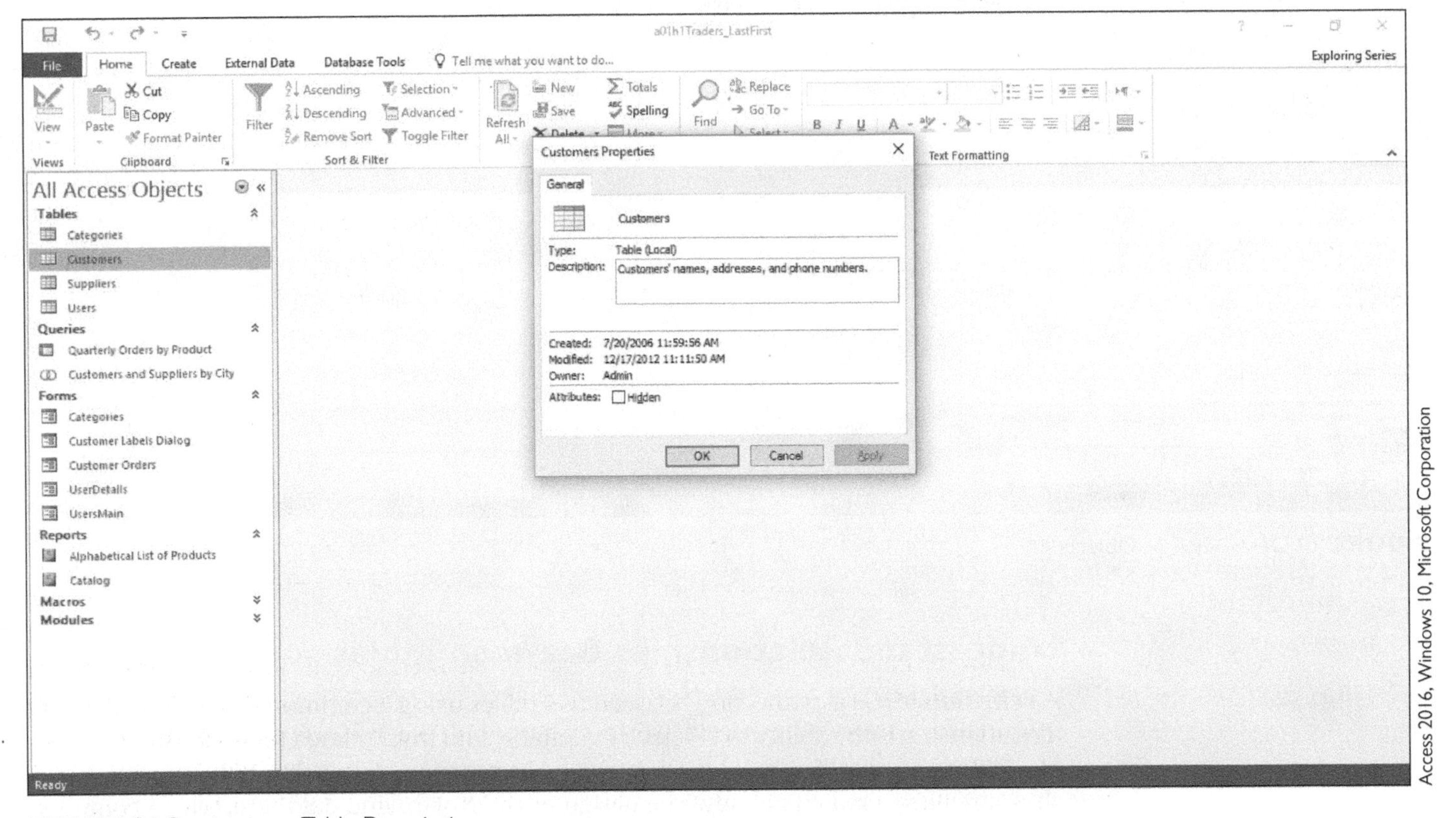

FIGURE 21 Previewing a Table Description

To enter a table description, complete the following steps:

1. Right-click the table name in the Navigation Pane.
2. Select Table Properties on the shortcut menu.
3. Type the description in the Table Properties dialog box and click OK.

TIP: SHOWING OBJECT DETAILS

Most users will not need to see a description frequently. However, if necessary, you can change the Navigation Pane to display details by default. The details include the creation date, modification date, and description of the object. You may need to increase the size of the Navigation Pane to see the full description, so this works better on wider screens.

To show object details, right-click All Access Objects in the Navigation Pane and click View By. Select Details to display the full details. Resize the Navigation Pane so you can view the complete descriptions, if necessary. Figure 22 shows a view of objects with descriptions.

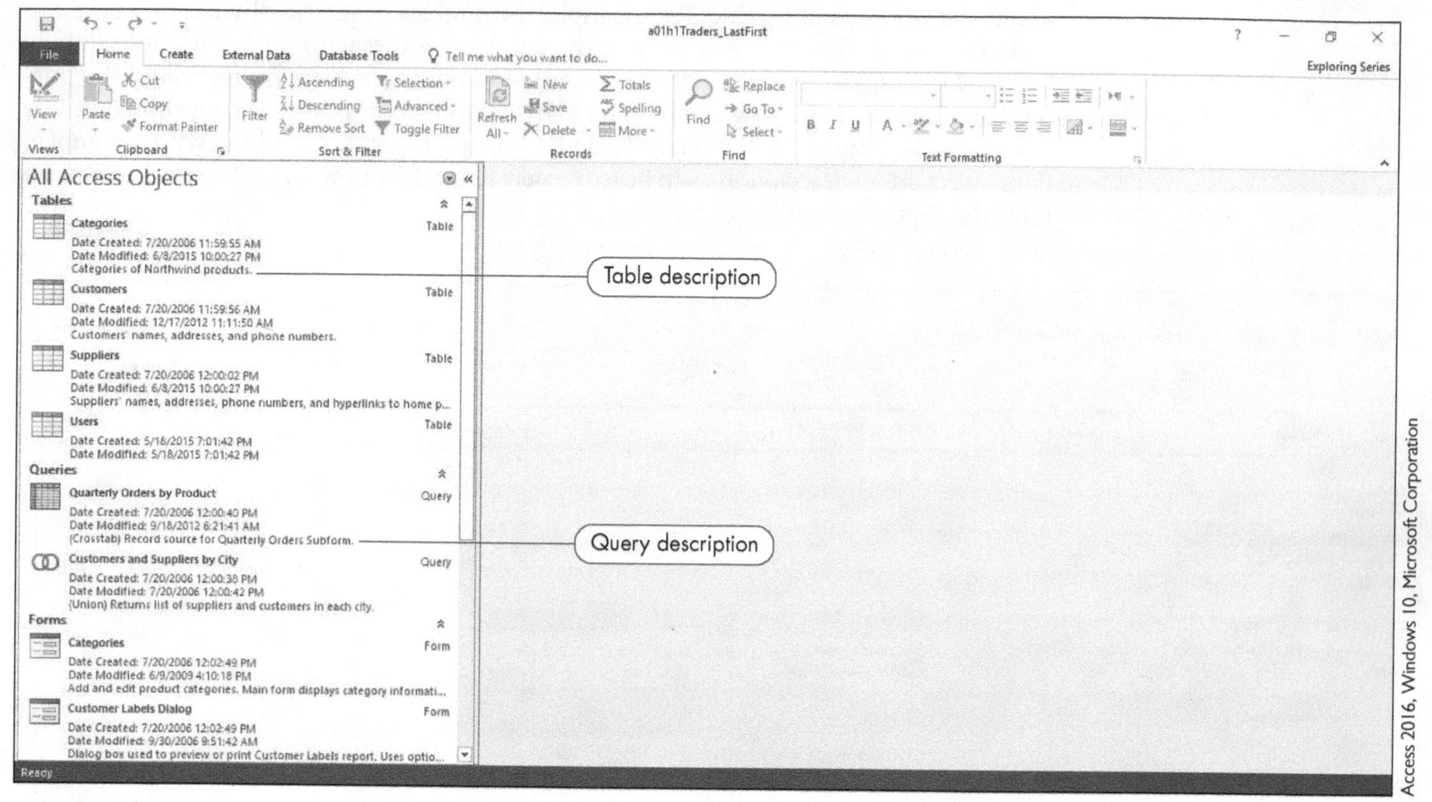

FIGURE 22 Detail View of Objects

Understand Relationships Between Tables

A ***relationship*** is a connection between two tables using a common field. The benefit of a relationship is the ability to efficiently combine data from related tables for the purpose of creating queries, forms, and reports. If you are using an existing database, relationships are likely created already. The design of the Northwind database, which contains multiple tables, is illustrated in Figure 23. The tables have been created, the field names have been added, and the data types have been set. The diagram shows the relationships that were created between tables using join lines. Join lines enable you to create a relationship between two tables using a common field. For example, the Suppliers table is joined to the Products table using the common field SupplierID. These table connections enable you to query the database for information stored in multiple tables. This feature gives the manager the ability to ask questions like "What products are produced by the supplier Exotic Liquids?" In this case, the name of the supplier (Exotic Liquids) is stored in the Supplier table, but the products are stored in the Products table. Notice in Figure 24, you can tell there is a table related to the Supplier table, because a plus sign ⊞ appears to the left of each Supplier. If you click the plus sign, you will see a list of products produced by this company.

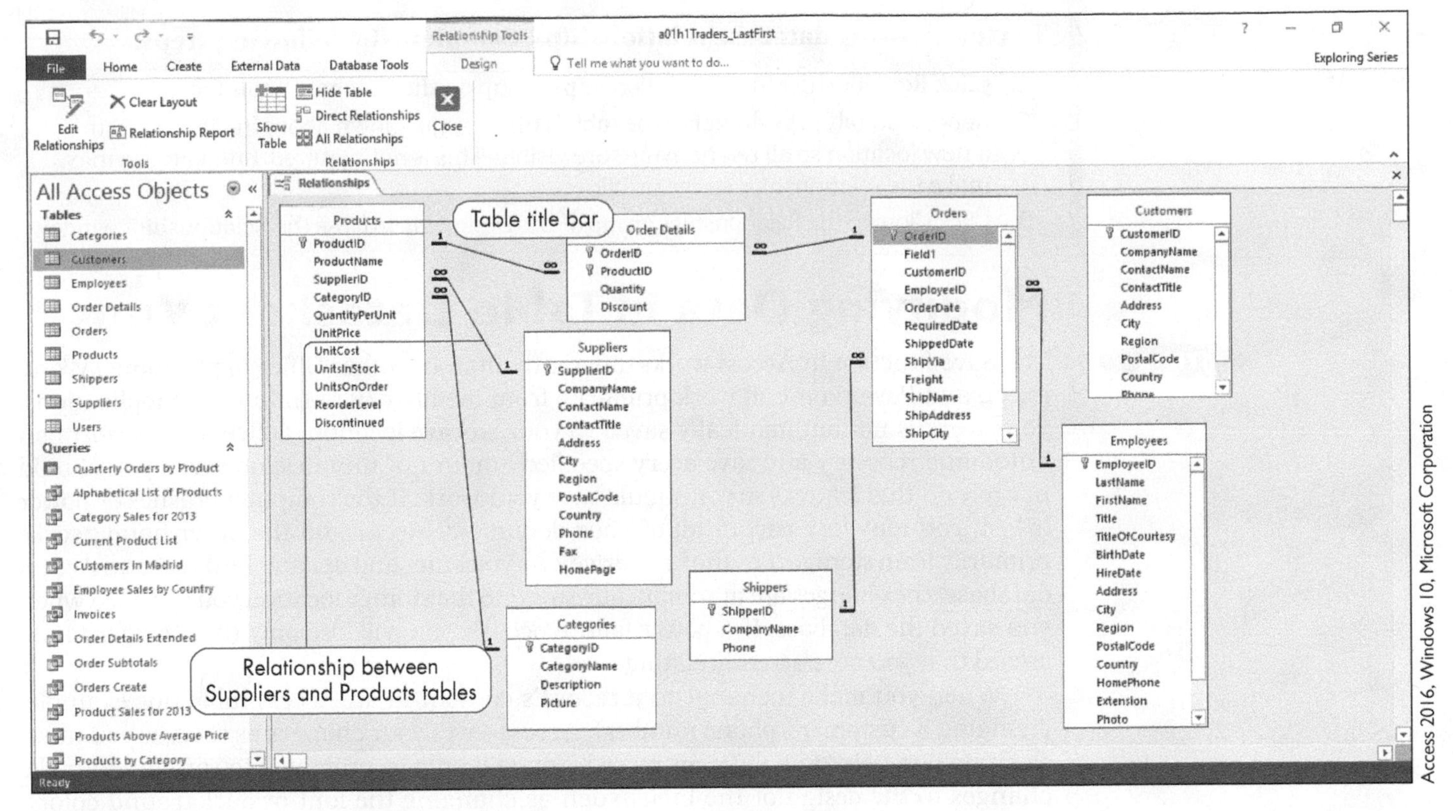

FIGURE 23 Northwind Database Relationships

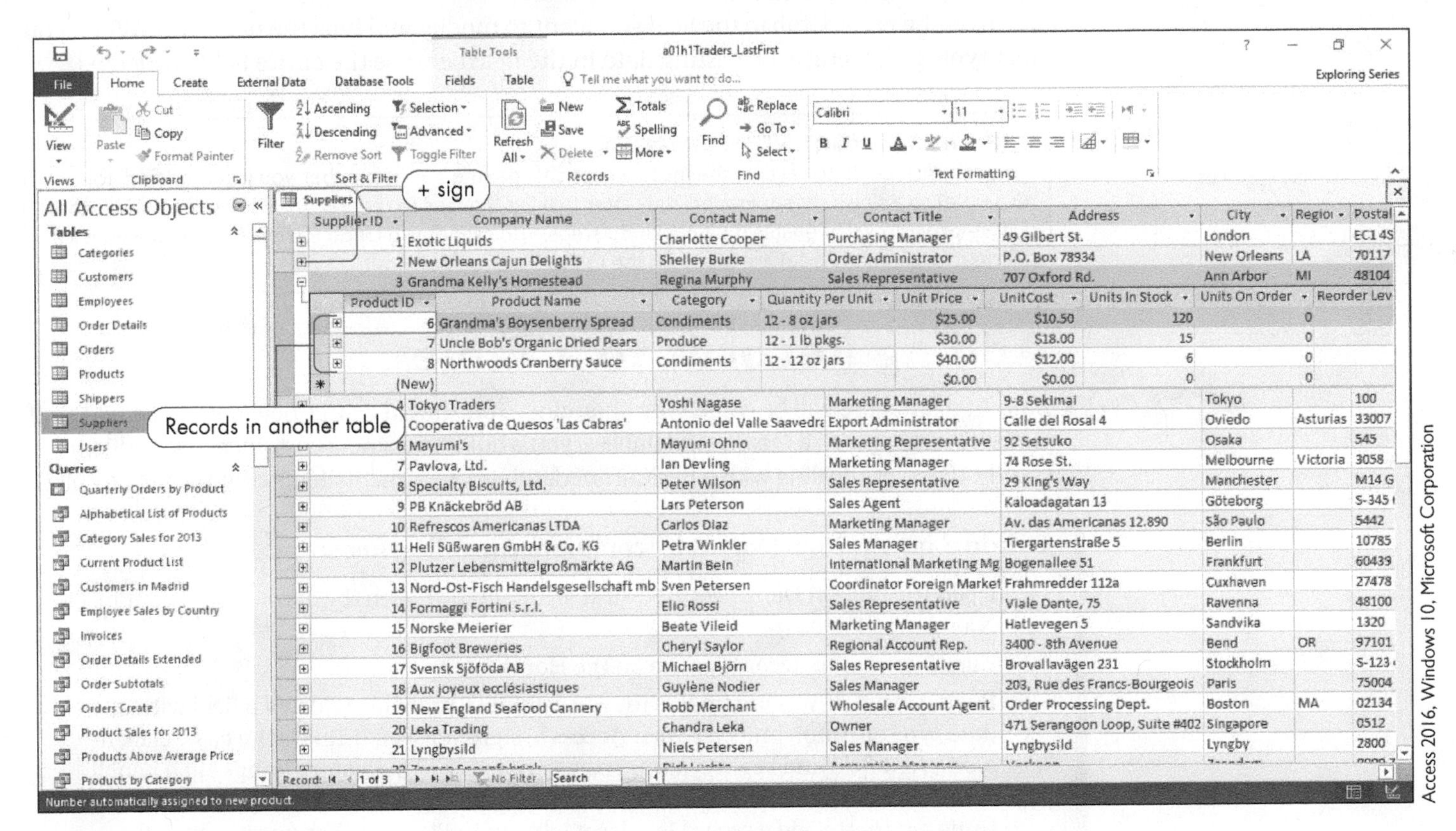

FIGURE 24 Related Tables

However, you can view the existing relationships in any database to familiarize yourself with the way tables work together.

To view existing database relationships, complete the following steps:

1. Click Relationships in the Relationships group on the Database Tools tab.
2. Reposition tables by dragging the table's title bar (as shown above in Figure 23) to a new location so all relationships are visible. This is not required, but doing so may make the relationships easier to follow.
3. Click Close in the Relationships group of the Design tab to close the Relationships window.

Modifying Data in Table Datasheet View

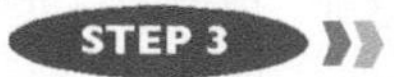

The Save function in Access works differently than the other Office applications. Word, Excel, and PowerPoint all work primarily from memory (RAM). In those applications, your work is not automatically saved to your storage location. Office may perform an automatic recovery and save every specified amount of minutes; however, you should not rely on that feature, so you should save your work. If the computer crashes or power is lost, you may lose part or all of your document. Access, on the other hand, works primarily from storage (i.e., the hard drive). As you enter and update the data in an Access database, the changes are automatically saved to the storage location you specified when you saved the database. If a power failure occurs, you will lose only the changes to the record that you are currently editing.

When you make a change to a record's content in an Access table (for example, changing a customer's phone number), Access saves your changes as soon as you move the insertion point to a different record. You will only be prompted to save if you make changes to the design of the table (such as changing the font or background color). Editing data is done similarly in queries and forms. Recall that reports cannot change data, so changes to data cannot be done there.

To edit a record, tab to the field you want to modify and type the new data. When you start typing, you erase all existing data in the field because the entire field is selected.

TIP: UNDO WORKS DIFFERENTLY

You can click Undo to reverse the most recent change (the phone number you just modified, for example) to a single record immediately after making changes to that record. However, unlike other Office programs that enable multiple Undo steps, you cannot use Undo to reverse multiple edits in Access. Undo (and Redo) are found on the Quick Access Toolbar.

Adding Records to a Table

Data in a database will be constantly changing. You should expect new data to be added. If you are working with a Customer database, you would expect new customers to be added constantly. If you are dealing with a Restaurant database, new menu items could be added daily.

To add a new record to a table, complete the following steps:

1. Open the table in Datasheet view (if it is not already open) by double-clicking it in the Navigation Pane.
2. Click New in the Records group on the Home tab.
3. Begin typing. If you are unable to type, you have probably selected a field with a data type of AutoNumber, which Access assigns for you. If this is the case, click in a different field and begin typing. The asterisk record indicator changes to a pencil symbol to show that you are in editing mode (see Figure 25). Note: you can follow the same process to add a record in a form (shown in Figure 26) or query.
4. Press Tab to move to the following field and enter data, and repeat this step until you have input all required data for this record.
5. Move to another record by clicking elsewhere or pressing Tab in the last field in a record. As soon as you move to another record, Access automatically saves the changes to the record you created or changed.

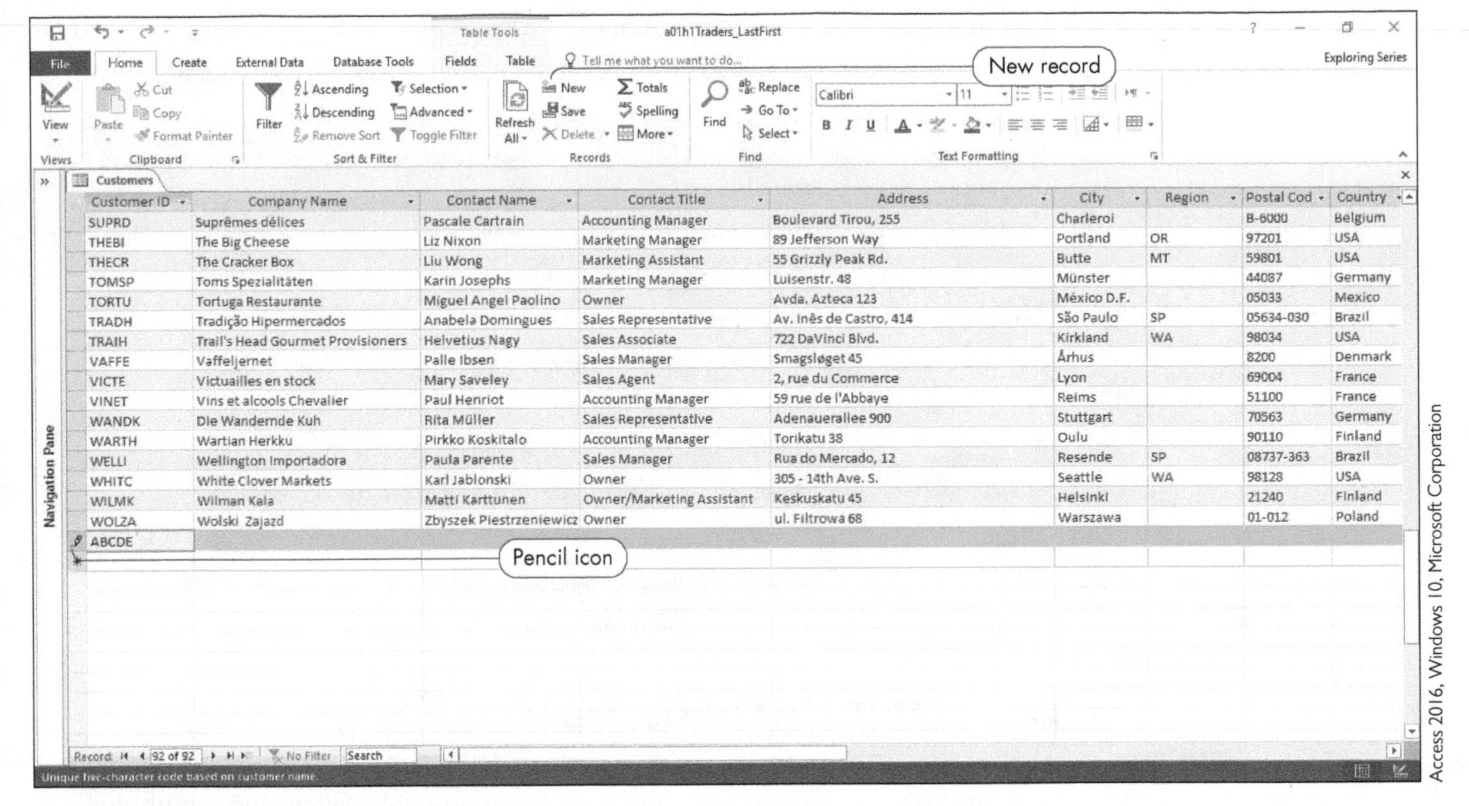

FIGURE 25 Adding a Record Using a Table

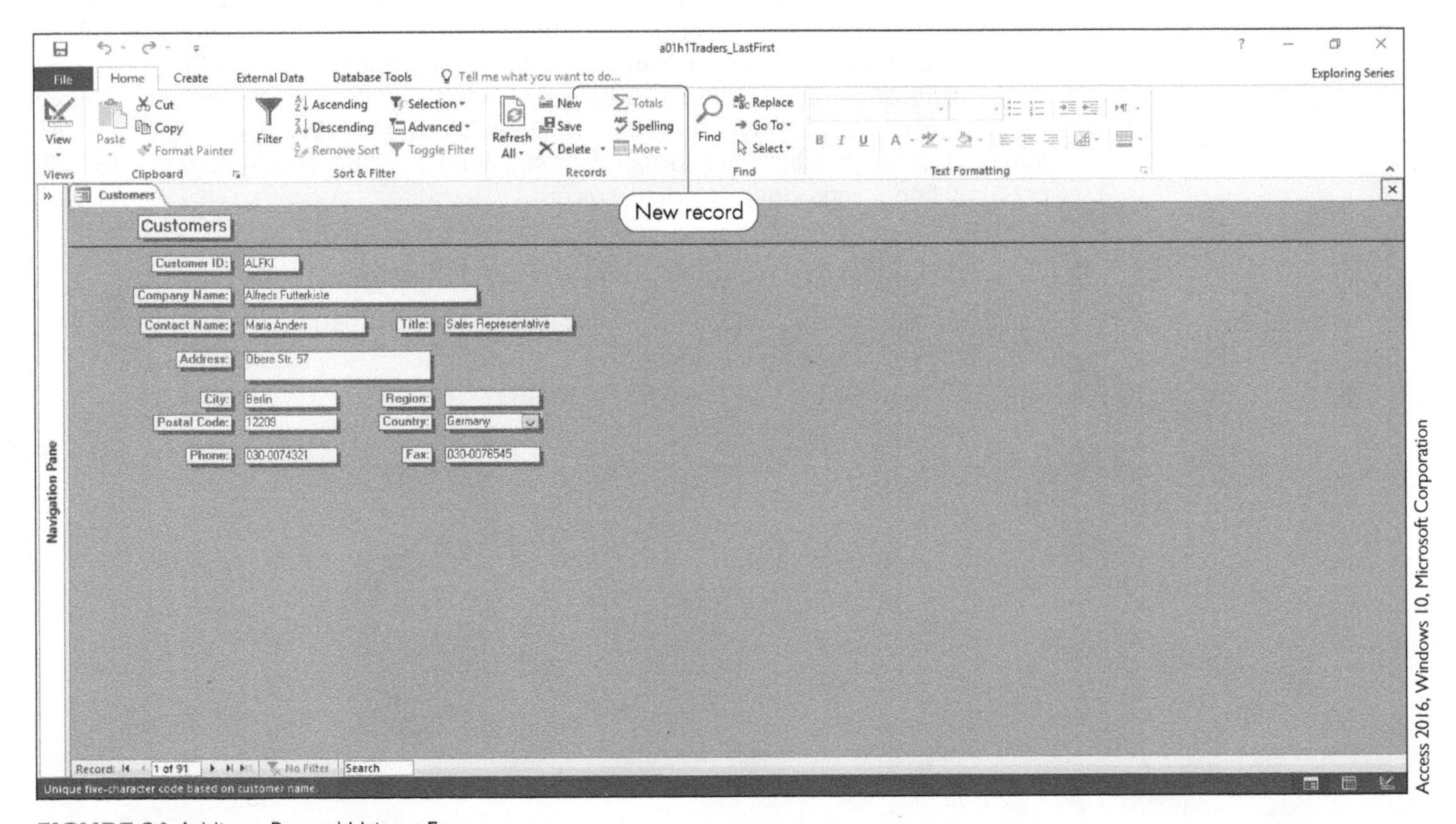

FIGURE 26 Adding a Record Using a Form

As with most of Office, there are a number of ways to perform the same task. Data entry is the same. See Table 1 for a list of some shortcuts you can use when performing data entry.

TABLE 1 Keyboard Shortcuts for Entering Data

Keystroke	Result
Up arrow (↑)	Moves insertion point up one row.
Down arrow (↓)	Moves insertion point down one row.
Left arrow (←)	Moves insertion point left one field in the same row.
Right arrow (→)	Moves insertion point right one field in the same row.
Tab or Enter	Moves insertion point right one field in the same row.
Shift+Tab	Moves insertion point left one field in the same row.
Home	Moves insertion point to the first field in the current row.
End	Moves insertion point to the last field in the current row.
Esc	Cancels any changes made in the current field while in Edit mode.
Ctrl+Z	Reverses the last unsaved edit.

Deleting Records from a Table

STEP 5 Deciding to delete records is not a simple decision. Many times, deleting records is a bad idea. Say you are working in the database for an animal shelter. Once an animal has been adopted, you may be tempted to delete the animal from the database. However, you would then lose any record of the animal ever existing, and if the owner calls asking if the animal has had its shots, or how old the animal is, you would no longer be able to provide that information. Often, instead of deleting information, you would create a yes/no field indicating that a record is no longer relevant. For example, the shelter database might have a check box for adopted. If the adopted box is checked yes, the animal is no longer at the shelter, but the information is still available. That said, sometimes you will certainly find it appropriate to delete a record.

To delete a record from a table, complete the following steps:

1. Click the record selector for the record you want to delete (see Figure 27).
2. Click Delete in the Records group on the Home tab. Click Yes in the warning dialog box. Note that you can take similar steps in queries and forms.

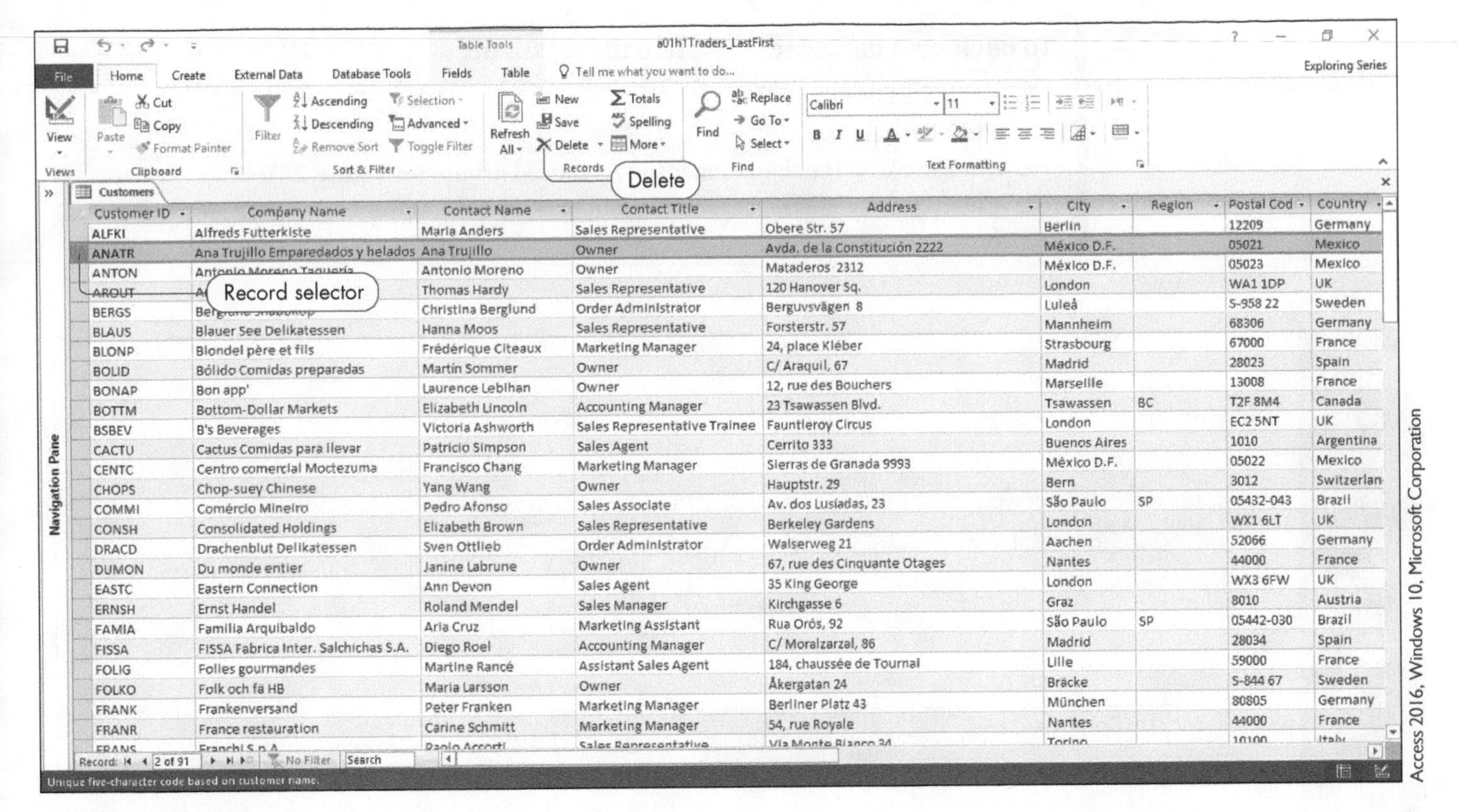

FIGURE 27 Deleting a Record

If you attempt to delete a record, you may get an error message. For example, if you try to delete a customer who has adopted pets, you may get a message stating *You cannot delete this record because another table has related records*. Even though the customer may have moved, they cannot be deleted because related records exist in another table, in this case, animals the customer has adopted.

Using Database Utilities

Database administrators spend a lot of time maintaining databases. Software utility programs make this process simpler. As Access is a database management utility, there are a number of tools that can be used to protect, maintain, and improve performance of a database.

Back Up a Database

STEP 6 »» ***Back Up Database*** is a utility that creates a duplicate copy of the entire database to protect from loss or damage. Imagine what would happen to a firm that loses track of orders placed, a charity that loses the list of donor contributions, or a hospital that loses the digital records of its patients. Making backups is especially important when you have multiple users working with the database. When you use the Back Up Database utility, Access provides a file name for the backup that uses the same file name as the database you are backing up, an underscore, and the current date. This makes it easy for you to keep track of databases by the date they were created.

Keep in mind, backing up a database on the same storage device as the original database can leave you with no protection in the event of hardware failure. Backups are typically stored on a separate device, such as an external hard drive or network drive.

To back up a database, complete the following steps:

1. Click the File tab.
2. Click Save As.
3. Click Back Up Database under the Advanced group (see Figure 28).
4. Click Save As. Revise the location and file name if you want to change either and click Save.

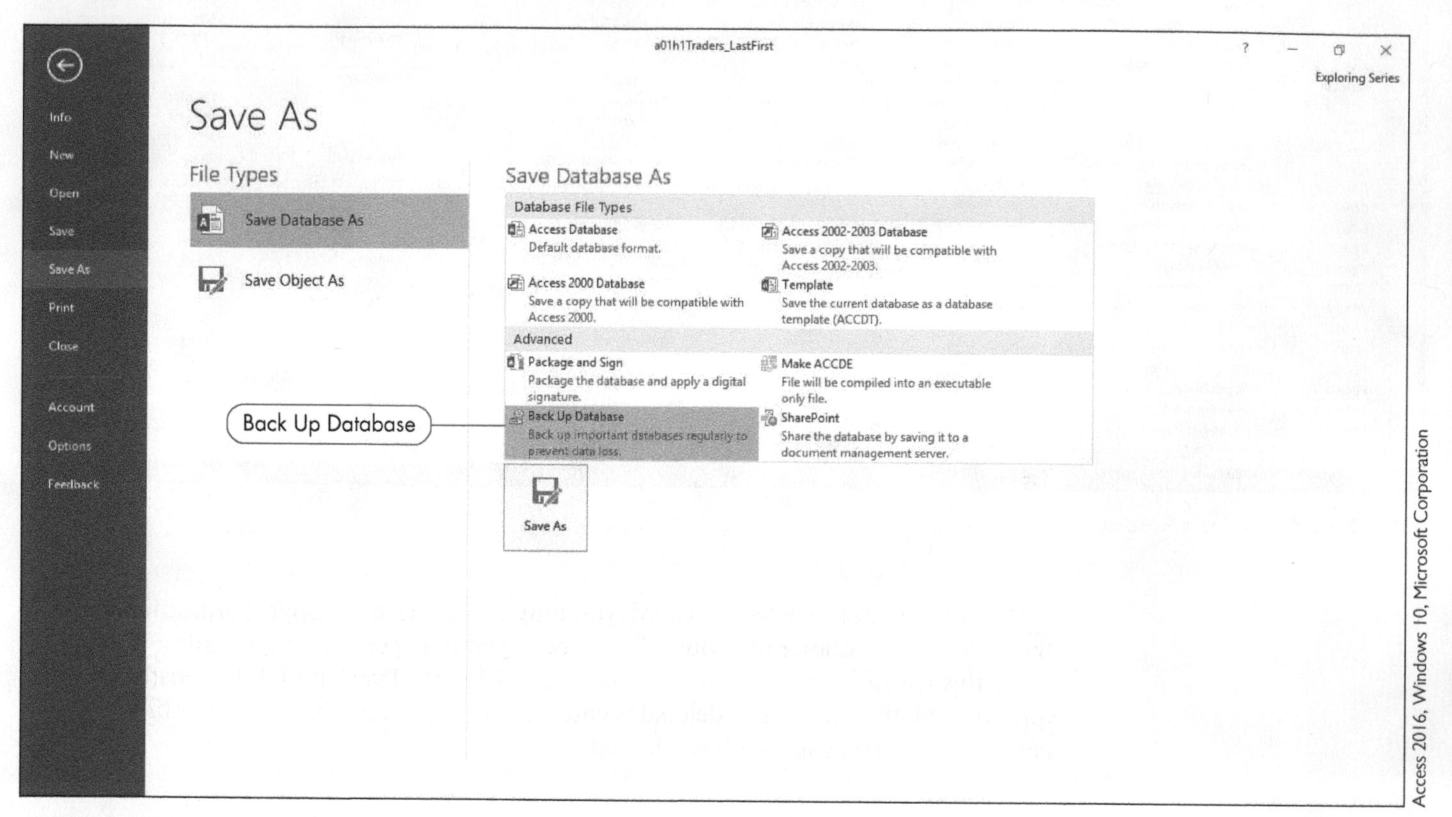

FIGURE 28 Back Up Database Option

Compact and Repair a Database

Databases have a tendency to expand with everyday use and may become corrupt, so Access provides the ***Compact and Repair Database*** utility. Compact and Repair Database reduces the size of a database and fixes any errors that may exist in the file.

To compact and repair an open database, complete the following steps:

1. Click the File tab.
2. Click Compact and Repair Database in the Info options. If you have any unsaved design changes, you will be prompted to save before the compact and repair can complete.

Alternately, you can have Access perform a Compact and Repair automatically.

To have Access compact and repair a database each time you close the database, complete the following steps:

1. Click the File tab.
2. Click Options.
3. Click Current Database.
4. Click the Compact on Close check box under Application Options in the Options for the current database pane.
5. Click OK.

TIP: SPLIT DATABASES

Another utility built into Access is the ***Database Splitter*** tool, which puts the tables in one file (the back-end database), and the queries, forms, and reports in a second file (the front-end database). This way, each user can create their own queries, forms, and reports without potentially changing an object someone else needs.

To split a database, click the Database Tools tab and click Access Database in the Move Data group. Click Split Database and click OK.

Encrypt a Database

To protect a database from unauthorized access, you can encrypt the database, which enables you to password-protect the stored information. Adding a password requires that the database be opened in exclusive mode. Open Exclusive mode guarantees that you are the only one currently using the database.

To open a database in exclusive mode, complete the following steps:

1. Ensure that the database is closed. You cannot open a database with exclusive access unless it is currently closed.
2. Click the File tab.
3. Click Open.
4. Click Browse to display the Open dialog box.
5. Locate and click the database you want to open, and click the Open arrow at the bottom of the dialog box. Make sure you click the arrow next to the word Open, and not the Open button.
6. Select Open Exclusive from the list. The database opens in exclusive mode.

To add a password once the database has been opened in exclusive mode, complete the following steps:

1. Click the File tab.
2. Click Encrypt with Password. The Set Database Password dialog box opens.
3. Type a password, and re-enter the password in the Verify box. Click OK.

Print Information

Though Access is primarily designed to store data electronically, you may want to produce a print copy of your data.

To print information from any object (table, query, form, report) in your database, complete the following steps:

1. Click the File tab.
2. Click Print. The right panel display changes to enable you to choose a print option.
3. Click Print.
4. Change any settings that may need changing (for example, the print range or number of copies).
5. Click OK.

It is good practice to preview your work before printing a document. This way, if you notice an error, you can fix it and not waste paper.

To preview your work before printing, complete the following steps:

1. Click the File tab.
2. Click Print.
3. Click Print Preview.
4. Click Close Print Preview on the Print Preview tab to exit without printing, or click Print to open the Print dialog box (see Figure 29).

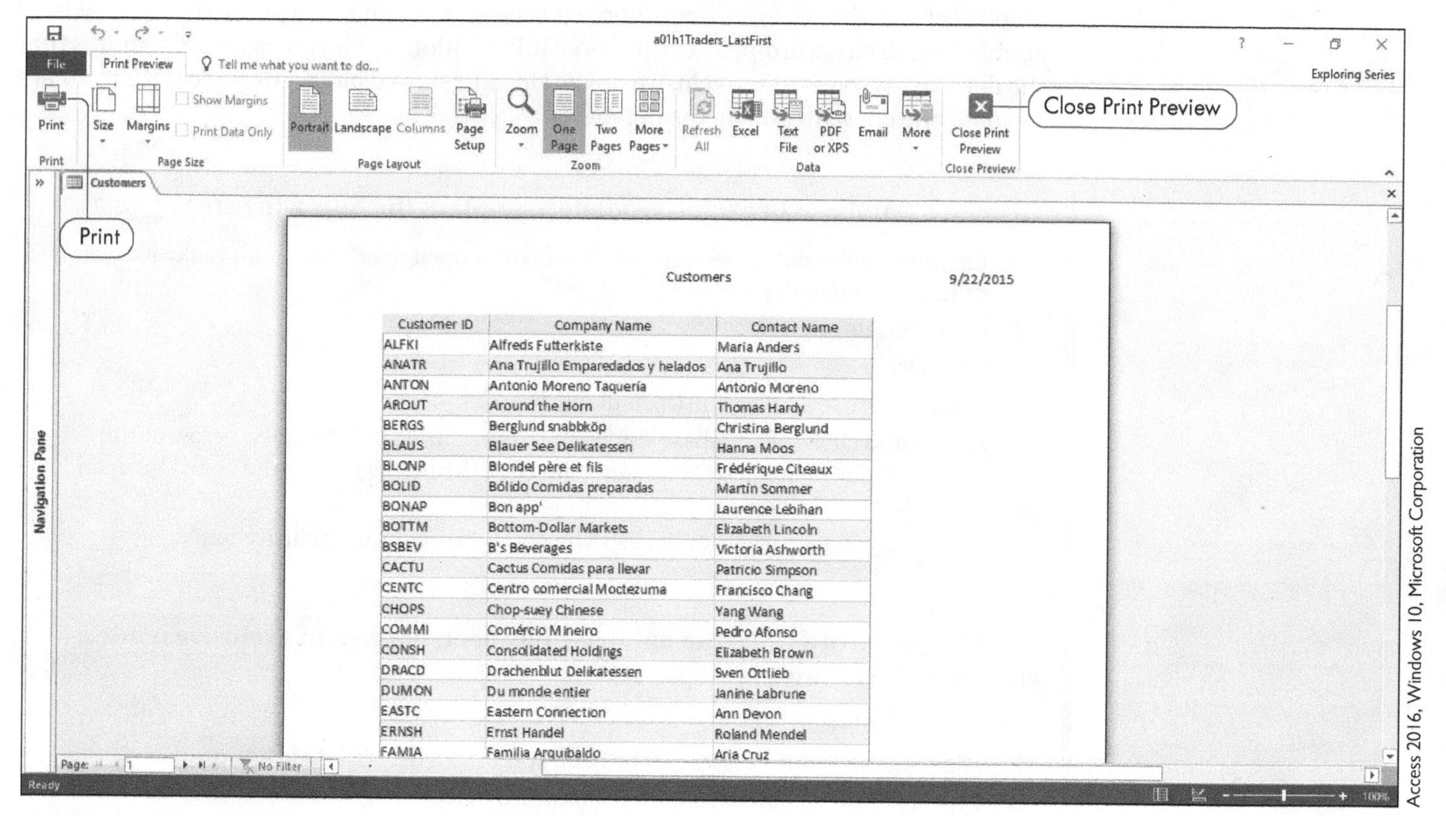

Customer ID	Company Name	Contact Name
ALFKI	Alfreds Futterkiste	Maria Anders
ANATR	Ana Trujillo Emparedados y helados	Ana Trujillo
ANTON	Antonio Moreno Taquería	Antonio Moreno
AROUT	Around the Horn	Thomas Hardy
BERGS	Berglund snabbköp	Christina Berglund
BLAUS	Blauer See Delikatessen	Hanna Moos
BLONP	Blondel père et fils	Frédérique Citeaux
BOLID	Bólido Comidas preparadas	Martín Sommer
BONAP	Bon app'	Laurence Lebihan
BOTTM	Bottom-Dollar Markets	Elizabeth Lincoln
BSBEV	B's Beverages	Victoria Ashworth
CACTU	Cactus Comidas para llevar	Patricio Simpson
CENTC	Centro comercial Moctezuma	Francisco Chang
CHOPS	Chop-suey Chinese	Yang Wang
COMMI	Comércio Mineiro	Pedro Afonso
CONSH	Consolidated Holdings	Elizabeth Brown
DRACD	Drachenblut Delikatessen	Sven Ottlieb
DUMON	Du monde entier	Janine Labrune
EASTC	Eastern Connection	Ann Devon
ERNSH	Ernst Handel	Roland Mendel
FAMIA	Familia Arquibaldo	Aria Cruz

FIGURE 29 Table Print Preview

1. Name the four main types of objects in an Access database and briefly describe the purpose of each.
2. What is the difference between Datasheet view and Design view in a table?
3. How does Access handle saving differently than other Office programs such as Excel?
4. How do relationships benefit a database user?

Hands-On Exercises

Skills covered: Open a Database • Save a Database with a New Name • Enable Content in a Database • Examine the Access Interface • Explore Table Datasheet View • Navigate Through Records • Explore Table Design View • Rename and Describe Tables • Understand Relationships Between Tables • Understand the Difference Between Working in Storage And Memory • Change Data in Table Datasheet View • Add Records to a Table • Delete Records from A Table • Back Up a Database • Compact and Repair a Database • Encrypt a Database • Print Information

1 Databases Are Everywhere!

Northwind purchases food items from suppliers around the world and sells them to restaurants and specialty food shops. Northwind depends on the data stored in its Access database to process orders and make daily decisions. You will open the Northwind database, examine the Access interface, review the existing objects in the database, and explore Access views. You will add, edit, and delete records using both tables and forms. Finally, you will back up the database.

STEP 1 » OPEN, SAVE, AND ENABLE CONTENT IN A DATABASE

As you begin your job, you first will become familiar with the Northwind database. This database will help you learn the fundamentals of working with database files. Refer to Figure 30 as you complete Step 1.

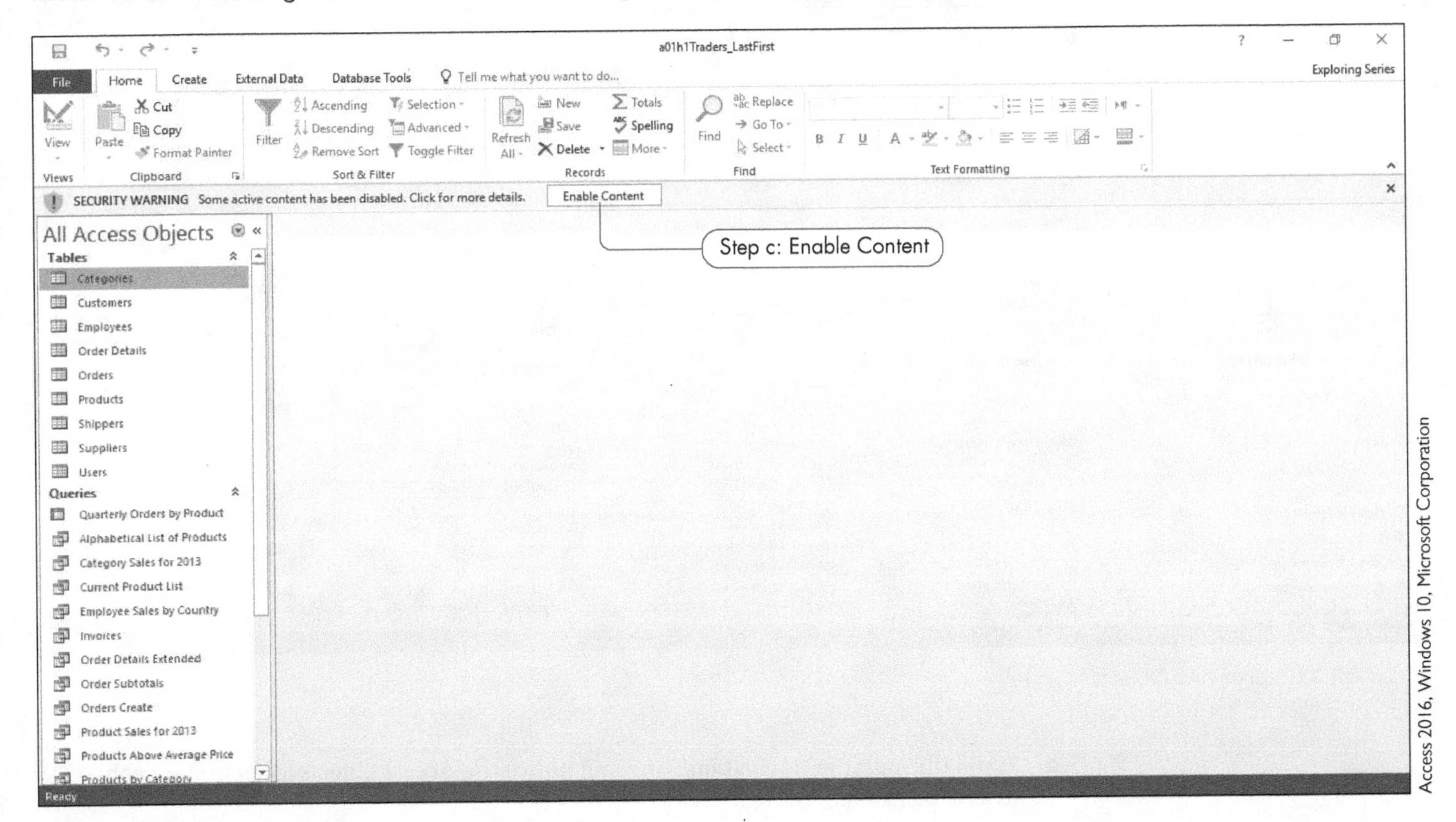

FIGURE 30 Northwind Database

a. Open Access, click **Open Other Files**, and click **Browse** . Navigate to the folder location designated by your instructor. Click *a01h1Traders* and click **Open**.

> **TROUBLESHOOTING:** If you make any major mistakes in this exercise, you can close the file, open a*01h1Traders* again, and then start this exercise over.

b. Click the **File tab** and click **Save As.** Click **Save As** and save the file as **a01h1Traders_LastFirst**.

When you save files, use your last and first names. For example, as the Access author, I would save my database as "a01h1Traders_CameronEric."

The Security Warning message bar appears below the Ribbon, indicating that some database content is disabled.

c. Click **Enable Content** on the Security Warning message bar.

When you open an Access file, you should enable the content.

STEP 2 » RECOGNIZE DATABASE OBJECT TYPES

Now that you have opened the Northwind database, you examine the Navigation Pane, objects, and views to become familiar with these fundamental Access features. Refer to Figure 31 as you complete Step 2.

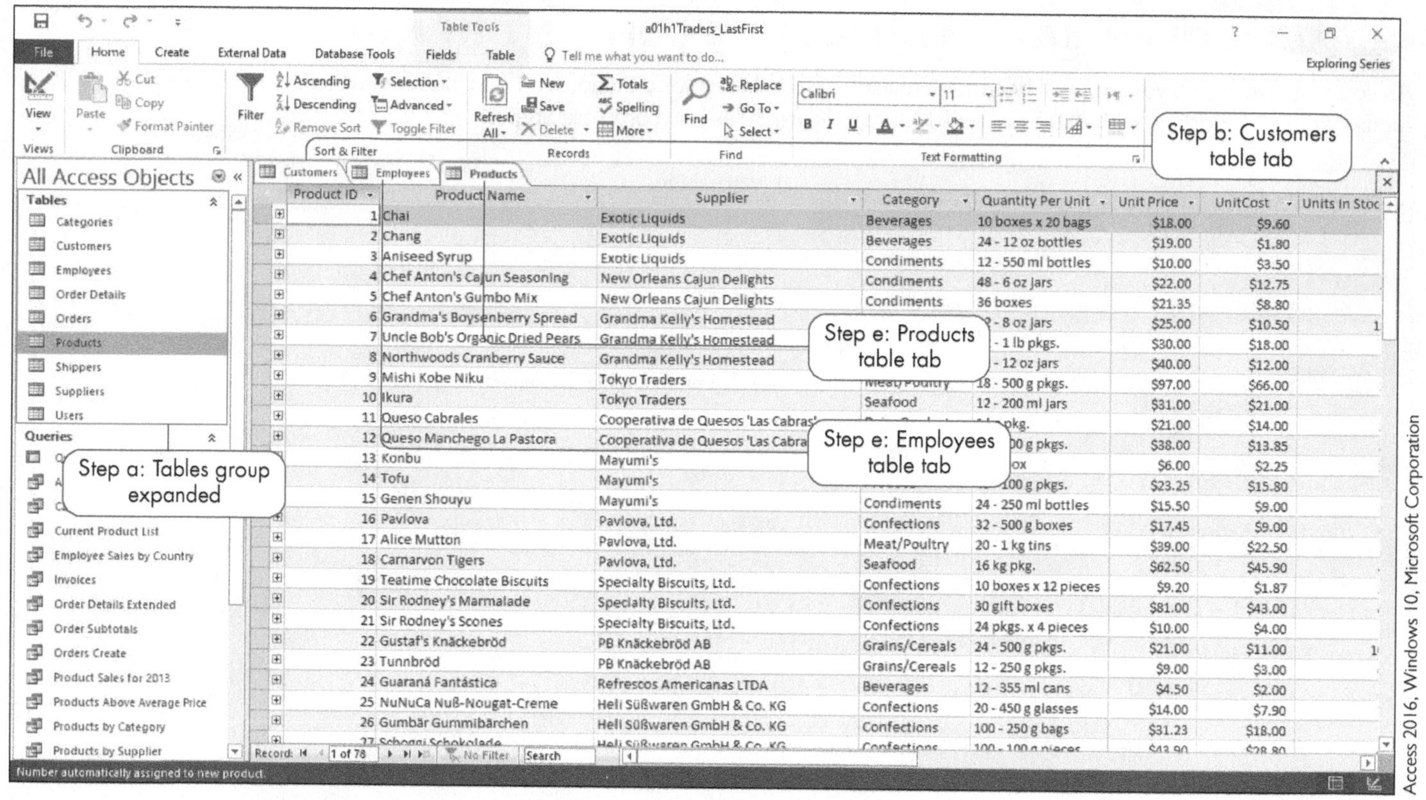

FIGURE 31 Northwind Objects

a. Scroll through the Navigation Pane and notice the Access objects listed under each expanded group.

The Tables group and the Forms group are expanded, displaying all of the table and form objects. The Queries, Reports, Macros, and Modules groups are collapsed so that the objects in those groups are not displayed.

b. Double-click the **Customers table** in the Navigation Pane.

The Customers table opens in Datasheet view, showing the data contained in the table. The Customers tab displays below the Ribbon indicating the table object is open. Each customer's record displays on a table row. The columns of the table display the fields that comprise the records.

c. Click **View** in the Views group on the Home tab.

The view of the Customers table switches to Design view. The top portion of Design view displays each field that comprises a customer record, the field's data type, and an optional description of what the field should contain. The bottom portion of Design view displays the field properties (details) for the selected field.

d. Click **View** in the Views group on the Home tab again.

Because the View button is a toggle, your view returns to Datasheet view, which shows the data stored in the table.

e. Double-click **Employees** in the Tables group of the Navigation Pane. Double-click **Products** in the same location.

The Employees and Products tables open. The tabs for three table objects display below the Ribbon: Customers, Employees, and Products.

f. Click **Shutter Bar Open/Close** « on the title bar of the Navigation Pane to hide the Navigation Pane. Click again to » show the Navigation Pane.

Shutter Bar Open/Close toggles to allow you to view more in the open object window, or to enable you to view your database objects.

g. Scroll down in the Navigation Pane and click **Reports**.

The Reports group expands, and all report objects display.

h. Scroll up until you can see Forms. Click **Forms** in the Navigation Pane.

The Forms group collapses and individual form objects no longer display.

STEP 3 » MODIFY DATA IN TABLE DATASHEET VIEW

You want to learn to edit the data in the Northwind database, because data can change. For example, employees will change their address and phone numbers when they move, and customers will change their order data from time to time. Refer to Figure 32 as you complete Step 3.

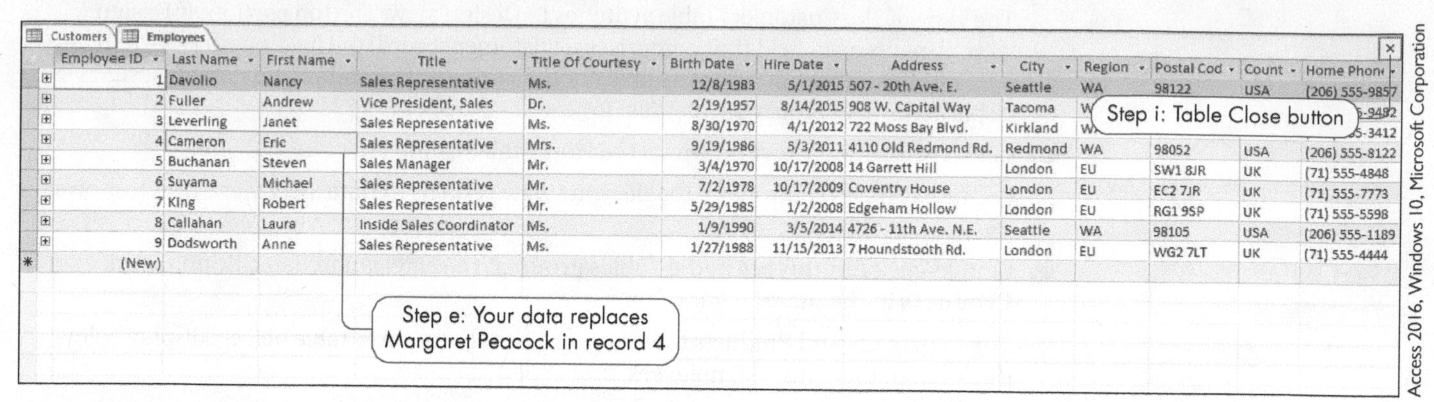

Employee ID	Last Name	First Name	Title	Title Of Courtesy	Birth Date	Hire Date	Address	City	Region	Postal Cod	Count	Home Phon
1	Davolio	Nancy	Sales Representative	Ms.	12/8/1983	5/1/2015	507 - 20th Ave. E.	Seattle	WA	98122	USA	(206) 555-9857
2	Fuller	Andrew	Vice President, Sales	Dr.	2/19/1957	8/14/2015	908 W. Capital Way	Tacoma	W			5-9482
3	Leverling	Janet	Sales Representative	Ms.	8/30/1970	4/1/2012	722 Moss Bay Blvd.	Kirkland	W			5-3412
4	Cameron	Eric	Sales Representative	Mrs.	9/19/1986	5/3/2011	4110 Old Redmond Rd.	Redmond	WA	98052	USA	(206) 555-8122
5	Buchanan	Steven	Sales Manager	Mr.	3/4/1970	10/17/2008	14 Garrett Hill	London	EU	SW1 8JR	UK	(71) 555-4848
6	Suyama	Michael	Sales Representative	Mr.	7/2/1978	10/17/2009	Coventry House	London	EU	EC2 7JR	UK	(71) 555-7773
7	King	Robert	Sales Representative	Mr.	5/29/1985	1/2/2008	Edgeham Hollow	London	EU	RG1 9SP	UK	(71) 555-5598
8	Callahan	Laura	Inside Sales Coordinator	Ms.	1/9/1990	3/5/2014	4726 - 11th Ave. N.E.	Seattle	WA	98105	USA	(206) 555-1189
9	Dodsworth	Anne	Sales Representative	Ms.	1/27/1988	11/15/2013	7 Houndstooth Rd.	London	EU	WG2 7LT	UK	(71) 555-4444
(New)												

FIGURE 32 Northwind Employees Table

a. Click the **Employees tab** to view the Employees table.

b. Double-click **Peacock** (the value of the Last Name field in the fourth row); the entire name highlights. Type your last name to replace Peacock.

The pencil symbol in the record selector box indicates that the record is being edited but has not yet been saved.

c. Press **Tab** to move to the next field in the fourth row. Replace Margaret with your first name and press **Tab**.

You have made changes to two fields in the same record.

d. Click **Undo** on the Quick Access Toolbar.

Your first and last names revert back to Margaret Peacock because you have not yet left the record.

e. Type your first and last names again to replace Margaret Peacock. Press **Tab**.

You should now be in the title field and the title, Sales Representative, is selected. The record has not been saved, as indicated by the pencil symbol in the record selector box.

f. Click anywhere in the third row where Janet Leverling's data is stored.

The pencil symbol disappears, indicating that your changes have been saved.

g. Click the **Address field** in the first row, Nancy Davolio's record. Select the entire address and then type **4004 East Morningside Dr.** Click anywhere on the second record, Andrew Fuller's record.

h. Click **Undo**.

Nancy Davolio's address reverts back to 507 - 20th Ave. E. However, the Undo command is now faded. You can no longer undo the change that you made replacing Margaret Peacock's name with your own.

i. Click **Close** [X] at the top of the table to close the Employees table.

The Employees table closes. You are not prompted to save your changes; they have already been saved for you because Access works in storage, not memory. If you reopen the Employees table, you will see your name in place of Margaret Peacock's name.

STEP 4 » ADD RECORDS TO A TABLE

You have been asked to add new information about a new line of products to the Northwind database. Refer to Figure 33 as you complete Step 4.

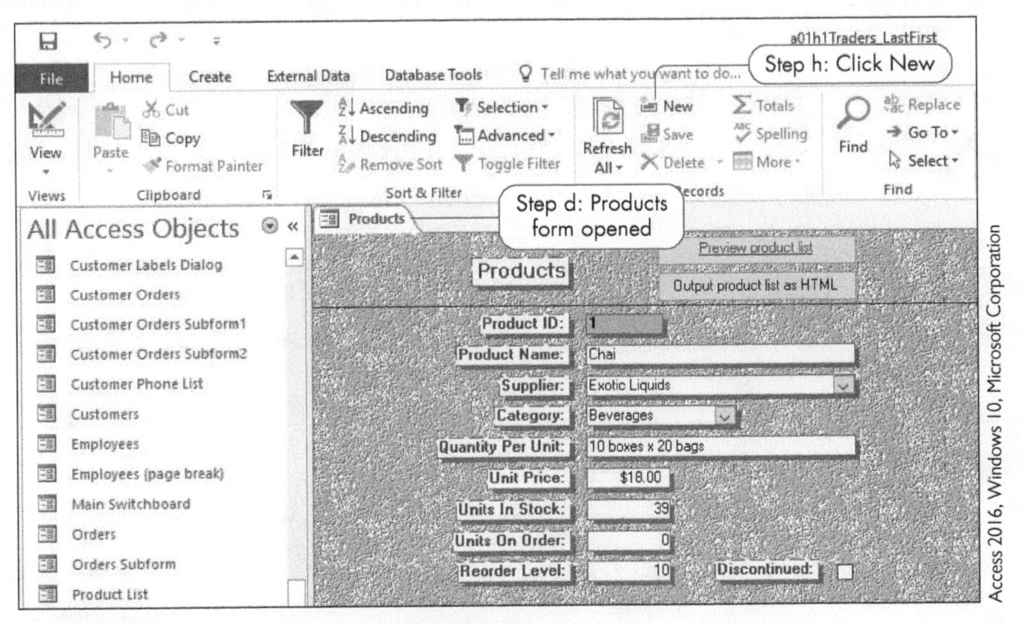

FIGURE 33 Adding Data Using Products Form

a. Right-click the **Customers tab** and click **Close All.**

b. Click the **Tables group** in the Navigation Pane to collapse it. Click the **Reports group** in the Navigation Pane to collapse it as well.

c. Click the **Forms group** in the Navigation Pane to expand the list of available forms.

d. Double-click the **Products form** to open it.

e. Click the **Next record** arrow. Click **Last record**, click **Previous record**, and then click **First record**.

f. Click **Find** in the Find group on the Home tab, type **Grandma** in the **Find box**, click the **Match arrow**, and then select **Any Part of Field**. Click **Find Next**.

You should see the data for Grandma's Boysenberry Spread. Selecting the Any Part of Field option will return a match even if it is contained in the middle of a word.

g. Close the Find dialog box.

h. Click **New** in the Records group of the Home tab.

i. Type the following information for a new product. Click, or press **Tab**, to move into the next cell. Notice as soon as you begin typing, Access will assign a ProductID to this product.

Field Name	Value to Type
Product Name	***Your names* Pecan Pie** (replacing Your name with your last name)
Supplier	**Grandma Kelly's Homestead** (click the arrow to select from the list of Suppliers)
Category	**Confections** (click the arrow to select from the list of Categories)
Quantity Per Unit	**1**
Unit Price	**15.00**
Units in Stock	**18**
Units on Order	**50**
Reorder Level	**20**
Discontinued	**No** (leave the check box unchecked)

j. Click anywhere on the Pecan Pie record you just typed. Click the **File tab**, click **Print**, and then click **Print Preview**.

   The first four records display in the Print Preview.

k. Click **Last Page** in the navigation bar and click **Previous Page** to show the new record you entered.

   The beginning of the Pecan Pie record is now visible. The record continues on the next page.

l. Click **Close Print Preview** in the Close Preview group.

m. Close the Products form.

STEP 5 » DELETE RECORDS FROM A TABLE

To help you understand how Access stores data, you verify that the new product is in the Products table. You also attempt to delete a record. Refer to Figure 34 as you complete Step 5.

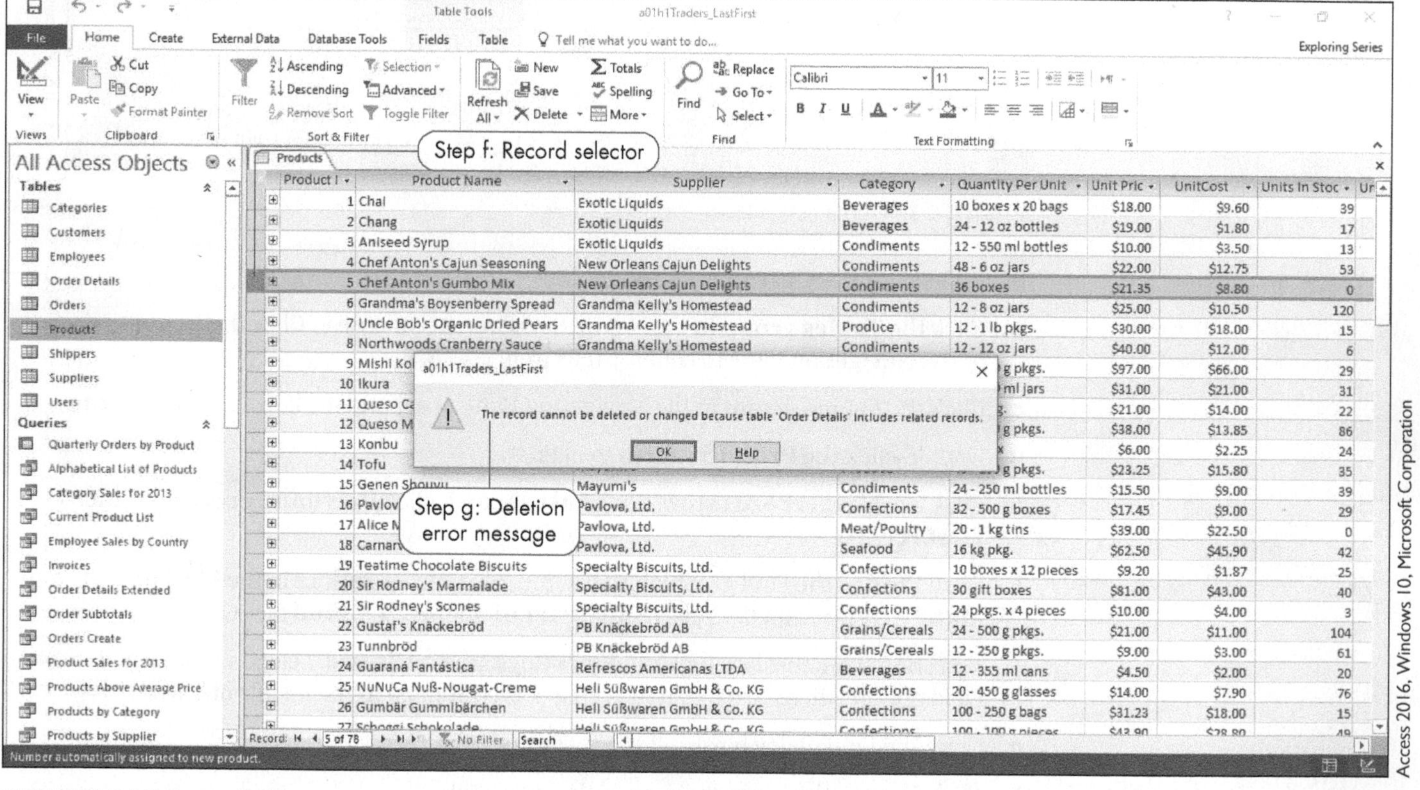

FIGURE 34 Deleting Data

a. Click the **Forms group** in the Navigation Pane to collapse it. Expand the **Tables group**.

b. Double-click the **Products table** to open it.

c. Click **Last record** in the navigation bar.

   The Pecan Pie record you entered in the Products form is listed as the last record in the Products table. The Products form was created from the Products table. Your newly created record, Pecan Pie, is stored in the Products table even though you added it using the form.

d. Navigate to the fifth record in the table, Chef Anton's Gumbo Mix.

e. Use the horizontal scroll bar to scroll right until you see the Discontinued field.

   The check mark in the Discontinued check box tells you that this product has been discontinued.

f. Click the **record selector** to the left of the fifth record.

A border surrounds the record and the record is shaded, indicating it is selected.

g. Click **Delete** in the Records group and read the error message.

The error message that displays tells you that you cannot delete this record because the table 'Order Details' has related records. (Customers ordered this product in the past.) Even though the product is now discontinued and no stock remains, it cannot be deleted from the Products table because related records exist in the Order Details table.

h. Click **OK**.

i. Navigate to the last record and click the **record selector** to highlight the entire row.

The Pecan Pie record you added earlier is displayed.

j. Click **Delete** in the Records group. Read the warning.

The warning box that displays tells you that this action cannot be undone. Although this product can be deleted because it was just entered and no orders were created for it, you do not want to delete the record.

k. Click **No**. You do not want to delete this record. Close the Products table.

> **TROUBLESHOOTING:** If you clicked Yes and deleted the record, return to Step 4d. Re-open the form and re-enter the information for this record. This will be important later in this lesson.

STEP 6 » USE DATABASE UTILITIES

You will protect the Northwind database by using the Back Up Database utility. Refer to Figure 35 as you complete Step 6.

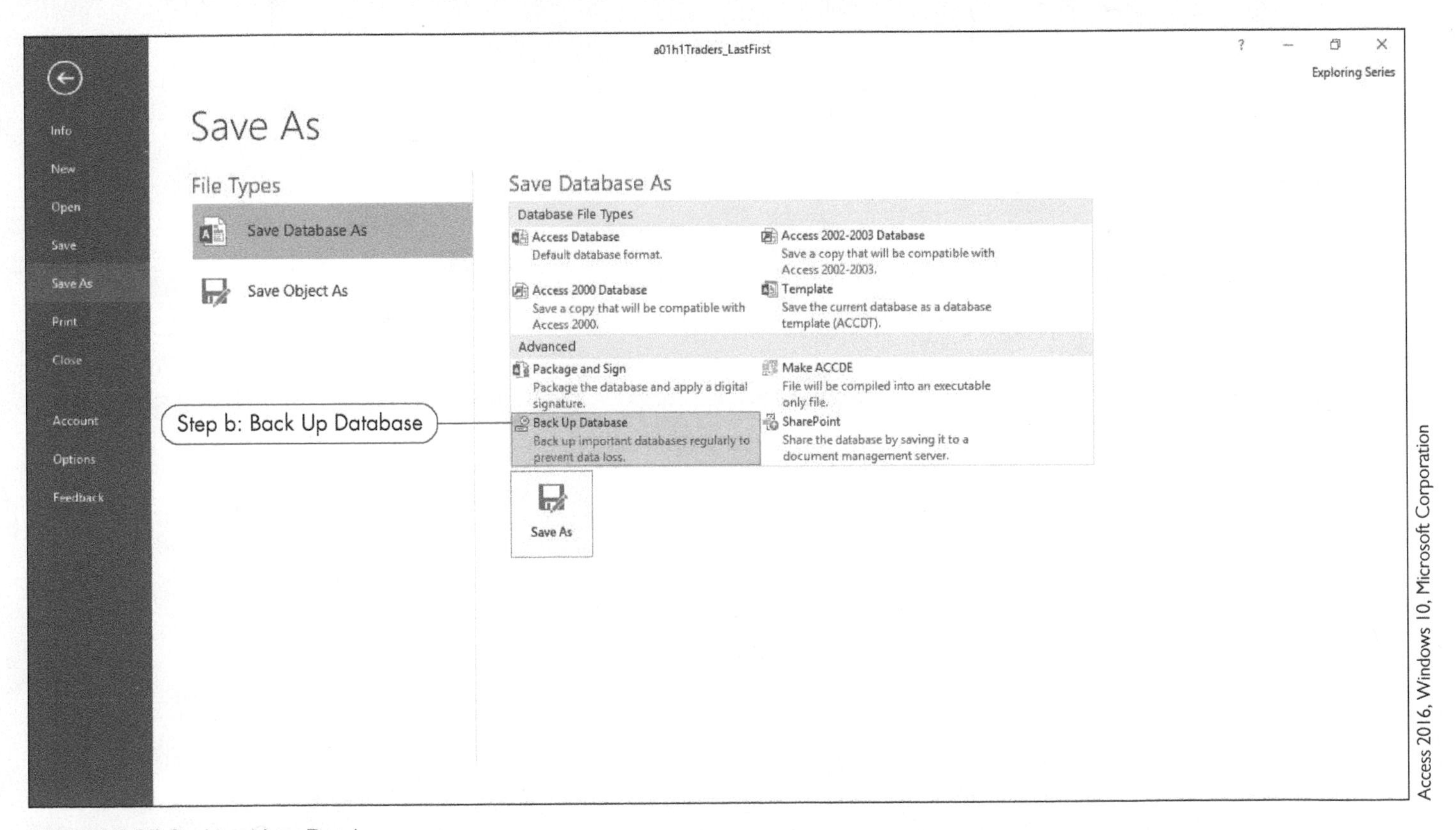

FIGURE 35 Backing Up a Database

a. Click the **File tab** and click **Save As.**

b. Double-click **Back Up Database** under the Advanced section to open the Save As dialog box.

The backup utility assigns the default name by adding a date to your file name.

c. Verify that the Save in folder displays the location where you want your file saved and click **Save**.

You just created a backup of the database after completing Hands-On Exercise 1. The original database file remains onscreen.

d. Keep the database open if you plan to continue with Hands-On Exercise 2. If not, close the database and exit Access.

Filters and Sorts

Access provides you with many tools that you can use to change the order of information and to identify and extract only the data needed at the moment. You may want to find specific information, such as which suppliers are located in Denton, TX, or which customers have placed orders in the last seven days. There may be other times you simply want to sort information rather than extract information.

In this section, you will learn how to sort information and to isolate records in a table based on criteria.

Working with Filters

Suppose you wanted to see a list of the products in the Confections category in the Northwind database. To obtain this list, you would open the Products table in Datasheet view and create a filter. A ***filter*** allows you to specify conditions to display only those records that meet those conditions. These conditions are known as criteria (or criterion, singular), and are a number, a text phrase, or an expression (such as >50) used to select records from a table. Therefore, to view a list of all Confections, you would filter the Products table, displaying only records with a Category value of Confections. In this case, Category being equal to Confections is the criterion.

You can use filters to analyze data quickly. Applying a filter does not delete any records; filters only hide records that do not match the criteria. Two types of filters are discussed in this section: Selection filter and Filter By Form.

Use a Selection Filter to Find Exact Matches

STEP 1 »» A ***Selection filter*** displays only the records that match a criterion you select. You can use a Selection filter to find records that equal a criterion. For example, if you filter a name field and you select "equals Eric", you would only find customers who have a name of Eric (but not any other variation). Selection filters are not case sensitive, so any variation of capitalization (ERIC, eric) would also appear in the search results.

To use a Selection filter to find an exact match, complete the following steps:

1. Click in any field that contains the criterion on which you want to filter.
2. Click Selection in the Sort & Filter group on the Home tab.
3. Select Equals "criterion" from the list of options (*criterion* will be replaced by the value of the field).

Figure 36 displays a Customers table with 91 records. The records in the table are displayed in sequence according to the CustomerID. The navigation bar at the bottom indicates that the active record is the second row in the table. Owner in the Job Title field is selected.

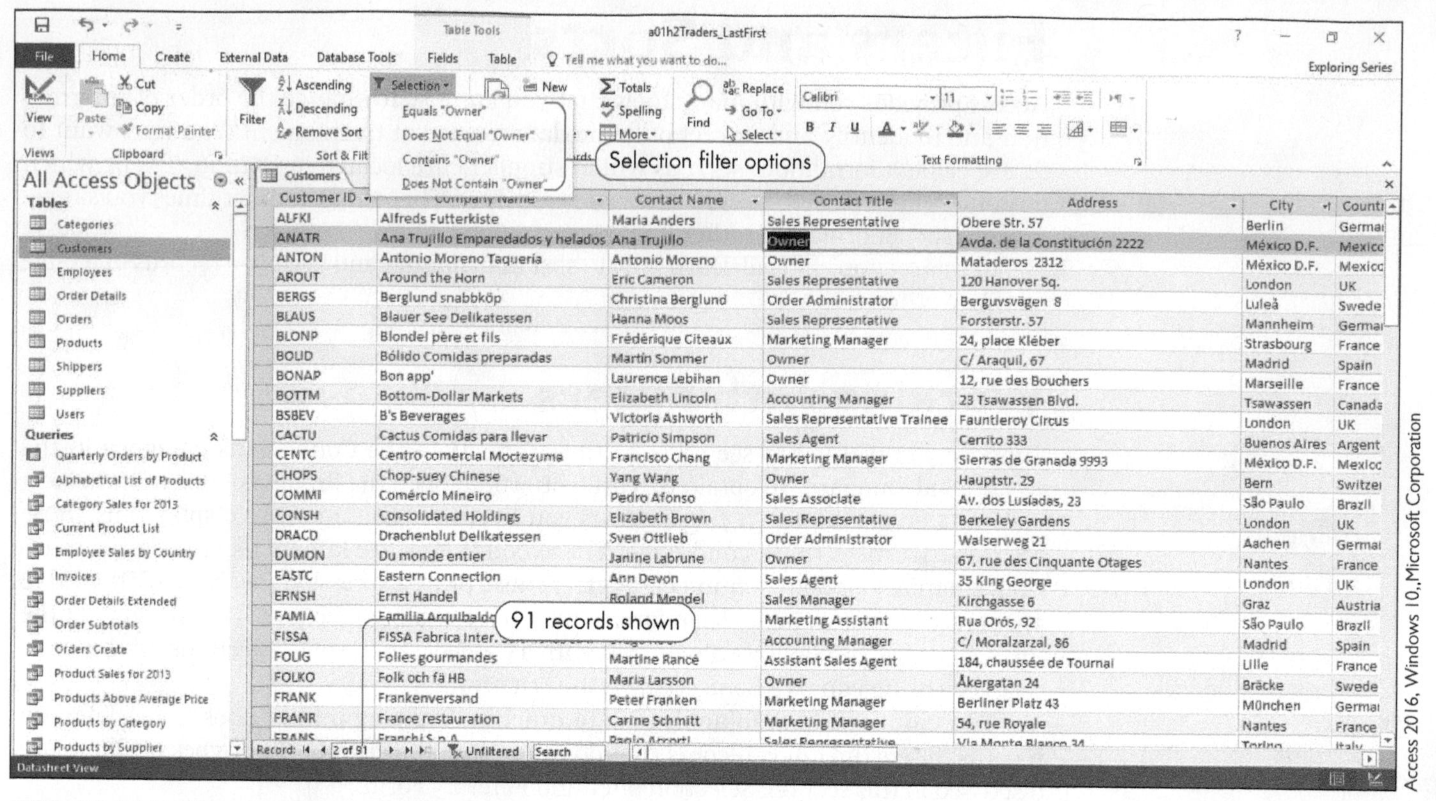

FIGURE 36 Unfiltered Customers Table

Figure 37 displays a filtered view of the Customers table, showing records with the job title Owner. The navigation bar shows that this is a filtered list containing 17 records matching the criterion. The Customers table still contains the original 91 records, but only 17 records are visible with the filter applied.

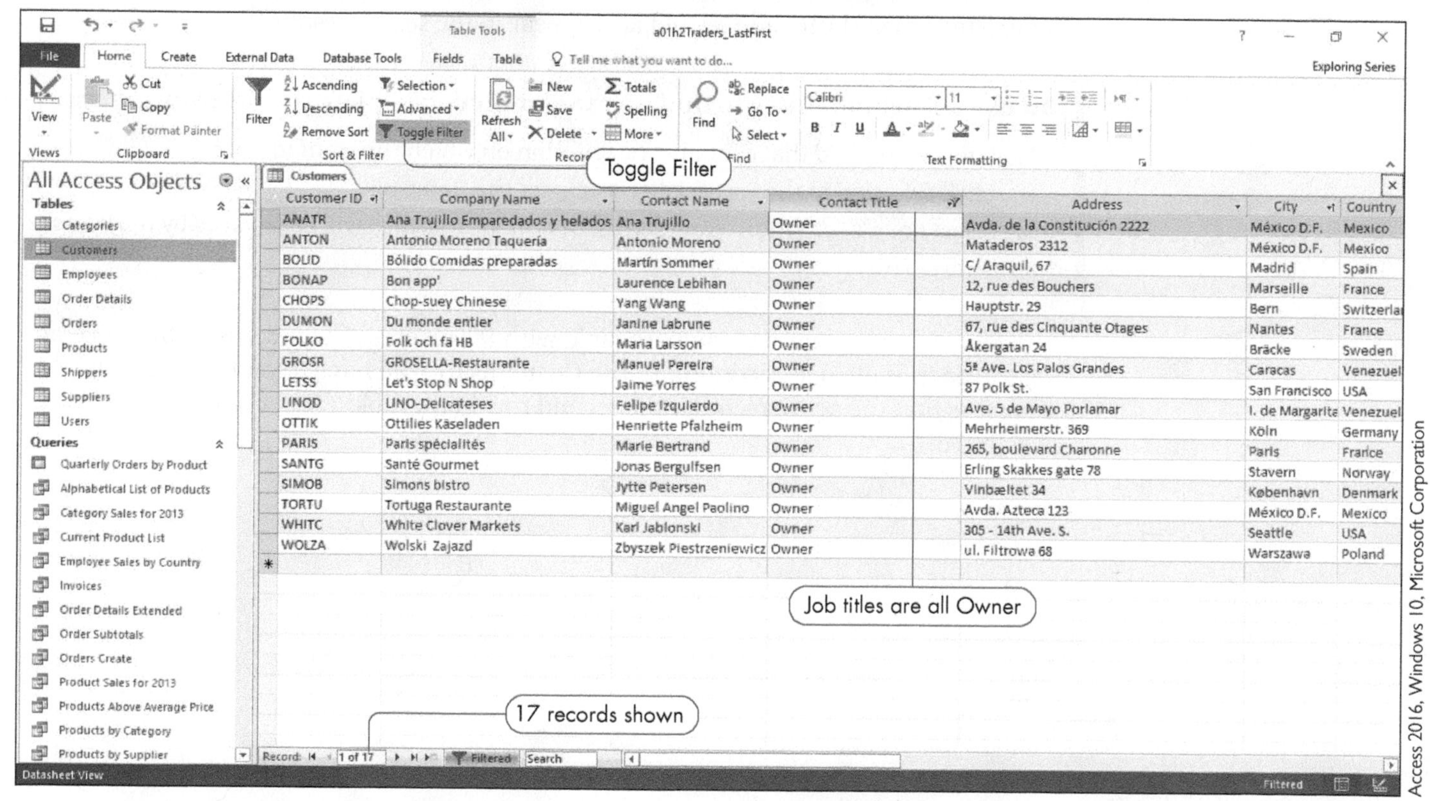

FIGURE 37 Filtered Customers Table

You can click Toggle Filter (refer to Figure 37) at any time to remove all filters and display all the records in the table. Filters are a temporary method for examining table data. If you close the filtered table and reopen it, the filter will be removed and all of the records will be visible again. You can at any point click Toggle Filter to display the results of the last saved filter.

Use a Selection Filter to Find Records Containing a Value

STEP 2 You can also use a Selection filter to find records that contain a criterion. For example, if you filter a name field and you select "contains Eric", it would find Eric, as well as names containing Eric (such as Erica, Erich, Erick, and even Broderick, Frederick, and Frederica). As with the exact match, this is not case sensitive, as shown in the results in Figure 38.

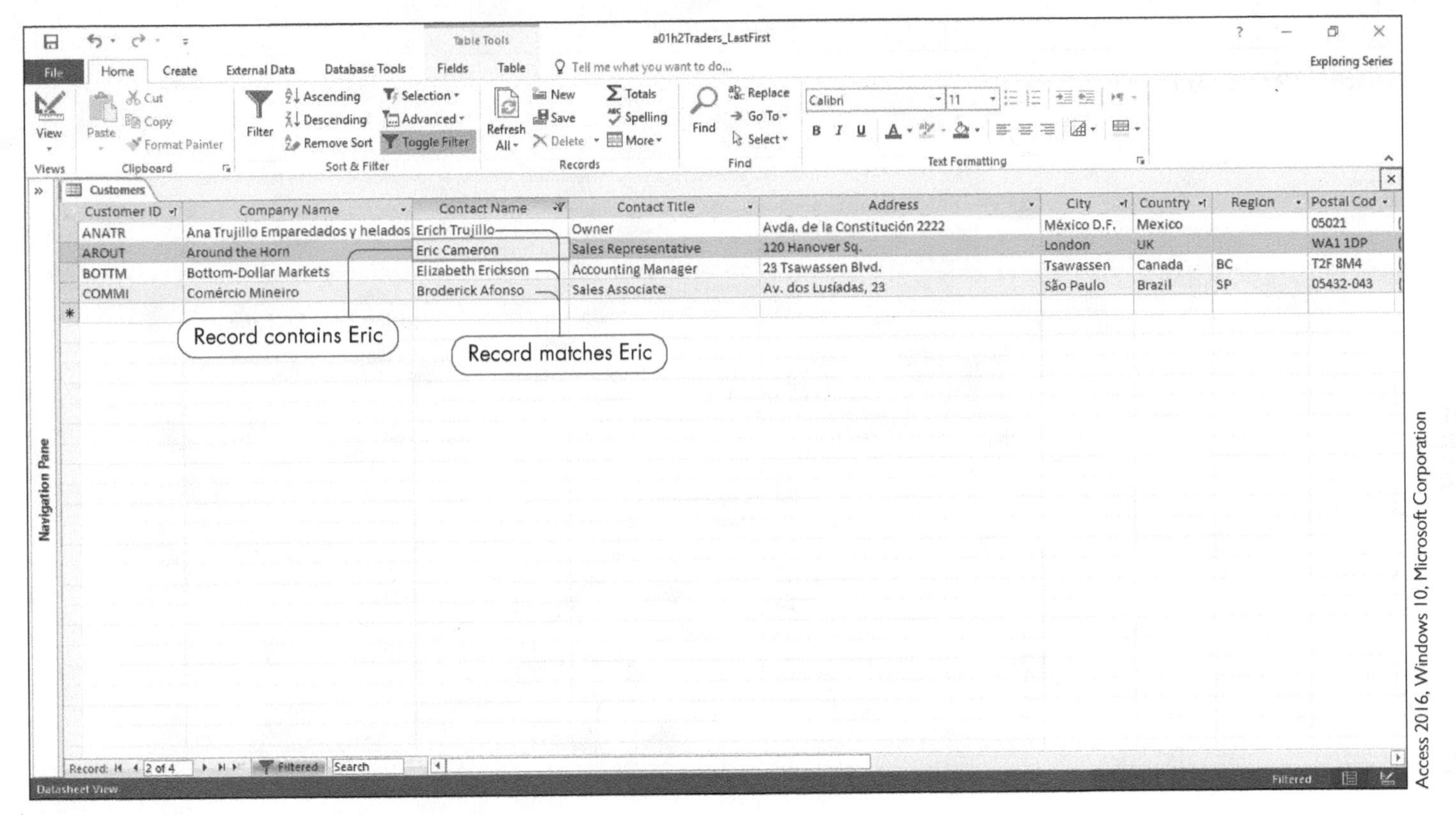

FIGURE 38 Finding Records Containing a Value

> **To use a Selection filter to find all values containing certain text, complete the following steps:**
>
> 1. Click in any field that contains the criterion on which you want to filter.
> 2. Click Selection in the Sort & Filter group on the Home tab.
> 3. Select Contains "criterion" from the list of options (*criterion* will be replaced by the value of the field).

Your results will show all records containing a partial or full match.

Use Filter By Form

Filter By Form is a more versatile method of selecting data because it enables you to display records based on multiple criteria. When you use Filter By Form, all of the records are hidden and Access creates a blank form in a design grid. You see only field names with an arrow in the first field. Figure 39 shows Filter By Form in Datasheet view, and Figure 40 shows Filter By Form in a form view.

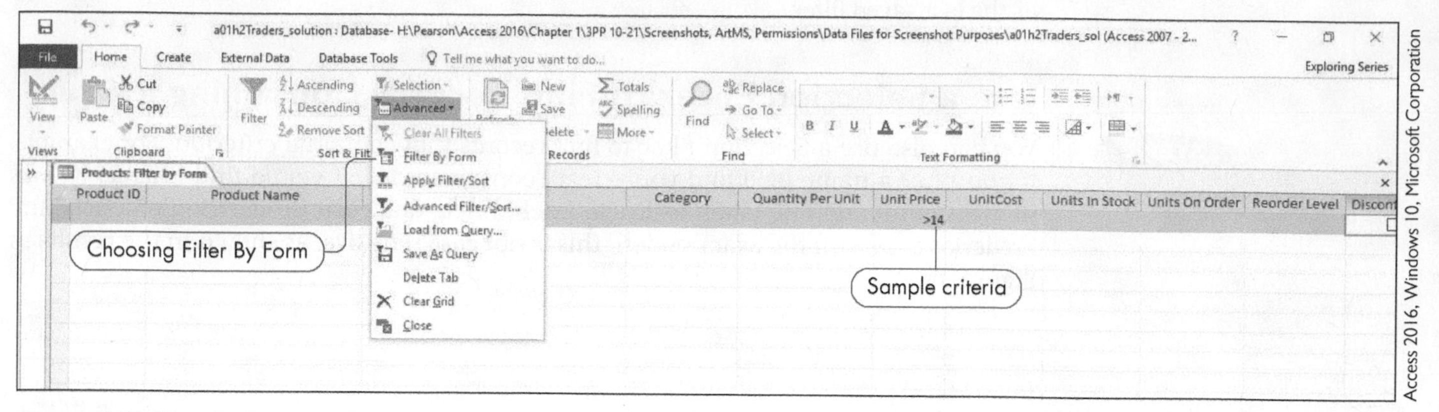

FIGURE 39 Filter By Form in a Table

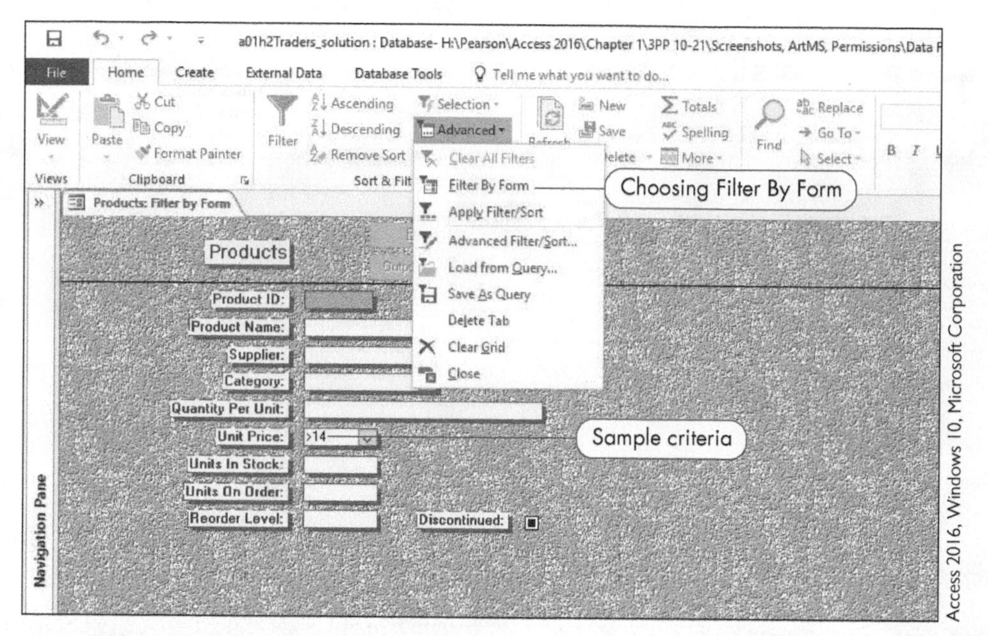

FIGURE 40 Filter By Form in a Form

An advantage of using this filter method is that you can specify AND and OR logical operators. If you use the AND operator, a record is included in the results if all the criteria are true. If you use the OR operator, a record is included if at least one criterion is true. Another advantage of Filter By Form is that you can use a comparison operator such as equal (=), not equal (<>), greater than (>), less than (<), greater than or equal to (>=), and less than or equal to (<=).

To use Filter By Form, complete the following steps:

1. Click Advanced in the Sort & Filter group on the Home tab.
2. Click Filter By Form.
3. Click in the field you want to use as a criterion. Click the arrow to select the criterion from existing data.
4. Add additional criterion and comparison operators as required.
5. Click Toggle Filter in the Sort & Filter group on the Home tab to apply the filter.

Performing Sorts

You can change the order of information by sorting one or more fields. A ***sort*** lists records in a specific sequence, such as alphabetically by last name or by ascending EmployeeID.

Sort Table Data

STEP 4 Ascending sorts a list of text data in alphabetical order or a numeric list in lowest to highest order. Descending sorts a list of text data in reverse alphabetical order or a numeric list in highest to lowest order. You can equate this to these terms outside of a database. When you are coming down from a high place (such as the top of a ladder), you are said to be descending, and when you are climbing a ladder, you are ascending. Figure 41 shows the Customers table sorted in ascending order by city name.

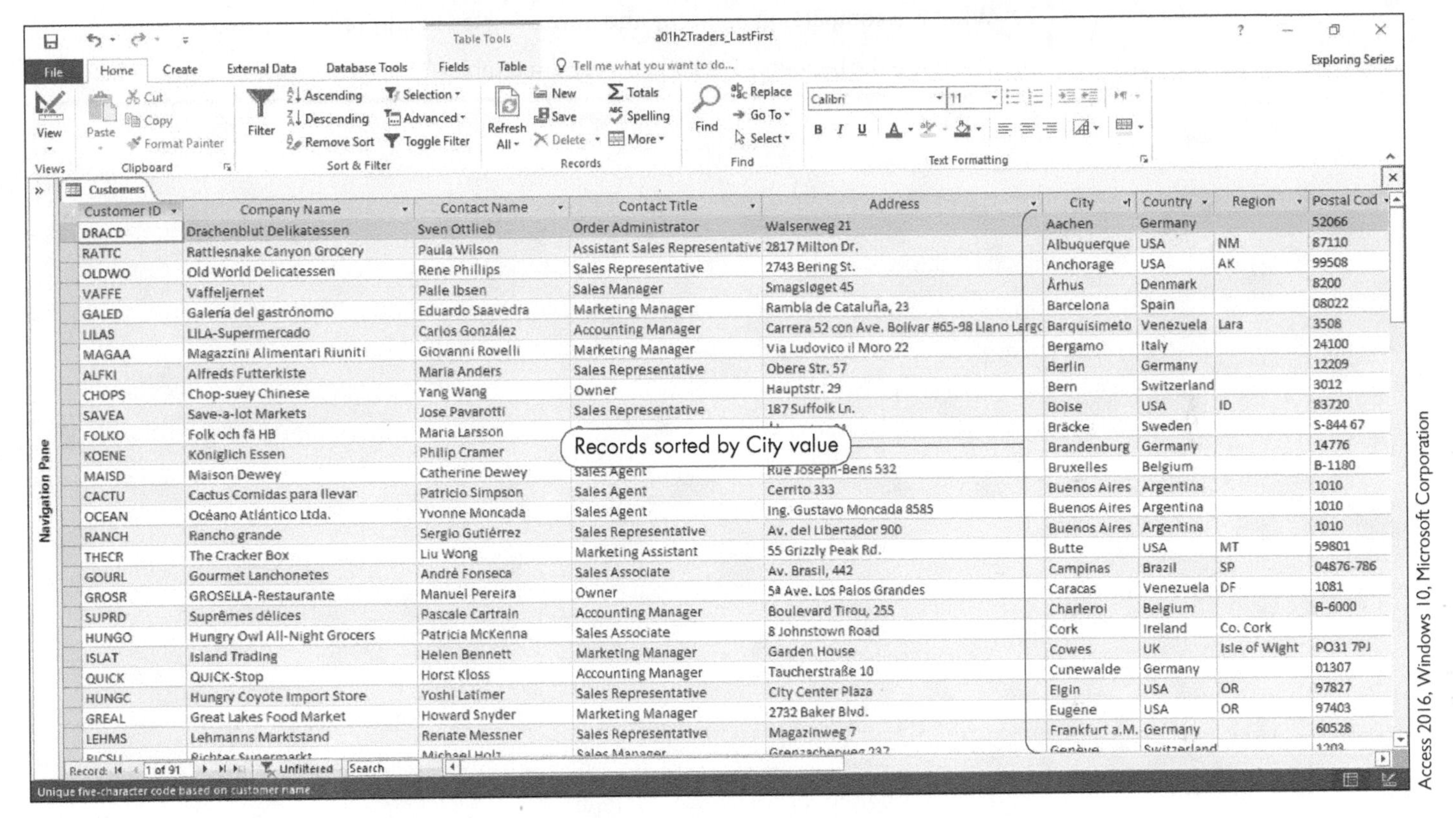

FIGURE 41 Sorted Customers Table

To sort a table on one criterion, complete the following steps:

1. Click in the field that you want to use to sort the records.
2. Click Ascending or Descending in the Sort & Filter group on the Home tab.

Access can sort records by more than one field. When sorting by multiple criteria, Access first sorts by the field located on the left. It is important to understand that in order to sort by multiple fields, you must arrange your columns in this order. This may lead to moving a field to the left so it is sorted first.

To move a field, complete the following steps:

1. Click the column heading and hold down the left mouse button. A thick line appears to the left of the column.
2. Drag the field to the appropriate position.

Once the column has been moved, you can perform a sort by selecting the field to the left, sorting, and then doing the same for the secondary sort column.

5. What is the purpose of creating a filter?
6. What is the difference between a Selection filter and a Filter By Form?
7. What is a comparison operator and how is it used in a filter?
8. What are the benefits of sorting records in a table?

Hands-On Exercises

Skills covered: Use a Selection Filter to Find Exact Matches • Use a Selection Filter to Find Records Containing a Value • Use Filter By Form • Sort Table Data

2 Filters and Sorts

The sales manager at Northwind Traders wants quick answers to her questions about customer orders. You use the Access database to filter tables to answer these questions, then sort the records based on the manager's requirements.

STEP 1 » USE A SELECTION FILTER TO FIND EXACT MATCHES

The sales manager asks for a list of customers who live in London. You use a Selection filter with an equal condition to locate these customers. Refer to Figure 42 as you complete Step 1.

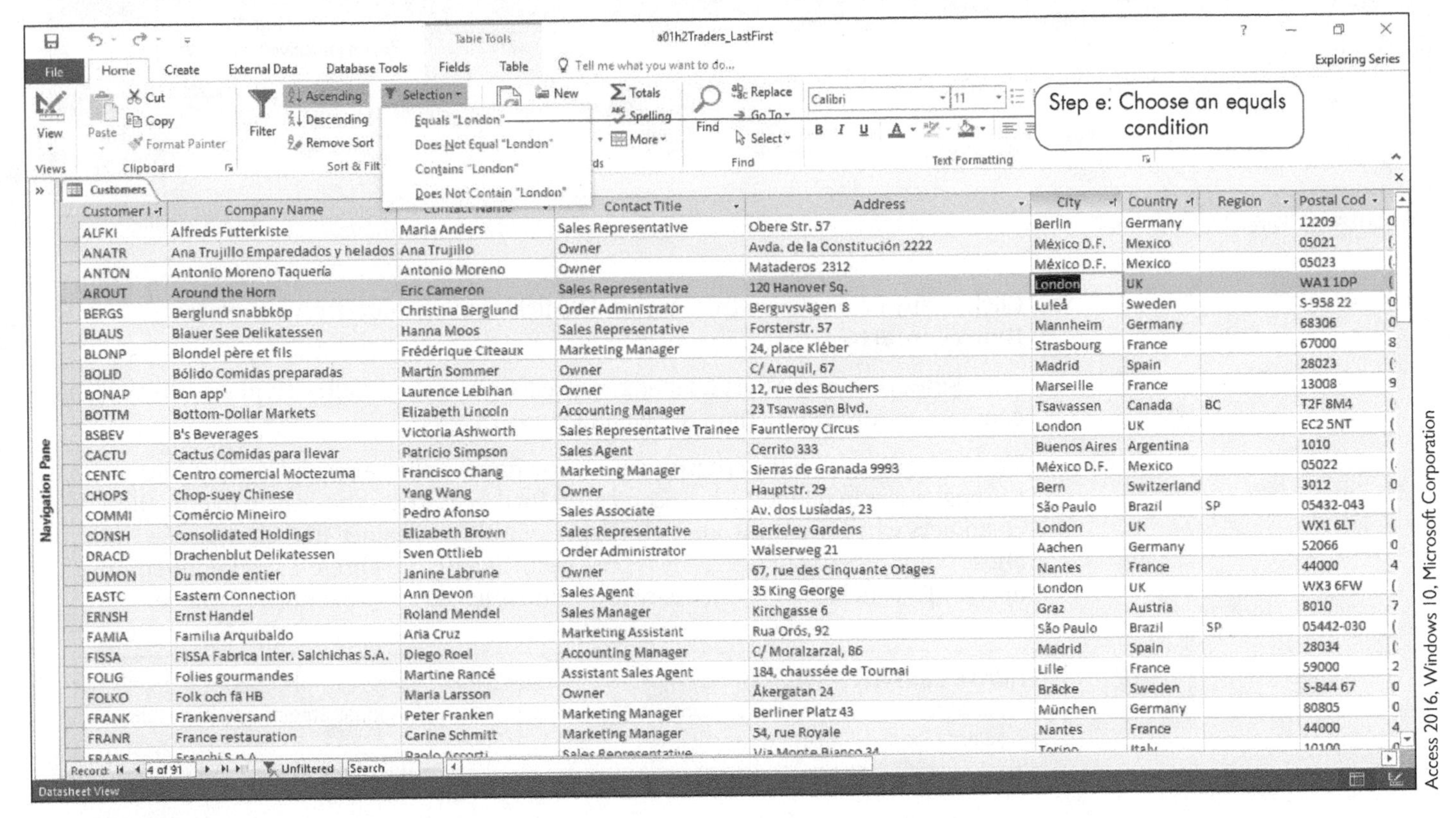

Access 2016, Windows 10, Microsoft Corporation

FIGURE 42 Filtering the Customers Table

a. Open the *a01h1Traders_LastFirst* database if you closed it after the last Hands-On Exercise and save it as **a01h2Traders_LastFirst**, changing h1 to h2. Click **Enable Content**.

b. Double-click the **Customers table** in the Navigation Pane, navigate to record 4, and then replace Thomas Hardy with your name in the Contact Name field.

c. Scroll right until the City field is visible. The fourth record has a value of London in the City field. Click the field to select it.

d. Click **Selection** in the Sort & Filter group on the Home tab.

e. Select **Equals "London"** from the menu. Six records are displayed.

The navigation bar display shows that six records that meet the London criterion are available. The other records in the Customers table are hidden. The Filtered icon also displays on the navigation bar and column heading, indicating that the Customers table has been filtered.

f. Click **Toggle Filter** in the Sort & Filter group to remove the filter.

g. Click **Toggle Filter** again to reset the filter.

STEP 2 » USE A SELECTION FILTER TO FIND RECORDS CONTAINING A VALUE

The sales manager asks you to narrow the list of London customers so that it displays only Sales Representatives. To accomplish this task, you add a second layer of filtering using a Selection filter. Refer to Figure 43 as you complete Step 2.

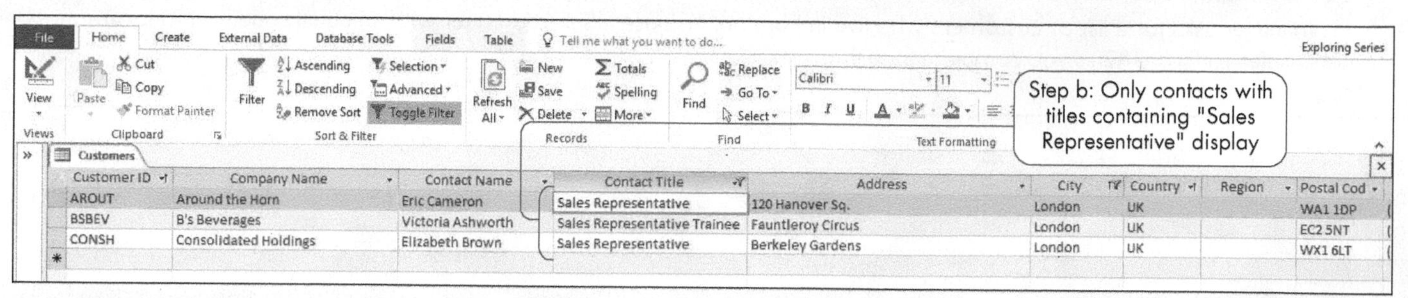

FIGURE 43 Filtered Customers

a. Click in any field value in the Contact Title field that contains the value **Sales Representative**.

b. Click **Selection** in the Sort & Filter group, click **Contains "Sales Representative"**, and compare your results to those shown in Figure 43.

Three records match the criteria you set. You have applied a second layer of filtering to the customers in London. The second layer further restricts the display to only those customers who have the words Sales Representative contained in their titles. Because you chose Contains as your filter, any representatives with the phrase Sales Representative appear. This includes Victoria Ashworth, who is a Sales Representative Trainee.

> **TROUBLESHOOTING:** If you do not see the record for Victoria Ashworth, you selected Equals "Sales Representative" instead of Contains "Sales Representative". Repeat Steps a and b, making sure you select Contains "Sales Representative".

c. Close the Customers table. Click **Yes** when prompted to save the design changes to the Customers table.

STEP 3 » USE FILTER BY FORM

You are asked to provide a list of records that do not match just one set of criteria. You will provide a list of all extended prices less than $50 for a specific sales representative. Use Filter By Form to provide the information when two or more criteria are necessary. You also preview the results in Print Preview to see how the list would print. Refer to Figure 44 as you complete Step 3.

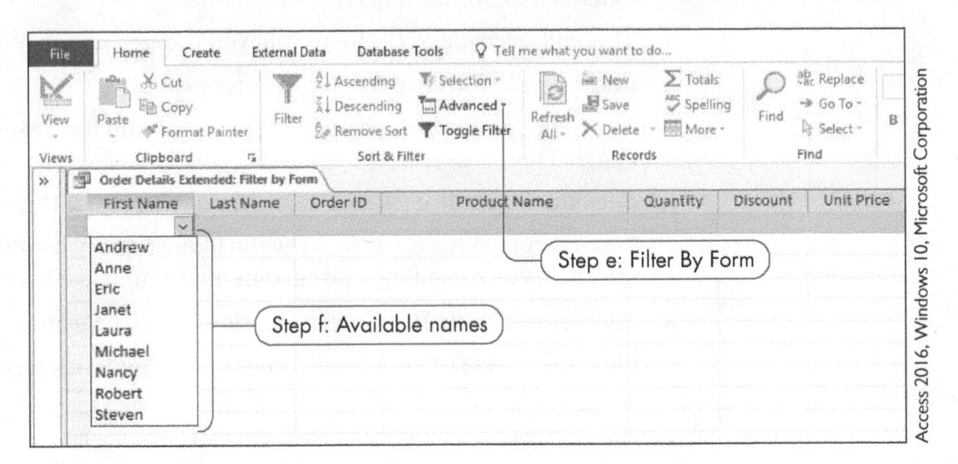

FIGURE 44 Using Filter By Form

a. Click the **Tables group** in the Navigation Pane to collapse the listed tables.

b. Click the **Queries group** in the Navigation Pane to expand the list of available queries.

c. Locate and double-click **Order Details Extended** to open it.

This query contains information about orders. It has fields containing information about the sales person, the Order ID, the product name, the unit price, quantity ordered, the discount given, and an extended price. The extended price is a field used to total order information.

d. Click **Advanced** in the Sort & Filter group and select **Filter By Form** from the list. The first field, First Name, is active by default.

All of the records are now hidden, and you see only field names and an arrow in the first field. Although you are applying Filter By Form to a query, you can use the same process as applying Filter By Form to a table. You are able to input more than one criterion using Filter By Form.

e. Click the **First Name arrow.**

A list of all available first names appears. Your name should be on the list. Figure 44 shows *Eric Cameron*, which replaced Margaret Peacock in Hands-On Exercise 1.

> **TROUBLESHOOTING:** If you do not see your name and you do see Margaret on the list, you probably skipped steps in Hands-On Exercise 1. Close the query without saving changes, return to the first Hands-On Exercise, and then rework it, making sure not to omit any steps. Then you can return to this location and work the remainder of this Hands-On Exercise.

f. Select your first name from the list.

g. Click in the first row under the Last Name field to reveal the arrow. Locate and select your last name by clicking it.

h. Scroll right until you see the Extended Price field. Click in the first row under the Extended Price field and type **<50**.

This will select all of the items that you ordered where the total was less than 50.

i. Click **Toggle Filter** in the Sort & Filter group.

You have specified which records to include and have executed the filtering by clicking Toggle Filter.

j. Click the **File tab**, click **Print**, and then click **Print Preview**.

You instructed Access to preview the filtered query results. The preview displays the query title as a heading. The current filter is applied, as well as page numbers.

k. Click **Close Print Preview** in the Close Preview group.

l. Close the Order Details Extended query. Click **Yes** when prompted to save your changes.

STEP 4 » SORT TABLE DATA

The Sales Manager is pleased with your work; however, she would like some of the information to appear in a different order. You will now sort the records in the Customers table using the manager's new criteria. Refer to Figure 45 as you complete Step 4.

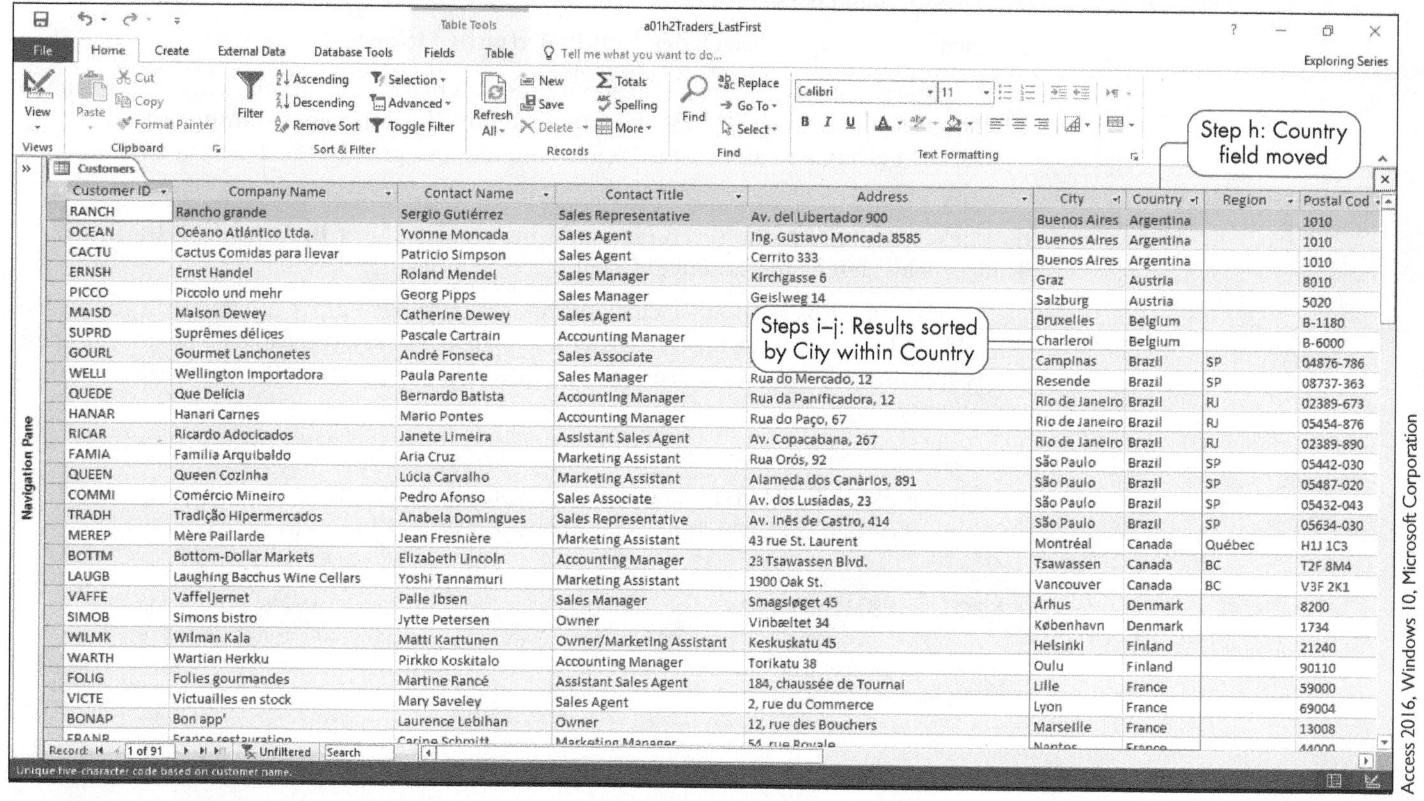

FIGURE 45 Updated Customers Table

a. Click the **Queries group** in the Navigation Pane to collapse the listed queries.

b. Click the **Tables group** in the Navigation Pane to expand the list of available tables and double-click the **Customers table** to open it.

This table contains information about customers. The table is sorted in alphabetical order by Company Name.

c. Click **Shutter Bar Open/Close** in the Navigation Pane to hide the Navigation Pane.

   It will be easier to locate fields in the Customer table if the Navigation Pane is hidden.

d. Click any entry in the Customer ID field. Click **Descending** in the Sort & Filter group on the Home tab.

   Sorting in descending order on a text field produces a reverse alphabetical order.

e. Scroll right until you can see both the Country and City fields.

f. Click the **Country column heading**.

   The entire field is selected.

g. Click the **Country column heading** again and hold down the **left mouse button**.

   A thick line displays on the left edge of the Country field.

h. Check to make sure that you see the thick line. Drag the **Country field** to the left until the thick line moves between the City and Region fields. Release the mouse button and the Country field position moves to the right of the City field.

   You moved the Country field next to the City field so that you can easily sort the table based on both fields.

i. Click any city name in the City field and click **Ascending** in the Sort & Filter group.

   The City field displays the cities in alphabetical order.

j. Click any country name in the Country field and click **Ascending**.

   The countries are sorted in alphabetical order. The cities within each country also are sorted alphabetically. For example, the customer in Graz, Austria, is listed before the customer in Salzburg, Austria.

k. Close the Customers table. Click **Yes** to save the changes to the design of the table.

l. Click **Shutter Bar Open/Close** in the Navigation Pane to show the Navigation Pane.

STEP 5 » VIEW RELATIONSHIPS

To further familiarize yourself with the database, you examine the connections between the tables in the Northwind database. Refer to Figure 46 as you complete Step 5.

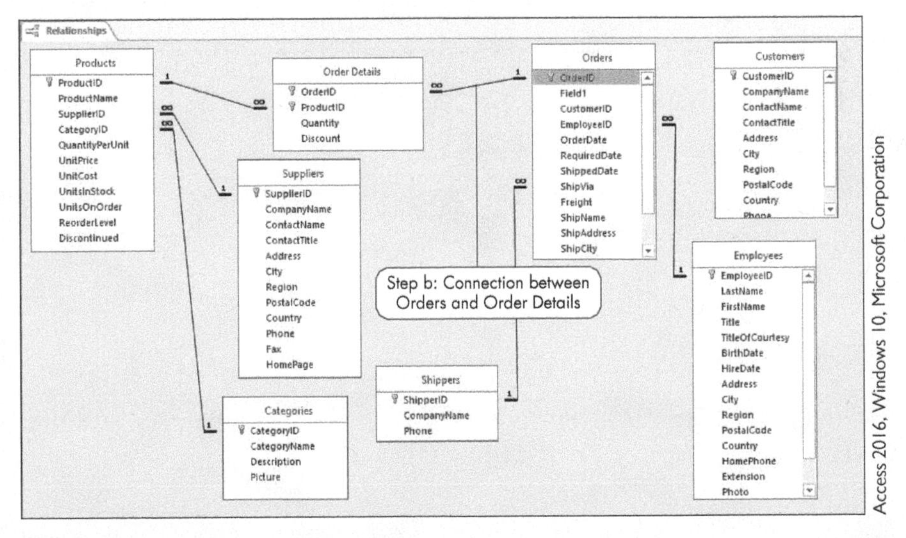

FIGURE 46 Northwind Relationships

a. Click the **Database Tools tab** and click **Relationships** in the Relationships group.

b. Examine the join lines showing the relationships that connect the various tables. For example, the Orders table is connected to the Order Details table using the OrderID field as the common field.

c. Close the Relationships.

d. Close the database. You will submit this file to your instructor at the end of the last Hands-On Exercise.

Access Database Creation

Now that you have examined the fundamentals of an Access database and explored the power of databases, it is time to create one! In this section, you explore the benefits of creating a database using each of the methods discussed in the next section.

Creating a Database

When you first start Access, Backstage view opens and provides you with three methods for creating a new database. These methods are:

- Create a blank desktop database
- Create a database from a template (note: there will be many templates shown)
- Create a custom web app

Creating a blank desktop database lets you create a database specific to your requirements. Rather than starting from scratch by creating a blank desktop database, you may want to use a template to create a new database. An Access ***template*** is a predefined database that includes professionally designed tables, forms, reports, and other objects that you can use to jumpstart the creation of your database. Creating a ***custom web app*** enables you to create a database that you can build and then use and share with others through the Web.

Figure 47 shows the options for creating a custom web app, a blank desktop database, and multiple templates from which you can select the method for which you want to create a database.

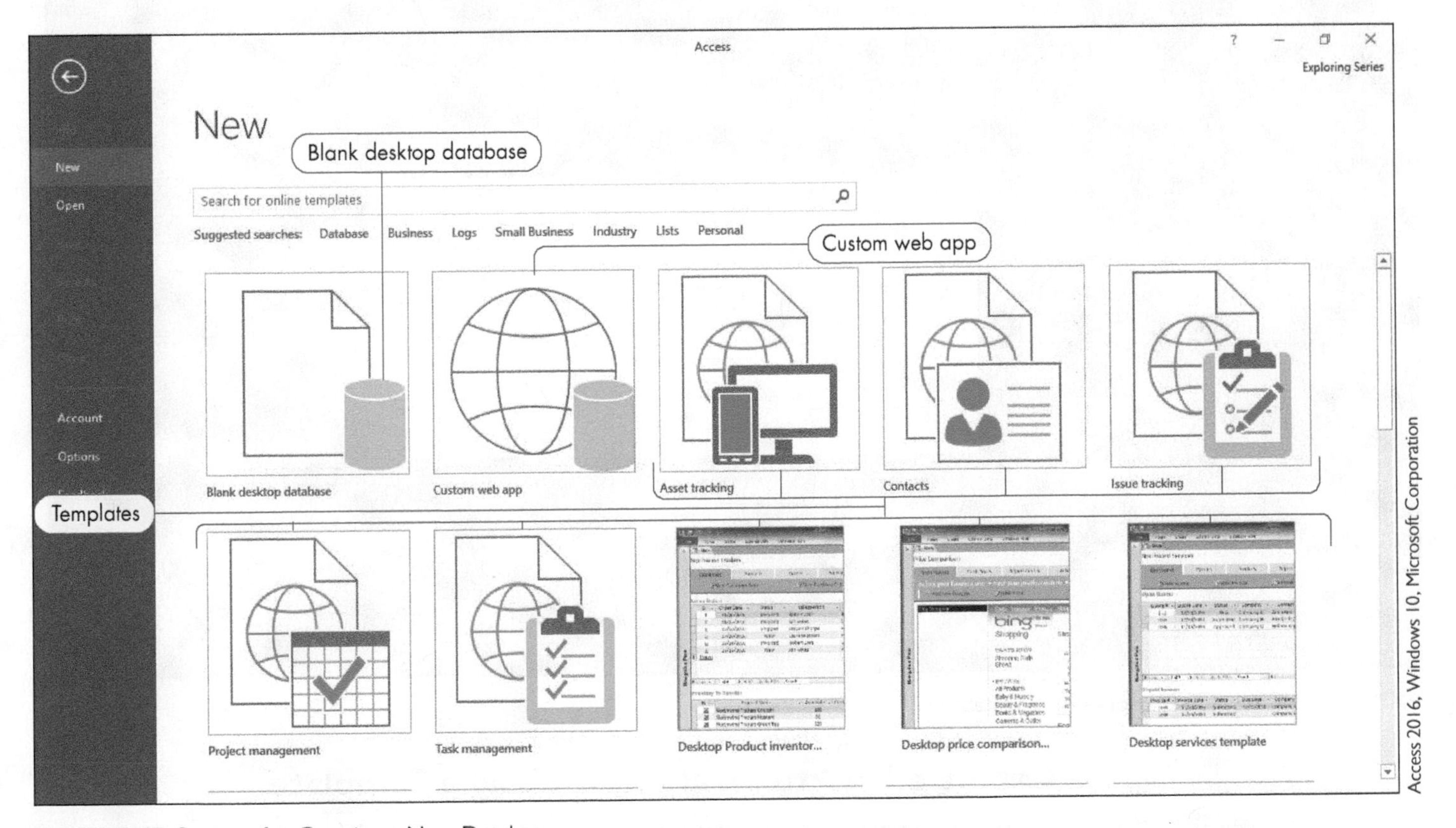

FIGURE 47 Options for Creating a New Database

Create a Blank Desktop Database

Often, if you are migrating from Excel to Access, you would start by creating a blank desktop database. At that point, you could import your existing structure and data into a new table. Another time you might use a blank desktop database is when you are starting a project and want to design your own tables.

When you create a blank desktop database, Access opens to a blank table in Datasheet view where you can add fields or data. You can also refine the table in Design view. You would then create additional tables and objects as necessary. Obviously, this task requires some level of Access knowledge, so unless you have requirements to follow, you may be better served using a template.

To create a blank desktop database, complete the following steps:

1. Open Access. (If Access is already open, click the File tab to open Backstage view and click New.)
2. Click the Blank desktop database tile.
3. Type the file name for the file in the text box, click Browse to navigate to the folder where you want to store the database file, and then click OK.
4. Click Create (see Figure 48).
5. Type data in the empty table that displays.

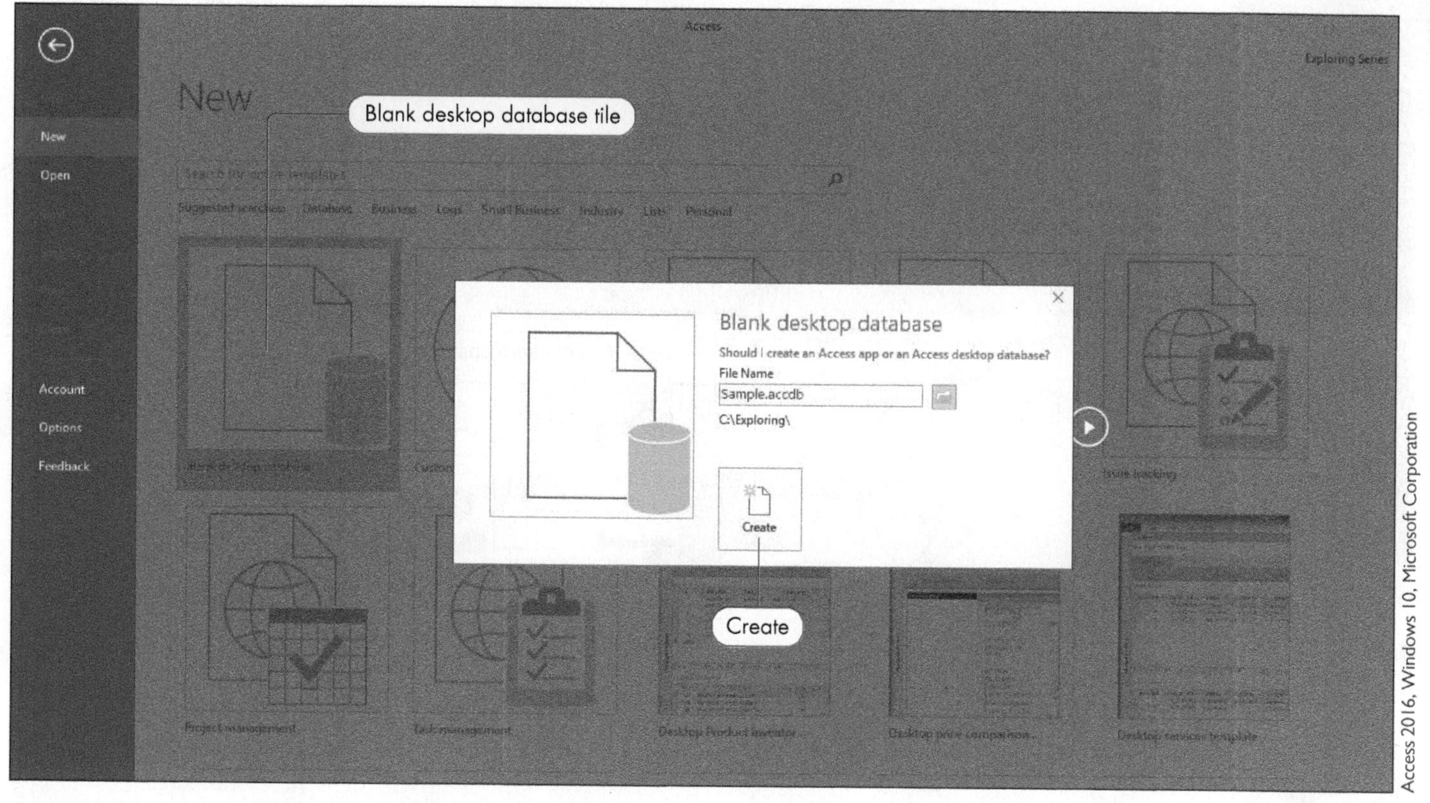

FIGURE 48 Creating a Blank Desktop Database

Create a Desktop Database Using a Template

Using a template to start a database saves you a great deal of creation time. Working with a template can also help a new Access user become familiar with database design. Templates are available from Backstage view, where you can select from a variety of templates or search online for more templates.

Access also provides templates for desktop use.

To create a desktop database from a template, complete the following steps:

1. Open Access. (If Access is already open, click the File tab to open Backstage view and click New.)
2. Click the desktop database template you want to use, or use the search box at the top of the page. Figure 49 shows some examples of templates.
3. Type the file name for the file in the text box, click Browse to navigate to the folder where you want to store the database file, and then click OK.
4. Click Create to download the template.

   The database will be created and will open.
5. Click Enable Content in the Security Warning message bar.

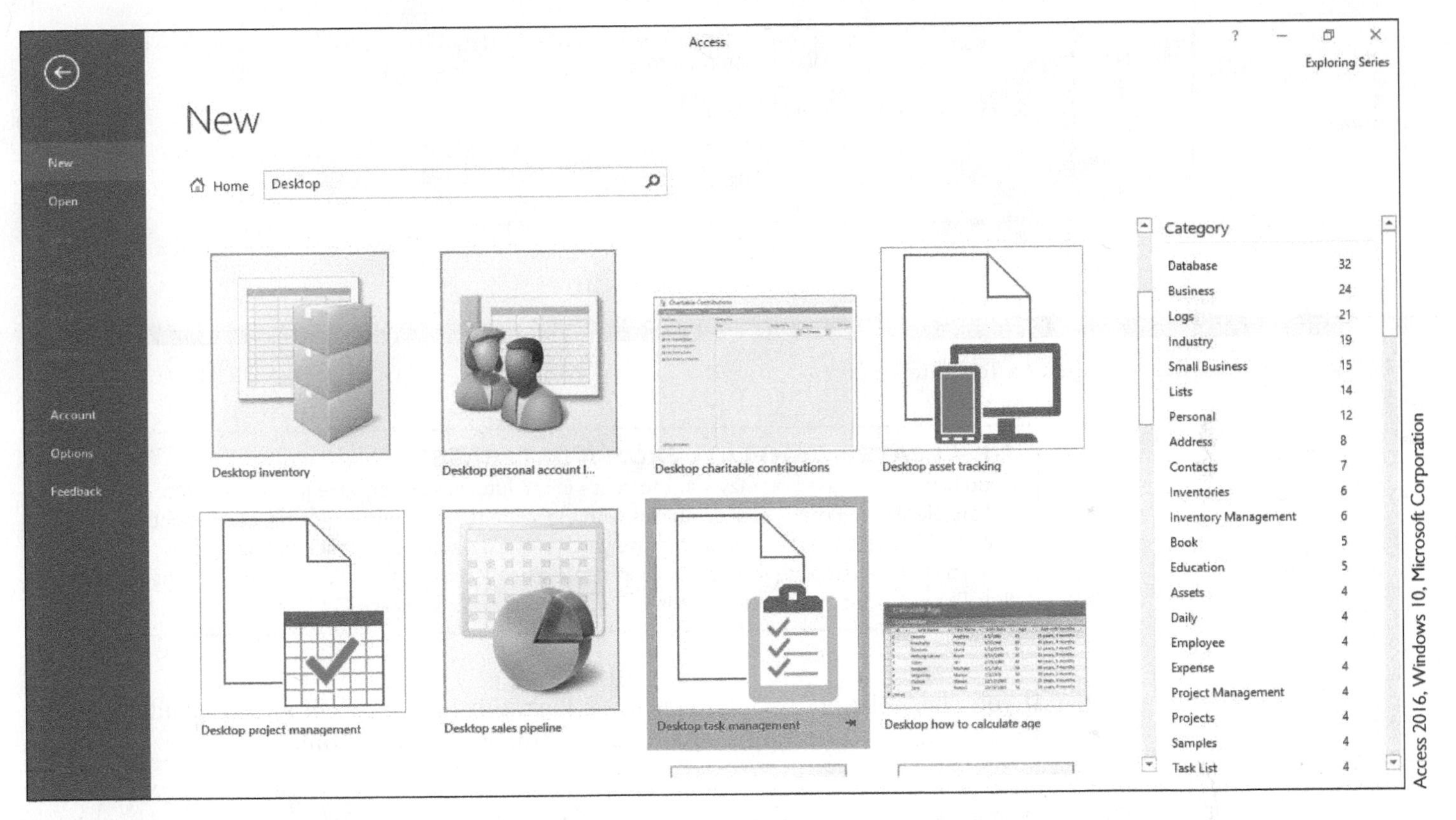

FIGURE 49 Database Templates

Once the database is open, you may see a Getting Started page that includes links you can use to learn more about the database. When finished reviewing the learning materials, close the Getting Started page to view the database. Figure 50 displays the Getting Started page included with the Desktop task management template. Notice the hyperlink to import contacts from Microsoft Outlook. If you use Outlook, this is a nice feature. Close the Getting Started page to return to the database. Because you downloaded a template, some objects will have already been created. You can work with these objects just as you did in the first three sections of this chapter. Edit any object to meet your requirements.

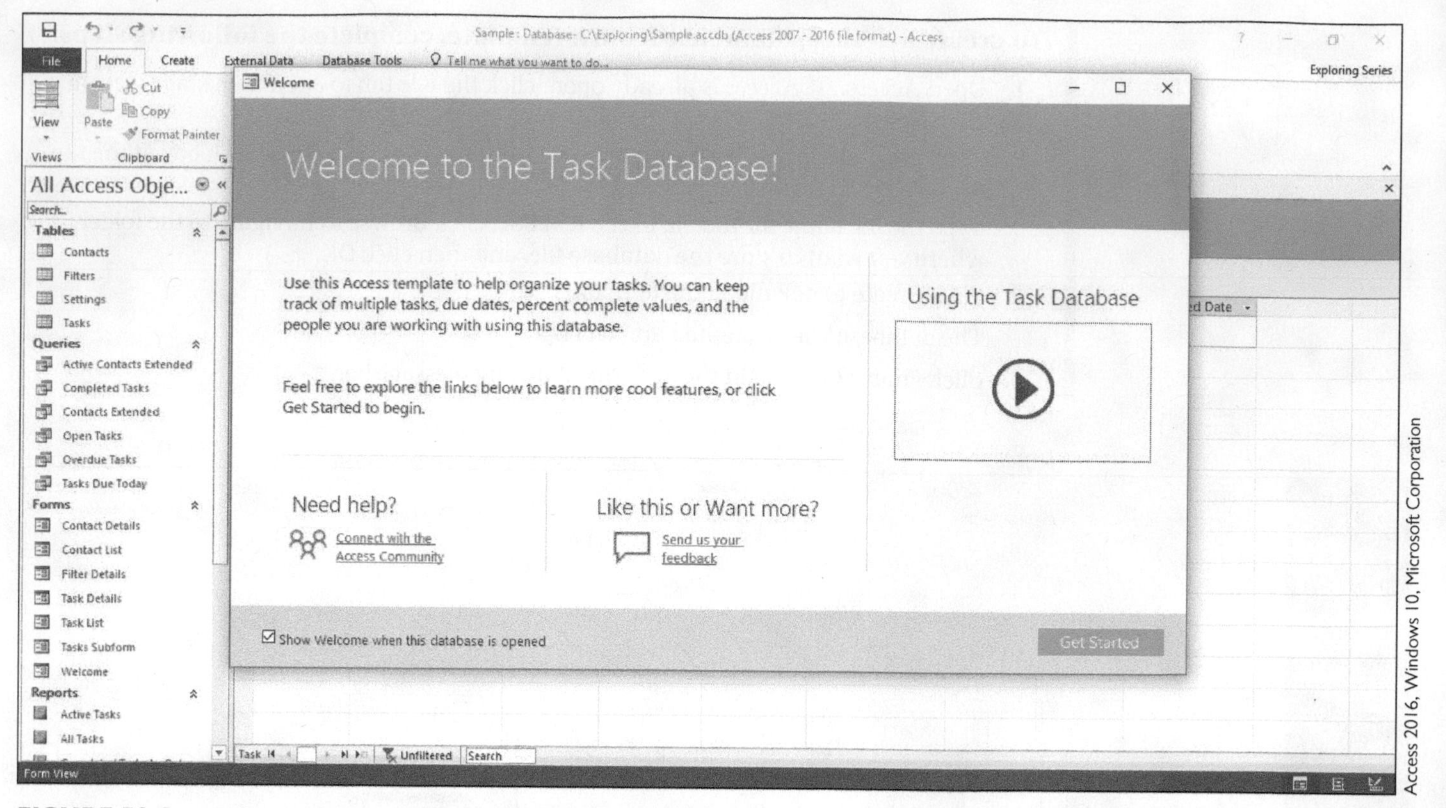

FIGURE 50 Getting Started Page for a Template

> **TIP: CREATE A TEMPLATE FROM A DATABASE**
> If you have a database you may want to reuse in the future, you can save it as a template. Doing so will enable you to create new databases with the same tables, queries, forms, and reports as the one you have created. You can also reuse parts of the database as application parts.
> To create a template from an existing database, click the File tab, click Save As, and then double-click Template. Set options such as the name and description and click OK.

If you check the option for Application Part, this template will also be available under User Templates on the Application Parts menu on the Create tab.

Add Records to a Downloaded Desktop Database

STEP 2 Once a desktop database template has been downloaded, you can use it as you would use any Access database. Figure 51 shows the Desktop Task Management template. Review the objects listed in the Navigation Pane. Once you are familiar with the database design, you can enter your data using a table or form.

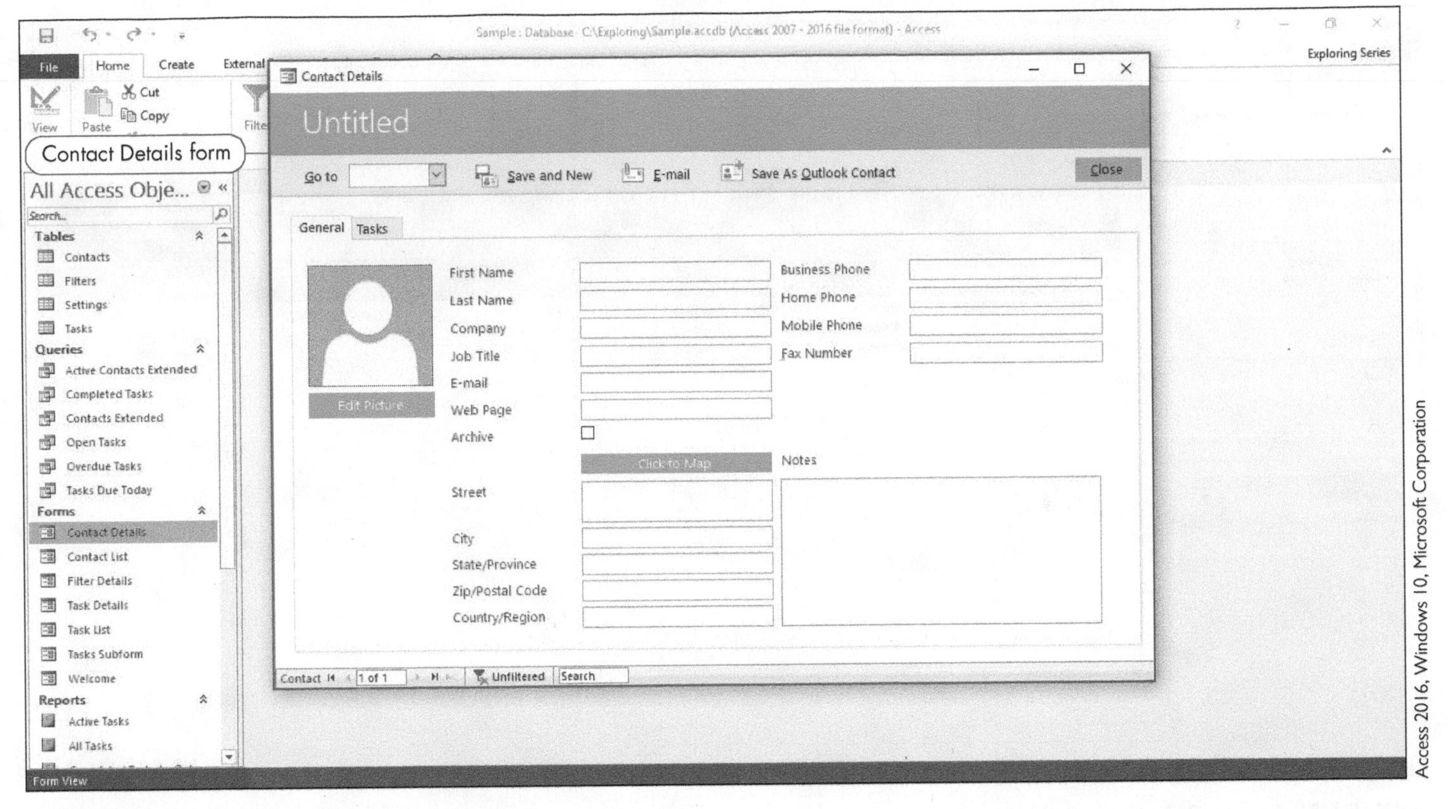

FIGURE 51 Desktop Task Management Database

Explore the Database Objects in a Downloaded Desktop Database Template

One of the reasons to use a template is so you do not have to create any of the objects. Therefore, you will notice each template comes with a varying amount of predefined queries, forms, and reports. Familiarize yourself with the unique features of a template; as they are professionally designed, they are typically well thought out.

Create a Table Using an Application Part

An ***application part*** enables you to add a set of common Access components to an existing database, such as a table, a form, and a report for a related task. These are provided by Microsoft and offer components (for example, a Contacts table) you can add to an existing database, rather than creating an entirely new database, as shown in Figure 52.

To add an application part to a database, complete the following steps:

1. Click Application Parts in the Templates group on the Create tab.
2. Select one of the options from the list.
3. Respond to the dialog boxes. For example, if you insert an Issues application part, you may be prompted to create a relationship between Issues and an existing table (such as Customers). Setting up a relationship is not required, but may be appropriate.
4. Check the Navigation Pane to verify that the new components were created.

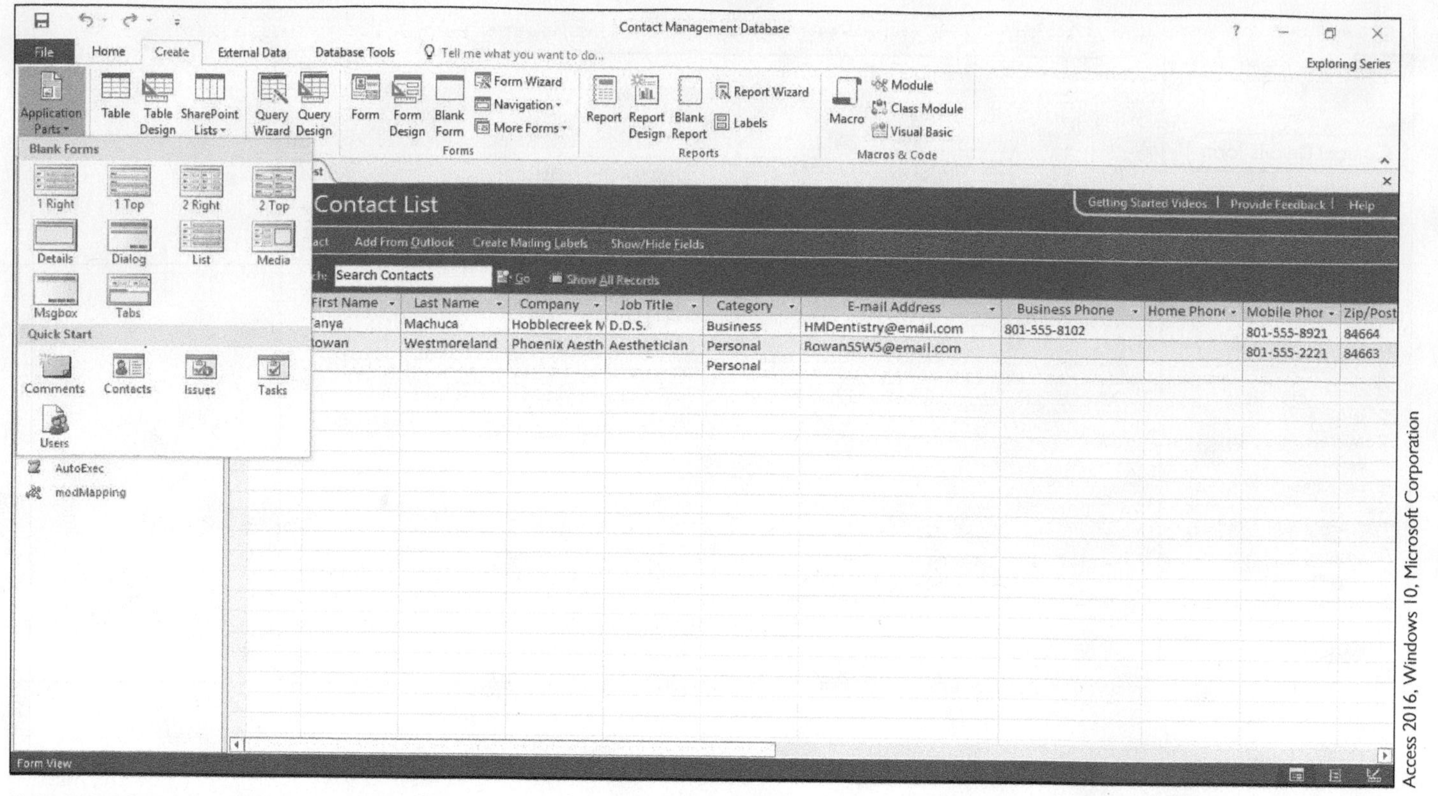

FIGURE 52 Adding an Application Part

Create a Web App Using a Template

An Access Web app (or application) is a type of database that lets you build a browser-based database app. You can create a database in the cloud that you and others can access and use simultaneously. This requires that you use a host server such as SharePoint (a Web app platform developed by Microsoft) or Office 365 (a cloud service edition of SharePoint).

Before creating a Web app, ensure that you have access to a host server. In a business environment, this would likely be set up and maintained by your Information Technology department. Your college or university may not give students access to this server. If they do, your professor can give you the information you will need.

To create a Web app using SharePoint, complete the following steps:

1. Click the File tab.
2. Click New.
3. Click Custom web app.
4. Type an App Name.
5. Input the web location (which will be provided by your company's technology professionals or by your professor, if available).
6. Click Create.
7. Create tables. This can be done manually, from a template, or from an existing data source.

In a business environment (and on the Microsoft Office Specialist examination for Access) you may need to migrate the database you have created to a SharePoint server. Doing so is similar to the Save operation covered earlier in the chapter.

To migrate an existing database to a SharePoint server, complete the following steps:

1. Click the File tab.
2. Click Save As.
3. Click SharePoint.
4. Click Save As.
5. Select the location on the SharePoint server where you wish to save your database, and click Save.

As mentioned earlier, SharePoint is typically used more in a corporate environment, so you may not have a SharePoint server available at your college or university.

9. What is a custom web app, and what is required to build a custom web app?
10. What are two benefits of using a template to create a database?
11. If you want to add a component to an existing database (such as a Contacts table), what would you use?

Hands-On Exercises

Skills covered: Create a Database Using a Template • Add Records to a Downloaded Desktop Database • Explore the Database Objects in a Downloaded Desktop Database Template

3 Access Database Creation

After working with the Northwind database on the job, you decide to use Access to create a personal contact database. Rather than start from a blank table, you use an Access Contact Manager desktop template to make your database creation simpler.

STEP 1 » CREATE A DATABASE USING A TEMPLATE

You locate an Access desktop template that you can use to create your personal contact database. This template not only allows you to store names, addresses, telephone numbers, and other information, but also lets you categorize your contacts, send email messages, and create maps of addresses. You download and save the template. Refer to Figure 53 as you complete Step 1.

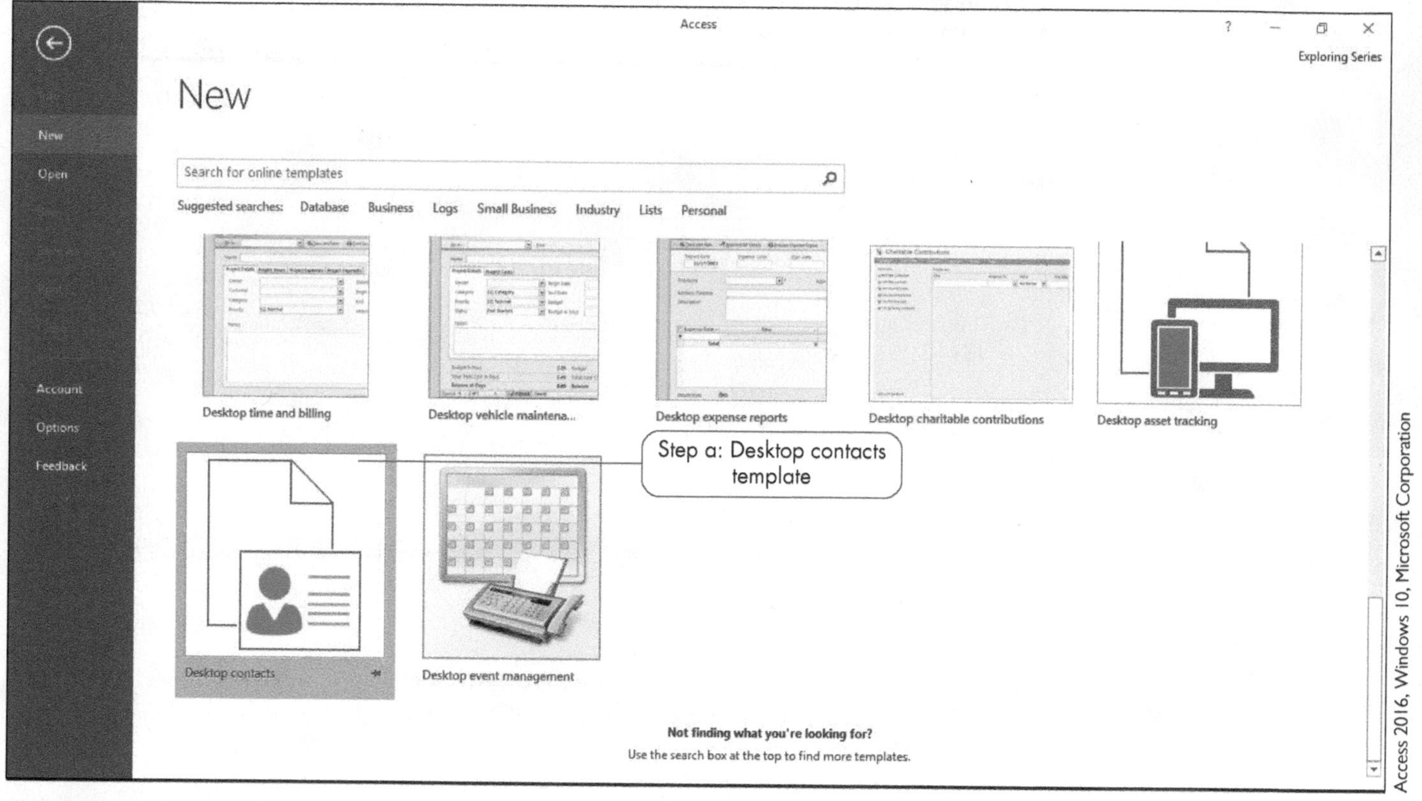

FIGURE 53 Database Templates

a. Open Access. Scroll down and click the **Desktop contacts** template tile.

> **TROUBLESHOOTING:** If the Desktop contacts template is not visible, you can use the search box at the top of the screen.

b. Click **Browse** to navigate to the folder where you are saving your files, type **a01h3Contacts_LastFirst** as the file name, and then click **OK**.

c. Click **Create** to download the template.

d. Click the *Show Getting Started when this database is opened* check box to deselect it, and close the Getting Started with Contacts page.

The database displays the Contact List form.

e. Click **Enable Content** on the Security Warning message bar.

STEP 2 » ADD RECORDS TO A DOWNLOADED DESKTOP DATABASE

Because the database opens in the Contact List form, you decide to begin by entering a contact in the form. Refer to Figure 54 as you complete Step 2.

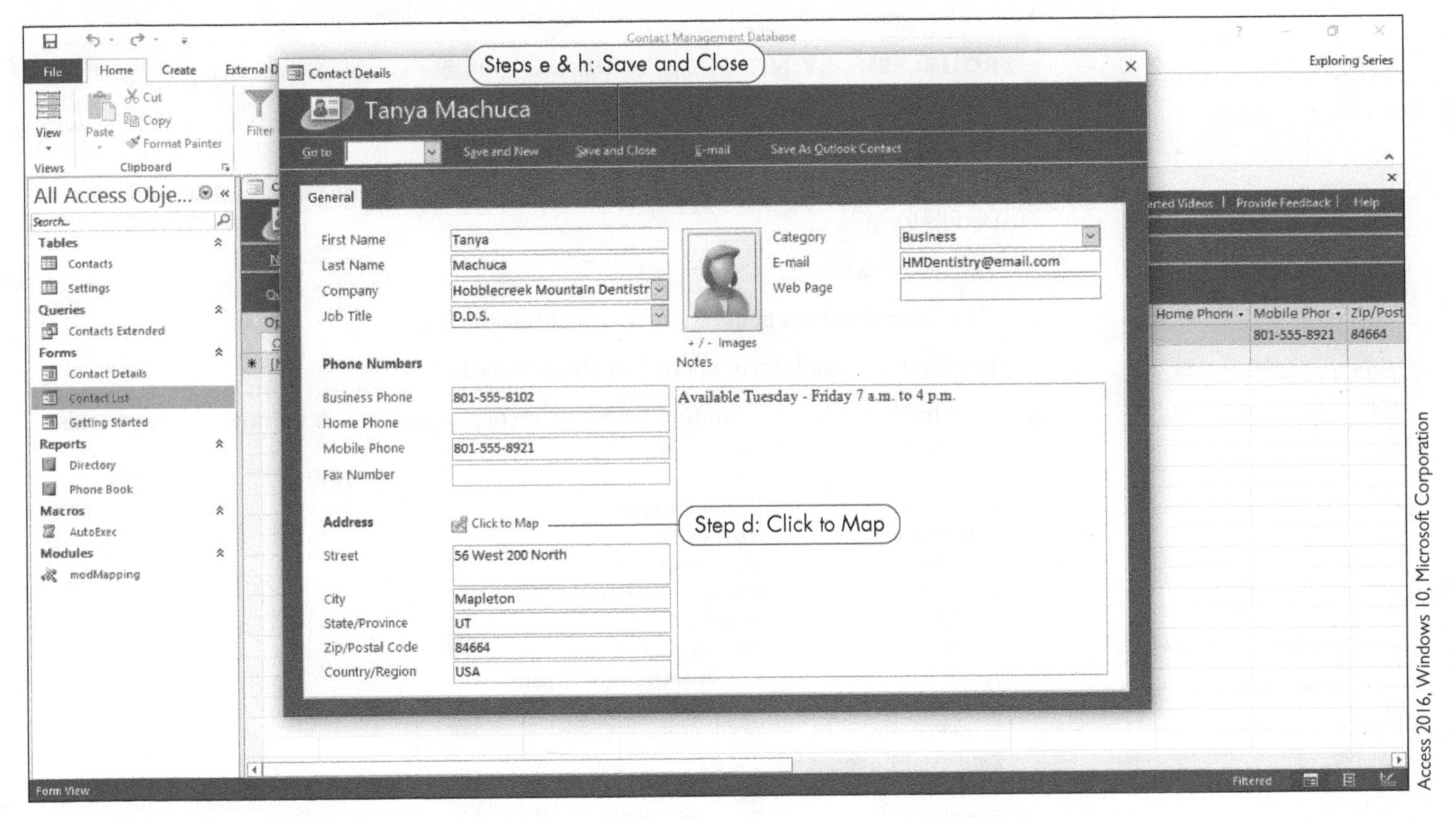

FIGURE 54 Contact Details for Tanya Machuca

a. Click in the First Name field of the first record. Type the following information, pressing **Tab** between each entry. Do not press Tab after entering the ZIP/Postal Code.

Field Name	Value to Type
First Name	**Tanya**
Last Name	**Machuca**
Company	**Hobblecreek Mountain Dentistry**
Job Title	**D.D.S.**
Category	**Business** (select from list)
E-mail	**HMDentistry@email.com**
Business Phone	**801-555-8102**
Home Phone	(leave blank)
Mobile Phone	**801-555-8921**
Zip/Postal Code	**84664**

b. Click **Open** in the first field of Dr. Machuca's record.

Open is a hyperlink to a different form in the database. The Contact Details form opens, displaying Dr. Machuca's information. More fields are available for you to use to store information. (Note that this form could also be opened from the Navigation Pane.)

c. Type the following additional information to the record:

Field Name	Value to Type
Street	**56 West 200 North**
City	**Mapleton**
State/Province	**UT**
Country/Region	**USA**
Notes	**Available Tuesday - Friday 7 a.m. to 4 p.m.**

d. Click the **Click to Map** hyperlink to view a map to Dr. Machuca's office.

Bing displays a map to the address in the record. You can get directions, locate nearby businesses, and use many other options.

> **TROUBLESHOOTING:** You may be prompted to choose an application. Select any Web browser such as Microsoft Edge from the list.

e. Close the map. Click **Save and Close** in the top center of the form to close the Contact Details form.

The record is saved.

f. Click **New Contact** beneath the Contact List title bar.

The Contact Details form opens to a blank record.

g. Type the following information for a new record, pressing **Tab** to move between fields. Some fields will be blank.

Field Name	Value to Type
First Name	**Rowan**
Last Name	**Westmoreland**
Company	**Phoenix Aesthetics**
Job Title	**Aesthetician**
Mobile Phone	**801-555-2221**
Street	**425 North Main Street**
City	**Springville**
State/Province	**UT**
Zip/Postal Code	**84663**
Category	**Personal**
E-mail	**Rowan55W5@email.com**
Notes	**Recommended by Michelle**

h. Click **Save and Close**.

STEP 3 » EXPLORE THE DATABASE OBJECTS IN A DOWNLOADED DESKTOP DATABASE TEMPLATE

You explore the objects created by the template so that you understand the organization of the database. Refer to Figure 55 as you complete Step 3.

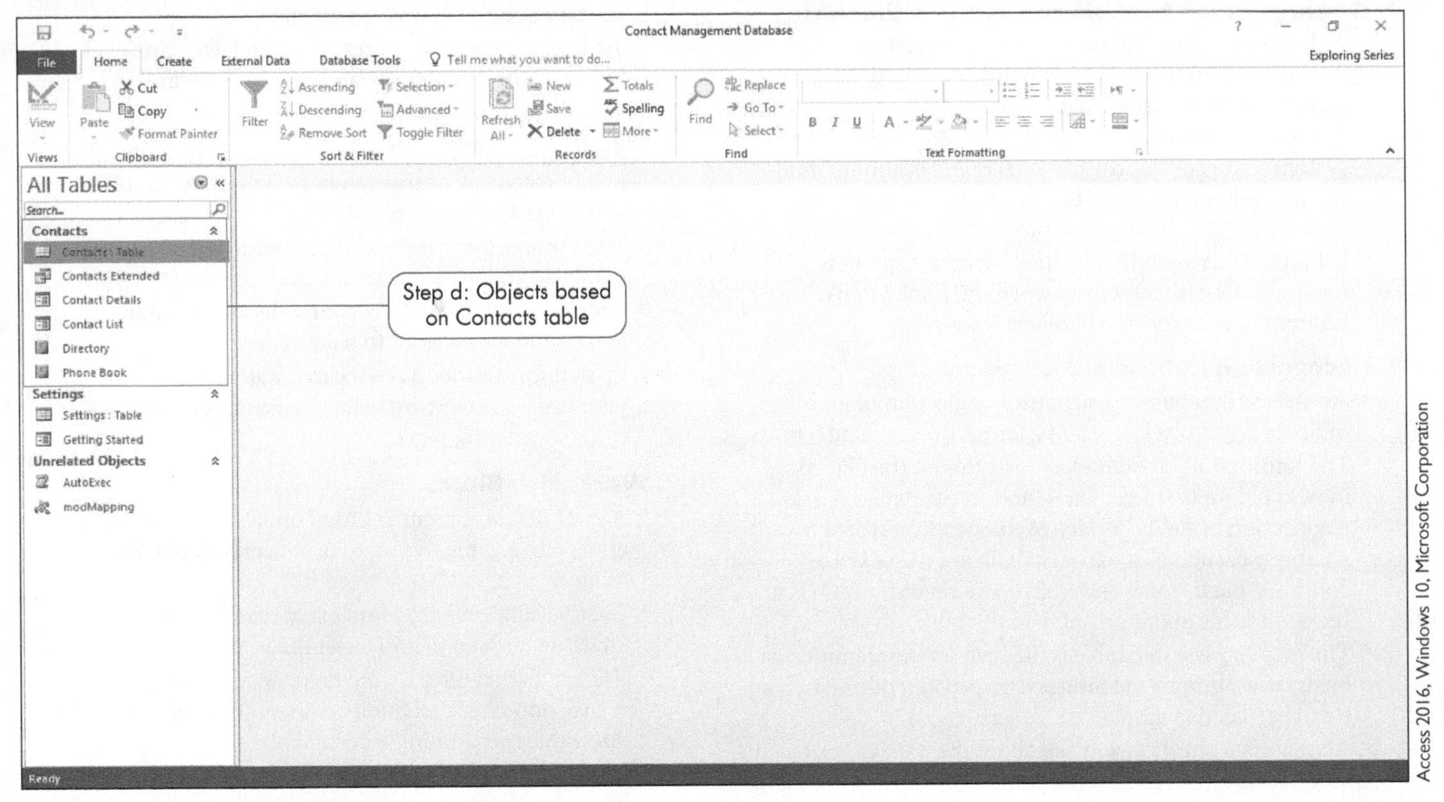

FIGURE 55 Tables and Related Views

a. Double-click the **Contacts table** in the Navigation Pane.

The information you entered using the Contact List form and the Contact Details form displays in the Contacts table.

b. Double-click the **Phone Book report** in the Navigation Pane.

The Phone Book report opens displaying the contact name and phone information organized by category.

c. Double-click the **Directory report** in the Navigation Pane.

The Directory report opens, displaying a full alphabetical contact list. The Directory report was designed to display more fields than the Phone Book, but it is not organized by category.

d. Click **All Access Objects** on the Navigation Pane and select **Tables and Related Views**.

You can now see the objects that are based on the Contacts table.

e. Right-click the **Directory report tab** and select **Close All**.

f. Close the database and exit Access. Based on your instructor's directions, submit the following:

a01h1Traders_LastFirst_*CurrentDate*

a01h2Traders_LastFirst

a01h3Contacts_LastFirst

Chapter Objectives Review

After reading this chapter, you have accomplished the following objectives:

1. Open, save, and enable content in a database.
- A database is a collection of data organized as meaningful information that can be accessed, managed, stored, queried, sorted, and reported.
- A database management system (DBMS) is a software system that provides the tools to create, maintain, and use a database. Access is the database management system found in business versions of Microsoft Office.
- When a database is first opened, Access displays a message bar with a security warning. Click Enable Content if you trust the database's source.

2. Recognize database object types.
- An Access database is a structured collection of four major types of objects—tables, forms, queries, and reports.
- The foundation of a database is its tables, the objects in which data is stored. Each table in the database has a collection of fields (a piece of information stored in a database, such as a name), which are displayed as columns. Each row is referred to as a record, which is a set of all fields about an entry in the table.
- The primary key in a table is the field (or combination of fields) that uniquely identifies a record in a table (such as a driver's license number).
- A query is a question you ask about the data in your database.
- A form enables simplified entry and modification of data.
- A report contains professional-looking formatted information from underlying tables or queries.
- Examine the Access interface: Objects are organized and listed in the Navigation Pane. Access also uses a Tabbed Documents interface in which each object that is open has its own tab.
- Explore table Datasheet view: Datasheet view is a grid containing fields (columns) and records (rows).
- Navigate through records: Navigation arrows enable you to move through records, with arrows for the first, previous, next, and last records, as well as one to add a new record.
- Explore table Design view: Design view gives you a detailed view of the table's structure and is used to create and modify a table's design by specifying the fields it will contain, the fields' data types, and their associated properties.
- Rename and describe tables: Tables can be renamed as necessary and a description can be added. The description gives the user more information about what an object does.

3. Modify data in table Datasheet view.
- Access works primarily from storage. Records can be added, modified, or deleted in the database, and as the information is entered, it is automatically saved. Undo cannot reverse edits made to multiple records.

4. Add records to a table.
- A pencil symbol displays in the record selector box to indicate when you are in editing mode. Moving to another record saves the changes.

5. Delete records from a table.
- To delete a record, click the record selector and click Delete in the Records group on the Home tab.

6. Use database utilities.
- Back up a database: The Back Up Database utility creates a duplicate copy of the database. This may enable users to recover from failure.
- The Compact and Repair utility reduces the size of a database and fixes any errors that may exist in the file.
- Encrypt a database: Encrypting databases enables you to add a password to a database.
- Print information: Access can create a print copy of your data. Previewing before printing is a good practice to avoid wasting paper.

7. Work with filters.
- A filter displays records based on a set of criteria that is applied to a table to display a subset of records in that table.
- Use a selection filter to find exact matches: A selection filter can be used to find exact matches.
- Use a selection filter to find records containing a value: A selection filter can find partial matches, for example, find values containing a certain phrase.
- Use filter by form: Filter By Form displays records based on multiple criteria and enables the user to apply logical operators and use comparison operators.

8. Perform sorts.
- Sort table data: Sorting changes the order of information, and information may be sorted by one or more fields.
- Data can be sorted ascending (low to high) or descending (high to low).

9. Create a database.
- Creating a blank desktop database: Creating a blank desktop database enables you to create a database specific to your requirements.
- Create a desktop database using a template: A template is a predefined database that includes professionally designed tables, forms, reports, and other objects that you can use to jumpstart the creation of your database.
- Add records to a downloaded desktop database: Once a database has been created, it can be used as any other database is.
- Explore the database objects in a downloaded database template: Once you create a database using a template, explore it and become familiar with the contents.
- Create a table using an application part: If you require a certain type of table (such as Contacts) you can add them using an application part.
- Create a Web app using a template: Creating a custom web app enables you to create a database that you can build and use and share with others through the Web.

Key Terms Matching

Match the key terms with their definitions. Write the key term letter by the appropriate numbered definition.

a. Application part
b. Database
c. Database Management System (DBMS)
d. Datasheet view
e. Design view
f. Field
g. Filter
h. Filter By Form
i. Form
j. Navigation Pane
k. Object
l. Primary key
m. Query
n. Record
o. Relationship
p. Report
q. Selection filter
r. Sort
s. Table
t. Template

1. ______ A filtering method that displays only records that match selected criteria.

2. ______ A filtering method that displays records based on multiple criteria.

3. ______ A main component that is created and used to make a database function, such as a table or form.

4. ______ A method of listing records in a specific sequence (such as alphabetically).

5. ______ A predefined database that includes professionally designed tables, forms, reports, and other objects.

6. ______ A question you ask about the data in your database.

7. ______ An Access interface element that organizes and lists database objects in a database.

8. ______ An Access object that simplifies entering, modifying, and deleting table data.

9. ______ A set of common Access components that can be added to an existing database.

10. ______ An object that contains professional-looking formatted information from underlying tables or queries.

11. ______ An object used to store data, organizing data into columns and rows.

12. ______ Complete set of all the fields about one person, place, event, or concept.

13. ______ The field (or combination of fields) that uniquely identifies each record in a table.

14. ______ View that enables you to create and modify a table design.

15. ______ A collection of data organized as meaningful information that can be accessed, managed, stored, queried, sorted, and reported.

16. ______ A connection between two tables using a common field.

17. ______ A grid that enables you to add, edit, and delete the records of a table.

18. ______ A piece of information stored in a table, such as a company name or city.

19. ______ A software system that provides the tools needed to create, maintain, and use a database.

20. ______ Enables you to specify conditions to display only those records that meet certain conditions.

Multiple Choice

1. Which of the following is an example of an Access object?

(a) Database
(b) Field
(c) Form
(d) Record

2. Where is data in a database stored?

(a) Form
(b) Query
(c) Report
(d) Table

3. You edit several records in an Access table. When should you execute the Save command?

(a) Immediately after you edit a record
(b) Once at the end of the session
(c) Records are saved automatically; the save command is not required
(d) When you close the table

4. Which of the following is *not* true of an Access database?

(a) Each field has a data type that establishes the kind of data that can be entered.
(b) Every record in a table has the same fields as every other record.
(c) Every table in a database contains the same number of records as every other table.
(d) A primary key uniquely identifies a record.

5. Which of the following is true regarding table views?

(a) You can add, edit, and delete records using Design view.
(b) Datasheet view shows a detailed view of the table design.
(c) Datasheet view provides access to more field properties than Design view.
(d) Changes made in Datasheet view are automatically saved when you move the insertion point to a different record.

6. Which of the following utilities is used to recover in the event of loss or damage?

(a) Back Up Database
(b) Compact and Repair Database
(c) Database Splitter
(d) Encrypt Database

7. Which of the following would be matched if you use a Selection filter's exact match option for the name Ann?

(a) Ann, ANN, and ann
(b) Danny, Ann, and Anny
(c) Ann (but not ANN)
(d) Both a and b

8. Which of the following conditions is available through a Selection filter?

(a) Equal condition
(b) Delete condition
(c) AND condition
(d) OR condition

9. All of the following statements are true about creating a database *except*:

(a) Creating a custom web app requires that you use a server (such as SharePoint).
(b) When creating a blank desktop database, Access opens to a blank table in Datasheet view.
(c) Using a template to create a database saves time because it includes predefined objects.
(d) The objects provided in a template cannot be modified.

10. To add a predefined table to an existing database, you should use which of the following?

(a) Application part
(b) Blank desktop database
(c) Custom web app
(d) Database template

Practice Exercises

1 Replacement Parts

As a recent hire at Replacement Parts, you are tasked with performing updates to the customer database. You have been asked to open the company's database, save it with a new name, and then modify, add, and delete records. You will then back up the database, apply filters and sorts, and use an application part to add a new table that will be used to track customer shipping and receiving complaints. Refer to Figure 56 as you complete the exercise.

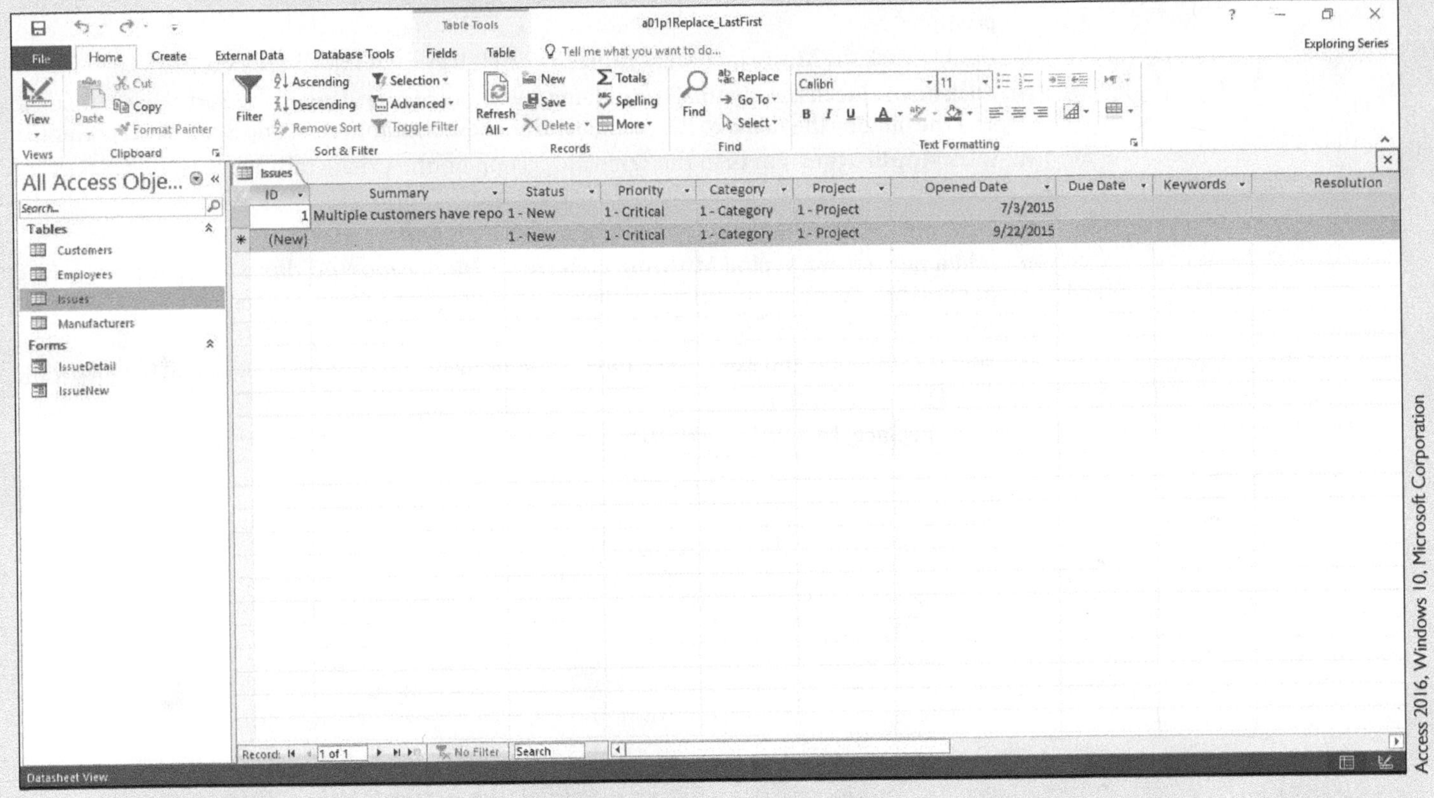

Access 2016, Windows 10, Microsoft Corporation

FIGURE 56 Issues Table Added to Replacement Parts Database

a. Open the *a01p1Replace* file. Save the database as **a01p1Replace_LastFirst**. Click **Enable Content** on the message bar.

b. Double-click the **Manufacturers table** to open the table in Datasheet view. Locate record 800552 (Haas). Change the name to **Haas International** and the CountyOfOrigin to **Austria**.

c. Type the following new records:

MfgID	ManufacturerName	CountryOfOrigin	EmployeeID
801411	Bolshoy Fine China	Russia	817080
801422	Tejada and Sons	Dominican Republic	816680
801433	Lubitz UK	England	817580

d. Delete record **800661** (John Bradshaw).

e. Close the Manufacturers table.

f. Click the **File tab**, click **Save As**, and then double-click **Back Up Database**. Accept the default backup file name and click **Save**.

g. Double-click the **Customers table** to open the table in Datasheet view.

h. Click the **State field** for the first record (Diego Martinez). Click **Selection** in the Sort & Filter group, and then click **Equals "OR"** to display the two customers in Oregon. Close the table, selecting **Save** when prompted.

i. Double-click the **Employees table** to open the table in Datasheet view.

j. Click the **plus sign** ⊞ next to Alfonso Torres. Notice he is assigned as the representative for the manufacturer Antarah.

   This information is available due to the relationship already created in the database between Employees and Manufacturers.

k. Click **Advanced** in the Sort & Filter group on the Home tab, and select **Filter By Form.** Click in the Salary field. Type **>60000** and click **Toggle Filter** in the Sort & Filter group on the Home tab to apply the filter. Six employees are displayed. Close the table, selecting **Save** when prompted.

l. Double-click the **Manufacturers table** to open the table in Datasheet view.

m. Click any value in the Manufacturer Name field. Click **Ascending** in the Sort & Filter group to sort the table by the name of the manufacturer. Close the table, selecting **Save** when prompted.

n. Click **Application Parts** in the Templates group on the Create tab. Select **Issues**. Select the option for "There is no relationship." Click **Create**.

o. Double-click the **Issues table** to open the table in Datasheet view.

p. Add a new record, typing **Multiple customers have reported damaged goods received in Denton, Texas.** in the Summary field. Leave all other fields as the default values. Compare your results to Figure 56.

q. Close the database and exit Access. Based on your instructor's directions, submit the following:

   a01p1Replace_LastFirst

   a01p1Replace_LastFirst_*CurrentDate*

2 Custom Coffee

The Custom Coffee Company provides coffee, tea, and snacks to offices in Miami. Custom Coffee also provides and maintains the equipment for brewing the beverages. To improve customer service, the owner recently had an Access database created to keep track of customers, orders, and products. This database will replace the Excel spreadsheets currently maintained by the office manager. The company hired you to verify and input all the Excel data into the Access database. Refer to Figure 57 as you complete the exercise.

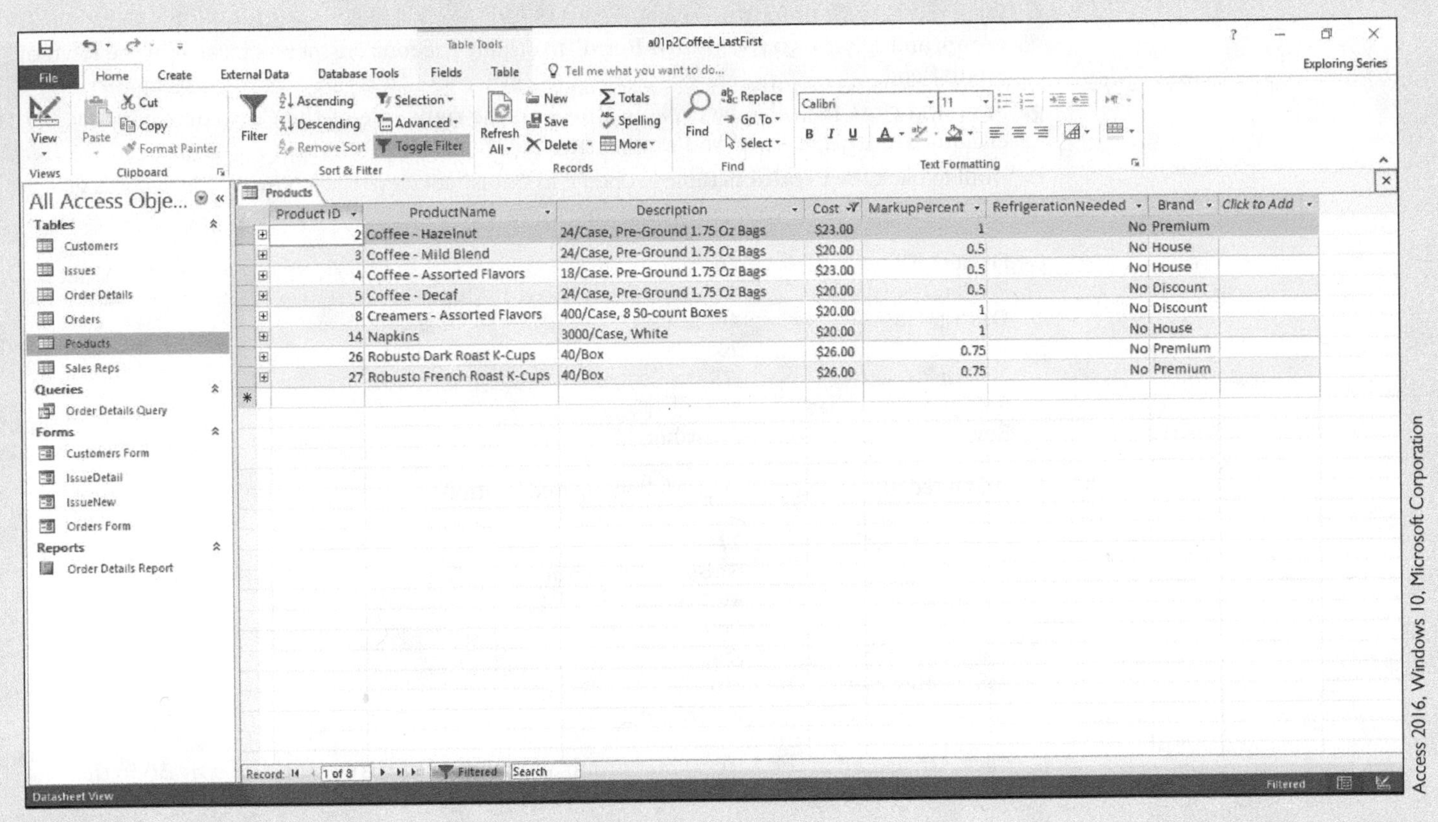

Product ID	ProductName	Description	Cost	MarkupPercent	RefrigerationNeeded	Brand
2	Coffee - Hazelnut	24/Case, Pre-Ground 1.75 Oz Bags	$23.00	1	No	Premium
3	Coffee - Mild Blend	24/Case, Pre-Ground 1.75 Oz Bags	$20.00	0.5	No	House
4	Coffee - Assorted Flavors	18/Case. Pre-Ground 1.75 Oz Bags	$23.00	0.5	No	House
5	Coffee - Decaf	24/Case, Pre-Ground 1.75 Oz Bags	$20.00	0.5	No	Discount
8	Creamers - Assorted Flavors	400/Case, 8 50-count Boxes	$20.00	1	No	Discount
14	Napkins	3000/Case, White	$20.00	1	No	House
26	Robusto Dark Roast K-Cups	40/Box	$26.00	0.75	No	Premium
27	Robusto French Roast K-Cups	40/Box	$26.00	0.75	No	Premium

FIGURE 57 Filtered Products Table

a. Open the *a01p2Coffee* file and save the database as **a01p2Coffee_LastFirst**. Click **Enable Content** on the message bar.

b. Click the **Database Tools tab** and click **Relationships** in the Relationships group. Review the table relationships. Notice the join line between the Customers and Orders tables.

c. Click **Close** in the Relationships group.

d. Double-click the **Sales Reps table** to open it in Datasheet view. For rep number 2, replace **YourFirstName** and **YourLastName** with your first and last names. For example, as the Access author, I would type *Eric* in place of YourFirstName and *Cameron* in place of YourLastName. Close the table by clicking **Close** on the right side of the Sales Reps window.

e. Double-click the **Customers table** to open it in Datasheet view. Click **New** in the Records group. Add a new record by typing the following information; press **Tab** after each field:

Customer Name:	**Bavaro Driving School**
Contact:	**Ricky Watters**
Address1:	**1 Clausen Way**
Address2:	**Floor 2**
City:	**South Bend**

State:	**IN**
Zip Code:	**46614**
Phone:	**(857) 519-6661**
Credit Rating:	**A**
Sales Rep ID:	**2**

Notice the pencil symbol in the record selector for the new row. This symbol indicates the new record has not been saved. Press **Tab**. The pencil symbol disappears, and the new customer is automatically saved to the table.

f. Click the **City field** for the second record (South Bend). Click **Selection** in the Sort & Filter group, and select **Equals "South Bend"** to display the four customers located in the town of South Bend.

g. Save and close the table by clicking **Close** on the right side of the Customers window, and clicking **Yes** when asked if you want to save the changes.

h. Double-click the **Products** table to open it in Datasheet view. Click **New** in the Records group. Add a new record by typing the following information:

Product ID:	**26**
ProductName:	**Robusto Dark Roast K-Cups**
Description:	**40/Box**
Cost:	**26**
MarkupPercent:	**.75**
RefrigerationNeeded	**No**
Brand	**Premium**

i. Add a second product using the following information:

Product ID:	**27**
ProductName:	**Robusto French Roast K-Cups**
Description:	**40/Box**
Cost:	**26**
MarkupPercent:	**.75**
RefrigerationNeeded	**No**
Brand	**Premium**

j. Click **Advanced** in the Sort & Filter group and select **Filter By Form**. Type **>=20** in the Cost field and click **Toggle Filter** in the Sort & Filter group.

All products costing $20 or more (there will be 8) display. See Figure 57.

k. Save and close the table by clicking **Close** on the right side of the Products window, and clicking Yes when asked if you want to save the changes.

l. Click the **File tab**, click **Save As**, and then double-click **Back Up Database**. Accept the default backup file name and click **Save.**

m. Click **Application Parts** in the Templates group of the Create tab. Select **Issues**. Click **Next** to accept the default relationship. Select **CustomerName** as the Field from 'Customers', select **Sort Ascending** from Sort this field, and then type **Customer** as the name for the lookup column. Click Create.

n. Double-click the **Issues table** to open it in Datasheet view.

o. Select **Advantage Sales** for the Customer and type **Customer reports hazelnut coffee delivered instead of decaf.** in the Summary field. Leave all other fields as the default values.

p. Close the database and exit Access. Based on your instructor's directions, submit the following:

a01p2Coffee_LastFirst

a01p2Coffee_LastFirst_*CurrentDate*

3 Healthy Living

FROM SCRATCH

You and two friends from your gym have decided to use Access to help you reach your weight goals. You decide to use the Access Nutrition template to help you get organized. Refer to Figure 58 as you complete this exercise.

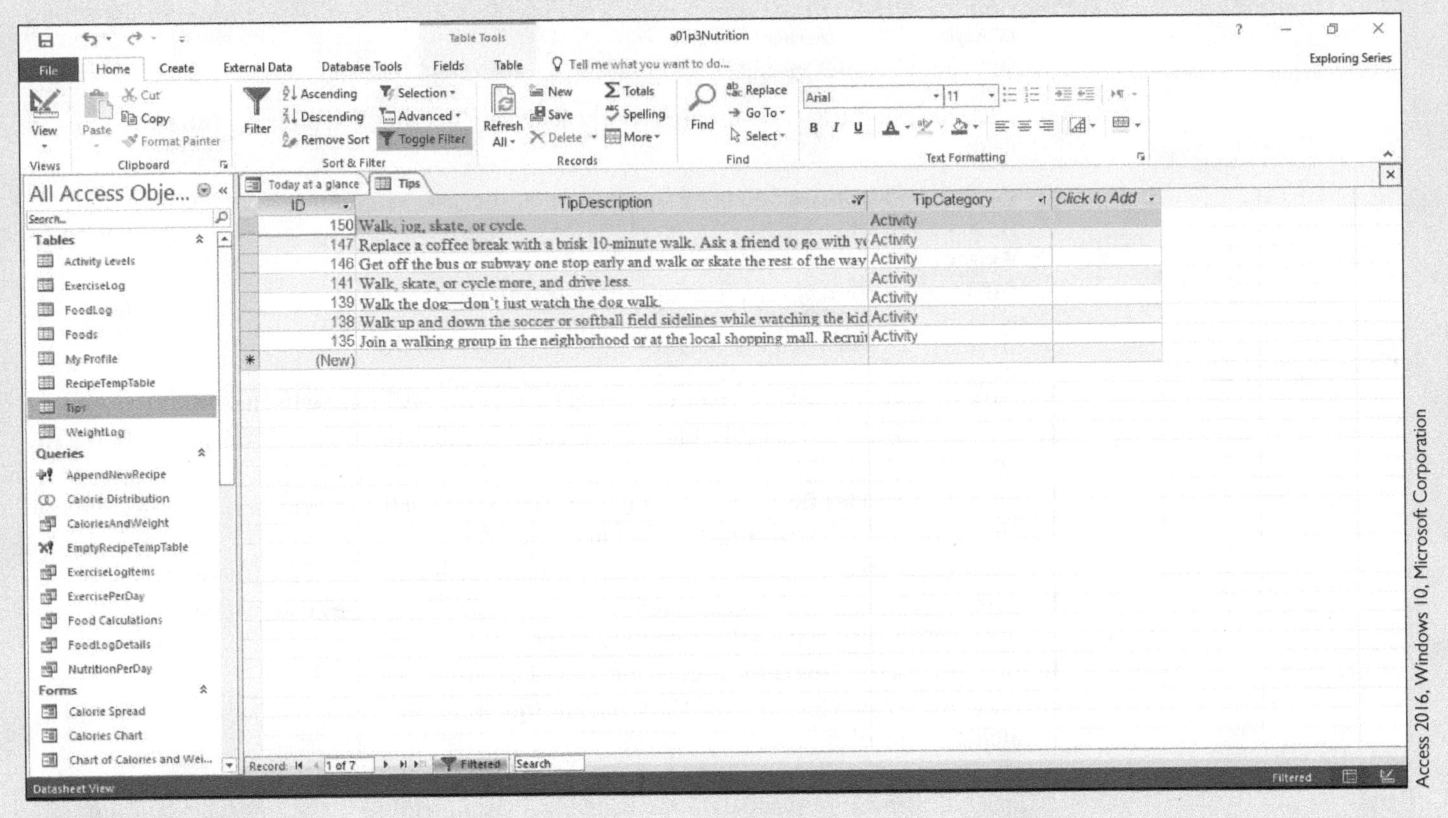

Access 2016, Windows 10, Microsoft Corporation

FIGURE 58 Filtered Tips Table

a. Open Access and click the **Desktop Nutrition tracking** template in Backstage view.

b. Type **a01p3Nutrition_LastFirst** in the File name box. Click **Browse**. Navigate to the location where you are saving your files in the File New Database dialog box, click **OK** to close the dialog box, and then click **Create** to create the new database.

c. Click **Enable Content** on the message bar. Double-click the **My Profile** table in the Navigation Pane to open it in Datasheet view.

d. Delete the existing record.

e. Type the following information in as a new record, pressing **Tab** between each field:

Sex:	**Male**
Height:	**64**
Weight:	**190**
Age:	**48**
Lifestyle:	**Lightly Active**
Goal:	**Lose weight**

f. Click **New** in the Records group. Type the following information, pressing **Tab** between each field:

Sex:	**Male**
Height:	**69**
Weight:	**140**
Age:	**45**
Lifestyle:	**Moderately Active**
Goal:	**Gain weight**

g. Click **New** in the Records group. Type the following information, pressing **Tab** between each field:

Sex:	**Female**
Height:	**66**
Weight:	**140**
Age:	**40**
Lifestyle:	**Moderately Active**
Goal:	**Maintain my weight**

h. Close the table by clicking **Close** on the right side of the My Profile window.

i. Double-click the **Foods table**. Click **Advanced** in the Records group and then select **Filter By Form**.

j. Click the **Calories field** for the first record. Type **<200** in the Calories field and **>=15** in the Fiber [grams] field. Click **Toggle Filter** in the Sort & Filter group.

   You will have a list of all high = fiber, low = calorie foods in the database (there are three).

k. Save and close the table by clicking **Close** on the right side of the Foods window, and clicking **Yes** when asked if you want to save the changes.

l. Double-click the **Tips table** to open it in Datasheet view.

m. Click in the first **TipCategory**. Click **Ascending** in the Sort & Filter group to sort the tips in alphabetical order.

n. Highlight the word **Walk** in the fifth record (ID #138). Make sure you do not highlight the space after the word Walk when you highlight. Click **Selection** in the Sort & Filter group, and select **Contains "Walk"**.

   Seven tips appear that contain the word walk. See Figure 58.

o. Save and close the table by clicking **Close** on the right side of the Tips window, and clicking **Yes** when asked if you want to save the changes.

p. Click the **File tab**, click **Save As**, and then double-click **Back Up Database**. Use the default backup file name.

q. Close the database and exit Access. Based on your instructor's directions, submit the following:

   a01p3Nutrition_LastFirst

   a01p3Nutrition _LastFirst_*CurrentDate*

Mid-Level Exercises

1 Sunshine Mental Health Services

Sunshine Mental Health Services provides counseling and medication services. They have recently expanded their database to include patients in addition to the staff. You were hired to replace their former Information Technology support staff member. You will work to update the data in the database, familiarize yourself with the table relationships, filter and sort a table, and add a table to keep track of user accounts.

a. Open the *a01m1Sunshine* file and save the database as **a01m1Sunshine_LastFirst**. Click **Enable Content** on the Security Warning message bar.

b. Open the **Staff table** in Datasheet view.

c. Locate the record for Kovit Ang (StaffID 80073). Replace his Address with **11 Market Street**, replace his City with **Harrison**, and his ZIPCode with **04040**. Leave all other fields with their current values.

d. Add yourself as a new staff member. Type a StaffID of **99999** and type your name in the FullName field. Type **1 Clinton Terrace** for your Address, **Harrison** as your City, **ME** as your State, and **04040** as your ZIP. Type a JobCode of **300**, a Salary of **48500**, and a 401k contribution of **0.02**. Click the box in the Active field so a check box appears in the box.

e. Delete record **80399** (Stan Marsh).

f. Sort the table by Salary in descending order. Save and close the table.

g. Click **Relationships** in the Relationships group on the Database Tools tab and notice the relationship between the Position table and the Staff table, and the relationship between the Staff table and Patients table. Each position has staff associated with it, and staff members have patients associated with them. Close the Relationships window.

h. Rename the **Pos table** to **Position**. Add a description to the table stating **This table contains a list of all available job titles at the company**. Click **OK**.

i. Open the **Position table** in Datasheet view. Click the **plus sign** next to JobCode 100 (Social Worker). Notice seven social workers are employed by the company. Click the **plus sign** next to JobCode 300 (IT Support). Only your name should appear. Close the table.

j. Open the **Patients table** in Datasheet view. Use a Selection filter to show all patients associated with StaffID **80073**. Save and close the table.

k. Open the **Staff table** in Datasheet view. Use Filter By Form to display all staff members who earn a salary of more than **80000**. Toggle the filter to verify the results. Save and close the table.

l. Back up the database. Accept the default file name.

m. Add a **Users application part** to the database. Change the relationship so there is One 'Staff' to many 'Users' by clicking the arrow next to Patients and selecting **Staff**. Click **Next**. Select the **FullName** field from 'Staff', choose the **Sort Ascending** option, and name the lookup column **User**. Click **Create**.

n. Open the **Users table** in Datasheet view.

o. Select **Adolfo Ortiz** in the User field. Type **aortiz@sunshinementalhealth.org** for Email and **aortiz** for Login. Leave the FullName blank. Close the table.

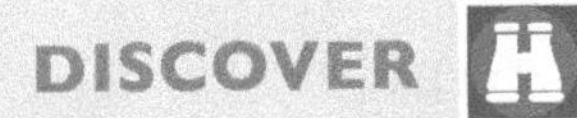

p. Create a form based on the Patients table using the Form button in the Forms group of the Create tab. Save the form as **Patient Data Entry.**

q. Switch to Form view of the form. Delete the phone number for PatientID **1** (Minoru Kobayashi). Close the form.

r. Close the database and exit Access. Based on your instructor's directions, submit the following:

a01m1Sunshine_LastFirst

a01m1Sunshine_LastFirst_*CurrentDate*

2 National Conference

ANALYSIS CASE 

The Association of Higher Education will host its National Conference on your campus next year. To facilitate the conference, the Information Technology department has replaced last year's Excel spreadsheets with an Access database containing information on the rooms, speakers, and sessions. Your assignment is to create a room itinerary that will list all of the sessions, dates, and times for each room. The list will be posted on the door of each room for the duration of the conference.

a. Open the *a01m2NatConf* file and save the database as **a01m2NatConf_LastFirst**. Click **Enable Content** on the Security Warning message bar.

b. Open **Relationships**.

c. Review the objects and relationships in the database. Notice that there is a relationship between Speakers and SessionSpeaker. Close the relationships.

d. Open the **SessionSpeaker table**. Scroll to the first blank record at the bottom of the table and type a new record using SpeakerID **99** and SessionID **09**. (Note: Speaker 99 does not exist.) How does Access respond? Press **Escape** twice to cancel your change.

e. Open the **Speakers table**. Replace *YourFirstName* with your first name and *YourLastName* with your last name. Close the Speakers table.

f. Open the **Sessions table** and use a Selection filter to identify the sessions that take place in room 101.

g. Sort the filtered results in ascending order by the **SessionTitle** field. Save and close the table.

h. Open the **Master List - Sessions and Speakers** report. Right-click the **Master List - Sessions and Speakers** tab and select **Report View**.

DISCOVER 

i. Apply a filter that limits the report to sessions in **Room 101** only. The process will be similar to applying a filter to a table.

j. View the report in Print Preview. Close Print Preview and close the report.

k. Back up the database. Use the default backup file name.

l. Open the *a01m2Analysis* document in Word and save as **a01m2Analysis_LastFirst**. Use the database objects you created to answer the questions. Save and close the document.

m. Close the database and exit Access. Based on your instructor's directions, submit the following:

a01m2NatConf_LastFirst
a01m2NatConf_LastFirst_*CurrentDate*
a01m2Analysis_LastFirst

3 New Castle County Technical Services

RUNNING CASE

New Castle County Technical Services (NCCTS) provides technical support for a number of companies in the greater New Castle County, Delaware, area. They are working to move their record keeping to an Access database. You will add, update, and delete some records, add filters, and create a backup.

This project is a running case.

a. Open the database *a01m3NCCTS* and save the database as **a01m3NCCTS_LastFirst**. Click **Enable Content** on the Security Warning message bar.

b. Open the **Call Types table** in Datasheet view. Type the following rates for the HourlyRate field and then close the table:

Description	HourlyRate
Hardware Support	30
Software Support	25
Network Troubleshooting	40
Network Installation	40
Training	50

Description	HourlyRate
Security Camera Maintenance	40
Virus Removal	25
Disaster Recovery	60
VoIP Service	45
Other	35

c. Open the **Reps table** in Datasheet view. Add a new record, filling in the value **8** for the RepID field, your last name as the rep's last name, and your first name as the rep's first name.

d. Sort the Reps table by **LastName** in ascending order. Close the table.

e. Open the **Customers table** in Datasheet view. Locate the record for **Edwin VanCleef** (PC030). Delete the entire record.

f. Click in the **City field** for SVC Pharmacy. Use the Selection filter to only show customers who are located in the city of **Newark**. Save and close the table.

g. Open the **Calls table** in Datasheet view. Use **Filter By Form** to filter the HoursLogged field so only calls with 10 or more hours logged on the call (**>=10**) are displayed. Save and close the table.

h. Back up the database, using the default name.

i. Close the database and exit Access. Based on your instructor's directions, submit the following:

a01m3NCCTS_LastFirst

a01m3NCCTS_LastFirst_*CurrentDate*

Beyond the Classroom

Creating a Student Database

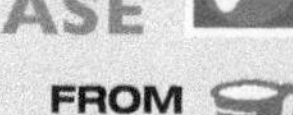

Create a new blank desktop database, name the file **a01b1Students_LastFirst**, and then save the database in the location where you are saving your files. Create a new table using the Contacts application part. Delete the Company, JobTitle, BusinessPhone, HomePhone, FaxNumber, Country/Region, WebPage, Attachments, ContactName, and FileAs fields from the Company table. Save the table, then switch to Datasheet view. Enter the information about at least five students, fictional or real, including your own information. Enter their major in the Notes field. Sort the table by last name in ascending order. Create a filter to display students with your major. Delete all queries, forms, and reports. Close the database and exit Access. Based on your instructor's directions, submit a01b1Students_LastFirst.

Lugo Web Hosting

Your Access database has become corrupted and you are in the process of restoring it from a backup from two weeks ago. In the last two weeks, there have been only a few changes. All users who previously had a 900 GB quota have had their quotas increased to 1 TB. In addition, all users who were previously on the server named Aerelon have been moved to another server, Caprica. You have determined you can use filters to help fix the data in the Users table. Open the *a01b2Lugo_Backup* file and save the database as **a01b2Lugo_LastFirst**. Apply filters to show users who meet the conditions above and then manually change the data for each user. Sort the table by the server in ascending order. Close the database and exit Access. Based on your instructor's directions, submit a01b2Lugo_LastFirst.

Capstone Exercise

You are employed as a technical supervisor at a chain of bookstores. One of the store managers has expressed confusion about Access. You have offered to train her on the basics of Access. To avoid mistakes in the main database, you will save the file with a new name. You will then train her on the basics of the database system, including making data modifications, sorting and filtering, adding a table using an application part, and creating a backup.

Modify Data in a Table

You will open an original database file and save the database with a new name. You will then demonstrate adding, updating, and deleting information.

a. Open the *a01c1Books* file and save the database as **a01c1Books_LastFirst**.

b. Open the **Publishers table** in Datasheet view. Notice that some of the publisher city and state information is missing. Update the database with the information below and close the table.

PubID	PubName	PubCity	PubState
DC	DC Comics	New York	NY
SM	St. Martin	Boston	MA
TB	Triumph Books	Chicago	IL
TL	Time Life	Pueblo	CO

c. Change the PubCity for Pearson to **Hoboken**.

d. Close the Publishers table.

e. Open the **Author table** in Datasheet view.

f. Navigate to the last record (Author ID of XXXX01) and replace **YourFirstName** with your first name and **YourLastName** with your last name. Close the table.

g. Open the **Author table** again and notice the changes you made have been stored.

h. Click the **plus sign** next to your name. Notice the book Social Media: A Student's View is listed. Close the table again.

i. Open the **Books table** in Datasheet view. Notice the book with ISBN 9780809400775 (American Cooking: The Northwest) has no items in stock. Delete this record.

j. Close the table.

Sort a Table and Apply a Selection Filter

You will sort the publisher's table by name and then apply a filter to display only publishers located in New York.

a. Open the **Publishers table** in Datasheet view. Notice Time Life appears after Triumph Books. This is because the table is sorted by the PubID field.

b. Click in any record in the PubName field and sort the field in ascending order.

c. Apply a Selection filter to display only publishers with a PubCity equal to **New York**.

d. Close the table and save the changes.

Use Filter By Form

You will obtain a list of all books with more than 50 units in stock. This will help the management decide on what books to put on sale. You will use Filter By Form to accomplish this. You will also demonstrate how filters are saved.

a. Open the **Books table** in Datasheet view.

b. Use Filter By Form to display books with more than **50** units in stock. Save and close the table.

c. Open the **Books table** in Datasheet view. Click **Toggle Filter** in the Sort & Filter group to demonstrate that the filter is saved.

Back Up a Database and Add an Application Part

You will demonstrate adding an application part to the manager to show how tables are created. You will first back the database up to reinforce the importance of backing up the data.

a. Create a backup copy of your database, accepting the default file name.

b. Add a Comments application part, selecting the option **One 'Books' to many 'Comments'**. Select the **Title field** for the Field from Books and **Sort Ascending** for Sort this field. Name the lookup column **Book**.

c. Open the **Comments table** in Datasheet view. Add a new comment. Select **Social Media: A Student's View** for the Book. Use the current date and add **A fun and insightful book!** for the Comment field.

d. Close the database and exit Access. Based on your instructor's directions, submit the following:

a01c1Books_LastFirst
a01c1Books_LastFirst_*CurrentDate*

Glossary

Access The database management system included in the Office suite.

Application part A feature that enables you to add a set of common Access components to an existing database, such as a table, a form, and a report for a related task.

Back Up Database A utility that creates a duplicate copy of the entire database to protect from loss or damage.

Compact and Repair Database A utility that reduces the size of a database and fixes any errors that may exist in the file.

Custom Web app A feature which enables users to create a database that you can build and then use and share with others through the Web.

Database A collection of data organized as meaningful information that can be accessed, managed, stored, queried, sorted, and reported.

Database Management System (DBMS) A software system that provides the tools needed to create, maintain, and use a database.

Database Splitter A utility that puts the tables in one file (the back-end database), and the queries, forms, and reports in a second file (the front-end database).

Datasheet view A grid containing fields (columns) and records (rows) used to view, add, edit, and delete records.

Design view A view which gives users a detailed view of the table's structure and is used to create and modify a table's design by specifying the fields it will contain, the fields' data types, and their associated properties.

Field A category of information stored in a table (such as Customer ID or Company Name).

Field Property A feature which defines the characteristics of a field in more detail.

Filter A feature which allows users to specify conditions to display only those records that meet those conditions.

Filter By Form A more versatile method of selecting data, enabling users to display records based on multiple criteria.

Form An object which simplified entry and modification of data.

Macro A stored series of commands that carry out an action; often used to automate simple tasks.

Module An advanced object written using the VBA (Visual Basic for Applications) programming language.

Navigation Pane An Access interface element that organizes and lists the objects in an Access database.

Object A component created and used to make the database function (such as a table, query, form, or report).

Primary key The field (or combination of fields) that uniquely identifies each record in a table.

Query A question users ask about the data in a database.

Record A complete set of all the fields about one person, place, event, or concept.

Relationship A connection between two tables using a common field.

Report An object which contains professional-looking formatted information from underlying tables or queries.

Selection Filter A method of selecting that displays only the records that match a criterion you select.

Sort A feature which lists records in a specific sequence.

Table The location where all data is stored in a database; organizes data into columns and rows.

Template A predefined database that includes professionally designed tables, forms, reports, and other objects that you can use to jumpstart the creation of your database.

Tables and Queries in Relational Databases

Access

Tables and Queries in Relational Databases

LEARNING OUTCOMES
- **You will create and modify tables for data input and organization.**
- **You will develop queries to extract and present data.**

OBJECTIVES & SKILLS: After you read this chapter, you will be able to:

Table Design, Creation, and Modification

OBJECTIVE 1: DESIGN A TABLE

OBJECTIVE 2: CREATE AND MODIFY TABLES AND WORK WITH DATA
Create a Table in Datasheet View, Delete a Field, Set a Table's Primary Key, Work with Field Properties, Create a New Field in Design View, Modify the Table in Datasheet View

HANDS-ON EXERCISE 1:
Table Design, Creation, and Modification

Multiple-Table Databases

OBJECTIVE 3: SHARE DATA
Import Excel Data, Import Data from an Access Database, Modify an Imported Table's Design, Add Data to an Imported Table

OBJECTIVE 4: ESTABLISH TABLE RELATIONSHIPS
Establish Table Relationships, Enforce Referential Integrity

HANDS-ON EXERCISE 2:
Multiple-Table Databases

Single-Table Queries

OBJECTIVE 5: CREATE A SINGLE-TABLE QUERY
Create a Single-Table Query

OBJECTIVE 6: USE THE QUERY WIZARD
Use the Query Wizard

OBJECTIVE 7: SPECIFY QUERY CRITERIA FOR DIFFERENT DATA TYPES
Specify Query Criteria

OBJECTIVE 8: UNDERSTAND QUERY SORT ORDER
Specify Query Sort Order

OBJECTIVE 9: RUN, COPY, AND MODIFY A QUERY
Run, Copy, and Modify a Query; Change Query Data

HANDS-ON EXERCISE 3:
Single-Table Queries

Multitable Queries

OBJECTIVE 10: CREATE A MULTITABLE QUERY
Add Additional Tables to a Query, Create a Multitable Query

OBJECTIVE 11: MODIFY A MULTITABLE QUERY
Modify a Multitable Query, Summarize Data Using a Multitable Query

HANDS-ON EXERCISE 4:
Multitable Queries

CASE STUDY | Bank Audit

During a year-end review, a bank auditor uncovers mishandled funds at Commonwealth Federal Bank in Wilmington, Delaware. In order to analyze the data in more detail, the auditor asks you to create an Access database so he can review the affected customers, the compromised accounts, and the branches involved.

As you begin, you realize that some of the data are contained in external Excel and Access files that you decide to import directly into the new database. Importing from Excel and Access is fairly common, and will help to avoid errors that are associated with data entry. Once the data have been imported, you will use queries to determine exactly which records are relevant to the investigation.

This chapter introduces the Bank database case study to present the basic principles of table and query design. Once the new database is created and all the data are entered, you will help the auditor answer questions by creating and running queries. The value of that information depends entirely on the quality of the underlying data—the tables.

Syda Productions/
Shutterstock

Designing Databases and Extracting Data

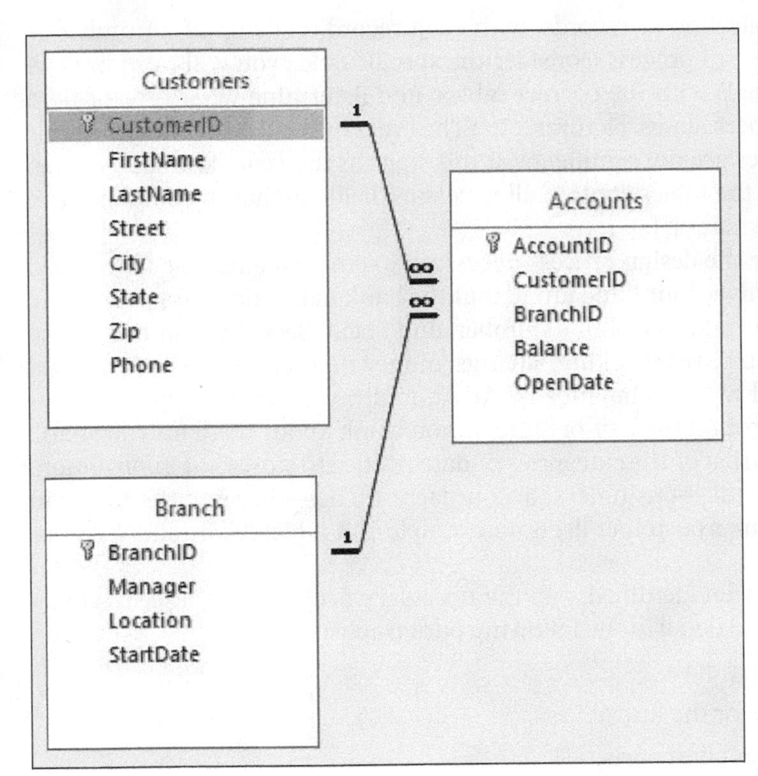

Number of Customer Accounts

Customer ID	Number of Accounts
30001	5
30002	1
30003	4
30004	4
30005	4
30006	1
30007	2
30009	2
30010	2
30011	3

Access 2016, Windows 10, Microsoft Corporation

FIGURE I Bank Audit Database

CASE STUDY | Bank Audit

Starting Files	File to be Submitted
Blank desktop database **a02h2Accounts** **a02h2Customers**	**a02h4Bank_LastFirst**

Table Design, Creation, and Modification

Good database design begins with the tables. Tables provide the framework for all of the activities you perform in a database. If the framework is poorly designed, the database will not function as expected. Whether you are experienced in designing tables or are a new database designer, the process should not be done haphazardly. You should follow a systematic approach when creating tables for a database.

In this section, you will learn the essentials of good table design. After developing and analyzing the table design on paper, you will implement that design in Access. In this chapter you will learn to refine them by changing the properties of various fields.

Designing a Table

Recall that a table is a collection of records, with each record made up of a number of fields. During the table design process, consider the specific fields you will need in each table; list the proposed fields with the correct tables, and determine what type of data each field will store (numbers, dates, pictures, etc.) The order of the fields within the table and the specific field names are not significant at this stage as they can be changed later. What is important is that the tables contain all necessary fields so that the database can produce the required information later.

For example, consider the design process necessary to create a database for a bank. Most likely you have a bank account and know that the bank maintains data about you. Your bank has your name, address, phone number, and Social Security number. It also knows which accounts you have (checking, savings, money market), if you have a credit card with that bank, and what its balance is. Additionally, your bank keeps information about its branches around the city or state. If you think about the data your bank maintains, you can make a list of the categories of data needed to store that information. These categories for the bank—customers, accounts, branches—become the tables in the bank's database. A bank's customer list is an example of a table; it contains a record for each bank customer.

After the tables have been identified, add the necessary fields using these six guidelines, which are discussed in detail in the following paragraphs:

- Include the necessary data.
- Design for now and for the future.
- Store data in their smallest parts.
- Determine primary keys.
- Link tables using common fields.
- Design to accommodate calculations.

Figure 2 shows a customer table and two other tables found in a sample Bank database. It also lists fields that would be needed in each table.

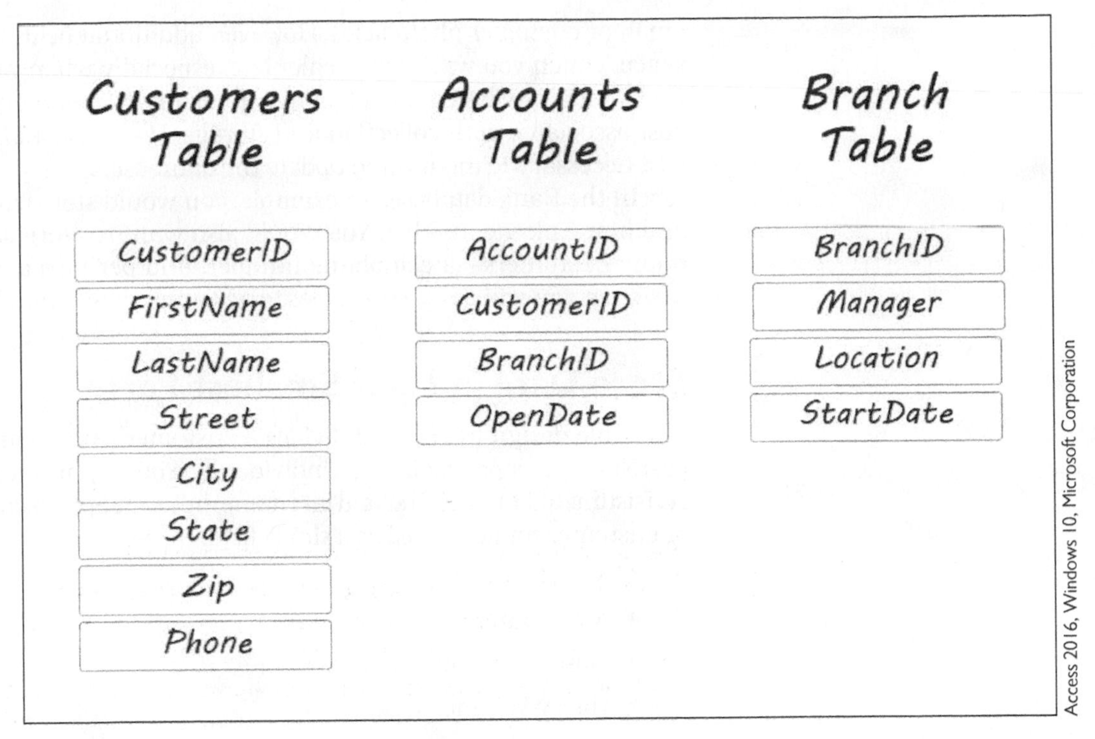

FIGURE 2 Rough Draft of Tables and Fields in a Sample Bank Database

Include Necessary Data

A good way to determine what data are necessary in tables is to consider the output you will need from your database. You will probably need to create professional-looking reports for others, so begin by creating a rough draft of the reports you will need. Then design tables that contain the fields necessary to create those reports. In other words, ask yourself what information will be expected from the database (output) and determine the data required (input) to produce that information. Consider, for example, the tables and fields in Figure 2. Is there required information that could not be generated from those tables?

- You will be able to determine how long a customer has banked with the branch because the date he or she opened the account is stored in the Accounts table, which will connect to the Customers and Branch tables.
- You will be able to determine which branch a customer uses because the Accounts table includes both the CustomerID and the BranchID. The Accounts table will eventually connect to both the Customers and Branch tables, making it possible to gather this information.
- You will not be able to generate the monthly bank statement. In order to generate a customer bank statement (showing all deposits and withdrawals for the month), you would need to add an additional table—to track activity for each account.
- You will not be able to email a customer because the Customers table does not contain an email field at this time.

If you discover a missing field, such as the email field, you can add it during the initial design process or later.

Design for Now and for the Future

As the information requirements of an organization evolve over time, the database systems that hold the data must change as well. When designing a database, try to anticipate the future needs of the system and build in the flexibility to satisfy those demands. For example, you may also decide to create additional fields for future use (such as an email or customer photo field). However, additional fields will also require more storage space, which you will need to calculate, especially when working with larger databases. Good database design must balance the data collection needs of the company with the cost associated with collection and storage. Plans must also include the frequency and cost necessary to modify and update the database.

In the Bank database, for example, you would store each customer's name, address, and home phone number. You would also want to store additional phone numbers for many customers—a cell phone number, and perhaps a work number. As a database designer, you will design the tables to accommodate multiple entries for similar data.

Store Data in Their Smallest Parts

The table design in Figure 2 divides a customer's name into two fields (FirstName and LastName) to store each value individually. You might think it easier to use a single field consisting of both the first and last name, but that approach is too limiting. Consider a list of customer names stored as a single field:

- Sue Grater
- Rick Grater
- Nancy Gallagher
- Harry Weigner
- Barb Shank
- Pete Shank

The first problem in this approach is the lack of flexibility: You could not easily create a salutation for a letter using the form *Dear Sue* or *Dear Ms. Gallagher* because the first and last names are not accessible individually.

A second difficulty is that the list of customers cannot be easily displayed in alphabetical order by last name because the last name begins in the middle of the field. The most common way to sort names is by the last name, which you can do more efficiently if the last name is stored as a separate field.

Think of how an address might be used. The city, state, and postal code should always be stored as separate fields. You may need to select records from a particular state or postal code, which will be easier if you store the data as separate fields.

Determine Primary Keys

When designing your database tables, it is important to determine the primary key, the field that will uniquely identify each record in a table. For example, in Figure 2, the CustomerID field will uniquely identify each customer in the database.

Plan for Common Fields Between Tables

As you create the tables and fields for the database, keep in mind that some tables will be joined in relationships using common fields. Creating relationships will help you to extract data from more than one table when creating queries, forms, and reports. For example, you will be able to determine which customers have which accounts by joining the Customers and Accounts tables. For now, you should name the common fields the same (although that is not a firm requirement in Access). For example, CustomerID in the Customers table will join to the CustomerID field in the Accounts table. Draw a line between common fields to indicate the joins, as shown in Figure 3. These join lines will be created in Access when you learn to create table relationships later in the chapter.

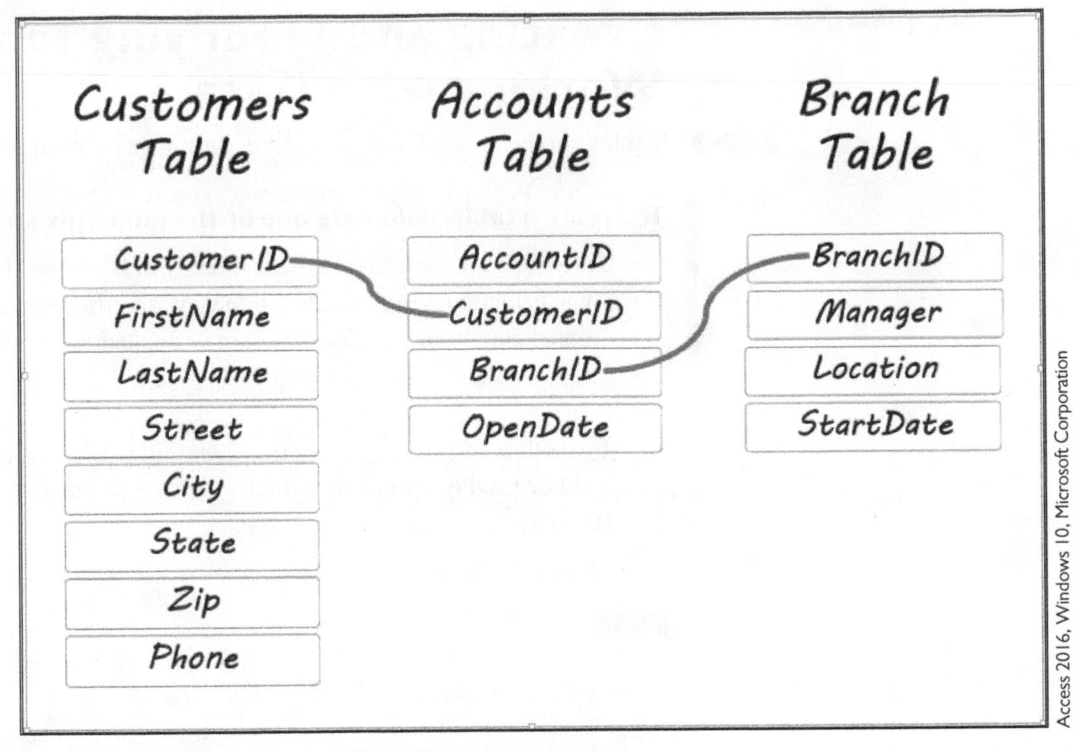

FIGURE 3 Determine Relationships Using Common Fields

Avoid ***data redundancy***, which is the unnecessary storing of duplicate data in two or more tables. Having redundant or duplicate data in multiple tables can lead to serious errors. Suppose the customer address data were stored in both the Customers and Accounts tables. If a customer moved to a new address, it is possible that the address would be updated in only one of the two tables. The result would be inconsistent and unreliable information. Depending on which table you would use to check an address, either the new or the old one might be given to someone requesting the information. Storing the address in only one table is more reliable; if it changes, it only needs to be updated one time (in the Customers table) and can be referenced again and again from that table.

TIP: ADD CALCULATED FIELDS TO A TABLE

A calculated field produces a value from an expression or function that references one or more existing fields. Access enables you to store calculated fields in a table using the calculated data type, and to include those fields in queries, forms, and reports. However, many Access users prefer to create calculated fields in their query designs rather than in the tables themselves.

Design to Accommodate Calculations

Calculated fields are frequently created in database objects with numeric data, such as a monthly interest field that multiplies the balance in a customer's account by 1% each month (Balance*.01). You can also create calculated fields using date/time data. For example, if you want to store the length of time a customer has had an account, you can create a calculated field that subtracts the opening date from today's date. The result will be the number of days each customer has been an account holder.

A person's age is another example of a calculated field using date arithmetic—the date of birth is subtracted from today's date and the result is divided by 365 (or 365.25 to account for leap years). It might seem easier to store a person's age as a number rather than the birth date and avoid the calculated field, but that would be a mistake because age changes over time and the field would need to be updated each time it changes. You can use date arithmetic to subtract one date from another to find out the number of days, months, or years that have elapsed between them.

Creating and Modifying Tables and Working with Data

STEP 1 »» Tables can be created in a new blank database or in an existing database.

To create a table, complete one of the following steps:

- Enter field names and table data directly in Datasheet view.
- Type field names in rows in Design view and then enter the data in Datasheet view.
- Import data from another database or application, such as Excel.
- Use a template.

Regardless of how a table is first created, you can always modify it later to include a new field or modify an existing field. Figure 4 shows a table created by entering fields in Design view.

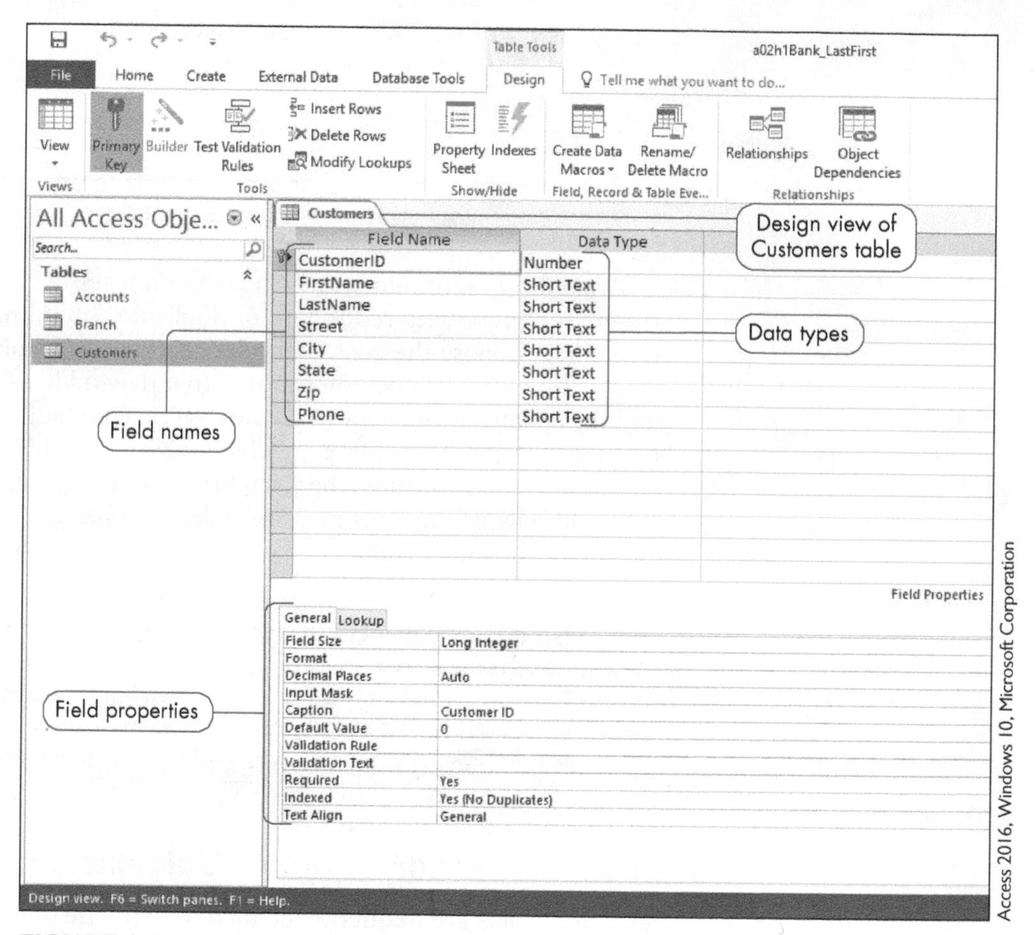

FIGURE 4 Customers Table Created in Design View

When you add a new field to a table, the field must be given an appropriate name to identify the data it holds. The field name should be descriptive of the data and can be up to 64 characters in length, including letters, numbers, and spaces. Field names cannot begin with a leading blank space. Database developers sometimes use Pascal Case notation for field names. Instead of spaces in multiword field names, you can use uppercase letters to distinguish the first letter of each new word, for example, ProductCost or LastName (sometimes developers use Camel Case, which is similar to Pascal Case, where the first letter of the first word is lowercase). It is sometimes preferable to avoid spaces in field names, because spaces can cause naming conflicts with other applications that may use these fields, such as Microsoft Visual Basic for Applications.

Fields can be added, deleted, or renamed either in Design view or Datasheet view. To delete a field in Datasheet view, select the field and press Delete. Click Yes in the message box.

To delete a field in Design view, complete the following steps:

1. Click the record selector of the field you want to delete to select it.
2. Click Delete Rows in the Tools group on the Design tab.
3. Click Yes in the message box that displays to confirm that you want to permanently delete the field and the data in it. Click No if you do not want to delete the field.
4. Click Yes in the second message box that displays if the selected field you are deleting is a primary key. Click No if you do not want to delete the primary key.

To rename a field, double-click the field name you want to change, type the new field name, press Enter, and then save the table.

TIP: HIDE FIELDS IN AN ACCESS DATASHEET

To hide a field in a datasheet, right-click the column selector that displays the field name and from the shortcut menu, select Hide Fields. To make the field visible again, right-click any column selector, select Unhide Fields, and select the appropriate column's check box.

Determine Data Type

Every field has an assigned ***data type*** that determines the type of data that can be entered and the operations that can be performed on that data. Access recognizes 12 data types. Table 1 lists these data types, their uses, and examples of each. You can change a data type after you have entered data into your table, but do so with caution. Be aware of messages from Access indicating that you may lose data when you save your changes. In some cases, changing data types is inconsequential; for example, you may want to convert a number to a currency value. This type of change would only affect the formatting displayed with the values, but not the underlying values themselves. In any case, when designing tables, choose the initial data type carefully, and be sure to back up your database before changing data types.

TABLE 1 Data Types and Uses

Data Type	Description	Example
Short Text	Stores alphanumeric data, such as a customer's name or address. It can contain alphabetic characters, numbers, and/or special characters (e.g., an apostrophe in O'Malley). Social Security numbers, telephone numbers, and postal codes should be designated as text fields because they are not used in calculations and often contain special characters such as hyphens and parentheses. A short text field can hold up to 255 characters.	2184 Walnut Street
Long Text	Lengthy text or combinations of text and numbers, such as several sentences or paragraphs; used to hold descriptive data. Long text controls can display up to 64,000 characters.	A description of product packaging
Number	Contains a value that can be used in a calculation, such as the number of credits a course is worth. The contents are restricted to numbers, a decimal point, and a plus or minus sign.	12
Date/Time	Stores dates or times that can be used in date or time arithmetic.	10/31/2018 1:30:00 AM
Currency	Used for fields that contain monetary values.	$1,200

TABLE 1	Continued	
Data Type	**Description**	**Example**
AutoNumber	A special data type used to assign the next consecutive number each time you add a record. The value of an AutoNumber field is unique for each record in the table.	1, 2, 3
Yes/No	Only one of two values can be stored, such as Yes or No, True or False, or On or Off (also known as a Boolean). For example, is a student on the Dean's list: Yes or No.	Yes
OLE Object	Contains an object created by another application. OLE objects include pictures and sounds.	JPG image
Hyperlink	Stores a Web address (URL) or the path to a folder or file. Hyperlink fields can be clicked to retrieve a webpage or to launch a file stored locally.	http://www.irs.gov
Attachment	Used to store multiple images, spreadsheet files, Word documents, and other types of supported files.	An Excel workbook
Calculated	The results of an expression that references one or more existing fields.	[Price]*.05
Lookup Wizard	Creates a field that enables you to choose a value from another table or from a list of values by using a list box or a combo box.	Accounts table with a CustomerID field that looks up the customer from the records in the Customers table

Set a Table's Primary Key

STEP 2 The primary key is the field (or possibly a combination of fields) that uniquely identifies each record in a table. Access does not require that each table have a primary key. However, a good database design usually includes a primary key in each table. You should select unique and infrequently changing data for the primary key. For example, a credit card number may seem to be unique, but would not make a good primary key because it is subject to change when a new card is issued due to fraudulent activity.

You probably would not use a person's name as the primary key, because several people could have the same name. A value like CustomerID, as shown in the Customers table in Figure 5, is unique and is a better choice for the primary key. When no field seems to stand out as a primary key naturally, you can create a primary key field with the AutoNumber data type. The ***AutoNumber*** data type is a number that automatically increments each time a record is added.

Figure 6 depicts a Speakers table, where no unique field can be identified from the data itself. In this case, you can identify the SpeakerID field with an AutoNumber data type. Access automatically numbers each speaker record sequentially with a unique ID as each record is added.

Customers

	Customer ID	FirstName	LastName	Street	City	State	Zip	Phone	Click to Add
⊞	30001	Allison	Millward	2732 Baker Blvd.	Greensboro	NC	27492	(555) 334-5678	
⊞	30002	Bernett	Fox	12 Orchestra Terrace	High Point	NC	27494	(555) 358-5554	
⊞	30003	Clay	Hayes	P.O. Box 555	Greensboro	NC	27492	(555) 998-4457	
⊞	30004	Cordle	Collins	2743 Bering St.	Winston-Salem	NC	27492	(555) 447-2283	
⊞	30005	Eaton	Wagner	2743 Bering St.	Greensboro	NC	27492	(555) 988-3346	
⊞	30006	Kwasi	Williams	89 Jefferson Way	High Point	NC	27494	(555) 447-5565	
⊞	30007	Natasha	Simpson	187 Suffolk Ln.	Greensboro	NC	27493	(555) 775-3389	
⊞	30008	Joy	Jones	305 - 14th Ave. S.	Winston-Salem	NC	27493	(555) 258-7655	
⊞	30009	John	Nunn	89 Chiaroscuro Rd.	Greensboro	NC	27494	(555) 998-5557	
⊞	30010	Laura	Peterson	120 Hanover Sq.	Winston-Salem	NC	27492	(555) 334-6654	
⊞	30011	YourName	YourName	800 University Ave.	High Point	NC	27494	(555) 447-1235	
*	0								

FIGURE 5 Customers Table with a Natural Primary Key

Speakers

SpeakerID	First Name	Last Name	Address	City	Sta	Zip Co	Phone Num	Email	AreaOfExpertise	Click to Add
1	Jerri	Williams	10000 SW 59 Court	Miami	FL	33146	(305) 777-8888	cahsley@um.edu	Student Life	
2	Warren	Brasington	9470 SW 25 Street	Philadelphia	PA	19104	(215) 888-7654	wbrasington@up.edu	Residence Halls	
3	James	Shindell	14088 Malaga Avenue	Miami	FL	33146	(305) 773-4343	jshindell@um.edu	Administration	
		od	400 Roderigo Avenue	Gainesville	FL	32611	(352) 555-5555	ewood@uf.edu	Student Life	
			9290 NW 59 Steet	Athens	GA	30602	(706) 777-1111	kpark@ug.edu	Student Life	
		iamson	108 Los Pinos Place	Tuscaloosa	AL	35487	(205) 888-4554	wwilliamson@ua.edu	Deans' Office	
7	Holly	Davis	8009 Riviera Drive	Gainesville	FL	32611	(352) 388-7676	hdavis.uf.edu	Residence Halls	
8	David	Tannen	50 Main Street	Philadelphia	PA	19104	(215) 777-2211	dtannen@up.edu	Student Life	
9	Jeffrey	Jacobsen	490 Bell Drive	Athens	GA	30602	(706) 388-9999	jjacobsen@ug.edu	Wellness	
10	Jerry	Masters	2000 Main Highway	Miami	FL	33146	(305) 777-8998	jmasters@um.edy	Wellness	
11	Kevin	Kline	2980 SW 89 Street	Gainesville	FL	32611	(352) 877-8900	kkline@uf.edu	Student Life	
			110 Center Highway	Athens	GA	30602	(706) 893-8872	jwithers@ug.edu	Wellness	
			2987 SW 14 Avenue	Philadelphia	PA	19104	(215) 558-7748	ballman@up.edu	Counseling Center	
			1008 West Marine Road	Miami	FL	33146	(305) 877-4993	mmiller@um.edu	Student Life	
15	Nancy	Vance	1878 W. 6 Street	Gainesville	FL	32611	(352) 885-4330	nvance@uf.edu	Counseling Center	
16	George	Jensen	42-15 81 Street	Elmhurst	NY	11373	(718) 555-6666	gjensen@school.edu	Residence Halls	
(New)										

SpeakerID (AutoNumber data type) is the primary key

Next record will be assigned SpeakerID 17

Access 2016, Windows 10, Microsoft Corporation

FIGURE 6 Speakers Table with an AutoNumber Primary Key

Explore a Foreign Key

In order to share data between two tables, the tables must share a common field. The common field will generally be the primary key in one table; the same field in the adjoining table is denoted as the ***foreign key***. The CustomerID is the primary key (identified with a primary key icon) in the Customers table and uniquely identifies each customer in the database. It also displays as a foreign key in the related Accounts table. The Accounts table contains the CustomerID field to establish which customer owns the account. A CustomerID can be entered only one time in the Customers table, but it may be entered multiple times in the Accounts table because one customer may own several accounts (checking, savings, credit card, etc.). Therefore, the CustomerID is the primary key in the Customers table and a foreign key in the Accounts table, as shown in Figure 7.

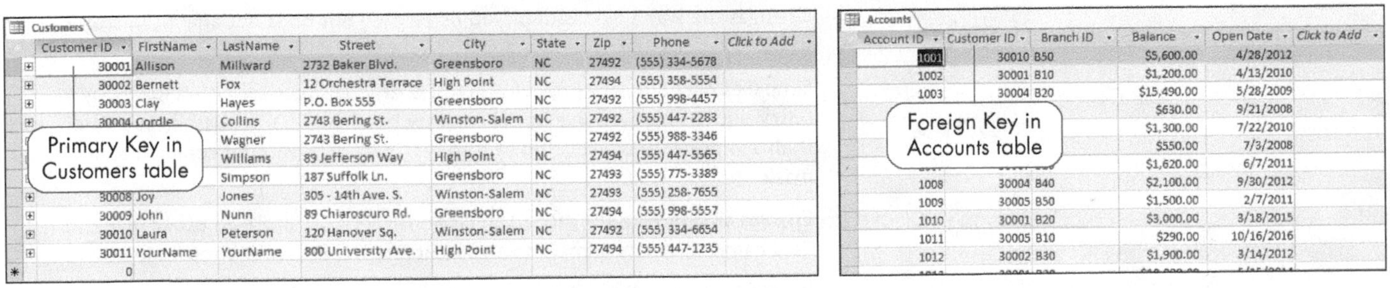

Customers

Customer ID	FirstName	LastName	Street	City	State	Zip	Phone	Click to Add
30001	Allison	Millward	2732 Baker Blvd.	Greensboro	NC	27492	(555) 334-5678	
30002	Bernett	Fox	12 Orchestra Terrace	High Point	NC	27494	(555) 358-5554	
30003	Clay	Hayes	P.O. Box 555	Greensboro	NC	27492	(555) 998-4457	
30004	Cordle	Collins	2743 Bering St.	Winston-Salem	NC	27492	(555) 447-2283	
		Wagner	2743 Bering St.	Greensboro	NC	27492	(555) 988-3346	
		Williams	89 Jefferson Way	High Point	NC	27494	(555) 447-5565	
		Simpson	187 Suffolk Ln.	Greensboro	NC	27493	(555) 775-3389	
30008	Joy	Jones	305 - 14th Ave. S.	Winston-Salem	NC	27493	(555) 258-7655	
30009	John	Nunn	89 Chiaroscuro Rd.	Greensboro	NC	27494	(555) 998-5557	
30010	Laura	Peterson	120 Hanover Sq.	Winston-Salem	NC	27492	(555) 334-6654	
30011	YourName	YourName	800 University Ave.	High Point	NC	27494	(555) 447-1235	
0								

Primary Key in Customers table

Accounts

Account ID	Customer ID	Branch ID	Balance	Open Date	Click to Add
1001	30010	B50	$5,600.00	4/28/2012	
1002	30001	B10	$1,200.00	4/13/2010	
1003	30004	B20	$15,490.00	5/28/2009	
			$630.00	9/21/2008	
			$1,300.00	7/22/2010	
			$550.00	7/3/2008	
			$1,620.00	6/7/2011	
1008	30004	B40	$2,100.00	9/30/2012	
1009	30005	B50	$1,500.00	2/7/2011	
1010	30001	B20	$3,000.00	3/18/2015	
1011	30005	B10	$290.00	10/16/2016	
1012	30002	B30	$1,900.00	3/14/2012	

Foreign Key in Accounts table

Access 2016, Windows 10, Microsoft Corporation

FIGURE 7 Two Tables Illustrating Primary and Foreign Keys

> **TIP: BEST FIT COLUMNS**
>
> If a field name is cut off in Datasheet view, you can adjust the column width by positioning the pointer on the vertical border on the right side of the column. When the pointer displays as a two-headed arrow, double-click the border. You can also click More in the Records group on the Home tab, select Field Width, and then click Best Fit in the Column Width dialog box.

Work with Field Properties

STEP 3 While a field's data type determines the type of data that can be entered and the operations that can be performed on that data, its ***field properties*** determine how the field looks and behaves. The field properties are set to default values according to the data type, but you can modify them if necessary. Field properties are commonly set in Design view, as shown in Figure 4; however, certain properties can be set in Datasheet view, on the Table Tools Fields tab. Common property types are defined in Table 2.

Field Size is a commonly changed field property. The field size determines the amount of space a field uses in the database. A field with a Short Text data type can store up to 255 characters; however, you can limit the characters by reducing the field size property. For example, you might limit the State field to only two characters because all state abbreviations are two letters. When setting field sizes, you may want to anticipate any future requirements of the database that might necessitate larger values to be stored.

You can set the ***Caption property*** to create a label that is more understandable than a field name. While Pascal Case is often preferred for field names, adding a space between words is often more readable. When a caption is set, it displays at the top of a table or query column in Datasheet view (instead of the field name), and when the field is used in a report or form. For example, a field named CustomerID could have the caption *Customer Number*.

Set the Validation Rule property to restrict data entry in a field to ensure that correct data are entered. The validation rule checks the data entered when the user exits the field. If the data entered violate the validation rule, an error message displays and prevents the invalid data from being entered into the field. For example, if you have set a rule on a date field that the date entered must be on or after today, and a date in the past is entered in the field, an error message will display. You can customize the error message (validation text) when you set the validation rule.

The Input Mask property simplifies data entry by providing literal characters that are typed for every entry, such as hyphens in a Social Security number (- -), or dashes in a phone number. Input masks ensure that data in fields such as these are consistently entered and formatted.

TABLE 2 Common Access Table Property Types and Descriptions

Property Type	Description
Field Size	Determines the maximum number of characters of a text field or the format of a number field.
Format	Changes the way a field is displayed or printed but does not affect the stored value.
Input Mask	Simplifies data entry by providing literal characters that are typed for every entry, such as hyphens in a Social Security number (- -) or slashes in a date. It also imposes data validation by ensuring that data entered conform to the mask.
Caption	Enables an alternate (or more readable) name to be displayed other than the field name; alternate name displays in datasheets, forms, and reports.
Default Value	Enters automatically a predetermined value for a field each time a new record is added to the table. For example, if most customers live in Los Angeles, the default value for the City field could be set to Los Angeles to save data entry time and promote accurate data entry.
Validation Rule	Requires data entered to conform to a specified rule.
Validation Text	Specifies the error message that is displayed when the validation rule is violated.
Required	Indicates that a value for this field must be entered. Primary key fields always require data entry.
Allow Zero Length	Allows entry of zero length text strings ("") in a Hyperlink, or Short or Long Text fields.
Indexed	Increases the efficiency of a search on the designated field.
Expression	Used for calculated fields only. Specifies the expression you want Access to evaluate and store.
Result Type	Used for calculated fields only. Specifies the format for the calculated field results.

TIP: FREEZE FIELDS IN AN ACCESS DATABASE

To keep a field viewable while you are scrolling through a table, select the field or fields you want to freeze, right-click, and then select Freeze Fields. If you want the field(s) to remain frozen when you are finished working, save the changes when you close the table. To unfreeze all fields, right-click the field(s) and select Unfreeze All Fields.

Create a New Field in Design View

STEP 4 ›› At times, it may be necessary to add table fields that were not included in the original design process. While it is possible to add fields in Datasheet view (using the Click to Add arrow at the top of an empty column), Design view, as shown in Figure 4, offers more flexibility in setting field properties.

To add a new field in Design view, complete the following steps:

1. Click in the first empty field row in the top pane of the table's Design view.
2. Enter the Field Name, Data Type, and Description (optional), and then set the Field Properties.
3. Click the row selector, and then click and drag the new field to place it in a different position in the table.
4. Click Save on the Quick Access Toolbar, and then switch to Datasheet view to enter or modify data.

Modify the Table in Datasheet View

STEP 5 ›› Whereas Design view is commonly used to create and modify the table structure by enabling you to add and edit fields and set field properties, Datasheet view is used to add, edit, and delete records. Datasheet view of an Access table displays data in a grid format—rows represent records and columns represent fields. You can select a record by clicking the record selector on the left side of each record. Use the new blank record (marked with an asterisk) at the end of the table to add a new record, or click the New (blank) record button on the navigation bar at the bottom of the table.

1. What is meant by "Store data in its smallest parts" when designing database tables?
2. What is the difference between a primary key and a foreign key?
3. Which field property creates a more readable label that displays in the top row in Datasheet view and in forms and reports?

Hands-On Exercises

Skills covered: Create a Table in Datasheet View • Delete a Field • Set a Table's Primary Key • Work with Field Properties • Create a New Field in Design View • Modify the Table in Datasheet View

1 Table Design, Creation, and Modification

Creating a database for the bank auditor at Commonwealth Federal Bank as he investigates the mishandled funds will be a great opportunity for you to showcase your database design and Access skills.

STEP 1 » CREATE A TABLE IN DATASHEET VIEW

You create a new desktop database to store information about the mishandled funds. You enter the data for the first record (BranchID, Manager, and Location). Refer to Figure 8 as you complete Step 1.

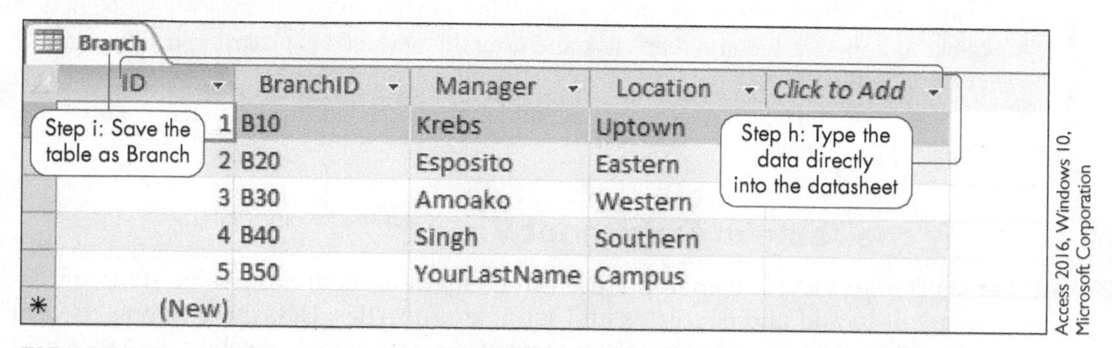

FIGURE 8 Create the Branch Table in Datasheet View

a. Start Microsoft Office Access 2016 and click **Blank desktop database**.

b. Type **a02h1Bank_LastFirst** into the File Name box.

c. Click **Browse** to find the folder location where you will store the database and click **OK**. Click **Create** to create the new database.

   Access will create the new database named a02h1Bank_LastFirst and a new table will automatically open in Datasheet view. There is already an ID field in the table by default.

d. Click **Click to Add** and select **Short Text** as the Data type.

   Click to Add changes to Field1. Field1 is selected to make it easier to change the field name.

e. Type **BranchID** and press **Tab**.

   A list of data types for the third column opens so that you can select the data type for the third column.

f. Select Short Text in the Click to Add window, type **Manager**, and then press **Tab**.

g. Select Short Text in the Click to Add window, and then type **Location**.

h. Click in the first column (the ID field) next to the New Record asterisk, press **Tab**, and then type the data for the new table as shown in Figure 8, letting Access assign the ID field for each new record (using the AutoNumber data type). Replace *YourLastName* with your own last name.

i. Click **Save** on the Quick Access Toolbar. Type **Branch** in the Save As dialog box and click **OK**.

   Entering field names, data types, and data directly in Datasheet view provides a simplified way to create the table initially.

STEP 2 » DELETE A FIELD AND SET A TABLE'S PRIMARY KEY

It is possible to modify tables even after data have been entered; however, be alert to potential messages from Access after you make design changes that may affect your data. In this step, you will modify the Branch table. You examine the design of the table and realize that the BranchID field is a unique identifier, making the ID field redundant. You delete the ID field and make the BranchID field the primary key field. Refer to Figure 9 as you complete Step 2.

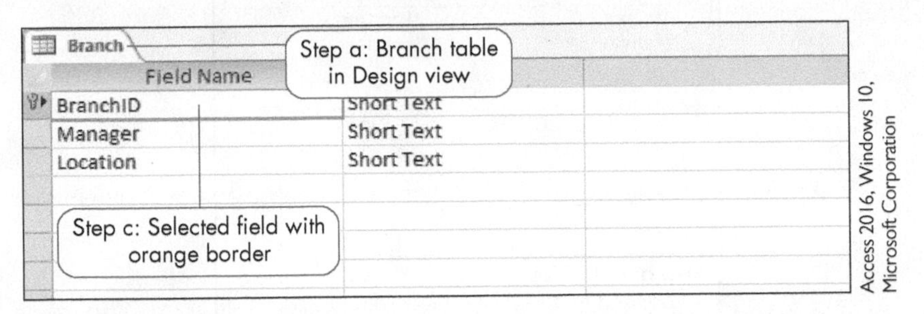

FIGURE 9 Branch Table in Design View

a. Click **View** in the Views group on the Home tab to switch to Design view of the Branch table.

The field name for each of the four fields displays along with the data type.

b. Ensure that the ID field selected, click **Delete Rows** in the Tools group on the Design tab. Click **Yes** to both warning messages.

Access responds with a warning that you are about to permanently delete a field and a second warning that the field is the primary key. You delete the field because you will set the BranchID field as the primary key.

c. Ensure that the BranchID field is selected, as shown in Figure 9.

d. Click **Primary Key** in the Tools group on the Design tab.

You set BranchID as the primary key. The Indexed property in the Field Properties section at the bottom of the design window displays Yes (No Duplicates).

e. Click **Save** on the Quick Access Toolbar to save the table.

> **TIP: SHORTCUT MENU**
> You can right-click a row selector to display a shortcut menu to copy a field, set the primary key, insert or delete rows, or access table properties. Use the shortcut menu to make these specific changes to the design of a table.

STEP 3 » WORK WITH FIELD PROPERTIES

You will modify the table design further to comply with the bank auditor's specifications. Refer to Figure 10 as you complete Step 3.

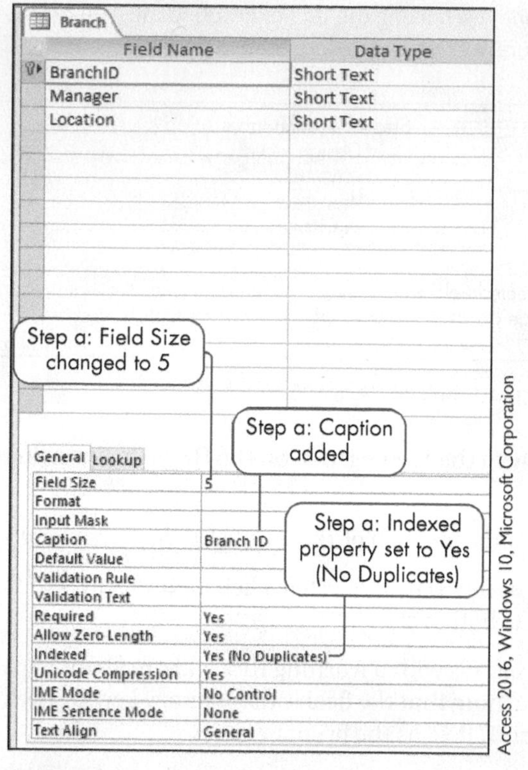

FIGURE 10 Changes to the Field Properties of the Branch Table in Design View

a. Click in the **BranchID field name**; modify the BranchID field properties by completing the following steps:

- Click in the **Field Size box** and change 255 to **5**.
- Click in the **Caption box** and type **Branch ID**. Make sure Branch and ID have a space between them.
  A caption provides a more descriptive field name. It will display as the column heading in Datasheet view.
- Check the Indexed property; confirm it is Yes (No Duplicates).

b. Click the **Manager field name**; modify the Manager field properties by completing the following steps:

- Click in the **Field Size box** in the Field Properties pane, and change 255 to **30**.
- Click in the **Caption box** in the Field Properties pane, and type **Manager's Name**.

c. Click the **Location field name** and modify the following Location field properties by completing the following steps:

- Click in the **Field Size box** and change 255 to **30**.
- Click in the **Caption box** and type **Branch Location**.

> **TIP: F6 FUNCTION KEY TO SWITCH TO FIELD PROPERTIES**
> With a field name selected in the top pane of the Design window, you can press the F6 function key to toggle to the field properties for the selected field. Continue to press F6 to cycle through the additional elements of the Access screen.

STEP 4 » CREATE A NEW FIELD IN DESIGN VIEW

You notify the auditor that a date field is missing in your new table. Modify the table to add the new field. Refer to Figure 11 as you complete Step 4.

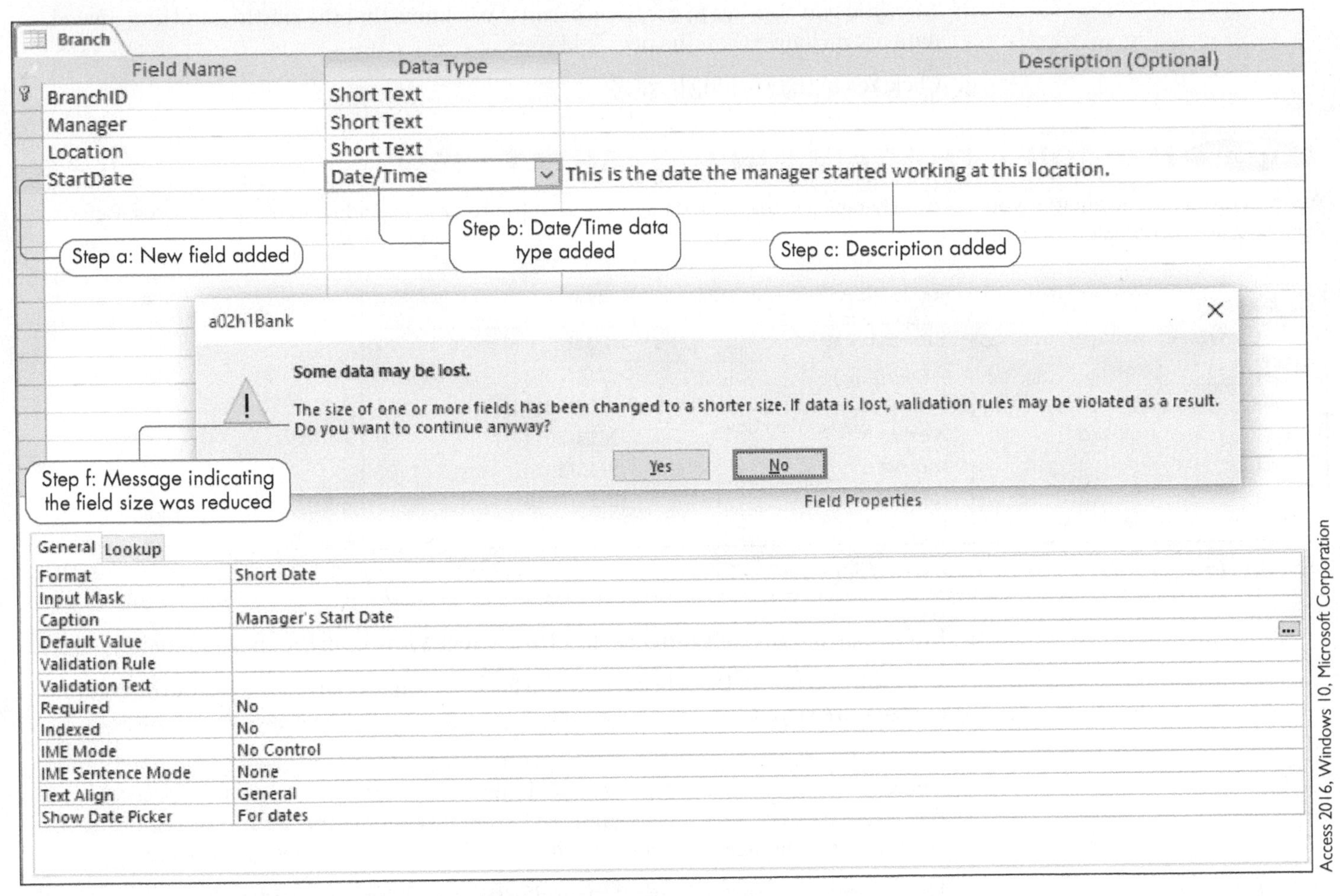

FIGURE 11 Adding a New Field to the Branch Table in Design View

a. Click in the first blank field row below the Location field name and type **StartDate**.

You added a new field to the table.

b. Press **Tab** to move to the Data Type column. Click the **Data Type arrow** and select **Date/Time**.

> **TIP: KEYBOARD SHORTCUT FOR DATA TYPES**
> You also can type the first letter of the data type, such as d for Date/Time, s for Short Text, or n for Number. To use the keyboard shortcut, click in the field name and press Tab to advance to the Data Type column. Next, type the first letter of the data type.

c. Press **Tab** to move to the Description column and type **This is the date the manager started working at this location.**

d. Click in the **Format box** in the Field properties pane, click the **arrow**, and then select **Short Date** from the list of date formats.

e. Click in the **Caption box** and type **Manager's Start Date**.

f. Click **Save** on the Quick Access Toolbar.

   A warning dialog box opens to indicate that "Some data may be lost" because the size of the BranchID, Manager, and Location field properties were shortened (in the previous step). It asks if you want to continue anyway. Always read the Access warning! In this case, you can click Yes to continue because you know that the existing and anticipated data are no longer than the new field sizes.

g. Click **Yes** in the warning box.

STEP 5 » MODIFY THE TABLE IN DATASHEET VIEW

As you work with the auditor, you will modify tables in the Bank database from time to time and add and modify records. Refer to Figure 12 as you complete Step 5.

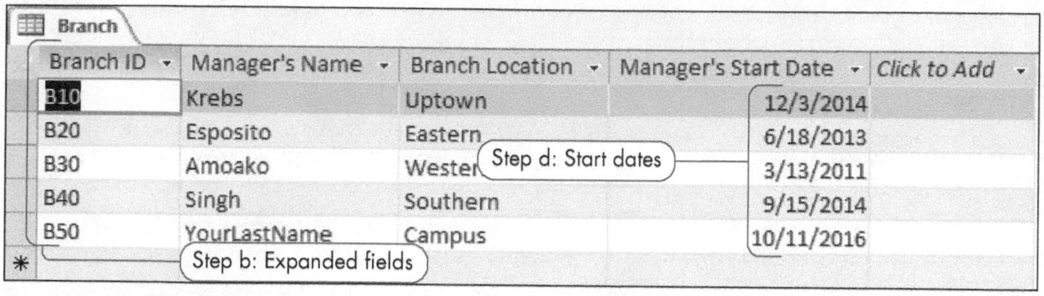

Branch

Branch ID	Manager's Name	Branch Location	Manager's Start Date	Click to Add
B10	Krebs	Uptown	12/3/2014	
B20	Esposito	Eastern	6/18/2013	
B30	Amoako	Wester	3/13/2011	
B40	Singh	Southern	9/15/2014	
B50	YourLastName	Campus	10/11/2016	
*				

Step d: Start dates

Step b: Expanded fields

Access 2016, Windows 10, Microsoft Corporation

FIGURE 12 Start Dates Added to the Branch Table

a. Right-click the **Branch tab** and click **Datasheet View** from the shortcut menu.

   The table displays in Datasheet view. The field captions display at the top of the columns, but they are cut off.

b. Position the pointer over the border between Branch ID and Manager's Name so that it becomes a double-headed arrow, and double-click the border. Repeat the process for the border between Manager's Name and Branch Location, the border between Branch Location and Manager's Start Date, and the border after Manager's Start Date.

   The columns contract or expand to display the best fit for each field name.

c. Click inside the **Manager's Start Date** in the first record and click the **Date Picker** next to the date field. Use the navigation arrows to find and select **December 3, 2014** from the calendar.

   You can also enter the dates by typing them directly into the StartDate field.

d. Type the start date directly in each field for the rest of the managers, as shown in Figure 12.

e. Click the **Close** [X] at the top-right corner of the datasheet, below the Ribbon. Click **Yes** to save the changes.

> **TROUBLESHOOTING:** If you accidentally click Close on top of the Ribbon, you will exit Access completely. To start again, launch Access and click the first file in the Recent list.

f. Double-click the **Branch table** in the Navigation Pane to open the table. Check the start dates.

g. Click the **File tab**, click **Print**, and then click **Print Preview**.

   Occasionally, users will print an Access table. However, database developers usually create reports to print table data.

h. Click **Close Print Preview** and close the Branch table.

i. Keep the database open if you plan to continue with the Hands-On Exercise. If not, close the database and exit Access.

Multiple-Table Databases

In Figure 2, the sample Bank database contains three tables—Customers, Accounts, and Branch. You created one table, the Branch table, in the previous section using Datasheet view and modified the table fields in Design view. You will create the two remaining tables using different methods—by importing data from external sources.

In this section, you will learn how to import data from Excel and Access, modify tables, create indexes, create relationships between tables, and enforce referential integrity.

Sharing Data

Most companies and organizations store some type of data in Excel spreadsheets. Often, the data stored in those spreadsheets can be more efficiently managed in an Access database. At other times, importing data from Excel and other applications can reduce the data entry effort for your database.

Import Excel Data

STEP 1 ›› Access provides you with a wizard that guides you through the process of importing data from Excel.

To import an Excel spreadsheet to Access, complete the following steps:

1. Click the External Data tab.
2. Click Excel in the Import & Link group. The Get External Data – Excel Spreadsheet dialog box opens, as shown in Figure 13.

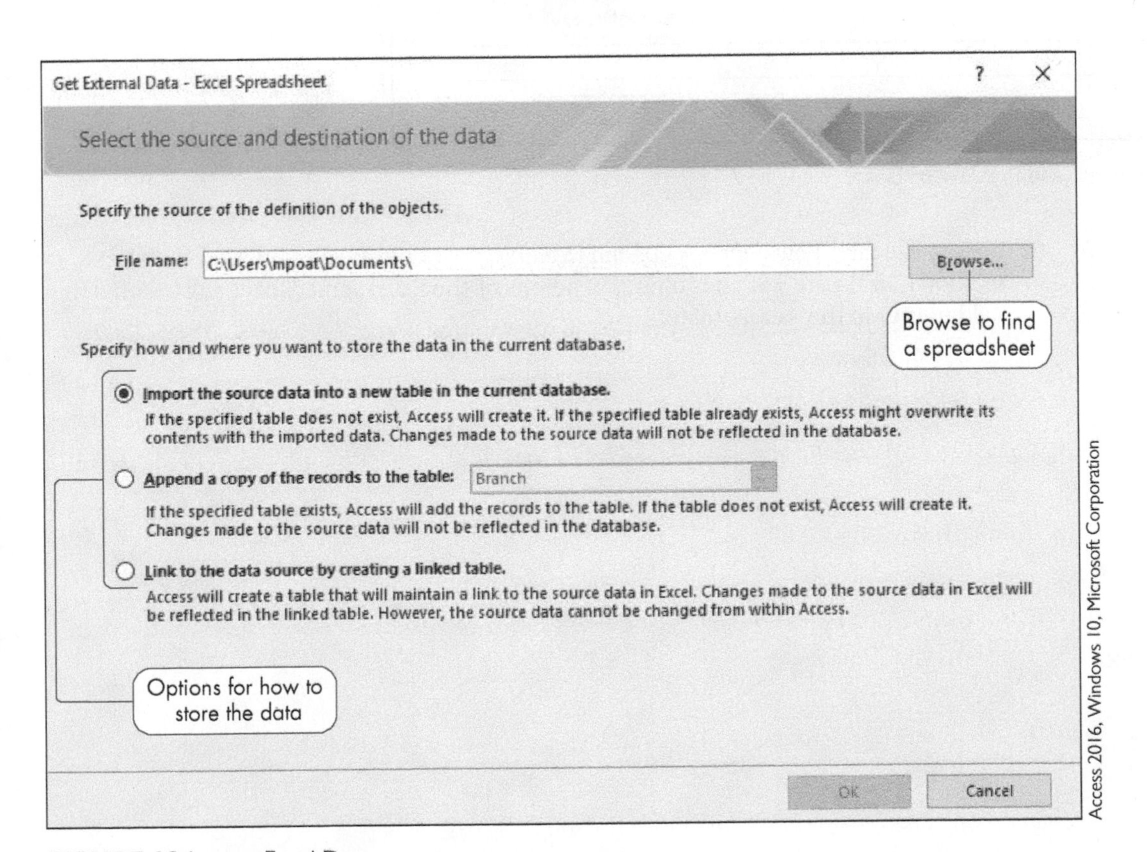

FIGURE 13 Import Excel Data

3. Click Browse to locate the Excel file you want to import, click the file to select it, and then click Open to specify this file as the source of the data.
4. Ensure the *Import the source data* option is selected, and click OK. The Import Spreadsheet Wizard launches.
5. Select the worksheet from the list of worksheets shown at the top of the dialog box, as shown in Figure 14 and then click Next.

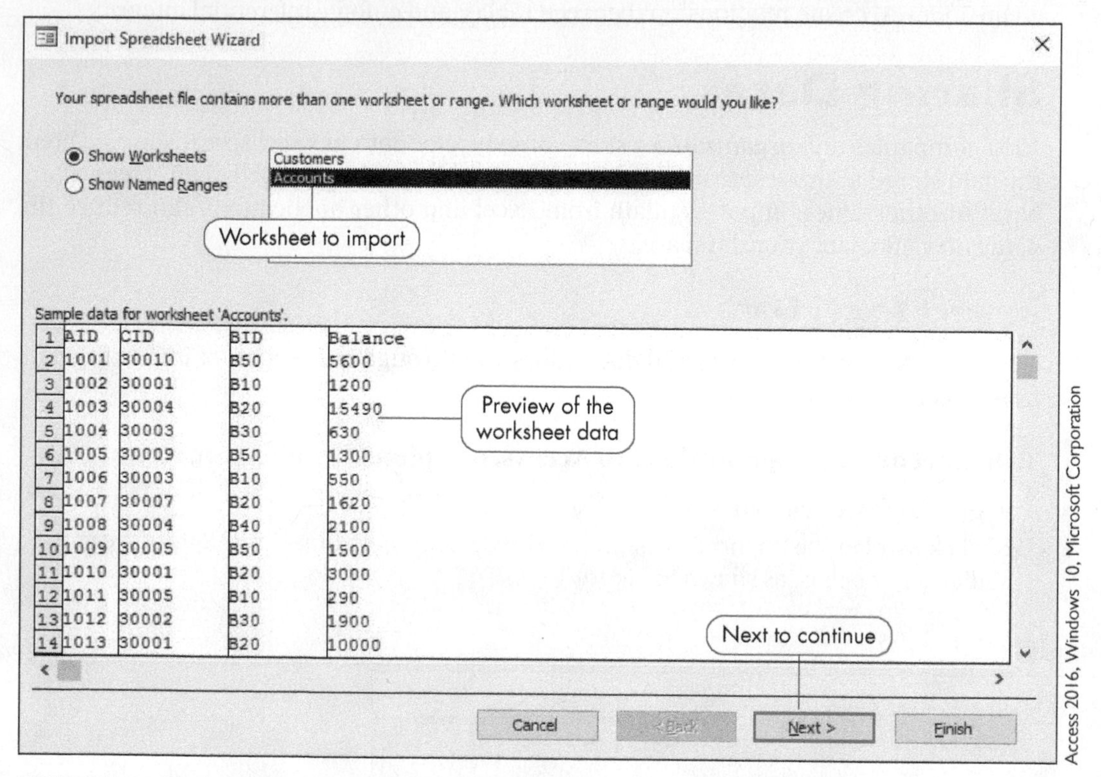

FIGURE 14 Available Worksheets and Preview of Data

6. Ensure the *First Row Contains Column Headings* check box is selected, and click Next, as shown in Figure 15. The column headings of the Excel spreadsheet will become the field names in the Access table.

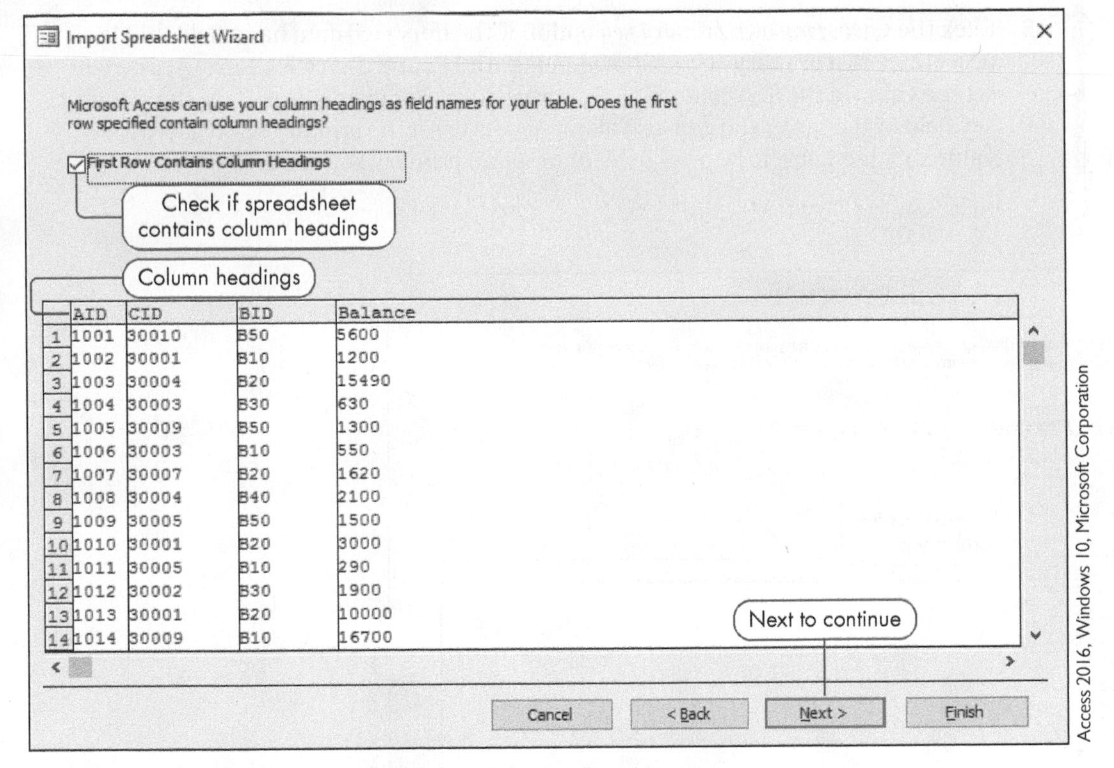

FIGURE 15 Excel Column Headings Become Access Field Names

7. Change the field options for the imported data, as shown in Figure 16, and then click Next.

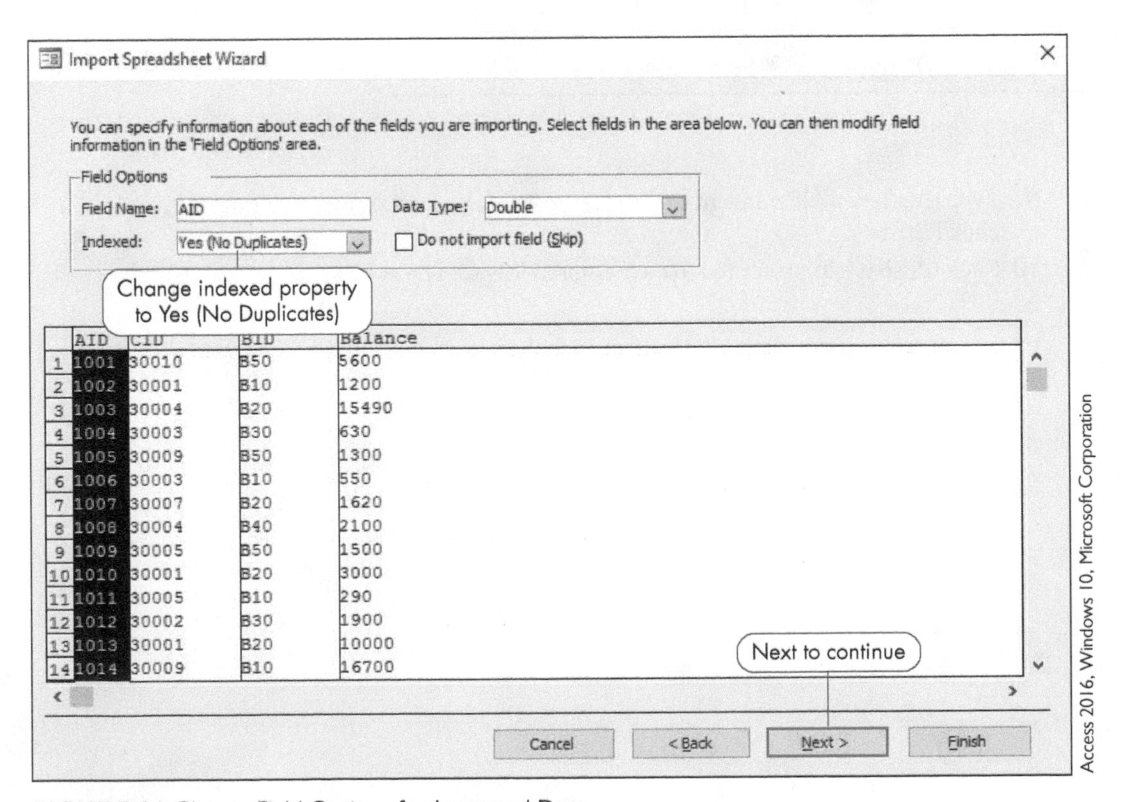

FIGURE 16 Change Field Options for Imported Data

8. Click the *Choose my own primary key* option if the imported data has a field that is acceptable as a primary key, as shown in Figure 17, and then click Next. Access will set the value in the first column of the spreadsheet (for example, AID) as the primary key field of the table. You can also allow Access to set the primary key if there is no value that is eligible to be a key field, or to set no primary key at all.

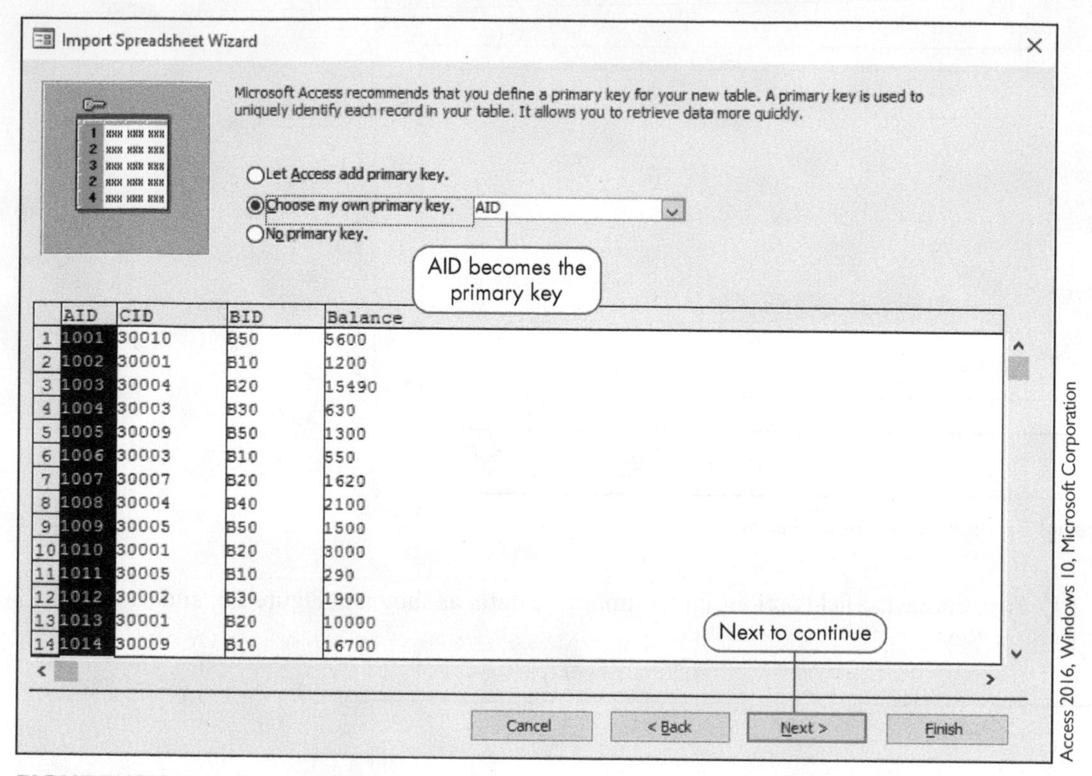

FIGURE 17 Set the Primary Key

9. Type the new table name in the Import to Table box, as shown in Figure 18, and then click Finish.
10. Click Close when prompted to Save Import Steps.

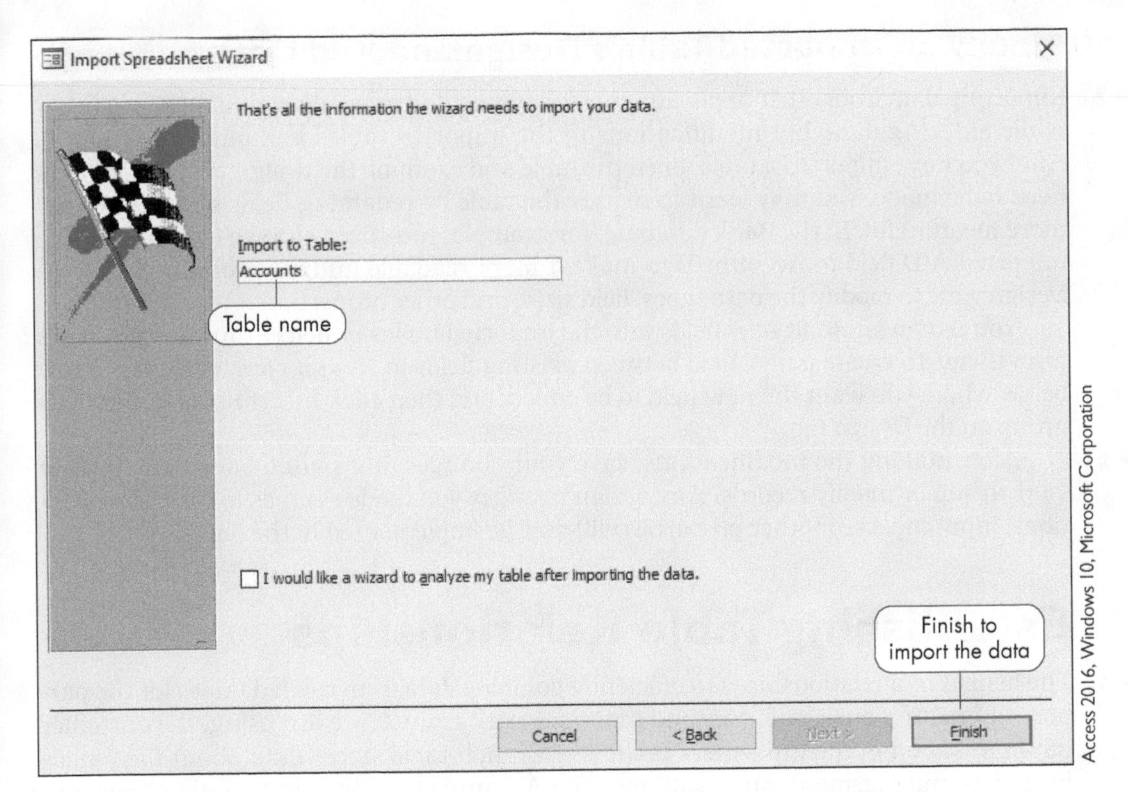

FIGURE 18 Enter a Table Name

> **TIP: LINKING TO EXTERNAL DATA**
> At times you might need to include a table in your database that already exists in another database. Instead of importing the data from this external source, you can create a link to it from within your database, and the table remains in the original database. You will be able to use the linked data as usual, without being able to modify the original table's design. You can also link to existing spreadsheets from your database without having to copy a large amount of data into your file.

Import Access Data

A wizard can also guide you as you import data from Access databases. You can import tables, queries, forms, reports, pages, macros, and modules from other databases. You can also modify the design of objects that are imported into your database.

To import an Access table into an existing database, complete the following steps:

1. Click the External Data tab.
2. Click Access in the Import & Link group. The Get External Data – Access Database dialog box opens.
3. Ensure that the *Import tables, queries, forms, reports, macros, and modules into the current database* option is selected.
4. Click Browse to locate the Access database you want to import.
5. Click the file to select it, and then click Open to specify this file as the source of the data.
6. Select the table you want to import, and then click OK. (Click Select All if the database contains multiple tables and you want to import all of them, and then click OK.)

Modify an Imported Table's Design and Add Data

STEP 3 Importing data from other applications saves typing and prevents errors that may occur while entering data, but modifications to the imported tables will often be required. After you have imported a table, open the table and examine the design to see if changes need to be made. You may want to modify the table by renaming fields so that they are more meaningful. In the Bank database, for example, you could change the name of the imported AID field to AccountID to make it more readable and meaningful. Switch to Design view to modify the data types, field sizes, and other properties.

You may want to fit new fields into the imported tables or delete unnecessary fields from them. To create a new field between existing fields in Design view, click in the row below where you want the new field to be added, and then click Insert Rows in the Tools group on the Design tab.

STEP 4 After making the modifications, save your changes and switch back to Datasheet view to add or modify records. Any design changes you made such as to field sizes, captions, input masks, or other properties will now be implemented in the datasheet.

Establishing Table Relationships

STEP 5 The benefit of a relationship is to efficiently combine data from related tables for the purpose of creating queries, forms, and reports. In the example we are using, the customer data are stored in the Customers table. The Branch table stores data about the bank's branches, management, and locations. The Accounts table stores data about account ownership and balances.

The common fields that were determined in the design phase of the tables can now be used to establish relationships between them.

To create the relationship between the common fields of two tables, complete the following steps:

1. Click the Database Tools tab.
2. Click Relationships in the Relationships group.
3. Drag the primary key field name from one table to the foreign key field name of the related table (for example, CustomerID in the Customers table to CustomerID in the Accounts table).
4. Set the desired options in the Edit Relationships dialog box, and click OK. Figure 19 shows the Bank database with relationships created by joining common fields.

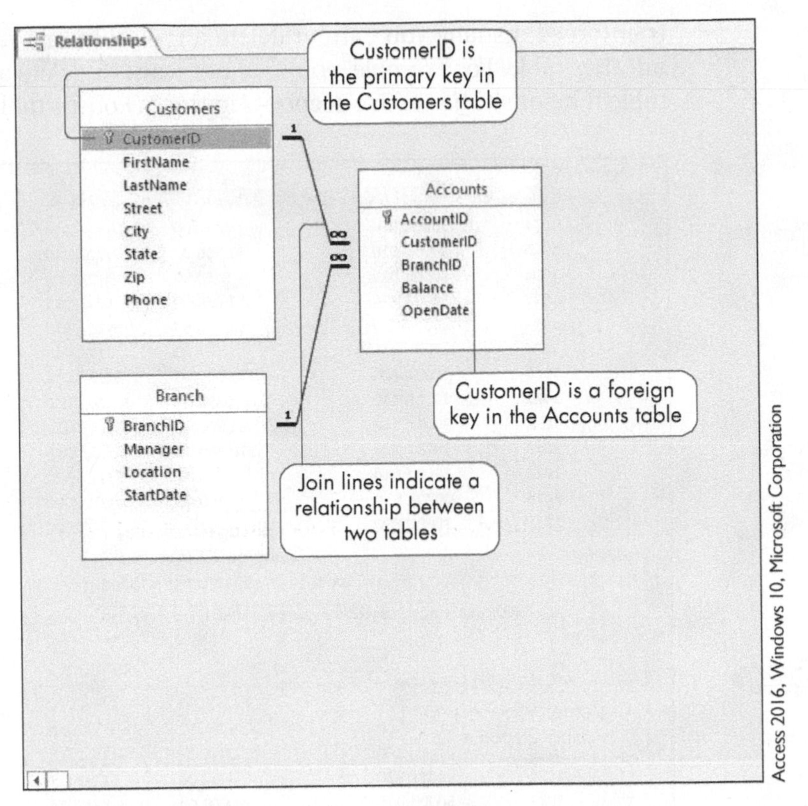

FIGURE 19 Relationships in the Bank Database

> **TIP: RETRIEVE DATA QUICKLY WITH INDEXING**
> When you set the primary key in Access, the Indexed property is automatically set to Yes (No Duplicates). The indexed property setting enables quick sorting in primary key order and quick retrieval based on the primary key. For non-primary key fields, it may be beneficial to set the Indexed property to Yes (Duplicates OK). Again, Access uses indexing to sort and retrieve data quickly based on the indexed field.

The primary key of a table plays a significant role when setting relationships. You cannot join two tables unless a primary key has been set in the primary table, which is one side of the relationship's join line. The other side of the relationship join line is most often the foreign key of the related table. A foreign key is a field in one table that is also the primary key and common field of another table. In the Bank database, CustomerID has been set as the primary key in the Customers table and also exists in the Accounts table. Therefore, a relationship can be set between the Customers table and the Accounts table, where CustomerID is the foreign key. Similarly, the Branch table can be joined to the Accounts table because BranchID has been set as the primary key in the Branch table, and BranchID is the foreign key in the Accounts table.

Enforce Referential Integrity

STEP 6 When you begin to create a relationship in Access, the Edit Relationships dialog box displays. The first check box, Enforce Referential Integrity, should be checked in most cases. ***Referential integrity*** enforces rules in a database that are used to preserve relationships between tables when records are changed.

When referential integrity is enforced, you cannot enter a foreign key value in a related table unless the primary key value exists in the primary table. In the case of the Bank database, the customer information is first entered into the Customers table before a customer's account information (which also includes CustomerID) can be entered into the Accounts table. If you attempt to enter an account prior to entering the customer information, an error will display, as shown in Figure 20. When referential integrity is enforced, usually you cannot delete a record in one table if it has related records in another table. For example, you may not want to delete a customer from the Customers table if he or she has active accounts in the Accounts table.

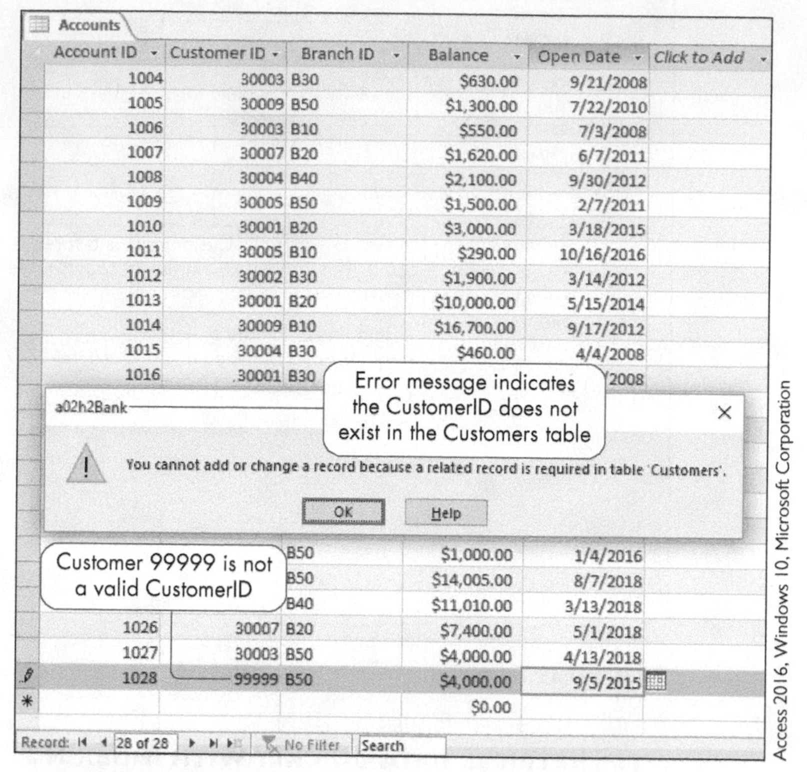

FIGURE 20 Error Message for Referential Integrity Violation

Set Cascade Options

When you create a relationship in Access and click the Enforce Referential Integrity check box, Access presents two additional options: Cascade Update Related Fields and Cascade Delete Related Records (see Figure 21). Check the ***Cascade Update Related Fields*** option so that when the primary key value is modified in a primary table, Access will automatically update all foreign key values in a related table. If a CustomerID is updated for some reason, all of the matching CustomerID values in the Accounts table will update automatically.

Check the ***Cascade Delete Related Records*** option so that when a record containing a primary key value is deleted in a primary table, Access will automatically delete all records in related tables that match the primary key. If one branch of a bank closes and its record is deleted from the Branch table, any account that is associated with this branch would then be deleted. Access will give a warning first to enable you to avoid the action of deleting records inadvertently.

Setting the Cascade Update and Cascade Delete options really depends on the business rules of an organization, and they should be set with caution. For example, if a branch of a bank closes, do you really want the accounts at that branch to be deleted? Another option might be to assign them to a different branch of the bank.

Establish a One-to-Many Relationship

Figure 21 also shows that the relationship that will be created will be a one-to-many relationship. Access provides three different relationships for joining tables: one-to-one, one-to-many, and many-to-many. The most common type by far is the one-to-many relationship. A ***one-to-many relationship*** is established when the primary key value in the primary table can match many of the foreign key values in the related table.

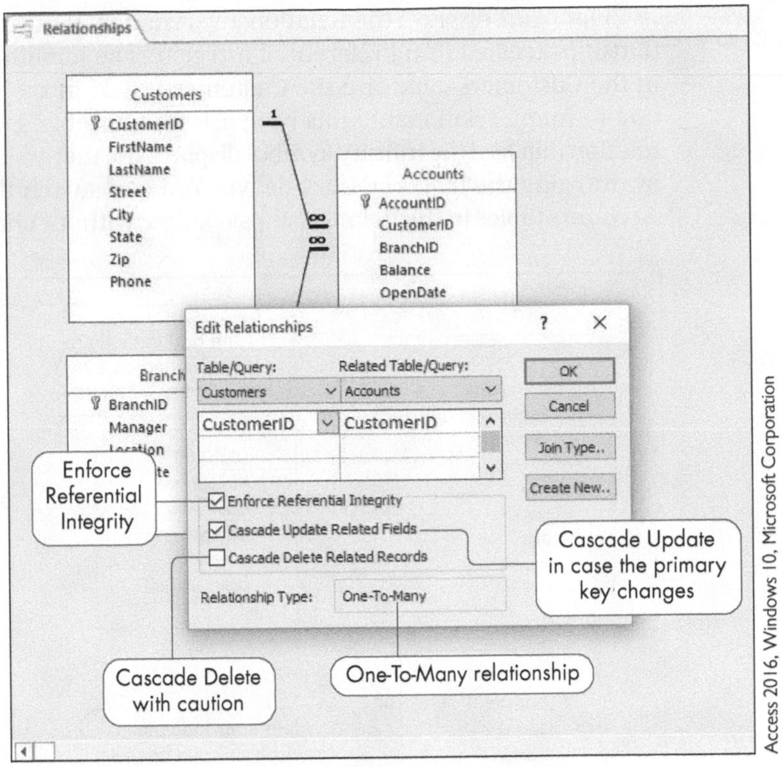

Access 2016, Windows 10, Microsoft Corporation

FIGURE 21 Cascade Update and Delete Options

For example, a bank customer will be entered into the Customers table one time only. The primary key value, which is the CustomerID number, might be 1585. That same customer could set up a checking, savings, and credit card account. With each account, the CustomerID (1585) is required and therefore will occur three times in the Accounts table. The value is entered one time in the Customers table and three times in the Accounts table. Therefore, the relationship between Customers and Accounts is described as one-to-many. Table 3 lists and describes all three types of relationships you can create between Access tables.

TABLE 3 Relationship Types

Relationship Type	Description
One-to-Many	The primary key table must have only one occurrence of each value. For example, each customer must have a unique identification number in the Customers table. The foreign key field in the related table may have repeating values. For example, one customer may have many different account numbers.
One-to-One	Two different tables use the same primary key. Exactly one record exists in the second table for each record in the first table. Sometimes security issues require a single table to be split into two related tables. For example, in an organization's database anyone in the company might be able to access the Employee table and find the employee's office number, department assignment, or telephone extension. However, only a few people need to have access to the employee's network login password, salary, Social Security number, performance review, or marital status, which would be stored in a second table. Tables containing this information would use the same unique identifier to identify each employee.
Many-to-Many	This is an artificially constructed relationship allowing many matching records in each direction between tables. It requires construction of a third table called a junction table. For example, a database might have a table for employees and one for projects. Several employees might be assigned to one project, but one employee might also be assigned to many different projects.

Pearson Education, Inc.

Figure 22 displays the Relationships window for the Bank database and all the relationships created using referential integrity. The join line between the CustomerID field in the Customers table and the CustomerID field in the Accounts table indicates that a one-to-many relationship has been set. The number 1 displays on the one side of the relationship and the infinity symbol displays the many side. You can rearrange the tables by dragging the tables by the title bar. You can switch the positions of the Branch and Accounts tables in the Relationships window without changing the relationship itself.

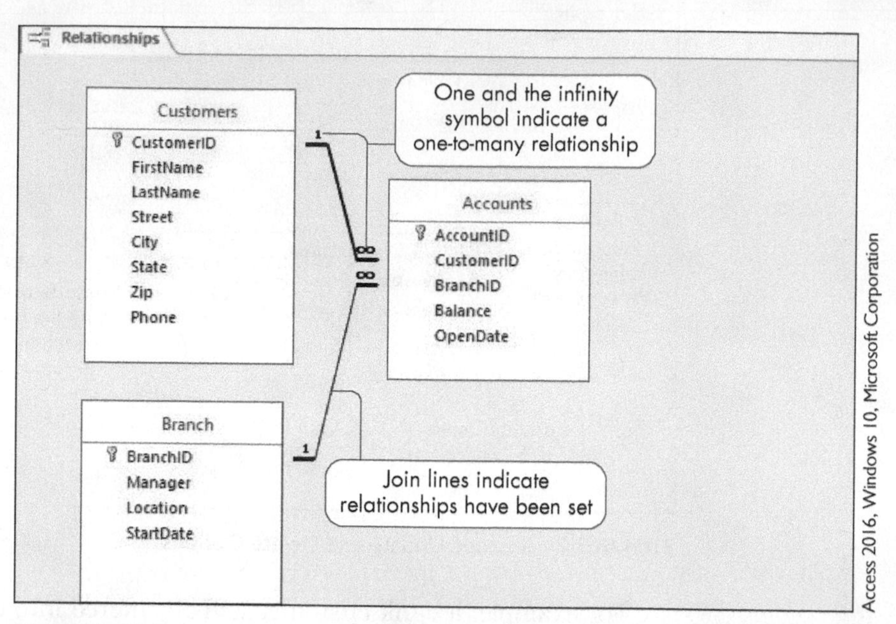

FIGURE 22 Relationships Window Displaying One-to-Many Relationships

TIP: NAVIGATING BETWEEN THE RELATIONSHIPS WINDOW AND A TABLE'S DESIGN

When you right-click a table's title bar in the Relationships window, the shortcut menu offers you the option to open the table in Design view. This is a convenient feature because if you want to link one table to another table, the joined fields must have the same data type. This shortcut enables you to check the fields and revise them if a table contains a field with the wrong data type.

Quick Concepts

4. Describe a scenario that may require you to import Excel data into Access.
5. What is the purpose of setting a relationship between two tables?
6. Why would you decide to use the Cascade Delete option (or not) when setting a relationship?
7. Specify two database tables that you might design that would contain a one-to-many relationship. Describe the relationship.

Hands-On Exercises

Watch the Video for this Hands-On Exercise!

MyITLab® HOE2 Training

Skills covered: Import Excel Data • Import Data from an Access Database • Modify an Imported Table's Design • Add Data to an Imported Table • Establish Table Relationships • Enforce Referential Integrity

2 Multiple-Table Databases

You created a new Bank database, and a new Branch table. Now you are ready to import additional tables—one from an Excel spreadsheet and one from an Access database. Assume that the data are formatted correctly and are structured properly so that you can begin the import process.

STEP 1 ›› IMPORT EXCEL DATA

You and the auditor have discovered several of Commonwealth's files that contain customer data. These files need to be analyzed, so you decide to import the data into Access. In this step, you import an Excel spreadsheet into the Bank database. Refer to Figure 23 as you complete Step 1.

All Access Obje...

Search...

Tables

Branch

Customers

Step e: Imported column headings

Customers

CID	FirstName	LastName	Street	City	State	Zip	Phone	Click to Add
30001	Allison	Millward	2732 Baker Blvd.	Greensboro	NC	27492	5553345678	
30002	Bernett	Fox	12 Orchestra Terrace	High Point	NC	27494	5553585554	
30003	Clay	Hayes	P.O. Box 555	Greensboro	NC	27492	5559984457	
30004	Cordle	Collins	2743 Bering St.	Winston-Salem	NC	27492	5554472283	
30005	Eaton	Wagner	2743 Bering St.	Greensboro	NC	27492	5559883346	
30006	Kwasi	Williams	89 Jefferson Way	High Point	NC	27494	5554475565	
30007	Natasha	Simpson	187 Suffolk Ln.	Greensboro	NC	27493	5557753389	
30008	Joy	Jones	305 - 14th Ave. S.	Winston-Salem	NC	27493	5552587655	
30009	John	Nunn	89 Chiaroscuro Rd.	Greensboro	NC	27494	5559985557	
30010	Laura	Peterson	120 Hanover Sq.	Winston-Salem	NC	27492	5553346654	
*								

FIGURE 23 Imported Customers Table

a. Open *a02h1Bank_LastFirst* if you closed it at the end of Hands-On Exercise 1, and save it as **a02h2Bank_LastFirst**, changing h1 to h2.

b. Click **Enable Content** below the Ribbon to indicate that you trust the contents of the database.

c. Click the **External Data tab** and click **Excel** in the Import & Link group to launch the Get External Data – Excel Spreadsheet feature. Ensure that the *Import the source data into a new table in the current database* option is selected.

> **TROUBLESHOOTING:** Ensure that you click Excel in the Import & Link group to import the spreadsheet and not the Excel command in the Export group.

d. Click **Browse** and navigate to your student data files. Select the *a02h2Customers* workbook. Click **Open** and click **OK** to open the Import Spreadsheet Wizard.

e. Ensure that the *First Row Contains Column Headings* check box is checked to indicate to Access that column headings exist in the Excel file.

The field names CID, FirstName, LastName, Street, City, State, ZIP, and Phone will import from Excel along with the data stored in the rows in the worksheet. You will modify the field names later in Access.

f. Click **Next**.

g. Ensure that CID is displayed in the Field Name box in Field Options. Click the **Indexed arrow** and select **Yes (No Duplicates)**. Click **Next**.

The CID (CustomerID) will become the primary key in this table. It needs to be a unique identifier, so you must change the property to No Duplicates.

h. Click the **Choose my own primary key option**. Make sure that the CID field is selected. Click **Next**.

The final screen of the Import Spreadsheet Wizard asks you to name your table. The name of the Excel worksheet is Customers, and Access defaults to the worksheet name. It is an acceptable name.

i. Click **Finish** to accept Customers as the table name.

A dialog box opens prompting you to save the steps of this import to use again. If this is data that is to be collected in Excel and updated to the database on a regular basis, saving the import steps would save time. You do not need to save the import steps in this example.

j. Click **Close**.

The new table displays in the Navigation Pane of the Bank database.

k. Open the imported Customers table in Datasheet view and double-click the border between each of the field names to adjust the columns to Best Fit. Compare your table to Figure 23.

l. Save and close the table.

STEP 2 » IMPORT DATA FROM AN ACCESS DATABASE

The auditor asks you to import an Access database table that contains account information related to the accounts you are analyzing. You use the Import Wizard to import the database table. Refer to Figure 24 as you complete Step 2.

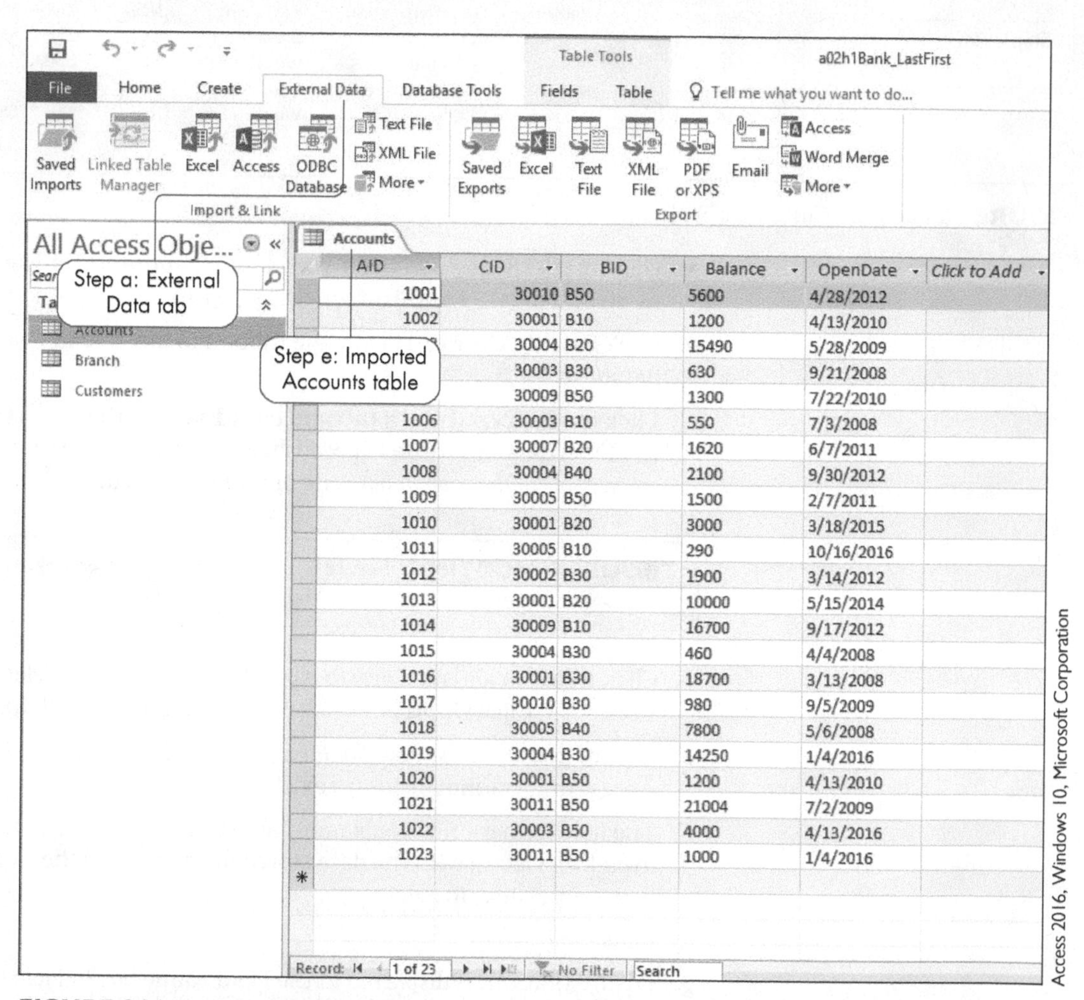

AID	CID	BID	Balance	OpenDate	Click to Add
1001	30010	B50	5600	4/28/2012	
1002	30001	B10	1200	4/13/2010	
	30004	B20	15490	5/28/2009	
	30003	B30	630	9/21/2008	
	30009	B50	1300	7/22/2010	
1006	30003	B10	550	7/3/2008	
1007	30007	B20	1620	6/7/2011	
1008	30004	B40	2100	9/30/2012	
1009	30005	B50	1500	2/7/2011	
1010	30001	B20	3000	3/18/2015	
1011	30005	B10	290	10/16/2016	
1012	30002	B30	1900	3/14/2012	
1013	30001	B20	10000	5/15/2014	
1014	30009	B10	16700	9/17/2012	
1015	30004	B30	460	4/4/2008	
1016	30001	B30	18700	3/13/2008	
1017	30010	B30	980	9/5/2009	
1018	30005	B40	7800	5/6/2008	
1019	30004	B30	14250	1/4/2016	
1020	30001	B50	1200	4/13/2010	
1021	30011	B50	21004	7/2/2009	
1022	30003	B50	4000	4/13/2016	
1023	30011	B50	1000	1/4/2016	

FIGURE 24 Imported Accounts Table

a. Click the **External Data tab** and click **Access** in the Import & Link group to launch the Get External Data – Access Database feature. Ensure that the *Import tables, queries, forms, reports, macros, and modules into the current database* option is selected.

b. Click **Browse** and navigate to your student data files. Select the *a02h2Accounts* database. Click **Open** and click **OK** to open the Import Objects dialog box.

c. Click the **Accounts table** for importing and click **OK**.

d. Click **Close** in the Save Import Steps dialog box.

The Navigation Pane now contains three tables: Accounts, Branch, and Customers.

e. Open the imported Accounts table in Datasheet view and compare it to Figure 24.

f. Close the table.

STEP 3 ›› MODIFY AN IMPORTED TABLE'S DESIGN

When importing tables from either Excel or Access, the fields may have different data types and property settings than required to create table relationships. You will modify the tables so that each field has the correct data type and field size. Refer to Figure 25 as you complete Step 3.

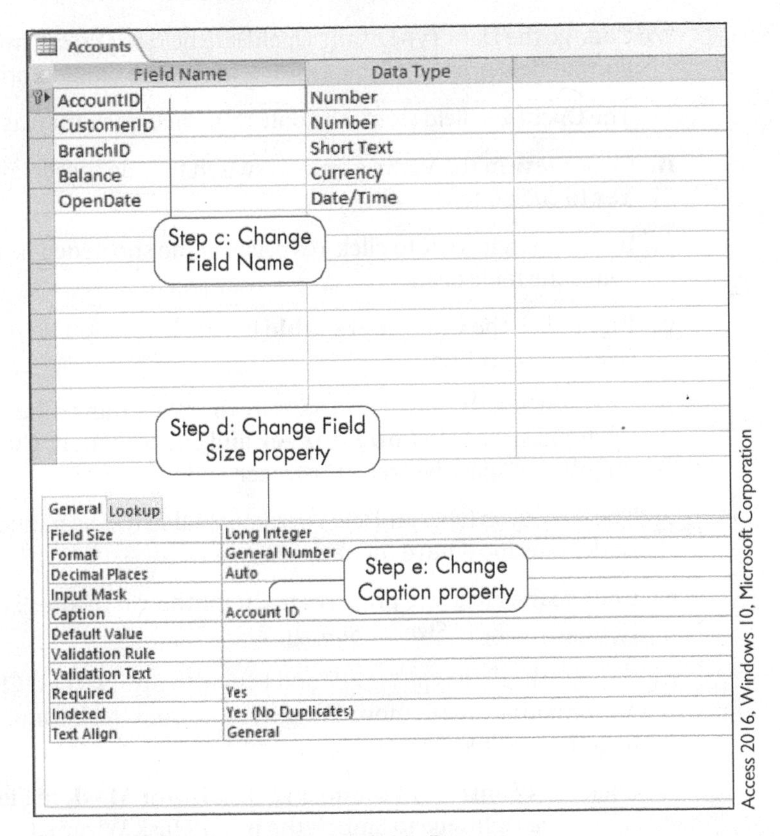

FIGURE 25 Modified Accounts Table Design

a. Right-click the **Accounts table** in the Navigation Pane.

b. Select Design view from the shortcut menu to open the table in Design view.

The Accounts table displays with the primary key AID selected.

c. Change the AID field name to **AccountID**.

d. Change the Field Size property to **Long Integer**.

Long Integer ensures that there will be enough numbers as the number of customers grows over time and may exceed 32,768 (the upper limit for Integer values).

e. Type **Account ID** in the Caption box for the AccountID field. The caption contains a space between Account and ID.

f. Click the **CID** field. Change the CID field name to **CustomerID**.

g. Change the Field Size property to **Long Integer**.

You can select the Field Size option using the arrow, or you can type the first letter of the option you want. For example, type l for Long Integer or s for Single. Make sure the current option is completely selected before you type the letter.

h. Type **Customer ID** in the Caption box for the CustomerID field. The caption contains a space between Customer and ID.

i. Click the **BID field**. Change the BID field name to **BranchID**.

j. Type **5** in the Field Size property box in the Field Properties.

k. Type **Branch ID** in the Caption property box for the Branch ID field.

l. Change the Data Type of the Balance field to **Currency**.

The Currency data type is used for fields that contain monetary values. In this case, changing the data type is not consequential; formatting the imported Balance field as Currency will not change the original data values.

m. Change the Data Type of the OpenDate field to **Date/Time** and set **Short Date** in the Format field property. Type **Open Date** in the Caption property box.

The OpenDate field stores the date that each account was opened.

n. Click **View** in the Views group to switch to Datasheet view. Read the messages and click **Yes** to each one.

In this case, it is OK to click Yes because the shortened fields will not cut off any data. Leave the table open.

o. Right-click the **Customers table** in the Navigation Pane and from the shortcut menu, select **Design View**.

p. Change the CID field name to **CustomerID**. Change the Field Size property of the CustomerID field to **Long Integer** and add a caption, **Customer ID**. Take note of the intentional space between Customer and ID.

The Accounts table and the Customers table will be joined using the CustomerID field. Both fields must have the same data type.

q. Change the Field Size property to **20** for the FirstName, LastName, Street, and City fields. Change the Field Size for State to **2**.

r. Change the data type for ZIP and Phone to **Short Text**. Change the Field Size property to **15** for both fields. Remove the @ symbol from the Format property where it exists for all fields in the Customers table.

s. Click the **Phone field name** and click **Input Mask** in Field Properties. Click the **ellipsis** [...] on the right side to launch the Input Mask Wizard. Click **Yes** to save the table and click **Yes** to the *Some data may be lost* warning. Click **Finish** to apply the default phone number input mask.

The phone number input mask enables users to enter 6105551212 in the datasheet, and Access will display it as (610) 555-1212.

t. Click **Save** to save the design changes to the Customers table.

STEP 4 » ADD DATA TO AN IMPORTED TABLE

Now that you have created the Access tables, you discover that you need to add another customer and his account records to them. Refer to Figure 26 as you complete Step 4.

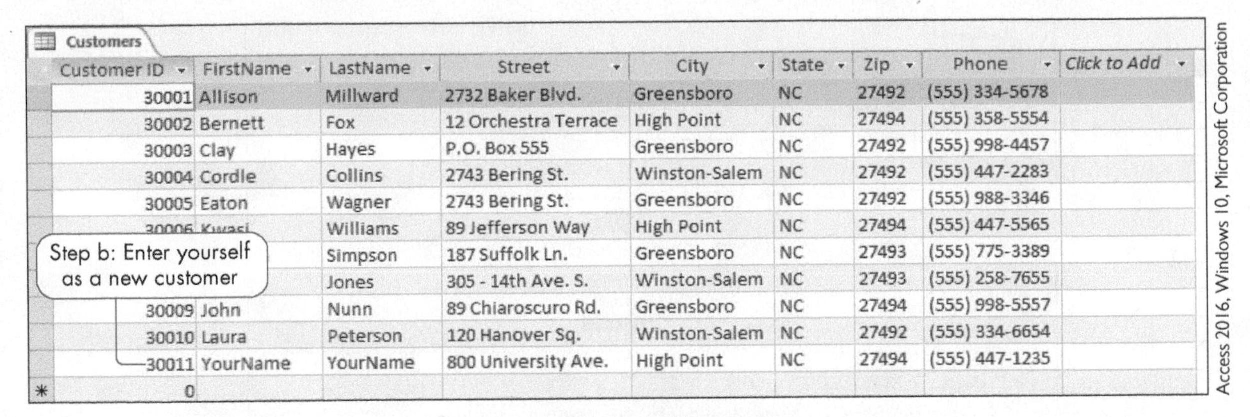

Customers

Customer ID	FirstName	LastName	Street	City	State	Zip	Phone	Click to Add
30001	Allison	Millward	2732 Baker Blvd.	Greensboro	NC	27492	(555) 334-5678	
30002	Bernett	Fox	12 Orchestra Terrace	High Point	NC	27494	(555) 358-5554	
30003	Clay	Hayes	P.O. Box 555	Greensboro	NC	27492	(555) 998-4457	
30004	Cordle	Collins	2743 Bering St.	Winston-Salem	NC	27492	(555) 447-2283	
30005	Eaton	Wagner	2743 Bering St.	Greensboro	NC	27492	(555) 988-3346	
30006	Kwasi	Williams	89 Jefferson Way	High Point	NC	27494	(555) 447-5565	
		Simpson	187 Suffolk Ln.	Greensboro	NC	27493	(555) 775-3389	
		Jones	305 - 14th Ave. S.	Winston-Salem	NC	27493	(555) 258-7655	
30009	John	Nunn	89 Chiaroscuro Rd.	Greensboro	NC	27494	(555) 998-5557	
30010	Laura	Peterson	120 Hanover Sq.	Winston-Salem	NC	27492	(555) 334-6654	
30011	YourName	YourName	800 University Ave.	High Point	NC	27494	(555) 447-1235	
* 0								

FIGURE 26 Customers Table Displaying the Added Customer ID 30011

a. Click **View** in the Views group to display the Customers table in Datasheet view.

The asterisk at the bottom of the table data in the row selector area is the indicator of a place to enter a new record.

b. Click next to the * in the **Customer ID field** in the new record row below 30010. Type **30011**. Fill in the rest of the data using your personal information as the customer. You may use a fictitious address and phone number.

Note the phone number format. The input mask you set formats the phone number.

c. Close the Customers table. The Accounts table tab is open.

> **TROUBLESHOOTING:** If the Accounts table is not open, double-click Accounts in the Navigation Pane.

d. Click next to the * in the **Account ID field** in the new record row. Type **1024**. Type **30011** as the Customer ID and **B50** as the Branch ID. Type **14005** for the Balance field value. Type **8/7/2018** for the Open Date.

e. Add the following records to the Accounts table:

Account ID	Customer ID	Branch ID	Balance	Open Date
1025	30006	B40	$11,010	3/13/2018
1026	30007	B20	$7,400	5/1/2018

f. Close the Accounts table, but keep the database open.

STEP 5 ›› ESTABLISH TABLE RELATIONSHIPS

The tables for the bank investigation have been designed and populated. Now you will establish connections between the tables. Look at the primary and foreign keys as a guide. Refer to Figure 27 as you complete Step 5.

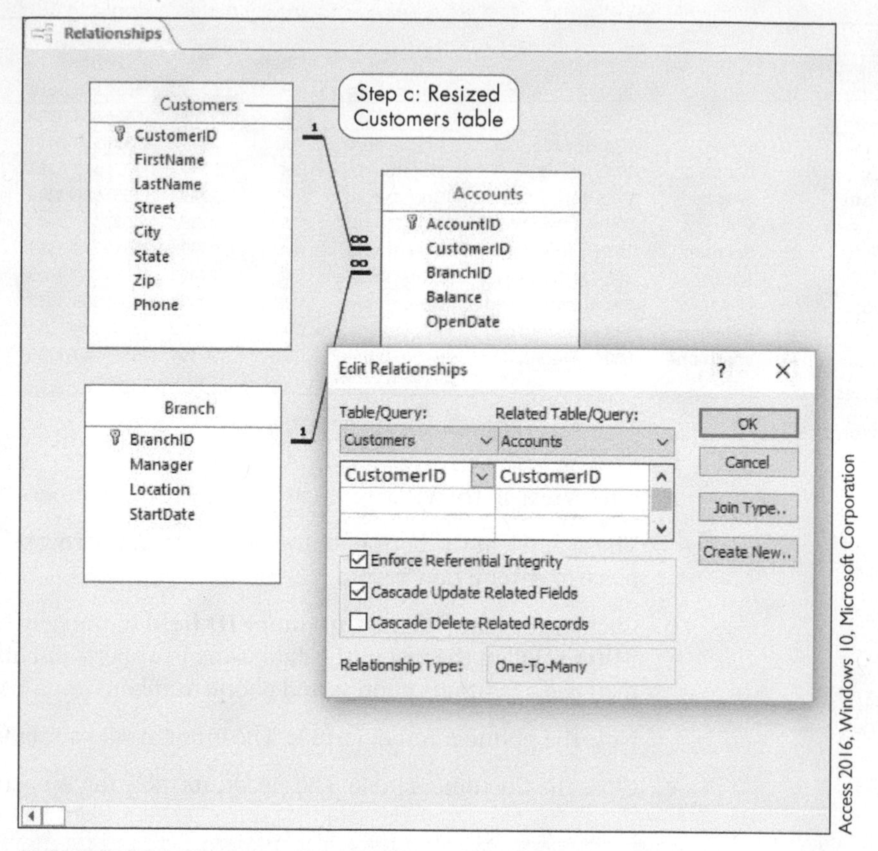

FIGURE 27 Relationships Between Tables

a. Click the **Database Tools tab** and click **Relationships** in the Relationships group.

The Relationships window opens and the Show Table dialog box displays.

TROUBLESHOOTING: If the Show Table dialog box does not open, click Show Table in the Relationships group on the Relationship Tools Design tab.

b. Double-click each of the three tables displayed in the Show Table dialog box to add them to the Relationships window. Click **Close** in the Show Table dialog box.

TROUBLESHOOTING: If you have a duplicate table, click the title bar of the duplicated table and press Delete.

c. Click and drag the border of the Customers table field list to resize it so that all of the fields are visible. Arrange the tables as shown in Figure 27.

d. Drag the **BranchID field** (the primary key) in the Branch table onto the BranchID field (the foreign key) in the Accounts table. The Edit Relationships dialog box opens. Click the **Enforce Referential Integrity** and **Cascade Update Related Fields check boxes** to select them. Click **Create**.

A black line displays, joining the two tables. It has a 1 at the end near the Branch table and an infinity symbol on the end next to the Accounts table. You have established a one-to-many relationship between the Branch and Accounts tables. Each single branch is connected with many accounts.

e. Drag the **CustomerID field** (the primary key) in the Customers table onto the CustomerID field (the foreign key) in the Accounts table. The Edit Relationships dialog box opens. Click the **Enforce Referential Integrity** and **Cascade Update Related Fields check boxes** to select them. Click **Create**.

You have established a one-to-many relationship between the Customers and Accounts tables. A customer will have only a single CustomerID number. The same customer may have many different accounts: Savings, Checking, Credit Card, and so forth.

> **TROUBLESHOOTING:** If you get an error message when you click Create, verify that the data types of the joined fields are the same. To check the data types from the Relationships window, right-click the title bar of a table and select Table Design from the shortcut menu. Modify the data type of the join fields, if necessary. Customer ID should be Number and Branch ID should be Short Text in both tables.

f. Click **Save** on the Quick Access Toolbar to save the changes to the relationships. Close the Relationships window.

STEP 6 » ENFORCE REFERENTIAL INTEGRITY

The design of the Bank database must be 100% correct; otherwise, data entry may be compromised. Even though you are confident that the table relationships are set correctly, you decide to test them by entering some invalid data. If referential integrity is enforced, the invalid data will be rejected by Access. Refer to Figure 28 as you complete Step 6.

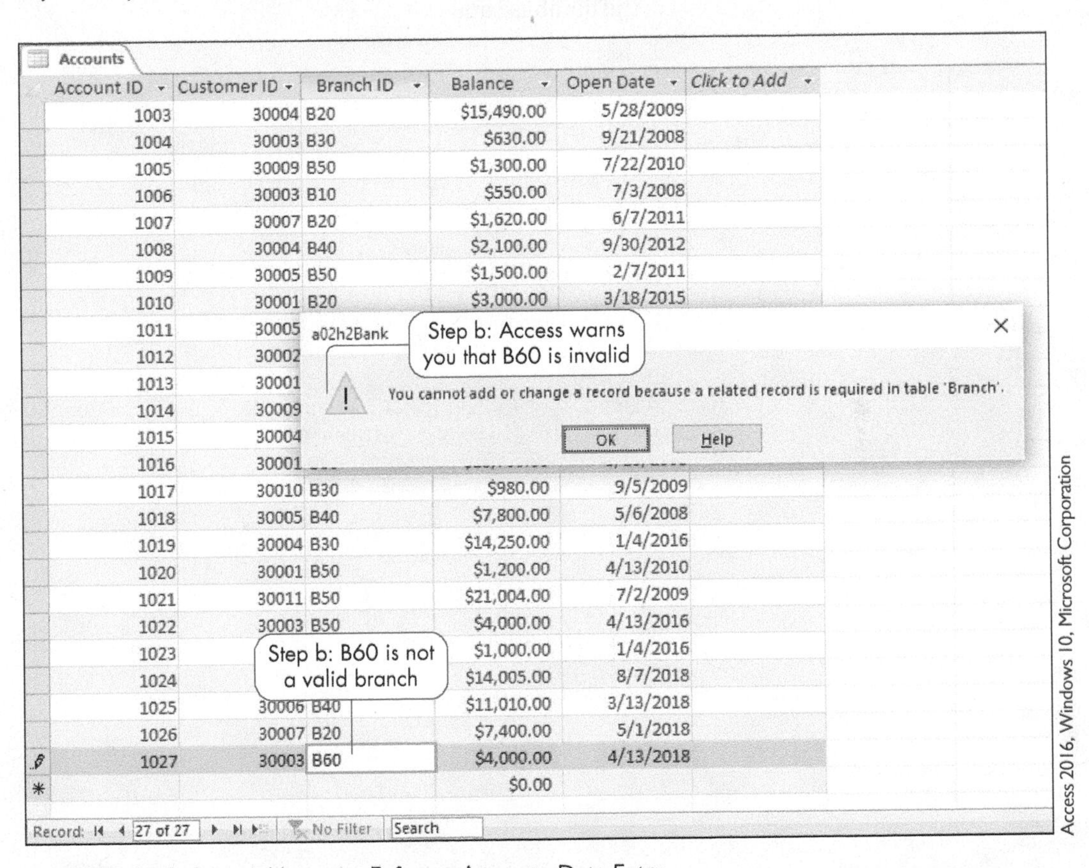

FIGURE 28 Referential Integrity Enforces Accurate Data Entry

a. Double-click the **Accounts table** to open it in Datasheet view.

b. Add a new record, pressing **Tab** after each field: Account ID: **1027**, Customer ID: **30003**, Branch: **B60**, Balance: **4000**, Open Date: **4/13/2018**. Press **Enter**.

   You attempted to enter a nonexistent BranchID (B60) and were not allowed to make that error. A warning message is telling you that a related record in the Branch table is required, because the Accounts table and the Branch table are connected by a relationship with Enforce Referential Integrity checked.

c. Click **OK**. Double-click the **Branch table** in the Navigation Pane and examine the data in the BranchID field. Notice the Branch table has no B60 record. Close the Branch table.

d. Replace B60 with **B50** in the new Accounts record and press **Tab** three times. As soon as the focus moves to the next record, the pencil symbol disappears and your data are saved.

   You successfully identified a BranchID that Access recognizes. Because referential integrity between the Accounts and Branch tables has been enforced, Access looks at each data entry item in a foreign key and matches it to a corresponding value in the table where it is the primary key. In Step b, you attempted to enter a nonexistent BranchID and were not allowed to make that error. In Step d, you entered a valid BranchID. Access examined the index for the BranchID in the Branch table and found a corresponding value for B50.

e. Close the Accounts table.

f. Close any open tables.

g. Keep the database open if you plan to continue with the Hands-On Exercise. If not, close the database and exit Access.

Single-Table Queries

A ***query*** enables you to ask questions about the data stored in a database and then provides the answers to the questions by creating subsets or summaries of data in a datasheet. If you wanted to see which customers currently have an account with a balance over $5,000, you could find the answer by creating an Access query.

In this section, you will use the Simple Query Wizard and Query Design view to create single-table queries that display only data that you select. Multitable queries will be covered in the next section.

Creating a Single-Table Query

Because data are stored in tables in a database, you always begin a query by determining which table (or tables) contain the data that you need. For the question about account balances over $5,000, you would use the Accounts table. You can create a single-table query in two ways—by using the Simple Query Wizard or the Query Design tool in the Queries group on the Create tab. While the Simple Query Wizard offers a step-by-step guide to creating a query, the Query Design tool allows for more flexibility and customization, and is often the preferred method for creating queries.

After you design a query, you run it to display the results in a datasheet. A query's datasheet looks like a table's datasheet, except that it is usually a subset of the fields and records found in the table on which it is based. The subset shows only the records that match the criteria that were added in the query design. The subset may contain different sorting of the records than the sorting in the underlying table. You can enter new records in a query, modify existing records, or delete records in Datasheet view. Any changes made in Datasheet view are reflected in the underlying table on which the query is based.

Create a Single-Table Select Query

Select queries are a type of query that displays only the fields and records that match criteria entered in the query design process.

To create a select query using the Query Design tool, complete the following steps:

1. Click the Create tab.
2. Click Query Design in the Queries group on the Design tab.
3. Select the table you want for your query from the Show Table dialog box.
4. Click Add to add the table to the top pane of the query design and close the Show Table dialog box.
5. Drag the fields needed from the table's field list to the query design grid (or alternatively, double-click the field names); then add criteria and sorting options.
6. Click Run in the Results group on the Design tab to show the results in Datasheet view.

Use Query Design View

Query Design view is divided into two sections: The top pane displays the tables from which the data will be retrieved, and the bottom pane (known as the query design grid) displays the fields and the criteria that you set. In the query design grid, you select only the fields that contain the data you want in the query and arrange them in the order that you want them displayed in the query results. You add criteria to further limit (or filter) the records to display only those that you require in the results. The design grid also enables you to sort the records based on one or more fields. You can create calculated fields to display data based on expressions that use the fields in the underlying table. For example, you could calculate the monthly interest earned on each bank account by multiplying the Balance by an interest rate. If a query contains more than one table, the join lines between tables display as they were created in the Relationships window.

The query design grid (the bottom pane) contains columns and rows. Each field in the query has its own column and contains multiple rows. The rows allow you to control the query results.

- The Field row displays the field name.
- The Table row displays the data source (in some cases, a field occurs in more than one table, for example, when it is a join field; therefore, it is often beneficial to display the table name in the query design grid).
- The Sort row enables you to sort in ascending or descending order (or neither).
- The Show row controls whether the field will be displayed or hidden in the query results.
- The ***Criteria row*** is used to set the rules that determine which records will be selected, such as customers with account balances greater than $5,000.

Figure 29 displays the query design grid with the Show Table dialog box open. The Accounts table has added from the Show Table dialog box. Figure 30 shows Design view of a sample query with four fields, with a criterion set for one field and sorting set on another. The results of the query display in Datasheet view, as shown in Figure 31.

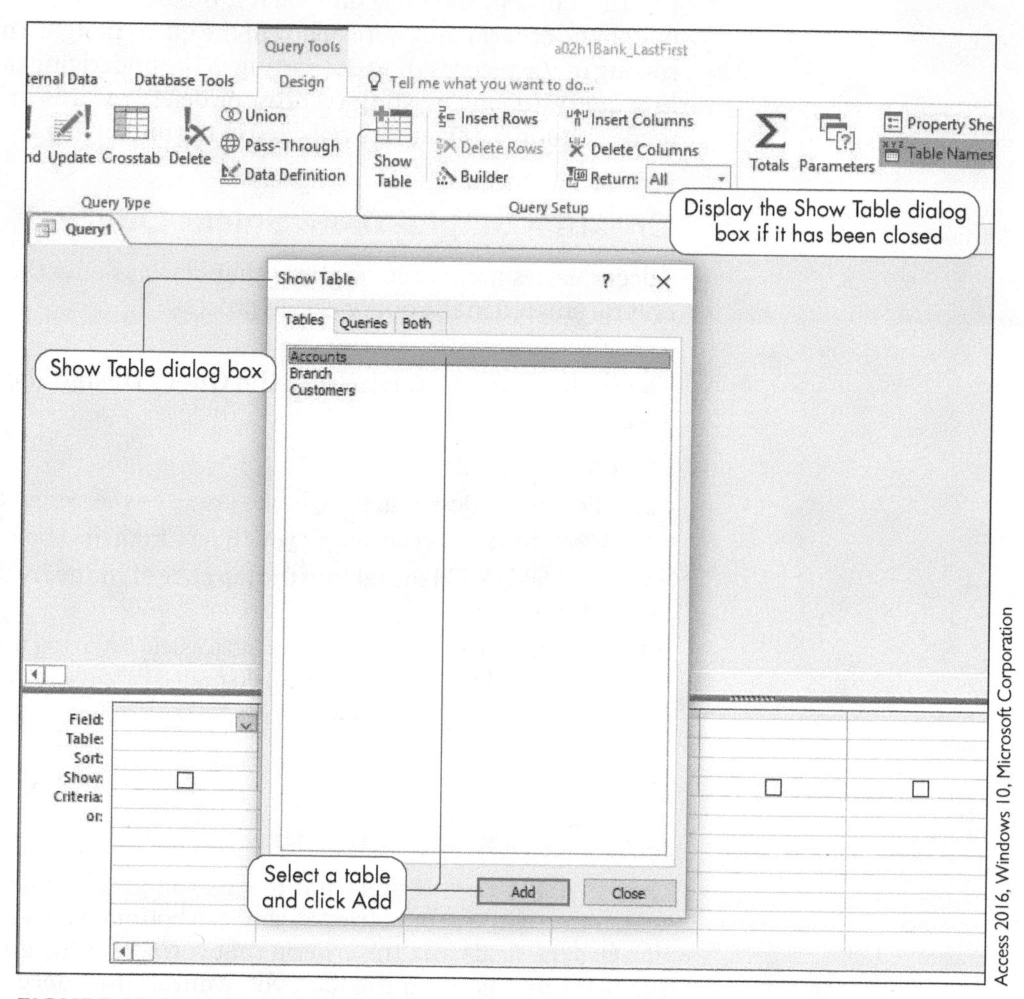

FIGURE 29 Query Design View with Show Table Dialog Box

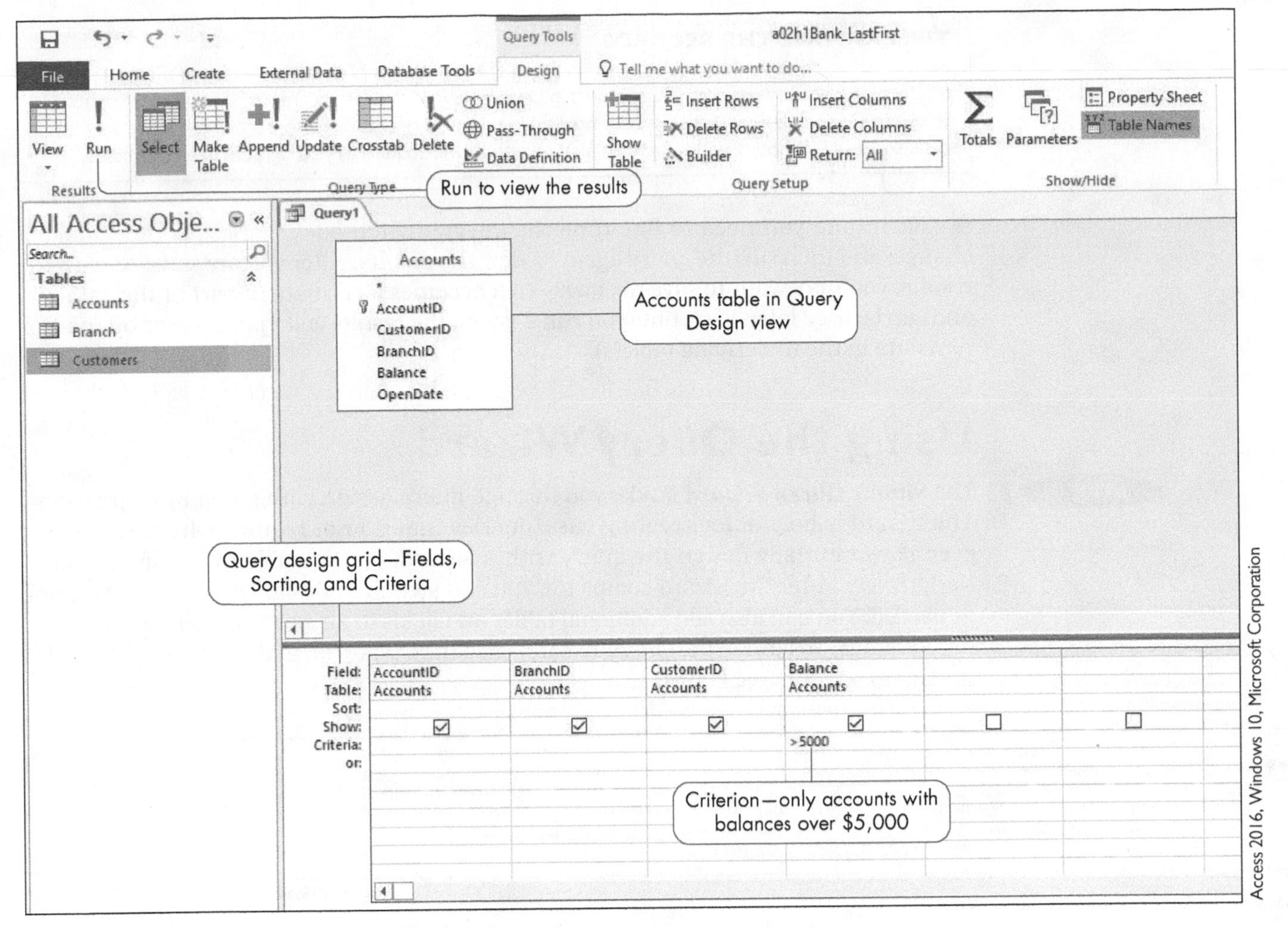

FIGURE 30 Query Design View with Sample Criterion

Query1

Account ID	Branch ID	Customer ID	Balance
1014	B10	30009	$16,700.00
1026	B20	30007	$7,400.00
1013	B20	30001	$10,000.00
1003	B20	30004	$15,490.00
1019	B30	30004	$14,250.00
1016	B30	30001	$18,700.00
1025	B40	30006	$11,010.00
1018	B40	30005	$7,800.00
1028	B50	30005	$8,000.00
1024	B50	30011	$14,005.00
1021	B50	30011	$21,004.00
1020	B50	30001	$12,000.00
1001	B50	30010	$5,600.00
*			$0.00

Query results in Datasheet view

Only accounts with a balance over $5,000

Record: 1 of 13 No Filter Search

FIGURE 31 Query Results in Datasheet View

TIP: EXAMINE THE RECORDS

Be sure to examine the records returned in the query results. Verify that the records in the query results match the criteria that you specified in Design view. If the results are not what you anticipated, return to Design view, and check your criteria. Unexpected results can also occur from inaccurate data, so troubleshooting your queries is a skill that you will acquire as your experience progresses.

Each time you need to fine-tune the query, switch back to Design view, make a change, and then run the query again to view the results. After you are satisfied with the results, you may want to save the query so it becomes a permanent part of the database and can be used later. Each time you run a query, the results will update based on the current data in the underlying table(s).

Using the Query Wizard

The ***Simple Query Wizard*** guides you through query design with a step-by-step process. The wizard is helpful for creating basic queries that do not require criteria. However, even if you initially design the query with a wizard, you are able to modify it later in Design view. After the wizard completes, you can switch to Design view and add criteria as needed. You can also add additional tables and fields to an existing query when conditions change. To launch the Query Wizard, click the Create tab and click Query Wizard in the Queries group (see Figure 32).

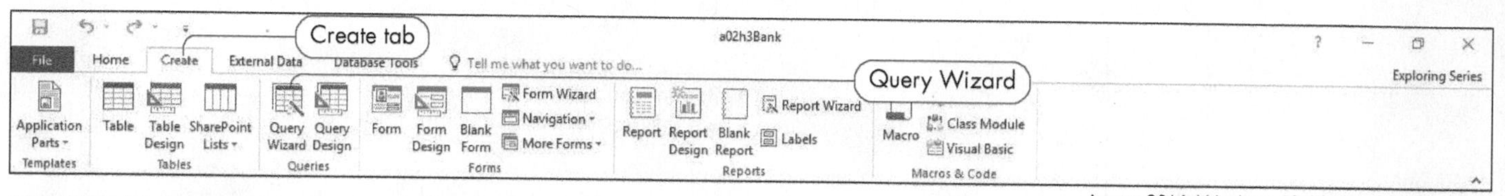

FIGURE 32 Launching the Query Wizard

Access 2016, Windows 10, Microsoft Corporation

Select Simple Query Wizard in the New Query dialog box, as shown in Figure 33.

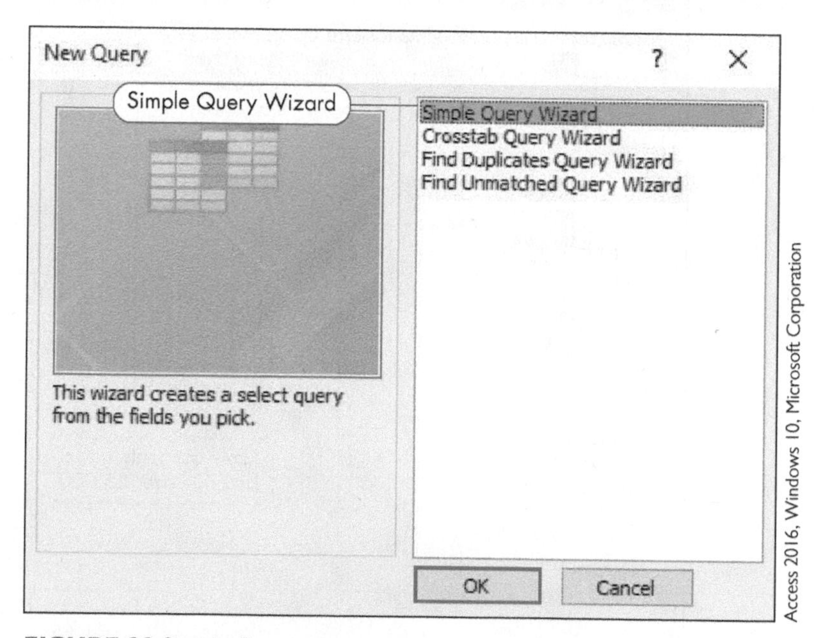

FIGURE 33 Simple Query Wizard

In the first step of the Simple Query Wizard dialog box, you specify the tables or queries and fields required in your query. When you select a table from the Tables/Queries arrow (queries can also be based on other queries), a list of the table's fields displays in the Available Fields list box (see Figures 34 and 35).

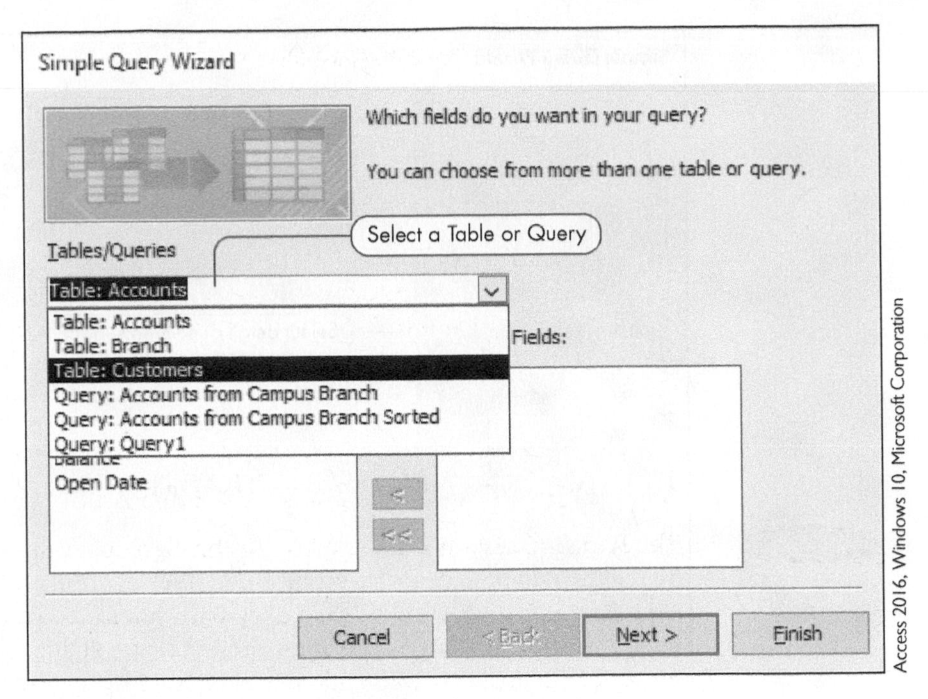

FIGURE 34 Specify Which Tables or Queries to Use

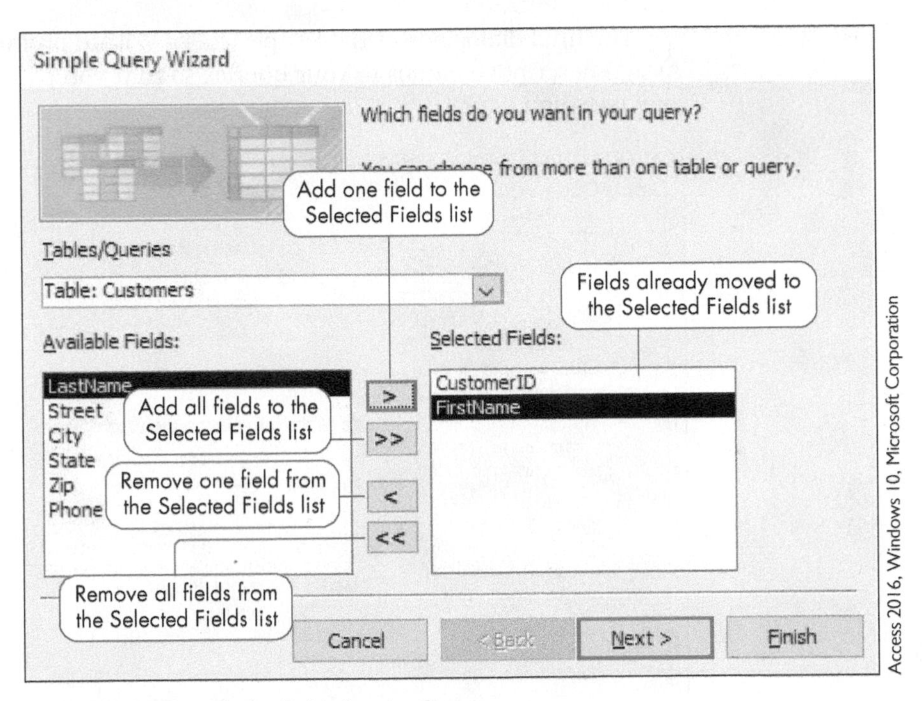

FIGURE 35 Specify the Fields for the Query

Select the necessary fields and add them to the Selected Fields list box using the directional arrows shown in Figure 35. In the next screen (shown in Figure 36), you choose between a detail and a summary query. The detail query shows every field of every record in the result. The summary query enables you to group data and view only summary records. For example, if you were interested in the total funds deposited at each of the bank branches, you would set the query to Summary, click Summary Options, and then click Sum on the Balance field. Access would then sum the balances of all accounts for each branch.

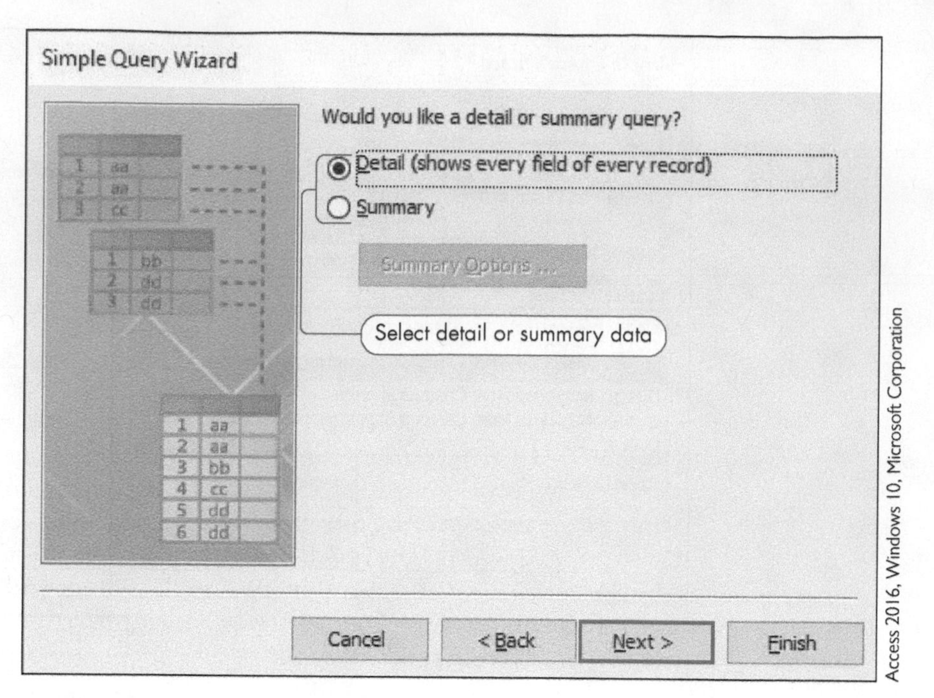

FIGURE 36 Choose Detail or Summary Data

The final dialog box of the Simple Query Wizard prompts for the name of the query. Assign descriptive names to your queries so that you can easily identify what each one does (see Figure 37).

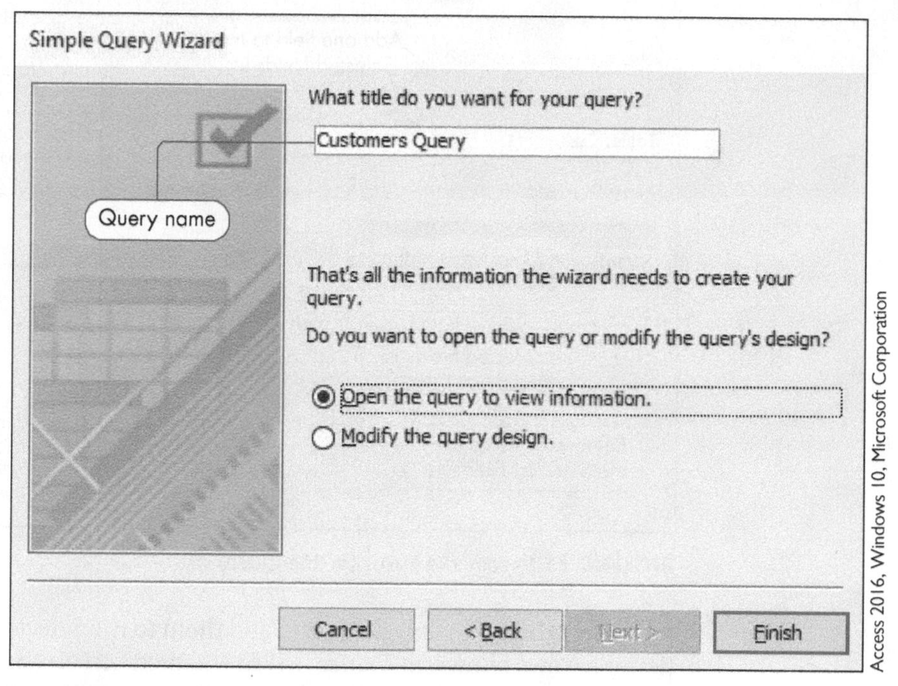

FIGURE 37 Name the Query

Specifying Query Criteria for Different Data Types

STEP 2 » You set criteria to limit the records to display only those that you require in the query results. When specifying a criterion for a query, you may need to include a delimiter—a special character that surrounds a criterion's value. The delimiter required is determined by the field data type. Text fields require quotation marks before and after the text; for example, "Campus" could be used to display customers from the Campus branch in the Bank database. Access automatically adds the quotation marks around text, but to ensure that the correct delimiter is used, you may want to include the delimiters yourself.

When the criterion is in a date field, you enclose the criterion in pound signs, such as #10/14/2018#. Access automatically adds the pound signs around dates, but to ensure that the correct delimiter is used, you may want to include the delimiters yourself. A date value can be entered using any allowed format, such as February 2, 2018, 2/2/2018, or 2-Feb-18. Use plain digits (no delimiter) for the criteria of a numeric field, currency, or AutoNumber. You can enter numeric criteria with or without a decimal point and with or without a minus sign. Commas and dollar signs are not allowed. You enter criteria for a Yes/No field as Yes or No. See Table 4 for query criteria and examples.

TABLE 4 Query Criteria

Data Type	Criteria	Example
Text	"Harry"	For a FirstName field, displays only text that matches Harry exactly. The quotation marks can be typed, or Access will add them automatically.
Numeric	5000	For a Quantity field, displays only numbers that match 5000 exactly (do not specify commas, currency symbols, etc.).
Date	#2/2/2018#	For a ShippedDate field, shows orders shipped on February 2, 2018.
Yes/No	Yes	For a Discontinued field, returns records where the check box is selected, denoting Yes.

Use Wildcards

Wildcards are special characters that can represent one or more characters in a text value. Suppose you want to use a criterion to search for the last name of a customer, but you are not sure how to spell the name; however, you know that the name starts with the letters *Sm*. You can use a wildcard with a text value (such as Sm*) to search for the name.

You enter wildcard characters in text values in the Criteria row of a query. Therefore, if you want to search for names that start with the letters *Sm*, specify the criterion in the LastName field as *Sm**. All last names that begin with *Sm* would display in the results. Wildcard characters can be placed in the beginning, middle, or end of a text string. Table 5 shows more query criterion examples that use wildcards.

TABLE 5 Query Criteria Using Wildcards

Character	Description	Example	Result
*	Matches any number of characters in the same position as the asterisk	Sm*	Small, Smiley, Smith, Smithson
?	Matches a single character in the same position as the question mark	H?ll	Hall, Hill, Hull
[ ]	Matches any single character within the brackets	F[ae]ll	Fall and Fell, but not Fill or Full
[!]	Matches any character not in the brackets	F[!ae]ll	Fill and Full, but not Fall or Fell

Use Comparison Operators in Queries

Comparison operators, such as equal (=), not equal (<>), greater than (>), less than (<), greater than or equal to (>=), and less than or equal to (<=), can be used in query criteria. Comparison operators enable you to limit the query results to only those records that meet the criteria. For example, if you only want to see accounts that have a balance greater than $5,000, you would type >5000 in the Criteria row of the Balance field. Table 6 shows more comparison operator examples.

TABLE 6 Comparison Operators in Queries

Expression	Example
=10	Equals 10
<>10	Not equal to 10
>10	Greater than 10
>=10	Greater than or equal to 10
<10	Less than 10
<=10	Less than or equal to 10

Work with Null

Sometimes finding null values is an important part of making a decision. For example, if you need to know which orders have been completed but not shipped, you would create a query to find the orders with a null (missing) ShipDate. The term that Access uses for a blank field is ***null***. Table 7 provides two examples of when to use the null criterion in a query.

TABLE 7 Establishing Null Criteria Expressions

Expression	Description	Example
Is Null	Use to find blank fields	For a SalesRepID field in the Customers table when the customer has not been assigned to a sales representative.
Is Not Null	Used to find fields with data	For a ShipDate field; a value has been entered to indicate that the order was shipped to the customer.

Establish AND, OR, and NOT Criteria

Remember the earlier question, "Which customers currently have an account with a balance over $5,000?" This question was answered by creating a query with a single criterion. At times, questions are more focused and require queries with multiple criteria. For example, you may need to know "Which customers from the Eastern branch currently have an account with a balance over $5,000?" To answer this question, you specify two criteria in different fields using the ***AND condition***. This means that the query results will display only records that match *all* criteria. When the criteria are in the same row of the query design grid, Access interprets this as an AND condition. You can also use the AND logical operator to test two criteria in the same field, as shown in Table 8.

When you have multiple criteria and you need to satisfy only one, not all of the criteria, use the ***OR condition***. The query results will display records that match any of the specified criteria. You can use the OR logical operator, and type the expression into the Criteria row, separating the criteria with the OR keyword. Table 8 shows an example of an OR condition created using this method. You can also type the first criterion into the Criteria row and then type the next criterion by using the Or row in the same field or a different field in the design grid (see Figure 38).

The NOT logical operator returns all records except the specified criteria. For example, "Not Eastern" would return all accounts except those opened at the Eastern branch.

TABLE 8 AND, OR, and NOT Queries

Logical Operator	Example	Result
AND	>5000 AND <10000	For a Balance field, returns all accounts with a balance greater than $5,000 and less than $10,000.
OR	"Eastern" OR "Campus"	For a Location field, returns all accounts that are at the Eastern or the Campus branch.
NOT	Not "Campus"	For a Location field, returns all records except those in the Campus branch.

Pearson Education, Inc.

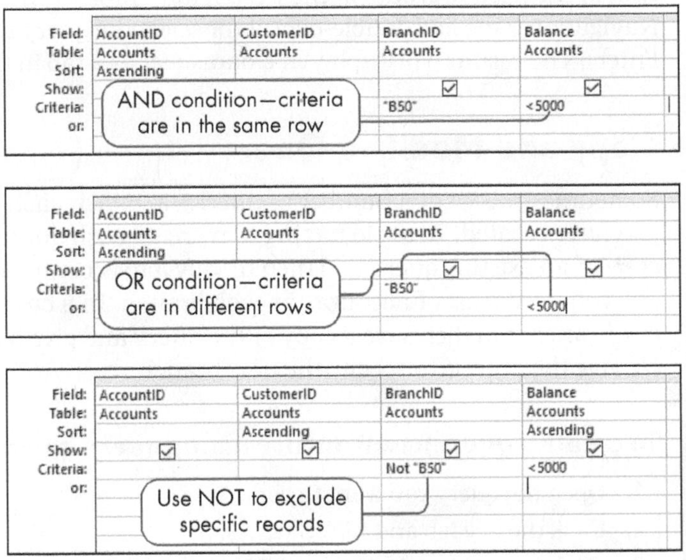

Access 2016, Windows 10, Microsoft Corporation

FIGURE 38 Query Design Views Showing the AND, OR, and NOT Operators

TIP: FINDING VALUES IN A DATE RANGE

To find the values contained within a date range, use the greater than (>) and less than (<) operators. For example, to find the values of dates on or after January 1, 2018, and on or before December 31, 2018, use the criterion >=1/1/2018 and <=12/31/2018. You can also use the BETWEEN operator to find the same inclusive dates, for example, BETWEEN 1/1/2018 and 12/31/2018.

Understanding Query Sort Order

The query sort order determines the order of records in a query's Datasheet view. You can change the order of records by specifying the sort order in Design view. When you want to sort using more than one field, the sort order is determined from left to right. The order of columns should be considered when first creating the query. For example, a query sorted by LastName and then by FirstName must have those two fields in the correct order in the design grid. When modifying sort order, it is sometimes necessary to rearrange fields, or add and delete columns in the query design grid.

To change order, add, or delete fields in the query design grid, complete one of the following steps:

- Change the order of a field: select the column you want to move by clicking the column selector. Click again and drag the selected field to its new location.
- Insert an additional column in the design grid: select a column and click Insert Columns in the Query Setup group on the Design tab. The additional column will insert to the left of the selected column.
- Delete a column: click the column selector to select the column and click Delete Columns in the Query Setup group, or press Delete on the keyboard.

Running, Copying, and Modifying a Query

Once your query is designed and saved, you run it to view the results. After you create a query, you may want to create a duplicate copy to use as the basis for creating a similar query. Duplicating a query saves time when you need the same tables and fields but with slightly different criteria.

Run a Query

There are several ways to run a query. One method is from within Design view; click Run in the Results group on the Design tab. Another method is to locate the query in the Navigation Pane and double-click it (or select the query in the Navigation Pane and press Enter). The results will display in a datasheet as a tab in the main window.

Copy and Modify a Query

Sometimes you want a number of queries in which each query is similar to another that you have created. To avoid having to recreate each query from scratch, you can create a copy of an existing query and then modify it to accommodate the new criteria. For example, you need a list of accounts in each branch. In a case like this, you create a query for one branch and then save a copy of the query and give it a new name. Finally, you would change the criteria to specify the next branch.

To create a query based on an existing query, complete the following steps:

1. Open the query you want to copy.
2. Click the File tab and click Save As.
3. Click Save Object As in the File Types section.
4. Ensure that Save Object As is selected in the Database File Types section and click Save As.
5. Type the name you want to use for the new query in the Save As dialog box and click OK (see Figure 39).
6. Switch to Design view of the copied query and modify the query criteria, as necessary.
7. Save and run the modified query.

TIP: COPYING THE QUERY IN THE NAVIGATION PANE

You can also right-click the original query in the Navigation Pane and from the shortcut menu, select Copy. Right-click in the empty space of the Navigation Pane again and then select Paste. Type a name for the new query in the Paste As dialog box and click OK.

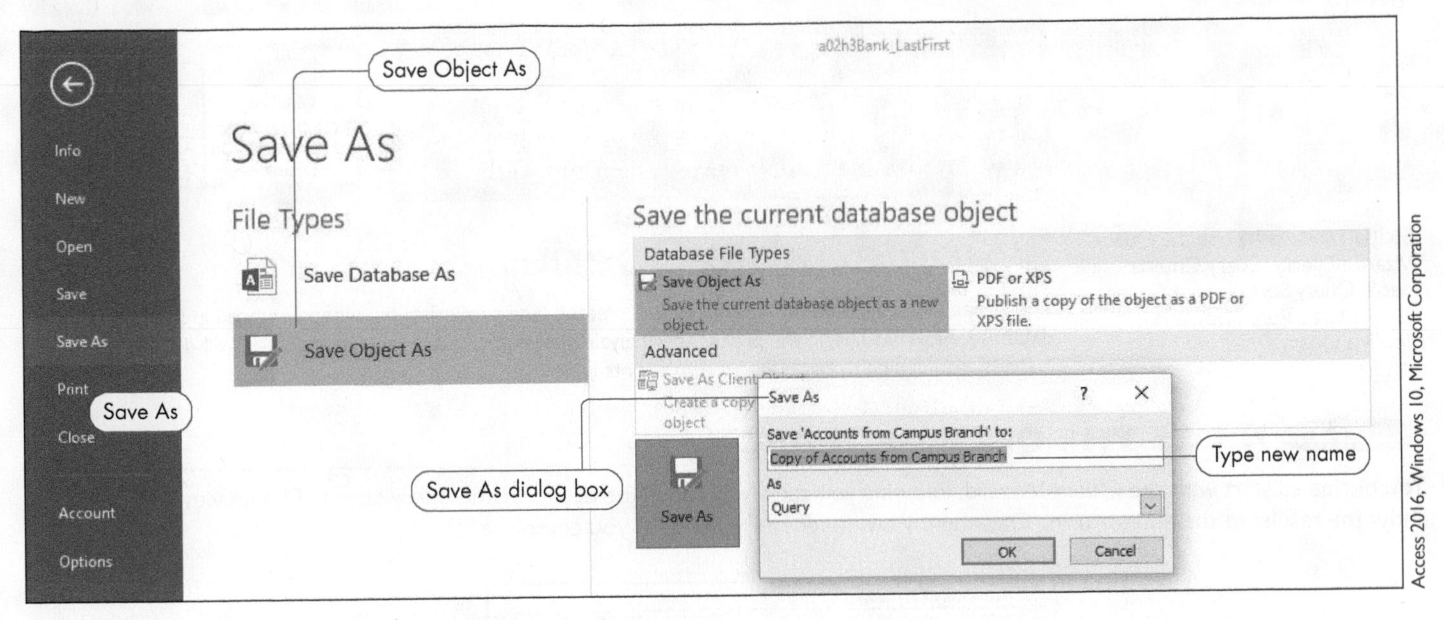

FIGURE 39 Using Save Object As to Save a Copy of a Query

Change Query Data

Be aware that query results in the datasheet display the actual records that are stored in the underlying table(s). Being able to correct an error immediately while it is displayed in the query datasheet is an advantage. You can save time by not having to close the query, open the table, find the error, fix it, and then run the query again. However, use caution when editing records in query results since you will be changing the original table data.

Quick Concepts

8. Define a single-table query. Give an example.
9. Give an example of how to use the Criteria row to find certain records in a table.
10. Why would you use an OR condition in a query?
11. Why would you want to copy an existing query?

Hands-On Exercises

Skills covered: Use the Query Wizard • Specify Query Criteria • Specify Query Sort Order • Change Query Data • Run, Copy, and Modify a Query

3 Single-Table Queries

The tables and table relationships have been created, and some data have been entered in the Bank database. Now, you begin the process of analyzing the bank data for the auditor. You will do so using queries. You decide to begin with the Accounts table.

STEP 1 ›› USE THE QUERY WIZARD

You decide to start with the Query Wizard, knowing you can always alter the design of the query later in Design view. You will show the results to the auditor using Datasheet view. Refer to Figure 40 as you complete Step 1.

Accounts from Campus Branch

Account ID	Customer ID	Branch ID	Balance
1001	30010	B50	$5,600.00
1002	30001	B10	$1,200.00
			$15,490.00
1004	30003	B30	$630.00
1005	30009	B50	$1,300.00
1006	30003	B10	$550.00
1007	30007	B20	$1,620.00
1008	30004	B40	$2,100.00
1009	30005	B50	$1,500.00
1010	30001	B20	$3,000.00
1011	30005	B10	$290.00
1012	30002	B30	$1,900.00
1013	30001	B20	$10,000.00
1014	30009	B10	$16,700.00
1015	30004	B30	$460.00
1016	30001	B30	$18,700.00
1017	30010	B30	$980.00
1018	30005	B40	$7,800.00
1019	30004	B30	$14,250.00
1020	30001	B50	$1,200.00
1021	30011	B50	$21,004.00
1022	30003	B50	$4,000.00
1023	30011	B50	$1,000.00
1024	30011	B50	$14,005.00
		B40	$11,010.00
1026	30007	B20	$7,400.00
1027	30003	B50	$4,000.00

Record: 1 of 27 No Filter Search

FIGURE 40 Query Results Before Criteria Are Applied

a. Open *a02h2Bank_LastFirst* if you closed it at the end of Hands-On Exercise 2, and save it as **a02h3Bank_LastFirst**, changing h2 to h3.

b. Click the **Create tab** and click **Query Wizard** in the Queries group.

   The New Query dialog box opens. Simple Query Wizard is selected by default.

c. Click **OK**.

d. Verify that Table: Accounts is selected in the Tables/Queries box.

e. Click **AccountID** in the Available Fields list, then click **Add One Field** [>] to move it to the Selected Fields list. Repeat the process with **CustomerID**, **BranchID**, and **Balance**.

   The four fields should now display in the Selected Fields list box.

f. Click **Next**.

g. Confirm that Detail (shows every field of every record) is selected and click **Next**.

h. Name the query **Accounts from Campus Branch**. Click **Finish**.

This query name describes the data in the query results. Your query should have four fields: AccountID, CustomerID, BranchID, and Balance. The Navigation bar indicates that 27 records meet the query criteria.

STEP 2 » SPECIFY QUERY CRITERIA AND SORT ORDER

The auditor indicated that the problem seems to be confined to the Campus branch. You use this knowledge to revise the query to display only Campus accounts. Refer to Figure 41 as you complete Step 2.

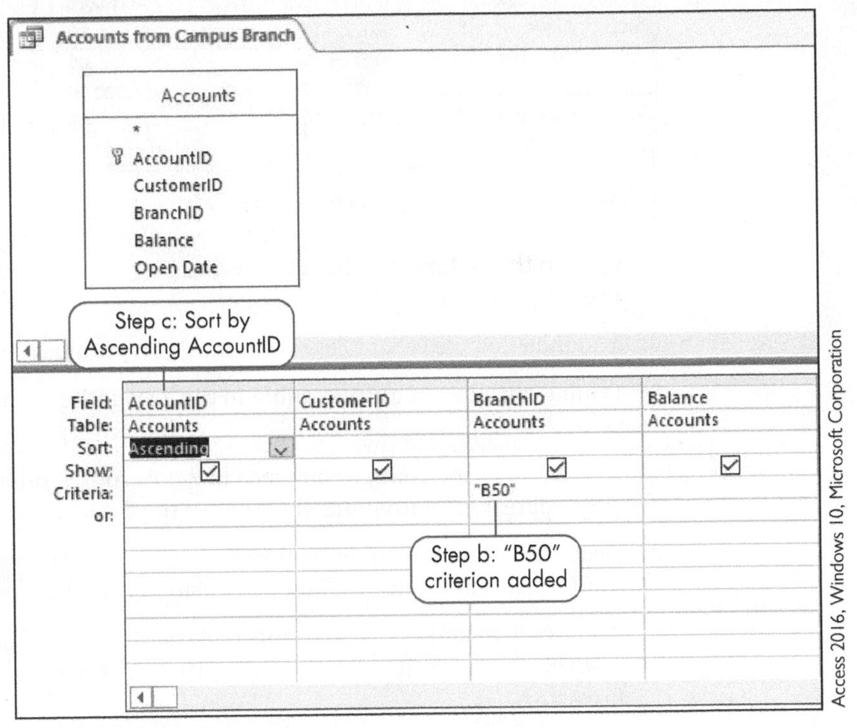

FIGURE 41 Enter Criteria and Add Sort Order

a. Click the **Home tab** and click **View** in the Views group.

The Accounts from Campus Branch query opens in Design view. You have created this query to view only those accounts at the Campus branch. However, other branches' accounts also display. You need to limit the query results to only the records of interest.

b. Click in the **Criteria row** (fifth row) in the BranchID column, type **B50**, and press **Enter**.

B50 is the BranchID for the Campus branch. Access queries are not case sensitive; therefore, b50 and B50 will produce the same results. Access adds quotation marks around text criteria after you press Enter, or you can type them yourself.

c. Click in the **Sort row** (third row) in the AccountID column and select **Ascending**.

d. Click **Run** in the Results group.

You should see nine records in the query results, all from Branch B50, sorted in ascending order by Account ID.

CHANGE QUERY DATA AND RUN, COPY, AND MODIFY A QUERY

When the query results are on the screen, the auditor notices that some of the data are incorrect, and one of the accounts is missing. From your experience with Access, you explain to the auditor that the data can be changed directly in a query rather than switching back to the table. Refer to Figure 42 as you complete Step 3.

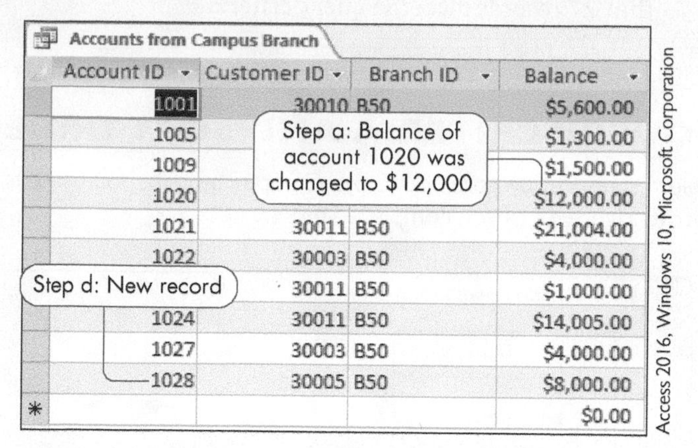

Accounts from Campus Branch

Account ID	Customer ID	Branch ID	Balance
1001	30010	B50	$5,600.00
1005			$1,300.00
1009			$1,500.00
1020			$12,000.00
1021	30011	B50	$21,004.00
1022	30003	B50	$4,000.00
	30011	B50	$1,000.00
1024	30011	B50	$14,005.00
1027	30003	B50	$4,000.00
1028	30005	B50	$8,000.00
*			$0.00

FIGURE 42 Changes Made in the Query Datasheet

a. Click in the **Balance field** in the record for account 1020. Change $1,200 to **$12,000**. Press **Enter**. Save and close the query.

You modified the record directly in the query results.

b. Double-click the **Accounts table** in the Navigation Pane

Only one account shows a $12,000 balance. The Account ID is 1020 and the Customer ID is 30001. The change you made in the Accounts table from the Campus Branch query datasheet automatically changed the data stored in the underlying table.

c. Open the Customers table. Notice the name of the customer whose CustomerID is 30001, Allison Millward. Close the Customers table.

d. Add a new record to the Accounts table with the following data: **1028** (Account ID), **30005** (Customer ID), **B50** (Branch ID), **8000** (Balance), and **8/4/2018** (Open Date). Press **Tab**.

> **TROUBLESHOOTING:** If the Accounts table is not open, double-click Accounts in the Navigation Pane.

The new record is added to the Accounts table.

e. Double-click the **Accounts from Campus Branch query** in the Navigation Pane.

Customer 30005 now shows two accounts: one with a balance of $1,500 and one with a balance of $8,000.

f. Click the **File tab**, click **Save As**, click **Save Object As**, and then click **Save As**. Type **Accounts from Campus Branch Sorted** as the query name. Click **OK**.

g. Click **View** in the Views group to return to Design view of the copied query.

h. Click in the **Sort row** of the AccountID field and select **(not sorted)**. Click in the **Sort row** of the CustomerID field and select **Ascending**. Click in the **Sort row** of the BalanceID field and select **Ascending**.

i. Click **Run** in the Results group.

Customer 30005 now shows two accounts with the two balances sorted in ascending order. Likewise, all other customers with more than one account are listed in ascending order by balance.

j. Save the query. Close the Accounts from Campus Branch Sorted query and close the Accounts table.

k. Keep the database open if you plan to continue with the Hands-On Exercise. If not, close the database and exit Access.

Multitable Queries

Multitable queries contain two or more tables, and enable you to take advantage of the relationships that have been set in your database. When you extract information from a database with a query, often you will need to pull data from multiple tables. One table may contain the core information that you want, while another table may contain the related data that make the query provide the complete results.

For example, the sample Bank database contains three tables: Customers, Accounts, and Branch. You connected the tables through relationships in order to store data efficiently and to enforce consistent data entry between them. The Customers table provides the information for the owners of the accounts. However, the Accounts table includes the balances of each account—the key financial information. Therefore, both the Customers and Accounts tables are needed to provide the information that you want: which Customers own which Accounts.

Creating a Multitable Query

There are several ways to create multitable queries. The simplistic method is to add tables to an existing query, or to copy an existing query and then add to it. You can also create a multitable query from scratch either using the Query Wizard or the Query Design tool.

Add Additional Tables to a Query

STEP 1 » One way to create a multitable query is to add tables and fields to an existing query, for example to add branch or customer data to a query that includes account information.

To add tables to a saved query, complete the following steps:

1. Open the existing query in Design view.
2. Add additional tables to a query by dragging tables from the Navigation Pane directly into the top pane of the query design window.
3. Add fields, criteria, and sorting options in the query design grid.
4. Run and save the query.

For example, the Branch and Customers tables were added to the query, as shown in Figure 43. The join lines between tables indicate that relationships were previously set in the Relationships window. With the additional tables and fields available, you can now add the customer's name (from Customers) and the branch location name (from Branch) rather than using CustomerID and BranchID in your results. The datasheet will contain more readily identifiable information than ID numbers for customers and locations.

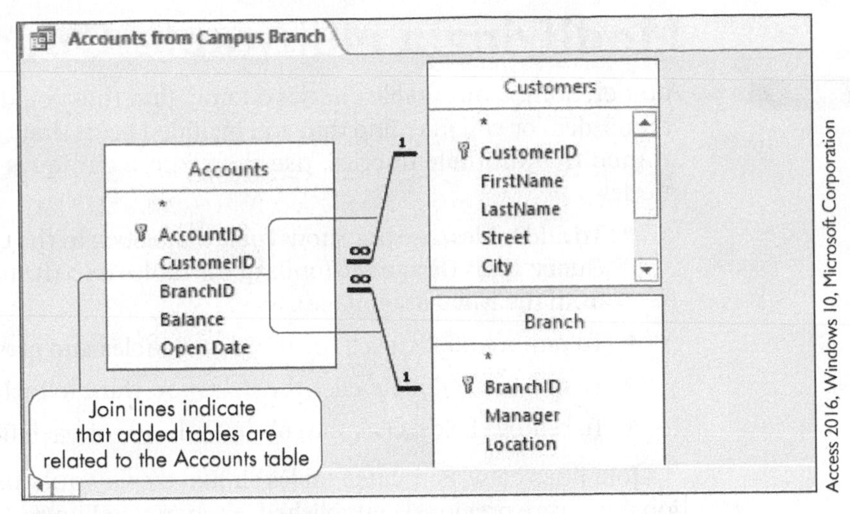

FIGURE 43 Two Additional Tables Added to a Query

Create a Multitable Query

STEP 2 Creating a multitable query from scratch is similar to creating a single-table query; however, choosing the right tables and managing the relationships in the query might require some additional skills. First, you should only use related tables in a multitable query. Related tables are tables that are joined in a relationship using a common field. Generally, related tables should already be joined in the Relationships window when you begin to create a multitable query. Using Figure 43 as a guide, creating a query with the Accounts and Branch tables would be acceptable, as would using Accounts and Customers tables, or Accounts, Branch, and Customers tables. All three scenarios include related tables. However, creating a query with only the Branch and Customers tables would not be acceptable because these tables are not directly related to one another (in other words, they do not have a common field).

To create a multitable query, complete the following steps:

1. Click the Create tab.
2. Click Query Design in the Queries group.
3. Add the tables you want in your query from the Show Table dialog box. Close the Show Table dialog box.
4. Drag the fields you want to display from the tables to the query design grid (or alternatively, double-click the field names); then add criteria and sorting options.
5. Click Run in the Results group on the Design tab to show the results in Datasheet view.

TIP: PRINT THE RELATIONSHIP REPORT TO HELP CREATE A MULTITABLE QUERY

When you create a multitable query, you only include related tables. As a guide, when the Relationships window is open, you can print the Relationship Report. Click the Database Tools tab, then click Relationship Report in the Tools group on the Relationship Tools Design tab. This report will provide a diagram that displays the tables, fields, and relationships in your database. The report is exportable to other formats such as Word if you want to share it with colleagues.

Modifying a Multitable Query

After creating a multitable query, you may find that you did not include all of the fields you needed, or you may find that you included fields that are unnecessary to the results. To modify multitable queries, use the same techniques you learned for single-table queries.

- To add tables, use the Show Table dialog box in the Query Setup group on the Query Tools Design tab (or drag the tables into the top pane of the query design from the Navigation Pane).
- To remove tables, click the unwanted tables and press Delete.
- To add fields, double-click the fields you want to include.
- To remove fields, click the column selector of each field and press Delete.

Join lines between related tables should display automatically in a query if the relationships were previously established, as shown in Figure 43.

> **TIP: MULTITABLE QUERIES INHERIT RELATIONSHIPS**
> When you add two or more related tables to a query, join lines display automatically. You can delete a join line in a query with no impact on the relationship set in the database. Deleting a join line only affects the relationship in the individual query. The next time you create a query with the same tables, the relationships will be inherited from the database. And, if you open the Relationships window, you will find the join lines intact.

Add and Delete Fields in a Multitable Query

In Figure 44, three tables, as well as the join lines between the tables, display in the top pane of Design view. All the fields from each of the tables are now available for use in the query design grid. Figure 44 shows that Location (from the Branch table) replaced BranchID and LastName (from the Customers table) replaced CustomerID to make the results more useful. BranchID was deleted from the query; therefore, the "B50" criterion was removed as well. "Campus" was added to the Location field's Criteria row in order to extract the names of the branches rather than their BranchID numbers. Because criteria values are not case sensitive, typing "campus" is the same as typing "Campus" and both will return the same results. The results of the revised query are shown in Figure 45.

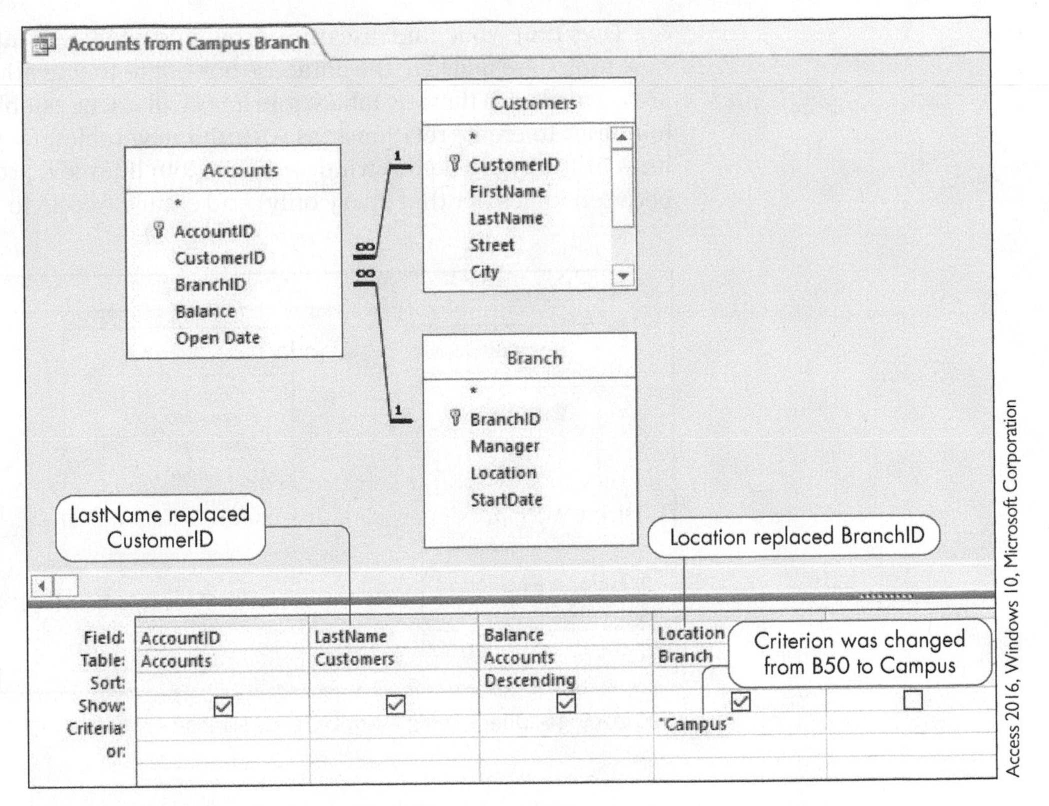

FIGURE 44 Modify the Query Design

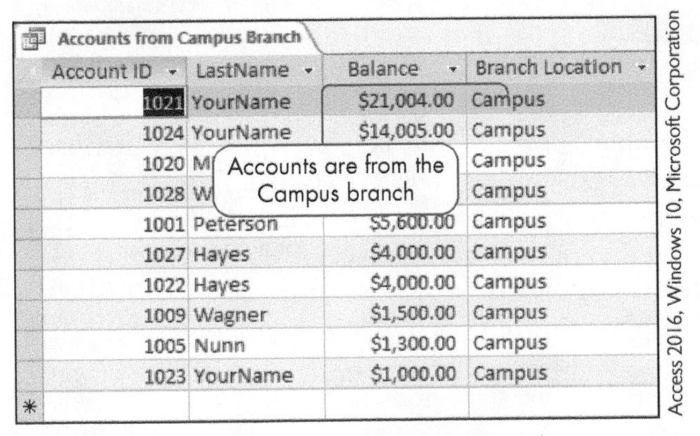

Account ID	LastName	Balance	Branch Location
1021	YourName	$21,004.00	Campus
1024	YourName	$14,005.00	Campus
1020	M		Campus
1028	W		Campus
1001	Peterson	$5,600.00	Campus
1027	Hayes	$4,000.00	Campus
1022	Hayes	$4,000.00	Campus
1009	Wagner	$1,500.00	Campus
1005	Nunn	$1,300.00	Campus
1023	YourName	$1,000.00	Campus

FIGURE 45 Datasheet View of a Multitable Query

Add Join Lines in a Multitable Query

In Figure 46, two tables are added to the query design, but no join line connects them. The results of the query will be unpredictable and will display more records than expected. The Customers table contains 11 records, and the Branch table contains 5 records. Because Access does not know how to interpret the unrelated tables, the results will show 55 records—every possible combination of customer and branch (11 × 5). See Figure 47.

To fix this problem, you can create join lines using existing tables if the tables contain a common field with the same data type. In this example, in which there is no common field, you can add an additional table that provides join lines between all three tables. You can add the Accounts table, which provides join lines between the two existing tables, Customers and Branch, and the added Accounts table. As soon as the third table is added to the query design, the join lines display automatically.

Over time, your databases may grow, and additional tables will be added. Occasionally, new tables are added to the database but not to the Relationships window. When queries are created with the new tables, join lines will not be established. When this happens, add join lines to create relationships with the new tables. Or you can create temporary join lines in the query design window. These join lines will provide a temporary relationship between tables (for that query only) and enable Access to interpret the query properly.

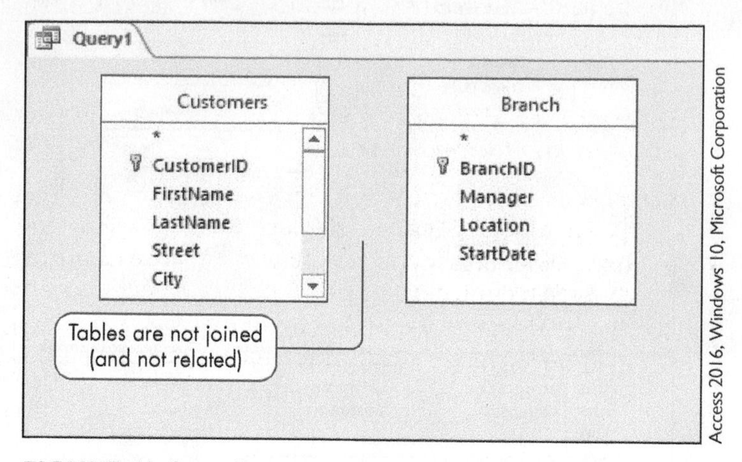

FIGURE 46 Query Design with Unrelated Tables

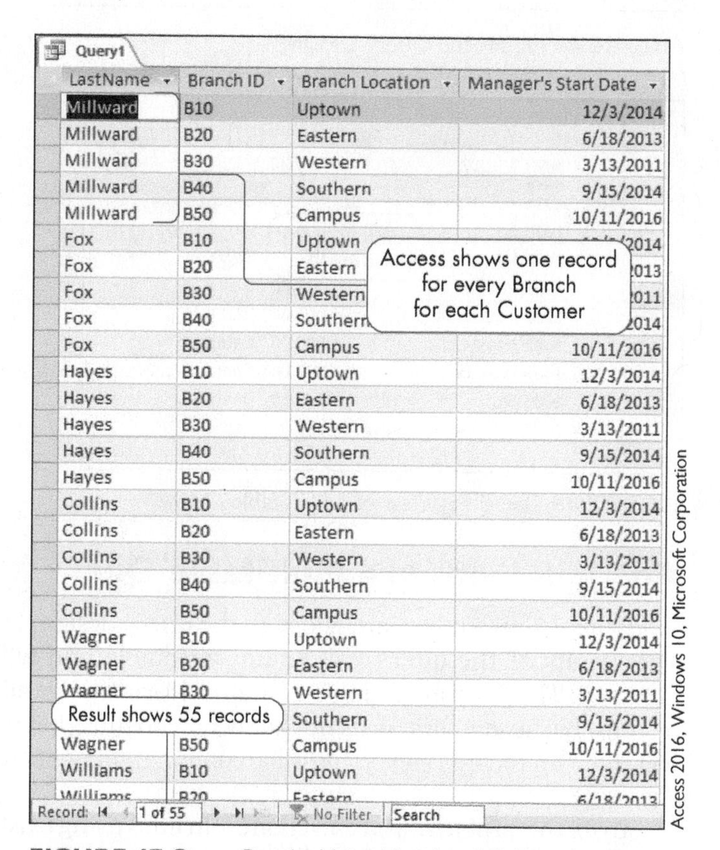

LastName	Branch ID	Branch Location	Manager's Start Date
Millward	B10	Uptown	12/3/2014
Millward	B20	Eastern	6/18/2013
Millward	B30	Western	3/13/2011
Millward	B40	Southern	9/15/2014
Millward	B50	Campus	10/11/2016
Fox	B10	Uptown	[illegible]
Fox	B20	Eastern	[illegible]
Fox	B30	Western	[illegible]
Fox	B40	Southern	[illegible]
Fox	B50	Campus	10/11/2016
Hayes	B10	Uptown	12/3/2014
Hayes	B20	Eastern	6/18/2013
Hayes	B30	Western	3/13/2011
Hayes	B40	Southern	9/15/2014
Hayes	B50	Campus	10/11/2016
Collins	B10	Uptown	12/3/2014
Collins	B20	Eastern	6/18/2013
Collins	B30	Western	3/13/2011
Collins	B40	Southern	9/15/2014
Collins	B50	Campus	10/11/2016
Wagner	B10	Uptown	12/3/2014
Wagner	B20	Eastern	6/18/2013
Wagner	B30	Western	3/13/2011
[illegible]	[illegible]	Southern	9/15/2014
Wagner	B50	Campus	10/11/2016
Williams	B10	Uptown	12/3/2014
Williams	B20	Eastern	6/18/2013

FIGURE 47 Query Results Using Unrelated Tables

Summarize Data Using a Multitable Query

You can get valuable information from your database using a multitable query. For example, if you want to know how many accounts each customer has, you would create a new query and add both the Customers and Accounts tables to Design view. After you verify that the join lines are correct, you add the CustomerID field from the Customers table and the AccountID field from the Accounts table to the query design grid. When you initially run the query, the results show duplicates in the CustomerID column because some customers have multiple accounts.

To summarize this information (how many accounts each customer has), complete the following steps:

1. Switch to Design view and click Totals in the Show/Hide group on the Query Tools Design tab. The Total row displays. Both fields show the Group By option in the Total row. The Total row enables you to summarize records by using functions such as Sum, Average, Count, etc.
2. Click in the Total row of the AccountID field, select Count from the list of functions, and run the query again. This time the results show one row for each customer and the number of accounts for each customer.

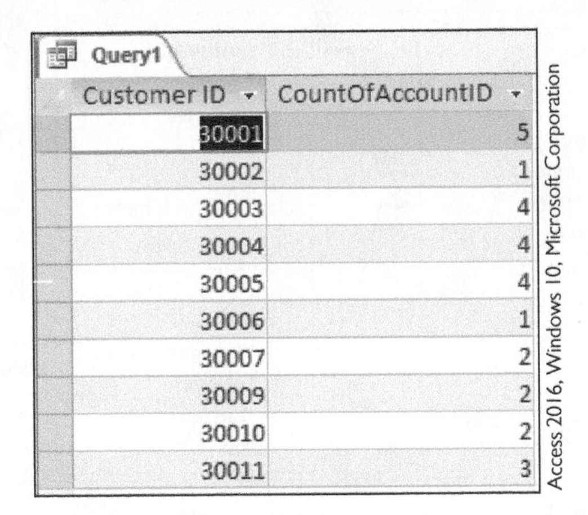
Query1

Customer ID	CountOfAccountID
30001	5
30002	1
30003	4
30004	4
30005	4
30006	1
30007	2
30009	2
30010	2
30011	3

Access 2016, Windows 10, Microsoft Corporation

FIGURE 48 Datasheet Results with the Count of Accounts per Customer

12. What is the advantage of creating a multitable query?
13. What is the benefit of summarizing data in a multitable query?
14. What is the result of creating a query with two unrelated tables?

Hands-On Exercises

Skills covered: Add Additional Tables to a Query • Create a Multitable Query • Modify a Multitable Query • Summarize Data Using a Multitable Query

4 Multitable Queries

Based on the auditor's request, you will evaluate the data further. This requires creating queries that are based on multiple tables rather than on a single table. You decide to open an existing query, add additional tables, and then save the query with a new name.

STEP 1 » ADD ADDITIONAL TABLES TO A QUERY

The previous query was based on the Accounts table, but now you need to add information to the query from the Branch and Customers tables. You will add the Branch and Customers tables to the query. Refer to Figure 49 as you complete Step 1.

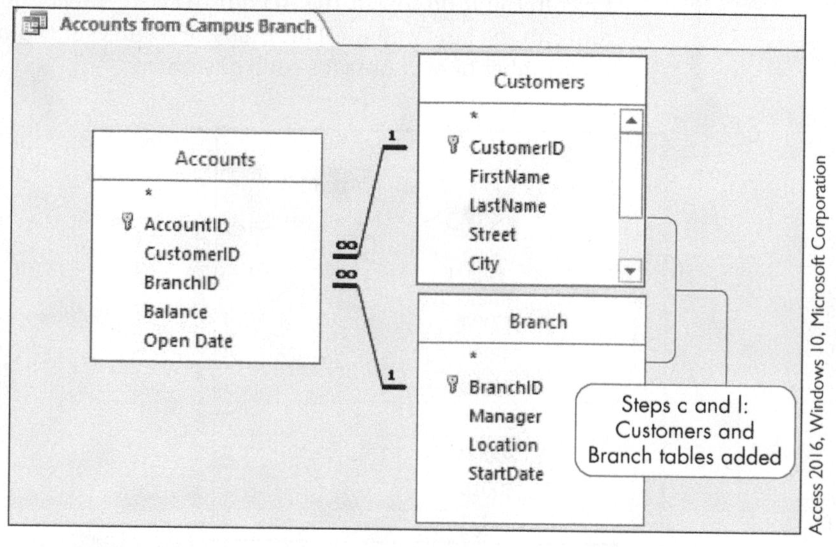

FIGURE 49 Add Tables to an Existing Query

a. Open *a02h3Bank_LastFirst* if you closed it at the end of Hands-On Exercise 3, and save it as **a02h4Bank_LastFirst**, changing h3 to h4.

b. Right-click the **Accounts from Campus Branch query** in the Navigation Pane and select **Design View** from the shortcut menu.

c. Drag the **Branch table** from the Navigation Pane to the top pane of the query design grid to the right of the Accounts table.

A join line connects the Branch table to the Accounts table. The tables in the query inherit the relationship created earlier in the Relationships window.

d. Drag the **Location field** from the Branch table to the first empty column in the design grid.

The Location field should be positioned to the right of the Balance field.

e. Click the **Show check box** below the BranchID field to clear the check box and hide this field from the results.

The BranchID field is no longer needed in the results because the Location field provides the branch name instead. Because you deselected the BranchID Show check box, the BranchID field will not display the next time the query is run.

f. Delete the B50 criterion in the BranchID field.

g. Type **Campus** as a criterion in the Location field and press **Enter**.

   Access adds quotation marks around Campus for you because Campus is a text criterion. You are substituting the Location criterion *(Campus)* in place of the BranchID criterion (B50).

h. Click in the AccountID field **Sort row**, click the arrow, and then click **(not sorted)**. Click in the **Sort row** of the Balance field. Click the arrow and select **Descending**.

i. Click **Run** in the Results group.

   The BranchID field does not display in Datasheet view because you hid the field in Step e. Only Campus accounts display in the datasheet (10 records). Next, you will add the Customers LastName field to and delete the CustomerID field from the query.

j. Save the changes to the query design.

k. Click **View** in the Views group to return to Design view. Point over the column selector at the top of the BranchID field, and when a downward arrow displays, click to select it. Press **Delete**.

   The BranchID field has been removed from the grid.

l. Drag the **Customers table** from the Navigation Pane to the top pane of the query design grid and reposition the tables so that the join lines are not blocked (see Figure 49).

   The join lines automatically connect the Customers table to the Accounts table (similar to Step c above).

m. Drag the **LastName field** in the Customers table to the second column in the design grid.

   The LastName field should be positioned to the right of the AccountID field.

n. Click the **column selector** in the CustomerID field to select it. Press **Delete**.

   The CustomerID field is no longer needed in the results because we added the LastName field instead.

o. Click **Run** in the Results group.

   The last names of the customers now display in the results.

p. Save and close the query.

STEP 2 » CREATE A MULTITABLE QUERY

After discussing the query results with the auditor, you realize that another query is needed to show those customers with account balances of $1,000 or less. You create the query and view the results in Datasheet view. Refer to Figure 50 as you complete Step 2.

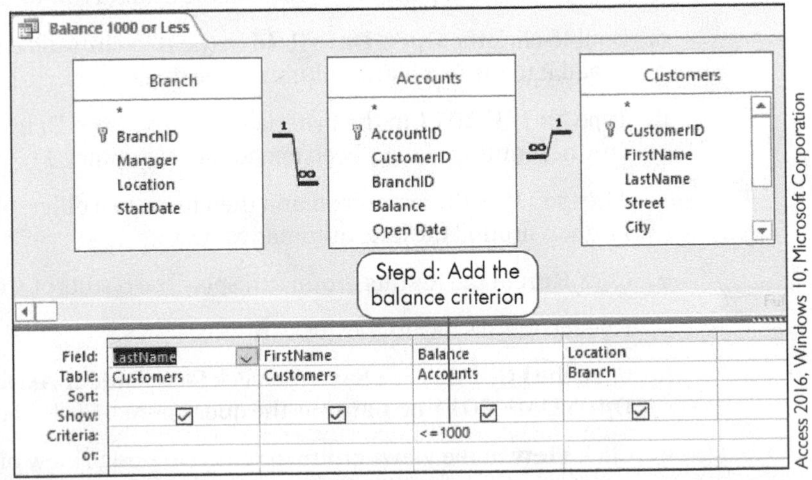

FIGURE 50 Create a Multitable Query

a. Click the **Create tab** and click **Query Design** in the Queries group.

b. Double-click the **Branch table name** in the Show Table dialog box. Double-click **Accounts** and **Customers** so that all three are added to Design view. Click **Close** in the Show Table dialog box.

   Three tables are added to the query.

c. Double-click the following fields to add them to the query design grid: **LastName**, **FirstName**, **Balance**, and **Location**.

d. Type **<=1000** in the Criteria row of the Balance column.

e. Click **Run** in the Results group to see the query results.

   Six records that have a balance of $1,000 or less display.

f. Click **Save** on the Quick Access Toolbar and type **Balance 1000 or Less** as the Query Name in the Save As dialog box. Click **OK**.

STEP 3 » MODIFY A MULTITABLE QUERY

The auditor requests additional changes to the Balance 1000 or Less query you just created. You will modify the criteria to display the accounts that were opened on or after January 1, 2011, with balances of $2,000 or less. Refer to Figure 51 as you complete Step 3.

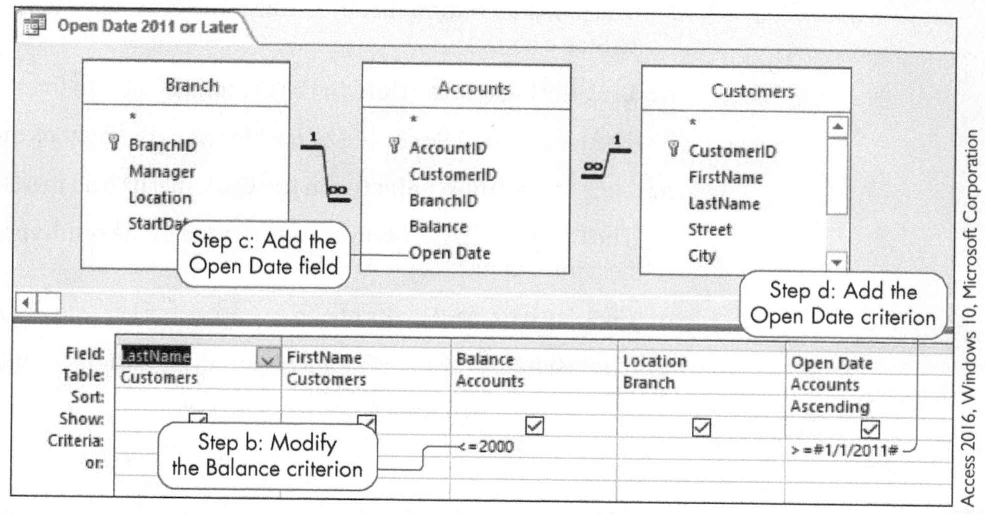

FIGURE 51 Query Using the And Condition

a. Click **View** in the Views group to switch the Balance 1000 or Less query to Design view.

b. Type **<=2000** in place of <=1000 in the Criteria row of the Balance field and press **Enter**.

c. Double-click the **Open Date field** in the Accounts table in the top pane of Design view to add it to the first blank column in the design grid.

d. Type **>=1/1/2011** in the Criteria row of the Open Date field and press **Enter** to extract only accounts that have been opened since January 1, 2011.

   After you type the expression and then move to a different column, Access will add the # symbols around the date automatically.

e. Click **Run** in the Results group to display the results of the query.

   Five records display in the query results.

f. Click the **File tab**, click **Save As**, click **Save Object As**, and then click **Save As**. Type **Open Date 2011 or Later** as the query name. Click **OK**.

g. Click **View** in the Views group to return to Design view of the copied query.

h. Click in the **Sort row** of the Open Date field and select **Ascending**.

i. Click **Run** in the Results group.

The records are sorted from the earliest open date on or after January 1, 2011, to the most recent open date.

j. Save and close the query.

STEP 4 » SUMMARIZE DATA USING A MULTITABLE QUERY

The auditor wants to know the number of accounts each customer has opened. You create a query using a Total row to obtain these data. Refer to Figure 52 as you complete Step 4.

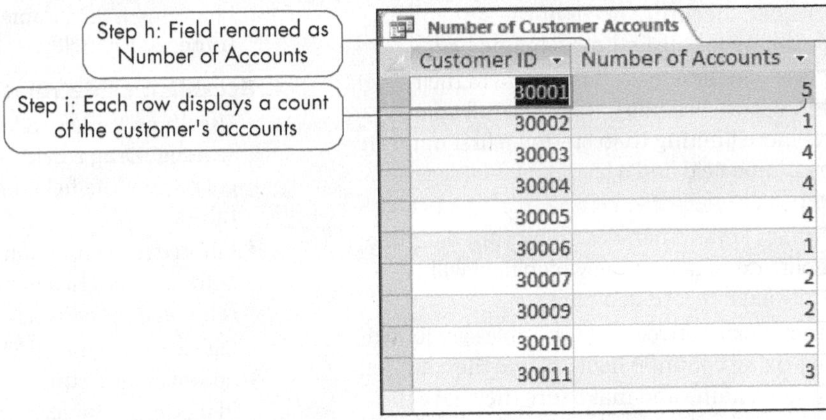

Step h: Field renamed as Number of Accounts

Step i: Each row displays a count of the customer's accounts

Number of Customer Accounts

Customer ID	Number of Accounts
30001	5
30002	1
30003	4
30004	4
30005	4
30006	1
30007	2
30009	2
30010	2
30011	3

Access 2016, Windows 10, Microsoft Corporation

FIGURE 52 Number of Accounts per Customer

a. Click the **Create tab** and click **Query Design** in the Queries group.

b. Add the **Accounts table** and the **Customers table** to the top section of Design view. Click **Close** in the Show Table dialog box.

c. Double-click the **CustomerID** in the Customers table in the top section of Design view to add it to the first blank column in the design grid, and double-click the **AccountID** in the Accounts table to add it to the second column.

d. Click **Run** in the Results group.

The results show there are 28 records. Every account a customer has opened is displayed. The auditor wants only the total number of accounts a customer has, so you modify the query.

e. Click **View** in the Views group to return to Design view of the query.

f. Click **Totals** in the Show/Hide group.

Both columns show the Group By option in the Total row.

g. Click **Group By** in the Total row of the AccountID field and select **Count**.

h. Modify the AccountID field to read **Number of Accounts: AccountID**.

You typed a new field name followed by a colon that will display Number of Accounts in the datasheet when you run the query.

i. Click **Run** in the Results group. Resize the columns of the datasheet to fully display the results.

The results show one row for each customer and the number of accounts each customer has opened since the database was created.

j. Click **Save** on the Quick Access Toolbar and type **Number of Customer Accounts** as the query name. Close the query.

k. Close the database and exit Access. Based on your instructor's directions, submit a02h4Bank_LastFirst.

Chapter Objectives Review

After reading this chapter, you have accomplished the following objectives:

1. Design a table.

- Include necessary data: Consider the output requirements when creating table structure. Determine the data required to produce the expected information.
- Design for now and for the future: When designing a database, anticipate the future needs of the system and build in the flexibility to satisfy those demands.
- Store data in their smallest parts: Store data in their smallest parts for more flexibility. Storing a full name in a Name field is more limiting than storing a first name in a separate FirstName field and a last name in a separate LastName field.
- Determine primary keys: When designing your database tables, it is important to determine which field will uniquely identify each record in a table.
- Plan for common fields between tables: Tables are joined in relationships using common fields. Name the common fields with the same name and make sure they have the same data type.
- Design to accommodate calculations: Calculated fields are frequently created with numeric data. You can use date arithmetic to subtract one date from another to find the number of days, months, or years that have elapsed between them.

2. Create and modify tables and work with data.

- You can create tables in Datasheet view or Design view. Alternatively, you can import data from another database or an application such as Excel to create tables in an Access database.
- Determine data type: Data type properties determine the type of data that can be entered and the operations that can be performed on that data. Access recognizes 12 data types.
- Set a table's primary key: The primary key is the field that uniquely identifies each record in a table.
- Explore a foreign key: A foreign key is a field in one table that is also the primary key of another table.
- Work with field properties: Field properties determine how the field looks and behaves. Examples of field properties are the Field Size property and the Caption property.
- Create a new field in Design view: It may be necessary to add table fields that were not included in the original design process. While it is possible to add fields in Datasheet view, Design view offers more flexibility.
- Modify the table in Datasheet view: Datasheet view is used to add, edit, and delete records. Design view is used to create and modify the table structure by enabling you to add and edit fields and set field properties.

3. Share data.

- Import Excel data: You can import data from other applications such as an Excel spreadsheet.
- Import Access data: You can import data from another database by using the Import Wizard.
- Modify an imported table's design and add data: After importing a table, examine the design and make necessary modifications. Modifications may include changing a field name, adding new fields, or deleting unnecessary fields.

4. Establish table relationships.

- Use Show Table to add tables to the Relationships window. Drag a field name from one table to the corresponding field name in another table to join the tables.
- Enforce referential integrity: Referential integrity enforces rules in a database that are used to preserve relationships between tables when records are changed.
- Set cascade options: The Cascade Update Related Fields option ensures that when the primary key is modified in a primary table, Access will automatically update all foreign key values in a related table. The Cascade Delete Related Records option ensures that when the primary key is deleted in a primary table, Access will automatically delete all records in related tables that reference the primary key.
- Establish a one-to-many relationship: A one-to-many relationship is established when the primary key value in the primary table can match many of the foreign key values in the related table. One-to-one and many-to-many are also relationship possibilities, but one-to-many relationships are the most common.

5. Create a single-table query.

- Create a single-table select query: A single-table select query uses fields from one table to display only those records that match certain criteria.
- Use Query Design view: Use Query Design view to create and modify a query. The top portion of the view contains tables with their respective field names and displays the join lines between tables. The bottom portion, known as the query design grid, contains columns and rows that you use to control the query results.

6. Use the Query Wizard.

- The Query Wizard is an alternative method for creating queries. It enables you to select tables and fields from lists. The last step of the wizard prompts you to save the query.

7. Specify query criteria for different data types.

- Different data types require different syntax. Date fields are enclosed in pound signs (#) and text fields in quotations (" "). Numeric and currency fields require no delimiters.
- Use wildcards: Wildcards are special characters that can represent one or more characters in a text value. A question mark (?) is a wildcard that stands for a

single character in the same position as the question mark, while an asterisk (*) is a wildcard that stands for any number of characters in the same position as the asterisk.

- Use comparison operators in queries: Comparison operators such as equal (=), not equal (<>), greater than (>), less than (<), greater than or equal to (>=), and less than or equal to (<=) can be used in the criteria of a query to limit the query results to only those records that meet the criteria.
- Work with null: Access uses the term null for a blank field. Null criteria can be used to find missing information.
- Establish AND, OR, and NOT criteria: The AND, OR, and NOT conditions are used when queries require logical criteria. The AND condition returns only records that meet all criteria. The OR condition returns records meeting any of the specified criteria. The NOT logical operator returns all records except the specified criteria.

8. Understand query sort order.

- The query sort order determines the order of records in a query's Datasheet view. You can change the order of records by specifying the sort order in Design view.
- The sort order is determined from the order of the fields from left to right. Move the field columns to position them in left to right sort order.

9. Run, copy, and modify a query.

- Run a query: To obtain the results for a query, you must run the query. To run the query, click Run in the Results group in Design view. Another method is to locate the query in the Navigation Pane and double-click it. A similar method is to select the query and press Enter.
- Copy and modify a query: To save time, after specifying tables, fields, and conditions for one query, copy the query, rename it, and then modify the fields and criteria in the second query.
- Change query data: You can correct an error immediately while data is displayed in the query datasheet. Use caution when editing records in query results because you will be changing the original table data.

10. Create a multitable query.

- Add additional tables to a query: Open the Navigation Pane and drag the tables from the Navigation Pane directly into the top section of Query Design view.
- Create a multitable query: Multitable queries contain two or more tables enabling you to take advantage of the relationships that have been set in your database.

11. Modify a multitable query.

- Add and delete fields in a multitable query: Multitable queries may need to be modified. Add fields by double-clicking the field name in the table you want; remove fields by clicking the column selector and pressing Delete.
- Add join lines in a multitable query: If the tables have a common field, create join lines by dragging the field name of one common field onto the field name of the other table. Or you can add an additional table that will provide a join between all three tables.
- Summarize data using a multitable query: Use the total row options of a field such as Count to get answers.

Key Terms Matching

Match the key terms with their definitions. Write the key term letter by the appropriate numbered definition.

a. AND condition
b. AutoNumber
c. Caption property
d. Cascade Delete Related Records
e. Cascade Update Related Fields
f. Comparison Operator
g. Criteria row
h. Data redundancy
i. Data type
j. Field property
k. Foreign key
l. Multitable query
m. Null
n. One-to-many relationship
o. OR condition
p. Query
q. Referential Integrity
r. Simple Query Wizard
s. Wildcard

1. _____ Special character that can represent one or more characters in the criterion of a query.

2. _____ Characteristic of a field that determines how it looks and behaves.

3. _____ Returns only records that meet all criteria.

4. _____ A row in the Query Design view that determines which records will be selected.

5. _____ Determines the type of data that can be entered and the operations that can be performed on that data.

6. _____ Used to create a more understandable label than a field name label that displays in the top row in Datasheet view and in forms and reports.

7. _____ Enables you to ask questions about the data stored in a database and provides answers to the questions in a datasheet.

8. _____ The term Access uses to describe a blank field.

9. _____ A number that automatically increments each time a record is added.

10. _____ The unnecessary storing of duplicate data in two or more tables.

11. _____ When the primary key value in the primary table can match many of the foreign key values in the related table.

12. _____ A field in one table that is also the primary key of another table.

13. _____ An option that directs Access to automatically update all foreign key values in a related table when the primary key value is modified in a primary table.

14. _____ Rules in a database that are used to preserve relationships between tables when records are changed.

15. _____ Contains two or more tables, enabling you to take advantage of the relationships that have been set in your database.

16. _____ Returns records meeting any of the specified criteria.

17. _____ Provides a step-by-step guide to help you through the query design process.

18. _____ When the primary key value is deleted in a primary table, Access will automatically delete all foreign key values in a related table.

19. _____ Uses greater than (>), less than (<), greater than or equal to (>=), and less than or equal to (<=), etc. to limit query results that meet these criteria.

Multiple Choice

1. All of the following are suggested guidelines for table design *except*:
   (a) Include all necessary data.
   (b) Store data in its smallest parts.
   (c) Avoid date arithmetic.
   (d) Link tables using common fields.

2. Which of the following determines how the field names can be made more readable in table and query datasheets?
   (a) Field size
   (b) Data type
   (c) Caption property
   (d) Normalization

3. When entering, deleting, or editing input masks:
   (a) The table must be in Design view.
   (b) The table must be in Datasheet view.
   (c) The table may be in either Datasheet or Design view.
   (d) Data may only be entered in a form.

4. With respect to importing data into Access, which of the following statements is *true?*
   (a) The Import Wizard works only for Excel files.
   (b) The Import Wizard is found on the Create tab.
   (c) You can assign a primary key while you are importing Excel data.
   (d) Imported table designs cannot be modified in Access.

5. The main reason to set a field size in Access is to:
   (a) Limit the length of values in a table.
   (b) Make it possible to delete records.
   (c) Keep your database safe from unauthorized users.
   (d) Keep misspelled data from being entered into a table.

6. An illustration of a one-to-many relationship would be:
   (a) An employee listed in the Employees table earns a raise so the Salaries table must be updated.
   (b) A customer may have more than one account in an accounts table.
   (c) Each employee in an Employees table has a matching entry in the Salaries table.
   (d) An employee leaves the company so that when he is deleted from the Employees table, his salary data will be deleted from the Salaries table.

7. A query's specifications as to which tables to include must be entered on the:
   (a) Table row of the query design grid.
   (b) Show row of the query design grid.
   (c) Sort row of the query design grid.
   (d) Criteria row of the query design grid.

8. When adding date criteria to the Query Design view, the dates you enter must be delimited by:
   (a) Parentheses ().
   (b) Pound signs (#).
   (c) Quotes (" ").
   (d) At signs (@).

9. It is more efficient to make a copy of an existing query rather than to create a new query when which of the following is *true?*
   (a) The existing query contains only one table.
   (b) The existing query and the new query use the same tables and fields.
   (c) The existing query and the new query have the exact same criteria.
   (d) The original query is no longer being used.

10. Which of the following is *true* for the Query Wizard?
   (a) No criteria can be added as you step through the Wizard.
   (b) You can only select related tables as a source.
   (c) Fields with different data types are not allowed.
   (d) You are required to summarize the data.

Practice Exercises

1 Philadelphia Bookstore

Tom and Erin Mullaney own and operate a bookstore in Philadelphia, Pennsylvania. Erin asked you to help her create an Access database to store the publishers and the books that they sell. The data for the publishers and books is currently stored in Excel worksheets that you decide to import into a new database. You determine that a third table—for authors—is also required. Your task is to create and populate the three tables, set the table relationships, and enforce referential integrity. You will then create queries to extract information from the tables. Refer to Figure 53 as you complete this exercise.

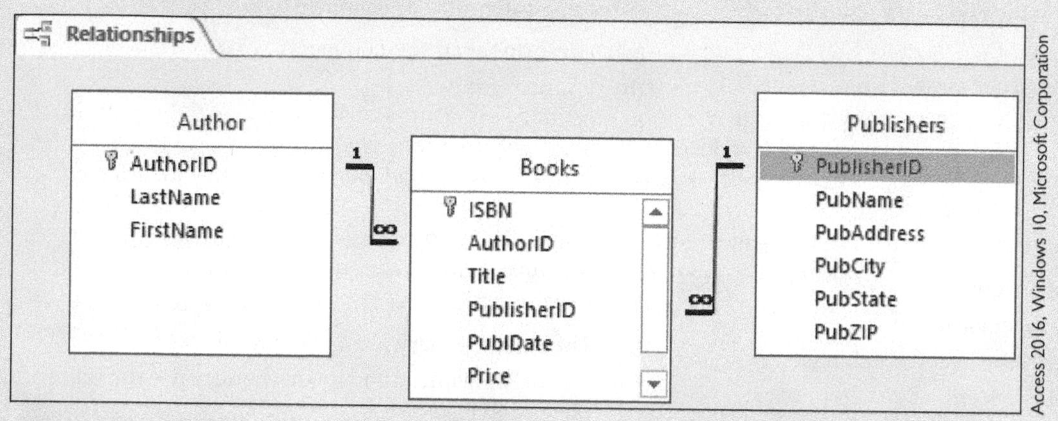

FIGURE 53 Books Relationships Window

a. Open Access and click **Blank desktop database**. Type **a02p1Books_LastFirst** in the **File Name box**. Click **Browse** to navigate to the location where you are saving your files in the File New Database dialog box, click **OK** to close the dialog box, and then click **Create** to create the new database.

b. Type **11** in the Click to Add column and click **Click to Add**. The field name becomes Field1, and *Click to Add* now displays as the third column. In the third column, type **Beschloss**, and then press **Tab**. Repeat the process for the fourth column; type **Michael R.** and press **Tab** two times. The insertion point returns to the first column where (New) is selected.

c. Press **Tab**. Type the rest of the data using the following table. These data will become the records of the Author table.

ID	Field1	Field2	Field3
1	11	Beschloss	Michael R.
(New)	**12**	**Turow**	**Scott**
	13	**Rice**	**Anne**
	14	**King**	**Stephen**
	15	**Connelly**	**Michael**
	16	**Rice**	**Luanne**
	17	*your last name*	*your first name*

d. Click **Save** on the Quick Access Toolbar. Type **Author** in the Save As dialog box and click **OK**.

e. Click **View** in the Views group to switch to Design view of the Author table.

f. Select **Field1**—in the second row—in the top portion of the table design and type **AuthorID** to rename the field. In the Field Properties section in the lower pane of the table design, type **Author ID** in the Caption box and verify that Long Integer displays for the Field Size property.

g. Select **Field2** and type **LastName** to rename the field. In the Field Properties section in the bottom portion of Design view, type **Author's Last Name** in the Caption box and type **20** as the field size.

h. Select **Field3** and type **FirstName** to rename the field. In the Field Properties section in the bottom portion of the table design, type **Author's First Name** as the caption and type **15** as the field size.

i. Click the **ID field row selector** (which displays the primary key) to select the row, and then click **Delete Rows** in the Tools group. Click **Yes** two times to confirm both messages.

j. Click the **AuthorID row selector**, and then click **Primary Key** in the Tools group to set the primary key.

k. Click **Save** on the Quick Access Toolbar to save the design changes. Click **Yes** to the *Some data may be lost* message. Close the table.

l. Click the **External Data tab** and click **Excel** in the Import & Link group to launch the Get External Data – Excel Spreadsheet feature. Verify that the *Import the source data into a new table in the current database* option is selected, click **Browse**, and then navigate to your student data folder. Select the *a02p1Books* workbook, click **Open**, and then click **OK**. This workbook contains two worksheets. Follow the steps below:
   - Select the **Publishers worksheet** and click **Next**.
   - Click the **First Row Contains Column Headings check box** to select it and click **Next**.
   - Ensure that the PubID field is selected, click the **Indexed arrow**, select **Yes (No Duplicates)**, and then click **Next**.
   - Click the **Choose my own primary key arrow**, ensure that PubID is selected, and then click **Next**.
   - Accept the name Publishers for the table name, click **Finish**, and then click **Close** without saving the import steps.

m. Use the Import Wizard again to import the Books worksheet from the *a02p1Books* workbook into the Access database. Follow the steps below:
   - Ensure that the Books worksheet is selected and click **Next**.
   - Click the **First Row Contains Column Headings check box** to select it, and click **Next**.
   - Click the **ISBN column**, click the down arrow, set the Indexed property box to **Yes (No Duplicates)**, and then click **Next**.
   - Click the **Choose my own primary key arrow**, select **ISBN** as the primary key field, and then click **Next**.
   - Accept the name Books as the table name. Click **Finish** and click **Close** without saving the import steps.

n. Right-click the **Books table** in the Navigation Pane and select **Design View**. Make the following changes:
   - Click the **PubID field** and change the name to **PublisherID**.
   - Set the caption property to **Publisher ID.**
   - Change the PublisherID Field Size property to **2**.
   - Click the **ISBN field** and change the Field Size property to **13**.
   - Change the AuthorCode field name to **AuthorID**.
   - Change the AuthorID Field Size property to **Long Integer**.
   - Click the **ISBN field row selector** (which displays the primary key) to select the row. Click and drag to move the row up to the first position in the table design.
   - Click **Save** on the Quick Access Toolbar to save the design changes to the Books table. Click **Yes** to the *Some data may be lost* warning.
   - Close the table.

o. Right-click the **Publishers table** in the Navigation Pane and select **Design View**. Make the following changes:
   - Click the **PubID field** and change the name to **PublisherID**.
   - Change the PublisherID Field Size property to **2**.
   - Change the Caption property to **Publisher's ID**.
   - Change the Field Size property to **50** for the PubName and PubAddress fields.

- Change the Pub Address field name to **PubAddress** (remove the space).
- Change the PubCity Field Size property to **30**.
- Change the PubState Field Size property to **2**.
- Change the Pub ZIP field name to **PubZIP** (remove the space).
- Click **Save** on the Quick Access Toolbar to save the design changes to the Publishers table. Click **Yes** to the *Some data may be lost* warning. Close all open tables.

p. Click the **Database Tools tab** and click **Relationships** in the Relationships group. Click **Show Table**, if the Show Table dialog box does not open automatically. Follow the steps below:

- Double-click each table name in the Show Table dialog box to add it to the Relationships window and close the Show Table dialog box.
- Drag the **AuthorID field** from the Author table onto the AuthorID field in the Books table.
- Click the **Enforce Referential Integrity** and **Cascade Update Related Fields check boxes** in the Edit Relationships dialog box to select them. Click **Create** to create a one-to-many relationship between the Author and Books tables.
- Drag the **PublisherID field** from the Publishers table onto the PublisherID field in the Books table.
- Click the **Enforce Referential Integrity** and **Cascade Update Related Fields check boxes** in the Edit Relationships dialog box to select them. Click **Create** to create a one-to-many relationship between the Publishers and Books tables.
- Click **Save** on the Quick Access Toolbar to save the changes to the Relationships window, then in the Relationships group, click **Close**.

q. Click the **Create tab**, and then click **Query Wizard** in the Queries group. With Simple Query Wizard selected, click **OK**.

- Select the Publishers table, double-click to add **PubName**, **PubCity**, and **PubState** to the Selected Fields list. Click **Next**, and then click **Finish**. In Datasheet view, double-click the border to the right of each column to set the column widths to Best Fit. Click **Save** on the Quick Access Toolbar.

r. Click the **File tab**, click **Save As**, and then double-click **Save Object As**. Modify the copied query name to **New York Publishers Query**, and then click **OK**.

- Click **View** in the Views group on the Home tab to switch to Design view of the query. Click and drag the **Books table** from the Navigation Pane into the top pane of the query design window.
- Select the Books table, double-click **Title** and **PublDate** to add the fields to the query design grid.
- Click in the Criteria row of the PubState field, and type **NY**. Click the **Sort** cell of the PublDate field, click the arrow, and then click **Descending**.
- Click **Run** in the Results group (12 records display in the Datasheet sorted by PublDate in descending order). Double-click the border to the right of each column to set the column widths to Best Fit.
- Save and close the query.

s. Close the database and exit Access. Based on your instructor's directions, submit a02p1Books_LastFirst.

2 Employee Salary Analysis

The Morgan Insurance Company offers a full range of insurance services. They store all of the firm's employee data in an Access database. This file contains each employee's name and address, job performance, salary, and title, but needs to be imported into a different existing database. A database file containing two of the tables (Location and Titles) already exists; your job is to import the employee data from Access to create the third table. Once imported, you will modify field properties and set new relationships. The owner of the company, Victor Reed, is concerned that some of the Atlanta and Boston salaries may be below the guidelines published by the national office. He asks that you investigate the salaries of the two offices and create a separate query for each city. Refer to Figure 54 as you complete this exercise.

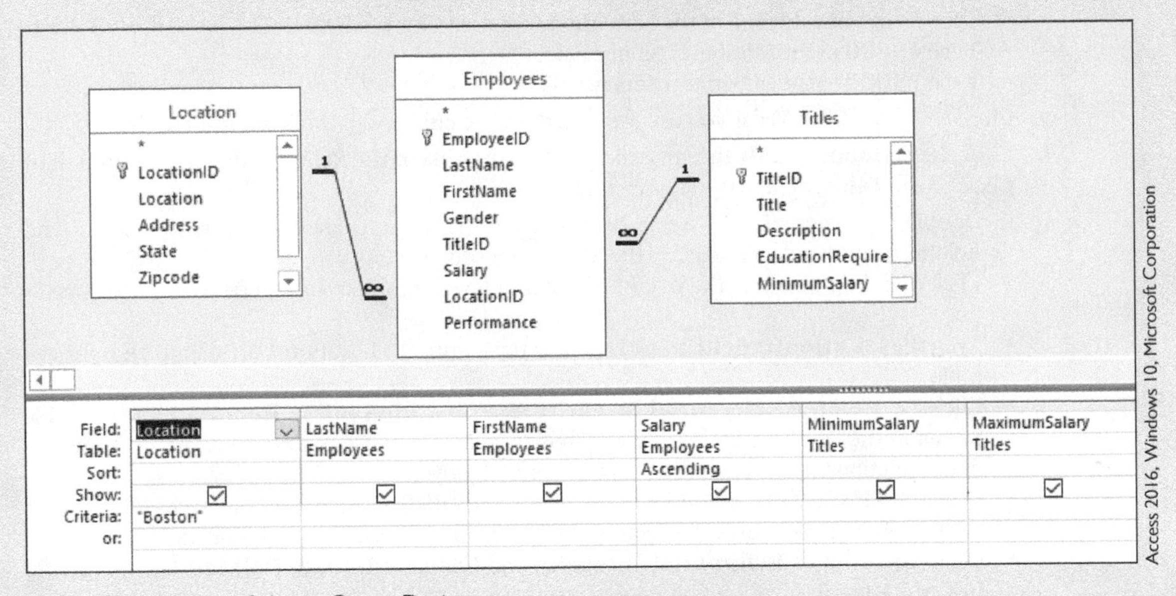

FIGURE 54 Boston Salaries Query Design

a. Open *a02p2Insurance* and save it as **a02p2Insurance_LastFirst**. Double-click the **Location table** and review the data to become familiar with the field names and the type of information stored in the table. Review the Titles table. Close both tables.

b. Click the **External Data tab**, click **Access** in the Import & Link group, and then complete the following steps:
   - Click **Browse** and navigate to the *a02p2Employees* database in the location of your student data files. Select the file, click **Open**.
   - Click **OK** in the Get External Data – Access Database dialog box.
   - Select the **Employees table**, and then click **OK**.
   - Click **Close** without saving the import steps.

c. Double-click the **Employees table** in the Navigation Pane, then click **View** in the Views group on the Home tab to switch to Design view of the Employees table. Make the following changes:
   - Ensure that the EmployeeID field is selected, and then click **Primary Key** in the Tools group.
   - Click the **LastName field** and change the Field Size property to **20**.
   - Change the Caption property to **Last Name**.
   - Click the **FirstName field** and change the Field Size property to **20**.
   - Change the Caption property to **First Name**.
   - Click the **LocationID field** and change the Field Size property to **3**.
   - Change the Caption property to **Location ID**.
   - Click the **TitleID field** and change the Field Size property to **3**.
   - Change the Caption property to **Title ID**.
   - Change the Salary field data type to **Currency** and change General Number in the Format property in field properties to **Currency**.
   - Save the design changes. Click **Yes** to the *Some data may be lost* warning.

d. Click **View** in the Views group to view the Employees table in Datasheet view and examine the data. Click any record in the Title ID and then click **Ascending** in the Sort & Filter group on the Home tab. Multiple employees are associated with the T01, T02, T03, and T04 titles.

e. Double-click the **Titles table** in the Navigation Pane to open it in Datasheet view. Notice that the T04 title is not in the list.

f. Add a new record in the first blank record at the bottom of the Titles table. Use the following data:
   - Type **T04** in the TitleID field.
   - Type **Senior Account Rep** in the Title field.
   - Type **A marketing position requiring a technical background and at least three years of experience** in the Description field.
   - Type **Four year degree** in the Education Requirements field.
   - Type **45000** in the Minimum Salary field.
   - Type **75000** in the Maximum Salary field.

g. Close all tables. Click **Yes** if you are prompted to save changes to the Employees table.

h. Click the **Database Tools tab** and click **Relationships** in the Relationships group, and then Click **Show Table**. Follow the steps below:
   - Double-click each of the three table names in the Show Table dialog box to add it to the Relationships window and close the Show Table dialog box.
   - Click and drag to adjust the height of the Employees table so that all fields display in each one.
   - Drag the **LocationID field** in the Location table onto the LocationID field in the Employees table.
   - Click the **Enforce Referential Integrity** and **Cascade Update Related Fields check boxes** in the Edit Relationships dialog box to select them. Click **Create** to create a one-to-many relationship between the Location and Employees tables.
   - Drag the **TitleID field** in the Titles table onto the TitleID field in the Employees table (move the field lists by clicking and dragging their title bars as needed so that they do not overlap).
   - Click the **Enforce Referential Integrity** and **Cascade Update Related Fields check boxes** in the Edit Relationships dialog box to select it. Click **Create** to create a one-to-many relationship between the Titles and Employees tables.
   - Click **Save** on the Quick Access Toolbar to save the changes to the Relationships window and close the Relationships window.

i. Click the **Create tab** and click the **Query Wizard** in the Queries group. Follow the steps below:
   - Select **Simple Query Wizard** and click **OK**.
   - Select **Table: Employees** in the Tables/Queries box.
   - Double-click **LastName** in the Available Fields list to move it to the Selected Fields list.
   - Double-click **FirstName** in the Available Fields list to move it to the Selected Fields list.
   - Double-click **LocationID** in the Available Fields list to move it to the Selected Fields list.
   - Click **Next**.
   - Type **Employees Location** as the query title and click **Finish**.
   - Click **View** in the Views group on the Home tab to switch to Design view of the query. Click and drag the **Titles** table from the Navigation Pane into the top pane of the query design window.
   - Double-click **Title** in the Titles table to add the field to the query design grid.
   - Click the **Sort** cell of the LocationID field, click the arrow, and then click **Ascending**.
   - Click **Run** in the Results group (311 records display in the Datasheet sorted by LocationID in ascending order). Double-click the border to the right of each column to set the column widths to Best Fit.
   - Save and close the query.

j. Click the **Create tab** and click the **Query Wizard** in the Queries group. Follow the steps below:
   - Select **Simple Query Wizard** and click **OK**.
   - Select **Table: Location** in the Tables/Queries box.
   - Double-click **Location** in the Available Fields list to move it to the Selected Fields list.
   - Select **Table: Employees** in the Tables/Queries box.

- Double-click **LastName**, **FirstName**, and **Salary**.
- Select **Table: Titles** in the Tables/Queries box.
- Double-click **MinimumSalary** and **MaximumSalary**. Click **Next**.
- Ensure that the *Detail (shows every field of every record)* option is selected, and click **Next**.
- Type **Atlanta Salaries** as the query title and click **Finish**.

k. Click **View** in the Views group on the Home tab to switch to Design view of the Atlanta Salaries query.
- Click in the Criteria row of the Location field, and type **Atlanta**. Click the **Sort cell** of the Salary field, click the arrow, and then click **Ascending**.
- Click **Run** in the Results group. Review the data to determine if any of the Atlanta employees have a salary less than the minimum or greater than the maximum when compared to the published salary range. These salaries will be updated later.
- Save and close the query.

l. Right-click the **Atlanta Salaries query** in the Navigation Pane and from the shortcut menu, select **Copy**. Right-click a blank area in the Navigation Pane and select **Paste**. In the Paste As dialog box, type **Boston Salaries** for the query name. Click **OK**.

m. Right-click the **Boston Salaries query** in the Navigation Pane and select **Design View**. In the Criteria row of the Location field, replace Atlanta with **Boston**.
- Click **Run** in the Results group. Review the data to determine if any of the Boston employees have a salary less than the minimum or greater than the maximum when compared to the published salary range.
- Modify some data that have been incorrectly entered. In the query results, for the first employee, Frank Cusack, change the salary to **$48,700.00**; for Brian Beamer, **$45,900.00**; for Lorna Weber, **$45,700.00**; for Penny Pfleger, **$45,800.00**.
- Save and close the query.

n. Close the database and exit Access. Based on your instructor's directions, submit a02p2Insurance_LastFirst.

Mid-Level Exercises

1 My Game Collection

Over the years, you have collected quite a few video games, so you have cataloged them in an Access database, in the Games table. After opening the database, you will create two more tables—one to identify the game system (System) that runs your game and the other to identify the category or genre of the game (Category). Then, you will join each table in a relationship so that you can query the database.

a. Open *a02m1Games* and save the database as **a02m1Games_LastFirst**. Open the Games table and review the fields containing the game information. Close the table.

b. Click the **Create tab** and click **Table Design** in the Tables group.

c. Type **SystemID** for the first Field Name and select **AutoNumber** as the Data Type.

d. Type **SystemName** for the second Field Name and accept **Short Text** as the Data Type.

e. Set **SystemID** as the primary key. Add the caption **System ID**.

f. Change the SystemName Field Size property to **15**. Add the caption **System Name**, making sure there is a space between System and Name. Save the table as **System**. Switch to Datasheet view.

g. Add the system names to the System table as shown below, letting Access use AutoNumber to create the SystemID values. Close the table when finished.

System ID	System Name
1	**XBOX 360**
2	**PS3**
3	**Wii**
4	**NES**
5	**PC Game**
6	**Nintendo 3DS**

h. Click the **Create tab** and click **Table Design** in the Tables group. Type **CategoryID** for the first Field Name and select **AutoNumber** as the Data Type. Set the CategoryID as the primary key.

i. Type **CategoryDescription** for the second Field Name and accept **Short Text** as the Data Type. Change the Field Size property to **25**. Add the caption **Category Description**, making sure there is a space between Category and Description. Save the table as **Category**, saving the changes to the table design. Switch to Datasheet view.

j. Add the category descriptions to the Category table as shown below, letting Access use AutoNumber to create the CategoryID values. Close the table when finished.

CategoryID	Category Description
1	**Action**
2	**Adventure**
3	**Arcade**
4	**Racing**
5	**Rhythm**
6	**Role-playing**
7	**Simulation**
8	**Sports**

k. Click the **Database Tools tab** and click **Relationships** in the Relationships group. Display all three tables in the Relationships window and close the Show Table dialog box. Create a one-to-many relationship between CategoryID in the Category table and CategoryID in the Games table. Enforce referential integrity and cascade update related fields.

l. Create a one-to-many relationship between SystemID in the System table and SystemID in the Games table. Enforce referential integrity and cascade update related fields. Close the Relationships window, saving the changes.

m. Use the Query Wizard to create a simple query using the Games table. Add the following fields in the query (in this order): GameName, Rating. Save the query as **Ratings Query**.

n. Switch to Design view. Sort the Rating field in ascending order and run the query. Close the query, saving the changes.

o. Create a multitable query in Design view using all three tables. Add the following fields (in this order): GameName, CategoryDescription, Rating, SystemName, and DateAcquired.

p. Sort the query in ascending order by GameName and run the query. Save the query as **Game List Query** and close the query.

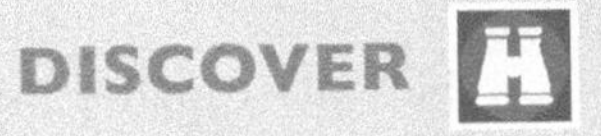

q. Copy the **Game List Query** and paste it into the Navigation Pane using the name **PS3 Games**. Modify the query in Design view by using **PS3** as the criterion for SystemName. Remove the sort by GameName and sort in ascending order by Rating. The query results should include 7 records.

r. Close the PS3 Games query, saving the changes. Assume you are going home for Thanksgiving and you want to take your **Wii** gaming system and games home with you—but you only want to take home games with a rating of **Everyone**.

s. Create a query named **Thanksgiving Games** that shows the name of the game, its rating, the category description of the game, and the system name for each. Run the query. The results of the query will tell you which games to pack. Close the query.

t. Close the database and exit Access. Based on your instructor's directions, submit a02m1Games_LastFirst.

2 The Prestige Hotel

The Prestige Hotel chain caters to upscale business travelers and provides state-of-the-art conference, meeting, and reception facilities. It prides itself on its international, four-star cuisine. Last year, it began a member reward club to help the marketing department track the purchasing patterns of its most loyal customers. All of the hotel transactions are stored in the database. Your task is to help the managers of the Prestige Hotels in Denver and Chicago identify their customers who stayed in a room last year and who had three persons in their party.

a. Open *a02m2Hotel* and save the file as **a02m2Hotel_LastFirst**. Review the data contained in the three tables. Specifically, study the tables and fields containing the data you need to analyze: dates of stays in Denver and Chicago suites, the members' names, and the numbers in the parties.

b. Import the location data from the Excel file *a02m2Location* into your database as a new table. The first row of the worksheet contains column headings. Set the LocationID Indexed property to **Yes (No Duplicates)** and set the Data Type to **Long Integer**. Select the **LocationID field** as the primary key. Name the table **Location**. Do not save the import steps.

c. Open the Relationships window and create a relationship between the Location table and the Orders table using the LocationID field. Enforce referential integrity and cascade update related fields. Create a relationship between the Orders and Members tables using the MemNumber field, ensuring that you enforce referential integrity and cascade update related fields. Create a relationship between the Orders and Service tables using the ServiceID field, ensuring that you enforce referential integrity and cascade update related fields. Save and close the Relationships window.

d. Open the Members table and use the Find command to locate Bryan Gray's name. Replace his name with your own first and last names. Locate Nicole Lee's name and replace it with your name. Close the table.

e. Create a query using the following fields: ServiceDate (Orders table), City (Location table), NoInParty (Orders table), ServiceName (Service table), FirstName (Members table), and LastName (Members table). Set the criteria to limit the output to **Denver**. Use the Between operator to show services only from **7/1/2017** to **6/30/2018**. Set the NoInParty criterion to **3**. Sort the results in ascending order by the ServiceDate.

f. Run the query and examine the number of records in the status bar at the bottom of the query. It should display 155. If your number of records is different, examine the criteria and make corrections.

g. Change the order of the query fields so that they display as FirstName, LastName, ServiceDate, City, NoInParty, and ServiceName. Save the query as **Denver Rooms 3 Guests**. Close the query.

DISCOVER

h. Copy the **Denver Rooms 3 Guests** query and paste it, renaming the new query **Chicago Rooms 3 Guests**.

i. Open the Chicago Rooms 3 Guests query in Design view and change the criterion for City to **Chicago**. Run the query and save the changes. It should display 179 results. Close the query.

DISCOVER

j. Review the criteria of the two previous queries and then create a third query named **Denver and Chicago Rooms 3 Guests**. Use the criteria from the two individual queries as a basis to create a combination AND–OR condition. The results will display guests in **Denver** or **Chicago** with **3** guests and service dates between **7/1/2013** and **6/30/2018**. The records returned in the results should equal the sum of the records in the two individual queries (334 records). Run, save, and close the query.

k. Close the database and exit Access. Based on your instructor's directions, submit a02m2Hotel_LastFirst.

3 New Castle County Technical Services

RUNNING CASE

New Castle County Technical Services (NCCTS) provides technical support for a number of companies in the greater New Castle County, Delaware area. Once you have completed the changes to the database tables and set the appropriate relationships, you will be ready to extract information by creating queries.

a. Open the database *a01m3NCCTS_LastFirst* and save it as a02m3NCCTS_LastFirst changing 01 to 02.

b. Open the Call Types table in Design view. Before you create your queries, you want to modify some of the table properties:
   - Set the caption of the HourlyRate field to **Hourly Rate**.
   - View the table in Datasheet view, and save the changes when prompted.

c. Close the table.

d. Make the following additional changes to the tables:
   - Open the Calls table in Design view. Change the data type of the CallTypeID field to **Number**.
   - Set the caption of the HoursLogged field to **Hours Logged**.
   - Set the caption of the OpenedDate field to **Opened Date** and set the format to **Short Date**.
   - Set the caption of the ClosedDate field to **Closed Date** and set the format to **Short Date**.
   - Set the caption of the CustomerSatisfaction field to **Customer Satisfaction**.
   - View the table in Datasheet view, and save the changes when prompted. You will not lose any data by making this change, so click **Yes** in the message box when prompted. Close the table.
   - Open the Customers table in Design view. Set the field size of CompanyName to **50** and the caption to **Company Name**. View the table in Datasheet view, and save the changes when prompted. You will not lose any data by making this change, so click **Yes** in the message box when prompted. Close the table.
   - Open the Reps table in Design view. Set the caption of the RepFirst field to **Rep First Name**. Set the caption of the RepLast field to **Rep Last Name**. View the table in Datasheet view, and save the changes when prompted. Close the table.

e. Open the Relationships window. Create a join line between the Call Types and Calls tables, ensuring that you enforce referential integrity and cascade update related fields. Set a relationship between Reps and Calls and between Customers and Calls using the same options. Save and close the Relationships window.

f. Create a multitable query, following the steps below:

- Add the following fields (in this order): **CallID** (from Calls), **Description** (from Call Types), **CompanyName** (from Customers), and **RepFirst** and **RepLast** (from Reps).
- Run the query, and then modify it to add **HoursLogged** (from Calls).
- Sort the query by HoursLogged in ascending order. Set the criteria of the HoursLogged field to **Is Not Null** and run the query again.
- Modify the criteria of the HoursLogged field to **>=5** and **<=10**, the description to **Disaster Recovery**, and the rep to **Barbara**.
- Save the query as **Complex Disaster Recovery Calls_Barbara**. Run and then close the query.

g. Create a copy of the **Complex Disaster Recovery Calls_Barbara** query, and modify it following the steps below:

- Save the copy of the query as **Complex Network Installation Calls_Barbara**.
- Modify the query so that the description displays Barbara's network installation calls that logged between 5 and 10 hours.
- Save, run, and then close the query.

h. Close the database and exit Access. Based on your instructor's directions, submit a02m3NCCTS_LastFirst.

Beyond the Classroom

Database Administrator Position

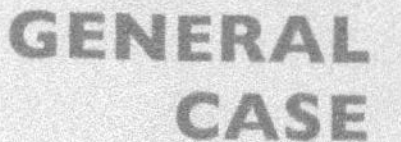

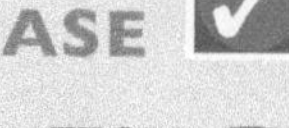

Create a database to keep track of candidates for open positions at Secure Systems, Inc., database management experts. Use the Internet to search for information about database management positions. One useful site is published by the federal government's Bureau of Labor Statistics. It compiles an Occupational Outlook Handbook describing various positions, the type of working environment, the education required, salary information, and the projected growth. The website is http://www.bls.gov/ooh. Research the necessary information in order to create the database using these requirements:

a. Create a new database named **a02b1Admin_LastFirst**.

b. Create three tables including the field names as follows, and in the specified orders:
   - **Candidates (CandidateID, FirstName, LastName, Phone, Email).**
   - **JobOpenings (JobOpeningID, JobName, RequiredSkill, HourlyPayRate, DataPosted, Supervisor).**
   - **Interviews (InterviewSequenceID, CandidateID, JobOpeningID, InterviewedBy, DateOfInterview, Rank).**

c. Set the data types, field properties, and a primary key for each table.

d. Set table relationships, and be sure to enforce referential integrity between them. Cascade update related fields

e. Add 10 candidates to the Candidates table.

f. Add a **Database Administrator** job and four other sample jobs to the JobOpenings table.

g. Add eight sample interviews—four for the Database Administrator position and four others. Rank each candidate on a scale of 1 to 5 (with 5 as the highest).

h. Create a query that lists the LastName, FirstName, JobOpeningID, InterviewedBy, DateOfInterview, and Rank fields. Display only Database Administrator interviews with a ranking of 3 or lower. Sort by LastName and then by FirstName. Run and save the query as **Database Admin Low Rank**. Close the query

i. Close the database and exit Access. Based on your instructor's directions, submit a02b1Admin_LastFirst.

May Beverage Sales

A coworker explained that he was having difficulty with queries that were not returning correct results, and asked you to help diagnose the problem. Open *a02b2Traders* and save it as **a02b2Traders_LastFirst**. It contains two queries, *May 2018 Orders of Beverages and Confections* and *2018 Beverage Sales by Ship Country*. The May 2018 Orders of Beverages and Confections query is supposed to contain only information for orders shipped in May 2018. You find other shipped dates included in the results. Change the criteria to exclude the other dates. Run and save the query. Close the query.

The 2018 Beverage Sales by Ship Country query returns no results. Check the criteria in all fields and modify so that the correct results are returned. Run and save the query. Close the query.

Close the database and exit Access. Based on your instructor's directions, submit a02b2Traders_LastFirst.

Capstone Exercise

MyITLab® Grader

The Morris Arboretum in Chestnut Hill, Pennsylvania tracks donors in Excel. They also use Excel to store a list of plants in stock. As donors contribute funds to the Arboretum, they can elect to receive a plant gift from the Arboretum. These plants are both rare plants and hard-to-find old favorites, and they are part of the annual appeal and membership drive to benefit the Arboretum's programs. The organization has grown, and the files are too large and inefficient to handle in Excel. You will begin by importing the files from Excel into a new Access database. Then you will create a table to track donations, create a relationship between the two tables, and create some baseline queries.

Create a New Database

You will examine the data in the Excel worksheets to determine which fields will become the primary keys in each table and which fields will become the foreign keys.

a. Open the *a02c1Donors* Excel workbook, examine the data, and close the workbook.

b. Open the *a02c1Plants* Excel workbook, examine the data, and close the workbook.

c. Create a new, blank database named **a02c1Arbor_LastFirst**. Close the new blank table created automatically by Access without saving it.

Import Data from Excel

You will import two Excel workbooks into the database.

a. Click the **External Data tab** and click **Excel** in the Import & Link group.

b. Navigate to and select the *a02c1Donors* workbook to be imported.

c. Select the **First Row Contains Column Headings** option.

d. Set the DonorID field Indexed option to **Yes (No Duplicates)**.

e. Choose **DonorID** as the primary key when prompted and accept the table name Donors.

f. Import the *a02c1Plants* workbook, set the **ID field** as the primary key, and then change the indexing option to **Yes (No Duplicates)**.

g. Accept the table name Plants.

h. Change the ID field name in the Plants table to **PlantID**.

i. Open each table in Datasheet view to examine the data. Close the tables.

Create a New Table

You will create a new table to track the donations as they are received from the donors.

a. You will create a new table in Design view and save the table as **Donations**.

b. Add the following fields in Design view and set the properties as specified:

- Add the primary key field as **DonationID** with the **Number Data Type** and a field size of **Long Integer**.
- Add **DonorID** (a foreign key) with the **Number Data Type** and a field size of **Long Integer**.
- Add **PlantID** (a foreign key) as a **Number** and a field size of **Long Integer**.
- Add **DateOfDonation** as a **Date/Time** field.
- Add **AmountOfDonation** as a **Currency** field.

c. Switch to Datasheet view, and save the table when prompted. You will enter data into the table in a later step. Close the table.

Create Relationships

You will create the relationships between the tables using the Relationships window.

a. Open the Donors table in Design view and change the Field Size property for DonorID to **Long Integer** so it matches the Field Size property of DonorID in the Donations table. Save and close the table.

b. Open the Plants table in Design view and change the Field Size property for PlantID to **Long Integer** so it matches the Field Size property for PlantID in the Donations table. Save and close the table.

c. Identify the primary key fields in the Donors table and the Plants table and join them with their foreign key counterparts in the related Donations table. Enforce referential integrity and cascade and update related fields. Save and close the Relationships window.

Add Sample Data to the Donations Table

You will add 10 records to the Donations table.

a. Add the following records to the Donations table:

Donation ID	Donor ID	Plant ID	Date of Donation	Amount of Donation
10	8228	611	3/1/2018	$150
18	5448	190	3/1/2018	$ 55
6	4091	457	3/12/2018	$125
7	11976	205	3/14/2018	$100
1	1000	25	3/17/2018	$120
12	1444	38	3/19/2018	$ 50
2	1444	38	4/3/2018	$ 50
4	10520	49	4/12/2018	$ 60
5	3072	102	4/19/2018	$ 50
21	1204	25	4/22/2018	$120

b. Sort the Donations table by the AmountOfDonation field in descending order. Close the table.

Use the Query Wizard

You will create a query of all donations greater than $100 in the Donations table.

a. Add the DonorID and AmountOfDonation fields from Donations (in that order).

b. Save the query as **Donations Over 100**.

c. Add criteria to include only donations of more than $100.

d. Sort the query results in ascending order by AmountOfDonation.

e. Run the query.

f. Save and close the query.

Create a Query in Design View

You will create a query that identifies donors and donations.

a. Create a query that identifies the people who made a donation after April 1, 2018. This list will be given to the Arboretum staff so they can notify the donors that a plant is ready for pickup. The query should list the date of the donation, donor's full name (LastName, FirstName), phone number, the amount of the donation, and name of the plant they want (in that order). Add the tables and fields necessary to produce the query.

b. Sort the query by date of donation in descending order, then by donor last name in ascending order.

c. Run, close, and save the query as **Plant Pickup List**.

Copy and Modify a Query in Design View

You will copy a query and modify it to add and sort by a different field.

a. Copy the Plant Pickup List query and paste it using **ENewsletter** as the query name.

b. Open the ENewsletter query in Design view and delete the DateofDonation column.

c. Add the ENewsletter field to the first column of the design grid and set it to sort in ascending order, so that the query sorts first by ENewsletter and then by LastName.

d. Run, save, and close the query. Close the database and exit Access. Based on your instructor's directions, submit a02c1Arbor_LastFirst.

Glossary

AND condition In a query, returns only records that meet all criteria.

AutoNumber A number that automatically increments each time a record is added.

Caption property Used to create a more readable label that displays in the top row in Datasheet view and in forms and reports.

Cascade Delete Related Records When the primary key value is deleted in a primary table, Access will automatically delete all foreign key values in a related table.

Cascade Update Related Fields An option that directs Access to automatically change all foreign key values in a related table when the primary key value is modified in a primary table.

Comparison Operators Use greater than (>), less than (<), greater than or equal to (>=), and less than or equal to (<=), etc. to limit query results that meet these criteria.

Criteria row A row in Query Design view that determines which records will be selected.

Data redundancy The unnecessary storing of duplicate data in two or more tables.

Data type Determines the type of data that can be entered and the operations that can be performed on that data.

Field properties Characteristics of fields that determine how they look and behave.

Foreign key A field in a related table that is the primary key of another table.

Multitable queries Results contain fields from two or more tables, enabling you to take advantage of the relationships that have been set in your database.

Null The term Access uses to describe a blank field value.

One-to-many relationship When the primary key value in the primary table can match many of the foreign key values in the related table.

OR condition In a query, returns records meeting any of the specified criteria.

Query A question about the data stored in a database answers provided in a datasheet.

Referential Integrity Rules in a database that are used to preserve relationships between tables when records are changed.

Simple Query Wizard Provides a step-by-step guide to help you through the query design process.

Wildcards Special characters that can represent one or more characters in the criterion of a query.

Index

E

F

G

H

I

J

K

L

M

T

U

V

W

X

Z